LIVING OFF YOUR MONEY

The Modern Mechanics of Investing During Retirement with Stocks and Bonds

MICHAEL H. McCLUNG

Living Off Your Money
The Modern Mechanics of Investing During Retirement with Stocks and Bonds

ISBN-13: 978-0-9974034-1-1 (Hardback)
ISBN-13: 978-0-9974034-0-4 (Softback)
ISBN-13: 978-0-9974034-2-8 (E-Book)

DISCLAIMER
The information in this book is provided for education and informational purposes, without any expressed or implied warranty of any kind, including warranties of accuracy, completeness, or fitness for any particular purpose.

The contents are based on my personal experience, my interpretations of the data, and my computer simulations. Although I made every reasonable attempt to achieve accuracy, I can assume no responsibility for errors or omissions.

Use this information as you see fit and at your own risk. Your particular situation may not be suited to the examples illustrated or recommendations provided, so adjust your use accordingly. Your financial decisions must be based on your own independent due diligence, including consulting with a professional as needed.

Investing in stocks and bonds, or any other security, has potential rewards and risks. You much assess the risks yourself or seek independent professional advice.

Visit www.LivingOffYourMoney.com

For my dear wife, Sheila,
whose support never wavered through
what appeared to be a never-ending book,
and to my children,
Craig, Sheldon, Honor, and Jadzia,
who add to the meaning of it all.

ACKNOWLEDGEMENTS

A special thanks to Global Financial Data who subsidized access to their United Kingdom and Japan datasets for this book. These datasets were invaluable in verifying and comparing the performance of retirement strategies.

I am grateful to my expert reviewers, who generously gave their time: Harold Evensky of Evensky & Katz, Steve Evanson of Evanson Asset Management, Joseph Tomlinson of Tomlinson Financial Planning, and Larry Swedroe of Buckingham Asset Management.

I want to acknowledge Yale's Robert Shiller, who for many years has posted and updated his US market data from his own research. Access to his dataset was an invaluable asset to this book, especially in the early days when the initial soundness of ideas and approaches were being tested.

Special thanks also go to Sheila, my wife, whose finance degree came in handy when she was the first reader of each chapter, sometime multiple times. I appreciate Debra Murray, my sister, providing helpful advice for the introductory chapters. I also appreciate the expertise and support from Bob Rich, my copyeditor, as well as Liz Dexter, my proofreader, whose remarkable attention to detail provided an exceptional last line of defense against my many mistakes. Finally, I want to thank my book designer, Stephanie Anderson of Jera Publishing, who not only helped make up for my slipped schedule, but exceeded my design expectations.

CONTENTS

I have too many unread books on my shelves, so why should I buy yours?

WALTER E. GOH

WHAT'S GOOD TO KNOW FIRST

This preface distinguishes what's different about this book compared to others on investing during retirement. In doing so, it introduces the purpose, the problem, and the approach. Most importantly, it helps you decide if this book is right for you.

THE PURPOSE

It's common knowledge few Americans save enough for retirement. The surprising part is, those who do then rarely invest it well *during* retirement. This is unfortunate. To a degree, it squanders what has been diligently saved. Why does this happen? Investing during retirement is more difficult for sure, but that's not the root of the problem

Our brain doesn't deal well with ambiguity, conflicting opinions, and a constant bombardment of misleading information…the domain of investing during retirement. Ultimately, there is too much wrong guidance and not enough right guidance, and it's difficult to discern which is which. No wonder so many get it wrong.

Adding to the problem, the investing landscape has changed significantly over the past 20 years, outdating practices once considered correct. Financial economics has been and still is in a state of transition. Old theories are known to be lacking, but there is no consensus on what should take their place. Without clear unified guidance from economists, many retirees stick to what was deemed best in the past; unfortunately, this seemingly conservative stance is not a good one.

This book consolidates exactly what you need to know to invest well in retirement. It provides an updated set of best practices. There is no ambiguity or incomplete answers. All recommendations are supported with proper evidence to understand not only what works but why, including side-by-side comparisons of alternatives. Today's retirees can do appreciably better than previous generations by applying these updated practices—this means more income with less risk.

What kind of numbers are we talking about? It's impossible to provide guarantees, but I'll estimate adhering to this book's recommendations will increase your retirement income by 15% to 50%, depending on previous practices. Of course it also depends on what is happening in the markets, but the recommendations are generally most valuable during poor to moderate markets…when it matters most. At the extreme end, when all this book's recommendations are combined (as shown in Chapter 10), the average annual income under a global benchmark increased 87% over specific practices still used by some retirees.

Be clear this book is not about tricks and wishful thinking, but about applying rational evidence-based practices. Considering the magnitude of the payoff, investing well in retirement is a rare life opportunity.

The Scope of the Problem

Anyone aiming to create a top-performing plan for investing during retirement quickly encounters a host of barriers, making the task extremely difficult.

The literature varies in its usefulness. On topics like risk the discussion rarely provides objective help for the hardest decisions to be made. Other well-covered topics, like asset allocation, generally apply but without retirement specifics (e.g., what fund combinations are most suitable; what are the appropriate stock-bond ratios; what are the tradeoffs). Specialized topics, like income-harvesting and variable-withdrawal strategies (explained later in depth), have reasonably good coverage if you can find it, but no means to compare alternatives—performance comparisons are difficult or impossible to make. When precise studies and comparisons can be found, the assumptions* don't support the needs of today's retirees.

Unsubstantiated claims are perhaps hardest to deal with. Outside academic studies, conclusions and advice are frequently handed out with minimal supporting data. When evidence is provided, even in academic studies, it's typically based either on one set of United States historical data, or computer simulations lacking a resemblance to true markets. This isn't enough.

It's also important to understand academic standards aren't aimed at the pragmatic needs of retirees. Early on I believed academic research set the highest standard for retirement guidance: a combination of scientific method, mathematical rigor, logical analysis, and peer reviews. As my own research progressed, I became aware of the extent academia's goals for original research differed from my need for pragmatic guidance. To begin with, fundamental truths aren't always practical and practical solutions don't always lead to fundamental truths. I also found caveats are a well-honed tool within academic writings, often used to address ambiguities that are crucial to the pragmatist, or to equivocate on practical implications. Completeness is also not a criterion, given the research goal is often narrow, independent from how it might be applied. However, this is not a critique of academia but a reality for investors to understand—the goals of academia within financial economics are generally its own, with too rare of focus on pragmatic guidance.

This book is concerned with real people investing their savings in real markets, tangibly affecting their lives for better or worse. Proper guidance in this context must sort through the ambiguities, deal with what's lacking, verify assumptions, and compare alternatives, all to arrive at balanced judgments. For anyone publishing retirement guidance, there is an implicit obligation to provide one's best—incomplete coverage accompanied by caveats or equivocating, whether in a conclusion or a footnote, cannot soften poor outcomes.

Another problem is biases are pervasive within the investing domain. Again, this isn't a critique, but an acknowledgement of the effects incentives have on human nature. Biases aren't from intent, but from a lack of self-awareness. Biases arise out of the subtle influences incentives exert on our thoughts and actions. The magnitude of a bias generally correlates to the magnitude of the incentive, even when unconscious.

Strong incentives contribute to biases in the retirement industry. The financial media is generally biased towards investment news that best captures an audience. Financial planners and money managers are generally biased towards

---

* Common assumptions are a US-based market portfolio, annual rebalancing, and inflation-adjusted fixed withdrawals.

investment strategies that aid their business, either through simplifying their operations or generating more revenue. Financial authors are generally biased for a diversity of reasons—it may stem from their business or career interests, or a mindset that reinforces their actions, reputation, or esteem. Some professionals are much more objective than others, some admirably so, but no one is totally immune.

Luigi Zingales, an economist as well as a professor at the Chicago Booth School of Business, wrote a revealing paper[1] on how economics as a profession has pervasive biases. He discusses how economists who support business interests have better career opportunities, resulting in biases. From the opposite side, some economists are rewarded for being anti-business, forming an opposing set of biases. Zingales also describes* how papers supporting certain research conclusions are more likely to be published in leading journals due to editor bias (driven by a different set of incentives). This implies biases even play a role in deciding who is awarded university tenure. The implications of this are sobering. While we can expect economists to be more objective than the average person, their incentives to varying degrees shape the financial industry.

I can easily say this book is freer than most from biases. I'm not exposed to industry incentives. My aim isn't to grow a financial business or attract new clients. My dominant goal is to write a worthwhile book, and sell enough to write another worthwhile book; however, avoiding biases is not that straightforward. I'm not bias free. While researching this book I noticed a subtle predisposition to favor concepts and strategies I originated or supported. I found it necessary to deliberatively counterbalance these natural biases by focusing on the data, continually questioning the results, and giving attention to proper research methods.

We can't eliminate our biases, as a producer or a consumer, but we can substantially reduce them with conscious effort and discipline. The best advice I can give for reading this book is to temporarily put all investing mindsets on hold, taking a careful look at the data presented, only then forming your conclusions.

THE TARGET AUDIENCE

This book is for those living off their money, planning to, or helping others to do so. It applies to individual investors from non-financial careers as well as financial advisors or investment managers, basically anyone interested in taking a careful look at the data and the best practices it implies.

The common investing scenario is a retiree drawing annual income from a combination of retirement accounts (e.g., 401Ks, IRAs), taxable brokerage accounts, and perhaps other investments like annuities or individual bonds. Additional income may come from a pension, Social Security, or other sources; however, to apply this book's guidance a significant portion of income must stem from market assets directly controlled.

Unfortunately, this book cannot be considered a proper guide for beginning investors. It too often digs into topics with the depth and pace to satisfy more experienced investors. Also, a substantial portion focuses on the supporting evidence, which tends to be more difficult to understand than the recommendations. Less experienced investors can still profit from this book if they are dedicated readers, but it will take extra effort and occasional Internet queries to fill in background knowledge.

Fortunately, once understood investing well during retirement is not difficult. This brings us to the challenge this book presents.

---

* Luigi Zingales talks about his paper in an October 20, 2014 interview on EconTalk, economist Russ Roberts' excellent and readily available podcast series.

THE READER'S CHALLENGE

This book is best approached by setting aside some time. The coverage is pragmatic, but a complete reading takes a level of involvement beyond what most books on investing require.

Only a small percentage of retirees are motivated enough to actively seek how to invest well in retirement. If you fall into this group, this book will be easier to read, perhaps even providing an enjoyable foray through what the data shows. However, many more retirees are sitting on the fence—they want to invest well but find it burdensome and formidable. If you fall into this larger group, consider the following: there's a large payoff for investing well in retirement (remember the earlier numbers!) and you can take advantage of it.

The average lifetime includes 2000 work weeks—I estimate it'll take one week of studying this book to substantially magnify the benefits of what you've worked long and hard to save. It's all doable: *if you had the forethought and discipline to save well for retirement, you have what it takes to benefit from this book.* You don't have to be a genius or have a degree in economics. What you need is a strong dose of emotional intelligence—that's what sustains our motivation to follow through when our best interests are at stake.

It's been said there is more benefit from reading one good book five times, than from five average books once. It takes an uncommon amount of effort to gain the full benefits of a good book. I believe this is a good book. You needn't read it multiple times, but there may be parts requiring more than one read to fully gain the benefit. I suggest you start by flipping through the book a time or two to orient yourself before settling into a more serious read.

Despite the challenge, you can take shortcuts if you want to substantially reduce your effort. Conceptually, there are two books here: a 75-page how-to book wrapped in a much larger why-it's-so book. A Chapter Guide before the start of each chapter explains what is essential (i.e., the how-to portion) versus the broader explanations more suitable to in-depth readers. To profit, a reader need only understand the recommendations, even though the essence of the book is in the why-it's-so parts.

Fortunately, very little ongoing effort is needed once a plan is put in place, with the benefits continuing throughout retirement.

A COMPANION SPREADSHEET

Despite the reader challenge, there is no need for retirees to do their own calculations to follow the recommendations. Applying the recommendations doesn't even require a lot of calculations, but it's still better to avoid the possibility of errors. As an aid, a downloadable spreadsheet is provided for free on the book's website: www.livingoffyourmoney.com.

THE INVESTING ASSUMPTIONS

A set of assumptions underlie every approach to the market. This book's primary assumptions are listed below.

a. Complex investment instruments rarely make good investments; they are usually created to benefit the industry, not investors.

b. Low-cost index funds are generally the best instruments for stocks and bonds, although managed funds are sometimes a reasonable choice.

c. Retirees want their investments to perform well during retirement, but only at a level of risk they are comfortable with.

d. Top retirement plans don't need frequent attention, typically annual or semi-annual maintenance is sufficient.

AN EVIDENCE-BASED GUIDE — APPLYING SCIENCE TO DATA

It has already been said the recommendations in this book are supported by proper evidence. Now is the time to clarify what this means, but a quick story will set the stage.

Recently, a bestselling author on investing told financial advisors they lose potential clients by providing too much data. He explained, clients make their decisions based on emotional connections; the data only clutters up the process. Regrettably, this reflects the prevailing norm: emotions, sound bites, and sales pitches drive key financial decisions more than knowledge. This book takes an opposing approach, emphasizing the power of data and the knowledge it conveys.

The market data we have in hand is an excellent guide, showing what works and what doesn't investing during retirement. This data spans long periods of time, multiple countries, and different asset classes. Properly used it provides the best possible answers. However, we must tread carefully through the data to reach correct conclusions.

Campbell Harvey, a Duke professor of economics and expert on data mining, argues along with his coauthors[2] that "most claimed research findings in financial economics are likely false" due to improper data techniques — this is especially startling considering he is talking about experienced researchers.

This book applies the science of analyzing data[*] to form answers, following an approach known as evidence-based research. Wikipedia defines evidence-based research in the following words:

> Evidence is comprised of research findings derived from the systematic collection of data through observation and experiment. All practical decisions made should be based on research studies selected and interpreted according to some specific norms. Typically, such norms disregard theoretical studies and qualitative studies and consider quantitative studies according to a narrow set of criteria of what counts as evidence.

Wikipedia continues with the definition of an evidence-based practice.

> An evidence-based practice develops individualized guidelines of best practices to inform the improvement of whatever professional task is at hand. Evidence-based practice is a philosophical approach that is in opposition to rules of thumb, folklore, and tradition. Examples of a reliance on "the way it was always done" can be found in almost every profession, even when those practices are contradicted by new and better information.[3]

---

* The word *data science* is avoided due to its overuse and broader connotations. Certainly data science is applied in this book, but its better known facets, including machine learning and Bayesian analysis, are less applicable to investing during retirement compared to more classical statistical approaches.

The above definitions, along with a skeptical mindset, capture the approach and philosophy of this book. The only thing missing is a clear statement of the specific norms for proper evidence within the domain of investing during retirement.

The following four criteria define the norms to comply with for all recommendations in this book— if for some reason a recommendation cannot fully comply with these norms then it's clearly stated.

1. Recommendations must be verified with real market data (i.e., market simulations alone are not sufficient... we don't know how to fully model markets).

2. Recommendations must be based on methods supporting independent confirmation by other researchers (i.e., results that cannot be replicated are not sufficient).

3. All recommendations must be verified using at least one independent data source but preferably several; testing with independent data is the only way to insure correct results, preventing a data-mining bias (which is thoroughly defined later).

4. All recommendations must hold up to robust testing, designed to seek out counterevidence or identify weaknesses. Typically this requires a diversity of tests, cross-verifying conclusions across multiple contexts and datasets. Only by consciously seeking to identify flaws in favored strategies can the natural biases in research be counterbalanced.

A brief example makes the above clearer. A new strategy, Prime Harvesting, is recommended in Chapter 3; however, before it's recommended it has to satisfy the norms of evidence-based research. For this particular case, it means showing satisfactory performance (compared to its peers) under the following diverse conditions: multiple real markets (US, UK, and Japan), varying withdrawal rates, varying retirement lengths, several thousand randomly-generated portfolios, several thousand simulated markets, and varying risk metrics (e.g., worse-case scenario, top-90% performance, average performance). These tests are explained later, but as a whole they reflect the primary premise: a strong dose of due diligence, applied according to the norms of evidence-based research, produces exceptionally strong answers.

THE MODERN MECHANICS — WHAT'S NEW HERE?

Modern Mechanics in the title of this book corresponds to the best practices that will be identified. *Modern* fits because the recommendations are mostly based on research from the last 20 years. *Mechanics* fits because the recommendations are detailed and complete, delving into the nuts and bolts of all it takes to invest well in retirement.

So what's new? For a start, very few retirees apply anything close to the ideas covered, mostly because they have not been systemically sorted through and presented with sufficient data. It's like all the parts have been lying around but never assembled — certainly there is no up-to-date evidence-based retirement plan circulating in the general literature. More specifically, several new strategies are recommended, ones you won't find elsewhere, plus a couple of existing strategies are enhanced to perform better. Additionally, new metrics are introduced to help compare alternatives...the most important supports comparing which portfolios are best suited for retirement.

Finally the form of the book is new. This book follows the data, directly compares alternatives, and delivers a complete set of step-by-step recommendations.

It's safe to say there are no comparable books focusing on data. It may be due to timing, the lack of author incentives, or publishers not believing there are enough savvy readers to justify books like this. Whatever the reason, providing pragmatic in-depth well-verified complete answers for investing well during retirement is new.

THE PAST VERSUS THE FUTURE

We are all familiar with some form of the common investment disclaimer: past performance does not guarantee future results. This disclaimer is certainly true, but it's also true (and will be shown) that the historical data is the best guide we have to future markets.

The market exhibits fundamental behavior in the form of real returns. Although real returns vary greatly year to year, they also maintain some forms of consistency across diverse conditions over long time periods. I call these consistent behaviors *market invariants*. Market invariants have influenced real market returns throughout history. Just as important, there is no reason to believe these invariants will cease to exert their influence in the future.

Market invariants play a role in financial economics. Fama and French's three-factor model of the market is based on invariants. Shiller's valuation work based on price-earnings ratios (i.e., CAPE-10) is also based on invariants. There appears to be consensus that momentum is an invariant.

The existence of market invariants support the rationale of defining a set of best practices for the future, based on what has been observed in the past. Certainly not all market influences are invariants and invariants can be difficult to directly leverage; nevertheless, the data makes clear invariants persist across extremely diverse circumstances, exerting their influence to keep the markets as a whole within certain boundaries. The outcome is past market characteristics, when prudently considered, provide the best approximation we have of future market characteristics.

On the other hand, acknowledging and considering the influence of market invariants doesn't preclude planning for extreme scenarios never encountered before; however, this type of planning, based on speculation beyond known bounds, is best served by supplementing with guaranteed income...the topic of the last chapter.

SYSTEMIC WITHDRAWALS AND THE RETIREMENT-INCOME PHILOSOPHY

This final topic before officially starting the book concerns the philosophy taken towards retirement income.

Jeremy Cooper and Wade Pfau in their paper, *The Yin and Yang of Retirement Income Philosophies*, explain that retirement strategies fall into two main camps: probability-based and safety-first. The probability-based camp focuses on a portfolio of volatile stock and bond funds to meet income needs. The safety-first camp focuses on a portfolio of guaranteed-income (e.g., annuities, bond ladders) to meet income needs. Neither of these camps is pure, though: the probability-based camp often supplements with guaranteed-income in a secondary role; the safety-first camp often supplements with stock and bond funds in a secondary role. Nevertheless, the differences are major.

Philosophically, the safety-first camp makes complete sense; however, this book fits squarely into the probability-based camp for several reasons outlined below.

First, the data shows by using an updated set of probability-based best practices (the topic of this book) there is significantly lower risk than traditionally estimated—most retirees will find the risk acceptable and the reward worthwhile.

There's another reason, often overlooked. The risk of insufficient income can come from poor markets *or unexpected expenses*. In both cases the result is not enough income to meet expenses. When stocks make up a substantial portion of the portfolio, there is typically surplus value from the stocks (over 90% of the time historically). This frequent surplus value from stocks can help or fully cover unexpected expenses, essentially providing an extra hedge.

In contrast, a safety-first solution often costs significantly more than traditionally estimated because of longer life spans—low returns from guaranteed-income solutions rarely support long retirements well. Also, a safety-first solution doesn't generally have the built-in hedge for unexpected expenses —the bulk of the portfolio is more likely to be allocated to guaranteed income, limiting both the stock allocation and the potential for surplus value to cover any unexpected expenses.

Ultimately, it will become clear that many retirees can't afford a pure safety-first approach, or if they can, they aren't willing to pay the price, or sacrifice the loss in flexibility, or accept the exposure to unexpected expenses. Guaranteed income still has an optional role, but it must be a balanced one.

From within the probability-based camp, this book focuses on what is called *systemic withdrawals*[*]...a conglomerate of strategies generating sustainable income from a portfolio of stock and bond funds. The first 10 chapters identify and verify the best practices for systemic withdrawals. The last chapter, almost a book in itself, shows how guaranteed income can supplement systemic withdrawals to handle cases worse than we've seen in the past.

§

Once you've completed this book, you'll be well prepared to form your own plan and put it into action. The downloadable spreadsheet will aid you, plus the book's website can keep you abreast of updates, but everything you have to have is here.

---

[*]   A similar term, systematic withdrawals, is commonly used in the literature, but its definitions vary and sometimes misalign with the solutions covered.

THE ONE-PAGE REFERENCE GUIDE
FOR INVESTING WELL DURING RETIREMENT
The downloadable spreadsheet supports this guide.

▶ Form a plan by iterating through the following steps until satisfied.

1. Pick your target retirement length based on life expectancy, typically 30 to 40 years. Websites such as https://personal.vanguard.com/us/insights/retirement/plan-for-a-long-retirement-tool can identify the age where the life-expectancy probability is between the recommended amounts of 1% to 5%.

2. Make sure you are comfortable with income-harvesting in Chapter 3, specifically Prime Harvesting (or Alternate Prime as an alternative).

3. Make sure you are comfortable with variable withdrawals in Chapter 4, specifically EM (or ECM as an alternative).

4. Pick your initial stock percentage. See Chapter 7 recommendations.

5. Pick one of the portfolios from the recommendations in Chapter 8. Or optionally, define your own well-diversified portfolio using the Harvesting Ratio (defined in Chapter 5 and applied in Chapter 8).

6. Identify your initial withdrawal rate, following the example in Chapter 9.

7. Consider Figure 141 in Chapter 10 to make any needed adjustments to the stock percentage or withdrawal rate based on your primary retirement parameters.

8. Optionally consider using guaranteed income, based on Chapter 11's recommendations and the following steps.
    i. Determine your essential-income rate (factoring in all income sources)
    ii. Compare GI options (i.e., TIPS ladders, I Bonds, inflation-adjusted SPIAs) and their payouts
    iii. Choose a GI strategy, considering the essential-income rate, stock-valuation level, bequest motivation, and the various payout rates for different options
    iv. Calculate and consider the total income rate from combining the guaranteed-income plan and systemic-withdrawal plan.

▶ At the start of retirement:

1. For systemic-withdrawals
    i. Start Prime Harvesting (or the alternative) to manage income harvesting, following the step-by-step example in Chapter 3.
    ii. Start EM (or the alternative) to determine annual withdrawal amounts, following the step-by-step example in Chapter 4.

2. Begin the guaranteed-income plan (if any), possibly purchasing bonds and annuities.

▶ Once a year, do plan maintenance, which is essentially adhering to Prime Harvesting and EM, plus any guaranteed-income requirements.

▶ Every 5 to 10 years, reevaluate your goals and outlook. For major changes, reiterate on the plan if needed. If merited, review the guidance on restarting systemic withdrawals in Chapter 10. Also consider reviewing the examples in the last chapter.

CHAPTER I GUIDE

This chapter explains why investing during retirement requires new concepts and strategies. Advances in financial economics are described as the underpinnings for the modern mechanics of investing during retirement. The mechanics are introduced, essentially outlining the core contents of this book.

Less interested readers can skim the chapter focusing on the "The Modern Mechanics".

INVESTING DURING RETIREMENT IS DIFFERENT
THE RETIREMENT LANDSCAPE
THE REVOLUTION IN FINANCIAL ECONOMICS
THE MODERN MECHANICS
THE POINT

Our financial descendants will look back to this time and wonder, "What were they thinking?"

WALTER E. GOH*, 1991
NATIONAL CONFERENCE OF ACADEMIC RETIREMENT PLANNERS

CHAPTER 1

INVESTING DURING RETIREMENT IS DIFFERENT

THE TOP PRIORITY FOR INVESTING during retirement must be to provide sufficient, if not ample, income for as long as we live. Running out of money late in life, when our earnings potential has dwindled, certainly qualifies as a financial disaster—recovery would be difficult if not impossible. Retirement is not a time to learn from investment mistakes.

Investing *during* retirement is different from investing during the accumulating years. Periodically selling stocks and bonds to support sustainable income add a new dimension to the problem. A strained duality is created: while our money must never run out, it must continually fund our standard of living. This duality creates a different investment dynamic, one requiring checks and balances beyond investing in the accumulating years.

Regrettably, investing during retirement in the media or practical literature is too often reduced to tactical planning for IRAs and 401Ks, a dose of annuities, and boosting bond levels to cut "risk"—all followed by a return to investing as usual with no strategic changes. Usually, there is little or no emphasis on the differences stemming from the portfolio withdrawals that provide income.

A plan for investing during retirement should answer several key questions, all revolving around withdrawals. What asset allocation is most likely to support sustainable withdrawals? What assets should be sold each year to fund withdrawals? When and how should the portfolio be rebalanced to minimize risk from withdrawals? How might future unknowns be hedged to protect withdrawals? And of course, how much can be safely withdrawn each year? The correctness of these answers strongly correlates to financial success in retirement.

A tenet of this book is the global market data provides the answers, showing us how to invest well during retirement. Alone, though, the data isn't enough. As outlined in the preface, evidence-based practices ensure correct answers are pulled from the data. Likewise, the science of data plays a part, leveraging what has been learned before to properly analyze and interpret the data in hand. Done right, this combination produces exceptionally good answers, directly aligned to the needs of retirees.

---

* A quote from Walter E. Goh introduces each chapter. You can find out more about Walter on the book's website.

What about financial economics? By itself, it hasn't gone far enough in supporting the needs of retirement investors. This lack is in part because financial economics is in a state of transition, reforming its core theories. It may also be the pragmatic needs of retirees extend too far beyond theory and narrow empirical research. Whatever the reasons, it's clear from the data, better solutions are possible than now proposed by financial economics alone. This should change as the field evolves, but probably not for this generation of retirees.

Nevertheless, the rigor of financial economics can ultimately provide a depth to investment answers that is not obtainable otherwise. This is why investors care about financial economics. It's also why it's reassuring when retirement guidance (even when derived from the data) can be mapped back to a defendable position within financial economics. In other words, financial economics can't provide complete answers yet, but we should still pay attention, gleaning what we can from what it does well. Before looking more at financial economics, it's helpful to first consider the landscape of investing during retirement.

THE LANDSCAPE

During the accumulating years preceding retirement, especially early on, time is greatly on the side of the investor's portfolio. The long-term compounding of investment returns provides powerful fuel for portfolio growth. When ill markets are significantly down, holding fast eventually provides the cure. With proper diversification and enough time, good market performance follows the bad. The ability to wait through bear markets and global crises is the great simplifier for the long-term investor saving for retirement.

In retirement with periodic withdrawals, we can no longer fully depend on compound investment growth or the restoration of our portfolio value from market recoveries. The underlying characteristics are still at play, but not with enough power to eliminate the additional risk from withdrawals. Withdrawals can erode portfolio value during down markets. When depressed stocks are sold to support withdrawals, losses are permanently locked in, even during normal market cycles. Said another way, a market recovery cannot return value to assets that had to be sold at reduced prices to fund living expenses. Sells at depressed prices increase the odds of running out of money and necessitate a defensive posture for making withdrawals.

The right asset allocation combined with careful management of the overall portfolio (explored in depth later) can provide a buffer to selling at depressed prices to support withdrawals, adding time for losses to recover before being locked in though sells. Still, there is a limit for how long poor performance in retirement can be handled without adverse retirement effects — 10 to 15 years may be around the maximum. In contrast, during the accumulating years, 20 to 30 years of poor performance might be handled with no ill effect on starting retirement.

Another distinction stems from starting with a lump sum under varying market conditions. Investing during the accumulating years is typically based on dollar-cost-averaging over many years, but retirement kicks off under specific market conditions managing a lump sum. The initial market valuation of the shares held at the start of retirement can significantly affect the expected rate of safe withdrawals. When valuations are attractive (i.e., stocks are cheap), then the outlook for a high income rate is excellent. When valuations are unattractive (i.e., stocks are expensive), then a low income rate is more probable. History shows the sustainable withdrawal rate varies depending on when stocks are cheap versus expensive, such as 8% annual withdrawals versus 4%. To some extent, the starting portfolio value will balance the expected rate (when stocks are expensive, the portfolio value is typically higher to help compensate), but this income-balancing effect is often incomplete and unpredictable. Ultimately, we can't reliably predict future markets, or time markets well, but modest adjustments based on market conditions can improve overall results.

Although the average lifespan is now in the upper seventies, the probability of a 65 year old living into their nineties is now 20% for males and 31% for females[4]. There is even an 18% chance that one member of a retiring couple will live beyond 95. These percentages make it prudent to plan for a long life, which comes with unexpected expenses and often a growing reliance on savings.

The longer we live, the more income we need and the less flexibility we have to obtain it. We need income at a minimum to cover essentials and unforeseeable expenses. Shortfalls may occur due to our personal affairs, our health, or our income sources. Before retirement, shortfalls could be alleviated by saving more or working longer. In retirement, although some retirees work part-time, we must assume this ability to earn income eventually disappears with waning health.

Restating the above, during the accumulating years, risks could be alleviated outside the investment portfolio (again, such as saving more or retiring later); however, in retirement, as life-options narrow with age, risk must be alleviated from within the portfolio — there must be a reliable income stream with no outside aid. This implies risk must be kept very low in retirement.

The adage "form follows function" applies here. During the accumulating years, what matters most is increasing portfolio value safely for retirement. In retirement, what matters most is generating income safely throughout retirement. Different aims require solutions of different forms. The result is investing during retirement requires more forethought and distinct strategies, extending well beyond what was required for the accumulating years.

With this in mind, let's return to financial economics for a moment.

THE REVOLUTION IN FINANCIAL ECONOMICS

"The last 15 years have seen a revolution in the way financial economists understand the investment world." This statement was made in 1999 by Professor John Cochrane, a leading financial economist from the University of Chicago, in his succinct appraisal of where the field stood.[5] The revolution Cochrane refers to is still in progress; however, a line can now be drawn between the old pre-revolutionary thinking in financial economics and the new post-revolutionary thinking. This division is important for retirement planning: the old thinking led to weak retirement plans while the new thinking opened the door to better performing and safer plans.

Below is an outline of the old thinking: how most financial economists understood the investment world before the revolutionary shift Cochrane describes.

a. In compliance with the capital asset pricing model (CAPM), all investors should operate from a two-fund world. One fund is composed of risk-free assets (e.g., treasury bills); the other fund is made up of risky assets (e.g., stocks), approximating the market portfolio (i.e., a portfolio proportionally invested across all the risky assets in the market).

b. The "market portfolio" is the optimal portfolio for risky assets — no additional risky asset can be added to the market portfolio to improve the return-to-risk ratio (as defined by the Sharpe Ratio). This means the market portfolio is the safest possible allocation of risky assets for all investors, including retirees.

c. An investor's risk aversion determines how little or much of the risky fund (the market portfolio) should be held. For example, an investor with a high risk aversion holds more of the risk-free bond fund; an investor with a low risk aversion holds more of the risky total-market fund.

d. Return should be increased only by raising the allocation to the risky fund (the market portfolio). To increase return above what 100% in the risky fund can deliver, money is borrowed at the risk-free rate and invested in the risky fund, essentially buying more total-market funds on margin.

e. Stock and bond market prices (from the risky market) are independent from earlier years, forming a sequence of random returns (i.e., a random walk). Likewise, stock and bond prices are unpredictable in the short and long-term. Stock market valuations tell us nothing about future market performance.

f. Periodic rebalancing maintains the correct portfolio, realigning the stock-bond ratio to match the investor's risk aversion.

Few investors today adhere to a pure form of the above thinking, but there is no doubt these old thoughts still have an influence on what "good" investing during retirement looks like. Exactly how this old thinking manifests in retirement plans is periodically explored throughout this book, but in short, the market portfolio with annual rebalancing performs poorly in retirement.

Below is an outline of the new thinking: how most financial economists now see the investment world *after* the revolutionary shift Cochrane references. This thinking is much more conducive to strong retirement planning. Most important here, it properly aligns to the long-term global market behavior observed in the data.

a. Multiple factors explain portfolio returns, meaning the two-fund portfolio (i.e., the risk-free fund and the total-market fund) is insufficient. There are many factors, although the best known are size, value, and momentum.

b. In a multi-factor world, retirees should operate in a multi-fund world (e.g., value stocks, small stocks) beyond the capital asset pricing model's recommendations. Likewise, "riskier" high-return funds may be on a retirement portfolio's efficient frontier (i.e., the optimal allocation for a targeted return rate).

c. Stock-market prices are not independent from earlier years. While prices remain unpredictable over the short term, they have a component of predictability over long periods. Market valuations do tell us something about the future—high valuations are on average followed by low stock returns and low valuations by high stock returns.

d. Since stock prices aren't totally random, there is no longer a single static asset allocation to cover all situations. For example, the best stock-bond ratio can shift over time. Likewise, periodic rebalancing is no longer a simple conclusion; when and how to rebalance the portfolio can depend on portfolio conditions and market conditions.

e. The time horizon for the investor does make a difference. Short-term and long-term investors usually shouldn't hold the same portfolio.

Although notable critics of the above new thinking can be found, relatively few economists now dispute these market characteristics in their most basic form. Nevertheless, a major dispute continues around the why, the extent, and the implications. The result is, surprisingly little relevant pragmatic advice has trickled out to retirees.

Fortunately there is no need to wait for a consensus around a new encompassing theory. Some of the most pragmatic results coming out of financial economics in the last 25 years stem from Fama and French's work on the value and size effect on stock returns. Notably, this work is essentially empirical without a strong theoretical foundation—it's based on the data. Recommendations for investing during retirement can progress in the same way, focusing on the data to update retirement strategies while the debates are being resolved and the theory catches up.

Keep in mind, investing during retirement isn't possible without following a set of strategies, whether old or new, whether implicit or explicit. Even doing only the minimal is a strategy. Living off your money requires decisions for each step of the process—these decisions form your strategies. The question is what strategies will you choose, and if you don't actively choose, then most likely the choice is being made for you based on tradition...doing what has "always" been done with at best mediocre results.

Every one of the strategies recommended in this book is shown to have a long-standing verifiable track record along with rational underpinnings. More specifically, the recommendations come from well-established market patterns found in the global data when applying the science of data, adhering to evidence-based research. In addition, wherever applicable, the recommendations are well-rooted in new economic thinking.

THE MODERN MECHANICS

Modern mechanics are simply the working pieces of the best practices for systemic withdrawals. (As a reminder, the term *systemic withdrawals* refers to the complete set of strategies for generating sustainable income from a portfolio of stock and bond funds.) The mechanics are defined with a pragmatic level of precision, including the hands-on steps retirees must follow to enact their retirement plan. These mechanics might be organized several ways, but here they are grouped into the following components:

1. An Income-Harvesting Strategy

2. A Variable-Withdrawal Strategy

3. A Baseline Market and Portfolio

4. A Retirement-Portfolio Metric

5. A Strategy for Setting the Initial Withdrawal Rate

As mentioned in the preface, these mechanics are new to most retirees, rarely put into practice and then only partially. Acceptance in investment circles of the better known aspects has been slow in part due to the lasting debates surrounding the new economic thinking, coupled with a lack of sufficient verification. The lesser or unknown aspects, like the retirement-portfolio metric or a Baseline Market, haven't before been adequately addressed for retirement planning.

Each component of the new mechanics is outlined below. The mechanics are generally independent from each other—each can be used without the others—although only together do they form a complete plan.

1. An Income-Harvesting Strategy

An income-harvesting strategy defines exactly how to manage the portfolio during retirement to minimize the impact of periodic withdrawals.

Every retirement investor has an income-harvesting strategy, most just don't realize it. Traditional rebalancing, the default, is one of the simplest of strategies. The problem is, traditional rebalancing doesn't perform well in retirement. It's not the worst strategy, but far from efficient.

There are a diverse set of existing income-harvesting strategies to choose from in the literature. All strategies, at least implicitly, define rebalancing rules (how and when to rebalance) and what assets are sold to fund withdrawals. Some affect the stock-bond ratio, others affect the broader asset allocation. Setting the withdrawal rate, though, is outside the domain of an income-harvesting strategy.

The new thinking in financial economics reflects the need for a smart income-harvesting strategy. When retirement performance is simulated using old market assumptions, the smart income-harvesting strategies have a much smaller advantage over annual rebalancing (although still an advantage). In contrast, when performance is simulated using new market assumptions, the advantages of smart income-harvesting strategies are substantially boosted. More importantly, this boost from smart harvesting consistently shows up in real historical data, outperforming all forms of traditional rebalancing.

Chapter 3 covers income-harvesting strategies in depth.

2. A Variable-Withdrawal Strategy

A variable-withdrawal strategy determines how much can be withdrawn annually. It can increase withdrawals during strong markets and lower withdrawals during poor markets. Ideally, the portfolio never runs out of money, with rates lowered as much as necessary to handle market shortfalls.

Despite the flexibility of variable-withdrawal strategies, a fixed, inflation-adjusted withdrawal rate is the de facto standard within the industry and the retirement literature: the same inflation-adjusted amount is withdrawn every year. Certainly, a fixed rate is easier to discuss, compare, and plan with, but it matches neither retirees' true spending patterns nor the reality of changing market conditions. Fixed withdrawals force a low rate to handle the worst possible case, almost always resulting in income lower than necessary (with a large portion of assets left untouched throughout retirement). More dramatic, fixed withdrawals will run out of money during an unforeseeably poor market—a retiree would almost certainly compensate if required by lowering the rate, but a fixed-rate strategy ignores the possibility and provides no guidance for effectively doing so.

The best known variable-withdrawal strategies vary significantly, but overall their performance is strong. Every strategy has its own metric to monitor the retirement state and adapt accordingly. A higher withdrawal rate is specified when there are signs the portfolio is strong, and a lower withdrawal rate when there are signs the portfolio is weak. Often, floor and ceiling amounts are used to set boundaries on the annual amount withdrawn. While these strategies don't directly depend on the new thinking in financial economics, they must be verified with the real market data (embodying the new thinking).

Chapter 4 covers variable-withdrawal strategies in depth.

3. A Retirement Portfolio Metric: The Harvesting Ratio

Post-revolutionary thinking in financial economics indicates retirees are not limited to the market portfolio, but how can a retiree know what asset allocation works well in retirement?

There are obstacles to looking in the literature to find the right portfolio for retirement. First, who are you going to believe? Expert advice is very diverse. Much of it's subjective, not meeting the standard for evidence-based guidance, again making the right answers difficult to discern from the wrong ones. Also, the overwhelming majority of portfolio advice revolves around the accumulation phase of investing, with relatively little distinction made for investing during retirement.

What the new mechanics contribute is help in identifying strong retirement portfolios. The Harvesting Ratio, a new portfolio metric, measures the suitability of a portfolio to support a specific withdrawal rate. The higher a portfolio's Harvesting Ratio for a specified withdrawal rate, the more likely the portfolio will be successful in retirement.

The Harvesting Ratio works by measuring the correct balance between portfolio return and volatility necessary to support a specific withdrawal rate. While this simple relationship might not appear sufficient, it is. Matching the portfolio allocation to retirement withdrawals substantially pays off in safety and income.

The evidence is carefully reviewed in Chapter 5, showing the Harvesting Ratio as a reliable metric for comparing retirement portfolios. Chapter 8 applies the Harvesting Ratio to a well-known set of "Lazy Portfolios", bringing to light the strong (as well as weak) portfolios for retirement. These same results are then used to create a new set of specific portfolio recommendations for retirement.

The Harvesting Ratio is not intended to supplant the fundamentals of asset allocation (all retirement portfolios should first be composed of a well-diversified mix of low-cost funds of high-quality assets), but it aids asset selection by removing most of the arbitrary decision-making from the process.

4. A Baseline Market and Portfolio

Virtually all results from retirement research are either relative, or only valid within a specific market context. This is acceptable for testing and comparing strategies, but at some point a retiree wants to know the income and risk levels to expect for his or her own retirement. A baseline market and a baseline portfolio are defined in the new mechanics to provide realistic estimates of income and risk for retirement planning.

A baseline market acts as a proxy for future markets. To be effective, it must have certain characteristics: it must be globally oriented; it must support a variety of asset classes for proper diversification; it must include a sufficiently long history encompassing the best and worst market periods. It should also be based on real market data, insuring it conforms to the new thinking in financial markets. Unfortunately, no existing dataset meets these criteria and we don't know how to properly model markets.

The solution taken is to fabricate a baseline market by starting with the best real data available and scaling it to align with long-term global stock and bond returns. The process and rationale for this are fully explained later, but for now accept the resulting baseline market will satisfy the criteria, providing an appropriate proxy for future markets.

A baseline portfolio is also needed, representing an average retiree's portfolio when following best practices. A simple but effective baseline portfolio can be composed using the Harvesting Ratio. The result is a portfolio representative of what most retirees should use for their retirement portfolio.

The combination of a baseline market with a baseline portfolio provides realistic estimates of the performance and risk retirees can expect using a globally diversified portfolio. There is no crystal ball, but prudently using these baselines fills an existing gap in retirement planning.

Chapter 6 covers the Baseline Market and Baseline Portfolio.

5. A Strategy for Setting the Initial Withdrawal Rate

Most variable-withdrawal strategies must be seeded with an initial rate, or baseline rate, which affects how well the strategy performs. Withdrawals typically revolve around this initial rate, moving above it during good times and below it during bad times. When the initial rate is properly set, the demands on the variable-withdrawal strategy are lowered and the results better.

The new thinking in financial economics acknowledges that long-term stock prices have an element of predictability. The problem is the data shows a strong reliance on market predictions is risky; however, the data also shows long-term predictions can be *moderately* applied to improve the selection of the initial withdrawal rate.

This aspect of the new mechanics deploys a moderate but effective approach by modestly tilting the initial withdrawal rate based on long-term market predictions. The result is much better than sailing blind, with a worthwhile boost in both performance and risk avoidance.

Chapter 9 covers the complete rationale and steps for seeding the initial withdrawal rate using market valuations.

§

These five components of the modern mechanics will form a complete solution to the systemic withdrawals problem. Their exact makeup is determined in later chapters by what reliably works and what is essential, filtering out lots of invalid or extraneous investment trends, opinions, and techniques. The final result is an updated set of best practices for systemic withdrawals.

THE POINT

Investing during retirement is different, requiring new strategies. Financial economics alone doesn't provide enough guidance, but it's evolving and should still be considered. The data is now our best guide. Following the data, adhering to evidence-based research, this book defines a new set of best practices. Compared to traditional approaches, these best practices lower risk while increasing income.

CHAPTER 2 GUIDE

This chapter defines risk during retirement, how it's estimated, how it's broken down, and how it's applied. The factors causing risk are also identified.

There is latitude in how well the reader should understand this chapter before moving forward. While it's essential from the investigative perspective (i.e., what, why, how), much less is essential for carrying out an individual plan. Less interested readers may skim the chapter for highlights, although a careful reading is worthwhile.

This chapter completes the foundation, with the rest of the book more directly oriented toward defining a retirement plan.

Some investors are entangled in their study of risk whereas the purpose of studying risk is to keep investors out of entanglements.

WALTER E. GOH

UNDERSTANDING RISK DURING RETIREMENT

RISK HAS A STRONG TENDENCY to stay opaque. It's one of those rare topics we can easily grasp intuitively, but quickly becomes obscure when trying to comprehend at a deeper level. To make matters worse, the financial media bombards retirees with risk-related assertions that are ill-suited for retirement planning.

There are many well-studied discussions of risk in the literature, coming from many perspectives. While risk discussions can be engaging and thought-provoking, they can also be distracting and difficult to apply. Each outlook depends on perspective, goals, and starting assumptions. To avoid becoming bogged down, it's important here to methodically refine what is known about the risk of investing during retirement, which is a lot, and then focus on applying it.

An appropriate starting place is to define exactly what investing risk means during retirement. Or more specifically, what risk means within the context of systemic withdrawals.

DEFINING THE RISK

Generally, risk is defined as exposure to danger, but in the context of investing, risk is usually defined by economists as exposure to loss. This exposure to loss is measured as the volatility in an asset's return. (Volatility resulting in a negative return is a loss, hence the equating of investment risk to volatility.)

Volatility as it's typically measured is oriented to short-term market happenings and a type of investing style no retiree should depend on. Investing during retirement extends decades into the future, where the short-term spikes and troughs gauged by volatility aren't always relevant. In retirement, it's best to put aside discussions on what might happen to portfolio value. It's not the loss of portfolio value retirees should care most about; it's the loss of retirement income. This distinction between value and income is important because tests show portfolio values often rise and fall (incur paper gains and losses) with no effect on retirement income.

The real risk in retirement is insufficient income to cover living expenses, with the extreme case being running out of money. However, insufficient income is cumbersome to meaningfully estimate — it's less intuitive and, depending on how it's defined, might vary between retirees. The extreme case, the probability of running out of money, turns out to be the best working definition for risk during retirement. It's easy to understand and can be precisely estimated (with caveats). Also, the risk of running out of money generally correlates well with the risk of insufficient income, making the simpler definition adequate for retirement planning.

This risk of running out of money is determined by several factors. For example, the withdrawal rate is a fundamental factor. Without withdrawals there is virtually no risk (the portfolio cannot run out of money). Increasing withdrawals always increases risk; lowering withdrawals always lowers risk. Likewise, retirement length is another fundamental factor for similar reasons. This is why the retirement literature contains many statements like "there is a 90% chance of retirement success (i.e., the probability of not running of money) for a 4% withdrawal rate for 30 years." Still, other factors affect risk, as the next section will show.

In summary, a simplified pragmatic definition for risk is the probability of running out of money before the end of retirement. A complete breakdown of what drives risk is covered in the next few sections. The discussion afterward turns to measuring risk, and finally to effectively monitoring and controlling risk.

BREAKING DOWN RISK

Risk can be broken down to into different facets and the factors that determine it. The aim of this breakdown is to align with retirement planning, identifying those areas essential to specific decision points. What is defined is conceptual; however, this is not an academic exercise. Retirement planning depends on an exploration of the underlying risk.

Figure 1 shows a breakdown of the elements of risk during retirement using systemic withdrawals. This breakdown is the focus of the rest of the chapter, but to start off, a quick summary is given below.

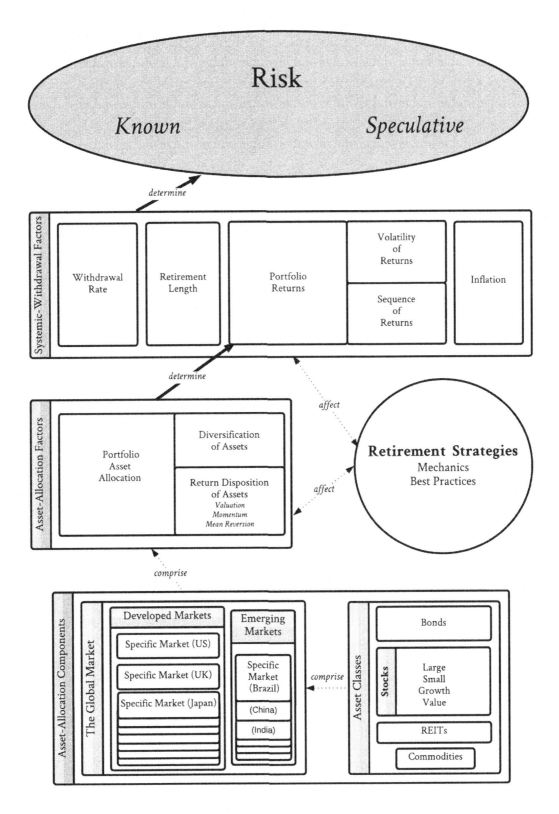

FIGURE 1

*Risk during retirement using systemic-withdrawals, including the
factors, components, and strategies that affect it.*

There are two facets to systemic-withdrawal risk: known risk and speculative risk. Known risk is what retirees commonly face. It's based on the historical data, measurable, well understood, and at the center of retirement planning. In contrast, speculative risk corresponds to the possibility of markets worse than we've ever seen. It's rare and hopefully will never be encountered. It's unmeasurable, ill understood, and can only be planned for in an indirect manner.

Moving down a level, six interrelated factors drive all retirement risk: the withdrawal rate, the retirement length, portfolio returns, return volatility, the sequence of returns, and inflation. The factors are not equal in their importance — their potency in affecting risk varies as well as their ability to be manipulated.

One more level down, three asset allocation factors also have a major effect on retirement risk, but only indirectly by affecting the three return factors. The pragmatic reality at this level is a retiree's global asset allocation drives portfolio returns, volatility of returns, and the sequence of returns, which in turn partially drive retirement risk.

Notice in the same diagram how retirement strategies affect and are affected by the direct and indirect factors of retirement risk. Conceptually, the retirement strategies of the new mechanics are a set of rules for monitoring and manipulating the risk factors (in varying degrees), all with the aim of generating a sufficient amount of income for the least risk. The same can be said of investing during retirement as a whole — it's about the proper monitoring and manipulation of the risk factors affecting income.

Known and Speculative Risk

As mentioned earlier, all retirement risk can be subdivided into two facets: known risk and speculative risk. Known retirement risk encapsulates everything we know from the historical market data. Conversely, speculative retirement risk is outside the boundaries of what has been seen in market history and thus can only be discussed in speculative terms.

From another perspective, speculative risk can be said to pick up where known risk leaves off. Consider this case: in the US market the known risk of failure for a 3% withdrawal rate is 0% — there is no instance of failure anywhere in the US data for such a low withdrawal rate. Does this mean it's impossible to run out of money withdrawing 3% annually? Yes, if based on known risk within the US, but not based on speculative risk, where the possibility of a failure always exists. Speculative risk extends indefinitely beyond what has been experienced in the past, although we can say the more extreme the case, the lower the risk (i.e., speculative risk for a 1% withdrawal rate has to be lower than for a 2% withdrawal rate, even though neither is measurable). The logical existence of this speculative risk is very clear: virtually anything can happen in the future, but always keep in mind it's truly speculative without a clear foundation for estimating or planning.

There are important but subtle reasons for distinguishing known risk from speculative risk. The line separating what we know about markets (known risk) from what we don't know (speculative risk) is too often blurred in discussions. This blurring can cause risk to be treated as if it has no distinct characteristics, leading some to conclude there is very little market behavior we can plan on, with the extreme opinion being markets are too risky for retirement. With well over 100 years of global market data, speculative risk becomes an anomaly that should not obscure what is known about the markets. Speculative risk is indeed speculative and should be classified as such. Quite distinctly, known risk can be methodically measured, based on our substantial historical record. Planning can be based on it.

This concept of speculative risk parallels the following thoughts on uncertainty made by University of Chicago economist Frank Knight in his 1921 book *Risk, Uncertainty, and Profit*:

> Uncertainty must be taken in a sense radically distinct from the familiar notion of Risk, from which it has never been properly separated. [...] The essential fact is that 'risk' means in some cases a quantity susceptible of measurement, while at other times it's something distinctly not of this character. [...] It will appear that a measurable uncertainty, or 'risk' proper, as we shall use the term, is so far different from an unmeasurable one that it's not in effect an uncertainty at all.

Similar to Knight's thoughts above, known risk is the measureable uncertainty or "risk" proper in retirement. Compared to speculative risk, known risk provides a level of understanding that is not uncertain at all, with clear boundaries drawn by historical markets. Known risk forms the basis for most of the retirement planning in this book. In contrast, speculative risk is the unmeasurable uncertainly in retirement, and as such is difficult to plan for except generally. Speculative risk is also the source of most disagreements surrounding retirement risk, and as such is better separated—we can only speculate on its future magnitude and frequency.

Nevertheless, speculative risk as defined must be small—the risk's existence starts beyond the market events of the last 100 years, spanning depressions, recessions, world wars, market bubbles, and high inflation. Known risk is bad enough and big enough to encompass all but the most extreme cases the future can throw at our retirements. Still, speculative risk is real and will periodically be given separate attention, distinct from the methodical focus best applied to known risk.

Risk going forward generally refers to the known risk of systemic withdrawals.

The Risk Factors

Distinguishing a risk factor from risk itself is the starting point for learning how to effectively control risk.

Figure 1 shows that six direct factors and three indirect factors determine retirement risk. Some of these factors can only be observed or monitored, while others can be manipulated to our advantage, lowering retirement risk. Most factors have established metrics for measurement, but a few do not. Some factors are distinct, affecting risk on their own, and some act in combination. Some only have meaning in terms of others.

The analysis of risk factors, which will be ongoing throughout this book, is not meant to be complete, but sufficient enough to serve the needs of retirement planning.*

The Direct Factors

The six direct factors of risk are described below, each in its most common form.

1. **Withdrawal Rate**

   The withdrawal rate refers to the percentage of the portfolio periodically pulled out for income. Typically, the withdrawal is made annually. For example, a 4.2% annual withdrawal rate for a $500,000 portfolio is $21,000.

   The withdrawal rate is the single most important factor of retirement risk. A low rate can push risk down to zero and a high rate can push it up to 100%. This is the only direct factor a retiree may claim to completely control. For this reason, a variable-withdrawal strategy plays a crucial role within a strong retirement plan, dynamically keeping risk in check by adjusting the withdrawal rate.

---

* As defined and broken down, retirement risk could be calculated as a single formula based on the six direct factors of retirement risk. While this approach would be interesting and insightful, the data is not readily available, plus it doesn't serve the needs of investing during retirement as well as historical simulations. However, the Harvesting Ratio in Chapter 5 does define a single formula with four factors to aid asset allocation, especially where the historical data is insufficient.

2. **Retirement Length**

Retirement length is the number of years a retiree lives in retirement. For a couple (e.g., husband and wife) the longer-living person determines the length of retirement. As the length increases, retirement risk increases, because sustainable withdrawals must last longer. Generally, retirement length is a secondary factor of retirement risk, in part because the total length is fixed for planning and in part because its effect on risk doesn't change substantially between longer retirement plans.

Over 30 years, the risk stemming from the retirement length flattens out. For example, where a 30-year retirement can support a 4.3% sustainable withdrawal rate, a 40-year retirement supports 4.0%—a 7% decrease in sustainable income for a 33% increase in retirement length. Somewhere above 45 years, the effect on known risk becomes completely flat (e.g., a 45 year, 50 year, and 55 year retirement plan all support a 3.8% sustainable withdrawal rate).

Occasionally, the length of retirement has an indirect impact on retirement planning. For example, some income-harvesting and variable-withdrawal strategies take into account the years remaining in retirement; for these strategies the retirement length has a substantial indirect effect on annual income later in life. Also, when using guaranteed income, outside of systemic withdrawals, the impact of planning for a 30-year versus a 40-year retirement is much larger.

The retiree's part concerning the retirement length is relatively simple: the retirement length is picked once at the start of retirement roughly based on the maximum remaining life expectancy, with planning then proceeding accordingly.

3. **Portfolio Returns**

Portfolio returns correspond to the total return of all assets in the systemic-withdrawal portfolio. Portfolio returns make up the second most important factor of retirement risk, behind the withdrawal rate. Low portfolio returns increase retirement risk; high portfolio returns decrease retirement risk.

The retiree has no direct control over returns, but a substantial amount of indirect control through asset allocation (as shown in Chapter 5). Referring back to Figure 1, returns and its related factors are determined by the three indirect factors of asset allocation. Also, income-harvesting strategies affect asset allocation in order to increase portfolio return.

Return can be measured in different forms. When using historical datasets, return is in annual terms and nominal (i.e., no inflation adjustment). This simple form is most often used discussing return values. It's also the form commonly used to measure volatility (the next factor). Portfolio return is commonly stated as an average (i.e., arithmetic mean), such as the 10-year average, a 30-year average, or a complete dataset average. Although less common and therefore less practical, the return metric with the highest direct correlation to retirement risk is the annualized real return (the geometric mean after inflation).

The effects of asset allocation on return and how it maps to retirement risk is discussed in depth in Chapter 5's coverage of the Harvesting Ratio.

4. **Volatility of Returns**

The volatility of returns refers to the variance of the portfolio returns (the previous factor). Volatility is typically measured as the standard deviation using nominal annual portfolio returns over a long time period, like 20 years or more. No doubt, higher volatility generally increases retirement risk; however, volatility is not one of the dominant factors of retirement risk.

Consider the following two sets of retirement returns:

Annual Returns for Retirement 1: 10% 10% 10% 10%...10% 10% 10% 10%
Annual Returns for Retirement 2: 20% 0% 20% 0%...20% 0% 20% 0% 20% 0%

The average annual return for both cases above is identical at 10%, but the volatility for the first case is zero, and 10% for the second case. Nevertheless, both cases have the exact same sustainable withdrawal when using an appropriate income-harvesting strategy.

Also, one of the most volatile periods in the US market began in 1929 at the start of the Great Depression; however, a 30-year retirement starting in 1929 didn't do too poorly, with a sustainable rate of 4.6% using annual rebalancing.

Short-term volatility has little effect on retirement risk, especially using a smart income-harvesting strategy. Nevertheless, a significant amount of long-term volatility will always increase retirement risk, just not by as much as returns.

Like with returns, the retiree has no direct control over volatility, but a substantial amount of indirect control through asset allocation. These two factors share the same relationship to the three factors of asset allocation.

It's also well-known that return and volatility are coupled: the more return, the higher the volatility. Less known is the right mix of portfolio return and volatility, to reduce retirement risk. Again, this is covered in depth in Chapter 5's coverage of the Harvesting Ratio.

For now, keep in mind that retirees often pay too much attention to volatility.

5. **Sequence of Returns**

The sequence of returns factor is based on the order in which returns occur during retirement. Generally, lower returns early in retirement have more risk than lower returns later in retirement. To be clear, the same set of returns with identical levels of volatility can have a different level of risk due only to the sequence of returns. The following two sets of retirement returns illustrate the point well.

Annual Returns for Retirement 1: 1% 2% 3% 4% 5%...26% 27% 28% 29% 30%
Annual Returns for Retirement 2: 30% 29% 28% 27% 26%...5%, 4%, 3%, 2%, 1%

The return and volatility are identical, but the first retirement period sustains a withdrawal rate of 7.7%, while the second a withdrawal rate of 9%, only because of the difference in the sequence of returns.

The sequence of returns is the only direct factor of risk that has no established metric, which is unfortunate since its effects are difficult to discern by looking at a series of return numbers, especially with all the other risk factors at play.

Although this factor is defined in terms of portfolio returns, sequencing effects may come from inflation too. Ultimately, it's the sequence of the real return that matters. It doesn't matter if poor real returns are due to low nominal returns or high inflation.

Although the sequence of returns is emphasized for its negative effects, a good sequence of returns (lowering retirement risk) is just as probable as a poor sequence of returns (raising retirement risk).

To some degree, the sequence of returns is a random event depending on short-term market happenings; however the sequence of returns can be partially affected by asset allocation, since high volatility has more potential for a poor sequence of returns. It's notable in the historical data that a poor sequence of returns coupled with high volatility doesn't overpower the advantages of high returns, but it comes close to nullifying the advantages. This is in part due to the ability of an efficient income-harvesting strategy.

Based on US data back to 1928, the sequence of returns had a noticeably negative affect on retirement risk in less than 10% of the retirement periods, but in none of these periods did the sequence of returns dominate retirement results. Still, even without dominating, a poor sequence can contribute to distorted retirement results. The worst retirement periods in US history, starting in the late 1960s, were partly due to poor sequencing.

The sequence of returns can only be classified as a secondary factor of return risk. It can't be controlled, and its effects are generally limited, although in rare cases it has the potential to distort retirement results for better or worse. For planning purposes, it demands no special attention, given best practices handle it.

6. **Inflation**

Inflation determines the purchasing power of retirement income. As inflation increases, the purchase power decreases, requiring a higher withdrawal rate to cover the same amount of expenses. Depending on perspective, inflation can erode portfolio value or it can inflate the withdrawal rate (to maintain equivalent value), but the outcome is identical. This makes inflation equivalent to the withdrawal rate in affecting retirement risk; however it remains a secondary factor of retirement risk in terms of planning.

There are three reasons inflation requires little direct focus when planning for systemic withdrawals. First, a retiree has no direct control over the inflation rate, except perhaps to a small degree through discretional spending. Second, its effects are automatically accounted for by inflation-adjusting the withdrawal rate. Third, stocks as an essential component of systemic withdrawals provide an excellent long-term hedge against inflation. The result is that a systemic withdrawal plan naturally balances out and incorporates the worst effects of inflation with no special attention from the retiree. (In contrast, inflation is a dominant factor affecting guaranteed-income planning.)

Inflation is typically measured by annual changes in the US Consumer Price Index (CPI)*, or its equivalent outside the US.

Summarizing, the withdrawal rate and portfolio returns are the two dominant factors for retirement planning. The withdrawal rate can be fully controlled, and returns are partially controlled indirectly through asset allocation. Volatility and sequence of returns are less important due to their smaller impact, but they are still significant and partially controlled indirectly through asset allocation. Retirement length is usually set once at the beginning of retirement to its maximum value, and then treated as a constant with little attention afterward. Inflation can have a potent effect, but it's typically handled indirectly through annual income adjustments plus hedged by stock returns.

The Indirect Factors

Three asset-allocation factors indirectly affect portfolio returns, volatility of returns, and sequencing of returns. As such, they become the indirect factors of retirement risk and important levers for controlling it. Retirees for the most part are very familiar with the asset-allocation factors, although they might not think of them of in such terms. They are described below.

1. **The Portfolio Asset Allocation**

The portfolio asset allocation determines exactly what assets make up the portfolio and in what proportion. Asset allocation has a dominant effect on portfolio returns. It's also completely under the control of the retiree. This makes it a key factor, albeit an indirect one, for controlling retirement risk. As such, a significant portion of this book focuses on controlling the asset allocation to reduce retirement risk.

---

* More specifically, Consumer Price Index-All Urban Consumers (CPI-U) is used.

2. **The Diversification of Asset Allocation**

Diversification simply means that the asset allocation is partitioned across multiple markets and asset classes. There are no well-established metrics for measuring or evaluating retirement diversification, but it's relatively simple to adjust for. Diversification should span a significant number of developed markets and emerging markets. It should also span a significant number of asset classes. The details are covered thoroughly under portfolio construction in Chapter 8.

3. **The Return Disposition of Asset Allocation**

Return disposition is the state of the market that affects future returns. It runs hand in hand with return predictability. With a positive disposition, a higher than average portfolio return is more likely; with a negative disposition, a lower than average portfolio return is more likely. It directly depends on the specific asset allocation. It can be a potent factor of return risk; nevertheless, it's difficult to efficiently leverage.

Mean reversion, market valuations, and momentum are all forms of return disposition. Financial economists have yet to agree on the extent and reliability of these forms of return disposition, only their existence to some degree. At any particular moment, the market can be positively or negatively predisposed. Return disposition pulls market behavior back from extreme positions in either direction.

Some forms of return disposition, such as market valuations, have accepted metrics and will be discussed later, but generally there is no well-established metric for measuring return disposition.

Return disposition cannot be controlled for a given asset allocation, only monitored. It can however be indirectly controlled through the makeup of the asset allocation. This indirect control and monitoring enables it to be leveraged, although without precision. Because it's imprecise, return disposition in many ways should be ignored in retirement, but with proper care it can be considered in certain contexts (topics covered in Chapters 9 and 11).

Figure 1 also shows the components which comprise the asset allocation. As already mentioned, these components include many markets (e.g., developed and emerging) and many asset classes. There are index funds for every component shown, whether by market or asset class or both. The proportions of these components and how they operate as a whole are more important than the individual components. Over half of the retirement problem is solved if a retiree knows how to allocate and maintain assets in the proper portions (indirectly balancing return with volatility to minimize risk).

MEASURING THE RISK

Measuring risk is at the heart of retirement planning. It means estimating the probability of running out of money before the end of retirement. Measuring risk enables the direct comparison of retirement strategies. For example, if strategy A has less retirement risk than strategy B for a specific amount of income, then it's a better retirement strategy (all other things being equal). Measuring risk supports the definition of a set of best practices across the spectrum of retirement mechanics. Then, with best practices in place, measuring risk optimizes final planning—ultimately a retiree wants to know how much income to expect for a minimum amount of risk, given selected parameters.

Risk measurements are well suited to computer simulation. There are generally two simulation approaches: backtesting simulations and Monte Carlo simulations, with bootstrapping simulations providing a composite third approach (see sidebars for each). Backtesting simulations fully rely on historical market data; Monte Carlo simulations randomly create data using by modeling markets; bootstrapping randomly resamples the historical data to create new data.

Backtesting is the primary method of simulation used in this book, and the focus here, because it's based on real market data. Jim Otar in his book *Unveiling the Retirement Myth*[6] makes this point well: "A man-made simulator is still a man-made simulator. It's still not the real thing. Do yourself a favor; use the actual history." General Monte Carlo techniques are not used because the underlying models to create the data are either not sophisticated enough or have no agreed standards for modeling markets in a realistic way. However, bootstrapping is used occasionally when needing to broaden the results past what backtesting can provide.

In a nutshell, backtesting uses *past* retirements to provide a risk estimate for the future. Here's the general rationale: if a percentage (e.g., 5%) of past retirements failed over the last 100 years for a given portfolio, withdrawal rate, and market (e.g., the US), then the same percentage can be used as an estimate for future failures with the same portfolio, withdrawal rate, and market.

Backtesting is sometimes criticized or undervalued because it can be used improperly (discussed later as a data-mining bias). The problem stems from drawing too many conclusions from too little data (against the norms of evidence-based research). Today the best datasets usually contain from 80 to 140 years of data for their specific markets, with varying levels of detail. More data would be ideal, but what's in hand is sufficient (for comparing risk) because backtesting can be applied to *multiple* independent datasets, cross-validating the results. Fortunately, in the past 20 years the number of historical datasets has greatly increased, expanding beyond US markets into many international markets.

Figure 2 shows backtesting results using different withdrawal rates within the US market. For example, the risk estimate for a 4.5% inflation-adjusted withdrawal rate (e.g., $45,000 the first year for a $1 million portfolio) is a 20% probability of failure (i.e., running out of money), or the equivalent 80% probability of success (having money left over). To arrive at this estimate, backtesting found 11 of the 53 retirement periods failed by running out of money prematurely and 42 succeeded. Every risk measurement is always within the context of a specific set of strategies and parameters. This time, it's annual rebalancing with a 60% stock percentage and a fixed inflation-adjusted withdrawal rate. Note this single backtesting estimate of retirement risk is not enough to draw conclusions from, but when coupled with other risk estimates, it becomes part of a complete answer.

Withdrawal Rate	Risk Estimate (Positive Form): Percentage of Backtesting Successes	Risk Estimate (Negitive Form): Percentage of Backtesting Failures
3.0%	100%	0%
3.5%	100%	0%
4.0%	93%	7%
4.5%	80%	20%
5.0%	63%	37%
5.5%	52%	48%
6.0%	39%	61%
6.5%	32%	69%
7.0%	20%	80%

FIGURE 2

Backtesting risk estimates for 53 30-year retirement periods
spanning from 1928 through 2010 in the US market.

Distinct from measuring probability, another form for measuring risk is the Maximum Sustainable Withdrawal Rate (MSWR). MSWR represents the highest inflation-adjusted fixed withdrawal rate that can be used without running out of money during a retirement period. For example, if backtesting a specific 30-year retirement period fails (i.e., runs out of money) with a 4.4% withdrawal rate, but succeeds with a 4.3% withdrawal rate, then the MSWR is 4.3%.

A more enhanced form of MSWR combines multiple measurements across all the retirement periods in a dataset. For example, MSWR-100% is the MSWR across all the retirement periods, where 100% of the backtested retirement periods in the dataset are successful. Likewise, MSWR-80% is the MSWR across periods where at least 80% of the periods are successful.

Figure 3 graphs 54 MSWR values for 30-year retirements starting from 1928 to 1981 using the US dataset. For example, a retirement starting in 1930 supports a 5.1% MSWR, meaning a maximum of 5.1% (of the starting portfolio value with inflation adjustment) can be withdrawn each year of retirement (from 1930 to 1959) without running out of money. A retirement starting in 1949 supports a 7.5% MSWR, meaning a maximum of 7.5% can be withdrawn each year of retirement (from 1949 to 1978) without running out of money.

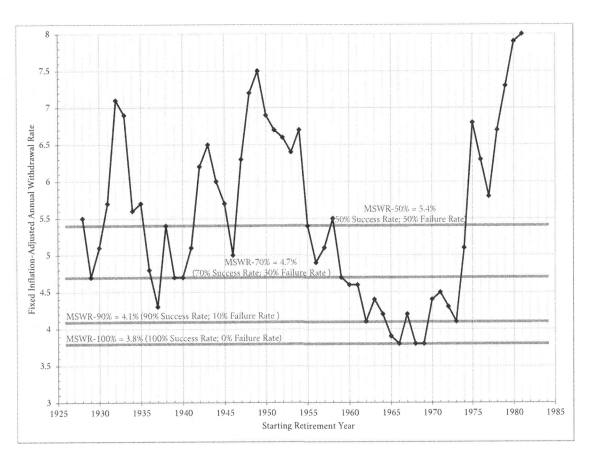

FIGURE 3

*Maximum Sustainable Withdrawal Rates for the US Market. Annual rebalancing
is used for a portfolio with 55% in a total-market stock fund and 45% in an
intermediate-treasury bond fund. The retirement length is 30 years.*

Figure 3 also shows the enhanced form of MSWR, with measurements spanning the complete dataset. For example, MSWR-100% equals 3.8% because all the retirement periods (i.e., 100%) ranging from 1928 to 1981 have a MSWR of at least 3.8%. MSWR-90% equals 4.1%, because 90% of the retirement periods have a MSWR of at least 4.1%. MSWR-70% equals 4.7%. MSWR-50%, representing half the backtested retirements, equals 5.4%. This nomenclature is used throughout the book.

Few conclusions, based on one set of parameters for a single dataset, can be drawn from any of these numbers yet. Just understanding how the risk estimates are made, their intent, and their nomenclature is the aim for now.

Backtesting Simulation

Backtesting shows exactly how a strategy performs when set in the past. The historical market data, primarily annual returns from stock and bond indexes, drive backtesting by encapsulating the market behaviors most cared about. While some of these behaviors are reasonably well understood, others are not, giving backtesting the great advantage of side-stepping the need to model that which is not well understood, instead using the real data factors in everything (e.g., asset allocation, return disposition, sequence of returns, volatility, inflation).

Backtesting works as if the retiree had gone back in time to start retirement in a specific year, such as 1928. Each year of the retirement thereafter (e.g., 1929, 1930, 1931, etc.) is based on the corresponding historical data. The portfolio's value grows and shrinks according to the historical returns as annual withdrawals are simulated. If the portfolio value lasts through the complete retirement period (i.e., the money does not run out), then the test is marked as "successful" for the year the retirement began in; if the portfolio value drops to zero before the end of retirement period, then the test is marked as "failed".

After the completion of one retirement period, the starting year is bumped up by one (e.g., 1928 to 1929) and the complete sequence is restarted for the new period with the result again recorded as either a success or failure. This continues for every retirement period up to the one ending at the last year of the dataset (e.g., 2010). The percentage of successful retirements across all the retirement periods measures the known risk.

For example, using historical data from 1928 through 2010, the following 53 retirement periods can be backtested assuming a 30-year retirement, with the final pass-fail statistics forming the risk measurement.

Period 1: 30-Year Retirement from 1928-1957
Period 2: 30-Year Retirement from 1929–1958
Period 3: 30-Year Retirement from 1930-1959

. . .

Period 51: 30-Year Retirement from 1979–2008
Period 52: 30-Year Retirement from 1980–2009
Period 53: 30-Year Retirement from 1981–2010

As just illustrated above, the historical data from 1928 to 2010 supports 53 30-year test periods starting with the 1928-1957 period and ending with the 1981-2010 period. If every one of the test cycles completed without running out of money, then the success rate is 100%. If 10 of the cycles failed, leaving 43 successful, the success rate is 81% (i.e., 43/53). If half the cycles failed, the success rate would be 50%. This final measure provides a quantitative metric for evaluating and comparing the performance of investment strategies.

Monte Carlo Simulation

An alternate approach to estimating risk is using a Monte Carlo simulation. A Monte Carlo simulation uses randomization to generate an unlimited amount of test data according to the model of choice as defined by the researcher. Although this technique is a valuable tool for certain classes of problems, for retirement it's only as good as the underlying model of the markets. Building a complete model of the market is problematic, given there are gaps in our understanding of how markets function.

A simple model might include only inflation and return data within the confines of historical averages and volatility. A more advanced model might include correlation between assets. An even more advanced model may include mean reversion and momentum. How far to go is up to the researcher, but this ad hoc nature of Monte Carlo modeling makes it hard for others to confirm or interpret the results of all but the simplest models.

Until a standardized model for markets is defined and agreed on, general Monte Carlo simulations are not attractive for estimating retirement risk.

Bootstrapping Simulation

There is one limited but well-defined form of Monte Carlo simulation, bootstrapping, which randomly resamples the historical data. Bootstrapping has a few advantages: its results are repeatable, it maintains the correlation between assets, and it produces an almost unlimited amount of data through resampling. Unfortunately, bootstrapping also strips out all forms of return disposition (i.e., autocorrelation) and produces return and volatility characteristics far beyond the historical market boundaries. Still, as long as its shortfalls are considered, bootstrapping can add another dimension to testing retirement strategies.

A modified bootstrapping technique called simple-block bootstrapping helps to partially preserve return disposition while maintaining return and volatility characteristics. Instead of randomly resampling return data from the complete dataset, returns are instead randomly permutated within multi-year blocks (e.g., 5-year). For example, using SBBI data starting in 1928, the returns are randomly scrambled for years 1928-1932, then for years 1933-1937, and so on to generate a new unique set of market data while bounding the degree of reordering.

SPECIFIC MARKETS VERSUS THE GLOBAL MARKET

Before going further, a quick review is helpful. The concept of known (measurable) risk was introduced and distinguished from speculative (unmeasurable) risk. This known risk can be measured using backtesting. In addition, known risk is typically represented in one of two forms: 1) the measured probability of success (i.e., not running out of money) for a given withdrawal rate; or 2) the measured maximum sustainable withdrawal rate for a given success rate, such as MSWR-100% (the sustainable rate with 100% success) or MSWR-90% (the sustainable rate with 90% success).

What hasn't been emphasized yet is that known risk varies, depending on the specific dataset used for backtesting or the specific strategy being backtested. For example, MSWR-100% for a total-market portfolio with 60% stocks in the US using annual rebalancing is 3.7%, but the same in the UK is only 3.0%. Likewise, the same case using a smart income-harvesting strategy is 3.8% in the US and 3.7% in the UK. Again, the risk measured depends on the market and the strategy.

Measuring specific-market risks is important for testing and comparing strategies; however, global-market risk is also important. What ultimately matters most to retirees is their own retirement plan's performance. Assuming best practices, retirees should be investing globally, which implies the most realistic estimate of future retirement performance comes from measuring known global-market risk. (Comprehensive estimates of future retirement performance are one of this book's deliverables, covered in Chapter 10.)

An important implication of the above is final planning should not be distracted by extreme examples of specific-market risk. Consider that Austria's real stock market return for the last 113 years is only 0.6%. Such low returns will translate to extremely poor retirement results (i.e., MSWR-100% is under 1.5%); however, this case can be removed from final consideration. Retirement planning does not and should not depend on the risk of any specific market in isolation—this benefit comes with global investing.

The above doesn't eliminate a pragmatic dependency on specific-market risk. The historical datasets are almost all based on specific markets. As mentioned, these datasets support independent domains for verifying retirement strategies. More specifically, the independent datasets of specific markets are needed to reduce the chance of a data-mining bias, which is explained in the next section.

This book uses the following four specific-market datasets* for backtesting.

1. United States Market from 1928 through 2010, based on 2011 Ibbotson's Stocks, Bonds, Bills, and Inflation (SBBI) Yearbook

2. United States S&P Market from 1871 through 2010, based on Robert Shiller's dataset at Yale

3. United Kingdom Market from 1923 through 2010, based on Global Financial Data's FTSE and T-Bill datasets

4. Japan Market from 1950 through 2010, based on Global Financial Data's Topix and T-Bill datasets

Also used is the small but significant global market data from 1972 through 2010, based on Simba's spreadsheet of international mutual-fund returns.

A couple of caveats are now necessary. First, although all retirees should invest globally, it's also reasonable to give some tilt to the US market (more on this later), so the US is one specific market deserving extra attention. Also, as discussed earlier, data is lacking for a sufficiently complete long-term global dataset to measure global-market risk, so a Baseline Market must be created (fusing real market data from other sources) as a substitute for the global market (exactly why and how are covered in detail in Chapter 6).

For now, it's only important to keep in mind that known risk depends on its context: it may be for specific markets to compare strategies, or for the global market for final planning using best practices.

THE HAZARD OF A DATA-MINING BIAS

Data mining is extracting patterns from data. This book mines the data using backtesting and to a lesser extent using bootstrap simulations. Used well, data mining leads to new understandings of market behavior and better strategies

---

* The historical datasets are fully described in Appendix A.

(i.e., more income for less risk); used improperly, it leads to a data-mining bias where wrong conclusions are drawn and poor strategies recommended (with less income or more risk). Following the norms of evidence-based research, with ample cross-validation, greatly reduces the hazard of a data-mining bias.

A data-mining bias stems from mistaking random or temporary patterns in the market data as fundamental ongoing market characteristics, causing risk to be incorrectly measured. A data-mining bias always underestimates risk—a dangerous thing because a strategy looks better than it really is. The process of iteratively backtesting and tuning a specific strategy for a specific market always has a risk of a data-mining bias. The way to reduce the risk is by verifying results using an independent dataset (i.e., out-of-sample data) without tuning the strategy. Going further, testing with multiple independent datasets can nearly eliminate the risk of a data-mining bias.

Here's a simplistic example of a data-mining bias. Let's assume all the retirement periods across a dataset were backtested. A close examination of the measured risk for each period shows retirements starting in odd years on average support a higher MSWR than those starting in even years. It could then be accurately stated that according to the data, retiring in odd-years improves retirement results (i.e., it's a good strategy). While this "truth" holds for the specific dataset, it's no doubt due to random behavior (a data-mining bias) as opposed to market fundamentals that will reliably hold true in the future. Testing with other datasets, distinct from the dataset used to form the strategy, will show retiring in odd years isn't a reliable strategy to improve performance.

In practice, a data-mining bias is much less obvious. Here's a more realistic example. Let's assume a new income-harvesting strategy is being tested. The strategy rebalances the portfolio only when annualized 30-year trailing returns are above 12%. Backtesting with a 5% withdrawal rate shows a success rate of 72% compared to annual rebalancing's 63% success rate. Encouraged by the results, a researcher tunes the new strategy to instead rebalance when trailing returns are above 11%. This improves the backtesting success rate to 74%. The researcher continues tuning and backtesting the trailing return value until the optimal trailing return is found at 7.6%, producing an 81% success rate. Next, the researcher starts tuning the length of the trailing-return interval. Starting at a 30-year trailing returns and moving downward, the researcher finds a 23-year trailing-return interval produces the best backtesting results, boosting performance to an 86% success rate. The researcher then publishes a paper showing that rebalancing when 23-year trailing returns exceed 7.6% is a strong retirement strategy.

The above approach by the researcher almost certainly contains a data-mining bias and underestimates the risk of the strategy. The strategy tested is better than annual rebalancing for the given dataset, but it remains unclear how the strategy will perform with an independent dataset (one the strategy wasn't tuned for). It's fair to tune a strategy to improve empirical results, especially when based on an underlying rationale or theory, but turning for optimal performance almost always introduces some bias for the dataset used.

The above examples illustrate why independent datasets are critical for verifying strategies. Many retirement strategies developed in the last 20 years were originally backtested and tuned with either the US SBBI or US Shiller dataset (described in the next section). For this reason, whenever possible, I also verify strategies using UK and Japan datasets. If a strategy is a top performer across the US, UK, and Japan markets, it's likely to be a top performer for a future retirement in a global market (everything else being equal). Going further using simulated data, a bootstrapping simulation of many different markets is also used when deemed necessary to provide one more layer of protection against a data-mining bias.

In addition, the following supplementary guidelines are followed to further reduce the chance of a data-mining bias.

1. Ensure a strategy is consistent across different asset allocations.

2. Favor methods with underlying theories, or at least a firm rationale.

3. Keep It Simple — complex strategies with many parameters are more prone to overtuning.

4. Distrust unstable strategies whose results are sensitive to minor parameter changes.

PUTTING RISK FACTORS TO USE

It's worth coming back to why we should bother with identifying the factors of risk. Any factor that can be controlled is a potential lever for affecting risk; any factor that can be monitored is a potential guide for controlling other risk factors. Retirement strategies both monitor and control risk factors to affect risk, then backtesting indicates how well different strategies perform when doing so. Best practices are essentially those strategies and parameters known to most reliably leverage the risk factors to lower risk while generating sufficient income.

The risk factors vary substantially in their usefulness though — some are more effective and reliable than others. Also, there are innumerable ways to raise risk though inappropriate choices that adversely affect the risk factors. Investing during retirement is not an easy puzzle to figure out, but understanding the risk factors makes the path more coherent.

The following provides a sampling of how the risk factors are understood and applied throughout the rest of the book. This is in part a recap and in part a preview of what is to come.

a. There is a fundamental tradeoff between the risk of running out of money and the level of income generated. If income is lowered enough, risk will eventually drop to zero. Likewise, if income is raised enough, risk will eventually rise to 100%...certain failure. A goal is to identify the income levels with a small enough level of risk to satisfy most retirees without needlessly sacrificing income.

b. Known specific-market risk can be high even at low income levels, but diversification is able to mute specific market risk. Known global-market risk can be kept reasonably small for an acceptable level of income. It turns out, known global-market risk roughly aligns with known US market risk, but is a little higher (i.e., supports a little lower amount of income).

c. Of all the factors, the withdrawal rate (the level of income) is the most accessible and powerful factor affecting retirement risk. To exploit this advantage, it's prudent to let withdrawals vary with the state of the portfolio and markets — this is the focus of the variable-withdrawal strategies.

d. Portfolio returns, volatility of returns, and sequence of returns are all factors of risk that cannot be directly controlled, but they can be indirectly controlled through their own underlying factors...the asset-allocation factors. After the withdrawal rate, asset allocation (i.e., the asset allocation factors) provides the best path to reducing retirement risk.

e. The retirement length can't be controlled directly or indirectly. As such, it's treated more as a constant of investing during retirement. However, some strategies effectively monitor an estimate of the remaining retirement length to reduce risk.

f. The inflation factor can't be controlled, and there is little advantage to monitoring it independently. Inflation is most easily handled by incorporating it into the withdrawal rate (i.e., working with an inflation-adjusted withdrawal rate), then letting the variable-withdrawal strategy compensate for it.

g. The volatility of returns is important, but still a secondary factor of risk. Correctly done, asset allocation creates the optimal balance between return and volatility, keeping risk low while supporting sufficient income. This relationship is captured and applied by the Harvesting Ratio in Chapter 5.

h. The makeup of the stock allocation (e.g., small, value, emerging markets) provides a powerful asset-allocation level for controlling risk, again considered by the Harvesting Ratio in Chapter 5.

i. The stock percentage is a weaker asset-allocation lever than usually realized. The most effective stock percentage is typically limited to relatively narrow boundaries around 50% — a too high or too low percentage will usually increase risk. Lowering the stock percentage below its optimal point lowers risk only when the withdrawal rate is correspondingly lowered, but keep in mind guaranteed-income is often a better approach to reducing overall risk (known and speculative) than lowering the stock percentage along with the withdrawal rate.

j. Return disposition as an indirect factor is difficult to use, but also too important to ignore. Market valuations as a measure of return disposition are used to set the initial withdrawal rate, and also discussed in the last chapter on planning with guaranteed income. Beyond these limited uses, there is insufficient evidence to support putting return disposition to more direct use, despite its broad potential. However, there are indirect methods of using return disposition that can safely reduce risk, such as smart rebalancing within the income-harvesting strategies.

k. Beyond the identified factors, retirement risk can only be affected outside the domain of systemic withdrawals*.

---

* The most common investment during retirement that falls outside systemic withdrawal is guaranteed-income (e.g., bond ladders, annuities), addressed in the last chapter. Another common alternative, completely outside this book's scope although viable in the right markets, is direct real-estate ownership with rental income.

THE POINT

Breaking down risk identifies the facets and the factors useful for understanding and controlling risk during retirement. Speculative risk is unmeasurable, but known risk based on the data can be measured to find the right strategies, the right portfolios, and suitable initial withdrawal rates. Known specific-market risk supports comparing strategies and avoiding a data-mining bias. However, only known global-market risk (measured from a baseline market) can provide realistic estimates of future retirement performance.

Considering the specifics, retirees usually pay too much attention to volatility; the withdrawal rate and portfolio returns are the two dominant factors affecting risk in retirement; half the systemic-withdrawal problem is solved by knowing how to allocate and maintain assets in their proper portions, indirectly balancing returns with volatility.

This chapter covers income-harvesting strategies: what these strategies do, and how various strategies perform relative to each other. The outcome is one recommended strategy, Prime Harvesting, with precise instructions for applying it.

Less interested readers need only skim the chapter, carefully focusing on the Prime Harvesting section in the introductory survey, the recommendation section, and the example at the end.

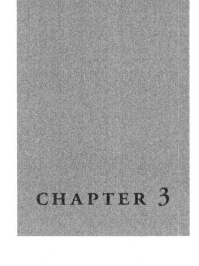

If I'm confident I could entrust you with raising my children, and I'm dazzled by your brilliance, then I might trust your investment strategy without seeing your data.

Walter E. Goh

CHAPTER 3

Surveying and Selecting an Income-Harvesting Strategy

INCOME-HARVESTING STRATEGIES MANAGE THE RETIREMENT portfolio to minimize the impact of periodic withdrawals. They specify what's sold to fund withdrawals, what triggers rebalancing, and how rebalancing takes place. Some strategies also affect the stock-bond ratio, although usually not directly. Income-harvesting strategies may not be natural attention-getters for investors, but don't mistake them as mere accounting details—the effects can be considerable, perhaps even making or breaking a retirement plan in certain circumstances.

This chapter surveys a dozen income-harvesting strategies, including side-by-side performance comparisons under diverse conditions. More than 30 strategies were originally tested before narrowing the list. The survey aims to provide a representative sampling of all strategies*, including the best performing and best known. The final outcome is to reduce the set of strategies down to a single income-harvesting recommendation.

Consistently strong strategies appear to be relatively rare, so don't expect better choices to show up each year in the literature. To avoid gambling with retirement assets, retirees should not change from one strategy to another without solid evidence of better performance, preferably shown by direct comparison adhering to evidence-based research. Chasing strategies can be almost as bad as chasing returns.

Some of the strategies tested are documented in retirement books; others in financial journals; a few on the Web. Most are defined by financial professionals. A few perform rather well; most moderately well; a few poorly.

Why bother with a survey? Why not just tell the best strategy and move on? A survey is useful for several reasons:

a. It documents the performance of the poor strategies, helping to reduce their use in retirement. Some have long-standing and dedicated advocates.

b. Broad coverage helps reduce the likelihood that some retirees will later be diverted (from what works well) in search of greener pastures.

---

* Valuation-based strategies are not included in the survey, but are discussed later in the chapter.

c. The "best" income-harvesting strategies are the ones which perform well *relative* to the alternatives. This is realized only through side-by-side comparisons.

It's also helpful to understand upfront what this chapter does *not* do. It does not recommend a safe withdrawal rate or a retirement portfolio. These are independent topics covered in later chapters.

THE BACKTESTING DETAILS

Given this survey revolves around backtesting, the default parameters and how to interpret the results are best explained first.

The Default Parameters and Assumptions

There will be a diversity of tests; however, every backtesting simulation uses the following default parameters unless otherwise noted.

1. A 30-year retirement period.

2. An initial allocation of 60% stocks and 40% bonds. Some strategies override this initial allocation and others use it as the starting point, varying it as needed throughout retirement.

3. Fixed-rate inflation-adjusted withdrawals.

4. A default market based on the US SBBI dataset spanning from 1928 to 2010.

5. A default portfolio using the following allocation (intended to be somewhat representative of what today's retirees often use):
   - For bonds, 100% intermediate-term treasuries
   - For stocks, a moderately diversified allocation:
     - 70% Total Market Stocks
     - 10% Small Company Stocks
     - 10% Large Value Stocks
     - 10% Small Value Stocks

6. Reinvested dividends—the focus is always on total return throughout this book.

No special consideration is given to taxes. Taxes differ depending on circumstances; nevertheless, the behaviors of the top-ranked strategies are reasonable when it comes to tax considerations (i.e., taxes are unlikely to affect the ranking).

Interpreting the Results

A Maximum Sustainable Withdrawal Rate (MSWR) graph, as described in Chapter 2 (Figure 3), is shown for each surveyed strategy. This graph provides a snapshot of a strategy's performance. Keep in mind when comparing strategies, the performance during the poorest retirement periods (i.e., the lower MSWR values) is what matters most for bounding risk—during strong retirement periods, virtually every strategy is a winner.

When results are listed in tabular form, the following values are included (depending on the specific table and the strategy):

a. **Withdrawal Rate**—the annual withdrawal percentage (fixed rate, inflation-adjusted).

b. **Stock**—the initial percentage of the portfolio held in stocks.

c. **Average Remaining**—the average, in millions of dollars, remaining at the end of the backtested retirement periods (i.e., at the end of 30 years) based on a starting portfolio value of $1 million dollars; however, the relationship of the starting value to the "average remaining" applies to any starting portfolio value.

d. **Average Year of Failure**—for the retirement periods that fail, the average retirement year when the failure occurred out of a 30-year retirement period.

e. **Lowest-Bond Average**—the average of the lowest bond percentage reached for each retirement period. For example, if during one 30-year retirement period the percentage of bonds in the portfolio ranged from 15% to 55%, the lowest percentage, 15%, goes into the average for all the retirement periods backtested. This value provides an indication of how low the bond percentage drops during a typical retirement period.

f. **Highest-Bond Average**—the average of the highest bond percentage reached for each retirement period. For example, if during one retirement period, the percentage of bonds in the portfolio ranged from 15% to 55%, the highest percentage, 55%, goes into the average for all the retirement periods backtested.

g. **Bond Average**—the overall average percentage of bonds for all retirement years over all retirement periods backtested.

h. **Success Rate**—the percentage of retirement periods ending successfully with assets remaining.

Required Caveats

A few caveats are required to fairly set the stage for this survey, as well as the one in the next chapter.

a. The aim of modeling each strategy is to accurately and faithfully match the originator's intent. A large amount of retesting and crosschecking was done to reinforce this aim. Also, the core software infrastructure was calibrated by comparing traditional rebalancing results with FireCalc[7], a popular retirement calculator on the Web. While I believe all results are correct, with proper due diligence taken, there is no path to complete confidence when writing software to interpret the ideas of others.

b. A couple of strategies explicitly state a financial advisor or money manager should be monitoring performance and making adjustments as needed. This aspect of any strategy is too open-ended for modeling. Whenever there were ambiguities or incompleteness in a strategy, I chose an interpretation that performed well with the sample portfolio using the SBBI dataset, making a best effort to provide a fair representation of each strategy.

c. For each of the referenced strategies, I use the same sources I believe retirees are using; however, these sources may not represent the originators' latest thinking. Also, some of the strategies that are not top performers today may have been innovative and the best in their class when they were introduced. Hindsight provides an enormous research advantage.

d. Ultimately, this survey (and the next) can only claim to compare my interpretation and modeling of the strategies defined in the referenced sources. It's not intended to judge how well any particular money manager or financial advisor might have fared with their own interpretations, latest thoughts, or custom adjustments to a specific client's portfolio.

e. Finally, throughout the survey and the rest of the book, the numbers sometimes show a decimal-point precision that can't apply to the future. The data is our best guide, but it's never a precise guide to the future.

TRADITIONAL REBALANCING — THE BASELINE INCOME-HARVESTING STRATEGY

When surveying income-harvesting strategies, it's helpful to have a known reference point for comparison. Traditional rebalancing provides this reference point as a baseline strategy, given its use by most investors. In the introductory survey, the performance of every strategy will be compared to traditional rebalancing's performance.

Traditional rebalancing is simply restoring asset values back to their target percentages at periodic intervals by buying and selling as needed. Traditional rebalancing brings to mind the old computer sales adage, "no one gets fired for buying IBM". No advisor, portfolio manager, or financial writer can be faulted for assuming or advocating traditional rebalancing during retirement. Traditional rebalancing is so dominant, it's not considered a strategy, but a part of "good" portfolio maintenance. Nevertheless, its use in retirement makes it an income-harvesting strategy by default. As will be shown, it does not compare well with the top-performing alternatives. It's not a bad strategy, but also not a good one. Annual rebalancing fits the assumptions of pre-revolutionary economics outlined in Chapter 1, but not the assumptions of post-revolutionary economics.

Push-back against traditional rebalancing is rare though, making it understandable that many retirees consider it the safest option and are hesitant to veer from it; however, evidence against traditional rebalancing does exists in the literature. For example, Duke University economist Campbell Harvey and his coauthors in their 2014 paper, Rebalancing Risk[8], show traditional rebalancing increases risk during sharp market downturns. The authors explain that traditional rebalancing becomes a kind of "anti-momentum" strategy during these poor markets, where under-performing assets are bought and outperforming assets are sold. They point out that other factors (momentum in their study) can better guide rebalancing to lower risk. The point is, traditional rebalancing should not be assumed to be the safest retirement choice.

Traditional rebalancing comes in several forms, although annual rebalancing is the dominant form. Rebalancing over longer periods of several years is common, as well as rebalancing when the portfolio values drift outside a specific range. Generally, the evidence isn't clear for favoring one form of traditional rebalancing over another. For example, backtesting using US SBBI data from 1928 to 2010 shows rebalancing every four or five years improves retirement performance, but the improvements disappear when backtesting with Shiller's US data as well as with UK and Japan data. Longer rebalancing periods usually result in a higher average percentage of stocks and therefore a higher return, but don't always map to the best retirement performance. Throughout this survey, as well as the rest of the book, annual rebalancing is used to represent all the forms of traditional rebalancing.

The income-harvesting steps below describe precisely how annual rebalancing works in retirement when making annual withdrawals. Following the complete set of steps, annual rebalancing's initial backtesting results are then shown. (This same form—a set of implementation steps followed by initial backtesting results—is used throughout the survey for each income-harvesting strategy.)

Income-Harvesting Steps with Annual Rebalancing

1. Sell enough portfolio assets to fund the next withdrawal (which assets don't matter in theory, because the portfolio is rebalanced at the end).

2. Withdraw the annual living expenses from the portfolio's cash.

3. Buy and sell as needed to rebalance back to target values:
   a. The stock and bond percentages are restored to their target percentages.
   b. Individual stock assets are rebalanced to their target values within the stock allocation.
   c. Individual bond assets are rebalanced to their target values within the bond allocation.

In the above steps (for annual rebalancing as well as other harvesting strategies), selling assets to withdraw funds is listed as a step distinct from selling assets to rebalance. In practice, only one step is used with all transactions taking place in conjunction to reduce fees. Both ways, the resulting portfolio allocation is the same.

Backtesting Results

Figure 4 shows annual rebalancing's Maximum Sustainable Withdrawal Rate (MSWR) for 54 30-year retirement periods, the first period starting in 1928 (extending to 1957) and the last starting in 1981 (extending to 2010).

Figure 5 shows the results for various withdrawal percentages and stock ratios.

None of these results are very interesting by themselves, but they form the baseline for comparing other strategies.

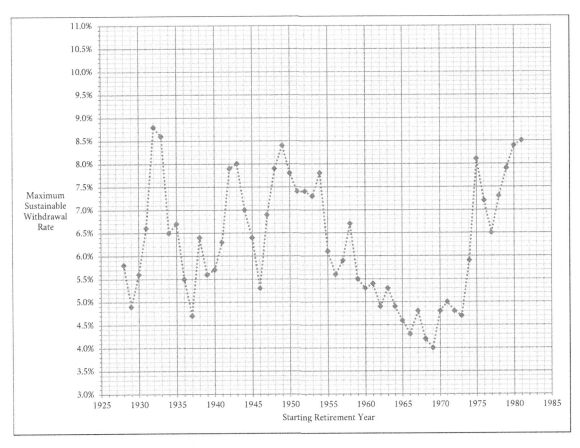

FIGURE 4

Maximum Sustainable Withdrawal Rates with annual rebalancing.

Withdraw Rate	Stock	Average Remaining	Average Year of Failure	Lowest-Bond Average	Highest-Bond Average	Bond Average	Success Rate
4.0%	10%	0.6M	26.2	90.00%	90.00%	90.00%	42.60%
4.0%	20%	1.2M	27.1	80.00%	80.00%	80.00%	77.80%
4.0%	30%	2.1M	29.7	70.00%	70.00%	70.00%	94.40%
4.0%	40%	3.4M	NA	60.00%	60.00%	60.00%	100.00%
4.0%	50%	4.8M	NA	50.00%	50.00%	50.00%	100.00%
4.0%	60%	6.6M	NA	40.00%	40.00%	40.00%	100.00%
4.0%	70%	8.8M	NA	30.00%	30.00%	30.00%	100.00%
4.0%	80%	11.3M	29	20.00%	20.00%	20.00%	98.10%
4.0%	90%	14.2M	26.5	10.00%	10.00%	10.00%	96.30%
4.5%	10%	0.4M	23.4	90.00%	90.00%	90.00%	24.10%
4.5%	20%	0.6M	25.1	80.00%	80.00%	80.00%	42.60%
4.5%	30%	1.2M	26.2	70.00%	70.00%	70.00%	68.50%
4.5%	40%	2.2M	26.9	60.00%	60.00%	60.00%	87.00%
4.5%	50%	3.5M	25	50.00%	50.00%	50.00%	94.40%
4.5%	60%	5.1M	25.3	40.00%	40.00%	40.00%	94.40%
4.5%	70%	7.0M	25.3	30.00%	30.00%	30.00%	94.40%
4.5%	80%	9.3M	25	20.00%	20.00%	20.00%	92.60%
4.5%	90%	12.0M	21.3	10.00%	10.00%	10.00%	94.40%
5.0%	10%	0.2M	21.2	90.00%	90.00%	90.00%	14.80%
5.0%	20%	0.4M	22.9	80.00%	80.00%	80.00%	22.20%
5.0%	30%	0.7M	24.2	70.00%	70.00%	70.00%	40.70%
5.0%	40%	1.4M	24.9	60.00%	60.00%	60.00%	59.30%
5.0%	50%	2.4M	24.6	50.00%	50.00%	50.00%	75.90%
5.0%	60%	3.7M	25.5	40.00%	40.00%	40.00%	77.80%
5.0%	70%	5.5M	24.6	30.00%	30.00%	30.00%	83.30%
5.0%	80%	7.6M	22.7	20.00%	20.00%	20.00%	87.00%
5.0%	90%	10.1M	21.6	10.00%	10.00%	10.00%	87.00%

FIGURE 5

Annual rebalancing results for varying withdrawal rates and stock percentages.

Annual rebalancing's withdrawals are funded each year from the asset classes with the highest growth, or if there is no growth, then from the asset classes with the least loss. At the same time, the higher performing assets supplement the lower performing assets, bringing all back to their target percentage. While this buy-low and sell-high approach seems reasonable, there is more to a strong income-harvesting strategy. (It's also the basis for the anti-momentum effect previously mentioned.) The general problem with annual rebalancing is lack of consideration of what is happening to the overall portfolio over time—the target allocation is adhered to, no matter what.

Again, annual rebalancing isn't a poor solution, it just isn't strong. Later comparisons show it performs somewhere in the upper-middle range of the surveyed strategies.

An Introductory Survey of Income-Harvesting Strategies

This section surveys the selected incoming-harvesting strategies, showing how each works, with a preliminary look at performance. Each strategy is introduced, its rules for portfolio management broken down into precise individual steps, then its backtesting results shown. Following the introductory survey, the strategies are more thoroughly compared side-by-side.

When describing the steps for implementing a strategy, the most straightforward explanation is given to accomplish what it requires. For simplicity, no attention is given to minimizing the number of buy or sell transactions to reduce broker expenses.

Most of these strategies manage the portfolio at the highest asset-class level (e.g., stocks, bonds, cash) as opposed to the finer-grain subclass levels (e.g., large value stocks, small stocks, growth stocks). One may wonder if strategies operating at this higher level may be unnecessarily inefficient, but tentative results show this doesn't appear to be the case. Finer-grain management was backtested for a couple of cases without finding a substantial improvement in performance.

Bonds-First Strategy

Spitzer and Singh, professors of economics and finance respectively, published a paper[9] comparing strategies in the June 2007 issue of the Journal of Financial Planning. While the goal of their paper was to explore the effects of rebalancing on a retirement portfolio, in a broader sense they were comparing a set of income-harvesting strategies.

Here's their description of the four strategies examined in their paper:

1. Withdraw money from the asset that had the highest return during the year and do not rebalance. This will be referred to as "High First."

2. Withdraw money from the asset that had the lowest return during the year and do not rebalance. This will be referred to as "Low First."

3. Take withdrawals from bonds first and do not rebalance. This will be referred to as "Bonds First."

4. Take withdrawals from stocks first and do not rebalance. This will be referred to as "Stocks First."

Spitzer and Singh found the Bonds-First strategy (the third strategy above) performed best of the four strategies, making it an attractive choice for this survey.

The Steps

1. Sell enough bond assets to fund the next withdrawal; if bonds are depleted, sell from stocks.

2. Withdraw the annual living expenses from the portfolio's cash (from the previous sell).

3. Buy and sell as needed to rebalance individual stock assets to their target stock values (without modifying the portfolio's stock percentage).

4. Buy and sell as needed to rebalance individual bond assets to their target bond values (without modifying the portfolio's bond percentage).

Backtesting Results

Figure 6 shows the strategy's MSWR values compared to annual rebalancing. Bonds-First does significantly better in almost every retirement period. Only during the most difficult periods starting in the mid-1960s did Bonds-First merely tie with annual rebalancing.

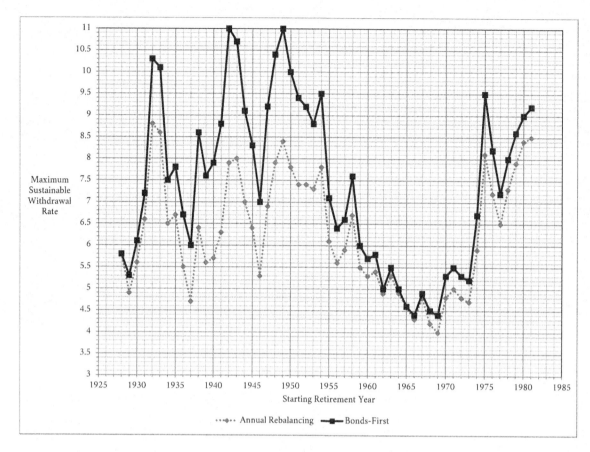

FIGURE 6

Bonds-First Strategy compared to annual rebalancing.

Figure 7 shows the results for various withdrawal percentages and stock ratios. Not only is the performance strong (again in relation to annual rebalancing), but also, the average remaining portfolio value at the end of retirement is high…actually the highest for all the strategies included in the survey.

Withdraw Rate	Stock	Average Remaining	Average Year of Failure	Lowest-Bond Average	Highest-Bond Average	Bond Average	Success Rate
4.0%	10%	2.1M	29	2.10%	89.80%	47.10%	96.30%
4.0%	20%	4.8M	NA	0.30%	79.60%	33.00%	100.00%
4.0%	30%	7.4M	NA	0.00%	69.30%	23.80%	100.00%
4.0%	40%	9.8M	NA	0.00%	59.00%	17.00%	100.00%
4.0%	50%	11.9M	NA	0.00%	48.60%	11.80%	100.00%
4.0%	60%	13.8M	NA	0.00%	38.00%	7.60%	100.00%
4.0%	70%	15.4M	NA	0.00%	27.40%	4.40%	100.00%
4.0%	80%	16.5M	NA	0.00%	16.50%	2.10%	100.00%
4.0%	90%	17.3M	26	0.00%	5.90%	0.60%	96.30%
4.5%	10%	1.3M	26.5	0.70%	89.40%	44.40%	66.70%
4.5%	20%	3.5M	27.1	0.00%	79.30%	30.40%	87.00%
4.5%	30%	5.8M	28.3	0.00%	68.80%	21.80%	94.40%
4.5%	40%	7.9M	29	0.00%	58.50%	15.60%	98.10%
4.5%	50%	9.9M	30	0.00%	48.00%	10.70%	98.10%
4.5%	60%	11.7M	28	0.00%	37.40%	6.90%	96.30%
4.5%	70%	13.1M	26.3	0.00%	26.70%	4.00%	94.40%
4.5%	80%	14.2M	24.3	0.00%	15.90%	1.90%	94.40%
4.5%	90%	14.9M	20	0.00%	5.40%	0.60%	94.40%
5.0%	10%	0.7M	23.7	0.00%	89.40%	44.20%	44.40%
5.0%	20%	2.5M	24.8	0.00%	78.70%	29.30%	66.70%
5.0%	30%	4.4M	25.8	0.00%	68.60%	20.60%	77.80%
5.0%	40%	6.3M	24.7	0.00%	58.30%	14.70%	87.00%
5.0%	50%	8.1M	25.1	0.00%	47.80%	10.10%	87.00%
5.0%	60%	9.7M	23.4	0.00%	37.20%	6.50%	90.70%
5.0%	70%	11.0M	23.8	0.00%	25.90%	3.70%	88.90%
5.0%	80%	12.0M	21.2	0.00%	15.10%	1.80%	90.70%
5.0%	90%	12.6M	19.8	0.00%	4.80%	0.50%	88.90%

FIGURE 7

Bonds-First Strategy results for varying withdrawal rates and stock percentages.

Bonds-First's strength stems from giving stocks years of insulated growth before starting to withdraw from them, as many as 15 years. Another factor is the average stock percentage during retirement is very high, contributing both to strong performance and the large remaining balance at the end of retirement.

However, Bonds-First has several limitations. Later when other data sets are backtested, its performance isn't as consistent as desired. Just as important, the portfolio will always end with 100% in stocks. This creates an uncomfortable exposure to speculative risk for most retirees. Also, like annual rebalancing, there is no consideration for what is occurring to the portfolio, limiting flexibility in extreme markets.

While Bonds-First works surprisingly well, the smarter strategies do better.

Age-Based Strategies: 100-Age, 120-Age, and Glidepath

Outside annual rebalancing, age-based strategies may be the best known. They are certainly often recommended in the media. While they are not described as "income-harvesting strategies", their use in retirement again makes them just that.

These strategies determine each year's stock percentage by using the retiree's current age. Here's the general idea: as we age, we cannot handle as much investment risk, so we should progressively lower our portfolio's stock ownership. To some extent, the underlying idea might also be, we need less growth from stocks as we age because our remaining life is shorter.

The most common age-based strategy is 100-Age, where the retiree's age is subtracted from 100 to determine the stock percentage. For example, if you are 65 years old, you would have 35% (i.e., 100 - 65) invested in stocks with the balance in bonds. When you turn 66, your stock allocation should drop to 34% (i.e., 100 - 66) and so on.

A 30-year retirement using 100-Age would have the following stock percentages from the beginning to the end of retirement.

35%, 34%, 33%, 32%, 31%, 30%...10%, 9%, 8%, 7%, 6%, 5%

Over the last decade or two, 120-Age* has surfaced as an alternative to 100-Age. Here, the stock percentage is 120 minus the retiree's age as seen in the following percentages for a 30-year retirement for a 65 year old retiree.

55%, 54%, 53%, 52%, 51%, 50%...30%, 29%, 28%, 27%, 26%, 25%

Another age-based strategy is Glidepath[10], where the stock percentages taper off slowly at the beginning of retirement and accelerate at the end†. A 65 year old retiree's 30-year retirement would have the following series of annual stock percentages using Glidepath.

54%, 53%, 52%, 51%, 49%, 48%, 46%, 45%, 43%, 41%, 40%, 38%, 6%, 34%,
32%, 30%, 28%, 26%, 23%, 20%, 18%, 15%, 11%, 8%, 4%, 0%, 0%, 0%, 0%, 0%

The irony is, while age-based strategies appear conservative and sensible, they have the distinction of being the poorest performing income-harvesting strategies. The dichotomy between recommendation and result is so large that the term "urban myth" is appropriate for the attractiveness of these strategies in retirement.

The source of these strategies is not clear, although Jack Bogle, former CEO and founder of Vanguard, has for many years been a proponent of putting your age in bonds (i.e., age = percentage) as a rough guide for retirement. Mr. Bogle's advice is heeded by many for good reason: perhaps more than anyone else in the twentieth century, he greatly aided individual investors with innovation, fair dealings, and straight talk (his sterling reputation is well deserved). At the same time, his recommendation illustrates how apparently sensible, well-intentioned advice from an industry expert can falter when the criteria for evidence-based guidance are not met.

The Steps

1. Sell enough portfolio assets to fund the next withdrawal.

2. Withdraw the annual living expenses from the portfolio's cash.

3. Buy and sell as needed to rebalance according to the following rules:
   a. Total stock and bond allocations are set to the current year's age-based percentage.
   b. Individual stock assets are rebalanced to their target stock values (without modifying the portfolio's stock percentage).
   c. Individual bond assets are rebalanced to their target bond values (without modifying the portfolio's bond percentage).

---

* Recently I've also noticed more references to 110-Age.
† The Glidepath function for the stock percentage is $\text{Log}_{10}(100 - \text{current-age}) - 1$.

Backtesting Results

Figure 8 shows the MSWR values for the age-based strategies, compared to annual rebalancing. The age-based strategies perform significantly worse than annual rebalancing—the graph lines for each of the age-based strategies fall significantly under the line for annual rebalancing. For example, annual rebalancing in the 30-year retirement period starting in 1937 supported a withdrawal rate of 4.7% annually, where 100-Age only supported a rate of 3.4% (28% less income), 120-Age a rate of 4.1% (13% less income), and Glidepath a rate of 4% (15% less income).

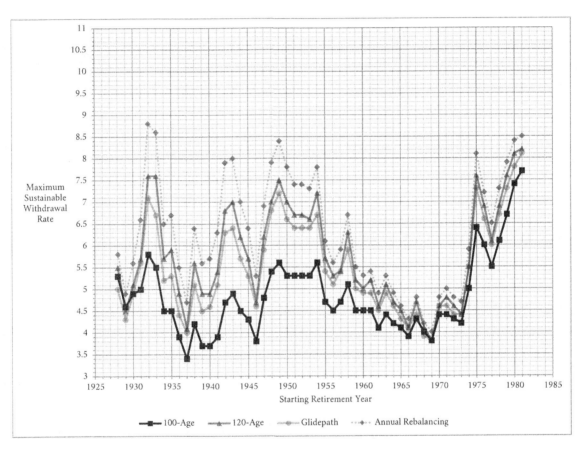

FIGURE 8

Age-based Strategies compared to annual rebalancing.

Figure 9 shows the results for various withdrawal percentages and stock ratios. Except for the lowest withdrawal rates, the performance is poor compared to other strategies. (Backtesting results using different stock percentages are not included, since the age-based strategies control the stock-bond ratio.) Advocates may still claim the age-based strategies are safer as long as the withdrawal rate is kept appropriately low; however, the evidence does not support this claim. Exceptionally poor markets can stress any withdrawal rate, making an efficient income-harvesting strategy always important.

Age-Based Strategy	Withdraw Rate	Average Remaining	Average Year of Failure	Lowest-Bond Average	Highest-Bond Average	Bond Average	Success Rate
Age-100	4.0%	1.8M	28.5	65.00%	94.00%	78.30%	85.20%
Age-120	4.0%	4.2M	28	45.00%	74.00%	58.30%	98.10%
Glidepath	4.0%	3.0M	29	45.60%	100.00%	70.40%	96.30%
Age-100	4.5%	1.0M	26	65.00%	94.00%	77.70%	63.00%
Age-120	4.5%	3.0M	25.2	45.00%	74.00%	58.20%	90.70%
Glidepath	4.5%	2.0M	26.8	45.60%	100.00%	70.00%	83.30%
Age-100	5.0%	0.6M	24.1	65.00%	94.00%	76.80%	37.00%
Age-120	5.0%	2.1M	24.9	45.00%	74.00%	57.70%	68.50%
Glidepath	5.0%	1.4M	24.9	45.60%	100.00%	68.70%	61.10%

FIGURE 9

Age-based Strategies results for varying withdrawal rates.

Why do these strategies perform so poorly? The main reason is, they all overweight the allocation to bonds. Also, selling stocks each year according to an age formula is blind to the market's behavior and the overall performance of the portfolio.

It turns out the optimal age-based formula is around "140 Minus Age" (for the default portfolio using the SBBI dataset). While this extreme age-based strategy is much better than the others in its group, often surpassing traditional rebalancing, it still underperforms annual rebalancing in the most difficult retirement periods...when a strategy counts the most.

The Guyton PMR Strategy

Jonathan Guyton, principal of Cornerstone Wealth Advisors, is well known for his early innovative work on income-harvesting and variable-withdrawals strategies (under different terminology).

Guyton's PMR Strategy for income-harvesting* is defined in the 2004 issue of the *Journal of Financial Planning*[11], and then refined in a follow-up paper in 2006 co-authored with William Klinger[12].

Below are Guyton's words describing PMR:

- Following years in which an equity asset class has a positive return that produced a weighting in excess of its target allocation, the excess allocation is "sold" and the proceeds invested in cash to meet future withdrawal requirements.

- Portfolio withdrawals are funded each year on January 1 using assets in the following order: (1) cash from rebalancing any over-weighted equity asset classes from the prior year-end, (2) cash from rebalancing any over-weighted fixed income assets from the prior year-end, (3) withdrawals from remaining cash, (4) withdrawals from remaining fixed income assets, (5) withdrawals from remaining equity assets in order of the prior year's performance.

- No withdrawals are taken from an equity asset class following a year in which it had a negative return so long as cash or fixed income assets are sufficient to fund the withdrawal requirement.

Guyton's PMR strategy is reframed into the below steps for backtesting.

---

* Guyton combines income-harvesting with variable-withdrawals, but in this survey and the next the strategies are broken apart for comparison.

The Steps

1. If an individual stock or bond asset has a positive return for the year, move the excess return to cash. Excess return is the amount that exceeds the asset's target allocation based on each year's total portfolio value.

2. Withdraw first from cash (i.e., as much as possible), then from bonds, and lastly from stocks. No withdrawals are taken from bonds if sufficient cash is available; likewise, no withdrawals are taken from stocks if sufficient cash or bonds are available.

There is no direct rebalancing of stocks and bonds; rebalancing occurs indirectly only though selling to transfer excess value to cash.

Backtesting Results

Klinger, Guyton's co-author, in a later 2007 paper[13] essentially states PMR is not significantly better than annual rebalancing, but backtesting using SBBI historical data does show a modest improvement over traditional rebalancing*. Still, the improvement is moderate and not consistent across all the datasets.

Figure 10 shows the strategy's MSWR values compared to annual rebalancing, with moderate gains in almost all the retirement periods. Figure 11 shows the results for various withdrawal percentages and stock ratios, also an improvement compared to traditional rebalancing.

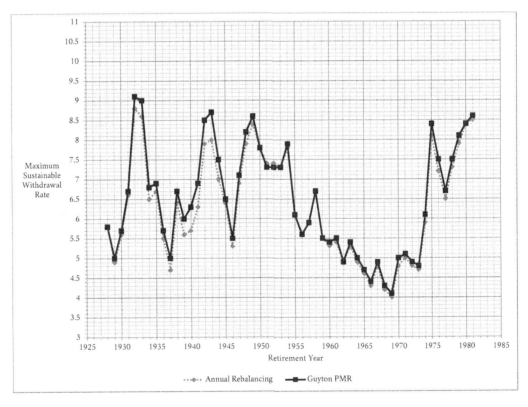

FIGURE 10

Guyton PMR Strategy compared to annual rebalancing.

---

*   It's unusual for backtesting performance to exceed an author's estimation.

Withdraw Rate	Stock	Average Remaining	Average Year of Failure	Lowest-Bond Average	Highest-Bond Average	Bond Average	Success Rate
4.0%	10%	0.6M	26.5	66.40%	93.40%	85.60%	44.40%
4.0%	20%	1.1M	27.9	58.40%	85.80%	76.50%	83.30%
4.0%	30%	1.8M	NA	55.30%	77.30%	68.30%	100.00%
4.0%	40%	2.4M	NA	49.80%	69.00%	58.10%	100.00%
4.0%	50%	2.8M	NA	38.80%	59.70%	46.90%	100.00%
4.0%	60%	3.3M	NA	27.70%	49.20%	35.50%	100.00%
4.0%	70%	3.9M	NA	17.40%	36.30%	24.10%	100.00%
4.0%	80%	4.7M	28	8.60%	22.10%	13.00%	98.10%
4.0%	90%	6.6M	25.5	1.70%	8.20%	3.40%	96.30%
4.5%	10%	0.4M	23.7	64.80%	94.00%	84.40%	24.10%
4.5%	20%	0.6M	26	57.60%	85.70%	73.20%	42.60%
4.5%	30%	1.0M	27.1	50.80%	76.90%	65.10%	70.40%
4.5%	40%	1.6M	26.6	43.80%	68.40%	56.30%	90.70%
4.5%	50%	2.2M	25.3	37.10%	59.30%	45.90%	94.40%
4.5%	60%	2.6M	26	27.10%	49.00%	34.70%	94.40%
4.5%	70%	3.2M	24	16.80%	36.00%	23.20%	96.30%
4.5%	80%	3.9M	25	8.10%	21.40%	12.10%	94.40%
4.5%	90%	5.8M	20.3	1.50%	7.60%	2.90%	94.40%
5.0%	10%	0.2M	21.6	66.00%	93.40%	82.90%	14.80%
5.0%	20%	0.4M	23.7	57.40%	87.30%	71.60%	22.20%
5.0%	30%	0.6M	24.2	43.40%	77.10%	62.40%	50.00%
5.0%	40%	1.1M	26	44.00%	67.80%	53.40%	61.10%
5.0%	50%	1.6M	25	32.60%	58.70%	43.90%	79.60%
5.0%	60%	2.0M	25.5	24.50%	48.60%	32.90%	85.20%
5.0%	70%	2.5M	24.3	15.00%	35.60%	21.90%	88.90%
5.0%	80%	3.2M	24.3	7.10%	21.10%	11.00%	87.00%
5.0%	90%	5.0M	22	1.30%	7.10%	2.50%	85.20%

FIGURE 11

Guyton PMR Strategy results for varying withdrawal rates and stock percentages.

PMR is essentially a three-pool strategy, dividing assets between cash, bonds, and stocks. The cash and bonds provide a buffer to volatility in stocks. Also, past performance is indirectly considered by comparing the current asset allocation to the target allocation. Then why doesn't the strategy perform better?

The problem is, comparing current allocation to target allocation does not reflect well how stocks are doing over a multi-year period, causing stocks' "excess returns" to be shifted to cash during periods when stocks as a whole are still actually underperforming, ultimately lowering the portfolio's return.

In the end, PMR is not a top performer in this survey, but it appears better than annual rebalancing. To Guyton and Klinger's credit, their total strategy was both innovative and well tested, using Monte Carlo techniques.

The Parker Strategy

Zachary Parker is Vice President of Income Distribution & Product Strategy at Securities America. In 2011, he received the Practitioner Thought Leadership Award from the Retirement Income Industry Association. His income-harvesting strategy surveyed here is described in the August 2008 issue of the *Journal of Financial Planning*[14]. The original study defining his strategy was a Judge's Grant winner in the 2007 Financial Frontiers Award competition.

Parker's strategy is the most complex in this survey. He divides the portfolio into four accounts, each playing a part in the harvesting strategy:

1. The Income Guarantee Account is invested in bonds. This account is the source of all annual withdrawals.

2. The Equity Harvest Account is invested in stocks. This account annually transfers a percentage of its growth to the Income Guarantee Account.

3. The Equity Withdrawal Account is also invested in stocks. This account annually transfers a percentage of its total value to the Income Guarantee Account.

4. The Derivative Protection Account is also invested in bonds. This account has a one-time purpose…if there is ever a drastic drop in equity values, transfer all of this account to the Equity Harvest Account.

As with most studies, some adaptation from Parker's study is necessary for this survey. Parker assumes 3% inflation with adjustments every 5 years, where this survey adjusts inflation every year based on CPI. Parker's asset allocation is different; nevertheless, what is used in this survey is comparable. Also, Parker assumes a fixed growth rate for bonds, where this survey uses historical returns. Finally, Parker states as a key assumption that an advisor periodically reviews the strategy and adjusts the portfolio as necessary to stay with the philosophy; here backtesting uses only the explicitly defined steps for the strategy as described below.

The Steps
Initially fill the strategy's four accounts to match their target values. Parker's most aggressive, but best performing, parameters are approximated: allocate 26% of the portfolio to bonds in the Income Guarantee Account, 30% to stocks in the Equity Withdrawal Account, 34% to stocks in the Equity Harvest Account, and finally 10% to bonds in the Derivative Protection Account.

1. If the Equity Withdrawal Account's underlying value did not decline by 5% during the year, transfer a portion of the account's assets to the Income Guarantee Account. The portion to be transferred is 7.5% of the account's assets if a transfer was made the previous year; if no transfer was made the previous year, then transfer the higher of two numbers: 7.5% of the account's assets or the amount of the most recent transfer.

2. If the Equity Harvest Account's underlying value grew over the last year, transfer a portion of the growth to the Income Guarantee Account. The portion to transfer is 60% of growth up to the Income Guarantee Account's target value; otherwise, 25% of the growth is transferred.

3. If the Equity Harvest Account's underlying value declined 30% or more over the previous two years, do a one-time transfer of all the assets in the Derivative Protection Account to the Equity Harvest Account.

4. Sell enough bonds from the Income Guarantee Account to fund the next withdrawal. If the account does not have sufficient funds, make up the shortfall by selling from the Equity Harvest Account. If the Equity Harvest Account is short, make up the shortfall by selling from the Equity Withdrawal Account.

5. Withdraw the annual living expenses from the portfolio's cash.

6. Buy and sell as needed to rebalance individual stock assets to their target stock values (without modifying the portfolio's stock percentage).

7. Buy and sell as needed to rebalance individual bond assets to their target bond values (without modifying the portfolio's bond percentage).

Backtesting Results
Figure 12 shows the strategy's MSWR values compared to annual rebalancing. Figure 13 shows the harvesting results for different withdrawal rates using five different portfolio makeups defined in Parker's paper, ranging from aggressive to conservative.

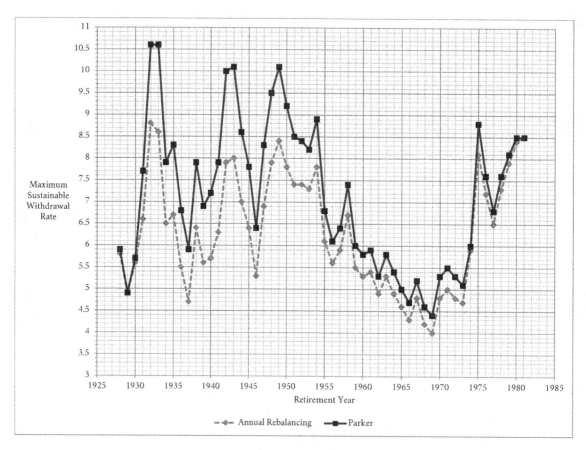

FIGURE 12

Parker Strategy compared to annual rebalancing.

Parker's Adjusted Models	Withdraw Rate	Stock	Average Remaining	Average Year of Failure	Lowest-Bond Average	Highest-Bond Average	Bond Average	Success Rate
Aggressive	4.0%	63%	8.0M	NA	24.70%	42.90%	36.30%	100.00%
Moderate Aggressive	4.0%	56%	6.9M	NA	30.20%	46.00%	40.70%	100.00%
Moderate	4.0%	52%	6.3M	NA	32.50%	49.30%	43.10%	100.00%
Moderate Conservative	4.0%	49%	5.9M	NA	33.60%	50.60%	44.40%	100.00%
Conservative	4.0%	45%	5.4M	NA	35.90%	53.50%	47.30%	100.00%
Aggressive	4.5%	63%	6.7M	NA	21.80%	39.40%	33.40%	98.10%
Moderate Aggressive	4.5%	56%	5.7M	NA	26.40%	42.70%	37.50%	98.10%
Moderate	4.5%	52%	5.2M	24	27.60%	45.90%	39.20%	98.10%
Moderate Conservative	4.5%	49%	4.8M	25	27.60%	48.00%	40.20%	98.10%
Conservative	4.5%	45%	4.3M	26	28.40%	51.30%	42.70%	98.10%
Aggressive	5.0%	63%	5.5M	23.7	17.60%	36.10%	29.90%	92.60%
Moderate Aggressive	5.0%	56%	4.6M	26	21.10%	39.80%	33.40%	92.60%
Moderate	5.0%	52%	4.1M	25.8	20.70%	43.50%	34.80%	92.60%
Moderate Conservative	5.0%	49%	3.9M	25.4	20.00%	45.90%	35.60%	92.60%
Conservative	5.0%	45%	3.4M	25	20.80%	49.80%	37.80%	88.90%

FIGURE 13

Parker Strategy results for varying withdrawal rates and models.

The strategy's MSWR values and success rates are high, the bond averages are reasonable, and the average remaining dollars are solid; overall the strategy's performance is excellent using the US data. Unfortunately, it isn't as strong with non-US datasets.

As a preview of what's ahead, when the broader results (e.g., UK, Japan) are considered at the end of this chapter (e.g., Figure 30 and Figure 31), one may wonder if Parker's results include some amount of an unintended data-mining bias. Keep in mind a data-mining bias is hard to discern, but its risk is ever present when developing investment strategies, especially strategies with several parameters tuned for optimal performance. If there is a bias, the strategy's full strengths will not carry into the future.

Parker does address the risk of overtuning in the following caveat for a particular parameter: "Although this optimal point was based on historical performance, there is no reason to assume it will remain optimal into the future; but the assumption can be made that this optimal point would remain fairly stable and could be adjusted throughout the life of the plan." I believe his point is that a financial planner or money manager could dynamically adjust the parameters throughout the plan to counter any weaknesses, although how to do this is not clear.

Even if there is some bias to US data, the strategy is still a strong performer. As such it provides another benchmark to compare other strategies against.

The Weiss Strategy

Gerald Weiss is a Certified Financial Planner, heading his own firm, Weiss Financial Planning. He outlined his harvesting strategy in a 2001 paper, "Dynamic Rebalancing"[15], published in the *Journal of Financial Planning*. This older strategy is a solid performer, as is Weiss' paper, identifying many of the core issues concerning income harvesting.

Weiss' strategy is simple but effective. In up years when stocks perform well, traditional annual rebalancing takes place as normal with withdrawals mainly coming from stocks. However, in down years when stocks underperform, no rebalancing occurs, with withdrawals coming only from bonds until the market improves. "Up Years" are those where the cumulative return from the start of retirement is above the expected average; "Down Years" are those where the cumulative return is below the expected average. The strategy also rebalances annually if bonds are completely depleted, or if stocks are underrepresented in the portfolio due to a bear market.

Cumulative real return is the trigger for rebalancing during up markets—it's calculated as the inflation-adjusted geometric mean from the start of retirement. Weiss did not specify what the expected cumulative return should be, but 5% is used given it performs best with backtesting, although up to 7% performs almost as well.

The Steps

1. Sell enough bond assets to fund the next withdrawal; if bonds are depleted, sell from stocks.

2. Withdraw the annual living expenses from the portfolio's cash.

3. Buy and sell as needed to rebalance according to the following rules:
   a. Rebalance back to target stock and bond ratios if any of the following criteria are true:
      i. If stocks are under their target allocation (i.e., a low percentage of the portfolio).
      ii. If cumulative stock returns from the start of retirement are greater than 5%.
      iii. If the bonds are depleted.
   b. Individual stock assets are rebalanced to their target stock values (without modifying the portfolio's stock percentage).
   c. Individual bond assets are rebalanced to their target bond values (without modifying the portfolio's bond percentage).

Backtesting Results

Figure 14 shows the strategy's MSWR values compared to annual rebalancing. The figure illustrates how the strategy matches annual rebalancing during strong retirement periods, but boosts performance during the worst years by using bonds to buffer the sale of stocks.

Figure 15 shows the results for various withdrawal percentages and stock ratios.

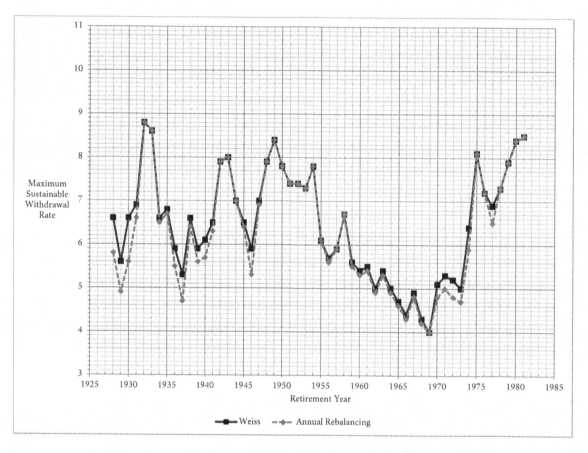

FIGURE 14

Weiss Strategy compared to annual rebalancing.

Withdraw Rate	Stock	Average Remaining	Average Year of Failure	Lowest-Bond Average	Highest-Bond Average	Bond Average	Success Rate
4.0%	10%	0.8M	26.1	70.50%	90.00%	86.90%	51.90%
4.0%	20%	1.6M	27.8	54.70%	80.00%	76.20%	83.30%
4.0%	30%	2.7M	NA	46.60%	70.00%	66.10%	100.00%
4.0%	40%	4.0M	NA	38.00%	60.00%	56.50%	100.00%
4.0%	50%	5.6M	NA	30.30%	50.00%	47.10%	100.00%
4.0%	60%	7.5M	NA	23.00%	40.00%	37.60%	100.00%
4.0%	70%	9.5M	NA	16.30%	30.00%	27.80%	100.00%
4.0%	80%	11.7M	25	10.60%	20.00%	18.70%	98.10%
4.0%	90%	14.5M	28	4.90%	10.00%	9.50%	96.30%
4.5%	10%	0.4M	24	77.40%	90.00%	86.50%	25.90%
4.5%	20%	0.8M	26	61.40%	80.00%	75.90%	50.00%
4.5%	30%	1.5M	27.6	47.80%	70.00%	66.30%	83.30%
4.5%	40%	2.7M	29	38.80%	60.00%	56.80%	96.30%
4.5%	50%	4.2M	26.3	31.20%	50.00%	47.20%	94.40%
4.5%	60%	5.8M	26.3	23.80%	40.00%	37.30%	94.40%
4.5%	70%	7.5M	24	16.70%	30.00%	27.90%	96.30%
4.5%	80%	9.8M	23	10.70%	20.00%	18.70%	92.60%
4.5%	90%	12.3M	21	4.90%	10.00%	9.60%	94.40%
5.0%	10%	0.2M	21.6	76.70%	90.00%	86.60%	16.70%
5.0%	20%	0.5M	23.8	66.50%	80.00%	76.20%	24.10%
5.0%	30%	0.9M	26.2	56.40%	70.00%	66.70%	44.40%
5.0%	40%	1.6M	27.2	43.30%	60.00%	56.90%	75.90%
5.0%	50%	2.9M	25.4	33.00%	50.00%	47.20%	87.00%
5.0%	60%	4.2M	24.7	24.50%	40.00%	37.40%	88.90%
5.0%	70%	5.9M	22.8	17.40%	30.00%	28.10%	90.70%
5.0%	80%	7.9M	20.4	11.00%	20.00%	18.90%	90.70%
5.0%	90%	10.2M	22	5.10%	10.00%	9.70%	87.00%

FIGURE 15

Weiss Strategy results for varying withdrawal rates and stock percentages.

While Weiss' strategy is not a top performer in this survey, it does well and is consistently better than annual rebalancing. Weiss' early paper and analysis is a significant contribution to the income-harvesting literature.

The OmegaNot Strategy

David Lee developed the OmegaNot Strategy[16] around 2001. He derived it while trying to interpret and backtest columnist Scott Burns' Omega strategy. Here are Lee's words describing it:

> Scott [Burns] was not specific about how this strategy would be implemented and (to my knowledge) no one has ever done any back-testing on this approach. This was intended to be the subject of this chapter. The truth is that I ended up (partly through my own misinterpretations) simulating a strategy that is fundamentally different than what Scott was trying to describe, although at a high level it matches his description as I stated it above.

David Lee's resulting strategy, OmegaNot, is a strong performer...one of the best. Its downside, fully realized by Lee, is the strategy's low bond average. Like the Bonds-First strategy, bonds are never replenished; however, withdrawals come from bonds only when the inflation-adjusted stock growth is insufficient to support them.

Lee's approach to using the inflation-adjusted target stock value as a metric for real growth is both simple and effective. A variation is successfully put to use later in the Prime Harvesting Strategy.

The Steps

1. Each year, adjust the targeted stock value by the inflation rate. The first year's targeted stock value is set to the initial stock allocation (e.g., 60% of the portfolio value, given 60% is initially allocated to stocks).

2. If the current stock value is greater than the targeted stock value, sell enough from the excess to fund the annual withdrawal. If the stock's excess value does not fully fund the withdrawal, sell bonds to make up the shortfall. If bonds become depleted, sell stocks to complete the amount needed for the withdrawal.

3. Withdraw the annual living expenses from the portfolio's cash.

4. Buy and sell as needed to rebalance individual stock assets to their target stock values (without modifying the portfolio's stock percentage).

5. Buy and sell as needed to rebalance individual bond assets to their target bond values (without modifying the portfolio's bond percentage).

Backtesting Results

Figure 16 shows the strategy's MSWR values compared to annual rebalancing. The figure shows OmegaNot significantly outperforming annual rebalancing for every backtested retirement period.

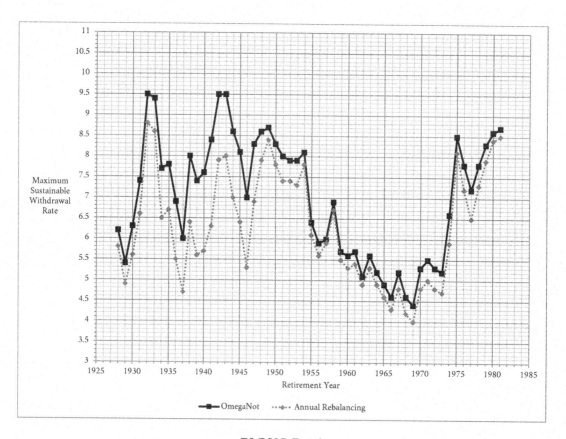

FIGURE 16

OmegaNot Strategy compared to annual rebalancing.

Figure 17 shows the results for various withdrawal percentages and stock ratios. Again, performance is strong, but bond averages are generally low. For example, a 5% withdrawal rate with an initial stock allocation of 60% has a 92.6% success rate, but the overall bond average is only 20.7% with the low-bond average 4.9%. Higher averages are seen with lower withdrawal rates though: a 4.5% withdrawal rate with a 50% initial stock allocation produces a 98.1% success rate with an overall bond average of 30.4% and a low-bond average of 14%.

Withdraw Rate	Stock	Average Remaining	Average Year of Failure	Lowest-Bond Average	Highest-Bond Average	Bond Average	Success Rate
4.0%	10%	0.7M	27.6	41.80%	93.30%	76.60%	57.40%
4.0%	20%	1.6M	NA	41.00%	84.70%	68.60%	100.00%
4.0%	30%	2.8M	NA	40.70%	77.40%	58.30%	100.00%
4.0%	40%	4.8M	NA	25.40%	66.50%	43.80%	100.00%
4.0%	50%	7.3M	NA	15.70%	54.60%	31.60%	100.00%
4.0%	60%	9.9M	NA	9.40%	43.10%	21.90%	100.00%
4.0%	70%	12.4M	NA	5.60%	31.50%	14.20%	100.00%
4.0%	80%	14.6M	NA	3.00%	19.70%	7.90%	100.00%
4.0%	90%	16.5M	26	1.10%	8.40%	2.90%	96.30%
4.5%	10%	0.4M	24.9	59.60%	94.00%	74.60%	25.90%
4.5%	20%	0.8M	27.7	27.10%	84.60%	62.00%	70.40%
4.5%	30%	1.7M	28	33.90%	76.80%	54.50%	90.70%
4.5%	40%	3.3M	29.5	22.30%	66.80%	42.20%	96.30%
4.5%	50%	5.6M	30	14.00%	54.80%	30.40%	98.10%
4.5%	60%	8.0M	27	8.40%	43.10%	21.00%	98.10%
4.5%	70%	10.3M	24	5.20%	31.00%	13.60%	98.10%
4.5%	80%	12.5M	22.5	2.70%	19.50%	7.40%	96.30%
4.5%	90%	14.2M	20.3	0.90%	8.20%	2.70%	94.40%
5.0%	10%	0.2M	22.2	46.90%	93.40%	73.80%	18.50%
5.0%	20%	0.4M	25.6	37.80%	86.00%	59.20%	33.30%
5.0%	30%	1.0M	26.1	28.30%	75.60%	51.90%	66.70%
5.0%	40%	2.2M	25	23.40%	67.10%	41.30%	87.00%
5.0%	50%	4.1M	23.8	13.50%	55.50%	30.00%	92.60%
5.0%	60%	6.2M	24.3	8.30%	43.00%	20.70%	92.60%
5.0%	70%	8.4M	21	4.90%	30.80%	13.20%	94.40%
5.0%	80%	10.4M	19.8	2.60%	19.10%	7.20%	92.60%
5.0%	90%	12.0M	17.3	0.80%	7.90%	2.60%	92.60%

FIGURE 17

OmegaNot Strategy results for varying withdrawal rates and stock percentages.

Although OmegaNot is not recommended, it's a top-performing strategy with consistent performance across multiple datasets. The downside is that its low bond averages carry a higher exposure to speculative risk; nevertheless, if there weren't better alternatives, it would still be worth considering.

The Three-Bucket Strategy

The best known three-bucket strategy is Ray Lucia's, described in his *Buckets of Money* books. The Three-Bucket Strategy surveyed here tries to adhere to Lucia's description as much as possible.

Mr. Lucia has a Wikipedia page[17], containing the following snippets:

Raymond Joseph Lucia, Sr. is an American former Certified Financial Planner, former Registered Investment Advisor, author, radio personality and television host. He is host of The Ray Lucia Show, a nationally syndicated radio and television financial talk show on the Global American Broadcasting Radio Network and the Biz Television Network.

On July 8, 2013, The United States Securities and Exchange Commission (SEC) banned him from associating with an investment adviser, broker or dealer, revoked his license and that of his former company, and slapped both with a fine — $50,000 to Lucia and $250,000 to his former firm.

The Buckets of Money strategy was promoted for over ten years before the SEC accused Mr. Lucia of misleading investors by portraying his strategy as successfully backtested when it was not. Here, the backtesting data is explored.

Although Mr. Lucia goes into considerable details on asset allocation, I found his income-harvesting ideas less clear in his books. I could not find precise guidance for handling unexpected situations, such as prematurely running out of a bucket's assets. I was also unable to find backtesting performance data in any of Mr. Lucia's publications, although a previous version of his website indicated his strategy was successfully backtested for the bear market of 1973-74. However, I could not recreate the performance described.

The Bucket of Money Strategy uses the following division of assets into three "buckets".

1. The first bucket contains safe-money investments, enough to fund seven years of withdrawals.

2. The second bucket contains moderately safe investments, enough to refill bucket one for another seven years when it empties.

3. The third bucket contains higher risk assets, typically equities, to refill the first two buckets when they are both depleted after approximately fourteen years.

The essential idea is to live off the first bucket for seven years while the second and third grows, then shift the second bucket to the first, living off it while the third keeps growing for a second seven years, finally starting all over again after a total of fourteen years with the accumulated assets of the third bucket used to refill the first two buckets.

The historical datasets contain good data for assets to fill bucket one and bucket three, but there is not good data for assets going into bucket two. Corporate bonds generally fulfill Lucia's criteria for bucket two (and are listed as a possible bucket two asset in his third book), but their poor backtesting results make their exclusive use questionable for a fair test of the strategy. To get past this barrier, bucket two's contents are simulated, essentially guaranteeing a solid bucket-two return during backtesting. Using simulated data, bucket two's return is annually set to 3% over the T-bill rate. This is a generous return for "moderately safe" investments during the worst of markets, given the return is derived from the safest asset, T-bills. From 1926 to 2010, adding 3% to the T-bill rate provides an annual return ranging from 2.98% to 17.71%, with the average of 6.67% and an annualized return of 6.01%. For those years where there is no T-Bill Rate (e.g., before 1926 for US data), Shiller's long interest rate is substituted for the T-bill rate.

The generous simulation of bucket two's return is emphasized so that any poor backtesting results cannot be a side effect of how bucket two is simulated; however, stronger than should be expected backtesting results are likely a side effect in extremely poor markets.

The Steps

To start, allocate to bucket one the withdrawal amount times seven (i.e., years), allocate to bucket two the withdrawal amount times six, and to bucket three allocate the remaining money. (This allocation for buckets one and two works as well as any in the 5-7 year ranges when backtesting with the US SBBI data.)

1. Each year, sell assets from bucket one to fund the withdrawal, and then pull the annual living expenses from the resulting cash. If there is not enough in bucket one to cover the withdrawal, then refill bucket one using all the contents of bucket two.

2. When bucket one and bucket two are depleted, refill them from the contents of bucket three using the starting guidelines, but this time use the updated inflation-adjusted withdrawal amount when calculating bucket sizes. If bucket three cannot refill buckets one and two, then divide the assets between bucket one and bucket two (and bucket three disappears).

3. Individual assets are rebalanced annually within their buckets.

Backtesting Results

Figure 18 shows the strategy's MSWR values compared to annual rebalancing. Figure 19 shows the results for various withdrawal percentages and bucket sizes.

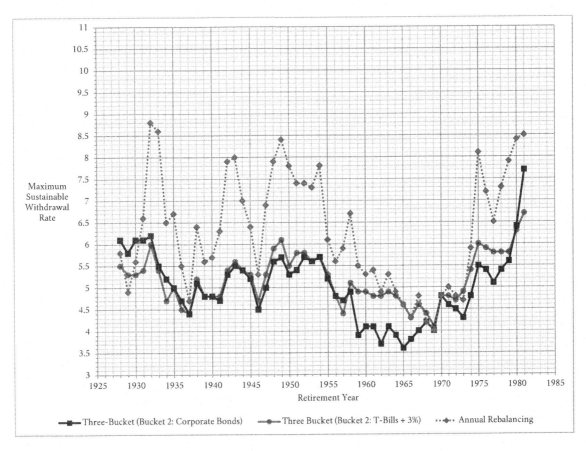

FIGURE 18

Three-Bucket Strategy with 7-year bucket sizes compared to annual rebalancing.
Bucket two is shown with two different assets: 1) corporate bonds; 2) a simulated
asset with a return rate equal to the current T-Bill rate plus 3%.

Withdraw Rate	Bucket Size	Average Remaining	Average Year of Failure	Lowest-Bond Average	Highest-Bond Average	Bond Average	Success Rate
4.0%	7 Years	8.3M	NA	1.60%	65.10%	32.20%	100.00%
4.0%	6 Years	10.0M	NA	1.10%	56.70%	25.50%	100.00%
4.0%	5 Years	11.4M	NA	0.80%	46.80%	19.60%	100.00%
4.5%	7 Years	4.9M	28.6	2.40%	75.50%	43.40%	90.70%
4.5%	6 Years	6.7M	26.8	1.40%	64.30%	33.70%	88.90%
4.5%	5 Years	8.4M	27	1.10%	52.70%	25.80%	90.70%
5.0%	7 Years	2.3M	26.4	2.50%	79.60%	54.70%	55.60%
5.0%	6 Years	4.0M	25.4	1.50%	68.20%	43.70%	66.70%
5.0%	5 Years	5.7M	23.4	1.10%	57.00%	32.10%	77.80%

FIGURE 19

Three-Bucket results (using a simulated bucket 2) for varying withdrawal rates and bucket sizes.

Overall the performance is weak, even with a generous return for bucket two. More is needed in a strategy than simply bucketing to effectively insulate stock volatility from withdrawals. Specifically, using "years" to calculate bucket sizes can cause imbalances during difficult markets by resulting in too many bonds—as previously stated, using a percentage of the overall portfolio performs better than "years". Also, blindly refilling the buckets when they are depleted does not perform well; a smarter rebalancing trigger is needed to raise the performance.

The Enhanced Two-Bucket Strategy

The Enhanced Two-Bucket Strategy (ETBS) tries to leverage the ideas from the Grangaard Strategy™. Paul Grangaard is an author and consultant on retirement planning. His harvesting strategy is outlined in his book[18] along with papers on his website[19]. To be clear, ETBS isn't Grangaard's strategy, because there are too many differences (described below); however, ETBS is a strategy an individual retiree might come up with by reading the book and making the necessary changes to adapt it to an income-harvesting strategy based wholly on index funds.

Grangaard recommends allocating to a "bond bucket" enough to fund 10 years of withdrawals; the rest of the portfolio is allocated to stocks. Grangaard's core idea is for the bond bucket to fund all withdrawals for 10 years, insulating the withdrawals from the volatility of stocks (i.e., the risk of having to sell low). As has been seen before, insulating stocks is generally good advice, but the details matter greatly. The book also suggests bonds might be replenished before 10 years (e.g., at 5 years) if the return objectives are met—also generally good advice as reflected in Weiss' work.

ETBS veers from Grangaard's recommendation primarily by how the bond bucket is formed. For ETBS the bond bucket is always composed of an intermediate-treasury bond index (as opposed to a ladder), matching the assumptions of this survey to enable direct comparison with the other strategies. In contrast, Grangaard recommends bond ladders* for the bond bucket. Briefly, the advantage of ladders is that the income rate is locked in during difficult markets and the income is guaranteed; however, what is lost is the negative correlation between bond funds and stock funds during those same difficult markets (i.e., the extra returns from a bond fund can help compensate for poor stock returns).

Grangaard's goals as well as his characterization of the problems of investing during retirement are clear at a high level, but implementing the concept using bond funds raises several questions. Also, like a few other strategies,

---

*   Using bond ladders with systemic withdrawals is explored in Appendix B. There is significant added complexity and the historical results appear mixed, but it can sometimes improve results. I didn't find the case for ladders compelling though.

Grangaard leaves some details fluid for the investor or investment advisor (which he recommends) to customize and adjust as needed. To complete ETBS, the following interpretations are necessary.

The first interpretation requires deciding how much should be allocated to bonds to cover withdrawals for a 10-year period. The simplest approach is to multiply the current year's withdrawal amount by 10. This is reasonable, given high-quality bonds often do little more than keep up with inflation; in fact, with the SBBI data, this approach with intermediate treasury bonds resulted on average of around 10.5 years of withdrawals.

The next interpretation is exactly how to manage the bonds earmarked to fund 10 years of withdrawals. Questions arose such as what to do if bonds are depleted before 10 years, or what to do if significant bonds are left at the end of the 10 years. Backtesting performance did not show a substantial difference between various options, so the simplest choice is used: replenish bonds from stock sells when there is not enough to fund the next annual withdrawal, whether or not more or less than 10 years have elapsed. This means a shortfall in the bond fund (due to low returns or high inflation) will trigger early selling of stocks to replenish bonds in as few as 7, 8, or 9 years; likewise a surplus in the bond fund due to strong returns and low inflation may delay replenishing up to 15 years.

The last interpretation is, if and when to replenish bonds early because the portfolio's return objective has been met. The following criterion is used: replenish bonds when the real stock return (i.e., inflation adjusted geometric return) from the start of retirement is greater than 7%, and at least 5 years have passed since the last replenish. The long-term market average of 7% is used as the trigger because it's known to perform relatively well (although 6% or 8% also perform relatively well). A minimum 5-year period is used because Grangaard suggested it, plus it also performs relatively well.

All these interpretations are included in the following steps defining ETBS.

The Steps

Initially fill the bond bucket with 10 years of withdrawals (i.e., 10 times the initial withdrawal amount).

1. If there are not enough bonds to fund the current year's withdrawal, sell enough stocks to replenish bonds with another 10 years of withdrawals (i.e., 10 times the current year's withdrawal amount).

2. If 5 years have elapsed since bonds were replenished and the real return for stocks (since the start of retirement) is greater than 7%, sell enough stocks to replenish bonds early for another 10 years (using the bonds already in place).

3. Withdraw from bonds.

4. Buy and sell as needed to rebalance individual stock assets to their target stock values (without modifying the portfolio's stock percentage).

5. Buy and sell as needed to rebalance individual bond assets to their target bond values (without modifying the portfolio's bond percentage).

Backtesting Results

Figure 20 shows the strategy's MSWR values compared to annual rebalancing. Figure 21 shows the results for varying withdrawal percentages. It's clear that ETBS consistently underperforms annual rebalancing.

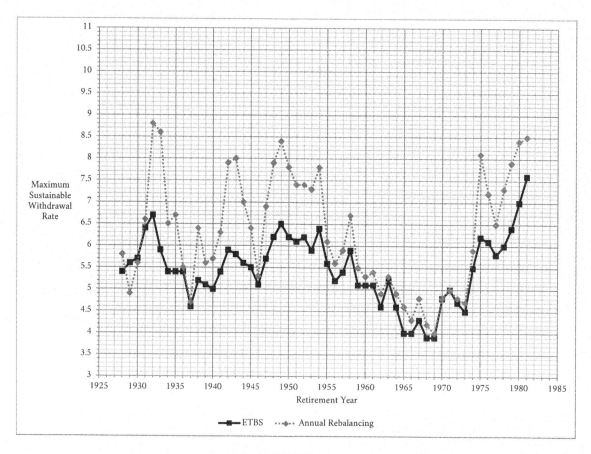

FIGURE 20

ETBS compared to annual rebalancing.

Withdraw Rate	Average Remaining	Average Year of Failure	Lowest-Bond Average	Highest-Bond Average	Bond Average	Success Rate
4.0%	9.9M	29.5	3.50%	46.20%	23.60%	96.30%
4.5%	6.7M	23	5.20%	54.90%	30.40%	90.70%
5.0%	4.0M	21.8	9.80%	63.20%	40.00%	79.60%

FIGURE 21

ETBS results for varying withdrawal rates.

Although ETBS has strong points (e.g., using bonds to insulate stocks; setting a return goal), the results when compared to traditional rebalancing indicate that the strategy's weaknesses overpower its strengths. The weaknesses stem from two interrelated problems:

- Calculating the bond allocation using years is less efficient than using the percentage of the portfolio. In some markets, the 10-year allocation for bonds can become a disproportionately large part of the overall portfolio, possibly even driving the stock percentage to zero. Varying the number of years in bonds by a couple of years in either direction did not result in significantly better performance.

- Replenishing bonds when they are depleted causes a large portion of stocks to be immediately sold independently of what is happening in the market—selling at a bad time can drive the portfolio to failure.

What can be learned from this exercise? Good general ideas don't necessarily translate to effective income-harvesting strategies—the details greatly matter. Also, it can be difficult to translate high-level goals into well-specified individual plans. Finally, it appears difficult to squeeze strong harvesting performance out of a bucket strategy based on time intervals (versus portfolio percentage).

The Rational Strategy

The Rational Strategy covers another set of income-harvesting steps circulating within the literature, although it may be known under different names and includes variations. As the name I give to it implies, the strategy is based on rational ideas that are individually sound, although again the results show this is not enough.

The following overlapping concepts guide the makeup of the strategy:

- Stocks fuel portfolio growth.

- Stocks should not be sold when they are down if at all possible.

- Bonds buffer stocks during bad years by funding withdrawals.

- Bonds are replenished from stock sales during good years.

More specifically, bonds support withdrawals but they are only replenished from nominal stock growth. All the concepts are realized in the following steps defining the Rational Strategy.

The Steps

Initially calculate the bond allocation by multiplying the initial withdrawal amount by a target number of years (5 to 7 years are recommended, but 5 is used as the best-performing); the rest of the portfolio is allocated to stocks.

1. Each year, recalculate the targeted bond allocation by multiplying the current annual withdrawal amount by the targeted years in bonds (e.g., 5).

2. Sell enough bond assets to fund the next withdrawal; if bonds are depleted, sell from stocks.

3. Withdraw the annual living expenses from the portfolio's cash.

4. Buy and sell as needed to rebalance according to the following criteria:
   a. If stocks are up for the year and bonds are less than their target allocation, then make up as much as possible of the bonds' shortage from the year's stock growth (by selling stocks to buy bonds).
   b. Individual stock assets are rebalanced to their target stock values (without modifying the portfolio's stock percentage).
   c. Individual bond assets are rebalanced to their target bond values (without modifying the portfolio's stock percentage).

Backtesting Results

Figure 22 shows the strategy's MSWR values compared to annual rebalancing. Figure 23 shows the results for various withdrawal percentages and years set aside in bonds (i.e., the target bond allocation).

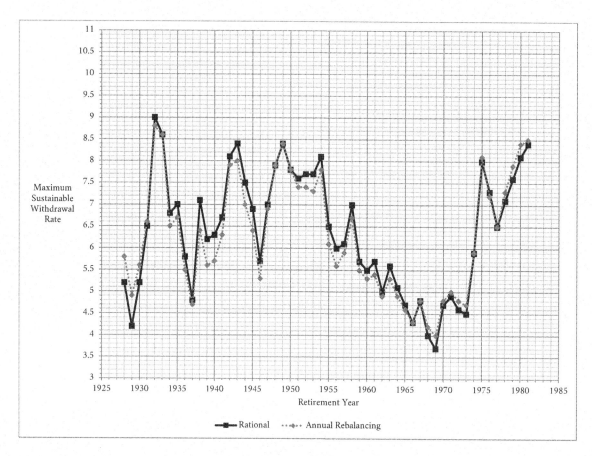

FIGURE 22

Rational Strategy compared to annual rebalancing.

Withdraw Rate	Bond Target	Average Remaining	Average Year of Failure	Lowest-Bond Average	Highest-Bond Average	Bond Average	Success Rate
4.0%	5 Years	12.6M	25	6.20%	25.20%	14.90%	98.10%
4.0%	6 Years	11.5M	25	8.70%	30.40%	18.60%	98.10%
4.0%	7 Years	10.4M	25	11.30%	35.60%	22.50%	98.10%
4.5%	5 Years	9.8M	24.3	7.50%	29.10%	18.40%	92.60%
4.5%	6 Years	8.7M	25.4	10.00%	34.50%	22.70%	90.70%
4.5%	7 Years	7.6M	25.6	12.10%	40.30%	26.90%	90.70%
5.0%	5 Years	7.5M	23.9	7.10%	30.20%	19.60%	79.60%
5.0%	6 Years	6.4M	23.5	10.70%	36.50%	24.60%	77.80%
5.0%	7 Years	5.3M	23.4	15.50%	42.80%	30.00%	75.90%

FIGURE 23

Rational Strategy results for varying withdrawal rates and bond-target years.

Overall, the results are not strong. For some retirement periods, the performance is better than annual rebalancing, but during difficult periods (e.g., retirements starting in 1929, 1968, and 1969) when it matters most, the strategy underperforms. What's surprising is the similarity between this strategy and some top performers (e.g., OmegaNot, Prime Harvesting) — it seems like this strategy should perform much better than it does.

The strategy's weakness is primarily due to measuring stock growth without considering inflation. The result is that cumulative stock performance isn't accurately measured, and stocks are sometimes sold at a loss in real terms. In addition, the immediate sells from nominal stock growth can sometime lose out on momentum (compared to alternatives). It's also notable that although allocating bonds by years (instead of percentage) typically results in too many bonds, this time there were on average too few bonds because of how they were replenished.

The details and how they interoperate matter greatly, making it very difficult to anticipate how a strategy will perform without a complete verification. Good concepts combined with rational thinking and individually sound rules aren't enough.

The Prime Harvesting Strategy – A New Strategy

Prime Harvesting is formed out of the top-performing characteristics of the preceding strategies. However, as already shown it's the composite behavior that ultimately matters. Picking and choosing what works best together, the following characteristics (i.e., what works) are included in Prime Harvesting:

1. Withdrawals are always funded by bonds, providing a buffer from stock volatility.

2. The bond allocation is based on a percentage of the total portfolio, as opposed to setting aside a fixed number of years of income.

3. Bonds are replenished from stock sells only when the total market is up (i.e., stocks are never sold at a loss if possible).

4. A comprehensive metric is used to identify when the market is up, covering multiple years as opposed to the most recent performance.

The comprehensive metric for identifying when markets are up is adapted from Dave Lee's OmegaNot Strategy. This metric is an essential part of Prime Harvesting: if stock values are greater than 120% of their inflation-adjusted initial value, then the market is considered "up" and a portion of stocks are transferred to bonds. Triggering off 120%, instead of 100%, takes more advantage of market momentum.

Another distinguishing characteristic is, once the initial stock percentage is set, additional stocks are never purchased throughout retirement (the only exception is dividend reinvestment within funds). The stock percentage can only rise passively by stock growth, or indirectly by lowering bonds (by selling to fund withdrawals). Again, stocks are only sold to replenish bonds and then bonds are only sold to fund withdrawals. This means, the original stock allocation fuels growth throughout retirement with no potential for anti-momentum (i.e., continuing to buy stocks as prices drop over multiple years).

Prime Harvesting is very simple, but effective. It's also the strategy recommended in this book for income-harvesting. The reason will eventually become clear. The strategy comes in two forms: Prime Harvesting and Alternate-Prime Harvesting. Both forms are defined in the following steps. The only difference between the two strategies is highlighted in bold in Step 1.

The Steps with Prime Harvesting (With Spreadsheet Support)

1. If stock assets are greater than 120% of their initial value after annually adjusting for inflation, **sell 20% of stocks to buy additional bonds**.

2. Sell enough bond assets to fund the next withdrawal; if bonds are depleted, sell enough from stocks to cover the withdrawal.

3. Withdraw the annual living expenses from the portfolio's cash.

4. Buy and sell as needed to rebalance individual stock assets to their target stock values (without modifying the portfolio's stock percentage).

5. Buy and sell as needed to rebalance individual bond assets to their target bond values (without modifying the portfolio's bond percentage).

When stocks are doing well, Prime Harvesting captures the gain, transferring stocks to bonds. As stocks continue to increase in value, more gain is captured and the bond percentage increases. With Prime Harvesting, there is no limit to the bond percentage. This sometimes loses out on extra return, but it reduces risk.

When stocks are underperforming, Prime Harvesting waits for the market to recover before selling. As long as bonds are available, this prevents stocks from ever being sold while they are down (locking in a loss).

The Steps with Alternate-Prime Harvesting (With Spreadsheet Support)

1. If the stock assets are greater than 120% of their initial value after annually adjusting for inflation, then **sell enough stocks to replenish the target bond allocation (i.e., the initial bond percentage)**.

2. Sell enough bond assets to fund the next withdrawal; if bonds are depleted, sell enough from stocks to cover the withdrawal.

3. Withdraw the annual living expenses from the portfolio's cash.

4. Buy and sell as needed to rebalance individual stock assets to their target stock values (without modifying the portfolio's stock percentage).

5. Buy and sell as needed to rebalance individual bond assets to their target bond values (without modifying the portfolio's bond percentage).

When stocks are doing well, Alternate-Prime always replenishes bonds back to their target level, no more or less. This typically increases income for a small increase in risk.

Both forms of Prime Harvesting work with any initial stock percentage.

Backtesting Results

Figure 24 and Figure 25 show the Prime and Alternate-Prime strategies' MSWR values respectively with each compared to annual rebalancing. Figure 26 and Figure 27 show the Prime Harvesting and Alternate-Prime results respectively for various withdrawal percentages and stock ratios.

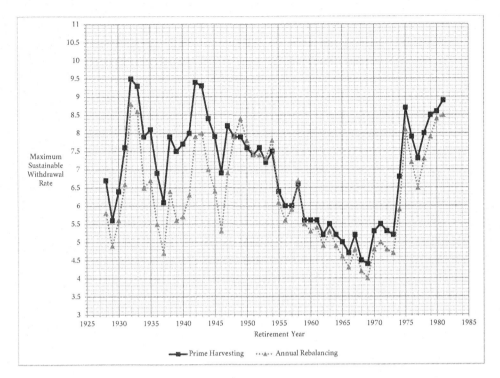

FIGURE 24

Prime Harvesting compared to annual rebalancing.

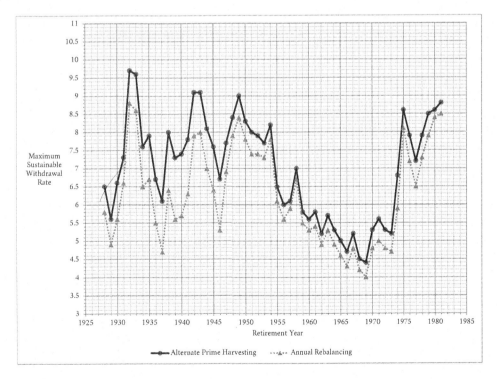

FIGURE 25

Alternate-Prime Harvesting compared to annual rebalancing.

Withdraw Rate	Stock	Average Remaining	Average Year of Failure	Lowest-Bond Average	Highest-Bond Average	Bond Average	Success Rate
4.0%	10%	0.8M	28.1	40.50%	92.70%	75.20%	61.10%
4.0%	20%	1.6M	NA	39.50%	84.60%	68.40%	100.00%
4.0%	30%	2.6M	NA	43.50%	78.70%	63.00%	100.00%
4.0%	40%	3.6M	NA	37.40%	74.90%	57.90%	100.00%
4.0%	50%	4.6M	NA	30.30%	72.40%	53.20%	100.00%
4.0%	60%	5.5M	NA	23.70%	70.40%	48.90%	100.00%
4.0%	70%	6.5M	NA	17.40%	69.10%	44.90%	100.00%
4.0%	80%	7.3M	NA	11.40%	67.80%	41.20%	100.00%
4.0%	90%	8.0M	26	6.60%	67.90%	37.80%	96.30%
4.5%	10%	0.4M	25.4	63.30%	93.70%	72.90%	25.90%
4.5%	20%	0.9M	27.6	26.00%	84.60%	61.50%	74.10%
4.5%	30%	1.7M	28	33.40%	77.10%	56.80%	92.60%
4.5%	40%	2.6M	29	30.10%	72.10%	52.40%	98.10%
4.5%	50%	3.6M	30	25.70%	69.20%	48.50%	98.10%
4.5%	60%	4.5M	27	20.60%	67.70%	44.90%	98.10%
4.5%	70%	5.4M	25.5	15.60%	67.00%	41.40%	96.30%
4.5%	80%	6.2M	22	10.30%	65.60%	38.10%	96.30%
4.5%	90%	6.9M	20	5.60%	64.50%	35.30%	94.40%
5.0%	10%	0.2M	22.5	51.80%	93.20%	72.20%	18.50%
5.0%	20%	0.5M	25.8	37.30%	85.70%	58.10%	35.20%
5.0%	30%	1.0M	26.1	26.40%	76.60%	52.40%	70.40%
5.0%	40%	1.8M	25.3	26.40%	70.30%	48.10%	87.00%
5.0%	50%	2.7M	24.5	22.80%	67.30%	44.40%	92.60%
5.0%	60%	3.6M	22.3	18.60%	65.30%	41.10%	94.40%
5.0%	70%	4.4M	20.7	13.80%	63.60%	37.90%	94.40%
5.0%	80%	5.1M	20	9.30%	62.40%	35.10%	92.60%
5.0%	90%	5.7M	19.8	5.20%	60.50%	32.50%	90.70%

FIGURE 26

Prime Harvesting results for varying withdrawal rates and stock percentages.

Withdraw Rate	Stock	Average Remaining	Average Year of Failure	Lowest-Bond Average	Highest-Bond Average	Bond Average	Success Rate
4.0%	10%	0.7M	27	49.50%	92.70%	80.70%	53.70%
4.0%	20%	1.5M	29	37.30%	83.30%	70.90%	98.10%
4.0%	30%	2.6M	NA	42.10%	75.40%	63.60%	100.00%
4.0%	40%	3.9M	NA	37.30%	66.40%	55.10%	100.00%
4.0%	50%	5.6M	NA	30.30%	55.70%	45.50%	100.00%
4.0%	60%	7.7M	NA	22.50%	43.90%	35.70%	100.00%
4.0%	70%	10.0M	NA	15.00%	32.50%	25.60%	100.00%
4.0%	80%	12.6M	NA	7.80%	20.50%	15.80%	100.00%
4.0%	90%	15.4M	26	2.10%	9.10%	6.50%	96.30%
4.5%	10%	0.4M	24.2	62.10%	93.20%	78.70%	25.90%
4.5%	20%	0.8M	27.7	32.90%	84.30%	65.50%	53.70%
4.5%	30%	1.6M	28	28.70%	74.40%	58.30%	90.70%
4.5%	40%	2.8M	29	31.00%	65.40%	50.80%	98.10%
4.5%	50%	4.3M	30	26.90%	54.80%	42.70%	98.10%
4.5%	60%	6.2M	27	20.40%	43.20%	33.50%	98.10%
4.5%	70%	8.4M	25.5	13.40%	32.00%	24.20%	96.30%
4.5%	80%	10.8M	22	7.00%	20.00%	14.80%	96.30%
4.5%	90%	13.3M	20	1.80%	8.80%	6.00%	94.40%
5.0%	10%	0.2M	21.9	48.30%	93.00%	78.20%	18.50%
5.0%	20%	0.4M	24.9	43.30%	86.20%	63.00%	25.90%
5.0%	30%	0.9M	26.5	24.60%	74.60%	52.90%	61.10%
5.0%	40%	1.9M	25.9	28.10%	65.10%	46.70%	85.20%
5.0%	50%	3.2M	24.3	24.00%	54.50%	39.20%	92.60%
5.0%	60%	4.9M	22.3	18.50%	42.90%	31.20%	94.40%
5.0%	70%	6.9M	20.3	11.80%	31.20%	22.40%	94.40%
5.0%	80%	9.1M	19.8	6.30%	19.30%	13.70%	92.60%
5.0%	90%	11.3M	20.2	1.60%	8.50%	5.50%	88.90%

FIGURE 27

Alternate-Prime Harvesting results for varying withdrawal rates and stock percentages.

Alternate-Prime always outperformed annual rebalancing. Prime Harvesting always outperformed annual rebalancing during difficult retirement periods, but underperformed in the 1950s when MSWR values were above 6% and performance mattered less for hedging risk.

Based on this US data, Alternate-Prime outpaces Prime Harvesting, but additional data will also show Prime Harvesting is ultimately a little safer than Alternate-Prime. This extra margin of safety comes from sacrificing return during peak stock performance to build up a larger bond reserve. Further analysis will show Prime Harvesting to be the overall top performer.

Prime Harvesting can sometimes have a seemingly undesirable side effect: during long periods of low stock returns, bond levels can go below their preferred limits because they are continuing to fund withdrawals with no stock sells to replenish them. Bond levels do not strongly correlate to systemic-withdrawal risk, but when maintained within preferred limits, they do generally reduce exposure to speculative risk. However, Prime Harvesting has a strong counterbalance to these occasional low bond levels—these periods correspond to attractive stock valuations. Discussed more in a later chapter, attractive stock valuations substantially reduce exposure to known risk. It's important to understand that growing stock percentages using Prime Harvesting is not an anomaly, but a response to the market, trying to minimize overall risk*. It's always important to understand that stocks are never purchased after retirement starts. Instead, bond attrition is the cause of a rising stock percentage.

Briefly mentioned before, it's worth noting that additional tests were run using Prime Harvesting to manage individual asset subclasses (e.g., small stocks, large value stocks) as opposed to stocks as a whole. Performance only improved a little. Although the data wasn't available to also test broader assets like US stocks, developed market stocks, and emerging market stocks, there appears to be significant latitude in the tracking. Further study (with more data) may show the extra complexity of finer tracking is worthwhile for some retirees; however, with the data in hand it's easier and reasonable to avoid the additional complexity.

Other Strategies Investigated But Not Included

Below are the more noteworthy additional strategies tested but not included in the survey.

- Variations of traditional rebalancing.

- More variations of bucket strategies.

- Rebalancing based on trailing real returns.

- Many combinations of strategies, combining the best features of each.

A Rising Glidepath strategy as outlined by Pfau and Kitces[20] was also preliminarily tested after this survey was complete (because of the media attention it received). While age-based strategies lower the stock percentage each successive retirement year, a Rising Glidepath strategy increases the stock percentage, depending on a variety of possible formulas. A Rising Glidepath strategy is generally much better than an age-based strategy. Pfau and Kitces point out, this is partly due to avoiding sequence-of-returns risk early in retirement, an interesting observation. Still, performance is ultimately limited because what is happening in the portfolio (or the market) is not factored in. A Rising Glidepath strategy showed a moderate improvement over traditional rebalancing for some realistic retirement cases when based on equivalent stock-bond averages, but this improvement was not consistent over broader testing. When Rising Glidepath was started with the same initial stock percentage as annual rebalancing but then moved upward each year (e.g., starting

---

* OmegaNot's low bond average has this same compensating counterbalance, but it's a matter of degree—its bond average is significantly lower than Prime Harvesting's.

at 60% and moving to 89% over 30 years), it did increase performance; however, much of this increase maps back to a higher average stock percentage. Overall, one might say, Rising Glidepath improves performance over annual rebalancing, but the variations tested did not perform at the level of the top harvesting strategies. One important takeaway of the Rising Glidepath paper is, we should not be fretting too much about a high stock percentage late in retirement.

COMPARING THE STRATEGIES

This section has two goals: 1) comparing the surveyed strategies side by side to show relative performance; 2) exposing each strategy to a substantially broader set of data.

Coming back to the risk of a data-mining bias, it's only by testing with independent (out-of-sample) data can a mature assessment of a strategy's performance be made. So far, all the backtesting has been with the US SBBI data. Now, three other datasets will also be used:

1. Shiller's US data from 1871 to 2010 with a portfolio of S&P stocks (i.e., large stocks). Bonds are based on the US long interest rate (10-year treasury bonds).

2. United Kingdom data from 1923 to 2010 with a portfolio of the UK's total-market stocks. The UK's treasury bills are used for bonds.

3. Japan data from 1950 to 2010 with a portfolio of Japan's total-market stocks. Japan's treasury bills are used for bonds.

Also, bootstrapping will be used to add further diversity (explained in the previous chapter).

The goal is to find consistently strong performance under diverse circumstances. Prime Harvesting is not perfect, but it will be shown to generally meet this goal—certainly better than the alternatives.

Identifying the Top Performers

The primary unit of comparison is first MSWR-100%, documenting performance during the worst retirement period. MSWR-90% is shown next, providing a better view into more typical performance: the top 90% of the retirement periods. Next, bootstrapping results will be shown in a couple of different forms, testing success rates using fixed withdrawal amounts. Finally, a relative ranking of the strategies is shown, providing a succinct snapshot of performance across all the tests.

To start, Figure 28 shows a summary of MSWR-100% backtesting results using US SBBI data, with the default portfolio for 30-year retirements. Again, MSWR-100% corresponds to the worst-case historical scenario within the dataset. All the top performers sustain a 4.4% annual withdrawal rate while the other strategies support progressively lower rates from 4.1% down to 3.4%. Also significant are the bond averages. For example, Prime Harvesting across the 53 retirement periods maintains a bond average of 45.7%, but its average lowest bond percentage was 30.8% and its average for the highest bond percentage was 67.8%. For the top performing strategies, the bond average inversely correlates with the average remaining values at the end of retirement, ranging from Prime Harvesting's 4.7 million average-remaining value to Bonds-First's 12.1 million average-remaining value. One might expect the top strategies to have the most remaining funds at the end of retirement, but this usually isn't the case for a couple of reasons. The top performers support higher withdrawal rates, leaving less value at the end of retirement, but more significantly, the top performers favor lower risk over higher returns. (How to safely boost the assets remaining at the end of retirement is discussed later.)

United States SBBI Data 1928-2010	MSWR-100%	Average Remaining	Lowest-Bond Average	Highest-Bond Average	Bond Average
Prime	4.4	4.7M	20.8%	67.8%	45.7%
Alternate Prime	4.4	6.5M	20.6%	43.3%	33.9%
Parker	4.4	6.4M	24.5%	41.3%	36.2%
OmegaNot	4.4	8.3M	8.6%	43.1%	21.2%
Bonds-First	4.4	12.1M	0.0%	37.5%	7.1%
Three Buckets	4.1	7.6M	1.7%	67.5%	34.1%
Guyton	4.1	3.2M	27.3%	49.1%	35.3%
Weiss	4	7.5M	23.0%	40.0%	37.6%
Annual Rebalancing	4	6.6M	40.0%	40.0%	40.0%
ETBS	3.9	10.6M	3.3%	46.8%	22.4%
Age-120	3.8	4.7M	45.0%	74.0%	58.4%
Rational	3.7	14.3M	5.1%	23.0%	13.1%
GlidePath	3.7	3.3M	45.6%	100.0%	71.8%
Age-100	3.4	3.0M	65.0%	94.0%	78.4%

FIGURE 28

MSWR-100% comparison of income-harvesting strategies using US SBBI data from 1928 to 2010.

Figure 29 shows a summary of MSWR-100% backtesting results using the US Shiller data for large stocks. Parker's strategy is the top performer this time, with a MSWR-100% of 3.8%. Prime and Alternate-Prime strategies fall into third place, behind Parker and OmegaNot, but also behind Guyton and Annual Rebalancing.

United States Shiller Data 1871-2010	MSWR-100%	Average Remaining	Lowest-Bond Average	Highest-Bond Average	Bond Average
Parker	3.8	3.2M	24.6%	41.0%	39.9%
OmegaNot	3.7	4.1M	13.9%	44.5%	26.9%
Guyton	3.7	2.1M	28.1%	48.0%	36.7%
Annual Rebalancing	3.7	3.3M	40.0%	40.0%	40.0%
Prime	3.6	3.3M	21.6%	67.4%	47.0%
Alternate Prime	3.6	3.9M	20.4%	44.8%	34.4%
Bonds-First	3.6	5.6M	0.0%	37.9%	9.3%
Weiss	3.6	3.7M	20.3%	40.0%	35.9%
Age-120	3.6	2.5M	45.0%	74.0%	58.4%
Rational	3.5	5.5M	7.5%	23.9%	14.6%
GlidePath	3.4	2.1M	45.6%	100.0%	71.8%
ETBS	3.4	5.1M	2.4%	43.5%	20.4%
Age-100	3.3	1.8M	65.0%	94.0%	78.4%
Three Buckets	3.3	4.9M	1.5%	56.6%	28.4%

FIGURE 29

MSWR-100% comparison of income-harvesting strategies using US Shiller data from 1871 to 2010.

This is the type of data a researcher hates to see. It breaks an anticipated pattern and introduces ambiguities. It raises the question of a data-mining bias. Perhaps Prime Harvesting is a top performer only with the SBBI data. More data will overcome these concerns; however, this case stands as a reminder that any strategy can underperform in the wrong market circumstances. This time, Prime Harvesting's and Alternate Prime's poor performance comes from one exceedingly poor retirement period starting in 1966, while invested only in US large stocks.

Looking further, every other metric using Shiller's data shows Prime Harvesting as the top performer, including every MSWR test (e.g., MSWR-95%, MSWR-80%, MSWR-50%), along with success rates from fixed rates withdrawals (4%, 4.5%, and 5%).

Two important points surface from backtesting the US Shiller data. First, picking an investment strategy is about probabilities: a strategy can never guarantee future performance. Second, the metric shapes the results—change the metric and you can change the results. Both points reinforce why a single test metric on a single dataset should not be considered a reliable indicator of future performance one way or another. Still, Prime Harvest did underperform in this case and this should be considered in the broader comparison.

Figure 30 shows a summary of the MSWR-100% backtesting results using United Kingdom data. OmegaNot outperforms all other strategies this time, with Prime, Alternate-Prime, and Bonds-First coming close. Parker's Strategy does significantly worse in this case. The age-based strategies do exceptionally poorly with the UK data. Annual rebalancing also performs surprisingly poorly.

United Kingdom 1923-2010	MSWR-100%	Average Remaining	Lowest-Bond Average	Highest-Bond Average	Bond Average
OmegaNot	3.8	8.1M	5.9%	45.4%	19.5%
Prime	3.7	6.6M	11.2%	66.7%	37.5%
Alternate Prime	3.7	7.7M	10.4%	51.7%	31.1%
Bonds-First	3.7	10.6M	0.0%	38.1%	7.9%
Weiss	3.4	10.3M	12.5%	40.0%	34.6%
Parker	3.2	8.0M	26.9%	49.8%	42.4%
Guyton	3.2	4.5M	26.7%	53.1%	36.1%
Rational	3.1	13.9M	6.6%	22.0%	13.8%
ETBS	3.1	12.3M	1.6%	40.0%	18.6%
Three Buckets	3.1	10.1M	1.4%	55.9%	27.6%
Annual Rebalancing	3	10.5M	40.0%	40.0%	40.0%
Age-120	2.6	8.8M	45.0%	74.0%	58.4%
GlidePath	2.4	6.9M	45.6%	100.0%	71.8%
Age-100	2.2	6.2M	65.0%	94.0%	78.4%

FIGURE 30

MSWR-100% comparison of income-harvesting strategies using UK data from 1923 to 2010.

Figure 31 shows a summary of the MSWR-100% backtesting results using the Japan data. Surprisingly, the Three-Bucket strategy comes in well ahead of the other strategies—an anomaly* due to Japan's specific market conditions. Prime and Alternate-Prime are the next top performers, significantly ahead of the others.

---

* Some but not all of this high performance for the Three-Bucket Strategy with Japanese data is due to simulating bucket 2 returns (i.e., T-bill rate plus 3%). Using the Japanese T-bill rate instead for the second bucket resulted in 3.8% MSWR-100%—still in first place with Prime Harvesting but no longer outstanding.

Japan 1950-2010	MSWR-100%	Average Remaining	Lowest-Bond Average	Highest-Bond Average	Bond Average
Three Buckets	4.3	5.6M	2.2%	65.5%	36.4%
Prime	3.8	6.2M	24.8%	76.4%	53.5%
Alternate Prime	3.8	10.6M	24.9%	45.5%	36.8%
OmegaNot	3.5	16.1M	9.2%	40.3%	23.4%
Bonds-First	3.5	21.5M	0.0%	35.7%	7.4%
Weiss	3.4	11.3M	27.5%	40.0%	37.7%
Guyton	3.3	3.3M	22.3%	50.5%	37.3%
ETBS	3.3	21.1M	1.6%	34.8%	15.4%
Annual Rebalancing	3.3	11.2M	40.0%	40.0%	40.0%
Parker	3.2	9.6M	29.6%	56.2%	46.4%
Age-120	3.1	7.4M	45.0%	74.0%	58.4%
GlidePath	3.1	4.6M	45.6%	100.0%	71.8%
Rational	3	27.3M	2.8%	15.7%	8.6%
Age-100	3	3.5M	65.0%	94.0%	78.4%

FIGURE 31

MSWR-100% comparison of income-harvesting strategies using Japan data from 1950 to 2010.

Up until this point, all the comparisons have been using MSWR-100%, which captures behavior for each dataset's worst retirement period. While Prime and Alternate-Prime's performance has been strong, neither has been outstanding for MSWR-100%.

Figure 32 shows MSWR-90% for the same four datasets, capturing more common retirement cases (i.e., top 90%). Prime is a top performer in every case, and Alternate-Prime second in every case but one—both strategies start to stand out as the tests are broadened.

	US SBBI	US Shiller	UK	Japan
Prime	5.2	4.5	4.2	5.6
Alternate Prime	5.2	4.5	4.2	5.5
Parker	5.1	4.3	3.9	4.8
OmegaNot	5.2	4.4	4.2	5.2
Bonds-First	5	4.4	4.2	5.2
Weiss	4.9	4.4	4.1	5
Guyton	4.9	4.4	3.8	4.8
Rational	4.6	4.3	3.8	4.9
ETBS	4.5	3.9	3.5	4.4
Annual Rebalancing	4.7	4.3	3.8	4.6
Three Buckets	4.5	3.9	3.5	4.6
Age-120	4.5	4.1	3.4	4.2
GlidePath	4.2	3.9	3	3.8
Age-100	3.9	3.8	2.6	3.6

FIGURE 32

Combined MSWR-90% for US, UK, and Japan datasets.

Given its prominence as a research method, bootstrapping results are shown next. As previously outlined, bootstrapping randomly resamples the data (i.e., the SBBI data) in different sequences to produce many new sets of market data. Given that the same data can be resampled multiple times in a single simulation, the overall return and volatility characteristics vary substantially when a large number of simulations are performed. This extreme diversity adds a new dimension to the testing, although reordering the data also filters out return disposition (e.g., momentum, valuation effects) and in effect reduces the performance difference between strategies.

Figure 33 shows the average success rate for backtesting 5000 simulated markets using bootstrapping. The resampled data is narrowed down to only include annualized total-market returns between 3% and 10% over the complete dataset to keep the tests somewhat realistic. The success rate is shown this time, as opposed to MSWR-100%, only because it's faster and easier to calculate during bootstrapping simulations. Keep in mind that, because of the nature of the test, including a quarter million individual retirement periods with semi-random data, small percentage differences are more significant. Prime Harvesting is the top performer.

	Success Rate	Average Remaining	Lowest-Bond Average	Highest-Bond Average	Bond Average
Prime	86.01%	3.7M	25%	72%	48%
Alternate Prime	85.46%	5.9M	23%	45%	34%
Parker	84.86%	5.8M	23%	47%	16%
Weiss	84.42%	5.7M	23%	40%	37%
OmegaNot	84.15%	8.1M	10%	43%	24%
Annual Rebalancing	83.64%	5.4M	40%	40%	40%
Guyton	83.55%	2.1M	24%	50%	36%
Age-120	82.20%	3.3M	45%	74%	58%
Three Buckets	81.00%	6.2M	2%	70%	43%
Rational	80.47%	10.8M	6%	27%	17%
Bonds-First	80.46%	11.9M	0%	36%	8%
GlidePath	78.40%	2.1M	46%	100%	71%
ETBS	78.36%	8.1M	4%	52%	32%
Age-100	76.30%	1.4M	65%	94%	78%

FIGURE 33

*Bootstrapping simulation (i.e., resampling with replacement) for 5000
random markets using a 4.5% inflation-adjusted withdrawal rate.*

Simple-block bootstrapping helps to partially preserve return disposition by randomly rearranging the return data only in 5-year blocks (e.g., 1928 to 1932).

Figure 34 and Figure 35 show the results using simple-block bootstrapping to simulate 1000 different markets, then averaging the backtesting results using a 4.5% and 5% fixed withdrawal rate respectively.

	Success Rate	Average Remaining	Lowest-Bond Average	Highest-Bond Average	Bond Average
OmegaNot	97.92%	9.3M	9%	42%	21%
Prime	97.85%	4.7M	23%	69%	46%
Alternate Prime	97.82%	6.7M	22%	43%	34%
Bonds-First	96.92%	13.8M	0%	38%	7%
Weiss	95.71%	6.2M	26%	40%	38%
Parker	95.60%	6.7M	23%	43%	37%
Guyton	94.86%	2.7M	26%	49%	35%
Annual Rebalancing	93.65%	5.7M	40%	40%	40%
Three Buckets	93.42%	6.0M	2%	72%	41%
Rational	90.50%	12.0M	7%	28%	17%
ETBS	90.08%	8.1M	5%	50%	30%
Age-120	89.99%	3.3M	45%	74%	58%
GlidePath	82.80%	2.0M	46%	100%	71%
Age-100	71.46%	1.1M	65%	94%	78%

FIGURE 34

Simple-block bootstrapping simulation for 1000 markets using a 4.5% inflation-adjusted withdrawal rate.

	Success Rate	Average Remaining	Lowest-Bond Average	Highest-Bond Average	Bond Average
Prime	91.83%	3.7M	21%	64%	43%
Alternate Prime	91.82%	5.3M	21%	42%	32%
OmegaNot	91.32%	7.5M	9%	41%	21%
Bonds-First	89.87%	11.8M	0%	37%	6%
Weiss	88.55%	4.7M	27%	40%	38%
Parker	87.60%	5.6M	20%	39%	34%
Guyton	86.36%	2.2M	24%	46%	33%
Annual Rebalancing	84.97%	4.3M	40%	40%	40%
Rational	82.60%	9.3M	7%	31%	19%
ETBS	77.33%	4.9M	9%	58%	39%
Age-120	76.69%	2.3M	45%	74%	58%
Three Buckets	70.81%	2.9M	2%	82%	52%
GlidePath	65.10%	1.3M	46%	100%	70%
Age-100	43.50%	0.6M	65%	94%	77%

FIGURE 35

Simple-block bootstrapping simulation for 1000 markets using a 5% inflation-adjusted withdrawal rate.

Figure 36 shows simple-block bootstrapping again using a 4.5% withdrawal rate, but for a 40-year retirement (as opposed to the default 30-years).

	Success Rate	Average Remaining	Lowest-Bond Average	Highest-Bond Average	Bond Average
Alternate Prime	88.42%	11.4M	22%	43%	33%
Prime	88.27%	6.1M	23%	70%	45%
OmegaNot	87.77%	19.6M	7%	42%	17%
Bonds-First	86.65%	35.0M	0%	37%	5%
Weiss	83.03%	9.7M	30%	40%	38%
Parker	82.42%	12.5M	21%	46%	34%
Rational	78.15%	27.0M	5%	28%	17%
Annual Rebalancing	77.09%	9.0M	40%	40%	40%
Guyton	76.49%	2.9M	23%	49%	33%
Age-120	71.75%	6.1M	35%	74%	53%
ETBS	67.45%	12.3M	7%	53%	36%
GlidePath	63.41%	3.4M	35%	100%	61%
Three Buckets	53.03%	6.1M	1%	79%	49%
Age-100	29.95%	0.5M	55%	94%	71%

FIGURE 36

Simple-block bootstrapping simulation for 1000 markets using a 5%
inflation-adjusted withdrawal rate for 40-year retirement.

Prime Harvesting, Alternate-Prime, and OmegaNot are consistently the top performers across these tests. However, so much data with varying results can be hard to assimilate. A clearer pattern can be seen by stepping back to focus on the relative rank of the strategies across the results.

Figure 37 shows the relative rank of all the strategies across all the tests plus MSWR-80% and MSWR-50%. The top three rankings are highlighted for each case to form a clearer visual picture. A rank of "1" indicates a strategy is a top performer for the case (or tied for it); a rank of "2" indicates a second place ranking, and so on.

	US SBBI MSWR				US Shiller MSWR				UK MSWR				Japan MSWR				Bootstrapping Success Rate			
	100%	90%	80%	50%	100%	90%	80%	50%	100%	90%	80%	50%	100%	90%	80%	50%	Test 1	Test 2	Test 3	Test 4
Prime	1	1	2	3	3	1	1	1	2	1	1	2	2	1	1	2	1	2	1	2
Alternate Prime	1	1	1	3	3	1	1	1	2	1	1	1	2	2	2	2	2	3	2	1
Parker	1	2	3	4	1	3	2	2	4	3	2	3	6	6	5	4	3	6	6	6
OmegaNot	1	1	3	2	2	2	1	1	1	1	1	2	3	3	3	3	5	1	3	3
Bonds-First	1	3	4	1	3	2	2	1	2	1	2	2	3	3	2	1	11	4	4	4
Three Buckets	2	7	8	10	6	5	5	8	5	5	6	6	1	7	9	8	9	9	12	13
Guyton	2	4	5	6	2	2	2	5	4	4	3	5	5	6	6	5	7	7	7	9
Weiss	3	4	4	5	3	2	2	4	3	2	2	4	4	4	4	5	4	5	5	5
Annual Rebalancing	3	5	6	7	2	3	3	5	6	4	3	5	5	7	7	5	6	8	8	8
ETBS	4	7	7	9	5	5	5	6	5	5	4	6	5	6	8	7	13	11	10	11
Age-120	5	7	8	8	3	4	4	7	7	6	5	7	7	8	10	6	8	12	11	10
Rational	6	6	6	6	4	3	2	3	5	4	3	4	5	5	4	4	10	10	9	7
GlidePath	6	8	9	11	5	5	6	8	8	7	7	8	7	9	11	9	12	13	13	12
Age-100	7	9	10	12	6	6	7	9	9	8	8	9	8	10	12	10	14	14	14	14

FIGURE 37

Summary of relative ranking of income-harvesting strategies.

Prime Harvesting and Alternate-Prime Harvesting are the most consistent strategies, usually ranking in the first or second position and always in the top three ranks. No other strategies are consistently in the top three ranks. OmegaNot and Weiss' strategy are always in the top 5 ranks. Parker's strategy is always in the top 6 ranks. All the other strategies including annual rebalancing come in considerably behind.

Considering Different Asset Allocations

The emphasis so far has been on comparing strategies across multiple datasets. It's also important to ensure the top-performers work well across different asset allocations.

This section examines a variety of allocations, with a narrower focus on the top performers: Prime Harvesting and Alternate-Prime. Annual rebalancing is included as the baseline as well as Parker's strategy as another alternative for comparison.

The next few figures compare performance using 5000 randomly generated portfolios. The portfolios are formed from the US SBBI dataset, since it breaks down asset returns. The stock percentage is randomly varied from 25% to 75%, with the balance going into bonds. The stock allocation is divided into 10% portions and randomly allocated to each of the asset classes (e.g., small, large value) allowing duplicates (i.e., the same asset class can be randomly reselected more than once for an additional 10% allocation). This same approach is used for bonds: the allocation is divided into 10% portions and randomly allocated to the available bond categories with duplicates possible. (Appendix A shows all stock and bond categories.) This random selection creates a diverse set of 5000 portfolios.

Figure 38 compares Prime Harvesting's and annual rebalancing's backtesting results for the 5000 portfolios—each portfolio (along the x-axis) is backtested once with Prime Harvesting and once with annual rebalancing with both MSWR-100% results recorded (on the y-axis). So some sense can be made of the data, the results are sorted by Prime Harvesting's MSWR-100% values, descending from 5.7% down to 3.1%. For example, for the portfolio numbers around 1000 (on the horizontal axis), Prime Harvesting's MSWR-100% values are all at 4.5%, and annual rebalancing's MSWR-100% values for the same set of portfolios ranging from 4.2% down to 3.7%, with most results coming in around 4%. (Each small point, representing one of the 5000 portfolios' MSWR-100% values, is displayed with an element of transparency, so darker points represent a higher number of clustered results around a specific value.)

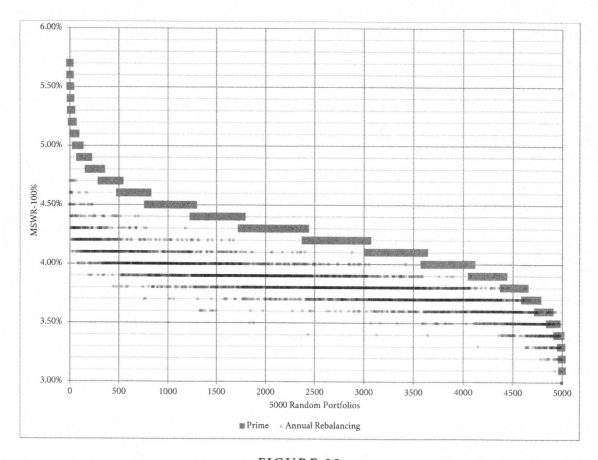

FIGURE 38

Prime Harvesting versus annual rebalancing backtesting performance for 5000 random portfolios.

What does Figure 38 show? Prime Harvesting performs significantly better (i.e., a higher MSWR-100%) than annual rebalancing for virtually all the 5000 retirement portfolios. Only in rare cases for the poorest portfolios did annual rebalancing beat Prime Harvesting (this can only be seen in the raw data). Specifically, annual rebalancing beat Prime Harvesting only 12 times out of the 5000 portfolios, each with very poor retirement portfolios (at the far right-end of the figure) that should not be used.

Figure 39 compares Prime Harvesting's and Parker's backtesting results for the same 5000 portfolios. Prime Harvesting's results are again the stronger of the two. Prime Harvesting comes out ahead of Parker's strategy approximately 50% of the time, ties around 30% of the time, and comes out behind 20% of the time. As seen with annual rebalancing, Prime Harvesting's relative performance drops for the poorer portfolios. Also notable, when Prime Harvesting comes out behind, it's usually close.

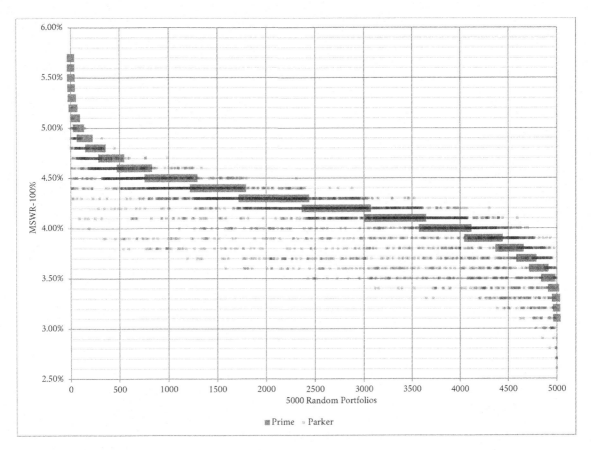

FIGURE 39

Prime Harvesting versus the Parker Strategy for 5000 random portfolios.

Figure 40 compares Prime Harvesting's and Alternate-Prime-Harvesting's backtesting results for the same 5000 portfolios. Again, Prime Harvesting is the top performer, but this time the results are much closer. For 86% of the cases, the strategies have the same results; 10% of the time Prime Harvesting wins (usually by 0.1%); 4% of the time Alternate-Prime Harvesting wins. The closeness illustrates why Alternate-Prime Harvesting is a viable alternative for gaining extra income for a small amount of additional risk; however, under extreme market conditions Prime Harvesting could perform significantly better.

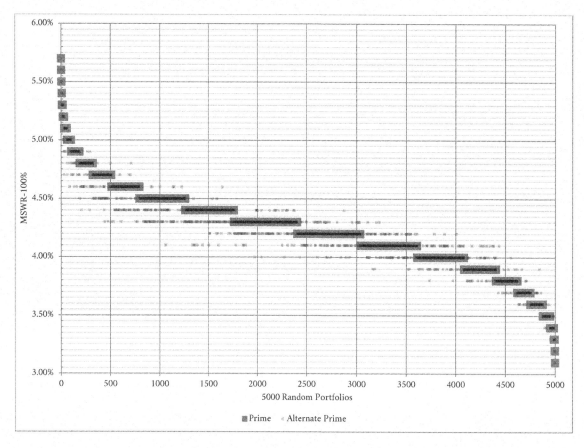

FIGURE 40

Prime Harvesting versus Alternate-Prime for 5000 random portfolios.

Not shown are the same comparisons using OmegaNot and Bonds-First. OmegaNot performs very well across different allocations, coming in very close to Prime Harvesting. Bonds-First also does very well in comparison, but weaker than OmegaNot. Again, the main reason OmegaNot and Bonds-First are not viable contenders is their lower average bond percentages compared to Prime Harvesting.

For one last look at asset allocation, Figure 41 again compares Prime Harvesting to annual rebalancing using the 5000 portfolio, but this time MSWR-90% is shown (as opposed to MSWR-100%). This graph shows that, for the more common cases (as opposed to the worst-case) the disparity in performance grows even larger, with Prime Harvesting doing substantially better.

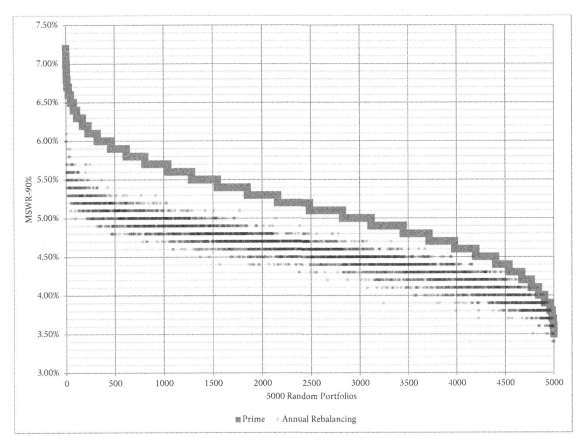

FIGURE 41

MSWR-90% for Prime Harvesting versus annual rebalancing for 5000 random portfolios.

A Closer Look at Bond Levels

The previous sections establish Prime Harvesting as the top income-harvesting strategy; however, it's important for the retiree to clearly understand and accept there's a possibly of a wide range of stock and bond percentages during a "normal" 30-year retirement.

Figure 42 compares the 30-year average bond percentage for Prime, Alternate-Prime, Parker, and annual rebalancing strategies using a 5% withdrawal rate with the SBBI dataset. For example, the average bond percentage using Prime Harvesting for the 30-year retirement period starting in 1935 is 48%; for the retirement period starting in 1955 is 44%; for the retirement period starting in 1968 is a mere 8%.

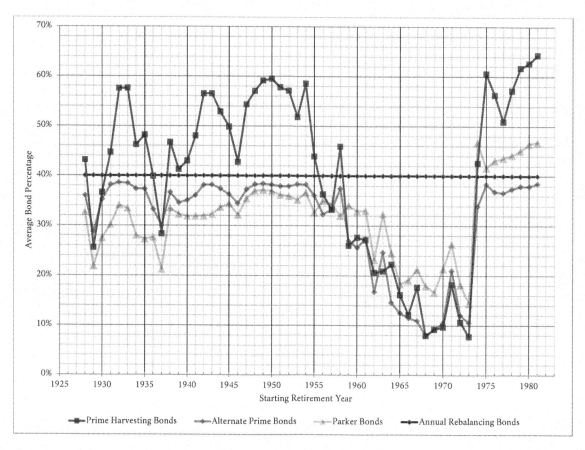

FIGURE 42

Average bond percentage at 5% withdrawal rate.

The low bond averages extend through the difficult retirement periods from the late 1960s to the early 1970s; during these difficult times the strategies were essentially waiting for stock prices to recover before selling to rebalance to a lower stock level. It's interesting and reassuring that during this period (when the stock percentages where very high) the corresponding stock valuations were very attractive. Generally when Prime Harvesting is heavy with stocks, prices are depressed. This makes the risk of further loss lower and the probability of strong stock returns higher. *Remember, Prime Harvesting never buys additional stock after retirement starts—high stock percentages can occur only when bonds are being sold to insulate stocks.*

This variation in the stock-bond ratio will make some retirees uncomfortable. Nevertheless, this exact behavior lowers risk. This isn't just true for Prime Harvesting; it applies to OmegaNot, Parker's Strategy, Weiss' strategy, and others. Backtesting clearly shows that eliminating this occasional tilt toward a high stock percentage *increases* known risk. If a retiree chooses to hedge speculative risk, generally the best approach is supplementing systemic withdrawal with guaranteed income, not by tweaking Prime Harvesting.

With these large variations in the stock-bond ratio, it's interesting to examining how much of an income-harvesting strategy's performance might be due simply to the average stock or bond level.

To consider this, each of the strategies is configured to produce the same bond average, approximately 40%. For most strategies, a 40% average in bonds is obtained by setting the starting stock-bond ratio, but for some an alternate approach is required: instead of 100-Age or 120-Age, 137-Age must be used to achieve a 40% bond average; Glidepath's starting retirement age must be 45; Rational must use 9 years for the targeted time in bonds; Three-Buckets must use 5.7 years as the bucket size in years.

Figure 43 shows the SBBI results with a 5% withdrawal rate when all strategies are configured to have near a 40% bond average. For some strategies, there is little change in performance, for others there is a large change. Notably, Prime Harvesting, Alternate-Prime, and Parker continue as the top performers. In contrast, Bonds-First with its simplistic strategy has a large drop in performance. OmegaNot's performance drops some. The implication is, some strategies perform well primarily due to the stock-bond ratio they maintain, while for others it's more due to their overall strategy. The top-performing strategies all fit in the latter category, with behavior due to more than raw stock percentages. Ultimately, the top-performing strategies are smarter, delivering more income per unit of volatility.

Equalized Bonds United States SBBI Data 1928-2010	Success Rate	Initial Stock Allocation	Average Remaining	Average Year of Failure	Lowest Bond Average	Highest Bond Average	Bond Average
Prime	94.4%	64%	3.9M	21.7	17%	65%	40%
Alternate-Prime	92.6%	49%	3.1M	24.3	25%	56%	40%
Parker	92.6%	47%	3.3M	24.5	21%	46%	40%
Weiss	90.7%	56%	3.8M	23.6	27%	43%	40%
OmegaNot	87.0%	41%	2.3M	25.3	22%	66%	40%
Age-137	79.6%	NA	4.3M	23.7	28%	57%	41%
Guyton PMR	79.6%	53%	1.7M	25.5	31%	56%	41%
ETBS	79.6%	NA	4.0M	21.8	10%	63%	40%
Glidepath (Age: 45 to 74)	79.6%	13%	4.1M	23.4	26%	59%	41%
Annual Rebalancing	77.8%	60%	3.7M	25.5	40%	40%	40%
Rational (9-Year)	74.1%	NA	3.4M	22.9	21%	54%	41%
Three-Buckets (5.7 years)	70.4%	NA	4.4M	24.1	1%	66%	40%
Bonds-First	61.1%	13%	1.3M	23.2	2%	86%	39%

FIGURE 43

Results after normalizing bond averages for a 5% withdrawal rate.

A closer consideration of Prime Harvesting and Alternate-Prime make their bond-handling characteristics clear. Starting with Alternate-Prime, the more straightforward case, Figure 44 shows bond averages over 30-year retirements. These averages come from backtesting 100 randomly generated high-performing portfolios* over a range of starting stock percentages. For example, the figure shows that, with a starting bond percentage of 50%, the average bond percentage across all the backtested retirement periods for the 100 portfolios ranged from an average low of 34% to an average high of 56%, with an overall average of 46% in bonds.

---

*   Five thousand random portfolios were generated with the top one hundred selected based on their performance.

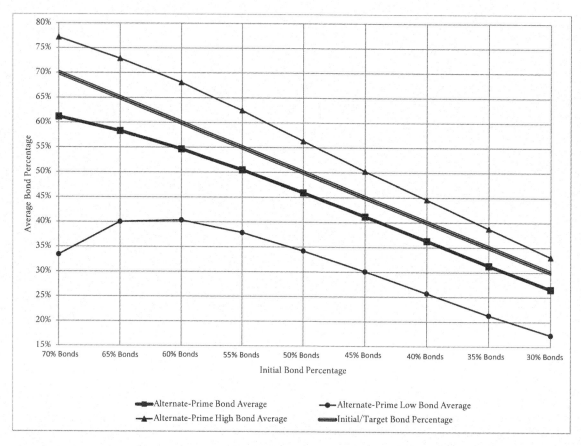

FIGURE 44

Alternate-Prime Harvesting bond averages for 100 top-performing portfolios.

For Prime Harvesting, Figure 45 shows the same results. With an initial bond percentage of 50%, the average bond percentage for 30-year retirements across the 100 portfolios ranged from an average low of 34% to an average high of 73%, with an overall average of 56% in bonds. Unlike Alternate-Prime, Prime Harvesting has no upper bound for bonds, allowing the bond percentage to continue upward as long as it's supported by sufficient stock growth.

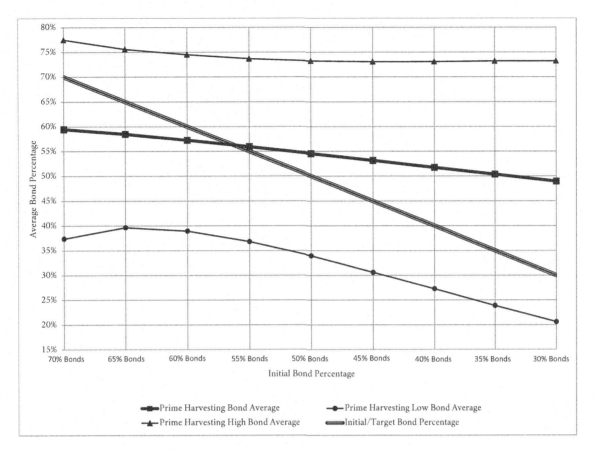

FIGURE 45

Prime Harvesting bond averages for 100 top-performing portfolios.

Although it's tidier and more comforting to have a fixed stock-bond ratio, it comes at a cost. The data indicates, allowing income-harvesting strategies to float the ratio produces a substantial income premium. If the stock returns are up, the bond percentage will typically rise as stock gains are locked in; if the stock returns are down, the bond percentage will typically reduce to insulate stocks. However, the average is still dependent on the initial rate. A higher initial withdrawal rate results in a higher stock average; likewise a lower initial rate results in a lower stock average.

Despite the data, retirees can still choose to maintain a bond floor, selling stocks as needed to maintain a minimum bonds percentage. Figure 46 shows this case: a 30% bond floor is enforced using Prime Harvesting with a 60% initial stock percentage. There is a moderate but consistent loss in income based on the SBBI data. While this is a viable option for retirees who are uncomfortable with a low bond percentage, it's important to understand that across four datasets (SBBI, Shiller, UK, Japan) this consistently *lowered* performance during difficult retirement periods. On the other hand, when combined with a variable-withdrawal strategy, the loss in income is divided across many years without a major impact—this is briefly revisited in Chapter 10. Bounding the lower bond level isn't recommended based on the data, but an otherwise strong retirement plan can handle it.

FIGURE 46

Prime Harvest comparison without and with 30% bond floor.

VALUATION-BASED STRATEGIES

For completeness, it is worth briefly diverging to discuss valuation-based strategies. Valuation-based strategies are at the extreme end of the conventionality spectrum; however, they are commonly discussed in the literature and sometimes perform extremely well. These strategies dynamically adjust the stock-bond ratio based on market valuations. The exact parameters vary depending on the specific strategy, but the same basic formula usually applies: if stock valuations are attractive, increase the portfolio's stock allocation, but if stock valuations are unattractive, decrease the portfolio's stock allocation.

Given a philosophy of following the data wherever it leads, I spent an inordinate amount of time researching valuation-based strategies for this book, with the assumption that they would be included in this survey. Backtesting was done using multiple valuation metrics, including CAPE-10, Peak-PE, and the Q Ratio. These "enhanced" strategies were also combined with the conventional income-harvesting strategies to explore synergies. Overall, the results were promising, beating out all other strategies, although ultimately too problematic, and with a tendency to be misleading.

The fundamental problem for valuation-based strategies is that they can't meet the guidelines for evidence-based research. Sometimes this is due to a lack of data, sometimes it's due to a strategy's metrics require tuning across datasets (which leads to a data-mining bias), and sometimes to a set of specific red flags in the data. Generally the strategies have substantial evidence within the confines of the US historical data, but not enough for a global portfolio; however, it's not even clear if the evidence is sufficient for a US-only portfolio.

Their omission is in no way from the standpoint of purism…there is simply not enough data available to form a strategy that can be used without undue risk when compared to the alternatives. Good odds are not the same as safe odds.

For readers seeking more details, here's a brief rundown on some of the CAPE-10 issues encountered. Each valuation metric has its own specific problems, but this list is representative of problems across all the valuation-based income-harvesting strategies.

1. CAPE-10 strategies must be carefully tuned, which increases the risk of a data-mining bias. This might be okay if sufficient out-of-sample data were available for verification, but CAPE-10 long-term data is limited.

2. When CAPE-10 was tested with the UK data (the only other available dataset with long-term PE data) it did no better than Prime Harvesting for MSWR-100% and significantly poorer for MSWR-80%. The UK Price-Earnings data was for the FTSE-32 index, while the return data was for the full FTSE index, but a similar limitation did not degrade performance using US data (i.e., Shiller's PE values are used for the SBBI dataset).

3. Short-term studies in the literature indicate PE characteristics can shift between countries, adding to the overall challenge of ever having an out-of-sample test.

4. The most successful US strategies could not generally be applied in a small way for top performance. For example, a pure CAPE-10 strategy outperformed Prime Harvesting in the US, only using a 100% stock allocation for attractive valuations and less than a 20% stock allocation for unattractive valuations. Smaller tilts generally underperformed Prime Harvesting.

5. The 2000-era PE data is extreme, which skews the overall results when calibrating a strategy, plus it introduces questions about the stability of the metric. For example, performing a regression analysis on CAPE-10 to predict the supported withdrawal rate, a *negative* withdrawal rate was predicted for retirements starting around 2000.

6. The strategy can significantly raise taxes for retirement accounts that are not tax-advantaged.

Valuations are used elsewhere in this book, but in a limited fashion to roughly gauge long-term market performance. This limited use of valuations is fundamentally distinct from using an income-harvesting strategy to dynamically adjusting the year-to-year stock-bond ratio.

RECOMMENDATIONS WITH CONCLUDING THOUGHTS

In light of the data, Prime Harvesting is the recommended income-harvesting strategy, with Alternate-Prime remaining an attractive alternative. Both strategies operate with any reasonable set of retirement parameters. Both strategies are also, for the most part, independent from the other retirement mechanics, although as the strategies of choice here they will be put to use throughout the rest of this book.

A few concluding thoughts will help fill in loose ends.

- There is nothing exceptional about waiting until stocks reach precisely 120% of their original inflation-adjusted value before rebalancing; however this specific trigger performs very well across a diverse range of market conditions. Rebalancing at 110% or 100% of the original stock value also works, although with a little poorer historical performance. The key, which is more difficult to find than one might expect, is to sell when stocks are up and to take advantage of market momentum.

- Some retirees might conclude, annual rebalancing is good enough because they plan on taking a lower than necessary withdrawal rate. After all, annual rebalancing had a 100% success rate for 4% annual withdrawals using the default portfolio with the SBBI data. There's a problem with this thinking though—the potential effects of speculative risk are unknown, in theory stressing any withdrawal rate. It's always safer to have an efficient income-harvesting strategy.

- Deploying Prime Harvesting should be independent of a retiree's risk tolerance. However, for those uncomfortable with a varying stock percentage (which is distinct from risk), an upper bound can be enforced as long as the withdrawal rate is lowered to compensate. It is worth noting though, a guaranteed-income solution as outlined in the final chapter of this book always provides a stronger hedge against speculative risk than suboptimally bounding the stock percentage.

- Alternate-Prime will usually outperform Prime Harvesting when valuations are attractive at the start of retirement. It's also fair to note, the same is probably true for OmegaNot and Bonds-First, although their exposure to speculative risk is higher. Valuation levels are defined and applied in Chapter 9; however, valuations certainly need not be considered to put Prime Harvesting to use.

- Very stable stock prices (i.e., low standard deviation) reduce the advantages of most harvesting strategies over traditional rebalancing, as does a very low stock percentage. At the far end, income-harvesting is not applicable to a portfolio of only bonds.

- Prime Harvesting and Alternate-Prime can both work well with bond ladders, because the assets allocated to bonds will never be later needed to buy stocks. Although this is not one of this book's recommendations, the tradeoffs are explored in Appendix B.

- Resiliency is an important characteristic not emphasized in the tables and graphs, but it can be attributed to all top-performing strategies including Prime Harvesting. Resiliency means a small change in parameters does not greatly affect the results. It also means results are generally strong across a variety of conditions. Finally, it means that results taper off slowly as conditions worsen, with no drastic drops in performance from small parameter changes.

- A smart harvesting strategy like Prime Harvesting provides a significant advantage when setting the initial stock percentage at the start of retirement. This is covered in Chapter 7.

A PRIME HARVESTING EXAMPLE

An example below clarifies how to apply Prime Harvesting, although the spreadsheet from the book's website will perform the calculations. To recap, here are the Prime Harvesting steps:

1. If stock assets are greater than 120% of their initial value after annually adjusting for inflation, sell 20% of stocks to buy additional bonds.

2. Sell enough bond assets to fund the next withdrawal; if bonds are depleted, sell enough from stocks to cover the withdrawal.

3. Withdraw the annual living expenses from the portfolio's cash.

4. Buy and sell as needed to rebalance individual stock assets to their target stock values (without modifying the portfolio's stock percentage).

5. Buy and sell as needed to rebalance individual bond assets to their target bond values (without modifying the portfolio's bond percentage).

For the example, assume a retiree has a starting portfolio value of $500,000 and an initial withdrawal rate of 5%. Also, assume the portfolio is evenly split between 50% stocks and 50% bonds.

At the start of retirement, the following steps are taken.

a. Calculate the first year withdrawal: $500,000 * 5% = $25,000.

b. Withdraw (transfer to a bank or money market account) the $25,000, leaving a portfolio value of $475,000. Half of the portfolio ($237,500) is invested in stocks, and half in bonds.

c. Record the initial value of the stocks ($237,500).

After the first year, assume stocks have risen 10% to $261,250, bonds have risen 5% to $249,375, and inflation is 3%.

a. Adjust the withdrawal amount by inflation: $25,000 + ($25,000 * 3%) = $25,750.

b. Adjust the recorded initial value of stock by inflation: $237,500 + ($237,500 * 3%) = $244,625.

c. Check if stock value is greater than 120% of the initial stock value adjusted for inflation.

> 120% of the initial stock value adjusted for inflation is 120% * $244,625 = $293,550. Therefore, the current stock value ($261,250) is not greater than the adjusted initial stock value ($293,550). This means, no stocks are sold to buy bonds this year.

d. Sell enough bonds to fund the next withdrawal of $25,750. The bond amount drops from $249,375 to $223,625 and the stock amount remains at $261,250.

e. $25,750 is transferred out of the portfolio for living expenses.

f. Individual stock assets are rebalanced to their target values within the current $261,250 stock allocation.

g. Individual bond assets are rebalanced to their target values within the current $223,625 bond allocation.

After the second year, assume stocks have risen 22% from $261,250 to $318,725, bonds have risen 4% from $223,625 to $232,570, and inflation is 4%.

a.   Adjust the previous withdrawal amount by inflation: $25,750 + ($25,750 * 4%) = $26,780.

b.   Adjust the recorded initial value of stock by inflation: $244,625 + ($244,625* 4%) = $254,410.

c.   Check if stock value is great then 120% of the initial stock value adjusted for inflation.

   120% of the initial stock value adjusted for inflation is 120% * $254,410 = $305,292; therefore, the current stock value ($318,725) is greater than the adjusted initial stock value ($305,292), so 20% of stocks (i.e., 20% * $318,725) are sold to buy bonds this year.

   The stock value decreases to $254,980 and the bond value increases to $296,315.

d.   Sell enough bonds to fund the next withdrawal of $26,780. The bond amount drops from $296,315 to $269,535 and the stock amount remains at $254,980.

e. $26,780 is transferred out of the portfolio for living expenses.

f.   Individual stock assets are rebalanced to their target values within the current $254,980 stock allocation.

g.   Individual bond assets are rebalanced to their target values within the current $269,535 bond allocation.

This same pattern continues after each year of retirement. The only difference from a real retirement scenario is that the annual withdrawal amount will be calculated by a separate variable-withdrawal strategy.

The Point

Prime Harvesting is the overall safest income-harvesting strategy identified, clearly performing substantially better than traditional rebalancing. Alternate-Prime Harvesting is a close second with a little more risk for higher income. These strategies perform well across different markets, portfolios, retirement lengths, and withdrawal rates.

This chapter covers variable-withdrawal strategies: how they determine the amount to withdraw annually, and how various strategies perform relative to each other. The outcome is two recommended strategies, EM and ECM, with precise instructions for applying both.

Less interested readers need only skim the chapter, carefully focusing on the EM and ECM section in the introductory survey and the example toward the end.

SURVEYING AND SELECTING A VARIABLE-WITHDRAWAL STRATEGY

THE BACKGROUND DETAILS

THE BASELINE—FIXED-RATE INFLATION-ADJUSTED WITHDRAWALS

AN INTRODUCTORY SURVEY OF VARIABLE-WITHDRAWAL STRATEGIES

COMPARING THE STRATEGIES

RECOMMENDATIONS WITH CONCLUDING THOUGHTS

AN EM EXAMPLE

THE POINT

Crowds believe or disbelieve in generalities; it takes an individual to know exactly what and when to trust.

Walter E. Goh

CHAPTER 4

SURVEYING AND SELECTING A VARIABLE-WITHDRAWAL STRATEGY

T HE TRADITIONAL APPROACH TO RETIREMENT withdrawals, at least in the literature, is to pick a single fixed inflation-adjusted withdrawal rate to use throughout retirement. This usually means picking a rate that can survive the worst known case based on historical markets (i.e., MSWR-100%). The best known fixed inflation-adjusted rate is 4%, which comes from Bengen's classic 1994 paper[21] using annual rebalancing with a 50% US total-market stock allocation.

Inflation-adjusted fixed withdrawals have an undesirable characteristic: they almost always leave a significant portion of the potential income unused. For example, MSWR-100% using Prime Harvesting with this chapter's default portfolio is 4.4%, while the *average* withdrawal rate using the same data is 7%. This means, on average the retiree doesn't have access to 60% of the potential retirement income.

While a fixed rate typically leaves a lot of unused assets, it can also leave the retiree more exposed to failure: any future retirement period with a sustainable rate lower than the selected rate leaves the retiree broke. This exposure to failure is small, but it's also unnecessary and stressful for many retirees. Some rightly point out that during tough times, no one would rigidly stick to a fixed withdrawal rate to blindly drain the portfolio, but this is part of the point. It makes little sense to stick with a fixed withdrawal rate, essentially ignoring how markets affect the portfolio during retirement, for better or worse.

The solution is a variable-withdrawal strategy, one that dynamically adjusts withdrawals to match market and portfolio conditions. During good times, the retiree pulls out more; during poor times, less. Of course, no strategy can deliver all the potential income (without perfect foreknowledge of the future), but the best strategies do well, far better than a fixed rate. This idea of varying the withdrawal rate is intuitive for most retirees who spent a lifetime of budgeting and saving. When our financial times are going well, we splurge if we choose to, but when the times are not so good, we cut back on our spending—it doesn't take an economist to figure this out.

Retirees can and will use variable-withdrawal strategies differently though. Some will carefully abide by their recommendations, annually using all that can be safely withdrawn. Others will use the recommended withdrawal amount only as a rough upper bound for spending during the year. From a different angle, some will also use the withdrawal amount as a gauge for how the portfolio is doing and to provide reassurance that market volatility is being compensated for. Finally, some will use a variable-withdrawal strategy to compensate for extra withdrawals due to unexpected expenses. Any of the recommended strategies transparently handle all these uses well with no extra management burden.

The withdrawal rate is the only direct risk factor the retiree has complete control over. Intelligently controlling the annual withdrawal rate is likely the most powerful lever available to the retiree for balancing risk with the reward of retirement income. However, efficiently and safely varying the withdrawal rate is a challenging problem, but one easily managed with the right guidance.

This chapter surveys a set of the best known variable-withdrawal strategies, similar to the previous survey on income harvesting. The outcome is two recommended strategies, the best choice depending on the needs and orientation of the retiree.

It's worth noting a variable-withdrawal strategy is generally independent from the underlying income harvesting strategy. Still, the numbers in this chapter are based on the recommended income-harvesting strategy, Prime Harvesting.

The Background Details

Surveying the performance of variable-withdrawal strategies is more difficult than surveying income-harvesting strategies. The amount and detailed nature of the data is one challenge. Also, the complexity of some of the strategies is higher. On the other hand, there are fewer known variable-withdrawal strategies than income-harvesting strategies, even though variable-withdrawal strategies are arguably more important.

Comparing the strategies is made easier by introducing a new metric, Harvesting-Rate Efficiency (HREFF), which is introduced after the preliminary survey.

Below is the background for understanding the preliminary survey.

Backtesting Specifics

Generally, the same backtesting assumptions used for the income-harvesting survey are used here. As mentioned, Prime-Harvesting is the underlying income-harvesting strategy. The default retirement length is 30 years.

Another consideration for most of the strategies is providing an initial withdrawal rate…a starting point to work from. The initial rate often defines the baseline from which variable-withdrawal strategies operate, lowering the rate below the baseline during weak markets and raising it above the baseline during strong markets.

The initial rate used throughout the preliminary survey is 5%, well above the MSWR-100% rate of 4.4%. This rate ensures that each strategy must handle a variety of situations: what starts as an unsustainable rate for a few retirement periods will be conservative for other periods. (Chapter 9 specifies how to appropriately pick an initial withdrawal rate for a variable-withdrawal strategy.)

For the strategies that use age to determine withdrawals, the starting retirement age is 65 unless stated otherwise.

Interpreting the Survey Backtesting Results

Figure 47 shows a small sample of how backtesting results are displayed in the initial survey (only the first three 30-year retirement periods are shown). Each column has the following meaning:

- The "Year" column identifies the starting retirement year, typically for a 30-year retirement.

- The 'Y' columns (e.g., Y1, Y2…Y30) show each year's inflation-adjusted withdrawal rate, for every year of retirement. For example, the 2nd year of a retirement starting in 1929 (i.e., the "1929" row, "Y2" column) has a withdrawal rate equivalent to a 3.8% inflation-adjusted withdrawal rate (based on starting portfolio value). The 10th year (i.e., the "1929" row, "Y10" column) has a withdrawal rate equivalent to a 5.2% inflation-adjusted withdrawal rate.

- The "Remaining" column shows the dollar amount remaining at the end of each retirement period, assuming a starting portfolio value of $1,000,000.

- The "MSWR" column shows the Maximum Sustainable Withdrawal Rate for the retirement period, assuming fixed inflation-adjusted withdrawals—the limit of how much the retirement period could have consistently supported with knowledge of the future.

- "Avg" is the average annual withdrawal rate for the retirement period. Although unusual, the average can sometimes exceed the MSWR value by starting with low early withdrawals, letting the portfolio value grow to generate extra income later.

- The "HREFF-3" column stands for a specific measure of a new metric, Harvesting-Rate Efficiency. The metric is explained thoroughly when the strategies are compared later in the chapter, but included now for future reference. It indicates the efficiency of the variable-withdrawal strategy in providing income, relative to the MSWR for the period, based on a 3% minimum rate (i.e., income floor).

Year	Y1	Y2	Y3	Y4	Y5	Y6	Y7	Y8	Y9	Y10	Y11	Y12	Y13	Y14	Y15	Y16	Y17	Y18	Y19	Y20	Y21	Y22	Y23	Y24	Y25	Y26	Y27	Y28	Y29	Y30	Remaining	MSWR	Avg	HREFF-3
1928	6.1	5.1	4.4	3.9	4.3	5.2	5.3	6.3	6.3	6	6.3	6.2	6.3	5	4.8	6.2	6.2	6.2	6.3	6.2	6.3	6.2	6.3	6.2	6.3	6.3	6.3	6.3	6.3	6.3	1,439,999	6.7	5.8	85.5%
1929	4.1	3.8	3.6	3.8	4	4.1	5	6.3	4.3	5.2	5.4	4.6	4	4	4.7	6.3	6.3	6.2	6.1	5.2	6.2	6.2	6.2	6.3	6.3	6.2	6.3	6.3	6.3	6.3	1,579,581	5.6	5.3	95.4%
1930	4.1	3.8	3.8	4.4	4.4	5.9	6.3	4.9	6.3	6.3	5.7	4.2	4.4	6.2	6.3	6.3	6.2	6.2	6.3	6.2	6.2	6.2	6.3	6.3	6.2	6.3	6.3	6.3	6.3	6.3	2,107,401	6.4	5.7	87.6%

FIGURE 47

Example backtesting results for variable-withdrawal strategies.

Also, the background for each year's withdrawal rate is grayscaled according to the rate's value—withdrawal rates below 4% gradually have darker fill, making the lowest rates stand out visually. There is no shading for withdrawal rates above 5%. This supports a broad visual overview of the withdrawal results.

Key Definitions

The following three key values recur throughout the definitions of the variable-withdrawal strategies, so it's helpful to define them here for reference. Anytime one of these values is used in a definition, it's highlighted in **bold**. (Again, less interested readers can skip or skim over each strategy definition. Plus, a spreadsheet is available to perform the calculations for the top strategies.)

1. **Initial Withdrawal Rate**: The Initial Withdrawal Rate is the percentage of the *first* withdrawal in relation to the total portfolio value. The Initial Withdrawal Rate is determined once, at the start of retirement.

2. **Inflation-Adjusted Withdrawal Amount**: For the first withdrawal (at the beginning of retirement), the Inflation-Adjusted Withdrawal Amount is the **Initial Withdrawal Rate** times the starting portfolio value. At the end of each year, the new Inflation-Adjusted Withdrawal Amount is the previous year's amount

adjusted for the year's inflation. For example, if the first withdrawal amount was $52,000, then at the end of the first year, with an inflation rate of 3.1%, the Inflation-Adjusted Withdrawal Amount is $52,000 + (3.1% *$52,000) = $53,612. For the next year with an inflation rate of 3.8%, the Inflation-Adjusted Withdrawal Amount is $53,612 + ($53,612 * 3.8%) = $55,649.

3. **Current Withdrawal Rate (CWR)**: Each year's CWR is the **Inflation-Adjusted Withdrawal Amount** divided by the portfolio's current value. For example, if the Inflation-Adjusted Withdrawal Amount is $68,500 and the current portfolio value is $1,200,500, then CWR is $68,500 / $1,200,500 = 5.7%.

Italics are also used to identify key values within a strategy's definition, but those values have no meaning outside the specific strategy being defined.

The Baseline: Fixed-Rate Inflation-Adjusted Withdrawals

Fixed-rate inflation-adjusted withdrawals are the baseline for comparing variable-withdrawal strategies (similar to the use of annual rebalancing as the baseline for income-harvesting). Fixed-rate inflation-adjusted withdrawals are certainly the most commonly referenced withdrawal-rate strategy in the literature. While the withdrawal amount changes with inflation, its real value remains constant.

The Steps
1. Calculate the **inflation-adjusted withdrawal amount** (see Key Definitions above).

2. Withdraw for the year the **inflation-adjusted withdrawal amount**.

Backtesting Results
Figure 48 shows all fixed-rate inflation-adjusted withdrawals for every retirement period when backtesting with the default portfolio, using the SBBI dataset. Not surprisingly, the annual withdrawals are a precise 5% (i.e., the initial rate) each year, except where retirements failed in 1966, 1968, and 1969 by prematurely running out of money.

Year	Y1	Y2	Y3	Y4	Y5	Y6	Y7	Y8	Y9	Y10	Y11	Y12	Y13	Y14	Y15	Y16	Y17	Y18	Y19	Y20	Y21	Y22	Y23	Y24	Y25	Y26	Y27	Y28	Y29	Y30	Remaining	MSWR	Avg	HREFF-3
1928	5	5	5	5	5	5	5	5	5	5	5	5	5	5	5	5	5	5	5	5	5	5	5	5	5	5	5	5	5	5	1,833,026	6.7	5.0	74.4%
1929	5	5	5	5	5	5	5	5	5	5	5	5	5	5	5	5	5	5	5	5	5	5	5	5	5	5	5	5	5	5	1,743,583	5.6	5.0	89.1%
1930	5	5	5	5	5	5	5	5	5	5	5	5	5	5	5	5	5	5	5	5	5	5	5	5	5	5	5	5	5	5	2,167,532	6.4	5.0	77.9%
1931	5	5	5	5	5	5	5	5	5	5	5	5	5	5	5	5	5	5	5	5	5	5	5	5	5	5	5	5	5	5	2,745,958	7.6	5.0	65.6%
1932	5	5	5	5	5	5	5	5	5	5	5	5	5	5	5	5	5	5	5	5	5	5	5	5	5	5	5	5	5	5	4,449,300	9.5	5.0	52.5%
1933	5	5	5	5	5	5	5	5	5	5	5	5	5	5	5	5	5	5	5	5	5	5	5	5	5	5	5	5	5	5	4,588,176	9.3	5.0	53.6%
1934	5	5	5	5	5	5	5	5	5	5	5	5	5	5	5	5	5	5	5	5	5	5	5	5	5	5	5	5	5	5	3,629,515	7.9	5.0	63.1%
1935	5	5	5	5	5	5	5	5	5	5	5	5	5	5	5	5	5	5	5	5	5	5	5	5	5	5	5	5	5	5	3,730,662	8.1	5.0	61.6%
1936	5	5	5	5	5	5	5	5	5	5	5	5	5	5	5	5	5	5	5	5	5	5	5	5	5	5	5	5	5	5	3,362,281	6.9	5.0	72.3%
1937	5	5	5	5	5	5	5	5	5	5	5	5	5	5	5	5	5	5	5	5	5	5	5	5	5	5	5	5	5	5	2,788,640	6.1	5.0	81.8%
1938	5	5	5	5	5	5	5	5	5	5	5	5	5	5	5	5	5	5	5	5	5	5	5	5	5	5	5	5	5	5	3,868,583	7.9	5.0	63.1%
1939	5	5	5	5	5	5	5	5	5	5	5	5	5	5	5	5	5	5	5	5	5	5	5	5	5	5	5	5	5	5	3,940,829	7.5	5.0	66.5%
1940	5	5	5	5	5	5	5	5	5	5	5	5	5	5	5	5	5	5	5	5	5	5	5	5	5	5	5	5	5	5	3,540,996	7.7	5.0	64.8%
1941	5	5	5	5	5	5	5	5	5	5	5	5	5	5	5	5	5	5	5	5	5	5	5	5	5	5	5	5	5	5	4,080,728	8	5.0	62.3%
1942	5	5	5	5	5	5	5	5	5	5	5	5	5	5	5	5	5	5	5	5	5	5	5	5	5	5	5	5	5	5	4,809,274	9.4	5.0	53.1%
1943	5	5	5	5	5	5	5	5	5	5	5	5	5	5	5	5	5	5	5	5	5	5	5	5	5	5	5	5	5	5	4,724,190	9.3	5.0	53.6%
1944	5	5	5	5	5	5	5	5	5	5	5	5	5	5	5	5	5	5	5	5	5	5	5	5	5	5	5	5	5	5	3,470,820	8.4	5.0	59.4%
1945	5	5	5	5	5	5	5	5	5	5	5	5	5	5	5	5	5	5	5	5	5	5	5	5	5	5	5	5	5	5	2,880,411	7.9	5.0	63.1%
1946	5	5	5	5	5	5	5	5	5	5	5	5	5	5	5	5	5	5	5	5	5	5	5	5	5	5	5	5	5	5	2,629,943	6.9	5.0	72.3%
1947	5	5	5	5	5	5	5	5	5	5	5	5	5	5	5	5	5	5	5	5	5	5	5	5	5	5	5	5	5	5	3,594,900	8.2	5.0	60.8%
1948	5	5	5	5	5	5	5	5	5	5	5	5	5	5	5	5	5	5	5	5	5	5	5	5	5	5	5	5	5	5	3,049,792	7.9	5.0	63.1%
1949	5	5	5	5	5	5	5	5	5	5	5	5	5	5	5	5	5	5	5	5	5	5	5	5	5	5	5	5	5	5	3,180,177	7.9	5.0	63.1%
1950	5	5	5	5	5	5	5	5	5	5	5	5	5	5	5	5	5	5	5	5	5	5	5	5	5	5	5	5	5	5	3,310,271	7.6	5.0	65.6%
1951	5	5	5	5	5	5	5	5	5	5	5	5	5	5	5	5	5	5	5	5	5	5	5	5	5	5	5	5	5	5	3,182,738	7.4	5.0	67.4%
1952	5	5	5	5	5	5	5	5	5	5	5	5	5	5	5	5	5	5	5	5	5	5	5	5	5	5	5	5	5	5	3,190,603	7.6	5.0	65.6%
1953	5	5	5	5	5	5	5	5	5	5	5	5	5	5	5	5	5	5	5	5	5	5	5	5	5	5	5	5	5	5	3,413,782	7.2	5.0	69.3%
1954	5	5	5	5	5	5	5	5	5	5	5	5	5	5	5	5	5	5	5	5	5	5	5	5	5	5	5	5	5	5	4,252,178	7.5	5.0	66.5%
1955	5	5	5	5	5	5	5	5	5	5	5	5	5	5	5	5	5	5	5	5	5	5	5	5	5	5	5	5	5	5	2,703,765	6.4	5.0	77.9%
1956	5	5	5	5	5	5	5	5	5	5	5	5	5	5	5	5	5	5	5	5	5	5	5	5	5	5	5	5	5	5	2,678,386	6	5.0	83.1%
1957	5	5	5	5	5	5	5	5	5	5	5	5	5	5	5	5	5	5	5	5	5	5	5	5	5	5	5	5	5	5	3,054,983	6	5.0	83.1%
1958	5	5	5	5	5	5	5	5	5	5	5	5	5	5	5	5	5	5	5	5	5	5	5	5	5	5	5	5	5	5	3,936,583	6.6	5.0	75.6%
1959	5	5	5	5	5	5	5	5	5	5	5	5	5	5	5	5	5	5	5	5	5	5	5	5	5	5	5	5	5	5	2,332,247	5.6	5.0	89.1%
1960	5	5	5	5	5	5	5	5	5	5	5	5	5	5	5	5	5	5	5	5	5	5	5	5	5	5	5	5	5	5	2,449,780	5.6	5.0	89.1%
1961	5	5	5	5	5	5	5	5	5	5	5	5	5	5	5	5	5	5	5	5	5	5	5	5	5	5	5	5	5	5	2,132,609	5.6	5.0	89.1%
1962	5	5	5	5	5	5	5	5	5	5	5	5	5	5	5	5	5	5	5	5	5	5	5	5	5	5	5	5	5	5	1,332,266	5.2	5.0	95.9%
1963	5	5	5	5	5	5	5	5	5	5	5	5	5	5	5	5	5	5	5	5	5	5	5	5	5	5	5	5	5	5	2,715,508	5.5	5.0	90.7%
1964	5	5	5	5	5	5	5	5	5	5	5	5	5	5	5	5	5	5	5	5	5	5	5	5	5	5	5	5	5	5	1,806,936	5.2	5.0	95.9%
1965	5	5	5	5	5	5	5	5	5	5	5	5	5	5	5	5	5	5	5	5	5	5	5	5	5	5	5	5	5	5	440,240	5	5.0	99.8%
1966	5	5	5	5	5	5	5	5	5	5	5	5	5	5	5	5	5	5	5	5	5	5	5	5	0	0	0	0	0	0	0	4.7	4.2	2.3%
1967	5	5	5	5	5	5	5	5	5	5	5	5	5	5	5	5	5	5	5	5	5	5	5	5	5	5	5	5	5	5	1,920,795	5.2	5.0	95.9%
1968	5	5	5	5	5	5	5	5	5	5	5	5	5	5	5	5	5	0	0	0	0	0	0	0	0	0	0	0	0	0	0	4.5	3.7	0.0%
1969	5	5	5	5	5	5	5	5	5	5	5	5	5	5	5	0	0	0	0	0	0	0	0	0	0	0	0	0	0	0	0	4.4	3.3	0.0%
1970	5	5	5	5	5	5	5	5	5	5	5	5	5	5	5	5	5	5	5	5	5	5	5	5	5	5	5	5	5	5	3,636,124	5.3	5.0	94.1%
1971	5	5	5	5	5	5	5	5	5	5	5	5	5	5	5	5	5	5	5	5	5	5	5	5	5	5	5	5	5	5	4,090,684	5.5	5.0	90.7%
1972	5	5	5	5	5	5	5	5	5	5	5	5	5	5	5	5	5	5	5	5	5	5	5	5	5	5	5	5	5	5	3,054,988	5.3	5.0	94.1%
1973	5	5	5	5	5	5	5	5	5	5	5	5	5	5	5	5	5	5	5	5	5	5	5	5	5	5	5	5	5	5	1,507,187	5.2	5.0	95.9%
1974	5	5	5	5	5	5	5	5	5	5	5	5	5	5	5	5	5	5	5	5	5	5	5	5	5	5	5	5	5	5	6,869,798	6.8	5.0	73.3%
1975	5	5	5	5	5	5	5	5	5	5	5	5	5	5	5	5	5	5	5	5	5	5	5	5	5	5	5	5	5	5	10,366,568	8.7	5.0	57.3%
1976	5	5	5	5	5	5	5	5	5	5	5	5	5	5	5	5	5	5	5	5	5	5	5	5	5	5	5	5	5	5	8,228,397	7.9	5.0	63.1%
1977	5	5	5	5	5	5	5	5	5	5	5	5	5	5	5	5	5	5	5	5	5	5	5	5	5	5	5	5	5	5	6,582,138	7.3	5.0	68.3%
1978	5	5	5	5	5	5	5	5	5	5	5	5	5	5	5	5	5	5	5	5	5	5	5	5	5	5	5	5	5	5	7,628,847	8	5.0	62.3%
1979	5	5	5	5	5	5	5	5	5	5	5	5	5	5	5	5	5	5	5	5	5	5	5	5	5	5	5	5	5	5	7,712,702	8.5	5.0	58.7%
1980	5	5	5	5	5	5	5	5	5	5	5	5	5	5	5	5	5	5	5	5	5	5	5	5	5	5	5	5	5	5	6,636,052	8.6	5.0	58.0%
1981	5	5	5	5	5	5	5	5	5	5	5	5	5	5	5	5	5	5	5	5	5	5	5	5	5	5	5	5	5	5	6,621,648	8.9	5.0	56.0%
																																Avg	4.93	68.7%

FIGURE 48

Fixed-Rate Inflation-Adjusted Withdrawals backtesting results.

The advantage of fixed-rate inflation-adjusted withdrawal is regularity and constant spending power. The disadvantage for difficult markets is the possibility of running out of money. The disadvantage for good markets is drawing out much less than possible, leaving a large pool of untapped income. Notice that for successful retirement periods, a large amount of unused income usually remains at the end of retirement.

An Introductory Survey of Variable-Withdrawal Strategies

This section surveys nine variable-withdrawal strategies. Each strategy is introduced, its rules identified for determining annual withdrawals, and its backtesting results shown.

The goal of the survey and the following comparisons is only to recommend a strategy, not to identify what income the retiree should expect. Later chapters, using a baseline market and baseline portfolio, focus on estimating future income.

All the variable-withdrawal strategies are reasonably good, unlike some of the strategies in the income-harvesting survey. Still, some are better than others. One aim is preventing the portfolio from running out of money. Another aim is maximizing income, or at least making sure it's sufficient. Fulfilling both aims well is the challenge, which each strategy approaches differently. (It's also worth noting the same caveats apply as stated in Chapter 3: while I do my best to accurately model each strategy, I don't know the latest thinking of the originators, or how they might customize a particular strategy for a specific client considering market conditions.)

Keep in mind, the examples shown cover only a small range of what a strategy might need to handle. Here, the goal is not to severely stress the strategies (that comes later), but to provide a representative sample of each strategy's behavior based on the historical US market.

Strategy 1: Fixed-Percent Withdrawals

Fixed-Percent Withdrawals pull out the same fixed percentage of the total portfolio value every year. Considering its simplicity, ignoring the effects of inflation, it performs better than might be expected. Also, since the percentage is based on the current portfolio value, it takes into account the state of the portfolio.

For example, with a 5% withdrawal rate and a portfolio of $400,000, the withdrawal is $20,000. If the portfolio drops to a value of $320,000 the next year, then the withdrawal becomes $16,000 (i.e., 5% of $320,000). If the portfolio value goes up to $500,000 the year after, the withdrawal becomes $25,000...always a straight 5% with no adjustments for inflation.

Fixed-Percent is the simplest of all the withdrawal-rate strategies. With no floor value, it will never run out of money, although withdrawals may get very small during poor market conditions.

The Steps

Annual withdrawals always follow the same simple steps.

1. Calculate the *current withdrawal amount* by multiplying the **Initial Withdrawal Rate** (e.g., an unchanging 5%) by the current portfolio value.

2. Withdraw for the year the *current withdrawal amount*.

Backtesting Results

Figure 49 shows the fixed-percent withdrawals. (Although the annual withdrawal rate is fixed, the values shown are constantly changing due to changing portfolio values from varying investment returns and inflation adjustments.)

Year	Y1	Y2	Y3	Y4	Y5	Y6	Y7	Y8	Y9	Y10	Y11	Y12	Y13	Y14	Y15	Y16	Y17	Y18	Y19	Y20	Y21	Y22	Y23	Y24	Y25	Y26	Y27	Y28	Y29	Y30	Remaining	MSWR	Avg	HREFF-3
1928	5.9	5.1	4.5	3.8	4.2	4.8	4.7	5.5	6.3	4.8	5.3	5.2	4.8	3.9	3.8	4.4	5	6	4.6	4.1	3.9	4.3	4.8	4.9	5	4.7	6.2	6.8	6.5	5.8	1,827,069	6.7	5.0	73.0%
1929	4.3	3.7	3.1	3.3	3.9	3.8	4.5	5.3	3.9	4.4	4.3	3.9	3.2	3.2	3.7	4.2	5.5	4.2	3.7	3.5	4	4.4	4.5	4.6	4.4	5.7	6.3	6	5.4	6.2	1,996,375	5.6	4.4	63.5%
1930	4.3	3.4	3.7	4.4	4.3	5.2	6.1	4.5	5	4.9	4.5	3.6	3.6	4.4	5	6.2	4.7	4.2	4	4.5	5	5.1	5.3	5	6.3	6.8	6.5	5.9	6.7	6.6	2,157,593	6.4	5.0	74.9%
1931	3.8	4	5.1	5	6.1	7.2	5.3	6	5.8	5.3	4.3	4.3	5.1	5.6	6.5	5	4.4	4.2	4.7	5.1	5.1	5.3	5	6.5	7	6.7	6	6.9	6.9	6.9	2,447,747	7.6	5.5	71.2%
1932	5.2	7.1	7	8.2	9.3	7.2	7.9	7.8	7.2	5.9	5.7	6.5	7	8	6.2	5.4	5.2	5.6	6	6	6.1	5.7	7.3	7.9	7.5	6.8	7.7	7.7	7.7	8.1	3,243,873	9.5	6.9	71.9%
1933	6.8	6.7	7.9	8.9	6.9	7.6	7.5	6.9	5.7	5.5	6.3	6.7	7.7	6	5.2	5	5.4	5.8	5.8	5.9	5.6	7.1	7.7	7.3	6.6	7.5	7.5	7.5	7.9	7.4	3,301,916	9.3	6.7	71.9%
1934	4.9	6	7	5.2	5.8	5.7	5.2	4.2	4.2	4.9	5.6	6.7	5.2	4.6	4.3	4.8	5.2	5.2	5.3	5	6.4	6.9	6.6	6	6.8	6.8	6.6	7.2	6.7	6.9	3,078,212	7.9	5.7	71.6%
1935	6.1	7	5.3	5.9	5.8	5.3	4.3	4.3	5	5.6	6.8	5.2	4.6	4.4	4.9	5.2	5.2	5.3	5	6.4	6.9	6.6	5.9	6.8	6.7	6.6	7.2	6.6	6.9	7.1	3,102,686	8.1	5.8	71.1%
1936	5.9	4.3	4.9	4.8	4.3	3.5	3.5	4.1	4.7	5.7	4.4	3.9	3.7	4.1	4.6	4.7	4.8	4.5	6	6.6	6.4	5.7	6.6	6.7	6.6	7.1	6.6	6.7	7	7.2	3,125,022	6.9	5.3	74.2%
1937	3.6	4.1	4	3.7	2.9	3	3.5	4.1	5.3	4	3.6	3.4	3.9	4.3	4.4	4.6	4.3	5.6	6.2	5.9	5.3	6.1	6.2	6	6.6	6	6.3	6.6	6.8	6.1	2,716,875	6.1	4.9	54.4%
1938	5.8	5.6	5.1	4.2	4.2	4.9	5.4	6.4	4.9	4.3	4.1	4.5	4.9	5	5.1	4.8	6.3	6.8	6.5	5.9	6.8	6.8	6.6	7.2	6.6	6.9	7.2	7.4	6.7	7.2	3,285,850	7.9	5.8	72.3%
1939	4.9	4.4	3.6	3.6	4.4	5	6.2	4.8	4.2	4	4.5	4.9	4.9	5.1	4.8	6.2	6.7	6.4	5.7	6.6	6.6	6.5	7	6.5	6.8	7	7.2	6.5	7	7.1	3,420,668	7.5	5.6	73.1%
1940	4.5	3.7	3.7	4.4	5.1	6.3	4.8	4.2	4	4.5	4.9	4.9	5.1	4.8	6.1	6.7	6.4	5.7	6.5	6.5	6.4	7	6.4	6.7	6.9	7.2	6.5	7	7	5.8	2,995,197	7.7	5.7	71.8%
1941	4	4.1	4.9	5.4	6.4	4.9	4.3	4.1	4.5	5	5	5.1	4.8	6.3	6.9	6.6	5.9	6.8	6.9	6.8	7.2	6.7	6.9	7.2	7.3	6.6	7.1	7.3	6.1	6	3,214,011	8	5.9	72.5%
1942	5	6	6.6	7.8	6	5.3	5.1	5.6	5.9	5.8	6	5.7	7.1	7.6	7.3	6.6	7.4	7.4	7.4	7.8	7.3	7.4	7.7	7.7	7	7.5	7.6	6.4	6.3	6.5	3,211,094	9.4	6.7	70.7%
1943	5.8	6.4	7.4	5.7	5	4.8	5.2	5.7	5.7	5.8	5.5	7.1	7.7	7.4	6.6	7.6	7.6	7.5	8	7.5	7.7	7.9	8.1	7.4	7.7	7.9	6.6	6.5	6.6	6.6	3,161,410	9.3	6.8	72.1%
1944	5.5	6.5	5	4.4	4.2	4.6	5	5	5.2	4.9	6.4	6.9	6.6	5.9	6.8	6.8	6.8	7.2	6.7	6.9	7.2	7.3	6.6	7.1	7.2	6	6	6.1	6.1	4.9	2,497,241	8.4	6.1	71.3%
1945	6	4.6	4	3.9	4.3	4.7	4.8	4.9	4.7	6.1	6.7	6.4	5.7	6.6	6.6	6.5	7.1	6.5	6.8	7.1	7.3	6.6	7.1	7.2	6	6	6.1	6.1	5	3.9	2,157,298	7.9	5.8	72.6%
1946	3.8	3.4	3.2	3.6	4	4.2	4.3	4	5.6	6.3	6.1	5.4	6.4	6.5	6.4	6.9	6.4	6.6	6.9	7.1	6.4	6.8	7	5.8	5.7	5.8	5.9	4.7	3.6	3.9	2,266,232	6.9	5.4	72.2%
1947	4.4	4.2	4.7	5.2	5.3	5.4	5	6.7	7.3	7	6.3	7.3	7.3	7.2	7.7	7.2	7.4	7.7	7.8	7.1	7.5	7.6	6.4	6.3	6.4	6.4	5.2	4	4.3	4.8	2,482,942	8.2	6.2	74.6%
1948	4.8	5.3	5.5	5.5	5.6	5.3	6.7	7.2	6.8	6.2	7	7	6.8	7.4	6.8	7.1	7.3	7.5	6.8	7.3	7.4	6.1	6	6.1	6.2	4.9	3.7	4.1	4.6	4.1	2,065,705	7.9	6.1	75.9%
1949	5.5	5.7	5.7	5.8	5.5	6.9	7.3	7	6.3	7.1	7.1	7	7.5	7	7.2	7.4	7.6	6.9	7.4	7.4	6.2	6	6.2	6.2	5	3.8	4.2	4.6	4.2	3.9	2,097,565	7.9	6.2	76.8%
1950	5.3	5.3	5.5	5.2	6.6	7.1	6.7	6.1	6.9	6.9	6.8	7.3	6.8	7	7.3	7.5	6.8	7.2	7.3	6.1	5.9	6.1	6.1	4.9	3.7	4.1	4.6	4.1	3.8	3.8	2,381,198	7.6	6.0	76.5%
1951	5	5.2	4.9	6.3	6.8	6.5	5.9	6.7	6.7	6.6	7.2	6.6	6.9	7.1	7.3	6.6	7.1	7.2	6	5.8	6	6	4.8	3.6	4	4.5	4	3.8	3.8	4	2,570,725	7.4	5.8	75.7%
1952	5.1	4.8	6.4	7	6.7	6	7	7	6.9	7.4	6.9	7.1	7.3	7.5	6.8	7.2	7.3	6.1	6	6.2	6.2	5	3.9	4.2	4.6	4.2	3.9	3.8	3.9	3.5	2,383,897	7.6	5.9	74.5%
1953	4.7	6.1	6.6	6.3	5.7	6.5	6.5	6.4	7	6.4	6.7	6.9	7.2	6.5	7	7.1	5.8	5.7	5.9	5.9	4.7	3.5	3.9	4.4	4	3.7	3.7	3.9	3.5	4	2,773,606	7.2	5.5	73.7%
1954	6.4	7	6.6	6	6.8	6.8	6.7	7.3	6.7	7	7.2	7.5	6.8	7.2	7.3	6.1	6.1	6.2	6.2	5.1	4	4.3	4.7	4.2	3.9	3.8	3.9	3.5	4	4.5	3,215,913	7.5	5.8	74.6%
1955	5.4	5.2	4.5	5.5	5.6	5.4	6	5.5	5.8	6.1	6.4	5.7	6.3	6.4	5.3	5.3	5.4	5.4	4.3	3.3	3.6	4	3.7	3.4	3.3	3.5	3.1	3.6	4.1	4	2,977,027	6.4	4.8	64.5%
1956	4.8	4.2	5.2	5.3	5.1	5.7	5.2	5.5	5.8	6.1	5.5	6.1	6.2	5.1	5.1	5.2	5.2	4.2	3.2	3.5	3.9	3.5	3.3	3.2	3.4	3	3.5	3.9	3.9	4.6	3,536,638	6	4.6	56.2%
1957	4.4	5.3	5.4	5.2	5.8	5.3	5.6	5.9	6.2	5.5	6.1	6.2	5.1	4.9	5.1	5.1	4	2.9	3.3	3.8	3.4	3.2	3.3	3.5	3.1	3.6	4	4	4.6	5	3,826,586	6	4.6	53.3%
1958	6.1	6.2	6.1	6.6	6.1	6.4	6.7	6.9	6.2	6.7	6.8	5.6	5.5	5.6	5.7	4.5	3.4	3.7	4.2	3.8	3.5	3.5	3.7	3.3	3.8	4.2	4.1	4.9	5.3	4.8	3,710,074	6.6	5.1	72.0%
1959	5.1	4.9	5.5	5	5.3	5.6	5.9	5.3	5.8	6	4.9	4.7	4.8	4.9	3.8	2.8	3.1	3.6	3.3	3.1	3.1	3.4	3	3.4	3.9	3.8	4.5	4.8	4.4	4.7	3,694,324	5.6	4.4	41.4%
1960	4.9	5.4	4.9	5.2	5.5	5.7	5.1	5.7	5.9	4.9	4.8	4.9	4.9	3.9	2.9	3.2	3.7	3.3	3.1	3.1	3.3	3	3.4	3.9	3.8	4.5	4.8	4.4	4.6	5.1	4,196,659	5.6	4.4	42.8%
1961	5.5	5.1	5.3	5.7	5.9	5.3	5.8	6	4.9	4.8	4.9	5	3.9	2.9	3.2	3.7	3.3	3.1	3.1	3.3	3	3.4	3.9	3.8	4.5	4.9	4.5	4.7	5.2	4.5	3,860,780	5.6	4.4	43.2%
1962	4.5	4.8	5.1	5.4	4.7	5.5	5.7	4.6	4.5	4.7	4.7	3.7	2.7	3	3.5	3.1	2.9	3	3.2	2.9	3.2	3.7	3.6	4.3	4.7	4.3	4.5	4.9	4.3	5.1	4,428,902	5.2	4.2	25.6%
1963	5.3	5.6	5.9	5.3	5.8	6	4.9	4.7	4.9	4.9	3.8	2.8	3.2	3.6	3.3	3.1	3.1	3.4	3	3.5	3.9	3.8	4.5	4.9	4.4	4.7	5.2	4.5	5.3	5.5	4,866,890	5.5	4.4	43.9%
1964	5.3	5.6	5	5.6	5.8	4.7	4.5	4.6	4.7	3.6	2.6	3	3.5	3.1	3	3.1	3.4	3	3.4	3.9	3.8	4.5	4.9	4.5	4.7	5.2	4.5	5.3	5.5	5.8	5,162,833	5.2	4.3	32.6%
1965	5.3	4.6	5.3	5.6	4.5	4.4	4.5	4.6	3.6	2.6	3	3.4	3.1	2.9	2.9	3.1	2.8	3.2	3.7	3.6	4.2	4.6	4.2	4.5	4.9	4.3	5	5.2	5.5	4.9	4,512,403	5	4.1	24.1%
1966	4.4	5	5.3	4.3	4.1	4.2	4.3	3.3	2.3	2.7	3.2	2.9	2.7	2.8	3.1	2.7	3.1	3.6	3.5	4.1	4.4	4.1	4.3	4.8	4.2	4.9	5.1	5.3	4.8	5.7	5,270,860	4.7	4.0	16.4%
1967	5.6	5.8	4.8	4.7	4.8	4.9	3.8	2.9	3.2	3.6	3.3	3	3	3.2	2.9	3.3	3.8	3.7	4.4	4.7	4.3	4.5	5	4.3	5.1	5.3	5.5	5	6	6.1	5,611,469	5.2	4.4	35.3%
1968	5.2	4.2	4	4.1	4.2	3.2	2.2	2.6	3.1	2.8	2.6	2.8	3	2.7	3.1	3.5	3.5	4.1	4.4	4	4.3	4.7	4.1	4.9	5	5.3	4.8	5.7	5.8	6.6	5,906,336	4.5	4.0	13.2%
1969	4.1	3.9	4	4.1	3.1	2.3	2.6	3	2.7	2.6	2.6	2.9	2.6	2.9	3.4	3.2	3.9	4.2	3.8	4	4.5	3.9	4.6	4.8	5	4.6	5.5	5.7	6.5	6.9	6,000,122	4.4	3.9	8.1%
1970	4.8	5	5.1	3.9	2.8	3.2	3.7	3.4	3.2	3.2	3.6	3.2	3.7	4.2	4.1	4.8	5.2	4.8	4.9	5.4	4.8	5.6	5.7	6	5.4	6.4	6.5	7.3	7.7	7.6	6,469,081	5.3	4.8	61.7%
1971	5.2	5.3	4.2	3.2	3.5	3.9	3.5	3.3	3.3	3.5	3.1	3.6	4.1	4	4.7	5.1	4.7	4.9	5.4	4.7	5.5	5.6	5.9	5.3	6.4	6.5	7.3	7.8	7.7	7.4	6,164,719	5.5	5.0	73.5%
1972	5.1	3.9	2.9	3.3	3.7	3.4	3.2	3.2	3.5	3.1	3.5	4	3.9	4.6	5	4.5	4.8	5.2	4.5	5.4	5.5	5.8	5.2	6.1	6.2	7	7.3	7.4	7	6.8	5,577,515	5.3	4.8	61.1%
1973	3.9	2.9	3.3	3.7	3.3	3.1	3.1	3.4	3	3.4	3.9	3.8	4.6	4.9	4.5	4.7	5.2	4.5	5.3	5.5	5.7	5.2	6.1	6.1	6.9	7.3	7.3	7	6.8	6.3	5,115,508	5.2	4.8	51.9%
1974	3.7	4.2	4.8	4.3	4	4.1	4.2	3.8	4.4	4.8	4.8	5.5	6	5.5	5.7	6.1	5.4	6.3	6.5	6.8	6.1	7.1	7.1	7.8	8.3	8.2	7.9	7.7	7.1	7.6	5,705,610	6.8	5.9	83.5%
1975	5.7	6.5	5.8	5.4	5.2	5.4	4.9	5.7	6.1	6	7	7.5	7	7.1	7.6	6.9	7.9	8	8.3	7.4	8.5	8.5	9.4	9.9	9.7	9.3	9.2	8.7	9.1	8.9	6,156,539	8.7	7.4	83.9%
1976	5.7	5.1	4.8	4.6	4.8	4.4	5	5.5	5.5	6.4	6.9	6.3	6.5	7	6.3	7.2	7.4	7.7	6.9	8	8.1	8.9	9.4	9.2	8.9	8.7	8.3	8.6	8.4	7.9	5,363,074	7.9	6.9	86.1%
1977	4.5	4.2	4.1	4.4	4	4.6	5	5	5.8	6.3	5.8	5.9	6.4	5.7	6.6	6.8	7.1	6.4	7.4	7.5	8.3	8.7	8.6	8.3	8.2	7.7	8	7.9	7.4	7.5	4,912,047	7.3	6.5	86.5%
1978	4.6	4.6	4.8	4.3	5	5.5	5.4	6.3	6.8	6.3	6.4	6.9	6.3	7.2	7.3	7.6	6.8	7.8	7.8	8.6	9.1	8.9	8.6	8.5	8	8.3	8.2	7.7	7.8	7.6	4,852,229	8	7.0	85.5%
1979	4.9	5	4.6	5.3	5.8	5.7	6.6	7.2	6.6	6.8	7.3	6.6	7.5	7.6	8	7.1	8.1	8.1	8.9	9.4	9.2	8.9	8.8	8.3	8.6	8.5	8	8	7.7	6.6	3,881,789	8.5	7.3	84.9%
1980	5.1	4.6	5.3	5.7	5.7	6.6	7.1	6.6	6.7	7.2	6.6	7.5	7.6	7.9	7.1	8.2	8.2	9	9.4	9.2	8.8	8.6	8.1	8.5	8.4	7.9	8	7.8	6.8	6.8	3,580,179	8.6	7.4	84.6%
1981	4.6	5.3	5.7	5.7	6.6	7.2	6.6	6.7	7.2	6.6	7.5	7.6	8	7.1	8.3	8.3	9.1	9.6	9.4	9.1	9	8.6	8.9	8.6	8.1	8.2	7.9	6.8	6.9	7.2	3,472,769	8.9	7.5	83.8%
																																Avg	5.51	63.9%

FIGURE 49

Fixed-Rate Withdrawals backtesting results.

Besides the simplicity, the main advantage is there's no chance of running out of money. For a 5% withdrawal rate, 95% of the portfolio is always left. The disadvantage is the overall lack of efficiency: withdrawals can vary greatly and sometimes unnecessarily, plus a relatively large portfolio is usually left at the end of life (unused income).

For retirements starting in the 1960s, withdrawals commonly dropped below 3%. Withdrawals at 3.5% or below are also frequent, occurring in approximately half of the retirement periods.

Fixed-percentage withdrawals are mediocre, neither being exceptionally strong or weak.

Strategy 2: The 95% Rule

Bob Clyatt semi-retired when he was 42, and starting living partly from his savings. Afterward, he wrote a popular book for early retirees, *Work Less, Live More: The Way to Semi-Retirement*. In his book, partially devoted to investing during retirement, he defines the 95% Rule, a variable-withdrawal strategy.

The 95% Rule is an improved version of Fixed-Percent withdrawal, maintaining at least 95% of the previous year's withdrawal amount. This prevents sharp drops in income from temporary losses in portfolio value. Withdrawals can still get very low using the 95% Rule, but it takes longer.

The portfolio can in theory run out of money using the 95% Rule, but this strategy is very good at balancing extremely poor market conditions.

The Steps

At the start of retirement, the initial withdrawal amount is calculated by multiplying the initial withdrawal rate by the portfolio value. Initially, set the *minimum amount* to 95% of this initial withdrawal amount. The remaining annual withdrawals are calculated at the end of each retirement year using the following steps.

1. Calculate the *current withdrawal amount* by multiplying the **Initial Withdrawal Rate** (e.g., 5%) by the current portfolio value.

2. If the *current withdrawal amount* is less than the *minimum amount*, then change it to the *minimum amount*.

3. Reset the *minimum amount* (for use next year) to 95% of the *current withdrawal amount*.

4. Withdraw for the year the *current withdrawal amount*.

Backtesting Results

Figure 50 shows the 95% Rule withdrawals. Note the withdrawals sometimes appear to be less than 95% of the previous year because of the effects of inflation.

Year	Y1	Y2	Y3	Y4	Y5	Y6	Y7	Y8	Y9	Y10	Y11	Y12	Y13	Y14	Y15	Y16	Y17	Y18	Y19	Y20	Y21	Y22	Y23	Y24	Y25	Y26	Y27	Y28	Y29	Y30	Remaining	MSWR	Avg	HREFF-3
1928	5.9	5.6	5.7	6.1	6.4	5.9	5.5	5.1	5.8	5.5	5.3	5.1	4.8	4.1	3.6	4	4.6	5.6	4.5	3.9	3.6	4	4.5	4.6	4.8	4.5	6	6.6	6.3	5.8	1,768,502	6.7	5.123	74.7%
1929	4.8	4.9	5.1	5.4	5	4.6	4.3	4.9	4.6	4.4	4.2	4	3.4	3	3.3	3.8	5.1	4.1	3.5	3.3	3.7	4.2	4.2	4.4	4.2	5.5	6.1	5.8	5.3	6	1,943,333	5.6	4.503	63.3%
1930	4.7	5	5.3	4.9	4.5	4.9	5.9	5.6	5.4	5.1	4.8	4.1	3.6	4	4.7	5.9	4.7	4.1	3.8	4.2	4.8	5	5.1	4.8	6.2	6.6	6.3	5.8	6.5	6.5	2,115,707	6.4	5.093	78.0%
1931	4.8	5	5	4.9	6	7.1	6.7	6.4	6.2	5.8	4.9	4.4	4.8	5.3	6.3	5.1	4.4	4.1	4.5	4.9	5	5.2	4.9	6.3	6.9	6.6	6	6.8	6.8	6.8	2,410,607	7.6	5.597	72.7%
1932	5.2	7.1	7	8.2	9.3	8.7	8.4	8.1	7.5	6.4	5.7	6.4	6.8	7.8	6.3	5.4	5.1	5.5	5.9	5.9	6	5.7	7.2	7.8	7.5	6.8	7.7	7.7	7.6	8.1	3,215,492	9.5	6.96	72.5%
1933	6.8	6.7	7.9	8.9	8.4	8.1	7.8	7.3	6.2	5.5	6.1	6.6	7.6	6.1	5.2	4.9	5.3	5.7	5.7	5.8	5.5	7	7.6	7.2	6.6	7.4	7.4	7.4	7.8	7.3	3,270,362	9.3	6.793	72.3%
1934	4.9	6	7	6.6	6.3	6	5.7	4.8	4.3	4.7	5.4	6.6	5.3	4.6	4.3	4.7	5.1	5.1	5.2	4.9	6.3	6.8	6.5	6	6.7	6.7	6.6	7.1	6.7	6.8	3,042,224	7.9	5.79	72.5%
1935	6.1	7	6.6	6.4	6.1	5.7	4.9	4.3	4.8	5.4	6.6	5.3	4.6	4.3	4.7	5.1	5.1	5.2	4.9	6.3	6.8	6.5	6	6.7	6.7	6.5	7.1	6.7	6.8	7	3,069,120	8.1	5.873	71.7%
1936	5.9	5.5	5.3	5.1	4.8	4.1	3.6	4	4.6	5.6	4.5	3.9	3.6	4	4.5	4.6	4.7	4.5	6	6.6	6.3	5.8	6.6	6.6	6.5	7	6.5	6.7	6.9	7.1	3,094,128	6.9	5.38	75.7%
1937	4.7	4.6	4.4	4.1	3.5	3.1	3.4	3.9	5.2	4.1	3.6	3.4	3.8	4.2	4.3	4.5	4.2	5.6	6.1	5.8	5.3	6.1	6.1	5.9	6.5	6.1	6.3	6.5	6.7	6.2	2,681,551	6.1	4.94	71.5%
1938	5.8	5.6	5.3	4.5	4.1	4.9	5.4	6.3	5.1	4.4	4.1	4.5	4.9	5	5.1	4.8	6.3	6.8	6.5	6	6.7	6.7	6.6	7.2	6.7	6.9	7.2	7.4	6.8	7.2	3,270,757	7.9	5.827	72.6%
1939	4.9	4.6	3.9	3.6	4.3	5	6.2	5	4.3	4	4.5	4.8	4.9	5	4.8	6.1	6.7	6.4	5.8	6.6	6.6	6.4	7	6.6	6.7	7	7.2	6.6	7	7.1	3,404,523	7.5	5.653	73.6%
1940	4.7	4.1	3.7	4.4	5.1	6.3	5	4.3	4.1	4.5	4.8	4.9	5	4.7	6.1	6.6	6.3	5.8	6.5	6.5	6.4	7	6.5	6.7	6.9	7.1	6.5	6.9	7	6.3	2,965,456	7.7	5.69	72.5%
1941	4.8	4.2	4.8	5.3	6.3	5.1	4.4	4.1	4.5	4.9	5	5.1	4.8	6.3	6.9	6.6	6	6.8	6.8	6.8	7.2	6.8	6.9	7.2	7.3	6.7	7.1	7.2	6.5	5.9	3,182,344	8	5.943	73.2%
1942	5	6	6.6	7.8	6.3	5.4	5.1	5.6	5.8	5.8	6	5.6	7.1	7.6	7.2	6.6	7.4	7.4	7.3	7.7	7.3	7.4	7.6	7.7	7.1	7.5	7.6	6.8	6.3	6.4	3,190,162	9.4	6.7	70.8%
1943	5.8	6.4	7.4	6	5.1	4.8	5.2	5.7	5.7	5.8	5.5	7.1	7.7	7.3	6.7	7.6	7.6	7.5	8	7.5	7.6	7.9	8	7.4	7.7	7.8	7	6.4	6.6	6.6	3,141,488	9.3	6.78	72.3%
1944	5.5	6.5	5.2	4.5	4.2	4.6	5	5	5.2	4.9	6.4	6.9	6.6	6.1	6.8	6.8	6.8	7.2	6.8	6.9	7.1	7.2	6.7	7.1	7.2	6.4	5.9	6.1	6	5.3	2,467,693	8.4	6.097	71.8%
1945	6	4.8	4.1	3.9	4.2	4.7	4.8	4.9	4.6	6.1	6.6	6.4	5.8	6.6	6.6	6.5	7.1	6.6	6.8	7	7.3	6.7	7.1	7.2	6.4	5.9	6.1	6.1	5.3	4.5	2,107,446	7.9	5.89	73.4%
1946	4.8	4.1	3.8	3.7	3.9	4.1	4.2	4	5.5	6.2	6	5.5	6.3	6.4	6.3	6.8	6.4	6.5	6.8	7	6.4	6.7	6.9	6.2	5.6	5.7	5.8	5	4.3	3.8	2,189,186	6.9	5.49	77.4%
1947	4.7	4.5	4.6	5.1	5.2	5.3	5	6.6	7.3	7	6.4	7.2	7.3	7.2	7.7	7.2	7.4	7.6	7.8	7.1	7.5	7.6	6.8	6.2	6.4	6.4	5.5	4.7	4.2	4.7	2,432,265	8.2	6.273	75.3%
1948	4.8	5.3	5.5	5.5	5.6	5.3	6.7	7.2	6.8	6.3	7	7	6.8	7.4	6.9	7.1	7.3	7.5	6.9	7.3	7.3	6.6	5.9	6.1	6.1	5.3	4.5	4	4.5	4.1	2,020,534	7.9	6.153	76.7%
1949	5.5	5.7	5.7	5.8	5.5	6.9	7.3	7	6.4	7.1	7.1	7	7.5	7	7.2	7.4	7.6	7	7.4	7.4	6.6	6	6.2	6.2	5.4	4.6	4.1	4.6	4.1	3.8	2,054,704	7.9	6.237	77.6%
1950	5.3	5.3	5.5	5.2	6.6	7.1	6.7	6.2	6.9	6.9	6.8	7.3	6.9	7	7.3	7.5	6.9	7.2	7.3	6.6	5.9	6.1	6.1	5.3	4.5	4	4.5	4	3.8	3.7	2,334,826	7.6	6.013	77.3%
1951	5	5.2	4.9	6.3	6.8	6.5	6	6.7	6.7	6.6	7.1	6.7	6.9	7.1	7.3	6.7	7.1	7.2	6.4	5.8	5.9	6	5.2	4.4	3.9	4.4	3.9	3.7	3.7	3.9	2,526,203	7.4	5.8	76.3%
1952	5.1	4.8	6.4	7	6.7	6.1	6.9	7	6.9	7.4	6.9	7.1	7.3	7.5	6.9	7.2	7.3	6.5	6	6.1	6.1	5.3	4.5	4.1	4.5	4.1	3.8	3.7	3.9	3.5	2,349,156	7.6	5.887	74.8%
1953	4.8	6.1	6.6	6.3	5.8	6.5	6.5	6.4	7	6.5	6.7	6.9	7.1	6.6	6.9	7	6.3	5.7	5.8	5.9	5.1	4.3	3.8	4.3	3.9	3.6	3.6	3.8	3.4	3.9	2,719,621	7.2	5.57	73.9%
1954	6.4	7	6.6	6.1	6.8	6.8	6.7	7.3	6.8	7	7.2	7.5	6.8	7.2	7.3	6.6	6.1	6.2	6.2	5.4	4.6	4.2	4.6	4.1	3.8	3.7	3.8	3.5	4	4.4	3,176,458	7.5	5.823	74.8%
1955	5.4	5.2	4.8	5.5	5.6	5.4	6	5.7	5.8	6.1	6.4	5.9	6.3	6.4	5.7	5.2	5.4	5.4	4.7	4	3.5	4	3.6	3.3	3.3	3.4	3.1	3.5	4	3.9	2,928,731	6.4	4.883	65.1%
1956	4.8	4.4	5.1	5.2	5	5.7	5.4	5.5	5.8	6.1	5.6	6	6.2	5.5	5	5.1	5.2	4.5	3.8	3.4	3.8	3.4	3.2	3.2	3.3	3	3.4	3.9	3.8	4.5	3,478,660	6	4.627	56.1%
1957	4.8	5.3	5.4	5.2	5.8	5.5	5.6	5.9	6.1	5.6	6	6.2	5.5	5	5	5.1	4.4	3.8	3.3	3.7	3.3	3.1	3.2	3.4	3.1	3.5	3.9	3.8	4.5	4.8	3,677,127	6	4.66	59.8%
1958	6.1	6.2	6.1	6.6	6.2	6.4	6.7	6.9	6.3	6.7	6.8	6.1	5.5	5.6	5.6	4.9	4.2	3.7	4.1	3.7	3.5	3.5	3.7	3.3	3.7	4.2	4.1	4.8	5.2	4.8	3,649,656	6.6	5.173	73.3%
1959	5.1	4.9	5.5	5.2	5.3	5.6	5.9	5.4	5.8	6	5.3	4.8	4.8	4.9	4.2	3.6	3.2	3.5	3.2	3	3.1	3.3	3	3.4	3.9	3.8	4.5	4.8	4.4	4.6	3,674,359	5.6	4.467	46.3%
1960	4.9	5.4	5.1	5.2	5.5	5.7	5.2	5.7	5.9	5.3	4.8	4.9	4.9	4.3	3.6	3.2	3.6	3.2	3	3	3.2	2.9	3.3	3.8	3.7	4.4	4.7	4.3	4.5	5	4,118,491	5.6	4.407	39.6%
1961	5.5	5.2	5.3	5.6	5.9	5.4	5.8	6	5.3	4.8	4.9	4.9	4.3	3.6	3.2	3.6	3.2	3	3	3.3	2.9	3.3	3.8	3.7	4.4	4.8	4.4	4.6	5	4.5	3,772,903	5.6	4.44	40.7%
1962	4.8	4.8	5.1	5.4	4.9	5.4	5.7	5.1	4.6	4.6	4.7	4	3.4	3.1	3.4	3	2.9	2.9	3.1	2.8	3.2	3.7	3.6	4.2	4.6	4.2	4.4	4.9	4.4	5	4,380,290	5.2	4.197	30.2%
1963	5.3	5.6	5.9	5.4	5.8	6	5.3	4.8	4.8	4.9	4.3	3.6	3.2	3.5	3.2	3	3.1	3.3	3	3.4	3.9	3.8	4.5	4.9	4.5	4.7	5.1	4.6	5.3	5.5	4,852,718	5.5	4.473	47.2%
1964	5.3	5.6	5.2	5.6	5.8	5.2	4.7	4.6	4.7	4.1	3.5	3.1	3.3	3	2.9	3	3.3	2.9	3.3	3.8	3.7	4.4	4.8	4.4	4.6	5	4.5	5.2	5.3	5.6	5,019,181	5.2	4.347	34.9%
1965	5.3	4.8	5.3	5.5	5	4.5	4.5	4.6	4	3.4	3	3.3	3	2.8	2.8	3.1	2.7	3.1	3.6	3.5	4.1	4.5	4.1	4.4	4.8	4.3	4.9	5.1	5.3	4.9	4,400,588	5	4.14	25.1%
1966	4.8	5	5.3	4.7	4.2	4.2	4.3	3.7	3.2	2.8	3	2.8	2.6	2.7	3	2.6	3	3.5	3.4	4	4.3	4	4.2	4.6	4.2	4.7	4.9	5.1	4.8	5.6	5,114,038	4.7	3.973	13.8%
1967	5.6	5.8	5.2	4.7	4.8	4.8	4.2	3.6	3.2	3.5	3.2	3	3	3.2	2.8	3.2	3.7	3.6	4.3	4.6	4.3	4.5	4.9	4.4	5	5.2	5.5	5	5.9	6	5,538,416	5.2	4.357	40.4%
1968	5.2	4.6	4.2	4.1	4.2	3.6	3.1	2.8	3	2.7	2.5	2.7	2.9	2.6	3	3.4	3.3	3.9	4.3	3.9	4.2	4.6	4.1	4.7	4.8	5.1	4.7	5.5	5.6	6.3	5,669,476	4.5	3.987	12.8%
1969	4.8	4.3	4	4.1	3.5	3	2.7	2.9	2.6	2.5	2.5	2.8	2.5	2.8	3.3	3.1	3.8	4.1	3.7	3.9	4.4	3.9	4.5	4.6	4.9	4.5	5.3	5.5	6.3	6.7	5,824,284	4.4	3.917	8.6%
1970	4.8	5	5.1	4.4	3.7	3.3	3.6	3.3	3.1	3.2	3.5	3.1	3.6	4.1	4	4.7	5.1	4.7	4.9	5.3	4.8	5.5	5.6	5.9	5.5	6.3	6.4	7.2	7.6	7.6	6,394,406	5.3	4.83	70.1%
1971	5.2	5.3	4.6	3.9	3.5	3.9	3.5	3.3	3.2	3.4	3.1	3.5	4	3.9	4.7	5	4.6	4.8	5.3	4.8	5.5	5.6	5.8	5.4	6.3	6.5	7.3	7.7	7.7	7.3	6,108,843	5.5	4.953	74.5%
1972	5.1	4.4	3.7	3.3	3.7	3.3	3.1	3.2	3.4	3.1	3.5	3.9	3.8	4.5	4.8	4.4	4.6	5.1	4.5	5.2	5.3	5.6	5.2	6	6.1	6.8	7.1	7.2	6.8	6.6	5,421,913	5.3	4.777	68.8%
1973	4.8	4	3.6	3.6	3.2	3	3	3.3	2.9	3.3	3.8	3.7	4.4	4.8	4.4	4.6	5	4.5	5.2	5.4	5.6	5.2	6.1	6.2	7	7.4	7.4	7.1	6.9	6.4	5,209,022	5.2	4.86	49.9%
1974	4.8	4.2	4.7	4.2	4	4	4.2	3.8	4.3	4.7	4.7	5.5	5.9	5.4	5.6	6.1	5.5	6.3	6.4	6.7	6.2	7	7.1	7.8	8.2	8.2	7.8	7.6	7.1	7.5	5,654,540	6.8	5.85	83.6%
1975	5.7	6.5	5.8	5.4	5.2	5.4	4.9	5.7	6.1	6	7	7.5	7	7.1	7.6	6.9	7.9	8	8.3	7.7	8.5	8.5	9.3	9.8	9.6	9.3	9.2	8.7	9.1	8.9	6,147,220	8.7	7.42	83.9%
1976	5.7	5.1	4.8	4.6	4.8	4.4	5	5.5	5.5	6.4	6.9	6.3	6.5	7	6.3	7.2	7.4	7.7	7.1	8	8.1	8.9	9.4	9.1	8.9	8.7	8.3	8.6	8.4	7.9	5,356,443	7.9	6.95	86.2%
1977	4.7	4.2	4.1	4.3	4	4.5	5	5	5.8	6.3	5.8	5.9	6.4	5.7	6.6	6.8	7.1	6.5	7.4	7.5	8.3	8.7	8.6	8.3	8.1	7.7	8	7.9	7.4	7.5	4,899,664	7.3	6.47	86.5%
1978	4.8	4.6	4.7	4.3	5	5.5	5.4	6.3	6.8	6.3	6.4	6.9	6.3	7.2	7.3	7.6	7	7.8	7.8	8.6	9.1	8.9	8.6	8.4	8	8.3	8.2	7.7	7.8	7.5	4,842,149	8	6.97	85.6%
1979	4.9	5	4.6	5.3	5.8	5.7	6.6	7.2	6.6	6.8	7.3	6.6	7.5	7.6	8	7.3	8.1	8.1	8.9	9.4	9.2	8.9	8.7	8.3	8.6	8.4	7.9	8	7.7	7.3	3,851,134	8.5	7.343	85.2%
1980	5.1	4.6	5.3	5.7	5.7	6.6	7.1	6.6	6.7	7.2	6.6	7.5	7.6	7.9	7.3	8.2	8.2	9	9.4	9.2	8.8	8.6	8.1	8.5	8.3	7.9	8	7.7	7.4	6.8	3,557,412	8.6	7.387	84.9%
1981	4.7	5.3	5.7	5.7	6.6	7.1	6.6	6.7	7.2	6.5	7.5	7.6	7.9	7.3	8.3	8.3	9.1	9.6	9.4	9.1	8.9	8.6	8.8	8.6	8.1	8.2	7.9	7.5	6.9	7.2	3,444,116	8.9	7.563	84.0%
																																Avg	5.543	65.3%

FIGURE 50

The 95% Rule backtesting results.

The 95% Rule meets its goal of improving on fixed-percent withdrawals by slowing down the rate of income decreases during poor markets. Still, its disadvantages are similar.

The withdrawals vary significantly as the market goes up and down, with the potential for small withdrawals during years of normal market gyrations. Again, the high remaining values at the end of retirement indicate withdrawals are generally lower than necessary throughout retirement. For retirements starting in the 1960s, withdrawals commonly dropped near or below 3%. Withdrawals at 3.5% or below occur in close to half of the retirement periods.

Strategy 3: Decision Rules

Jonathan Guyton's variable-withdrawal strategy, Decision Rules, is defined in the same paper[22] as his income-harvesting strategy.

Guyton's strategies have received a significant amount of attention in the last decade, in good part because he early on correctly pointed out the potential for higher withdrawals. Michael Finke, a professor at Texas Tech University, made the following statement: "[Mr. Guyton] was the first to make the point that a dynamic strategy is relatively easy to implement. It's intuitively appealing to financial planning clients, and it did a good job of improving retirement income sustainability."[23]

Only the variable-withdrawal portion of Guyton's broader strategy is used here (the rest is related to income-harvesting).

The Steps

At the start of retirement, the initial withdrawal is calculated by multiplying the initial withdrawal rate by the portfolio value. The remaining annual withdrawals are calculated at the end of each retirement year using the following steps.

1. Set the *current withdrawal amount* to the previous year's withdrawal amount (for the first year, use the initial withdrawal amount).

2. Calculate the *current rate* by dividing the *current withdrawal amount* by the current portfolio value.

3. Conditionally apply the Prosperity Rule.

    If the *current rate* is less than 80% of the initial withdrawal rate, then add 10% to the *current withdrawal amount*, then recalculate the *current rate* by dividing the *current withdrawal amount* by the current portfolio value.

4. Apply the Modified Withdrawal Rule

    Calculate the *total return* as the current portfolio value minus the portfolio value from a year ago (right after the last year's withdrawal).

    Do the following if either of the following two conditions is true: 1) if the *total return* is positive; 2) if the *current rate* is less than the initial withdrawal rate:
    a. Adjust the *current withdrawal amount* for inflation up to a maximum of 6% annually (e.g., with an amount of $48,000 and 3.1% inflation, the adjusted amount is $48,000 * (1 + 0.031) = $49,488).
    b. Recalculate the *current rate* by dividing the *current withdrawal amount* by the current portfolio value. (Any missed inflation increases, due to skipping the previous steps, are never made up.)

5. Conditionally apply the Capital Preservation Rule.

    If the *current rate* is more than 20% above the initial withdrawal rate, reduce the *current withdrawal amount* by 10%.

    This rule is active only when there are more than 15 years left before the end of planned retirement.

6. Withdraw for the year the *current withdrawal amount*.

Backtesting Results

Figure 51 shows Decision-Rules withdrawals.

Year	Y1	Y2	Y3	Y4	Y5	Y6	Y7	Y8	Y9	Y10	Y11	Y12	Y13	Y14	Y15	Y16	Y17	Y18	Y19	Y20	Y21	Y22	Y23	Y24	Y25	Y26	Y27	Y28	Y29	Y30	Remaining	MSWR	Avg	HREFF-3
1928	5	5	5.4	5.4	4.8	4.8	4.8	4.8	5.3	5.3	5.3	5.3	5.2	4.2	4.2	4.2	4.2	4.6	4.1	3.9	3.9	3.9	4.2	4.2	4.2	4.2	4.7	5.1	5.7	5.7	1,971,948	6.7	4.7	69.4%
1929	5	4.8	4.8	4.4	4.4	3.9	3.9	4.3	4.3	4.3	4.3	4.2	3.4	3.4	3.4	3.4	3.7	3.7	3.5	3.5	3.5	3.8	3.8	3.8	3.8	4.2	4.6	5	5	5.5	2,137,356	5.6	4.1	67.3%
1930	4.8	4.8	4.4	4.4	4.4	4.4	4.8	4.8	4.8	4.8	4.7	4.2	4.2	4.2	4.2	4.6	4.1	3.9	3.9	3.9	4.2	4.2	4.2	4.2	4.7	5.1	5.7	5.7	5.7	5.7	2,241,040	6.4	4.6	70.6%
1931	5	4.5	4.5	4.5	5	5.4	5.4	5.4	5.4	5.4	4.9	4.8	4.8	4.8	5.3	4.7	4.5	4.5	4.5	4.5	4.5	4.5	4.5	4.9	5.4	5.9	5.9	6.5	6.5	6.5	2,664,915	7.6	5.1	66.5%
1932	5.5	6.1	6.1	6.7	7.4	7.4	7.4	7.4	7.4	6.6	6.5	6.5	6.5	7.2	6.4	6.2	6.2	6.2	6.1	6.1	6.1	6.1	6.1	6.7	6.7	6.7	6.7	6.7	6.7	7.3	3,403,695	9.5	6.6	69.2%
1933	5.5	6	6.7	7.3	7.3	7.3	7.3	7.3	6.5	6.4	6.4	6.4	7.1	6.3	6.1	6.1	6.1	6	6	6	6	6	6.6	6.6	6.6	6.6	6.6	6.6	7.2	7.2	3,463,771	9.3	6.5	70.1%
1934	5	5	5.5	5.5	5.5	5.5	5.4	4.8	4.8	4.8	4.8	5.2	4.7	4.5	4.5	4.5	4.9	4.9	4.9	4.9	5.4	5.9	5.9	5.9	5.9	5.9	5.9	6.5	6.5	6.5	3,406,964	7.9	5.3	67.0%
1935	5	5.5	5.5	5.5	5.5	5.5	4.9	4.8	4.8	4.8	5.3	4.8	4.6	4.6	4.6	4.9	4.9	4.9	4.9	5.4	6	6	6	6	6	6	6.6	6.6	6.6	6.6	3,413,822	8.1	5.4	66.6%
1936	5	5	5	5	4.9	4	3.9	3.9	3.9	4.3	3.8	3.7	3.7	3.7	4	4.4	4.4	4.4	4.8	5.3	5.8	5.8	5.8	5.8	5.8	6.4	6.4	6.4	6.4	6.4	3,445,042	6.9	4.9	69.4%
1937	4.5	4.5	4.5	4	3.2	3.2	3.2	3.5	3.8	3.4	3.3	3.3	3.3	3.6	3.9	3.9	3.9	4.3	4.7	5.2	5.2	5.7	5.7	5.7	5.7	5.7	5.7	6.3	6.3	6.3	3,036,397	6.1	4.5	58.8%
1938	5	5	5	4.5	4.4	4.4	4.9	5.4	4.8	4.6	4.6	4.6	4.5	4.5	4.5	4.5	5	5.5	6	6	6	6	6	6.6	6.6	6.6	6.6	6.6	6.6	6.6	3,553,267	7.9	5.4	67.5%
1939	5	4.9	4	3.9	3.9	4.3	4.7	4.3	4.1	4.1	4.1	4.4	4.4	4.4	4.4	4.9	5.3	5.9	5.9	5.9	5.9	5.9	6.5	6.5	6.5	6.5	6.5	6.5	6.5	7.1	3,770,517	7.5	5.2	68.3%
1940	4.9	4	3.9	3.9	4.3	4.7	4.3	4.1	4.1	4.1	4.4	4.4	4.4	4.4	4.9	5.3	5.9	5.9	5.9	5.9	5.9	6.5	6.5	6.5	6.5	6.5	6.5	6.5	7.1	6.7	3,329,426	7.7	5.3	67.2%
1941	4.5	4.4	4.4	4.4	4.9	4.4	4.2	4.2	4.2	4.5	4.5	4.5	4.5	5	5.5	6	6	6	6	6.6	6.6	6.6	6.6	6.6	6.6	6.6	6.6	7.3	6.9	6.9	3,644,823	8	5.5	67.9%
1942	4.9	5.4	6	6.6	5.9	5.7	5.7	5.7	5.5	5.5	5.5	5.5	6.1	6.7	6.7	6.7	6.7	6.7	6.7	6.7	6.7	6.7	6.7	7.4	7.4	7.4	7.4	7.4	7.4	7.4	3,513,695	9.4	6.4	68.0%
1943	5	5.5	6	5.4	5.2	5.2	5.2	5.1	5.1	5.1	5.1	5.6	6.2	6.8	6.8	6.8	6.8	6.8	7.5	7.5	7.5	7.5	7.5	7.5	7.5	7.5	7.5	7.5	7.5	7.5	3,480,979	9.3	6.5	68.7%
1944	5	5.5	4.9	4.7	4.7	4.7	4.7	4.7	4.7	4.7	5.1	5.6	6.2	6.2	6.2	6.2	6.2	6.2	6.2	6.2	6.8	6.8	6.8	6.8	6.8	6.8	6.8	6.8	6.8	6.2	2,703,047	8.4	5.9	69.2%
1945	5	4.5	4.3	4.3	4.3	4.2	4.2	4.2	4.2	4.7	5.1	5.6	5.6	5.6	6.2	6.2	6.2	6.2	6.2	6.2	6.8	6.8	6.8	6.8	6.8	6.8	6.8	6.8	6.2	5.6	2,246,630	7.9	5.6	70.2%
1946	4.2	4.1	3.7	3.7	3.6	3.6	3.6	3.6	4	4.3	4.8	4.8	5.3	5.8	5.8	6.4	6.4	6.4	6.4	6.4	6.4	6.4	7	6.6	6.6	6.6	6.6	6	5.4	5.4	2,471,793	6.9	5.3	74.0%
1947	4.8	4.8	4.8	4.7	4.7	4.7	4.7	5.2	5.7	6.3	6.3	6.3	6.3	6.3	6.9	6.9	6.9	6.9	6.9	6.9	6.9	7.6	7.2	7.2	7.2	7.2	6.5	5.8	5.8	5.8	2,647,174	8.2	6.1	74.1%
1948	5	5	4.9	4.9	4.9	4.9	5.4	5.9	5.9	5.9	5.9	5.9	6.5	6.5	6.5	6.5	6.5	7.2	7.2	7.2	7.2	6.8	6.8	6.8	6.8	6.2	5.5	5.5	5.5	5.4	2,160,800	7.9	6.0	75.8%
1949	5	4.9	4.9	4.9	4.9	5.4	5.9	6.5	6.5	6.5	6.5	6.5	6.5	6.5	6.5	6.5	7.2	7.2	7.2	7.2	7.2	7.2	7.2	7.2	6.6	5.9	5.8	5.8	5.8	5.6	2,063,794	7.9	6.3	78.5%
1950	4.9	4.9	4.9	4.9	5.4	5.9	5.9	5.9	5.9	5.9	5.9	6.5	6.5	6.5	6.5	7.2	7.2	7.2	7.2	6.8	6.8	6.8	6.8	6.2	5.5	5.5	5.5	5.4	5.3	4.9	2,363,508	7.6	6.0	78.7%
1951	5	5	5	5.5	6.1	6.1	6.1	6	6	6.1	6	6.1	6.1	6	6.7	6.7	6.7	6.7	6.6	6.6	6.6	6.6	6.1	5.4	5.4	5.4	5.4	5.2	4.8	4.6	2,467,625	7.4	5.9	79.1%
1952	5	5	5.5	6	6.1	6	6.1	6	6	6.7	6.7	6.7	6.7	6.7	6.7	6.7	6.7	6.6	6.6	6.6	6.6	6.1	5.4	5.4	5.4	5.4	5.2	4.8	4.6	4.5	2,289,111	7.6	6.0	77.7%
1953	5	5	5.5	5.5	5.5	5.5	5.5	5.5	6.1	6.1	6.1	6.1	6.7	6.7	6.7	6.7	6.6	6.6	6.6	6.6	6.1	5.4	5.4	5.4	5.4	5.2	4.8	4.6	4.5	4.5	2,543,857	7.2	5.7	79.0%
1954	5.5	6.1	6	6.1	6.1	6.1	6.1	6.7	6.7	6.7	6.7	6.7	6.7	6.7	6.7	6.6	6.6	6.6	6.6	6.1	5.4	5.4	5.4	5.4	5.2	4.8	4.6	4.5	4.5	4.5	3,048,908	7.5	5.9	78.3%
1955	5	5	4.8	4.8	4.8	4.8	5.3	5.3	5.3	5.3	5.8	5.8	5.8	5.8	5.8	5.8	5.8	5.8	5.3	4.8	4.7	4.7	4.7	4.6	4.2	4	3.9	3.9	3.9	3.9	2,727,742	6.4	5.0	76.7%
1956	5	4.8	4.8	4.8	4.8	4.8	4.8	4.8	4.8	5.3	5.3	5.3	5.8	5.5	5.5	5.5	5.5	5	4.5	4.5	4.5	4.4	4.3	4	3.8	3.7	3.7	3.7	3.7	3.7	3,321,633	6	4.7	76.2%
1957	4.8	4.8	4.8	4.8	4.8	4.8	4.8	5.3	5.3	5.3	5.3	5.8	5.5	5.5	5.5	5.5	5	4.5	4.5	4.5	4.4	4.3	4	3.8	3.7	3.7	3.7	3.7	3.7	4.1	3,748,222	6	4.7	76.0%
1958	5	5.5	5.5	5.5	5.5	5.5	6	6.1	6.1	6	6.1	6	6	6	6	5.5	4.9	4.9	4.9	4.9	4.7	4.4	4.2	4.1	4.1	4.1	4.1	4.1	4.5	4.5	3,757,485	6.6	5.2	77.1%
1959	5	5	5	5	5	5	5	5	5	5.5	5.2	5.2	5.2	5.2	4.3	3.8	3.8	3.8	3.8	3.6	3.4	3.2	3.1	3.1	3.5	3.5	3.8	4.2	4.2	4.2	3,862,662	5.6	4.4	61.9%
1960	5	5	4.9	4.9	4.9	4.9	4.9	4.9	5.4	5.1	5.1	5.1	5.1	4.7	3.8	3.7	3.7	3.7	3.6	3.3	3.2	3.1	3.1	3.4	3.4	3.8	4.1	4.1	4.1	4.5	4,310,872	5.6	4.3	59.5%
1961	5	5	5	5	5	5	5	5.5	5.2	5.2	5.2	5.2	4.7	3.8	3.8	3.8	3.8	3.6	3.4	3.2	3.1	3.1	3.5	3.5	3.8	4.2	4.2	4.2	4.6	4.6	3,986,886	5.6	4.3	61.7%
1962	4.9	4.9	4.9	4.9	4.8	4.8	5.2	4.9	4.9	4.9	4.9	4.1	3.3	3.3	3.3	3.2	3.1	2.9	2.8	2.7	2.7	3	3.3	3.6	4	4	4	4.3	4.3	4.8	4,726,700	5.2	4.0	22.1%
1963	5	5	5	5	5	5.5	5.2	5.2	5.2	5.2	4.3	3.4	3.4	3.4	3.4	3.3	3.1	3.2	3.1	3.1	3.4	3.4	3.8	4.1	4.1	4.1	4.6	4.6	4.6	5	5,145,564	5.5	4.2	53.5%
1964	5	5	5	5	5	5	5	5	5	4.6	3.7	3.6	3.6	3.6	3.5	3.3	3.1	3	3	3	3	3.3	3.7	3.7	4	4.4	4.4	4.4	4.9	4.9	5,197,900	5.2	4.1	34.1%
1965	5	4.8	4.8	4.8	4.8	4.8	4.8	4.8	4	3.2	3.2	3.2	3.1	3.1	2.8	2.7	2.6	2.6	2.9	3.2	3.5	3.9	3.9	3.9	4.2	4.2	4.7	4.7	5.1	5.1	4,825,057	5	3.9	18.1%
1966	4.8	4.8	4.8	4.6	4.6	4.6	4.6	3.7	3	3	3	3	2.9	2.7	2.5	2.5	2.7	3	3	3.3	3.6	3.6	4	4.4	4.2	4.2	4.6	4.6	4.6	5	5,529,300	4.7	3.8	6.3%
1967	5	5	5	5	5	5	4.6	3.7	3.6	3.6	3.6	3.5	3.3	3.1	3	3	3.3	3.3	3.7	4	4	4	4.4	4.4	4.4	4.9	4.9	4.9	5.4	5.4	5,880,858	5.2	4.2	48.7%
1968	5	4.7	4.7	4.7	4.7	3.9	3.1	2.8	2.8	2.8	2.7	2.5	2.6	2.5	2.5	2.8	2.8	3.1	3.4	3.4	3.7	4.1	4.1	4.1	4.5	4.5	4.5	5	5.5	6	6,245,004	4.5	3.8	5.0%
1969	4.7	4.2	4.2	4.2	3.5	2.8	2.8	2.8	2.8	2.7	2.5	2.6	2.5	2.5	2.8	2.8	3.1	3.4	3.4	3.7	4.1	4.1	4.1	4.1	4.5	4.5	5	5	5.5	6	6,415,205	4.4	3.7	3.9%
1970	5	5	5	4.6	3.7	3.7	3.7	3.6	3.5	3.3	3.1	3	3	3.3	3.7	4	4.4	4.4	4.4	4.9	4.9	4.9	5.4	5.4	5.4	5.9	5.9	6.5	7.2	7.2	6,887,471	5.3	4.6	53.6%
1971	5	5	4.6	3.7	3.7	3.7	3.6	3.5	3.3	3.1	3	3	3.3	3.7	4	4.4	4.4	4.4	4.9	4.9	4.9	5.4	5.4	5.4	5.9	5.9	6.5	7.2	7.2	7.2	6,807,013	5.5	4.7	52.4%
1972	5	4.6	3.7	3.7	3.7	3.6	3.5	3.3	3.1	3	3	3.3	3.3	3.7	4	4	4.4	4.9	4.9	4.9	4.9	5.4	5.4	5.4	5.9	6.5	6.5	7.2	7.2	7.2	6,216,590	5.3	4.6	52.6%
1973	4.6	3.7	3.7	3.7	3.6	3.5	3.3	3.1	3	3	3.3	3.3	3.7	4	4	4	4.4	4.4	4.9	4.9	5.4	5.4	5.4	5.9	6.5	6.5	7.2	7.2	7.2	7.2	5,782,416	5.2	4.7	53.7%
1974	4	4	4.4	4.4	4.2	3.9	3.7	3.7	4	4.4	4.4	4.9	5.3	5.3	5.3	5.9	5.9	5.9	5.9	6.5	6.5	6.5	6.5	7.1	7.8	7.8	7.8	7.8	7.8	7.8	6,399,824	6.8	5.6	80.1%
1975	5	5.5	5.4	5.3	4.9	5.1	5	5	5.5	5.5	6	6.6	6.6	6.6	7.3	7.3	7.3	7.3	8	8	8	8	8.8	9.7	9.7	9.7	9.7	9.7	9.7	9.7	7,052,268	8.7	7.2	80.7%
1976	5	5	4.8	4.5	4.2	4.2	4.6	5	5	5.5	6.1	6.1	6.1	6.7	6.7	6.7	6.7	7.4	7.4	7.4	7.4	8.1	8.9	8.9	8.9	8.9	8.9	8.9	8.9	8.9	6,095,072	7.9	6.7	82.9%
1977	5	4.8	4.5	4.2	4.2	4.2	4.6	4.6	5	5.5	5.5	5.5	5.5	5.5	6.1	6.1	6.1	6.1	6.7	6.7	7.4	8.1	8.1	8.1	8.1	8.1	8.1	8.1	8.1	8.1	5,408,490	7.3	6.2	83.2%
1978	4.8	4.5	4.3	4.2	4.6	5.1	5.1	5.6	6.1	6.1	6.1	6.1	6.1	6.7	6.7	6.7	6.7	7.4	7.4	8.2	8.2	8.2	8.2	8.2	8.2	8.2	8.2	8.2	8.2	8.2	5,599,107	8	6.7	81.8%
1979	4.7	4.4	4.3	4.7	5.2	5.2	5.7	6.3	6.3	6.3	6.9	6.9	6.9	6.9	7.6	7.6	7.6	7.6	8.4	9.2	9.2	9.2	9.2	9.2	9.2	9.2	9.2	9.2	9.2	9.2	4,610,324	8.5	7.4	84.4%
1980	4.7	4.6	4.6	5.1	5.1	5.6	6.2	6.2	6.2	6.8	6.8	6.8	6.8	7.5	7.5	7.5	7.5	8.2	9	9	9	9	9	9	9	9	9	9	9	9	3,997,249	8.6	7.4	84.2%
1981	4.9	4.9	4.9	4.9	5.4	5.9	5.9	5.9	6.5	6.5	7.2	7.2	7.2	7.2	7.9	7.9	8.7	8.7	8.7	8.7	8.7	8.7	8.7	8.7	8.7	8.7	8.7	8.7	8.7	8.7	4,042,027	8.9	7.4	81.8%
																																Avg	5.34	64.3%

FIGURE 51

Decision Rules backtesting results.

The strategy is strong at preventing the portfolio from running out of money, although it doesn't guarantee it.

As seen before, the primary weakness is that withdrawal rates sometimes drop unnecessarily low. For example, look at the middle band of years for the retirement starting from 1959 through 1973. The withdrawal rate in each period dropped near 3% or below for an extended period, although significant funds are left in the portfolio at the end of retirement.

There is some irony in Guyton's conservative handling of variable withdrawals, since he was sometimes criticized for advocating too high of withdrawals. His strategy does well at balancing poor market conditions.

Strategy 4: Floor-to-Ceiling Rule

William Bengen is well-known as an early leader in setting safe withdrawal rates using historical backtesting (he might be called the father of fixed 4% withdrawals). More recently, he defined the "Floor-to-Ceiling" Rule, a variable-withdrawal strategy[*].

Basically, as the portfolio rises, the withdrawal amount will rise until it hits a ceiling; as the portfolio value drops, the withdrawal amount lowers until it hits a floor. Annual withdrawals will always fall between the floor and the ceiling values.

Although different values can be used for the floor and ceiling, it appears Bengen most commonly defines the floor as 10% below the inflation-adjusted withdrawal amount (defined in Key Definitions) and the ceiling at 25% above the inflation-adjusted withdrawal amount.

The Steps

At the start of retirement, the *initial withdrawal* is calculated by multiplying the initial withdrawal rate by the portfolio value. The remaining annual withdrawals are calculated at the end of each retirement year using the following steps.

1. Calculate the **inflation-adjusted withdrawal amount** (see Key Definitions earlier in the chapter for full description).

2. Calculate the *floor amount* by multiplying the **inflation-adjusted withdrawal amount** by 0.90.

3. Calculate the *ceiling amount* by multiplying the **inflation-adjusted withdrawal amount** by 1.25.

4. Calculate the *current withdrawal amount* by multiplying the initial withdrawal rate (e.g., 5%) by the current portfolio value.

5. If the *current withdrawal amount* is less than the *floor amount*, then reset it to the *floor amount*.

6. If the *current withdrawal amount* is greater than *ceiling amount*, then reset it to the *ceiling amount*.

7. Withdraw for the year the *current withdrawal amount*.

Backtesting Results

Figure 52 shows the Floor-to-Ceiling withdrawals. Given the target withdrawal rate as 5%, the floor becomes an inflation-adjusted 4.5% and the ceiling an inflation-adjusted 6.25% (shown rounded up to 6.3%).

---

[*] Unfortunately the best reference I found for Bengen Floor-to-Ceiling strategy disappeared from the Web, but a search should turn up a brief description. Bengen also published a book in 2006, *Conserving Client Portfolios During Retirement*.

Year	Y1	Y2	Y3	Y4	Y5	Y6	Y7	Y8	Y9	Y10	Y11	Y12	Y13	Y14	Y15	Y16	Y17	Y18	Y19	Y20	Y21	Y22	Y23	Y24	Y25	Y26	Y27	Y28	Y29	Y30	Remaining	MSWR	Avg	HREFF-3
1928	5.9	5.2	4.6	4.5	4.5	4.7	4.7	5.4	6.3	4.7	5.2	5.1	4.7	4.5	4.5	4.5	4.9	5.9	4.5	4.5	4.5	4.5	4.7	4.8	4.9	4.6	6.1	6.3	6.3	5.8	1,807,674	6.7	5.0	74.4%
1929	4.5	4.5	4.5	4.5	4.5	4.5	4.5	5	4.5	4.5	4.5	4.5	4.5	4.5	4.5	4.5	4.9	4.5	4.5	4.5	4.5	4.5	4.5	4.5	4.5	5.2	5.7	5.5	4.9	5.8	1,853,160	5.6	4.7	83.0%
1930	4.5	4.5	4.5	4.5	4.5	5	6	4.5	4.9	4.8	4.5	4.5	4.5	4.5	4.8	6	4.6	4.5	4.5	4.5	4.8	5	5.1	4.8	6.2	6.3	6.3	5.8	6.3	6.3	2,138,182	6.4	5.0	77.9%
1931	4.5	4.5	5	4.9	6.1	6.3	5.3	6	5.8	5.3	4.5	4.5	5.1	5.6	6.3	5	4.5	4.5	4.6	5	5.1	5.3	5	6.3	6.3	6.3	6.1	6.3	6.3	6.3	2,512,382	7.6	5.4	70.5%
1932	5.2	6.3	6.3	6.3	6.3	6.3	6.3	6.3	6.3	6.3	6.3	6.3	6.3	6.3	6.3	6	5.7	6.1	6.3	6.3	6.3	6.2	6.3	6.3	6.3	6.3	6.3	6.3	6.3	6.3	3,687,077	9.5	6.2	65.0%
1933	6.3	6.3	6.3	6.3	6.3	6.3	6.3	6.3	6.1	6	6.3	6.3	6.3	6.3	5.6	5.4	5.8	6.1	6.1	6.2	5.9	6.3	6.3	6.3	6.3	6.3	6.3	6.3	6.3	6.3	3,726,177	9.3	6.1	66.0%
1934	4.9	6	6.3	5.2	5.8	5.7	5.2	4.5	4.5	4.9	5.6	6.3	5.2	4.6	4.5	4.9	5.2	5.2	5.3	5	6.3	6.3	6.3	6	6.3	6.3	6.3	6.3	6.3	6.3	3,202,350	7.9	5.6	69.9%
1935	6.1	6.3	5.3	5.9	5.8	5.3	4.5	4.5	5	5.6	6.3	5.2	4.6	4.5	4.9	5.2	5.2	5.4	5.1	6.3	6.3	6.3	6	6.3	6.3	6.3	6.3	6.3	6.3	6.3	3,247,774	8.1	5.6	69.1%
1936	5.9	4.5	4.8	4.7	4.5	4.5	4.5	4.5	4.6	5.6	4.5	4.5	4.5	4.5	4.5	4.5	4.7	4.5	5.9	6.3	6.2	5.5	6.3	6.3	6.3	6.3	6.3	6.3	6.3	6.3	3,158,086	6.9	5.3	75.5%
1937	4.5	4.5	4.5	4.5	4.5	4.5	4.5	4.5	4.9	4.5	4.5	4.5	4.5	4.5	4.5	4.5	4.5	5.2	5.7	5.5	4.9	5.7	5.8	5.6	6.2	5.7	6	6.3	6.3	5.9	2,620,172	6.1	5.1	82.0%
1938	5.8	5.6	5.1	4.5	4.5	4.9	5.4	6.3	4.9	4.5	4.5	4.5	4.9	4.9	5.1	4.8	6.3	6.3	6.3	5.9	6.3	6.3	6.3	6.3	6.3	6.3	6.3	6.3	6.3	6.3	3,465,415	7.9	5.6	70.0%
1939	4.9	4.5	4.5	4.5	4.5	4.9	6.1	4.7	4.5	4.5	4.5	4.8	4.8	5	4.7	6.1	6.3	6.3	5.7	6.3	6.3	6.3	6.3	6.3	6.3	6.3	6.3	6.3	6.3	6.3	3,543,239	7.5	5.5	72.3%
1940	4.6	4.5	4.5	4.5	5	6.2	4.7	4.5	4.5	4.5	4.8	4.8	5	4.7	6.1	6.3	6.3	5.7	6.3	6.3	6.3	6.3	6.3	6.3	6.3	6.3	6.3	6.3	6.3	6	3,104,380	7.7	5.5	71.0%
1941	4.5	4.5	4.8	5.3	6.3	4.9	4.5	4.5	4.5	4.9	5	5.1	4.8	6.3	6.3	6.3	5.9	6.3	6.3	6.3	6.3	6.3	6.3	6.3	6.3	6.3	6.3	6.3	6.3	6.3	3,459,834	8	5.6	70.0%
1942	5	6	6.3	6.3	6.1	5.4	5.1	5.7	5.9	5.9	6.1	5.7	6.3	6.3	6.3	6.3	6.3	6.3	6.3	6.3	6.3	6.3	6.3	6.3	6.3	6.3	6.3	6.3	6.3	6.3	3,796,952	9.4	6.1	64.4%
1943	5.8	6.3	6.3	5.8	5.1	4.8	5.3	5.7	5.8	5.9	5.5	6.3	6.3	6.3	6.3	6.3	6.3	6.3	6.3	6.3	6.3	6.3	6.3	6.3	6.3	6.3	6.3	6.3	6.3	6.3	3,832,514	9.3	6.0	64.7%
1944	5.5	6.3	5	4.5	4.5	4.6	5	5	5.2	4.9	6.3	6.3	6.3	6	6.3	6.3	6.3	6.3	6.3	6.3	6.3	6.3	6.3	6.3	6.3	6.3	6.3	6.3	6.3	5.4	2,727,693	8.4	5.8	68.7%
1945	6	4.6	4.5	4.5	4.5	4.6	4.7	4.9	4.6	6.1	6.3	6.3	5.7	6.3	6.3	6.3	6.3	6.3	6.3	6.3	6.3	6.3	6.3	6.3	6.3	6.3	6.3	6.3	5.3	4.5	2,293,902	7.9	5.7	71.3%
1946	4.5	4.5	4.5	4.5	4.5	4.5	4.5	4.5	5.3	6	5.8	5.1	6.2	6.3	6.1	6.3	6.2	6.3	6.3	6.3	6.3	6.3	6.3	5.8	5.7	5.8	5.8	4.7	4.5	4.5	2,205,451	6.9	5.5	78.1%
1947	4.5	4.5	4.6	5.1	5.2	5.4	5	6.3	6.3	6.3	6.3	6.3	6.3	6.3	6.3	6.3	6.3	6.3	6.3	6.3	6.3	6.3	6.3	6.3	6.3	6.3	6.1	4.8	5.1	5.6	2,875,421	8.2	5.8	70.6%
1948	4.8	5.3	5.5	5.5	5.6	5.3	6.3	6.3	6.3	6.3	6.3	6.3	6.3	6.3	6.3	6.3	6.3	6.3	6.3	6.3	6.3	6.3	6.3	6.3	6.3	5.5	4.5	4.6	5.1	4.6	2,304,869	7.9	5.8	73.5%
1949	5.5	5.7	5.7	5.8	5.5	6.3	6.3	6.3	6.3	6.3	6.3	6.3	6.3	6.3	6.3	6.3	6.3	6.3	6.3	6.3	6.3	6.3	6.3	6.3	5.7	4.5	4.8	5.3	4.8	4.5	2,374,774	7.9	5.9	74.1%
1950	5.3	5.3	5.5	5.2	6.3	6.3	6.3	6.2	6.3	6.3	6.3	6.3	6.3	6.3	6.3	6.3	6.3	6.3	6.3	6.3	6.3	6.3	6.3	5.4	4.5	4.5	5	4.5	4.5	4.5	2,561,522	7.6	5.8	75.3%
1951	5	5.2	4.9	6.3	6.3	6.3	5.9	6.3	6.3	6.3	6.3	6.3	6.3	6.3	6.3	6.3	6.3	6.3	6.3	6.3	6.3	6.3	5.2	4.5	4.5	4.8	4.5	4.5	4.5	4.5	2,632,650	7.4	5.7	76.1%
1952	5.1	4.8	6.3	6.3	6.3	6	6.3	6.3	6.3	6.3	6.3	6.3	6.3	6.3	6.3	6.3	6.3	6.3	6.3	6.3	6.3	5.6	4.5	4.7	5.1	4.6	4.5	4.5	4.5	4.5	2,522,495	7.6	5.7	74.3%
1953	4.7	6.1	6.3	6.3	5.7	6.3	6.3	6.3	6.3	6.3	6.3	6.3	6.3	6.3	6.3	6.3	6.1	6	6.2	6.2	4.9	4.5	4.5	4.5	4.5	4.5	4.5	4.5	4.5	4.5	2,684,620	7.2	5.6	76.8%
1954	6.3	6.3	6.3	6	6.3	6.3	6.3	6.3	6.3	6.3	6.3	6.3	6.3	6.3	6.3	6.3	6.3	6.3	6.3	5.6	4.5	4.7	5.2	4.6	4.5	4.5	4.5	4.5	4.5	4.7	3,356,971	7.5	5.7	75.0%
1955	5.4	5.2	4.6	5.5	5.6	5.4	6.1	5.5	5.8	6.1	6.3	5.7	6.3	6.3	5.4	5.3	5.4	5.4	4.5	4.5	4.5	4.5	4.5	4.5	4.5	4.5	4.5	4.5	4.5	4.5	2,445,789	6.4	5.2	80.0%
1956	4.8	4.5	5.1	5.2	5	5.7	5.1	5.5	5.8	6.1	5.4	6	6.2	5.1	5	5.2	5.2	4.5	4.5	4.5	4.5	4.5	4.5	4.5	4.5	4.5	4.5	4.5	4.5	4.5	2,705,352	6	5.0	82.4%
1957	4.5	5.3	5.4	5.2	5.8	5.3	5.6	5.9	6.2	5.5	6.1	6.2	5.1	4.9	5.1	5.1	4.5	4.5	4.5	4.5	4.5	4.5	4.5	4.5	4.5	4.5	4.5	4.5	4.5	4.5	3,005,707	6	5.0	82.7%
1958	6.1	6.2	6.1	6.3	6.1	6.3	6.3	6.3	6.3	6.3	6.3	5.7	5.6	5.8	5.8	4.6	4.5	4.5	4.5	4.5	4.5	4.5	4.5	4.5	4.5	4.5	4.5	4.5	4.9	4.5	3,426,841	6.6	5.3	79.4%
1959	5.1	4.9	5.5	5	5.3	5.6	5.9	5.3	5.8	6	4.9	4.7	4.9	4.9	4.5	4.5	4.5	4.5	4.5	4.5	4.5	4.5	4.5	4.5	4.5	4.5	4.5	4.5	4.5	4.5	2,627,206	5.6	4.9	86.0%
1960	4.9	5.4	4.9	5.2	5.5	5.7	5.1	5.7	5.9	4.9	4.8	4.9	4.9	4.5	4.5	4.5	4.5	4.5	4.5	4.5	4.5	4.5	4.5	4.5	4.5	4.5	4.5	4.5	4.5	4.5	2,939,286	5.6	4.8	85.2%
1961	5.6	5.1	5.3	5.7	5.9	5.3	5.8	6	4.9	4.8	4.9	5	4.5	4.5	4.5	4.5	4.5	4.5	4.5	4.5	4.5	4.5	4.5	4.5	4.5	4.5	4.5	4.5	4.5	4.5	2,561,514	5.6	4.8	85.6%
1962	4.5	4.8	5.1	5.4	4.7	5.5	5.7	4.7	4.5	4.7	4.7	4.5	4.5	4.5	4.5	4.5	4.5	4.5	4.5	4.5	4.5	4.5	4.5	4.5	4.5	4.5	4.5	4.5	4.5	4.5	2,532,858	5.2	4.7	89.0%
1963	5.4	5.6	5.9	5.3	5.8	6	4.9	4.7	4.9	4.9	4.5	4.5	4.5	4.5	4.5	4.5	4.5	4.5	4.5	4.5	4.5	4.5	4.5	4.5	4.5	4.5	4.5	4.5	4.5	4.5	3,452,111	5.5	4.8	86.1%
1964	5.3	5.6	5	5.6	5.8	4.7	4.5	4.6	4.7	4.5	4.5	4.5	4.5	4.5	4.5	4.5	4.5	4.5	4.5	4.5	4.5	4.5	4.5	4.5	4.5	4.5	4.5	4.5	4.5	4.5	2,920,839	5.2	4.7	89.2%
1965	5.3	4.6	5.3	5.6	4.5	4.5	4.5	4.6	4.5	4.5	4.5	4.5	4.5	4.5	4.5	4.5	4.5	4.5	4.5	4.5	4.5	4.5	4.5	4.5	4.5	4.5	4.5	4.5	4.5	4.5	2,175,418	5	4.6	91.3%
1966	4.5	5	5.3	4.5	4.5	4.5	4.5	4.5	4.5	4.5	4.5	4.5	4.5	4.5	4.5	4.5	4.5	4.5	4.5	4.5	4.5	4.5	4.5	4.5	4.5	4.5	4.5	4.5	4.5	4.5	998,962	4.7	4.5	96.0%
1967	5.7	5.8	4.8	4.7	4.8	4.9	4.5	4.5	4.5	4.5	4.5	4.5	4.5	4.5	4.5	4.5	4.5	4.5	4.5	4.5	4.5	4.5	4.5	4.5	4.5	4.5	4.5	4.5	4.5	4.5	3,654,735	5.2	4.6	88.2%
1968	5.2	4.5	4.5	4.5	4.5	4.5	4.5	4.5	4.5	4.5	4.5	4.5	4.5	4.5	4.5	4.5	4.5	4.5	4.5	4.5	4.5	4.5	4.5	4.5	4.5	4.5	4.5	4.5	4.5	1.9	0	4.5	4.4	72.6%
1969	4.5	4.5	4.5	4.5	4.5	4.5	4.5	4.5	4.5	4.5	4.5	4.5	4.5	4.5	4.5	4.5	4.5	4.5	4.5	4.5	4.5	4.5	4.5	4.5	4.5	4.5	3.4	0	0	0	0	4.4	4.0	14.1%
1970	4.8	5	5.1	4.5	4.5	4.5	4.5	4.5	4.5	4.5	4.5	4.5	4.5	4.5	4.5	4.5	4.5	4.5	4.5	4.5	4.5	4.5	4.5	4.5	4.5	4.9	5.1	5.8	6.2	6.2	5,272,948	5.3	4.7	88.6%
1971	5.2	5.3	4.5	4.5	4.5	4.5	4.5	4.5	4.5	4.5	4.5	4.5	4.5	4.5	4.5	4.5	4.5	4.5	4.5	4.5	4.5	4.5	4.7	4.5	5.2	5.4	6.1	6.3	6.3	6.1	5,065,078	5.5	4.8	86.9%
1972	5.1	4.5	4.5	4.5	4.5	4.5	4.5	4.5	4.5	4.5	4.5	4.5	4.5	4.5	4.5	4.5	4.5	4.5	4.5	4.5	4.5	4.5	4.5	4.9	5.1	5.8	6.2	6.3	5.9	5.7	4,669,212	5.3	4.8	89.6%
1973	4.5	4.5	4.5	4.5	4.5	4.5	4.5	4.5	4.5	4.5	4.5	4.5	4.5	4.5	4.5	4.5	4.5	4.5	4.5	4.5	4.5	4.5	4.6	4.8	5.6	6	6.1	5.7	5.6	5	4,052,866	5.2	4.7	90.5%
1974	4.5	4.5	4.7	4.5	4.5	4.5	4.5	4.5	4.5	4.6	4.5	5.3	5.7	5.2	5.5	5.9	5.2	6.1	6.2	6.3	5.9	6.3	6.3	6.3	6.3	6.3	6.3	6.3	6.3	6.3	6,058,966	6.8	5.4	79.1%
1975	5.7	6.3	5.8	5.4	5.2	5.4	4.9	5.7	6.1	6	6.3	6.3	6.3	6.3	6.3	6.3	6.3	6.3	6.3	6.3	6.3	6.3	6.3	6.3	6.3	6.3	6.3	6.3	6.3	6.3	8,283,191	8.7	6.1	69.4%
1976	5.7	5.1	4.8	4.6	4.8	4.5	5	5.5	5.5	6.3	6.3	6.3	6.3	6.3	6.3	6.3	6.3	6.3	6.3	6.3	6.3	6.3	6.3	6.3	6.3	6.3	6.3	6.3	6.3	6.3	6,793,353	7.9	5.9	74.2%
1977	4.5	4.5	4.5	4.5	4.5	4.5	5	4.9	5.7	6.2	5.7	5.8	6.3	5.7	6.3	6.3	6.3	6.3	6.3	6.3	6.3	6.3	6.3	6.3	6.3	6.3	6.3	6.3	6.3	6.3	5,731,015	7.3	5.7	77.9%
1978	4.7	4.6	4.8	4.5	5	5.5	5.4	6.3	6.3	6.3	6.3	6.3	6.3	6.3	6.3	6.3	6.3	6.3	6.3	6.3	6.3	6.3	6.3	6.3	6.3	6.3	6.3	6.3	6.3	6.3	6,236,743	8	5.9	73.8%
1979	4.9	5	4.6	5.3	5.8	5.8	6.3	6.3	6.3	6.3	6.3	6.3	6.3	6.3	6.3	6.3	6.3	6.3	6.3	6.3	6.3	6.3	6.3	6.3	6.3	6.3	6.3	6.3	6.3	6.3	5,981,717	8.5	6.0	70.8%
1980	5.1	4.6	5.3	5.7	5.7	6.3	6.3	6.3	6.3	6.3	6.3	6.3	6.3	6.3	6.3	6.3	6.3	6.3	6.3	6.3	6.3	6.3	6.3	6.3	6.3	6.3	6.3	6.3	6.3	6.3	5,149,594	8.6	6.1	70.6%
1981	4.6	5.3	5.8	5.7	6.3	6.3	6.3	6.3	6.3	6.3	6.3	6.3	6.3	6.3	6.3	6.3	6.3	6.3	6.3	6.3	6.3	6.3	6.3	6.3	6.3	6.3	6.3	6.3	6.3	6.3	5,120,295	8.9	6.1	68.7%
																																Avg	5.35	76.1%

FIGURE 52

Floor-to-Ceiling Withdrawals backtesting results.

The results are generally excellent in terms of consistent income matched to the state of the portfolio. The salient flaw is that the strategy ran out of money at the end of the 1968 and 1969 retirements. A lower initial rate, such as 4.5%, would have fared better, but the aim here is to see how a strategy handles an unsustainable initial rate since the floor to the market's future behavior is unknown. Also, during strong retirement periods, even with higher withdrawals, a large amount of remaining funds is left at the end of retirement. Despite these weaknesses, the strategy remains an overall strong performer.

Strategy 5: Sensible Withdrawals

Peter Ponzo is a retired math professor from the University of Waterloo. For several years, he published excellent analysis and commentary on investment topics, all under the Internet name of "gummy". Since then, Professor Ponzo has moved on to explore other interests, but his Sensible Withdrawals remains a notable variable-withdrawal strategy to include in this survey.

The general approach for Sensible Withdrawals is to start with a core withdrawal rate, 80% of the initial withdrawal rate, then add to it a portion of the "extra" return, based on how well the portfolio is doing. Extra return is the increase in portfolio value after factoring in inflation and the upcoming withdrawal. The strategy doesn't specify exactly how much of the extra income to add to the annual withdrawal amount, but Ponzo provides a spreadsheet for retirees to make their own choice (based on US data).

Ponzo's recommendation with an initial rate to cover just the core spending needs (e.g., 3%) should make the risk of running out of money negligible, although with substantially reduced income. The gummy website[24] gives many more details for anyone interested in examining Sensible Withdrawals in more depth.

The steps below use 31% of the extra return to boost the withdrawal amount, selected so Sensible Withdrawals provides its best showing in the survey, given the initial withdrawal rate. Any higher percentage, or higher initial withdrawal rate, causes a failure in 1969 similar to the Floor-to-Ceiling strategy.

The Steps

At the start of retirement, the initial withdrawal is calculated by multiplying the initial withdrawal rate by the portfolio value. Also, set the *previous portfolio amount* to the starting portfolio value minus the initial withdrawal. The remaining annual withdrawals are calculated at the end of each retirement year using the following steps.

1. Calculate the **inflation-adjusted withdrawal amount** (see Key Definitions earlier in the chapter for full description).

2. Set the *current withdrawal amount* to 80% of the **inflation-adjusted withdrawal amount**.

3. Calculate the *extra return* as follows.
   a. The *base portfolio value* is set to the current portfolio value minus the *current withdrawal amount*.
   b. Adjust the *previous portfolio amount* by this year's inflation rate (e.g., with a value of $480,000 and 3.1% inflation, the adjusted value is $480,000 * (1 + 0.031) = $494,880).
   c. Set the *extra return* to the *base portfolio value* minus the adjusted *previous portfolio amount*.

4. If the *extra return* is greater than zero, add 31% of the *extra return* to the *current withdrawal amount*.

5. Withdraw for the year the *current withdrawal amount*.

6. For use the next year, set the *previous portfolio amount* to the current portfolio value (after the withdrawal).

Backtesting Results

Figure 53 shows the Sensible-Withdrawals results.

Year	Y1	Y2	Y3	Y4	Y5	Y6	Y7	Y8	Y9	Y10	Y11	Y12	Y13	Y14	Y15	Y16	Y17	Y18	Y19	Y20	Y21	Y22	Y23	Y24	Y25	Y26	Y27	Y28	Y29	Y30	Remaining	MSWR	Avg	HREFF-3
1928	9.9	4	4	4	5.9	7.9	4	8.8	9.6	4	7.2	4	4	4	7.8	7.6	11	4	4	4	6.3	7.2	5	5.2	4	13	8.1	4	4	1,283,352	6.7	6.0	83.3%
1929	4	4	4	5.3	7.4	4	8.1	8.9	4	6.5	4	4	4	7.3	6.8	10	4	4	4	5.5	5.9	4.6	4.5	4	10	7	4	4	10	1,027,069	5.6	5.6	94.2%
1930	4	4	5.5	8.5	4	9.3	10	4	7.4	4	4	4	4.4	8.4	7.8	11	4	4	4	6.4	7.1	4.9	5.1	4	12	7.9	4	4	10	4.9	1,549,971	6.4	6.1	88.9%
1931	4	5.4	11	4	11	11	4	8	4	4	4.4	8.9	7.5	11	4	4	4	6.4	7.2	5	5.3	4	13	8.2	4	4	10	5	4	1,934,528	7.6	6.3	76.9%
1932	5.6	16	4	13	12	4	9.2	4.2	4	4	9.4	7.8	11	4	4	4	7.1	7	4.8	5.1	4	14	8.6	4	4	11	5.1	4.8	8	3,225,703	9.5	6.9	66.0%
1933	16	4	12	12	4	9	4.1	4	4	9.2	7.6	11	4	4	4	6.9	6.9	4.8	5.1	4	14	8.5	4	4	11	5	4.7	7.8	4	3,278,590	9.3	6.8	65.8%
1934	4	11	11	4	8	4	4	4.1	8.6	8.3	12	4	4	4	7	6.6	4.7	5.2	4	13	7.9	4	4	9.8	4.8	4	8.2	4	6.5	2,673,466	7.9	6.3	73.2%
1935	11	11	4	8	4	4	4.1	8.5	8.3	12	4	4	4	6.9	6.6	4.7	5.2	4	13	7.8	4	4	9.7	4.8	4	8.2	4	6.5	6.2	2,730,551	8.1	6.3	72.3%
1936	9.6	4	7.3	4	4	4	7.8	7.6	11	4	4	4	6.3	7.4	5.1	5.3	4	13	8.3	4	4	11	5.1	4	7.5	4	6	6.2	5.8	2,565,533	6.9	6.1	82.1%
1937	4	6.8	4	4	4	7.3	7.1	11	4	4	6.1	6.8	5.1	5	4	13	8.1	4	4	10	5	4	8.3	4	6.6	6	6.5	4	2,012,410	6.1	5.8	89.6%
1938	9	4	4	4.1	8.8	7.4	10	4	4	4	6.4	6.9	4.8	5.3	4	13	8.1	4	4	10	4.9	4	8.5	4	6.7	6.3	6.5	4	8.1	3,023,365	7.9	6.1	72.4%
1939	4	4	4	4.2	8.6	8.3	12	4	4	6.9	6.7	4.7	5.2	4	13	7.9	4	4	9.8	4.8	4	8.2	4	6.5	6.1	6.3	4	7.9	5.6	3,049,366	7.5	6.0	74.9%
1940	4	4	4.1	8.5	8.2	12	4	4	6.9	6.7	4.7	5.1	4	12	7.8	4	4	9.7	4.8	4	8.1	4	6.4	6.7	6.3	4	7.8	5.5	4	2,722,322	7.7	6.0	72.8%
1941	4	4.2	9	7.5	11	4	4	6.5	7.1	4.9	5.4	4	13	8.3	4	4	10	5	4.1	7.5	4	6	6.4	5.8	4	8.3	5.8	4	4.2	3,113,139	8	6.0	70.5%
1942	4.6	10	8.6	12	4	4	4	7.5	6.5	4.6	5.4	4	13	8.1	4	4	10	4.9	4.8	7.6	4	6.7	6.6	5.6	4	8	5.8	4	5	5.8	3,603,708	9.4	6.5	62.6%
1943	9.5	7.9	11	4	4	4	7	7.2	5	5.1	4	14	8.7	4	4	11	5.2	4.6	8	4	6.3	6.9	4	7.3	6.1	4	4.8	6	4.9	3,558,164	9.3	6.3	63.6%
1944	7.4	11	4	4	6.5	6.9	4.8	5.3	4	13	8.1	4	4	10	4.9	4.2	7.5	4	6.7	6.4	6.5	4	8.2	5.7	4	4.4	5.5	4.7	4	2,652,905	8.4	5.9	66.4%
1945	10	4	4	6.4	6.9	4.8	5.3	4	13	8.1	4	4	10	4.9	4	8.5	4	6.7	6.3	6.5	4	8.1	5.7	4	4.2	5.4	4.6	4	2,109,078	7.9	5.8	68.9%
1946	4	4	6	6.5	5.3	5	4	14	8.7	4	4	11	5.2	4	7.8	4	6.2	6.5	6	4	7.4	6	4	5.3	4.7	4	4	5.9	1,959,556	6.9	5.6	77.1%
1947	4	6.9	7.4	5.1	5.1	4	14	8.8	4	4	11	5.2	4.4	8	4	6.3	6.8	6	7.3	6.1	4	4.6	5.9	4.9	4	4	6.1	7.4	2,736,098	8.2	5.9	68.2%
1948	4	7.3	6.2	4.5	5.3	4	13	7.8	4	4	9.7	4.8	4.2	8.3	4	6.5	6.4	6.3	4	7.7	5.6	4	4.4	5.9	5	4	6.3	7.5	4	2,366,791	7.9	5.8	69.1%
1949	7.3	6.1	4.4	5.3	4	13	7.8	4	4	9.6	4.7	4.4	8.4	4	6.5	6.5	6.2	4	7.7	5.6	4	4.5	6	4	6.3	7.6	4	4	2,478,262	7.9	5.8	66.6%
1950	6.4	4.5	5.3	4	13	7.9	4	4	9.8	4.8	4.1	8.4	4	6.6	6.4	6.3	4	7.8	5.7	4	4.3	5.9	5	4	6.3	7.5	4	4	4	2,646,684	7.6	5.7	70.6%
1951	4.6	5.3	4	13	8	4	4	9.9	4.8	4	8.4	4	6.6	6.4	6.4	4	7.9	5.7	4	4.1	5.8	4	4	6.3	7.4	4	4	4	5.3	2,678,068	7.4	5.6	71.9%
1952	5	4	14	8.6	4	4	11	5.1	4.4	7.8	4	6.2	6.7	5.9	4	7.2	6	4	4.6	5.8	4.8	4	4	6	7.2	4	4	4	4.8	4	2,585,802	7.6	5.6	69.7%
1953	4	13	7.9	4	4	9.8	4.8	4	8.3	4	6.5	6.3	6.3	4	7.9	5.6	4	4	5.7	5	4	6.2	7.2	4	4	5.4	4	6.9	2,638,536	7.2	5.6	73.7%
1954	13	8	4	4	10	4.9	4	8.5	4	6.7	6.5	6.4	4	8	5.7	4	4.8	5.7	4.7	4	5.7	7.1	4	4	4.5	4	7.5	7	3,268,843	7.5	5.8	72.6%
1955	7	4	4	10	5	4	8.4	4	6.6	6.2	6.5	4	8.2	5.2	4	4.6	5.6	6.5	4	4	4.9	4	5.9	6.4	4	2,225,131	6.4	5.3	79.3%
1956	4	4	10	5	4	8.4	4	6.7	6.1	6.5	4	8.3	5.7	4	4	5.1	4.5	4	4	5.6	6.3	4	4	5	5.5	6	4	6.7	2,222,034	6	5.3	83.9%
1957	4	9.9	4.9	4	8.2	4	6.5	6.1	6.4	4	8	5.6	4	4	5.3	4.8	4	4	6.1	6.7	4	4	4.4	5.4	4	5.5	6	4	6.8	5.1	2,306,232	6	5.3	85.4%
1958	11	5.3	4	8	4	6.3	6.7	6.1	4	7.6	5.5	4	4	5.5	4.8	4	4	7	4	4	5.2	4	6.5	7.2	4	8.3	6.2	4	3,109,729	6.6	5.5	79.8%
1959	4.9	4	8.2	4	6.5	6	6.3	4	8	5.5	4	4	5.2	4.8	4	4	6.1	6.6	4	4	4.4	5.3	4	5.4	5.8	4	6.5	5	4	5	2,034,755	5.6	5.1	88.6%
1960	4	7.6	4	6.3	5.9	4	8.6	5.8	4	4	5.1	4.6	4	4	5.7	6.3	4	4	4.1	5.3	4	5.4	5.8	4	6.5	5	4	5	5.7	2,286,213	5.6	5.1	88.1%
1961	7.7	4	6.1	6.3	6	4	7.4	5.9	4	5.2	4.6	4	5.8	6.4	4	4	4.1	5.3	4	5.5	5.9	4	6.7	5.1	4	5.1	5.9	4	1,933,096	5.6	5.1	88.4%
1962	4	6.1	6.2	5.9	4	8.8	5.9	4	4	5	4.6	4	5.7	6.2	4	4	4.2	5	4	5.4	5.9	4.6	4	4.5	5.1	4	5.8	1,576,268	5.2	4.9	92.2%
1963	6.5	6	6.3	4	8	5.6	4	4	5.3	4.8	4	4	6.1	6.6	4	4	4.4	5.3	4	5.4	5.9	4	6.6	5	4	5	5.8	4	6.9	4.5	2,292,218	5.5	5.1	90.8%
1964	6.1	6.5	4	8.2	5.6	4	4	5.2	4.8	4	4	6.2	6.6	4	4	4.2	5	4	5.1	5.4	4	6	4.7	4	4.6	5.2	4	5.9	4	4.1	1,687,878	5.2	4.9	91.9%
1965	5.9	4	8.7	5.8	4	4	5	4.6	4	4	5.7	6.2	4	4	4.2	4.9	4	5	5.3	4	5.8	4.5	4	4.5	5	4	5.6	4	4	1,290,453	5	4.8	92.5%
1966	4	7.7	6	4	4	4.6	4	5.8	6.2	4	4	4	4.6	4	4.6	4.8	4	5.1	4.1	4	4.3	4	4.5	4	5.6	4	457,537	4.7	4.5	93.3%
1967	8.4	5.7	4	4	5.1	4.5	4	4	5.6	6.2	4	4	4	5.1	4	5.4	5.8	4	6.5	5	4	5	5.7	4	6.7	4.4	4.5	4	7	5	2,444,622	5.2	5.0	93.2%
1968	5.5	4	4	5	4.7	4	4	6	6.3	4	4	4	4.6	4	4.6	4.8	4	5.1	4.1	4	4.3	4	4.5	4	4	4	4	4	164,842	4.5	4.4	95.1%
1969	4	4	4.9	4.5	4	5.6	6	4	4	4	4.6	4	4.6	4.8	4	5.1	4.1	4	4.3	4	4.5	4	4	4	4	41,309	4.4	4.3	95.6%
1970	4	5.4	4.9	4	6.3	6.9	4	4.5	5.5	4	5.6	6.1	4	7	5.3	4	5.3	6.2	4	7.5	4.7	4.9	4	8	5.2	8.5	6	5.9	3,662,480	5.3	5.3	97.4%
1971	5.5	5	4	4	5.8	6.6	4	4	5.2	4	5.8	6.3	4	7.3	5.4	4	5.5	6.5	4	7.8	4.9	5	4	8.7	5.6	8.3	6.2	5.4	4	3,583,593	5.5	5.4	94.3%
1972	4.8	4	4	6.1	6.7	4	4.4	5.5	4	5.7	6.2	4	7	5.3	4	5.3	6.2	4	7.5	4.7	4.9	4	8	5.3	6.1	5.9	4	4	3,049,196	5.3	5.3	96.3%
1973	4	4	5.8	6.5	4	4.1	5.3	4	5.6	6.1	4	6.9	5.2	4	5.2	6	4	7.3	4.6	4.8	4	7.7	5.4	8.2	5.9	5.7	4	4	1,908,804	5.2	5.1	95.8%
1974	4	6.9	7.7	4	4	4.6	6.2	4	6.7	4	8.5	6.6	4	5.7	6.9	4	9.4	5.3	6.1	4	10	5.3	8.9	7.1	5.6	4	4	7.5	4,871,457	6.8	5.9	82.4%
1975	9	9.1	4	4	4	5.5	4	9	6.9	4.4	10	8.1	4	5.8	8.3	4	11	5.8	7.3	4	12	5.1	11	8.8	4.6	4.1	5	4	7.5	4.4	7,206,766	8.7	6.5	70.0%
1976	8.6	4	4	4	5.4	4	8.3	7.3	4.2	9.7	7.5	4	5.6	7.8	4	10	5.8	6.8	4	12	5.6	10	8.2	4.6	4	4.7	4	7.2	4.3	4	6,020,644	7.9	6.1	72.9%
1977	4	4	4	5.5	4	7.7	7.1	4	9.1	7	4	5.5	7.5	4	9.6	5.6	6.4	4	11	5.6	9.7	7.7	4.7	4	4.3	4	7.2	4.3	4	5.6	5,177,916	7.3	5.8	70.5%
1978	4	4	5.5	4	8.3	7.4	4.1	9.8	7.6	4	5.6	7.9	4	10	5.6	6.8	4	11	5.1	10	8.2	4.7	4	4.6	4	7.3	4.4	4	5.8	4.2	5,710,189	8	6.0	70.9%
1979	4	5.4	4	8.7	7.5	4.3	10	7.9	4	5.7	8.1	4	11	5.7	7.1	4	12	5	10	8.5	4.6	4	4.8	4	7.3	4.3	4	5.8	4.5	4	5,410,223	8.5	6.1	67.8%
1980	4.9	4	8.6	7.1	4.5	9.9	7.8	4	6	7.8	4	10	5.8	7	4	12	5.4	10	8.4	4.2	4	4.6	4	7.9	4.6	4	6.1	4.2	4	4.2	4,705,167	8.6	6.1	66.0%
1981	4	8.6	7.4	4.3	10	7.8	4	5.6	8	4	11	5.9	7.1	4	12	5.6	10	8.5	4.5	4.1	4.9	4	7.2	4.3	4	5.8	4.2	4	4.5	7.9	4,577,580	8.9	6.2	66.0%
																																Avg	5.68	79.3%

FIGURE 53

Sensible Withdrawals backtesting results.

The strategy overall does well, although the minimum withdrawal rate (i.e., 4%) consistently recurs throughout all the retirement periods, including the best and worst. This is due to the "starting" income being the "floor", with extra income only added during years when there is portfolio growth, all independent from the overall state of the portfolio. For example, 1932 was an exceptionally strong year to retire in a MSWR of 9.5%, but a third of the annual withdrawals are still 4%. (A retiree could partly account for this by stockpiling extra income, but this isn't so easy during a series of low-performing years.) On the flip side, 1969 was an exceptionally poor year to retire with an MSWR of 4.4%, putting the 4% "floor" uncomfortably close to the failure rate.

Sensible Withdrawals is very good at balancing withdrawals during typical market conditions. Unfortunately, unless the initial rate is moderate, it runs out of money easier than might be expected during poor market conditions. While Sensible Withdrawals can be tuned to perform better in strong markets or weak markets, it cannot be tuned to do better in both.

Strategy 6: Endowment Formula

Bob Carlson is editor of the newsletter *Retirement Watch*. He has also written two books: *The New Rules of Retirement* and *Invest Like a Fox…Not Like a Hedgehog*.

Carlson's Endowment Formula[25] takes a middle ground approach, combining Fixed-Rate Inflation-Adjusted Withdrawals with Fixed-Percentage Withdrawals. Simply put, 70% comes from the first strategy and 30% from the second. This combined approach is an improvement over both independent strategies.

The Steps

At the start of retirement, the initial withdrawal is calculated by multiplying the initial withdrawal rate by the portfolio value. The remaining annual withdrawals are calculated at the end of each retirement year using the following steps.

1. Calculate the **inflation-adjusted withdrawal amount** by adjusting its previous value by inflation (see Key Definitions for full description on page 120).

2. Calculate the *fixed-percent amount* by multiplying the initial withdrawal rate (e.g., 5%) by the current portfolio value.

3. Calculate the *current withdrawal amount* by adding 70% of the **inflation-adjusted withdrawal amount** to 30% of the *fixed-percent amount*.

4. Withdraw for the year the *current withdrawal amount*.

Backtesting Results

Figure 54 shows Endowment Formula withdrawals.

Year	Y1	Y2	Y3	Y4	Y5	Y6	Y7	Y8	Y9	Y10	Y11	Y12	Y13	Y14	Y15	Y16	Y17	Y18	Y19	Y20	Y21	Y22	Y23	Y24	Y25	Y26	Y27	Y28	Y29	Y30	Remaining	MSWR	Avg	HREFF-3
1928	5.3	5.2	5	4.7	4.5	4.6	4.6	4.8	5.3	5.1	5.2	5.2	5.1	4.7	4.4	4.4	4.6	5	4.9	4.6	4.4	4.4	4.5	4.6	4.7	4.7	5.2	5.7	6	6	1,872,370	6.7	4.9	72.8%
1929	4.8	4.5	4	3.8	3.8	3.7	3.9	4.3	4.2	4.2	4.2	4.1	3.8	3.6	3.6	3.7	4.2	4.2	4	3.9	3.9	4	4.2	4.3	4.3	4.7	5.2	5.5	5.5	5.7	2,053,929	5.6	4.3	73.5%
1930	4.8	4.4	4.1	4.2	4.2	4.5	5	4.8	4.9	4.9	4.8	4.4	4.2	4.2	4.4	4.9	4.9	4.7	4.5	4.4	4.5	4.7	4.8	4.8	5.2	5.7	5.9	5.9	6.1	6.3	2,171,177	6.4	4.8	74.7%
1931	4.6	4.4	4.6	4.7	5.1	5.8	5.7	5.8	5.8	5.7	5.3	5	5	5.2	5.6	5.4	5.2	4.9	4.8	4.9	4.9	5	5	5.4	5.9	6.2	6.2	6.4	6.6	6.8	2,513,902	7.6	5.4	70.5%
1932	5.1	5.7	6.1	6.8	7.6	7.6	7.8	7.9	7.8	7.3	6.9	6.8	6.9	7.2	7	6.5	6.1	6	6	6	6	5.9	6.3	6.8	7	7	7.2	7.4	7.5	7.8	3,311,955	9.5	6.8	71.2%
1933	5.6	5.9	6.5	7.3	7.3	7.5	7.6	7.4	7	6.6	6.5	6.6	7	6.7	6.3	5.9	5.8	5.8	5.8	5.8	5.7	6.1	6.6	6.8	6.8	7	7.2	7.3	7.5	7.5	3,375,039	9.3	6.6	71.2%
1934	5	5.3	5.8	5.6	5.7	5.7	5.6	5.2	4.9	4.9	5.1	5.6	5.5	5.2	4.9	4.9	5	5	5.1	5.1	5.5	5.9	6.2	6.1	6.4	6.5	6.6	6.8	6.8	6.9	3,159,156	7.9	5.6	70.8%
1935	5.3	5.9	5.7	5.8	5.8	5.7	5.3	5	5	5.2	5.6	5.5	5.2	5	4.9	5	5	5.1	5.1	5.5	5.9	6.1	6.1	6.3	6.5	6.6	6.8	6.8	6.9	7	3,184,141	8.1	5.7	70.2%
1936	5.3	5	4.9	4.9	4.7	4.3	4.1	4.1	4.2	4.7	4.6	4.4	4.1	4.1	4.2	4.4	4.5	4.5	5	5.5	5.8	5.8	6.1	6.3	6.4	6.7	6.7	6.8	6.9	7.1	3,231,371	6.9	5.2	74.0%
1937	4.6	4.4	4.3	4.1	3.7	3.4	3.4	3.6	4	4	3.9	3.7	3.7	3.9	4	4.2	4.2	4.6	5.1	5.4	5.4	5.7	5.8	5.9	6.2	6.2	6.3	6.5	6.6	6.5	2,813,198	6.1	4.8	73.8%
1938	5.2	5.4	5.3	5	4.7	4.8	4.9	5.4	5.2	5	4.7	4.6	4.7	4.8	4.9	4.9	5.3	5.8	6	6	6.3	6.5	6.5	6.8	6.8	6.9	7	7.2	7.1	7.2	3,376,365	7.9	5.7	71.3%
1939	5	4.8	4.4	4.2	4.2	4.4	4.9	4.9	4.7	4.5	4.5	4.6	4.7	4.8	4.8	5.2	5.7	5.9	5.9	6.1	6.3	6.4	6.6	6.7	6.7	6.9	7	6.9	7	7.1	3,516,938	7.5	5.5	72.5%
1940	4.9	4.5	4.2	4.3	4.5	5	5	4.7	4.5	4.5	4.6	4.7	4.8	4.8	5.2	5.7	5.9	5.9	6.1	6.3	6.4	6.6	6.6	6.7	6.8	7	6.9	7	7	6.7	3,061,763	7.7	5.6	71.6%
1941	4.7	4.5	4.6	4.8	5.3	5.2	4.9	4.7	4.6	4.7	4.8	4.9	4.9	5.3	5.8	6.1	6.1	6.3	6.5	6.7	6.9	6.9	7	7.1	7.2	7.1	7.2	7.3	7	6.7	3,275,109	8	5.9	72.2%
1942	5	5.3	5.7	6.4	6.3	6	5.8	5.7	5.8	5.8	5.9	5.8	6.2	6.7	6.9	6.8	7.1	7.2	7.3	7.5	7.5	7.5	7.6	7.7	7.6	7.6	7.7	7.3	7.1	6.9	3,245,991	9.4	6.7	70.4%
1943	5.2	5.6	6.2	6.1	5.8	5.5	5.4	5.5	5.6	5.7	5.6	6.1	6.6	6.9	6.8	7.1	7.3	7.4	7.7	7.7	7.8	7.9	8	7.9	7.9	8	7.6	7.3	7.1	7	3,197,347	9.3	6.7	71.9%
1944	5.1	5.5	5.4	5.1	4.8	4.7	4.8	4.9	5	4.9	5.4	5.9	6.1	6.1	6.4	6.5	6.7	6.9	6.9	7	7.1	7.2	7.1	7.1	7.2	6.9	6.7	6.5	6.4	6	2,498,083	8.4	6.1	71.7%
1945	5.3	5.1	4.8	4.5	4.4	4.5	4.5	4.7	4.6	5.1	5.6	5.8	5.8	6.1	6.3	6.4	6.6	6.6	6.7	6.8	7	6.9	7	7.1	6.8	6.6	6.5	6.4	6	5.3	2,093,136	7.9	5.9	73.3%
1946	4.7	4.3	3.9	3.8	3.8	3.9	4	4	4.4	5	5.3	5.4	5.7	6	6.1	6.4	6.4	6.5	6.7	6.9	6.8	6.9	7	6.7	6.4	6.3	6.2	5.8	5.1	4.7	2,197,842	6.9	5.5	77.8%
1947	4.8	4.6	4.6	4.8	4.9	5	5.1	5.5	6.1	6.4	6.4	6.7	6.9	7.1	7.3	7.4	7.4	7.6	7.7	7.6	7.7	7.7	7.4	7.1	6.9	6.8	6.4	5.7	5.2	5.1	2,405,011	8.2	6.3	76.2%
1948	4.9	5	5.2	5.3	5.4	5.4	5.8	6.2	6.5	6.4	6.6	6.8	6.9	7.1	7.1	7.1	7.3	7.4	7.3	7.3	7.4	7.1	6.8	6.6	6.5	6	5.3	4.9	4.8	4.5	1,971,350	7.9	6.2	78.1%
1949	5.1	5.3	5.4	5.6	5.6	6	6.4	6.6	6.6	6.8	6.9	7	7.2	7.2	7.3	7.4	7.5	7.4	7.5	7.5	7.2	6.9	6.7	6.6	6.1	5.4	5	4.9	4.6	4.3	1,985,043	7.9	6.3	79.3%
1950	5.1	5.2	5.3	5.2	5.6	6.1	6.3	6.3	6.5	6.7	6.7	7	7	7	7.2	7.3	7.2	7.3	7.4	7	6.7	6.6	6.5	6	5.3	4.9	4.8	4.5	4.3	4.1	2,252,831	7.6	6.1	79.3%
1951	5	5.1	5	5.4	5.8	6.1	6	6.3	6.4	6.5	6.8	6.8	6.8	7	7.1	7	7.1	7.2	6.9	6.6	6.4	6.3	5.9	5.2	4.8	4.7	4.4	4.2	4	3.9	2,447,782	7.4	5.9	78.3%
1952	5	5	5.4	5.9	6.2	6.1	6.4	6.6	6.8	7	7	7.1	7.2	7.4	7.3	7.3	7.4	7	6.8	6.6	6.5	6.1	5.4	5	4.8	4.6	4.3	4.1	4	3.8	2,240,888	7.6	6.0	77.5%
1953	4.9	5.3	5.7	5.9	5.9	6.1	6.3	6.3	6.6	6.6	6.7	6.8	7	6.9	6.9	7	6.7	6.4	6.3	6.2	5.7	5.1	4.7	4.5	4.3	4.1	3.9	3.9	3.7	3.7	2,613,282	7.2	5.7	76.8%
1954	5.4	5.9	6.2	6.1	6.4	6.6	6.7	6.9	6.9	7	7.1	7.3	7.2	7.3	7.3	7	6.8	6.7	6.6	6.1	5.5	5.1	4.9	4.7	4.4	4.2	4	3.8	3.8	3.9	3,046,717	7.5	5.9	77.2%
1955	5.1	5.2	5	5.1	5.3	5.3	5.6	5.6	5.7	5.8	6	6	6.1	6.2	6	5.8	5.7	5.6	5.3	4.7	4.3	4.2	4	3.8	3.6	3.5	3.3	3.3	3.5	3.6	2,828,307	6.4	4.9	71.2%
1956	4.9	4.7	4.8	5	5	5.2	5.2	5.3	5.5	5.7	5.6	5.8	5.9	5.7	5.5	5.4	5.4	5	4.5	4.1	4	3.8	3.6	3.4	3.4	3.2	3.2	3.4	3.5	3.7	3,398,955	6	4.6	67.1%
1957	4.8	5	5.1	5.1	5.3	5.3	5.4	5.6	5.8	5.7	5.9	6	5.7	5.5	5.4	5.3	4.9	4.3	4	3.9	3.7	3.5	3.4	3.4	3.3	3.3	3.5	3.6	3.9	4.2	3,809,661	6	4.7	70.1%
1958	5.3	5.6	5.8	6.1	6.1	6.2	6.4	6.6	6.5	6.6	6.7	6.4	6.2	6	5.9	5.5	4.9	4.5	4.4	4.2	3.9	3.8	3.7	3.5	3.5	3.7	3.8	4.1	4.5	4.6	3,727,444	6.6	5.2	75.0%
1959	5	5	5.2	5.1	5.2	5.3	5.5	5.4	5.6	5.7	5.5	5.2	5.1	5.1	4.7	4.1	3.8	3.7	3.5	3.3	3.2	3.2	3.1	3.2	3.3	3.4	3.7	4	4.2	4.3	3,675,993	5.6	4.4	60.0%
1960	5	5.1	5	5.1	5.2	5.4	5.3	5.4	5.6	5.4	5.2	5.1	5.1	4.7	4.2	3.8	3.7	3.6	3.4	3.2	3.2	3.1	3.1	3.3	3.4	3.6	3.9	4	4.2	4.4	4,144,141	5.6	4.4	58.1%
1961	5.2	5.1	5.2	5.3	5.5	5.5	5.6	5.7	5.5	5.3	5.2	5.1	4.7	4.2	3.9	3.8	3.6	3.4	3.3	3.2	3.1	3.1	3.3	3.4	3.7	4	4.1	4.2	4.4	4.4	3,766,251	5.6	4.4	59.9%
1962	4.9	4.8	4.9	5.1	5	5.1	5.3	5.1	4.9	4.8	4.8	4.4	3.9	3.6	3.5	3.4	3.2	3.1	3.1	2.9	3	3.1	3.2	3.5	3.8	3.9	4	4.3	4.2	4.5	4,373,799	5.2	4.1	39.2%
1963	5.1	5.3	5.5	5.4	5.6	5.7	5.5	5.3	5.1	5.1	4.7	4.1	3.8	3.7	3.5	3.3	3.2	3.2	3.1	3.2	3.4	3.5	3.7	4.1	4.2	4.3	4.6	4.5	4.8	5	4,923,721	5.5	4.4	61.6%
1964	5.1	5.2	5.2	5.3	5.5	5.2	5	4.9	4.8	4.5	3.9	3.6	3.5	3.3	3.2	3.1	3.1	3	3.1	3.3	3.4	3.6	4	4.1	4.2	4.4	4.4	4.7	4.9	5.1	5,102,057	5.2	4.2	48.9%
1965	5.1	4.9	5.1	5.2	5	4.8	4.7	4.7	4.3	3.8	3.5	3.4	3.3	3.1	3	3	2.9	2.9	3.1	3.2	3.4	3.7	3.8	3.9	4.2	4.1	4.4	4.6	4.8	4.8	4,438,928	5	4.0	29.8%
1966	4.8	4.9	5	4.8	4.6	4.4	4.4	4	3.5	3.2	3.1	3	2.8	2.8	2.8	2.7	2.8	2.9	3	3.3	3.5	3.6	3.8	4	4	4.2	4.4	4.7	4.7	5	5,296,137	4.7	3.8	12.2%
1967	5.2	5.4	5.2	5.1	5	5	4.6	4.1	3.8	3.7	3.5	3.3	3.2	3.1	3	3	3.2	3.3	3.5	3.8	3.9	4.1	4.3	4.3	4.5	4.8	5	5	5.3	5.5	5,661,564	5.2	4.2	46.1%
1968	5.1	4.8	4.5	4.4	4.3	4	3.4	3.1	3	2.9	2.8	2.7	2.7	2.6	2.7	2.9	2.9	3.2	3.5	3.6	3.7	3.9	3.9	4.1	4.3	4.5	4.6	4.9	5.1	5.6	5,938,027	4.5	3.8	9.0%
1969	4.7	4.5	4.3	4.2	3.9	3.4	3.1	3	2.9	2.7	2.6	2.6	2.6	2.6	2.8	2.8	3.1	3.3	3.4	3.6	3.8	3.8	4	4.2	4.4	4.5	4.8	5	5.4	5.8	6,010,440	4.4	3.7	7.4%
1970	4.9	4.9	5	4.6	4.1	3.8	3.7	3.6	3.4	3.3	3.3	3.2	3.3	3.5	3.6	3.8	4.2	4.3	4.4	4.7	4.7	4.9	5.1	5.4	5.4	5.7	5.9	6.3	6.8	7.1	6,676,996	5.3	4.6	73.8%
1971	5.1	5.1	4.8	4.3	4.1	4	3.8	3.6	3.5	3.4	3.3	3.3	3.5	3.6	3.9	4.2	4.3	4.5	4.7	4.7	4.9	5.2	5.4	5.4	5.7	6	6.4	6.9	7.2	7.4	6,419,464	5.5	4.7	78.0%
1972	5	4.7	4.1	3.8	3.8	3.6	3.4	3.3	3.3	3.2	3.3	3.5	3.6	3.9	4.2	4.3	4.4	4.7	4.7	4.9	5.1	5.4	5.4	5.7	6	6.4	6.9	7.2	7.3	7.4	6,151,574	5.3	4.8	76.4%
1973	4.7	4.1	3.8	3.8	3.6	3.4	3.3	3.3	3.1	3.2	3.3	3.4	3.7	4	4.1	4.3	4.5	4.5	4.7	4.9	5.2	5.2	5.5	5.7	6.2	6.6	6.9	7	7	6.8	5,128,337	5.2	4.7	71.1%
1974	4.6	4.5	4.5	4.4	4.3	4.2	4.2	4.1	4.1	4.3	4.4	4.7	5.1	5.2	5.4	5.6	5.6	5.8	6	6.3	6.3	6.6	6.8	7.2	7.6	7.9	8	8	7.8	7.9	5,962,175	6.8	5.7	81.8%
1975	5.2	5.6	5.7	5.6	5.5	5.5	5.3	5.4	5.6	5.8	6.2	6.6	6.8	6.9	7.2	7.2	7.5	7.7	8	7.9	8.2	8.4	8.8	9.3	9.5	9.6	9.6	9.5	9.6	9.5	6,490,828	8.7	7.3	82.4%
1976	5.2	5.2	5.1	4.9	4.9	4.7	4.8	5	5.2	5.5	5.9	6.1	6.2	6.5	6.5	6.8	7	7.3	7.2	7.6	7.8	8.2	8.7	8.9	9.1	9.1	9	9	9	8.8	5,615,909	7.9	6.8	84.7%
1977	4.9	4.7	4.5	4.4	4.3	4.3	4.5	4.6	5	5.4	5.5	5.6	5.9	5.9	6.1	6.4	6.6	6.6	6.9	7.1	7.6	8	8.3	8.4	8.4	8.4	8.4	8.3	8.2	8	5,096,896	7.3	6.4	85.2%
1978	4.9	4.8	4.8	4.6	4.7	4.9	5.1	5.5	5.9	6	6.2	6.5	6.5	6.7	7	7.2	7.2	7.5	7.6	8	8.5	8.7	8.8	8.8	8.7	8.8	8.7	8.5	8.4	8.2	5,046,987	8	6.9	84.8%
1979	5	5	4.9	5	5.2	5.4	5.8	6.2	6.4	6.6	6.8	6.8	7.1	7.3	7.6	7.6	7.8	8	8.4	8.8	9.1	9.2	9.2	9.1	9.1	9	8.8	8.7	8.5	8.2	4,303,228	8.5	7.4	85.0%
1980	5	4.9	5	5.2	5.4	5.8	6.2	6.4	6.5	6.8	6.8	7.1	7.3	7.6	7.5	7.8	8	8.4	8.9	9.1	9.1	9.1	9	9	8.9	8.7	8.6	8.5	8.1	7.8	3,705,392	8.6	7.4	84.9%
1981	4.9	5	5.2	5.4	5.8	6.2	6.4	6.5	6.8	6.8	7.1	7.3	7.6	7.6	7.9	8.1	8.5	9	9.2	9.4	9.4	9.3	9.3	9.3	9.1	8.9	8.7	8.3	7.9	7.8	3,585,005	8.9	7.6	84.3%
																																Avg	5.47	68.3%

FIGURE 54

Endowment Formula backtesting results.

While the Endowment Formula successfully combines and balances the strengths of the fixed-rate and fixed-percentage strategies, it's still susceptible to their underlying limitations.

The weaknesses tend toward those seen in the fixed-percent strategy. There is the potential for small withdrawals during years of normal market volatility. Also, the high remaining values at the end of retirement indicate withdrawals are generally lower than necessary throughout retirement. For example, retirements starting in the mid-1950s through the early 1970s commonly had withdrawals below 3.5%, while finishing with a relatively large remaining portfolio.

The Endowment Formula will never run out of money, although rates can be very low.

Strategy 7: Mortality Updating Failure Percentage

In 2012, the Retirement Income Industry Association's Academic Thought Leadership Award was awarded to Morningstar researchers Blanchett[*], Kowara, and Chen for their paper, *Optimal Withdrawal Strategy for Retirement Income Portfolios*[26]. This paper makes two significant contributions: the first is a metric to measure and compare the efficiency of variable withdrawals using different strategies (more on this later); the second is a top-performing variable-withdrawal strategy: Mortality Updating Failure Percentage (MUFP).

The basic idea of MUFP is elegantly straightforward: estimate the years of life remaining, then estimate the sustainable withdrawal rate for those remaining years of life. For example, if a retiree is 65 years old with a life expectancy of 22 years, then the annual withdrawal corresponds to the estimated sustainable rate for those 22 years. The next year, the annual withdrawal corresponds to the estimated sustainable rate for the remaining 21 years. If the retiree reaches 80 years old, then the life expectancy is 10 years, so the annual withdrawal corresponds to the estimated sustainable rate for 10 years.

MUFP is an exceptionally strong strategy, but there are several reasons it's not viable for individual investors in its pure form:

- Every retiree has a different portfolio, so how to estimate the sustainable rate for the remaining years is not clear for individuals. (Fortunately, it turns out there is significant latitude in estimating the sustainable rate, but a retiree still needs a well-defined approach with readily assessable numbers.)

- MUFP works well for 30-year retirement, but it breaks down in it raw form for 40-year retirements. (A workaround is to scale back the retiree's age so the planned retirement never exceeds an age of 95.)

- MUFP starts with relatively aggressive withdrawal rates during the early retirement years. This has an advantage of providing extra income when retirees often want it, but these high early rates mean income can also be pushed excessively low (e.g., less than 1.5%) during poor markets. While this isn't seen during typical cases based on the SBBI data, it's not uncommon under broader testing.

Because of the above limitations, MUFP is not recommended in its pure form. However, to my knowledge it's still generally the top performing variable-withdrawal strategy found in the literature. As such, it provides an excellent benchmark to compare other strategies against. Also, MUFP is the basis for the strategy eventually recommended.

For this initial survey and the follow-up comparisons, the estimated sustainable withdrawal rates are custom calculated to match the corresponding historical dataset. This type of accuracy based on historical data is not possible for real retirements, but again, it provides a top-performing benchmark for comparison.

The selected MUFP parameters follow the original paper's guidelines: a 10% target probability[†] of outliving the estimated years of life remaining (when using a 60% stock portfolio) and a 10% target probability of failure (the "global" optimal probability value) when determining the withdrawal-rate estimate for the years of life left. The paper outlines other options (e.g., 50% mortality figures, 50% probability of failure), but the selected numbers provide the best backtesting performance.

Two tables are needed to follow the strategy in the steps below. Figure 55 shows the mortality table used to estimate the years of life remaining for a retiree. Figure 56 shows the withdrawal-rate estimates for the different

---

[*]   Blanchett is the Head of Retirement Research for Morningstar.

[†]   The mortality figures are based on total US population (male and female) using National Vital Statistics Reports, United States Life Tables, 2007. *NVSR* Vol. 59 No. 9, p. 61.

datasets. The first set of estimates, SBBI-Estimated Withdrawal Rate, matches the default portfolio and SBBI data used in this survey. Notice that the withdrawal-rate estimates vary significantly for the datasets early in retirement, but tend to converge later.

Age	45	46	47	48	49	50	51	52	53	54	55	56	57	58	59	60	61	62	63	64	65	66	67	68	69	70	71	72	73	74	75	76	77	78	79	80	81	82	83	84	85	86	87	88	89	90	91	92	93	94	95	96	97	98	99	100
Estimated Years of Life	40	39	39	38	37	36	35	34	33	32	31	30	29	28	27	26	25	24	23	23	22	21	20	19	18	17	16	16	15	14	13	13	12	11	11	10	9	9	8	8	7	7	6	6	6	5	5	4	4	4	3	3	3	3	3	3

FIGURE 55

Mortality table based on US total population, with a 10% probability of outliving the estimated years of life.

Estimated Years of Life	40	39	38	37	36	35	34	33	32	31	30	29	28	27	26	25	24	23	22	21	20	19	18	17	16	15	14	13	12	11	10	9	8	7	6	5	4	3
SBBI-Estimated Withdrawal Rate	5.0%	5.0%	5.0%	5.0%	5.0%	5.0%	5.1%	5.1%	5.2%	5.2%	5.2%	5.3%	5.3%	5.4%	5.5%	5.5%	5.6%	5.6%	5.7%	5.8%	5.9%	6.0%	6.2%	6.4%	6.6%	6.9%	7.2%	7.6%	8.0%	8.4%	9.0%	9.7%	10.7%	11.7%	13.1%	14.7%	17.9%	22.2%
Shiller-Estimated Withdrawal Rate	4.1%	4.2%	4.2%	4.2%	4.2%	4.3%	4.3%	4.3%	4.4%	4.5%	4.5%	4.6%	4.6%	4.7%	4.7%	4.8%	4.8%	4.9%	5.0%	5.1%	5.3%	5.5%	5.7%	5.9%	6.0%	6.2%	6.5%	6.8%	7.3%	7.8%	8.4%	9.2%	10.4%	11.8%	13.5%	15.6%	18.5%	23.2%
UK-Estimated Withdrawal Rate	3.9%	4.1%	4.1%	4.1%	4.1%	4.1%	4.2%	4.2%	4.2%	4.2%	4.3%	4.4%	4.5%	4.5%	4.6%	4.7%	4.7%	4.9%	5.0%	5.0%	5.1%	5.3%	5.4%	5.6%	5.9%	6.2%	6.5%	6.8%	7.3%	7.7%	8.4%	9.4%	10.6%	12.0%	13.5%	15.4%	18.2%	22.6%
Japan-Estimated Withdrawal Rate	3.8%	3.9%	3.9%	3.9%	3.9%	3.9%	4.0%	4.0%	4.0%	4.0%	4.1%	4.1%	4.2%	4.2%	4.3%	4.3%	4.4%	4.5%	4.6%	4.8%	4.9%	5.1%	5.2%	5.4%	5.6%	5.9%	6.1%	6.7%	7.2%	7.7%	8.4%	9.2%	10.4%	11.8%	15.6%	15.6%	18.5%	23.8%

FIGURE 56

Withdrawal-rate estimates for estimated years of life for the SBBI, Shiller, UK, and Japan datasets based on backtesting with a 10% failure rate.

The Steps

1. The retiree's current age is used with the mortality table (Figure 55) to look up the estimated years of life remaining. This value will be known as *estimated-years-of-life*.

2. Use *estimated-years-of-life* to index into the withdrawal-rate table (SBBI row in Figure 56) to find the *estimated sustainable withdrawal rate*. This is the rate with a 90% chance of success for the estimated years of life remaining.

3. Multiply the *estimated sustainable withdrawal rate* by the current portfolio value to get the *current withdrawal amount*.

4. Withdraw for the year the *current withdrawal amount*.

Backtesting Results

Figure 57 shows MUFP withdrawals for every retirement period, backtesting with the default portfolio using the SBBI dataset, assuming a 65 year old retiree.

Year	Y1	Y2	Y3	Y4	Y5	Y6	Y7	Y8	Y9	Y10	Y11	Y12	Y13	Y14	Y15	Y16	Y17	Y18	Y19	Y20	Y21	Y22	Y23	Y24	Y25	Y26	Y27	Y28	Y29	Y30	Remaining	MSWR	Avg	HREFF-3
1928	6.7	5.9	5.3	4.4	4.9	5.8	5.8	6.7	8.1	6.1	7.1	6.7	6.2	5.1	5	6.3	7.7	9.4	7.4	6.1	6	6.5	7.9	7.8	7.6	7.2	9.6	12	11	7.2	544,796	6.7	7.0	101.8%
1929	4.9	4.3	3.5	3.9	4.7	4.7	5.7	6.6	4.9	5.7	5.7	5	4.1	4.3	5.1	6.3	8.8	6.2	5.8	5.1	6.2	6.8	7.5	7.3	6.2	9.4	10	11	7.4	9.1	706,928	5.6	6.2	106.1%
1930	4.9	3.9	4.3	5.2	5.2	6.4	7.8	5.4	6.4	6.4	5.9	4.6	4.8	6.2	7.1	9.5	7.3	6.2	6.1	6.7	8.2	8	8.8	7.5	10	12	11	9.3	11	11	825,066	6.4	7.2	108.8%
1931	4.3	4.6	6	5.8	7.4	8.9	6.6	7.3	7.4	6.8	5.6	5.6	7	8	9.4	7.4	6.7	6.1	7.3	8	8.6	8.5	8.2	11	12	12	8.9	13	12	9.8	840,606	7.6	8.0	102.4%
1932	6	8.2	8.1	9.6	11	8.8	9.8	9.5	9	7.5	7.6	8.6	9.7	12	8.5	7.7	7.6	8.1	9.6	9.3	9.9	8.6	13	14	12	11	13	15	12	13	1,208,369	9.5	9.9	102.3%
1933	7.8	7.7	9.2	11	8.2	9.3	9.3	8.4	7	7.1	8.5	9	11	8.4	7.1	7	8.1	8.7	9.4	9.1	8.7	12	14	12	9.6	13	12	13	13	9.7	1,047,440	9.3	9.6	101.5%
1934	5.6	6.9	8.1	6	6.9	6.9	6.4	5.1	5.2	6.4	7.6	9.3	7.2	6.4	5.9	7	8.1	7.9	8.7	7.6	11	12	12	9.2	11	12	9.8	13	9.5	9.4	1,008,021	7.9	8.2	101.6%
1935	6.9	8.1	6.1	6.9	6.9	6.4	5.3	5.2	6.3	7.4	9.5	7	6.3	6.1	6.7	7.7	8.1	8.1	7.9	10	12	11	9.6	11	11	10	11	11	10	9.9	1,042,156	8.1	8.3	100.6%
1936	6.7	5	5.6	5.6	5.2	4.3	4.3	5.1	6	7.7	6	5.2	5	5.8	6.6	7.1	7.7	6.8	10	11	11	8.8	12	11	10	12	9.4	12	11	11	1,120,338	6.9	7.8	108.5%
1937	4.1	4.7	4.7	4.3	3.5	3.6	4.4	5.1	6.9	5.3	4.9	4.5	5.4	6.4	6.5	7	6.7	9.4	11	10	9	11	12	10	11	9.9	10	12	12	8.4	894,255	6.1	7.5	114.1%
1938	6.6	6.5	6	4.9	5	6	6.8	8	6.3	5.6	5.5	6	6.9	7.2	7.3	7	10	11	11	8.8	11	11	11	12	9.3	11	11	13	9.4	10	1,119,599	7.9	8.4	102.3%
1939	5.6	5.1	4.1	4.2	5.2	6.2	7.9	5.9	5.4	5.2	6.2	6.6	6.9	7.3	6.6	9.3	11	9.9	9	11	11	9.8	12	9.5	9.8	11	11	10	11	10	1,193,156	7.5	8.1	104.0%
1940	5.2	4.2	4.3	5.2	6.1	7.8	6	5.2	5.1	5.9	6.7	6.7	7.1	6.8	8.8	10	10	8.4	11	10	10	11	10	10	10	12	9	12	12	7.6	934,375	7.7	8.2	101.9%
1941	4.6	4.7	5.7	6.3	7.7	6	5.4	5	5.8	6.6	6.9	7	6.8	9.4	10	10	9.1	11	11	10	12	9.9	11	11	11	9.5	11	13	8.3	6.4	818,594	8	8.4	101.3%
1942	5.7	6.9	7.7	9.2	7.2	6.5	6.3	6.9	7.5	7.7	8.2	7.5	10	11	10	9.4	12	11	11	12	11	11	12	12	9.6	12	12	9.9	7.7	7	832,360	9.4	9.3	96.6%
1943	6.6	7.3	8.6	6.7	6	5.8	6.5	7	7.3	7.7	7.4	9.7	11	11	9.1	11	12	11	13	11	12	12	13	11	11	12	8.6	8.5	7.7	7	789,671	9.3	9.3	97.3%
1944	6.3	7.4	5.8	5.1	5	5.6	6.3	6.3	6.7	6.4	8.8	9.5	9.3	8.4	9.7	10	10	11	10	10	11	11	10	11	11	8.9	7.3	8.4	7.6	4.5	544,049	8.4	8.3	96.5%
1945	6.8	5.3	4.7	4.5	5.1	5.8	6	6.1	5.9	8.1	9.3	8.7	7.8	9.6	9.4	9.3	11	9.3	11	11	12	9.5	12	11	8.2	7.8	7.4	8.4	5	2.7	355,825	7.9	7.9	80.9%
1946	4.4	3.9	3.7	4.2	4.8	5.1	5.4	5	7.3	8.5	8.5	7.2	9.1	9.4	8.9	10	9.5	9.6	11	11	9.7	10	12	8.3	7	7.5	7.1	5.4	2.9	3.1	434,176	6.9	7.3	80.2%
1947	5	4.8	5.4	6.1	6.3	6.6	6.3	8.4	9.5	9.3	8.5	9.9	10	10	11	10	11	11	12	10	12	12	9.6	8.2	7.8	8.4	5.2	3.6	3.9	4	496,967	8.2	8.2	95.1%
1948	5.4	6.1	6.4	6.5	6.8	6.5	8.4	9	8.8	8.1	9.6	9.4	9.4	11	9.2	10	11	11	10	11	12	8.6	8.2	7.9	7.6	5.4	3	4.2	4.4	3.4	398,683	7.9	7.9	82.6%
1949	6.3	6.6	6.6	6.8	6.6	8.5	9.2	8.7	8	9.4	9.7	9.2	10	9.6	9.8	11	12	9.7	11	11	9.1	7.9	8.6	8.2	5.2	3.3	3.8	5	3.9	3.1	397,626	7.9	7.9	88.4%
1950	6.1	6.1	6.4	6	7.9	8.7	8.5	7.5	8.9	9.1	9.1	9.8	9.1	9.8	9.9	11	9.9	11	12	8.6	8.3	8	8.7	5.5	3.2	4.1	4.5	4.4	3.5	3.1	462,463	7.6	7.6	85.8%
1951	5.7	6	5.7	7.4	8.2	8	7.3	8.3	8.6	8.6	9.8	8.6	9.4	10	10	9.3	11	11	8.9	7.8	8.4	8.1	5.9	3.4	3.9	4.8	3.9	4	3.5	3.3	508,747	7.4	7.3	90.3%
1952	5.8	5.5	7.4	8.2	8.1	7.3	8.7	8.7	8.8	9.7	9.2	9.3	10	11	9.1	10	11	8.5	8.6	8.3	8.8	5.9	4	4.6	5.1	4.7	4	4.5	4.2	3.2	516,187	7.6	7.4	89.8%
1953	5.4	7	7.7	7.4	6.8	8	8.2	7.9	8.9	8.3	9.1	9.2	9.9	8.9	9.6	10	8.5	7.6	8.3	8.1	5.9	3.4	4.5	5	4.1	4	3.7	4.4	3.3	3.2	541,527	7.2	6.9	85.1%
1954	7.3	8	7.7	7	8.2	8.4	8.3	9	8.5	9.1	9.8	9.9	9.1	10	10	8.6	8.6	8.4	9	6.4	4.6	5.1	6.2	5.1	4.4	4.7	4.6	4.4	4.3	4.3	733,775	7.5	7.3	94.1%
1955	6.2	6	5.3	6.5	6.7	6.6	7.6	6.7	7.4	8	8.7	7.5	8.7	9.2	7.2	7.2	7.7	7.4	5.8	3.8	4.6	5.2	4.8	4.2	3.9	4.4	3.5	4.3	4.3	3.5	634,537	6.4	6.1	90.8%
1956	5.5	4.8	6	6.2	6.1	7	6.4	6.8	7.4	8	7.3	8.1	8.6	7.1	6.6	7.1	7.5	5.3	3.8	4.3	5.3	4.4	4.4	4.1	4.1	3.7	3.8	4.7	3.9	4	754,294	6	5.7	92.2%
1957	5	6.1	6.3	6.1	7	6.5	7	7.3	7.9	7.2	8.3	8.3	6.9	6.6	6.6	7	5.3	3.2	4.3	4.9	4.5	4	4.3	4.3	3.5	4	4.1	4.3	4.5	4.2	760,649	6	5.7	87.3%
1958	7	7.2	7.1	7.8	7.3	7.8	8.4	8.5	7.9	8.8	9.4	7.4	7.4	7.7	7.6	5.9	4.3	4.8	6	5	4.9	4.7	5.4	4.3	4.5	5.3	4.5	5.9	5.5	4.3	787,198	6.6	6.4	94.8%
1959	5.8	5.6	6.4	5.8	6.4	6.9	7.4	6.4	7.4	7.9	6.5	6	6.4	6.7	4.7	3.2	4.1	4.8	4.5	4	4.3	4.3	4	4.1	4.3	4.3	4.6	5.4	4.2	3.9	741,789	5.6	5.3	89.3%
1960	5.5	6.2	5.7	6.1	6.6	7	6.3	7.1	7.6	6.3	6.3	6.3	6.6	5.1	3.4	4.2	5.1	4.4	4.3	4.2	4.7	3.9	4.6	4.8	4.2	5.2	5	4.9	4.6	4.5	884,241	5.6	5.4	92.8%
1961	6.3	5.8	6.2	6.6	7.1	6.5	7.2	7.4	6.2	6.1	6.5	6.4	5	3.6	4	4.9	4.6	4.1	4.5	4.6	4.2	4.4	5.3	4.6	5.1	5.6	4.5	5.4	5.2	3.6	742,527	5.6	5.4	93.6%
1962	5.2	5.6	6	6.3	5.7	6.7	7.1	5.7	5.6	6	6.3	4.6	3.3	4	4.5	4.2	4.1	4.1	4.7	3.9	4.5	4.8	4.8	5.2	5.2	4.8	4.7	5.8	4	4.3	896,689	5.2	5.1	93.5%
1963	6.1	6.5	6.9	6.2	7	7.4	6.1	5.7	6.1	6.3	4.9	3.3	4	4.9	4.2	4.1	4.4	4.6	4.3	4.6	5.4	4.8	6	5.9	4.9	5.4	5.5	4.8	5.2	4.7	1,008,434	5.5	5.3	93.5%
1964	6	6.5	5.8	6.6	6.9	5.7	5.5	5.6	5.9	4.5	3.1	3.7	4.6	4.2	3.8	4.1	4.7	3.9	4.7	5	5	5.5	6.2	5.1	5.1	5.9	4.2	5.8	5.2	4.8	1,033,516	5.2	5.1	90.3%
1965	6	5.3	6.2	6.5	5.4	5.3	5.6	5.6	4.4	3.2	3.8	4.4	4	3.9	3.9	4.4	4	4.3	5.2	4.7	5.8	5.8	5.5	5.4	5.6	4.6	5.2	5.9	5.4	4.3	947,210	5	5.0	94.2%
1966	5.1	5.8	6.1	5	4.9	5.2	5.4	3.9	2.8	3.4	4.2	3.7	3.6	3.8	4	3.7	4.3	4.7	4.7	5.3	5.9	4.9	5.6	5.8	4.2	5.4	5.1	5.9	4.7	5.1	1,120,445	4.7	4.7	81.1%
1967	6.4	6.7	5.6	5.5	5.8	5.9	4.7	3.4	3.9	4.6	4.3	3.9	4.1	4.5	3.9	4.6	5.4	4.9	6.2	6.3	5.8	5.9	6.9	5.1	5.8	6.3	6	6	6.5	6	1,333,524	5.2	5.4	100.1%
1968	5.9	4.8	4.6	4.8	5.1	3.8	2.6	3.1	3.9	3.6	3.5	3.5	4	3.6	3.9	4.7	4.6	5.3	6	5	5.6	5.9	4.9	5.7	5.4	5.9	4.9	6.7	6.2	6.6	1,428,327	4.5	4.8	77.7%
1969	4.6	4.5	4.7	4.8	3.7	2.7	3.2	3.7	3.4	3.3	3.6	3.8	3.5	4	4.4	4.4	5.4	5.6	5.3	5.4	6.2	4.7	6.1	5.8	5.7	5.3	6	7.1	7.5	7.1	1,486,516	4.4	4.9	81.1%
1970	5.5	5.7	5.9	4.5	3.3	3.9	4.6	4.1	4	4.2	4.8	4.1	4.8	5.6	5.2	6.5	7.2	6.2	7.1	7.5	6.3	7.3	8	7.8	6.6	8.4	8.2	11	10	9.9	2,018,561	5.3	6.3	111.5%
1971	5.9	6.1	4.8	3.7	4.1	4.8	4.4	4	4.2	4.6	4.2	4.6	5.5	5.3	6.1	6.9	6.4	6.6	7.8	5.9	7.5	7.4	8.1	6.8	7.8	8.7	9.6	11	11	7.9	1,598,625	5.5	6.4	111.6%
1972	5.8	4.5	3.3	3.8	4.5	4.1	3.9	4	4.5	4.1	4.8	5.3	5.3	6.4	6.7	6.3	7	7.4	6.3	7.4	8	7.9	7.5	8.6	8.5	11	11	13	9.3	7.4	1,452,071	5.3	6.6	115.1%
1973	4.5	3.3	3.8	4.3	4	3.8	3.9	4.2	3.8	4.4	5.2	5	6	6.6	5.8	6.5	7.5	5.8	7.6	7.4	8.1	6.9	9	8.8	9.9	11	11	9.8	7.8	4.9	963,185	5.2	6.3	113.0%
1974	4.2	4.8	5.5	5	4.8	5	5.3	4.7	5.5	6.2	6.3	7.2	8	7.4	7.5	8.5	7.4	8.6	9.3	9.2	8.6	9.9	11	12	12	13	10	11	6.7	7.4	1,346,757	6.8	7.7	109.1%
1975	6.5	7.5	6.8	6.3	6.3	6.6	6.1	6.9	7.8	7.9	9.5	10	9.4	9.8	10	9.4	11	11	12	10	13	12	15	14	14	13	11	9.3	10	9.2	1,528,203	8.7	9.7	108.4%
1976	6.5	5.9	5.5	5.4	5.8	5.4	6.2	6.8	6.9	8.2	9.1	8.2	8.6	9.5	8.1	9.8	10	10	9.9	11	12	13	14	14	11	11	7.1	10	9.1	7.6	1,238,120	7.9	8.9	108.9%
1977	5.1	4.8	4.8	5.1	4.7	5.6	6.3	6.1	7.3	8.1	7.6	7.7	8.6	7.7	8.7	9.3	10	8.6	11	11	13	13	14	11	9.5	7.4	8.6	9.9	8.2	7.7	1,212,799	7.3	8.3	109.9%
1978	5.3	5.2	5.5	5.1	6	6.7	6.7	7.7	8.6	8.1	8.6	9.1	8.2	9.7	9.6	10	9.7	11	12	13	14	14	13	11	8.8	11	9.8	10	9.7	7.7	1,185,071	8	9.2	111.2%
1979	5.5	5.8	5.3	6.2	6.9	7	8.2	8.8	8.3	8.7	9.7	8.4	10	10	10	9.7	12	12	14	14	15	13	13	9.9	10	11	9.4	11	8.8	4.4	627,220	8.5	9.5	108.2%
1980	5.8	5.3	6.1	6.7	6.8	8	8.8	8	8.5	9.3	8.7	9.7	10	11	9.3	11	12	13	14	13	13	11	9.8	11	10	9.9	9.6	9.7	4.9	5.2	658,467	8.6	9.3	104.9%
1981	5.2	6.1	6.7	6.7	7.9	8.7	8.2	8.2	9.1	8.4	9.9	9.9	11	9.7	11	12	14	14	14	13	13	10	12	11	9.8	11	8.8	5.6	6	5.8	675,827	8.9	9.5	103.7%
																																Avg	7.28	97.9%

FIGURE 57

MUFP backtesting results.

MUFP results are generally the best seen up until this point in the survey (Sensible Withdraws had higher numbers but came close to running out of money). This establishes a strong baseline for comparison. The withdrawal rates are up when the market is strong and appropriately down when the market is weak. The relatively small remaining amounts at the end of retirement show that a large portion of the portfolio is made available for income without coming too close to running out of money. In fact, MUFP will never run out of money, although rates can be very low.

The only discernible weakness in these results is MUFP's annual withdrawals occasionally, although not frequently, dropping to unnecessarily low values. Five retirement periods had a withdrawal below 3%; more often, withdrawals dropped below 3.5%, but usually not in consecutive years.

Strategy 8: Extended Mortality Updating Failure Percentage (EM and ECM)

EM and ECM are newly defined, extended versions of the previous Mortality Updating Failure Percentage Strategy. These strategies work around the obstacles individual retirees encounter when applying MUFP. EM is the general extended version and ECM is the more conservative extended version[*]. EM and ECM share the same core definition, but rely on different constant values for calculations.

The core idea from MUFP remains the same, but there are several enhancements.

- The mortality table and failure-percentage table have been combined into one table for all retirees and portfolios. This addresses most of the pragmatic problems for individual retirees deploying MUFP. This table, shown in Figure 58, defines the annual withdrawal percentage based on the number of years left in the planned retirement. This one table works independently of gender, and is independent from whether a couple or an individual is involved. It also works for long retirements. The underlying failure-percentage is based on MSWR-90% for a well-diversified global portfolio (i.e., the Baseline Market and Portfolio introduced in Chapter 6), but it applies to all retirement portfolios, independent of the exact allocation.

- The resulting withdrawal percentages (for all versions of MUFP) are sometimes too aggressive to handle the complete range of market conditions, so a scaling function is added to dampen the withdrawal rate when it exceeds the initial withdrawal rate (note, with pure MUFP, no initial withdrawal rate is specified). This scaling provides an adaptable soft ceiling for the withdrawal rates. The closer the default percentage is above the initial withdrawal rate, the more downward pressure is applied, but as the default percentage rises significantly above the initial rate, then less downward pressure is applied (i.e., excess portfolio value makes it safer to withdraw more).

- An income floor, by default a very low one, is added to partially smooth out the more radical drops in annual income. The more withdrawal rates are scaled back in the previous step, the safer it is to raise the income floor. This is why the default income floor for EM is 2.25%, but for the more conservative ECM it's a higher 2.5%. These low floor defaults are intended to handle extreme market conditions—the SBBI dataset can handle up to a 4% floor without failure. (It makes sense for retirees to set the income floor to their essential-income rate, but more on this later.)

Estimated Years Left in Retirement	50+	49	48	47	46	45	44	43	42	41	40	39	38	37	36	35	34	33	32	31	30	29	28	27	26
Withdrawal Rate Percentage	5.1%	5.1%	5.1%	5.2%	5.2%	5.2%	5.2%	5.2%	5.3%	5.3%	5.4%	5.4%	5.4%	5.5%	5.5%	5.6%	5.6%	5.7%	5.8%	5.8%	5.9%	6.0%	6.1%	6.3%	6.4%

Estimated Years Left in Retirement	25	24	23	22	21	20	19	18	17	16	15	14	13	12	11	10	9	8	7	6	5	4	3	2	1
Withdrawal Rate Percentage	6.6%	6.9%	6.9%	7.1%	7.5%	7.9%	7.9%	8.3%	8.7%	8.7%	9.2%	9.7%	9.7%	10.3%	10.3%	11.3%	11.3%	13.0%	13.0%	13.0%	14.3%	14.3%	17.7%	17.7%	17.7%

FIGURE 58

Extended MUFP Table.

---

[*] EMUFP and ECMUFP would be the full acronyms, but they are almost unpronounceable.

The Steps (With Spreadsheet Support)

1. Establish the key values (i.e., constants) to be used later.
   a. For EM use the following
      i. Set the *scale rate* to 95%.
      ii. Set the *floor rate* to 2.25%.
   b. For ECM use the following
      i. Set the *scale rate* to 60%.
      ii. Set the *floor rate* to 2.5%.
   c. Set the *cap rate* (the default is 150% of initial rate, but no cap is used in the initial survey).
   (The option and tradeoffs of raising the above *floor rate* are also discussed in Chapter 10.)

2. Look up the *withdrawal rate percentage* based on the estimated years left in retirement in the Extended MUFP Table (see Figure 58).

3. Calculate the initial current withdrawal amount
   a. *Current withdrawal amount = withdrawal rate percentage * portfolio value*

4. Calculate the *scale boundary*
   a. *scale boundary = 75% * **inflation-adjusted withdrawal amount***

5. If the *current withdrawal amount* is greater than the *scale boundary* then scale it down
   a. *scale diff = current withdrawal amount – scale boundary*
   b. *scale ratio = scale diff / scale boundary*
   c. *If scale ratio is greater than 1 then set it to 1.*
   d. *current withdrawal amount = scale boundary + (scale diff * scale ratio * scale rate)*

6. if a cap is defined and the current withdrawal amount is too big, then cap it
   a. *Set the cap amount = (cap rate / initial withdrawal rate) * **inflation-adjusted withdrawal amount***
   b. If the *current withdrawal amount* > cap amount, then set it to the *cap amount.*

7. If the *current withdrawal amount* is too small, then set it to the floor value
   a. *floor value = (floor rate / initial withdrawal rate) * **inflation-adjusted withdrawal amount***
   b. If *current withdrawal amount* < *floor value*, then set it to the *floor value.*

8. Withdraw for the year the *current withdrawal amount.*

Backtesting Results

Figure 59 shows EM withdrawals for every retirement period, backtesting with the default portfolio using the SBBI dataset for a 30-year retirement assuming a 65 year old retiree (like for MUFP).

Year	Y1	Y2	Y3	Y4	Y5	Y6	Y7	Y8	Y9	Y10	Y11	Y12	Y13	Y14	Y15	Y16	Y17	Y18	Y19	Y20	Y21	Y22	Y23	Y24	Y25	Y26	Y27	Y28	Y29	Y30	Remaining	MSWR	Avg	HREFF-3
1928	6	5	4.4	3.9	4.3	5.2	5.2	6.7	8.3	5.7	7.4	6.9	6.1	4.6	4.6	6.4	8.1	9.7	7.7	5.8	5.7	6.8	8.6	8.5	8.3	7.9	11	13	12	8	626,229	6.7	7.0	101.0%
1929	4.1	3.8	3.6	3.8	4	4.1	4.9	6.2	4.3	5.1	5.3	4.6	4	4	4.7	6.3	9.3	6.2	5.6	4.8	6.7	7.7	8.5	8.4	6.9	11	11	12	8.5	11	849,886	5.6	6.3	105.9%
1930	4.1	3.8	3.8	4.3	4.4	5.8	7.8	4.7	6	6.1	5.5	4.2	4.4	6	7.5	9.8	7.6	5.8	5.9	7.1	8.7	8.6	9.4	8	11	13	11	11	13	12	958,994	6.4	7.3	107.4%
1931	3.8	4	5.1	5	7.4	8.9	6.1	7.4	7.5	6.7	5	4.9	7.1	8.2	9.5	7.5	6.5	5.6	7.5	8.2	8.8	8.7	8.4	11	12	12	9.3	14	13	10	921,721	7.6	8.0	100.6%
1932	5	8	7.9	9.4	11	8.6	9.7	9.4	8.9	7.5	7.6	8.5	9.6	11	8.5	7.7	7.6	8.1	9.5	9.3	9.9	8.6	13	14	12	11	13	15	12	13	1,277,870	9.5	9.8	101.0%
1933	7.6	7.5	8.9	10	8.1	9.1	9.1	8.3	6.6	6.8	8.4	8.9	11	8.4	7	6.8	8.1	8.6	9.3	9.1	8.7	12	14	12	9.7	13	12	13	13	10	1,118,578	9.3	9.5	100.4%
1934	4.6	6.3	8	5.2	6.6	6.7	5.9	4.4	4.6	6.1	7.8	9.4	7.4	6.1	5.4	7.3	8.3	8.1	8.8	7.8	11	12	12	9.4	11	12	10	13	9.9	9.8	1,095,790	7.9	8.2	99.5%
1935	6.3	7.9	5.2	6.4	6.5	5.8	4.5	4.5	5.9	7.6	9.5	6.9	5.8	5.6	6.7	7.9	8.3	8.2	8.1	11	12	11	9.9	12	11	11	12	11	11	10	1,136,330	8.1	8.3	98.5%
1936	5.9	4.2	4.7	4.7	4.4	3.9	3.9	4.5	5.5	7.9	5.5	4.6	4.5	5.5	6.6	7.4	8.1	7.1	11	11	11	9.2	12	12	10	12	9.7	12	11	11	1,222,790	6.9	7.7	104.9%
1937	3.8	4	4	3.8	3.6	3.7	3.9	4.3	6.7	4.5	4.2	4	4.8	6	6	7	6.6	9.2	11	9.9	8.8	10	11	9.7	11	9.5	9.8	12	12	8.4	923,343	6.1	7.1	106.9%
1938	5.8	5.7	5.1	4.1	4.2	5.4	6.6	8	5.7	5	4.9	5.6	7.1	7.5	7.5	7.3	10	11	9.1	12	11	11	12	9.6	11	11	13	9.8	11		1,221,826	7.9	8.3	99.8%
1939	4.6	4.3	3.8	3.8	4.4	5.6	8	5.2	4.6	4.6	5.8	6.5	7.1	7.6	6.6	9.6	11	10	9.3	11	11	10	12	9.8	10	11	11	11	12	11	1,308,260	7.5	8.1	101.3%
1940	4.3	3.8	3.8	4.4	5.4	7.8	5.3	4.5	4.4	5.4	6.7	6.5	7.4	6.8	9	10	10	8.6	11	11	10	11	11	11	12	9.3	13	12	7.9		1,004,997	7.7	8.1	99.3%
1941	3.9	4	4.7	5.6	7.7	5.3	4.6	4.4	5.2	6.3	7	6.6	9.5	10	10	9.2	11	11	11	12	10	11	11	9.7	11	13	8.8	6.5			918,457	8	8.3	98.3%
1942	4.7	6.4	7.6	9.1	7	5.8	5.6	6.6	7.6	7.7	8.2	7.6	10	11	10	9.4	12	11	11	12	11	11	12	9.8	12	12	10	8	7.4		907,510	9.4	9.2	95.4%
1943	5.9	7.1	8.4	6	5.2	5	6.1	6.9	7.4	7.7	7.5	9.7	11	11	9.1	11	12	11	13	11	12	12	13	11	11	13	8.9	8.9	8.1	7.4	867,056	9.3	9.2	96.2%
1944	5.3	7.3	4.8	4.3	4.2	4.9	5.7	5.8	6.5	6.1	9	9.6	9.5	8.9	10	11	10	11	12	12	11	11	12	9.2	7.7	8.8	8.1	4.1			620,499	8.4	8.3	94.3%
1945	6.1	4.4	4	3.9	4.4	5	5.4	5.6	5.4	8.4	9.5	8.9	8.1	9.7	9.5	9.5	11	9.5	11	11	12	9.7	12	12	8.5	8.2	7.7	8.9	4.5	3.1	405,745	7.9	7.9	88.6%
1946	3.8	3.8	3.8	3.8	4.1	4.3	4.6	4.3	7.4	8.5	8.5	7.3	9.1	9.5	8.9	10	9.6	9.7	11	11	9.9	11	12	8.5	7.2	7.9	7.4	4.8	3.2	3.5	488,999	6.9	7.3	93.9%
1947	4.2	4.1	4.5	5.3	5.7	6.2	5.8	8.4	9.5	9.4	8.6	9.9	10	10	11	10	11	12	10	12	9.8	8.5	8.2	8.7	4.6	3.8	3.8	4			595,714	8.2	8.1	93.1%
1948	4.5	5.2	5.7	5.8	6.4	6.1	8.5	9	8.8	8.1	9.6	9.4	9.4	11	9.3	10	11	11	10	11	12	8.7	8.5	8.2	7.9	4.8	3.4	4	4.1	3.8	483,141	7.9	7.8	93.4%
1949	5.3	5.9	6	6.4	6.1	8.4	9.2	8.6	8	9.4	9.6	9.2	10	9.7	9.8	11	12	9.8	12	11	9.2	8.1	8.8	8.5	4.6	3.7	3.8	4.6	3.9	3.8	477,399	7.9	7.9	94.3%
1950	5.1	5.3	5.6	5.3	7.9	8.7	8.4	7.5	8.8	9	9.1	9.8	9.2	9.9	10	11	10	11	12	8.7	8.5	8.3	8.9	4.9	3.5	3.9	4.1	4.2	3.8	3.8	574,913	7.6	7.5	92.9%
1951	4.8	5.1	4.8	7.4	8.2	8	7.3	8.3	8.5	8.5	9.7	8.7	9.4	10	10	9.3	11	11	8.9	8	8.6	8.3	5.3	3.7	3.8	4.4	3.9	4	3.8	3.8	649,650	7.4	7.2	91.8%
1952	4.9	4.6	7.4	8.1	8	7.2	8.6	8.6	8.7	9.6	9.2	9.3	10	11	9.2	10	11	8.6	8.7	8.5	8.9	5.4	3.9	4.2	4.9	4.6	4.1	4.6	4.5	3.8	720,385	7.6	7.3	91.8%
1953	4.4	6.6	7.4	7.3	6.3	8	8.1	7.8	8.8	8.3	9	9.1	9.8	8.9	9.6	10	8.5	7.7	8.4	8.2	5.3	3.8	4.2	4.7	4	4	3.9	4.6	3.9	3.9	760,374	7.2	6.8	90.1%
1954	7	7.8	7.5	6.5	8.1	8.2	8.2	8.8	8.4	9	9.6	9.8	9	10	10	8.6	8.7	8.5	9	4.1	4.5	6.2	4.7	4.2	4.6	4.6	4.7	4.8			1,041,739	7.5	7.2	92.5%
1955	5.3	5.1	4.4	5.9	6.3	6.2	7.7	6.5	7.5	8.1	8.8	7.7	8.8	9.2	7.4	7.4	7.9	7.6	5.3	3.8	4.2	4.8	4.5	4.1	4	4.5	3.9	4.7	4.8	4.1	932,708	6.4	6.0	90.5%
1956	4.5	4.1	5.2	5.4	5.4	7	6	6.7	7.6	8.2	7.5	8.2	8.7	7.3	6.5	7.3	7.7	4.7	3.8	5	4.2	4.2	4.1	4.2	4	4.1	5.6	4.5	4.9		1,138,812	6	5.7	91.5%
1957	4.1	5.2	5.5	5.4	6.8	6	7	7.4	8	7.3	8.4	8.4	6.7	6.4	6.5	7.3	4.7	3.7	4	4.6	4.3	4	4.3	4.3	4.6	5.1	5.6	5.3			1,175,737	6	5.6	91.0%
1958	6.4	6.8	6.7	7.7	7.2	7.7	8.3	8.4	7.8	8.7	9.3	7.4	7.4	7.7	7.6	5.2	3.9	4.2	5.6	4.6	4.5	4.5	5.5	4.3	4.6	6.1	4.9	7.7	7.2	4.8	1,113,037	6.6	6.4	94.7%
1959	4.8	4.7	5.7	5	5.9	6.7	7.5	6	7.6	8	6.2	5.5	6.2	6.8	4.3	3.7	4	4.4	4.3	4	4.2	4.4	4.2	4.4	4.8	4.9	5.6	7.6	5.2	4.9	1,163,653	5.6	5.4	93.6%
1960	4.6	5.4	4.8	5.3	6.2	6.9	5.8	7.2	7.7	5.9	5.9	6.1	6.6	4.6	3.8	4	4.1	4.2	4.2	4.8	4.1	4.9	5.4	4.7	6.6	6.4	6.4	5.9	5.9		1,343,735	5.6	5.4	95.2%
1961	5.4	4.9	5.4	6.1	6.9	5.9	7.3	7.5	5.6	5.6	6.3	6.2	4.5	3.8	3.9	4.5	4.3	4	4.3	4.6	4.3	4.6	6.2	5.1	6.1	7.5	5.3	7.4	7.1	4.2	1,102,908	5.6	5.5	95.8%
1962	4.2	4.6	5.1	5.7	4.9	6.4	7.2	5	5	5.6	6.1	4.2	3.8	3.9	4.2	4	4	4	4.6	4	4.7	5.3	5.4	6.5	6.5	5.8	5.7	8	4.7	5.6	1,386,127	5.2	5.2	96.8%
1963	5.1	5.7	6.4	5.4	6.8	7.4	5.3	5.5	5.6	6.4	4.4	3.7	3.9	4.4	4	4	4.2	4.5	4.3	4.7	6.2	7.2	7.6	5.6	7	7.2	5.8	6.9	5.9		1,466,663	5.5	5.5	98.0%
1964	5.1	5.7	4.9	6	6.7	4.9	4.8	5	5.5	4.1	3.6	3.8	4.2	4	3.9	4	4.5	4.7	5.4	5.4	6.7	7.9	6	6.1	7.8	4.8	7.9	7.2	6.2		1,508,645	5.2	5.4	99.9%
1965	5	4.4	5.4	5.9	4.6	4.6	5	5	4	3.7	3.8	4.1	3.9	3.9	3.9	4.2	4	4.2	5.4	4.8	6.9	7.1	6.4	6.4	7	5.1	6.4	7.9	7.3	5	1,364,618	5	5.2	100.3%
1966	4.2	4.8	5.3	4.2	4.2	4.5	4.7	3.8	3.2	3.8	3.9	3.8	3.8	3.8	3.9	3.8	4.1	4.5	4.7	5.7	7	5.2	6.7	7.2	4.5	6.8	6.3	7.9	5.6	6.8	1,613,346	4.7	5.0	97.7%
1967	5.6	6.1	4.7	4.6	5	5.3	4.2	3.7	3.8	4.1	4	3.8	3.9	4.1	3.8	4.2	5.3	4.8	7.1	7.3	6.4	6.7	8.2	5.3	6.9	7.7	7.4	7.5	8.1	7.6	1,740,085	5.2	5.6	102.9%
1968	4.9	4.1	4	4.1	4.3	3.8	2.9	3.4	3.8	3.8	3.7	3.8	3.9	4.1	3.8	4.2	4.3	5	6.3	5	6.1	6.8	5.1	6.6	6.3	7.4	5.4	8.6	8.1	8.6	1,931,318	4.5	5.1	89.4%
1969	3.9	3.9	4	4.1	3.8	2.9	3.4	3.8	3.6	3.5	3.7	3.8	3.6	3.8	4	4	4.9	5.2	4.9	5.2	6.9	4.5	6.9	6.6	6.3	5.9	7.4	8.8	9.3	8.9	1,932,692	4.4	5.1	89.5%
1970	4.5	4.8	5	4	3.5	3.8	4	3.8	3.8	3.9	4.3	3.9	4.4	5.5	5.1	7.3	8.2	6.9	7.9	8.4	7.2	8.3	9.1	8.8	7.5	9.6	9.4	13	12	12	2,450,692	5.3	6.6	115.7%
1971	4.9	5.2	4.1	3.8	3.8	4.1	3.9	3.8	3.9	4.1	3.9	4.2	5.1	5.1	6.5	7.7	7.3	7.4	8.6	6.5	8.6	8.5	9.3	7.9	9.1	10	11	13	13	9.2	1,921,383	5.5	6.8	114.4%
1972	4.8	3.9	3.4	3.8	3.8	3.8	3.8	4	3.8	4.2	4.8	4.8	6.6	7.2	6.5	7.5	8	6.9	8.2	8.8	8.7	8.3	9.5	9.4	12	11	14	10	8.1		1,657,264	5.3	6.8	116.8%
1973	3.9	3.4	3.8	3.8	3.8	3.8	3.9	4.5	4.3	5.7	6.8	5.5	6.7	8	6	8.3	8.2	8.9	7.9	9.9	9.8	11	12	12	11	11	9				1,193,988	5.2	6.6	115.3%
1974	3.8	4	4.6	4.3	4.2	4.3	4.6	4.1	5	6.1	6.4	7.7	8.5	8	8.1	9.1	8.1	9.2	10	9.9	9.3	11	11	12	12	13	11	11	6.7	7.9	1,478,351	6.8	7.8	108.3%
1975	5.7	7.3	6.2	5.5	5.5	6.1	5.5	6.9	7.8	7.9	9.5	10	9.4	9.9	10	9.5	11	11	12	10	13	12	15	14	14	13	11	10	11	9.8	1,690,324	8.7	9.7	107.6%
1976	5.6	5	4.6	4.6	5	4.6	5.9	6.8	7.1	8.6	9.5	8.6	9	9.8	9.1	11	10	12	13	13	15	14	11	11	12	11	13	11	11	8.8	1,493,362	7.9	9.2	111.3%
1977	4.2	4.1	4.1	4.3	4.1	4.9	5.9	5.7	7.7	8.5	8.1	8.1	9	8.1	9.1	9.7	11	9.1	12	11	13	14	12	10	8.2	9.3	11	9.1	8.6		1,394,856	7.3	8.5	111.0%
1978	4.4	4.4	4.7	4.3	5.3	6.5	6.7	8	8.8	8.4	8.8	9.3	8.5	10	9.9	11	10	11	12	13	14	13	13	12	9.1	11	10	11	10	8	1,284,666	8	9.2	110.0%
1979	4.6	4.9	4.5	5.5	6.7	7	8.4	8.9	8.5	8.9	9.9	8.6	10	11	11	9.9	12	12	14	14	13	13	10	11	11	9.7	12	9.2	4		699,089	8.5	9.5	106.9%
1980	4.8	4.4	5.4	6.3	6.6	8.1	8.9	8.1	8.6	9.4	8.8	9.8	10	11	9.5	12	12	13	14	14	13	12	10	11	11	10	10	10	4.4	5	787,795	8.6	9.4	104.7%
1981	4.3	5.2	6.1	6.2	8	8.8	8.2	8.3	9.2	8.5	10	10	11	9.8	11	12	14	15	13	13	11	12	10	11	9.2	5.1	6	6			798,772	8.9	9.6	103.3%
																																Avg	7.32	99.7%

FIGURE 59

EM backtesting results.

Figure 60 shows ECM withdrawals for every retirement period, backtesting with the default portfolio using the SBBI dataset for a 30-year retirement assuming a 65 year old retiree.

Year	Y1	Y2	Y3	Y4	Y5	Y6	Y7	Y8	Y9	Y10	Y11	Y12	Y13	Y14	Y15	Y16	Y17	Y18	Y19	Y20	Y21	Y22	Y23	Y24	Y25	Y26	Y27	Y28	Y29	Y30	Remaining	MSWR	Avg	HREFF-3
1928	5.2	4.6	4.2	3.9	4.1	4.8	4.8	5.9	6.8	5.4	6.4	6.2	6	4.8	4.7	6.1	7	8	6.9	6.1	6.1	6.5	7.7	7.6	7.7	7.6	9.9	13	12	9.3	1,043,400	6.7	6.6	95.1%
1929	4	3.8	3.6	3.8	3.9	4	4.5	5.4	4.2	4.7	4.9	4.4	4	4	4.5	5.7	7.5	5.8	5.4	4.9	6.2	6.8	7.5	7.6	6.8	9.9	11	12	9.4	11	1,333,871	5.6	6.0	100.7%
1930	3.9	3.8	3.8	4.1	4.2	5.1	6.4	4.5	5.4	5.5	5.2	4.2	4.3	5.5	6.3	7.9	6.6	5.8	6	6.4	7.6	7.6	8.4	7.6	9.9	12	11	11	13	12	1,500,751	6.4	6.8	100.1%
1931	3.8	3.9	4.6	4.6	6.1	7.1	5.5	6.3	6.4	6.1	5	4.9	6.3	7	7.9	6.7	6.3	5.9	6.8	7.2	7.7	7.7	7.8	9.8	10	11	9.1	12	12	11	1,374,333	7.6	7.2	91.1%
1932	4.5	6.5	6.5	7.5	8.5	7.2	7.9	7.8	7.6	6.7	6.8	7.5	8.2	9.5	7.6	7.2	7.2	7.6	8.6	8.4	9	8.3	11	12	11	11	12	14	13	13	1,953,600	9.5	8.8	89.9%
1933	6.2	6.2	7.1	8	6.8	7.5	7.6	7.1	6.3	6.4	7.3	7.7	8.9	7.4	6.6	6.7	7.5	7.8	8.3	8.3	8.2	10	12	11	9.5	12	12	13	13	11	1,846,162	9.3	8.6	90.0%
1934	4.3	5.4	6.5	4.8	5.8	5.9	5.4	4.3	4.5	5.6	6.6	7.6	6.4	5.9	5.4	6.4	7.1	7.1	7.7	7.1	9.4	9.9	10	8.8	9.9	11	9.8	13	11	11	1,737,597	7.9	7.4	90.3%
1935	5.4	6.4	4.8	5.6	5.8	5.4	4.4	4.4	5.4	6.4	7.7	6.2	5.7	5.6	6.2	6.8	7.2	7.2	7.3	8.8	10	9.4	9.1	10	9.9	10	11	11	11	11	1,763,621	8.1	7.5	89.6%
1936	5.1	4	4.4	4.4	4.2	3.9	3.9	4.3	5	6.5	5.1	4.4	4.4	5.2	6	6.3	6.8	6.3	8.6	9.2	9.4	8.1	10	10	9.4	11	9.6	11	11	11	1,807,069	6.9	7.0	95.3%
1937	3.8	3.9	3.9	3.8	3.6	3.7	3.9	4.1	5.6	4.3	4.1	4	4.5	5.3	5.4	6.1	6	7.5	8.7	8.2	7.7	8.8	9.5	8.8	9.5	9.1	9.3	11	11	9.3	1,470,608	6.1	6.5	98.9%
1938	5	5	4.7	4	4.1	4.9	5.7	6.6	5.3	4.7	4.8	5.3	6.2	6.4	6.5	6.4	8.4	8.9	9.2	8.1	9.8	9.6	10	11	9.4	11	11	13	11	11	1,917,971	7.9	7.5	90.7%
1939	4.3	4.1	3.8	3.8	4.2	4.9	6.5	4.8	4.4	4.4	5.3	5.8	6.1	6.5	6.1	7.8	8.8	8.4	8.1	9	9.6	9	11	9.4	9.6	11	11	11	12	11	1,985,340	7.5	7.3	92.4%
1940	4.1	3.8	3.8	4.1	4.8	6.4	4.8	4.3	4.3	5	5.9	5.9	6.3	6.1	7.4	8.3	8.4	7.6	9.1	9	9.2	9.8	9.6	9.8	9.8	11	9.4	12	12	8.8	1,588,101	7.7	7.3	90.3%
1941	3.9	3.9	4.4	5	6.3	4.8	4.4	4.2	4.8	5.6	6.1	6.1	6	7.7	8.2	8.3	7.9	8.9	9.5	9.2	10	9.4	10	11	10	9.9	11	13	9.7	8.6	1,609,680	8	7.6	90.3%
1942	4.4	5.4	6.2	7.2	6.1	5.4	5.2	6	6.4	6.6	7	6.6	8.2	9	8.6	8.3	9.7	9.5	10	10	10	10	12	11	9.8	12	11	11	9.6	9.2	1,633,552	9.4	8.4	86.8%
1943	5.1	5.9	6.8	5.4	4.8	4.8	5.5	6.1	6.3	6.6	6.5	7.9	8.8	8.8	7.9	9.4	9.9	9.7	11	10	11	11	12	11	11	12	9.7	11	10	9.6	1,628,000	9.3	8.5	88.4%
1944	4.8	6	4.5	4.2	4.1	4.6	5.1	5.2	5.8	5.6	7.3	7.8	7.8	7.3	8.2	8.6	8.9	9.3	9.3	9.4	10	10	9.9	11	10	9.3	8.5	9.8	9.3	6.7	1,104,592	8.4	7.6	87.6%
1945	5.2	4.2	3.9	3.9	4.2	4.6	4.9	5.1	5	6.8	7.6	7.3	6.9	8	8	8.3	9.2	8.4	9.3	9.5	10	9.1	11	11	8.6	8.8	8.6	9.8	7.2	4.4	798,979	7.9	7.3	88.3%
1946	3.8	3.8	3.8	3.8	3.9	4.1	4.3	4.1	6.1	6.9	6.9	6.2	7.5	7.8	7.6	8.5	8.3	8.5	9.4	9.5	9.1	9.5	11	8.5	7.9	8.5	8.3	7.2	4.3	4.9	935,415	6.9	6.8	93.2%
1947	4	4	4.3	4.7	5.1	5.4	5.2	6.8	7.6	7.6	7.2	8.1	8.4	8.6	9.1	8.9	9.6	9.8	11	9.6	11	11	9.7	9.1	9	9.6	7.3	6.1	6.4	6.8	1,150,836	8.2	7.7	90.4%
1948	4.2	4.7	5	5.2	5.6	5.4	6.9	7.3	7.2	6.9	7.9	7.8	8	8.8	8.2	8.9	9.6	9.7	9.5	9.9	11	8.7	9	8.9	8.6	7.2	4.6	6.5	7	5.9	926,633	7.9	7.5	92.1%
1949	4.8	5.1	5.2	5.5	5.4	6.9	7.4	7.1	6.8	7.7	8	7.9	8.7	8.4	8.6	9.3	10	9	10	10	9	8.5	9.3	9.1	6.9	5.2	5.9	7.5	6.4	5.4	937,531	7.9	7.5	93.1%
1950	4.6	4.7	5	4.8	6.5	7	6.9	6.4	7.3	7.5	7.7	8.2	7.9	8.5	8.6	9.3	9	9.4	10	8.4	8.6	8.6	9.2	7.1	4.7	6.1	6.6	6.7	6	5.4	1,082,323	7.6	7.2	93.2%
1951	4.4	4.6	4.5	6.1	6.6	6.6	6.2	6.9	7.1	7.2	8	7.5	8	8.5	8.7	8.4	9.4	9.3	8.4	8	8.6	8.5	7.2	4.8	5.5	6.8	5.9	6.3	5.9	5.7	1,179,148	7.4	7.0	92.7%
1952	4.4	4.3	6.1	6.6	6.5	6.2	7.1	7.1	7.3	7.9	7.8	7.9	8.5	8.9	8.2	9	9.6	8.1	8.5	8.4	8.9	7.1	5.9	6.2	6.6	6.4	5.5	6.5	6.4	5	1,117,949	7.6	7.1	91.9%
1953	4.2	5.6	6.2	6.1	5.6	6.6	6.7	6.6	7.3	7.1	7.6	7.8	8.3	7.9	8.3	8.8	7.9	7.5	8.2	8.1	6.9	4.7	6.1	6.5	5.6	5.6	5.3	6.6	5.3	5.5	1,234,806	7.2	6.7	91.5%
1954	5.8	6.4	6.2	5.7	6.7	6.8	6.9	7.4	7.1	7.6	8.2	8.3	7.9	8.7	8.7	7.9	8.2	8.2	8.7	7.1	6	6.2	7.2	6.3	5.5	6	6.1	6.1	6.2	6.4	1,467,099	7.5	7.0	92.8%
1955	4.7	4.6	4.2	5.2	5.5	5.5	6.4	5.8	6.4	6.8	7.3	6.7	7.5	7.9	6.7	6.9	7.3	7.2	6.3	4.4	5.3	5.9	5.6	4.8	4.7	5.6	4.5	6.1	6.2	5.3	1,291,308	6.4	5.9	91.1%
1956	4.2	3.9	4.7	4.9	4.9	5.9	5.4	5.9	6.4	6.8	6.5	7	7.4	6.5	6.3	6.7	7.1	5.5	4.3	4.7	5.9	4.8	4.9	4.7	4.9	4.6	4.9	6.6	5.8	6.2	1,543,721	6	5.6	92.1%
1957	4	4.7	4.9	4.8	5.8	5.3	6	6.2	6.7	6.3	7	7.1	6.3	6.3	6.4	6.7	5.4	3.9	4.6	5.2	4.9	4.5	5	5.3	4.4	5.3	5.9	6.3	6.7	6.6	1,627,320	6	5.6	92.3%
1958	5.4	5.7	5.7	6.3	6.1	6.5	6.9	7	6.7	7.3	7.7	6.6	6.7	7	7	6	4.5	4.9	6.2	5.3	5.2	5.1	6.2	5	5.4	6.6	6.1	7.7	7.6	6.5	1,613,179	6.6	6.2	93.6%
1959	4.4	4.4	5	4.6	5.2	5.8	6.2	5.5	6.4	6.7	5.9	5.5	6.1	6.3	4.6	3.8	4.2	4.8	4.6	4.3	4.6	4.9	4.6	5	5.6	5.7	6.4	7.4	6.4	6.3	1,586,784	5.6	5.4	94.5%
1960	4.3	4.8	4.5	4.8	5.4	6	5.2	6.1	6.5	5.5	5.7	5.9	6.2	4.8	3.9	4.2	5	4.4	4.4	4.3	5	4.3	5.2	5.9	5.1	6.6	6.6	6.8	6.7	6.8	1,827,965	5.6	5.4	94.3%
1961	4.8	4.5	4.9	5.3	5.9	5.3	6.1	6.3	5.3	5.4	6	6	4.6	3.9	4.1	4.7	4.5	4.2	4.5	4.7	4.5	4.8	6.2	5.6	6.3	7	6.2	7.2	7.4	5.6	1,543,353	5.6	5.4	94.8%
1962	4.1	4.3	4.7	5	4.6	5.6	6.1	4.7	4.8	5.2	5.7	4.3	3.8	4	4.3	4.1	4.1	4.1	4.6	4.1	4.8	5.4	5.6	6.3	6.4	6.2	6.3	7.6	5.9	6.5	1,840,631	5.2	5.1	96.2%
1963	4.6	5	5.5	4.9	5.8	6.2	5	4.8	5.3	5.7	4.4	3.8	4	4.5	4.1	4.1	4.3	4.6	4.4	4.8	6.1	5.5	6.9	7.1	6.3	7	7.3	6.8	7.5	7.3	2,168,306	5.5	5.5	97.0%
1964	4.6	5	4.5	5.3	5.8	4.7	4.8	4.9	5.2	4.3	3.8	3.9	4.3	4.1	4	4	4.4	4	4.6	5.2	5.3	6.2	6.9	6.2	6.3	7.2	5.6	7.6	7.4	7.1	2,140,858	5.2	5.2	98.2%
1965	4.6	4.2	4.8	5.2	4.4	4.4	4.7	4.7	4	3.8	3.8	4	3.9	3.9	3.9	4.1	4	4.2	5.2	4.7	6.2	6.4	6.3	6.4	6.7	5.9	6.6	7.7	7.5	6.5	1,917,364	5	5.1	98.6%
1966	4	4.4	4.8	4.1	4.1	4.3	4.4	3.8	3.3	3.8	3.9	3.8	3.8	3.8	3.9	3.8	4.1	4.4	4.5	5.4	6.2	5.2	6.3	6.6	4.9	6.6	6.5	7.6	6.6	7.3	2,245,569	4.7	4.9	97.7%
1967	4.9	5.2	4.4	4.4	4.7	4.9	4.1	3.8	3.8	4.1	4	3.9	3.9	4.1	3.9	4.2	5.1	4.7	6.3	6.5	6.2	6.4	7.4	6	6.8	7.5	7.4	7.7	8.6	8.5	2,741,068	5.2	5.4	100.7%
1968	4.5	4	3.9	4	4.1	3.8	2.9	3.4	3.8	3.8	3.8	3.8	3.8	3.8	3.8	4.1	4.1	4.7	5.7	4.8	5.7	6.2	5.2	6.3	6.3	6.8	6.1	8	7.9	8.7	2,752,661	4.5	4.9	87.2%
1969	3.9	3.9	3.9	4	3.8	2.9	3.4	3.8	3.6	3.5	3.7	3.8	3.6	3.8	3.9	3.9	4.5	4.7	4.6	4.9	6.1	4.5	6.2	6.2	6.2	6.1	6.8	8.1	8.8	8.8	2,724,567	4.4	4.9	86.4%
1970	4.2	4.4	4.6	3.9	3.5	3.8	4	3.8	3.8	3.9	4.1	3.9	4.3	5	4.8	6.2	6.9	6.3	6.9	7.3	6.7	7.5	8.2	8.3	7.4	9.2	9.2	12	12	11	3,591,251	5.3	6.2	109.1%
1971	4.5	4.7	4	3.8	3.8	4	3.9	3.8	3.8	4	3.9	4.1	4.7	4.8	5.8	6.5	6.3	6.5	7.4	6.4	7.7	7.7	8.5	7.6	8.7	9.6	11	13	12	10	3,197,570	5.5	6.4	108.2%
1972	4.4	3.9	3.4	3.8	3.9	3.8	3.8	3.8	3.9	3.8	4	4.4	4.5	5.7	6.1	5.9	6.4	6.8	6.4	7.2	7.7	7.8	7.7	8.8	8.8	11	11	13	11	9.3	2,701,032	5.3	6.3	109.9%
1973	3.8	3.4	3.8	3.8	3.8	3.8	3.8	3.8	3.8	3.9	4.2	4.1	5	5.9	5	6	6.7	5.8	7.1	7.1	7.8	7	8.7	8.7	9.5	11	10	11	9.4	7.1	1,927,481	5.2	6.1	108.8%
1974	3.8	3.9	4.3	4.1	4	4.1	4.3	4	4.6	5.4	5.7	6.5	7.1	6.8	7	7.7	7.3	8.1	8.8	9	8.6	9.7	11	11	11	12	11	12	9.7	10	2,830,396	6.8	7.4	102.5%
1975	5	6	5.4	5	5.1	5.4	5.1	6.1	6.6	6.8	7.9	8.4	8.1	8.5	9	8.6	10	10	11	10	12	12	14	14	14	14	13	13	13	13	3,294,232	8.7	9.3	101.9%
1976	4.9	4.5	4.3	4.3	4.6	4.4	5.3	5.9	6.1	7.1	7.8	7.3	7.7	8.4	7.7	9	9.6	9.8	9.6	11	12	12	14	13	12	13	11	14	13	11	2,841,247	7.9	8.8	104.9%
1977	4.1	4	4	4.1	4	4.5	5.2	5.1	6.4	7	6.8	6.9	7.6	7.1	7.9	8.4	9.2	8.3	10	10	12	12	13	12	11	11	11	13	11	11	2,611,049	7.3	8.2	105.9%
1978	4.1	4.1	4.3	4.1	4.8	5.6	5.8	6.6	7.2	7	7.4	7.8	7.5	8.6	8.6	9.4	9	10	11	12	13	12	13	12	11	12	12	12	12	11	2,493,998	8	8.8	104.0%
1979	4.3	4.5	4.2	4.9	5.8	6	6.9	7.3	7.1	7.4	8.2	7.5	8.7	9.1	9.4	8.9	11	10	12	13	13	12	13	12	12	13	11	13	12	8	1,608,472	8.5	9.1	102.7%
1980	4.4	4.2	4.8	5.4	5.7	6.7	7.3	6.8	7.2	7.9	7.6	8.4	8.8	9.4	8.5	10	11	11	13	12	12	12	12	12	12	12	12	13	9.2	9.2	1,738,215	8.6	9.1	102.2%
1981	4.1	4.7	5.3	5.4	6.5	7.1	6.9	6.9	7.6	7.3	8.4	8.5	9.2	8.6	9.7	10	12	12	13	12	13	12	13	12	11	12	11	10	10	10	1,759,833	8.9	9.3	100.9%
																																Avg	6.93	95.6%

FIGURE 60

ECM backtesting results.

The results show that both versions inherit the strengths of MUFP, but there are key differences. Both versions start retirement with significantly smaller withdrawal rates, although ECM more so. A smaller initial rate helps the strategies adapt to future poor market conditions with less severe drops in income. However, both strategies can also quickly ramp up the rate when justified, so overall income remains comparable.

Later in the chapter, more testing illustrates the flexibility of these two top-performing strategies, but overall, the results are exceptionally strong.

Strategy 9: Delta-Prime: A New Strategy

Delta-Prime is born out of the research for this book.

Three sources contributed to the formation of this strategy. The first is Wade Pfau's 2010 paper[27], published in the *Journal of Investing*, showing the predictive ability of the current withdrawal rate (defined in Key Definitions) in determining the final outcome of a retirement. The second is the use of life-expectancy through mortality tables, as seen in Blanchett et al.'s MUFP. The third is the "floor" concept used in Bengen's strategy, the Floor-to-Ceiling Rule. As will be shown, these concepts help make Delta-Prime a top performing strategy in this survey.

Delta-Prime generally works in three steps:

- First, establish a base withdrawal amount, using an enhanced "floor rule" based on the current withdrawal rate.

- Second, calculate the "delta ratio", incorporating life expectancy and the current withdrawal rate to gauge the state of the portfolio within the retirement.

- Third, use the delta ratio to calculate how much the base withdrawal amount can be boosted without undue risk.

The one mortality table, defined below, should work well for most retirees. Still, for longer retirement periods, Delta-Prime must be calibrated to never have a retirement age over 95, the same as for MUFP. This can be done with a simple adjustment: modify the current retirement age so the last year ends at 95. For example, for a retirement plan to live to 100, a retiree simply subtracts 5 from their current age. If planning to live to 105, simply subtract 10 from the current age. If planning to live to 95 or less, no change is needed—use the correct current age.

The Steps

At the start of retirement, the initial withdrawal is calculated by multiplying the initial withdrawal rate by the portfolio value. The remaining annual withdrawals are calculated at the end of each retirement year using the following steps.

The following mortality table[28], based on a 50% chance of survivability for the total US population, provides life-expectancy estimates based on age (used during backtesting).

Age	45	46	47	48	49	50	51	52	53	54	55	56	57	58	59	60	61	62	63	64	65	66	67	68	69	70	71	72	73	74	75	76	77	78	79	80	81	82	83	84	85	86	87	88	89	90	91	92	93	94	95	96	97	98	99	100
Years Left	35	35	34	33	32	31	30	29	28	27	27	26	25	24	23	23	22	21	20	19	19	18	17	16	16	15	14	14	13	12	12	11	10	10	9	9	8	8	7	7	6	6	6	5	5	5	4	4	4	3	3	3	3	3	2	2

Calculate the **inflation-adjusted withdrawal amount** by adjusting its previous value by inflation (see Key Definitions for full description on page 120). This value will be used later.

1. Initially set the **current withdrawal amount** to a base withdrawal amount using the following steps.
   a. Calculate the **current withdrawal amount** by multiplying the initial withdrawal rate (e.g., 5%) by the current portfolio value.
   b. If the **current withdrawal amount** is less than 90% of the **inflation-adjusted withdrawal amount**, then recalculate the **current withdrawal amount** using the following steps:
      i. Calculate the **current withdrawal rate** by dividing the **inflation-adjusted withdrawal amount** by the current portfolio value.

    ii.   Calculate *scalar* using the following steps.

        a.   Set *scalar* equal to: 1.14 – (3.38 X **current withdrawal rate**).

        b.   If *scalar* is less than 0.5 then reset it to 0.5.

    iii.   Set **current withdrawal amount** to **scalar** * **inflation-adjusted withdrawal amount**.

Under Steps ii and iii above, the equation setting **scalar** adjusts **current withdrawal amount** according to the magnitude of **current withdrawal rate** (CWR). A higher CWR leads to a more conservative base withdrawal. For example, if the CWR is 8%, then the calculated base withdrawal amount is 87% of the Inflation-Adjusted-Withdrawal amount. If the CWR is 10%, then the base withdrawal amount is 80% of the Inflation-Adjusted-Withdrawal amount. If the CWR is 12%, then base withdrawal amount is 73% of the Inflation-Adjusted-Withdrawal amount.

2.   Calculate the delta ratio using the following steps:

    a.   Calculate the *baseline years left* by dividing the current portfolio value by the **inflation-adjusted withdrawal amount** (i.e., the inverse of the **current withdrawal rate**).

    b.   For the retiree's current age, look up the estimated years of life left in the mortality table and set estimated years left to this value.

    c.   Calculate the *delta ratio*, where *b* is the *baseline years left*, and *e* is the *estimated years left* from the mortality table.

$$delta\ ratio = \frac{10 + b}{3 \times e^3}$$

The delta ratio's constants and exponent are used to scale 'b' and 'e' appropriately. The next step uses the result to determine how much the withdrawal can be boosted without undue risk.

3.   Multiple the *delta ratio* by the current portfolio value, then add the resulting product to the **current withdrawal amount**.

4.   Withdraw for the year the **current withdrawal amount**.

Backtesting Results

Figure 61 shows Delta-Prime withdrawals for every retirement period, backtesting with the default portfolio using the SBBI dataset, assuming a 65 year old retiree (like for the MUFP strategy and its enhancements).

Year	Y1	Y2	Y3	Y4	Y5	Y6	Y7	Y8	Y9	Y10	Y11	Y12	Y13	Y14	Y15	Y16	Y17	Y18	Y19	Y20	Y21	Y22	Y23	Y24	Y25	Y26	Y27	Y28	Y29	Y30	Remaining	MSWR	Avg	HREFF-3
1928	6.1	5.3	4.7	4.7	4.8	4.9	4.9	5.7	6.8	5.1	5.7	5.7	5.6	5.1	5.3	5.6	6.2	7.8	6.7	6.1	6.6	7	7.5	9.7	9.5	8.2	17	17	14	16	538,182	6.7	7.5	104.2%
1929	4.8	4.7	4.4	4.5	4.7	4.7	5	5.3	4.8	5	5	4.9	4.5	4.4	5	5.3	6.5	5.5	5.5	5.2	6.3	6.8	6.8	8.6	7.4	9.8	16	13	8.5	19	632,983	5.6	6.7	111.5%
1930	4.8	4.5	4.6	4.9	4.9	5.3	6.4	5	5.2	5.1	5.1	4.8	4.9	5.3	5.7	7.3	6.2	5.7	6	6.3	8.2	8.2	8.1	9.4	13	14	19	12	15	26	778,138	6.4	8.1	113.3%
1931	4.7	4.8	5.2	5.1	6.4	7.6	5.6	6.3	6.2	5.7	5.1	5.2	5.7	6.3	8.2	5.9	6	5.8	6.7	7.1	8.4	8.4	7.7	14	14	12	14	17	15	20	729,265	7.6	8.3	101.4%
1932	5.4	7.4	7.3	8.7	9.9	7.6	8.6	8.4	7.8	6.4	6.2	7.4	8.3	9.7	7.5	6.4	6.4	7	8.7	8.5	10	8.7	12	18	15	11	21	18	13	26	957,690	9.5	10.2	100.8%
1933	7.1	6.9	8.3	9.5	7.2	8.1	8.1	7.3	6	6	6.9	7.7	9.4	6.9	6.2	5.8	6.9	7.4	8.4	8.3	8.9	12	13	16	11	14	20	15	15	20	886,847	9.3	9.8	99.6%
1934	5	6.2	7.3	5.4	6.1	6	5.5	4.9	5	5.3	6	7.7	5.9	5.5	5.6	5.9	6.6	6.5	7.5	7.1	11	12	11	11	13	12	16	16	11	20	903,782	7.9	8.5	100.0%
1935	6.3	7.3	5.5	6.2	6	5.5	5	5	5.3	6.1	7.5	5.8	5.5	5.4	5.7	6.1	6.6	6.7	7.2	9.4	13	11	8.6	14	13	11	18	13	12	22	923,292	8.1	8.6	98.9%
1936	6	4.9	5	4.9	4.9	4.6	4.6	4.9	5.1	6.1	5.1	5	5	5.2	5.7	5.7	6.3	6	8.7	9.7	11	8.6	10	14	11	12	15	14	13	23	961,409	6.9	8.2	108.3%
1937	4.6	4.8	4.8	4.6	4.3	4.3	4.6	4.8	5.3	4.9	4.7	4.6	5	5.3	5.6	5.6	5.7	7.2	9.3	8.6	8.6	11	10	12	13	10	16	15	14	17	779,049	6.1	7.8	116.9%
1938	5.9	5.8	5.3	4.9	4.8	5.1	5.7	6.8	5.2	5.1	5	5.3	5.6	5.6	6.1	5.9	8.4	9.2	9.7	8	12	11	9.8	15	11	12	18	16	11	22	970,725	7.9	8.7	101.2%
1939	5	4.9	4.6	4.6	4.9	5.1	6.6	4.9	5	5	5.1	5.3	5.5	5.7	5.9	7.5	9	8.3	8	9.5	11	10	11	12	12	12	18	12	14	23	1,046,102	7.5	8.5	103.9%
1940	4.7	4.6	4.7	4.9	5.2	6.6	5	4.9	4.9	5.2	5.1	5.3	5.7	5.6	7.5	8.2	8.4	7.1	9.7	9.3	11	11	9.2	13	12	12	15	15	14	15	828,733	7.7	8.3	100.6%
1941	4.8	4.8	5	5.6	6.6	5.1	5	4.9	5.1	5.3	5.4	5.6	5.4	7.4	8.7	8.1	7.6	9.1	10	9.6	13	10	10	14	13	10	18	16	9.7	13	767,144	8	8.5	99.8%
1942	5.2	6.2	6.9	8.3	6.3	5.6	5.3	5.9	6.3	6.4	6.6	6.3	8.6	9.2	9.2	8	10	9.9	11	11	12	12	12	16	11	13	19	12	8.9	14	767,877	9.4	9.4	95.1%
1943	6	6.6	7.8	6	5.2	5	5.6	6	6.2	6.4	6	8.2	9.4	8.8	8.2	9.6	11	10	12	11	13	13	13	14	14	13	14	11	9.6	15	760,304	9.3	9.5	97.1%
1944	5.7	6.7	5.2	4.9	4.9	5	5.2	5.3	5.6	5.3	7	8	7.9	6.8	8.6	8.5	9	9.6	9.5	9.8	12	12	9.3	14	13	9.5	12	11	9.5	9	546,006	8.4	8.3	95.2%
1945	6.2	4.7	4.8	4.7	4.9	4.8	5	5.2	4.9	6.7	7.4	7.2	6.6	7.8	8.2	7.8	9.6	8.3	9.9	10	13	10	11	15	10	8.9	13	11	6.3	5.6	364,465	7.9	7.9	95.7%
1946	4.7	4.5	4.4	4.6	4.7	4.8	4.9	4.8	5.8	6.7	6.4	5.7	7.3	7.4	7.6	8.2	8	8.3	9.9	9.9	10	11	11	11	9.1	8.8	12	7	4	6.3	457,423	6.9	7.3	100.8%
1947	4.9	4.8	4.8	5.3	5.4	5.6	5.3	7.1	8	7.8	6.8	8.4	8.8	8.5	9.8	8.8	9.9	10	12	9.8	13	13	8.8	11	10	9.7	9.3	4.7	5.2	9	569,210	8.2	8.2	95.9%
1948	4.9	5.4	5.8	5.8	5.9	5.6	7.2	7.7	7.5	6.8	7.8	8	8.1	8.8	8.5	8.7	9.9	10	9.8	11	13	8.9	8.3	11	10	6.9	5.4	5.9	6.1	7.4	472,395	7.9	7.8	96.9%
1949	5.7	5.9	5.9	6.1	5.7	7.3	7.9	7.5	6.8	8	7.9	7.9	9.1	8.1	9	9.2	10	8.8	11	11	9.6	8.5	8.6	11	7.7	4.9	7.4	7.6	5.8	7.3	496,479	7.9	7.9	98.4%
1950	5.5	5.5	5.7	5.4	6.9	7.5	7.2	6.5	7.5	7.7	7.5	8.4	8	8.3	9.1	9.3	8.9	9.6	11	8.1	8.9	8.8	8.5	8.3	5.5	6	8.9	6.8	5.4	7.5	599,343	7.6	7.6	98.6%
1951	5.2	5.4	5.1	6.6	7.2	6.9	6.2	7.2	7.3	7.3	8	7.4	8.2	8.4	9.2	8	9.6	9.5	8.2	7.5	9.2	8.8	6.8	5.9	6.4	6.9	7.9	6.3	5.5	8.2	666,510	7.4	7.3	98.0%
1952	5.3	5	6.7	7.4	7	6.3	7.5	7.5	7.5	8.3	7.6	8.1	8.8	8.9	8.4	8.8	9.9	7.6	8.2	8.1	9.6	7.4	5.6	7.1	7.5	6.4	7.5	6.5	6	7.1	627,623	7.6	7.5	97.1%
1953	4.8	6.3	6.9	6.7	5.9	6.9	7	6.8	7.6	7.1	7.4	7.9	8.6	7.5	8.7	8.7	7.4	6.9	8	7.8	7.3	5.5	5.8	7.7	6.5	5.8	7.2	6.7	4.9	7.7	697,577	7.2	7.0	96.4%
1954	6.6	7.2	6.9	6.3	7.2	7.2	7.2	7.8	7.3	7.8	8	8.6	7.9	8.6	9.2	7.3	7.7	7.7	8.6	6.8	6.4	6.5	6.8	7.4	6.5	6.1	8.3	6.1	6	9.7	847,754	7.5	7.4	97.9%
1955	5.6	5.4	4.7	5.8	5.8	5.7	6.5	5.8	6.3	6.7	7.1	6.4	7.4	7.6	6.4	6.1	6.8	6.7	6.4	5.2	6.1	6.4	5.7	6.2	5.8	5.8	6.2	6	5.9	7.6	742,878	6.4	6.2	96.4%
1956	4.9	4.8	5.3	5.5	5.2	6	5.4	5.8	6.2	6.7	5.9	6.8	7.3	5.8	5.9	6	6.5	5.7	5.1	5.3	6.4	5.7	5.2	6	5.9	4.8	6.5	6.4	5.1	8.7	855,237	6	5.9	97.4%
1957	4.9	5.5	5.6	5.4	6.1	5.5	6	6.2	6.7	6	6.7	7	5.8	5.5	6	6	5.6	4.6	5.3	5.6	5.8	5.3	5.1	6.2	5.1	5.2	7.2	5.8	6	9.1	859,352	6	5.9	97.4%
1958	6.3	6.5	6.4	7	6.4	6.7	7.2	7.4	6.7	7.4	7.5	6.2	6.2	6.4	6.8	5.6	5.1	5.3	6.1	5.6	5.9	5.8	5.9	6.1	6.2	6.5	7.7	7.9	7.3	9.1	862,675	6.6	6.6	98.9%
1959	5.2	5.1	5.7	5.2	5.6	5.9	6.3	5.6	6.3	6.6	5.2	5.1	5.5	5.6	5.3	4.4	4.9	5.2	5.2	4.8	5.3	5.4	4.7	5.7	5.9	5.2	7.5	6.9	5.2	7.9	799,091	5.6	5.6	99.4%
1960	5	5.6	5.1	5.4	5.7	6	5.3	6.1	6.4	5.3	5.1	5.4	5.6	5.1	4.6	4.8	5.3	4.9	5	4.9	5.6	4.8	5	6.3	5.6	6	8	6.1	5.7	8.9	909,879	5.6	5.6	99.3%
1961	5.7	5.2	5.5	5.9	6.2	5.6	6.1	6.4	5.2	5.2	5.3	5.5	5.2	4.5	4.8	5.1	5	4.7	5	5.1	5	5.2	5.5	6	6.5	6.4	7.1	6.6	6.4	6.9	766,965	5.6	5.6	99.8%
1962	4.6	5	5.3	5.6	4.9	5.7	6.1	4.9	5.1	5	5	4.9	4.3	4.5	4.9	4.6	4.6	4.5	5	4.4	5.1	5.4	5	6.4	6.3	5.3	6.9	6.7	4.5	7.8	880,295	5.2	5.3	100.3%
1963	5.5	5.8	6.1	5.5	6.1	6.3	5.1	4.9	5.2	5.4	4.9	4.3	4.6	4.9	4.8	4.6	4.8	4.9	4.7	4.9	5.9	5.4	5.9	7.2	6.1	6.1	8.4	5.7	6.2	9	1,000,714	5.5	5.6	101.1%
1964	5.4	5.8	5.2	5.9	6	4.9	5	4.9	5	4.8	4.1	4.4	4.8	4.5	4.5	4.4	4.8	4.3	4.8	5.1	5.3	5.7	5.8	6.1	6	6.2	6	6.5	5.8	8.6	972,196	5.2	5.4	101.6%
1965	5.4	4.8	5.5	5.8	4.7	5	5.1	5.1	4.7	4.2	4.3	4.6	4.5	4.3	4.4	4.5	4.2	4.4	5	4.7	5.7	5.7	5.1	6.1	6.2	4.7	7	6.2	5.6	7.1	842,323	5	5.2	101.8%
1966	4.9	5.1	5.5	4.9	4.8	4.9	5	4.5	3.8	4.1	4.4	4.2	4	4	4.2	3.8	4.1	4.4	4.4	4.7	5.3	4.7	4.7	5.7	4.2	4.8	6	5.4	4.3	7.3	877,539	4.7	4.7	98.9%
1967	5.8	6	5	4.9	5	5.1	4.8	4.3	4.5	4.7	4.5	4.4	4.4	4.5	4.3	4.5	5	4.8	5.5	5.6	5.8	5.9	6.1	5.9	6.6	6.3	8.3	6.5	7	11	1,190,152	5.2	5.6	104.6%
1968	5.3	4.8	4.8	4.8	4.8	4.4	3.7	4	4.3	4.1	3.9	3.9	4.1	3.7	4	4.2	4.1	4.4	4.8	4.3	4.8	5	3.9	5.2	5	4.8	5.1	5.6	5.1	9	1,010,063	4.5	4.7	100.8%
1969	4.8	4.7	4.8	4.8	4.4	3.7	4	4.2	4	3.8	3.8	4	3.6	3.8	4.1	3.9	4.4	4.5	4.3	4.3	5	3.9	4.4	5.1	4.9	4	6	5.5	5.9	9	981,436	4.4	4.6	100.6%
1970	4.9	5.1	5.3	4.8	4.2	4.5	4.7	4.5	4.4	4.5	4.6	4.4	4.7	4.9	4.9	5.3	5.8	5.4	6	6.3	6.1	6.9	6.8	8.6	7.4	8.3	12	13	12	20	1,714,888	5.3	6.7	116.8%
1971	5.3	5.5	4.8	4.5	4.6	4.8	4.6	4.5	4.5	4.6	4.4	4.6	4.9	4.8	5.3	5.5	5.5	5.6	6.5	5.6	7.2	7.2	7.2	8	9	8.9	15	14	13	16	1,440,019	5.5	6.8	115.9%
1972	5.2	4.7	4.3	4.5	4.6	4.5	4.4	4.4	4.5	4.3	4.5	4.8	4.8	5.1	5.5	5.2	5.6	5.9	5.6	6.3	7.3	7.3	6.6	9.5	9.4	11	16	15	10	14	1,270,336	5.3	6.8	119.2%
1973	4.7	4.3	4.4	4.6	4.5	4.3	4.3	4.4	4.2	4.4	4.6	4.6	5	5.1	5.1	5.2	5.8	5.2	6.2	6.3	7.4	6.7	7.5	9.8	11	11	16	11	8.8	8.8	892,854	5.2	6.5	117.4%
1974	4.6	4.8	4.8	4.9	4.8	4.8	4.9	4.7	5	5.2	5.2	5.7	6.5	5.8	6.4	6.9	6.3	7.5	8.6	8.8	9	11	10	16	15	14	17	13	8.1	16	1,286,628	6.8	8.2	110.6%
1975	5.9	6.7	6.1	5.6	5.4	5.7	5.2	6	6.5	6.6	7.7	8.6	8.2	8.3	9.6	8.2	11	11	13	10	15	14	15	21	18	14	18	12	12	20	1,399,053	8.7	10.4	111.6%
1976	5.9	5.3	4.9	4.8	5	5	5.3	5.8	5.9	7	7.6	7.1	7.6	8.2	7.6	8.8	9.8	10	9.8	12	14	15	15	19	15	12	15	14	12	18	1,278,814	7.9	9.8	115.0%
1977	4.6	4.8	4.8	4.9	4.8	5	5.2	5.1	6.1	6.7	6.1	6.4	7.3	6.3	7.9	8	9.1	7.8	11	11	15	15	14	15	12	9.3	16	13	11	18	1,221,022	7.3	9.0	114.1%
1978	4.8	4.7	4.9	4.9	5.2	5.7	5.8	6.7	7.4	6.9	7	7.9	7.2	8.4	9	9.3	8.8	10	12	13	17	15	13	15	11	12	17	13	12	17	1,144,904	8	9.7	113.5%
1979	5	5.2	4.7	5.5	6	6	7.1	7.7	7.2	7.5	8.1	7.4	9	9	10	8.6	11	11	14	14	17	14	13	14	14	12	16	14	11	8.5	631,338	8.5	9.9	110.3%
1980	5.2	4.8	5.5	6	6	7	7.7	7	7.3	8.1	7.2	8.6	9.1	9.4	8.7	10	11	12	15	14	15	13	10	15	13	11	17	13	6.1	11	688,808	8.6	9.8	108.8%
1981	4.7	5.5	6	6	7	7.6	7.1	7.2	7.9	7.2	8.3	8.7	9.6	8.3	11	10	13	13	15	13	15	12	13	16	13	12	16	7.5	7.9	13	726,031	8.9	10.0	107.7%
																																Avg	7.53	103.4%

FIGURE 61

Delta-Prime backtesting results.

The Delta-Prime results are excellent—the best seen in the initial survey. The withdrawal rates are higher, the most difficult periods perform relatively well, and the portfolio never comes close to running out of money. The annual rate never drops below 3.6% in any of the 54 retirement periods. Also, the annual rate only drops below 4% in 1966, 1968, and 1969, the three most difficult retirement periods with MSWRs of 4.7%, 4.5%, and 4.4% respectively.

Still, coming back to the guidelines for evidence-based research, much more evidence is needed to support a claim that Delta-Prime is the best variable-withdrawal strategy for retirement. The following sections show Delta-Prime has weaknesses, ultimately preventing its recommendation, given the alternatives.

COMPARING THE STRATEGIES

The previous section initially surveyed the withdrawal-rate strategies and provided a detailed look at their withdrawals from 1928 through 2010 using SBBI data. Now the strategies will be compared side-by-side, using additional datasets and portfolios.

There's an obstacle though. It's difficult to compare the mass of data involved. For 30-year retirements starting from 1928 to 1981, there are 1620 distinct withdrawal values (30 withdrawals for each of the 54 retirement periods). Multiply this number of withdrawal values by the number of strategies, and the volume balloons. Multiply it again by the datasets covering other countries, and well over 50,000 annual withdrawals become involved. With so much data, a complete comparison is impractical.

The solution is to use a special metric designed to compare variable-withdrawal strategies.

Introducing the Harvesting-Rate Efficiency Metric (HREFF)

A new metric, Harvesting-Rate Efficiency (HREFF), supports the direct comparison of variable-rate strategies. Before examining HREFF, let's first briefly look at its precursor (the idea HREFF is built on).

As mentioned earlier in this chapter, in 2012 the Retirement Income Industry Association's Academic Thought Leadership Award was awarded to Morningstar researchers Blanchett, Kowara, and Chen for their paper, *Optimal Withdrawal Strategy for Retirement Income Portfolios*. In addition to the MUFP strategy, their paper introduces a new metric, Withdrawal Efficiency Rate (WER), to compare the efficiency of variable-withdrawal strategies. Here's the author's description:

> "Withdrawal Efficiency Rate" (WER) can be used to evaluate different withdrawal strategies and thus determine the optimal income maximizing strategy for a retiree. The main idea behind WER is the calculation of how well, on average, a given withdrawal strategy compares with what the retiree(s) could have withdrawn if they possessed perfect information on both the market returns, including their sequencing, and the precise time of death. It is intuitively clear that, given a choice between two withdrawal strategies, the one that on average captures a higher percentage of what was feasible in a perfect foresight world should be preferred."[29]

Figure 62 shows the WER values for all the strategies, with Delta-Prime as the top-performer, MUFP in second place, and EM and ECM coming in close behind.

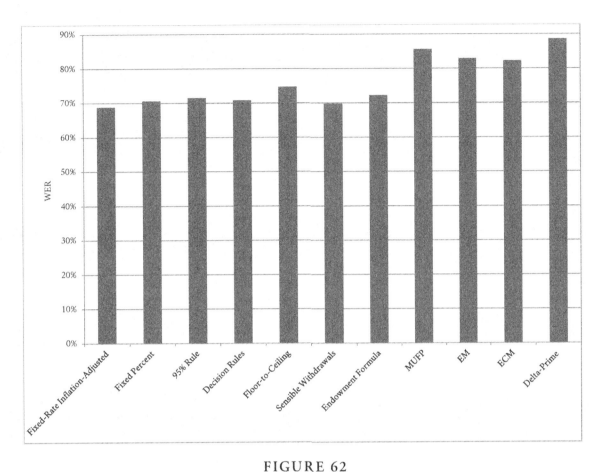

FIGURE 62

WER values for strategies based on SBBI data and 5% initial withdrawal rate.

While WER is a significant contribution, it doesn't support the concept of a minimum acceptable rate[*]. If a retiree has essential expenses that are not considered discretionary, then any withdrawal lower than this amount would preferably be penalized by the metric. For example, if a retiree needs a minimum of 3% to cover living expenses, then ideally the metric would start to penalize annual withdrawals as they approach 3%, then fully penalize them as they go below 3%. In other words, an ideal metric would take into consideration the risk of insufficient income.

The problem of not considering a minimum withdrawal rate can be seen by looking again at Figure 62. The WER value for the 95% Rule is a little higher than for Sensible Withdrawals, although the preceding survey data shows the 95% Rule drops withdrawals below 3% many times, while Sensible Withdrawals never goes below 3%. Although this may not matter for all retirees, it certainly matters for a retiree whose essential expenses are covered by a 3% withdrawal rate.

HREFF essentially provides the same functionality as WER, but also considers a minimum rate. As with WER, HREFF is the ratio of the "average" of a retirement's annual withdrawal rates compared to the Maximum Sustainable Withdrawal Rate (i.e., the largest inflation-adjusted fixed withdrawal rate without a failure). The distinctive part is that annual withdrawals only contribute to the average value when above a minimum rate parameter. As the annual

---

[*]   WER penalizes variations in the withdrawal rate, but this does not correspond well enough with the idea of a minimum acceptable withdrawal rate.

withdrawal rate approaches the minimum rate, its contribution to HREFF diminishes toward zero, then turns negative as the amount goes below the minimum rate (values below the minimum rate count against the average). The minimum rate can represent the minimum amount a retiree can live on for the year, so the penalty corresponds to real-life hardship.

The precise definitions of HREFF and WER are included in their respective technical notes in this chapter. As the formulas show, HREFF differs from WER in other ways too, beyond adding a minimum rate; however, it's still based on the original concepts introduced by WER.

In the following section, the strategies are compared using HREFF, with multiple minimum-rate parameters.

Technical Note: Withdrawal Efficiency Rate (WER)

Blanchett, Kowara, and Chen's definition of the Withdrawal Efficiency Rate is shown in the following formula:

$$WER = \frac{\left(\frac{1}{N}\gamma\sum_1^N \frac{w_i^{-\gamma}}{\gamma}\right)^{-\frac{1}{\gamma}}}{M}$$

where

- N is the retirement length with annual withdrawals w_1, w_2...w_N.

- M is the MSWR value—the inflation-adjusted maximum successful withdrawal rate for the N-year retirement (e.g., 5.6%).

- Gamma (γ) is a constant (e.g., 3) controlling how much variations in the withdrawal rate are penalized.

WER leverages exponents on w_i within the above formula to penalize variations in the withdrawal rate (in lieu of a minimum withdrawal rate).

Technical Note: Harvesting-Rate Efficiency (HREFF)

The Harvesting-Rate Efficiency metric is defined by the following formula:

$$HEFF = \frac{\left(\frac{1}{N}\sum_1^N f(w_i)^{\frac{1}{\gamma}}\right)^\gamma}{M}$$

where for all $w_i \leq$ MR:

$$f(w_i) = w_i - MR$$

where for all $w_i >$ MR:

$$f(w_i) = w_i - \frac{MR}{1 + \epsilon(w_i - MR)^3}$$

where

- *N* is the retirement length (e.g., 30 years) with annual withdrawals w_1, w_2...w_N (e.g., 5%, 4.8%)

- *M* is the MSWR value—the inflation-adjusted maximum successful withdrawal rate for the N-year retirement (e.g., 5.6%).

- MR is the minimum rate acceptable for the withdrawals (e.g., 3%).

- Gamma (γ) is a constant affecting how $f(w_i)$ is valued: variations in withdrawals are penalized, especially when the variations approach the minimum rate. HREFF's γ differs from WER's γ, generally having a much smaller effect on withdrawal variations well above the minimum rate. Gamma must be odd to properly support negative $f(w_i)$ values. Gamma defaults to 5 unless otherwise specified.

- Epsilon (ϵ) is a constant controlling the rate that $f(w_i)$ converges to zero as w_i approaches MR. The effects can be seen in the following diagram with minimum rate set to 3%. Epsilon defaults to 30 unless otherwise specified.

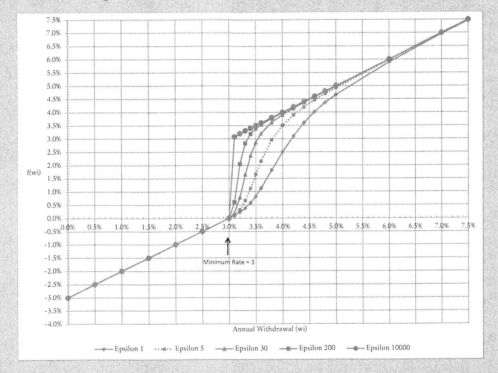

HREFF's definition doesn't normally penalize variations in withdrawal rates sufficiently above MR—the rationale is, variations at high withdrawal rates are less important than variations around MR.

As epsilon is increased (possibly with corresponding increases in gamma) the "penalty zone" above MR is expanded upward, causing variations to be penalized more. For this book, a relatively low epsilon value of 30 is used.

While varying HREFF's parameters affects what is being measured, the rankings between strategies are generally consistent across a wide range of parameters.

Comparing the Strategies — An Initial Take

Figure 63 shows the HREFF results for the default portfolio, using SBBI data between 1928 and 2010. Keep in mind that withdrawal values lose their HREFF rating as they approach the minimum rate, and take away from the overall efficiency rating as they go below the minimum. This implies, high HREFF values for a given minimum rate must be made up of withdrawals coming in *above* the minimum rate.

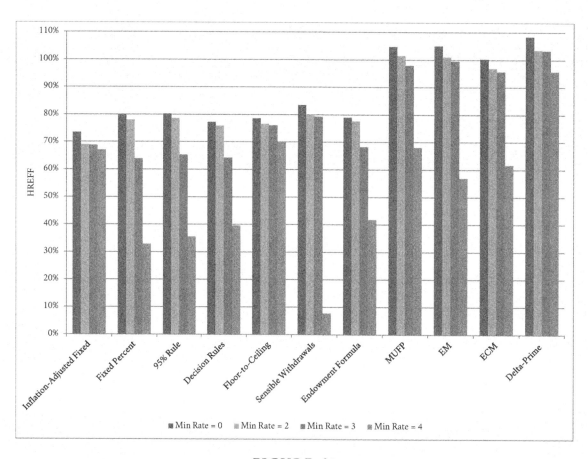

FIGURE 63

HREFF values for strategies based on SBBI data and 5% initial withdrawal rate.

For example, EM maintains a high value up through a minimum rate of 3%, then tapers off significantly at a minimum rate of 4%. This implies that the overwhelming majority of EM's withdrawals are well above 3%, but a significant number are less than or a little above 4%. Although not fully shown, MUFP's HREFF values show consistently high numbers up to 3%, but then the efficiency starts to taper off quickly at 3.5%, implying a significant number of withdrawal values come in not far above 3.5%. In contrast, while the overall efficiency for Inflation-Adjusted Fixed-Rate withdrawals is not strong, as expected its values are consistent across all the minimum rate values (the small variations are due to higher penalties for rates further below the minimum).

The last four strategies stand out in the comparison: MUFP, EM, ECM, and Delta-Prime as the top performer.

Figure 64 shows the HREFF results across the four main datasets, with higher HREFF values highlighted with darker shading. Like with the SBBI dataset, the initial withdrawal rate is set 0.6% above the sustainable rate. This means an initial rate of 4.2% for the US Shiller dataset, 4.3% for the UK, and 4.4% for Japan. Note that across these other datasets, HREFF drops substantially with a minimum rate of 4% due to overall lower returns. Specifically, a 4% variable rate can't be maintained when MSWR-100% is less than 4%. The figure shows across all the datasets that Delta-Prime is consistently the top-performing strategy, but MUFP, EM, and ECM also regularly do well.

		Inflation-Adj Fixed	Fixed Percent	95% Rule	Decision Rules	Floor-to-Ceiling	Sensible Withdrawals	Endowment Formula	MUFP	EM	ECM	Delta-Prime
SBBI	MR=0	73%	80%	80%	77%	79%	83%	79%	105%	105%	100%	108%
	MR=2	69%	78%	79%	76%	77%	80%	78%	101%	101%	97%	104%
	MR=3	69%	64%	65%	64%	76%	79%	68%	98%	100%	96%	103%
	MR=4	67%	33%	36%	40%	70%	8%	42%	68%	57%	62%	96%
Shiller	MR=0	70%	76%	77%	74%	75%	82%	76%	107%	104%	102%	109%
	MR=2	66%	66%	68%	69%	74%	78%	70%	101%	99%	98%	104%
	MR=3	65%	39%	41%	48%	72%	67%	43%	76%	75%	88%	101%
	MR=4	15%	20%	20%	22%	20%	1%	23%	49%	42%	37%	63%
UK	MR=0	81%	77%	78%	75%	81%	88%	77%	106%	104%	103%	107%
	MR=2	74%	68%	68%	64%	79%	82%	71%	99%	100%	98%	104%
	MR=3	73%	20%	22%	23%	77%	69%	28%	76%	76%	83%	99%
	MR=4	35%	8%	8%	5%	7%	1%	9%	26%	19%	19%	50%
Japan	MR=0	66%	76%	77%	78%	71%	82%	76%	106%	104%	100%	107%
	MR=2	63%	73%	74%	77%	70%	73%	74%	97%	98%	95%	102%
	MR=3	62%	62%	64%	69%	69%	66%	68%	86%	88%	90%	100%
	MR=4	43%	19%	20%	35%	20%	0%	25%	65%	59%	42%	89%

FIGURE 64

HREFF values across the SBBI, Shiller, UK, and Japan datasets.

Capping Withdrawal Rates

Looking closely at the yearly withdrawals of the top performing strategies, one might wonder if their performance is being skewed by dispersing excess portfolio value during strong markets (i.e., occasional very high withdrawal rates). For example, it's not unusual for Delta-Prime to surpass 10% withdrawals in the second half of strong retirement periods. To understand the potential effect of occasional high rates on the results, all annual withdrawals for the strategies can be capped.

Figure 65 shows the HREFF results with income rates capped at 6.25% annually (matching the same cap used in the Floor-to-Ceiling strategy with a 5% initial rate). The figure shows that a significant portion of the top-performing strategies' performance does stem from high rates from portfolio surpluses; however, it's also clear that this is not the only source of the strategies' strong performance. Even with capped rates, the top performers do significantly better than the other strategies.

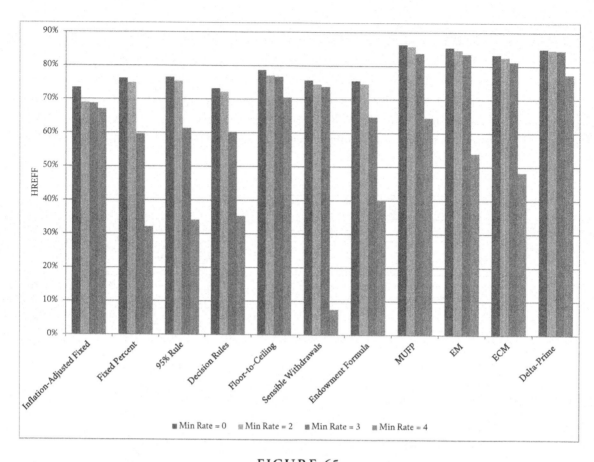

FIGURE 65

HREFF values with income capped at 6.25% using SBBI data.

However, Delta-Prime's lead over the other top performing strategies is blunted. MUFP comes out ahead for the minimum rate of 0% and 2% with EM, with Delta-Prime very close behind. For the 3% minimum rate, Delta-Prime is ahead, with MUFP and EM nearly as good. Delta-Prime remains well ahead for a 4% minimum rate.

The question remains whether or not capping withdrawals is a good idea. Generally, some cap is wise, but, surprisingly, it doesn't help as much as one might expect. The reason is, during the worst retirement periods, the withdrawal amount rarely (if ever) rises above the capped value, therefore capping usually doesn't make a difference. Based on the historical data in hand, capping income at 150% of the initial withdrawal rate reaps most of the benefits of limiting high income rates.

Another approach is to only occasional cap annual income. This means, when calculated rates are very high, withdraw the full amount when it's needed or can be put to good use; otherwise, leave the unneeded portion in the portfolio. The withdrawal strategy will always automatically account for any income not withdrawn. There is no extra management burden. A good perspective is to view the withdrawal rate as the *maximum* allowable rate for the year, allowing one to responsibly withdraw up to that amount but use a lower rate when the extra income is not needed.

Of course, limited withdrawals will also increase the amount remaining at the end of retirement. If leaving assets to heirs is a priority, as opposed to spending or giving surplus funds away while living, then an easy plan is to cap the rate, leaving unneeded income in place to boost the assets remaining at the end of retirement.

Capped rates are briefly revisited in Chapter 10.

Considering the Bernicke Effect

Ty Bernicke published an influential paper[30] in 2005 whose premise is we spend less in retirement as we age. The Bogleheads website[31] provides a summary of Bernicke's conclusions as well as other papers showing similar results: we spend less in retirement as we age. The numbers vary across papers, and others even argue that spending does not decrease in retirement. Whether or not Bernicke is right cannot be answered here, but his assertion provides another angle for comparing variable-withdrawal strategies.

Figure 66 compares normal HREFF values to Bernicke-Scaled HREFF values (both with a minimum rate of zero), where the first 10 years of withdrawals are overweighted, the middle 10 years are neutral weighted, and the last 10 years are underweighted[*].

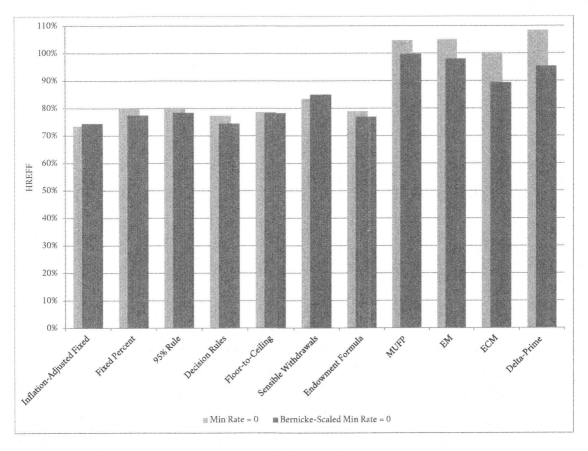

FIGURE 66

HREFF (with no minimum rate) compared to Bernicke-Scaled HREFF using SBBI data.

---

* The overweighting is by 65% and the underweighting by −65%, although these large values are somewhat misleading because some of the effects are reduced by the HREFF calculation. Ultimately, the weights are subjectively selected in order to intuitively convey what a closer examination of the numbers reflects.

A moderate change in the results can be seen, but there is no major realignment. The same four strategies remain as the top performers, although MUFP now comes out first, EM second, and Delta-Prime third. It's worth noting that virtually any strategy can be tuned to boost early income, but this generally increases risk later in retirement. The challenge is in finding a proper balance.

A Focus on the Markets' Poorest Retirement Periods

With any metric there is a possibility of important details lying hidden, plus averages often obscure the worst performance. To examine the poorest performance, the overall HREFF value is recalculated to include only the bottom 10% of the retirement periods: those with the lowest individual HREFF values.

Figure 67 shows these HREFF results for the bottom 10%, using a 2% minimum rate to accentuate very low income. Some strategies show substantially worse performance, although the same four strategies remain at the top. MUFP is affected most from among the top performers, dropping significantly for all but the SBBI dataset. It's not surprising that ECM does relatively better in this context, since it's more oriented to handling poor markets. Delta-Prime is again the top performer. Interestingly, performance below 30% usually reflects that some of the retirement periods ran out of money before the end of retirement.

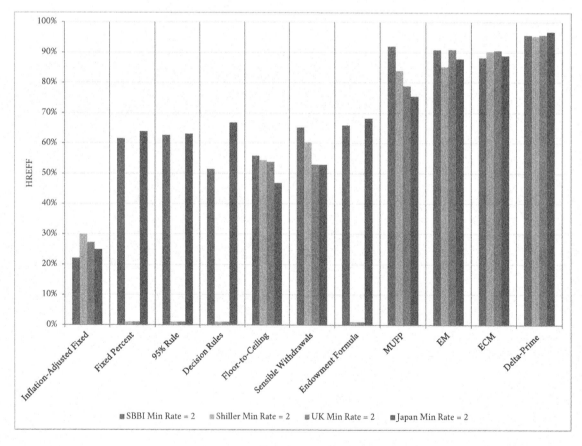

FIGURE 67

HREFF for the bottom 10% of the retirement periods.

To be fair, however, several of the strategies could certainly have their parameters better tuned to boost performance during poor markets. This was done when creating EM and ECM, based on MUFP's definition. Also, keep in mind that an unsustainable initial withdrawal rate was picked for each dataset to intentionally stress the strategies. What is important to understand is with the wrong starting parameters under the wrong market conditions, some strategies do very poorly.

The Top Three Strategies with Long Retirements

The focus now shifts to the three top performers: EM, ECM, and Delta-Prime (again MUFP isn't fully viable in its pure form). Chapter 10 will show that 40-year retirement plans are best for many retirees given current life expectancies. This section takes an initial look at these longer plans, with later chapters completing the discussion.

Figure 68, Figure 69, and Figure 70 show 40-year results with an 8% cap for the default portfolio using EM, ECM, and Delta-Prime respectively. The initial withdrawal rate is 4.8% (as before, 0.6% above MSWR-100%). Delta-Prime maintains a significantly higher floor value; nevertheless, the average withdrawal numbers are comparable across the three strategies. The average income over the first 10 years is more representative of differences between the strategies: 5.3% for Delta-Prime, 5.2% for EM, and 4.7% for ECM. For the toughest retirement period starting in 1969, the average over the first 10 years varies more: 4.2% for Delta-Prime, 3.4% for EM, and 3.4% for ECM.

Year	Y1	Y2	Y3	Y4	Y5	Y6	Y7	Y8	Y9	Y10	Y11	Y12	Y13	Y14	Y15	Y16	Y17	Y18	Y19	Y20	Y21	Y22	Y23	Y24	Y25	Y26	Y27	Y28	Y29	Y30	Y31	Y32	Y33	Y34	Y35	Y36	Y37	Y38	Y39	Y40	Remaining	MSWR	Avg	1st 10Y	HREFF-3
1928	5.7	4.6	4.1	3.7	3.9	4.5	4.5	5.7	7.3	4.7	5.6	5.6	5.0	4.1	4.1	5.0	6.5	8.0	5.6	4.9	4.8	5.6	7.2	7.5	7.4	7.1	8.0	8.0	8.0	8.0	8.0	8.0	8.0	8.0	8.0	8.0	8.0	8.0	8.0	8.0	1,864,199	6.4	6.4	4.9	96.5%
1929	3.9	3.7	3.3	3.6	3.7	3.7	4.2	5.2	3.9	4.2	4.2	4.0	3.6	3.7	4.0	4.7	7.3	4.6	4.2	4.1	5.1	5.9	6.5	7.2	6.0	8.0	8.0	8.0	8.0	8.0	8.0	8.0	8.0	8.0	8.0	8.0	8.0	8.0	8.0	8.0	1,787,386	5.4	5.9	3.9	100.7%
1930	3.9	3.6	3.6	4.0	4.0	5.0	6.6	4.2	5.0	4.9	4.4	3.8	3.8	4.6	5.8	7.9	5.7	4.6	4.5	5.7	7.4	7.4	7.8	7.4	8.0	8.0	8.0	8.0	8.0	8.0	8.0	8.0	8.0	8.0	8.0	8.0	8.0	8.0	8.0	8.0	2,038,424	6.2	6.3	4.5	97.8%
1931	3.7	3.8	4.6	4.6	6.4	7.9	5.1	6.4	6.3	5.4	4.2	4.3	5.4	6.7	8.0	5.8	5.0	4.6	5.5	7.0	7.4	7.4	7.1	8.0	8.0	8.0	8.0	8.0	8.0	8.0	8.0	8.0	8.0	8.0	8.0	8.0	8.0	8.0	8.0	8.0	1,887,921	7.2	6.7	5.4	90.9%
1932	4.7	7.5	7.3	8.0	8.0	7.9	8.0	8.0	8.0	6.3	6.2	7.5	8.0	8.0	7.5	6.5	6.3	7.1	7.8	8.0	8.0	7.8	8.0	8.0	8.0	8.0	8.0	8.0	8.0	8.0	8.0	8.0	8.0	8.0	8.0	8.0	8.0	8.0	8.0	8.0	2,791,715	8.9	7.7	7.4	85.7%
1933	7.2	7.0	8.0	8.0	7.4	8.0	8.0	7.6	5.8	5.5	7.1	7.7	8.0	7.1	5.7	5.5	6.9	7.3	7.5	7.9	7.6	8.0	8.0	8.0	8.0	8.0	8.0	8.0	8.0	8.0	8.0	8.0	8.0	8.0	8.0	8.0	8.0	8.0	8.0	8.0	2,892,608	8.7	7.6	7.3	86.6%
1934	4.3	5.8	7.4	4.8	5.7	5.7	5.0	4.0	4.1	4.9	6.1	7.9	5.5	4.8	4.6	5.6	6.7	6.5	7.1	6.8	8.0	8.0	8.0	8.0	8.0	8.0	8.0	8.0	8.0	8.0	8.0	8.0	8.0	8.0	8.0	8.0	8.0	8.0	8.0	8.0	1,689,419	7.5	6.8	5.2	89.2%
1935	6.0	7.4	4.8	5.8	5.7	5.1	4.0	4.1	4.9	6.0	7.8	5.4	4.6	4.5	5.4	6.2	6.7	6.9	6.3	8.0	8.0	8.0	8.0	8.0	8.0	8.0	8.0	8.0	8.0	8.0	8.0	8.0	8.0	8.0	8.0	8.0	8.0	8.0	8.0	5.1	1,091,194	7.6	6.8	5.4	87.9%
1936	5.6	3.9	4.4	4.4	4.0	3.7	3.6	4.0	4.6	6.3	4.3	3.9	3.8	4.3	5.1	5.4	6.0	5.3	8.0	8.0	8.0	8.0	8.0	8.0	8.0	8.0	8.0	8.0	8.0	8.0	8.0	8.0	8.0	8.0	8.0	8.0	8.0	8.0	6.6	7.1	1,366,591	6.5	6.4	4.5	94.4%
1937	3.6	3.8	3.8	3.7	3.3	3.3	3.6	3.9	5.3	3.9	3.7	3.7	3.9	4.5	4.6	5.1	4.9	7.5	8.0	8.0	7.5	8.0	8.0	8.0	8.0	8.0	8.0	8.0	8.0	8.0	8.0	8.0	8.0	8.0	8.0	8.0	5.9	3.9	4.3	4.8	1,129,850	5.8	6.0	3.8	93.7%
1938	5.4	5.3	4.7	3.9	3.9	4.7	5.4	7.2	4.8	4.2	4.1	4.6	5.2	5.6	6.0	5.6	8.0	8.0	8.0	8.0	8.0	8.0	8.0	8.0	8.0	8.0	8.0	8.0	8.0	8.0	8.0	8.0	8.0	8.0	8.0	8.0	6.5	8.0	8.0	7.1	1,475,506	7	6.8	5.0	94.0%
1939	4.4	4.0	3.6	3.6	4.0	4.8	6.8	4.5	4.1	3.9	4.5	5.0	5.2	5.7	5.3	7.9	8.0	8.0	7.6	8.0	8.0	8.0	8.0	8.0	8.0	8.0	8.0	8.0	8.0	8.0	8.0	8.0	8.0	8.0	7.8	4.4	5.4	8.0	6.1	4.6	1,274,948	6.9	6.4	4.4	89.5%
1940	4.1	3.6	3.6	4.1	4.7	6.9	4.5	4.0	4.0	4.4	4.9	5.1	5.5	5.2	7.7	8.0	8.0	7.4	8.0	8.0	8.0	8.0	8.0	8.0	8.0	8.0	8.0	8.0	8.0	8.0	8.0	8.0	8.0	7.8	4.0	5.4	6.5	6.7	4.8	4.4	1,407,475	6.9	6.4	4.4	88.8%
1941	3.8	3.8	4.3	5.1	6.8	4.6	4.0	4.0	4.4	5.0	5.2	5.5	5.1	7.8	8.0	8.0	7.8	8.0	8.0	8.0	8.0	8.0	8.0	8.0	8.0	8.0	8.0	8.0	8.0	8.0	8.0	8.0	8.0	5.8	6.4	7.9	6.0	6.8	5.6	5.3	1,778,863	6.9	6.6	4.6	93.2%
1942	4.5	5.8	7.0	8.0	6.1	5.1	4.8	5.7	6.4	6.3	6.8	6.2	8.0	8.0	8.0	8.0	8.0	8.0	8.0	8.0	8.0	8.0	8.0	8.0	8.0	8.0	8.0	8.0	8.0	8.0	8.0	8.0	7.8	7.9	8.0	7.6	6.0	7.5	7.1	4.6	1,605,506	7.4	7.2	6.0	96.6%
1943	5.5	6.5	7.8	5.5	4.6	4.5	5.0	5.9	6.1	6.3	5.8	8.0	8.0	8.0	8.0	8.0	8.0	8.0	8.0	8.0	8.0	8.0	8.0	8.0	8.0	8.0	8.0	8.0	8.0	8.0	8.0	7.5	8.0	8.0	8.0	7.6	7.0	8.0	6.4	6.3	1,843,844	7.5	7.3	5.8	95.7%
1944	5.0	6.7	4.4	4.0	3.9	4.3	4.8	5.0	5.4	4.9	7.5	8.0	7.9	7.2	8.0	8.0	8.0	8.0	8.0	8.0	8.0	8.0	8.0	8.0	8.0	8.0	8.0	8.0	8.0	7.5	5.0	5.5	7.7	5.9	4.8	5.3	5.3	5.4	5.5	5.6	1,770,006	6.8	6.6	4.8	94.2%
1945	5.8	4.1	3.8	3.7	4.0	4.4	4.5	4.8	4.6	7.1	7.7	7.5	6.5	8.0	8.0	8.0	8.0	8.0	8.0	8.0	8.0	8.0	8.0	8.0	8.0	8.0	8.0	8.0	7.3	4.3	5.5	6.3	6.0	4.9	4.7	5.6	4.2	6.2	6.3	4.8	1,619,917	6.6	6.4	4.7	93.4%
1946	3.7	3.6	3.5	3.6	3.8	3.9	4.0	3.9	6.0	7.2	6.9	5.6	7.5	7.8	7.7	8.0	8.0	8.0	8.0	8.0	8.0	8.0	8.0	8.0	8.0	8.0	8.0	5.9	3.9	4.4	5.9	4.6	4.9	4.7	4.9	4.4	4.6	7.2	5.3	5.8	1,856,000	6	6.0	4.3	95.4%
1947	4.0	3.8	4.2	4.8	5.0	5.3	4.9	7.5	8.0	7.9	7.2	8.0	8.0	8.0	8.0	8.0	8.0	8.0	8.0	8.0	8.0	8.0	8.0	8.0	8.0	8.0	8.0	5.4	6.7	7.4	6.8	5.4	6.6	6.7	4.8	6.1	6.7	7.4	7.6	7.2	1,772,304	6.9	6.9	5.5	97.8%
1948	4.2	4.8	5.2	5.3	5.5	5.2	7.4	8.0	7.7	6.9	8.0	8.0	7.9	8.0	8.0	8.0	8.0	8.0	8.0	8.0	8.0	8.0	8.0	8.0	8.0	7.0	4.3	4.9	6.5	5.0	5.0	4.9	6.7	4.8	5.2	7.0	5.4	8.0	7.8	5.5	1,454,203	6.8	6.7	6.0	96.6%
1949	5.0	5.4	5.4	5.8	5.3	7.6	8.0	7.8	7.1	8.0	8.0	7.9	8.0	8.0	8.0	8.0	8.0	8.0	8.0	8.0	8.0	8.0	8.0	8.0	6.7	4.3	5.3	6.3	5.4	4.7	5.3	5.7	5.4	5.9	6.6	6.3	7.2	8.0	6.9	6.2	1,597,512	6.9	6.8	6.5	97.7%
1950	4.8	4.9	5.1	4.8	7.1	7.8	7.4	6.5	7.8	7.7	7.6	8.0	7.8	8.0	8.0	8.0	8.0	8.0	8.0	8.0	8.0	8.0	8.0	6.4	4.0	4.7	6.2	4.9	4.7	4.7	5.9	4.5	6.3	7.1	5.6	7.6	7.4	7.5	7.1	6.9	1,788,382	6.7	6.7	6.4	98.4%
1951	4.5	4.7	4.4	6.7	7.4	7.2	5.9	7.5	7.5	7.3	8.0	7.5	7.9	8.0	8.0	8.0	8.0	8.0	7.6	7.6	8.0	7.9	5.6	3.9	4.3	5.6	4.9	4.4	4.8	5.1	4.7	5.2	7.4	6.2	7.3	7.9	6.0	8.0	7.8	4.6	1,417,462	6.6	6.5	6.3	96.7%
1952	4.6	4.3	6.6	7.5	7.2	6.1	7.6	7.7	7.7	8.0	7.7	8.0	8.0	8.0	8.0	8.0	8.0	7.6	7.6	8.0	8.0	5.9	4.1	4.8	5.6	5.0	4.7	4.6	5.3	4.3	5.5	6.4	6.9	7.6	7.6	6.8	6.6	8.0	5.5	6.6	1,696,322	6.7	6.7	6.7	97.4%
1953	4.2	6.0	7.0	6.6	5.5	7.1	7.1	7.1	7.8	7.1	7.5	7.9	8.0	7.6	8.0	8.0	7.3	6.8	7.2	7.6	5.3	3.8	4.2	5.3	4.4	4.3	4.6	5.0	4.4	5.0	6.9	5.7	8.0	8.0	6.5	7.4	7.6	6.6	7.4	6.6	1,752,763	6.4	6.5	6.6	98.8%
1954	6.6	7.3	6.9	5.9	7.3	7.4	7.2	8.0	7.4	7.7	8.0	8.0	7.7	8.0	8.0	7.4	7.5	7.6	7.7	5.9	4.3	4.6	5.7	5.0	4.4	4.5	5.1	4.2	5.1	6.0	6.0	7.3	8.0	7.1	7.1	8.0	5.2	8.0	7.8	7.2	1,864,492	6.7	6.7	7.2	98.3%
1955	5.0	4.7	4.1	5.3	5.5	5.4	6.5	5.6	6.4	6.9	7.4	6.4	7.4	7.8	6.0	6.1	6.8	6.6	4.6	3.8	4.2	4.7	4.3	4.1	4.1	4.5	4.1	4.5	5.7	5.0	7.3	7.4	7.2	7.1	7.4	5.3	6.8	8.0	7.6	5.4	1,667,653	5.7	5.8	5.5	99.8%
1956	4.3	3.8	4.7	5.0	4.7	5.9	5.0	5.7	6.4	7.0	5.8	7.1	7.3	5.6	5.5	6.0	6.5	4.4	3.7	4.0	4.7	4.1	4.0	4.1	4.2	3.9	4.6	5.3	5.2	6.6	7.6	6.0	7.6	7.9	5.1	7.5	7.2	8.0	6.8	7.5	2,071,783	5.5	5.7	5.3	99.9%
1957	3.9	4.9	5.0	4.9	5.9	5.2	5.7	6.4	7.1	5.7	7.0	7.2	5.3	5.2	5.6	6.0	4.3	3.6	3.8	4.4	4.1	3.9	4.0	4.6	4.0	4.7	6.0	5.4	7.3	7.5	7.1	7.2	8.0	6.4	7.7	8.0	7.9	8.0	8.0	8.0	2,407,983	5.5	5.9	5.5	103.3%
1958	6.0	6.2	6.0	7.2	6.2	6.9	7.3	7.6	6.9	7.4	7.6	5.8	5.7	6.3	6.5	4.6	3.7	3.9	4.5	4.3	4.1	4.1	4.6	4.2	4.7	6.1	6.0	7.4	8.0	6.8	7.8	8.0	7.1	8.0	7.9	8.0	7.1	8.0	8.0	8.0	3,105,449	6.1	6.4	6.8	101.6%
1959	4.6	4.4	5.2	4.6	5.1	5.7	6.2	5.3	6.4	6.7	4.9	4.7	5.1	5.4	4.0	3.6	3.7	4.0	3.8	3.8	3.9	4.2	3.9	4.5	5.3	5.3	7.2	7.5	6.7	7.1	8.0	5.6	8.0	8.0	8.0	7.5	8.0	8.0	8.0	8.0	3,408,459	5.3	5.7	5.4	104.2%
1960	4.3	5.0	4.4	4.9	5.3	5.9	4.9	6.1	6.7	4.8	4.8	5.1	5.3	4.1	3.6	3.7	4.1	3.8	3.7	3.8	4.1	3.8	4.2	5.2	4.8	6.7	7.5	6.1	7.2	7.6	5.8	7.5	8.0	8.0	7.2	8.0	8.0	8.0	8.0	8.0	4,033,716	5.2	5.7	5.2	105.1%
1961	5.1	4.5	4.9	5.5	5.9	5.2	5.9	6.5	4.8	4.7	5.0	5.2	4.0	3.6	3.7	4.0	3.8	3.7	3.7	4.0	3.8	4.1	5.1	5.0	6.4	7.4	6.6	7.0	7.9	5.8	8.0	7.9	8.0	7.8	8.0	8.0	8.0	8.0	8.0	8.0	3,760,544	5.3	5.8	5.3	104.9%
1962	4.0	4.3	4.7	5.2	4.4	5.4	5.8	4.5	4.4	4.6	4.8	3.8	3.4	3.6	3.8	3.7	3.7	3.7	3.8	3.7	4.0	4.5	4.6	6.2	6.7	5.9	7.0	7.4	5.5	7.3	7.9	7.9	7.8	8.0	8.0	8.0	8.0	8.0	8.0	8.0	3,287,971	5	5.6	4.7	105.5%
1963	4.9	5.2	5.7	5.0	5.8	6.3	4.6	4.5	4.8	4.9	3.9	3.4	3.6	3.9	3.7	3.7	3.7	3.9	3.7	4.1	5.1	4.7	6.6	7.5	6.2	7.1	8.0	6.0	8.0	7.9	8.0	7.5	8.0	8.0	8.0	8.0	8.0	8.0	8.0	8.0	2,590,886	5.2	5.9	5.2	107.2%
1964	4.8	5.3	4.5	5.5	5.8	4.5	4.4	4.7	4.8	3.9	3.5	3.6	3.8	3.7	3.6	3.6	3.7	3.6	3.8	4.4	4.4	5.5	6.7	5.8	6.3	7.5	6.0	7.5	7.9	7.9	7.5	8.0	8.0	8.0	8.0	8.0	8.0	8.0	8.0	8.0	3,198,792	5	5.8	4.8	108.5%
1965	4.7	4.1	4.9	5.4	4.2	4.2	4.3	4.5	3.7	3.2	3.6	3.7	3.6	3.6	3.6	3.7	3.6	3.7	4.1	4.1	5.3	5.9	5.3	6.2	7.0	5.2	7.5	7.4	8.0	6.8	8.0	8.0	8.0	8.0	8.0	8.0	8.0	8.0	8.0	8.0	3,167,824	4.8	5.6	4.3	106.9%
1966	4.0	4.5	4.8	4.0	3.9	4.0	4.1	3.6	2.8	3.3	3.6	3.5	3.3	3.5	3.6	3.5	3.7	3.9	3.8	4.7	5.6	4.7	5.4	6.9	4.9	7.1	7.5	7.5	6.9	8.0	8.0	8.0	8.0	8.0	8.0	8.0	7.6	8.0	8.0	8.0	2,831,173	4.5	5.5	3.9	91.7%
1967	5.3	5.6	4.3	4.3	4.5	4.6	3.8	3.4	3.6	3.7	3.6	3.6	3.6	3.7	3.6	3.7	4.1	4.0	5.0	6.1	5.5	6.0	7.3	5.9	7.4	7.8	8.0	7.2	8.0	8.0	8.0	8.0	8.0	8.0	8.0	8.0	8.0	8.0	8.0	8.0	3,444,066	5	5.9	4.3	109.5%
1968	4.7	3.8	3.7	3.9	3.9	3.6	2.5	3.0	3.6	3.2	3.1	3.3	3.6	3.3	3.6	3.8	3.8	4.2	4.8	4.5	5.3	6.1	4.9	7.0	7.1	7.6	7.0	8.0	8.0	8.0	8.0	8.0	8.0	8.0	7.8	8.0	8.0	8.0	8.0	8.0	2,649,154	4.3	5.6	3.6	78.8%
1969	3.8	3.7	3.8	3.9	3.5	2.6	2.9	3.5	3.1	2.9	3.0	3.4	3.0	3.5	3.6	3.6	4.0	4.3	4.0	4.6	5.7	4.2	6.0	6.7	7.0	6.1	8.0	8.0	8.0	8.0	8.0	8.0	8.0	8.0	8.0	8.0	8.0	8.0	8.0	3.9	1,328,806	4.2	5.4	3.4	48.3%
1970	4.3	4.5	4.6	3.7	3.2	3.6	3.7	3.6	3.6	3.6	3.7	3.6	3.8	4.2	4.2	5.4	6.6	5.5	6.1	7.4	6.3	7.6	8.0	8.0	7.6	8.0	8.0	8.0	8.0	8.0	8.0	8.0	8.0	8.0	8.0	8.0	8.0	8.0	7.7	8.0	2,291,244	5.1	6.2	3.8	110.1%
1971	4.7	4.8	3.9	3.6	3.6	3.8	3.6	3.6	3.6	3.7	3.6	3.7	4.1	4.1	5.1	6.0	5.5	5.8	7.1	5.9	7.8	7.8	8.0	7.8	8.0	8.0	8.0	8.0	8.0	8.0	8.0	8.0	8.0	8.0	8.0	8.0	8.0	8.0	8.0	8.0	2,851,406	5.3	6.2	3.9	110.3%
																																										Avg	6.3	5.2	96.4%

FIGURE 68

EM withdrawals for 40-year retirement starting at 65 with a 4.8% initial withdrawal rate using SBBI data and an 8% income cap.

Year	Y1	Y2	Y3	Y4	Y5	Y6	Y7	Y8	Y9	Y10	Y11	Y12	Y13	Y14	Y15	Y16	Y17	Y18	Y19	Y20	Y21	Y22	Y23	Y24	Y25	Y26	Y27	Y28	Y29	Y30	Y31	Y32	Y33	Y34	Y35	Y36	Y37	Y38	Y39	Y40	Remaining	MSWR	Avg	1st 10Y	HREFF-3
1928	4.9	4.3	3.9	3.7	3.8	4.3	4.2	5.1	6.0	4.5	5.2	5.2	4.8	4.1	4.1	4.8	5.8	6.6	5.3	4.8	4.8	5.4	6.2	6.5	6.5	6.4	8.0	8.0	8.0	7.9	8.0	8.0	8.0	8.0	8.0	8.0	8.0	8.0	8.0	8.0	2,129,060	6.4	6.1	4.5	91.8%
1929	3.8	3.6	3.3	3.6	3.7	3.7	4.0	4.7	3.8	4.0	4.1	3.9	3.6	3.7	3.9	4.4	6.0	4.4	4.1	4.1	4.8	5.4	5.8	6.1	5.7	7.4	8.0	7.8	7.3	8.0	8.0	8.0	8.0	8.0	8.0	8.0	8.0	8.0	8.0	8.0	1,991,977	5.4	5.7	3.8	97.0%
1930	3.8	3.6	3.6	3.9	3.9	4.5	5.6	4.1	4.6	4.5	4.3	3.8	3.8	4.4	5.2	6.5	5.2	4.5	4.4	5.3	6.2	6.3	6.6	6.5	7.8	8.0	8.0	7.7	8.0	8.0	8.0	8.0	8.0	8.0	8.0	8.0	8.0	8.0	8.0	8.0	1,893,157	6.2	6.1	4.2	93.3%
1931	3.6	3.7	4.2	4.2	5.4	6.4	4.7	5.6	5.7	5.0	4.2	4.2	5.1	5.9	6.7	5.5	4.9	4.6	5.3	6.1	6.4	6.5	6.3	8.0	8.0	8.0	8.0	8.0	8.0	8.0	8.0	8.0	8.0	8.0	8.0	8.0	8.0	8.0	8.0	8.0	2,229,779	7.2	6.4	4.9	86.2%
1932	4.3	6.1	6.0	7.0	7.7	6.5	7.0	7.1	6.8	5.9	5.8	6.4	6.9	7.8	6.5	6.0	6.0	6.3	6.8	7.0	7.4	7.0	8.0	8.0	8.0	8.0	8.0	8.0	8.0	8.0	8.0	8.0	8.0	8.0	8.0	8.0	8.0	8.0	8.0	8.0	3,408,681	8.9	7.2	6.4	80.4%
1933	5.9	5.8	6.6	7.5	6.2	6.8	6.7	6.5	5.6	5.4	6.2	6.6	7.4	6.2	5.7	5.5	6.2	6.4	6.6	6.9	6.8	8.0	8.0	8.0	8.0	8.0	8.0	8.0	8.0	8.0	8.0	8.0	8.0	8.0	8.0	8.0	8.0	8.0	8.0	8.0	3,581,687	8.7	7.1	6.3	81.5%
1934	4.1	5.0	6.0	4.5	5.1	5.1	4.7	4.0	4.0	4.6	5.4	6.5	5.2	4.6	4.5	5.2	5.9	5.9	6.1	6.1	7.6	8.0	8.0	7.5	8.0	8.0	8.0	8.0	8.0	8.0	8.0	8.0	8.0	8.0	8.0	8.0	8.0	8.0	8.0	8.0	2,163,510	7.5	6.5	4.7	85.0%
1935	5.1	6.0	4.4	5.2	5.1	4.7	4.0	4.0	4.6	5.4	6.5	5.1	4.5	4.4	5.1	5.7	5.9	6.0	5.9	7.3	8.0	7.7	7.3	8.0	8.0	8.0	8.0	8.0	8.0	8.0	8.0	8.0	8.0	8.0	8.0	8.0	8.0	8.0	8.0	6.4	1,520,114	7.6	6.6	4.9	84.2%
1936	4.8	3.8	4.1	4.1	3.9	3.6	3.6	3.9	4.3	5.4	4.1	3.9	3.8	4.2	4.7	5.0	5.4	4.9	6.7	7.5	7.5	6.8	8.0	8.0	8.0	8.0	8.0	8.0	8.0	8.0	8.0	8.0	8.0	8.0	8.0	8.0	8.0	8.0	6.7	6.9	1,776,994	6.5	6.2	4.2	90.7%
1937	3.6	3.7	3.7	3.6	3.3	3.3	3.6	3.8	4.7	3.8	3.7	3.6	3.8	4.2	4.3	4.6	4.5	6.1	6.7	6.8	6.4	7.2	7.4	7.5	8.0	7.7	8.0	8.0	8.0	8.0	8.0	8.0	8.0	8.0	8.0	8.0	6.4	4.9	5.8	6.2	1,576,587	5.8	5.8	3.7	91.5%
1938	4.8	4.7	4.3	3.8	3.8	4.3	4.8	6.0	4.5	4.1	4.0	4.4	4.8	5.1	5.4	5.2	6.9	7.3	7.2	6.9	8.0	7.9	8.0	8.0	8.0	8.0	8.0	8.0	8.0	8.0	8.0	8.0	8.0	8.0	8.0	8.0	6.4	7.8	8.0	7.0	1,951,234	7	6.5	4.5	89.7%
1939	4.1	3.9	3.6	3.6	3.9	4.4	5.7	4.3	4.0	3.9	4.2	4.6	4.8	5.2	4.9	6.5	7.2	6.9	6.5	7.5	7.8	7.6	8.0	8.0	8.0	8.0	8.0	8.0	8.0	8.0	8.0	8.0	8.0	8.0	7.2	5.7	6.1	7.8	6.7	6.0	1,743,546	6.9	6.3	4.1	87.2%
1940	3.9	3.6	3.6	3.9	4.3	5.7	4.2	3.9	3.9	4.2	4.6	4.7	5.0	4.8	6.4	6.9	6.9	6.3	7.2	7.5	7.6	8.0	7.8	8.0	8.0	8.0	8.0	8.0	8.0	8.0	8.0	8.0	8.0	7.3	5.1	6.2	6.7	6.9	6.2	5.8	1,958,017	6.9	6.2	4.1	86.8%
1941	3.7	3.7	4.1	4.6	5.7	4.3	3.9	3.9	4.2	4.6	4.7	5.0	4.7	6.4	7.0	6.9	6.6	7.3	7.5	7.7	8.0	8.0	8.0	8.0	8.0	8.0	8.0	8.0	8.0	8.0	8.0	8.0	8.0	6.3	6.5	7.4	6.5	6.9	6.6	6.5	2,518,640	6.9	6.4	4.3	90.2%
1942	4.2	5.0	5.8	6.7	5.4	4.7	4.5	5.2	5.7	5.7	5.9	5.7	6.9	7.5	7.3	6.9	7.9	7.8	8.0	8.0	8.0	8.0	8.0	8.0	8.0	8.0	8.0	8.0	8.0	8.0	8.0	8.0	7.4	7.5	7.8	7.5	6.7	7.5	7.4	6.2	2,324,210	7.4	7.0	5.3	92.9%
1943	4.8	5.5	6.3	5.0	4.3	4.3	4.7	5.3	5.5	5.6	5.4	6.8	7.3	7.3	6.8	7.8	8.0	8.0	8.0	8.0	8.0	8.0	8.0	8.0	8.0	8.0	8.0	8.0	8.0	8.0	8.0	6.9	8.0	8.0	7.4	7.3	6.9	8.0	7.0	7.1	2,672,809	7.5	7.0	5.1	91.7%
1944	4.5	5.6	4.2	3.9	3.8	4.1	4.4	4.6	4.9	4.6	6.2	6.7	6.5	6.2	6.9	7.1	7.3	7.7	7.4	7.9	8.0	8.0	8.0	8.0	8.0	8.0	8.0	8.0	8.0	7.0	6.0	6.2	7.3	6.5	5.9	6.1	6.1	6.2	6.4	6.6	2,430,531	6.8	6.4	4.5	92.3%
1945	5.0	3.9	3.7	3.7	3.8	4.1	4.2	4.5	4.3	5.9	6.3	6.2	5.8	6.7	6.7	6.9	7.5	7.0	7.4	7.9	8.0	7.6	8.0	8.0	7.5	7.7	8.0	8.0	6.8	5.2	6.1	6.4	6.4	5.8	5.5	6.1	5.0	6.5	6.8	6.1	2,213,264	6.6	6.2	4.3	91.0%
1946	3.7	3.6	3.5	3.6	3.7	3.8	3.9	3.8	5.1	5.9	5.8	5.1	6.2	6.4	6.5	7.0	6.8	7.0	7.4	7.9	7.6	7.9	8.0	7.4	7.2	7.6	7.8	6.3	4.8	5.3	6.4	5.7	5.8	5.6	5.8	5.2	5.6	7.1	6.4	6.8	2,623,991	6	5.9	4.1	94.8%
1947	3.8	3.8	4.0	4.4	4.5	4.7	4.5	6.2	6.7	6.5	6.1	6.9	7.0	7.2	7.7	7.5	7.9	8.0	8.0	8.0	8.0	8.0	8.0	8.0	8.0	8.0	7.4	5.9	6.5	6.9	6.7	6.1	6.6	6.6	5.8	6.5	6.9	7.6	8.0	8.0	2,799,509	6.9	6.7	4.9	94.6%
1948	4.0	4.4	4.6	4.7	4.9	4.7	6.1	6.6	6.4	6.0	6.6	6.7	6.8	7.4	7.0	7.4	7.9	8.0	7.6	8.0	8.0	7.5	7.6	8.0	7.9	6.8	5.5	5.9	6.6	6.0	6.0	5.8	6.6	5.8	6.1	7.0	6.5	8.0	8.0	7.2	2,285,473	6.8	6.6	5.2	95.2%
1949	4.5	4.8	4.8	5.1	4.8	6.2	6.6	6.4	6.1	6.6	6.7	6.8	7.3	7.1	7.3	7.7	8.0	7.5	8.0	8.0	7.6	7.4	7.8	8.0	6.7	5.4	6.1	6.5	6.2	5.7	6.0	6.1	6.0	6.4	6.8	6.8	7.4	8.0	7.8	7.8	2,592,998	6.9	6.7	5.6	95.7%
1950	4.4	4.4	4.6	4.4	5.9	6.3	6.1	5.8	6.5	6.5	6.5	7.0	6.7	7.1	7.4	7.7	7.4	7.8	8.0	7.2	7.3	7.4	7.7	6.6	4.9	5.8	6.5	5.9	5.7	5.5	6.2	5.2	6.5	7.0	6.5	7.8	7.9	8.0	8.0	8.0	3,123,515	6.7	6.6	5.5	96.6%
1951	4.2	4.3	4.1	5.6	6.1	6.0	5.4	6.2	6.3	6.3	6.8	6.5	6.8	7.1	7.4	7.0	7.7	7.7	6.8	7.0	7.4	7.3	6.3	4.8	5.4	6.3	5.9	5.3	5.5	5.8	5.4	5.9	7.1	6.7	7.3	8.0	7.1	8.0	8.0	7.2	2,488,088	6.6	6.4	5.5	95.8%
1952	4.2	4.1	5.5	6.1	6.0	5.5	6.3	6.4	6.5	6.8	6.6	6.8	7.1	7.4	7.0	7.5	7.9	6.8	6.9	7.3	7.6	6.4	5.1	5.8	6.2	5.9	5.7	5.3	5.8	4.9	6.0	6.5	6.9	7.6	7.8	7.5	7.5	8.0	7.6	8.0	3,012,247	6.7	6.5	5.7	96.2%
1953	4.0	5.1	5.8	5.7	5.0	6.0	6.0	6.0	6.5	6.2	6.4	6.7	7.0	6.6	7.1	7.3	6.6	6.4	6.7	7.0	6.1	4.4	5.1	6.0	5.3	5.1	5.3	5.6	5.0	5.6	6.5	6.2	7.7	7.8	7.0	7.6	8.0	7.8	8.0	8.0	3,121,282	6.4	6.3	5.6	97.3%
1954	5.5	6.0	5.8	5.2	6.1	6.2	6.1	6.6	6.4	6.6	6.9	7.1	6.7	7.3	7.4	6.6	6.9	7.0	7.1	6.3	5.2	5.5	6.2	5.9	5.2	5.2	5.7	4.8	5.9	6.3	6.5	7.1	8.0	7.4	7.5	8.0	7.1	8.0	8.0	8.0	3,588,188	6.7	6.5	6.1	96.7%
1955	4.5	4.3	3.9	4.7	4.9	4.8	5.6	5.1	5.7	5.9	6.2	5.8	6.3	6.6	5.8	5.9	6.2	6.2	5.0	4.1	4.5	5.1	4.7	4.5	4.3	4.7	4.3	4.9	6.0	5.6	6.8	7.0	7.0	7.2	7.6	6.8	7.6	8.0	8.0	7.8	2,936,611	5.7	5.7	4.9	98.9%
1956	4.0	3.7	4.3	4.5	4.4	5.1	4.6	5.1	5.6	5.9	5.3	6.0	6.2	5.4	5.4	5.8	6.0	4.6	3.8	4.2	4.9	4.3	4.2	4.3	4.4	4.1	4.8	5.6	5.6	6.3	7.0	6.3	7.3	7.7	6.4	7.8	7.7	8.0	8.0	8.0	3,643,253	5.5	5.6	4.7	98.4%
1957	3.8	4.4	4.5	4.5	5.1	4.7	5.1	5.6	5.9	5.3	6.0	6.2	5.1	5.1	5.5	5.8	4.5	3.7	3.9	4.5	4.3	4.0	4.2	4.7	4.1	4.8	5.8	5.4	6.5	6.8	6.6	6.7	8.0	6.7	7.5	8.0	8.0	8.0	8.0	8.0	3,879,825	5.5	5.6	4.9	99.5%
1958	5.1	5.3	5.2	5.9	5.5	5.9	6.1	6.4	6.0	6.3	6.5	5.7	5.7	6.0	6.1	4.9	4.0	4.2	4.9	4.6	4.5	4.4	4.8	4.4	5.0	6.1	6.1	6.8	7.5	6.8	7.4	7.9	7.5	8.0	8.0	8.0	8.0	8.0	8.0	8.0	5,266,782	6.1	6.1	5.8	98.7%
1959	4.2	4.1	4.6	4.3	4.6	5.0	5.4	4.8	5.7	5.8	4.6	4.6	4.9	5.2	4.1	3.6	3.8	4.1	3.9	3.9	4.0	4.2	4.0	4.5	5.2	5.3	6.4	6.7	6.4	6.5	7.4	6.4	8.0	8.0	8.0	7.7	8.0	8.0	8.0	8.0	5,321,611	5.3	5.5	4.9	100.8%
1960	4.1	4.5	4.1	4.5	4.8	5.2	4.5	5.4	5.8	4.6	4.6	4.8	5.0	4.1	3.6	3.8	4.2	3.9	3.8	3.9	4.1	3.8	4.3	5.2	4.9	6.1	6.7	6.1	6.5	6.9	6.4	7.2	8.0	8.0	7.3	8.0	8.0	8.0	8.0	8.0	5,562,074	5.2	5.5	4.8	101.9%
1961	4.6	4.2	4.5	4.9	5.2	4.7	5.3	5.7	4.6	4.5	4.8	4.9	4.0	3.6	3.7	4.1	3.9	3.8	3.8	4.0	3.9	4.2	5.0	5.0	6.0	6.6	6.3	6.4	7.1	6.2	7.5	7.5	8.0	7.6	8.0	8.0	8.0	8.0	8.0	8.0	5,476,586	5.3	5.6	4.8	101.4%
1962	3.9	4.1	4.3	4.6	4.1	4.8	5.1	4.3	4.2	4.4	4.5	3.8	3.6	3.7	3.8	3.7	3.7	3.7	3.8	3.7	4.0	4.4	4.5	5.8	6.0	5.8	6.2	6.5	6.0	6.7	7.2	7.3	7.4	8.0	8.0	8.0	8.0	8.0	8.0	8.0	4,464,183	5	5.4	4.4	102.2%
1963	4.4	4.7	5.0	4.5	5.1	5.5	4.4	4.3	4.6	4.7	3.9	3.6	3.7	3.9	3.7	3.7	3.8	3.9	3.7	4.1	4.8	4.6	5.9	6.4	5.9	6.3	6.9	6.0	7.1	7.1	7.8	7.0	8.0	8.0	8.0	8.0	8.0	8.0	8.0	8.0	4,099,123	5.2	5.6	4.7	103.1%
1964	4.3	4.7	4.2	4.8	5.1	4.2	4.2	4.4	4.5	3.8	3.6	3.6	3.8	3.7	3.6	3.7	3.7	3.6	3.8	4.3	4.4	5.2	6.0	5.6	5.9	6.5	6.0	6.7	7.1	7.2	7.0	8.0	8.0	8.0	8.0	8.0	8.0	8.0	8.0	8.0	4,380,836	5	5.5	4.4	104.3%
1965	4.3	3.9	4.5	4.8	4.0	4.0	4.1	4.2	3.7	3.3	3.6	3.7	3.6	3.6	3.6	3.7	3.6	3.7	4.0	4.0	5.0	5.4	5.0	5.8	6.1	5.6	6.6	6.7	7.1	6.4	7.9	8.0	8.0	8.0	8.0	8.0	8.0	8.0	8.0	8.0	4,326,751	4.8	5.4	4.1	104.5%
1966	3.8	4.2	4.4	3.9	3.8	3.9	4.0	3.6	2.9	3.3	3.6	3.6	3.4	3.5	3.6	3.5	3.6	3.8	3.8	4.4	5.0	4.5	5.0	5.9	4.8	6.1	6.5	6.6	6.3	7.2	7.9	8.0	8.0	8.0	8.0	8.0	7.6	8.0	8.0	8.0	4,028,890	4.5	5.3	3.8	89.6%
1967	4.7	4.9	4.1	4.1	4.2	4.3	3.8	3.6	3.6	3.7	3.6	3.6	3.6	3.7	3.6	3.7	4.0	4.0	4.7	5.5	5.2	5.4	6.2	5.6	6.4	6.7	7.2	6.5	7.8	7.9	8.0	8.0	8.0	8.0	8.0	8.0	8.0	8.0	8.0	8.0	4,751,687	5	5.6	4.1	105.7%
1968	4.3	3.8	3.7	3.8	3.8	3.6	2.6	3.1	3.6	3.3	3.1	3.3	3.6	3.3	3.6	3.7	3.7	4.1	4.4	4.3	4.7	5.3	4.6	5.9	6.0	6.5	6.1	7.0	7.5	8.0	8.0	8.0	8.0	8.0	7.4	8.0	8.0	8.0	8.0	8.0	3,660,419	4.3	5.3	3.6	82.2%
1969	3.7	3.7	3.7	3.8	3.5	2.6	3.0	3.5	3.2	3.0	3.1	3.4	3.0	3.5	3.6	3.6	3.9	4.1	3.9	4.3	5.0	4.1	5.3	5.8	6.0	5.7	6.8	6.9	8.0	8.0	8.0	8.0	8.0	7.3	7.9	8.0	7.8	8.0	8.0	5.0	1,860,084	4.2	5.2	3.4	59.0%
1970	4.0	4.2	4.3	3.7	3.2	3.6	3.7	3.6	3.6	3.6	3.7	3.6	3.7	4.0	4.0	4.9	5.7	5.0	5.5	6.2	5.8	6.5	6.9	7.3	6.7	8.0	8.0	8.0	8.0	8.0	8.0	8.0	8.0	8.0	8.0	8.0	8.0	8.0	8.0	8.0	3,545,429	5.1	5.9	3.8	105.8%
1971	4.3	4.4	3.8	3.6	3.6	3.7	3.6	3.6	3.6	3.6	3.6	3.7	3.9	4.0	4.6	5.3	5.0	5.3	6.0	5.5	6.6	6.6	7.1	6.7	7.7	8.0	8.0	8.0	8.0	8.0	8.0	8.0	8.0	8.0	8.0	8.0	8.0	8.0	8.0	8.0	4,037,942	5.3	6.0	3.8	105.5%
																																										Avg	6.1	4.7	93.8%

FIGURE 69

ECM withdrawals for 40-year retirement starting at 65 with a 4.8% initial withdrawal rate using SBBI data and an 8% income cap.

Year	Y1	Y2	Y3	Y4	Y5	Y6	Y7	Y8	Y9	Y10	Y11	Y12	Y13	Y14	Y15	Y16	Y17	Y18	Y19	Y20	Y21	Y22	Y23	Y24	Y25	Y26	Y27	Y28	Y29	Y30	Y31	Y32	Y33	Y34	Y35	Y36	Y37	Y38	Y39	Y40	Remaining	MSWR	Avg	1st 10Y	HREFF-3
1928	5.8	5.0	4.4	4.5	4.6	4.6	4.6	5.4	6.2	4.7	5.2	5.2	4.8	4.6	4.6	4.8	5.1	6.2	4.8	4.9	4.8	5.1	5.3	5.4	5.8	5.7	8.0	8.0	8.0	8.0	8.0	8.0	8.0	8.0	8.0	8.0	8.0	8.0	8.0	8.0	2,115,019	6.4	6.1	5.0	93.1%
1929	4.6	4.5	4.2	4.3	4.5	4.5	4.6	5.0	4.5	4.6	4.6	4.5	4.2	4.2	4.4	4.6	5.2	4.7	4.5	4.5	4.7	5.0	5.2	5.3	5.3	6.3	7.7	7.2	6.9	8.0	8.0	8.0	8.0	8.0	8.0	8.0	8.0	8.0	8.0	8.0	1,883,871	5.4	5.8	4.5	104.3%
1930	4.6	4.4	4.4	4.6	4.6	4.9	5.9	4.7	4.8	4.7	4.7	4.5	4.5	4.7	4.8	6.1	4.7	4.8	4.7	5.0	5.1	5.5	5.9	5.4	7.7	8.0	8.0	7.3	8.0	8.0	8.0	8.0	8.0	8.0	8.0	8.0	8.0	8.0	8.0	8.0	1,858,172	6.2	6.1	4.8	96.2%
1931	4.5	4.5	4.9	4.8	6.0	7.0	5.2	5.9	5.8	5.3	4.7	4.7	5.1	5.6	6.6	5.1	4.9	4.8	4.8	5.4	5.4	5.8	5.6	7.5	8.0	8.0	7.9	8.0	8.0	8.0	8.0	8.0	8.0	8.0	8.0	8.0	8.0	8.0	8.0	8.0	2,213,263	7.2	6.4	5.4	87.7%
1932	5.1	7.0	6.8	8.0	8.0	7.2	7.9	7.8	7.3	6.0	5.8	6.6	7.2	8.0	6.4	5.6	5.4	5.9	6.4	6.6	6.6	6.4	8.0	8.0	8.0	8.0	8.0	8.0	8.0	8.0	8.0	8.0	8.0	8.0	8.0	8.0	8.0	8.0	8.0	8.0	3,312,888	8.9	7.3	7.1	81.5%
1933	6.7	6.5	7.8	8.0	6.9	7.6	7.5	6.9	5.7	5.6	6.3	6.9	7.9	6.1	5.4	5.1	5.7	6.1	6.2	6.4	6.0	8.0	8.0	8.0	8.0	8.0	8.0	8.0	8.0	8.0	8.0	8.0	8.0	8.0	8.0	8.0	8.0	8.0	8.0	8.0	3,466,087	8.7	7.2	6.9	82.5%
1934	4.7	5.8	6.8	5.1	5.7	5.6	5.1	4.6	4.6	4.9	5.5	6.8	5.2	4.6	4.8	4.9	5.3	5.4	5.6	5.4	7.0	7.9	7.8	6.8	8.0	8.0	8.0	8.0	8.0	8.0	8.0	8.0	8.0	8.0	8.0	8.0	8.0	8.0	8.0	8.0	2,104,412	7.5	6.6	5.3	86.3%
1935	5.9	6.9	5.2	5.8	5.7	5.2	4.7	4.7	4.9	5.6	6.8	5.2	4.6	4.8	4.9	5.3	5.4	5.5	5.3	7.0	7.6	7.4	6.9	7.9	8.0	8.0	8.0	8.0	8.0	8.0	8.0	8.0	8.0	8.0	8.0	8.0	8.0	8.0	8.0	8.0	1,368,138	7.6	6.7	5.5	86.4%
1936	5.7	4.6	4.7	4.6	4.6	4.4	4.4	4.6	4.5	5.6	4.7	4.6	4.5	4.7	4.8	4.6	4.8	4.9	6.2	7.1	6.7	6.1	7.6	7.6	8.0	8.0	8.0	8.0	8.0	8.0	8.0	8.0	8.0	8.0	8.0	8.0	8.0	8.0	8.0	8.0	1,492,534	6.5	6.4	4.8	95.3%
1937	4.4	4.6	4.5	4.4	4.1	4.1	4.3	4.5	4.9	4.5	4.4	4.3	4.5	4.7	4.7	4.8	4.7	5.4	6.1	6.0	5.2	6.4	6.8	6.5	7.7	6.8	7.9	8.0	8.0	8.0	8.0	8.0	8.0	8.0	8.0	8.0	8.0	5.9	6.4	8.0	1,149,274	5.8	6.0	4.4	101.1%
1938	5.6	5.5	5.0	4.6	4.6	4.8	5.3	6.3	4.8	4.7	4.6	4.8	4.9	5.0	5.2	4.9	6.5	7.1	6.9	6.3	7.3	7.6	7.7	8.0	8.0	8.0	8.0	8.0	8.0	8.0	8.0	8.0	8.0	8.0	8.0	8.0	8.0	8.0	8.0	8.0	1,712,569	7	6.7	5.1	93.1%
1939	4.7	4.6	4.4	4.4	4.6	4.8	6.1	4.6	4.6	4.6	4.7	4.7	4.8	5.0	4.7	6.3	6.9	6.6	6.0	7.1	7.1	7.1	8.0	7.4	8.0	8.0	8.0	8.0	8.0	8.0	8.0	8.0	8.0	8.0	8.0	6.1	8.0	8.0	7.7	8.0	1,206,646	6.9	6.5	4.7	91.9%
1940	4.4	4.4	4.4	4.6	4.9	6.1	4.7	4.6	4.6	4.7	4.7	4.8	5.0	4.8	6.2	6.8	6.6	5.9	6.9	7.1	6.9	7.8	7.4	7.7	8.0	8.0	8.0	8.0	8.0	8.0	8.0	8.0	8.0	8.0	6.2	6.6	8.0	8.0	6.5	8.0	1,233,860	6.9	6.5	4.7	91.9%
1941	4.5	4.5	4.7	5.2	6.2	4.8	4.6	4.6	4.7	4.9	4.9	5.1	4.8	6.4	7.0	6.8	6.1	7.1	7.3	7.4	7.9	7.5	8.0	8.0	8.0	8.0	8.0	8.0	8.0	8.0	8.0	8.0	7.8	7.4	7.6	7.9	8.0	7.7	6.8	8.0	1,581,015	6.9	6.7	4.9	95.3%
1942	4.9	5.9	6.5	7.7	5.9	5.2	5.0	5.5	5.9	5.9	6.0	5.7	7.3	7.9	7.5	6.8	7.9	7.8	7.9	8.0	8.0	8.0	8.0	8.0	8.0	8.0	8.0	8.0	8.0	8.0	8.0	8.0	6.9	8.0	8.0	8.0	8.0	8.0	8.0	8.0	1,598,816	7.4	7.3	5.8	97.1%
1943	5.7	6.2	7.3	5.6	4.9	4.7	5.2	5.6	5.7	5.8	5.5	7.2	7.9	7.6	6.8	7.9	8.0	8.0	8.0	8.0	8.0	8.0	8.0	8.0	8.0	8.0	8.0	8.0	8.0	8.0	8.0	7.2	7.4	8.0	8.0	7.7	8.0	8.0	7.8	8.0	1,913,182	7.5	7.2	5.7	95.6%
1944	5.3	6.3	4.9	4.6	4.6	4.5	4.9	5.0	5.2	4.9	6.4	7.0	6.7	6.1	7.0	7.1	7.1	7.6	7.2	7.6	7.8	8.0	7.7	8.0	8.0	7.3	7.7	7.8	8.0	6.8	6.4	6.6	7.0	7.7	6.7	6.3	8.0	6.6	6.4	8.0	1,523,698	6.8	6.7	5.0	96.8%
1945	5.8	4.5	4.6	4.5	4.6	4.5	4.6	4.8	4.6	6.1	6.6	6.4	5.7	6.7	6.7	6.8	7.3	6.7	7.2	7.6	7.9	7.3	8.0	8.0	7.2	7.0	7.8	7.6	6.9	5.7	6.8	7.1	6.3	7.0	6.5	6.5	7.2	7.0	6.9	8.0	1,338,081	6.6	6.5	4.9	96.7%
1946	4.5	4.3	4.3	4.4	4.5	4.6	4.6	4.5	5.3	6.0	5.8	5.1	6.3	6.4	6.3	6.9	6.4	6.7	7.2	7.6	6.7	7.5	8.0	6.4	6.6	6.7	7.3	6.0	5.5	5.7	7.0	6.2	5.7	6.7	6.7	5.6	7.7	7.6	6.2	8.0	1,594,694	6	6.1	4.7	100.8%
1947	4.6	4.6	4.5	5.0	5.1	5.3	5.0	6.6	7.3	7.0	6.2	7.3	7.4	7.4	7.9	7.5	7.8	8.0	8.0	7.8	8.0	8.0	7.5	7.3	7.9	7.8	6.4	5.5	6.4	6.7	7.1	6.5	6.3	7.9	6.6	6.8	8.0	8.0	8.0	8.0	1,908,953	6.9	6.9	5.5	98.4%
1948	4.6	5.1	5.4	5.4	5.6	5.3	6.6	7.2	6.8	6.2	7.0	7.0	7.0	7.7	7.0	7.4	7.8	8.0	7.3	8.0	8.0	6.8	6.9	7.0	7.5	5.6	5.4	5.6	6.6	6.0	6.5	6.3	6.4	6.9	7.1	7.4	8.0	8.0	8.0	8.0	1,548,541	6.8	6.8	5.8	98.5%
1949	5.3	5.6	5.6	5.7	5.4	6.8	7.3	6.9	6.3	7.2	7.1	7.1	7.7	7.2	7.4	7.8	8.0	7.3	8.0	8.0	6.7	6.7	7.2	7.2	5.8	5.2	5.7	6.0	6.2	5.8	6.6	6.7	5.9	7.6	7.9	7.1	8.0	8.0	8.0	8.0	1,833,731	6.9	6.9	6.2	98.5%
1950	5.2	5.2	5.4	5.1	6.5	7.0	6.7	6.0	6.9	6.9	6.8	7.4	6.9	7.3	7.5	7.8	7.1	7.7	7.9	6.6	6.4	6.8	7.1	5.4	5.1	5.3	6.0	5.6	5.9	5.7	6.8	6.0	6.3	8.0	7.5	8.0	8.0	8.0	8.0	8.0	2,244,447	6.7	6.7	6.1	99.0%
1951	4.9	5.1	4.8	6.2	6.7	6.4	5.8	6.7	6.7	6.6	7.2	6.7	7.0	7.3	7.6	6.9	7.5	7.6	6.3	6.3	6.5	6.7	5.3	4.9	5.3	5.6	5.6	5.4	5.8	5.9	6.1	6.4	6.8	7.9	8.0	8.0	8.0	8.0	8.0	8.0	1,670,886	6.6	6.6	6.0	98.5%
1952	5.0	4.7	6.2	6.9	6.6	5.9	6.9	6.9	6.9	7.4	6.9	7.2	7.5	7.7	7.0	7.5	7.8	6.4	6.4	6.7	6.7	5.4	5.1	5.2	5.7	5.4	5.5	5.4	6.0	5.4	6.6	7.0	6.5	8.0	8.0	7.9	8.0	8.0	8.0	8.0	2,193,585	6.7	6.7	6.3	98.4%
1953	4.6	6.0	6.5	6.2	5.6	6.4	6.5	6.4	7.0	6.5	6.7	7.0	7.3	6.7	7.2	7.4	6.1	5.9	6.2	6.4	4.9	4.8	5.1	5.3	5.3	5.1	5.3	5.5	5.5	5.7	7.1	6.7	7.3	8.0	8.0	8.0	8.0	8.0	8.0	8.0	2,349,971	6.4	6.5	6.2	99.8%
1954	6.3	6.8	6.5	5.9	6.7	6.7	6.6	7.3	6.7	7.1	7.3	7.6	6.9	7.5	7.6	6.4	6.4	6.5	6.6	5.4	4.9	5.1	5.2	5.2	5.3	5.1	5.5	5.1	5.9	6.3	7.0	7.7	7.8	8.0	8.0	8.0	8.0	8.0	8.0	8.0	2,673,682	6.7	6.7	6.7	98.6%
1955	5.3	5.1	4.4	5.4	5.5	5.3	6.0	5.5	5.8	6.1	6.4	5.8	6.4	6.6	5.5	5.4	5.6	5.6	4.9	4.6	4.7	5.0	4.9	4.7	4.8	4.9	4.8	5.0	5.7	5.5	6.9	7.0	6.2	7.9	8.0	6.2	8.0	8.0	8.0	8.0	1,645,571	5.7	5.9	5.4	101.8%
1956	4.7	4.6	5.0	5.1	5.0	5.6	5.1	5.5	5.8	6.1	5.4	6.1	6.3	5.2	5.1	5.3	5.4	4.8	4.5	4.6	4.8	4.7	4.6	4.6	4.8	4.5	4.9	5.2	5.4	5.8	6.9	6.2	6.3	8.0	6.4	7.1	8.0	8.0	7.3	8.0	1,986,985	5.5	5.7	5.3	101.5%
1957	4.6	5.2	5.3	5.1	5.7	5.2	5.6	5.8	6.1	5.5	6.1	6.3	5.1	5.0	5.2	5.3	4.8	4.3	4.5	4.7	4.6	4.5	4.6	4.7	4.6	4.8	5.3	5.1	6.1	6.3	6.6	6.8	7.1	7.3	8.0	7.9	8.0	8.0	8.0	8.0	2,636,197	5.5	5.8	5.4	103.5%
1958	6.0	6.1	6.0	6.5	6.0	6.3	6.6	6.9	6.2	6.7	6.8	5.6	5.6	5.8	5.8	4.6	4.5	4.7	4.9	4.8	4.6	4.7	4.9	4.6	5.0	5.3	5.5	6.0	6.9	6.4	7.6	8.0	6.7	8.0	8.0	8.0	8.0	8.0	8.0	8.0	4,382,982	6.1	6.2	6.3	100.3%
1959	4.9	4.8	5.4	4.9	5.3	5.5	5.8	5.2	5.8	6.0	4.9	4.7	4.9	5.0	4.6	4.2	4.4	4.6	4.4	4.3	4.3	4.5	4.4	4.5	5.0	4.8	5.5	5.6	5.7	5.9	7.2	6.0	6.7	8.0	8.0	7.2	8.0	8.0	8.0	8.0	3,604,203	5.3	5.6	5.4	103.9%
1960	4.7	5.3	4.8	5.1	5.4	5.6	5.0	5.7	5.9	4.9	4.8	4.9	5.0	4.7	4.2	4.4	4.6	4.4	4.3	4.3	4.4	4.2	4.5	4.7	4.7	5.1	5.5	5.2	5.8	6.1	6.0	6.8	6.7	8.0	7.4	8.0	8.0	8.0	8.0	8.0	4,044,981	5.2	5.6	5.2	105.0%
1961	5.4	4.9	5.2	5.6	5.8	5.2	5.7	5.9	4.9	4.8	4.9	5.0	4.6	4.2	4.4	4.5	4.4	4.3	4.3	4.4	4.2	4.4	4.8	4.6	5.1	5.3	5.3	5.4	6.3	5.4	7.0	6.9	7.0	7.8	8.0	8.0	8.0	8.0	8.0	8.0	3,404,292	5.3	5.6	5.3	104.2%
1962	4.4	4.7	5.0	5.3	4.7	5.4	5.6	4.6	4.5	4.7	4.7	4.5	4.1	4.3	4.4	4.3	4.2	4.2	4.3	4.1	4.3	4.5	4.5	4.8	5.1	4.8	5.2	5.5	5.3	5.8	6.8	6.8	6.2	8.0	8.0	8.0	8.0	8.0	8.0	8.0	2,890,285	5	5.4	4.9	106.0%
1963	5.2	5.5	5.8	5.2	5.8	5.9	4.8	4.7	4.8	4.9	4.6	4.1	4.3	4.5	4.3	4.2	4.3	4.4	4.2	4.4	4.6	4.6	5.0	5.1	5.1	5.2	5.9	5.3	6.4	6.5	7.8	6.9	7.9	8.0	8.0	8.0	8.0	8.0	8.0	8.0	2,920,143	5.2	5.7	5.3	107.0%
1964	5.1	5.5	4.9	5.5	5.7	4.6	4.4	4.6	4.7	4.5	4.0	4.2	4.4	4.3	4.1	4.2	4.3	4.1	4.3	4.5	4.4	4.8	5.0	4.8	5.1	5.3	5.1	5.6	6.3	6.4	6.9	7.8	7.9	8.0	8.0	8.0	8.0	8.0	8.0	8.0	3,125,959	5	5.6	5.0	108.4%
1965	5.1	4.5	5.2	5.5	4.5	4.7	4.5	4.5	4.5	4.0	4.2	4.4	4.2	4.1	4.1	4.2	4.0	4.1	4.3	4.3	4.5	4.7	4.6	4.7	5.1	4.7	5.4	5.4	6.1	5.6	7.4	7.5	8.0	8.0	8.0	8.0	8.0	8.0	8.0	8.0	3,064,486	4.8	5.5	4.7	110.2%
1966	4.6	4.9	5.1	4.6	4.6	4.6	4.6	4.3	3.8	4.0	4.2	4.0	3.9	3.9	4.0	3.7	3.9	4.1	4.0	4.3	4.4	4.2	4.4	4.6	4.2	4.6	4.9	4.9	5.0	5.5	6.5	7.2	7.4	8.0	8.0	7.2	6.7	7.5	6.8	8.0	1,398,306	4.5	5.1	4.5	109.9%
1967	5.5	5.7	4.7	4.6	4.8	4.8	4.5	4.2	4.3	4.4	4.3	4.2	4.2	4.2	4.0	4.2	4.4	4.3	4.6	4.8	4.6	4.8	5.1	4.7	5.3	5.4	5.9	5.5	7.0	7.1	8.0	8.0	8.0	8.0	8.0	8.0	8.0	8.0	8.0	8.0	3,782,042	5	5.7	4.8	109.6%
1968	5.0	4.6	4.5	4.6	4.6	4.2	3.6	3.9	4.1	3.9	3.8	3.8	3.9	3.6	3.8	4.0	3.9	4.1	4.2	4.1	4.2	4.4	4.0	4.3	4.5	4.6	4.5	5.0	5.5	6.1	7.3	7.6	6.5	7.3	5.2	5.9	7.8	6.4	5.9	7.3	1,135,003	4.3	4.9	4.3	109.8%
1969	4.6	4.5	4.5	4.6	4.2	3.7	3.9	4.1	3.9	3.7	3.7	3.8	3.5	3.7	3.9	3.8	4.1	4.1	3.9	4.1	4.2	3.8	4.2	4.3	4.4	4.2	4.8	4.9	5.9	6.0	7.3	6.2	5.6	4.9	5.6	5.4	6.3	5.9	4.4	4.4	493,027	4.2	4.6	4.2	105.0%
1970	4.7	4.9	5.0	4.5	4.1	4.3	4.4	4.3	4.2	4.2	4.3	4.2	4.3	4.5	4.4	4.7	4.8	4.7	4.8	5.1	4.8	5.2	5.2	5.5	5.6	6.3	7.1	8.0	8.0	8.0	8.0	8.0	8.0	8.0	8.0	8.0	8.0	8.0	8.0	8.0	2,506,213	5.1	5.9	4.5	111.1%
1971	5.0	5.2	4.6	4.3	4.4	4.5	4.4	4.3	4.3	4.3	4.2	4.3	4.5	4.5	4.7	4.8	4.7	4.8	5.0	4.8	5.1	5.1	5.6	5.4	6.4	6.6	8.0	8.0	8.0	8.0	8.0	8.0	8.0	8.0	8.0	8.0	8.0	8.0	8.0	8.0	2,672,515	5.3	5.9	4.5	108.7%
																																										Avg	6.2	5.3	99.3%

FIGURE 70

Delta-Prime withdrawals for 40-year retirement starting at 65 with a 4.8% initial withdrawal rate using SBBI data and an 8% income cap.

Although Delta-Prime is a consistent top-performer for long retirements up to 50 years, it's not foolproof using the historical data. For a 40-year UK retirement starting in 1937 with a MSWR of 3.3%, Delta-Prime ended up with a very low portfolio value for the last 3 years and virtually ran out of money in the last year. For a 50-year retirement starting the same year in the UK with a MSWR of 3.1%, the result was much worse, running out of money five years before the end of retirement. Neither EM nor ECM came close to running out of money in either case for the same period. The Delta-Prime numbers are often exceptionally strong, but they may come with some price in resiliency. A tougher look at the top strategies is needed.

Pushing Harder on the Top Three Strategies

The focus stays on the three top performers: EM, ECM, and Delta-Prime. The aim is to expose these strategies to significantly different performance characteristics, including some abnormally poor returns, based on the historical data. Keep in mind that these results are not based on a well-diversified portfolio, so volatility and down markets are sometimes substantially worse than that a retiree should expect to encounter.

To do this well, the following conditions are tested. The Baseline Market definition is pulled from a future chapter to represent the global market with all returns scaled down so the total-market real return equals 5%. The retirement length is again 40 years. Plus, the historical data is wrapped (i.e., used in a circular fashion with 1928 data following 2010 data as illustrated at the start of Chapter 10) to increase the number of 40-year backtesting periods. Multiple portfolios based on non-diversified individual asset classes (e.g., small value, large growth) are backtested. These non-diversified highly volatile markets are difficult for variable-withdrawal strategies. Also, no cap is set on annual income, which in these cases would have helped. Most significantly, only the three worst retirement periods out of a total of 73 are included in the HREFF average. The result is a much harsher set of test characteristics and measurements, designed to stress the top three strategies.

Figure 71 summarizes the findings. Delta-Prime is no longer consistently the top performer. Certainly, these tests are difficult ones, but generally still in a range we'd hope to see handled by a variable-withdrawal strategy.

	MSWR-100%	EM HREFF	ECM HREFF	Delta-Prime HREFF
Small Growth	2.3%	46%	40%	4%
Large Value	2.7%	21%	31%	12%
Micro-Cap	2.9%	88%	89%	67%
Large Growth	3.0%	75%	89%	35%
Large	3.1%	57%	78%	39%
Total Market	3.1%	81%	92%	66%
Low-Cap	3.8%	91%	89%	94%
Mid-Cap	3.9%	91%	90%	94%
Small	4.0%	94%	88%	93%
Small Value	5.0%	91%	86%	91%

FIGURE 71

HREFF for three worst retirement periods for undiversified portfolios (of individual asset classes) using global-market baseline. The minimum rate is 2.

To make the impact clearer, Figure 72, Figure 73, and Figure 74 show the full results for a portfolio of Large Growth Stocks using EM, ECM, and Delta-Prime respectively (with everything else equal). Note that MSWR is *below* 3.5% in thirteen retirement periods and drops as low as 3% in 1966 and 1968, certainly an abnormally tough case. What's startling is that EM and ECM never run out of money, but Delta-Prime runs out 6 times.

Year	Remaining	MSWR	Avg	HREFF-2
1928	298,900	5.1	5.7	106.8%
1929	251,400	4.2	4.8	109.8%
1930	245,500	4.8	5.4	107.1%
1931	204,000	5.2	5.6	103.0%
1932	253,500	6	6.2	100.7%
1933	274,000	6.1	6.2	97.7%
1934	154,800	5.4	5.5	98.2%
1935	82,900	5.2	5.4	96.6%
1936	91,500	4.5	4.8	95.8%
1937	88,500	4.1	4.5	99.0%
1938	72,600	5	5.3	92.7%
1939	50,400	4.5	4.7	91.4%
1940	36,900	4.3	4.5	88.1%
1941	43,100	4.6	4.8	87.4%
1942	35,100	5.1	5.2	85.5%
1943	46,200	5.1	5.1	81.6%
1944	17,800	5	4.8	75.2%
1945	26,400	4.6	4.7	80.7%
1946	25,700	4.3	4.3	75.5%
1947	54,000	5	5.0	79.3%
1948	67,400	4.8	4.7	75.7%
1949	78,600	5.3	5.2	81.1%
1950	97,100	5	4.8	76.6%
1951	93,800	4.8	4.7	84.0%
1952	123,500	4.8	4.7	85.7%
1953	117,300	4.6	4.4	85.0%
1954	114,900	4.6	4.4	88.7%
1955	93,900	3.9	3.7	83.8%
1956	112,400	3.6	3.4	79.4%
1957	128,800	3.8	3.6	84.0%
1958	169,100	4	3.9	89.2%
1959	203,500	3.6	3.4	81.9%
1960	226,500	3.4	3.3	78.5%
1961	204,100	3.6	3.6	80.7%
1962	141,500	3.2	3.3	87.3%
1963	114,000	3.4	3.5	87.2%
1964	130,400	3.3	3.4	89.2%
1965	112,700	3.1	3.2	78.6%
1966	112,400	3	3.2	84.2%
1967	136,300	3.3	3.6	92.6%
1968	121,100	3	3.3	84.2%
1969	93,700	3.1	3.5	88.9%
1970	135,700	3.5	4.1	108.9%
1971	155,800	3.7	4.4	109.8%
1972	202,700	3.3	3.9	105.5%
1973	145,600	3.2	3.8	104.6%
1974	130,200	4	4.8	112.2%
1975	109,300	5.5	6.0	102.6%
1976	100,300	5.1	5.7	102.7%
1977	119,800	4.9	5.3	100.3%
1978	128,300	5.6	6.1	101.2%
1979	179,800	6.1	6.4	99.5%
1980	287,900	6.6	6.9	99.7%
1981	166,300	6.6	6.8	98.8%
1982	263,000	7.5	7.6	98.3%
1983	255,500	6.9	6.8	95.9%
1984	202,700	6.9	6.9	96.5%
1985	144,100	7	6.9	95.3%
1986	130,200	6.4	6.2	93.3%
1987	142,100	6.2	6.0	93.2%
1988	149,300	6.4	6.1	91.8%
1989	184,200	6.3	6.0	92.9%
1990	121,300	5.7	5.4	92.4%
1991	114,100	6.1	5.7	89.7%
1992	97,500	5.1	4.8	89.7%
1993	116,900	5.2	4.8	89.0%
1994	128,600	5.2	4.8	89.8%
1995	156,800	5.6	5.2	89.0%
1996	146,100	4.8	4.5	87.1%
1997	136,500	4.7	4.2	86.8%
1998	161,300	4.1	3.7	87.4%
1999	146,200	3.4	3.1	81.9%
2000	93,400	3	2.8	75.2%
Avg		4.8		91.4%

FIGURE 72

EM Strategy for large growth stocks using global-market baseline.

The table below lists, for each starting year, the annual withdrawal values (Y1–Y40) together with the Remaining balance, MSWR, Avg, and HREFF-2 summary columns.

Year	Remaining	MSWR	Avg	HREFF-2
1928	501,100	5.1	5.4	101.7%
1929	416,900	4.2	4.7	106.6%
1930	413,600	4.8	5.2	104.2%
1931	315,300	5.2	5.3	99.0%
1932	371,300	6	6.0	97.2%
1933	401,400	6.1	5.9	95.0%
1934	237,500	5.4	5.3	94.8%
1935	128,400	5.2	5.1	95.7%
1936	130,000	4.5	4.6	99.5%
1937	129,900	4.1	4.4	103.0%
1938	123,500	5.1	5.1	95.6%
1939	86,000	4.5	4.5	96.4%
1940	65,800	4.3	4.4	96.6%
1941	103,500	4.6	4.6	95.5%
1942	90,800	5.1	5.0	93.9%
1943	96,500	5.1	4.9	92.7%
1944	80,500	5	4.6	87.6%
1945	79,700	4.6	4.6	93.9%
1946	77,400	4.3	4.3	93.5%
1947	133,300	5	4.9	94.1%
1948	135,000	5.3	5.1	93.4%
1949	133,700	5.3	5.1	93.2%
1950	143,300	5	4.8	93.3%
1951	132,900	4.8	4.7	94.6%
1952	179,900	4.8	4.7	94.9%
1953	167,500	4.6	4.4	94.0%
1954	151,600	4.6	4.5	94.4%
1955	108,200	3.9	3.8	92.3%
1956	121,700	3.6	3.5	90.4%
1957	147,000	3.8	3.6	91.8%
1958	216,900	4	3.8	93.3%
1959	241,700	3.6	3.4	91.4%
1960	269,000	3.4	3.3	92.2%
1961	270,800	3.6	3.6	95.1%
1962	163,500	3.2	3.2	95.0%
1963	143,700	3.4	3.5	98.2%
1964	155,700	3.3	3.4	96.5%
1965	120,600	3.1	3.1	92.2%
1966	125,000	3	3.1	94.9%
1967	206,900	3.3	3.6	101.2%
1968	137,300	3	3.2	97.1%
1969	122,600	3.1	3.4	101.2%
1970	209,900	3.5	4.1	111.3%
1971	233,200	3.7	4.3	109.8%
1972	271,600	3.3	3.8	107.7%
1973	192,000	3.2	3.7	106.8%
1974	222,700	4	4.7	113.0%
1975	184,300	5.5	6.0	104.9%
1976	158,800	5.1	5.6	105.6%
1977	202,900	4.9	5.3	103.4%
1978	341,000	5.6	6.2	106.5%
1979	470,400	6.1	6.6	105.8%
1980	595,300	6.6	7.2	106.2%
1981	378,900	6.6	7.1	105.3%
1982	574,100	7.5	8.0	105.2%
1983	490,000	6.9	7.2	102.8%
1984	426,800	6.9	7.2	103.5%
1985	319,800	7	7.3	102.6%
1986	265,500	6.4	6.5	100.3%
1987	304,800	6.2	6.4	101.0%
1988	319,300	6.4	6.4	99.0%
1989	373,900	6.3	6.4	100.4%
1990	242,800	5.7	5.7	99.4%
1991	233,800	6.1	6.0	97.6%
1992	181,700	5.1	5.0	97.3%
1993	224,200	5.2	5.0	95.8%
1994	241,800	5.2	5.1	96.6%
1995	282,500	5.6	5.5	96.6%
1996	261,300	4.9	4.7	94.3%
1997	241,400	4.7	4.5	93.6%
1998	288,400	4.1	3.9	93.5%
1999	202,400	3.4	3.2	93.3%
2000	98,900	3	2.9	87.7%
Avg			4.9	98.1%

FIGURE 73

ECM Strategy for large growth stocks using global-market baseline.

Year	Y1-Y40 (40 annual withdrawal-rate columns)	Remaining	MSWR	Avg	HREFF-2
1928	(grid values)	261,200	5.1	5.9	108.8%
1929		176,700	4.2	4.7	108.3%
1930		205,500	4.8	5.5	109.4%
1931		185,400	5.2	5.8	107.9%
1932		210,400	6	6.4	104.2%
1933		217,200	6.1	6.3	101.5%
1934		132,000	5.4	5.5	100.8%
1935		74,600	5.2	5.5	103.8%
1936		49,000	4.5	4.7	102.7%
1937		51,000	4.1	4.3	104.0%
1938		73,200	5.1	5.2	100.0%
1939		41,800	4.5	4.7	101.2%
1940		31,600	4.3	4.5	102.3%
1941		55,700	4.6	4.7	100.0%
1942		46,000	5.1	5.1	98.1%
1943		39,000	5.1	5.1	97.6%
1944		48,200	5	4.9	97.0%
1945		34,100	4.6	4.6	98.9%
1946		23,300	4.3	4.3	98.6%
1947		75,900	5	4.9	97.1%
1948		66,500	5.3	5.2	96.6%
1949		67,500	5.3	5.2	96.1%
1950		68,600	5	4.9	96.0%
1951		75,600	4.8	4.7	96.5%
1952		95,100	4.8	4.7	95.6%
1953		98,000	4.6	4.5	95.5%
1954		56,100	4.6	4.5	94.4%
1955		28,400	3.9	3.8	93.3%
1956		0	3.6	3.5	63.9%
1957		28,600	3.8	3.6	89.5%
1958		87,300	4	3.9	92.7%
1959		79,800	3.6	3.4	87.1%
1960		79,300	3.4	3.3	81.3%
1961		105,300	3.6	3.5	89.9%
1962		37,600	3.2	3.1	76.0%
1963		41,500	3.4	3.4	91.4%
1964		28,500	3.3	3.2	82.8%
1965		11,500	3.1	3.0	70.5%
1966		12,000	3	2.9	74.9%
1967		11,500	3.3	3.2	89.6%
1968		0	3	3	60.8%
1969		0	3.1	3.0	1.4%
1970		36,900	3.5	3.6	101.0%
1971		34,900	3.7	3.7	98.9%
1972		0	3.3	3.1	61.3%
1973		0	3.2	2.9	41.0%
1974		66,500	4	4.2	103.7%
1975		97,300	5.1	5.5	106.0%
1976		78,400	5.1	5.5	106.1%
1977		80,600	4.9	5.2	103.6%
1978		172,700	5.6	6.1	104.0%
1979		233,200	6.1	6.5	104.0%
1980		307,200	6.6	7.3	108.0%
1981		200,800	6.6	7.2	107.7%
1982		251,200	7.5	8.1	106.2%
1983		231,400	6.9	7.3	103.7%
1984		213,000	6.9	7.4	105.9%
1985		155,100	7	7.4	104.4%
1986		143,200	6.4	6.6	102.5%
1987		155,800	6.2	6.4	102.0%
1988		173,600	6.4	6.5	100.3%
1989		194,400	6.3	6.5	101.6%
1990		145,600	5.7	5.9	103.2%
1991		136,300	6.1	6.2	100.1%
1992		118,900	5.1	5.3	102.1%
1993		149,900	5.2	5.3	100.9%
1994		162,400	5.2	5.3	101.0%
1995		188,200	5.6	5.7	101.0%
1996		175,600	4.9	5.0	100.3%
1997		159,300	4.7	4.7	99.7%
1998		153,900	4.1	4.1	98.1%
1999		1,800	3.4	3.2	75.7%
2000		0	3	2.6	6.%
			Avg	4.9	94.3%

FIGURE 74

Delta-Prime Strategy for large growth stocks using global-market baseline.

Recommendations with Concluding Thoughts

Delta-Prime is the top performer in most tests. However, its performance under abnormally poor market conditions is worrisome. Digging deeper into the data shows Delta-Prime does its best when MSWR values are above 3.5%; it's less reliable as sustainable rates drop under 3.5% and approach the 3% range. Most worrisome is that Delta-Prime runs out of money significantly more often than EM or ECM when times are extremely tough.

A big advantage for any variable-withdrawal strategy is properly handling unexpectedly poor markets (i.e., speculative risk). Such poor markets are rare, but virtually every retiree appreciates knowing their withdrawal strategy can compensate during such markets. This one criterion makes it difficult to recommend Delta-Prime.

Also significant when looking at a variety of asset allocations, Delta-Prime's sensitivity to the initial withdrawal rate varies more than EM's and ECM's. Delta-Prime is usually successful managing an initial rate well above the sustainable level (i.e., MSWR-100%), but occasionally it can only handle a rate slightly above the sustainable level. Delta-Prime doesn't show this weakness with the SBBI data, implying some of this sensitivity may reflect a data-mining bias (Delta-Prime was originally tuned using the default portfolio with SBBI data). Even with a substantial amount of testing with multiple datasets (out of sample testing), the possibility of some amount of data-mining bias remains and can be difficult to discern, especially with variable-withdrawal strategies. More testing with additional data can eventually show if a bias exists, but either way, EM and ECM outperform Delta-Prime in abnormally severe markets.

Considering all the results, EM is recommended as the best overall strategy for balancing income with risk[*]. ECM is recommended as the safest overall strategy for those willing to sacrifice some income for extra safety. No other strategy handles poor markets nearly as well as EM and ECM when backtesting MSWR rates between 2.5% to 3.5%. Also important, EM and ECM are top performers during typical markets, coming in only behind Delta-Prime. In addition, EM and ECM are based on a much simpler model than Delta-Prime, which is generally a good characteristic for avoiding a data-mining bias. Finality, EM and ECM are derived from Blanchett et al.'s work, which includes independent Monte Carlo testing.

The one possible downside of both EM and ECM is they are sometimes too conservative early in retirement, occasionally specifying a low withdrawal rate when the market will soon recover and can support much more. On the other hand, this is only clear from hindsight: this same behavior protects retirees from abnormally harsh markets. Still, Chapter 10 shows that EM and ECM adapt well to a variety of income floors, effectively providing retirees a range of choices (with corresponding speculative-risk tradeoffs) [†].

Without a high income floor, what then should a retiree do when the annual income is too low using a variable-withdrawal strategy such as EM or ECM? In a real retirement, the answer becomes obvious: a retiree will and should go ahead and withdraw what they must have to cover essential expenses. Yes, this will increase risk, but it's a small increase (as long as reasonable amounts are involved). Investing during retirement done correctly deals with minimizing many small risks (i.e., big risks are stayed away from); therefore, no retirement decision should be only a step away from failure. The point is, when a strategy isn't fully adhered to, a retiree is usually only exposed to one more small risk. With a little luck, all will be fine. Retirement strategies should have substantial leeway and a

---

[*] Some readers may be questioning why a significant portion of this chapter was dedicated to a new strategy, Delta-Prime, when it ultimately isn't recommended. There is still value in analysis even when it doesn't result in a recommendation. The process makes clear that test results under limited conditions are truly tentative. The process also indirectly makes clear that selected tests can slant the results one direction or another—without the tests that pushed harder on the top three strategies, Delta-Prime would clearly be the strategy to recommend. These facts also reflect the importance of maintaining the proper mindset of evidence-based research, which implies, no investigator should grow too fond of their own creations.

[†] To be fair, other strategies given the same options for configurability will also perform better; however, EM and ECM are exceptional in their adaptability.

built-in margin for error. Occasionally overdrawing by a relatively small amount in a variable-withdrawal strategy is not a problem, so take what is needed. However, this flexibility doesn't negate the fact that consistent and significant income shortages over a span of years (e.g., 5 years) signal major portfolio stress that must be dealt with as well as possible, downsizing if needed to reduce essential income needs.

As mentioned earlier, another pragmatic option using EM is to set the income floor (which defaults to 2.25%) to match the retiree's essential-income rate (a topic covered in the last chapter). Based on market history, this compromise will serve the retiree well. Figure 75 shows an example by raising EM's income floor to 4% (note 4% is extremely high for an essential-income rate, but it fully illustrates EM's capability for a higher floor). EM readily handles this as well or better than Delta-Prime, but understand a higher income floor brings back the small but real risk (depending on the floor value) the floor will exceed the sustainable rate, causing a failure. Still, this illustrates EM functions well with a range of income floors.

Year	Y1	Y2	Y3	Y4	Y5	Y6	Y7	Y8	Y9	Y10	Y11	Y12	Y13	Y14	Y15	Y16	Y17	Y18	Y19	Y20	Y21	Y22	Y23	Y24	Y25	Y26	Y27	Y28	Y29	Y30	Remaining	MSWR	Avg	HREFF-3
1928	6	5	4.4	4	4.3	5.2	5.2	6.7	8.3	5.7	7.4	6.9	6.1	4.6	4.6	6.4	8.1	9.7	7.7	5.8	5.7	6.8	8.6	8.5	8.3	7.9	11	13	12	8	626,156	6.7	7.0	101.1%
1929	4.1	4	4	4	4	4	4.8	6.1	4.3	5.1	5.2	4.5	4	4	4.7	6.3	9.3	6.1	5.5	4.8	6.6	7.7	8.5	8.3	6.9	11	11	12	8.5	11	847,579	5.6	6.3	106.4%
1930	4.1	4	4	4.3	4.4	5.8	7.8	4.7	6	6	5.5	4.2	4.4	6	7.4	9.7	7.6	5.8	5.9	7.1	8.7	8.6	9.3	8	11	13	11	11	13	12	958,139	6.4	7.3	107.7%
1931	4	4	5	5	7.4	8.8	6.1	7.4	7.5	6.6	5	4.9	7.1	8.2	9.5	7.5	6.5	5.6	7.5	8.2	8.8	8.7	8.4	11	12	12	9.3	14	13	10	921,818	7.6	8.0	100.7%
1932	5	8	7.9	9.4	11	8.6	9.7	9.4	8.9	7.5	7.6	8.5	9.6	11	8.5	7.7	7.6	8.1	9.5	9.3	9.9	8.6	13	14	12	11	13	15	12	13	1,277,870	9.5	9.8	101.0%
1933	7.6	7.5	8.9	10	8.1	9.1	9.1	8.3	6.6	6.8	8.4	8.9	11	8.4	7	6.8	8.1	8.6	9.3	9.1	8.7	12	14	12	9.7	13	12	13	13	10	1,118,578	9.3	9.5	100.4%
1934	4.6	6.3	8	5.2	6.6	6.7	5.9	4.4	4.6	6.1	7.8	9.4	7.4	6.1	5.4	7.3	8.3	8.1	8.8	7.8	11	12	12	9.4	11	12	10	13	9.9	9.8	1,095,790	7.9	8.2	99.5%
1935	6.3	7.9	5.2	6.4	6.5	5.8	4.5	4.5	5.9	7.6	9.5	6.9	5.8	5.6	6.7	7.9	8.3	8.2	8.1	11	12	11	9.9	12	11	11	12	11	11	10	1,136,330	8.1	8.3	98.5%
1936	5.9	4.2	4.7	4.7	4.4	4	4	4.4	5.5	7.9	5.5	4.5	4.5	5.5	6.6	7.4	8.1	7.1	11	11	11	9.2	12	12	10	12	9.7	12	11	11	1,222,380	6.9	7.7	105.0%
1937	4	4	4	4	4	4	4	4.2	6.5	4.5	4.2	4	4.7	5.9	5.9	7	6.6	9.2	11	9.9	8.8	10	11	9.7	11	9.4	9.7	12	12	8.4	926,205	6.1	7.1	108.0%
1938	5.8	5.7	5.1	4.1	4.2	5.4	6.6	8	5.7	5	4.9	5.6	7.1	7.5	7.5	7.3	10	11	11	9.1	12	11	11	12	9.6	11	11	13	9.8	11	1,221,826	7.9	8.3	99.8%
1939	4.6	4.3	4	4	4.4	5.5	8	5.2	4.6	4.6	5.7	6.5	7	7.6	6.5	9.5	11	10	9.3	11	11	10	12	9.8	10	11	11	11	12	11	1,307,388	7.5	8.1	101.5%
1940	4.3	4	4	4.3	5.4	7.8	5.3	4.5	4.4	5.4	6.6	6.5	7.3	6.8	9	10	10	8.6	11	11	10	11	10	11	11	12	9.3	13	12	7.9	1,004,474	7.7	8.1	99.5%
1941	4	4	4.7	5.6	7.7	5.2	4.6	4.4	5.2	6.3	7	7	6.6	9.5	10	10	9.2	11	11	11	12	10	11	11	11	9.7	11	13	8.8	6.5	918,348	8	8.3	98.4%
1942	4.7	6.4	7.6	9.1	7	5.8	5.6	6.6	7.6	7.7	8.2	7.6	10	11	10	9.4	12	11	11	12	11	11	12	12	9.8	12	12	10	8	7.4	907,510	9.4	9.2	95.4%
1943	5.9	7.1	8.4	6	5.2	5	6.1	6.9	7.4	7.7	7.5	9.7	11	11	9.1	11	12	11	13	11	12	12	13	11	11	13	8.9	8.9	8.1	7.4	867,056	9.3	9.2	96.2%
1944	5.3	7.3	4.8	4.3	4.2	4.9	5.7	5.8	6.5	6.1	9	9.6	9.5	8.6	9.8	10	10	11	10	11	12	12	11	12	11	9.2	7.7	8.8	8.1	4.1	620,499	8.4	8.3	94.3%
1945	6.1	4.4	4	4	4.3	5	5.4	5.6	5.4	8.4	9.5	8.9	8.1	9.7	9.5	9.5	11	9.5	11	11	12	9.7	12	12	8.5	8.2	7.7	8.9	4.5	4	376,557	7.9	7.9	94.8%
1946	4	4	4	4	4	4.3	4.6	4.3	7.4	8.5	8.5	7.2	9.1	9.4	8.9	10	9.6	9.7	11	11	9.9	11	12	8.5	7.1	7.8	7.4	4.8	4	4	438,746	6.9	7.3	99.3%
1947	4.2	4.1	4.5	5.3	5.7	6.2	5.8	8.4	9.5	9.4	8.6	9.9	10	10	11	10	11	11	12	10	12	12	9.8	8.5	8.2	8.7	4.6	4	4	4	577,315	8.2	8.1	93.5%
1948	4.5	5.2	5.7	5.8	6.4	6.1	8.5	9	8.8	8.1	9.6	9.4	9.4	11	9.3	10	11	11	10	11	12	8.7	8.5	8.2	7.9	4.8	4	4	4	4	448,431	7.9	7.9	94.8%
1949	5.3	5.9	6	6.4	6.1	8.4	9.2	8.6	8	9.4	9.6	9.2	10	9.7	9.8	11	12	9.8	12	11	9.2	8.1	8.8	8.5	4.6	4	4	4.5	4	4	445,829	7.9	7.9	95.1%
1950	5.1	5.3	5.6	5.3	7.9	8.7	8.4	7.5	8.8	9	9.1	9.8	9.2	9.9	10	11	10	11	12	8.7	8.5	8.3	8.9	4.9	4	4	4	4.1	4	4	525,322	7.6	7.5	94.1%
1951	4.8	5.1	4.8	7.4	8.2	8	7.3	8.3	8.5	8.5	9.7	8.7	9.4	10	10	9.3	11	11	8.9	8	8.6	8.3	5.3	4	4	4.3	4	4	4	4	592,459	7.4	7.2	92.8%
1952	4.9	4.6	7.4	8.1	8	7.2	8.6	8.6	8.7	9.6	9.2	9.3	10	11	9.2	10	11	8.6	8.7	8.5	8.9	5.4	4	4.2	4.8	4.5	4	4.6	4.5	4	711,520	7.6	7.3	91.9%
1953	4.4	6.6	7.6	7.3	6.3	8	8.1	7.8	8.8	8.3	9	9.1	9.8	8.9	9.6	10	8.5	7.7	8.4	8.2	5.3	4	4.1	4.7	4	4	4	4.5	4	4	731,995	7.2	6.8	90.5%
1954	7	7.8	7.5	6.5	8.1	8.2	8.2	8.8	8.4	9	9.6	9.8	9	10	10	8.6	8.7	8.5	9	6	4.1	4.5	6.2	4.7	4.2	4.6	4.6	4.6	4.7	4.8	1,041,739	7.5	7.2	92.5%
1955	5.3	5.1	4.4	5.9	6.3	6.2	7.7	6.5	7.5	8.1	8.8	7.7	8.8	9.2	7.4	7.4	7.9	7.6	5.3	4	4.2	4.7	4.5	4.1	4	4.5	4	4.6	4.8	4.1	923,592	6.4	6.0	90.7%
1956	4.5	4.1	5.2	5.4	5.4	7	6	6.7	7.6	8.2	7.5	8.2	8.7	7.3	6.5	7.3	7.7	4.7	4	4	4.9	4.2	4.2	4.1	4.2	4	4.1	5.6	4.5	4.9	1,134,780	6	5.7	91.6%
1957	4.1	5.2	5.5	5.4	6.8	6	7	7.4	8	7.3	8.4	8.4	6.7	6.4	6.5	7.3	4.7	4	4	4.5	4.3	4	4.3	4.4	4	4.3	4.6	5	5.5	5.2	1,163,700	6	5.6	91.2%
1958	6.4	6.8	6.7	7.7	7.2	7.7	8.3	8.4	7.8	8.7	9.3	7.4	7.4	7.7	7.6	5.2	4	4.2	5.6	4.6	4.5	4.5	5.5	4.3	4.6	6	4.9	7.7	7.2	4.8	1,112,260	6.6	6.4	94.7%
1959	4.8	4.7	5.7	5	5.9	6.7	7.5	6	7.6	8	6.2	5.5	6.2	6.8	4.3	4	4	4.4	4.3	4	4.2	4.4	4.2	4.4	4.8	4.8	5.6	7.6	5.1	4.9	1,157,080	5.6	5.4	93.9%
1960	4.6	5.4	4.8	5.3	6.2	6.9	5.8	7.2	7.7	5.9	5.9	6.1	6.6	4.6	4	4	4.7	4.1	4.2	4.1	4.8	4.1	4.9	5.4	4.7	6.6	6.4	6.4	5.9	5.8	1,340,757	5.6	5.4	95.2%
1961	5.4	4.9	5.4	6.1	6.9	5.9	7.3	7.5	5.6	5.6	6.3	6.2	4.5	4	4	4.5	4.3	4	4.3	4.6	4.2	4.6	6.1	5.1	6.1	7.4	5.3	7.4	7.1	4.2	1,099,547	5.6	5.5	96.0%
1962	4.2	4.6	5.1	5.7	4.9	6.4	7.2	5	5	5.6	6.1	4.2	4	4	4.2	4	4	4	4.6	4	4.6	5.2	5.3	6.4	6.4	5.7	5.7	8	4.7	5.5	1,381,550	5.2	5.1	96.8%
1963	5.1	5.7	6.4	5.4	6.8	7.4	5.3	5	5.6	6	4.4	4	4	4.4	4	4	4.2	4.5	4.3	4.6	6.1	5.2	7.6	7.5	5.5	6.9	7.2	5.7	6.9	5.9	1,462,518	5.5	5.5	98.1%
1964	5.1	5.7	4.9	6	6.7	4.9	4.8	5	5.5	4.1	4	4	4.2	4	4	4	4.5	4	4.6	5.3	5.3	6.5	7.8	5.9	6	7.7	4.7	7.8	7	6.1	1,496,712	5.2	5.3	100.0%
1965	5	4.4	5.4	5.9	4.6	4.6	5	5	4	4	4	4	4	4	4	4.1	4	4.2	5.3	4.7	6.7	6.8	6.2	6.3	6.8	5	6.3	7.9	7.2	5	1,355,460	5	5.1	100.2%
1966	4.2	4.8	5.3	4.2	4.2	4.5	4.7	4	4	4	4	4	4	4	4	4	4	4.2	4.3	5.1	6.2	4.8	6	6.5	4.3	6.3	5.8	7.6	5.3	6.4	1,570,256	4.7	4.8	100.0%
1967	5.6	6.1	4.7	4.6	5	5.3	4.2	4	4	4.1	4	4	4	4.1	4	4.2	5.2	4.7	6.9	7.2	6.3	6.6	8.2	5.3	6.9	7.7	7.4	7.4	8	7.6	1,728,878	5.2	5.6	103.7%
1968	4.9	4.1	4	4.1	4.3	4	4	4	4	4	4	4	4	4	4	4	4	4.3	5.1	4.3	5	5.5	4.5	5.5	5.4	6.4	4.9	8	7.6	8	1,795,758	4.5	4.8	103.1%
1969	4	4	4	4.1	4	4	4	4	4	4	4	4	4	4	4	4	4.1	4.2	4.1	4.3	5.2	4	5.3	5.2	5.1	4.9	6.1	8	8.4	8	1,743,650	4.4	4.7	102.8%
1970	4.5	4.8	5	4	4	4	4	4	4	4	4.2	4	4.3	5.3	4.9	7	8	6.7	7.8	8.2	6.9	8.1	8.9	8.7	7.4	9.4	9.2	12	12	11	2,404,396	5.3	6.6	115.8%
1971	4.9	5.2	4.1	4	4	4.1	4	4	4	4	4	4.1	5	5	6.4	7.6	7.1	7.3	8.5	6.3	8.6	8.4	9.2	7.8	9	9.9	11	13	12	9.1	1,897,741	5.5	6.7	114.3%
1972	4.8	4	4	4	4	4	4	4	4	4	4.1	4.6	4.6	6.2	6.8	6.1	7.5	7.9	6.9	8.1	8.7	8.6	8.2	9.4	9.3	12	11	14	10	8.3	1,691,319	5.3	6.8	119.0%
1973	4	4	4	4	4	4	4	4	4	4	4.3	4.2	5.3	6.3	5.1	6.2	7.7	5.3	8	7.9	8.6	7.4	9.6	9.4	10	11	11	11	8.7	4.7	1,150,928	5.2	6.4	115.2%
1974	4	4	4.6	4.2	4.1	4.3	4.6	4.1	5	6	6.4	7.7	8.5	8	8.1	9.1	8.1	9.2	10	9.9	9.3	11	11	12	12	13	11	11	6.7	7.9	1,477,171	6.8	7.8	108.3%
1975	5.7	7.3	6.2	5.5	5.5	6.1	5.5	6.9	7.8	7.9	9.5	10	9.4	9.9	10	9.5	11	11	12	10	13	12	15	14	14	13	11	10	11	9.8	1,690,324	8.7	9.7	107.6%
1976	5.6	5	4.6	4.6	5	4.6	5.9	6.8	7.1	8.6	9.5	8.6	9	9.9	8.6	10	11	11	10	12	13	13	15	14	12	12	9	12	11	8.8	1,493,362	7.9	9.2	111.3%
1977	4.2	4.1	4.1	4.3	4.1	4.9	5.9	5.7	7.7	8.5	8.1	8.1	9	8.1	9.1	9.7	11	9.1	12	11	13	13	14	12	10	8.2	9.3	11	9.1	8.6	1,394,856	7.3	8.5	111.0%
1978	4.4	4.4	4.7	4.3	5.3	6.5	6.7	8	8.8	8.4	8.8	9.3	8.5	10	9.9	11	10	11	12	13	14	13	13	12	9.1	11	10	11	10	8	1,284,666	8	9.2	110.0%
1979	4.6	4.9	4.5	5.5	6.7	7	8.4	8.9	8.5	8.9	9.9	8.6	10	11	11	9.9	12	12	14	14	14	13	13	10	11	11	9.7	12	9.2	4	699,089	8.5	9.5	106.9%
1980	4.8	4.4	5.4	6.3	6.6	8.1	8.9	8.1	8.6	9.4	8.8	9.8	10	11	9.5	12	12	13	14	14	13	12	10	11	11	10	10	10	4.4	5	787,795	8.6	9.4	104.7%
1981	4.3	5.2	6.1	6.2	8	8.8	8.2	8.3	9.2	8.5	10	10	11	9.8	11	12	14	14	15	13	13	11	13	12	10	11	9.2	5.1	6	6	798,772	8.9	9.6	103.3%
																																Avg	7.30	100.7%

FIGURE 75

EM with income floor set to 4%.

To reduce risk further, not fully depending on EM to produce the essential-income rate, guaranteed income can be used. ECM is an outstanding choice when combined with guaranteed income because its conservative orientation supports a firmer income floor (which defaults to 2.5%) during adverse markets (again, more on this in the last chapter).

EM and ECM also work well if a retiree must unexpectedly withdraw additional funds to handle unforeseen expenses. There is little difference between pulling out an extra $20,000 to cover an unexpected expense versus the market dropping the portfolio value an additional $20,000 — variable-withdrawal strategies handle both cases. Fortunately, market history shows that extra income is often available when circumstances dictate it must be taken. Still, withdrawing no more than needed always provides the largest buffer against speculative risk.

More EM and ECM examples, emulating a global portfolio under a global market, are provided in Chapter 10, Putting It All Together. The final chapter also explores performance under a failure market, combined with guaranteed income.

As a final note, up until this point it has been assumed Prime Harvesting (i.e., the recommended income-harvesting strategy) is the best strategy to underlie a variable-withdrawal strategy. Although the results are not shown, this assumption was confirmed by comparing results using five different underlying income-harvesting strategies: Prime Harvesting, Alternate-Prime Harvesting, the Parker Strategy, Traditional Annual Rebalancing, and the 100-Age strategy. As expected, Prime Harvesting produced the highest HREFF values during the poorest retirement periods.

An EM Example

An example clarifies EM's use, although the available spreadsheet will do the calculations. The steps from the earlier EM definition are referenced.

For this example assume a retiree has a starting portfolio value of $500,000, an initial withdrawal rate of 5%, and is planning a 40-year retirement. The first withdrawal at the start of retirement is calculated by the initial withdrawal rate: $500,000 * 5% = $25,000.

At the end of the first year, there are 39 years left in the planned retirement. Assume the portfolio value is now $520,000 and the previous year's inflation rate is 3% (used to calculate **inflation-adjusted withdrawal amount**).

1. For EM:
   a. Set *scale rate* to 95%.
   b. Set *floor rate* to 2.25%.
   c. Set *cap rate* to 150% of the initial withdrawal rate (e.g., 6% for 4% initial rate).

2. Look up the *withdrawal rate percentage* based on the estimated years left in retirement in the Extended MUFP Table (see Figure 58).

   Since there are 39 years left in retirement, the *withdrawal rate percentage* is 5.4%.

3. Calculate the initial *current withdrawal amount*:

   Current withdrawal amount = withdrawal rate percentage * portfolio value = 5.4% * $520,000 = $28,080

4. Calculate the *scale boundary:*

    scale boundary = 75% * **inflation-adjusted withdrawal amount**

    since the **inflation-adjusted withdrawal amount** is ($25,000 + ($25,000 * 3%)) = $25,750

    scale boundary = 75% * $25,750 = $19,312

5. If the *current withdrawal amount* is greater than the *scale boundary,* then scale it down.

    $28,080 is greater than $19,312, so scale it down:

    a. *scale diff = current withdrawal amount – scale boundary = $28,080 - $19,312 = $8,768*
    b. *scale ratio = scale diff / scale boundary = $8,768 / $19,312 = 0.4540*
    c. *If scale ratio is greater than 1 then set it to 1.*

       0.4540 is not greater than 1, so left unchanged

    d. *current withdrawal amount = scale boundary + (scale diff * scale ratio * scale rate)*

       current withdrawal amount = $19,312 + ($8,767 * 0.4540 * 95%) = $23,093

6. If a cap is defined and the current withdrawal amount is too big, then cap it:
    a. *Set the cap amount = (cap rate / initial withdrawal rate)* * **inflation-adjusted withdrawal amount**

       cap amount = (7.5% / 5%) * $25,750 = $38,626

    b. If the *current withdrawal amount* > cap amount, then set it to the *cap amount.*

       $23,093 is not greater than $38,626, so no cap is set.

7. If the *current withdrawal amount* is too small, then set it to the floor value:
    a. *floor value = (floor rate / initial withdrawal rate)* * **inflation-adjusted withdrawal amount**

       floor value = 2.25% / 5% * $25,750 = $11,587

    b. If *current withdrawal amount* < *floor value,* then set it to the *floor value.*

       $23,093 is not less than $11,587, so it's not reset.

8. Withdraw for the year the *current withdrawal amount,* which is $23,093.

This same pattern continues after each year of retirement, using new input values for the years left in retirement, the **inflation-adjusted withdrawal amount**, and the portfolio value.

The Point

Fixed withdrawals do not match real retirement needs given the variability of long-term markets. A variable-withdrawal strategy is safer and typically produces more income.

EM is the best overall variable-withdrawal strategy, balancing income and risk. ECM is the overall safest strategy, producing solid but less income. Both strategies perform well across different markets, asset allocations, and time periods.

If additional income, beyond what EM or ECM recommends, is needed, then it can be taken; occasional extra withdrawals of reasonable amounts will be compensated for with only a small increase in risk.

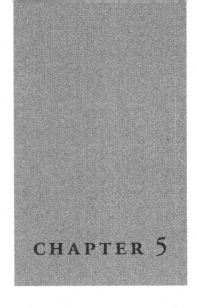

The efficient-market hypothesis greatly enhanced our understanding of equity markets and evolved our investment strategies. After that, the efficient-market hypothesis greatly stymied our understanding of the equity markets and put a drag on the evolution of investment strategies.

Walter E. Goh

CHAPTER 5

INTRODUCING THE HARVESTING RATIO — A RETIREMENT PORTFOLIO METRIC

VIRTUALLY EVERY INDIVIDUAL INVESTOR STRUGGLES with asset allocation at some time. Asset allocation determines exactly what assets make up your portfolio and in what proportion. However, the correct allocation for retirement is not obvious even after perusing the literature.

Figure 1 in Chapter 2 shows that asset allocation (or more specifically the three factors of asset allocation) determines three risk factors: portfolio returns, volatility of returns, and sequence of returns. Of these, only portfolio returns and volatility can be effectively controlled. The implication is, retirement asset allocation is primarily about affecting portfolio returns and volatility to minimize risk.

Modern Portfolio Theory (MPT) teaches us that the characteristics of the overall portfolio are what matters most, not the individual assets. Done right, the sum of the whole performs better than the sum of the individual parts: well-diversified assets complement and balance each other, lowering the overall volatility for a given amount of return. This same principle applies to retirement, but the specifics are different; as later shown, bringing the withdrawal rate into the picture pushes beyond the scope of MPT. For now, take it on faith that the proper balance between return and volatility is distinct for retirement.

It would be simpler if our brains could naturally intuit the right balance between portfolio return and portfolio volatility in retirement, but this is far from possible. What happens instead is our "gut feel" and comfort level are often at odds with what the numbers show. Even if it's well understood that a significant amount of volatility is required to produce enough return to sustain withdrawals, humans just aren't good enough with numbers to see the right balance. For example, which is safer for a 4.5% withdrawal rate: Portfolio One with an average return of 9.5% and a standard deviation of 10.1%, or Portfolio Two with an average return of 10.75% and a standard deviation of 12.4%? Who knows, right? This is too complex to mentally model.

This chapter defines a new retirement portfolio metric, the Harvesting Ratio, to gauge the best balance between a portfolio's return and volatility to minimize risk. Those portfolios with stronger Harvesting Ratios are more likely to succeed in retirement for a specified withdrawal rate. As will be shown, the benefits of taking this approach are substantial. The end result is, the Harvesting Ratio goes a long way in guiding retirees to correct asset allocations.

It will be shown that the Harvesting Ratio can indirectly estimate risk using less data than required for backtesting, homing in on what can be controlled without dealing with the noise in the data. Working off less data in this case enables guidance for portfolios of newer asset classes (e.g., REITs, international value stocks, emerging-market stocks) that don't have long-term data. The Harvesting Ratio brings another perspective to risk, distinct from backtesting.

The effectiveness of the Harvesting Ratio bypasses many of the debates surrounding asset allocation and portfolio construction. This is not to imply that at least some of these debates aren't of interest or shouldn't be considered, but straightforward pragmatic evidence-based guidance is what retirees currently need most to invest well.

Before defining the Harvesting Ratio, it makes sense to first examine why a new retirement metric is needed. After all, well-established portfolio metrics have been around for a long time.

RETURN, VOLATILITY, AND MODERN PORTFOLIO THEORY

At the core of Model Portfolio Theory is Harry Markowitz's Nobel-Prize winning mathematical work, Mean-Variance Optimization (MVO). MVO calculates an "optimal" set of portfolios, each with the highest return for a given level of volatility (or the lowest volatility for a given return). This optimal set is called the *efficient frontier*. Very few investors directly apply MVO to invest on the efficient frontier (due to pragmatic limitations), but many rely on MVO indirectly by adhering to portfolio guidance based on it.

How then does MVO relate to investing during retirement? Figure 76 shows the efficient frontier calculated for the 14 asset classes defined in the SBBI dataset. Also shown are the backtesting results for five portfolios along this efficient frontier (the specific allocations are unimportant here). What's important is that not all the portfolios on the frontier do well in retirement: the portfolios around the upper middle portion of the frontier appear to perform best, with the portfolios on the edges performing not as well, even poorly for some cases. The point is, MVO provides no direct guidance for retirement—retirement planning is beyond the scope of MVO.

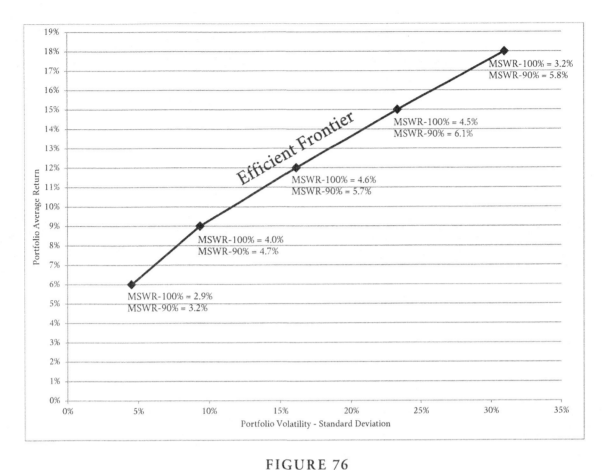

FIGURE 76

*Efficient Frontier for SBBI assets with 30-year retirement
backtesting results for 5 portfolios on the frontier.*

A look at the underlying ratio used by MVO provides insight into the extent of the problem. As its name implies, MVO optimizes (i.e. maximizes) portfolio return per unit of volatility, here represented as R/V, either for a specified level of return (R) or a specific level of volatility (V). How then does the R/V ratio correspond to retirement success? Backtesting a large set of portfolios with varying R/V values answers this question.

Figure 77 examines 5000 randomly generated portfolios (along the horizontal axis), showing for each portfolio the R/V ratio (on the right vertical axis) and the success rate (on the left vertical axis) for a 30-year retirement using a 5% withdrawal rate. The small individual dashes forming the solid line represent the R/V values for the 5000 portfolios, sorted by R/V to ascend, forming a solid line. The squared dots represent the backtesting success-rate values for each of the portfolios. This means there is one dash and one dot on the vertical axis for each of the 5000 portfolios along the horizontal axis, comparing R/V to success rate. The notable part is a surprising trend: as the R/V values ascend, supposedly improving, the corresponding retirement success rates descend. Portfolios with strong R/V values are shown as weak retirement portfolios; likewise portfolios with weak R/V values are shown as strong retirement portfolios. This is contrary to what might be expected, and counterintuitive on the surface.

What's clear is that maximum return per unit of volatility is not the characteristic we are looking for when seeking strong retirement portfolios. The problem is due to the highest R/V portfolios having insufficient returns for supporting most withdrawal rates. As portfolio returns increase, volatility increases faster, positioning all the high-return portfolios at the right of the graph with low R/V values.

Given the results in Figure 77, why not just pick a portfolio with a low R/V ratio, or select a high-return portfolio ignoring volatility? This works moderately well, but without a better gauge, the odds are high you'll end up with unnecessary volatility contributing indirectly to unnecessary risk. It's possible to do better.

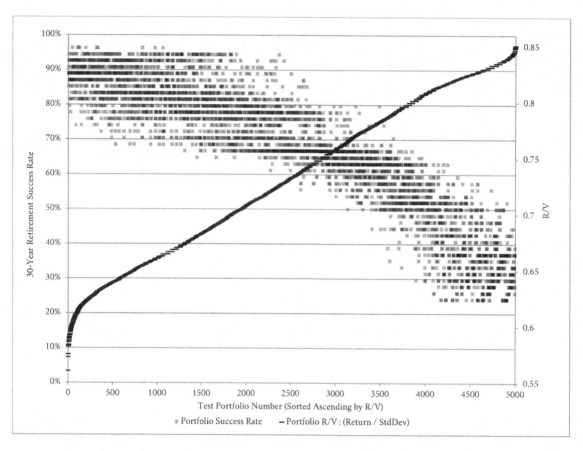

FIGURE 77

Retirement success rate versus the return per unit of volatility (R/V) for 5000 randomly generated portfolios based on Shiller and SBBI data. Each portfolio is randomly composed of eleven stock asset classes in 10% increments with no more than 30% per asset. Stock percentages range from 25% to 75%. Intermediate Treasury Bonds are used for all bond allocations. Backtesting uses a 5% inflation-adjusted withdrawal rate with annual rebalancing. The portfolios are sorted by R/V values.

Moving ahead, MPT evolved to include the capital asset pricing model (CAPM). CAPM goes further, defining the *market portfolio* as the single best portfolio on the Efficient Frontier (when combined with a risk-free asset). The market portfolio, a theoretical entity, represents a global portfolio proportionally weighted over all the assets in the world market. CAPM tells us the market portfolio is the only portfolio of risky assets needed to efficiently satisfy any investor's needs, including retirees[*].

The market portfolio is noteworthy as the portfolio with the highest Sharpe Ratio. The Sharpe Ratio is perhaps the best known of all portfolio metrics. It measures excess return, over the risk-free rate, per unit of volatility.

$$Sharpe\ Ratio = \frac{portfolio\ return\ -\ risk\ free\ rate}{portfolio\ volatility}$$

The Sharpe Ratio is CAPM's own version of the desired return and volatility characteristics of a portfolio. This implies that a portfolio with a higher Sharpe Ratio should be a better retirement portfolio than one with a lower Sharpe Ratio, right? Again, let's look at the data.

Figure 78 examines the same 5000 portfolios, this time comparing the Sharpe Ratio (on the right vertical axis) to the retirement success rate (on the left vertical axis), similar to the previous graph on R/V in Figure 77. Again, what we see is not expected: there is little to no relationship between the Sharpe Ratio[†] of a portfolio and its retirement success rate. If the Sharpe Ratio was a valid metric for retirement portfolios, then retirement success rate should clearly rise as the Sharpe Ratio rises. The inconsistency in this data is rooted in the pre-revolutionary thinking discussed in Chapter 1.

---

[*]   The One-Fund Theorem indicates that the most efficient portfolio for any investor, including retirees, can always be composed from a combination of the Market Portfolio and risk-free assets such as treasury bills.

[†]   Like R/V, the portfolio's Sharpe Ratio is calculated using the portfolio's complete historical return and volatility data from 1928 to 2010. The risk-free rate is the historical average for T-Bill returns for the same period.

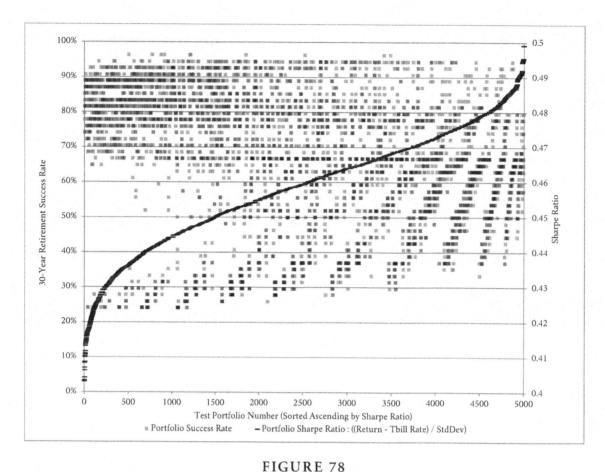

FIGURE 78

*Retirement success rate versus the Sharpe Ratio for 5000 randomly generated
portfolios. The portfolios are sorted by their Sharpe Ratio.*

Despite the revolution in financial economics and poor empirical results, the market portfolio with the highest
Sharpe Ratio continues to be commonly recommended to retirees through total-market funds. The rationale is, a
total-market fund approximates the theoretical market portfolio and is therefore safer for retirement. However, the
data clearly indicates otherwise.

The Harvesting Ratio, defined in the next section, reorients what is being measured to the needs of the retiree.

DEFINING THE HARVESTING RATIO

Retirement portfolios work best with returns that are sufficiently large to fund withdrawals, but with volatility that
can still be safely managed.

The Harvesting Ratio (HR) captures the correct return and volatility relationship for retirement portfolios.
Portfolios with high HR values consistently perform better in retirement than portfolios with low HR values. HR
opens the door for retirees to directly compare the suitability of different portfolios to support a specified withdrawal
rate with the lowest risk of running out of money.

HR corresponds to early work in portfolio theory. Markowitz in *The Early History of Portfolio Theory: 1600 - 1960* noted that the British economist A.D. Roy deserves an equal share of the credit for forming Modern Portfolio Theory. Distinct from Markowitz, Roy specified the formula *(portfolio return – disastrous return) / volatility* for portfolio selection. Roy's ratio, SFRatio, notably stands for Safety-First. The Harvesting Ratio is akin to Roy's proposal for portfolio selection, oriented to retirement.

HR measures excess return per unit of volatility. Excess return is defined as the return above that sufficient to support a specific retirement withdrawal rate. What is distinct is not the concept[*], but the pragmatic orientation toward retirement[†], coupled with rigorous verification. The conceptual formula for HR follows:

$$harvesting\ ratio = \frac{portfolio\ return\ -\ sufficient\ return}{portfolio\ volatility}$$

Sufficient return is the minimum level of return needed to safely support a retiree's withdrawal rate, given the variabilities of the market.

Conceptually, the Harvesting Ratio is a risk metric, implying that the remaining risk factors might be incorporated into the calculation of sufficient return, including the sequence of returns, inflation, withdrawal rate, and retirement length. However, the simpler the better, as long as effectiveness isn't sacrificed. Empirical tests show a strong approximation for *sufficient return* is the sum of the anticipated inflation rate and the anticipated annual withdrawal rate.

The above leads to the following formula for the Harvesting Ratio:

$$HR = \frac{R - (I + WR)}{\sigma}$$

"R" is the portfolio's average annual return, "I" is the expected average annual inflation rate, "WR" is the anticipated inflation-adjusted annual withdrawal rate, and sigma ("σ") is the portfolio volatility as measured by standard deviation[‡] of the portfolio return. This approximation for sufficient return is effective within the typical retirement boundaries, such as 20 to 40 year retirement periods with inflation-adjusted withdrawal rates ranging from 3.5% to 6%.

The example referenced earlier, comparing two portfolios return and volatility for 4.5% withdrawals, can be revisited using HR. Portfolio One has an average annual return of 9.5% based on historical returns, with a standard deviation of 10.1%. Inflation can be estimated at 3% based on past values—a rough estimate works well enough. The target withdrawal rate is fixed at 4.5% (assuming annual inflation adjustments).

---

[*] The Sortino Ratio is another related ratio, where "sufficient return" is similar to "minimum expected return", but the Sortino Ratio emphasizes down-side risk, which is not as readily available for individual investors. Also, preliminary testing shows it slightly underperforms the simpler Harvesting Ratio.

[†] After forming HR for this book, I found sketches of Lowell Herr's related work on the Retirement Ratio (RR). As far as I can tell, Herr is the first to apply a ratio with roughly the same general inputs toward retirement planning. He uses RR to estimate whether or not a portfolio will run out of money before the end of retirement at a specified withdrawal rate.

[‡] There is a general consensus in the literature that the standard deviation, based on a normal distribution of stock returns plus both upward and downward price movements, is not the best measure for stock volatility; nevertheless, it works well for HR, and is readily availability for most assets.

Portfolio One's Harvesting Ratio = (9.5% - (3% + 4.5%)) / 10.1% = 0.198.

Portfolio Two has an average annual return of 10.75%, standard deviation of 12.4%, the same 3% inflation rate, and the same 4.5% target withdrawal rate.

Portfolio Two's Harvesting Ratio = (10.75% - (3% + 4.5%)) / 12.4% = 0.262.

Other things being equal, Portfolio Two's significantly higher Harvesting Ratio, 0.262, compared to 0.198, indicates it's better suited to support a 4.5% withdrawal rate.

HR can now be applied to the same example of 5000 random portfolios, the exact scenario previously applied to R/V and the Sharpe Ratio in Figure 77 and Figure 78. If HR is an effective measure, there should be a clear correlation between HR values and retirement success rates.

Figure 79 does just this, showing a high correlation between HR (on the right vertical axis) and retirement success rate (on the left vertical axis) for the 5000 random portfolios (along the horizontal axis). The extent of the correlation will be explained later, but it's clear the portfolios with high HR values did better in retirement than portfolios with low HR values. The HR value for each portfolio is calculated with long-term historical returns and standard deviations from the datasets (the same as for R/V and the Sharpe Ratio). A fixed 3% is used as the estimated annual inflation rate and a fixed 5% as the annual withdrawal rate. Using only the long-term return and volatility characteristics of portfolios, HR effectively identifies the portfolios best suited to retirement—those in the far top-right portion of the graph with the highest HR values and success rates.

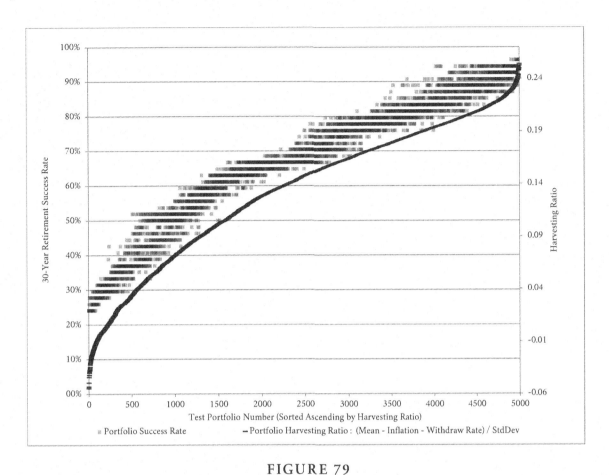

FIGURE 79

Retirement success rate versus the Harvesting Ratio for 5000 randomly generated portfolios. The portfolios are sorted by their Harvesting Ratio values.

A few of questions may be coming to mind now: How reliable is HR for future planning? Does it work well for today's portfolios? What does it take to calculate it correctly? Ultimately, does it really address the problem of retirement asset allocation? Long answers will follow, but here are short answers: HR is strong and consistent as a retirement planning aid; it applies to today's portfolios; it can also be calculated from a moderate amount of historical return data (unlike backtesting), expanding its applicability. The bottom line is HR, when combined with accepted asset-allocation practices, identifies a set of strong retirement portfolios.

Note HR as defined is a dimensionless metric[*], similar to Sharpe's Ratio. This means, HR values can only be compared across identical time periods. For example, a HR value calculated using average return and volatility data from 1928 to 1980 for one portfolio should not be compared to a HR value calculated using average return and volatility data from 1960 to 2010 for another portfolio. Using identical time periods ensures that differences in HR values between portfolios are due to asset allocation, as opposed to varying markets.

The rest of this chapter is devoted to providing evidence that HR is reliable and can be pragmatically applied. Chapter 8 uses HR on a set of well-known portfolios with interesting results, adding general conclusions for what makes strong retirement portfolios, and specific recommendations.

---

[*] Normalizing HR to a baseline may have some advantages, but a goal here is to keep HR's application straightforward.

THE EVIDENCE SUPPORTING HR

This section validates HR. Doing so requires a heavy dose of methodical precision, perhaps to the point of being laborious; nevertheless, it's imperative to have confidence in what makes for strong retirement portfolios. Different approaches are applied in multiple contexts to thoroughly verify HR, well past what has already been shown in Figure 79.

One approach to verification is a simple scatter diagram for retirement portfolios, with backtesting results shown along the vertical axis and HR values shown along the horizontal axis. Used in multiple contexts, this diagram visually represents the relationship between HR and retirement results. This should consistently show that portfolios with higher HR values have improved retirement results.

Another approach is a common statistical technique, linear regression analysis. Regression analysis measures how one set of data corresponds to a second set of data. Specifically here, it's used to determine how well HR identifies strong retirement portfolios. Based on the data, regression analysis also generates a function for HR to predict retirement results: how well retirement results are predicted provides another view of HR's effectiveness.

The most important output[*] of regression analysis here is R^2, the underlying metric which indicates to what degree HR successfully maps to retirement results (success rates or sustainable withdrawal rates). For simple regression based on one variable like HR, R^2 is actually the square of the statistical correlation between the predicting variable (HR) and the predicted variable (e.g., success rate, sustainable withdrawal rate). For example, if the correlation between HR and the retirement success rate is 0.7 for a set of test results, then R^2 is 49% (i.e., 0.7 x 0.7). A high R^2 means HR is a strong predictor of retirement results. Another common description for R^2 is that it determines how much of the movement in the variable of interest is due to the movement in the predicting variable. For example, an R^2 of 80% indicates that 80% of the movement in the retirement success rate (or sustainable withdrawal rate) is due to movement in the HR value. An R^2 of 100%, while never attainable here, would mean the predicting variable flawlessly correlates to the variable of interest, with perfect forecasting ability within the dataset.

What constitutes a strong R^2 value depends on what is being compared, so a rough rule of thumb is helpful in interpreting the HR analysis. An R^2 of 50% is lower than desired for HR although still considerable (i.e., the correlation is still above 0.7). R^2 values above 70% are preferred to reflect a substantial and strong relationship. An R^2 above 80% is the goal, reflecting more than enough strength and precision for planning. In rare cases, with an extremely high R^2 above 90%, the results fall in the exceptionally strong category; however for statistical reasons it's best to think of the predictive powers never exceeding the 90% range—there can be no such thing as high precision regarding future market predictions. Also keep in mind, there will always be more at play than what is reflected in R^2, but it's a useful and well-established statistical measure suitable for verifying HR.

HR is validated by subdividing the problem into four claims and verifying each claim separately. All four claims must be true, at least in part, for HR to be effective and pragmatic for retirees to leverage. The four claims follow.

1. Retirement portfolios with higher Harvesting Ratios tend to have higher success rates, and support higher withdrawal rates.

2. The Harvesting Ratio can be effectively calculated with relatively small amounts of historical data, making it applicable to asset classes with limited histories.

3. The Harvesting Ratio works for modern portfolios, including a diverse set of asset classes.

---

[*] When verifying HR, regression analysis's p-values are always extremely low (i.e., strong), making it acceptable to ignore them, focusing on the predictive power captured by R^2.

4. During poor markets, portfolios with higher Harvesting Ratios are generally safer for retirement than portfolios with lower Harvesting Ratios.

Except where stated otherwise, the following inputs and parameters are used when verifying the claims.

a. Backtesting is based on 30-year retirements.

b. For randomly generated portfolios, the stock percentage is restricted to fall from 25% to 75% to better match retirement portfolios. Random allocation to stock asset classes is done in 10% increments, with no more than 30% allocated to a single asset class.

c. US data from 1928 to 2010 are used based on a combination of the Shiller and SBBI datasets.
   - The stock allocation is between eleven stock asset classes: Shiller's S&P, Large, Small, Mid, Low, Micro, Total Market, Large Growth, Large Value, Small Growth, and Small Value.
   - When the bond allocation is held constant, all bonds are Intermediate Treasury Bonds (5-Year Maturity).
   - When the bond allocation is varied, it's between Long-Term High-Grade Corporate Bonds, Long-Term Government Bonds (20-Year Maturity), Intermediate-Term Government Bonds (5-Year Maturity), and US Treasury Bills (30-Day Maturity).

d. Annual rebalancing is the default harvesting strategy, because it's simple and best known; nevertheless, the general conclusions are also confirmed using Prime Harvesting. For the most part, the results of this chapter are independent from the income-harvesting strategy.

Claim 1: Retirement portfolios with higher Harvesting Ratios tend to have higher success rates and support higher withdrawal rates.

This claim has two parts: 1) portfolios with higher HR values tend to have higher success rates; 2) portfolios with higher HR values tend to support higher withdrawal rates. The first part is verified first.

Figure 80 is a scatter diagram showing higher HR values corresponding to higher success rates for 5000 randomly generated portfolios. For this case, the stock-bond ratio, the stock allocation, and the bond allocation are all randomly selected. Each dot on the graph represents a unique portfolio. HR is calculated using the 83-year return averages and volatility for each portfolio. For the inflation estimate in the HR calculation, 3% is used, and 5% is the target withdrawal rate. As HR values for the portfolios increase along the horizontal axis, the corresponding success rates rise along the vertical axis. Regression analysis shows a strong R^2 of 90%, indicating 90% of the variation in the success rate can be explained by the variation in the HR value. This generally illustrates that a higher-HR portfolio has a significantly better success rate than a lower-HR portfolio[*].

---

[*] Many of the tests in this chapter use the full SBBI 83-year averages for return and volatility, although the 30-year retirement periods being backtesting also come from the same 83-year period. In theory, this could boost the observed correlation between portfolio success and HR. Still, the 30-year retirement periods vary greatly from the long-term average. Also, HR must still correctly rank the portfolios for retirement. Nevertheless, later tests do use return and volatility data independent from the backtested retirement periods, with equivalent results.

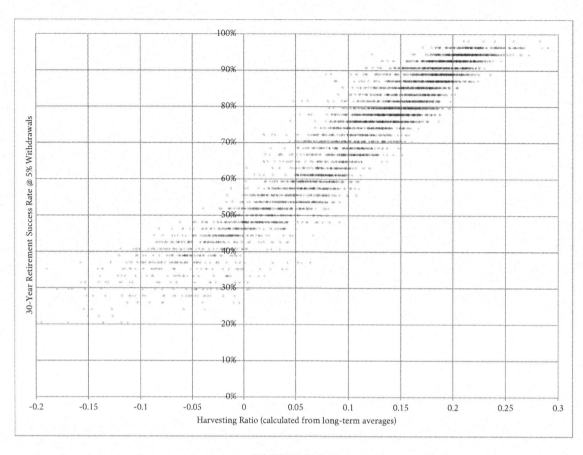

FIGURE 80

*5000 random portfolios plotted by HR and retirement success rate. Stocks,
bonds, and the stock-bond ratio are all randomly varied.*

Still, even with the high R^2, for any given HR value there is more variance in the success rate than preferred. As will be shown in the next example, HR is more accurate when the bond allocation is held constant.

Figure 81 shows HR results using a new set of 5000 portfolios with the bond allocation held constant (only intermediate treasury bonds) while randomly varying both the stock allocation and the stock-bond ratio for a 5% withdrawal rate. Again, retirement success clearly increases as HR increases, but this time, a much tighter and more pronounced relationship is shown. R^2 is also extremely strong at 97.5%[*]. Again, this reflects that HR is more accurate when comparing portfolios where only the stocks are varied, holding the bonds allocation constant.

---

[*] Such a high R^2 raises the question of whether spurious significance is being included in the regression (e.g., autocorrelation might be boosting the number). While this could be true, the graph still clearly shows the strong relationship between HR and success rates.

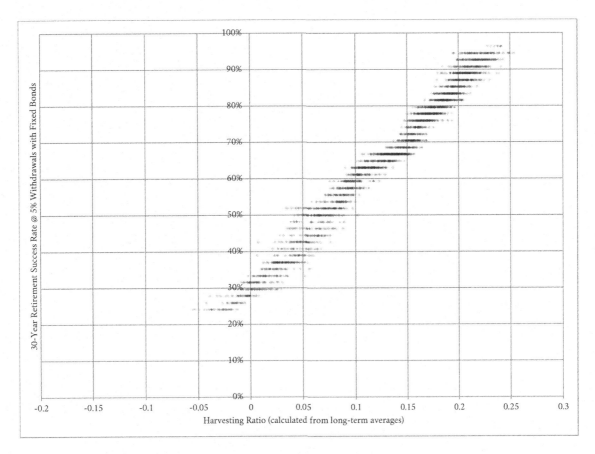

FIGURE 81

5000 random portfolios plotted by HR and retirement success rate. The bond allocation is held constant, while stocks and the stock-bond ratio are randomly varied.

Figure 82 further narrows the focus, using another set of 5000 portfolios, holding both the bond allocation and the stock-bond ratio constant, varying only the underlying stock allocation for a 5% withdrawal rate. Again, portfolio success clearly increases as HR increases, although holding the stock-bond ration constant doesn't make the relationship any tighter than when holding only the bond allocation fixed. Actually, for this case, R^2 drops a little to 84.7%, although this is still high. Not shown with another 5000 portfolios, a 4% withdrawal rate (as opposed to 5%) reflects the same results with a R^2 of 83.8% varying only the stock allocation using a 40% stock percentage and all bonds in intermediate treasuries.

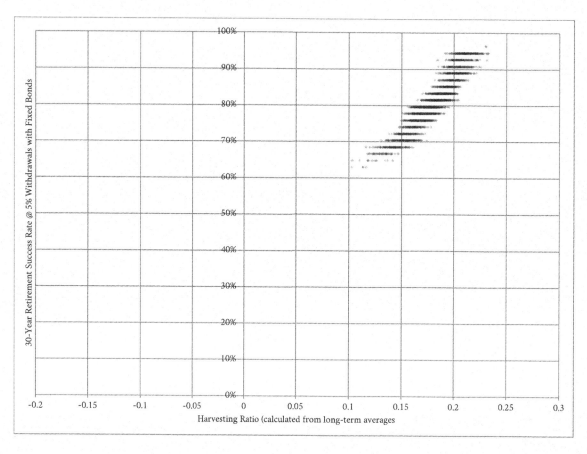

FIGURE 82

5000 random portfolios plotted by HR and retirement success rate. The bond allocation is held constant and the stock percentage is fixed at 60%, while the stock allocation is randomly varied.

As mentioned, regression analysis can be used to predict the retirement success rate directly from a HR value. An accurate prediction better illustrates HR's effectiveness.

Figure 83 graphically compares the success rate predicted by HR (using the regression function) to the actual backtesting success rate for the same 5000 portfolios, holding the bonds allocation constant while varying the stock allocations and stock-bond ratio for a 5% withdrawal rate. (Again HR is calculated using each asset's historical average for return and volatility, a 3% estimated inflation rate, and a 5% withdrawal rate.)

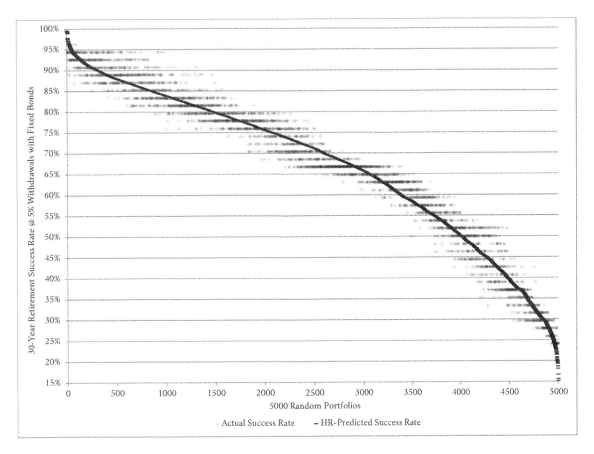

FIGURE 83

HR-predicted success rates compared to the actual success rates for 5000 random portfolios. Bonds are fixed with stocks and the stock-bond ratio randomly varied.

The predicted success rates are impressively close to the true success rates:

- 53% of the time, HR predicts the 30-year retirement success rate within ±2% of the actual rate. For example, if the predicted retirement success rate is 92%, then the actual rate falls anywhere from 90% to 94% in 53% of the cases.

- 91% of the time, HR predicts the 30-year retirement success rate within ±5% of the actual value (i.e., 4585 out of 5000 portfolios).

- 99.8% of the time, HR predicts the 30-year retirement success rate within ±10% of the actual value (all but 11 cases out of 5000).

Although not shown, the same test, predicting the success rate using HR, but varying only the stock allocation (i.e., fixed stock percentage and fixed bond allocation) does even better: 56% of the predictions are within ±2%, 94.3% of the predictions are within ±5% of the actual 30-year success rate and 99.9% within ±10%.

The previous cases confirm the first half of the claim: portfolios with higher HR values tend to have higher success rates. The data also shows that HR's results are refined by narrowing what is being measured.

Now the second part of the claim must be verified: portfolios with higher HR values tend to support higher withdrawal rates. (With the initial results now in hand, less data will be shown for this part of the claim.) The verification is done by showing the correlation between HR and the maximum sustainable withdrawal rate, calculated as MSWR-90%. MSWR-90% captures a portfolio's more typical characteristics. (Claim 4 focuses on MSWR-100% to examine worst-case characteristics). As before, 3% is the estimated inflation rate.

Figure 84 shows higher HR values corresponding to higher MSWR-90% values for 5000 randomly generated portfolios. As HR values for the portfolios increase along the horizontal axis, the corresponding MSWR-90% values rise along the vertical axis. A regression analysis indicates a strong R^2 of 87% between HR and MSWR-90%[*].

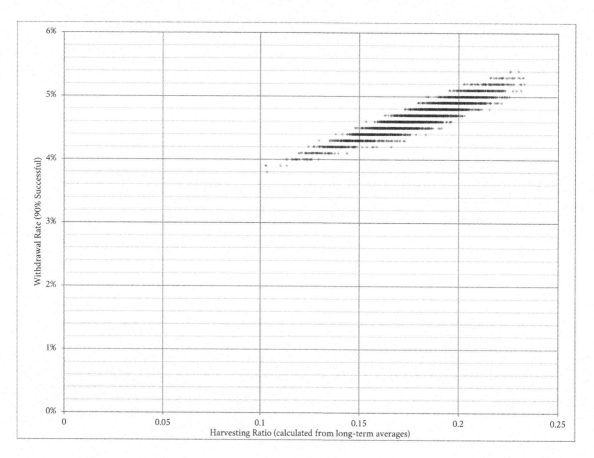

FIGURE 84

5000 random portfolios plotted by HR and MSWR-90%. The bond allocation is held constant and the stock percentage is fixed at 60%, while the stock allocation is randomly varied.

---

[*] For the same case, using Prime Harvesting the R^2 is 91%. This improvement is likely due to reducing the noise introduced by the sequence of returns, given that bonds are used to buffer stocks from volatility.

In addition, as done for the success rate, regression analysis can also predict MSWR-90% for a 30-year retirement using only HR. Doing this for the same 5000 random portfolios, varying only the stock allocation, the predicted results are again impressively close to the actual results.

- 75% of the time, HR predicts MSWR-90% within ±0.1%. For example, if the predicted MSWR-90% is 4.6% for the period, then the actual rate will typically fall from 4.5% to 4.7% in 75% of the cases.

- Likewise, 97% of the time HR predicts MSWR-90% within ±0.2%.

- Finally, 99.9% of the time, (i.e., 4998 out of 5000) HR predicts MSWR-90% within ±0.3%.

The above sufficiently verifies the second part of the claim and completes the overall verification for Claim 1: portfolios with higher Harvesting Ratios tend to have higher success rates plus tend to support higher withdrawal rates.

It's worth noting in light of the above strong results predicting sustainable rates, HR's strength is in making relative comparisons between portfolios; it's not intended as an absolute predictor of sustainable withdrawal rates. Estimating the sustainable withdrawal is useful, but better alternatives are presented in Chapter 9.

Claim 2: The Harvesting Ratio can be effectively calculated with relatively small amounts of historical data, making it applicable to asset classes with limited histories.

For the Harvesting Ratio to be broadly applicable, it needs to work with a relatively small amount of historical data, not just those asset classes with 80 years or more of data.

An interesting initial test for this claim is to calculate HR using only the first 30 years of US data from 1928 to 1957 (spanning the Great Depression and World War II) and then use these HR values to predict MSWR-90% for retirements spanning 1958 through 2010. This corresponds more closely to a typical retiree scenario where a limited amount of asset data is used to predict future retirement performance.

Figure 85 shows the above case for 1000 random portfolios with a fixed 60% allocation to stocks (the results are virtually the same varying stock percentages). Although only 30 years of data is used to calculate HR, the same general results can be seen—as HR values for the portfolios increase along the horizontal axis, the corresponding success rates rise along the virtual axis. Not surprising, R^2 for this regression is weaker, but still strong at 75.9%.

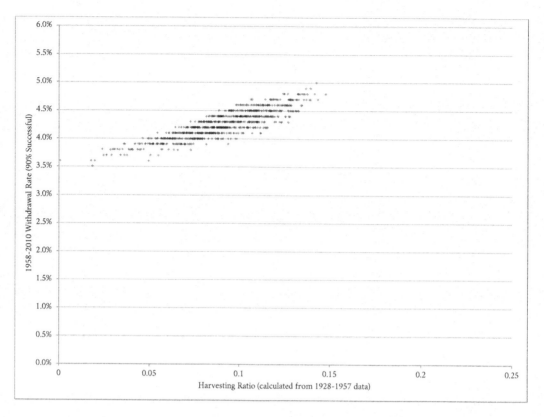

FIGURE 85

*1000 random portfolios plotted by HR and MSWR-90% with fixed bonds and
60% stocks. HR is calculated from 1928-1957 data (with 3% inflation estimate and
5% target withdrawal rate). The backtested periods are from 1958 to 2010.*

Again going a step further with the regression analysis, the Harvesting Ratio based on 1928 to 1957 data is able to predict MSWR-90% for retirements spanning 1958 to 2010 with the following precision:

- 58% of the time, HR predicts the 30-year retirement success rate, MSWR-90%, within ±0.1. As before, if the actual MSWR-90% is 4.6% for the period then the predicted MSWR-90% is within 4.5% to 4.7%.

- 91% of the time, HR predicts MSWR-90% within ±0.2.

- 99.3% of the time (i.e., 993 out of 1000), HR predicts MSWR-90% within ±0.3.

The above results are impressive, illustrating HR can work well with a small amount of data; however, additional analysis shows 30 years of historical data does not always have the same strong results.

Figure 86 shows six scatter diagrams for the same 1000 portfolios, with backtesting results from 1928 to 2010. The only difference in each diagram is which 30-year historical data period is used to calculate each portfolio's average return and standard deviation in the HR calculation. Notice that the scatter diagrams vary, with diagrams 2, 3, and 4 being stronger predictors and diagrams 1, 5, and 6 weaker. With weaker predictors, there is a larger margin of error; however, even then the HR predictions do not steer investors in the wrong direction. In all the diagrams, the very highest HR values still correspond to the top withdrawal rates. (To be clear, a low R^2 value doesn't imply that a high-HR portfolio will do poorly in retirement, it only means it can't accurately predict how it will do.)

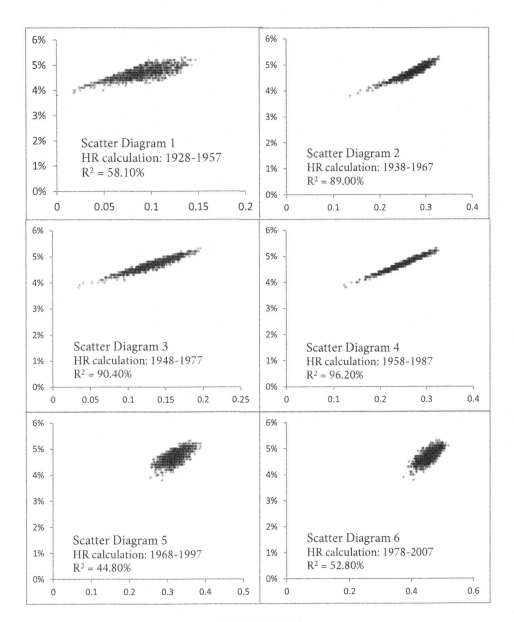

FIGURE 86

HR calculated for 1000 random portfolios using historical averages from six different 30-year periods. Each of the six measures is compared to the same backtesting results (i.e., MSWR-90%) spanning 1928 to 2010. The stock allocation for each portfolio is 60%.

A broader analysis, shown in Figure 87, clarifies how the amount of historical data used in calculating HR affects the accuracy of HR predictions. There is no precise cut-off for what constitutes a good or bad R^2 value, but there is cause for concern as R^2 drops below 50%. While 30 years of data does moderately well, 40 years is more reliable. Based on this chart, one could say 40 years of historical data is the desired minimum for calculating HR, but 30 years will suffice if more data is not available. As the amount of data decreases to 20 and even 10 years, the reliability becomes inconsistent. The implication is, it takes as much as 40 years for an asset class's return and volatility characteristics to fully manifest.

Starting Sample Year	83-Year HR Sample	40-Year HR Sample	30-Year HR Sample	20-Year HR Sample	10-YEAR HR Sample
1928	86.9%	66.0%	58.1%	51.6%	22.1%
1938		93.4%	89.0%	88.5%	78.2%
1948		85.9%	90.4%	84.0%	15.3%
1958		81.0%	96.2%	91.9%	85.1%
1968		71.2%	44.8%	81.4%	91.9%
1978			53.5%	19.5%	69.8%
1988				33.1%	6.9%
1998					56.2%

FIGURE 87

R^2 values for HR calculated with varying amounts of historical data. Calculated using MSWR-90% values from 5000 random portfolios backtested from 1928-2010 with 60% stocks.

The claim has been verified with caveats. The Harvesting Ratio can be calculated from a relatively small amount of historical data; however, 40 years or more is desired. Data covering as little as 30 years is generally sufficient, but any less significantly increases the probability of misleading results. As we shall see in the next section, 30 to 40 years of data is available for the most widely used asset classes, both domestic and international*.

Claim 3: The Harvesting Ratio works for modern portfolios, including a diverse set of asset classes.

This section verifies that HR works for a broader set of asset classes, covering what many retirees invest in today. Simba's dataset is used to verify the claim, which includes global mutual fund data going back to 1972. While Simba's dataset is small, containing only 39 years of data, it's sufficient as a secondary source. It also provides another checkmark, verifying HR with an independent dataset.

Figure 88 lists the eleven mutual funds used from Simba's data. These funds make up a set of randomly generated portfolios. Only the first three selected funds are traditional US-based stock asset classes.

Total US Market	VTSMX	Vanguard Total Stock Market Index Fund
Large Cap Blend	VFINX	Vanguard 500 Index Fund
Mid-Cap Blend	VIMSX	Vanguard Mid-Cap Index Fund
REIT	VGSIX	Vanguard REIT Index Fund
International Developed - EAFE	VDMIX	Vanguard Developed Markets Index Fund
Emerging Markets	VEIEX	Vanguard Emerging Markets Index Fund
Total International	VGTSX	Vanguard Total International Index Fund
International -- Pacific	VPACX	Vanguard Pacific Stock Index Fund
International -- Europe	VEURX	Vanguard European Stock Index Fund
International -- Value	VTRIX	Vanguard International Value Fund
International -- Small	VFSVX	Vanguard FTSE All-Word ex-US Small Cap Index Fund

FIGURE 88

Vanguard mutual funds in Simba data used to build 1000 random portfolios for verifying HR.

---

* Interestingly, although the data shows that a 10-year performance record is not a reliable measurement for an asset class or fund, it's the most common "long-term" metric made available to investors.

Similar to before, HR is verified examining the backtesting results of 1000 randomly generated portfolios. The stock ratio is fixed at 50%. For the bond allocation, Vanguard Total Bond Market Index Fund (VBMFX) is used. HR is calculated for each portfolio using average fund returns from 1972 to 2010 in Simba's data.

Figure 89 shows the results, comparing each portfolio's HR value to its maximum withdrawal rate. The results are consistent: as HR increases, the maximum withdrawal rate also increases. R^2 is also high at 83.7%.

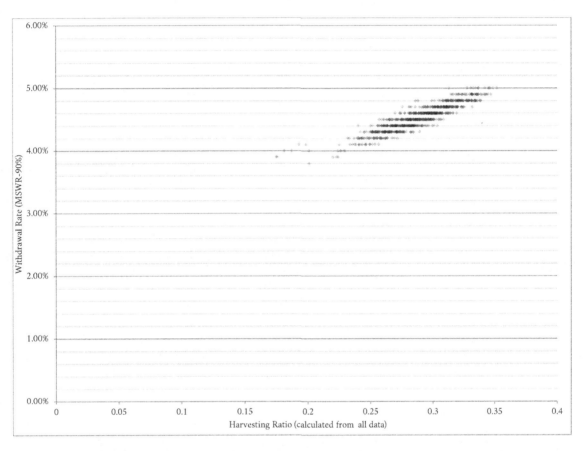

FIGURE 89

1000 random portfolios plotted by HR and retirement success rate using Simba's data. The bond allocation is held constant and the stock percentage is fixed at 50%, while the stock allocation is randomly varied.

For the same case, regression analysis is used to predict MSWR-90% for a 30-year retirement using only HR. The predicted results are again impressively close to the actual results[*].

- 78% of the time, HR predicts MSWR-90% within ±0.1%. For example, if the actual MSWR-90% is 4.6% for the period, then 78% of the time the predicted rate will fall with 4.5% to 4.7%.

- Likewise, 98% of the time, HR predicts MSWR-90% within ±0.2%.

- Finally, 99.9% of the time (i.e., 4998 out of 5000), HR predicts MSWR-90% within ±0.3%.

The above results are enough to verify the Claim 3: HR works for modern portfolios, including a diverse set of asset classes.

There is one caveat. Preliminary testing shows HR results do not apply to commodity funds. This is likely due to differences in commodities' long-term real-return characteristics compared to stocks. Adding only two commodity funds to the portfolio mix significantly degraded the clarity of HR results—this small percentage of non-conforming behavior was noticeable. A retiree may choose to use commodity funds, but they should not be included in HR calculations and related portfolio comparisons.

Claim 4: During poor markets, portfolios with higher Harvesting Ratios are generally safer for retirement than portfolios with lower Harvesting Ratios.

The first claim states high-HR portfolios tend to have higher success rates and support higher withdrawal rates, but this is not equivalent to saying portfolios with higher HR values are safer. It's possible for higher-HR portfolios to generally do better, but underperform during poor market conditions. To confirm higher-HR portfolios are generally safer, the focus now turns to performance during the most difficult cases in the data.

This claim is more complex to verify than the first three. It's necessary to look at the problem from several different angles, digging through and cross-referencing results, to ensure a complete answer. To keep the complexity manageable, verification focuses on the portfolio's stock allocation, keeping the bond allocation and percentage constant (although these other cases are addressed at the end of the discussion).

To start, Figure 90 shows the relationship between HR and several different MSWR measurements (MSWR-100%, MSWR-95%, MSWR-90%, and MSWR-80%) for 5000 random portfolios. Clearly, HR performs well for the more general cases captured by MSWR-95%, MSWR-90%, and MSWR-80%, but it blurs for the worst case captured by MSWR-100%—the key case for this claim. R^2 for MSWR-100% is only 14.8%, reflecting a low correlation between HR and strong portfolios during the worst retirement period. This first impression with the low R^2 indicates the claim could be false. Nevertheless, a deeper look at the data will resolve this concern.

---

[*] Because there are only 39 years of data, the HR calculation is almost guaranteed to have accurate return and volatility estimates as input, something that is not assured in future retirements; however, HR must still accurately rank the portfolios—the point of this test.

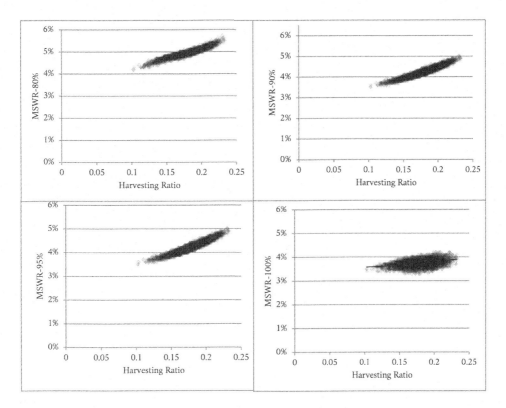

FIGURE 90

*MSWR-100%, MSWR-95, MSWR-90, MSWR-80 for 5000 random portfolios
varying the stock allocation – bonds are fixed as well as the stock percentage
at 60%. R² is 14.8%, 90.3%, 90.2%, and 88.7% respectively.*

Figure 91 reexamines the MSWR-100% case more closely, adding several annotations.

a. As HR rises, there is still a small upward movement in MSWR-100%. This is reflected by the double-edged trend line shown through the center of the data. The upward trend shows that higher-HR portfolios are still generally performing a little better.

b. The top 10% of the portfolios ranked by HR, enclosed in the boxed area, are still the best performing in the group, albeit only by a little.

c. The high-HR portfolios outperform all variations of the total-market portfolios shown.

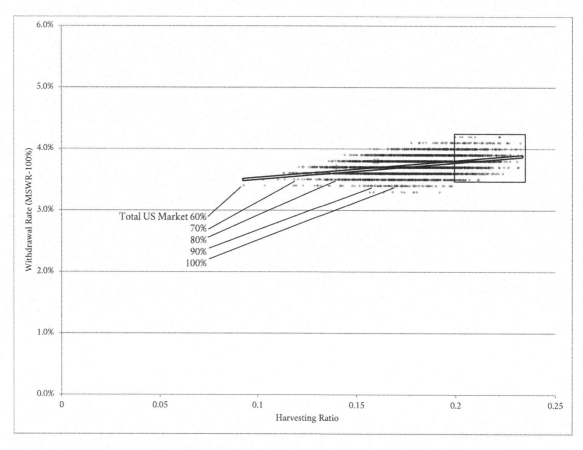

FIGURE 91

MSWR-100% for 5000 random portfolios varying the stock allocation. Bonds are fixed as well as the stock percentage at 60% (except total-market portfolios with varying stock percentages). The boxed area encloses portfolios with HR values in the top 10%.

What's surprising with the low R^2 is that HR still predicts MSWR-100% reasonably well with the regression function.

- 53% of the time, HR predicts MSWR-100% within ±0.1%. For example, if the actual MSWR-100% is 4.6% for the period, then overall 53% of the time the predicted rate will fall with 4.5% to 4.7%.

- Likewise, 85% of the time, HR predicts MSWR-100% within ±0.2%.

- Finally, 98% of the time (4888 out of 5000), HR predicts MSWR-100% within ±0.3%.

The accuracy of the above predictions is due in part to all portfolio performance falling into the narrow range of 3.3% to 4.2%. This essentially means all the portfolios are underperforming, leaving the high-HR portfolios less potential for distinction. Nevertheless, the predictions show HR is still working, just not as well. Understanding why is the next step.

Instead of looking at all the retirement periods between 1928 to 2010 as a group using MSWR-100%, individual retirement periods can be examined one by one for the same 5000 portfolios. A regression analysis is done on each of the 54 30-year retirement periods in the US SBBI data, again looking at the relationship between HR and the withdrawal rate.

Figure 92 shows R^2 and backtesting results for each of these individual retirement periods (with the left vertical axis measuring R^2 and the right vertical axis MSWR-100%). As before, a high R^2 indicates HR is effective for the retirement period and a lower R^2 indicates it's less effective. For this analysis Prime Harvesting, as opposed to annual rebalancing, is used to filter out avoidable noise due to inefficient portfolio management. Also shown are the results from four specific portfolios: a high-HR portfolio, a medium-HR portfolio, a low-HR portfolio, and the US market portfolio. The figure shows high R^2 values in approximately 85% of the retirement periods (in 46 of the 54 periods, the R^2 value was over 50%). In the remaining 15% of the retirement periods, HR was not as effective, although still sufficient.

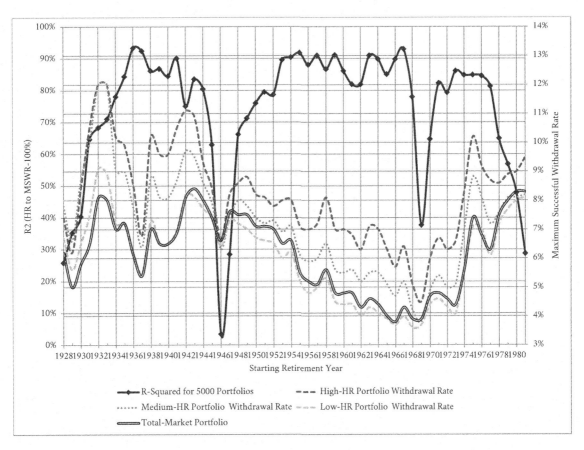

FIGURE 92

R^2 and backtesting results for each of the 54 retirement periods spanning 1928 to 2010 for 5000 random portfolios.

The reason for HR's occasionally drop in effectiveness is found by examining the four most distinct periods in Figure 92 with low R^2 values: retirement periods starting in 1928, 1946, 1969, and 1981.

- In 1928, with the impending Crash of 1929 and Great Depression, the sequence of returns significantly distorted retirement results. Deflation partly compensated, but it wasn't enough.

- In 1946, the period started with very high inflation and five years of poor returns. Again, this poor sequencing hurt retirement income and caused HR projections to be less accurate; however, returns recovered after the initial five years, leaving retirement income with a supported withdrawal rate above 6% using Prime Harvesting.

- In 1969, the problem was again poor sequencing. Over the first 10 years of retirement, inflation was running twice its average at 6.7%, with annualized US stock market returns at only 2.7%.

- Although 1981 started with poor sequencing (high inflation and poor returns), the dominant cause this time appears to be that asset classes significantly veered from their historical norms; a "tracking error" caused HR's predictions to be less accurate. Interestingly, the high-HR portfolios were less affected by the tracking errors than medium to low-HR portfolios.

To summarize, HR's occasional weakness stems from two sources. The primary source is poor sequencing, occurring in three out of the four US cases above. The secondary source is asset classes veering from their historical averages, occurring in one of the four cases. However, in no case does HR point the retiree in the wrong direction.

Figure 93 shows that in the four years where HR's correlation is at its lowest, there is still an upward trend line indicating high-HR portfolio performing better.

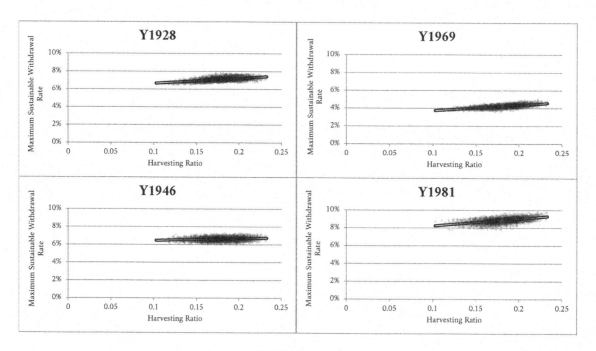

FIGURE 93

Comparison of MSWR versus Harvesting Ratio for those years with lowest R^2
for 5000 random portfolios with 60% stocks using Prime Harvesting.

When critiquing HR, it makes sense to also look at the alternatives. Figure 94 compares the R^2 values for HR, the Sharpe Ratio, and R/V across the 15 poorest retirement periods (based on the average sustainable withdrawal rate). As before, the higher the R^2 value, the higher the correlation to strong retirement portfolios. HR is the most effective ratio with a R^2 over 50% in 14 out of the 15 toughest periods using Prime Harvesting. The only exception is in the first period, 1969; however, the high R^2 for the Sharpe Ratio is misleading, because it captures a *negative* correlation, meaning the higher the Sharpe Ratio, the *worse* the portfolio performed. In the end, HR was the best predictor of strong retirement portfolios in every one of the 15 most difficult retirement periods.

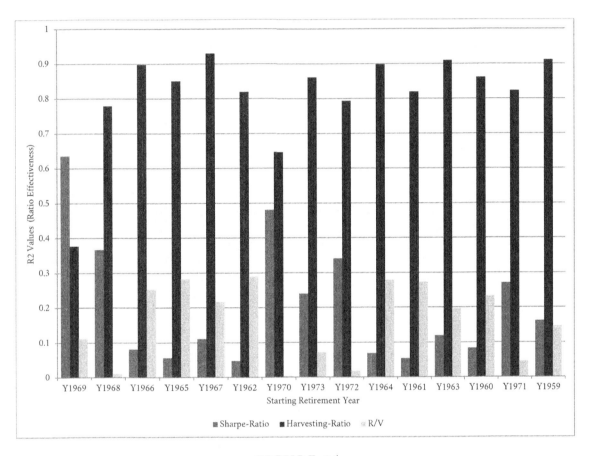

FIGURE 94

R^2 comparison of Sharpe Ratio, Harvesting Ratio, and R/V for the 15 poorest retirement periods in SBBI dataset.

Let's review what the US data shows. HR is fully effective in approximately 85% of the retirement periods. For the other 15%, HR is still effective but to a lesser extent. This occasional drop in effectiveness is due to a combination of poor sequencing and tracking errors.

What about the same case using Simba's data (US and International funds from 1972-2011)? Figure 95 shows a clear HR relationship with no significant noise for MSWR-100% with the stock percentage fixed at 50%. R^2 is high at 81%. Also, the total-market portfolios, evenly split between US and international markets (VTSMX and

VGTSX), again come in toward the bottom in performance with correspondingly low HR values. Why didn't the anomalies in the US data show up in the Simba data? It just depends on the market and the timeframe, plus the data set is small, reducing the likelihood of anomalies.

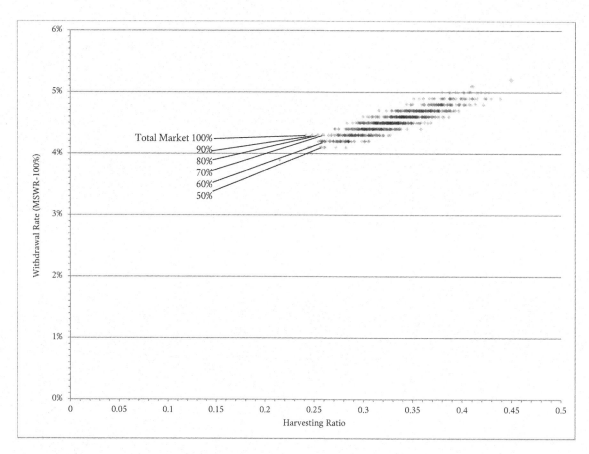

FIGURE 95

1000 Portfolios backtested with Simba data for MSWR-100%.

There is one last and perhaps more intuitive way to examine HR's effectiveness, bypassing the opaqueness of regression analysis. The 5000 portfolios can be sorted into quintiles based on their HR value, allowing average back-testing results between quintiles to be compared. The first quintile contains the portfolios with the top HR values, the second with the next set of HR values, and so on till the fifth quintile with the lowest HR values.

Figure 96 shows the average supported MSWR for each retirement period (with bond fixed and 60% stocks), divided into the first, third, and fifth quintiles. The total-market MSWR is also included for comparison. It's clear in this simple analysis that the higher-HR quintiles consistently support higher withdrawal rates across all markets, although the advantages can become minimal during difficult markets.

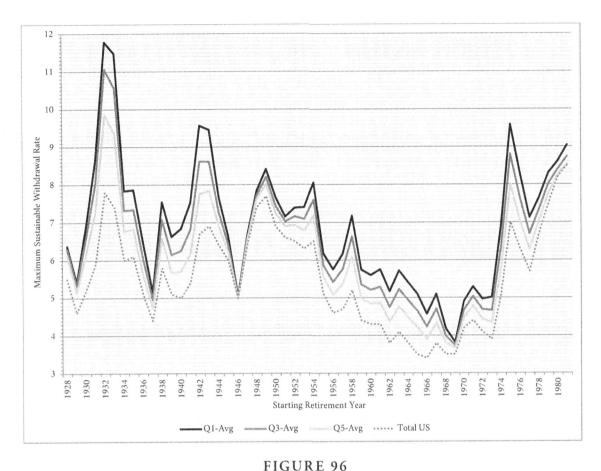

FIGURE 96

Average retirement results based on 5000 random portfolios subdivided into quintiles by HR.

Figure 97 graphs the *smallest* supported withdrawal rate from each of 1000 portfolios in each quintile. This illustrates that HR's rankings are not unduly affected by market anomalies producing erratic results. For the retirement period starting in 1937, the smallest withdrawal rate is 5% for the 1000 portfolios in the top quintile, 4.8% for the portfolios in the third quintile, and 4.4% for the portfolios in the fifth quintile, while the market portfolio's withdrawal rate is 4.4%.

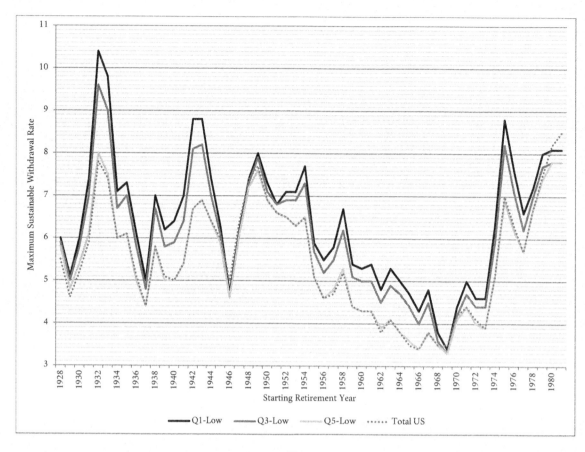

FIGURE 97

Lowest MSWR per quintile based on 5000 random portfolios subdivided by HR.

The verification of Claim 4 is complete and successful, but a couple of loose ends remain. Claim 4 does generally hold when varying the bond allocation, although as seen before, with less precision. In contrast, Claim 4 does *not* generally hold for HR when varying the stock-bond ratios. This is because the HR relationship loses accuracy as the stock percentage rises, resulting in high-stock portfolios (e.g., 70% and above) being overvalued by HR.

Certainly, HR can be used for initial portfolio comparisons with different stock percentages, but for final planning it's best to use a fixed stock percentage, focusing only on the fund allocations within the stock portion of the portfolio.

Chapter 7 takes another route to set the stock-bond ratio in retirement.

A Few More Details

There are still a few remaining topics to complete the coverage of HR. Given that the viability of HR has been established by verifying the four claims, this section will be brief.

Retirement Lengths

The previous analysis is based on 30-year retirements. Figure 98 shows R^2 between HR and MSWR-90% for retirement lengths ranging from 15 to 40 years. These consistently high R^2 values indicate that HR is generally independent of the length of typical retirement plans. Moving under 15 years, though, HR starts to become less effective for planning.

	R^2
10-Year Retirement Length	0.465
15-Year Retirement Length	0.829
20-Year Retirement Length	0.888
30-Year Retirement Length	0.870
40-Year Retirement Length	0.842

FIGURE 98

R^2 values for varying retirement lengths.

Withdrawal Rates

Analysis shows the withdrawal rate parameter is significant in the HR calculation, but the parameter value usually comes with significant leeway. This leeway explains why the 5% withdrawal rate is a good overall value when using HR to estimate the maximum supported withdrawal rate. It also explains why there is no problem applying HR when a variable-withdrawal strategy will be used.

On the other hand, if the HR value drops significantly when the withdrawal rate is increased by a moderate amount (e.g., from 4% to 5%), this indicates that the portfolio is at a boundary. Given that markets stray from their historical norms, it's safer to stay away from any such boundary. This is easy to do though: pick portfolios with strong HR values across a reasonable range of withdrawal rates.

Inflation Estimates

Tests show HR is more accurate when true inflation numbers are used; however, as with the withdrawal rate, there is a significant amount of latitude. A 3% inflation estimate works well overall. It's recommended as the default inflation value when calculating HR.

CONCLUDING THOUGHTS

It's always easier to present a case as if it's black and white, but doing so rarely tells the whole story. The following concerns surrounding HR each have some validity, but they don't ultimately change HR's applicability. They are acknowledged as part of the pragmatic realities of retirement planning.

- There is no guarantee that past asset-class returns will carry into the future.

  The future remains unknown, but historical data show asset-class characteristics to rarely change over the long term in a relative sense—if an asset class has exhibited certain characteristics for 40 years or more compared to other asset classes, most often these characteristics will carry into the future. Still, long-term characteristics have changed on rare occasions; most notably emerging markets have performed substantially better since the 1950s than in earlier periods[32]. Nevertheless, any asset class can have an exceptionally poor or strong run over 10, 20, or perhaps even 30 years, but there is no way to know when this might happen. (Outside of index funds, HR applies to actively managed funds the same way, as long as the investing style doesn't change. If a fund's style alters, perhaps due to a manager change, then past performance numbers may no longer be fully relevant.) Despite these caveats, the data still shows a high-HR portfolio has the highest probability of future success.

- A high-HR portfolio made up of higher-volatility assets could have more downside risk.

  A high-HR may have more downside volatility over the short term, but this is not equivalent to risk in retirement. If higher-HR portfolios are truly damaged more than lower-HR portfolios during poor markets, then the sustainable withdrawal should decrease as HR increases, but this was shown not to be the case.

  Still, it's reasonable to speculate that a high-HR portfolio during a poor market could damage a retirement more than a low-HR portfolio, but for a well-diversified portfolio this falls into the domain of speculative risk. This chapter has shown it's much more likely that a low-HR portfolio will underperform during a poor market.

- More data is needed to verify HR.

  More data for verification is desirable. While the first dataset is substantial, covering US data from 1928 to 2010, the second dataset based on global mutual funds is small, only spanning 1972 through 2010. An additional long-term dataset, with returns broken down by asset classes, would support a more thorough verification, but currently this is not available. Of course, any alternative to HR should conform to the same standard HR is evaluated against.

  The pragmatic path is to proceed according to the best available data, updating plans when needed as new research becomes available. As it stands now, HR does meet the standard of evidence-based research set forth in this book, which is higher than most standards for verifying investment strategies.

An underlying theme is that retirees operate off probabilities, not absolutes, but there are viable hedges. The first and best hedge is diversification (covered in Chapter 6 and Chapter 8). Outside diversification, the data show only two paths for effectively lowering risk through asset allocation, neither of which depends on using a subpar allocation for stocks*. The first is to decrease the portfolio's stock-bond ratio a moderate amount in conjunction with lowering the withdrawal rate, a topic discussed in Chapter 7. The second and strongest solution is to move a portion of assets outside systemic withdrawals into guaranteed income, the topic of the last chapter.

THE POINT

The Harvesting Ratio measures the correct relationship between portfolio return and volatility to reduce risk for a specified level of income. This capability is a strong guide for retirement asset allocation, as will be demonstrated in Chapter 8.

---

* Maintaining the proper stock allocation is the essence of Tobin's Separation Theorem: the stock asset allocation remains constant with only the total allotment to stocks changing to suit different levels of risk tolerance.

CHAPTER
6 GUIDE

This chapter defines the Baseline Market and Baseline Portfolio in order to provide realistic numbers for retirement planning.

Understanding why these baselines are needed is essential, which is explained in the introduction. How the baselines are created is less important.

Less interested readers need only skim the chapter (after the introduction), but if needed make sure to understand the justification for a global portfolio. The section on considering a low-return world is also worth the attention of retirees concerned by the forecasts for a generation of low market returns.

Investing should be a science, but pragmatism requires we dabble in its arts.

Walter E. Goh

CHAPTER 6

Defining a Baseline Market and Portfolio

At some point, retirees want realistic income and risk estimates for their own retirement plans. Backtesting can supply these numbers with the right market data, but unfortunately this data is not available for global markets. The global stock data tends to be total-market data, tilted towards large growth stocks, which the previous chapter shows is not suitable for retirement portfolios.

A Baseline Market and Baseline Portfolio are defined in this chapter to provide the correct data for realistic estimates. A Baseline Market will be the proxy for future global markets. A Baseline Portfolio will be the proxy for the high-HR portfolios retirees should be using. Neither baseline is perfect, but together they support an improved and reasonable estimate of what to expect for future retirements using best practices.

After defining the baselines, this chapter then shows initial backtesting results using them. The rest of the book leverages these baselines to complete the estimates. As a start though, it's worth taking a closer look at why a global baseline is essential for retirement planning.

Global Diversification

Global diversification may or may not have been worthwhile a few decades ago, given limited choices, but the abundance of global funds today make it an important part of bounding overall risk. Still, retirees in countries with strong market histories such as the US may wonder if global diversification is truly worth it—US real return since 1900 is 6.3%, while global real return for the same period is a more modest 5.0%[33]. A clear rationale for global diversification is needed. One is outlined below.

As introduced in Chapter 2, specific markets have substantial risks independent from the global economy, just like specific stocks have substantial risks independent from their market. Consider the following extreme facts.[34]

- After World War II, the Japan stock market lost 96% of its real value, mostly due to hyperinflation.

- Belgium's real stock market return for the last 113 years is 2.5%.

- Austria's real stock return for the last 113 years is 0.6%.

- Market values dropped to zero in 1917 in Russia and 1949 in China with the onset of communism.

Global diversification essentially filters out of known risk the extreme and distracting cases. Specific-market risk has always been the source of the worse stock returns. This implies known risk, when based on a global well-diversified portfolio, need not directly consider the returns in places like Austria, Belgium, Japan, Germany, and Switzerland... only the global averages. These global averages still present a tough market, although without the overpowering distortions from individual countries.

Still, the US market is different, right? US historical returns are stronger and more consistent than most countries'. The US's geography keeps it free from the geopolitics some markets have suffered under. Its free-market economy and stable government provides a satisfactory environment for economic growth. Certainly, the worst market examples above fall well into the realm of speculative risk for the US market. Data from 1871 to the present shows nothing comparable. Also, US stocks today comprise about 45% of the global market and strongly affect what is happening in other countries...investing in totally uncorrelated markets is near impossible.

While the above may all be true in varying degrees, other markets are still distinct from the US market and do lower risk through diversification.

- The global market exhibits a little less of a downside and a little less volatility. For example, over the past century, the worst annualized 10-year real return for the US market was -8.9%, compared to -7.5%[35] for a global portfolio. Also, the global market's standard deviation has been below 18% where the US's has been above 20%.

- Global markets are interconnected with the US market, but they still operate with varying degrees of independence. Even during the exceptional market contagion of 2007, some of the global problems did not map back to the US subprime-mortgage crisis. Problems in Ireland, Spain, and the UK, while similar, appear to be independently rooted, not side effects from the US[36]. More concretely, Australian real stock returns were 4.3% from 2000-2012, while for the same period US real stock returns were -0.2%.

- Even though real return is 25% higher in US markets compared to global markets since 1900, backtesting shows sustainable income is only 10% higher.

- Finally, some economists believe future US returns will not be as strong as past returns. Dimson et al. capture this point well in their *Credit Suisse Global Investment Returns Yearbook 2013* summary: "Extrapolating from such a successful market can lead to 'success' bias. Investors can gain a misleading view of equity returns elsewhere, or of future equity returns for the USA itself. That is why this Yearbook focuses on global returns, rather than just those from the USA."

Frankly though, it's difficult to make a compelling case for global diversification based purely on the data. Substantial counterexamples show that a pure US-based portfolio has worked well for the last 150 years.

What is perhaps the best direct evidence for investing globally is neither from long-term historical returns nor speculative. HR comparisons indicate that retirement portfolios are significantly stronger using the global funds available today. New global funds contributing to higher HR values have become available in the last couple of decades, opening up potential that is not reflected in the long-term historical numbers. Now investors can choose from international REITs, international small value stocks, and even emerging-market small-cap and value stocks. Global diversification looks not only safer, it appears to pay better.

If global diversification is good, then why not totally diversify across world markets without any preference for a single market like the US? It turns out that the top HR numbers come from combining a strong market, like the US market (or Australian market), with broader world market funds. Still, to gain the full benefits of diversification, no single market should be allowed to overpower the portfolio during a crisis.

Figure 99 outlines one of many US-based retirement portfolio breakdowns with appropriate global diversification. In this example, specific-market risk from US stocks is limited to 15% of the portfolio. Of course, there are many other portfolio breakdowns with appropriate levels of diversification, but the point is, the most benefit is gained when both diversification and performance (i.e., the Harvesting Ratio) are considered. Although not the focus here, the data also show it's just as important to diversify across multiple asset classes (e.g., small stocks, large value stocks). It's impossible to know where future fault lines may lie.

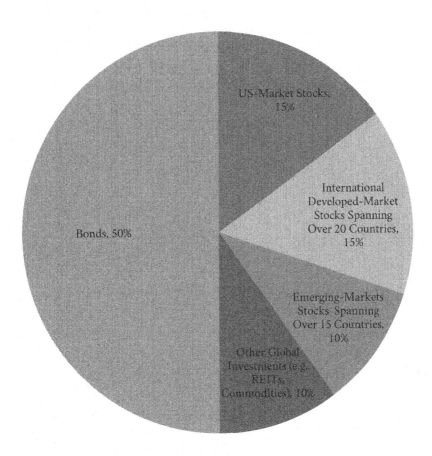

FIGURE 99

Sample retirement-portfolio diversification, limiting specific-market risk.

The relative ease of full diversification across multiple countries and asset classes makes it possible for retirees to stay out of the market forecasting business. Broad diversification with an eye on HR is the safest approach.

DEFINING A BASELINE MARKET

The Baseline Market must represent the global market. It must support a variety of asset classes for complete diversification. It must support backtesting, encompassing the best and worst market periods of known risk for a well-diversified portfolio. It must be based on real market data to avoid the pitfalls of simulated data. As mentioned before, there's no existing dataset which meets all these criteria.

The solution is to fabricate a baseline by scaling the US SBBI dataset to align with long-term global stock and bond returns. This satisfies all the essential criteria, in part because the US data starts with the right global characteristics.

Figure 100 compares global total-market retirement results to US total-market retirement results. The global MSWR values comes from Wade Pfau's backtesting numbers[37] spanning 17 developed markets back to 1900. The second set of MSWR values comes from Pfau's backtesting numbers for the same period, using only US data. The average MSWR is 5.9% for the global case and 5.6% for the US case. Both show similar swings in the retirement results, at times supporting a MSWR of 10% and above and at other times 4% and below. While these are total-market tests (again the underlying global data doesn't included asset-class breakdowns), they show the US market as a reasonable starting point for creating a global baseline. The details come next.

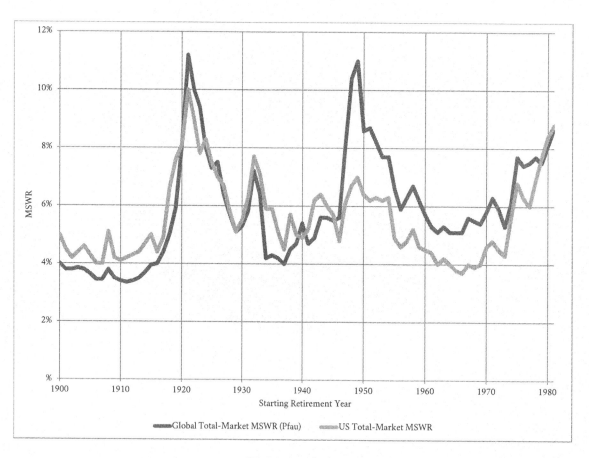

FIGURE 100

*MSWR comparison between Global Total-Market and US
Total-Market with 50% stocks and 50% bonds.*

Below is the checklist for creating a Baseline Market, along with how the US SBBI data is used to satisfy each requirement.

A. The Baseline Market should include sufficient asset breakdowns to support diverse portfolios.

Since the Baseline Market is formed from the SBBI dataset, it inherits the best available long-term breakdown of asset classes (shown in Appendix A).

B. The Baseline Market should include enough data to support backtesting.

Again by inheriting the SBBI history from 1928 to 2010, there is sufficient data for backtesting.

C. The Baseline Market should reflect global stock returns for developed and emerging markets.

Since 1900, the annualized real total-market global stock return for both developed and emerging markets is 5% (again based on the *Credit Suisse Yearbook*). The annualized real total-market return for the US market using the SBBI dataset from 1928 to 2010 is 6.15%. By starting with the SBBI total-market data and scaling down every year's return by 6.055%, the resulting Baseline-Market total-market real return becomes 5.0%, exactly matching the global return from 1900 to 2012. The same proportion (i.e., a 6.055% reduction) is also used to scale down returns for each stock asset class in the dataset (e.g., Large Company Stocks, Mid-Cap Stocks, Small Value Stocks).

D. The Baseline Market should reflect global bond returns.

Although retirees usually don't invest in bonds globally, the global numbers work well for the baseline for a couple of reasons. The average numbers are a reasonable estimate of future performance for most developed markets. Also, the global equity premium is maintained by scaling both bonds and stocks, which is a good attribute to keep in the baseline[*].

The annualized real global bond returns for the 1900 to 2012 period are 1.8%. The annualized real return for intermediate-term treasury bonds in the US SBBI dataset from 1928 to 2010 is 2.07%. By taking the SBBI intermediate-term treasury data and scaling down every year's return by 4.8%, the resulting bond return for the Baseline Market becomes 1.8%, exactly matching the global bond return from 1900 to 2012.

E. The Baseline Market's stock volatility should reflect global stock volatility.

The standard deviation for the global market real return from 1900 to 2010 is 17.7%[38], while the standard deviation for total-market real return of the Baseline Market is 20.2%. This is close enough, especially considering volatility is not a dominant risk factor. The higher volatility provides a modestly more conservative approximation.

---

[*] The equity premium can indirectly affect the optimal stock-bond ratio, plus it can have subtle effects on other strategies.

F. The Baseline Market should reasonably represent the remaining risk factors where this matters.

    i. Inflation effects are already factored into the Baseline Market by scaling to real returns.

    ii. The sequence of returns should be adequately represented in the Baseline Market, given the global market has a little smaller historical downside risk based on 10-year returns. Also, US retirements starting in the late 1960s suffered through a poor sequence of returns, which should provide a conservative slant.

    iii. The remaining risk factors, retirement length and withdrawal rate, are independent from the Baseline Market.

Combined, this makes the Baseline Market a suitable proxy for the global market.

CONSIDERING A LOW-RETURN WORLD

In recent years, much has been written about lower prospects for future market returns. Most notably, economists Dimson, Marsh, and Staunton wrote the following in the *Credit Suisse Global Investment Returns Yearbook 2013*:

> We have seen that an investor with a 20–30 year horizon faces close to zero real returns on inflation-protected government bonds. The expected real return on conventional long bonds is expected to be a little higher, so the annualized real return on a rolling investment in cash is likely to be negative by as much as ½% over, say, 20 years, and close to zero over 30 years. Adding an equity premium of 3%–3½% to these negative/low real expected cash returns gives an expected real equity return in the region of 3%–3½% over 20–30 years. We are indeed living in a low-return world.

What should be done to prepare for this possibility of a low-return world? Actually, very little should be done, if anything. The portfolio mechanics are designed to handle the situations encompassed in a low-return world, including the ups and downs of volatile markets. Concerning the data, history is filled with tough markets—the Baseline Market already includes the characteristics of a low-return world.

Compared to the numbers Dimson et al. quote above, consider the Baseline Market's 30-year forward real stock returns starting in 1955 dropped to 3.5%; for the same period real bond returns dropped to 0.6%. More drastically, starting in 1962, the Baseline Market's 20-year forward real stock returns dropped to 0.1% while real bond returns were -1.1%. Also, under a 40-year benchmark retirement case that will be used, which wraps the historical data (defined at the start of Chapter 10), the Baseline Market's 30-year real stock returns dropped to 0.3% with corresponding real bond returns of 2.3%.

It is worth restating, the low-return world as described by Dimson et al. is already part of known risk; it's included in the Baseline Market and as such factored into the backtesting results.

DEFINING A BASELINE PORTFOLIO

Virtually all retirement studies are based on a portfolio of total-market stocks, which is unfortunate since this type of portfolio was shown in Chapter 5 to perform poorly in retirement. A better choice is needed to represent the typical retiree's portfolio. This is the purpose of the Baseline Portfolio.

Since the Baseline Market is derived from the SBBI dataset, the portfolio can be composed from its corresponding asset classes. Chapter 8 shows that a simple pattern for a high-HR portfolio is to evenly distribute assets across the core high-performing asset classes. This is done to define the Baseline Portfolio using the following allocation.

Large	Mid-Cap	Low-Cap	Micro-Cap	Large Value	Small Value
16.67%	16.67%	16.67%	16.67%	16.67%	16.67%

The first four asset classes spread the stock allocation evenly across deciles 1 through 10*: Large Stocks are the S&P 500 approximating deciles 1 and 2; Mid-Cap Stocks are deciles 3 to 5; Low-Cap Stocks are deciles 6 to 8, and Micro-Cap Stocks are deciles 9 and 10. The last two choices, Large Value Stocks and Small Value Stocks, are high-HR asset classes well known from Fama and French's research on the three-factor model of stock returns[39]. (The two core SBBI asset classes, Large Growth and Small Growth, are excluded because of their long-term low-HR values.)

For some retirees, the Baseline Portfolio might seem extreme; however, Figure 101 shows another perspective by comparing Morningstar's breakdown of comparable index funds (for the Baseline Portfolio) to a similar breakdown for the US total-market fund VTSMX. These numbers show the Baseline Portfolio is much better diversified across the underlying asset classes than a total-market fund (this point is revisited in more depth in Chapter 8's coverage of portfolio construction).

Morningstar Asset Class Category	Approximation for Baseline Portfolio	US Total Market Fund (VTSMX)
Large Value	15.50%	24%
Large Blend	12.67%	22%
Large Growth	8.67%	26%
Mid Value	12.17%	6%
Mid Blend	11.17%	6%
Mid Growth	8.00%	7%
Small Value	12.17%	3%
Small Blend	10.83%	3%
Small Growth	8.33%	3%

FIGURE 101

Estimation of underlying asset allocation for Baseline Portfolio and Total-Market Portfolio based on Morningstar's breakdown of the related index funds.

The bond allocation for the Baseline Portfolio is straightforward, given there is only a single asset (based on intermediate-treasury bonds scaled to match global bond returns).

---

* The University of Chicago's Center for Research in Security Prices (CRSP) categorized stocks in deciles based on the capitalization size.

INITIAL BACKTESTING NUMBERS

To put the Baseline Market and Portfolio in perspective, Figure 102 compares their performance to the US default portfolio (used in the previous surveys), the US total-market portfolio, and each of the US individual asset classes. The results are sorted by MSWR-100%. Again, the US default portfolio has 70% Total-Market Stocks, 10% Small Stocks, 10% Large Value stocks, 10% Small Value Stocks. Coincidentally and ironically (it wasn't planned), the performance of the Baseline Market and Portfolio turn out to be close to the US default portfolio.

	MSGR-100%	MSGR-95%	MSGR-90%	MSGR-80%	MSGR-50%
US Small Value Stocks	5.20%	5.90%	6.50%	6.90%	7.90%
US Large Value Stocks	4.90%	5.10%	5.30%	5.60%	6.80%
US Default Portfolio	4.40%	4.70%	5.20%	5.50%	7.30%
Baseline Market and Portfolio	4.30%	4.80%	5.40%	5.60%	6.80%
US Mid-Cap Stocks	4.20%	4.40%	4.70%	5.00%	6.30%
US Low-Cap Stocks	4.00%	4.80%	5.20%	5.40%	6.60%
US Large Stocks	3.50%	3.70%	3.80%	4.10%	5.70%
US Total-Market	3.50%	3.70%	3.90%	4.20%	5.70%
US Micro-Cap Stocks	3.20%	4.30%	4.90%	5.40%	7.00%
US Large Growth Stocks	3.20%	3.30%	3.50%	3.70%	5.30%
US Small Growth Stocks	2.70%	3.40%	3.80%	4.40%	5.80%

FIGURE 102

Baseline Market and Portfolio's performance compared to US individual asset-class performance, the reference portfolio (i.e., US Default), and US Total-Market portfolio for 30-year retirements.

Figure 103 shows more of the Baseline Portfolio's performance under the Baseline Market.

		MSWR-100%	MSWR-95%	MSWR-90%	MSWR-80%	MSWR-50%
20 Years	45% Stock	5.00%	6.00%	6.10%	6.60%	8.10%
20 Years	50% Stocks	5.00%	6.00%	6.10%	6.60%	8.40%
20 Years	55% Stocks	4.90%	5.90%	6.10%	6.70%	8.60%
30 Years	45% Stock	4.30%	4.70%	5.30%	5.40%	6.50%
30 Years	50% Stocks	4.30%	4.80%	5.40%	5.60%	6.80%
30 Years	55% Stocks	4.30%	4.90%	5.40%	5.70%	7.00%
40 Years	45% Stock	4.00%	4.40%	4.80%	4.90%	5.60%
40 Years	50% Stocks	4.00%	4.50%	5.00%	5.10%	5.80%
40 Years	55% Stocks	4.00%	4.60%	5.10%	5.20%	6.10%

FIGURE 103

Variations of the Baseline Portfolio's performance with Baseline Market.

Chapter 11, Putting It All Together, shows additional Baseline Portfolio and Market results, applying the full set of best practices.

Final Thoughts

The important question isn't whether the Baseline Portfolio and Market will accurately predict future market characteristics—this is an unanswerable question. The important question is whether the baselines provide reasonable proxies for prudent retirement planning based on the available data. I believe this is true, more than for existing alternatives.

In one sense though, the baseline numbers are conservative. The HR value for the Baseline Portfolio is significantly lower than the HR values of the portfolios recommended in Chapter 8 (based on the global index funds now available). The implication is retirees should on average be able to outperform the baseline numbers; nevertheless, it takes more data than is available to adequately confirm this. While the baseline numbers are best suited for planning, it doesn't hurt to hope for better.

The Point

The Baseline Market and Baseline Portfolio provide realistic estimates of future retirement income and risk for planning based on a globally diversified high-HR portfolio.

CHAPTER 7 GUIDE

This chapter identifies the appropriate stock percentages for retirement portfolios. It starts by outlining the problem and finishes with a table of recommendations.

Less interested readers can skim the chapter and focus on the recommendations.

Readers who might want to veer from the core recommendations should also consider "Other Measures and Tradeoffs".

*Don't totally avoid risk, or swim in it with abandon; risk
should be appropriately embraced like a dear old aunt.*

WALTER E. GOH

SETTING THE STOCK PERCENTAGE

THE MOST DIFFICULT INVESTMENT DECISION for many retirees is setting the portfolio's stock percentage. Wade Pfau's international backtesting results[40] in Figure 104 illustrate the difficulty of the problem. Pfau shows the optimal stock percentage for 17 different developed markets. These optimal percentages range from 15% in Switzerland to 100% in Germany, Japan, and Spain. What works best for one specific market has little correlation with what works best for another. Trying to use these numbers as a guide is disorienting.

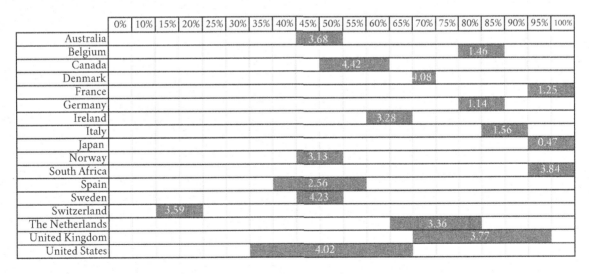

FIGURE 104

*The optimal stock-percentage range for 30-year retirements for each of 17 countries from 1900
through 2008 using annual rebalancing, fixed withdrawals, and total-market portfolio.
Shown with each highlighted range of stock percentages is MSWR-100% for each country.*

Surveying the literature for advice doesn't make the problem easier. Expert recommendations, when they are clearly stated, aren't consistent. A quick Internet query finds stock recommendations ranging from 30% to 60%. In other cases, the recommendations are very general, or based on a retiree's risk tolerance…a subjective value. Rarely is there any supporting data. It's all confusing.

This lack of clear answers partly stems from the traditional assumption of annual rebalancing. Annual rebalancing locks in the stock percentage, keeping it fixed no matter what is happening in the market or with the portfolio. The trouble is that as market conditions change, the best performing stock percentage changes with it.

In contrast, a smart income-harvesting strategy lets the stock percentage float. No longer are retirees picking one fixed percentage to last throughout retirement. They need only pick an initial stock percentage, letting the income-harvesting strategy manage it going forward. This is a much easier problem.

Figure 105 shows a snippet of the problem by comparing annual rebalancing's fixed stock percentage to Prime-Harvesting's *initial* stock percentage for the US, UK, and Japan markets. In each case, the optimal stock percentage is highlighted along with its MSWR-100%. Notice the optimal stock percentage is less consistent with annual rebalancing than with Prime Harvesting. For annual rebalancing, the optimal range (in the highlighted box) spans 50% (from 40% to 90%), but for Prime Harvesting, the optimal range spans only 25% (from 40% to 65%) while also boosting performance. Using Prime Harvesting, a 50% to 55% initial stock percentage works well across all three cases.

Annual Rebalancing	0% Stock	10% Stock	20% Stock	30% Stock	35% Stock	40% Stock	45% Stock	50% Stock	55% Stock	60% Stock	65% Stock	70% Stock	80% Stock	90% Stock	100% Stock
US SBBI Total-Market Portfolio (1928 - 2010)	2.2%	2.7%	3.1%	3.6%	3.7%	3.8%	3.8%	3.8%	3.8%	3.7%	3.7%	3.7%	3.6%	3.5%	3.4%
UK (1923 - 2010)	1.7%	2.0%	2.2%	2.4%	2.5%	2.6%	2.7%	2.8%	2.9%	3.0%	3.1%	3.2%	3.4%	3.4%	3.2%
Japan (1950 - 2010)	2.7%	2.9%	3.0%	3.1%	3.1%	3.2%	3.2%	3.2%	3.2%	3.3%	3.3%	3.3%	3.3%	3.3%	3.2%

Prime Harvesting	0% Stock	10% Stock	20% Stock	30% Stock	35% Stock	40% Stock	45% Stock	50% Stock	55% Stock	60% Stock	65% Stock	70% Stock	80% Stock	90% Stock	100% Stock
US SBBI Total-Market Portfolio (1928 - 2010)	2.2%	3.2%	3.7%	3.8%	3.8%	3.9%	3.9%	3.8%	3.8%	3.8%	3.7%	3.6%	3.6%	3.5%	3.4%
UK (1923 - 2010)	1.7%	2.3%	2.9%	3.2%	3.3%	3.4%	3.5%	3.6%	3.7%	3.7%	3.7%	3.6%	3.4%	3.4%	3.2%
Japan (1950 - 2010)	2.7%	3.0%	3.3%	3.5%	3.7%	3.8%	3.9%	3.8%	3.8%	3.8%	3.8%	3.7%	3.6%	3.4%	3.2%

FIGURE 105

The range of optimal stock percentage across three markets for Prime Harvesting and traditional annual rebalancing. The stock percentage with the highest MSWR-100% is highlighted for each dataset.

In fact though, the above only sets the stage—the precise problem to be solved has important differences. To start, a portfolio's initial stock percentage need only be based on what works well for a globally diversified portfolio, removing or at least strongly dampening the idiosyncratic nature of specific markets.

Picking the proper stock percentage in retirement must start with the right assumptions and the right goal, so let's first take a step back.

THE ASSUMPTIONS AND THE GOAL

The retirement portfolio's initial stock percentage should work well when following best practices. While this may sounds obvious, most examples in the literate revolve around poor practices: annual rebalancing with a total-market stock portfolio based on US markets. Here, the following starting assumptions guide selecting an appropriate initial stock percentage:

1. The portfolio is globally diversified, averaging performance across many markets and muting the anomalous behavior in specific markets.

2. A strong income-harvesting strategy (e.g., Prime Harvesting) is applied, letting the stock-bond percentage float as needed, reducing sensitivity to specific global market conditions and retirement parameters.

3. The portfolio has a high-HR, producing sufficient income as safely as possible from the stock allocation.

Also, the goal can't be to minimize *all* risk, which includes speculative risk. To do so would require lowering the withdrawal rate substantially and eliminating all stocks from the portfolio. The goal is to minimize known risk, which supports a healthy retirement income.

Additionally, it's judicious to assume fixed withdrawals to simplify the problem. This translates into the following: the optimal initial stock percentage is the one supporting the highest MSWR-100% using a smart income-harvesting strategy and strong retirement portfolio. (Later in the book, variable-withdrawals will be reincorporated.)

Other measures besides MSWR-100% should also be examined, but they are usually secondary. Optimizing the stock percentage based on MSWR-90% typically generates more income for a small increase in risk. Also, MSWR-50%, as the median MSWR value, helps to understand the typical tradeoffs between choosing one stock percentage over another.

Finally, although the word "optimal" is used throughout, picking the optimal for the future is impossible. Nevertheless, if the optimal (or near optimal) for the past can be shown to be stable and consistent, it is the right choice for the future.

FINDING AND SUBSTANTIATING THE RIGHT PERCENTAGE

A good starting place to look for the right stock percentage is to randomly generate many different portfolios and see how the stock percentage affects MSWR-100%.

Figure 106 shows MSWR-100% averages across three tests, each backtesting 25,000 random portfolios for a 30-year retirement. The results are broken up by deciles, based on each portfolio's initial stock percentage. Following are each test's parameters.

- Test 1: US data with the stock allocation randomly selected (bonds are held constant).

- Test 2: US data with both the stock and bond allocations randomly selected.

- Test 3: Baseline Market with the stock allocation randomly selected (bonds are held constant).

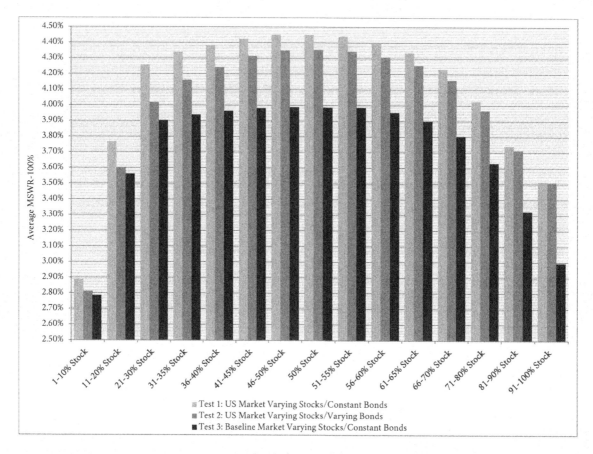

FIGURE 106

Average MSWR-100% by initial stock percentage across three tests of 25,000 random portfolios.

The focus should be on the Baseline Market, Test 3, but the other two cases help to ensure that the general results are not sensitive to one context.

Based on the averages, it's notable all three sets show 50% as the optimal initial stock percentage.

Averages sometimes hide important details, so another approach is used to look at individual results for high-HR portfolios. Figure 107 highlights the optimal stock-percentage range for 100 high-HR portfolios, with the data compressed for a visual overview. These 100 portfolios are randomly generated for diversity, but guaranteed to have a relatively high harvesting ratio*. The first line in the figure highlights the first portfolio's optimal stock percentage ranges from 40% to 55%; the second portfolio in the second line again ranges from 40% to 55%; the third from 45% to 55%. This continues for another 97 portfolios, one per line. There is a clear pattern: every one of the 100 portfolios includes 50% stocks within its optimal range.

Figure 107 does not show specific MSWR-100% values, but it's worth noting that outside the optimal range, performance does not drop off sharply, but slowly tappers off. For example, MSWR-100% is 4.1% at the optimal stock percentage of 50% to 55% stocks, but MSWR-100 only drops to 4.0% going down to 35% stocks or up to 65% stocks. This flexibility of going outside the optimal with only a small loss of income increases the likelihood of picking a percentage with a strong future performance.

---

* The 100 portfolios with the highest harvesting ratios are selected from a set of 1000 randomly generated portfolios.

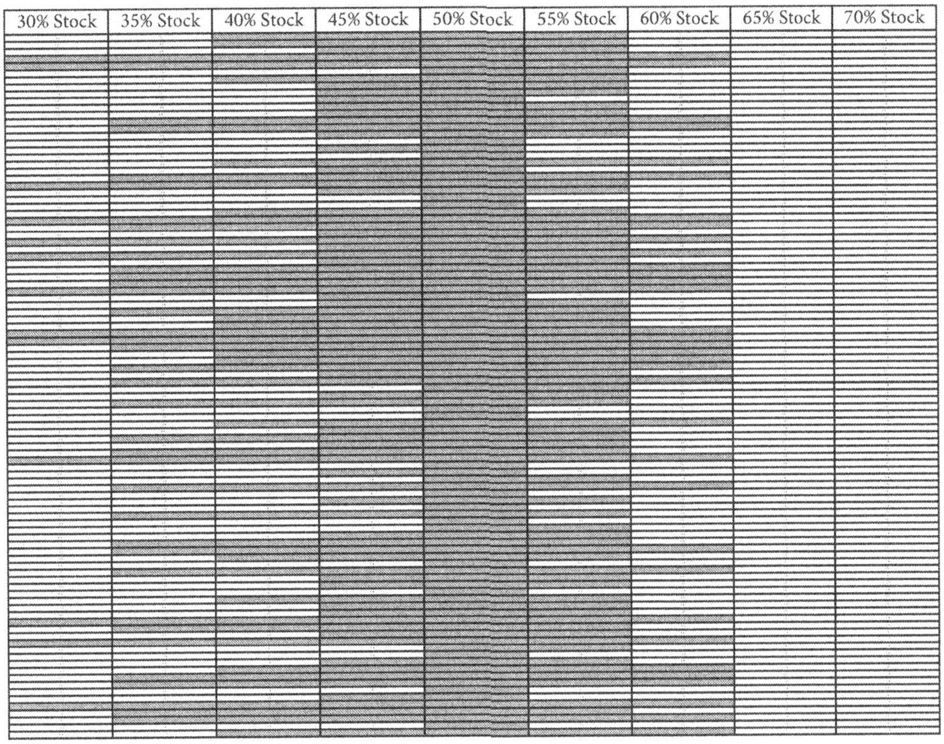

30% Stock	35% Stock	40% Stock	45% Stock	50% Stock	55% Stock	60% Stock	65% Stock	70% Stock

FIGURE 107

Prime Harvesting's optimal initial stock percentage range based on MSWR-100% for 100 randomly generated high-HR portfolios using the Baseline Market for 30-year retirements.

Sometimes, it's tempting to believe that lower stock percentages are always safer during poor markets, but actually, the opposite is sometimes true. Consider the following case using the previous numbers for a low-return world—an alternate baseline is created with real returns for total-market stocks reduced to 3.25% (down from the Baseline's 5%) and bonds real returns reduced to 0.5% (down from the Baseline's 1.8%). This reduces the equity premium to 2.75% from 3.2%. The other asset classes are also reduced by the same proportions. MSWR-100% also drops 2.9% (down from the Baseline's 3.5%). What's most notable in this case is the effect on the optimal initial stock percentage—Figure 108 shows it rises for the same 100 random portfolios. The exceptionally poor market increases the optimal initial stock allocation to 55%. Certainly, the optimal can drop for some poor markets, but a retiree cannot assume that a lower stock percentage is the best way to handle the risk of poor markets.

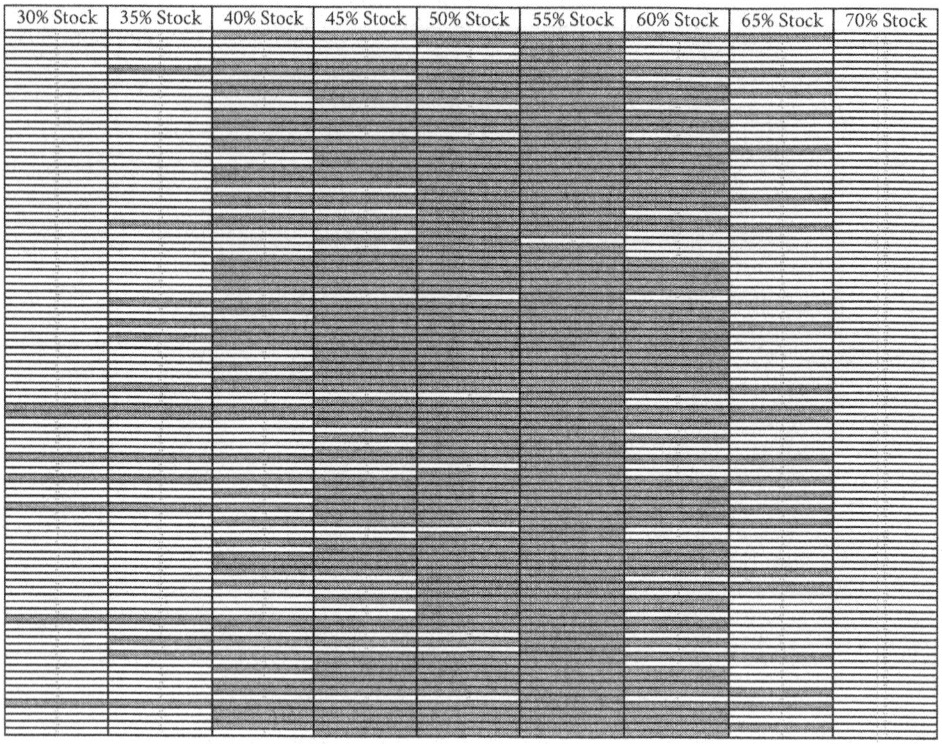

FIGURE 108

The optimal initial stock percentage range based on MSWR-100% for 100 randomly generated high-HR portfolios under a low-return world. Annualized stock returns are scaled down to 3.3% for total-market portfolio and annualized bond returns are scaled down to 0.5%, with other portfolios scaled proportionally.

Distinct from the known risk, speculative risk will attribute increased risk to more stocks. This implies retirees can use a stock percentage below the known-risk optimum in order to reduce speculative risk, but this should be done only in moderation and then *only* if the withdrawal rate is correspondingly lowered (which will be covered). While this simple option may suit some retirees, the most reliable approach to addressing speculative risk will always remain outside the boundaries of systemic withdraws using guaranteed income. As a general rule, let systemic withdrawals do what it does well (managing volatile portfolio, producing strong income) by providing it with the best possible parameters to work from, then use guaranteed income to reduce risk further if desired.

Coming back to known risk, the tentative conclusions up to this point follow. A 50% initial stock allocation is optimal for the Baseline Market. When markets stray from their normal behavior, it's impossible to know exactly how this will manifest—a higher or lower stock percentage may perform better. However, global diversification increases market consistency by averaging the behavior of many specific markets into one single global market. Also, when global market behavior does stray, there is reason to believe that a 50% stock percentage will still perform comparatively well because retirement performance from the stock allocation doesn't typically drop off sharply.

So far, the evidence for a 50% optimal stock percentage is based solely on MSWR-100%, which corresponds to the worst-case scenario. What happens when success rates are instead examined using fixed withdrawal rates (e.g., 4.5%, 5%)?

Generally, an upward push is exerted on the optimal stock percentage as fixed withdrawal rates rise: more income to support withdrawals requires more stocks. Using annual rebalancing, the optimal for a fixed 4% withdrawal rate ranges from 45% to 50%; the optimal for a 4.5% withdrawal rate is 60%; the optimal for a 5% withdrawal rate is 70%. (Again, these optimums are based on success rates.) In contrast, using Prime Harvesting, this upward push is partly compensated for with a floating stock percentage.

Figure 109, Figure 110, and Figure 111 highlight the optimum stock percentage for 4%, 4.5%, and 5% fixed withdrawals respectively, using Prime Harvesting. For the 4% and 4.5% percent cases, a 50% stock percentage remains optimal. For the 5% case, the optimum rises to 55%. What's important is 50% in stocks is a consistently strong initial allocation.

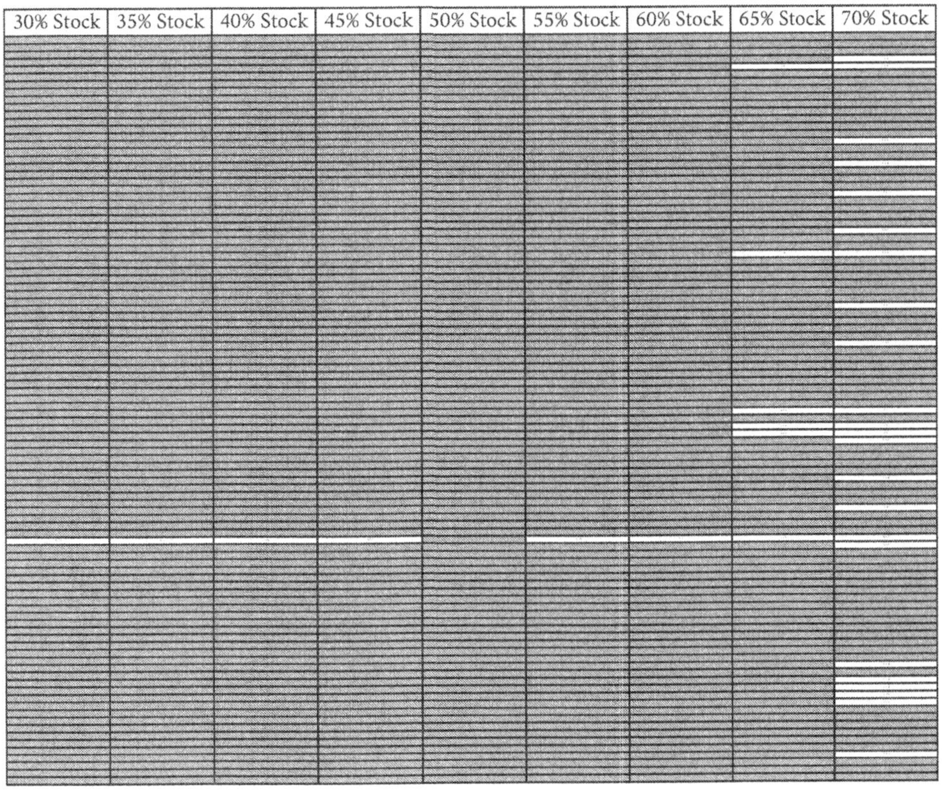

FIGURE 109

Prime Harvesting optimal initial stock percentage range based on success rate for 4% withdrawals for 100 random high-HR portfolios under Baseline Markets.

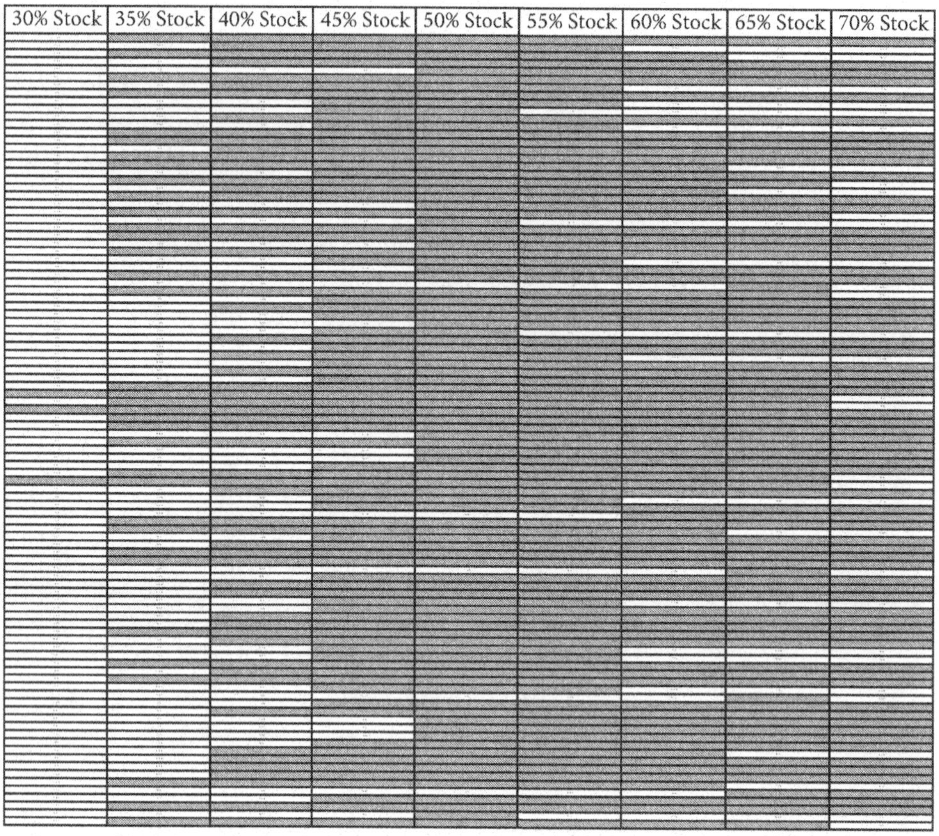

FIGURE 110

*Prime Harvesting optimal initial stock percentage range based on success rate for 4.5%
withdrawals for 100 random high-HR portfolios under Baseline Markets.*

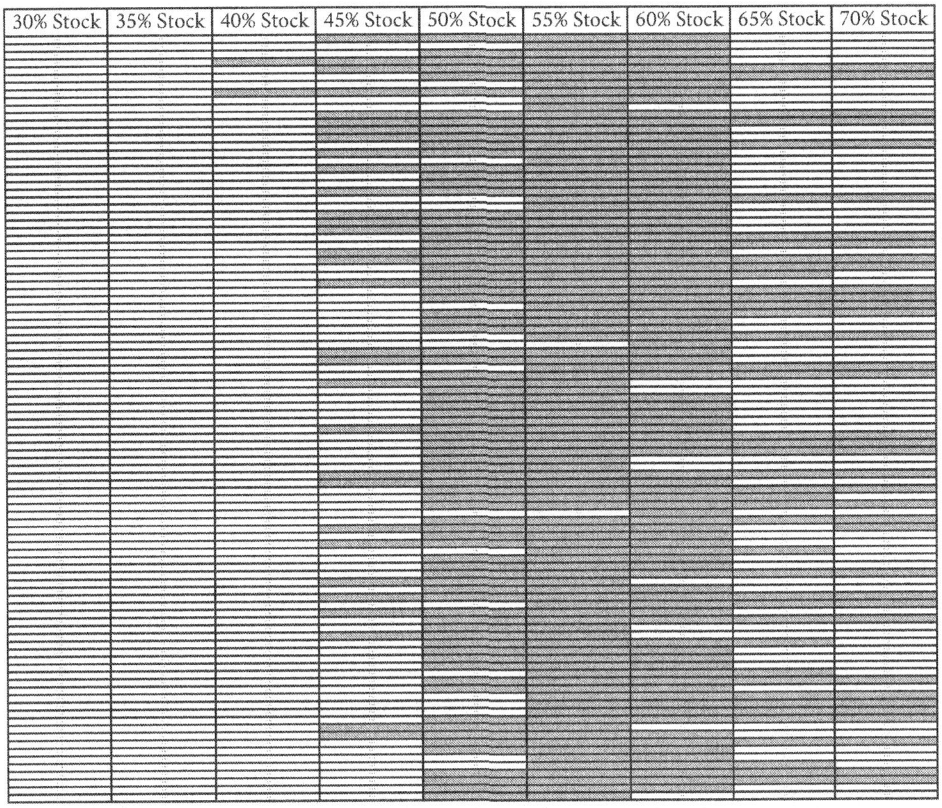

FIGURE 111

*Prime Harvesting optimal initial stock percentage range based on success rate for 5%
withdrawals for 100 random high-HR portfolios under Baseline Markets.*

Preliminary testing also shows the optimal stock percentage does not appear overly sensitive to the exact harvesting strategy as long as stock-bond percentages are allowed to efficiently float. Figure 112 shows the optimal stock percentages for four other top-performing income-harvesting strategies along with Prime Harvesting: Weiss, Parker, OmegaNot, and Alternate Prime. In every case, the initial stock percentage of 50% falls in the optimal range.

Initial Stock Percentage	Weiss	Parker	OmegaNot	Alternate Prime	Prime Harvesting
25%	3.7	4	4.1	3.8	4.1
30%	3.9	4.2	4.2	4.2	4.2
35%	4.1	4.2	4.2	4.3	4.2
40%	4.1	4.2	4.3	4.3	4.3
45%	4.1	4.2	4.3	4.3	4.3
50%	4.1	4.2	4.3	4.3	4.3
55%	4	4.2	4.3	4.3	4.3
60%	3.8	4.2	4.2	4.2	4.2
65%	3.8	4.2	4.2	4.2	4.2
70%	3.8	4.1	4.1	4.1	4.1
75%	3.6	3.9	3.9	3.9	3.9

FIGURE 112

Performance of different income-harvesting strategies with varying initial stock percentages using the Baseline Market and Portfolio. The optimal performance (in relation to 50%) is highlighted for each strategy.

Figure 113 focuses on Alternate-Prime's optimal stock range for the 100 random high-HR portfolios. Although less consistent than Prime Harvesting, Alternate-Prime's optimal stock percentage is still 50%. There is greater variance, because Alternate-Prime puts more emphasis on income (in contrast to Prime Harvesting's emphasis on safety). Even so, the performance cost when the optimal varies outside the 50% range remains consistently small, such as 4.1% instead of 4.2%.

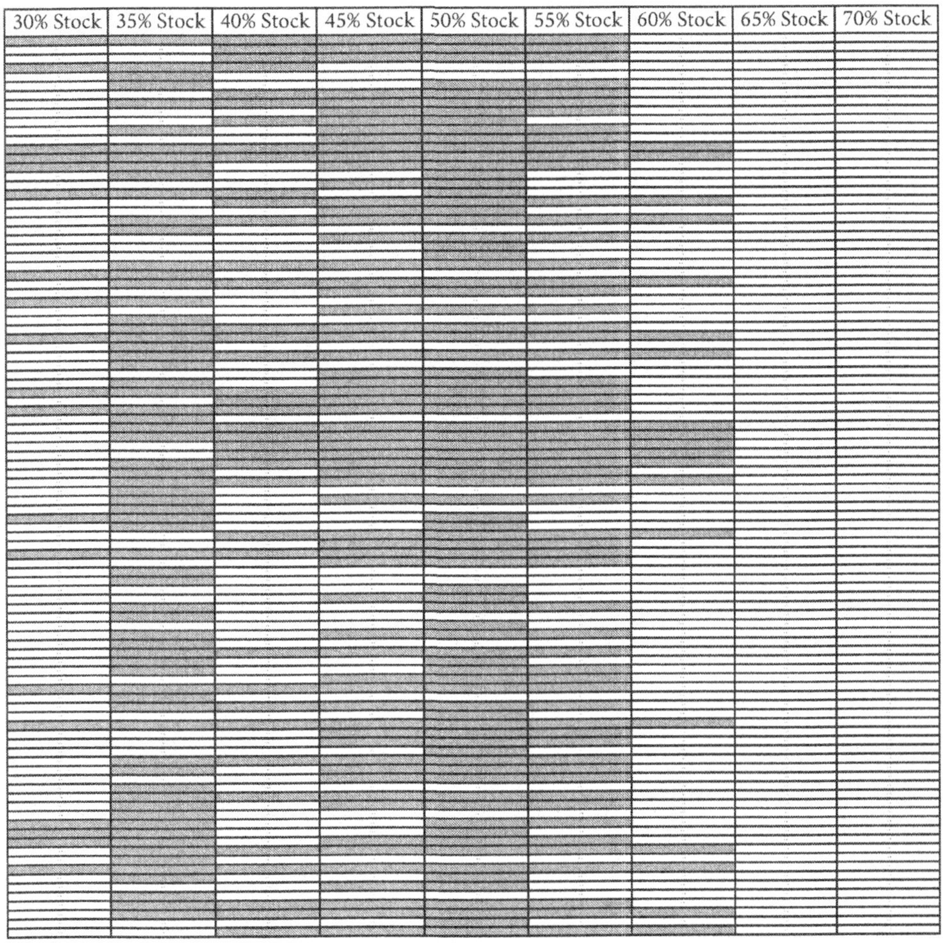

FIGURE 113

*Alternate-Prime Harvesting's optimal initial stock percentage range based on MSWR-100% for
100 randomly generated high-HR portfolios using the Baseline Market for 30-year retirements.*

The focus has been appropriately on the Baseline Market, but it's still a single dataset. To verify the optimal percentage across distinctly different markets, a bootstrapping simulation* is used. Previously used in Chapter 3, bootstrapping is a simple Monte Carlo simulation, which randomly resamples the SBBI data to produce many new sets of market data. This enables backtesting with significantly different return and volatility characteristics†. As before, the downside is that bootstrapping filters out all aspects of return disposition (hurting income-harvesting efficiency). While these results do not fully correspond to true markets, they provide an excellent sanity check for how a 50% stock allocation performs under many market variations.

Figure 114 shows the bootstrapping simulation results for backtesting across 1000 simulated markets. The average success rate is shown for varying stock percentages using three different withdrawal rates. The results are both significant and reassuring:

---

*   In this case, a bootstrap simulation is the best option for satisfying the evidence-based research criteria for an independent data source.

†   All the retirement risk factors can potentially affect the optimal initial stock percentage, plus the equity premium.

- For a 5% withdrawal rate, the success rate peaks at the 50% stock allocation: the optimum.

- For a 4.5% withdrawal rate, a 50% allocation comes within 99.7% of the performance of the 40% optimal success rate.

- For a 4.0% withdrawal rate, a 50% allocation comes within 99.1% of the performance of the 30% optimal success rate.

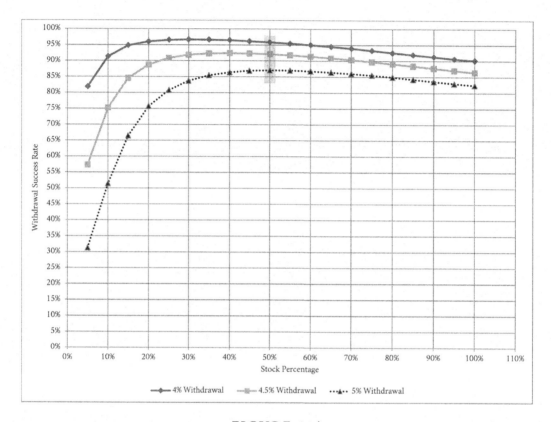

FIGURE 114

Average Prime Harvesting success rates across 1000 diverse markets from a bootstrapping simulation. The Baseline Portfolio is used for each of the market simulations.

Again, bootstrapping produces difficult cases for Prime Harvesting, nevertheless, the results show a 50% initial stock allocation typically performed at or near optimal across many diverse markets.

The conclusion using systemic withdrawals is so far clear: a 50% initial stock allocation is likely the safest initial stock allocation for the future when adhering to best practices for a 30-year retirement.

OTHER MEASURES AND TRADEOFFS

So far the focus has been on the safest stock allocation; however, putting all the data on the table may motivate some retirees to use a higher (or lower) stock allocation.

Figure 115 uses MSWR-100%, MSWR-90%, and MSWR-50% to consider the average effects of using a 60% stock allocation for the 100 high-HR portfolios. The tradeoffs aren't obvious at first glance, but examples will help. Again, MSWR-90% measures performance at the bottom 10 percentile (i.e., 90% do better), and MSWR-50% measures performance for the retirement period in the middle (the median rate). Examining MSWR-90% (the middle line in the figure) shows a 60% stock allocation to be optimal (after removing the worst 10% of the retirement periods). Using 60% stocks increases the withdrawal on average 0.2% compared to MSWR-90% with 50% in stocks (i.e., from 5.5% up to 5.7% as shown by Point A). This means 90% of the time 0.2% or more income will be gained (i.e., $2000 or more annually for a $1 million portfolio). Staying with 60% stock and looking at MSWR-50% on the top line shows the average increase is 0.6% or more 50% of the time (i.e., from 7% to 7.6% as shown by Point B). This means that 50% of the time, 0.6% or more income will be gained (i.e., $6000 or more annually for a $1 million portfolio). Going the other direction to MSWR-100%, 10% of the time the 60% allocation will on average decrease income 0.05% (from 4.3% to 4.25 as shown by Point C). This means 10% of the time, only a minimal amount up to 0.05% will be lost (i.e., up to $500 for a $1 million portfolio). Still, it's important to understand, the future may not conform to these numbers in general and almost certainly will not with the precision shown; nevertheless, this is the best data available to consider tradeoffs.

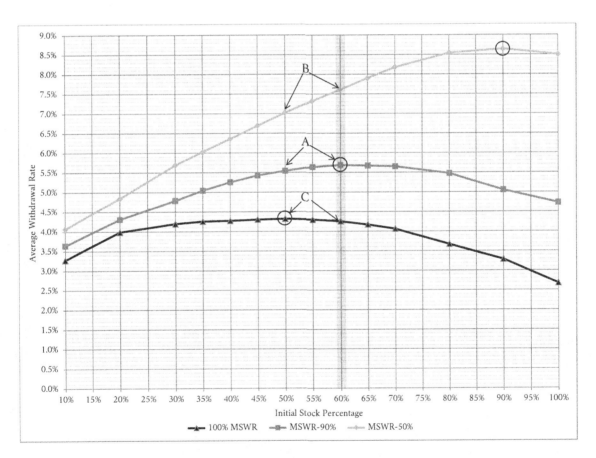

FIGURE 115

*Comparison of average MSWR-100%, MSWR-90%, and MSWR-50% for
100 randomly generated high-HR portfolios under the Baseline Market using
Prime Harvesting. The circle represents the optimal for each metric.*

Retirees can reach their own conclusions, but the benefit from raising the stock percentage above the optimal at 50% to 60% is an attractive alternative considering known risk (especially coupled with a variable-withdrawal strategy to compensate when needed). Yet, speculative risk forever exists as the unmeasurable entity, so the decision remains subjective.

An opposite consideration for some retirees is lowering the stock percentage under the MSWR-100% optimum to reduce speculative risk, but doing so will cause known risk to rise. The implication is to lower the stock allocation below the optimal requires a corresponding drop in the initial withdrawal rate. Figure 116 in the next section shows the percentage the initial withdrawal rate should drop as the initial stock percentage is lowered (the table values are calculated based on changes observed in MSWR-90%). As an example, lowering the initial stock percentage to 40% means that the retiree should correspondingly drop an initial income rate of 4.2% down by 5% to 4.0% (again, based on changes observed in MSWR-90%). Similarly, dropping the stock allocation to 30% should come with a 10% decrease in the initial income rate (e.g., dropping the initial rate from 4.2% to 3.8%). Pushing the initial stock percentage lower than 30% isn't recommended, because the decrease in income accelerates quickly.

Setting the initial withdrawal rate is discussed thoroughly in Chapter 9, but here it's important to understand that lowering the initial stock percentage below optimum should always be accompanied with a decrease in income, to keep known risk constant.

However, as mentioned before, lowering the stock allocations remains a limited and incomplete approach to reducing speculative risk when compared to using guaranteed income. Still, a modest drop in the stock percentage and the initial withdrawal rate will work well for some retirees.

THE RECOMMENDATIONS

Figure 116 summarizes the overall recommendations, now including other retirement lengths and alternative starting stock percentages. (Note the reference point for increasing or decreasing the withdrawal rate is a 30-year retirement with a 50% stock allocation.)

	15-Year Retirement	20-Year Retirement	30-Year Retirement	40+ Year Retirement
Viable Higher Percentage	45% Stock, Increase Withdrawal Rate by 20%	55% Stock, Increase Withdrawal Rate by 10%	60% Stock, No Change of Withdrawal Rate	65% Stock, Decrease Withdrawal Rate by 5%
Recommended Initial Stock	35% Stock, Increase Withdrawal Rate by 20%	45% Stock, Increase Withdrawal Rate by 10%	50% Stock, Withdrawal Rate Reference Point	55% Stock, Decrease Withdrawal Rate by 5%
Viable Lower Percentage	25% Stock, Increase Withdrawal Rate by 15%	35% Stock, Increase Withdrawal Rate by 5%	40% Stock, Decrease Withdrawal Rate by 5%	45% Stock, Decrease Withdrawal Rate by 10%
Minimum Percentage	15% Stock, Increase Withdrawal Rate by 10%	25% Stock, Withdrawal Rate Unchanged	30% Stock, Decrease Withdrawal Rate by 10%	35% Stock, Decrease Withdrawal Rate by 15%

FIGURE 116

Recommended initial stock percentages for different retirement lengths.

The recommended initial stock percentages in the highlighted row are all based on the optimal values using backtesting. The higher percentages shown, over the optimum, will boost income for a small increase in both known and speculative risk. The lower percentages shown, under the optimum, will reduce speculative risk, but at the cost of decreasing income to keep known risk constant. Both the optimal initial stock percentage and the initial withdrawal rate also change with the retirement length. For shorter retirements, the optimal percentage decreases and the income level increases. For longer retirements, the optimal percentage increases and the income level decreases.

These recommendations only apply to starting values. After the initial stock percentage is set, the income-harvesting strategy (i.e., Prime Harvesting) manages the stock percentage. After the initial withdrawal rate is set (the topic of Chapter 9), the variable-withdrawal strategy manages the annual withdrawal rate.

A few examples clarify. For a 40-year retirement, the optimal initial stock allocation is 55%, with the initial withdrawal rate decreasing by 5% (e.g., a default of 4.2% is lowered 5% down to 4%). For a 30-year retirement, a viable higher initial stock percentage is 60%, with no change to the initial rate (although year to year withdrawals will likely increase through the variable-withdrawal strategy by using the increased stock percentage). For a 15-year retirement, the minimum stock percentage is 15%, but it should be accompanied by a 10% drop in the initial withdrawal rate to compensate. Again, all values and adjustments are derived from backtesting.

As a final note, the risk stemming from the stock percentage is not always the same. It shifts with market valuations; therefore, one intuitively might expect the optimal initial stock percentage to also shift with market valuations. It does to some extent, but not as much as one might expect during tough markets. Therefore, it's sufficient to let the income-harvesting strategy and variable-withdrawal strategy compensate, without trying to adjust the initial stock percentage using valuations. However, this topic, along with the option to consider valuations, is revisited toward the end of Chapter 9.

The Point

A smart income-harvesting strategy supports the identification of an optimal initial stock percentage, which is 50% for a 30-year retirement using best practices. This optimum is easily adjusted for longer or shorter retirement plans. Optionally, for a small increase in known risk, the initial stock percentage can be raised (e.g., 10%) to moderately boost average income. Or conversely, a small decrease in speculative risk can be gained by lowering (e.g., 10%) the initial stock percentage under the optimum, but this requires a corresponding decrease in the initial withdrawal rate to keep known risk from rising.

This chapter focuses on what a retirement portfolio's asset allocation should look like and why. Specific portfolio recommendations with example funds are provided.

It's worth the read, although less interested readers can skim most of the chapter to focus on the recommendations.

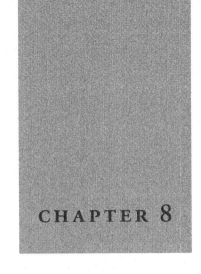

Some financial economists may benefit from putting aside their rigor and taking a random walk through the empirical data.

Walter E. Goh

CHAPTER 8

PORTFOLIO CONSTRUCTION USING THE HARVESTING RATIO

Chapter 5 verified the Harvesting Ratio (HR) for identifying which portfolios are more likely to succeed in retirement. This chapter applies HR to a variety of real portfolios. What works best is then refined into a small set of portfolio recommendations.

For some retirees, the recommendations may seem obvious, aligning with longstanding assumptions; for others the recommendations may seem iconoclastic, picking apart long-standing assumptions of what makes a safe retirement portfolio. What's distinct is the recommendations follow from the data. Certainly, no one can claim how a specific portfolio will perform for an upcoming retirement, but it is possible to identify those portfolios most likely to safely perform well across a diverse range of future possibilities.

APPLYING HR TO THE LAZY PORTFOLIOS

The Lazy Portfolios are a loosely defined set within the investment literature, pulled together from various sources. They are discussed on many websites and several books. Perhaps the best known advocate of Lazy Portfolios is Market Watch columnist Paul B. Farrell[41]. The purpose of the portfolios is to provide viable examples for individual investors to consider, compare, and potentially duplicate in their own portfolio. The bogleheads.org website has this to say: "Lazy portfolios are designed to perform well in most market conditions. Most contain a small number of low-cost funds that are easy to rebalance. They are 'lazy' in that the investor can maintain the same asset allocation for an extended period of time."

The Lazy Portfolios provides a good starting point for comparing the HR values of real portfolios. These portfolios may not be defined or advocated for retirement (I don't know the original intent of most), but no doubt some investors see the Lazy Portfolios as candidates for retirement, especially the stock breakdowns. Undoubtedly, the Lazy Portfolios provide a diverse range of choices and in doing so provide a good basis for examining HR values.

Simba's spreadsheet[42], the same referenced in Chapter 5 and Appendix A, conveniently includes a version of 24 Lazy Portfolios along with the data needed to calculate HR for each portfolio. The Lazy Portfolios and their composition as listed in Simba's spreadsheet are shown in Figure 117.

Fund	Ticker	Wellington	Wellesley	Taylor Larimore P3	Taylor Larimore 3 Fund	Taylor Larimore 4 Fund	Rick Ferri Core Four	Bill Berstein No Brainer Cowards	Bill Berstein No Brainer	Bill Bernstein Smart Money	Dilbert's Portfolio	Ted Aronson Family Taxable	Bill Schultheis Coffee House	FundAdvice Ultimate Buy & Hold	David Swensen Lazy Portfolio	David Swensen Yale Endowment	2nd Grader	Frank Armstrong Ideal Idx	Scott Burns Couch Portfolio	Scott Burns Margaritaville	Scott Burns Four Square	Scott Burns Five Fold	Scott Burns Six Ways from Sunday	Larry Swedroe Simple Portfolio	Larry Swedroe Minimize FatTails Portfolio
Total US Market	VTSMX			80%	50%	50%	48%	15%		15%	70%	5%	10%	6%	30%	30%	60%		50%	34%	25%	20%	16.67%		
Large Cap Value	VIVAX							10%		10%								9.25%						15%	
Large Cap Blend	VFINX								25%			15%	10%	6%				6.25%							
Large Cap Growth	VIGRX																								
Mid-Cap Blend	VIMSX																								
Small Cap Value	VISVX							10%		10%		5%	10%	6%				9.25%						15%	15%
Small Cap Blend	NAESX							5%	25%	5%			10%											13%	
Small Cap Growth	VISGX											5%						6.25%							
Micro Cap	BRSIX													6%											
REIT	VGSIX						8%	5%		5%			10%	6%	20%	20%		8%				20%	16.66%		
Intl Developed - EAFE	VDMIX							5%	25%	5%				6%	15%	15%									
Emerging Mkt	VEIEX											10%		6%	5%	5%								4%	15%
Total International	VGTSX				30%	30%	24%										30%	31%		33%	25%	20%	16.66%		
Intl Pacific	VPACX							5%		5%		15%													
Intl Europe	VEURX							5%		5%		5%													
Intl Value	VTRIX													6%											
VG Intl Small	VFSVX													12%										13%	
Wellington - Balanced	VWELX	100%																							
Wellesley - Balanced	VWINX		100%																						
Energy Fund	VGENX																								
Long Term Govt Bond	VUSTX													20%											
5 Yr T-Bills	VFITX										30%	10%	40%			15%									
Total Bond	VBMFX			20%	20%	10%	20%	40%		40%				8%	15%		10%		50%						
Synthetic TIPS	VIPSX					10%									15%	15%				33%	25%	20%	16.66%		35%
High Yield Corp	VWEHX											5%		12%											
2 Year ST Treasury	VFISX								25%			10%						30%						40%	35%
VG Extended Market	VEXMX																						16.66%		
Global Bond Fund	PIGLX																				25%	20%	16.66%		
ST Investment Grade	VFSTX																								
Stock Total		67%	40%	80%	80%	80%	80%	60%	75%	60%	70%	60%	60%	60%	70%	70%	90%	70%	50%	67%	50%	60%	67%	60%	30%
Bond Total		33%	60%	20%	20%	20%	20%	40%	25%	40%	30%	40%	40%	40%	30%	30%	10%	30%	50%	33%	50%	40%	33%	40%	70%

FIGURE 117

The Lazy Portfolios.

Simba's spreadsheet has two sets of historical portfolio data: the first, spanning 27 years from 1985 to 2011, includes more extensive asset choices; the second, spanning 40 years from 1972 to 2011, includes fewer asset choices. The Lazy Portfolios in Figure 117 use the shorter dataset spanning 27 years. Later, modifications will be made to the portfolios so the 40-year data can be used. In all cases, the spreadsheet supplies the portfolios' average return and standard deviation, making it easy* to calculate HR.

Figure 118 shows the HR values for each Lazy Portfolio, assuming a 3% inflation rate with both 4% and 5% withdrawal rates. As the graph shows, the portfolios' suitability for retirement as measured by HR varies significantly. Recall though that HR is a dimensionless metric, like the Sharpe Ratio, meaning it's hard to predict how these context-dependent measurements might translate into specific amounts of retirement income, but we can say history shows the high-HR portfolios perform significantly better than the low-HR portfolios in retirement.

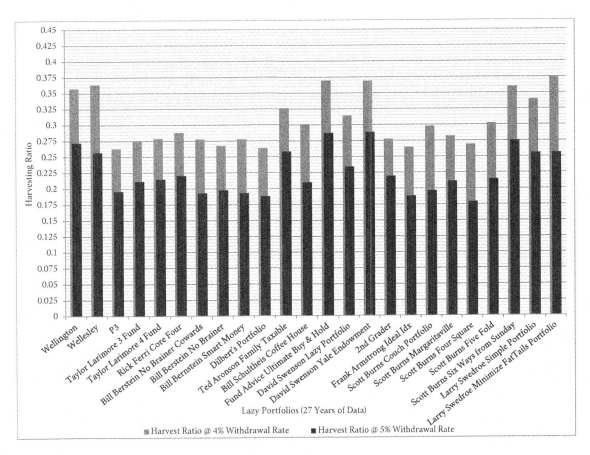

FIGURE 118

Harvesting Ratio for Lazy Portfolios using 27 years of data.

---

*   For those comfortable with Excel, it's a simple modification to add the HR calculation directly to Simba's spreadsheet.

However, as discussed in Chapter 5, calculating HR from 27 years of data is not ideal, especially when better data is in hand. With a few minor modifications to the Lazy Portfolios, the second, longer set of spreadsheet data can be used, supporting a more reliable HR calculation based on 40 years of data. The following modifications to four of the Lazy Portfolios are all that is needed to use the longer dataset.

- For Bill Bernstein's Smart Money Portfolio, 40% in ST Investment Grade Bond (VFSTX) is replaced by 40% in 2-Year ST Treasuries Bond (VFISX).

- For Ted Aronson's Family Taxable Portfolio, 5% in High Yield Corp Bond (VWEHX) is replaced with 5% in Total Bond (VBMFX); 10% in VG Extended Market (VEXMX) is replaced with a combination of 5% in Mid-Cap Blend (VIMSX) and 5% in Small-Cap Blend (NAESX).

- For Scott Burns' Four Square Portfolio, 25% in Global Bond Fund (PIGLX) is replaced with 25% in Total Bond (VBMFX)

- For Scott Burns' Five Fold Portfolio, 20% in Global Bond Fund (PIGLX) is replaced with 20% in Total Bond (VBMFX)

The above modifications result in a couple of duplicate portfolios. Two portfolios are dropped (one of Bill Bernstein's and one of Scott Burns') leaving a total of 22 Lazy Portfolios using the longer dataset.

Figure 119 shows the HR value for each Lazy Portfolio using the 40-year data, again assuming a 3% inflation rate with both 4% and 5% withdrawal rates. The 40-year data generally pushed up all the HR values, but most of the relative relationships remained the same. Still, there are some important differences. For example, for a 5% withdrawal rate, David Swenson's Yale Endowment Portfolio drops from first place down to eighth place with the larger dataset. For the same case, Larry Swedroe's Simple Portfolio moves from eighth place up to third. Most likely, the 40-year dataset is more accurate—shorter datasets can often reflect temporary asset behavior as opposed to fundamentals.

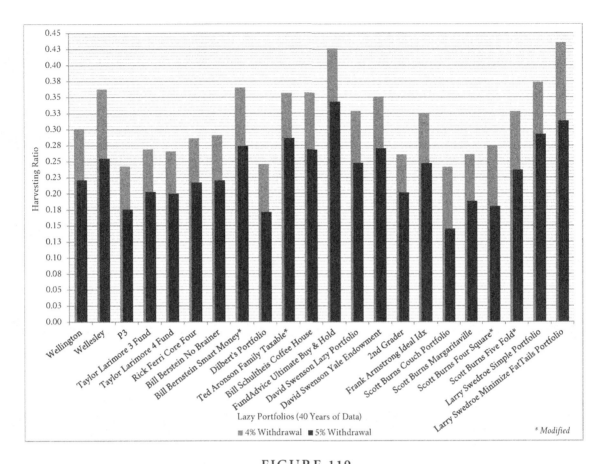

FIGURE 119

Harvesting Ratio for Lazy Portfolios modified to include 40 years of data.

Two distinct portfolios emerge with the highest HR values: FundAdvice's Ultimate Buy and Hold Portfolio, and Larry Swedroe's Minimize Fat Tails Portfolio—more will be said of these later.

Returning to the guidelines outlined in Chapter Five, HR provides more accurate portfolio comparisons if the same bond allocation and same stock-bond ratio are used. With this in mind, the bond allocation for all the Lazy Portfolios is normalized, so each uses the same bond allocation and percentage.

Figure 120 shows the new set of bond-normalized Lazy Portfolios. Every portfolio now has a 50% stocks allocation (while maintaining the same underlying stock proportions), and a 50% matching bond allocation. As before, duplicate portfolios were created, so now the list contains only 18 portfolios. *(For convenience, the same portfolio names are used, although they no longer match their creators' allocations.)* The Wellington and Wellesley portfolios can't be normalized because they are funds, but they are kept in the list for comparison. A substantial mix of stock allocations is left, roughly covering the spectrum of stock choices used by most index investors, including retirees.

		Wellington	Wellesley	Taylor Larimore Funds	Rick Ferri Core	Bill Berstein No Brainer	Bill Bernstein Smart Money	P3 & Dilbert's Portfolio	Ted Aronson Family Taxable	Bill Schultheis Coffee House	FundAdvice Ultimate Buy & Hold	David Swenson Lazy/Yale Portfolio	2nd Grader	Frank Armstrong Ideal Idx	Scott Burns Couch Portfolio	Scott Burns Margaritaville & Four Square	Scott Burns Five Fold	Larry Swedroe Simple Portfolio	Larry Swedroe Minimize FatTails Portfolio
Total US Market - TSM	VTSMX			31%	30%		13%	50%	3.57%			21.43%	33%		50%	25%	17%		
Large Cap Value - LCV	VIVAX						8%			8%	5%			6.61%				13%	
Large Cap Blend - LCB	VFINX					17%			10.71%	8%	5%			4.46%					
Large Cap Growth - LCG	VIGRX																		
Mid-Cap Blend - MCB	VIMSX								3.57%										
Small Cap Value - SCV	VISVX						8%		3.57%	8%	5%			6.61%				13%	25%
Small Cap Blend - SCB	NAESX					17%	4%		3.57%	8%								11%	
Small Cap Growth - SCG	VISGX								3.57%					4.46%					
Micro Cap	BRSIX										5%								
REIT	VGSIX				5%		4%			8%	5%	14.29%		5.71%			17%		
Intl Developed - EAFE	VDMIX										5%	10.71%							
Emerging Mkt - EM	VEIEX						4%		7.14%		5%	3.57%						3%	25%
Total International	VGTSX			19%	15%					8%			17%	22.14%		25%	17%		
Intl Pacific	VPACX						4%		10.71%										
Intl Europe	VEURX					17%	4%		3.57%										
Intl.Value	VTRIX										5%							11%	
VG Intl Small	VFSVX										10%								
Wellington - Balanced	VWELX	100%																	
Wellesley - Balanced	VWINX		100%																
Long Term Govt Bond - LTGB	VUSTX																		
5 Yr T-Bills	VFITX			12.5%	12.5%	12.5%	12.5%	12.5%	12.5%	12.5%	12.5%	12.5%	12.5%	12.5%	12.5%	12.5%	12.5%	12.5%	12.5%
Total Bond	VBMFX																		
Tbills/Treasury Money Mkt	VMPXX																		
Synthetic TIPS	VIPSX			25%	25%	25%	25%	25%	25%	25%	25%	25%	25%	25%	25%	25%	25%	25%	25%
2 Year ST Treasury	VFISX			12.5%	12.5%	12.5%	12.5%	12.5%	12.5%	12.5%	12.5%	12.5%	12.5%	12.5%	12.5%	12.5%	12.5%	12.5%	12.5%

FIGURE 120

Bond-normalized modified "Lazy Portfolios" with 50% stocks.

Figure 121 shows the corresponding HR results using the normalized definitions with 40-year data. This is the most accurate comparison HR is able to provide for the stock portion of the portfolios. (Using these same refinement steps, HR can compare the stock portions of any set of portfolios with approximately 30 years of data.)

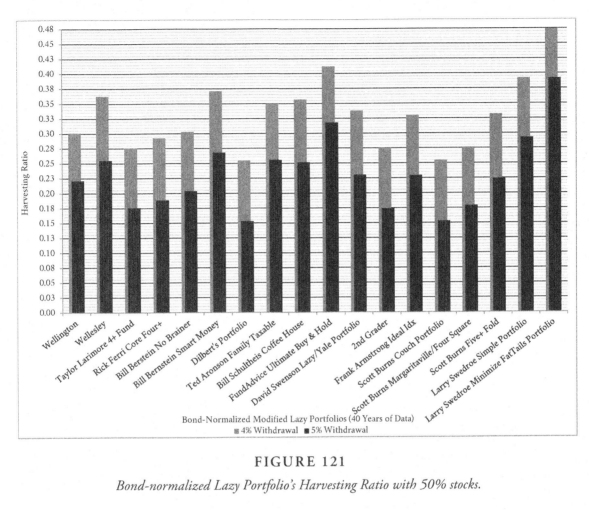

FIGURE 121

Bond-normalized Lazy Portfolio's Harvesting Ratio with 50% stocks.

The same two portfolios stand out. First place is held by the normalized Larry Swedroe Minimize FatTails Portfolio*: a powerful but relatively undiversified portfolio. Second is the normalized FundAdvice Ultimate Buy & Hold Portfolio: a strong and well-diversified portfolio. These two portfolios are examples of what generally works well from another perspective: they are both equally weighted stock allocations, which is explored in the next section.

Before continuing, some may wonder about using MVO to calculate the efficient frontier, then picking the highest-HR portfolio on the frontier. This should work, but MVO's recommendations are sensitive to the input parameters (asset return, variance, and correlation), making them difficult to apply. Even Harry Markowitz reportedly states[43] he invests in a diversified portfolio of half bonds and half stock index funds without applying his theory.

---

* The term "FatTails" refers to a fat-tailed probability distribution, where the "tails" (i.e., extremes) of the distribution are fatter (i.e., more likely). The "Minimize FatTails Portfolio" comes from Larry Swedroe's observation that high-return stock portfolios can use a lower stock percentage to generate a targeted level of return. The implication is risk (from fat tails) is lowered by holding a smaller percentage of volatile assets in the portfolio without sacrificing return. This portfolio is not intended to have 50% in stocks, but doing so provides a useful comparison.

Focusing on Equally-Weighted Stock Allocations

The top-performing FundAdvice and FatTails portfolios fall into the category of equally weighted stock allocations[*]. This simply means that the stock allocation is evenly divided between each of the portfolio's stock assets. It turns out, appropriately applied, equally weighted allocations produce high-HR portfolios.

Figure 122 shows a spectrum of equally weighted portfolios. On the left side, the 10x10 portfolio[†] is the most diversified, including 10 common stock asset classes with 10% allocated to each. (The FundAdvice portfolio is essentially the same as the 10x10 portfolio, with international small value stocks allocated to the international small stocks, most likely due to lack of fund choices in the recent past.) Moving to the right, the portfolios become less diversified by using HR comparisons to drop out the lowest performing asset classes from the portfolio. (Not every equally weighted portfolio is shown, only those with clean dividing lines and distinct performance differences.) Near the far right, the HR-2x50 portfolio, with only two stock asset classes, matches Swedroe's FatTails stock allocation.

Asset Class	10x10 (FundAdvice)	HR-8x12	HR-5x20	HR-4x25	HR-2x50 (Fattails)	HR-1x100
US Large	10%					
US Large Value	10%	12.50%	20.00%			
Small Blend/US Micro	10%	12.50%				
US Small Value	10%	12.50%	20.00%	25.00%	50.00%	
REITS	10%	12.50%	20.00%	25.00%		
Intl. Large	10%					
Intl. Large Value	10%	12.50%				
Intl. Small	10%	12.50%				
Intl. Small Value	10%	12.50%	20.00%	25.00%		
Emerging Markets	10%	12.50%	20.00%	25.00%	50.00%	100.00%

FIGURE 122

A spectrum of equally-weighted stock allocations defined using HR.

Equally weighted stock allocations tend to work well for a few reasons.

1. Only core assets with a proven track record are included in an equally weighted stock portfolio, enabling the simplicity of an equal allocation to work well. All the assets in the 10x10 portfolio have a long-term history going back a minimum of 40 years (most have substantially longer histories).

2. An equally weighted allocation can never tilt the portfolio toward a single underperforming asset. This may appear like a trivial distinction, but consider the market portfolio consistently underperforms in part due to the tilt towards large growth stocks.

3. An equally weighted allocation removes the burden of predicting which assets may be the next top performers. If an asset is chosen, then it gets a full allocation.

---

[*] Also known as a 1/N portfolio allocation.

[†] I'm not sure of the origin of the 10x10 portfolio. For now, the FundAdvice version from Paul Merriman is referenced. Steven Evanson also defines several variations of 10x10, one of which is used later in this chapter.

Figure 123 shows the equivalent equally weighted portfolios mapped to the funds available in Simba's data with 50% also in bonds. The only issue mapping to Simba's data is the lack of an international small value choice, but as done in the FundAdvice portfolio, this is handled by instead using international small (hence the double allocation in some cases).

Fund	Asset Class Category	10x10	HR-8x12	HR-5x20	HR-4x25	HR-2x50	1x100
VTSMX	Total US Market						
VIVAX	Large Cap Value	5.00%	6.25%	10.00%			
VFINX	Large Cap Blend	5.00%					
VIMSX	Mid-Cap Blend						
VISVX	Small Cap Value	5.00%	6.25%	10.00%	12.50%	25.00%	
NAESX	Small Cap Blend	5.00%	6.25%				
BRSIX	Micro Cap						
VGSIX	REIT	5.00%	6.25%	10.00%	12.50%		
VDMIX	Intl Developed - EAFE	5.00%					
VEIEX	Emerging Markets	5.00%	6.25%	10.00%	12.50%	25.00%	50.00%
VGTSX	Total International						
VTRIX	Intl.Value	5.00%	6.25%				
VFSVX	VG Intl Small	10.00%	12.50%	10.00%	12.50%		
VFITX	5 Yr T-Bills	12.5%	12.5%	12.5%	12.5%	12.5%	12.5%
VIPSX	Synthetic TIPS	25.0%	25.0%	25.0%	25.0%	25.0%	25.0%
VFISX	2 Year ST Treasury	12.5%	12.5%	12.5%	12.5%	12.5%	12.5%

FIGURE 123

Equally weighted stock allocations mapped into asset classes available in Simba's data.

Figure 124 shows both HR and backtesting results for the equally weighted portfolios using Simba's data. Undoubtedly, 40 years is too little historical data for reliable backtesting results, but combined with HR, the correlation is informative and clear. Notice that there is a tradeoff between diversification and HR, up to a point. Using less than four asset classes has an unclear advantage if any (HR's measurement should take precedence over backtesting with limited data). Based on these results, the top four candidate portfolios for retirement are 10x10, HR-8x12, HR-5x20, and HR-4x25.

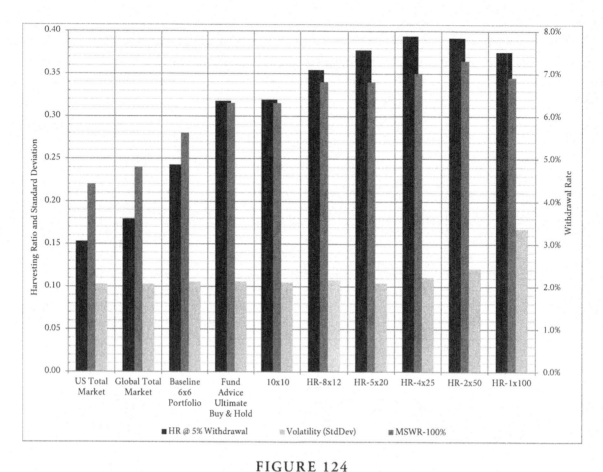

FIGURE 124

Portfolio comparison of HR, standard deviation, and MSWR-100%
with a 50% stock allocation using Simba's data.

Focusing only on the top four candidate portfolios, the tradeoff between diversification and HR is clear, but there's no proper way to measure how much diversification is appropriate without substantially more data than is available. It's not hard to image HR-4x25 as the top performer based on its highest HR, but it's also not hard to image underperformance due to one or two asset classes (out of four) temporarily doing poorly.

Other valid portfolios can be created through ad hoc combinations to increase HR. Still, it best not to go too far with fine tuning. HR is not intended to be a precise metric, but to position the retiree on the right page, or perhaps even the right position on the right page. There is a point where fine tuning portfolios becomes illusionary, although the exact dividing line is not clear. If a portfolio could be tuned with a high degree of accuracy, precisely mapping to future performance, then an equally weighted allocation would probably not be best. As it stands, equal weighting makes sense and is generally the most robust approach. Having said this, other criteria (still to be covered) can sometimes lead to portfolios that partially veer away from a pure equally weighted allocation.

CONSIDERING MARKET-SPECIFIC RISK

While the merits of international diversification are often heralded, the related risk of maintaining an overconcentration of stock in any single country is rarely mentioned, especially in the US. US retirees shouldn't assume the US market is immune to substantial market-specific risk.

There is a reasonably balanced approach to limiting the US allocation, while still giving it some extra weight based on past performance. In Chapter 6, Figure 99 provided an example of what such a well-diversified portfolio might look like, limiting the US allocation to 30% of stocks (i.e., 15% of the total portfolio with 50% bonds). This approach* is used as a guide to revise one the candidate portfolios.

Figure 125 shows a new portfolio, the Triad Portfolio, formed from the HR-8x12 portfolio by limiting the US portion of the stock allocation to 30%. The allocation to ex-US developed-market stocks is also limited to 30%. Still, HR remains high: about halfway between HR-8x12 and HR-5x20. The Triad Portfolio's name is derived from three key criteria: 1) strong diversification across core asset classes, 2) limited exposure to any specific stock market or subdivision, and 3) a high HR. Still, the Triad portfolio's 20% allocation to both REITs and emerging markets will give some investors pause, but for now hold any concerns…both these asset classes will be further subdivided.

Asset Class	HR-8x12	Triad Portfolio
US Large		
US Large Value	12.50%	10.00%
US Micro/Small blend	12.50%	10.00%
US Small Value	12.50%	10.00%
REIT	12.50%	20.00%
Intl. Large		
Intl. Large Value	12.50%	10.00%
Intl. Small	12.50%	10.00%
Intl. Small Value	12.50%	10.00%
Emerging Markets	12.50%	20.00%

FIGURE 125

Transitioning HR-8x12 portfolio to Triad Portfolio, balancing market-specific risk.

Figure 126 clarifies the point of creating the Triad Portfolio. The portfolio assets are subdivided into US stocks, international developed-market stocks, emerging markets, and global REITs (including US). Each of these subdivisions can to a degree be considered specific markets with distinct return characteristics and correlations (both of which are constantly changing). The Triad and HR-4x25 portfolios are the only two candidates with no more than 30% in any subdivision. Of these two, the Triad portfolio is the only one also strongly diversified across traditional asset classes.

---

* Another option is to shift a portion (e.g., one-third) of the US allocation to another market with a similar long-term performance and a comparable economic climate, such as the Australian market. Although fund choices are limited, suitable choices are available, such as Wisdom Tree Australia Dividend (AUSE).

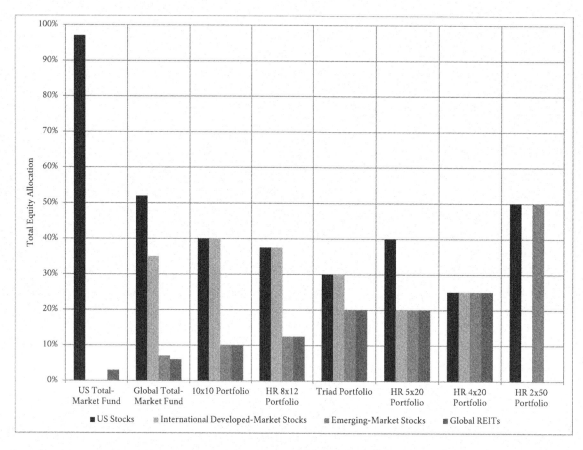

FIGURE 126

Diversification of equity allocations across portfolios.

The data is too limited for firm conclusions, but the Triad Portfolio adds another dimension of diversification that some retirees will find attractive and want to consider.

A LOOK AT THE UNDERLYING PORTFOLIO MAKEUP

Some retirees may be uncomfortable with the portfolios being considered, but a look at underlying fund breakdowns shows they are in some ways only a mundane realignment of assets. Examining the composition of each portfolio makes this clearer.

As a preliminary step, Figure 127 uses Morningstar's fund breakdown to show the underlying asset class allocation of the specific funds referenced in Simba's dataset. What may be surprising is index funds targeting specific asset classes do not purely represent their target allocation. For example, VIVAX, as a large value fund, actually contains 8% in large growth stocks as well as 12% spread across mid-caps. Likewise, NAESX, as a small-cap fund, contains over 40% in mid-cap stocks. These underlying asset breakdowns support a more accurate view into what makes up each of the candidate portfolios.

Asset Class Category	US Total Market Fund (VTSMX)	Intl Total Market Fund (VGTSX)	US Large-Cap Growth Fund (VIGRX)	US Large-Cap Blend Fund (VFINX)	US Large-Cap Value Fund (VIVAX)	US Small-Cap Growth Fund (VISGX)	US Small-Cap Blend Fund (NAESX)	US Small-Cap Value Fund (VISVX)	Intl Large-Cap Blend Fund (VDMIX)	Intl Large-Cap Value Fund (VTRIX)	Intl Small-Cap Blend Fund (VFSVX)	Intl Small-Cap Blend Fund (VINEX)	Intl Small-Cap Value Fund (DISVX)
Large Value	24%	28%	4%	30%	49%	0%	0%	0%	33%	29%	0%	3%	0%
Large Blend	22%	27%	20%	27%	32%	0%	0%	0%	31%	35%	1%	2%	1%
Large Growth	26%	24%	56%	31%	8%	0%	0%	0%	25%	25%	3%	5%	0%
Mid Value	6%	6%	2%	5%	8%	3%	12%	21%	4%	4%	21%	18%	28%
Mid Blend	6%	6%	7%	4%	4%	9%	14%	19%	4%	4%	23%	17%	22%
Mid Growth	7%	5%	10%	3%	0%	36%	19%	4%	3%	2%	22%	19%	9%
Small Value	3%	1%	0%	0%	0%	4%	17%	29%	0%	1%	13%	6%	20%
Small Blend	3%	1%	0%	0%	0%	17%	19%	21%	0%	0%	10%	14%	15%
Small Growth	3%	1%	0%	0%	0%	31%	18%	6%	0%	0%	7%	14%	5%

FIGURE 127

Underlying asset-class allocation of major index funds.

Figure 128 goes a step further, based on the previous index fund breakdowns, showing the complete underlying breakdown of the candidate portfolios, compared to a global total-market portfolio (based on Vanguard's Total-World Index VTWSX) and an estimate of the theoretical market portfolio. (The estimate of the theoretical market portfolio, which is constantly changing, is composed by combining data from three sources: a high-level breakdown of the market portfolio for 2011[44], a 2011 estimate of US stocks making up 49% of the global stock market[45], and a 2011 estimate of emerging-markets stocks making up 13% of the global stock market[46].)

Asset Class Category	Market Portfolio (1985-2012 Average)	Global Total-Market Portfolio (VTWSX)	10x10 Portfolio	HR-8x12 Portfolio	Triad Portfolio	HR-5x20 Portfolio	HR-4x20 Portfolio
US Large-Cap Value	5.73%	6.00%	3.95%	3.06%	2.45%	4.90%	0.00%
US Large-Cap Blend	5.98%	5.50%	2.95%	2.00%	1.60%	3.20%	0.00%
US Large-Cap Growth	6.23%	6.50%	1.95%	0.50%	0.40%	0.80%	0.00%
US Mid-Cap Value	1.49%	1.50%	2.30%	2.56%	2.05%	2.90%	2.63%
US Mid-Cap Blend	1.49%	1.50%	2.05%	2.31%	1.85%	2.30%	2.38%
US Mid-Cap Growth	1.74%	1.75%	1.30%	1.44%	1.15%	0.40%	0.50%
US Small-Cap Value	0.75%	0.75%	2.30%	2.88%	2.30%	2.90%	3.63%
US Small-Cap Blend	0.75%	0.75%	2.00%	2.50%	2.00%	2.10%	2.63%
US Small-Cap Growth	0.75%	0.75%	1.20%	1.50%	1.20%	0.60%	0.75%
International Large-Cap Value	5.22%	5.60%	3.10%	1.81%	1.45%	0.00%	0.00%
International Large-Cap Blend	5.22%	5.40%	3.40%	2.31%	1.85%	0.10%	0.13%
International Large-Cap Growth	4.64%	4.80%	2.80%	1.94%	1.55%	0.30%	0.38%
International Mid-Cap Value	1.16%	1.20%	2.50%	2.88%	2.30%	2.10%	2.63%
International Mid-Cap Blend	1.16%	1.20%	2.70%	3.13%	2.50%	2.30%	2.88%
International Mid-Cap Growth	0.97%	1.00%	2.45%	2.88%	2.30%	2.20%	2.75%
International Small-Cap Value	0.39%	0.20%	1.35%	1.69%	1.35%	1.30%	1.63%
International Small-Cap Blend	0.19%	0.20%	1.00%	1.25%	1.00%	1.00%	1.25%
International Small-Cap Growth	0.19%	0.20%	0.70%	0.88%	0.70%	0.70%	0.88%
Emerging Markets	6.61%	3.25%	5.00%	6.25%	10.00%	10.00%	12.50%
Real Estate / REITS	4.38%	1.90%	5.00%	6.25%	10.00%	10.00%	12.50%
Commodities	0.50%	0.00%	0.00%	0.00%	0.00%	0.00%	0.00%
Non-Government Bonds	14.63%	0.00%	0.00%	0.00%	0.00%	0.00%	0.00%
Government Bonds	29.65%	50.00%	50.00%	50.00%	50.00%	50.00%	50.00%

FIGURE 128

Underlying portfolio allocations based on Morningstar fund breakdowns.

The candidate portfolios are generally better diversified across all the distinct asset classes including small and value stocks. The market portfolios tilt more towards large stocks, especially large growth stocks. The result for those candidate portfolios towards the center is both high HR values and better diversification.

It will be hard for some retirees to part with a feeling that the market portfolio is somehow safer, but the data shows that the market portfolio is neither fundamentally different nor fundamentally safer.

The candidate portfolios are not radical ideas. Diversifying across asset classes, without weighting market capitalization, historically provides consistently strong retirement results. The emerging market and REITs allocation still stand out as relatively high in some portfolios, though. The next step is to look at how they can be effectively subdivided.

SUBDIVIDING EMERGING MARKETS AND REITs

Neither emerging markets nor REITs are homogeneous asset classes. Fund choices are now available for both to be subdivided into what are essentially new asset classes. Why and how is explained below.

Focusing first on REITs, multiple studies show the REIT market can be partitioned globally across independent regions.

- The Centre for European Economic Research[47] breaks the REIT markets into three regions: the Asia-Pacific region, the Anglo-Saxon Market (i.e., Canada, US, and UK Markets), and the Continental European Market. Other studies divide the REIT markets into US REITs, European REITs, and Asian REITs. However the boundaries are drawn, there appear to be three distinct REIT markets.

- Data[48] from January 2000 to May 2011 shows a correlation between US REITs and European REITS of 0.57; between US REITs and Asia-Pacific REITS of 0.46; between European REITS and Asia-Pacific REITS of 0.64. This relatively low correlation during tough global markets (including the dot-com crash and subprime crisis) supports treating REITS from the different regions as separate asset classes. Certainly, the subprime crisis starting in 2007 did affect all the REIT regions, but after a few years they returned to normal levels of correlation. One study[49] focusing on the subprime crisis found the REIT markets less susceptible to contagion from international shocks, guided more by market fundamentals.

- REITs within the countries making up the Asian region reflect a low correlation between each other[50], justifying some tilt toward Asian REITs.

- The correlation between the REIT regions generally appears to be lower than the correlation between broader stock markets[51].

In summary, global REIT markets function as three distinct regions with sufficiently low correlations. The key is to ensure a proper balance across these regions. One simple and pragmatic approach is to put half of the REIT allocation in a US REIT fund (e.g., Vanguard's VGSIX), and the other half in an international REIT fund (e.g., Vanguard's VGXRX). This provides sufficient exposure to all three regions, with a little tilt toward the Asia markets (with their own low correlations). For the Triad Portfolio with 50% in bonds and an even split between US and international REITs, the exposure to any REIT region should at most be 5% of the portfolio.

For emerging markets, the case is more straightforward. Emerging-market stocks fall under the same small and value factors identified by Fama and French for developed-market stocks[52], with similar diversification benefits. Recent emerging-market funds now support both these allocations. For example, WisdomTree's DGS is an emerging-market small-cap fund; likewise WisdomTree's DEM fund is an emerging-market large value fund. These same type funds typically also diversify across geographic regions (e.g., Asian, Latin America, Eastern Europe), further exhibiting characteristics of distinct markets[53]. For the Triad Portfolio with 50% in bonds and an even split between emerging-market small and large value funds, the exposure to any emerging-market asset class or geographic region should at most be 5% of the portfolio.

What About Bonds?

Not a lot will be said here about bonds, in part because the problem of allocating bonds for retirement is much less complex than for stocks. Also, there is little to add to what others have already said well in other books.

Still, keep in mind one of the primary purposes of bonds in retirement is buffering stocks during difficult times. Bonds are the ballast used to stabilize systemic withdrawal during times of high stock volatility. This means only the highest quality bond index funds should be used, preferably backed by the federal government. Very high quality municipal bond indexes with tax benefits may also work for some investors, but in general, other types of bonds should be used sparingly.

The following simple recommendation is an appropriate starting place for most retirees' bond allocation. Put approximately half of the allocation in a TIPS fund such as Vanguard's VIPSX. Split what's left across short-term (e.g., VFISX) and intermediate-term treasury-bond funds (e.g., VFITX).

The Recommendations

Despite the analysis, the final portfolio choice ultimately depends on individual judgment, sentiment, and preference.

Figure 129 shows the five candidate stock portfolios with the added breakdowns for REITs and emerging markets. The 10x10 now more closely mirrors Steven Evanson's version of the 10x10 portfolio, providing the most diversification across traditional asset classes. The other four portfolios progressively narrow in on the higher-HR assets while keeping diversification in mind. Interestingly, the Triad portfolio, after breaking down REITS and emerging markets, becomes a new form of 10x10. Any of these portfolios can form a strong retirement portfolio as is, or can be modified to fit a retiree's circumstances or preferences[*].

---

[*] Evidence-based recommendation could not be made for commodities, including precious metals, based on the data and techniques used in this book. For those who do prefer commodities, it's reasonable to put up to 10% of the stock allocation into a low-cost commodity fund.

Example Funds	Asset Class	10x10 (Evanson)	HR-8x12	Triad	HR-5x20	HR-4x20
VFINX	US Large	10.00%				
VIVAX	US Large Value	10.00%	12.50%	10.00%	20.00%	
NAESX/BRSIX	US Micro/small blend	10.00%	12.50%	10.00%		
VISVX	US Small Value	10.00%	12.50%	10.00%	20.00%	25.00%
VGSIX	REIT - US	5.00%	6.25%	10.00%	10.00%	12.50%
VGXRX	REIT - International	5.00%	6.25%	10.00%	10.00%	12.50%
VDMIX	Intl. Large	10.00%				
VTRIX	Intl. Large Value	10.00%	12.50%	10.00%		
VINEX/VFSVX	Intl. Small	10.00%	12.50%	10.00%		
DLS/GMISX/VF	Intl. Small Value	10.00%	12.50%	10.00%	20.00%	25.00%
DGS/EEMS	Emerging Markets - Small	5.00%	6.25%	10.00%	10.00%	12.50%
DEM/EVAL	Emerging Markets - Value	5.00%	6.25%	10.00%	10.00%	12.50%

FIGURE 129

Five candidate stock portfolios for retirement.

Figure 130 shows the same candidate portfolios with a 50% bond allocation.

Example Funds	Asset Class	10x10 (Evanson)	HR-8x12	Triad	HR-5x20	HR-4x20
VFINX	US Large	5.00%				
VIVAX	US Large Value	5.00%	6.25%	5.00%	10.00%	
NAESX/BRSIX	US Micro/small blend	5.00%	6.25%	5.00%		
VISVX	US Small Value	5.00%	6.25%	5.00%	10.00%	12.50%
VGSIX	REITS - US	2.50%	3.13%	5.00%	5.00%	6.25%
VGXRX	REITS - International	2.50%	3.13%	5.00%	5.00%	6.25%
VDMIX	Intl. Large	5.00%				
VTRIX	Intl. Large Value	5.00%	6.25%	5.00%		
VINEX/VFSVX	Intl. Small	5.00%	6.25%	5.00%		
DLS/GMISX/VFSVX	Intl. Small Value	5.00%	6.25%	5.00%	10.00%	12.50%
DGS/EEMS	Emerging Markets - Small	2.50%	3.13%	5.00%	5.00%	6.25%
DEM/EVAL	Emerging Markets - Value	2.50%	3.13%	5.00%	5.00%	6.25%
VFISX	Short-Term Treasury Bonds	12.5%	12.5%	12.5%	12.5%	12.5%
VFITX	Intermediate-Term Treasury Bonds	12.5%	12.5%	12.5%	12.5%	12.5%
VIPSX	Inflation-Protected Securities (TIPS)	25.0%	25.0%	25.0%	25.0%	25.0%

FIGURE 130

Five candidate portfolios with a 50% bond allocation.

To provide a final perspective, Figure 131 ranks the five portfolios according to four criteria:

1. Traditional diversification across stock asset classes (e.g., US small, international large value)

2. HR measured using Simba's data

3. Broad-based specific-market diversification shown in Figure 126

4. A comfort-level ranking, acknowledging that significant investments outside traditional norms may make some retirees uncomfortable, perhaps for good reason given shorter historical track records (e.g., 50 years instead of over 100 years).

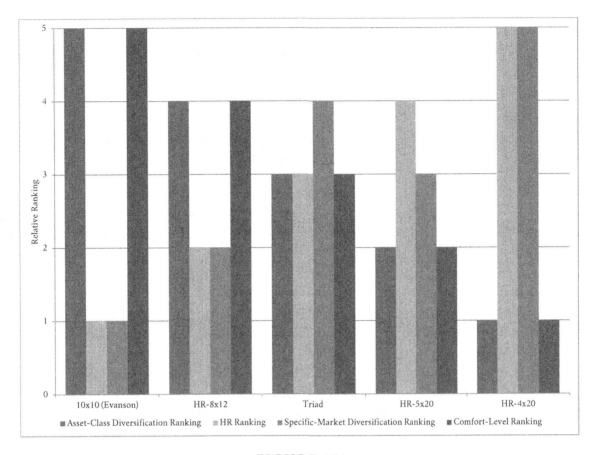

FIGURE 131

*Relative ranking of portfolios by four criteria: asset class diversification, HR,
broad-based diversification, and comfort level (higher rankings are better).*

These relative rankings are rough, in sweeping terms, but they clarify the broader criteria and the implicit tradeoffs between portfolios.

Base on my own judgment, sentiment, and preference, I favor the Triad portfolio. However, if I could make only one recommendation to meet the needs of a large set of retirees, I'd pick HR-8x12 because it's strong, has a longer set of historical data, and it's likely more retirees will be comfortable with it. Evanson's 10x10 is also a strong choice, perhaps satisfying the largest set of retirees' preferences with its more conventional asset-class allocation.

THE POINT

For strong and safe income it is important to diversity retirement portfolios broadly across asset classes and market subdivisions, while keeping HR high.

Three strong retirement portfolios stand out: Evanson's 10x10, HR-8x12, and the Triad portfolio. Any of these can be used as is or tuned to match a retiree's outlook and situation.

Chapter 9 Guide

This chapter starts by explaining why the initial withdrawal rate is important, and then focuses on how to appropriately pick it.

Included is the definition of a new metric, *valuation level,* which guides picking the initial withdrawal rate. The same metric is also considered in later chapters, so it's worth understanding why it's defined and how it's calculated.

Less interested readers can skim the chapter and focus on the section providing the step-by-step example for calculating the valuation level and then using it to set the initial withdrawal rate.

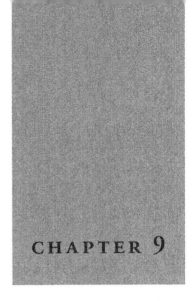

Reality trumps precision.

WALTER E. GOH

CHAPTER 9

USING VALUATIONS: PICKING THE INITIAL WITHDRAWAL RATE

A VARIABLE-WITHDRAWAL STRATEGY REDUCES THE pressure to pick the right withdrawal rate, but as mentioned before, picking the right *initial* rate is still important. An appropriate initial rate boosts the efficiency of a variable-withdrawal strategy, making income more evenly distributed throughout retirement. Set appropriately, an initial rate also lowers the risk of insufficient income. This applies to most variable-withdrawal strategies, including EM (i.e., the recommended strategy).

So what is an appropriate initial withdrawal rate? Without a better choice, many retirees use the worst-case rate, MSWR-100%. This is 4.3% for the Baseline Market and Baseline Portfolio for a 30-year retirement. While conservative, the 4.3% initial rate will usually be low...the Baseline's average sustainable rate is 6.7%. On the other hand, there are times when even a 4.3% initial rate looks too high (e.g., a retirement starting in 2000). The first step toward a solution is to accept that there is no single initial withdrawal rate that always works well—it depends on market conditions.

This is where market valuations help. Market valuations price the stock market as a whole, generally indicating if stocks are priced too high or too low when compared to their "fair" historical norm. An overpriced market indicates a lower sustainable withdrawal rate, so a lower initial rate should be selected; an underpriced market means a higher sustainable withdrawal rate, so a higher initial rate should be selected. Still, how to reliably make use of market valuations is not obvious.

Research over the last 20 years shows valuations can predict future long-term returns; however, the research also shows it's generally difficult to profit from these predictions because they aren't precise or consistent enough. In the context of retirement, Pfau shows[54] valuations are able to predict future withdrawal rates, but again the reliability of these predictions is not strong enough. In a nutshell, market valuations are too unpredictable to be considered reliable, while at the same time too reliable to ignore.

The key to effectively using valuations in retirement is aiming for modest results. Market valuations can modestly adjust the initial withdrawal rate, tilting the rate up a little when the future looks bright and tilting it down a little when it looks bleak. The data will show this is safe. In contrast, deploying valuations to achieve optimal

221

performance surpasses their point of reliability, with too much risk. The good news is, even modest results are a substantial improvement over the alternatives.

Starting with a US orientation and then extending to global markets, the rest of this chapter shows how to use valuations to select an appropriate initial withdrawal rate. It's debatable if the full criteria for evidence-based research can be met with the limited data, but considerable evidence is provided. Either way, an initial withdrawal rate must be picked, and in my opinion picking one with a valuation tilt is much better than without.

FORMING A RETIREMENT-VALUATION METRIC

The accuracy of a valuation metric depends on which valuation indicators are used and how they are combined into the metric. This section picks appropriate indicators and properly combines them into a retirement valuation metric. The next section then applies the valuation metric to tilt the initial withdrawal rate. (This initial analysis with standalone results uses only US indicators; global considerations are in later sections. Also, parts of this section may be difficult to follow, but understanding it all isn't required to pick an initial withdrawal rate at the end of the chapter.)

There is no obvious choice or path for forming a valuation metric, given the many possibilities and the mixed results reported in the literature. This made it necessary to test many indicators and compare their performance side by side, both alone and in combination. Although not fully shown here, this preliminary research included most if not all of the best-known indicators: various price-earnings ratios (CAPE10, CAPE20, Peak-PE, P/EXP5), the Q Ratio, dividend yields, various bond yields (as proxies for inflation), term spread, and various long-term trailing-return measurements (both real and nominal).

Figure 132 provides a high-level overview of the sustainable-withdrawal predictions using the indicators with the most potential. Although the end goal is not to precisely predict the future withdrawal rate (only to tilt towards it), the ability to accurate predict historical rates is the best gauge for evaluating and comparing metrics. Each solid line in the figure captures one prediction (i.e., a set of predicted MSWR values) using regression analysis with actual MSWR values shown by the dotted line. A prediction may come from a single valuation indicator, or a combination of several. For readability, the predictions are not labeled, there being too many to show, but the general trend is what matters here. Comparing the actual sustainable rates to the predicted sustainable rates shows substantial predictive powers by some of the indicators, even exceptional across some periods.

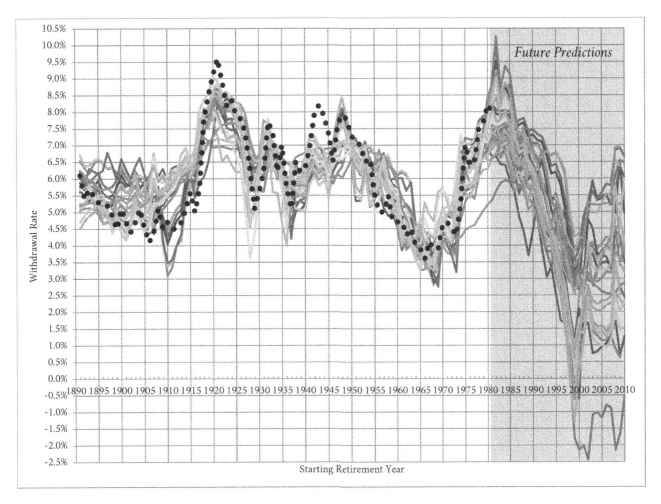

FIGURE 132

Comparison of actual and predicted 30-year sustainable withdrawal rates based on Shiller's US data using many different valuation indictors. The actual MSWR-100% values are represented by the dotted line.

Despite the generally strong results in Figure 132, two salient weaknesses reflect why only modest results are pragmatic.

1. The predictions don't always closely match the actual data. Too low of predictions would be okay (i.e., they are conservative), but predictions are just as likely to be too high. This is true for all the indicators: no valuation metric is reliable enough to predict the sustainable rate for an upcoming retirement.

2. As the dot-com bubble burst around 2000, the valuation indicators became distorted, losing much of their previous consistency. For example, retirements starting in 2002 have sustainable withdrawal-rate predictions ranging from 5% down to a nonsensical -2.5% (a distorted value predicted by a distorted PE ratio). This shows extra care must be taken to handle extreme market periods, even when seeking only modest results.

To counter the weaknesses, the following interrelated approaches are used to form a valuation metric.

a. Three independently strong indictors are used, preventing an overreliance on a single measure. The indicators, explained shortly, are CAPE10, Q, and iCAGR20.

b. Each indicator maps to one of four discrete valuation levels (Level 1 through Level 4) as opposed to an open-ended MSWR prediction. This implicitly sets boundaries to predictions and limits the ability of a single indicator to distort the result during a tumultuous period like after the dot-com bust.

c. The valuation indicators are equally weighted—simply a matter of averaging the three valuation levels. This contrasts with a less stable but closer "fitting" using regression analysis; again, no metric dominates the result this way.

The first indicator, CAPE10, is the 10-year Cyclically Adjusted Price-Earnings Ratio. The predictive capability of CAPE10 is well documented. CAPE10 averages the last 10 years of stock prices, then divides by current earnings. CAPE10 originated with Benjamin Graham and David Dodd in the 1930s. Nobel Laureate Robert Shiller (with others) revitalized and popularized the metric in the 1990s for valuing the market. Since then, CAPE10 has been the focus of many papers and blogs.

The second indicator, Q, is known as Tobin's Q or the Q Ratio. It's the relationship between the underlying assets composing the market and their replacement value. Q was defined by another Nobel Laureate, James Tobin, and William Brainard in the late 1960s. It's also known for its predictive power[*]. Q can be calculated by taking a company's net market value and dividing by its net book value. When used as a valuation metric, the Q calculation includes all companies in the market (exactly how is shown later). Unfortunately, the available historical data for Q goes back only to 1950 (for testing, valuations previous to 1950 are derived only from CAPE10 and iCAGR20, without Q).

The third indicator, iCAGR20, is the inflation-adjusted compound annual growth rate (i.e., the inflation-adjusted geometric mean, or real annualized returns) for the most recent 20 years of market returns. This metric does not have the well-established prominence of the other two, but the data supports its stand-alone predictive powers, plus it balances the input from CAPE10 and Q. Using Shiller's data, iCAGR20 alone has a R^2 of 50% for 30-year retirement results (i.e., MSWR-100%) compared to 49% for CAPE10. A similar iCAGR20 regression analysis in the UK and Japan showed an R^2 of 40% and 44% respectively, still significant values. Comparing the timeframe when Q data is available, 1950 to 2010, iCAGR20 has a R^2 of 70% for 30-year retirement results compared to CAPE10's 69% and Q's 83% using Shiller's data.

Figure 133 divides the historical MSWR values using Shiller's data[†] into four valuation levels. The approach is to use regression analysis to map each of the three indicators to a MSWR value, which is then mapped to a valuation level according to this figure. For example, Valuation Level 3 corresponds to sustainable withdrawal rates between 4% and 5.5%. The corresponding CAPE10 values, which map to the 4% withdrawal rate and the 5.5% withdrawal rate, define the range that falls into Valuation Level 3.

---

[*]   See Andrew Smithers' books.

[†]   Calibrating the valuation levels to Shiller's US data is convenient, because it enables Shiller's readily available values for CAPE10 and iCAGR20 to be used by a retiree at the start of retirement. The US Q data also works well with Shiller's data as a basis.

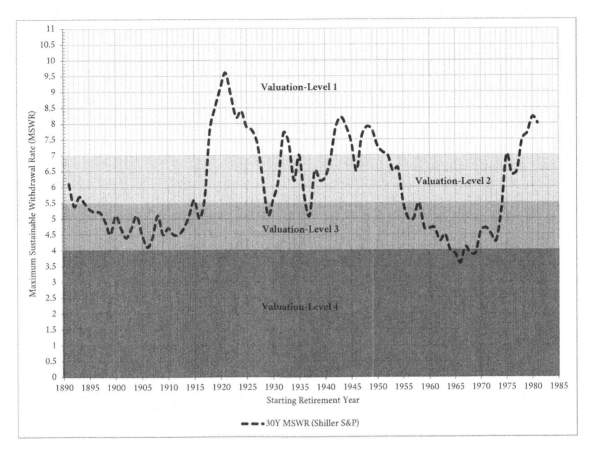

FIGURE 133

Valuation levels calibrated to Shiller's S&P data.

Figure 134 shows exactly how each indicator maps to one of the valuation levels shown in Figure 133. A retiree uses this figure to find the corresponding valuation level for each indicator, then averages the three valuation levels together to arrive at a single valuation metric. For example, a Q value of 0.5 falls into Valuation Level 2. An iCAGR20 value of 8% falls into Valuation Level 3. A CAPE20 value of 15 falls into Valuation Level 2. Averaging these three valuation levels, the result is 2.33 (the average of 2, 3, and 3).

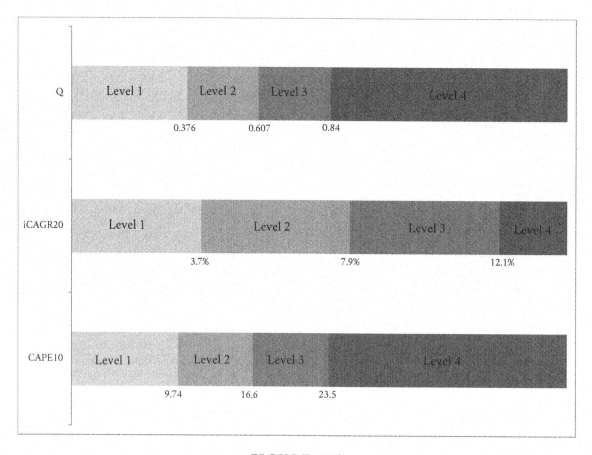

FIGURE 134

Three key valuation indicators and their mapping to valuation levels.

To provide a historical perspective, Figure 135 shows the valuation levels for CAPE10, iCAGR20, and Q along with their overall average going back to 1950. A later example walks through gathering the CAPE10, iCAGR20, and Q data, mapping them to valuation levels, and then using the average valuation level to identify a properly tilted initial withdrawal rate.

	1951	1952	1953	1954	1955	1956	1957	1958	1959	1960	1961	1962	1963	1964	1965	1966	1967	1968	1969	1970	1971	1972	1973	1974	1975	1976	1977	1978	1979	1980
CAPE10 Level	2	2	2	2	3	3	2	3	3	3	3	3	3	3	4	3	3	3	3	2	3	3	2	1	2	2	1	1	1	1
iCAGR20 Level	2	3	2	3	2	2	3	3	3	3	3	3	3	3	3	3	3	3	3	3	3	3	2	1	1	1	1	1	1	1
Q Level	2	2	1	2	2	2	2	2	3	3	3	3	4	4	4	3	4	4	4	3	3	3	3	2	2	2	2	1	1	2
Average Level	2.00	2.33	1.67	2.33	2.33	2.33	2.33	2.67	3.00	3.00	3.00	3.00	3.00	3.33	3.67	3.00	3.33	3.33	3.33	2.67	3.00	3.00	2.33	1.33	1.67	1.67	1.33	1.00	1.00	1.33

	1981	1982	1983	1984	1985	1986	1987	1988	1989	1990	1991	1992	1993	1994	1995	1996	1997	1998	1999	2000	2001	2002	2003	2004	2005	2006	2007	2008	2009	2010
CAPE10 Level	1	1	1	1	2	2	2	2	3	2	3	3	3	3	4	4	4	4	4	4	4	3	4	4	4	4	4	2	3	3
iCAGR20 Level	1	1	1	1	1	1	1	1	1	2	2	2	2	2	3	3	3	3	3	4	3	3	3	3	3	3	2	2	2	2
Q Level	1	1	2	2	2	2	2	2	2	2	3	4	4	4	4	4	4	4	4	4	4	4	4	4	4	4	4	3	3	4
Average Level	1.00	1.00	1.33	1.33	1.67	1.67	1.67	1.67	2.33	2.00	2.67	3.00	3.00	3.33	3.67	3.67	3.67	3.67	4.00	3.67	3.67	3.33	3.67	3.67	3.67	3.33	3.33	2.33	2.67	3.00

FIGURE 135

End-of-year valuation levels from 1951 to 2010.

Before moving on, it's important to verify that the final averaged valuation level is a good metric. Verification is again done by using the average valuation level to predict sustainable withdrawal rates for the Baseline Market and Portfolio. Again, the end goal is not to precisely predict MSWR, but this is a robust test of the metric accuracy. Figure 136 shows the predicted sustainable rate to be close enough to the actual sustainable rate, with a solid R^2 of 72%[*].

Also shown in Figure 136 is the simulated MSWR[†] for retirements starting in 1982 to 2010. Verifying the predicted rate for this timeframe, including the dot-com bubble in 2000, confirms that the valuation level is not distorted even when some of the underlying indicators are distorted.

---

[*]   For the same test, R^2 mapping directly back to Shiller's data is 80%. Both R^2 values compare favorably with Pfau's R^2 of 74.5% in the previously referenced study predicting MSWR with 10-year earnings yield, 10 year dividend yield, and bond yield (as a proxy for inflation).
[†]   The simulated MSWR comes from backtesting through generating data after 2010 by wrapping back to 1964 in the dataset (i.e., 2011 data came from 1964; 2012 from 1965, and so on). A "wrap date" of 1964 was picked for two reasons: 1) its CAPE10 value aligned well with the 2010 data; 2) the upcoming late 1960s were one of the worst historical retirement periods for the US, aligning with the many pessimistic forecasts for retiring after the dot-com bust. See the description of wrapping at the start of Chapter 10 for more information.

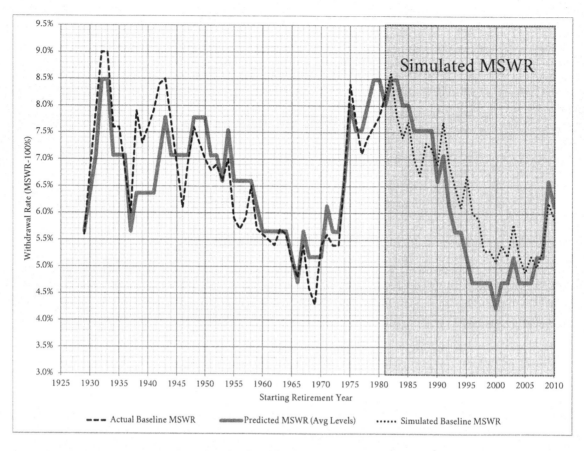

FIGURE 136

*Valuation Level predictions of MSWR for Baseline Market and Baseline Portfolio
for 30-year retirements. MSWR values are simulated after 1981.*

These tests show the average valuation-level provides a strong basis for tilting the initial withdrawal rate, which is shown in the next section.

TILTING THE INITIAL WITHDRAWAL RATE

Tilting the initial withdrawal rate means using the average valuation level (from the previous section) to modestly adjust the initial withdrawal rate up or down. The exact function* for applying the tilt is not so important, but the end results shown below are. Note, multiple tilts are provided, to give retirees a choice, although specific recommendations will be made.

---

* These tilts were initially calibrated by aligning the lowest valuation level (4) to the lowest withdrawal rate of 3.8% (as determined by the regression function from the previous section). As valuations increase from the lowest level, the withdrawal rate is tilted upward (accordingly to the degree of tilt and the increase in valuation).

Figure 137 shows six different withdrawal-rate tilts and how they correspond to the actual MSWR values for the Baseline Market and Portfolio. (Keep in mind these baseline-market tilts are all predicted purely from historical valuations using the valuation-level metric formed in the previous section.) For example, a 40% tilt for a 30-year retirement period starting in 1975 resulted in a 5.3% initial withdrawal rate, well under the actual baseline's sustainable rate of 8.4%. Higher tilts would fit the MSWR values more closely, but the goal is to intentionally underestimate the supported withdrawal rate. The more modest tilts leave significant room for error, while still improving the balance between risk and income. There was only one case in 1969 when the initial withdrawal rate using a 60% tilt was high enough to actually match the MSWR value.

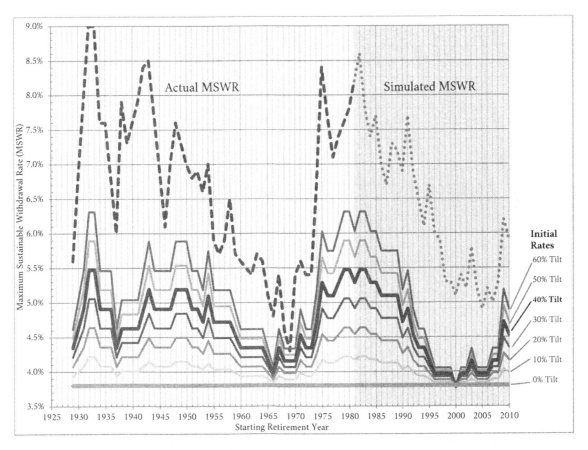

FIGURE 137

*Tilted initial withdrawal rates predicted using historical valuation levels, compared
to actual and simulated MSWR using Baseline Market and Portfolio.*

Figure 138 is the table of the various tilted initial withdrawal rates for each valuation level. After calculating the average valuation level using CAPE10, iCAGR20, and Q, a retiree simply uses this table to identify his or her initial withdrawal rate at the start of retirement. Again, the reference point is a 30-year retirement, but the rate is easily modified for longer or shorter retirements.

Valuation Level	60% Tilt	50% Tilt	40% Tilt	30% Tilt	20% Tilt	10% Tilt
1	6.3%	5.9%	5.5%	5.1%	4.6%	4.3%
1.1	6.2%	5.8%	5.4%	5.0%	4.6%	4.2%
1.2	6.1%	5.8%	5.4%	5.0%	4.6%	4.2%
1.3	6.1%	5.7%	5.3%	4.9%	4.5%	4.2%
1.4	6.0%	5.6%	5.2%	4.9%	4.5%	4.2%
1.5	5.9%	5.5%	5.2%	4.9%	4.5%	4.2%
1.6	5.8%	5.5%	5.1%	4.8%	4.4%	4.2%
1.7	5.7%	5.4%	5.1%	4.8%	4.4%	4.2%
1.8	5.6%	5.3%	5.0%	4.7%	4.4%	4.1%
1.9	5.5%	5.3%	5.0%	4.7%	4.4%	4.1%
2	5.5%	5.2%	4.9%	4.7%	4.3%	4.1%
2.1	5.4%	5.1%	4.9%	4.6%	4.3%	4.1%
2.2	5.3%	5.0%	4.8%	4.6%	4.3%	4.1%
2.3	5.2%	5.0%	4.7%	4.5%	4.2%	4.1%
2.4	5.1%	4.9%	4.7%	4.5%	4.2%	4.1%
2.5	5.0%	4.8%	4.6%	4.4%	4.2%	4.0%
2.6	5.0%	4.8%	4.6%	4.4%	4.2%	4.0%
2.7	4.9%	4.7%	4.5%	4.4%	4.1%	4.0%
2.8	4.8%	4.6%	4.5%	4.3%	4.1%	4.0%
2.9	4.7%	4.5%	4.4%	4.3%	4.1%	4.0%
3	4.6%	4.5%	4.3%	4.2%	4.1%	4.0%
3.1	4.5%	4.4%	4.3%	4.2%	4.0%	4.0%
3.2	4.4%	4.3%	4.2%	4.1%	4.0%	3.9%
3.3	4.4%	4.3%	4.2%	4.1%	4.0%	3.9%
3.4	4.3%	4.2%	4.1%	4.1%	3.9%	3.9%
3.5	4.2%	4.1%	4.1%	4.0%	3.9%	3.9%
3.6	4.1%	4.1%	4.0%	4.0%	3.9%	3.9%
3.7	4.0%	4.0%	3.9%	3.9%	3.9%	3.9%
3.8	3.9%	3.9%	3.9%	3.9%	3.8%	3.9%
3.9	3.9%	3.8%	3.8%	3.8%	3.8%	3.9%
4	3.8%	3.8%	3.8%	3.8%	3.8%	3.8%

FIGURE 138

Baseline market and portfolio tilts to the initial withdrawal rate for a 30-year retirement.

It's not difficult to come up with a safe tilt. A 10% tilt is extremely conservative with its highest value only reaching MSWR-100% for the Baseline Market and Portfolio. The challenge is determining how much tilt remains safe. Ultimately, the line of safety is subjective, but a low tilt should always be used. The question is, how low?

If investing only in US stocks, a 50% or 60% tilt in the initial withdrawal rate looks reasonable. But the best retirement portfolios are globally diversified with performance distinct from the US markets, so a lower tilt is needed. A 30% to 40% tilt appears right (i.e., very safe) for the needs of most retirees with a global portfolio, but more on this in the next section.

A Look at Global Markets

The previous section tilted the initial withdrawal rate using US valuation to match the Baseline Market and Portfolio. This approach has a potential weakness. The Baseline Market is the proxy for a globally diversified portfolio, but it's still derived from the US-based SBBI dataset and inherits a relationship to US valuations. This means additional evidence is desired to show a tilted initial withdrawal rate based only on US valuations appropriately applies to a real global portfolio. This evidence must be gathered indirectly, because the requisite global data is not available.

The starting rationale is that US markets correlate with global markets. CAPE10 and iCAGR20 are both calibrated to Shiller's S&P data, which is highly correlated with the US total market (well over 90%). The Q ratio is already calibrated to the total US market. Next, the correlation between the US total market and global developed markets is 66%; the correlation between the US total market and emerging markets is 57%; the correlation between the US total market and US REITs is 62%. All these correlations indicate that when the US market moves, the global markets usually move with it. This degree of correlation when mapped to long-term retirements should be enough to support the modest tilts in the initial withdrawal rate.

More specific evidence follows from Pfau's MSWR data for 17 global developed markets (earlier referenced in Figure 100 in Chapter 6). Pfau's data shows a clear correlation between US retirement results and global retirement results for developed markets. The R^2 is 59%. It's also noteworthy that, for the last 60 years, a globally diversified total-market portfolio in developed markets did as well or better supporting retirement than a US-based total-market portfolio.

Figure 139 is even more specific, comparing tilted initial withdrawal rates to the average "global" MSWR values from combining Pfau's global MSWR values (referenced above) with the Baseline Market and Portfolio MSWR values. All the tilted initial withdrawal rates should still fall conservatively below the resulting MSWR average for all the retirement periods. This is true, except for one 1936 case where a 60% tilt matches the MSWR value. One can also expect that modern global portfolios will perform better, given that Pfau's values are based on total-market portfolios.

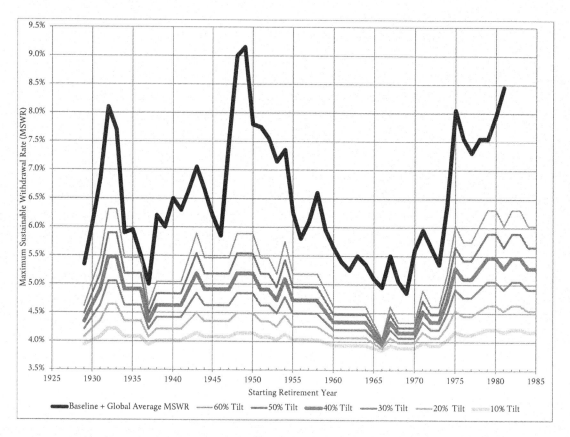

FIGURE 139

*Comparing tilted initial withdrawal rates to average MSWR values, from Pfau's global
developed-market data combined with Baseline Market and Portfolio data.*

To summarize, the correlation between US markets and global markets alone supports a modestly tilted initial withdrawal rate for a global portfolio. Still, it's worth trying to do a little better by adding global valuations—the next topic.

TILTING THE TILT — ADDING GLOBAL VALUATIONS

Limited historical data prevents global valuations from being approached with the same level of analysis used for the US valuations. Also, the last couple of decades haven't had the same level of research for global valuations, although that is starting to change.

To work with global valuations, it's necessary to build on early results, essentially interpreting global valuations from the stable reference point provided by the US data. This can be done only because there is credible evidence the global data as a whole (not individual countries) aligns with US data, as will be shown.

Joachim Klement, Chief Investment Officer at Wellershoff & Partners Ltd, published a 2012 report[55] showing that valuations predict future returns in both global developed market and emerging markets. Klement shows a R^2 of 46% between average CAPE10 and future 5-year real returns over 19 equally weighted developed markets. This comes close to the similar analysis done for the US with R^2 of 49%. Also, for 16 equally weighted emerging markets, Klement shows a R^2 of 29.1% between average CAPE10 and future 5-year real returns—a much smaller but still significant finding.

Mebane Faber, co-founder and the Chief Investment Officer of Cambria Investment Management, more recently wrote *Global Value: How to Spot Bubbles, Avoid Market Crashes, and Earn Big Returns in the Stock Market*[56]. Again focusing on CAPE10, he examines global valuations across 44 countries including developed markets and emerging markets. Partitioning CAPE10 values into quintiles, he shows that lower values correspond to substantially higher 10-year future returns; likewise, the quintiles with higher values correspond to substantially lower 10-year future returns.

Figure 140 summarizes Faber's results, comparing average CAPE10 in each quintile to future 10-year return returns. Overlying the figure are also the CAPE10 valuations levels from Figure 134. What is most important here is that Faber's partitioning of global CAPE10 levels generally maps[*] back to the previously established CAPE10 valuation levels. The key implication is it's reasonable to use the CAPE10 boundaries already defined to determine a global valuation level. For example, if CAPE10 is 15 for developed markets, referring back to Figure 134, the developed-market valuation level is 2. Keep in mind, absolute CAPE10 data varies by country, so only the average across many countries generally aligns with the established CAPE10 valuation levels.

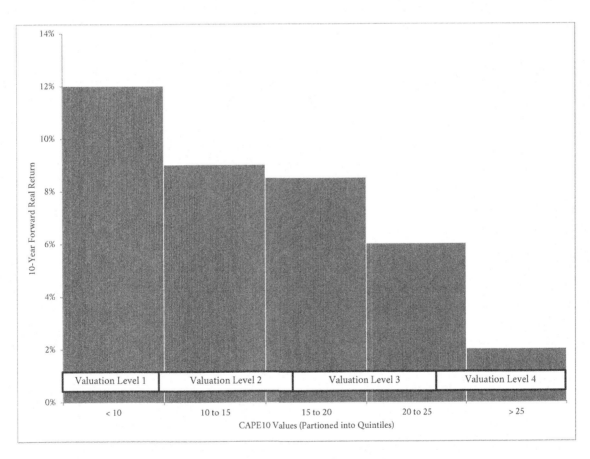

FIGURE 140

Average global CAPE10 versus average forward 10-year Real Return (Source: Mebane Faber). Overlaying the quintiles are this chapter's established CAPE10 valuations levels.

---

[*] Faber's use of 10-year forward returns correlates with MSWR-100% results, with an R^2 typically over 50%.

The question still remains as to how to use a global valuation level to tilt the initial withdrawal rate. To start, the global valuation level should be a weighted average of the developed market's CAPE10 valuation level and the emerging market's CAPE10 valuation level. Then in turn, the US valuation level can be averaged with the global valuation level. The final valuation level can then be tilted (as already defined) to arrive at the initial withdrawal rate. Examples will follow.

Keep in mind, global valuations likely do not have the accuracy of US valuations. This is why the global-level weight is limited to 50% (by straight averaging). It's also part of the reason why only a small final tilt is justified. As previously mentioned, where a 50% or 60% tilt may be reasonable for a purely US-based portfolio, a 30% or 40% tilt is more prudent for a global retirement portfolio. Still, Figure 139 shows, the initial withdrawal rate based purely on US valuations can do well for a global portfolio, because of the correlation between US markets the rest of the world—adding global valuations is a refinement to an already reasonable answer.

Conveniently, current valuations for global markets are now available online. A German company, Star Capital One, maintains a website* with detailed up-to-date global valuations, including CAPE10 values for the complete developed and emerging markets.

Here's an example for refining US valuations with global valuations. Assume the US valuation level (based on CAPE10, Q, and iCAGR20) is 3.2. Also assume CAPE10 for developed markets is 19.5 (looked up on Star Capital website) resulting in a valuation level of 3. Plus, assume CAPE10 for emerging markets is 15.2 (also looked up on Star Capital website) resulting in a valuation level of 2. With the Triad portfolio, 30% of the stock portfolio is in global developed markets and 20% in emerging markets, proportions of 3/5 and 2/5 respectively. (The REIT allocation is not considered because it has no clear and readily available valuation.)

a. US Level = 3.2

b. Global Level = (3/5 * Developed Markets Level 3) + (2/5 * Emerging Market Level 2) = 2.6

c. Overall Valuation Level = (1/2 * US Level 3.2) + (1/2 * Global Level 2.6) = 2.9

Referring back to Figure 138, the 40% tilt for Level 2.9 results in a 4.4% initial withdrawal rate (compared to 4.2% on US valuations).

Still, average global valuations won't drastically affect a US valuation, making the phase "tilting the tilt" apropos. Even if a US valuation level is 4 and both developed market and emerging markets valuation levels are very different at 2, the initial withdrawal rate would only rise from 3.8% to 4.5%. These types of variations are well within the range of what EM handles well. Plus, this appropriately maps back to the original premise that valuations can only be modestly applied.

A Step-by-Step Example

This book's website provides a spreadsheet for helping to tilt the initial withdrawal rate; however, the following steps also walk the retiree through the process. Fortunately, this needs to be done only once at the beginning of retirement. The assumed retirement start date for the example is September 2014.

---

*   http://www.starcapital.de/research/stockmarketvaluation

1. Gather the three US valuation indicators.
   A. The Q value comes from a simple calculation using data from the Federal Reserve. Download the Current Z.1 Release Balance sheet tables at http://www.federalreserve.gov/releases/z1/Current/z1r-5.pdf (or historical files can be found under the subdirectories at http://www.federalreserve.gov/releases/z1/ under the "Balance sheet tables" PDF). After opening the PDF, look up ***Market value of equities outstanding*** and divide it by ***Net worth (market value).*** For this example 21222.4 is divided by 19094.4 to arrive at a Q value of 1.11.
   B. iCAGR20 can be directly calculated from Shiller's data, but this is cumbersome. An easier approach is to use the tool at http://dqydj.net/sp-500-return-calculator/ to calculate iCAGR20. Just fill in the starting and ending dates (e.g., August 1995 and August 2014), check the box "Adjust for Inflation (CPI)", then hit the "Calculate" button to get iCAGR20 in the "Annualized S&P 500 Return (Dividends Reinvested)" field. This results in an iCAGR20 of 6.2%.
   C. Look up CAPE10 from Robert Shiller's downloadable spreadsheet at www.econ.yale.edu/~shiller/data.htm. All the historical values for "Cyclically Adjusted Price Earnings Ratio P/E10 or CAPE" are kept in the "data" tab in the spreadsheet. For example, the CAPE10 value for August 2014 is 25.69.

2. Take the three valuation indicators and cross-reference them against the level boundaries shown in Figure 134. A Q value of 1.11 has a valuation level of 4. An iCAGR20 value of 6.2% has a valuation level of 2. A CAPE10 of 25.69 has a valuation level of 4. (Looking up valuation levels, a retiree may optionally choose to interpolate when close to boundaries. For example, 2.5 could be used when close to the boundary between 2 and 3.)

3. Average the three valuation levels (i.e., 4, 2, and 4) to get an overall US valuation level of 3.33.

4. Gather CAPE10 for global developed markets and emerging markets. A developed-market CAPE10 of 19.5 and emerging-markets CAPE10 of 15.4 is found at http://www.starcapital.de/research/stockmarketvaluation.

5. Referring again to the level boundaries for CAPE10 in Figure 134, developed markets have a valuation level of 3 and emerging markets a valuation level of 2.

6. Use the developed-market and emerging-market valuation levels to calculate the global valuation level:

   Global Valuation Level = (3/5 * Developed Markets Level 3) + (2/5 * Emerging Market Level 2) = Level 2.6

7. Average US valuation level to the global valuation level to get the overall valuation level.

   (1/2 * US Level 3.33) + (1/2 * Global Level 2.6) = Overall Valuation Level 2.965

8. Looking up overall valuation level 2.965 (basically Level 3) on the tilt chart (Figure 138), use a 40% tilt to get a recommended initial withdrawal rate of 4.3%.

As a final step, the initial withdrawal rate is then sometimes adjusted to match other parameters (see Figure 116 in Chapter 7, which maps to Figure 141 in Chapter 10). For example, using the default recommendations for a 40-year retirement, the initial withdrawal rate is reduced by 5% to compensate for a long retirement. An initial withdrawal rate of 4.3% (found in the steps above) is reduced to 4.1% (i.e., 4.3% * 95%).

Concluding Thoughts

Although the initial withdrawal rate was gauged using 30-year retirement data, the general results apply to longer and short retirement periods. For US data, the correlation between valuation levels and retirement results remains strong across different retirement lengths: R^2 is 72% for a 30-year retirement under the Baseline Market and Portfolio; 65% for a 40-year retirement; 63% for a 50-year retirement. Also, EM indirectly adjusts the rate, based on the estimated duration of the retirement using mortality tables.

Another consideration already mentioned is, after the initial withdrawal rate is found (by applying the steps of this chapter), it must still be adjusted to match other parameters like the stock percentage or the retirement length. These adjustments were initially covered in the chapter on setting the initial stock percentage, but are reviewed in the summary of retirement parameters shown in Figure 141 at the start of the next chapter.

Valuation metrics should evolve and improve as more data become available. An ambitious and able retiree might even independently set the valuation level based on their own investigation and preferences, then apply the tilt table to arrive at their own initial withdrawal rate.

By necessity, tilts must always remain conservative due to the nature of market valuations; however part of investing well during retirement is having a variety of hedges. Following best practices, the tilts have three hedges for extra safety: 1) the HR for today's retirement portfolios should be significantly higher than the Baseline Portfolio; 2) diversification should also be significantly better in a modern retirement portfolio than in the Baseline Portfolio; 3) the variable-withdrawal strategy, EM, can usually handle initial rates well above the sustainable rate. All of these hedges can compensate for an errant tilt to the initial withdrawal rate.

Here's a concluding consideration for new retirees in the midst of planning. Poor valuations usually follow a market run-up, so when the initial rate is small, the portfolio value will often be big, potentially providing some solace for retirees disappointed with their initial withdrawal rate. Conversely, attractive valuations follow a poor market, so when the portfolio value is small, the initial rate will often be big, again potentially providing some solace for retirees disappointed with their portfolio value. This balance between valuations, portfolio value, and initial withdrawal rates is not perfect, but it should help to compensate during difficult times.

Broader Valuation Considerations

Two additional uses for valuations are briefly mentioned[*]. Both have only been tentatively verified, and their effects are limited. Also, both options apply only at the start of retirement, when systemic withdrawals are started.

Alternate Prime appears to reliably generate more income than Prime Harvesting when valuations are strong. This is not surprising, because Prime Harvesting is more oriented to handling the worst markets, which correspond to poor valuations. A retiree can optionally select an income-harvesting strategy using the following guide:

- Valuation Levels 1–2: Alternate-Prime

- Valuation Levels 2–3: Prime or Alternate-Prime

- Valuation Levels 3–4: Prime

---

[*] A third use for valuations, timing guaranteed-income purchases, is introduced in the final chapter.

As noted at the end of Chapter 7, the optimal stock percentage partially depends on valuations, but not as much as might be expected. Generally, it's sufficient to let the income-harvesting strategy and variable-withdrawal strategy handle market variations without trying to adjust the initial stock percentage based on market valuations. Nevertheless, for those inclined the initial stock percentage can be tilted a modest amount using the following guide.

- Valuation Levels 1–2: Increase the stock allocation by 5% to 10% of total portfolio value.

- Valuation Levels 2–3: No Change

- Valuation Levels 3–4: Decrease the stock allocation by 5% to 10% of total portfolio value.

Remember, these options only address known risk. While speculative risk probably increases with poor valuations and decreases with attractive valuations, it remains unpredictable and unmeasurable.

THE POINT

US valuations based on CAPE10, Q, and iCAGR20 coupled with global valuations based on CAPE10 can appropriately tilt the initial withdrawal rate, likely improving the efficiency of the variable-withdrawal strategy. Heeding poor valuations will also reduce risk.

This chapter is essential, demonstrating systemic-withdrawal best practices. It shows what is reasonable to expect exercising different options.

I've seen people with extremely high IQs miss the obvious point. We attribute too much common sense to brain power.

Walter E. Goh

CHAPTER 10

PUTTING IT ALL TOGETHER

THIS CHAPTER IS THE CULMINATION of the previous chapters, applying all the retirement mechanics and their best practices. The results provide realistic performance estimates, using representative plans.

The following best practices are used, with their default parameters used except where noted:

1. Prime Harvesting manages the portfolio.

2. The initial withdrawal rate is set according to the starting valuation level with a 40% tilt.

3. EM calculates the annual withdrawal amounts capped at 150% of the initial withdrawal rate.

4. The Baseline Market is the proxy for a globally diversified market.

5. The Baseline Portfolio is the proxy for a high-HR portfolio (such as Evanson's 10x10, HR-8x12, or the Triad portfolio).

6. The initial stock percentage is 50% for a 30-year retirement and 55% for a 40-year retirement.

As before, backtesting shows the results. There are a few differences worth noticing though, covered in the next section.

THE PRELIMINARY DETAILS

Figure 141 summarizes the recommended retirement parameters from the previous chapters — these are also the default parameters in this chapter. For example, the parameters for a 40-year retirement include a 55% initial stock percentage, a 40% tilt (or 30%) determining the initial withdrawal rate, and a 5% decrease in the determined initial withdrawal rate (from Chapter 9 Figure 138).

	15-Year Retirement	20-Year Retirement	30-Year Retirement	40+ Year Retirement
More Aggressive Recommendations	Valuation Tilt: 40% or 50% Increase Initial Rate by 20% 45% Initial Stock Allocation	Valuation Tilt: 40% or 50% Increase Initial Rate by 10% 55% Initial Stock Allocation	Valuation Tilt: 40% or 50% 60% Initial Stock Allocation	Valuation Tilt: 40% or 50% Decrease Initial Rate by 5% 65% Initial Stock Allocation
The Primary Recommendations	**Valuation Tilt: 30% or 40% Increase Initial Rate by 20% 35% Initial Stock Allocation**	**Valuation Tilt: 30% or 40% Increase Initial Rate by 10% 45% Initial Stock Allocation**	**Valuation Tilt: 30% or 40% 50% Initial Stock Allocation**	**Valuation Tilt: 30% or 40% Decrease Initial Rate by 5% 55% Initial Stock Allocation**
More Conservative Recommendations	Valuation Tilt: 30% Increase Initial Rate by 15% 25% Initial Stock Allocation	Valuation Tilt 30% Increase Initial Rate by 5% 35% Initial Stock Allocation	Valuation Tilt 30% Decrease Initial Rate by 5% 40% Initial Stock Allocation	Valuation Tilt 30% Decrease Initial Rate by 10% 45% Initial Stock Allocation
The Most Conservative Recommendations	Valuation Tilt: 30% Increase Initial Rate by 10% 15% Initial Stock Allocation	Valuation Tilt 30% 25% Initial Stock Allocation	Valuation Tilt 30% Decrease Initial Rate by 10% 30% Initial Stock Allocation	Valuation Tilt 30% Decrease Initial Rate by 15% 35% Initial Stock Allocation

FIGURE 141

The recommended retirement parameters.

Backtesting results include the following values…a few new.

1. *Initial* is the initial rate for the retirement period, typically set according to tilt and valuation level.

2. *Year* is the starting year of the retirement period.

3. *End* indicates the last year of historical data used for the retirement period. It's only shown when the historical data is wrapped (covered below).

4. *Y1, Y2*, etc., show the specific annual inflation-adjusted withdrawal rate for each year of the retirement. Similar to before, any year's withdrawal rate below 4% is highlighted using grayscale.

5. *%Left* is the percent of the starting portfolio left at the end of retirement after adjusting for inflation. For example, a *%Left* of 50% means the ending portfolio value is 50% of the starting portfolio value in real terms.

6. For comparing overall results:
   a. *Min* is the minimum annual withdrawal rate used over a retirement period, essentially the income floor. The cumulative "totals" field at the bottom of the column provides the minimum for all periods (i.e., the floor of all the retirement periods).
   b. *Avg* is the average annual withdrawal rate used over the retirement period. The "totals" field at the bottom of the column is the total average.
   c. *First 10Y* is the average annual withdrawal rate used over the first 10 years of the retirement period. The "totals" field at the bottom of the column is the related total average.

7. *MSWR* is the maximum sustainable withdrawal rate if inflation-adjusted fixed withdrawals are used.

Historical wrapping of the data is again used when backtesting longer retirements, although it is a little different from what was used in Chapter 9. Here, the first retirement year (i.e., 1928) repeats after the last retirement year (i.e., 2010) in an ongoing data sequence. Backtesting a 40-year retirement from 1928 to 2010 normally supports 44 retirement periods (from 1928 to 1981), while wrapping supports 73 retirement periods (1928 to 2000), and more diverse conditions. For example, the 40-year retirement period starting in 2000 will wrap the data after 2010 back to 1928 and continue up to 1956 with the following overall sequence:

2000 2001 2002 2003 2004 2005 2006 2007 2008 2009 2010 1928 1929 1930...1954 1955 1956

It is worth noting the special characteristics of the 40-year retirement period shown above, which is the last retirement period in many of this chapter's backtesting results. It starts with the dot-com crash in 2000, followed by the subprime crisis in 2007, and then 5 years later (with the data wrapping from 2010 to 1928) encounters the Depression-era market, all scaled to lower Baseline-Market global returns. This case will show the resiliency of systemic withdrawals following best practices.

REPRESENTATIVE PLANS AND THEIR NUMBERS

A variety of retirement plan are covered in this section, with their results compared to understand and evaluate the tradeoffs.

The parameters are never tuned to boost results for a specific scenario (taking advantage of historical foreknowledge). In this sense, the numbers are raw, providing a clear picture of how the different plans perform historically. Along the same lines, the default income floor for EM is defined at 2.25% (except where noted). This makes EM resilient to future unknowns, but it can also show occasionally low income.

The Benchmark 40-Year Retirement Plan with Variations

A 40-year plan is suitable for a retirement benchmark, given life expectancies and many retiring at age 65 or earlier. The numbers are worth reviewing. Based on a Society of Actuaries report[57], there is a 6% chance of a 65 year-old male outliving a 30-year retirement plan, a 12% chance for a 65 year old female, and an 18% chance for one member of a 65 year old couple. For a 35-year plan, again for age 65, there is a 1% chance of a male outliving the plan, a 3% chance for a female, and a 4% chance for one member of a couple. Also notable, research shows the factors contributing to a long life are difficult to predict, meaning anyone might be a candidate for a long life. This all points to a 40-year benchmark plan.

Figure 142 shows a 40-year benchmark plan using best practices, with the initial withdrawal rate now varying according to the starting valuation with a 40% tilt. The overall average income across all retirement periods is a strong 6% (shown in "totals" at the bottom); however, annual income drops under 4% a significant number of times and even under 3% a few times. Another important indicator is the overall average for the first 10 years, which is 5.3%, but this figure also dips below 4% in 10% of the retirement periods. Focusing on the lowest annual income, the floor briefly drops below 3% in 5 of the 73 retirement periods (i.e., in 7% of the cases). Still, most importantly, no retirement period is ever at risk of running out of money. The percentage-left values (i.e., %Left) range from 20% to 129%, all safe margins. Overall, income can be characterized as generally strong with temporary drops to low levels.

Initial	Year	End	Y1	Y2	Y3	Y4	Y5	Y6	Y7	Y8	Y9	Y10	Y11	Y12	Y13	Y14	Y15	Y16	Y17	Y18	Y19	Y20	Y21	Y22	Y23	Y24	Y25	Y26	Y27	Y28	Y29	Y30	Y31	Y32	Y33	Y34	Y35	Y36	Y37	Y38	Y39	Y40	%Left	Min	Avg	1st 10Y	MSWR
4.1%	1928	1967	6.1	4.5	3.7	3.4	3.7	4.6	4.5	5.9	6.1	4.6	5.6	5.4	4.8	3.8	3.8	5.0	6.1	6.1	6.1	5.1	4.9	5.6	6.1	6.1	6.1	6.1	6.1	6.1	6.1	6.1	6.1	6.1	6.1	6.1	6.1	6.1	6.1	6.1	6.1	6.1	103%	3.4	5.5%	4.7%	6.2%
4.1%	1929	1968	3.7	3.3	3.1	3.2	3.6	3.7	4.4	6.0	3.4	3.9	3.8	3.5	3.1	3.2	4.0	5.6	6.1	5.6	4.5	4.4	5.7	6.1	6.1	6.1	6.1	6.1	6.1	6.1	6.1	6.1	6.1	6.1	6.1	6.1	6.1	6.1	6.1	6.1	6.1	6.1	129%	3.1	5.1%	3.8%	5.2%
4.4%	1930	1969	3.7	3.3	3.5	4.2	4.1	5.6	6.6	4.4	5.3	5.0	4.5	3.6	3.7	5.1	6.6	6.6	6.6	5.6	5.2	6.6	6.6	6.6	6.6	6.6	6.6	6.6	6.6	6.6	6.6	6.6	6.6	6.6	6.6	6.6	6.6	6.6	6.6	6.6	6.6	6.6	95%	3.3	5.8%	4.6%	6.5%
4.7%	1931	1970	3.6	3.7	5.1	5.2	7.0	7.0	5.6	6.8	6.6	5.6	4.3	4.4	5.8	7.0	7.0	6.8	5.5	4.9	5.9	7.0	7.0	7.0	7.0	7.0	7.0	7.0	7.0	7.0	7.0	7.0	7.0	7.0	7.0	7.0	7.0	7.0	7.0	7.0	7.0	7.0	84%	3.6	6.4%	5.6%	7.7%
5.2%	1932	1971	4.8	7.8	7.8	7.8	7.8	7.8	7.8	7.8	7.8	7.8	7.8	7.8	7.8	7.8	7.8	7.8	7.8	7.8	7.8	7.8	7.8	7.8	7.8	7.8	7.8	7.8	7.8	7.8	7.8	7.8	7.8	7.8	7.8	7.8	7.8	7.8	7.8	7.8	7.8	7.8	101%	4.8	7.7%	7.5%	9.0%
5.2%	1933	1972	7.8	7.7	7.8	7.8	7.8	7.8	7.8	7.8	6.9	6.5	7.8	7.8	7.8	7.8	7.0	6.5	7.8	7.8	7.8	7.8	7.8	7.8	7.8	7.8	7.8	7.8	7.8	7.8	7.8	7.8	7.8	7.8	7.8	7.8	7.8	7.8	7.8	7.8	7.8	7.8	88%	6.5	7.7%	7.6%	9.0%
4.7%	1934	1973	4.4	6.2	7.0	4.9	5.8	5.6	4.9	4.0	4.1	5.2	6.7	7.0	6.0	5.0	4.6	5.5	6.9	6.8	7.0	6.5	7.0	7.0	7.0	7.0	7.0	7.0	7.0	7.0	7.0	7.0	7.0	7.0	7.0	7.0	7.0	7.0	7.0	7.0	7.0	7.0	65%	4.0	6.4%	5.2%	7.5%
4.7%	1935	1974	6.2	7.0	4.8	5.8	5.5	4.9	3.9	4.0	5.2	6.4	7.0	5.7	4.7	4.5	5.2	6.4	6.7	6.6	5.9	7.0	7.0	7.0	7.0	7.0	7.0	7.0	7.0	7.0	7.0	7.0	7.0	7.0	7.0	7.0	7.0	7.0	7.0	7.0	7.0	7.0	44%	3.9	6.3%	5.4%	7.3%
4.7%	1936	1975	6.0	3.8	4.2	4.2	3.9	3.5	3.5	4.0	5.0	7.0	4.7	4.1	3.9	4.5	5.5	5.7	6.3	5.3	7.0	7.0	7.0	7.0	7.0	7.0	7.0	7.0	7.0	7.0	7.0	7.0	7.0	7.0	7.0	7.0	7.0	7.0	7.0	7.0	7.0	7.0	47%	3.5	6.0%	4.5%	6.6%
4.1%	1937	1976	3.2	3.5	3.4	3.3	3.1	3.1	3.3	4.0	6.1	4.0	3.5	3.4	3.9	4.8	4.9	5.3	4.9	6.1	6.1	6.1	6.1	6.1	6.1	6.1	6.1	6.1	6.1	6.1	6.1	6.1	6.1	6.1	6.1	6.1	6.1	6.1	6.1	6.1	6.1	6.1	54%	3.1	5.2%	3.7%	5.7%
4.4%	1938	1977	5.8	5.4	4.7	3.7	3.8	5.3	6.5	6.6	6.2	4.8	4.5	5.4	6.1	6.2	6.4	5.8	6.6	6.6	6.6	6.6	6.6	6.6	6.6	6.6	6.6	6.6	6.6	6.6	6.6	6.6	6.6	6.6	6.6	6.6	6.6	6.6	6.6	6.6	6.6	6.6	51%	3.7	6.1%	5.3%	7.3%
4.4%	1939	1978	4.4	3.9	3.4	3.5	4.3	5.6	6.6	5.1	4.3	4.0	4.6	5.7	5.8	6.2	5.4	6.6	6.6	6.6	6.6	6.6	6.6	6.6	6.6	6.6	6.6	6.6	6.6	6.6	6.6	6.6	6.6	6.6	6.6	6.6	6.6	6.6	6.6	6.6	6.6	6.6	56%	3.4	5.9%	4.5%	6.8%
4.4%	1940	1979	4.1	3.4	3.5	4.5	5.7	6.6	5.2	4.4	4.1	4.7	5.8	5.9	6.2	5.6	6.6	6.6	6.6	6.6	6.6	6.6	6.6	6.6	6.6	6.6	6.6	6.6	6.6	6.6	6.6	6.6	6.6	6.6	6.6	6.6	6.6	6.6	6.6	6.6	6.6	6.6	60%	3.4	6.0%	4.6%	6.9%
4.4%	1941	1980	3.6	3.8	5.1	6.6	6.6	6.3	4.9	4.6	5.5	6.2	6.1	6.4	5.7	6.6	6.6	6.6	6.6	6.6	6.6	6.6	6.6	6.6	6.6	6.6	6.6	6.6	6.6	6.6	6.6	6.6	6.6	6.6	6.6	6.6	6.6	6.6	6.6	6.6	6.6	6.6	50%	3.6	6.2%	5.3%	6.9%
4.7%	1942	1981	4.7	6.3	7.0	7.0	6.8	5.5	5.0	5.9	6.6	6.3	6.6	5.9	7.0	7.0	7.0	7.0	7.0	7.0	7.0	7.0	7.0	7.0	7.0	7.0	7.0	7.0	7.0	7.0	7.0	7.0	7.0	7.0	7.0	7.0	7.0	7.0	7.0	7.0	7.0	7.0	35%	4.7	6.7%	6.1%	7.1%
4.9%	1943	1982	5.8	7.2	7.4	6.5	5.1	4.9	5.4	6.1	6.1	6.1	5.6	7.4	7.4	7.4	7.4	7.4	7.4	7.4	7.4	7.4	7.4	7.4	7.4	7.4	7.4	7.4	7.4	7.4	7.4	7.4	7.4	6.2	7.4	7.4	7.4	7.1	6.5	7.4	6.2	6.4	33%	4.9	6.9%	6.1%	7.2%
4.7%	1944	1983	5.4	7.0	4.8	4.1	3.9	4.4	5.0	5.1	5.3	4.7	7.0	7.0	7.0	6.8	7.0	7.0	7.0	7.0	7.0	7.0	7.0	7.0	7.0	7.0	7.0	7.0	7.0	7.0	7.0	7.0	6.2	6.7	7.0	7.0	6.5	7.0	6.8	7.0	7.0	7.0	34%	3.9	6.4%	5.0%	6.7%
4.7%	1945	1984	6.2	4.1	3.7	3.6	3.9	4.3	4.3	4.6	4.3	6.4	7.0	6.8	5.5	7.0	7.0	7.0	7.0	7.0	7.0	7.0	7.0	7.0	7.0	7.0	7.0	7.0	7.0	7.0	6.7	4.1	5.1	6.1	6.4	5.1	5.1	5.9	4.5	7.0	7.0	5.2	28%	3.6	5.9%	4.5%	6.1%
4.7%	1946	1985	3.6	3.5	3.4	3.5	3.6	3.7	3.7	3.6	5.0	5.8	5.5	4.5	6.2	6.6	6.1	7.0	6.6	6.9	7.0	7.0	7.0	7.0	7.0	7.0	7.0	7.0	7.0	5.0	3.7	4.1	5.4	4.6	5.0	5.1	5.0	4.6	5.1	7.0	6.0	6.4	32%	3.4	5.5%	3.9%	5.5%
4.7%	1947	1986	3.9	3.8	4.0	4.7	4.6	4.9	4.4	6.9	7.0	7.0	5.9	7.0	7.0	7.0	7.0	7.0	7.0	7.0	7.0	7.0	7.0	7.0	7.0	7.0	7.0	7.0	7.0	4.8	5.9	6.9	6.7	5.5	6.9	6.6	5.0	6.7	7.0	7.0	7.0	7.0	35%	3.8	6.3%	5.1%	6.4%
4.9%	1948	1987	4.2	4.6	5.2	5.3	5.4	5.1	7.2	7.4	7.3	5.7	7.4	7.4	7.4	7.4	7.4	7.4	7.4	7.4	7.4	7.4	7.4	7.4	7.4	7.4	7.4	6.7	4.6	5.0	6.4	5.3	5.2	5.0	6.2	4.9	5.4	7.4	5.5	7.4	7.4	5.3	29%	4.2	6.4%	5.7%	6.9%
4.9%	1949	1988	4.9	5.3	5.1	5.4	4.9	7.2	7.4	7.2	5.7	7.4	7.4	7.4	7.4	7.4	7.4	7.4	7.4	7.4	7.4	7.4	7.4	7.4	7.4	7.4	6.2	4.5	5.2	6.0	5.6	4.8	5.4	5.2	5.3	6.0	7.1	6.3	7.2	7.4	6.2	5.9	31%	4.5	6.5%	6.1%	6.6%
4.9%	1950	1989	4.8	4.7	4.8	4.6	6.5	7.3	6.6	5.5	7.2	7.1	6.8	7.4	6.8	7.4	7.4	7.4	7.4	7.4	7.4	7.4	7.4	7.4	7.4	5.5	4.0	4.5	5.5	4.8	4.6	4.6	5.2	4.4	6.3	7.3	5.5	7.4	7.2	6.8	6.3	5.8	31%	4.0	6.2%	5.9%	6.4%
4.7%	1951	1990	4.4	4.5	4.2	6.2	6.9	6.3	4.9	6.9	7.0	6.9	7.0	6.9	7.0	7.0	7.0	7.0	7.0	7.0	7.0	7.0	7.0	7.0	5.7	4.2	4.5	5.7	5.3	4.6	4.9	4.8	4.7	5.4	7.0	6.4	7.0	7.0	5.7	7.0	7.0	4.0	24%	4.0	6.1%	5.8%	6.2%
4.7%	1952	1991	4.6	4.2	6.3	7.0	6.7	5.4	7.0	7.0	7.0	7.0	6.9	7.0	7.0	7.0	7.0	7.0	7.0	7.0	7.0	7.0	7.0	5.8	4.2	4.9	5.8	5.5	5.2	5.1	5.7	4.7	6.5	7.0	7.0	7.0	7.0	7.0	7.0	7.0	5.3	6.5	32%	4.2	6.3%	6.2%	6.4%
4.5%	1953	1992	4.2	6.1	6.7	6.4	5.1	6.7	6.6	6.5	6.7	6.4	6.7	6.7	6.7	6.7	6.7	6.7	6.7	6.7	6.7	6.7	5.5	3.8	4.4	5.5	4.7	4.6	4.9	4.8	4.5	5.3	6.7	6.1	6.7	6.7	6.6	6.7	6.7	5.8	6.7	6.5	31%	3.8	6.0%	6.1%	6.1%
4.8%	1954	1993	6.4	7.1	6.4	5.4	6.9	7.1	6.6	7.3	6.7	7.0	7.3	7.3	7.2	7.3	7.3	7.3	7.3	7.3	7.3	5.2	4.1	4.3	5.4	5.0	4.5	4.8	5.2	4.5	5.7	7.0	6.7	7.3	7.3	7.2	7.3	7.3	4.6	7.3	7.3	7.2	35%	4.1	6.4%	6.7%	6.4%
4.5%	1955	1994	5.0	4.6	3.9	5.1	5.3	5.0	6.0	5.1	5.6	6.1	6.7	5.9	6.7	6.7	6.2	6.1	6.7	6.2	4.2	3.5	3.9	4.5	4.3	4.2	4.2	4.6	4.3	5.0	6.7	5.6	6.7	6.7	6.7	6.7	6.7	4.8	6.3	6.7	6.7	6.0	30%	3.5	5.5%	5.2%	5.5%
4.5%	1956	1995	4.3	3.7	4.6	4.9	4.6	5.6	4.7	5.2	5.8	6.6	5.5	6.7	6.7	5.9	5.7	6.1	6.2	4.0	3.4	3.7	4.5	4.1	4.0	4.3	4.4	4.1	5.3	6.5	6.0	6.7	6.7	6.3	6.7	6.7	4.6	6.7	6.7	6.7	6.7	6.7	36%	3.4	5.5%	5.0%	5.4%
4.5%	1957	1996	3.8	4.9	5.0	4.9	5.7	5.0	5.3	6.0	6.7	5.6	6.7	6.7	5.7	5.7	6.1	6.0	4.2	3.4	3.7	4.4	4.3	3.9	4.2	4.5	4.0	5.1	6.7	5.7	6.7	6.7	6.7	6.7	6.7	5.1	6.7	6.7	6.7	6.7	6.7	6.7	39%	3.4	5.6%	5.3%	5.5%
4.5%	1958	1997	6.5	6.6	6.3	6.7	6.3	6.7	6.7	6.7	6.7	6.7	6.7	6.7	6.6	6.7	6.7	4.7	3.7	4.0	4.8	4.6	4.5	4.4	4.7	4.4	5.3	6.7	6.7	6.7	6.7	6.7	6.7	6.7	6.7	6.7	6.7	6.7	6.7	6.7	6.7	6.7	62%	3.7	6.1%	6.6%	6.1%
4.3%	1959	1998	4.8	4.5	5.3	4.6	5.0	5.6	6.3	5.4	6.4	6.4	5.4	5.3	5.6	5.6	3.9	3.3	3.6	4.0	3.8	3.8	4.1	4.1	3.9	5.0	6.3	5.9	6.4	6.4	6.4	6.4	6.4	4.9	6.4	6.4	6.4	6.4	6.4	6.4	6.4	6.4	57%	3.3	5.4%	5.4%	5.3%
4.1%	1960	1999	4.5	5.3	4.5	4.9	5.3	6.1	5.2	6.1	6.1	5.5	5.3	5.7	5.6	3.8	3.1	3.4	4.1	3.8	3.7	4.0	4.5	3.9	5.1	6.1	5.9	6.1	6.1	6.1	6.1	6.1	6.1	6.1	6.1	6.1	6.1	6.1	6.1	6.1	6.1	6.1	72%	3.1	5.3%	5.4%	5.3%
4.1%	1961	2000	5.7	4.7	5.0	5.7	6.1	5.4	6.1	6.1	5.3	5.1	5.4	5.3	3.7	3.2	3.4	3.9	3.8	3.5	3.6	3.9	3.7	4.4	6.0	5.7	6.1	6.1	6.1	6.1	6.1	5.0	6.1	6.1	6.1	6.1	6.1	6.1	6.1	6.1	6.1	6.1	60%	3.2	5.3%	5.5%	5.2%
4.1%	1962	2001	4.1	4.4	4.8	5.9	4.7	6.1	6.1	5.2	5.0	5.3	5.2	3.6	3.1	3.3	3.8	3.6	3.6	3.7	4.0	3.9	5.1	6.1	6.0	6.1	6.1	6.1	6.1	6.1	6.1	6.1	6.1	6.1	6.1	6.1	6.1	6.1	6.1	6.1	6.1	6.1	69%	3.1	5.3%	5.2%	5.2%
4.1%	1963	2002	5.2	5.8	6.1	5.6	6.1	6.1	5.6	5.5	5.9	5.5	3.8	3.2	3.4	4.0	3.7	3.6	3.9	3.9	3.7	4.9	6.1	5.7	6.1	6.1	6.1	6.1	6.1	6.1	6.1	6.1	6.1	6.1	6.1	6.1	6.1	6.1	6.1	6.1	6.1	6.1	53%	3.2	5.4%	5.7%	5.5%
4.1%	1964	2003	5.2	6.1	5.0	6.1	6.1	5.4	5.0	5.4	5.4	3.6	3.1	3.3	3.7	3.6	3.5	3.7	4.0	3.7	4.5	6.1	6.0	6.1	6.1	6.1	6.1	6.1	6.1	6.1	6.1	6.1	6.1	6.1	6.1	6.1	6.1	6.1	6.1	6.1	6.1	6.1	74%	3.1	5.4%	5.3%	5.4%
4.0%	1965	2004	5.6	4.6	5.9	6.0	4.6	4.6	4.7	4.7	3.4	3.0	3.1	3.5	3.3	3.3	3.3	3.5	3.4	3.9	5.1	5.0	6.0	6.0	6.0	6.0	6.0	5.3	6.0	6.0	6.0	6.0	6.0	6.0	6.0	6.0	6.0	6.0	6.0	6.0	6.0	6.0	73%	3.0	5.1%	4.7%	4.9%
3.8%	1966	2005	4.2	5.6	5.7	4.3	4.1	4.5	4.3	3.2	2.9	2.9	3.2	3.1	3.0	3.1	3.3	3.1	3.8	4.8	4.5	5.7	5.7	5.7	5.7	5.7	4.9	5.7	5.7	5.7	5.7	5.7	5.7	5.7	5.7	5.7	5.7	5.7	5.7	5.7	5.7	5.7	74%	2.9	4.8%	4.2%	4.6%
4.1%	1967	2006	6.1	6.1	4.9	4.8	5.0	5.0	3.5	3.1	3.2	3.6	3.4	3.3	3.4	3.6	3.4	4.2	5.4	4.9	6.1	6.1	6.1	6.1	6.1	6.1	6.1	6.1	6.1	6.1	6.1	6.1	6.1	6.1	6.1	6.1	6.1	6.1	6.1	6.1	6.1	6.1	83%	3.1	5.3%	4.5%	5.2%
4.0%	1968	2007	5.6	3.8	3.7	4.0	3.9	3.1	2.8	3.0	3.1	3.1	3.0	3.1	3.1	3.1	3.3	4.1	4.0	5.1	5.8	4.9	6.0	6.0	4.4	6.0	6.0	6.0	6.0	6.0	6.0	6.0	6.0	6.0	6.0	6.0	6.0	6.0	6.0	6.0	6.0	6.0	60%	2.8	4.9%	3.6%	4.4%
4.0%	1969	2008	3.5	3.4	3.5	3.5	3.0	2.5	2.8	3.0	3.0	3.0	3.0	3.0	3.0	3.2	3.6	3.5	4.6	5.0	4.2	5.1	6.0	3.9	5.8	6.0	6.0	6.0	6.0	6.0	6.0	6.0	6.0	6.0	6.0	6.0	6.0	6.0	6.0	6.0	6.0	5.3	27%	2.5	4.7%	3.1%	4.0%
4.0%	1970	2009	4.6	4.8	4.7	3.3	3.0	3.1	3.4	3.3	3.3	3.4	3.6	3.4	4.2	5.2	5.0	6.0	6.0	6.0	6.0	6.0	6.0	6.0	6.0	6.0	6.0	6.0	6.0	6.0	6.0	6.0	6.0	6.0	6.0	6.0	6.0	6.0	6.0	6.0	6.0	6.0	69%	3.0	5.2%	3.7%	5.1%
4.3%	1971	2010	4.9	4.8	3.4	3.1	3.2	3.6	3.4	3.4	3.6	3.6	3.5	4.1	4.9	4.9	6.3	6.4	6.3	6.4	6.4	5.9	6.4	6.4	6.4	6.4	6.4	6.4	6.4	6.4	6.4	6.4	6.4	6.4	6.4	6.4	6.4	6.4	6.4	6.4	6.4	6.4	67%	3.1	5.5%	3.7%	5.4%
4.1%	1972	1928	4.7	3.3	3.0	3.1	3.4	3.3	3.2	3.3	3.5	3.3	3.9	4.9	4.7	6.1	6.1	6.1	6.1	6.1	5.8	6.1	6.1	6.1	6.1	6.1	6.1	6.1	6.1	6.1	6.1	6.1	6.1	6.1	6.1	6.1	6.1	6.1	6.1	6.1	6.1	6.2	90%	3.0	5.3%	3.4%	5.2%
4.1%	1973	1929	3.4	3.1	3.1	3.5	3.3	3.3	3.3	3.5	3.3	3.8	4.6	4.5	5.9	6.1	5.7	6.1	6.1	5.2	6.1	6.1	6.1	6.1	6.1	6.1	6.1	6.1	6.1	6.1	6.1	6.1	6.1	6.1	6.1	6.1	6.1	6.1	6.1	6.1	6.2	6.2	73%	3.1	5.3%	3.4%	5.2%
4.5%	1974	1930	3.5	3.8	4.7	4.4	4.1	4.3	4.3	4.0	5.1	5.9	5.8	6.7	6.7	6.7	6.7	6.7	6.7	6.7	6.7	6.7	6.7	6.7	6.7	6.7	6.7	6.7	6.7	6.7	6.7	6.7	6.7	6.7	6.7	6.7	6.7	6.7	6.7	6.8	6.8	6.8	83%	3.5	6.1%	4.4%	6.3%
5.0%	1975	1931	5.4	7.0	6.2	5.7	5.4	5.5	5.0	6.6	7.5	7.4	7.6	7.6	7.6	7.6	7.6	7.6	7.6	7.6	7.6	7.6	7.6	7.6	7.6	7.6	7.6	7.6	7.6	7.6	7.6	7.6	7.6	7.6	7.6	7.6	7.6	7.6	7.6	7.6	7.6	7.6	109%	5.0	7.2%	6.2%	7.6%
4.8%	1976	1932	5.5	5.0	4.6	4.7	4.7	4.4	5.5	6.5	6.5	7.3	7.3	7.3	7.3	7.3	7.3	7.3	7.3	7.3	7.3	7.3	7.3	7.3	7.3	7.3	7.3	7.3	7.3	7.3	7.3	7.3	7.3	7.3	7.3	7.3	7.3	7.4	7.4	7.4	7.4	7.4	98%	4.4	6.9%	5.5%	6.9%
4.8%	1977	1933	4.2	4.0	4.0	4.1	3.9	4.6	5.1	5.2	6.6	7.2	6.2	6.7	7.3	6.0	7.3	7.3	7.3	7.3	7.3	7.3	7.3	7.3	7.3	7.3	7.3	7.3	7.3	7.3	7.3	7.3	7.3	7.3	7.3	7.3	7.4	7.4	7.4	7.4	7.4	7.4	55%	3.9	6.6%	4.9%	6.2%
5.0%	1978	1934	4.2	4.2	4.3	4.1	4.8	5.5	5.4	6.9	7.6	6.6	7.0	7.6	6.2	7.6	7.6	7.6	7.6	7.6	7.6	7.6	7.6	7.6	7.6	7.6	7.6	7.6	7.6	7.6	7.6	7.6	7.6	7.6	7.6	7.6	7.6	7.6	7.6	7.6	7.6	7.6	62%	4.1	7.0%	5.4%	6.6%
5.2%	1979	1935	4.4	4.4	4.2	5.0	5.5	5.6	6.9	7.8	6.8	7.0	7.7	6.3	7.8	7.8	7.8	7.8	7.8	7.8	7.8	7.8	7.8	7.8	7.8	7.8	7.8	7.8	7.8	7.8	7.8	7.8	7.8	7.8	7.9	7.9	7.9	7.9	7.9	7.9	7.9	7.9	63%	4.2	7.3%	5.8%	6.9%
5.2%	1980	1936	4.4	4.2	4.8	5.5	5.4	6.9	7.7	6.6	7.1	7.6	6.0	7.8	7.8	7.8	7.8	7.8	7.8	7.8	7.8	7.8	7.8	7.8	7.8	7.8	7.8	7.8	7.8	7.8	7.8	7.8	7.8	7.9	7.9	7.9	7.1	7.9	7.9	7.9	7.9	7.9	81%	4.2	7.3%	6.0%	7.0%
5.0%	1981	1937	4.2	4.9	5.7	5.7	7.2	7.6	6.9	7.3	7.6	6.4	7.6	7.6	7.6	7.6	7.6	7.6	7.6	7.6	7.6	7.6	7.6	7.6	7.6	7.6	7.6	7.6	7.6	7.6	7.6	7.6	7.6	7.6	7.6	7.6	7.6	7.6	7.6	7.6	7.6	7.6	74%	4.2	7.3%	6.4%	7.3%
5.2%	1982	1938	5.2	5.8	5.8	7.4	7.8	7.1	7.3	7.8	6.7	7.8	7.8	7.8	7.8	7.8	7.8	7.8	7.8	7.8	7.8	7.8	7.8	7.8	7.8	7.8	7.8	7.8	7.8	7.8	7.8	7.9	7.9	7.9	7.9	7.9	7.9	7.9	7.9	7.9	7.9	7.9	75%	5.2	7.6%	6.9%	7.7%
5.2%	1983	1939	4.8	4.8	5.7	6.5	5.6	6.0	6.5	5.4	6.9	7.4	7.8	6.8	7.8	7.8	7.8	7.8	7.8	7.8	7.8	7.8	7.8	7.8	7.8	7.8	7.8	7.8	7.8	7.8	7.9	7.9	7.9	5.4	7.7	7.9	7.9	7.9	7.9	7.9	7.9	7.8	37%	4.8	7.3%	6.0%	7.0%
5.0%	1984	1940	4.3	5.1	5.6	5.0	5.3	5.9	4.8	6.1	6.8	7.4	6.1	7.6	7.6	7.6	7.6	7.6	7.6	7.6	7.6	7.6	7.6	7.6	7.6	7.6	7.5	7.6	7.6	7.6	7.6	6.3	4.9	5.4	7.6	7.6	7.6	7.6	6.6	7.6	7.6	5.1	29%	4.3	6.8%	5.6%	6.6%
5.0%	1985	1941	5.2	5.8	5.0	5.4	5.9	4.9	6.1	6.8	7.5	6.1	7.6	7.6	7.6	7.6	7.6	7.6	7.6	7.6	7.6	7.6	7.6	7.6	7.6	7.5	7.6	7.6	7.6	7.6	6.4	4.5	5.6	7.4	7.6	7.6	7.6	7.0	7.6	7.6	5.4	3.9	20%	3.9	6.8%	5.9%	6.8%
4.8%	1986	1942	4.8	4.3	4.5	5.0	4.2	5.1	5.6	6.3	5.3	6.6	6.8	7.3	7.3	7.3	7.3	7.3	7.3	7.3	7.3	7.3	7.3	7.3	5.7	7.0	7.3	7.4	7.4	4.8	3.9	4.1	6.1	5.4	7.4	7.4	5.3	7.3	5.6	5.5	3.8	3.8	20%	3.8	6.1%	5.2%	6.1%
4.8%	1987	1943	4.0	4.2	4.5	4.0	4.6	5.0	5.6	4.8	6.2	6.1	7.3	7.3	7.3	7.2	7.3	6.1	7.3	7.3	7.3	7.3	7.3	5.1	6.1	7.2	7.4	6.4	4.8	3.9	4.3	5.3	5.7	7.3	7.4	5.4	6.2	5.8	4.3	3.9	4.0	5.2	29%	3.9	5.8%	4.9%	5.8%
4.8%	1988	1944	4.7	5.1	4.2	5.2	5.7	6.4	5.3	7.0	7.1	7.3	7.3	7.3	7.3	7.3	7.3	7.3	7.3	7.3	7.3	7.3	6.1	6.7	7.3	7.4	7.2	5.4	4.3	4.7	6.8	6.1	7.4	7.4	7.2	7.4	6.4	5.3	3.8	4.8	7.2	7.4	39%	3.8	6.4%	5.8%	6.3%
4.8%	1989	1945	4.7	4.0	4.7	5.3	5.8	5.0	6.2	6.3	7.3	7.3	7.3	7.2	7.3	6.5	7.3	7.3	7.3	7.3	7.3	5.8	6.7	7.2	7.4	7.2	5.2	4.4	5.4	6.5	6.6	7.4	7.4	5.0	7.4	5.9	4.4	3.8	3.8	7.0	7.4	7.4	50%	3.8	6.3%	5.7%	6.2%
4.5%	1990	1946	3.8	4.6	4.9	5.6	4.7	6.2	6.1	6.7	6.7	6.7	6.7	6.7	5.7	6.7	6.7	6.7	6.7	6.7	5.0	6.0	6.7	6.8	6.7	5.1	3.8	4.5	6.4	5.8	6.8	6.8	6.2	6.8	6.8	5.2	3.6	4.0	6.2	6.8	6.8	6.8	41%	3.6	6.0%	5.6%	5.9%
4.7%	1991	1947	5.8	6.2	6.8	5.7	7.0	7.0	7.0	7.0	7.0	7.0	7.0	7.0	7.0	7.0	7.0	7.0	7.0	6.1	6.8	7.0	7.1	7.1	6.4	5.1	5.9	7.1	7.1	7.1	7.1	7.1	7.1	7.1	7.1	4.9	4.8	7.1	7.1	7.1	7.1	7.1	40%	4.8	6.7%	6.7%	6.7%
4.3%	1992	1948	5.1	5.7	4.7	6.2	6.1	6.4	6.4	6.4	6.4	6.4	6.3	6.4	6.4	6.4	6.4	6.4	5.8	6.2	6.4	6.5	6.5	5.6	4.6	5.8	6.5	6.5	6.5	6.5	6.5	6.5	6.5	6.5	5.0	4.8	6.5	6.5	6.5	6.5	6.5	6.5	35%	4.6	6.2%	6.0%	6.2%
4.1%	1993	1949	5.4	4.4	5.8	6.0	6.1	6.1	6.1	6.1	6.1	5.4	6.1	6.1	6.1	6.1	6.1	4.6	5.6	6.1	6.2	6.2	4.9	3.7	4.4	6.2	5.8	6.2	6.2	6.1	6.2	6.2	5.9	3.7	4.6	6.2	6.2	6.2	6.2	6.2	6.2	6.2	38%	3.7	5.8%	5.8%	5.8%
4.1%	1994	1950	4.1	5.1	5.1	6.1	6.1	6.1	6.0	6.1	5.2	6.1	6.1	6.1	6.1	6.1	4.5	5.1	6.1	6.2	5.0	3.9	3.2	3.4	4.8	4.9	6.2	6.2	5.2	6.2	5.9	4.4	3.5	3.7	6.2	6.2	6.2	6.2	6.2	6.2	6.2	6.2	42%	3.2	5.5%	5.6%	5.5%
4.0%	1995	1951	6.0	6.0	6.0	6.0	6.0	6.0	6.0	6.0	6.0	6.0	6.0	6.0	6.0	6.0	6.0	6.0	6.1	6.1	6.1	5.5	6.1	6.1	6.1	6.1	6.1	6.1	6.1	6.1	6.1	5.6	6.1	6.1	6.1	6.1	6.1	6.1	6.1	6.1	6.1	6.1	68%	5.5	6.0%	6.0%	6.2%
3.8%	1996	1952	5.1	5.7	5.7	5.7	5.7	5.7	5.0	5.7	5.7	5.7	5.7	5.7	4.4	5.1	5.7	5.8	5.8	4.5	3.7	4.7	5.8	5.8	5.8	5.8	5.4	5.8	5.8	5.1	3.7	3.8	5.8	5.8	5.8	5.8	5.8	5.8	5.8	5.8	5.8	5.8	59%	3.7	5.4%	5.6%	5.5%
3.8%	1997	1953	5.7	5.7	5.7	5.7	5.7	5.0	5.7	5.7	5.7	5.7	5.7	3.7	4.2	5.2	5.8	5.0	3.9	3.1	3.5	5.0	5.2	5.8	5.8	5.6	5.8	5.8	5.3	3.5	3.9	5.8	5.8	5.8	5.8	5.8	5.8	5.8	5.8	5.8	5.8	5.8	44%	3.1	5.3%	5.6%	5.4%
3.8%	1998	1954	5.1	5.3	4.5	4.9	3.7	5.2	5.4	5.1	5.6	4.7	3.2	3.6	4.2	5.8	4.1	3.3	2.9	3.0	3.8	4.0	5.8	5.8	4.3	5.6	4.9	4.2	3.3	3.4	5.5	5.8	5.8	5.8	5.8	5.8	5.8	5.8	5.8	5.8	5.8	5.8	60%	2.9	4.9%	5.0%	4.8%
3.8%	1999	1955	5.3	4.5	4.7	3.7	5.0	5.4	4.9	5.5	4.9	3.2	3.7	4.3	5.8	4.2	3.3	3.0	3.2	4.0	4.0	5.8	5.8	4.4	5.7	5.5	4.3	3.4	3.6	5.3	5.8	5.8	5.8	5.8	5.8	5.8	5.8	5.8	5.8	5.8	5.8	5.8	69%	3.0	4.9%	4.7%	4.8%
3.6%	2000	1956	4.7	4.9	3.8	5.2	5.4	5.1	5.4	4.7	3.0	3.4	4.1	5.5	3.9	3.1	2.8	2.9	3.7	3.6	5.2	5.5	4.2	5.2	5.0	4.2	3.1	3.4	5.5	5.5	5.5	5.5	5.5	5.5	5.5	5.5	5.5	5.5	5.5	5.5	5.5	5.5	79%	2.8	4.7%	4.6%	4.7%
																																										Totals	56%	2.5	6.0%	5.3%	6.2%

FIGURE 142

Benchmark backtesting results for recommended 40-year systemic withdrawal plan.

As mentioned before, low annual income rates are sometimes due to a pre-retirement run-up in asset prices. The portfolio value may be inflated under a market with high valuations. So, although a withdrawal percentage may be low, the actual income is sometimes more balanced than it looks because of initially inflated portfolio values. For example, 5% of a properly valued $500,000 portfolio is the same as 3.7% of an overvalued $675,000 portfolio. Most of the retirement periods containing low-income years started with a relative high valuation level of 3 or more*. Still, this doesn't completely compensate for low income levels.

* Normalizing retirement income to reflect this balancing effect is a worthwhile area for future study.

EM strives to maintain conservatively positioned portfolios, at the price of occasional low income. It's illuminating to see EM's performance without this conservative positioning.

Figure 143 shows exactly this, using the same 40-year retirement parameters, but with EM's income floor raised to 4% (up from its default of 2.25%, matching MSWR-100*). This level of performance comes with much more speculative risk, but the results are nevertheless impressive. Even with the high income floor, the percentage left at the end of retirement remains generally strong, coming in once at 8%, but otherwise at 20% and above. These results illustrate the full power of systemic-withdrawal best practices, although such a high EM floor is not recommended.

Initial	Year	End	Y1	Y2	Y3	Y4	Y5	Y6	Y7	Y8	Y9	Y10	Y11	Y12	Y13	Y14	Y15	Y16	Y17	Y18	Y19	Y20	Y21	Y22	Y23	Y24	Y25	Y26	Y27	Y28	Y29	Y30	Y31	Y32	Y33	Y34	Y35	Y36	Y37	Y38	Y39	Y40	%Left	Min	Avg	1st 10Y	MSWR
4.1%	1928	1967	6.1	4.5	4.0	4.0	4.0	4.5	4.4	5.8	6.1	4.5	5.4	5.3	4.7	4.0	4.0	4.9	6.1	6.0	5.0	4.8	5.5	6.1	6.1	6.1	6.1	6.1	6.1	6.1	6.1	6.1	6.1	6.1	6.1	6.1	6.1	6.1	6.1	6.1	6.1	6.1	102%	4.0	5.5%	4.8%	6.2%
4.1%	1929	1968	4.0	4.0	4.0	4.0	4.0	4.0	4.1	5.6	4.0	4.0	4.0	4.0	4.0	4.0	4.9	6.1	5.1	4.2	4.1	5.2	6.1	6.1	6.1	6.1	6.1	6.1	6.1	6.1	6.1	6.1	6.1	6.1	6.1	6.1	6.1	6.1	6.1	6.1	6.1	6.1	125%	4.0	5.2%	4.2%	5.2%
4.4%	1930	1969	4.0	4.0	4.0	4.1	4.1	5.4	6.6	4.3	5.2	4.9	4.4	4.0	4.0	4.9	6.6	6.6	6.6	5.5	5.0	6.5	6.6	6.6	6.6	6.6	6.6	6.6	6.6	6.6	6.6	6.6	6.6	6.6	6.6	6.6	6.6	6.6	6.6	6.6	6.6	6.6	83%	4.0	6.4%	5.7%	7.7%
4.7%	1931	1970	4.0	4.0	5.1	5.1	7.0	7.0	5.6	6.8	6.6	5.6	4.3	4.4	5.8	7.0	7.0	7.0	6.7	5.5	4.9	5.8	7.0	7.0	7.0	7.0	7.0	7.0	7.0	7.0	7.0	7.0	7.0	7.0	7.0	7.0	7.0	7.0	7.0	7.0	7.0	7.0	83%	4.0	6.4%	5.7%	7.7%
5.2%	1932	1971	4.8	7.8	7.8	7.8	7.8	7.8	7.8	7.8	7.8	7.8	7.8	7.8	7.8	7.8	7.8	7.8	7.8	7.8	7.8	7.8	7.8	7.8	7.8	7.8	7.8	7.8	7.8	7.8	7.8	7.8	7.8	7.8	7.8	7.8	7.8	7.8	7.8	7.8	7.8	7.8	101%	4.8	7.7%	7.5%	9.0%
5.2%	1933	1972	7.8	7.7	7.8	7.8	7.8	7.8	7.8	6.9	6.5	7.8	7.8	7.8	7.0	6.5	7.8	7.8	7.8	7.8	7.8	7.8	7.8	7.8	7.8	7.8	7.8	7.8	7.8	7.8	7.8	7.8	7.8	7.8	7.8	7.8	7.8	7.8	7.8	7.8	7.8	7.8	88%	6.5	7.7%	7.6%	9.0%
4.7%	1934	1973	4.4	6.2	7.0	4.9	5.8	5.6	4.9	4.0	4.1	5.2	6.7	7.0	6.0	5.0	4.6	5.5	6.9	6.8	6.9	6.5	7.0	7.0	7.0	7.0	7.0	7.0	7.0	7.0	7.0	7.0	7.0	7.0	7.0	7.0	7.0	7.0	7.0	7.0	7.0	7.0	65%	4.0	6.4%	5.2%	7.5%
4.7%	1935	1974	6.2	7.0	4.8	5.8	5.5	4.9	4.0	4.0	5.2	6.3	7.0	5.7	4.7	4.5	5.2	6.4	6.7	6.6	5.9	7.0	7.0	7.0	7.0	7.0	7.0	7.0	7.0	7.0	7.0	7.0	7.0	7.0	7.0	7.0	7.0	7.0	7.0	7.0	7.0	7.0	44%	4.0	6.3%	5.4%	7.3%
4.7%	1936	1975	6.0	4.0	4.2	4.2	4.0	4.0	4.0	4.0	4.9	7.0	4.6	4.0	4.0	4.4	5.4	5.6	6.2	5.2	7.0	7.0	7.0	7.0	7.0	7.0	7.0	7.0	7.0	7.0	7.0	7.0	7.0	7.0	7.0	7.0	7.0	7.0	7.0	7.0	7.0	7.0	46%	4.0	6.0%	4.6%	6.6%
4.1%	1937	1976	4.0	4.0	4.0	4.0	4.0	4.0	6.1	4.0	4.0	4.0	6.1	6.1	6.1	6.1	6.1	6.1	6.1	6.1	6.1	6.1	6.1	6.1	6.1	6.1	6.1	6.1	6.1	6.1	6.1	6.1	6.1	6.1	6.1	6.1	6.1	6.1	6.1	6.1	6.1	6.1	49%	4.0	5.3%	4.2%	5.7%
4.4%	1938	1977	5.8	5.4	4.7	4.0	4.0	5.2	6.5	6.6	6.2	4.8	4.5	5.3	6.1	6.2	6.4	5.8	6.6	6.6	6.6	6.6	6.6	6.6	6.6	6.6	6.6	6.6	6.6	6.6	6.6	6.6	6.6	6.6	6.6	6.6	6.6	6.6	6.6	6.6	6.6	6.6	50%	4.0	6.1%	5.3%	7.3%
4.4%	1939	1978	4.4	4.0	4.0	4.0	4.2	5.5	6.6	5.1	5.4	6.6	6.6	6.6	6.6	6.6	6.6	6.6	6.6	6.6	6.6	6.6	6.6	6.6	6.6	6.6	6.6	6.6	6.6	6.6	6.6	6.6	6.6	6.6	6.6	6.6	6.6	6.6	6.6	6.6	6.6	6.6	55%	4.0	6.0%	4.6%	6.8%
4.4%	1940	1979	4.1	4.0	4.0	4.4	5.6	6.6	5.2	4.3	4.1	4.7	5.7	5.8	6.1	5.5	6.6	6.6	6.6	6.6	6.6	6.6	6.6	6.6	6.6	6.6	6.6	6.6	6.6	6.6	6.6	6.6	6.6	6.6	6.6	6.6	6.6	6.6	6.6	6.6	6.6	6.6	59%	4.0	6.0%	4.7%	6.9%
4.4%	1941	1980	4.0	4.0	5.0	6.6	6.6	6.2	4.9	4.6	5.4	6.1	6.1	6.4	5.7	6.6	6.6	6.6	6.6	6.6	6.6	6.6	6.6	6.6	6.6	6.6	6.6	6.6	6.6	6.6	6.6	6.6	6.6	6.6	6.6	6.6	6.6	6.6	6.6	6.6	6.6	6.6	49%	4.0	6.2%	5.3%	7.1%
4.7%	1942	1981	4.7	6.3	7.0	6.8	5.5	5.0	5.9	6.6	6.3	6.9	7.0	7.0	7.0	7.0	7.0	7.0	7.0	7.0	7.0	7.0	7.0	7.0	7.0	7.0	7.0	7.0	7.0	7.0	7.0	7.0	7.0	7.0	7.0	7.0	7.0	7.0	7.0	7.0	7.0	7.0	35%	4.7	6.7%	6.1%	7.1%
4.9%	1943	1982	5.8	7.2	7.4	6.5	5.1	4.9	5.4	6.1	6.1	6.1	5.6	7.4	7.4	7.4	7.4	7.4	7.4	7.4	7.4	7.4	7.4	7.4	7.4	7.4	7.4	7.4	7.4	7.4	7.4	6.2	7.4	7.4	7.1	6.5	7.4	6.2	6.4	33%	4.9	6.9%	6.1%	7.2%
4.9%	1944	1983	5.4	7.0	4.8	4.1	4.0	4.4	5.0	5.1	5.3	4.7	7.0	7.0	6.8	7.0	7.0	7.0	7.0	7.0	7.0	7.0	7.0	7.0	7.0	6.1	7.0	7.0	6.5	7.0	6.8	7.0	7.0	7.0	7.0	7.0	7.0	7.0	7.0	34%	4.0	6.4%	5.0%	6.7%
4.7%	1945	1984	6.2	4.1	4.0	4.0	4.0	4.3	4.3	4.5	4.2	6.3	7.0	6.8	5.4	7.0	7.0	7.0	7.0	7.0	7.0	7.0	7.0	7.0	7.0	7.0	6.6	4.1	5.1	6.0	6.3	5.1	5.1	5.9	4.5	7.0	7.0	5.1	28%	4.0	5.9%	4.6%	6.1%
4.7%	1946	1985	4.0	4.0	4.0	4.0	4.0	4.0	4.8	5.5	5.2	4.3	5.9	6.3	5.9	7.0	6.4	6.7	7.0	7.0	7.0	7.0	7.0	7.0	7.0	7.0	4.8	4.0	4.0	5.2	4.5	4.8	4.9	4.8	5.0	7.0	5.8	6.2	31%	4.0	5.5%	4.2%	5.5%
4.7%	1947	1986	4.0	4.0	4.0	4.6	4.6	4.9	4.4	6.9	7.0	5.9	7.0	7.0	7.0	7.0	7.0	7.0	7.0	7.0	7.0	4.7	5.8	6.9	6.7	5.4	6.9	6.6	5.0	6.7	7.0	35%	4.0	6.3%	5.1%	6.4%
4.9%	1948	1987	4.2	4.6	5.2	5.3	5.4	7.2	7.4	7.4	7.4	7.4	7.4	7.4	7.4	7.4	7.4	7.4	7.4	7.4	7.4	7.4	6.2	4.6	5.0	6.4	5.3	5.2	5.0	5.4	7.4	5.5	7.4	7.4	31%	4.0	6.4%	5.7%	6.9%
4.9%	1949	1988	4.9	5.3	5.1	5.4	4.9	7.2	7.4	7.2	5.7	7.4	7.4	7.4	7.4	7.4	7.4	7.4	7.4	7.4	7.4	6.2	4.5	3.2	6.0	5.8	5.4	5.2	5.3	6.0	7.1	6.3	7.2	7.4	6.2	5.9	31%	4.5	6.5%	6.1%	6.6%
4.7%	1950	1989	4.8	4.7	4.8	4.6	6.3	7.3	6.5	7.1	6.8	7.4	6.8	7.4	7.4	7.4	7.4	7.4	7.4	7.4	7.4	4.5	3.5	4.8	4.6	4.3	7.3	5.5	7.4	7.2	6.8	6.3	5.8	31%	4.0	6.2%	5.9%	6.4%
4.7%	1951	1990	4.4	4.5	4.2	6.2	6.9	6.3	4.9	6.9	7.0	6.9	7.0	7.0	7.0	7.0	7.0	7.0	5.7	4.2	4.5	5.7	5.3	4.6	4.9	4.8	4.7	5.4	7.0	6.4	7.0	7.0	5.7	7.0	24%	4.0	6.1%	5.8%	6.2%
4.7%	1952	1991	4.6	4.2	6.3	7.0	6.7	5.4	7.0	7.0	7.0	6.9	7.0	7.0	7.0	7.0	7.0	5.8	4.2	4.9	5.8	5.5	5.2	5.1	5.7	4.7	6.5	7.0	7.0	7.0	7.0	7.0	5.3	6.5	32%	4.2	6.3%	6.2%	6.1%
4.5%	1953	1992	4.2	6.1	6.7	6.4	5.7	5.6	5.0	6.1	6.7	6.2	6.1	6.6	5.5	5.0	5.7	6.1	5.4	4.3	3.5	4.7	4.5	4.8	4.8	4.5	3.2	5.0	6.7	6.6	6.7	5.7	6.7	5.5	31%	4.0	6.0%	6.1%	6.1%
4.8%	1954	1993	6.4	7.1	6.4	5.4	6.9	7.1	6.6	7.3	6.7	7.0	7.3	7.3	7.2	7.3	7.3	7.3	7.3	7.3	5.2	4.1	3.3	5.4	5.0	4.5	4.8	4.5	4.2	5.0	6.7	7.3	7.2	7.3	4.6	7.3	7.3	7.2	35%	4.1	6.4%	6.7%	6.4%
4.5%	1955	1994	5.0	4.6	4.0	5.1	5.2	5.0	6.0	5.1	5.6	6.7	5.9	6.7	6.2	6.1	6.6	6.2	4.2	4.0	4.0	4.4	4.2	4.2	4.2	3.5	4.2	5.0	6.7	6.7	6.7	6.7	6.7	6.7	4.7	6.7	5.7	5.9	30%	4.0	5.5%	5.2%	5.5%
4.5%	1956	1995	4.3	4.0	4.6	4.9	4.6	5.6	4.7	5.1	5.8	6.6	5.5	6.7	6.7	5.9	5.6	6.1	6.2	4.0	4.0	4.4	4.0	4.2	4.3	4.1	5.4	5.0	6.4	5.9	6.7	6.7	6.7	6.7	4.5	6.7	6.7	6.7	36%	4.0	5.5%	5.0%	5.4%
4.5%	1957	1996	4.0	4.9	5.0	4.9	5.7	4.9	5.3	5.9	6.7	5.6	7.0	6.1	6.0	4.2	4.0	4.0	4.3	4.2	4.0	4.1	4.4	4.0	5.0	5.7	5.6	6.7	6.7	6.7	6.7	6.7	6.7	5.2	6.7	6.7	6.7	6.7	6.7	6.7	41%	4.0	5.6%	5.3%	5.5%
4.3%	1958	1997	6.5	6.6	6.3	6.7	6.3	6.7	6.7	6.7	6.7	6.7	6.7	6.7	6.7	4.7	4.0	4.0	4.8	4.6	4.5	4.4	4.7	4.4	5.3	6.7	6.7	6.7	6.7	6.7	6.7	6.7	6.7	6.7	61%	4.0	6.1%	6.6%	6.1%
4.3%	1959	1998	4.8	4.5	5.3	4.6	5.0	5.6	5.3	5.4	4.4	5.3	5.6	5.6	4.0	4.0	4.0	4.0	4.0	4.0	4.8	6.1	5.6	6.4	6.4	6.4	6.4	6.4	4.8	6.4	6.4	6.4	6.4	6.4	6.4	6.4	54%	4.0	5.4%	5.4%	5.3%
4.1%	1960	1999	4.5	5.3	4.5	4.9	5.3	6.1	5.2	6.1	6.1	5.5	5.3	5.7	5.6	4.0	4.0	4.0	4.0	4.0	4.3	4.0	4.9	6.1	5.6	6.1	6.1	6.1	5.9	6.1	6.1	6.1	6.1	6.1	6.1	6.1	6.1	6.1	69%	4.0	5.4%	5.4%	5.3%
4.1%	1961	2000	5.7	4.7	5.0	5.7	6.1	5.4	6.1	6.1	5.3	5.1	5.4	5.3	4.0	4.0	4.0	4.0	4.0	4.0	4.0	4.1	5.5	5.2	6.1	6.1	6.1	4.4	6.1	6.1	6.1	6.1	6.1	6.1	6.1	6.1	6.1	6.1	53%	4.0	5.3%	5.5%	5.2%
4.1%	1962	2001	4.1	4.4	4.8	5.9	4.7	6.1	6.1	5.2	5.0	5.3	5.2	4.0	4.0	4.0	4.0	4.5	6.0	5.3	6.1	6.1	6.1	5.6	5.7	5.4	6.1	6.1	6.1	6.1	6.1	6.1	6.1	6.1	6.1	6.1	6.1	6.1	63%	4.0	5.3%	5.2%	5.2%
4.1%	1963	2002	5.2	5.8	6.1	5.6	6.1	6.1	5.6	5.3	5.9	5.5	4.0	4.0	4.0	4.0	4.0	4.0	4.5	6.0	5.3	6.1	6.1	6.1	5.6	6.1	6.1	6.1	6.1	6.1	6.1	6.1	6.1	6.1	6.1	6.1	6.1	6.1	47%	4.0	5.5%	5.7%	5.5%
4.1%	1964	2003	5.2	6.1	5.0	6.1	6.1	5.4	5.0	5.4	4.0	4.0	4.0	4.0	4.0	4.0	4.0	4.5	6.1	6.1	6.1	6.1	6.1	5.9	6.1	6.1	6.1	6.1	6.1	6.1	6.1	6.1	6.1	6.1	6.1	6.1	6.1	6.1	67%	4.0	5.4%	5.4%	5.4%
4.0%	1965	2004	5.6	4.6	5.9	6.0	4.6	4.6	4.7	4.7	4.0	4.0	4.0	4.0	4.0	4.0	4.2	4.2	5.8	6.0	5.0	6.0	4.2	6.0	6.0	6.0	6.0	6.0	6.0	6.0	6.0	6.0	6.0	6.0	6.0	6.0	6.0	6.0	60%	4.0	5.2%	4.9%	4.9%
3.8%	1966	2005	4.2	5.6	5.7	4.3	4.3	4.3	4.0	4.0	4.0	4.0	4.0	4.0	4.0	4.0	4.2	5.2	5.7	4.0	5.6	5.7	5.7	5.7	5.7	5.7	5.7	5.7	5.7	5.7	5.7	53%	4.0	4.9%	4.5%	4.6%
4.1%	1967	2006	6.1	6.1	4.9	4.8	5.0	5.0	4.0	4.0	4.0	4.0	4.0	4.0	4.0	4.0	4.7	4.3	5.7	6.1	5.8	6.1	5.1	6.1	5.1	6.1	6.1	6.1	6.1	6.1	6.1	6.1	6.1	6.1	6.1	6.1	72%	4.0	5.3%	4.8%	5.2%
4.0%	1968	2007	5.6	4.0	4.0	4.0	4.0	4.0	4.0	4.0	4.0	4.0	4.0	4.0	4.0	4.0	4.4	4.0	4.5	5.0	6.0	5.2	6.0	6.0	6.0	6.0	5.6	6.0	6.0	6.0	6.0	6.0	6.0	39%	4.0	4.8%	4.2%	4.4%
4.0%	1969	2008	4.0	4.0	4.0	4.0	4.0	4.0	4.0	4.0	4.0	4.0	4.0	4.0	4.0	4.0	4.0	3.7	3.7	5.9	4.1	5.1	4.0	4.0	4.3	4.0	4.5	4.0	5.4	4.0	4.0	8%	4.0	4.2%	4.0%	4.0%
4.0%	1970	2009	4.6	4.8	4.7	4.0	4.0	4.0	4.0	4.0	4.0	4.5	4.2	5.7	6.0	5.3	5.9	6.0	5.4	6.0	6.0	6.0	6.0	6.0	6.0	6.0	6.0	6.0	6.0	6.0	6.0	55%	4.0	5.3%	4.2%	5.1%
4.3%	1971	2010	4.9	4.8	4.0	4.0	4.0	4.0	4.0	4.0	4.0	4.4	5.6	6.4	5.6	6.0	5.2	6.4	6.4	6.4	6.4	6.4	6.4	6.4	6.4	6.4	6.4	6.4	6.4	6.4	6.4	6.4	6.4	6.4	59%	4.0	5.5%	4.2%	5.4%
4.1%	1972	1928	4.7	4.0	4.0	4.0	4.0	4.0	4.0	4.0	4.0	4.2	4.1	5.4	5.1	5.2	6.0	6.1	4.8	6.1	6.1	6.1	6.1	6.1	6.1	6.1	6.1	6.1	6.1	6.1	6.1	6.1	6.1	6.1	6.1	6.2	6.2	60%	4.0	5.4%	4.1%	5.2%
4.1%	1973	1929	4.0	4.0	4.0	4.0	4.0	4.0	4.0	4.0	4.1	5.0	5.9	4.8	5.6	6.1	4.5	6.1	6.1	6.1	6.1	6.1	6.1	6.1	6.1	6.1	6.1	6.1	6.1	6.1	6.1	6.1	77%	4.0	5.4%	4.0%	5.2%
4.5%	1974	1930	4.0	4.0	4.6	4.4	4.1	4.3	4.2	4.0	5.0	5.9	5.8	6.7	6.7	6.7	6.7	6.7	6.7	6.7	6.7	6.7	6.7	6.7	6.7	6.7	6.7	6.7	6.7	6.7	6.7	6.7	6.7	6.7	6.7	6.8	6.8	6.8	82%	4.0	6.1%	4.5%	6.3%
5.0%	1975	1931	5.4	7.0	6.2	5.7	5.4	5.0	6.6	7.5	7.4	7.6	7.6	7.6	7.6	7.6	7.6	7.6	7.6	7.6	7.6	7.6	7.6	7.6	7.6	7.6	7.6	7.6	7.6	7.6	7.6	7.6	7.6	7.6	7.6	7.6	7.6	7.6	109%	5.0	7.2%	6.2%	7.6%
4.8%	1976	1932	5.5	5.0	4.6	4.7	4.7	4.4	5.5	6.5	6.5	7.3	7.3	7.3	7.3	7.3	7.3	7.3	7.3	7.3	7.3	7.3	7.3	7.3	7.3	7.3	7.3	7.3	7.3	7.3	7.3	7.4	7.4	7.4	7.4	7.4	98%	4.4	6.9%	5.5%	6.9%
4.8%	1977	1933	4.2	4.0	4.0	4.1	4.2	5.2	6.6	7.2	6.2	6.7	7.3	6.0	7.3	7.3	7.3	7.3	7.3	7.3	7.3	7.3	7.3	7.3	7.3	7.3	7.3	7.3	7.3	7.3	7.3	7.3	7.4	7.4	7.4	7.4	7.4	7.4	55%	4.0	6.6%	4.9%	6.6%
5.0%	1978	1934	4.2	4.2	4.3	4.1	4.8	5.5	5.4	7.0	6.6	7.0	6.2	7.6	7.6	7.6	7.6	7.6	7.6	7.6	7.6	7.6	7.6	7.6	7.6	7.6	7.6	7.6	7.6	7.6	7.6	7.6	7.6	7.6	7.6	7.6	7.6	7.6	62%	4.1	7.0%	5.4%	6.6%
5.2%	1979	1935	4.4	4.4	4.2	5.0	5.5	5.6	7.0	7.7	6.3	7.8	7.8	7.8	7.8	7.8	7.8	7.8	7.8	7.8	7.8	7.8	7.8	7.8	7.8	7.8	7.9	7.9	7.9	7.9	7.9	7.9	7.9	63%	4.2	7.3%	5.8%	6.9%
5.2%	1980	1936	4.4	4.2	4.8	5.5	5.4	6.9	7.7	6.6	7.1	7.6	6.0	7.8	7.8	7.8	7.8	7.8	7.8	7.8	7.8	7.8	7.8	7.8	7.8	7.8	7.9	7.9	7.9	7.9	7.9	81%	4.2	7.5%	6.0%	7.0%
5.0%	1981	1937	4.2	4.9	5.7	7.2	7.0	7.3	7.6	6.4	7.6	7.6	7.6	7.6	7.6	7.6	7.6	7.6	7.6	7.6	7.6	7.6	7.6	7.6	7.6	74%	4.2	7.3%	6.4%	7.3%
5.2%	1982	1938	5.2	5.8	5.8	7.4	7.8	7.1	7.3	7.4	7.8	7.8	7.8	7.8	7.8	7.8	7.8	7.8	7.8	7.8	7.8	7.9	7.9	5.4	7.7	7.9	7.9	7.9	7.9	75%	5.2	7.6%	6.9%	7.7%
5.0%	1983	1939	4.8	4.8	5.7	6.5	5.6	6.0	6.5	5.4	6.9	7.4	7.8	6.8	7.8	7.8	7.8	7.8	7.8	7.8	7.8	7.9	7.9	5.4	7.7	7.9	7.9	7.9	37%	4.8	7.3%	6.0%	7.7%
5.0%	1984	1940	4.3	5.1	5.0	5.3	5.0	4.9	6.1	6.8	7.5	6.1	7.6	7.6	7.6	7.6	7.6	7.6	7.6	7.6	7.5	7.6	7.6	7.6	6.6	4.5	5.6	7.4	7.6	7.6	7.0	7.6	7.6	5.4	4.0	20%	4.0	6.8%	5.6%	6.6%
4.8%	1985	1941	5.2	5.8	5.0	5.4	5.9	4.9	6.1	6.8	7.5	6.1	7.6	7.6	7.6	7.6	7.6	7.6	7.5	7.6	7.6	7.6	7.6	6.6	4.5	5.6	7.4	7.6	7.6	7.0	7.6	7.6	5.4	4.0	20%	4.0	6.8%	5.9%	6.8%
4.8%	1986	1942	4.8	4.3	4.5	5.0	4.2	5.1	5.6	6.3	6.6	6.8	7.3	7.3	7.3	7.3	5.7	7.0	7.3	7.4	7.4	7.3	7.3	5.6	5.4	4.0	4.1	6.1	5.4	7.3	7.3	5.6	4.0	4.0	18%	4.0	6.1%	5.2%	6.1%
4.8%	1987	1943	4.0	4.2	4.5	4.0	4.6	5.0	5.5	4.8	6.2	6.1	7.3	7.3	7.2	7.3	6.1	7.3	3.1	6.0	7.2	7.4	6.4	4.8	4.0	4.2	5.6	7.3	7.4	5.4	4.1	5.3	4.0	4.0	5.0	29%	4.0	5.8%	4.9%	5.8%
4.8%	1988	1944	4.7	5.1	4.2	5.2	4.8	5.5	4.8	6.2	6.1	7.4	7.4	7.3	7.3	7.3	7.3	3.5	6.0	7.2	7.4	7.2	5.4	4.7	7.4	5.5	4.0	4.7	7.0	4.8	38%	4.0	6.4%	5.8%	6.3%
4.8%	1989	1945	4.7	4.0	4.7	5.3	5.8	5.0	6.2	6.3	7.3	7.3	7.3	6.5	7.3	7.3	3.8	6.7	7.2	7.4	7.2	5.2	4.4	5.4	6.5	6.6	7.4	5.0	7.4	5.9	4.4	4.0	4.0	7.4	7.4	49%	4.0	6.3%	5.7%	6.2%
4.5%	1990	1946	4.0	4.5	4.9	5.6	4.7	5.9	6.1	6.7	6.7	6.7	5.7	6.7	6.7	6.7	4.0	6.0	6.8	6.8	6.1	6.8	5.1	4.0	5.8	6.8	6.8	6.8	4.0	6.8	5.9	40%	4.0	6.0%	5.6%	5.9%
4.7%	1991	1947	5.8	6.2	6.8	5.7	7.0	7.0	6.6	6.7	6.7	6.7	7.0	7.0	7.0	6.8	7.0	7.1	7.1	6.4	5.1	5.9	7.1	7.1	7.1	7.1	4.9	4.8	7.1	7.1	7.1	40%	4.8	6.7%	6.7%	6.7%
4.3%	1992	1948	5.1	5.7	4.7	6.2	6.1	6.4	6.4	6.4	6.4	6.3	6.4	6.4	6.4	6.3	6.4	6.3	6.4	6.5	6.5	6.5	6.5	6.5	6.5	5.0	4.8	6.5	6.5	6.5	6.5	4.3	35%	4.6	6.2%	6.0%	6.2%
4.1%	1993	1949	4.4	4.4	5.8	6.0	6.1	6.1	6.1	6.1	5.4	6.1	6.1	4.6	5.6	6.1	6.2	4.9	4.3	6.2	5.7	6.2	6.0	6.2	6.2	5.8	6.2	6.2	6.2	38%	4.0	5.8%	5.8%	5.8%
4.1%	1994	1950	4.1	5.1	5.1	6.1	6.1	6.1	6.0	6.1	5.2	6.1	6.1	6.1	4.5	5.1	6.1	6.2	3.0	4.0	4.0	4.6	4.7	6.2	6.2	3.0	5.6	4.2	4.0	4.0	6.2	6.2	6.2	6.2	6.2	6.2	41%	4.0	5.5%	5.6%	5.5%
4.0%	1995	1951	6.0	6.0	6.0	6.0	6.0	6.0	6.0	6.0	6.0	6.0	6.0	6.1	6.1	5.5	6.1	6.1	6.1	6.1	6.1	6.1	6.1	5.6	6.1	6.1	6.1	6.1	6.1	6.1	6.1	68%	5.5	6.0%	6.0%	5.5%
3.8%	1996	1952	5.1	5.7	5.7	5.7	5.7	5.7	5.0	5.7	5.7	5.7	4.4	5.1	5.7	5.8	5.8	4.5	4.0	5.8	5.8	5.8	5.3	5.8	5.8	4.0	4.0	5.8	5.8	5.8	5.8	5.8	5.8	5.8	58%	4.0	5.5%	5.6%	5.5%
3.8%	1997	1953	5.7	5.7	5.7	5.7	5.7	5.7	5.7	5.0	5.7	5.7	4.0	4.0	5.2	5.8	4.9	4.0	4.0	4.0	4.9	4.7	5.8	5.8	5.8	4.0	4.0	5.8	5.8	5.8	5.8	5.8	5.8	42%	4.0	5.3%	5.6%	5.4%
3.8%	1998	1954	5.1	5.3	4.5	4.9	4.0	5.2	5.4	5.1	5.5	4.7	4.0	4.1	5.8	4.0	4.0	4.0	5.1	5.8	4.8	4.2	4.0	4.0	4.0	4.6	5.8	5.8	5.8	5.8	5.8	5.8	5.8	52%	4.0	4.9%	5.0%	4.8%
3.8%	1999	1955	5.3	4.5	4.7	4.0	5.0	5.4	4.9	5.3	4.9	4.0	4.0	4.2	5.7	4.0	4.0	4.0	5.2	5.8	5.1	4.9	4.0	4.0	4.0	4.8	5.8	5.8	5.7	5.7	5.8	5.8	5.8	5.8	40%	4.0	4.9%	4.8%	4.8%
3.6%	2000	1956	4.7	4.9	4.0	5.2	5.4	5.1	5.3	4.7	4.0	4.0	4.0	4.0	4.0	4.0	4.2	5.4	4.0	4.2	4.1	4.0	4.0	4.0	4.5	5.5	5.5	5.5	5.0	5.5	5.5	5.5	5.5	5.5	5.5	5.5	67%	4.0	4.8%	4.7%	4.7%
																																											Totals	53%	4.0	6.0%	5.4%	6.2%

FIGURE 143

Benchmark backtesting results for 40-year systemic withdrawal plan with EM floor increased to 4%.

---

* A reader examining the 1969 results may be wondering how annual income peaks above MSWR-100%. The failure rate is approximately 4.1%, so the little saved early (i.e., 0.1% per year) compounds to boost later income and still leave some.

Figure 144 shows similar outstanding behavior with a more moderate and viable 3.5% EM floor. More than 20% is left for every retirement period—a significant margin of safety.

Initial	Year	End	Y1	Y2	Y3	Y4	Y5	Y6	Y7	Y8	Y9	Y10	Y11	Y12	Y13	Y14	Y15	Y16	Y17	Y18	Y19	Y20	Y21	Y22	Y23	Y24	Y25	Y26	Y27	Y28	Y29	Y30	Y31	Y32	Y33	Y34	Y35	Y36	Y37	Y38	Y39	Y40	%Left	Min	Avg	1st 10Y	MSWR
4.1%	1928	1967	6.1	4.5	3.7	3.5	3.7	4.6	4.5	5.9	6.1	4.6	5.5	5.4	4.7	3.8	3.8	5.0	6.1	6.1	6.1	5.1	4.9	5.6	6.1	6.1	6.1	6.1	6.1	6.1	6.1	6.1	6.1	6.1	6.1	6.1	6.1	6.1	6.1	6.1	6.1	6.1	103%	3.5	5.5%	4.7%	6.2%
4.1%	1929	1968	3.7	3.5	3.5	3.5	3.6	3.6	4.3	5.9	3.5	3.8	3.8	3.5	3.5	3.5	3.9	5.5	6.1	5.3	4.5	4.3	5.6	6.1	6.1	6.1	6.1	6.1	6.1	6.1	6.1	6.1	6.1	6.1	6.1	6.1	6.1	6.1	6.1	6.1	6.1	6.1	128%	3.5	5.1%	3.9%	5.2%
4.4%	1930	1969	3.7	3.5	3.5	4.2	4.1	5.5	6.6	4.4	5.3	5.0	4.4	3.6	3.7	5.1	6.6	6.6	6.6	5.6	5.1	6.6	6.6	6.6	6.6	6.6	6.6	6.6	6.6	6.6	6.6	6.6	6.6	6.6	6.6	6.6	6.6	6.6	6.6	6.6	6.6	6.6	95%	3.5	5.8%	4.6%	6.5%
4.7%	1931	1970	3.6	3.7	5.1	5.2	7.0	7.0	5.6	6.8	6.6	5.6	4.3	4.4	5.8	7.0	7.0	6.8	5.5	4.9	5.9	7.0	7.0	7.0	7.0	7.0	7.0	7.0	7.0	7.0	7.0	7.0	7.0	7.0	7.0	7.0	7.0	7.0	7.0	7.0	7.0	7.0	84%	3.6	6.4%	5.6%	7.7%
5.2%	1932	1971	4.8	7.8	7.8	7.8	7.8	7.8	7.8	7.8	6.9	6.5	7.8	7.8	7.8	7.8	7.0	6.5	7.8	7.8	7.8	7.8	7.8	7.8	7.8	7.8	7.8	7.8	7.8	7.8	7.8	7.8	7.8	7.8	7.8	7.8	7.8	7.8	7.8	7.8	7.8	7.8	101%	4.8	7.7%	7.5%	9.0%
5.2%	1933	1972	7.8	7.7	7.8	7.8	7.8	7.8	7.8	7.8	6.9	6.5	7.8	7.8	7.8	7.8	7.0	6.5	7.8	7.8	7.8	7.8	7.8	7.8	7.8	7.8	7.8	7.8	7.8	7.8	7.8	7.8	7.8	7.8	7.8	7.8	7.8	7.8	7.8	7.8	7.8	7.8	88%	6.5	7.7%	7.6%	9.0%
4.7%	1934	1973	4.4	6.2	7.0	4.9	5.8	5.4	4.9	4.0	4.1	5.2	6.7	7.0	6.0	5.0	4.6	5.5	6.9	6.8	7.0	6.5	7.0	7.0	7.0	7.0	7.0	7.0	7.0	7.0	7.0	7.0	7.0	7.0	7.0	7.0	7.0	7.0	7.0	7.0	7.0	7.0	65%	4.0	6.4%	5.2%	7.5%
4.7%	1935	1974	6.2	7.0	4.8	5.8	5.5	4.9	3.9	4.0	5.2	6.4	7.0	5.7	4.7	4.5	5.2	6.4	6.7	6.0	5.9	7.0	7.0	7.0	7.0	7.0	7.0	7.0	7.0	7.0	7.0	7.0	7.0	7.0	7.0	7.0	7.0	7.0	7.0	7.0	7.0	7.0	44%	3.9	6.3%	5.4%	7.3%
4.7%	1936	1975	6.0	3.8	4.2	4.2	3.9	3.5	3.5	4.0	5.0	7.0	4.7	4.1	3.9	4.5	5.5	5.7	6.3	5.3	7.0	7.0	7.0	7.0	7.0	7.0	7.0	7.0	7.0	7.0	7.0	7.0	7.0	7.0	7.0	7.0	7.0	7.0	7.0	7.0	7.0	7.0	47%	3.5	6.0%	4.5%	6.6%
4.1%	1937	1976	3.5	3.5	3.5	3.5	3.3	3.5	3.9	6.1	4.0	3.5	3.5	3.8	4.7	4.8	5.2	4.8	6.1	6.1	6.1	6.1	6.1	6.1	6.1	6.1	6.1	6.1	6.1	6.1	6.1	6.1	6.1	6.1	6.1	6.1	6.1	6.1	6.1	6.1	6.1	6.1	53%	3.5	5.2%	3.9%	5.7%
4.4%	1938	1977	5.8	5.4	4.7	3.7	3.8	5.3	6.5	6.6	6.2	4.8	4.5	5.4	6.1	6.2	6.4	5.8	6.6	6.6	6.6	6.6	6.6	6.6	6.6	6.6	6.6	6.6	6.6	6.6	6.6	6.6	6.6	6.6	6.6	6.6	6.6	6.6	6.6	6.6	6.6	6.6	51%	3.7	6.1%	5.3%	7.3%
4.4%	1939	1978	4.4	3.9	3.5	3.5	4.3	5.6	6.6	5.1	4.3	4.0	4.6	5.7	5.8	6.2	5.4	6.6	6.6	6.6	6.6	6.6	6.6	6.6	6.6	6.6	6.6	6.6	6.6	6.6	6.6	6.6	6.6	6.6	6.6	6.6	6.6	6.6	6.6	6.6	6.6	6.6	56%	3.5	5.9%	4.5%	6.8%
4.4%	1940	1979	4.1	3.5	3.5	4.5	5.7	6.6	5.2	4.4	4.1	4.7	5.8	5.9	6.2	5.6	6.6	6.6	6.6	6.6	6.6	6.6	6.6	6.6	6.6	6.6	6.6	6.6	6.6	6.6	6.6	6.6	6.6	6.6	6.6	6.6	6.6	6.6	6.6	6.6	6.6	6.6	60%	3.5	6.0%	4.6%	6.9%
4.4%	1941	1980	3.6	3.8	5.1	6.6	6.6	6.3	4.9	4.6	5.5	6.2	6.1	6.4	5.7	6.6	6.6	6.6	6.6	6.6	6.6	6.6	6.6	6.6	6.6	6.6	6.6	6.6	6.6	6.6	6.6	6.6	6.6	6.6	6.6	6.6	6.6	6.6	6.6	6.6	6.6	6.6	50%	3.6	6.2%	5.3%	6.9%
4.7%	1942	1981	4.7	6.3	7.0	7.0	6.8	5.5	5.0	5.9	6.6	6.3	6.6	5.9	7.0	7.0	7.0	7.0	7.0	7.0	7.0	7.0	7.0	7.0	7.0	7.0	7.0	7.0	7.0	7.0	7.0	7.0	7.0	7.0	7.0	7.0	7.0	7.0	7.0	7.0	7.0	7.0	35%	4.7	6.7%	6.1%	7.1%
4.9%	1943	1982	5.8	7.2	7.4	6.5	5.1	4.9	6.1	6.1	6.1	5.6	7.4	7.4	7.4	7.4	7.4	7.4	7.4	7.4	7.4	7.4	7.4	7.4	7.4	7.4	7.4	6.2	7.4	7.4	7.1	6.5	7.4	6.2	6.4								33%	4.9	6.9%	6.1%	7.2%
4.7%	1944	1983	5.4	7.0	4.8	4.1	3.9	4.4	5.0	5.1	5.3	4.7	7.0	7.0	0.8	7.0	7.0	7.0	7.0	7.0	7.0	7.0	7.0	7.0	7.0	7.0	7.0	7.0	7.0	7.0	7.0	7.0	7.0	5.3	6.5								34%	3.9	6.4%	5.0%	6.7%
4.7%	1945	1984	6.2	4.1	3.7	3.6	3.9	4.3	4.6	4.3	6.4	7.0	6.8	5.5	7.0	7.0	7.0	7.0	7.0	7.0	7.0	7.0	7.0	7.0	7.0	6.7	4.1	5.1	6.1	6.4	5.1	5.1	5.9	4.5	7.0	7.0	5.2						28%	3.6	5.9%	4.5%	6.1%
4.7%	1946	1985	3.6	3.5	3.5	3.5	3.6	3.7	3.7	3.6	5.0	5.8	5.5	4.5	6.1	6.6	6.1	7.0	6.6	6.9	7.0	7.0	7.0	7.0	7.0	7.0	5.0	3.7	4.8	3.9	6.9	6.7	5.5	5.0	4.6	5.1	7.0	6.0	6.4				32%	3.5	5.5%	4.0%	5.5%
4.7%	1947	1986	3.9	3.8	4.0	4.7	4.6	4.9	4.4	6.9	7.0	5.9	7.0	7.0	7.0	7.0	7.0	7.0	7.0	7.0	7.0	7.0	5.0	3.7	4.9	5.8	6.9	6.7	5.5	6.9	6.6	5.0	5.1	7.0	6.0	6.4							35%	3.8	6.3%	5.1%	6.4%
4.9%	1948	1987	4.2	4.6	5.2	5.3	5.4	5.1	7.2	7.4	5.7	7.4	7.4	7.4	7.4	7.4	7.4	7.4	7.4	7.4	7.4	7.4	7.4	7.4	6.4	5.3	5.2	5.0	6.2	4.9	5.4	7.4	7.4	5.5	7.3								31%	4.4	6.4%	5.7%	6.9%
4.9%	1949	1988	4.9	5.3	5.1	5.4	4.9	7.2	7.4	5.7	7.4	7.4	7.4	7.4	7.4	7.4	7.4	7.4	7.4	7.4	7.4	6.2	4.5	5.2	6.0	5.6	4.8	5.4	5.4	5.3	6.0	7.1	6.3	7.2	7.4	6.2	5.9						31%	4.5	6.5%	6.1%	6.6%
4.9%	1950	1989	4.8	4.7	4.8	4.6	6.5	7.3	6.5	7.2	7.1	6.8	7.4	6.8	7.4	7.4	7.4	7.4	7.4	7.4	7.4	4.4	4.5	4.6	4.6	5.2	4.4	6.3	7.3	5.5	7.4	7.2	6.8	6.3	5.8								50%	4.7	6.2%	5.9%	6.4%
4.7%	1951	1990	4.4	4.5	4.2	6.2	6.9	6.3	4.9	6.9	7.0	6.9	7.0	6.9	7.0	7.0	7.0	7.0	7.0	5.7	4.2	4.5	5.7	5.4	4.9	5.8	5.5	5.2	5.1	5.7	4.7	6.5	7.0	7.0	7.0	5.3	6.5						24%	4.0	6.1%	5.8%	6.2%
4.7%	1952	1991	4.6	4.2	6.3	7.0	6.7	5.0	7.0	7.0	6.9	7.0	7.0	7.0	7.0	5.8	4.2	4.9	5.8	5.5	5.2	5.1	5.7	4.7	6.5	7.0	7.0	7.0	5.3	6.5													32%	4.2	6.3%	6.2%	6.4%
4.5%	1953	1992	4.2	6.1	6.7	6.4	5.1	6.7	6.6	6.5	6.7	6.4	6.7	6.7	6.7	6.7	6.7	5.5	3.8	4.4	5.5	4.7	4.6	4.9	4.8	4.5	5.3	6.7	6.1	6.7	6.7	6.6	6.7	5.8	6.7	6.5	6.3						31%	3.8	6.0%	6.1%	6.1%
4.8%	1954	1993	6.4	7.1	6.4	6.9	7.1	6.6	7.3	6.7	7.0	7.3	7.3	7.3	7.3	7.3	7.3	4.1	4.3	5.4	5.0	4.5	4.8	5.2	4.5	5.7	7.0	6.7	7.3	7.3	7.2	7.3	7.3	4.6	7.3	7.3	7.2						35%	4.1	6.4%	6.7%	6.4%
4.5%	1955	1994	5.0	4.6	3.9	5.1	5.3	5.0	5.1	5.6	6.1	6.7	5.9	6.7	6.2	6.1	6.7	6.2	4.2	3.5	3.9	4.5	4.3	4.2	4.6	4.3	5.0	5.6	6.7	6.7	6.7	6.3	6.7	6.7	4.6	6.3	6.7	6.0					30%	3.5	5.8%	5.2%	5.5%
4.5%	1956	1995	4.3	3.7	4.6	4.9	4.6	5.6	4.7	5.2	5.8	6.6	5.5	6.7	5.9	5.7	6.7	6.2	6.1	6.2	4.0	3.5	3.7	4.5	4.1	4.0	4.3	4.4	5.2	6.5	6.0	6.7	6.3	6.7	6.7	4.6	6.7	6.7	6.0				36%	3.5	5.5%	5.0%	5.4%
4.5%	1957	1996	3.8	4.9	5.0	4.9	5.7	5.0	5.3	6.0	6.7	5.6	6.7	5.7	6.1	6.0	4.2	3.5	3.9	4.2	4.5	4.1	3.9	4.2	4.5	5.1	6.7	6.7	6.7	6.7	6.7	5.1	6.7	6.7	6.7	6.7	6.7	6.7	6.7				39%	3.5	5.6%	5.3%	5.5%
4.3%	1958	1997	6.5	6.6	6.3	6.7	6.3	6.7	6.7	6.7	6.7	6.6	7.0	6.7	4.7	3.7	4.0	4.8	4.6	4.5	4.4	4.4	5.3	6.7	6.7	6.7	6.7	6.7	6.7	6.7	6.7	6.7	6.7	6.7	6.7	6.7	6.7						62%	3.7	6.1%	6.6%	6.1%
4.3%	1959	1998	4.8	4.5	5.3	4.6	5.0	5.6	6.3	5.4	6.4	5.4	5.3	5.6	5.6	3.9	3.5	3.5	4.1	3.9	5.0	6.3	5.9	6.4	6.4	6.4	6.4	6.4	4.9	6.4	7.4	5.5	7.4	7.2	6.4	6.4	6.4	6.4	6.4				56%	3.5	5.4%	5.4%	5.3%
4.1%	1960	1999	4.5	5.3	4.5	4.9	5.3	6.1	5.2	6.1	5.5	5.3	5.3	5.6	3.8	3.5	3.5	4.1	3.8	3.6	3.0	4.4	4.0	3.9	5.1	6.1	5.9	6.1	6.1	6.1	6.1	6.1	6.1	6.1	6.1	6.1	6.1	6.1					73%	3.5	5.4%	5.4%	5.3%
4.1%	1961	2000	5.7	4.7	5.0	5.7	5.4	6.1	5.3	5.1	5.3	5.1	5.4	3.3	3.5	3.5	3.6	3.9	3.7	4.6	6.1	6.1	6.1	6.1	6.1	6.1	4.9	6.1	6.1	6.1	6.1	6.1	6.1	6.1	6.1	6.1	6.1						59%	3.5	5.3%	5.5%	5.2%
4.1%	1962	2001	4.1	4.4	4.8	5.9	4.7	6.1	5.2	5.0	5.3	3.6	3.5	3.5	3.6	3.9	3.7	4.0	3.8	3.9	3.7	4.0	3.6	5.6	6.1	6.1	6.1	6.1	6.1	6.1	6.1	6.1	6.1	6.1	6.1	6.1	6.1						68%	3.5	5.3%	5.2%	5.2%
4.1%	1963	2002	5.2	5.8	6.1	5.6	6.1	6.1	5.6	5.5	3.5	3.5	3.9	3.7	3.6	3.8	3.9	3.7	4.8	6.1	5.6	6.1	6.1	6.1	6.1	6.1	6.1	6.1	6.1	6.1	6.1	6.1	6.1	6.1	6.1	6.1	6.1						53%	3.5	5.4%	5.7%	5.4%
4.1%	1964	2003	5.2	6.1	5.0	6.1	6.1	5.4	5.0	5.4	5.4	3.6	3.5	3.5	3.7	3.6	3.5	3.7	4.0	4.5	6.0	6.1	6.1	6.1	6.1	6.1	6.1	6.1	6.1	6.1	6.1	6.1	6.1	6.1	6.1	6.1	6.1						73%	3.5	5.4%	5.3%	5.4%
4.0%	1965	2004	5.6	4.6	5.9	6.0	4.6	4.6	4.7	4.7	3.5	3.5	3.5	3.5	3.5	3.5	3.8	4.9	4.8	6.0	6.0	6.0	4.9	6.0	6.0	6.0	6.0	6.0	6.0	6.0	6.0	6.0	6.0	6.0	6.0	6.0	6.0						69%	3.5	5.1%	4.8%	4.9%
3.8%	1966	2005	4.2	5.6	5.7	4.2	4.1	4.2	4.2	3.5	3.5	3.5	3.5	3.5	3.5	3.6	3.5	4.1	5.3	4.8	6.1	5.7	5.7	4.4	5.7	5.7	5.7	5.7	5.7	5.7	5.7	5.7	5.7	5.7	5.7	5.7	5.7						68%	3.5	4.9%	4.3%	4.6%
4.1%	1967	2006	6.1	6.1	4.9	4.8	5.0	5.0	3.5	3.5	3.5	3.5	3.5	3.5	3.6	3.5	4.1	5.3	4.8	6.1	5.7	5.7	6.1	5.7	6.0	6.1	6.1	5.7	5.7	5.7	5.7	5.7	5.7	5.7	5.7	5.7	5.7						81%	3.5	5.3%	4.6%	5.2%
4.0%	1968	2007	5.6	3.8	3.7	4.0	3.9	3.5	3.5	3.5	3.5	3.5	3.5	3.5	3.5	3.6	3.5	4.0	5.2	4.8	6.0	6.0	6.0	6.0	6.0	6.0	6.0	6.0	6.0	6.0	6.0	6.0	6.0	6.0	6.0	6.0	6.0						64%	3.5	4.9%	3.9%	4.4%
4.0%	1969	2008	3.5	3.5	3.5	3.5	3.5	3.5	3.5	3.5	3.5	3.5	3.5	3.5	3.5	3.8	4.0	3.5	4.2	4.2	3.5	4.8	5.9	6.0	5.5	6.0	6.0	6.0	6.0	6.0	6.0	6.0	6.0	6.0	6.0	6.0	3.6						21%	3.5	4.6%	3.5%	4.0%
4.0%	1970	2009	4.6	4.8	4.7	3.5	3.5	3.5	3.5	3.5	3.5	3.5	3.5	3.5	3.5	4.0	5.0	4.7	6.0	6.0	6.0	6.0	6.0	6.0	6.0	6.0	6.0	6.0	6.0	6.0	6.0	6.0	6.0	6.0	6.0	6.0	6.0						63%	3.5	5.2%	3.9%	5.1%
4.3%	1971	2010	4.9	4.8	3.5	3.5	3.5	3.5	3.5	3.5	3.5	3.5	4.0	4.8	4.6	6.2	6.4	4.9	6.4	6.4	6.4	6.4	6.4	6.4	6.4	6.4	6.4	6.4	6.4	6.4	6.4	6.4	6.4	6.4									65%	3.5	5.5%	3.8%	5.4%
4.1%	1972	1928	4.7	3.5	3.5	3.5	3.5	3.5	3.5	3.6	4.2	6.0	4.2	6.1	6.1	6.1	5.4	6.1	6.1	6.1	6.1	6.1	6.1	6.1	6.1	6.1	6.1	6.1	6.1	6.1	6.1	6.1	6.1	6.2									85%	3.5	5.3%	3.6%	5.2%
4.1%	1973	1929	3.5	3.5	3.5	3.5	3.5	3.5	3.5	3.7	4.5	4.3	5.7	6.1	5.4	6.1	5.0	6.1	6.1	6.1	6.1	6.1	6.1	6.1	6.1	6.1	6.1	6.1	6.1	6.1	6.1	6.1	6.1	6.2									69%	3.5	5.3%	3.5%	5.2%
4.5%	1974	1930	3.5	3.8	4.7	4.4	4.1	4.3	4.0	5.1	5.9	5.8	6.7	6.7	6.7	6.7	6.7	6.7	6.7	6.7	6.7	6.7	6.7	6.7	6.7	6.7	6.7	6.7	6.7	6.7	6.8	6.8											83%	3.5	6.1%	4.4%	6.3%
5.0%	1975	1931	5.4	7.0	6.2	5.7	5.4	5.5	5.0	6.5	7.5	7.4	7.6	7.6	7.6	7.6	7.6	7.6	7.6	7.6	7.6	7.6	7.6	7.6	7.6	7.6	7.6	7.6	7.6	7.6	7.6	7.6											109%	5.0	7.2%	6.2%	7.6%
4.8%	1976	1932	5.5	5.0	4.6	4.7	4.7	4.4	5.5	6.5	6.5	7.3	7.3	7.3	7.3	7.3	7.3	7.3	7.3	7.3	7.3	7.3	7.3	7.3	7.3	7.3	7.3	7.3	7.3	7.3	7.4	7.4	7.4	7.4									98%	5.0	6.9%	5.5%	6.9%
4.8%	1977	1933	4.2	4.0	4.0	4.1	3.9	4.6	5.1	5.2	6.6	7.2	6.2	7.0	7.3	7.3	7.3	7.3	7.3	7.3	7.3	7.3	7.3	7.3	7.3	7.4	7.4	7.4	7.4	7.4	7.4	7.4											55%	3.9	6.5%	4.9%	6.2%
5.0%	1978	1934	4.2	4.2	4.3	4.1	4.8	5.5	5.4	6.9	7.6	6.6	7.0	6.2	7.6	7.6	7.6	7.6	7.6	7.6	7.6	7.6	7.6	7.6	7.6	7.6	7.6	7.6	7.6	7.6	7.6	7.6											62%	4.1	7.0%	5.4%	6.6%
5.2%	1979	1935	4.4	4.4	4.2	5.0	5.5	5.4	6.9	7.6	7.1	7.6	6.0	7.8	7.8	7.8	7.8	7.8	7.8	7.8	7.8	7.8	7.8	7.8	7.8	7.8	7.9	7.9	7.9	7.9	7.9	7.9											63%	4.2	7.3%	5.8%	6.9%
5.2%	1980	1936	4.4	4.2	4.8	5.5	5.4	6.9	7.6	7.1	7.6	6.0	7.8	7.8	7.8	7.8	7.8	7.8	7.8	7.8	7.8	7.8	7.8	7.8	7.8	7.9	7.9	7.9	7.9	7.9	7.9	7.9											81%	4.4	7.3%	6.0%	7.0%
5.0%	1981	1937	4.2	4.9	5.7	7.2	6.9	7.3	6.6	7.8	6.7	7.8	7.8	7.8	7.8	7.8	7.8	7.8	7.8	7.8	7.8	7.8	7.8	7.8	7.8	7.8	7.3	7.0	7.8	7.8	7.8	6.4											74%	4.2	7.3%	6.4%	7.3%
5.2%	1982	1938	5.2	5.8	5.8	7.4	7.8	7.1	7.8	6.7	7.8	7.8	7.8	7.8	7.8	7.8	7.8	7.8	7.8	7.8	7.8	7.8	7.9	7.9	5.4	7.7	7.9	7.9	7.9	7.9	7.9	7.7											75%	5.2	7.6%	6.9%	7.7%
5.2%	1983	1939	4.8	4.8	5.7	6.5	5.6	6.0	6.5	5.4	6.9	7.4	7.8	6.8	7.8	7.8	7.8	7.8	7.8	7.8	7.8	7.9	7.9	5.4	7.7	7.9	7.9	7.9	7.9	7.9	7.9	7.8											37%	4.8	7.3%	6.0%	7.0%
5.0%	1984	1940	4.3	5.1	5.0	5.3	5.9	4.8	6.1	6.8	7.4	6.1	7.6	7.6	7.6	7.6	7.6	7.6	7.6	7.6	7.6	7.6	6.4	4.5	5.6	7.4	7.6	7.6	7.0	7.6	7.6	5.4	3.9										29%	3.9	6.8%	5.6%	6.6%
5.0%	1985	1941	5.2	5.8	5.0	5.4	5.9	6.1	6.8	7.5	6.1	7.6	7.6	7.6	7.6	7.6	7.6	7.6	7.6	7.5	7.6	7.6	7.6	6.4	4.5	5.6	7.4	7.6	7.6	7.0	7.6	5.4	3.9										20%	3.9	6.8%	5.9%	6.8%
4.8%	1986	1942	4.8	4.3	4.5	5.0	4.2	5.1	5.6	6.3	6.8	7.3	7.3	7.3	7.3	7.3	7.3	7.3	7.3	7.3	5.1	6.1	7.2	7.4	6.4	4.4	5.4	7.4	7.4	5.3	3.8	3.8											20%	3.8	6.1%	5.2%	6.1%
4.8%	1987	1943	4.0	4.2	4.5	4.0	4.6	5.0	5.6	4.8	6.2	6.1	7.3	7.3	7.3	7.3	6.1	7.3	7.3	5.1	6.1	7.2	7.4	6.4	4.4	3.9	4.1	5.1	5.4	5.3	4.3	3.9	4.0	5.2									29%	3.9	6.4%	4.9%	5.8%
4.8%	1988	1944	4.7	5.1	4.6	5.3	5.8	5.0	7.0	7.1	7.3	7.3	7.3	7.4	7.2	5.4	6.1	7.8	7.4	7.2	7.4	6.5	4.4	3.9	4.1	5.1	5.4	5.3	4.3	3.8	4.8	7.2	7.4	3.9									39%	3.8	6.4%	5.8%	6.3%
4.8%	1989	1945	4.7	4.0	4.7	5.3	5.8	5.0	2.2	7.3	7.3	7.3	7.2	6.5	7.3	7.3	5.8	6.7	7.2	7.4	5.2	4.4	4.5	6.6	7.4	5.0	5.9	4.4	3.8	3.8	7.4	7.0											50%	3.5	6.3%	5.7%	6.2%
4.5%	1990	1946	3.8	4.6	4.9	5.6	4.7	6.2	6.1	6.7	6.7	6.7	6.7	5.7	6.7	6.7	6.7	5.0	6.0	6.7	5.1	3.8	4.5	6.4	5.8	6.8	6.2	6.8	6.8	3.6	4.0	6.2	6.8	6.8	6.8								41%	3.6	6.0%	5.6%	5.9%
4.7%	1991	1947	5.8	6.2	6.8	5.7	7.0	7.0	7.0	6.7	6.7	6.7	6.7	6.7	7.0	5.0	6.0	6.7	7.1	6.4	5.1	5.9	7.1	7.1	7.1	7.1	7.1	7.1	4.0	4.1	7.1	7.1	7.1										40%	3.6	6.4%	6.7%	6.7%
4.3%	1992	1948	5.1	5.7	6.4	6.4	6.4	6.4	6.1	6.4	6.4	6.3	6.4	6.4	6.4	5.8	6.5	6.5	6.5	6.5	5.0	4.8	6.5	6.5	6.5	6.5	6.5	6.5															35%	4.6	6.2%	6.0%	6.2%
4.1%	1993	1949	5.4	4.4	5.8	6.0	6.1	6.1	6.1	6.1	5.4	6.1	6.1	6.1	4.6	5.6	6.1	6.2	6.2	4.9	3.7	4.4	5.8	6.2	6.1	6.2	6.2	6.2	5.9														38%	3.7	6.2%	6.0%	6.2%
4.1%	1994	1950	4.1	5.1	5.1	6.1	6.0	6.1	6.1	5.2	6.1	6.1	4.5	5.1	6.1	5.0	3.9	3.5	3.5	4.7	4.8	6.2	6.2	5.1	5.8	4.3	3.5	3.6	6.2	6.2	6.2	6.2	6.2	6.2									42%	3.5	5.5%	5.6%	5.5%
4.0%	1995	1951	6.0	6.0	6.0	6.0	6.0	6.0	6.0	6.0	6.0	6.0	6.0	6.0	6.0	6.0	6.0	6.1	6.1	6.1	6.1	6.1	6.1	6.1	6.1	6.1	6.1	6.1	6.1	6.1	6.1	6.1	6.1	6.1									68%	3.5	6.0%	6.0%	6.2%
3.8%	1996	1952	5.1	5.7	5.7	5.7	5.7	5.7	5.0	5.7	5.7	5.7	5.7	5.7	4.4	5.1	5.7	5.8	4.5	3.7	4.7	5.8	5.8	5.8	5.4	5.8	5.1	3.7	3.8	5.8	5.8	5.8	5.8	5.8	5.8	5.8							59%	3.7	5.4%	5.6%	5.5%
3.8%	1997	1953	5.7	5.7	5.7	5.7	5.0	5.7	5.7	5.7	5.6	4.7	3.5	3.6	4.2	5.8	4.0	3.5	3.5	3.5	3.5	4.9	5.1	3.8	5.8	5.8	5.8	5.8	5.8	5.8	5.8	5.8											44%	3.5	5.3%	5.6%	5.4%
3.8%	1998	1954	5.1	5.3	4.5	4.9	3.7	5.2	5.4	5.1	5.6	4.7	3.5	3.6	4.2	5.8	4.0	3.5	3.5	3.5	3.9	3.9	5.7	5.8	4.3	5.6	5.3	4.2	3.5	3.5	3.5	5.8	5.8	5.8	5.8	5.8	5.8						58%	3.5	4.9%	5.0%	4.8%
3.8%	1999	1955	5.3	4.5	4.7	5.4	4.9	5.5	4.9	3.5	3.6	4.3	5.8	4.1	3.5	3.5	3.9	3.9	5.7	5.8	4.3	5.6	5.3	4.2	3.5	3.6	5.8	5.8	5.8	5.8	5.8	5.8											58%	3.5	4.9%	4.7%	4.8%
3.6%	2000	1956	4.7	4.9	3.8	5.2	5.4	5.1	5.4	4.7	3.5	3.6	4.0	5.5	3.8	3.3	3.5	3.6	5.3	4.8	5.5	4.0	4.8	4.6	4.0	3.5	3.5	5.3	5.3	5.5	5.5	5.5	5.5	5.5	5.5								76%	3.5	4.7%	4.6%	4.7%
		Totals																																									55%	3.5	6.0%	5.3%	6.2%

FIGURE 144

Benchmark backtesting results for 40-year systemic withdrawal plan with EM floor increased to 3.5%.

Going back to EM's *floor rate* definition in the Chapter 4 example, a retiree can select EM's income floor to suit their own preference: the default 2.25% floor is exceptionally safe; a 3% floor is very secure; a 3.5% floor is reasonable; a 4% floor covers (barely) Known Market Risk as proxied by the Baseline Market and Portfolio. Still, it's generally recommended to stay with EM's default of 2.25% (why is below).

It may sound contradictory, but there is no need for a retiree to endure income levels temporarily dropping below their essential needs. Just take out more if necessary and let EM automatically adjust for the extra withdrawal amount. (Note, temporarily shortfalls of a few years are distinct from regular long-term shortfalls.) Using a low floor still matters, however, because pulling out more than EM recommends becomes a very conscious decision, justifying frugality. Dealing with insufficient annual income was discussed in Chapter 4's recommendations, but the general idea is, risk doesn't usually substantially increase with occasionally pulling out extra funds to meet essential income needs. On the other hand, some retirees will prefer setting a higher income floor. Part of the difference is psychological, and part is the frequency of the "additional" withdrawals (i.e., higher floors usually pull out more and smooth income). Although keeping the 2.25% default floor rate is recommended (pulling out extra only when necessary), it is reasonable to increase the floor to a moderate rate (e.g., 3%, 3.5%).

What overall conclusions can be drawn from the 40-year benchmark? One reasonable conclusion is to plan for around 4.5% annual income (hoping for much more), while maintaining non-discretionary expenses at around 3% or below (if possible) to stay well-positioned for income cutbacks.

An even safer alternative is using the more conservative ECM for withdrawals. Figure 145 shows ECM's results with its lower gearing. While the total average income is unchanged compared to EM, the average over the first 10 years is annually 0.5% lower. This delayed income enables a portfolio to survive under a broader range of extremely poor market conditions. The use of ECM is revisited in the last chapter as an excellent pairing with guaranteed income. Although not shown, another variation is using ECM with a higher income floor. For example, ECM with a 3.5% floor still has 33% left at the end of its most difficult retirement period.

Initial	Year	End	Y1	Y2	Y3	Y4	Y5	Y6	Y7	Y8	Y9	Y10	Y11	Y12	Y13	Y14	Y15	Y16	Y17	Y18	Y19	Y20	Y21	Y22	Y23	Y24	Y25	Y26	Y27	Y28	Y29	Y30	Y31	Y32	Y33	Y34	Y35	Y36	Y37	Y38	Y39	Y40	%Left	Min	Avg	1st 10Y	MSWR
4.1%	1928	1967	5.0	4.0	3.6	3.3	3.6	4.2	4.2	5.0	5.7	4.3	5.0	5.0	4.6	3.8	3.8	4.7	5.5	6.1	5.3	4.9	4.8	5.1	5.7	5.9	5.9	5.7	6.1	6.1	6.1	6.1	6.1	6.1	6.1	6.1	6.1	6.1	6.1	6.1	6.1	6.1	113%	3.3	5.3%	4.3%	6.2%
4.1%	1929	1968	3.5	3.2	3.1	3.2	3.4	3.5	4.0	5.0	3.4	3.7	3.7	3.4	3.1	3.2	3.8	4.9	6.1	4.9	4.2	4.2	5.0	5.6	5.8	6.0	5.5	6.1	6.1	6.1	6.1	6.1	6.1	6.1	6.1	6.1	6.1	6.1	6.1	6.1	6.1	6.1	137%	3.1	4.9%	3.6%	5.2%
4.4%	1930	1969	3.5	3.3	3.4	3.8	3.8	4.8	5.8	4.1	4.7	4.6	4.2	3.6	3.7	4.7	5.6	6.6	5.8	5.1	4.9	5.6	6.2	6.1	6.4	6.2	6.6	6.6	6.6	6.6	6.6	6.6	6.6	6.6	6.6	6.6	6.6	6.6	6.6	6.6	6.6	6.6	104%	3.3	5.6%	4.2%	6.5%
4.7%	1931	1970	3.5	3.6	4.5	4.6	5.8	6.6	5.0	5.7	5.7	5.2	4.3	4.3	5.4	6.1	7.0	5.8	5.3	4.8	5.6	6.2	6.3	6.4	6.2	7.0	7.0	7.0	7.0	7.0	7.0	7.0	7.0	7.0	7.0	7.0	7.0	7.0	7.0	7.0	7.0	7.0	96%	3.5	6.1%	5.0%	7.7%
5.2%	1932	1971	4.5	6.9	6.8	7.8	7.8	7.4	7.8	7.8	7.8	6.7	6.7	7.5	7.8	7.8	7.7	7.1	7.0	7.3	7.6	7.7	7.8	7.6	7.8	7.8	7.8	7.8	7.8	7.8	7.8	7.8	7.8	7.8	7.8	7.8	7.8	7.8	7.8	7.8	7.8	7.8	111%	4.5	7.5%	7.1%	9.0%
5.2%	1933	1972	6.4	6.4	7.4	7.8	6.8	7.4	7.3	7.1	6.2	6.0	6.8	7.3	7.8	7.0	6.4	6.2	6.8	7.0	7.1	7.4	7.2	7.8	7.8	7.8	7.8	7.8	7.8	7.8	7.8	7.8	7.8	7.8	7.8	7.8	7.8	7.8	7.8	7.8	7.8	7.8	105%	6.0	7.4%	6.9%	9.0%
4.7%	1934	1973	4.1	5.2	6.2	4.5	5.1	5.1	4.6	3.9	4.0	4.8	5.7	6.7	5.4	4.7	4.5	5.2	5.9	5.9	6.0	5.9	7.0	7.0	7.0	7.0	7.0	7.0	7.0	7.0	7.0	7.0	7.0	7.0	7.0	7.0	7.0	7.0	7.0	7.0	7.0	7.0	77%	3.9	6.1%	4.8%	7.5%
4.7%	1935	1974	5.2	6.2	4.4	5.1	4.9	4.6	3.9	3.9	4.8	5.6	6.5	5.2	4.5	4.4	4.9	5.7	5.8	5.8	5.6	7.0	7.0	7.0	7.0	7.0	7.0	7.0	7.0	7.0	7.0	7.0	7.0	7.0	7.0	7.0	7.0	7.0	7.0	7.0	7.0	7.0	52%	3.9	6.1%	4.9%	7.3%
4.7%	1936	1975	5.1	3.7	4.0	4.0	3.8	3.5	3.5	3.8	4.5	5.9	4.4	3.9	3.8	4.3	5.0	5.1	5.6	5.0	6.7	7.0	7.0	6.6	7.0	7.0	7.0	7.0	7.0	7.0	7.0	7.0	7.0	7.0	7.0	7.0	7.0	7.0	7.0	7.0	7.0	7.0	55%	3.5	5.8%	4.2%	6.6%
4.1%	1937	1976	3.2	3.3	3.3	3.2	3.1	3.1	3.2	3.7	5.2	3.7	3.4	3.3	3.7	4.3	4.4	4.7	4.5	5.8	6.1	6.1	5.7	6.1	6.1	6.1	6.1	6.1	6.1	6.1	6.1	6.1	6.1	6.1	6.1	6.1	6.1	6.1	6.1	6.1	6.1	6.1	60%	3.1	5.1%	3.5%	5.7%
4.4%	1938	1977	4.9	4.7	4.2	3.6	3.7	4.6	5.4	6.5	5.3	4.5	4.3	4.9	5.4	5.4	5.5	5.4	6.6	6.6	6.6	6.2	6.6	6.6	6.6	6.6	6.6	6.6	6.6	6.6	6.6	6.6	6.6	6.6	6.6	6.6	6.6	6.6	6.6	6.6	6.6	6.6	61%	3.6	5.9%	4.7%	7.3%
4.4%	1939	1978	4.0	3.7	3.4	3.4	4.0	4.8	5.9	4.6	4.0	3.8	4.3	5.0	5.1	5.4	5.0	6.5	6.6	6.6	6.3	6.6	6.6	6.6	6.6	6.6	6.6	6.6	6.6	6.6	6.6	6.6	6.6	6.6	6.6	6.6	6.6	6.6	6.6	6.6	6.6	6.6	64%	3.4	5.8%	4.2%	6.8%
4.4%	1940	1979	3.8	3.4	3.4	4.1	4.9	6.0	4.6	4.1	3.9	4.3	5.1	5.2	5.3	5.1	6.4	6.6	6.6	6.3	6.6	6.6	6.6	6.6	6.6	6.6	6.6	6.6	6.6	6.6	6.6	6.6	6.6	6.6	6.6	6.6	6.6	6.6	6.6	6.6	6.6	6.6	58%	3.4	5.9%	4.3%	6.9%
4.4%	1941	1980	3.5	3.6	4.4	5.4	6.4	5.3	4.4	4.3	4.9	5.3	5.3	5.5	5.3	6.4	6.6	6.6	6.3	6.6	6.6	6.6	6.6	6.6	6.6	6.6	6.6	6.6	6.6	6.6	6.6	6.6	6.6	6.6	6.6	6.6	6.6	6.6	6.6	6.6	6.6	6.6	57%	3.5	6.0%	4.8%	6.9%
4.7%	1942	1981	4.2	5.3	5.9	7.0	5.7	4.9	4.6	5.3	5.7	5.6	5.7	5.5	6.6	7.0	6.8	6.4	7.0	7.0	7.0	7.0	7.0	7.0	7.0	7.0	7.0	7.0	7.0	7.0	7.0	7.0	7.0	7.0	7.0	7.0	7.0	7.0	7.0	7.0	7.0	6.7	43%	4.2	6.5%	5.4%	7.1%
4.9%	1943	1982	5.0	6.0	7.0	5.6	4.7	4.6	5.0	5.5	5.5	5.5	5.2	6.6	7.0	6.9	6.4	7.2	7.4	7.2	7.4	7.4	7.4	7.4	7.4	7.4	7.4	7.4	7.4	7.4	7.4	7.4	7.4	6.3	7.2	7.4	7.0	6.9	6.6	7.4	6.7	7.0	44%	4.6	6.7%	5.4%	7.2%
4.7%	1944	1983	4.7	5.9	4.4	4.0	3.8	4.1	4.6	4.6	4.8	4.5	6.0	6.4	6.3	5.8	6.6	6.8	6.9	7.0	6.8	7.0	7.0	7.0	7.0	7.0	7.0	7.0	7.0	7.0	7.0	6.9	6.0	6.2	7.0	6.8	6.3	6.6	6.5	6.8	7.0	7.0	51%	3.8	6.2%	4.5%	6.7%
4.7%	1945	1984	5.2	3.9	3.7	3.6	3.7	4.1	4.1	4.2	4.1	5.5	5.9	5.8	5.1	6.1	6.2	6.2	6.8	6.3	6.5	7.0	7.0	7.0	7.0	7.0	7.0	7.0	7.0	7.0	6.3	4.7	5.7	6.1	6.3	5.8	5.6	6.0	5.2	6.7	7.0	6.2	39%	3.6	5.8%	4.2%	6.1%
4.7%	1946	1985	3.6	3.5	3.4	3.5	3.6	3.6	3.7	3.6	4.5	5.0	4.8	4.2	5.3	5.6	5.5	6.1	5.8	5.9	6.3	6.9	6.6	7.0	7.0	6.8	6.6	6.9	6.9	5.5	4.1	4.5	5.7	5.1	5.5	5.4	5.3	5.0	5.6	7.0	6.2	6.6	42%	3.4	5.3%	3.8%	5.5%
4.7%	1947	1986	3.8	3.7	3.8	4.3	4.3	4.4	4.1	5.7	6.1	5.9	5.3	6.2	6.3	6.4	6.7	6.4	6.8	6.9	7.0	7.0	7.0	7.0	7.0	7.0	7.0	7.0	6.6	5.2	5.9	6.3	6.3	5.8	6.4	6.3	5.7	6.5	7.0	7.0	7.0	7.0	55%	3.7	6.1%	4.6%	6.4%
4.9%	1948	1987	4.0	4.3	4.7	4.8	4.9	4.7	6.0	6.3	6.2	5.3	6.4	6.5	6.5	7.0	6.7	6.9	7.3	7.4	7.1	7.4	7.4	7.3	7.4	7.4	7.4	6.5	5.3	5.6	6.4	5.9	5.8	5.5	6.2	5.3	6.0	7.0	6.3	7.4	7.4	6.6	42%	4.0	6.3%	5.1%	6.9%
4.9%	1949	1988	4.5	4.7	4.6	4.8	4.5	6.0	6.3	6.1	5.3	6.3	6.5	6.5	6.9	6.6	6.8	7.1	7.4	7.1	7.4	7.4	7.4	7.2	7.4	7.4	6.3	5.2	5.9	6.3	6.1	5.4	5.8	5.6	5.8	6.2	6.8	6.6	7.2	7.4	7.2	7.2	46%	4.5	6.3%	5.3%	6.6%
4.9%	1950	1989	4.4	4.4	4.5	4.3	5.6	6.1	5.8	5.1	6.1	6.1	6.1	6.5	6.2	6.4	6.7	7.1	6.8	7.3	7.4	6.8	7.0	7.0	7.1	6.1	4.5	5.1	6.1	5.5	5.2	5.1	5.6	4.8	6.4	6.9	6.3	7.4	7.3	7.4	7.4	7.3	47%	4.3	6.1%	5.2%	6.4%
4.7%	1951	1990	4.1	4.2	4.0	5.3	5.7	5.5	4.6	5.8	6.0	5.9	6.3	6.0	6.1	6.5	6.8	6.5	7.0	7.0	6.5	6.7	7.0	6.8	5.9	4.7	5.0	5.9	5.7	5.1	5.3	5.1	5.0	5.7	7.0	6.4	7.0	7.0	6.5	7.0	7.0	5.9	37%	4.0	5.9%	5.1%	6.2%
4.7%	1952	1991	4.2	4.0	5.3	5.9	5.6	4.9	5.9	6.0	6.0	6.3	5.9	6.2	6.4	6.8	6.4	7.0	7.0	6.6	6.6	7.0	7.0	5.9	4.7	5.4	5.9	5.8	5.6	5.4	5.7	5.0	6.2	6.6	6.9	7.0	7.0	7.0	7.0	7.0	6.8	7.0	52%	4.0	6.1%	5.4%	6.4%
4.5%	1953	1992	3.9	5.1	5.5	5.4	4.6	5.6	5.6	5.6	6.0	5.6	5.8	6.1	6.4	6.1	6.7	6.7	6.3	6.2	6.4	6.5	5.7	4.3	4.9	5.7	5.3	5.0	5.2	5.1	4.8	5.5	6.5	6.0	6.7	6.7	6.7	6.7	6.7	6.7	6.7	6.7	52%	3.9	5.8%	5.3%	6.1%
4.8%	1954	1993	5.4	5.9	5.5	4.9	5.9	6.0	5.9	6.3	6.0	6.1	6.4	6.7	6.3	7.0	7.3	6.4	6.6	6.7	6.7	5.8	4.6	4.9	5.9	5.6	5.0	5.2	5.5	4.8	6.0	6.4	6.4	7.0	7.3	7.0	7.1	7.3	6.2	7.3	7.3	7.3	59%	4.6	6.2%	5.8%	6.4%
4.5%	1955	1994	4.4	4.2	3.7	4.5	4.6	4.6	5.2	4.7	5.1	5.4	5.8	5.4	6.0	6.5	5.5	5.6	5.9	5.7	4.5	3.8	4.2	4.8	4.6	4.4	4.4	4.7	4.5	5.2	6.1	5.7	6.7	6.7	6.7	6.7	6.7	6.1	6.7	6.7	6.7	6.7	52%	3.7	5.4%	4.6%	5.5%
4.5%	1956	1995	3.9	3.6	4.2	4.4	4.2	4.9	4.3	4.7	5.2	5.6	5.1	5.9	6.2	5.4	5.4	5.6	5.7	4.2	3.6	3.9	4.7	4.3	4.2	4.4	4.4	4.3	5.4	5.8	5.6	6.2	6.7	6.1	6.7	6.7	5.7	6.7	6.7	6.7	6.7	6.7	59%	3.6	5.3%	4.5%	5.4%
4.5%	1957	1996	3.7	4.3	4.5	4.4	5.0	4.5	4.7	5.2	5.7	5.1	5.9	6.2	5.3	5.4	5.5	5.6	4.4	3.6	3.9	4.6	4.4	4.1	4.3	4.5	4.1	5.2	6.0	5.7	6.6	6.7	6.5	6.6	6.7	6.2	6.7	6.7	6.7	6.7	6.7	6.7	66%	3.6	5.4%	4.7%	5.5%
4.5%	1958	1997	5.3	5.5	5.4	5.8	5.4	5.6	5.8	6.2	5.8	6.3	6.7	5.8	5.8	6.0	6.0	5.0	4.1	4.3	5.1	4.9	4.8	4.6	4.8	4.6	5.4	6.2	6.1	6.7	6.7	6.6	6.7	6.7	6.7	6.7	6.7	6.7	6.7	6.7	6.7	6.7	89%	4.1	5.9%	5.7%	6.1%
4.3%	1959	1998	4.2	4.1	4.6	4.2	4.4	4.9	5.3	4.8	5.6	5.9	5.0	5.0	5.2	5.2	4.0	3.4	3.7	4.1	4.0	3.9	4.1	4.1	4.0	5.0	5.6	5.5	6.4	6.4	6.2	6.3	6.4	5.8	6.4	6.4	6.4	6.4	6.4	6.4	6.4	6.4	83%	3.4	5.2%	4.8%	5.3%
4.1%	1960	1999	4.0	4.5	4.0	4.3	4.6	5.2	4.6	5.5	5.9	4.9	4.9	5.1	5.1	3.9	3.2	3.5	4.2	3.9	3.8	4.0	4.4	4.0	5.0	5.6	5.4	6.1	6.1	6.0	6.1	6.1	6.0	6.1	6.1	6.1	6.1	6.1	6.1	6.1	6.1	6.1	93%	3.2	5.1%	4.8%	5.3%
4.1%	1961	2000	4.7	4.2	4.4	4.9	5.1	4.8	5.3	5.6	4.8	4.8	5.0	5.0	3.8	3.3	3.5	4.0	3.9	3.6	3.7	3.9	3.8	4.4	5.3	5.3	5.8	6.1	5.9	6.1	6.1	5.4	6.1	6.1	6.1	6.1	6.1	6.1	6.1	6.1	6.1	6.1	82%	3.3	5.1%	4.9%	5.2%
4.1%	1962	2001	3.7	3.9	4.2	4.9	4.2	5.3	5.6	4.7	4.6	4.8	4.8	3.6	3.1	3.3	3.8	3.7	3.6	3.7	3.9	3.8	4.9	5.3	5.3	6.1	6.1	6.0	6.1	6.1	5.8	6.1	6.1	6.1	6.1	6.1	6.1	6.1	6.1	6.1	6.1	6.1	92%	3.1	5.1%	4.6%	5.2%
4.1%	1963	2002	4.4	4.8	5.2	4.8	5.4	5.8	4.9	4.9	5.1	5.0	3.8	3.3	3.5	4.0	3.8	3.7	3.9	3.9	3.7	4.7	5.4	5.2	6.0	6.1	5.9	6.1	6.1	5.8	6.1	6.1	6.1	6.1	6.1	6.1	6.1	6.1	6.1	6.1	6.1	6.1	85%	3.3	5.2%	5.0%	5.5%
4.1%	1964	2003	4.4	5.0	4.4	5.3	5.6	4.7	4.6	4.9	4.9	3.6	3.2	3.3	3.7	3.6	3.5	3.7	3.9	3.6	4.4	5.3	5.3	5.8	6.1	6.0	6.1	6.1	5.9	6.1	6.1	6.1	6.1	6.1	6.1	6.1	6.1	6.1	6.1	6.1	6.1	6.1	99%	3.2	5.2%	4.7%	5.4%
4.0%	1965	2004	4.7	4.1	4.9	5.2	4.2	4.2	4.4	4.4	3.4	3.1	3.2	3.5	3.3	3.3	3.3	3.4	3.4	3.8	4.7	4.8	5.5	5.7	5.4	5.8	6.0	5.2	6.0	6.0	6.0	6.0	6.0	6.0	6.0	6.0	6.0	6.0	6.0	6.0	6.0	6.0	92%	3.1	4.9%	4.3%	4.9%
3.8%	1966	2005	3.7	4.6	4.9	3.9	3.8	4.1	4.0	3.2	2.9	3.0	3.2	3.1	3.1	3.1	3.2	3.1	3.7	4.4	4.3	5.1	5.6	5.1	5.4	5.7	4.9	5.7	5.7	5.7	5.7	5.7	5.7	5.7	5.7	5.7	5.7	5.7	5.7	5.7	5.7	5.7	90%	2.9	4.7%	3.8%	4.6%
4.1%	1967	2006	5.1	5.4	4.3	4.3	4.5	4.5	3.4	3.1	3.2	3.5	3.4	3.3	3.4	3.5	3.4	4.0	4.9	4.6	5.4	5.9	5.6	5.8	6.1	5.6	6.1	6.1	6.1	6.1	6.1	6.1	6.1	6.1	6.1	6.1	6.1	6.1	6.1	6.1	6.1	6.1	101%	3.1	5.1%	4.1%	5.2%
4.0%	1968	2007	4.6	3.6	3.5	3.7	3.6	3.1	2.9	3.0	3.1	3.1	3.0	3.1	3.1	3.1	3.3	3.8	3.8	4.6	5.0	4.6	5.1	5.3	4.5	5.5	5.7	6.0	5.8	6.0	6.0	6.0	6.0	6.0	6.0	6.0	6.0	6.0	6.0	6.0	6.0	6.0	76%	2.9	4.7%	3.4%	4.4%
4.0%	1969	2008	3.3	3.3	3.3	3.4	3.0	2.5	2.9	3.0	3.0	3.0	3.0	3.0	3.0	3.1	3.4	3.4	4.1	4.4	3.9	4.6	5.1	3.9	5.1	5.5	5.8	5.4	6.0	6.0	6.0	6.0	6.0	6.0	6.0	6.0	6.0	6.0	6.0	6.0	6.0	6.0	47%	2.5	4.5%	3.1%	4.0%
4.0%	1970	2009	4.0	4.2	4.1	3.2	3.0	3.1	3.3	3.2	3.2	3.3	3.4	3.3	3.9	4.6	4.5	5.3	5.7	5.3	5.5	6.0	5.5	6.0	6.0	6.0	6.0	6.0	6.0	6.0	6.0	6.0	6.0	6.0	6.0	6.0	6.0	6.0	6.0	6.0	6.0	6.0	86%	3.0	5.0%	3.5%	5.1%
4.3%	1971	2010	4.3	4.3	3.4	3.2	3.2	3.5	3.4	3.4	3.5	3.5	3.4	3.8	4.4	4.4	5.3	5.7	5.4	5.6	6.0	5.4	6.4	6.4	6.4	6.4	6.4	6.4	6.4	6.4	6.4	6.4	6.4	6.4	6.4	6.4	6.4	6.4	6.4	6.4	6.4	6.4	88%	3.2	5.3%	3.6%	5.4%
4.1%	1972	1928	4.1	3.3	3.1	3.1	3.3	3.2	3.2	3.3	3.4	3.3	3.7	4.3	4.2	5.2	5.5	5.2	5.5	5.7	5.2	6.0	6.1	6.1	6.1	6.1	6.1	6.1	6.1	6.1	6.1	6.1	6.1	6.1	6.1	6.1	6.1	6.1	6.1	6.1	6.1	6.2	110%	3.1	5.1%	3.3%	5.2%
4.1%	1973	1929	3.3	3.1	3.1	3.3	3.2	3.2	3.2	3.3	3.2	3.6	4.1	4.1	5.0	5.4	5.0	5.3	5.7	5.0	5.7	6.1	6.1	6.1	6.1	6.1	6.1	6.1	6.1	6.1	6.1	6.1	6.1	6.1	6.1	6.1	6.1	6.1	6.1	6.1	6.2	6.2	92%	3.1	5.2%	3.3%	5.2%
4.5%	1974	1930	3.4	3.7	4.2	4.1	3.9	4.0	4.0	3.8	4.6	5.2	5.2	5.9	6.3	6.0	6.2	6.6	6.1	6.7	6.7	6.7	6.7	6.7	6.7	6.7	6.7	6.7	6.7	6.7	6.7	6.7	6.7	6.7	6.7	6.7	6.7	6.7	6.7	6.8	6.8	6.8	107%	3.4	5.9%	4.1%	6.3%
5.0%	1975	1931	4.8	5.9	5.4	5.1	5.0	5.0	4.7	5.9	6.3	6.3	7.1	7.6	7.2	7.4	7.6	7.3	7.6	7.6	7.6	7.6	7.6	7.6	7.6	7.6	7.6	7.6	7.6	7.6	7.6	7.6	7.6	7.6	7.6	7.6	7.6	7.6	7.6	7.6	7.6	7.6	144%	4.7	7.0%	5.4%	7.6%
4.8%	1976	1932	4.8	4.5	4.3	4.4	4.3	4.2	4.9	5.7	5.7	6.4	6.8	6.5	6.6	7.0	6.4	7.3	7.3	7.3	7.3	7.3	7.3	7.3	7.3	7.3	7.3	7.3	7.3	7.3	7.3	7.3	7.3	7.3	7.3	7.3	7.3	7.4	7.4	7.4	7.4	7.4	139%	4.2	6.6%	4.9%	6.9%
4.8%	1977	1933	4.0	3.9	3.9	3.9	3.8	4.3	4.6	4.7	5.7	6.1	5.6	5.9	6.2	5.7	6.5	6.8	7.3	6.7	7.3	7.3	7.3	7.3	7.3	7.3	7.3	7.3	7.3	7.3	7.3	7.3	7.3	7.3	7.3	7.3	7.4	7.4	7.4	7.4	7.4	7.4	90%	3.8	6.4%	4.5%	6.2%
5.0%	1978	1934	4.0	4.1	4.1	4.0	4.4	4.9	4.9	5.9	6.4	5.9	6.2	6.5	5.9	6.8	7.0	7.5	7.1	7.6	7.6	7.6	7.6	7.6	7.6	7.6	7.6	7.6	7.6	7.6	7.6	7.6	7.6	7.6	7.6	7.6	7.6	7.6	7.6	7.6	7.6	7.6	100%	4.0	6.8%	4.9%	6.6%
5.2%	1979	1935	4.2	4.2	4.1	4.6	5.0	5.0	5.9	6.5	6.1	6.3	6.6	6.0	6.8	7.2	7.6	7.1	7.8	7.8	7.8	7.8	7.8	7.8	7.8	7.8	7.8	7.8	7.8	7.8	7.8	7.8	7.8	7.8	7.9	7.9	7.9	7.9	7.9	7.9	7.9	7.9	108%	4.1	7.0%	5.2%	6.9%
5.2%	1980	1936	4.2	4.1	4.5	4.9	4.9	5.9	6.4	5.9	6.3	6.5	5.7	6.7	7.0	7.5	6.9	7.8	7.8	7.8	7.8	7.8	7.8	7.8	7.8	7.8	7.8	7.8	7.8	7.8	7.8	7.8	7.8	7.9	7.9	7.9	7.9	7.9	7.9	7.9	7.9	7.9	122%	4.1	7.1%	5.4%	7.0%
5.0%	1981	1937	4.0	4.5	5.0	5.0	6.1	6.5	6.1	6.2	6.6	6.0	6.7	7.0	7.4	6.9	7.6	7.6	7.6	7.6	7.6	7.6	7.6	7.6	7.6	7.6	7.6	7.6	7.6	7.6	7.6	7.6	7.6	7.6	7.6	7.6	7.6	7.6	7.6	7.6	7.6	7.6	116%	4.0	7.0%	5.6%	7.3%
5.2%	1982	1938	4.8	5.1	5.2	6.3	6.6	6.3	6.4	6.7	6.2	6.9	7.1	7.5	7.0	7.8	7.8	7.8	7.8	7.8	7.8	7.8	7.8	7.8	7.8	7.8	7.8	7.8	7.8	7.8	7.8	7.9	7.9	7.9	7.9	7.9	7.9	7.9	7.9	7.9	7.9	7.9	123%	4.8	7.3%	6.1%	7.7%
5.2%	1983	1939	4.5	4.5	5.1	5.7	5.1	5.4	5.8	5.1	6.2	6.4	6.8	6.3	7.0	7.2	7.7	7.8	7.8	7.8	7.8	7.8	7.8	7.8	7.8	7.8	7.8	7.8	7.8	7.8	7.9	7.9	7.9	7.2	7.9	7.9	7.9	7.9	7.9	7.9	7.9	7.9	73%	4.5	7.1%	5.4%	7.0%
5.0%	1984	1940	4.1	4.6	5.0	4.6	4.8	5.3	4.5	5.5	6.0	6.3	5.6	6.6	6.6	7.2	7.4	7.4	7.5	7.6	7.3	7.6	7.6	7.6	7.6	7.6	7.0	7.4	7.6	7.6	7.6	7.1	6.6	7.1	7.6	7.6	7.6	7.6	7.6	7.6	7.6	7.6	56%	4.1	6.8%	5.1%	6.6%
5.0%	1985	1941	4.7	5.1	4.6	4.9	5.2	4.6	5.4	6.0	6.3	5.6	6.5	6.5	7.1	7.3	7.3	7.3	7.6	7.2	7.6	7.6	7.6	7.6	7.6	7.1	7.2	7.6	7.6	7.6	7.2	6.3	7.3	7.6	7.6	7.6	7.6	7.6	7.6	7.6	7.6	7.0	44%	4.6	6.8%	5.2%	6.8%
4.8%	1986	1942	4.4	4.1	4.2	4.5	4.0	4.7	5.0	5.6	4.9	5.8	5.9	6.4	6.6	6.7	6.6	6.8	6.6	7.1	7.2	7.2	7.3	7.1	6.2	6.6	6.9	7.4	7.1	6.2	5.3	5.9	7.0	6.8	7.4	7.4	6.9	7.4	7.3	7.4	5.9	5.7	35%	4.0	6.2%	4.7%	6.1%
4.8%	1987	1943	3.9	4.0	4.2	3.9	4.3	4.6	4.9	4.5	5.4	5.4	6.2	6.3	6.3	6.2	6.4	6.0	6.8	6.8	6.6	7.0	6.9	5.9	6.2	6.7	7.4	6.6	6.1	5.0	6.0	6.5	6.8	7.4	7.4	6.9	7.2	7.3	6.4	6.0	5.7	6.8	43%	3.9	6.0%	4.5%	5.8%
4.8%	1988	1944	4.3	4.6	4.0	4.7	5.0	5.6	4.8	5.9	6.0	6.4	6.6	6.6	6.5	6.8	6.5	7.1	7.3	7.0	7.2	7.1	6.3	6.4	7.0	7.4	6.9	6.4	5.9	6.4	7.2	7.0	7.4	7.4	7.4	7.4	7.4	7.4	6.1	7.0	7.4	7.4	63%	4.0	6.5%	5.1%	6.3%
4.8%	1989	1945	4.3	3.9	4.3	4.7	5.1	4.6	5.5	5.6	6.2	6.3	6.3	6.2	6.4	6.1	6.7	6.9	6.8	6.9	6.7	6.2	6.5	6.7	7.4	6.9	6.3	6.0	6.7	7.1	7.3	7.4	7.4	6.8	7.4	7.4	6.8	5.9	5.7	7.4	7.4	7.4	87%	3.9	6.3%	5.1%	6.2%
4.5%	1990	1946	3.6	4.1	4.4	4.9	4.3	5.3	5.3	5.8	5.9	5.9	5.7	5.9	5.5	6.2	6.3	6.2	6.6	6.2	5.4	5.8	6.3	6.8	6.3	5.9	5.0	5.9	6.6	6.5	6.8	6.8	6.8	6.8	6.8	6.8	5.7	5.9	6.7	6.8	6.8	6.8	63%	3.6	6.0%	5.0%	5.9%
4.7%	1991	1947	4.9	5.3	5.7	5.0	5.9	5.9	6.4	6.5	6.5	6.3	6.5	6.1	6.8	6.9	6.7	7.0	6.9	6.0	6.2	6.8	7.1	6.8	6.5	6.1	6.6	7.1	7.1	7.1	7.1	7.1	7.1	7.1	7.1	7.1	6.8	7.1	7.1	7.1	7.1	7.1	58%	4.9	6.6%	5.8%	6.7%
4.3%	1992	1948	4.4	4.8	4.2	5.2	5.2	5.7	5.8	5.9	5.7	5.9	5.5	6.1	6.2	6.1	6.3	6.2	5.5	5.6	6.0	6.5	6.3	5.8	5.5	6.2	6.5	6.5	6.5	6.5	6.5	6.5	6.5	6.5	6.5	6.4	6.5	6.5	6.5	6.5	6.5	6.5	53%	4.2	6.0%	5.3%	6.2%
4.1%	1993	1949	4.5	4.0	4.9	5.0	5.4	5.5	5.5	5.3	5.5	5.0	5.7	5.8	5.7	5.9	5.7	4.9	5.3	5.6	6.2	5.7	5.4	4.6	5.4	6.1	6.0	6.2	6.2	6.2	6.2	6.2	6.2	5.5	5.9	6.2	6.2	6.2	6.2	6.2	6.2	6.2	53%	4.0	5.7%	5.1%	5.8%
4.1%	1994	1950	3.7	4.4	4.4	5.1	5.2	5.3	5.1	5.3	4.9	5.4	5.6	5.4	5.6	5.5	4.8	5.1	5.5	6.0	5.2	4.6	3.9	4.4	5.5	5.5	6.2	6.2	5.8	6.2	6.2	5.7	5.0	5.0	6.2	6.2	6.2	6.2	6.2	6.2	6.2	6.2	64%	3.7	5.4%	4.9%	5.5%
4.0%	1995	1951	5.0	5.0	5.4	5.5	5.6	5.5	5.6	5.2	5.8	5.9	5.8	6.0	5.8	5.2	5.4	5.8	6.1	5.8	5.5	5.3	6.1	6.1	6.1	6.1	6.1	6.1	6.1	6.1	6.1	6.0	6.1	6.1	6.1	6.1	6.1	6.1	6.1	6.1	6.1	6.1	83%	5.0	5.8%	5.5%	6.2%
3.8%	1996	1952	4.3	4.9	4.9	5.0	4.8	5.0	4.6	5.1	5.3	5.1	5.3	5.2	4.5	4.8	5.1	5.7	5.2	4.8	4.3	5.1	5.7	5.6	5.8	5.8	5.6	5.8	5.8	5.7	5.0	5.0	5.8	5.8	5.8	5.8	5.8	5.8	5.8	5.8	5.8	5.8	75%	4.3	5.3%	4.9%	5.5%
3.8%	1997	1953	4.8	4.8	4.9	4.8	4.9	4.6	5.0	5.1	5.0	5.1	4.9	3.9	4.3	4.8	5.5	4.9	4.4	3.6	4.2	5.1	5.2	5.8	5.8	5.5	5.8	5.8	5.7	4.8	4.9	5.6	5.8	5.8	5.8	5.8	5.8	5.8	5.8	5.8	5.8	5.8	59%	3.6	5.2%	4.9%	5.4%
3.8%	1998	1954	4.3	4.4	4.0	4.3	3.5	4.6	4.7	4.6	4.7	4.4	3.3	3.6	4.1	5.0	4.1	3.5	3.1	3.4	4.2	4.4	5.3	5.8	4.8	5.3	5.1	4.9	4.0	4.0	5.2	5.8	5.8	5.8	5.8	5.4	5.8	5.8	5.8	5.8	5.8	5.8	79%	3.1	4.8%	4.4%	4.8%
3.8%	1999	1955	4.4	3.9	4.1	3.5	4.4	4.6	4.4	4.7	4.5	3.3	3.6	4.1	5.0	4.2	3.5	3.2	3.6	4.3	4.4	5.3	5.8	4.8	5.3	5.3	4.9	4.0	4.3	5.1	5.8	5.8	5.8	5.4	5.6	5.8	5.8	5.8	5.8	5.8	5.8	5.8	86%	3.2	4.8%	4.2%	4.8%
3.6%	2000	1956	4.0	4.2	3.5	4.4	4.5	4.4	4.5	4.3	3.1	3.4	4.0	4.8	3.9	3.3	2.9	3.1	4.0	4.0	4.8	5.5	4.6	4.9	4.9	4.7	3.6	3.9	5.1	5.5	5.5	5.5	5.5	5.2	5.5	5.5	5.5	5.5	5.5	5.5	5.5	5.5	93%	2.9	4.6%	4.0%	4.7%
																																										Totals	76%	2.5	5.9%	4.8%	6.2%

FIGURE 145

Benchmark backtesting results using ECM for recommended 40-year systemic withdrawal plan.

In contrast to the best practices, Figure 146 shows results using a traditional plan for a 40-year retirement under the Baseline Market. This means annual rebalancing, a total-market portfolio, a matching 55% stock percentage, and inflation-adjusted fixed withdrawals set to the portfolio's MSWR-100% value (any more triggers a failure). The numbers are starkly poor. Average income is 3.2% for this traditional plan compared to 6% following best practices as shown in Figure 142—an 87% increase in average income from best practices with a lower probability of running out of money.

Initial	Year	End	Y1	Y2	Y3	Y4	Y5	Y6	Y7	Y8	Y9	Y10	Y11	Y12	Y13	Y14	Y15	Y16	Y17	Y18	Y19	Y20	Y21	Y22	Y23	Y24	Y25	Y26	Y27	Y28	Y29	Y30	Y31	Y32	Y33	Y34	Y35	Y36	Y37	Y38	Y39	Y40	%Left	Min	Avg	1st 10Y	MSWR
3.2%	1928	1967	3.2	3.2	3.2	3.2	3.2	3.2	3.2	3.2	3.2	3.2	3.2	3.2	3.2	3.2	3.2	3.2	3.2	3.2	3.2	3.2	3.2	3.2	3.2	3.2	3.2	3.2	3.2	3.2	3.2	3.2	3.2	3.2	3.2	3.2	3.2	3.2	3.2	3.2	3.2	3.2	162%	3.2	3.2%	3.2%	4.5%
3.2%	1929	1968	3.2	3.2	3.2	3.2	3.2	3.2	3.2	3.2	3.2	3.2	3.2	3.2	3.2	3.2	3.2	3.2	3.2	3.2	3.2	3.2	3.2	3.2	3.2	3.2	3.2	3.2	3.2	3.2	3.2	3.2	3.2	3.2	3.2	3.2	3.2	3.2	3.2	3.2	3.2	3.2	78%	3.2	3.2%	3.2%	3.8%
3.2%	1930	1969	3.2	3.2	3.2	3.2	3.2	3.2	3.2	3.2	3.2	3.2	3.2	3.2	3.2	3.2	3.2	3.2	3.2	3.2	3.2	3.2	3.2	3.2	3.2	3.2	3.2	3.2	3.2	3.2	3.2	3.2	3.2	3.2	3.2	3.2	3.2	3.2	3.2	3.2	3.2	3.2	106%	3.2	3.2%	3.2%	4.2%
3.2%	1931	1970	3.2	3.2	3.2	3.2	3.2	3.2	3.2	3.2	3.2	3.2	3.2	3.2	3.2	3.2	3.2	3.2	3.2	3.2	3.2	3.2	3.2	3.2	3.2	3.2	3.2	3.2	3.2	3.2	3.2	3.2	3.2	3.2	3.2	3.2	3.2	3.2	3.2	3.2	3.2	3.2	155%	3.2	3.2%	3.2%	4.6%
3.2%	1932	1971	3.2	3.2	3.2	3.2	3.2	3.2	3.2	3.2	3.2	3.2	3.2	3.2	3.2	3.2	3.2	3.2	3.2	3.2	3.2	3.2	3.2	3.2	3.2	3.2	3.2	3.2	3.2	3.2	3.2	3.2	3.2	3.2	3.2	3.2	3.2	3.2	3.2	3.2	3.2	3.2	306%	3.2	3.2%	3.2%	5.9%
3.2%	1933	1972	3.2	3.2	3.2	3.2	3.2	3.2	3.2	3.2	3.2	3.2	3.2	3.2	3.2	3.2	3.2	3.2	3.2	3.2	3.2	3.2	3.2	3.2	3.2	3.2	3.2	3.2	3.2	3.2	3.2	3.2	3.2	3.2	3.2	3.2	3.2	3.2	3.2	3.2	3.2	3.2	288%	3.2	3.2%	3.2%	5.7%
3.2%	1934	1973	3.2	3.2	3.2	3.2	3.2	3.2	3.2	3.2	3.2	3.2	3.2	3.2	3.2	3.2	3.2	3.2	3.2	3.2	3.2	3.2	3.2	3.2	3.2	3.2	3.2	3.2	3.2	3.2	3.2	3.2	3.2	3.2	3.2	3.2	3.2	3.2	3.2	3.2	3.2	3.2	136%	3.2	3.2%	3.2%	4.7%
3.2%	1935	1974	3.2	3.2	3.2	3.2	3.2	3.2	3.2	3.2	3.2	3.2	3.2	3.2	3.2	3.2	3.2	3.2	3.2	3.2	3.2	3.2	3.2	3.2	3.2	3.2	3.2	3.2	3.2	3.2	3.2	3.2	3.2	3.2	3.2	3.2	3.2	3.2	3.2	3.2	3.2	3.2	103%	3.2	3.2%	3.2%	4.7%
3.2%	1936	1975	3.2	3.2	3.2	3.2	3.2	3.2	3.2	3.2	3.2	3.2	3.2	3.2	3.2	3.2	3.2	3.2	3.2	3.2	3.2	3.2	3.2	3.2	3.2	3.2	3.2	3.2	3.2	3.2	3.2	3.2	3.2	3.2	3.2	3.2	3.2	3.2	3.2	3.2	3.2	3.2	55%	3.2	3.2%	3.2%	3.9%
3.2%	1937	1976	3.2	3.2	3.2	3.2	3.2	3.2	3.2	3.2	3.2	3.2	3.2	3.2	3.2	3.2	3.2	3.2	3.2	3.2	3.2	3.2	3.2	3.2	3.2	3.2	3.2	3.2	3.2	3.2	3.2	3.2	3.2	3.2	3.2	3.2	3.2	3.2	3.2	3.2	3.2	3.2	23%	3.2	3.2%	3.2%	3.5%
3.2%	1938	1977	3.2	3.2	3.2	3.2	3.2	3.2	3.2	3.2	3.2	3.2	3.2	3.2	3.2	3.2	3.2	3.2	3.2	3.2	3.2	3.2	3.2	3.2	3.2	3.2	3.2	3.2	3.2	3.2	3.2	3.2	3.2	3.2	3.2	3.2	3.2	3.2	3.2	3.2	3.2	3.2	96%	3.2	3.2%	3.2%	4.4%
3.2%	1939	1978	3.2	3.2	3.2	3.2	3.2	3.2	3.2	3.2	3.2	3.2	3.2	3.2	3.2	3.2	3.2	3.2	3.2	3.2	3.2	3.2	3.2	3.2	3.2	3.2	3.2	3.2	3.2	3.2	3.2	3.2	3.2	3.2	3.2	3.2	3.2	3.2	3.2	3.2	3.2	3.2	47%	3.2	3.2%	3.2%	3.8%
3.2%	1940	1979	3.2	3.2	3.2	3.2	3.2	3.2	3.2	3.2	3.2	3.2	3.2	3.2	3.2	3.2	3.2	3.2	3.2	3.2	3.2	3.2	3.2	3.2	3.2	3.2	3.2	3.2	3.2	3.2	3.2	3.2	3.2	3.2	3.2	3.2	3.2	3.2	3.2	3.2	3.2	3.2	41%	3.2	3.2%	3.2%	3.8%
3.2%	1941	1980	3.2	3.2	3.2	3.2	3.2	3.2	3.2	3.2	3.2	3.2	3.2	3.2	3.2	3.2	3.2	3.2	3.2	3.2	3.2	3.2	3.2	3.2	3.2	3.2	3.2	3.2	3.2	3.2	3.2	3.2	3.2	3.2	3.2	3.2	3.2	3.2	3.2	3.2	3.2	3.2	62%	3.2	3.2%	3.2%	4.0%
3.2%	1942	1981	3.2	3.2	3.2	3.2	3.2	3.2	3.2	3.2	3.2	3.2	3.2	3.2	3.2	3.2	3.2	3.2	3.2	3.2	3.2	3.2	3.2	3.2	3.2	3.2	3.2	3.2	3.2	3.2	3.2	3.2	3.2	3.2	3.2	3.2	3.2	3.2	3.2	3.2	3.2	3.2	115%	3.2	3.2%	3.2%	4.9%
3.2%	1943	1982	3.2	3.2	3.2	3.2	3.2	3.2	3.2	3.2	3.2	3.2	3.2	3.2	3.2	3.2	3.2	3.2	3.2	3.2	3.2	3.2	3.2	3.2	3.2	3.2	3.2	3.2	3.2	3.2	3.2	3.2	3.2	3.2	3.2	3.2	3.2	3.2	3.2	3.2	3.2	3.2	142%	3.2	3.2%	3.2%	5.1%
3.2%	1944	1983	3.2	3.2	3.2	3.2	3.2	3.2	3.2	3.2	3.2	3.2	3.2	3.2	3.2	3.2	3.2	3.2	3.2	3.2	3.2	3.2	3.2	3.2	3.2	3.2	3.2	3.2	3.2	3.2	3.2	3.2	3.2	3.2	3.2	3.2	3.2	3.2	3.2	3.2	3.2	3.2	120%	3.2	3.2%	3.2%	4.7%
3.2%	1945	1984	3.2	3.2	3.2	3.2	3.2	3.2	3.2	3.2	3.2	3.2	3.2	3.2	3.2	3.2	3.2	3.2	3.2	3.2	3.2	3.2	3.2	3.2	3.2	3.2	3.2	3.2	3.2	3.2	3.2	3.2	3.2	3.2	3.2	3.2	3.2	3.2	3.2	3.2	3.2	3.2	101%	3.2	3.2%	3.2%	4.5%
3.2%	1946	1985	3.2	3.2	3.2	3.2	3.2	3.2	3.2	3.2	3.2	3.2	3.2	3.2	3.2	3.2	3.2	3.2	3.2	3.2	3.2	3.2	3.2	3.2	3.2	3.2	3.2	3.2	3.2	3.2	3.2	3.2	3.2	3.2	3.2	3.2	3.2	3.2	3.2	3.2	3.2	3.2	67%	3.2	3.2%	3.2%	3.9%
3.2%	1947	1986	3.2	3.2	3.2	3.2	3.2	3.2	3.2	3.2	3.2	3.2	3.2	3.2	3.2	3.2	3.2	3.2	3.2	3.2	3.2	3.2	3.2	3.2	3.2	3.2	3.2	3.2	3.2	3.2	3.2	3.2	3.2	3.2	3.2	3.2	3.2	3.2	3.2	3.2	3.2	3.2	180%	3.2	3.2%	3.2%	5.0%
3.2%	1948	1987	3.2	3.2	3.2	3.2	3.2	3.2	3.2	3.2	3.2	3.2	3.2	3.2	3.2	3.2	3.2	3.2	3.2	3.2	3.2	3.2	3.2	3.2	3.2	3.2	3.2	3.2	3.2	3.2	3.2	3.2	3.2	3.2	3.2	3.2	3.2	3.2	3.2	3.2	3.2	3.2	230%	3.2	3.2%	3.2%	5.6%
3.2%	1949	1988	3.2	3.2	3.2	3.2	3.2	3.2	3.2	3.2	3.2	3.2	3.2	3.2	3.2	3.2	3.2	3.2	3.2	3.2	3.2	3.2	3.2	3.2	3.2	3.2	3.2	3.2	3.2	3.2	3.2	3.2	3.2	3.2	3.2	3.2	3.2	3.2	3.2	3.2	3.2	3.2	258%	3.2	3.2%	3.2%	5.8%
3.2%	1950	1989	3.2	3.2	3.2	3.2	3.2	3.2	3.2	3.2	3.2	3.2	3.2	3.2	3.2	3.2	3.2	3.2	3.2	3.2	3.2	3.2	3.2	3.2	3.2	3.2	3.2	3.2	3.2	3.2	3.2	3.2	3.2	3.2	3.2	3.2	3.2	3.2	3.2	3.2	3.2	3.2	233%	3.2	3.2%	3.2%	5.4%
3.2%	1951	1990	3.2	3.2	3.2	3.2	3.2	3.2	3.2	3.2	3.2	3.2	3.2	3.2	3.2	3.2	3.2	3.2	3.2	3.2	3.2	3.2	3.2	3.2	3.2	3.2	3.2	3.2	3.2	3.2	3.2	3.2	3.2	3.2	3.2	3.2	3.2	3.2	3.2	3.2	3.2	3.2	203%	3.2	3.2%	3.2%	5.3%
3.2%	1952	1991	3.2	3.2	3.2	3.2	3.2	3.2	3.2	3.2	3.2	3.2	3.2	3.2	3.2	3.2	3.2	3.2	3.2	3.2	3.2	3.2	3.2	3.2	3.2	3.2	3.2	3.2	3.2	3.2	3.2	3.2	3.2	3.2	3.2	3.2	3.2	3.2	3.2	3.2	3.2	3.2	227%	3.2	3.2%	3.2%	5.2%
3.2%	1953	1992	3.2	3.2	3.2	3.2	3.2	3.2	3.2	3.2	3.2	3.2	3.2	3.2	3.2	3.2	3.2	3.2	3.2	3.2	3.2	3.2	3.2	3.2	3.2	3.2	3.2	3.2	3.2	3.2	3.2	3.2	3.2	3.2	3.2	3.2	3.2	3.2	3.2	3.2	3.2	3.2	213%	3.2	3.2%	3.2%	5.1%
3.2%	1954	1993	3.2	3.2	3.2	3.2	3.2	3.2	3.2	3.2	3.2	3.2	3.2	3.2	3.2	3.2	3.2	3.2	3.2	3.2	3.2	3.2	3.2	3.2	3.2	3.2	3.2	3.2	3.2	3.2	3.2	3.2	3.2	3.2	3.2	3.2	3.2	3.2	3.2	3.2	3.2	3.2	243%	3.2	3.2%	3.2%	5.3%
3.2%	1955	1994	3.2	3.2	3.2	3.2	3.2	3.2	3.2	3.2	3.2	3.2	3.2	3.2	3.2	3.2	3.2	3.2	3.2	3.2	3.2	3.2	3.2	3.2	3.2	3.2	3.2	3.2	3.2	3.2	3.2	3.2	3.2	3.2	3.2	3.2	3.2	3.2	3.2	3.2	3.2	3.2	118%	3.2	3.2%	3.2%	4.3%
3.2%	1956	1995	3.2	3.2	3.2	3.2	3.2	3.2	3.2	3.2	3.2	3.2	3.2	3.2	3.2	3.2	3.2	3.2	3.2	3.2	3.2	3.2	3.2	3.2	3.2	3.2	3.2	3.2	3.2	3.2	3.2	3.2	3.2	3.2	3.2	3.2	3.2	3.2	3.2	3.2	3.2	3.2	98%	3.2	3.2%	3.2%	4.0%
3.2%	1957	1996	3.2	3.2	3.2	3.2	3.2	3.2	3.2	3.2	3.2	3.2	3.2	3.2	3.2	3.2	3.2	3.2	3.2	3.2	3.2	3.2	3.2	3.2	3.2	3.2	3.2	3.2	3.2	3.2	3.2	3.2	3.2	3.2	3.2	3.2	3.2	3.2	3.2	3.2	3.2	3.2	116%	3.2	3.2%	3.2%	4.1%
3.2%	1958	1997	3.2	3.2	3.2	3.2	3.2	3.2	3.2	3.2	3.2	3.2	3.2	3.2	3.2	3.2	3.2	3.2	3.2	3.2	3.2	3.2	3.2	3.2	3.2	3.2	3.2	3.2	3.2	3.2	3.2	3.2	3.2	3.2	3.2	3.2	3.2	3.2	3.2	3.2	3.2	3.2	195%	3.2	3.2%	3.2%	4.5%
3.2%	1959	1998	3.2	3.2	3.2	3.2	3.2	3.2	3.2	3.2	3.2	3.2	3.2	3.2	3.2	3.2	3.2	3.2	3.2	3.2	3.2	3.2	3.2	3.2	3.2	3.2	3.2	3.2	3.2	3.2	3.2	3.2	3.2	3.2	3.2	3.2	3.2	3.2	3.2	3.2	3.2	3.2	112%	3.2	3.2%	3.2%	3.9%
3.2%	1960	1999	3.2	3.2	3.2	3.2	3.2	3.2	3.2	3.2	3.2	3.2	3.2	3.2	3.2	3.2	3.2	3.2	3.2	3.2	3.2	3.2	3.2	3.2	3.2	3.2	3.2	3.2	3.2	3.2	3.2	3.2	3.2	3.2	3.2	3.2	3.2	3.2	3.2	3.2	3.2	3.2	107%	3.2	3.2%	3.2%	3.8%
3.2%	1961	2000	3.2	3.2	3.2	3.2	3.2	3.2	3.2	3.2	3.2	3.2	3.2	3.2	3.2	3.2	3.2	3.2	3.2	3.2	3.2	3.2	3.2	3.2	3.2	3.2	3.2	3.2	3.2	3.2	3.2	3.2	3.2	3.2	3.2	3.2	3.2	3.2	3.2	3.2	3.2	3.2	96%	3.2	3.2%	3.2%	3.8%
3.2%	1962	2001	3.2	3.2	3.2	3.2	3.2	3.2	3.2	3.2	3.2	3.2	3.2	3.2	3.2	3.2	3.2	3.2	3.2	3.2	3.2	3.2	3.2	3.2	3.2	3.2	3.2	3.2	3.2	3.2	3.2	3.2	3.2	3.2	3.2	3.2	3.2	3.2	3.2	3.2	3.2	3.2	36%	3.2	3.2%	3.2%	3.4%
3.2%	1963	2002	3.2	3.2	3.2	3.2	3.2	3.2	3.2	3.2	3.2	3.2	3.2	3.2	3.2	3.2	3.2	3.2	3.2	3.2	3.2	3.2	3.2	3.2	3.2	3.2	3.2	3.2	3.2	3.2	3.2	3.2	3.2	3.2	3.2	3.2	3.2	3.2	3.2	3.2	3.2	3.2	68%	3.2	3.2%	3.2%	3.7%
3.2%	1964	2003	3.2	3.2	3.2	3.2	3.2	3.2	3.2	3.2	3.2	3.2	3.2	3.2	3.2	3.2	3.2	3.2	3.2	3.2	3.2	3.2	3.2	3.2	3.2	3.2	3.2	3.2	3.2	3.2	3.2	3.2	3.2	3.2	3.2	3.2	3.2	3.2	3.2	3.2	3.2	3.2	44%	3.2	3.2%	3.2%	3.5%
3.2%	1965	2004	3.2	3.2	3.2	3.2	3.2	3.2	3.2	3.2	3.2	3.2	3.2	3.2	3.2	3.2	3.2	3.2	3.2	3.2	3.2	3.2	3.2	3.2	3.2	3.2	3.2	3.2	3.2	3.2	3.2	3.2	3.2	3.2	3.2	3.2	3.2	3.2	3.2	3.2	3.2	3.2	15%	3.2	3.2%	3.2%	3.3%
3.2%	1966	2005	3.2	3.2	3.2	3.2	3.2	3.2	3.2	3.2	3.2	3.2	3.2	3.2	3.2	3.2	3.2	3.2	3.2	3.2	3.2	3.2	3.2	3.2	3.2	3.2	3.2	3.2	3.2	3.2	3.2	3.2	3.2	3.2	3.2	3.2	3.2	3.2	3.2	3.2	3.2	3.2	1%	3.2	3.2%	3.2%	3.2%
3.2%	1967	2006	3.2	3.2	3.2	3.2	3.2	3.2	3.2	3.2	3.2	3.2	3.2	3.2	3.2	3.2	3.2	3.2	3.2	3.2	3.2	3.2	3.2	3.2	3.2	3.2	3.2	3.2	3.2	3.2	3.2	3.2	3.2	3.2	3.2	3.2	3.2	3.2	3.2	3.2	3.2	3.2	48%	3.2	3.2%	3.2%	3.5%
3.2%	1968	2007	3.2	3.2	3.2	3.2	3.2	3.2	3.2	3.2	3.2	3.2	3.2	3.2	3.2	3.2	3.2	3.2	3.2	3.2	3.2	3.2	3.2	3.2	3.2	3.2	3.2	3.2	3.2	3.2	3.2	3.2	3.2	3.2	3.2	3.2	3.2	3.2	3.2	3.2	3.2	3.2	9%	3.2	3.2%	3.2%	3.3%
3.2%	1969	2008	3.2	3.2	3.2	3.2	3.2	3.2	3.2	3.2	3.2	3.2	3.2	3.2	3.2	3.2	3.2	3.2	3.2	3.2	3.2	3.2	3.2	3.2	3.2	3.2	3.2	3.2	3.2	3.2	3.2	3.2	3.2	3.2	3.2	3.2	3.2	3.2	3.2	3.2	3.2	3.2	0%	3.2	3.2%	3.2%	3.2%
3.2%	1970	2009	3.2	3.2	3.2	3.2	3.2	3.2	3.2	3.2	3.2	3.2	3.2	3.2	3.2	3.2	3.2	3.2	3.2	3.2	3.2	3.2	3.2	3.2	3.2	3.2	3.2	3.2	3.2	3.2	3.2	3.2	3.2	3.2	3.2	3.2	3.2	3.2	3.2	3.2	3.2	3.2	72%	3.2	3.2%	3.2%	3.7%
3.2%	1971	2010	3.2	3.2	3.2	3.2	3.2	3.2	3.2	3.2	3.2	3.2	3.2	3.2	3.2	3.2	3.2	3.2	3.2	3.2	3.2	3.2	3.2	3.2	3.2	3.2	3.2	3.2	3.2	3.2	3.2	3.2	3.2	3.2	3.2	3.2	3.2	3.2	3.2	3.2	3.2	3.2	85%	3.2	3.2%	3.2%	3.8%
3.2%	1972	1928	3.2	3.2	3.2	3.2	3.2	3.2	3.2	3.2	3.2	3.2	3.2	3.2	3.2	3.2	3.2	3.2	3.2	3.2	3.2	3.2	3.2	3.2	3.2	3.2	3.2	3.2	3.2	3.2	3.2	3.2	3.2	3.2	3.2	3.2	3.2	3.2	3.2	3.2	3.2	3.2	71%	3.2	3.2%	3.2%	3.6%
3.2%	1973	1929	3.2	3.2	3.2	3.2	3.2	3.2	3.2	3.2	3.2	3.2	3.2	3.2	3.2	3.2	3.2	3.2	3.2	3.2	3.2	3.2	3.2	3.2	3.2	3.2	3.2	3.2	3.2	3.2	3.2	3.2	3.2	3.2	3.2	3.2	3.2	3.2	3.2	3.2	3.2	3.2	46%	3.2	3.2%	3.2%	3.5%
3.2%	1974	1930	3.2	3.2	3.2	3.2	3.2	3.2	3.2	3.2	3.2	3.2	3.2	3.2	3.2	3.2	3.2	3.2	3.2	3.2	3.2	3.2	3.2	3.2	3.2	3.2	3.2	3.2	3.2	3.2	3.2	3.2	3.2	3.2	3.2	3.2	3.2	3.2	3.2	3.2	3.2	3.2	154%	3.2	3.2%	3.2%	4.3%
3.2%	1975	1931	3.2	3.2	3.2	3.2	3.2	3.2	3.2	3.2	3.2	3.2	3.2	3.2	3.2	3.2	3.2	3.2	3.2	3.2	3.2	3.2	3.2	3.2	3.2	3.2	3.2	3.2	3.2	3.2	3.2	3.2	3.2	3.2	3.2	3.2	3.2	3.2	3.2	3.2	3.2	3.2	279%	3.2	3.2%	3.2%	5.8%
3.2%	1976	1932	3.2	3.2	3.2	3.2	3.2	3.2	3.2	3.2	3.2	3.2	3.2	3.2	3.2	3.2	3.2	3.2	3.2	3.2	3.2	3.2	3.2	3.2	3.2	3.2	3.2	3.2	3.2	3.2	3.2	3.2	3.2	3.2	3.2	3.2	3.2	3.2	3.2	3.2	3.2	3.2	232%	3.2	3.2%	3.2%	5.3%
3.2%	1977	1933	3.2	3.2	3.2	3.2	3.2	3.2	3.2	3.2	3.2	3.2	3.2	3.2	3.2	3.2	3.2	3.2	3.2	3.2	3.2	3.2	3.2	3.2	3.2	3.2	3.2	3.2	3.2	3.2	3.2	3.2	3.2	3.2	3.2	3.2	3.2	3.2	3.2	3.2	3.2	3.2	230%	3.2	3.2%	3.2%	4.9%
3.2%	1978	1934	3.2	3.2	3.2	3.2	3.2	3.2	3.2	3.2	3.2	3.2	3.2	3.2	3.2	3.2	3.2	3.2	3.2	3.2	3.2	3.2	3.2	3.2	3.2	3.2	3.2	3.2	3.2	3.2	3.2	3.2	3.2	3.2	3.2	3.2	3.2	3.2	3.2	3.2	3.2	3.2	316%	3.2	3.2%	3.2%	5.6%
3.2%	1979	1935	3.2	3.2	3.2	3.2	3.2	3.2	3.2	3.2	3.2	3.2	3.2	3.2	3.2	3.2	3.2	3.2	3.2	3.2	3.2	3.2	3.2	3.2	3.2	3.2	3.2	3.2	3.2	3.2	3.2	3.2	3.2	3.2	3.2	3.2	3.2	3.2	3.2	3.2	3.2	3.2	455%	3.2	3.2%	3.2%	6.2%
3.2%	1980	1936	3.2	3.2	3.2	3.2	3.2	3.2	3.2	3.2	3.2	3.2	3.2	3.2	3.2	3.2	3.2	3.2	3.2	3.2	3.2	3.2	3.2	3.2	3.2	3.2	3.2	3.2	3.2	3.2	3.2	3.2	3.2	3.2	3.2	3.2	3.2	3.2	3.2	3.2	3.2	3.2	567%	3.2	3.2%	3.2%	6.7%
3.2%	1981	1937	3.2	3.2	3.2	3.2	3.2	3.2	3.2	3.2	3.2	3.2	3.2	3.2	3.2	3.2	3.2	3.2	3.2	3.2	3.2	3.2	3.2	3.2	3.2	3.2	3.2	3.2	3.2	3.2	3.2	3.2	3.2	3.2	3.2	3.2	3.2	3.2	3.2	3.2	3.2	3.2	431%	3.2	3.2%	3.2%	6.7%
3.2%	1982	1938	3.2	3.2	3.2	3.2	3.2	3.2	3.2	3.2	3.2	3.2	3.2	3.2	3.2	3.2	3.2	3.2	3.2	3.2	3.2	3.2	3.2	3.2	3.2	3.2	3.2	3.2	3.2	3.2	3.2	3.2	3.2	3.2	3.2	3.2	3.2	3.2	3.2	3.2	3.2	3.2	606%	3.2	3.2%	3.2%	7.7%
3.2%	1983	1939	3.2	3.2	3.2	3.2	3.2	3.2	3.2	3.2	3.2	3.2	3.2	3.2	3.2	3.2	3.2	3.2	3.2	3.2	3.2	3.2	3.2	3.2	3.2	3.2	3.2	3.2	3.2	3.2	3.2	3.2	3.2	3.2	3.2	3.2	3.2	3.2	3.2	3.2	3.2	3.2	492%	3.2	3.2%	3.2%	7.0%
3.2%	1984	1940	3.2	3.2	3.2	3.2	3.2	3.2	3.2	3.2	3.2	3.2	3.2	3.2	3.2	3.2	3.2	3.2	3.2	3.2	3.2	3.2	3.2	3.2	3.2	3.2	3.2	3.2	3.2	3.2	3.2	3.2	3.2	3.2	3.2	3.2	3.2	3.2	3.2	3.2	3.2	3.2	418%	3.2	3.2%	3.2%	6.8%
3.2%	1985	1941	3.2	3.2	3.2	3.2	3.2	3.2	3.2	3.2	3.2	3.2	3.2	3.2	3.2	3.2	3.2	3.2	3.2	3.2	3.2	3.2	3.2	3.2	3.2	3.2	3.2	3.2	3.2	3.2	3.2	3.2	3.2	3.2	3.2	3.2	3.2	3.2	3.2	3.2	3.2	3.2	344%	3.2	3.2%	3.2%	6.9%
3.2%	1986	1942	3.2	3.2	3.2	3.2	3.2	3.2	3.2	3.2	3.2	3.2	3.2	3.2	3.2	3.2	3.2	3.2	3.2	3.2	3.2	3.2	3.2	3.2	3.2	3.2	3.2	3.2	3.2	3.2	3.2	3.2	3.2	3.2	3.2	3.2	3.2	3.2	3.2	3.2	3.2	3.2	255%	3.2	3.2%	3.2%	6.1%
3.2%	1987	1943	3.2	3.2	3.2	3.2	3.2	3.2	3.2	3.2	3.2	3.2	3.2	3.2	3.2	3.2	3.2	3.2	3.2	3.2	3.2	3.2	3.2	3.2	3.2	3.2	3.2	3.2	3.2	3.2	3.2	3.2	3.2	3.2	3.2	3.2	3.2	3.2	3.2	3.2	3.2	3.2	233%	3.2	3.2%	3.2%	5.7%
3.2%	1988	1944	3.2	3.2	3.2	3.2	3.2	3.2	3.2	3.2	3.2	3.2	3.2	3.2	3.2	3.2	3.2	3.2	3.2	3.2	3.2	3.2	3.2	3.2	3.2	3.2	3.2	3.2	3.2	3.2	3.2	3.2	3.2	3.2	3.2	3.2	3.2	3.2	3.2	3.2	3.2	3.2	282%	3.2	3.2%	3.2%	6.1%
3.2%	1989	1945	3.2	3.2	3.2	3.2	3.2	3.2	3.2	3.2	3.2	3.2	3.2	3.2	3.2	3.2	3.2	3.2	3.2	3.2	3.2	3.2	3.2	3.2	3.2	3.2	3.2	3.2	3.2	3.2	3.2	3.2	3.2	3.2	3.2	3.2	3.2	3.2	3.2	3.2	3.2	3.2	307%	3.2	3.2%	3.2%	6.0%
3.2%	1990	1946	3.2	3.2	3.2	3.2	3.2	3.2	3.2	3.2	3.2	3.2	3.2	3.2	3.2	3.2	3.2	3.2	3.2	3.2	3.2	3.2	3.2	3.2	3.2	3.2	3.2	3.2	3.2	3.2	3.2	3.2	3.2	3.2	3.2	3.2	3.2	3.2	3.2	3.2	3.2	3.2	198%	3.2	3.2%	3.2%	5.5%
3.2%	1991	1947	3.2	3.2	3.2	3.2	3.2	3.2	3.2	3.2	3.2	3.2	3.2	3.2	3.2	3.2	3.2	3.2	3.2	3.2	3.2	3.2	3.2	3.2	3.2	3.2	3.2	3.2	3.2	3.2	3.2	3.2	3.2	3.2	3.2	3.2	3.2	3.2	3.2	3.2	3.2	3.2	217%	3.2	3.2%	3.2%	6.1%
3.2%	1992	1948	3.2	3.2	3.2	3.2	3.2	3.2	3.2	3.2	3.2	3.2	3.2	3.2	3.2	3.2	3.2	3.2	3.2	3.2	3.2	3.2	3.2	3.2	3.2	3.2	3.2	3.2	3.2	3.2	3.2	3.2	3.2	3.2	3.2	3.2	3.2	3.2	3.2	3.2	3.2	3.2	148%	3.2	3.2%	3.2%	5.2%
3.2%	1993	1949	3.2	3.2	3.2	3.2	3.2	3.2	3.2	3.2	3.2	3.2	3.2	3.2	3.2	3.2	3.2	3.2	3.2	3.2	3.2	3.2	3.2	3.2	3.2	3.2	3.2	3.2	3.2	3.2	3.2	3.2	3.2	3.2	3.2	3.2	3.2	3.2	3.2	3.2	3.2	3.2	160%	3.2	3.2%	3.2%	5.2%
3.2%	1994	1950	3.2	3.2	3.2	3.2	3.2	3.2	3.2	3.2	3.2	3.2	3.2	3.2	3.2	3.2	3.2	3.2	3.2	3.2	3.2	3.2	3.2	3.2	3.2	3.2	3.2	3.2	3.2	3.2	3.2	3.2	3.2	3.2	3.2	3.2	3.2	3.2	3.2	3.2	3.2	3.2	151%	3.2	3.2%	3.2%	5.1%
3.2%	1995	1951	3.2	3.2	3.2	3.2	3.2	3.2	3.2	3.2	3.2	3.2	3.2	3.2	3.2	3.2	3.2	3.2	3.2	3.2	3.2	3.2	3.2	3.2	3.2	3.2	3.2	3.2	3.2	3.2	3.2	3.2	3.2	3.2	3.2	3.2	3.2	3.2	3.2	3.2	3.2	3.2	195%	3.2	3.2%	3.2%	5.6%
3.2%	1996	1952	3.2	3.2	3.2	3.2	3.2	3.2	3.2	3.2	3.2	3.2	3.2	3.2	3.2	3.2	3.2	3.2	3.2	3.2	3.2	3.2	3.2	3.2	3.2	3.2	3.2	3.2	3.2	3.2	3.2	3.2	3.2	3.2	3.2	3.2	3.2	3.2	3.2	3.2	3.2	3.2	130%	3.2	3.2%	3.2%	4.7%
3.2%	1997	1953	3.2	3.2	3.2	3.2	3.2	3.2	3.2	3.2	3.2	3.2	3.2	3.2	3.2	3.2	3.2	3.2	3.2	3.2	3.2	3.2	3.2	3.2	3.2	3.2	3.2	3.2	3.2	3.2	3.2	3.2	3.2	3.2	3.2	3.2	3.2	3.2	3.2	3.2	3.2	3.2	109%	3.2	3.2%	3.2%	4.5%
3.2%	1998	1954	3.2	3.2	3.2	3.2	3.2	3.2	3.2	3.2	3.2	3.2	3.2	3.2	3.2	3.2	3.2	3.2	3.2	3.2	3.2	3.2	3.2	3.2	3.2	3.2	3.2	3.2	3.2	3.2	3.2	3.2	3.2	3.2	3.2	3.2	3.2	3.2	3.2	3.2	3.2	3.2	79%	3.2	3.2%	3.2%	4.0%
3.2%	1999	1955	3.2	3.2	3.2	3.2	3.2	3.2	3.2	3.2	3.2	3.2	3.2	3.2	3.2	3.2	3.2	3.2	3.2	3.2	3.2	3.2	3.2	3.2	3.2	3.2	3.2	3.2	3.2	3.2	3.2	3.2	3.2	3.2	3.2	3.2	3.2	3.2	3.2	3.2	3.2	3.2	41%	3.2	3.2%	3.2%	3.6%
3.2%	2000	1956	3.2	3.2	3.2	3.2	3.2	3.2	3.2	3.2	3.2	3.2	3.2	3.2	3.2	3.2	3.2	3.2	3.2	3.2	3.2	3.2	3.2	3.2	3.2	3.2	3.2	3.2	3.2	3.2	3.2	3.2	3.2	3.2	3.2	3.2	3.2	3.2	3.2	3.2	3.2	3.2	18%	3.2	3.2%	3.2%	3.4%
																																									Totals	169%	3.2	3.2%	3.2%	4.8%

FIGURE 146

Backtesting for 40-year systemic withdrawal plan using the Baseline Market, annual rebalancing, a total-market portfolio, and inflation-adjusted fixed withdrawal rates starting at MSWR-100% (i.e., 3.2%).

A Typical 30-Year Retirement Plan

Most retirement studies focus on the 30-year retirement plan. While this plan is shorter than many retirees should use, it provides familiar ground for looking at the numbers.

Figure 147 shows backtesting results for a 30-year retirement. As before, income is often above 5%, but occasionally drops below 4%, and in one case, below 3%. The average overall income is a little higher, 6.3% compared to 6% for the 40-year retirement. The average for the first 10 years increases more, 5.8% compared to 5.3% for the 40-year retirement.

Initial	Year	Y1	Y2	Y3	Y4	Y5	Y6	Y7	Y8	Y9	Y10	Y11	Y12	Y13	Y14	Y15	Y16	Y17	Y18	Y19	Y20	Y21	Y22	Y23	Y24	Y25	Y26	Y27	Y28	Y29	Y30	%Left	Min	Avg	1st 10Y	MSWR
4.3%	1928	6.5	5.1	4.4	3.9	4.6	5.7	6.0	6.4	6.5	6.3	6.5	6.4	6.3	4.6	4.4	6.3	6.4	6.4	6.4	5.7	5.5	6.2	6.5	6.5	6.5	6.4	6.5	6.5	6.5	6.5	48%	3.9	5.9%	5.5%	6.5%
4.3%	1929	4.1	3.7	3.4	3.8	4.5	4.6	6.1	6.4	4.2	5.3	5.3	4.4	3.6	3.8	5.1	6.5	6.5	6.5	6.0	4.9	6.5	6.4	6.5	6.5	6.5	6.4	6.5	6.5	6.5	6.4	74%	3.4	5.4%	4.6%	5.6%
4.6%	1930	4.1	3.6	4.0	5.1	5.1	6.9	6.9	5.4	6.8	6.8	6.0	4.2	4.5	6.8	6.9	6.9	6.9	6.9	6.4	6.9	6.9	6.9	6.9	6.9	6.9	6.9	6.9	6.9	6.9	6.9	75%	3.6	6.2%	5.5%	6.8%
4.9%	1931	3.9	4.2	6.0	6.2	7.3	7.4	7.2	7.3	7.4	7.3	5.5	5.3	7.4	7.4	7.4	7.3	7.3	6.7	7.4	7.4	7.4	7.4	7.4	7.3	7.4	7.3	7.3	7.4	7.4	7.4	70%	3.9	6.9%	6.4%	7.9%
5.5%	1932	5.3	8.3	8.3	8.3	8.3	8.3	8.2	8.3	8.3	8.2	8.3	8.2	8.3	8.3	8.3	8.2	8.2	8.3	8.2	8.2	8.3	8.3	8.3	8.3	8.3	8.3	8.3	8.3	8.3	8.2	96%	5.3	8.2%	8.0%	9.0%
5.5%	1933	8.3	8.2	8.2	8.2	8.3	8.3	8.3	8.2	8.0	8.1	8.3	8.3	8.3	8.3	8.3	8.1	8.2	8.3	8.2	8.3	8.3	8.2	8.3	8.3	8.3	8.3	8.3	8.3	8.2	8.3	75%	8.0	8.3%	8.2%	9.0%
4.9%	1934	4.9	6.9	7.3	5.6	6.7	6.6	6.0	4.4	4.5	6.5	7.3	7.3	7.3	6.2	5.3	6.6	7.3	7.4	7.4	6.6	7.4	7.3	7.3	7.4	7.4	7.4	7.4	7.4	7.4	7.3	68%	4.4	6.7%	5.9%	7.6%
4.9%	1935	6.7	7.4	5.3	6.6	6.3	5.7	4.5	4.5	6.0	7.3	7.4	7.1	5.7	5.4	6.0	7.4	7.3	7.3	6.7	7.4	7.4	7.4	7.3	7.4	7.4	7.4	7.3	7.4	7.4	7.4	69%	4.5	6.7%	6.0%	7.6%
4.9%	1936	6.5	4.2	4.7	4.7	4.4	3.8	3.9	4.6	5.9	7.3	6.1	4.7	4.6	5.5	6.7	7.1	7.4	5.9	7.3	7.4	7.3	7.4	7.4	7.4	7.3	7.4	7.4	7.4	7.3	7.4	77%	3.8	6.2%	5.0%	6.8%
4.3%	1937	3.6	4.0	3.9	3.7	3.3	3.3	3.9	4.7	6.4	5.1	4.4	3.9	4.9	6.3	5.9	6.4	5.7	6.5	6.4	6.5	6.4	6.5	6.5	6.5	6.5	6.4	6.5	6.4	6.5	6.5	64%	3.3	5.5%	4.2%	6.0%
4.6%	1938	6.4	6.1	5.3	4.2	4.3	6.1	6.9	6.9	6.9	6.0	5.7	6.5	6.9	6.9	6.9	6.8	6.9	6.9	6.9	6.9	6.9	6.9	6.9	6.9	6.9	6.9	6.9	6.9	6.9	6.9	82%	4.2	6.5%	5.9%	7.9%
4.6%	1939	4.9	4.4	3.7	3.8	4.9	6.5	6.9	5.9	4.8	4.7	5.8	6.9	6.9	6.9	6.2	6.9	6.9	6.9	6.9	6.9	6.9	6.9	6.9	6.9	6.9	6.9	6.9	6.9	6.9	6.9	101%	3.7	6.2%	5.1%	7.3%
4.6%	1940	4.5	3.7	3.8	5.1	6.5	6.9	6.3	4.9	4.6	5.7	6.9	6.9	6.9	6.7	6.9	6.9	6.9	6.9	6.9	6.9	6.9	6.9	6.9	6.9	6.9	6.9	6.9	6.9	6.9	6.9	81%	3.7	6.3%	5.2%	7.6%
4.6%	1941	4.0	4.1	5.6	6.9	6.9	6.9	5.8	5.1	6.2	6.9	6.9	6.9	6.9	6.9	6.9	6.9	6.9	6.9	6.9	6.9	6.9	6.9	6.9	6.9	6.9	6.9	6.9	6.9	6.9	6.9	70%	4.0	6.5%	5.8%	7.9%
4.9%	1942	5.1	6.9	7.4	7.4	7.3	6.1	5.8	6.6	7.3	7.4	7.3	6.9	7.4	7.3	7.3	7.4	7.4	7.3	7.4	7.3	7.3	7.4	7.3	7.4	7.3	7.4	7.4	7.3	7.4	7.4	65%	5.1	7.1%	6.7%	8.4%
5.2%	1943	6.3	7.7	7.8	7.1	5.6	5.4	6.4	6.9	6.8	7.5	6.9	7.8	7.8	7.8	7.8	7.8	7.8	7.8	7.8	7.8	7.8	7.8	7.8	7.8	7.8	7.8	7.8	7.8	7.8	7.8	57%	5.4	7.4%	6.8%	8.5%
4.9%	1944	5.9	7.4	5.2	4.5	4.3	4.9	5.9	5.7	6.0	5.6	7.3	7.3	7.4	7.4	7.4	7.4	7.3	7.4	7.3	7.3	7.4	7.3	7.4	7.4	7.4	7.4	7.4	7.4	7.4	7.3	39%	4.3	6.8%	5.5%	7.7%
4.9%	1945	6.7	4.5	4.0	3.9	4.2	4.8	5.0	5.2	4.8	7.4	7.4	7.3	6.9	7.4	7.3	7.4	7.4	7.4	7.4	7.4	7.4	7.4	7.4	7.3	7.4	7.4	7.3	7.4	5.6	3.7	17%	3.7	6.4%	5.1%	6.9%
4.9%	1946	3.8	3.7	3.7	3.7	3.9	4.0	4.3	4.0	5.9	7.3	7.1	5.2	7.4	7.3	7.1	7.4	7.4	7.3	7.4	7.4	7.4	7.3	7.4	7.3	7.4	7.3	6.8	4.3	2.9	3.4	16%	2.9	5.9%	4.4%	6.1%
4.9%	1947	4.2	4.1	4.5	5.2	5.2	5.5	5.2	7.3	7.4	7.3	7.4	7.4	7.4	7.4	7.4	7.4	7.3	7.3	7.4	7.4	7.4	7.4	7.4	7.3	7.3	7.4	6.8	4.7	5.4	6.4	32%	4.1	6.6%	5.6%	7.0%
5.2%	1948	4.6	5.1	5.8	5.9	6.1	5.7	7.8	7.8	7.8	7.1	7.8	7.8	7.8	7.8	7.8	7.8	7.8	7.8	7.8	7.8	7.8	7.8	7.8	7.8	7.8	6.1	4.0	5.2	5.9	4.7	27%	4.0	6.9%	6.4%	7.6%
5.2%	1949	5.3	5.8	5.6	6.0	5.5	7.8	7.8	7.8	6.6	7.8	7.8	7.8	7.8	7.8	7.8	7.8	7.8	7.8	7.8	7.8	7.8	7.8	7.8	7.8	5.8	4.2	4.5	7.1	5.3	4.5	26%	4.2	6.9%	6.6%	7.3%
5.2%	1950	5.2	5.1	5.3	5.1	7.4	7.8	7.8	6.2	7.8	7.8	7.8	7.8	7.8	7.8	7.8	7.8	7.8	7.8	7.8	7.8	7.8	7.8	7.8	4.8	3.9	4.1	4.5	5.0	4.3	4.2	24%	3.9	6.6%	6.6%	7.0%
4.9%	1951	4.8	5.0	4.7	7.0	7.4	7.2	5.9	7.4	7.3	7.4	7.4	7.4	7.4	7.4	7.3	7.4	7.4	7.4	7.3	7.4	7.4	7.3	6.3	3.9	4.2	5.4	4.6	5.2	4.9	4.6	26%	3.9	6.4%	6.4%	6.8%
4.9%	1952	5.0	4.7	7.1	7.3	7.3	6.2	7.4	7.3	7.3	7.4	7.3	7.4	7.4	7.3	7.3	7.4	7.4	7.4	7.3	7.3	7.3	6.0	4.4	4.9	5.8	5.5	4.7	6.5	5.7	4.3	25%	4.3	6.5%	6.7%	6.9%
4.7%	1953	4.6	6.8	7.1	7.0	5.8	7.0	7.1	7.0	7.1	7.1	7.1	7.1	7.0	7.0	7.1	7.1	7.1	7.0	7.1	7.1	5.8	3.8	4.8	5.6	4.6	4.6	4.6	6.2	4.5	4.7	27%	3.8	6.2%	6.7%	6.6%
5.1%	1954	6.9	7.6	7.1	6.0	7.6	7.7	7.7	7.6	7.6	7.7	7.7	7.7	7.7	7.7	7.6	7.7	7.7	7.6	7.6	5.1	4.1	4.3	5.9	4.9	4.4	5.0	4.8	5.2	5.5	5.8	32%	4.1	6.6%	7.4%	7.0%
4.7%	1955	5.5	5.1	4.3	5.8	6.0	5.8	7.1	5.8	6.4	7.1	7.1	7.0	7.1	7.1	7.0	7.1	7.0	6.8	4.3	3.5	3.8	4.2	4.5	4.0	4.1	4.5	3.9	5.4	5.8	4.3	25%	3.5	5.6%	5.9%	5.9%
4.7%	1956	4.7	4.0	5.2	5.6	5.3	6.5	5.7	6.0	6.8	7.0	7.0	7.1	7.1	7.0	6.5	7.0	6.9	4.1	3.5	3.6	4.4	4.0	4.2	4.3	4.2	4.0	4.3	6.9	4.8	5.2	29%	3.5	5.4%	5.7%	5.7%
4.7%	1957	4.2	5.5	5.7	5.6	6.6	5.7	6.5	6.9	7.1	6.9	7.1	7.1	7.1	7.0	6.9	6.8	4.4	3.5	3.8	4.2	4.2	3.9	4.6	4.6	3.9	4.8	5.4	5.9	6.3	5.5	30%	3.5	5.6%	6.1%	5.9%
4.7%	1958	6.9	7.1	7.0	7.1	7.0	7.1	7.1	7.1	7.1	7.0	7.1	7.1	7.1	7.0	7.1	5.7	4.1	4.4	5.6	4.7	4.7	4.7	5.8	4.6	5.1	7.0	5.2	7.0	7.0	4.9	28%	4.1	6.2%	7.1%	6.5%
4.5%	1959	5.3	5.1	6.1	5.3	5.7	6.6	6.8	6.3	6.7	6.8	6.7	6.4	6.7	6.7	4.1	3.5	3.7	4.2	4.1	3.8	4.2	4.3	4.4	4.9	5.7	5.2	6.0	6.7	5.2	5.0	27%	3.5	5.4%	6.1%	5.7%
4.3%	1960	5.1	6.0	5.2	5.7	6.2	6.4	6.4	6.4	6.5	6.4	6.4	6.5	6.5	4.3	3.3	3.7	4.6	4.1	4.0	4.1	4.9	4.1	5.9	6.5	5.1	6.5	6.4	6.4	5.9	5.3	28%	3.3	5.5%	6.0%	5.6%
4.3%	1961	6.2	5.3	5.7	6.4	6.5	6.2	6.5	6.5	6.2	6.3	6.5	6.3	4.2	3.4	3.6	4.3	4.1	3.7	4.0	4.0	3.9	4.4	6.4	5.1	6.1	6.4	4.5	6.5	6.1	3.4	19%	3.4	5.3%	6.2%	5.5%
4.3%	1962	4.6	5.0	5.5	6.5	5.5	6.4	6.4	6.2	5.9	6.5	6.5	4.0	3.3	3.6	4.2	4.1	4.0	4.1	4.7	4.0	5.4	6.4	6.5	6.4	6.4	5.9	5.9	6.4	4.2	5.0	27%	3.3	5.3%	5.9%	5.4%
4.3%	1963	5.8	6.4	6.5	6.3	6.5	6.4	6.4	6.3	6.5	6.5	4.5	3.4	3.8	4.7	4.2	4.1	4.4	4.4	4.1	4.8	6.5	5.6	6.4	6.5	5.9	6.5	6.4	5.1	6.3	5.8	29%	3.4	5.6%	6.4%	5.7%
4.3%	1964	5.8	6.4	5.6	6.5	6.4	6.2	6.2	6.3	6.1	4.1	3.4	3.6	4.4	4.2	3.9	4.2	4.7	4.0	5.2	6.3	6.1	6.4	6.4	6.4	6.5	6.5	4.1	6.5	6.5	6.4	31%	3.4	5.5%	6.0%	5.6%
4.2%	1965	6.2	5.2	6.3	6.3	5.3	5.3	5.8	5.4	3.8	3.3	3.5	4.0	3.8	3.7	3.7	4.0	3.8	4.4	6.0	4.9	6.3	6.3	6.3	6.3	6.3	4.0	5.1	6.3	6.3	4.8	26%	3.3	5.1%	5.3%	5.1%
4.0%	1966	4.7	6.0	6.0	5.0	4.8	5.2	5.3	3.5	3.0	3.3	3.9	3.6	3.5	3.7	3.7	3.6	4.5	5.5	5.1	6.0	6.0	5.3	6.0	6.0	3.9	6.0	6.0	6.0	6.0	6.0	30%	3.0	4.9%	4.7%	4.8%
4.3%	1967	6.5	6.5	5.5	5.4	5.8	5.7	4.0	3.3	3.5	4.2	4.1	3.8	4.0	4.4	3.9	4.9	6.4	5.4	6.5	6.5	6.4	6.4	6.4	4.9	6.5	6.5	6.5	6.5	6.5	6.5	38%	3.3	5.4%	5.0%	5.4%
4.2%	1968	6.2	4.3	4.2	4.6	4.5	3.5	3.2	3.2	3.5	3.5	3.4	3.4	3.6	3.5	3.9	5.1	4.8	6.0	6.3	4.9	6.3	6.3	4.4	5.9	6.0	6.3	5.1	6.3	6.3	6.3	38%	3.2	4.8%	4.1%	4.6%
4.2%	1969	3.9	3.8	4.0	4.1	3.3	3.0	3.2	3.3	3.3	3.2	3.3	3.4	3.3	3.8	4.5	4.3	5.9	6.0	4.8	5.3	6.3	3.9	6.3	6.3	6.3	5.8	6.3	6.3	6.3	6.3	37%	3.0	4.7%	3.5%	4.3%
4.2%	1970	5.2	5.6	5.5	3.8	3.2	3.4	4.1	3.8	3.7	4.1	4.5	4.0	5.3	6.3	5.7	6.3	6.3	6.3	6.3	6.3	6.2	6.3	6.3	6.3	6.3	6.3	6.3	6.3	6.3	6.3	64%	3.2	5.4%	4.2%	5.4%
4.5%	1971	5.5	5.4	3.8	3.4	3.5	4.0	4.0	3.8	4.0	4.3	4.1	4.9	6.3	6.1	6.8	6.7	6.8	6.8	6.7	5.4	6.7	6.8	6.8	6.7	6.8	6.8	6.7	6.7	6.8	6.8	55%	3.4	5.7%	4.2%	5.6%
4.3%	1972	5.2	3.7	3.2	3.4	3.9	3.7	3.7	3.8	4.0	3.9	5.0	6.1	5.9	6.5	6.5	6.4	6.5	6.5	5.8	6.5	6.5	6.5	6.5	6.5	6.4	6.5	6.5	6.5	6.4	6.4	59%	3.2	5.5%	3.9%	5.4%
4.3%	1973	3.8	3.3	3.4	3.9	3.7	3.6	3.8	3.9	3.7	4.7	6.2	5.5	6.4	6.5	6.4	6.4	6.5	5.6	6.5	6.5	6.5	6.4	6.5	6.4	6.5	6.5	6.4	6.5	6.5	6.5	46%	3.3	5.5%	3.8%	5.4%
4.7%	1974	3.8	4.2	5.3	5.0	4.6	4.8	5.0	4.5	5.8	7.1	7.1	7.1	7.0	7.1	7.1	7.1	7.1	7.1	7.1	7.1	7.0	7.0	7.0	7.1	7.1	7.1	7.1	7.1	7.0	7.1	76%	3.8	6.4%	5.0%	6.7%
5.3%	1975	5.9	7.7	6.8	6.3	6.0	6.1	5.8	7.4	8.0	8.0	7.9	8.0	7.9	8.0	8.0	8.0	8.0	8.0	7.9	8.0	8.0	7.9	8.0	8.0	7.9	8.0	8.0	8.0	7.9	8.0	102%	5.8	7.6%	6.8%	8.4%
5.1%	1976	6.0	5.5	5.1	5.2	5.2	4.9	6.6	7.4	7.3	7.6	7.7	7.7	7.7	7.6	7.7	7.7	7.7	7.7	7.7	7.7	7.7	7.7	7.7	7.7	7.6	7.7	7.6	7.7	7.7	7.6	84%	4.9	7.1%	6.1%	7.7%
5.1%	1977	4.5	4.3	4.4	4.5	4.3	5.1	6.2	5.9	7.6	7.7	7.7	7.6	7.7	7.3	7.6	7.6	7.6	7.7	7.7	7.7	7.7	7.6	7.7	7.6	7.7	7.6	7.7	7.6	7.6	7.6	67%	4.3	6.9%	5.5%	7.1%
5.3%	1978	4.5	4.5	4.6	4.5	5.4	6.3	6.5	7.9	8.0	8.0	8.0	8.0	7.6	8.0	7.9	7.9	8.0	8.0	8.0	8.0	8.0	8.0	8.0	8.0	8.0	8.0	8.0	8.0	8.0	8.0	61%	4.5	7.3%	6.0%	7.4%
5.5%	1979	4.7	4.7	4.6	5.5	6.2	6.4	8.2	8.3	7.9	8.2	8.2	7.5	8.2	8.3	8.3	8.3	8.3	8.2	8.3	8.3	8.3	8.3	8.3	8.2	8.3	8.3	8.2	8.3	8.2	7.0	36%	4.6	7.6%	6.5%	7.6%
5.5%	1980	4.7	4.5	5.4	6.2	6.2	8.1	8.2	7.8	8.2	8.3	7.8	8.2	8.2	8.3	8.3	8.3	8.3	8.2	8.2	8.3	8.3	8.2	8.3	8.3	8.3	8.2	8.3	8.3	8.2	8.3	47%	4.5	7.7%	6.8%	7.8%
5.3%	1981	4.5	5.5	6.5	6.6	8.0	7.9	7.9	8.0	8.0	7.9	8.0	7.9	8.0	8.0	8.0	8.0	7.9	8.0	8.0	8.0	8.0	8.0	8.0	8.0	8.0	7.9	8.0	8.0	8.0	8.0	68%	4.5	7.7%	7.1%	8.2%
																															Totals	49%	2.9	6.3%	5.8%	6.7%

FIGURE 147

Backtesting results for recommended 30-year systemic withdrawal plan.

Of course, a 30-year retirement can also use different EM income floors (as shown in the 40-year examples, up to the MSWR-100% value of 4.3%).

20-Year and 15-Year Plans

Figure 148 and Figure 149 show results for 20-year and 15-year retirements. These shorter plans are for retiring late in life (or perhaps restarting a plan late in life). The optimal initial stock allocation is 45% stocks for a 20-year retirement and 35% stocks for a 15-year retirement. However, if leaving a large bequest is a major consideration, or the portfolio will outlive the retiree, then a higher stock percentage (e.g., 50%) can be used.

Initial	Year	Y1	Y2	Y3	Y4	Y5	Y6	Y7	Y8	Y9	Y10	Y11	Y12	Y13	Y14	Y15	Y16	Y17	Y18	Y19	Y20	%Left	Min	Avg	1st 10Y	MSWR
4.7%	1928	7.1	7.1	6.6	5.6	6.6	7.1	7.1	7.1	7.1	7.1	7.1	7.1	7.1	5.0	4.7	7.1	7.1	7.1	7.1	6.7	33%	4.7	6.7%	6.9%	7.5%
4.7%	1929	6.3	5.1	4.6	5.7	6.5	6.7	7.1	7.1	5.5	6.3	6.3	4.8	4.1	4.1	5.7	7.1	7.1	7.1	7.1	5.2	29%	4.1	6.0%	6.1%	6.5%
5.1%	1930	6.2	4.8	5.9	7.6	7.3	7.6	7.6	7.4	7.6	7.6	7.2	4.6	5.5	7.6	7.6	7.6	7.6	7.6	7.5	7.6	36%	4.6	7.0%	7.0%	7.7%
5.4%	1931	5.2	5.9	8.1	8.1	8.1	8.1	8.1	8.1	8.1	8.1	6.8	6.2	8.1	8.1	8.1	8.1	8.1	8.1	8.1	8.1	48%	5.2	7.7%	7.6%	8.8%
6.1%	1932	8.0	9.1	9.1	9.1	9.1	9.1	9.1	9.1	9.1	9.1	9.1	9.1	9.1	9.1	9.1	9.1	9.1	9.1	9.1	9.1	69%	8.0	9.0%	9.0%	9.0%
6.1%	1933	9.1	9.1	9.1	9.1	9.1	9.1	9.1	9.1	9.1	9.1	9.1	9.1	9.1	9.1	9.1	9.1	9.1	9.1	9.1	9.1	53%	9.1	9.1%	9.1%	9.0%
5.4%	1934	7.3	8.1	8.1	8.0	8.1	8.1	7.8	5.1	5.4	7.3	8.1	8.1	8.1	6.9	5.5	7.1	8.1	8.1	8.1	6.6	35%	5.1	7.4%	7.3%	8.3%
5.4%	1935	8.1	8.1	7.9	8.1	8.1	7.7	5.5	5.3	7.8	8.1	8.1	8.0	7.1	5.6	6.1	8.1	7.8	8.1	7.1	8.1	50%	5.3	7.4%	7.5%	8.3%
5.4%	1936	8.1	5.5	6.7	6.6	5.5	4.6	4.7	5.7	7.9	8.1	7.2	5.2	5.4	6.0	7.4	8.0	7.2	7.4	8.1	8.1	53%	4.6	6.7%	6.3%	7.4%
4.7%	1937	5.1	5.6	5.6	5.1	3.9	4.0	5.1	6.3	7.1	6.1	5.2	4.4	6.4	7.1	7.0	7.1	5.7	7.1	7.1	7.1	52%	3.9	5.9%	5.4%	6.6%
5.1%	1938	7.6	7.6	7.6	5.7	5.5	7.6	7.6	7.6	6.9	6.6	7.3	7.6	7.6	7.6	7.6	7.6	7.6	7.6	7.6	7.6	52%	5.5	7.3%	7.1%	8.5%
5.1%	1939	7.5	6.0	4.7	4.9	6.5	7.6	7.6	7.5	6.0	5.1	6.6	7.6	7.6	7.6	6.3	7.6	7.6	7.6	7.6	7.6	62%	4.7	6.9%	6.3%	7.8%
5.1%	1940	6.8	4.7	5.0	7.2	7.6	7.6	7.6	5.9	5.5	6.1	7.6	7.6	7.6	7.2	7.6	7.6	7.6	7.6	7.6	7.6	65%	4.7	7.0%	6.4%	8.1%
5.1%	1941	5.6	5.4	7.6	7.6	7.6	7.6	6.2	7.6	7.6	7.6	7.6	7.6	7.6	7.6	7.6	7.6	7.6	7.6	7.6	7.6	54%	5.4	7.3%	7.0%	8.7%
5.4%	1942	7.5	8.1	8.1	8.1	8.1	8.1	7.5	8.0	8.1	8.1	8.1	7.3	8.1	8.1	8.1	8.1	8.1	8.1	8.1	8.1	60%	7.3	8.0%	8.0%	9.0%
5.7%	1943	8.6	8.6	8.6	8.6	7.3	6.9	8.1	8.4	8.4	7.9	7.4	8.6	8.6	8.6	8.6	8.6	8.6	8.6	8.6	8.6	46%	6.9	8.3%	8.1%	9.0%
5.4%	1944	8.1	8.1	7.3	5.9	5.2	6.2	7.6	6.9	7.4	5.9	8.1	8.1	8.1	8.1	8.1	8.1	8.1	8.1	8.1	8.1	49%	5.2	7.5%	6.9%	8.6%
5.4%	1945	8.1	5.9	5.1	4.9	5.3	6.3	6.4	6.3	5.8	8.1	8.1	8.1	8.1	8.1	8.1	8.1	8.1	8.1	8.1	8.1	42%	4.9	7.2%	6.2%	8.0%
5.4%	1946	4.9	4.3	4.3	4.6	4.8	5.0	5.4	4.7	8.0	8.1	8.1	5.8	8.1	8.1	7.5	8.1	6.6	8.1	8.1	8.1	45%	4.3	6.5%	5.4%	7.0%
5.4%	1947	5.9	5.3	6.2	7.4	6.8	7.2	6.4	8.1	8.1	8.1	8.1	8.1	8.1	8.1	8.1	8.1	8.1	8.1	8.1	8.1	48%	5.3	7.5%	7.0%	8.8%
5.7%	1948	6.4	7.0	8.3	8.2	7.8	7.1	8.6	8.6	8.6	8.6	8.6	8.6	8.6	8.6	8.6	8.6	8.6	8.6	8.6	8.6	63%	6.4	8.3%	7.9%	9.0%
5.7%	1949	8.0	7.9	7.7	8.1	6.8	8.6	8.6	8.6	8.0	8.6	8.6	8.6	8.6	8.6	8.6	8.6	8.6	8.6	8.6	8.6	60%	6.8	8.3%	8.1%	9.0%
5.7%	1950	7.5	6.8	7.3	6.7	8.6	8.6	8.6	7.6	8.6	8.6	8.6	8.6	8.6	8.6	8.6	8.6	7.8	8.6	8.6	7.9	39%	6.7	8.2%	7.9%	9.0%
5.4%	1951	7.1	6.9	6.4	8.1	8.1	8.1	7.7	8.1	8.1	8.1	8.1	8.1	8.1	8.1	8.1	8.1	8.1	8.1	8.1	8.0	38%	6.4	7.9%	7.7%	9.0%
5.4%	1952	7.5	6.3	8.1	8.1	8.1	8.1	8.1	8.1	8.1	8.1	8.1	8.1	8.1	8.1	8.1	8.1	8.1	8.1	8.1	8.1	44%	6.3	8.0%	7.9%	9.0%
5.2%	1953	6.9	7.8	7.8	7.8	7.8	7.8	7.8	7.8	7.8	7.8	7.8	7.8	7.8	7.8	7.8	7.8	7.8	7.8	7.8	7.8	39%	6.9	7.8%	7.7%	8.9%
5.6%	1954	8.4	8.4	8.4	8.4	8.4	8.4	8.4	8.4	8.4	8.4	8.4	8.4	8.4	8.4	8.3	8.4	4.3				23%	4.3	8.2%	8.4%	9.0%
5.2%	1955	7.8	7.1	5.9	7.8	7.7	7.4	8.1	6.9	7.7	7.7	7.8	7.3	7.8	7.8	7.3	6.6	6.1	7.5	3.9		11%	2.3	6.9%	7.4%	7.4%
5.2%	1956	7.0	5.3	7.5	7.7	6.7	7.8	7.0	7.1	7.8	7.8	7.6	7.8	7.8	7.6	5.9	6.6	5.6	4.1	2.7	3.1	14%	2.7	6.5%	7.2%	6.9%
5.2%	1957	6.2	7.7	7.8	7.8	7.8	7.4	7.8	7.8	7.8	7.4	7.8	7.8	7.8	6.9	6.4	6.4	3.9	3.2	3.9		19%	3.2	6.7%	7.5%	7.1%
5.2%	1958	7.8	7.8	7.8	7.8	7.8	7.8	7.8	7.8	7.8	7.8	7.8	7.8	7.8	7.8	6.3	4.0	5.3	5.9	4.7		27%	4.0	7.2%	7.8%	7.9%
5.0%	1959	7.4	7.3	7.4	7.4	7.4	7.4	7.4	7.4	7.4	7.4	6.8	7.4	6.9	4.0	3.3	3.7	4.4	3.9	3.7		19%	3.3	6.3%	7.4%	6.8%
4.7%	1960	7.1	7.1	7.1	7.1	7.1	7.1	7.1	7.1	7.1	7.1	7.1	7.1	7.1	4.6	3.5	3.8	4.3	4.9	4.1	4.0	23%	3.5	6.1%	7.1%	6.7%
4.7%	1961	7.1	7.1	7.1	7.1	7.1	7.1	7.1	7.1	7.1	7.1	7.1	5.1	3.6	3.8	4.5	4.0	4.4	4.2	4.0		23%	3.6	5.9%	7.1%	6.6%
4.7%	1962	7.1	7.0	7.1	7.1	7.1	7.1	7.1	7.1	7.1	7.1	3.6	3.7	4.2	4.2	3.8	4.7	4.4	3.7			21%	3.6	5.7%	7.1%	6.3%
4.7%	1963	7.1	7.1	7.1	7.1	7.1	7.1	7.1	7.1	5.5	3.8	4.6	5.4	4.5	4.5	4.5	6.0	4.4	4.6			26%	3.8	5.9%	7.1%	6.6%
4.7%	1964	7.1	7.1	7.1	7.1	7.1	7.1	7.1	4.7	3.7	4.0	5.6	4.7	4.1	4.7	4.6	5.0	5.2	5.6			30%	3.7	5.8%	6.9%	6.4%
4.6%	1965	6.9	6.9	6.9	6.9	6.9	6.9	6.9	6.9	4.5	3.5	3.9	4.3	4.5	4.0	4.0	4.4	3.8	5.2	5.6	4.2	25%	3.5	5.4%	6.3%	6.0%
4.4%	1966	6.6	6.6	6.6	6.6	6.6	6.6	6.6	4.2	3.4	3.6	4.4	3.9	4.1	4.1	4.0	3.8	4.1	6.6	4.6	5.0	27%	3.4	5.1%	5.7%	5.6%
4.7%	1967	7.1	7.1	7.1	7.1	7.1	5.1	3.7	4.1	4.7	4.2	5.0	4.9	4.1	5.1	5.8	6.4	6.8	5.8			30%	3.7	5.7%	6.0%	6.2%
4.6%	1968	6.9	6.1	6.2	6.6	5.9	4.2	3.5	3.6	4.2	3.8	3.8	3.8	4.4	3.8	4.1	5.2	4.2	6.8	5.8	4.0	23%	3.5	4.8%	5.1%	5.4%
4.6%	1969	5.8	5.3	5.8	5.8	3.9	3.5	3.6	3.9	3.8	3.6	3.8	3.8	3.9	4.2	4.7	4.4	5.0	6.9	4.4	4.4	25%	3.5	4.5%	4.5%	5.0%
4.6%	1970	6.9	6.9	6.9	5.2	3.7	4.2	5.4	4.7	4.6	4.6	5.5	4.5	6.6	6.9	5.8	6.9	6.9	6.9	6.9	6.2	31%	3.7	5.8%	5.3%	6.1%
5.0%	1971	7.4	7.4	5.0	3.9	4.2	5.3	5.0	4.5	5.0	5.1	4.9	5.7	7.4	6.7	7.4	7.4	5.8	7.4	7.4	4.2	24%	3.9	5.9%	5.3%	6.2%
4.7%	1972	7.1	4.9	3.9	4.3	5.0	4.8	4.6	4.6	5.0	4.3	5.7	6.7	7.0	7.1	7.1	6.1	6.2	7.1	4.4	5.3	29%	3.9	5.6%	4.9%	6.0%
4.7%	1973	5.5	3.9	4.4	5.5	4.8	4.6	4.8	4.8	4.5	5.2	7.1	5.8	7.1	7.1	6.1	7.1	7.1	5.2	6.4	6.0	31%	3.9	5.7%	4.8%	6.0%
5.2%	1974	5.1	5.7	7.7	7.0	5.9	6.2	6.2	5.2	6.9	7.6	7.7	7.8	7.8	7.8	7.8	7.8	5.2	7.8	7.8	7.8	40%	5.1	6.9%	6.4%	7.3%
5.8%	1975	8.7	8.7	8.7	8.6	7.5	7.0	8.5	8.7	8.7	8.7	8.7	8.7	8.7	8.7	8.3	8.7	8.7	8.7	8.7	8.7	42%	7.0	8.5%	8.3%	9.0%
5.6%	1976	8.4	7.5	6.9	7.0	6.4	6.0	8.0	8.4	8.3	8.4	8.4	8.4	8.4	8.4	6.6	8.4	8.4	8.4	8.4	8.4	46%	6.0	7.9%	7.5%	8.3%
5.6%	1977	6.4	5.6	5.7	5.7	5.1	6.6	7.9	7.0	8.4	8.4	8.3	8.4	8.4	6.3	7.7	8.4	8.4	8.4	8.4	8.4	40%	5.1	7.4%	6.7%	7.7%
5.8%	1978	6.2	5.8	6.0	5.7	6.9	8.2	8.1	8.7	8.7	8.3	8.7	8.7	8.7	8.7	8.7	7.2	8.7	8.7	8.7	8.7	51%	5.7	7.9%	7.3%	8.2%
6.1%	1979	6.4	6.1	5.8	7.6	8.0	8.2	9.1	9.1	9.1	9.0	9.1	7.1	9.1	9.1	9.1	8.9	9.1	9.1	9.1	9.1	50%	5.8	8.4%	7.8%	8.7%
6.1%	1980	6.4	5.7	7.5	8.8	8.0	9.1	9.1	9.1	9.1	9.1	8.1	9.1	9.1	9.1	8.9	9.1	9.1	9.1	9.1	9.1	56%	5.7	8.6%	8.2%	9.0%
5.8%	1981	6.3	7.9	8.7	8.7	8.7	8.7	8.7	8.7	8.7	8.7	8.7	8.7	8.7	8.7	8.7	8.7	8.7	8.7	8.7	8.7	64%	6.3	8.5%	8.4%	9.0%
6.1%	1982	8.9	9.0	9.1	9.1	9.1	9.1	9.1	9.1	9.1	9.1	9.1	9.1	9.1	9.1	9.1	9.1	9.1	9.1	9.1	9.1	65%	8.9	9.1%	9.1%	9.0%
6.1%	1983	7.5	7.1	9.1	9.1	8.5	9.0	9.1	7.2	9.1	9.1	9.1	9.1	9.1	9.1	9.1	9.1	9.1	9.1	9.1	5.5	32%	5.5	8.6%	8.5%	9.0%
5.8%	1984	6.8	8.2	8.7	8.3	8.1	8.7	7.1	8.6	8.7	8.7	8.6	8.7	8.7	8.7	8.7	8.7	8.7	5.9	8.3		40%	5.9	8.3%	8.2%	9.0%
5.8%	1985	8.6	8.7	8.1	8.6	8.7	7.0	8.7	8.7	8.7	8.0	8.7	8.7	8.7	8.7	8.7	8.7	8.7	8.7	8.7	8.7	46%	7.0	8.4%	8.3%	9.0%
5.6%	1986	8.1	6.4	7.1	8.1	5.8	7.9	8.4	8.4	7.5	8.4	8.4	8.4	8.4	8.4	8.4	6.2	8.4	8.4	8.4	8.3	40%	5.8	7.9%	7.6%	8.5%
5.6%	1987	6.1	6.2	7.0	5.8	6.9	7.9	8.4	6.7	8.4	8.3	8.4	8.4	8.4	8.3	5.6	7.8	8.4	8.2	7.3		37%	5.6	7.5%	7.2%	8.1%
5.6%	1988	7.5	7.8	6.4	8.4	8.4	8.2	8.4	8.4	8.4	8.4	8.4	7.5	8.4	8.4	8.4	8.4	6.8	8.4	6.1	6.8	36%	6.4	8.1%	8.0%	8.9%
5.6%	1989	7.8	5.8	7.8	8.4	8.4	7.6	8.4	8.4	8.4	8.4	8.4	7.6	8.4	8.4	8.3	8.4	7.8	7.8	3.9		18%	3.9	7.9%	7.9%	8.5%
5.2%	1990	6.1	7.5	7.8	7.8	7.3	7.8	7.8	7.8	7.8	7.8	7.8	7.8	7.8	7.8	7.8	7.8	7.8	7.8	4.3	5.1	29%	4.3	7.4%	7.6%	8.1%
5.4%	1991	8.1	8.1	8.1	8.1	8.1	8.1	8.1	8.1	8.1	8.1	8.1	8.1	8.1	8.1	8.1	8.1	8.1	8.1	8.1	8.1	40%	8.1	8.1%	8.1%	8.9%
																					Totals	38%	2.3	7.2%	7.1%	7.8%

FIGURE 148

Backtesting results for recommended 20-year systemic withdrawal plan.

Initial	Year	Y1	Y2	Y3	Y4	Y5	Y6	Y7	Y8	Y9	Y10	Y11	Y12	Y13	Y14	Y15	%Left	Min	Avg	1st 10Y	MSWR
5.2%	1928	7.7	7.7	7.7	7.6	7.7	7.7	7.7	7.7	7.7	7.7	7.7	7.7	7.7	5.6	4.9	28%	4.9	7.4%	7.7%	8.6%
5.2%	1929	7.7	7.7	6.3	7.7	7.7	7.7	7.7	7.7	7.0	7.4	7.0	5.1	4.6	4.4	5.7	31%	4.4	6.8%	7.5%	8.1%
5.5%	1930	8.2	7.0	8.2	8.3	8.3	8.3	8.3	8.3	8.3	8.3	7.9	4.9	6.1	8.0	8.3	44%	4.4	7.8%	8.2%	8.9%
5.9%	1931	6.8	8.7	8.8	8.8	8.8	8.8	8.8	8.8	8.8	8.8	6.6	5.9	8.8	8.8	8.8	64%	4.9	8.3%	8.6%	9.0%
6.6%	1932	9.8	9.9	9.9	9.9	9.9	9.9	9.9	9.9	9.9	9.9	9.9	9.9	9.9	9.9	9.9	61%	5.9	9.9%	9.9%	9.0%
6.6%	1933	9.9	9.9	9.9	9.9	9.9	9.9	9.9	9.9	9.8	8.2	9.9	9.9	9.9	9.9	6.8	39%	6.8	9.6%	9.7%	9.0%
5.9%	1934	8.8	8.8	8.8	8.8	8.8	8.8	7.5	6.1	5.6	7.0	8.8	8.8	8.8	5.6	4.8	27%	4.8	7.7%	7.9%	9.0%
5.9%	1935	8.8	8.8	8.8	8.8	8.8	8.6	5.6	6.3	7.6	8.4	8.8	6.6	6.4	5.1	5.3	31%	4.8	7.5%	8.1%	9.0%
5.9%	1936	8.8	7.3	7.8	7.7	6.2	5.2	4.9	6.7	7.7	8.8	6.3	4.9	5.2	5.4	6.1	34%	4.9	6.6%	7.1%	8.1%
5.2%	1937	6.7	7.7	7.0	6.3	4.5	4.7	5.2	7.6	7.7	5.6	4.8	4.2	5.9	6.6	5.6	31%	4.2	6.0%	6.3%	7.2%
5.5%	1938	8.3	8.3	8.3	6.8	6.1	8.3	8.3	8.3	8.3	6.0	5.7	6.0	8.3	8.3	7.2	37%	4.2	7.5%	7.7%	8.9%
5.5%	1939	8.3	8.2	5.5	5.5	6.8	8.3	8.3	8.1	5.5	4.8	5.7	6.4	8.3	7.0	5.0	29%	4.8	6.8%	6.9%	8.1%
5.5%	1940	8.3	6.1	5.6	7.5	8.2	8.3	6.9	6.2	5.5	7.3	6.4	8.3	5.7	8.3	8.3	43%	4.8	6.9%	6.8%	8.2%
5.5%	1941	6.8	6.8	8.2	8.3	8.3	8.3	6.2	6.4	6.8	7.0	7.2	6.6	7.0	8.3	8.3	48%	5.2	7.4%	7.3%	8.9%
5.9%	1942	8.7	8.8	8.8	8.8	8.8	7.7	6.3	8.6	8.2	6.9	7.5	5.8	8.8	8.8	8.8	44%	5.8	8.1%	8.2%	9.0%
6.2%	1943	9.4	9.4	9.4	9.4	6.9	6.8	7.0	9.0	7.5	6.9	6.4	9.3	9.4	9.4	6.1	35%	5.8	8.2%	8.2%	9.0%
5.9%	1944	8.8	8.8	7.6	6.2	5.5	6.5	6.8	7.7	6.9	5.5	8.8	8.8	8.8	6.7	8.8	43%	5.5	7.5%	7.0%	8.8%
5.9%	1945	8.8	7.2	5.5	5.3	5.5	6.5	5.9	7.0	5.6	8.1	8.8	7.6	6.9	8.8	7.6	39%	5.3	7.0%	6.5%	8.3%
5.9%	1946	5.9	5.1	4.8	5.1	5.2	5.4	5.3	5.4	7.8	8.1	7.6	5.2	8.8	8.2	5.7	33%	4.8	6.2%	5.8%	7.4%
5.9%	1947	7.0	6.6	6.9	7.7	6.8	7.5	6.0	8.8	8.8	8.8	7.0	8.8	8.8	8.6	8.5	41%	4.8	7.8%	7.5%	9.0%
6.2%	1948	7.8	8.9	8.6	8.4	7.7	7.4	9.4	9.4	9.4	7.5	9.4	9.4	9.4	9.4	7.2	39%	6.0	8.6%	8.5%	9.0%
6.2%	1949	9.3	9.3	8.0	8.3	6.9	9.4	9.4	9.4	7.1	9.1	9.4	7.5	9.4	7.3	6.8	38%	6.8	8.4%	8.6%	9.0%
6.2%	1950	8.6	8.1	7.6	7.1	9.2	9.4	8.7	8.0	9.1	8.0	7.6	7.9	7.9	7.2	6.9	38%	6.8	8.1%	8.4%	9.0%
5.9%	1951	8.4	8.6	7.0	8.8	8.8	8.8	6.8	8.8	8.8	8.2	8.8	6.9	8.8	8.6	8.4	41%	6.8	8.3%	8.3%	9.0%
5.9%	1952	8.8	8.2	8.8	8.8	8.8	8.7	8.8	8.8	8.8	8.8	8.2	7.7	8.8	8.8	6.8	37%	6.8	8.5%	8.7%	9.0%
5.6%	1953	8.4	8.5	8.5	8.5	8.3	8.5	8.5	8.5	8.5	8.4	8.5	8.0	8.5	8.0	8.5	43%	6.8	8.4%	8.4%	9.0%
6.1%	1954	9.2	9.2	9.2	9.1	9.2	9.2	9.1	9.2	8.9	8.2	9.2	9.1	8.9	9.2	9.2	45%	8.0	9.1%	9.1%	9.0%
5.6%	1955	8.5	8.5	6.7	8.5	7.9	7.9	8.3	7.8	7.3	7.1	8.5	5.9	8.5	8.5	5.5	31%	5.5	7.7%	7.9%	9.0%
5.6%	1956	8.3	7.0	8.1	8.3	7.0	8.5	6.6	8.3	7.9	8.1	6.5	8.2	8.5	6.1	4.8	28%	4.8	7.5%	7.8%	8.9%
5.6%	1957	7.9	8.5	8.5	8.5	8.5	8.1	7.6	8.5	8.5	6.7	8.5	8.5	7.3	5.4	5.0	29%	4.8	7.7%	8.1%	9.0%
5.6%	1958	8.5	8.5	8.5	8.5	8.5	8.5	8.5	8.5	8.5	8.5	8.5	8.4	8.5	8.1	6.2	34%	5.0	8.3%	8.5%	9.0%
5.4%	1959	8.1	8.1	8.1	8.1	8.1	8.1	8.1	8.1	8.1	8.1	8.1	7.2	5.7	7.5	5.8	18%	4.1	7.4%	8.1%	8.5%
5.2%	1960	7.7	7.7	7.7	7.7	7.7	7.7	7.7	7.7	7.7	7.7	7.7	6.9	7.7	4.1	2.9	13%	2.9	7.1%	7.7%	7.9%
5.2%	1961	7.7	7.7	7.7	7.7	7.7	7.7	7.7	7.7	7.7	7.1	7.6	6.1	4.7	3.7	3.8	18%	2.9	6.8%	7.6%	7.6%
5.2%	1962	7.7	7.7	7.7	7.7	7.7	7.7	7.7	7.7	7.5	6.7	6.7	4.0	3.7	3.9	4.0	21%	3.7	6.5%	7.6%	7.3%
5.2%	1963	7.7	7.7	7.7	7.7	7.7	7.7	7.7	7.7	7.7	7.6	4.9	3.9	4.3	4.7	4.1	23%	3.7	6.6%	7.7%	7.6%
5.2%	1964	7.7	7.7	7.7	7.7	7.7	7.7	7.7	7.7	7.7	4.6	3.9	4.0	5.2	4.3	4.0	21%	3.9	6.4%	7.4%	7.4%
5.0%	1965	7.6	7.6	7.6	7.6	7.6	7.6	7.4	7.6	4.7	3.8	4.0	4.1	4.4	4.0	3.9	21%	3.8	6.0%	6.9%	6.9%
4.8%	1966	7.2	7.2	7.2	7.2	7.2	7.2	7.1	5.1	3.7	3.8	4.4	3.9	4.2	4.0	3.9	22%	3.7	5.6%	6.3%	6.5%
5.2%	1967	7.7	7.7	7.7	7.7	7.7	7.7	5.1	4.3	4.4	4.8	4.6	4.2	5.0	4.7	4.0	22%	3.7	5.8%	6.5%	6.9%
5.0%	1968	7.6	7.6	7.3	7.5	6.6	4.9	3.9	4.3	4.5	4.1	4.0	3.9	4.4	3.9	3.9	22%	3.9	5.2%	5.8%	6.2%
5.0%	1969	7.4	7.3	6.9	6.7	4.4	3.9	4.0	4.7	4.2	3.9	4.0	4.1	4.2	4.4	4.2	25%	3.9	4.9%	5.3%	5.9%
5.0%	1970	7.6	7.6	7.6	6.8	4.4	5.2	5.9	6.1	5.0	4.8	5.3	4.4	6.5	6.8	4.9	28%	3.9	5.9%	6.1%	7.0%
5.4%	1971	8.1	8.1	6.1	4.6	4.8	6.2	5.2	5.4	5.2	5.1	4.8	5.2	8.0	5.8	6.2	34%	4.4	5.9%	5.9%	7.0%
5.2%	1972	7.7	6.7	4.6	5.1	5.6	5.5	4.7	5.4	5.1	4.3	5.3	5.8	6.6	7.1	6.2	33%	4.3	5.7%	5.5%	6.7%
5.2%	1973	7.0	5.1	5.2	6.3	5.2	5.1	4.8	5.5	4.6	5.0	6.5	5.2	7.7	7.5	4.8	28%	4.3	5.7%	5.4%	6.6%
5.6%	1974	6.3	7.4	8.3	7.4	6.1	6.4	5.7	5.8	6.6	6.9	6.8	7.5	8.5	6.7	6.3	34%	4.6	6.8%	6.7%	8.0%
6.4%	1975	9.5	9.5	9.5	8.8	7.3	7.5	6.3	9.3	9.1	7.6	9.5	9.3	9.3	8.0	7.2	39%	5.7	8.5%	8.4%	9.0%
6.1%	1976	9.2	9.2	7.4	7.2	6.3	6.2	7.2	9.2	8.0	8.8	9.2	9.2	8.4	7.2	5.0	29%	5.0	7.8%	7.9%	8.8%
6.1%	1977	7.6	6.8	6.1	6.2	5.4	7.2	7.4	8.3	9.0	8.7	7.3	6.9	9.2	5.5	6.2	35%	5.0	7.2%	7.3%	8.1%
6.4%	1978	7.3	7.0	6.3	6.0	7.0	8.5	7.5	9.5	9.5	7.6	8.4	7.9	7.1	7.9	7.3	40%	5.4	7.7%	7.6%	8.6%
6.6%	1979	7.4	7.1	6.2	8.1	8.1	8.7	9.7	9.9	9.2	8.3	9.4	6.2	9.8	8.6	7.7	42%	6.0	8.3%	8.3%	9.0%
6.6%	1980	7.4	6.9	8.3	9.5	8.5	9.9	9.9	9.9	9.9	9.4	7.2	8.2	9.9	9.9	6.7	38%	6.2	8.8%	9.0%	9.0%
6.4%	1981	7.6	9.5	9.5	9.5	9.5	9.5	9.5	9.5	9.5	9.4	9.5	9.5	9.5	9.5	9.5	51%	6.7	9.4%	9.3%	9.0%
6.6%	1982	9.9	9.9	9.9	9.9	9.9	9.9	9.9	9.9	9.9	9.9	9.9	9.9	9.9	9.9	9.9	55%	7.6	9.9%	9.9%	9.0%
6.6%	1983	8.8	9.1	9.9	9.9	9.2	9.9	9.7	8.6	9.6	8.9	9.9	7.0	9.9	9.5	9.3	45%	7.0	9.3%	9.4%	9.0%
6.4%	1984	8.5	9.5	9.5	9.5	9.0	9.5	7.4	9.5	9.5	9.5	8.0	9.0	9.5	9.5	8.9	44%	7.0	9.1%	9.1%	9.0%
6.4%	1985	9.5	9.5	9.4	9.5	9.5	8.2	9.3	9.5	9.5	7.8	9.5	9.0	9.5	9.5	9.4	45%	7.4	9.2%	9.2%	9.0%
6.1%	1986	9.2	8.5	8.0	9.0	6.5	9.0	8.5	9.2	7.7	8.8	9.0	9.1	9.2	9.2	6.5	36%	6.5	8.5%	8.4%	9.0%
6.1%	1987	7.4	7.8	7.8	6.6	7.6	8.7	8.6	8.0	9.0	7.7	9.2	8.3	9.2	7.4	6.4	36%	6.4	8.0%	7.9%	9.0%
6.1%	1988	8.9	9.2	7.2	9.2	9.0	9.2	7.7	9.2	9.2	9.2	9.2	9.2	9.2	8.3	5.1	30%	5.1	8.6%	8.8%	9.0%
6.1%	1989	9.2	7.6	9.0	9.2	9.2	8.3	9.2	9.2	9.2	9.2	7.4	9.2	9.2	5.6	6.8	39%	5.1	8.5%	8.9%	9.0%
5.6%	1990	7.8	8.5	8.5	8.5	8.1	8.5	8.5	8.5	8.5	8.5	8.5	8.5	7.9	8.5	8.1	39%	5.6	8.4%	8.4%	9.0%
5.9%	1991	8.8	8.8	8.8	8.8	8.8	8.8	8.8	8.8	8.8	8.8	8.8	8.8	8.8	8.8	8.8	47%	7.8	8.8%	8.8%	9.0%
5.4%	1992	8.1	8.1	8.1	8.1	8.1	8.1	8.1	8.1	8.1	8.1	8.1	8.1	8.1	8.1	8.1	44%	8.1	8.1%	8.1%	9.0%
5.2%	1993	7.7	7.7	7.7	7.7	7.7	7.7	7.7	7.7	7.7	7.7	7.7	7.7	7.7	7.7	7.7	40%	7.7	7.7%	7.7%	9.0%
5.2%	1994	7.7	7.7	7.7	7.7	7.7	7.7	7.7	7.7	7.7	7.7	7.7	7.7	7.7	7.7	3.9	18%	3.9	7.4%	7.7%	8.7%
5.0%	1995	7.6	7.6	7.6	7.6	7.6	7.6	7.6	7.6	7.6	7.6	7.6	7.6	7.6	7.6	7.6	47%	3.9	7.6%	7.6%	9.0%
4.8%	1996	7.2	7.2	7.2	7.2	7.2	7.2	7.2	7.2	7.2	7.2	7.2	7.2	7.2	7.2	7.2	38%	7.2	7.2%	7.2%	8.5%
																Totals	34%	2.9	7.6%	7.8%	8.4%

FIGURE 149

Backtesting results for recommended 15-year systemic withdrawal plan.

Systemic withdrawals are not the best solution for retirement plans of 10 years or less (again, unless the portfolio will outlive the retiree).

An Early-Retirement 50-Year Plan

Figure 150 shows a 50-year plan with the same parameters as the 40-year plan. The results aren't substantially different. The overall average is 5.9% compared to the 40-year benchmark's 6.0%. The first-10-year average is 5% compared to the 40-year benchmark's 5.3%.

FIGURE 150

Backtesting results for recommended 50-year systemic withdrawal plan.

Figure 151 shows the same 50-year plan, but with the EM floor set to 3.5%. Again, there are no problems handling the longer retirement. However, using an EM floor of 4% would fail in this case, given that MSWR-100% is 3.8%.

Initial	Year	End	Y1	Y2	Y3	Y4	Y5	Y6	Y7	Y8	Y9	Y10	Y11	Y12	Y13	Y14	Y15	Y16	Y17	Y18	Y19	Y20	Y21	Y22	Y23	Y24	Y25	Y26	Y27	Y28	Y29	Y30	Y31	Y32	Y33	Y34	Y35	Y36	Y37	Y38	Y39	Y40	Y41	Y42	Y43	Y44	Y45	Y46	Y47	Y48	Y49	Y50	%Left	Min	Avg	1st 10Y	MSWR
4.1%	1928	1977	5.6	4.2	3.6	3.5	3.6	4.2	4.2	5.2	6.1	4.2	5.1	4.8	4.3	3.5	3.5	4.2	5.2	6.1	4.9	4.0	3.8	4.3	5.2	5.4	5.8	5.2	6.1	6.1	6.1	6.1	6.1	6.1	6.1	6.1	6.1	6.1	6.1	6.1	6.1	6.1	6.1	6.1	6.1	6.1	6.1	6.1	6.1	6.1	6.1	6.1	53%	3.5	5.3%	4.4%	5.9%
4.1%	1929	1978	3.5	3.5	3.5	3.5	3.5	3.5	3.9	5.1	3.5	3.6	3.5	3.5	3.5	3.5	3.5	4.3	6.1	4.3	3.7	3.5	4.0	5.0	5.2	5.7	4.9	6.1	6.1	6.1	6.1	6.1	6.1	6.1	6.1	6.1	6.1	6.1	6.1	6.1	6.1	6.1	6.1	6.1	6.1	6.1	6.1	6.1	6.1	6.1	6.1	6.1	60%	3.5	5.1%	3.7%	5.1%
4.4%	1930	1979	3.5	3.5	3.5	3.9	3.9	4.9	6.6	4.0	4.7	4.5	4.1	3.5	3.5	4.4	5.7	6.6	5.4	4.5	4.2	4.9	5.8	5.8	6.1	5.6	6.6	6.6	6.6	6.6	6.6	6.6	6.6	6.6	6.6	6.6	6.6	6.6	6.6	6.6	6.6	6.6	6.6	6.6	6.6	6.6	6.6	6.6	6.6	6.6	6.6	6.6	48%	3.5	5.7%	4.3%	6.2%
4.7%	1931	1980	3.5	3.6	4.7	4.8	6.6	7.0	5.1	6.0	5.9	5.2	4.1	4.1	5.1	6.3	7.0	5.5	4.5	4.3	4.8	5.5	5.5	5.8	5.3	7.0	7.0	7.0	7.0	7.0	7.0	7.0	7.0	7.0	7.0	7.0	7.0	7.0	7.0	7.0	7.0	7.0	7.0	7.0	7.0	7.0	7.0	7.0	7.0	7.0	7.0	7.0	39%	3.5	6.2%	5.2%	6.7%
5.2%	1932	1981	4.5	7.8	7.8	7.8	7.8	7.8	7.8	7.8	7.8	7.4	7.2	7.8	7.8	7.8	7.8	7.1	6.4	7.4	7.8	7.4	7.6	6.9	7.8	7.8	7.8	7.8	7.8	7.8	7.8	7.8	7.8	7.8	7.8	7.8	7.8	7.8	7.8	7.8	7.8	7.8	7.8	7.8	7.8	7.8	7.8	7.8	6.7	7.8	7.8	5.4	31%	4.5	7.6%	7.4%	7.8%
5.2%	1933	1982	7.2	7.1	7.8	7.8	7.8	7.8	7.8	7.8	6.0	5.8	7.5	7.8	7.8	7.3	5.7	5.4	6.0	6.9	6.8	6.8	6.2	7.8	7.8	7.8	7.8	7.8	7.8	7.8	7.8	7.8	7.8	7.8	7.8	7.8	7.8	7.8	7.8	7.8	7.8	7.8	7.8	7.2	7.8	7.8	7.8	7.3	6.4	7.8	5.9	6.2	33%	5.4	7.3%	7.3%	7.7%
4.7%	1934	1983	4.2	5.6	7.0	4.6	5.4	5.1	4.6	3.8	3.9	4.7	5.9	7.0	5.1	4.4	4.1	4.7	5.4	5.4	5.7	5.0	7.0	7.0	7.0	7.0	7.0	7.0	7.0	7.0	7.0	7.0	7.0	7.0	7.0	7.0	7.0	7.0	7.0	7.0	7.0	7.0	7.0	7.0	7.0	7.0	7.0	7.0	7.0	7.0	7.0	7.0	43%	3.8	6.2%	4.9%	6.5%
4.7%	1935	1984	5.6	7.0	4.5	5.3	5.1	4.6	3.8	3.8	4.7	5.6	7.0	5.0	4.2	4.1	4.5	5.2	5.1	5.4	4.9	7.0	7.0	7.0	6.7	7.0	7.0	7.0	7.0	7.0	7.0	7.0	7.0	7.0	7.0	7.0	7.0	7.0	7.0	7.0	7.0	5.7	7.0	7.0	7.0	7.0	6.7	7.0	5.5	7.0	7.0	6.9	33%	3.8	6.2%	5.0%	6.4%
4.7%	1936	1985	5.4	3.7	4.0	4.0	3.8	3.5	3.5	3.8	4.5	6.5	4.3	3.8	3.7	4.0	4.6	4.7	4.8	4.5	7.0	7.0	7.0	6.2	7.0	7.0	7.0	7.0	7.0	7.0	7.0	7.0	7.0	7.0	7.0	7.0	7.0	7.0	7.0	7.0	5.8	6.4	7.0	7.0	7.0	7.0	6.9	6.1	6.7	7.0	7.0	7.0	38%	3.5	5.9%	4.3%	6.0%
4.1%	1937	1986	3.5	3.5	3.5	3.5	3.5	3.5	3.5	3.5	5.6	3.6	3.5	3.5	3.5	4.0	4.0	4.2	3.8	6.1	6.1	6.1	4.9	6.1	6.1	6.1	6.1	6.1	6.1	6.1	6.1	6.1	6.1	6.1	6.1	6.1	6.1	6.1	6.1	5.5	6.1	6.1	6.1	6.0	6.1	6.1	5.2	6.1	6.1	6.1	6.1	6.1	37%	3.5	5.2%	3.7%	5.4%
4.4%	1938	1987	5.2	5.0	4.4	3.6	3.7	4.8	6.0	6.6	5.5	4.4	4.2	4.8	5.3	5.3	5.4	5.0	6.6	6.6	6.6	6.0	6.6	6.6	6.6	6.6	6.6	6.6	6.6	6.6	6.6	6.6	6.6	6.6	6.6	6.6	6.6	6.6	6.5	6.6	6.6	6.6	6.6	6.3	6.6	5.7	6.4	6.6	6.5	6.6	6.6	6.6	31%	3.6	6.0%	4.9%	6.5%
4.4%	1939	1988	4.1	3.7	3.5	3.5	4.0	5.0	6.6	4.5	3.9	3.7	4.2	5.0	4.9	5.2	4.6	6.6	6.6	6.6	6.6	6.6	6.6	6.6	6.6	6.6	6.6	6.6	6.6	6.6	6.6	6.6	6.6	6.6	6.6	6.6	6.6	6.6	6.6	6.6	6.6	6.6	6.6	6.6	6.6	6.6	6.6	6.6	6.6	6.6	6.6	6.6	51%	3.5	5.9%	4.3%	6.2%
4.4%	1940	1989	3.8	3.5	3.5	4.2	5.2	6.6	4.7	4.0	3.8	4.3	5.2	5.1	5.3	4.8	6.6	6.6	6.6	6.6	6.6	6.6	6.6	6.6	6.6	6.6	6.6	6.6	6.6	6.6	6.6	6.6	6.6	6.6	6.6	6.6	6.6	6.6	6.6	6.6	6.6	6.5	6.6	5.5	6.6	6.6	6.6	6.6	6.6	6.6	6.6	6.6	44%	3.5	6.0%	4.4%	6.3%
4.4%	1941	1990	3.5	3.6	4.7	6.2	6.6	5.6	4.5	4.2	4.9	5.5	5.5	5.7	5.0	6.6	6.6	6.6	6.5	6.6	6.6	6.6	6.6	6.6	6.6	6.6	6.6	6.6	6.6	6.6	6.6	6.6	6.6	6.6	6.6	6.3	6.5	6.6	6.6	6.4	6.5	6.3	5.8	6.6	6.6	6.6	6.6	6.6	6.6	6.6	6.6	6.4	31%	3.5	6.2%	4.9%	6.2%
4.7%	1942	1991	4.3	5.7	6.9	7.0	6.3	5.0	4.6	5.2	5.9	5.6	6.0	5.3	7.0	7.0	7.0	6.7	7.0	7.0	7.0	7.0	7.0	7.0	7.0	7.0	7.0	7.0	7.0	7.0	7.0	7.0	7.0	7.0	5.0	5.9	6.9	6.2	5.7	5.4	5.8	4.8	6.7	7.0	7.0	7.0	7.0	7.0	7.0	7.0	5.6	6.9	33%	4.3	6.4%	5.7%	6.5%
4.9%	1943	1992	5.3	6.6	7.4	5.9	4.8	4.6	5.0	5.5	5.5	5.5	5.2	7.4	7.4	7.4	6.2	7.4	7.4	7.4	7.4	7.4	7.4	7.4	7.4	7.4	7.4	7.4	7.4	7.4	7.4	7.4	6.5	4.4	5.1	6.4	5.4	5.2	5.5	5.4	5.0	5.8	7.4	6.4	7.4	7.4	6.8	7.4	7.4	5.8	7.2	6.6	33%	4.4	6.5%	5.6%	6.5%
4.7%	1944	1993	4.9	6.9	4.4	4.0	3.8	4.1	4.6	4.6	4.8	4.4	6.8	7.0	6.9	5.6	7.0	7.0	7.0	7.0	7.0	7.0	7.0	7.0	7.0	7.0	7.0	7.0	7.0	7.0	7.0	5.8	4.2	4.6	6.0	5.5	4.8	5.2	5.6	4.7	6.2	7.0	7.0	7.0	7.0	7.0	7.0	7.0	4.9	7.0	7.0	7.0	38%	3.8	6.1%	4.7%	6.1%
4.7%	1945	1994	5.6	3.9	3.6	3.6	3.7	4.1	4.1	4.2	4.0	5.6	6.6	5.9	4.8	6.4	6.4	6.2	7.0	6.1	6.6	7.0	7.0	6.8	7.0	7.0	6.8	6.8	7.0	6.9	4.6	3.8	4.2	4.9	4.6	4.5	4.4	4.8	4.5	5.2	7.0	5.9	7.0	7.0	7.0	7.0	7.0	5.0	6.6	7.0	7.0	6.3	31%	3.6	5.7%	4.2%	5.6%
4.7%	1946	1995	3.5	3.5	3.5	3.5	3.5	3.6	3.6	3.5	4.5	5.1	4.9	4.1	5.2	5.5	5.1	6.2	5.2	5.7	6.4	7.0	6.0	7.0	7.0	6.2	6.0	6.5	6.5	4.3	3.6	3.9	4.7	4.3	4.2	4.4	4.4	4.2	5.3	6.6	6.1	7.0	7.0	6.3	7.0	7.0	4.7	7.0	7.0	7.0	7.0	7.0	37%	3.5	5.4%	3.8%	5.2%
4.7%	1947	1996	3.7	3.6	3.9	4.4	4.4	4.5	4.1	6.1	7.0	6.5	5.3	6.9	6.9	6.9	7.0	6.6	6.9	7.0	7.0	6.9	7.0	7.0	7.0	7.0	7.0	7.0	5.0	3.8	4.1	5.2	5.0	4.5	4.7	5.1	4.4	5.8	7.0	6.4	7.0	7.0	7.0	7.0	7.0	6.1	7.0	7.0	7.0	7.0	7.0	7.0	48%	3.6	6.0%	4.8%	5.9%
4.9%	1948	1997	4.0	4.3	4.9	5.0	5.1	4.7	6.5	7.1	6.5	5.3	7.2	7.2	6.9	7.4	6.8	7.2	7.4	7.4	7.2	7.4	7.4	6.5	6.5	7.0	6.7	4.8	4.0	4.2	4.8	4.7	4.5	4.4	4.6	4.4	5.1	6.8	6.3	7.4	7.4	6.4	7.4	7.4	5.8	7.4	7.4	7.4	6.9	7.4	7.4	7.4	50%	4.0	6.2%	5.3%	6.3%
4.9%	1949	1998	4.6	4.9	4.8	5.0	4.6	6.4	7.1	6.3	5.3	7.0	7.3	7.0	7.4	6.9	7.0	7.4	7.4	7.1	7.4	7.4	6.5	6.5	6.8	6.8	4.8	4.0	4.3	4.8	4.5	4.4	4.6	4.5	4.3	5.4	6.5	6.2	7.4	7.4	7.2	7.4	7.4	5.2	7.4	7.4	7.4	7.4	7.4	7.4	7.4	7.4	54%	4.0	6.3%	5.6%	6.1%
4.9%	1950	1999	4.5	4.4	4.6	4.4	6.0	6.6	6.0	5.0	6.4	6.4	6.3	7.1	6.1	6.5	6.9	7.4	6.4	7.4	7.4	6.0	6.0	6.4	6.2	4.6	3.9	4.1	4.8	4.4	4.2	4.3	4.6	4.2	5.1	6.8	5.8	7.4	7.4	7.0	7.4	7.4	5.5	7.4	7.4	7.4	7.4	7.4	7.4	7.4	7.4	7.4	59%	3.9	6.1%	5.4%	5.9%
4.7%	1951	2000	4.1	4.3	4.0	5.7	6.3	5.7	4.6	6.2	6.6	6.3	7.0	6.2	6.4	7.0	7.0	6.6	7.0	7.0	6.2	6.0	6.3	6.2	4.4	3.7	3.9	4.5	4.3	4.0	4.1	4.3	4.1	4.9	6.5	6.1	7.0	7.0	7.0	7.0	7.0	5.3	7.0	7.0	7.0	7.0	7.0	7.0	7.0	7.0	7.0	7.0	56%	3.7	6.0%	5.4%	5.8%
4.7%	1952	2001	4.3	4.0	5.8	6.8	6.1	5.0	6.5	6.5	6.5	7.0	6.2	6.6	6.9	7.0	6.6	7.0	7.0	6.4	6.4	6.6	6.4	4.4	3.7	3.9	4.6	4.3	4.2	4.2	4.4	4.2	5.5	6.5	6.4	7.0	7.0	7.0	7.0	7.0	6.6	7.0	7.0	7.0	7.0	7.0	7.0	7.0	7.0	7.0	7.0	7.0	66%	3.7	6.1%	5.9%	6.1%
4.5%	1953	2002	3.9	5.6	6.3	5.9	4.8	6.1	6.1	5.8	6.7	5.8	6.3	6.7	6.7	6.3	6.7	6.7	5.9	5.9	6.3	5.9	4.2	3.5	3.7	4.3	4.0	3.9	4.0	4.0	3.8	4.8	6.5	5.7	6.7	6.7	6.7	6.7	6.7	5.7	6.7	6.7	6.7	6.7	6.7	6.7	6.7	6.7	6.7	6.7	6.7	6.7	49%	3.5	5.8%	5.7%	5.7%
4.8%	1954	2003	5.8	6.5	5.9	5.1	6.4	6.4	6.1	7.0	6.1	6.4	7.1	7.3	6.4	7.3	7.3	6.2	6.0	6.4	6.3	4.4	3.8	4.0	4.4	4.3	4.1	4.1	4.3	4.0	4.8	6.0	6.1	7.3	7.3	7.2	7.3	7.3	6.3	7.3	7.3	7.3	7.3	7.3	7.3	7.3	7.3	7.3	7.3	7.3	7.3	7.3	55%	3.8	6.3%	6.2%	6.1%
4.5%	1955	2004	4.6	4.3	3.7	4.8	4.9	4.6	5.4	4.6	5.1	5.5	6.5	5.3	6.7	6.7	5.2	5.1	5.3	5.3	3.9	3.5	3.5	3.9	3.7	3.6	3.7	3.8	3.7	4.3	5.4	5.4	6.7	6.7	6.7	6.7	6.7	6.1	6.7	6.7	6.7	6.7	6.7	6.7	6.7	6.7	6.7	6.7	6.7	6.7	6.7	6.7	69%	3.5	5.5%	4.8%	5.3%
4.5%	1956	2005	4.0	3.5	4.3	4.6	4.3	5.1	4.4	4.6	5.2	5.9	5.1	6.5	6.7	5.0	4.9	5.2	5.0	3.8	3.5	3.5	3.8	3.6	3.5	3.6	3.7	3.6	4.3	5.0	4.9	6.6	6.7	6.1	6.7	6.7	5.4	6.7	6.7	6.7	6.7	6.7	6.7	6.7	6.7	6.7	6.7	6.7	6.7	6.7	6.7	6.7	61%	3.5	5.4%	4.6%	5.1%
4.5%	1957	2006	3.7	4.5	4.7	4.5	5.3	4.6	4.8	5.3	6.2	5.1	6.6	6.7	5.0	5.0	5.2	5.1	3.8	3.5	3.5	3.8	3.6	3.5	3.6	3.7	3.6	4.1	5.3	4.9	6.5	6.7	6.6	6.7	6.7	6.0	6.7	6.7	6.7	6.7	6.7	6.7	6.7	6.7	6.7	6.7	6.7	6.7	6.7	6.7	6.7	6.7	70%	3.5	5.5%	4.9%	5.2%
4.5%	1958	2007	5.9	6.1	5.8	6.7	5.8	6.1	6.6	6.7	6.3	6.7	6.7	5.9	5.7	6.1	5.8	4.2	3.5	3.7	4.2	3.9	3.7	3.8	3.8	3.7	4.4	5.5	5.5	6.7	6.7	6.7	6.7	6.7	6.6	6.7	6.7	6.7	6.7	6.7	6.7	6.7	6.7	6.7	6.7	6.7	6.7	6.7	6.7	6.7	6.7	6.7	73%	3.5	5.9%	6.3%	5.9%
4.3%	1959	2008	4.4	4.2	4.9	4.3	4.6	5.1	5.8	4.8	6.3	6.4	4.9	4.8	5.0	4.9	3.6	3.5	3.5	3.6	3.5	3.5	3.5	3.5	3.5	3.9	4.8	4.6	6.3	6.4	5.8	6.4	6.4	5.5	6.4	6.4	6.4	6.4	6.4	6.4	6.4	6.4	6.4	6.4	6.4	6.4	6.4	6.4	6.4	6.4	6.4	6.4	44%	3.5	5.3%	5.1%	5.1%
4.1%	1960	2009	4.2	4.8	4.2	4.5	4.9	5.8	4.7	6.1	6.1	4.9	4.9	5.1	4.9	3.5	3.5	3.5	3.5	3.5	3.5	3.5	3.5	3.5	3.9	4.8	4.6	6.1	6.1	5.9	6.1	6.1	6.0	6.1	6.1	6.1	6.1	6.1	6.1	6.1	6.1	6.1	6.1	6.1	6.1	6.1	6.1	6.1	6.1	6.1	6.1	6.1	59%	3.5	5.2%	5.0%	5.1%
4.1%	1961	2010	5.1	4.4	4.6	5.2	5.9	4.9	6.1	6.1	4.7	4.6	5.0	4.8	3.5	3.5	3.5	3.5	3.5	3.5	3.5	3.5	3.5	3.5	4.2	4.2	5.4	6.1	5.3	5.9	6.1	4.8	6.1	6.1	6.1	6.1	6.1	6.1	6.1	6.1	6.1	6.1	6.1	6.1	6.1	6.1	6.1	6.1	6.1	6.1	6.1	6.1	60%	3.5	5.2%	5.2%	5.0%
4.1%	1962	1928	3.8	4.1	4.4	5.4	4.4	6.1	6.1	4.6	4.5	4.8	4.8	3.5	3.5	3.5	3.5	3.5	3.5	3.5	3.5	3.5	3.7	4.5	4.4	5.9	6.1	5.6	6.1	6.1	5.0	6.1	6.1	6.1	6.1	6.1	6.1	6.1	6.1	6.1	6.1	6.1	6.1	6.1	6.1	6.1	6.1	6.1	6.1	6.1	6.1	6.2	85%	3.5	5.2%	4.8%	5.0%
4.1%	1963	1929	4.7	5.2	6.0	5.1	6.1	6.1	5.0	4.8	5.2	5.0	3.6	3.5	3.5	3.6	3.5	3.5	3.5	3.5	3.5	3.8	4.5	4.4	5.7	6.1	5.5	6.1	6.1	5.2	6.1	6.1	6.1	6.1	6.1	6.1	6.1	6.1	6.1	6.1	6.1	6.1	6.1	6.1	6.1	6.1	6.1	6.1	6.2	6.2	68%	3.5	5.3%	5.3%	5.3%
4.1%	1964	1930	4.7	5.6	4.6	6.1	6.1	4.8	4.6	4.8	4.8	3.5	3.5	3.5	3.5	3.5	3.5	3.5	3.5	3.5	3.8	4.4	4.3	5.6	6.1	5.4	6.0	6.1	5.2	6.1	6.1	6.1	6.1	6.1	6.1	6.1	6.1	6.1	6.1	6.1	6.1	6.1	6.1	6.1	6.1	6.1	6.1	6.2	6.2	6.2	49%	3.5	5.3%	5.0%	5.2%
4.0%	1965	1931	5.1	4.3	5.5	6.0	4.3	4.2	4.4	4.3	3.5	3.5	3.5	3.5	3.5	3.5	3.5	3.5	3.5	3.5	3.8	3.6	4.6	5.3	4.5	5.0	5.7	4.1	6.0	6.0	6.0	6.0	6.0	6.0	6.0	6.0	6.0	6.0	6.0	6.0	6.0	6.0	6.0	6.0	6.0	6.0	6.0	6.0	6.1	6.1	6.1	6.1	30%	3.5	5.1%	4.5%	4.7%
3.8%	1966	1932	3.9	5.1	5.7	4.0	3.9	4.1	4.0	3.5	3.5	3.5	3.5	3.5	3.5	3.5	3.5	3.5	3.5	3.5	3.5	4.1	4.7	4.0	4.5	5.2	3.7	5.3	5.7	5.7	5.7	5.7	5.7	5.7	5.7	5.7	5.7	5.7	5.7	5.7	5.7	5.7	5.7	5.7	5.7	5.7	5.7	5.8	5.8	5.8	5.8	5.8	34%	3.5	4.8%	4.1%	4.4%
4.1%	1967	1933	5.9	6.1	4.4	4.4	4.6	4.5	3.5	3.5	3.5	3.5	3.5	3.5	3.5	3.5	3.5	3.5	4.0	3.9	5.0	5.6	4.7	5.2	6.0	4.5	6.1	6.1	6.1	6.1	6.1	6.1	6.1	6.1	6.1	6.1	6.1	6.1	6.1	6.1	6.1	6.1	6.1	6.1	6.1	6.1	6.2	6.2	6.2	6.2	6.2	6.2	47%	3.5	5.3%	4.4%	4.9%
4.0%	1968	1934	5.0	3.6	3.5	3.7	3.7	3.5	3.5	3.5	3.5	3.5	3.5	3.5	3.5	3.5	3.5	3.5	3.5	3.6	4.0	3.5	3.8	4.3	3.5	4.4	5.1	5.9	5.1	6.0	6.0	6.0	6.0	6.0	6.0	6.0	6.0	6.0	6.0	6.0	6.0	6.0	6.0	6.0	6.0	6.1	6.1	3.9	3.5	3.5	3.5	3.5	15%	3.5	4.6%	3.7%	4.2%
4.0%	1969	1935	3.5	3.5	3.5	3.5	3.5	3.5	3.5	3.5	3.5	3.5	3.5	3.5	3.5	3.5	3.5	3.5	3.5	3.5	3.5	3.5	3.5	3.5	3.5	4.0	4.5	4.0	5.4	5.6	6.0	6.0	6.0	6.0	6.0	6.0	6.0	6.0	6.0	6.0	6.0	3.5	5.3	6.0	6.1	5.7	3.5	3.5	3.5	3.5	3.5	3.5	5%	3.5	4.4%	3.5%	3.8%
4.0%	1970	1936	4.2	4.4	4.3	3.5	3.5	3.5	3.5	3.5	3.5	3.5	3.5	3.5	3.5	4.1	3.9	5.1	5.7	4.8	5.3	5.9	4.5	6.0	6.0	6.0	6.0	6.0	6.0	6.0	6.0	6.0	6.0	6.0	6.0	6.0	6.0	6.0	6.0	6.0	6.0	6.0	6.0	6.1	6.1	6.1	6.1	6.1	6.1	6.1	6.1	6.1	88%	3.5	5.2%	3.7%	4.8%
4.3%	1971	1937	4.5	4.4	3.5	3.5	3.5	3.5	3.5	3.5	3.5	3.5	3.5	3.6	4.1	4.1	5.0	5.8	4.8	5.3	6.1	4.5	6.1	6.4	6.4	6.4	6.4	6.4	6.4	6.4	6.4	6.4	6.4	6.4	6.4	6.4	6.4	6.4	6.4	6.4	6.4	6.4	6.5	6.5	6.5	6.5	6.5	6.5	6.5	6.5	6.5	6.5	52%	3.5	5.5%	3.7%	5.1%
4.1%	1972	1938	4.3	3.5	3.5	3.5	3.5	3.5	3.5	3.5	3.5	3.5	3.5	4.1	3.9	5.0	5.6	4.8	5.1	5.8	4.5	5.8	6.1	6.1	6.1	6.1	6.1	6.1	6.1	6.1	6.1	6.1	6.1	6.1	6.1	6.1	6.1	6.1	6.1	6.1	6.1	6.2	6.2	6.2	6.2	6.2	6.2	6.2	6.2	6.2	6.2	6.2	69%	3.5	5.4%	3.6%	4.8%
4.1%	1973	1939	3.5	3.5	3.5	3.5	3.5	3.5	3.5	3.5	3.5	3.5	4.0	3.8	4.7	5.4	4.5	5.1	5.5	4.2	5.8	6.1	6.1	5.8	6.1	6.1	6.1	6.1	6.1	6.1	6.1	6.1	6.1	6.1	6.1	6.1	6.1	6.1	6.1	6.1	6.2	6.2	6.2	6.2	6.2	6.2	6.2	6.2	6.2	6.2	6.2	6.2	62%	3.5	5.4%	3.5%	4.8%
4.5%	1974	1940	3.5	3.7	4.3	4.1	3.9	4.0	4.0	3.8	4.6	5.3	5.3	6.6	6.7	6.5	6.7	6.7	5.8	6.7	6.7	6.7	6.7	6.7	6.7	6.7	6.7	6.7	6.7	6.7	6.7	6.7	6.7	6.7	6.7	6.7	6.7	6.7	6.7	6.8	6.8	6.8	6.8	6.8	6.8	6.8	6.8	6.8	6.8	6.8	6.8	6.8	91%	3.5	6.2%	4.1%	5.9%
5.0%	1975	1941	5.0	6.4	5.7	5.3	5.1	5.1	4.7	5.9	6.8	6.8	7.6	7.6	7.6	7.6	7.6	7.6	7.6	7.6	7.6	7.6	7.6	7.6	7.6	7.6	7.6	7.6	7.6	7.6	7.6	7.6	7.6	7.6	7.6	7.6	7.6	7.6	7.6	7.6	7.6	7.6	7.6	7.6	7.6	7.6	7.6	7.6	7.6	7.6	7.6	7.6	127%	4.7	7.2%	5.7%	7.3%
4.8%	1976	1942	5.0	4.6	4.4	4.5	4.4	4.2	5.0	5.7	5.8	7.2	7.3	7.2	7.2	7.3	6.3	7.3	7.3	7.3	7.3	7.3	7.3	7.3	7.3	7.3	7.3	7.3	7.3	7.3	7.3	7.3	7.3	7.3	7.3	7.3	7.3	7.4	7.4	7.4	7.4	7.4	7.4	7.4	7.4	7.4	7.4	7.4	7.4	7.4	7.4	7.4	83%	4.2	6.9%	5.1%	6.6%
4.8%	1977	1943	4.0	3.9	3.9	3.9	3.8	4.3	4.7	4.7	5.9	6.6	5.7	6.0	6.6	5.4	6.8	7.3	7.3	6.8	7.3	7.3	7.3	7.3	7.3	7.3	7.3	7.3	7.3	7.3	7.3	7.3	7.3	7.3	7.3	7.3	7.4	7.4	7.4	7.3	7.4	7.4	7.4	7.4	7.4	7.4	7.4	7.4	7.4	7.4	7.4	7.4	50%	3.8	6.7%	4.6%	6.0%
5.0%	1978	1944	4.0	4.0	4.1	4.0	4.5	5.0	5.0	6.1	7.1	6.0	6.4	7.0	5.6	7.3	7.6	7.6	7.0	7.6	7.6	7.6	7.6	7.6	7.6	7.6	7.6	7.6	7.6	7.6	7.6	7.6	7.6	7.6	7.6	7.6	7.6	7.6	7.6	7.6	7.6	7.6	7.6	7.6	7.6	7.6	7.6	7.6	7.6	7.6	7.6	7.6	66%	4.0	7.0%	5.0%	6.3%
5.2%	1979	1945	4.2	4.2	4.1	4.7	5.1	5.1	6.2	7.0	6.1	6.4	7.2	5.8	7.3	7.8	7.8	7.1	7.8	7.8	7.8	7.8	7.8	7.8	7.8	7.8	7.8	7.8	7.8	7.8	7.8	7.8	7.8	7.8	7.9	7.9	7.9	7.5	7.9	7.9	7.9	7.9	7.9	7.9	7.9	7.9	7.9	7.7	6.6	7.9	7.9	7.9	79%	4.1	7.2%	5.3%	6.6%
5.2%	1980	1946	4.2	4.1	4.5	5.1	5.1	6.2	6.9	5.9	6.4	6.9	5.7	7.2	7.7	7.8	6.9	7.8	7.8	7.8	7.8	7.8	7.8	7.8	7.8	7.8	7.8	7.8	7.8	7.8	7.8	7.8	7.8	7.9	7.9	7.9	6.2	7.9	7.9	7.9	7.9	7.9	7.9	7.9	7.9	7.9	6.0	6.7	7.9	7.9	7.9	7.9	57%	4.1	7.2%	5.5%	6.6%
5.0%	1981	1947	4.0	4.6	5.2	5.3	6.6	7.4	6.3	6.5	7.3	5.9	7.5	7.6	7.6	7.3	7.6	7.6	7.6	7.6	7.6	7.6	7.6	7.6	7.6	7.6	7.6	7.6	7.6	7.6	7.6	7.6	7.6	7.6	7.6	7.6	7.6	7.6	7.6	7.6	7.6	7.6	7.6	7.6	7.6	7.6	7.6	7.6	7.6	7.6	7.6	7.6	58%	4.0	7.3%	5.9%	6.9%
5.2%	1982	1948	4.9	5.4	5.4	6.8	7.7	6.5	6.7	7.3	6.1	7.7	7.8	7.8	7.3	7.8	7.8	7.8	7.8	7.8	7.8	7.8	7.8	7.8	7.8	7.8	7.8	7.8	7.8	7.8	7.8	7.9	7.9	7.9	7.9	7.9	7.9	7.9	7.9	7.9	7.9	7.9	7.9	7.9	7.9	7.9	7.9	7.9	7.9	7.9	7.9	7.9	43%	4.9	7.6%	6.5%	7.3%
5.2%	1983	1949	4.5	4.5	5.3	6.0	5.2	5.5	6.0	5.0	6.3	6.7	7.6	6.1	7.7	7.7	7.8	7.8	7.8	7.8	7.8	7.8	7.8	7.8	7.8	7.8	7.8	6.2	7.0	7.7	7.9	7.7	6.6	5.2	6.5	7.9	7.8	7.9	7.9	7.8	7.9	7.9	7.5	4.9	5.7	7.8	7.9	7.9	7.9	7.9	6.7	7.0	35%	4.5	7.0%	5.5%	6.6%
5.0%	1984	1950	4.1	4.7	5.2	4.7	5.0	5.4	4.5	5.5	6.1	6.7	5.7	7.2	7.0	7.6	7.6	7.6	7.6	7.6	7.4	7.6	7.6	7.6	7.6	7.6	5.5	6.1	7.4	7.6	6.7	5.7	4.9	5.7	7.5	7.5	7.6	7.6	7.5	7.6	7.6	6.2	4.9	4.8	7.6	7.6	7.6	7.6	7.2	7.6	7.6	7.6	39%	4.1	6.7%	5.2%	6.3%
5.0%	1985	1951	4.8	5.3	4.7	5.1	5.5	4.6	5.6	6.0	6.9	5.6	7.2	7.1	7.6	7.6	7.6	7.6	7.6	7.2	7.6	7.6	7.6	7.6	7.4	5.4	5.9	6.9	7.6	6.5	5.4	4.7	5.9	7.2	7.4	7.6	7.6	7.5	7.6	7.6	6.9	4.6	5.1	7.1	7.6	7.6	7.6	7.6	6.0	7.6	7.6	7.6	44%	4.6	6.7%	5.4%	6.4%
4.8%	1986	1952	4.5	4.1	4.3	4.7	4.0	4.7	5.1	5.6	4.9	6.0	6.2	7.2	7.2	7.3	6.8	7.2	6.0	7.3	7.3	6.9	7.2	6.5	4.6	5.2	5.9	7.4	6.0	4.7	4.1	4.8	6.4	6.1	7.4	7.4	6.2	7.4	7.4	5.8	4.5	4.4	7.1	7.4	7.4	7.4	7.1	6.4	7.1	7.4	7.4	7.4	44%	4.0	6.2%	4.8%	5.8%
4.8%	1987	1953	3.9	4.0	4.2	3.8	4.3	4.6	5.1	4.4	5.5	5.5	6.9	6.9	6.7	6.2	6.4	5.4	6.7	6.9	6.4	6.7	6.1	4.6	4.9	5.7	7.2	5.5	4.9	4.2	4.9	6.3	6.5	7.4	7.4	6.6	7.3	7.2	6.2	4.4	4.6	5.9	7.4	7.4	7.4	7.3	5.6	7.4	7.4	7.4	7.4	7.4	37%	3.8	6.0%	4.5%	5.6%
4.8%	1988	1954	4.4	4.7	4.0	4.9	5.3	5.8	4.9	6.2	6.3	7.3	7.3	7.3	7.0	7.3	6.3	7.3	7.3	7.1	7.3	6.5	4.7	5.1	5.9	7.4	5.7	4.9	4.3	4.9	6.2	6.5	7.4	7.4	6.9	7.4	7.4	6.6	4.8	4.7	7.0	7.4	7.4	7.4	7.4	6.1	6.9	7.4	7.4	7.4	7.4	7.4	58%	4.0	6.4%	5.4%	6.1%
4.8%	1989	1955	4.4	3.9	4.4	4.9	5.4	4.6	5.7	5.6	6.9	7.0	7.1	6.5	6.7	5.7	7.0	7.2	6.5	7.0	6.4	4.8	5.1	5.8	7.2	5.6	5.0	4.5	5.6	6.4	6.5	7.4	7.4	6.0	7.4	7.3	5.8	4.5	4.8	6.5	7.4	7.4	7.4	6.9	7.1	7.4	7.4	7.4	7.4	7.4	7.4	7.4	71%	3.9	6.3%	5.3%	6.0%
4.5%	1990	1956	3.6	4.2	4.6	5.2	4.4	5.5	5.5	6.5	6.7	6.6	6.1	6.4	5.1	6.6	6.6	6.3	6.6	5.9	4.3	4.6	5.3	6.8	5.1	4.4	3.8	4.5	5.8	5.6	6.8	6.8	6.4	6.8	6.8	6.2	4.3	4.5	6.5	6.8	6.8	6.8	6.5	5.2	6.8	6.8	6.8	6.8	6.8	6.8	6.8	6.8	63%	3.6	5.9%	5.3%	5.7%
4.7%	1991	1957	5.2	5.7	6.3	5.3	6.8	6.7	7.0	7.0	7.0	7.0	7.0	6.2	7.0	7.0	7.0	7.0	6.7	4.9	5.4	6.0	7.1	5.7	4.9	4.4	5.2	6.5	6.8	7.1	7.1	7.0	7.1	7.1	7.1	5.2	4.9	7.0	7.1	7.1	7.1	6.3	6.1	6.8	7.1	7.1	7.1	7.1	7.1	7.1	7.1	7.1	53%	4.4	6.5%	6.4%	6.5%
4.3%	1992	1958	4.6	5.2	4.3	5.7	5.6	6.4	6.4	6.4	6.4	6.4	5.6	6.4	6.4	6.4	6.4	6.3	4.5	4.9	5.6	6.5	5.2	4.5	3.9	4.8	5.8	6.0	6.5	6.5	6.2	6.5	6.5	6.4	4.7	4.8	6.3	6.5	6.5	6.5	6.5	5.7	6.5	6.5	6.5	6.5	6.5	6.5	6.5	6.5	6.5	6.5	88%	3.9	6.0%	5.7%	6.0%
4.1%	1993	1959	4.8	4.1	5.3	5.5	6.1	6.1	6.1	5.8	6.1	4.9	6.1	6.1	6.1	6.1	5.7	4.0	4.3	5.1	6.2	4.7	4.0	3.5	3.9	5.0	5.0	6.2	6.2	5.4	6.2	6.2	6.0	4.1	4.3	6.2	6.2	6.2	6.2	6.2	5.7	6.2	6.2	6.2	6.2	6.2	6.2	6.2	6.2	6.2	6.2	6.2	81%	3.5	5.6%	5.5%	5.6%
4.1%	1994	1960	3.8	4.7	4.7	6.0	6.0	6.0	5.4	5.7	4.7	6.0	6.1	5.7	6.0	5.5	4.0	4.3	4.8	6.1	4.4	3.5	3.5	3.5	4.1	4.2	5.7	6.2	4.7	5.5	5.3	4.8	3.8	3.8	5.7	6.2	6.2	6.2	6.2	5.5	6.2	6.2	6.2	6.2	6.2	6.2	6.2	6.2	6.2	6.2	6.2	6.2	87%	3.5	5.4%	5.3%	5.4%
4.0%	1995	1961	5.7	5.7	6.0	6.0	6.0	6.0	6.0	5.7	6.0	6.0	6.0	6.0	6.0	4.9	5.2	5.9	6.1	5.7	4.8	4.1	5.1	6.0	6.0	6.1	6.1	5.9	6.1	6.1	5.9	4.4	4.8	6.1	6.1	6.1	6.1	6.1	6.1	6.1	6.1	6.1	6.1	6.1	6.1	6.1	6.1	6.1	6.1	6.1	6.1	6.1	112%	4.1	5.8%	5.9%	6.1%
3.8%	1996	1962	4.6	5.7	5.7	5.7	5.5	5.6	4.5	5.7	5.7	5.6	5.7	5.5	3.8	4.2	4.8	5.8	4.5	3.9	3.5	3.9	4.8	4.8	5.8	5.8	4.5	5.6	5.6	4.6	3.5	3.8	5.8	5.8	5.8	5.8	5.8	5.8	5.8	5.8	5.8	5.8	5.8	5.8	5.8	5.8	5.8	5.8	5.8	5.8	5.8	5.8	96%	3.5	5.3%	5.4%	5.4%
3.8%	1997	1963	5.6	5.6	5.6	5.3	5.6	4.5	5.6	5.7	5.4	5.6	5.1	3.5	3.8	4.4	5.7	4.2	3.5	3.5	3.5	3.9	4.0	5.3	5.8	4.3	5.2	5.1	4.6	3.5	3.5	5.1	5.8	5.8	5.8	5.7	4.9	5.8	5.8	5.8	5.8	5.8	5.8	5.8	5.8	5.8	5.8	5.8	5.8	5.8	5.8	5.8	87%	3.5	5.1%	5.5%	5.3%
3.8%	1998	1964	4.6	4.8	4.2	4.6	3.5	4.7	4.9	4.6	5.0	4.4	3.5	3.5	3.9	5.3	3.7	3.5	3.5	3.5	3.5	3.5	4.4	5.8	3.6	4.4	4.2	3.8	3.5	3.5	4.2	5.8	5.8	5.8	5.0	4.6	5.4	5.8	5.8	5.8	5.8	5.8	5.8	5.8	5.8	5.8	5.8	5.8	5.8	5.8	5.8	5.8	90%	3.5	4.8%	4.5%	4.7%
3.8%	1999	1965	4.7	4.1	4.4	3.5	4.7	4.9	4.5	4.9	4.5	3.5	3.5	4.0	5.2	3.8	3.5	3.5	3.5	3.6	3.6	4.6	5.8	3.7	4.4	4.4	3.9	3.5	3.5	4.3	5.8	5.8	5.8	4.7	4.4	5.6	5.8	5.8	5.8	5.8	5.8	5.8	5.8	5.8	5.8	5.8	5.8	5.8	5.8	5.8	5.8	5.8	99%	3.5	4.8%	4.4%	4.8%
3.6%	2000	1966	4.3	4.5	3.6	4.8	5.1	4.6	4.9	4.3	3.5	3.5	3.8	5.2	3.5	3.5	3.5	3.5	3.5	3.5	4.1	5.5	3.5	3.9	3.8	3.5	3.5	3.5	4.0	5.5	5.5	5.5	4.9	4.2	5.4	5.5	5.5	5.5	5.5	5.5	5.5	5.5	5.5	5.5	5.5	5.5	5.5	5.5	5.5	5.5	5.5	5.5	99%	3.5	4.7%	4.3%	4.6%
																																																			Totals	63%	3.5	5.9%	5.0%	5.8%

FIGURE 151

Backtesting results for 50-year systemic withdrawal plan with 3.5% EM floor.

A Less Volatile but Affordable Plan

Some retirees prefer a lower stock percentage. There are two options for doing this. The first is by reducing the initial stock percentage. The second is by putting a cap on Prime Harvesting's maximum stock percentage. Neither is optimal based on known risk, but the withdrawal rate can be lowered to compensate.

Figure 152 shows the results for both options combined: the initial stock percentage is lowered to 45%, and a 70% upper stock limit is maintained in Prime Harvesting. The initial income is also lowered appropriately by 5%. The total income average drops to 5.6%, compared to the 6% for the benchmark cases. The income average for the first 10-years drops to 5.1% from 5.3%. The average percentage left drops to 38% from 56%. MSWR-100% also drops to 3.8% (triggering a failure if an EM floor of 4% was used). Unexpectedly, the income floor naturally rises with the lower volatility to 2.8%, up from the benchmark 2.5% floor.

FIGURE 152

*Backtesting results for 40-year retirement with 45% initial stock allocation, a
30% bond floor, and the initial withdrawal rate dropped by 10%.*

Only a small portion of the above reductions in Baseline Market performance comes from capping Prime Harvesting at 70% stocks, making the 70% cap a reasonable choice for some retirees. But keep in mind, in every one of the specific-market tests (i.e., SBBI, Shiller, UK, and Japan) Prime Harvesting performs better with no cap set on stocks.

An earlier general conclusion still stands: the best way to lower risk is by lowering the withdrawal rate, or incorporating guaranteed income (as described in the following chapter), not by lowering the stock percentage below the established optimal. However, some retirees will sleep better with lower stock exposure, making it then the proper choice.

A Plan to Boost Income without Excessive Risk

A more aggressive but still reasonable initial stock percentage is 65% — the 40-year optimal percentage when MSWR-90% is used to measure performance instead of MSWR-100%.

Figure 153 shows results for a 40-year retirement with an initial 65% stock allocation (Chapter 7 compares the tradeoffs more thoroughly). Two additional changes are included to boost income: the tilt for the initial withdrawal rate is increased to 50%, and EM's income cap is increased to 200% of the initial rate.

FIGURE 153

Backtesting results for more aggressive 40-year systemic withdrawal plan with 65% stock allocation, a 50% tilt for the initial withdrawal rate, and annual income capped at 200% of the initial withdrawal rate.

The extra volatility caused the overall floor to drop to 2.25% compared to 2.5% for the benchmark 40-year retirement. However, the average for the first 10 years increased to 5.5% from 5.3% for the benchmark. More notably, the overall average income increased to 7% from 6.0% for the benchmark. However, the higher income caused the percentage left at the end of retirement to decrease to 31% from the benchmark's 56%, with more retirements ending with less than 20% of the starting real value. This scenario did remain successful when a 4% EM floor was used.

Generally, a better approach to boosting income is using Alternate-Prime Harvesting in place of Prime Harvesting, especially when valuations are attractive. Figure 154 shows Alternate-Prime results for a 40-year retirement, starting with the same of set of more aggressive parameters: 65% in stock, a 50% initial-withdrawal-rate tilt, and an income cap of 200% of the initial rate. The floor still dropped to 2.25% but the average for the first 10 years increased to 5.7%, and the total income average climbed to 7.7% with the percentage left increasing a little. As before, this scenario was fully successful when a 4% EM floor was used.

FIGURE 154

Backtesting results for more aggressive 40-year systemic withdrawal plan using Alternate-Prime Harvesting with 65% stock allocation, a 50% tilt for the initial withdrawal rate, and annual income capped at 200% of the initial withdrawal rate.

Based on the above numbers, boosting the initial stock percentage might seem worthwhile, but keep in mind that most of the income gain comes from years when the portfolio was already doing well. During difficult periods, risk is a little higher. Ultimately though, if the need for extra income is high, the small increase in risk may well be worth it.

A retiree should be more cautious following an aggressive plan to boost income when valuations are high, although aggressive plans can still perform well with high valuations. For very high valuation levels (e.g., above 3.5) aggressive plans should be avoided.

A Plan for Increasing Bequest Value

Leaving a significant bequest is a priority for some retirees. The easiest approach to achieving this is to put a cap on annual income. Another easy approach is to use Alternate-Prime instead of Prime Harvesting. Increasing the initial stock percentage also works.

Figure 155 shows results of combining the three approaches: capping income at a 6% inflation-adjusted rate with Alternate-Prime Harvesting and an initial stock percentage of 65%. A 30-year retirement is shown, given it better reflects portfolio value over more typical life spans (the bequest value usually continues growing with time when income is capped). The average percentage left is boosted to 184%, up from 49% for the 30-year retirement using default parameters. All three options contributed significantly, so any can be used alone or paired for a partial increase in value.

Initial	Year	Y1	Y2	Y3	Y4	Y5	Y6	Y7	Y8	Y9	Y10	Y11	Y12	Y13	Y14	Y15	Y16	Y17	Y18	Y19	Y20	Y21	Y22	Y23	Y24	Y25	Y26	Y27	Y28	Y29	Y30	%Left	Min	Avg	1st 10Y	MSWR
4.3%	1928	6.0	4.8	3.7	3.2	3.4	4.4	4.5	6.0	6.0	5.0	6.0	6.0	5.1	3.8	4.0	5.9	5.9	6.0	6.0	6.0	6.0	5.9	6.0	6.0	6.0	6.0	5.9	6.0	5.9	6.0	88%	3.2	5.4%	4.7%	6.1%
4.3%	1929	3.9	3.3	3.1	3.2	3.6	3.7	5.0	6.0	3.5	4.4	4.3	3.6	3.3	3.4	5.0	5.9	5.9	5.9	5.9	5.4	6.0	6.0	5.9	5.9	6.0	5.9	5.9	6.0	6.0	5.9	93%	3.1	4.9%	4.0%	4.8%
4.6%	1930	3.8	3.5	3.5	4.4	4.4	6.0	6.0	4.9	6.0	6.0	5.6	4.0	4.4	6.0	5.9	5.9	5.9	5.9	5.9	6.0	6.0	5.9	5.9	6.0	5.9	5.9	6.0	6.0	5.9	5.9	136%	3.5	5.4%	4.9%	6.7%
4.9%	1931	3.7	3.8	5.9	6.0	6.0	6.0	6.0	5.9	6.0	6.0	6.0	6.0	6.0	6.0	5.9	5.9	6.0	6.0	6.0	6.0	6.0	5.9	6.0	6.0	6.0	6.0	6.0	6.0	6.0	6.0	232%	3.7	5.8%	5.5%	8.1%
5.5%	1932	5.2	6.0	6.0	6.0	6.0	5.9	6.0	5.9	6.0	5.9	6.0	5.9	5.9	5.9	6.0	6.0	6.0	5.9	6.0	6.0	6.0	6.0	6.0	5.9	6.0	6.0	6.0	5.9	6.0	5.9	771%	5.2	5.9%	5.9%	9.0%
5.5%	1933	5.9	6.0	6.0	6.0	5.9	6.0	6.0	6.0	5.9	5.9	5.9	6.0	5.9	6.0	5.9	6.0	5.9	6.0	6.0	6.0	6.0	6.0	6.0	6.0	5.9	6.0	6.0	5.9	6.0	6.0	612%	5.9	6.0%	6.0%	9.0%
4.9%	1934	4.9	5.9	5.9	5.8	6.0	6.0	5.9	4.6	5.0	5.9	5.9	5.9	5.9	5.9	5.9	6.0	6.0	5.9	5.9	5.9	5.9	6.0	6.0	6.0	6.0	6.0	5.9	5.9	6.0	6.0	222%	4.6	5.8%	5.6%	8.3%
4.9%	1935	6.0	6.0	5.5	6.0	6.0	6.0	4.6	4.9	6.0	6.0	6.0	5.9	6.0	5.9	6.0	6.0	5.9	5.9	6.0	6.0	6.0	6.0	6.0	6.0	6.0	6.0	6.0	6.0	6.0	6.0	247%	4.6	5.9%	5.7%	8.6%
4.9%	1936	6.0	4.0	4.6	4.5	4.1	3.7	3.9	5.0	5.9	6.0	6.0	6.0	6.0	6.0	5.9	6.0	6.0	5.9	5.9	5.9	6.0	6.0	6.0	6.0	6.0	5.9	6.0	6.0	6.0	6.0	191%	3.7	5.6%	4.8%	7.2%
4.3%	1937	3.4	3.7	3.6	3.4	3.2	3.3	3.9	5.2	5.9	6.0	5.4	4.7	6.0	6.0	6.0	6.0	5.9	6.0	6.0	6.0	6.0	5.9	6.0	5.9	5.9	5.9	6.0	6.0	6.0	6.0	131%	3.2	5.3%	4.2%	6.0%
4.6%	1938	5.9	6.0	5.3	4.1	4.5	5.9	6.0	6.0	6.0	6.0	6.0	5.9	5.9	6.0	6.0	6.0	5.9	6.0	5.9	6.0	6.0	6.0	6.0	5.9	6.0	6.0	6.0	6.0	5.9	5.9	334%	4.1	5.8%	5.6%	8.6%
4.6%	1939	4.8	4.2	3.6	3.8	5.5	5.9	6.0	5.9	5.9	5.9	6.0	5.9	5.9	6.0	5.9	6.0	5.9	5.9	6.0	6.0	6.0	6.0	6.0	6.0	6.0	6.0	6.0	6.0	5.9	6.0	257%	3.6	5.7%	5.2%	8.0%
4.6%	1940	4.4	3.7	3.8	5.7	5.9	5.9	6.0	6.0	6.0	6.0	6.0	6.0	6.0	5.9	6.0	6.0	5.9	5.9	5.9	5.9	6.0	6.0	5.9	6.0	5.9	6.0	5.9	6.0	5.9	6.0	230%	3.7	5.8%	5.3%	8.2%
4.6%	1941	3.9	4.2	6.0	6.0	5.9	6.0	5.9	5.9	6.0	6.0	6.0	6.0	5.9	6.0	6.0	6.0	6.0	5.9	6.0	5.9	5.9	5.9	6.0	6.0	6.0	6.0	6.0	6.0	5.9	6.0	289%	3.9	5.8%	5.6%	8.8%
4.9%	1942	5.3	5.9	5.9	6.0	5.9	5.9	6.0	6.0	6.0	6.0	6.0	5.9	5.9	5.9	5.9	5.9	6.0	6.0	6.0	5.9	6.0	6.0	6.0	5.9	6.0	6.0	6.0	6.0	6.0	6.0	473%	5.3	5.9%	5.9%	9.0%
5.2%	1943	6.0	5.9	6.0	6.0	6.0	6.0	5.9	6.0	6.0	5.9	6.0	5.9	6.0	6.0	6.0	5.9	5.9	6.0	6.0	6.0	5.9	6.0	5.9	6.0	5.9	6.0	5.9	6.0	5.9	6.0	420%	5.9	6.0%	6.0%	9.0%
4.9%	1944	5.9	5.9	6.0	5.4	5.0	6.0	6.0	5.9	5.9	5.9	5.9	5.9	6.0	5.9	6.0	5.9	6.0	6.0	6.0	5.9	5.9	6.0	5.9	6.0	5.9	6.0	5.9	6.0	5.9	6.0	180%	5.0	5.9%	5.8%	8.8%
4.9%	1945	6.0	4.8	4.2	4.1	4.6	6.0	6.0	5.9	6.0	6.0	6.0	6.0	6.0	6.0	6.0	6.0	6.0	5.9	5.9	6.0	6.0	6.0	5.9	6.0	6.0	5.9	5.9	5.9	5.9	6.0	95%	4.1	5.8%	5.4%	7.8%
4.9%	1946	3.8	3.7	3.7	3.8	4.1	4.3	4.7	4.3	6.0	5.9	5.9	6.0	5.9	6.0	6.0	5.9	5.9	5.9	6.0	5.9	6.0	5.9	6.0	6.0	6.0	6.0	6.0	6.0	5.9	6.0	63%	3.7	5.5%	4.4%	6.4%
4.9%	1947	4.2	4.1	4.6	5.9	6.0	5.9	6.0	5.9	6.0	6.0	5.9	5.9	6.0	6.0	6.0	5.9	5.9	6.0	6.0	5.9	6.0	5.9	6.0	6.0	5.9	6.0	6.0	5.9	6.0	5.9	151%	4.1	5.8%	5.5%	8.1%
5.2%	1948	4.5	5.2	5.9	6.0	6.0	6.0	5.9	5.9	6.0	5.9	5.9	6.0	6.0	6.0	5.9	6.0	6.0	6.0	6.0	6.0	6.0	5.9	6.0	5.9	6.0	6.0	6.0	6.0	6.0	6.0	205%	4.5	5.9%	5.7%	8.8%
5.2%	1949	5.5	5.9	6.0	5.9	5.9	5.9	6.0	6.0	6.0	5.9	5.9	6.0	6.0	6.0	5.9	6.0	5.9	5.9	5.9	6.0	5.9	5.9	5.9	5.9	6.0	5.9	6.0	5.9	6.0	6.0	219%	5.5	5.9%	5.9%	9.0%
5.2%	1950	5.5	5.7	5.9	5.6	6.0	5.9	6.0	6.0	6.0	6.0	6.0	6.0	6.0	6.0	5.9	6.0	6.0	6.0	6.0	6.0	6.0	5.9	6.0	5.9	6.0	5.9	6.0	6.0	5.9	5.9	178%	5.5	5.9%	5.9%	8.7%
4.9%	1951	4.9	5.3	4.8	6.0	6.0	6.0	6.0	6.0	6.0	6.0	5.9	5.9	5.9	6.0	6.0	5.9	6.0	6.0	6.0	5.9	6.0	6.0	6.0	6.0	5.9	6.0	5.9	5.9	6.0	6.0	137%	4.8	5.9%	5.7%	8.0%
4.9%	1952	5.1	4.7	6.0	6.0	5.9	6.0	6.0	5.9	5.9	5.9	6.0	6.0	5.9	6.0	5.9	6.0	6.0	6.0	6.0	6.0	6.0	6.0	6.0	6.0	6.0	6.0	5.9	6.0	6.0	6.0	132%	4.7	5.9%	5.7%	8.2%
4.7%	1953	4.5	5.9	6.0	6.0	6.0	5.9	5.9	5.9	6.0	6.0	5.9	5.9	6.0	6.0	5.9	6.0	5.9	6.0	6.0	5.9	5.9	6.0	5.9	6.0	6.0	6.0	6.0	5.9	6.0	6.0	137%	4.5	5.9%	5.8%	8.0%
5.1%	1954	6.0	5.9	6.0	6.0	6.0	6.0	5.9	6.0	6.0	6.0	5.9	6.0	6.0	5.9	6.0	5.9	5.9	5.9	6.0	6.0	5.9	6.0	6.0	6.0	6.0	6.0	5.9	5.9	6.0	6.0	192%	5.9	6.0%	6.0%	8.7%
4.7%	1955	5.8	5.5	4.2	6.0	6.0	6.0	6.0	5.9	5.9	6.0	6.0	6.0	5.9	6.0	5.9	5.9	5.9	5.9	6.0	5.8	6.0	6.0	6.0	6.0	5.9	5.9	6.0	6.0	5.9	5.9	76%	4.2	5.9%	5.7%	6.7%
4.7%	1956	4.7	3.9	5.6	6.0	5.7	5.9	5.9	5.9	5.9	6.0	5.9	6.0	6.0	6.0	6.0	6.0	5.9	5.9	4.4	5.5	5.9	6.0	6.0	5.9	6.0	6.0	5.9	6.0	6.0	5.9	60%	3.9	5.8%	5.6%	6.2%
4.7%	1957	4.1	5.8	6.0	5.9	5.9	6.0	6.0	5.9	6.0	5.9	5.9	5.9	6.0	5.9	6.0	5.9	6.0	4.6	6.0	6.0	6.0	5.9	6.0	6.0	6.0	5.9	5.9	6.0	6.0	5.9	80%	4.1	5.8%	5.8%	6.5%
4.7%	1958	6.0	5.9	5.9	5.9	5.9	6.0	6.0	6.0	6.0	6.0	5.9	5.9	5.9	6.0	5.9	6.0	5.9	6.0	5.9	6.0	6.0	5.9	5.9	5.9	6.0	5.9	6.0	6.0	6.0	5.9	130%	5.9	6.0%	6.0%	7.8%
4.5%	1959	5.5	5.1	5.9	5.4	6.0	5.9	5.9	5.9	5.9	6.0	6.0	6.0	6.0	6.0	6.0	3.9	5.1	6.0	6.0	5.8	6.0	6.0	6.0	6.0	6.0	5.9	5.9	5.9	5.9	5.9	54%	3.9	5.8%	5.8%	6.1%
4.3%	1960	4.9	6.0	5.0	5.9	6.0	6.0	6.0	6.0	6.0	6.0	6.0	5.9	6.0	5.4	3.4	4.3	5.9	5.6	5.5	5.9	6.0	5.5	6.0	6.0	5.9	6.0	6.0	5.9	5.9	6.0	49%	3.4	5.7%	5.8%	5.9%
4.3%	1961	6.0	5.3	6.0	5.9	6.0	5.9	6.0	5.9	6.0	6.0	6.0	6.0	5.9	3.8	4.7	6.0	6.0	5.9	5.9	6.0	5.9	5.9	6.0	6.0	5.9	6.0	5.9	5.9	6.0	5.9	45%	3.8	5.8%	5.9%	6.2%
4.3%	1962	4.4	5.0	5.7	6.0	6.0	6.0	6.0	6.0	6.0	6.0	6.0	4.4	3.3	3.9	5.1	5.1	5.0	5.4	6.0	5.0	6.0	6.0	6.0	6.0	6.0	6.0	6.0	6.0	6.0	6.0	43%	3.3	5.5%	5.7%	5.7%
4.3%	1963	6.0	6.0	6.0	6.0	5.9	5.9	6.0	6.0	6.0	6.0	6.0	3.7	4.7	6.0	6.0	6.0	6.0	6.0	6.0	5.9	6.0	6.0	6.0	6.0	6.0	5.9	5.9	6.0	6.0	5.9	77%	3.7	5.9%	6.0%	6.4%
4.3%	1964	5.9	6.0	6.0	5.9	6.0	5.9	5.9	6.0	6.0	4.5	3.3	3.8	5.5	5.3	4.8	5.9	6.0	5.4	6.0	6.0	6.0	5.9	5.9	6.0	6.0	5.9	6.0	5.9	5.9	6.0	72%	3.3	5.7%	5.8%	6.0%
4.2%	1965	6.0	5.3	6.0	6.0	6.0	6.0	5.9	6.0	3.8	3.2	3.5	4.4	4.4	4.4	4.8	5.6	5.0	6.0	5.9	5.9	6.0	6.0	5.9	5.9	6.0	6.0	5.9	6.0	6.0	5.9	47%	3.2	5.5%	5.4%	5.6%
4.0%	1966	4.6	5.9	6.0	5.3	4.8	5.4	5.6	3.3	2.8	3.1	3.9	3.7	3.7	4.3	4.6	4.2	5.6	5.9	5.9	6.0	5.9	6.0	5.9	6.0	5.1	6.0	5.9	6.0	6.0	6.0	43%	2.8	5.1%	4.7%	5.0%
4.3%	1967	6.0	6.0	5.9	5.7	6.0	5.9	3.8	3.2	3.4	4.4	4.4	4.2	4.9	5.7	4.7	6.0	6.0	5.9	5.9	6.0	6.0	5.9	6.0	6.0	6.0	6.0	6.0	6.0	6.0	6.0	79%	3.2	5.5%	5.0%	5.6%
4.2%	1968	6.0	4.2	3.9	4.3	4.3	3.2	2.6	3.2	3.4	3.4	3.4	3.6	4.0	3.8	4.4	6.0	5.5	5.9	6.0	5.8	6.0	6.0	5.4	5.9	6.0	6.0	6.0	5.9	6.0	5.9	51%	2.6	4.9%	3.9%	4.6%
4.2%	1969	3.8	3.6	3.8	3.9	3.2	2.5	3.1	3.2	3.2	3.2	3.4	3.5	3.4	4.0	4.9	4.6	5.9	6.0	5.2	5.7	5.9	4.0	6.0	6.0	6.0	5.9	6.0	5.9	5.9	6.0	43%	2.5	4.6%	3.4%	4.2%
4.2%	1970	5.0	5.4	5.4	3.5	3.0	3.3	4.0	3.8	3.7	4.4	5.2	4.4	5.9	6.0	5.9	6.0	6.0	6.0	5.9	6.0	6.0	6.0	5.9	6.0	6.0	6.0	6.0	6.0	6.0	5.9	90%	3.0	5.3%	4.2%	5.4%
4.5%	1971	5.6	5.6	3.7	3.2	3.5	4.0	4.0	3.9	4.4	4.7	4.5	5.5	5.9	5.9	6.0	6.0	6.0	6.0	5.9	5.9	6.0	6.0	6.0	5.9	6.0	6.0	5.9	6.0	5.9	6.0	103%	3.2	5.3%	4.3%	5.7%
4.3%	1972	5.3	3.5	3.1	3.3	3.8	3.8	3.8	4.0	4.5	4.4	5.9	6.0	6.0	6.0	6.0	6.0	6.0	5.9	5.9	6.0	6.0	6.0	5.9	6.0	6.0	6.0	6.0	5.9	6.0	5.9	106%	3.1	5.3%	4.0%	5.5%
4.3%	1973	3.6	3.2	3.3	3.9	3.7	3.7	4.1	4.4	4.1	5.4	6.0	5.9	6.0	5.9	5.9	6.0	6.0	6.0	6.0	6.0	6.0	6.0	6.0	6.0	5.9	6.0	6.0	5.9	5.9	5.9	83%	3.2	5.3%	3.9%	5.6%
4.7%	1974	3.7	4.2	5.6	5.4	5.1	5.7	5.9	5.3	6.0	6.0	6.0	5.9	6.0	5.9	6.0	5.9	6.0	6.0	6.0	6.0	6.0	5.9	6.0	5.9	5.9	6.0	5.9	5.9	6.0	6.0	206%	3.7	5.7%	5.3%	7.5%
5.3%	1975	6.0	6.0	6.0	5.9	6.0	6.0	5.9	5.9	5.9	5.9	6.0	6.0	5.9	5.9	6.0	6.0	6.0	6.0	6.0	5.9	6.0	6.0	5.9	5.9	6.0	6.0	6.0	6.0	5.9	6.0	508%	5.9	6.0%	6.0%	9.0%
5.1%	1976	6.0	5.9	5.6	6.0	6.0	5.8	6.0	5.9	6.0	6.0	6.0	5.9	6.0	6.0	6.0	5.9	6.0	6.0	6.0	5.9	5.9	6.0	6.0	6.0	6.0	5.9	6.0	5.9	5.9	6.0	298%	5.6	6.0%	5.9%	8.5%
5.1%	1977	4.6	4.4	4.7	4.9	4.6	5.8	5.9	6.0	5.9	5.9	5.9	6.0	5.9	5.9	5.9	5.9	6.0	6.0	6.0	5.9	6.0	6.0	6.0	6.0	5.9	5.9	5.9	5.9	6.0	6.0	227%	4.4	5.7%	5.3%	7.8%
5.3%	1978	4.6	4.8	5.0	4.8	6.0	6.0	6.0	6.0	6.0	6.0	6.0	6.0	6.0	6.0	5.9	5.9	6.0	6.0	6.0	6.0	6.0	6.0	6.0	6.0	6.0	6.0	6.0	6.0	6.0	6.0	253%	4.6	5.8%	5.5%	8.2%
5.5%	1979	4.9	5.1	4.8	6.0	6.0	6.0	5.9	6.0	6.0	6.0	5.9	6.0	5.9	6.0	6.0	5.9	6.0	6.0	5.9	6.0	6.0	6.0	6.0	6.0	6.0	6.0	6.0	6.0	5.9	5.9	202%	4.8	5.9%	5.7%	8.3%
5.5%	1980	4.8	4.6	5.5	6.0	6.0	6.0	5.9	6.0	6.0	6.0	5.9	6.0	5.9	6.0	5.9	5.9	5.9	6.0	5.9	6.0	6.0	6.0	5.9	6.0	5.9	6.0	6.0	6.0	6.0	6.0	232%	4.6	5.9%	5.7%	8.3%
5.3%	1981	4.5	5.5	6.0	6.0	6.0	6.0	6.0	5.9	6.0	6.0	5.9	6.0	6.0	6.0	6.0	5.9	6.0	6.0	5.9	6.0	6.0	6.0	5.9	5.9	5.9	6.0	6.0	5.9	5.9	6.0	270%	4.5	5.9%	5.8%	8.3%
																															Totals	184%	2.5	5.7%	5.3%	7.3%

FIGURE 155

Backtesting results for 30-year systemic withdrawal plan with 6% income cap using Alternate Prime and a 65% initial stock percentage.

Using Alternate-Prime and raising the initial stock percentage increases risk by a small amount, but then capping income slightly lowers risk (although it doesn't fully compensate for the other two).

Emergency Funding and Frontloading Income

The resiliency of EM for handling extra withdrawals has been mentioned several times. Here, that resiliency is demonstrated by simulating an emergency withdrawal: one 20% withdrawal is made in the 5th year of a benchmark 40-year retirement. This case is also roughly equivalent to frontloading income over several years, such as pulling out an extra 2% each year for the first 10 years.

Figure 156 shows the results: EM compensates without disproportionate stress later in the retirement. Still, this ability to smoothly compensate can't be guaranteed. There is no way to know when future market stresses may require a stockpile of extra resources. Also, other retirement parameters such as setting a higher income floor can reduce the overall resiliency of the portfolio. For example, coupled with the 20% emergency withdrawal, a 4% floor in EM will trigger failures in 8 retirement periods; a 3.5% floor will trigger one failure (only 25 years into the retirement); a 3% floor and below remain 100% successful with the 20% emergency withdrawal.

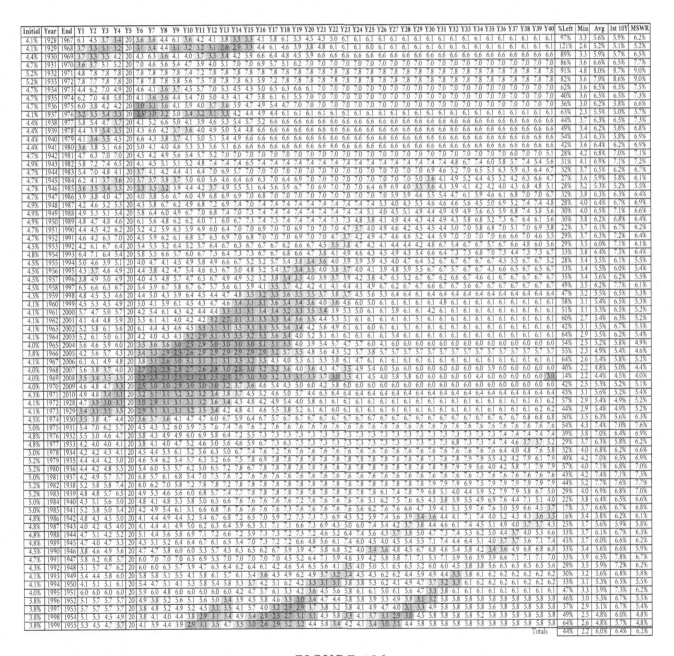

FIGURE 156

Backtesting results for 40-year systemic withdrawal plan with 20% emergency withdrawal taken in the 5th year of retirement.

Generally, the earlier income is taken, the more expensive it is. Nevertheless, when extra funds are seriously needed, a retiree should take them; everything will probably be okay, just not with the same likelihood as before.

An alternative is to set aside a separate pool of funds for frontloading or emergencies. In this case, the funds stay outside systemic withdrawals, probably in a bond fund*. During typical markets, this alternative will cost more, but it becomes more attractive as valuation levels rise.

RESTARTING SYSTEMIC WITHDRAWALS

Major changes in assumptions and circumstances during retirement might justify restarting a systemic withdrawal plan. Restarting means beginning the plan again with the current asset value and existing market conditions, as if retirement were just beginning. The need to restart should be rare, though—systemic withdrawals are oriented to handling major market changes as well as unexpected expenses.

Some may wonder about restarting as a strategy to ensure that the portfolio is always aligned with the current outlook. Restarting withdrawals ever 5 years was suggested as a strategy by DeMuth and Stein in their 2005 retirement book[58]. It works, but it also supplants the variable-withdrawal strategy (i.e., EM). Restarting can suddenly change income, potentially by a large amount and for a long time. A variable-withdrawal strategy is better positioned to handle these transitions as smoothly and safely as possible, especially with the ebbs and flows of volatile markets.

Restarting systemic withdrawals also introduces the temptation to cherry-pick the circumstances: restarting when temporary conditions support a boost in income. This can work, but ultimately there are no free gains. If income increases, so does risk; if income decreases, so does risk. There can never be the spontaneous generation of extra income without more risk. Again, variable-withdrawal strategies aim to smooth this out.

Related is the question of adjusting asset allocation as we age (with a much better approach than the age-based income-harvesting strategies). I have already make some related recommendations, such as using 35% as the initial stock allocation when starting a 15-year retirement, so shouldn't our target asset allocation change accordingly as we age? They could, but there are many variations, they haven't all been tested, and it doesn't appear to make a big difference. From another perspective, Pfau and Kitces have pointed out that there is merit in increasing the stock allocation as we age, although again there are many variations, which don't all show promise. My conclusion is that digging into all the intermediate retirement cases introduces more complexity for what doesn't appear to be a strong gain, if any. There is a point where added analysis and defining subcases does not have a good payoff. Still, speculative risk on its own can justify lowering the stock percentages near the end of retirement, so do so if you prefer.

Without clear evidence for or against restarting systemic withdrawals or making finer adjustments in the asset allocation as we age, retirees will likely find any sensible choice will fare reasonably well.

CONSIDERING TOTAL INCOME

Systemic withdrawals have been examined in isolation, although they rarely provide 100% of a retiree's income. In the US, most retirees receive Social Security benefits or another government pension. Some retirees still receive industry pensions. Other income sources are also common from investments outside financial markets. Additionally, retirees can allocate a portion of their assets to guaranteed-income solutions such as annuities or bond ladders, which generate income. The question here is, how do these other income sources affect withdrawals?

---

*   The concept of an even more resilient standby bond pool is covered in the last chapter.

Other income sources don't directly affect systemic withdrawals—this statement conflicts with a substantial amount of retirement literature, but the data doesn't point one direction or another. There are no objective evidence-based answers. Still, other income sources may affect how each retiree plans for speculative risk*, the subjective domain, which can have an indirect effect on systemic withdrawals. Below is a list of significant retirement options that are affected by perceptions of speculative risk in conjunction with other income sources.

- Prime Harvesting is recommended for income-harvesting, but Alternate-Prime normally performs better when starting valuations are attractive.

- The default income cap for EM is 150% of the initial withdrawal rate, but it can be reasonably increased to 200% to increase income during strong markets, or lowered to 125% to further decrease speculative risk.

- The recommended stock percentage is based on MSWR-100% (i.e., 50% for 30-year retirement and 55% for 40-year retirement), but it's reasonable to increase the percentage 10% to boost income or a lower percentage 10% to reduce speculative risk.

- There are three recommended portfolios: Evanson's 10x10, HR-8x12, and the Triad portfolio. The 10x10 is more diversified, but Triad has a higher HR, with HR-8x12 in the middle.

- The recommended tilt is 30% or 40% for picking the initial withdrawal rate. The higher tilt of 40%, or perhaps even 50%, usually produces more income, but a lower tilts of 30% or perhaps even 20% provides a stronger hedge against speculative risk.

As long as the overall plan remains sound, a retiree can follow their own preferences with reasonable safety and tradeoffs, taking into account other income sources, total income, and speculative risk.

FINAL THOUGHTS

With best practices identified and demonstrated, the study of systemic withdrawals is complete.

Retirement planning is no different from many aspects of life: we do our part, we have expectations of how it will go, and then deal with reality as it unfolds while endeavoring to make the most of what we have. Following best practices is about doing our part as retirement investors.

Still, there are times when guarantees can be obtained. Guarantees are luxuries though, with some remaining out of reach, and others only sometimes affordable. Surely it's best to accept some risk, but how much can be hard to determine. These are the topics of the final chapter.

THE POINT

The identified best practices produce superior retirement results with lower levels of risk. The plans and data shown provide reasonable estimates of what a retiree might expect in retirement. Comparing the plans and their tradeoffs will help a retiree form their own plan.

---

* This is distinct from guaranteed-income planning, where other income sources have a clearer influence.

This extensive chapter considers the use of guaranteed income to supplement systemic withdrawals. Readers with no interest in guaranteed income (e.g., annuities, bond ladders, I Bonds) can skip it, but are encouraged to read on if the valuation level of the markets (as defined in Chapter 9) is very high (e.g., 3.5).

Many retirees will find the consideration of GI worthwhile for the broader perspective it provides, even if they choose not to use it.

Less interested or partially interested readers can skim the chapter, focusing more on the sections covering the framework for considering GI, the top guaranteed-income instruments, the most viable basic strategies, the recommendations, and the examples.

Proper balance should be a comfortable position,
although it takes disciple to realize it.

<small>Walter E. Goh, 2013 International Windsurfer Convention</small>

<small>CHAPTER 11</small>

Underpinning Systemic Withdrawals with Guaranteed Income

This final chapter is practically a book on its own: when, why and how to use guaranteed-income (GI) investments to supplement systemic withdrawals. This is the final stage of retirement planning. For a few, this is even the most important stage.

GI by definition delivers reliable steady income, usually from individual bonds and annuities, independently from volatile assets. No investment is totally risk free, but by carefully selecting and applying GI, the risk in retirement can be reduced to its lowest level. However, GI usually comes at a significant cost, so tradeoffs must be balanced. Exactly how far to go with GI can't be objectively specified, but helpful boundaries can be drawn and the right instruments and strategies identified. After this chapter, some retirees will deem GI necessary; others will not, staying with 100% systemic withdrawals.

Most retirees use GI to ensure they are protected from market conditions which might cause systemic withdrawals to fail; however, perhaps surprisingly, using best practices, there are no systemic-withdrawal failures based on the known risk of a globally diversified portfolio[*]. Systemic withdrawals are stressed during the worst historical periods, but no retirement period comes close to running out of money while maintaining a reasonably steady income floor (more on this later). There is certainly risk of failure, but it's not captured in the global data, neither in the Baseline Market nor a composite of the international returns we have data for.

GI protects against extremely adverse market conditions, when even our best efforts with systemic withdrawal can fail. These extreme cases fall directly into the domain of speculative risk, which can't be measured because there is no representative data. This is why planning is difficult and no definitive answers can be given. Still, techniques are available to explore the likely characteristics of speculative risk in order to better understand the application and boundaries of GI, aiding the overall decision-making process.

Is it prudent for every retiree to use GI? No, not necessarily. This decision depends on the many interrelated strands that determine how GI fits and functions in retirement, one of which is affordability. I'll untangle these

---

[*]   There are many examples of failures from specific-market risk in an undiversified portfolio.

<small>263</small>

strands, pruning them, and then present what's left in a form that either leads to a straightforward GI plan, or a decision not to have one. Otherwise, mapping out a complete solution becomes unwieldy.

For readers outside the US, the bulk of details in this chapter are US-centric. Many developed markets and a few emerging markets have GI instruments analogous to those in the US, but not all, and there are always differences. Nevertheless, all retirees should be able to adapt the general guidelines to their own circumstances, wherever they live — the specifics vary but the concepts are the same.

A FRAMEWORK FOR CONSIDERING GUARANTEED INCOME

Virtually all retirees investing in financial markets should use systemic withdrawals, which provide a starting point for GI, not vice versa. GI will work in conjunction with systemic withdrawals, but as an independent solution. Assets invested in GI are invisible to systemic withdrawals, with the reverse also true. Once GI is purchased, it then produces "other income" like Social Security or a pension.

Regrettably, fluctuating interest rates continually change the cost of GI. Only by purchasing GI is a payout rate locked in. This means fixed numbers for GI planning can't be specified in a final analysis, although historical boundaries can be drawn and examples provided. The good news is that at purchase time, before a final decision is made, a retiree knows the payout GI will produce for the life of the instrument.

The lifespans of GI instruments vary. The life of an annuity usually matches the life of the retiree, or optionally two retirees when they are married. The life of a bond is usually defined by a fixed maturity date, which varies from less than one year up to 30 years. Coordinating multiple GI instruments with varying lifespans and payouts to support a steady income stream is part of the challenge of applying GI.

On the surface, decisions surrounding GI can appear straightforward: buy risk-free income with low expenses, low taxes, and strong payouts to build a guaranteed income floor. However, it doesn't take long for the decisions to become complex, to the point of becoming unmanageable without some form of simplification. To plan GI well, the problem must be broken down to make evaluation and decision-making easier. This is where a framework comes in.

A framework provides structure and boundaries to the problem. It defines a handful of concepts for evaluating GI. It also clarifies the essential requirements. It narrows down innumerable relationships and interconnections to a key set that matters most, making the overall problem simpler to consider. This section defines a framework for considering GI. Once it's in place, pragmatic evaluations and recommendations can follow. Before moving forward, though, clarification of a few terms is useful.

Longevity risk in retirement typically corresponds to outliving income: the portfolio runs out of money while trying to generate a fixed income rate. However, with EM or any good variable-withdrawal harvesting strategy, longevity risk becomes blurred. Toward the end of life, a retiree may not run out of money, but income may drop to insufficient levels (below the level of essential expenses). Accordingly, the concept of longevity risk should be expanded. Here it means the risk of insufficient income toward the end of life. Still, keep in mind that the risk of insufficient income also exists separately from longevity risk, potentially experienced early in retirement when a variable-withdrawal strategy drops income to compensate for extremely poor markets (far from the end of life).

A simply stated retirement goal is to always have sufficient income throughout retirement. This implies retirement's income floor (i.e., the lowest annual income amount) is always higher than a retiree's essential income needs.

The combination of systemic withdrawals with guaranteed income is also sometimes known as a floor-with-upside approach. This traditionally means the floor is covered by guaranteed income with the upside provided by systemic withdrawals. However, when planning for GI, a retiree may choose for a portion of the income floor to come from systemic withdrawals. In a theoretical sense, systemic withdrawals have no floor, but in practice it's reasonable to assume there is one[*] (although what it should be is a difficult question).

One can still easily argue that, in an ideal world, GI should lock in an income floor matching essential income needs, but many retirees will find this unaffordable. In practice, it's often better to use GI in moderation, locking in only a portion of the income floor, with systemic withdrawals providing the rest. The goal then isn't to eliminate the speculative risk that comes with systemic withdrawals, but to push it down another notch or two—below what is already a small amount.

A Realistic Systemic-Withdrawal Benchmark

The literature justifies the need for guaranteed income, because systemic withdrawals can fail. This conclusion is often reinforced by backtesting results assuming some variation of annual rebalancing, a total-market portfolio, and fixed withdrawal rates. These poor assumptions paint a much bleaker picture than necessary, skewing the overall problem and the conclusions. Under these assumptions, using a US total-market portfolio, there is a 7% failure rate for a 30-year retirement with an inflation-adjusted 4% withdrawal rate. The same assumptions for the Baseline Market increase the failure rate to 17%. These high failure rates appear to justify GI. In fact, results like these are the primary justification for the "safety first" philosophy where GI is applied first to cover essential expenses, then what's left of the portfolio (if anything) is allocated to systemic withdrawals. However, in order to properly evaluate the merits of GI, risk should be considered using best practices, not an outdated set of strategies with poor performance.

Figure 142 through Figure 145 in the previous chapter reflect variations of 40-year retirements based on best practices. Any of these can be a systemic-withdrawal benchmark. As mentioned earlier, what stands out is there are no retirement failures.

Do these systemic withdrawal numbers imply that the results are good enough to eliminate the need for guaranteed income? Based on known risk, yes, but not when considering speculative risk. Future markets might severely stress retirement plans to the point of failure, even using best practices.

Although best practices don't remove the justification for GI, they do remove any perceived mandate that existed for using it. A retiree can create a reasonable plan without GI. GI may be desirable at times, depending on a retiree's circumstances and current market conditions, but the numbers show it's optional.

The above reasoning is why the concept of GI affordability (explained fully later) is important. It makes little sense for a retiree to purchases a substantial amount of GI to reduce a small risk when the immediate result is a lower quality of life. Big risks justify large costs to hedge; little risks do not. On the other hand, speculative risk is real and always present, so protecting against it when it's affordable can be a sensible option.

A Failure-Market Benchmark

The main motivation for GI is surviving market conditions so poor they trigger systemic-withdrawal failures. Using known risk as an indicator the odds are, today's retirees will never see anything like a failure market. Nevertheless, the viability of GI solutions depends on successfully handling this type of market. This implies GI should be evaluated not under normal market conditions but under failure-market conditions.

Just as a Baseline Market was needed for testing realistic scenarios using systemic withdrawal, a failure-market benchmark is needed for testing realistic scenarios where GI is needed to supplement systemic withdrawals. Since there is no global market data meeting this criterion, again one must be created.

---

[*]   Financial consultant Michael Kitces points out the same in his May 2012 blog post "Annuities Versus Safe Withdrawal Rates: Comparing Floor/Upside Approaches".

A realistic failure market can be created like the Baseline Market by scaling down US SBBI return data. While the Baseline Market was formed by scaling down total-market stock returns from 6.3% to 5%, the failure market will scale total-market stock returns down to 3%, with related asset classes scaled proportionally. Likewise, where the Baseline Market scaled bonds returns down from 2.07% to 1.8%, the failure market will scale down bond returns to 0.5%.

The 3% total-market stock returns and 0.5% bond returns happen to correspond with the numbers Dimson et al. quote for a low-return world. However, here they represent a much worse set of conditions because they apply to the overall 83 years of SBBI data with substantial troughs. This includes both bear markets (i.e., low return and high volatility), and sequence-of-return risks, with both magnified. Most importantly, this degree of poor returns forces systemic withdrawal failures—the domain of GI.

Also, as used before, the failure-market benchmark is enhanced using historical data-wrapping (i.e., post-2010 data wraps back to 1928). This technique raises the bar for GI while significantly expanding the data for 40-year retirements.

Figure 157 shows the Baseline Portfolio's forward 30-year returns for the failure-market benchmark with data-wrapping. Also included for comparison are the Baseline Portfolio's 30-year returns for both the original US SBBI data, and the Baseline Market. The 30-year stock returns dip as low as 0%, although there is still a lot of diversity in returns.

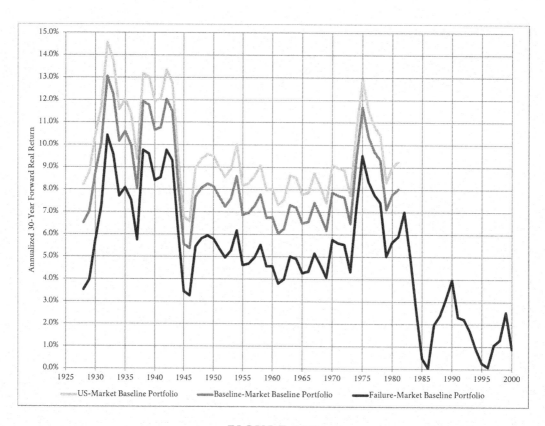

FIGURE 157

*Failure Market, Baseline Market, and US SBBI Market's 30-Year real forward
returns for Baseline Portfolio (with data wrapping after 1981).*

Figure 158 provides another perspective on the failure market by showing 40-year retirement results using traditional assumptions: a total-market portfolio, annual rebalancing, and inflation-adjusted 4% annual withdrawals. The portfolio runs out of money in 43 of the 83 retirement periods, this time with MSWR falling as low as 2.5%. *Note: the retirement figures now typically show age, starting at 65 (i.e., A65) and ending at 104 (i.e., A04), for each year in the retirement period.*

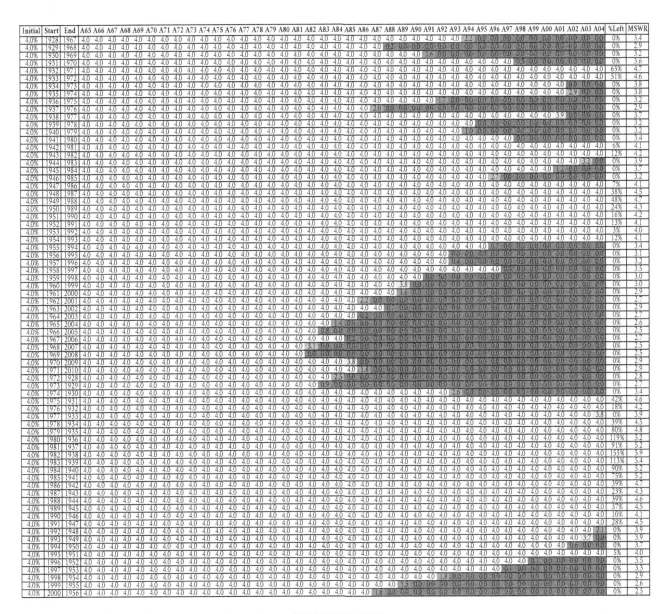

FIGURE 158

Systemic withdrawals for the failure-market benchmark using total-market portfolio (50% stocks), inflation-adjusted fixed income, and traditional rebalancing.

Figure 159 shows the primary aim of this exercise: the 40-year retirement results for the failure market using the recommended best practices (e.g., Prime Harvest, EM, and Baseline Portfolio). The portfolio runs out of money in 11 of the 83 retirement periods (although always late in retirement). The worst retirement period starts in 1987 with the portfolio running out of money five years early. EM can't fully compensate for such poor returns. In over half the retirement periods, the income floor drops below 3%, quite a few times in the first 20 years of retirement.

FIGURE 159

Systemic withdrawals for the failure-market benchmark using best practices for 40-year retirement using default parameters.

The salient point is, systemic withdrawal cannot adequately handle this failure market. Reducing the stock percentage to 30% doesn't fix the problem, but makes it worse. Likewise, increasing the stock percentage to 65% makes the problem worse. Changing the asset allocation will not fix the problem. Putting a fixed cap on EM helps some, but the portfolio still runs out of money until the cap gets down to 4%—and income still drops as low as 2.25%. Nothing truly fixes the problem. This is the domain of GI. Failure markets are what GI solutions must handle; therefore, failure markets are the context GI solutions should be tested under.

Some may still wonder about the severity of the failure market as defined. If it's significantly less severe, then systemic withdrawal can handle it (i.e., it's no longer a failure market), but should it be more severe? Why not scale overall stock returns back even further to 2%, 1%, or even 0%? This is easily done, but there are a few reasons not to. The failure market as defined is already substantially worse than any global market seen in data going back to 1900. As defined, it's severe enough to illustrate the points to be learned. Showing too much severity can negatively skew our perspective, which is already a potential problem. In addition, the risk of poor markets must be balanced with the possibility of unexpected expenses (discussed more below), which justify aiming for more income.

Some may also wonder if a 40-year failure-market benchmark is too long. Keep the earlier discussion in mind: there is an 18% chance that one member of a 65 year old couple will outlive a 30-year plan, plus a 4% chance one member of a 65 year old couple will outlive a 35-year plan. This 4% chance is enough to justify a 40-year benchmark; the likelihood of a long life appears to be higher than the likelihood of a failure market. Also, focusing on a 40-year benchmark provides more than adequate preparation for forming a shorter retirement plan, but the reverse is not true. Both the analysis and the recommendations for 40-year plans can be generally applied to 30-year plans or shorter, after adjusting for differences in the timeframes and payout rates.

Repositioning ECM Over EM

If a retiree chooses to use GI, then it's generally implied they are orienting their retirement plan to handle a failure market[*]. This decision is best coupled with one more choice: selecting ECM for variable withdrawals in place of EM.

ECM is a re-geared version of EM with lower early income, which is much better positioned for the domain of failure markets. While ECM's cost might be considered high (compared to EM) under normal markets, its cost is relatively low compared to what it takes to deploy GI to handle failure markets.

Figure 160 shows ECM's performance under a failure market (the other best practices are unchanged). ECM runs out of money only once, at age 103 in the 1987 retirement period. Otherwise, it consistently maintains a 2.5% floor. This ability to maintain a higher income floor by deploying a generally more conservative income distribution performs relatively well in the context of a failure market.

---

[*] Admittedly, there are a few exceptions to using GI only to handle failure markets, such as when interest rates are very high (i.e., GI is very cheap), or when purchasing an annuity later in life to boost income, but most often GI's primary purpose is to handle failure markets.

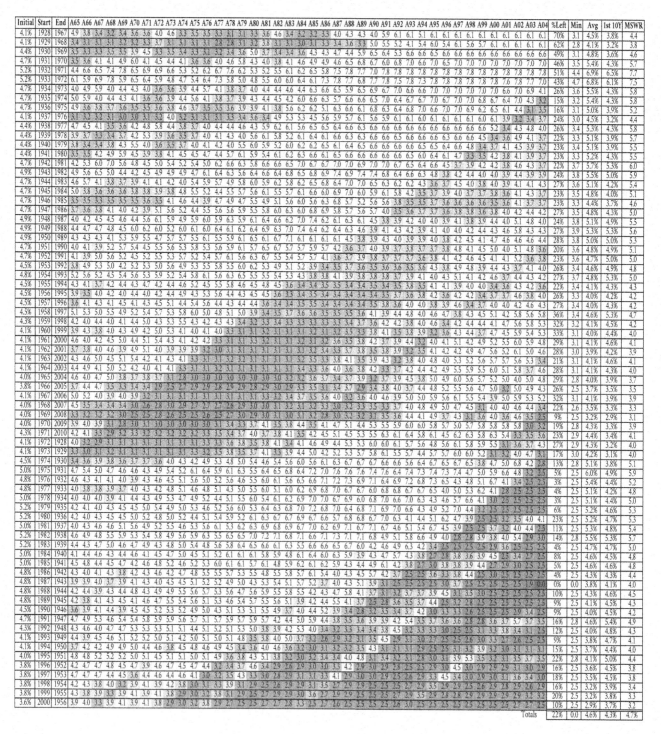

FIGURE 160

Systemic withdrawals for the failure-market benchmark using best practices with ECM.

These numbers, based on ECM with best practices under a failure market, will be used throughout the rest of the chapter to test GI with systemic withdrawals.

Requisite Inflation Protection

When inflation is low, investors tend to discount its risk, but it remains an ever-present threat[*]. Systemic withdrawals have a built-in inflation hedge, given stocks are probably the best inflation protection after inflation-adjusted bonds. GI doesn't have this natural hedge, however. It must explicitly carry its own inflation protection[†] to ensure viability during a failure market, when many economic parameters might be distorted.

It takes just one real example to make clear why inflation protection is essential. Figure 161 shows what happened to annuity income without inflation protection based on past annuity payouts[‡] and historical inflation rates. The Annuity Payout column shows the fixed payout rate when purchased at age 65 for the starting retirement year. The A66 column, when the retiree is 66 years old, shows the first payout in real terms (i.e., after inflation) one year into retirement. The A67 column, when the retiree is 67 years old, shows the second payout in real terms two years into retirement. The payouts continue for 30 years until age 95. Understand that the real rate of payout is changing only because of inflation. The annuity payout is fixed for life, exactly how annuities work today without explicit built-in inflation protection.

---

[*] One might argue that macroeconomics has somewhat tamed inflation in developed markets, but there is too little data to rely on this conclusion.

[†] Steven Evanson points out (private correspondence) that government statistics may be biased towards underreporting inflation. If so, this is one more reason to keep part of the portfolio in stocks as an inflation hedge.

[‡] The historical annuity payout is based on a www.bogleheads.org forum discussion with the following formula: (annuity yield) − 1 / (life expectancy) + (interest rate) / 2.

Year	Annuity Payout	A66	A67	A68	A69	A70	A71	A72	A73	A74	A75	A76	A77	A78	A79	A80	A81	A82	A83	A84	A85	A86	A87	A88	A89	A90	A91	A92	A93	A94	A95
1928	7.4%	7.4	7.4	8.0	8.8	9.6	9.4	9.1	9.0	8.8	8.7	8.8	8.9	8.8	7.8	7.2	7.0	6.8	6.7	5.5	4.9	4.8	4.9	4.5	4.3	4.3	4.3	4.3	4.3	4.2	4.0
1929	7.5%	7.5	8.0	8.8	9.7	9.5	9.2	9.0	8.8	8.8	8.9	9.0	8.8	7.8	7.2	7.0	6.9	6.7	5.5	4.9	4.9	5.0	4.6	4.4	4.4	4.3	4.3	4.3	4.3	4.2	4.0
1930	7.3%	7.9	8.6	9.5	9.3	9.0	8.9	8.7	8.6	8.7	8.8	8.7	7.7	7.1	6.9	6.7	6.6	5.4	4.8	4.8	4.9	4.5	4.3	4.3	4.2	4.2	4.2	4.1	4.0	3.9	3.9
1931	7.4%	8.1	8.9	8.7	8.4	8.3	8.1	8.1	8.2	8.2	8.1	7.2	6.6	6.4	6.3	6.2	5.0	4.5	4.5	4.6	4.2	4.0	4.0	4.0	4.0	4.0	3.8	3.7	3.7	3.6	3.6
1932	7.5%	8.3	8.1	7.8	7.7	7.5	7.5	7.6	7.7	7.5	6.7	6.2	6.0	5.9	5.7	4.7	4.2	4.2	4.2	3.9	3.7	3.7	3.7	3.7	3.7	3.6	3.4	3.4	3.4	3.3	3.3
1933	7.3%	7.2	7.0	6.9	6.7	6.7	6.8	6.8	6.7	5.9	5.5	5.3	5.3	5.2	5.1	4.2	3.8	3.8	3.5												
1934	7.3%	7.0	6.9	6.8	6.7	6.8	6.9	6.8	6.0	5.5	5.4	5.3	5.1	4.2	3.8	3.7	3.8	3.5	3.4												
1935	7.1%	7.0	6.8	6.8	6.9	6.9	6.8	6.1	5.6	5.4	5.3	5.2	4.2	3.8	3.8	3.8	3.5	3.4													
1936	7.0%	6.9	6.8	6.9	7.0	6.9	6.1	5.6	5.5	5.3	5.2	4.3	3.8	3.8	3.9	3.5	3.4	3.4	3.3												
1937	7.0%	7.0	7.1	7.1	7.0	6.2	5.8	5.6	5.5	5.3	4.4	3.9	3.9	4.0	3.6	3.5															
1938	7.0%	7.1	7.1	7.0	6.2	5.7	5.6	5.4	5.3	4.4	3.9	3.9	3.9	3.6	3.5																
1939	6.9%	6.9	6.8	6.0	5.6	5.4	5.3	5.2	4.2	3.8	3.8	3.8	3.5	3.4																	
1940	6.8%	6.7	5.9	5.5	5.3	5.2	5.1	4.2	3.7	3.8	3.8	3.5																			
1941	6.7%	5.9	5.5	5.3	5.2	5.1	4.1	3.7	3.7	3.7	3.4																				
1942	6.9%	6.4	6.2	6.1	5.9	4.9	4.4	4.3	4.4	4.0	3.9	3.8	3.8	3.8	3.8	3.7	3.6	3.5	3.4	3.4	3.4										
1943	6.9%	6.7	6.6	6.4	5.3	4.7	4.7	4.8	4.4	4.2	4.2	4.1	4.1	4.0	3.9	3.9	3.8	3.7	3.7	3.6											
1944	6.9%	6.8	6.6	5.4	4.9	4.8	4.9	4.5	4.3	4.3	4.2	4.3	4.3	4.1	4.0	3.9	3.9	3.8	3.8	3.7	3.7										
1945	6.9%	6.7	5.5	4.9	4.9	5.0	4.6	4.4	4.4	4.3	4.3	4.3	4.2	4.0	4.0	3.9	3.9	3.9	3.8	3.7	3.7										
1946	6.8%	5.6	5.0	4.9	5.0	4.6	4.4	4.4	4.4	4.4	4.4	4.2	4.1	4.0	4.0	3.9	3.9	3.8	3.8												
1947	6.8%	6.1	6.0	6.2	5.7	5.4	5.4	5.4	5.4	5.2	5.0	4.9	4.9	4.8	4.7	4.6	4.6	4.5	4.3	4.2	4.0	3.8	3.6	3.4	3.3	3.0	2.6	2.5			
1948	6.9%	6.8	7.0	6.4	6.1	6.1	6.0	6.1	6.1	5.9	5.7	5.6	5.5	5.4	5.4	5.3	5.2	5.2	5.1	4.9	4.7	4.5	4.2	4.0	3.9						
1949	6.8%	7.0	6.4	6.1	6.1	6.1	6.1	6.1	5.9	5.7	5.6	5.5	5.4	5.4	5.3	5.3	5.2	5.1	4.9	4.7	4.5	4.3	4.0	3.9	3.8	3.4	3.0				
1950	6.9%	6.3	6.0	6.0	5.9	6.0	6.0	5.8	5.6	5.5	5.4	5.3	5.3	5.2	5.1	5.1	5.0	4.8	4.7	4.4	4.2	4.0	3.8	3.7	3.3						
1951	7.0%	6.7	6.6	6.6	6.6	6.4	6.2	6.1	6.0	5.9	5.9	5.8	5.7	5.6	5.5	5.5	5.3	5.2	4.9	4.6	4.4	4.2	4.1	3.7							
1952	7.0%	7.0	6.9	7.0	7.0	6.7	6.5	6.4	6.3	6.2	6.2	6.1	6.0	6.0	5.8	5.6	5.4	5.2	4.9	4.6	4.5	4.3	3.9								
1953	7.1%	7.0	7.1	7.1	6.8	6.6	6.5	6.4	6.3	6.3	6.2	6.1	6.0	5.9	5.7	5.5	5.3	4.9	4.7	4.5	4.4	4.0									
1954	6.9%	7.0	7.0	6.7	6.6	6.4	6.3	6.2	6.1	6.0	6.0	5.8	5.6	5.4	5.2	4.9	4.6	4.5	4.3	3.9											
1955	7.0%	7.0	6.8	6.5	6.4	6.3	6.2	6.1	6.0	6.0	5.9	5.6	5.4	5.2	4.9	4.6	4.5	4.3	3.9												
1956	7.1%	6.9	6.7	6.6	6.5	6.4	6.4	6.3	6.2	6.1	6.0	5.8	5.6	5.3	5.0	4.7	4.6	4.4	4.0												
1957	7.4%	7.2	7.1	7.0	6.9	6.8	6.7	6.6	6.5	6.4	6.2	6.0	5.7	5.4	5.1	4.9	4.7	4.3	3.8												
1958	7.2%	7.1	7.1	6.9	6.9	6.8	6.7	6.6	6.5	6.3	6.0	5.8	5.4	5.1	4.8	4.3	3.8	3.6	3.4												
1959	7.7%	7.6	7.5	7.4	7.3	7.2	7.2	7.0	6.8	6.5	6.2	5.9	5.5	5.4	5.2	4.7	4.1	3.9	3.6												
1960	8.1%	7.9	7.9	7.8	7.6	7.6	7.4	7.2	6.9	6.6	6.2	5.9	5.7	5.5	4.9	4.4	4.1	3.9	3.6												
1961	7.6%	7.6	7.5	7.3	7.3	7.1	6.9	6.6	6.3	5.9	5.6	5.4	5.2	4.8	4.2	3.9	3.7														
1962	7.7%	7.6	7.5	7.4	7.3	7.0	6.8	6.5	6.1	5.8	5.6	5.4	4.9	4.3	4.0	3.8	3.5														
1963	7.6%	7.5	7.4	7.3	7.0	6.8	6.5	6.1	5.7	5.6	5.4	4.8	4.3	4.0	3.8																
1964	7.8%	7.7	7.6	7.3	7.0	6.7	6.3	6.0	5.8	5.6	5.0	4.4	4.1	3.9	3.7																
1965	7.8%	7.6	7.4	7.1	6.8	6.4	5.8	5.6	5.1	4.5	4.2	4.0																			
1966	8.0%	7.7	7.4	7.1	6.7	6.3	6.1	5.9	5.3	4.7	4.4	4.2	3.9																		
1967	8.0%	7.7	7.4	6.9	6.5	6.3	6.1	5.5	4.9	4.5	4.3	4.0	3.6																		
1968	8.5%	8.1	7.6	7.2	6.9	6.7	6.1	5.4	5.0	4.7	4.4	4.0																			
1969	8.7%	8.2	7.7	7.5	7.2	6.5	5.8	5.4	5.1	4.7	4.3																				
1970	9.6%	9.1	8.8	8.5	7.7	6.8	6.3	6.0	5.6	5.1	4.4	3.8																			
1971	8.8%	8.5	8.2	7.4	6.6	6.1	5.8	5.4	4.9	4.2	3.7																				
1972	8.7%	8.4	7.6	6.7	6.2	5.9	5.5	5.0	4.3	3.8	3.5																				
1973	8.9%	8.1	7.1	6.7	6.3	5.9	5.3	4.6	4.0	3.5																					
1974	9.2%	8.1	7.6	7.2	6.7	6.1	5.2	4.6	4.2	4.1	3.9	3.6	3.5																		
1975	9.4%	8.8	8.3	7.8	7.1	6.1	5.4	4.9	4.7	4.5	4.4	4.2	4.1	4.0	3.8	3.6															
1976	9.6%	9.1	8.4	7.6	6.8	5.8	5.3	5.1	4.9	4.7	4.6	4.5	4.3	4.1	3.9	3.7															
1977	9.3%	8.7	7.9	6.8	6.0	5.5	5.3	5.0	4.9	4.7	4.6	4.4	4.2	4.0	3.8																
1978	9.7%	8.8	7.6	6.7	6.1	5.9	5.6	5.4	5.2	5.1	4.9	4.7	4.5	4.2	4.1	4.0	3.9	3.8	3.7	3.5											
1979	10.2%	8.8	7.8	7.1	6.9	6.6	6.3	6.1	6.0	5.8	5.5	5.2	4.9	4.8	4.6	4.5	4.4	4.3	4.1	4.1	4.0	3.9	3.7	3.7	3.6	3.5	3.4	3.3	3.3	3.1	
1980	11.1%	9.8	9.0	8.6	8.3	8.0	7.7	7.6	7.2	6.9	6.5	6.2	6.0	5.8	5.7	5.5	5.4	5.2	5.1	5.0	4.9	4.7	4.7	4.5	4.5	4.3	4.1	4.1	3.9	3.9	3.8
1981	12.0%	11.0	10.6	10.1	9.8	9.4	9.2	8.9	8.5	8.0	7.6	7.4	7.1	6.9	6.8	6.6	6.4	6.3	6.2	6.0	5.8	5.7	5.6	5.5	5.3	5.1	5.0	4.8	4.8	4.6	4.6

FIGURE 161

*Historical annuity payouts in real terms for a 30-year retirement
starting at age 65 without inflation adjustments.*

The results are extremely poor. Based only on the real historical inflation levels, over half of the retirement periods end up with less than a 2% payout in real terms before the end of a 30-year retirement. Across all the retirement periods, the average annuity fixed payout is 7.5%, but finishes with a 2.3% average in real terms. This isn't about annuities, but about the erosion of value through inflation. There is too high a probability the same will happen to any type of GI than does not have explicit inflation protection.

Inflation protection is an essential requirement for selecting a GI instrument for retirement. This single requirement eliminates most forms of GI.

An Essential-Income Rate

After deciding to use GI, a retiree must decide on the amount to purchase. Since GI is often not cheap, the typical goal is to purchase only enough GI to ensure that essential expenses are covered. As previously mentioned, however, the amount of GI purchased doesn't have to match essential expenses. It's reasonable to count on systemic withdrawals to provide some income, even during a failure market.

A more refined goal is for guaranteed income combined with systemic-withdrawal income to be greater than essential expenses.

Each retiree must determine the amount needed to cover their essential expenses, which here will be called the *essential- income rate*. In this context "essential" is not about survival, but the basic expenses on which health, happiness, and comfort rely. Restated, the essential-income rate is the annual percentage of the portfolio a retiree needs to maintain their basic quality of life in retirement. It won't cover everything, but should cover everything needed to remain content for potentially long periods of time.

For example, Joe has $500,000 in assets saved for retirement. He hopes to generate $25,000 annually from these assets, which maps to a 5% inflation-adjusted withdrawal rate, but understands he cannot depend on this rate. He estimates that, after Social Security, he needs $15,000 a year to maintain his basic standard of living in retirement, covering housing expenses, food, utilities, minimal entertainment, and an allotment to support his avid interest in woodworking. This means, for Joe, the annual essential-income rate is 3% (i.e., $15,000 divided by 500,000).

Another example is Betty, who has $1,500,000 in assets saved for retirement. She'd be satisfied to generate around 4.5% a year of income from her assets, around $68,000, but also understands that she cannot fully depend on it. She estimates that, after Social Security, she requires another $30,000 a year to meet her essential income needs. This covers all the basic expenses similar to Joe's, but also includes other expenses she considers essential, such as travel costs to visit her grandchildren and annual dues to her social club. This means that, for Betty, the annual essential-income rate is 2% (i.e., $30,000 divided by 1,500,000).

Each retiree (or couple) defines their own individual essential-income rate. This important decision is one of the subjective parts of GI planning. The rate need not be exact, but it should approximate the income floor each retiree considers essential. Again, the goal is to make sure the guaranteed income rate plus systemic-withdrawal-income rate will match or be higher than the essential-income rate.

Of course the essential-income rate must be realistic. The performance of both GI and systemic withdrawals establish inherent boundaries for it. An essential-income rate of 2% or less is low, and easy to satisfy. An essential-income rate of 3% may on average be high for most retirees, but still reasonable and obtainable. An essential-income rate of 4% is high, and isn't obtainable under failure-market conditions (without drastic measures and other risks), but usually is obtainable under normal market conditions (depending on interest rates and market valuations). High essential-income rates, such as 4% and above, may require a retiree to downsize their expenses to create a GI plan, although circumstances vary. Lower essential-income rates always make planning easier, but it's important to be content with the rate chosen.

A Notion of Cost

Cost is defined here as the amount of income typically lost (or gained) using GI. The cost of GI is always attractive under a failure market, but a failure market is essentially the worst-case scenario, far from typical market conditions. It's the cost of GI during typical markets a retiree will most likely encounter. These typical costs provide a useful gauge for deciding how much, if any, GI to purchase.

Given that the Baseline Market encapsulates typical market conditions (as opposed to the failure-market benchmark), it's the proper basis for calculating GI cost. A year-by-year cost comparison of retirement income can be made by comparing Baseline-Market backtesting results with and without GI.

Figure 162 shows an example cost comparison for a single retirement period. The "100% Systemic Withdrawal" row shows annual income purely from systemic withdrawals without GI. The "GI Solution" row shows annual income when 50% of assets are initially allocated to an inflation-adjusted immediate annuity with a 4% payout, with the remaining 50% in systemic withdrawals. The "Cost of GI" row shows the annual withdrawal-rate difference between these two cases. A positive number indicates that annual income increases from using GI; a negative number that annual income decreases from using GI. The summary fields also show the differences, as does the %Left fields.

100% Systemic Withdrawals

A65	A66	A67	A68	A69	A70	A71	A72	A73	A74	A75	A76	A77	A78	A79	A80	A81	A82	A83	A84	A85	A86	A87	A88	A89	A90	A91	A92	A93	A94	A95	A96	A97	A98	A99	A00	A01	A02	A03	A04	%Left	AVG	1st 10Y
4.2	4.0	3.9	4.0	4.1	4.1	4.1	4.0	4.4	4.5	4.3	4.3	4.4	4.5	4.2	4.7	4.6	4.4	4.7	5.1	4.8	5.5	6.2	5.1	5.2	5.2	5.5	4.5	3.9	4.1	4.8	4.4	4.0	4.5	4.3	3.5	4.6	4.5	3.7	5.7	14%	4.5	4.1

GI Solution

A65	A66	A67	A68	A69	A70	A71	A72	A73	A74	A75	A76	A77	A78	A79	A80	A81	A82	A83	A84	A85	A86	A87	A88	A89	A90	A91	A92	A93	A94	A95	A96	A97	A98	A99	A00	A01	A02	A03	A04	%Left	AVG	1st 10Y
4.1	4.0	4.0	4.0	4.1	4.1	4.1	4.0	4.2	4.3	4.2	4.2	4.2	4.3	4.1	4.4	4.3	4.2	4.4	4.6	4.4	4.8	5.1	4.6	4.6	4.6	4.8	4.3	4.0	4.1	4.4	4.2	4.0	4.3	4.2	3.8	4.3	4.3	3.9	4.9	7%	4.3	4.2

Cost of GI

A65	A66	A67	A68	A69	A70	A71	A72	A73	A74	A75	A76	A77	A78	A79	A80	A81	A82	A83	A84	A85	A86	A87	A88	A89	A90	A91	A92	A93	A94	A95	A96	A97	A98	A99	A00	A01	A02	A03	A04	Bequest	AVG	1st 10Y
-0.1	0.0	0.1	0.0	0.0	0.0	0.0	0.0	-0.2	-0.2	-0.1	-0.1	-0.2	-0.2	-0.1	-0.3	-0.3	-0.2	-0.3	-0.5	-0.4	-0.7	-1.1	-0.5	-0.6	-0.6	-0.7	-0.2	0.1	0.0	-0.4	-0.2	0.0	-0.2	-0.1	0.3	-0.3	-0.2	0.2	-0.8	-7%	-0.3	0.1

FIGURE 162

*Example cost comparison without GI (i.e., 100% systemic withdrawals) and with
GI (i.e., allocating 50% to a 4% inflation-adjusted immediate annuity).*

Later in the chapter, the cost of GI is explored more fully over all the retirement periods for the GI recommendations. Retirees can use these cost estimates to better determine how much GI is affordable for their particular case.

A Notion of Affordability

Purchasing GI only makes sense if it's affordable. While this sounds straightforward, the concept of affordability is the catch-all for most of the ambiguity within the GI planning process. Affordability is determined by many interrelated factors, some nebulous.

Affordability extends well past cost and available assets. Consider the following example. I know the cost of a particular Mercedes-Benz sedan. I have funds available to buy the sedan. I believe the sedan is high quality. I would enjoy the sedan. I might even believe the sedan provides attractive automotive value for the cost. All of these factors count towards affordability, but I still don't consider the sedan affordable. My concept of affordability is personal. It extends into my life philosophy, tradeoffs with alternative uses for the assets, my own metrics of value, and so on. It's an ill-defined decision process only I can work though.

Risk tolerance is another factor of GI affordability. If a retiree can't sleep well at night without most of their essential-income rate locked in, then GI affordability almost becomes automatic (but not quite). If a retiree believes handling failure markets (i.e., the failure-market benchmark) is an important requirement, then GI becomes more affordable. If a retiree is comfortable reducing their expected annual income by a substantial percentage (e.g., 15%, 25%) to lock in the essential-income rate, then GI is generally more affordable. On the other hand, if a retiree is highly motivated to generate income well above their essential-income rate, then GI generally becomes less affordable.

Just as important to affordability is the essential-income rate. The essential-income rate combined with cost determines the percentage of total assets required for GI. GI maintains its affordability when it can protect the essential-income rate without negatively impacting a retiree's overall retirement plan. Consider the following example. A couple's initial withdrawal rate is 4.8% using systemic withdrawals (the valuation level is attractive at 1.7). Their essential-income rate is high at 3.9%. Fearful of the stock market, they form a plan to lock in the full 3.9% using an annuity. Unfortunately, GI costs are high because interest rates are low, so it takes 90% of total assets to implement the plan. The effect is, the couple is locked into little more than their essential-income rate for the rest of their lives. They lose their financial flexibility and increase their risk of unexpected expenses. This plan is not affordable as defined. While there isn't a precise dividing line, if more than 70% of total assets are required to fulfill a GI plan, then it's usually not affordable.

A bequest motive also has a large effect on GI affordability. If there is no bequest motive, GI is always more affordable. With a bequest motive, GI tradeoffs become cloudier. This factor more than any other steers retirees away from GI, even though a workable balance is usually possible.

Affordability shifts over time. As we change, our concept of affordability might change. One change is inevitable though—as we age, the cost of GI dramatically lowers. Annuity payouts escalate with age. Bond ladders built late in life pay significantly more because they are shorter (e.g., where a 30-year bond ladder built at age 75 pays 4.5%, a 15-year ladder built at age 90 pays 7.8%). Without a bequest motive, rising payouts will eventually always make GI affordable: a simple test late in retirement is to compare the current payout from systemic withdrawals to the current payout for GI.

Ultimately, for a GI plan to be accepted, it must pass a retiree's unique individual test for affordability.

Unexpected Expenses

Unexpected expenses can cause insufficient income as much as poor market returns. If there is not enough income to meet expenses, it doesn't matter if it's because the income is too low or the expenses too high—the results are the same. The risk of unexpected expenses may be as high as the risk of a failure market. There is no way to know. Neither have good measures. Both can be substantial.

Although both these risks lead to insufficient income, their hedges are very different. GI hedges the risk of a failure market, guaranteeing a fixed amount of income to cover essential expenses. The right hedge for unexpected expenses is less well defined. Living below one's means helps, as does setting aside an emergency fund. The root of a solution is having enough extra assets to cover extra expenses. This is where systemic withdrawal comes in.

During normal markets systemic-withdrawal assets grow faster than normal withdrawals, meaning portfolios often accumulate enough extra funds to cover unexpected expenses (especially when using an income cap). Although a retiree cannot rely on this growth, it's often the case with systemic withdrawal. It's virtually never the case with GI.

Liquidity might also be an issue. If GI is invested in an annuity, there is no way to pull out extra cash. A bond ladder can be cashed out, but interest-rate risk becomes an issue. Systemic withdrawal bonds (i.e., bond funds) will be the best source of cash to cover unexpected expenses[*].

The implication is, the more a retiree allocates to GI to hedge against failure markets, the higher the risk of not being able to cover unexpected expenses. One solution is to always maintain a certain percentage of assets in systemic withdrawals, but what that percentage should be is not clear. The lower bound may be 30% of total assets in order to maintain some flexibility. Undoubtedly, maintaining a much higher percentage of total assets in systemic withdrawals (e.g., 70%) will be much more flexible.

---

[*]   Maintaining liquidity could be a justification for maintaining a bond floor (e.g., 10%) in Prime Harvesting.

A Note on Taxes and Investing Expenses

Taxes and investing expenses are generally beyond the scope of this book, but they must be kept in mind.

Expenses can erode the value of GI instruments, so fully understand and weigh expenses before purchasing GI. Expenses usually aren't a problem if buying federal bonds, although they can be for other bonds including municipals. Then there are annuities, which are famous for high expenses (including commissions), but are starting to become more competitive, probably due to the Internet. Again, always confirm and compare GI expenses before purchasing.

For taxes, a quick summary of relevant 2014 US tax codes is provided as a reference point. When assets are held in tax-advantaged accounts such as IRAs or 401Ks, taxes are not an issue, but outside these accounts, taxes can have a significant influence. Generally, stock income is taxed at more favorable dividend and capital gain rates, while bond and annuity income are taxed as less favorable ordinary income. The exceptions are important though. Treasury bonds (excluding TIPS and STRIPS) are not taxed at the federal level, but are at the state level. Municipal bonds are not taxed at the federal level or the state and local level when issued within the retiree's state or local municipality. Corporate bonds, certificates of deposits (CDs), and mortgage-backed securities are generally fully taxed as ordinary income. Bonds with deferred income, such as TIPS and zero coupon bonds, have a portion of the deferred interest income taxed each year. Bonds resold on the secondary markets will also have associated capital gains (or losses). The list of top GI instruments is small, however, so the tax issues will be much less varied for most retirees.

When factoring in all the other criteria, taxes usually become an unavoidable investment cost with little to no effect on GI strategies. The salient exception is Treasury Inflation-Protected Securities used outside a tax-advantaged account, where taxes might affect whether they work or not.

THE TOP GUARANTEED-INCOME INSTRUMENTS

There are many fixed-income candidates for providing GI, but surprisingly few can satisfy the needs of retirement. The commonest problem is the lack of inflation protection, eliminating most of the choices.

Only three GI instruments make the final cut: TIPS Bond Ladders, Inflation-Adjusted SPIAs, and I Bonds. I'll explore each of these recommended instruments, then look at what didn't make the cut and why.

Considering terminology, a distinction is made between GI instruments and GI strategies. Here the discussion on GI instruments examines specific bonds or annuities, their characteristics, and how they are individually applied. Later, the discussion on GI strategies looks at broader plans, often examining combinations of GI instruments and how they operate in conjunction with systemic withdrawals.

TIPS Bond Ladder

Treasury Inflation-Protected Securities, commonly known as TIPS, are inflation-indexed government bonds. When bought individually, as opposed to in an index fund, they have little to no expenses, they are US-government backed (i.e., virtually no default risk during a failure market), and include a built-in inflation hedge. When maturity dates are staggered into a "ladder", TIPS provide a fixed steady real income stream. Overall, TIPS are uniquely effective in their ability to provide virtually riskless income when held under the right conditions in tax-advantaged accounts. However, they are far from perfect.

TIPS deliver a fixed real rate of return known as their *coupon rate*, with inflation adjustments matching CPI-U. Newly issued TIPS can be bought directly (known as buying "at auction") through online brokers* (e.g., Schwab, Fidelity). They are only offered a few times a year with maturities of 5, 10, 20, and 30 years. Longer maturities generally pay higher coupon rates.

TIPS can also be bought on the secondary market through online brokers. Given that these are previously owned TIPS being resold, a secondary-market TIPS can be bought with just about any remaining maturity up to the maximum of 30 years. (The reselling of TIPS as the current interest rate changes, establishing current market value, is what causes the yield of the older TIPS to be different from their coupon rate.)

Inflation-adjusted coupon payments are made twice a year based on the face value, and then a final payment on maturity returns the inflation-adjusted face value of the bond. For example, consider a TIPS with a face value of $1000, a 10-year maturity, and a 2% coupon rate. For 10 years, the retiree receives an inflation-adjusted 2% of $1000 (i.e., $20) split between two semi-annual payments. Then, on maturity 10 years later, the retiree receives back the $1000 face value, again adjusted for inflation.

A TIPS ladder holds TIPS bought with varying maturity dates and coupon rates to provide a steady fixed-income stream, such as a ladder built to provide an inflation-adjusted $10,000 a year for 30 years. Keep in mind when building a TIPS ladder that the income for any single year is composed of all the coupon payments for TIPS held in the ladder plus the face value of any individual TIPS maturing in the year. While the concept of a ladder is relatively straightforward, getting the details right to produce the desired income stream is more challenging.

This exploration of TIPS doesn't provide a retiree with all the details required to build a TIPS ladder. For example, TIPS usually don't sell at their face value (e.g., a TIPS with a $1000 face value may sell for $1020). This means that the actual yield usually doesn't match the coupon rate. Also, TIPS sold on the secondary market come at varying stages of maturity, again with yields different from the coupon rate. While these distinctions don't need to be made for high-level planning, they are crucial when buying TIPS to construct an actual ladder.

Freely available online sources explain everything it takes to build a TIPS ladder, although the reader has to piece some of the information together. Wade Pfau in 2013 wrote a blog article[59] on the pragmatic aspects of building a TIPS bond ladder, entitled "How Do I Build a TIPS Bond Ladder for Retirement Income?" Members of the Bogleheads forum continue the discussion[60], including Pfau's results, while producing a spreadsheet. Readers interested in building their own TIPS ladder are well served by this free advice, starting with Pfau's methodical work (which includes many helpful and astute reader comments), then filling in with the Bogleheads discussions†.

As a brief overview, a TIPS ladder is usually constructed working backward from the last year. For example, to build a 30-year ladder, first purchase a TIPS maturing in 30 years. The coupon payment plus principal payout at maturity should match the desired income. Then do the same for a 29-year TIPS (i.e., a 30-year TIPS with only 29 years left till maturity). Again, the coupon payment plus principal payout at maturity contribute to the desire income, but this time the coupon payment from the older 30-year TIPS is also included. Next, a 28-year TIPS is bought for year 28, with the older 30-year and 29-year TIPS contributing to the year's target income. This process continues down to the starting year, which receives coupon payments for all the succeeding years in the ladder. The calculations are tedious, but doable. Individual retirees do construct their own TIPS ladders using readily accessible tools. The good thing is, a ladder need only be constructed once or perhaps twice through retirement. Once built, a ladder requires no maintenance.

---

* TIPS can also be bought directly online through Treasury Direct, but not through a tax-advantaged account like an Individual Retirement Account (IRA).

† The TIPS discussions are generally high quality and helpful, but readers should confirm all information with at least one reputable independent source.

It's notable that a TIPS bond ladder always stays under the control of the retiree. This means all or part of a ladder can be liquidated early if required because of external circumstances. The secondary market is robust for reselling TIPS before maturity (although there is interest-rate risk when doing so). This also means if a retiree dies early, heirs receive the value remaining in the bond ladder.

It's important to understand that no assets are left at the end of TIPS ladder — the payout includes all the original assets forming the ladder. While this consumption of assets to produce income makes sense in retirement, keep in mind that it's different from traditional bond ladders oriented to preserving value outside of retirement (interest payments are then used to buy new bonds).

§

How much income will a TIPS ladder generate? A ladder's payout (essentially the supported withdrawal rate) is determined by its real internal rate of return (IRR). Think of the real IRR as a single composite coupon rate for all TIPS making up the ladder (more precisely the real IRR is the composite yield of the ladder, considering TIPS often do not sell at face value). The real IRR is conceptual, but it provides an easy shortcut for estimating the payout for a TIPS bond ladder.

Figure 163 shows the varying payouts based on the real IRR and length of a TIPS ladder. For example, a real IRR of 1% for a 30-year TIPS ladder supports an inflation-adjusted payout rate of 3.9%. A 2% real IRR for the same 30-year TIPS ladder will support a payout rate of 4.5%. TIPS maturity dates don't go past 30 years, but the figure shows what a retiree might expect for longer periods when using strategies (covered later) to extend a TIPS ladder past 30 years. A 1% real IRR for a simulated 40-year TIPS ladder supports a payout rate of only 3.0%.

Years in Ladder	Real Internal Rate of Return								
	0.0%	0.5%	1.0%	1.5%	2.0%	2.5%	3.0%	3.5%	4.0%
10	10.0%	10.3%	10.6%	10.8%	11.1%	11.4%	11.7%	12.0%	12.3%
11	9.1%	9.4%	9.6%	9.9%	10.2%	10.5%	10.8%	11.1%	11.4%
12	8.3%	8.6%	8.9%	9.2%	9.5%	9.7%	10.0%	10.3%	10.7%
13	7.7%	8.0%	8.2%	8.5%	8.8%	9.1%	9.4%	9.7%	10.0%
14	7.1%	7.4%	7.7%	8.0%	8.3%	8.6%	8.9%	9.2%	9.5%
15	6.7%	6.9%	7.2%	7.5%	7.8%	8.1%	8.4%	8.7%	9.0%
16	6.3%	6.5%	6.8%	7.1%	7.4%	7.7%	8.0%	8.3%	8.6%
17	5.9%	6.2%	6.4%	6.7%	7.0%	7.3%	7.6%	7.9%	8.2%
18	5.6%	5.8%	6.1%	6.4%	6.7%	7.0%	7.3%	7.6%	7.9%
19	5.3%	5.5%	5.8%	6.1%	6.4%	6.7%	7.0%	7.3%	7.6%
20	5.0%	5.3%	5.5%	5.8%	6.1%	6.4%	6.7%	7.0%	7.4%
21	4.8%	5.0%	5.3%	5.6%	5.9%	6.2%	6.5%	6.8%	7.1%
22	4.5%	4.8%	5.1%	5.4%	5.7%	6.0%	6.3%	6.6%	6.9%
23	4.3%	4.6%	4.9%	5.2%	5.5%	5.8%	6.1%	6.4%	6.7%
24	4.2%	4.4%	4.7%	5.0%	5.3%	5.6%	5.9%	6.2%	6.6%
25	4.0%	4.3%	4.5%	4.8%	5.1%	5.4%	5.7%	6.1%	6.4%
26	3.8%	4.1%	4.4%	4.7%	5.0%	5.3%	5.6%	5.9%	6.3%
27	3.7%	4.0%	4.2%	4.5%	4.8%	5.1%	5.5%	5.8%	6.1%
28	3.6%	3.8%	4.1%	4.4%	4.7%	5.0%	5.3%	5.7%	6.0%
29	3.4%	3.7%	4.0%	4.3%	4.6%	4.9%	5.2%	5.5%	5.9%
30	3.3%	3.6%	3.9%	4.2%	4.5%	4.8%	5.1%	5.4%	5.8%
31	3.2%	3.5%	3.8%	4.1%	4.4%	4.7%	5.0%	5.3%	5.7%
32	3.1%	3.4%	3.7%	4.0%	4.3%	4.6%	4.9%	5.2%	5.6%
33	3.0%	3.3%	3.6%	3.9%	4.2%	4.5%	4.8%	5.2%	5.5%
34	2.9%	3.2%	3.5%	3.8%	4.1%	4.4%	4.7%	5.1%	5.4%
35	2.9%	3.1%	3.4%	3.7%	4.0%	4.3%	4.7%	5.0%	5.4%
36	2.8%	3.0%	3.3%	3.6%	3.9%	4.2%	4.6%	4.9%	5.3%
37	2.7%	3.0%	3.2%	3.5%	3.9%	4.2%	4.5%	4.9%	5.2%
38	2.6%	2.9%	3.2%	3.5%	3.8%	4.1%	4.4%	4.8%	5.2%
39	2.6%	2.8%	3.1%	3.4%	3.7%	4.0%	4.4%	4.7%	5.1%
40	2.5%	2.8%	3.0%	3.3%	3.7%	4.0%	4.3%	4.7%	5.1%

FIGURE 163

Guaranteed withdrawal rates based on TIPS annualized real rates of return. The 2% column corresponds to the long-term average for TIPS. Since TIPS are not sold past 30 years, returns past 30 years are estimated to simulate extended ladders.

Once again, if the real IRR can be estimated, then a simple table lookup provides the corresponding payout for the TIPS ladder, without going through the complexity of building the ladder.

A rough estimate for real IRR can be simply calculated as 80% of the current yield for a TIPS maturing during the last year of the ladder. For example, the real IRR for a 30-year ladder is roughly 80% of the current yield for a 30-year TIPS. For TIPS sold at auction, the yield matches the coupon rate, but the US Treasury only auctions TIPS quarterly. The most up-to-date yield is usually provided by the secondary market, which is shown online at the Wall Street Journal's Market Data Center under the TIPS section[61]. For example, on March 2, 2015, the yield for a TIPS maturing on February 15, 2044 is 0.733%. Taking 80% of this yield value provides a real-IRR estimate of 0.59%. Looking up this estimate in Figure 163 maps to an inflation-adjusted payout of approximately 3.7% annually (interpolating between the 0.5% and 1% values) for a 30-year TIPS ladder. While this provides a convenient rough estimate for preliminary planning, an accurate estimate requires constructing the TIPS ladder on paper with actual TIPS prices.

When considering a ladder for the future, the historical data can show the typical range of payouts. Unfortunately, TIPS don't have a long history (especially 30-year TIPS), so some guesswork is required to anticipate future rates. Based on the historical TIPS rates shown in Figure 164, the 30-year rates tend to roughly run about 0.5% over the

10-year rates[62]. Looking at the longer 10-year rate, and making the 80% adjustment for the IRR, one might expect the real IRR for a 30-year TIP ladder to typically fall between 0% and 3%. (Although the 10-year coupon rate briefly exceeded 4% in the late 1990s, this was likely due to the perceived illiquidity of newly introduced TIPS and will probably never happen again[63].) Narrowing down to a more typical range, the "average" real IRR for retirees building a 30-year ladder is often somewhere around the middle between a 1% and 2% real IRR. This implies that the average payout for a 30-year TIPS ladder (again using Figure 163) is around 3.9% to 4.5%. It also implies that the average payout for a 40-year TIPS ladder is around 3.0% to 3.7%, which is not very attractive.

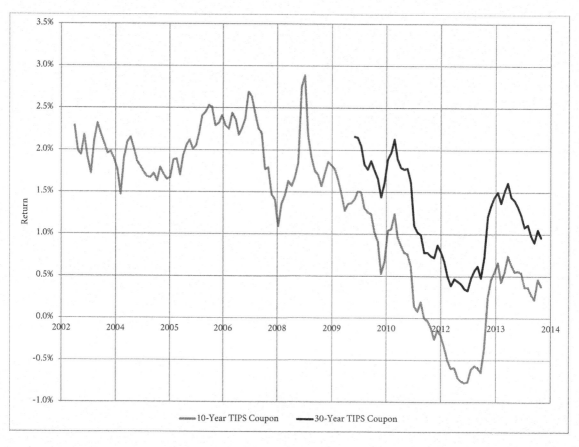

FIGURE 164

Historical TIPS coupon rates.

Although TIPS are exceptional in many ways, their disadvantages are significant. First, as already mentioned, setting up a ladder for a steady stream of income is not simple. Although it's certainly doable for individuals, many will find the extra layer of complexity a barrier. Second, TIPS are not tax efficient. When TIPS are held in a taxable account, the inflation adjustment to the principal (i.e., face value) of the TIPS is taxed each year. This is notable because the associated income is not received until maturity, although it could result in a large tax bill much earlier from high inflation. Third, the maximum maturity length is 30 years, meaning a TIPS bond ladder alone cannot provide GI for retirement periods over 30 years without a broader strategy. Related, the maturity of a TIPS ladder must match the longest possible life span of the retiree (or couple), because no assets remain after the ladder completes. Finally, and sometimes most importantly, the cost of TIPS can be high, even as reflected in the average payouts for long ladders.

In summary, TIPS are exceptional under the right conditions, but the pragmatic needs of retirees too often make them unattractive for GI. Their use is revisited in the sections on GI strategies, including comparisons with the alternatives.

Appendix B also covers a form of "asset dedication", where TIPS ladders are used in place of bond funds within systemic withdrawals. While not recommended, it's a viable option for retirees who are comfortable with the tradeoffs.

Inflation-Adjusted SPIAs

A Single Premium Immediate Annuity (SPIA) provides a stream of monthly income payments, starting immediately after purchase and lasting for life. This life stream of income is bought using a single upfront lump-sum payment (hence the name "single premium"). For an inflation-adjusted SPIA the income stream, the payout, is adjusted annually to match inflation based on CPI.* This income stream can be thought of as the inflation-adjusted withdrawal rate for the assets used to buy the SPIA, although in this case the income is fixed, guaranteed for life, and has no remaining value at the end of life.

Figure 165 shows actual inflation-adjusted SPIA payouts for September, 2014. For example, a 65 year old couple receives a 4.01% payout for the money invested; this means, for $100,000, there is an inflation-adjusted $4,010 annual payout (i.e., $334 per month) for as long as either member of the couple lives. A 75 year old female receives a 7.16% payout. For $100,000, this is an inflation-adjusted $7,016 annual payout as long as she lives. An 85 year-old male receives a 12.96% payout. For $100,000, this is an inflation-adjusted $12,960 annual payout as long as he lives. As shown, the rates are modest when purchased early in retirement, but grow to become exceptional when purchased later on in life.

Age	Joint Rate	Male Rate	Female Rate
65	4.01%	5.11%	4.72%
70	4.74%	6.13%	5.59%
75	5.75%	7.60%	7.16%
80	7.32%	10.28%	9.04%
85	9.07%	12.96%	11.20%

FIGURE 165

September 2014 payout rates for inflation-adjusted SPIA.

Annuities have the unique ability to pool risk across a group of retirees. This unique benefit is known as the "mortality premium", which essentially means that retirees dying earlier than expected will help support retirees dying later than expected. This not only protects an individual from outliving their purchased income stream, but also contributes to a higher income stream. Bought late in life, annuities generate a rate of guaranteed income higher than any other investment, eventually even outpacing the best systemic withdrawals performance.

---

* SPIAs with fixed increases for inflation (e.g., 3%) do not adequately cover inflation risk.

One potential problem with all annuities is default risk (the same risk carried by all corporate and municipal bonds); fortunately, there are reasons to believe the risk of a retiree not getting paid for an annuity is extremely small. Joe Tomlinson, a former actuary, provides a persuasive analysis for annuities being reasonably safe in his 2012 paper, *How Safe are Annuities?*[64] While thy are not perfect, he points out insurance companies as a group have a long and strong track record, delivering an extremely safe record for annuities. The industry is heavily regulated, in part to make sure individuals buying insurance products are protected. The insurance industry is also well capitalized, more so than the banking industry. This means that a company in trouble, which occasional happens, can be bought out by stronger companies if needed. Also, a significant portion of annuity income is guaranteed by states (more on this later), again to protect individuals. Tomlinson also considers the overall state of the insurance industry and its ability to handle a global financial crisis. He concludes with the following:

> One cannot forecast with certainty the financial health of the insurance industry 20 or 30 years from now. But I do not see any indications that the future for the insurance industry augurs serious problems for annuity owners. Unfortunately, there are no retirement decisions that are free from risk. Weighing the various risks, I remain comfortable recommending annuities.

Tomlinson goes on to discuss the unusual case of American International Group (AIG). AIG was a financially powerful, AAA-rated insurance company that essentially went bankrupt in 2008. The problem was triggered by subprime loans, which AIG backed with credit protection. This part of AIG's business resided in unregulated subsidiaries, independent from the traditional highly regulated parts of the insurance business, but the magnitude of the problem put the whole company at risk. Throughout the crisis, however, AIG never attempted to tap the financial reserves backing annuities or other regulated insurance products. Even if they had tried, state insurance regulators were in place to block the action—their task is guaranteeing that proper reserves are maintained to back all insurance products including annuities. The point is, the worst insurance company crisis to date in the US did not trigger an annuity default—the insurance industry as a whole has a vested interest in ensuring that annuity holders are always paid.

Another perspective comes from considering how the associated risks may overlap. It's reasonable to assume that SPIA defaults don't always occur with failure markets. In other words, a retirement failure market is distinct from a failure within the general economy that might trigger SPIA defaults by insurance companies. Certainly, they may be related, but they are not the same. If a failure market occurs but there is no SPIA default, then the SPIA solution works. If a SPIA default occurs outside a failure market, there is a strong chance the overall solution still works (i.e., the rest of the portfolio will provide the essential-income rate). The problem occurs when there is an SPIA default within a failure market. The point is simple: the probability of both events happening is real, but smaller than the already low probability of a failure market.

No doubt, annuities do increase risk above the level of government-backed bonds; nevertheless, many retirees will find annuity's unique advantages worth the small added risk. Admittedly, this is not completely clear without considering and comparing the costs—this comes later.

The position I take here is inflation-adjusted SPIAs ultimately satisfy essential GI requirements for safety (with SPIA-free solutions discussed later). However, retirees using SPIAs should take a few extra precautions* to make them safer. First, buy only from the highest-rated insurance companies. Second, lean toward buying from larger companies (despite the AIG case), given they are typically better diversified and have deeper financial backing. Third, when

---

* These precautions heavily draw on Tomlinson's recommendations, although they are not identical.

possible, spread annuity purchases across multiple companies (at least two). Fourth, consider the limits states place on guaranteeing annuities if a company defaults (e.g., $100,000 in Wyoming, $250,000 in Virginia, $500,000 in New York). Finally, never over invest in any single retirement instrument not backed by the government. Multiple forms of GI work well in combination, plus GI's purpose is to supplement systemic withdrawals, not to replace them.

Despite annuities' unique ability to pool risk to boost income for life, many retirees refuse to invest in them. While some of this refusal may be due to default risk, and some to a warranted reputation for excessive fees and commissions, the dominant reason appears to be that annuities lock up assets and prevent any remaining value from going to heirs*.

To counterbalance this aversion to annuities, keep in mind that a portion of an annuity's premium (i.e., the cost) is what supports retirees living longer. Any retiree living past the average life expectancy in effect pockets a portion of the premium paid by other retirees. Also, by eliminating the risk of outliving assets, annuities remove a potential liability for heirs if essential expenses can't be met. Finally, if systemic withdrawals are stressed, it's GI that relieves the pressure, potentially increasing the final bequest amount.

Annuities fit well into a GI solution when bought right† and used in moderation. The mortality premium compensates for the loss in flexibility and the loss in bequest value, given both should still be available from systemic withdrawals in ample amounts.

I Bonds

An I Bond is an inflation-adjusted, expense-free US-government bond. In several ways, I Bonds are the best overall GI instrument available. However, they come with one major constraint: only a limited amount can be purchased each year.

Only $10,000 in I Bonds can be purchased each year per US social security number, with an additional $5000 purchase from an IRS tax refund. This limits an individual to $15,000 per year, and a couple to $30,000 a year. This limit typically translates to a relatively small percentage of a retirement portfolio's value, making I Bonds harder to strategically apply. Still, bought over time, I Bonds can form a substantial reserve of GI. Also, with early planning, retirees can start purchasing I Bonds a few years before retirement. I Bonds can't provide an immediate income stream like an SPIA or TIPS ladder, but they uniquely excel at preserving real value, risk-free, for later use within other long-term strategies.

I Bonds are purchased online through Treasury Direct. They have no secondary market like TIPS, but none is needed, given their characteristics and limits on ownership. Their interest rate is set when issued, followed by inflation adjustments every six months.

Unlike TIPS, there is no annual coupon payment and no need for a ladder. All interest accrues and compounds tax free, as long as the bond is held, up to 30 years. When redeemed, the face value plus all accrued interest value is paid out. I Bonds can be redeemed any time after one year, although there is a 3-month interest penalty if held for less than 5 years. The amount redeemed is flexible, because I Bonds can be bought in any denomination from $25 to $10,000.

I Bonds have no fixed maturity date, and therefore no potential interest-rate risk (unlike TIPS sold before maturity on the secondary market). I Bonds can't be resold, but again there is no need, since they can be redeemed

---

* Annuities often provide an option for guaranteed payments for a set number of years, even on death, but this evidently comes at a cost that doesn't change the basic conclusions to buy or not.

† The choices for inflation-adjusted SPIAs are limited but sufficient, but it remains crucial for retirees to always shop carefully for good financial products with reasonable fees and expenses.

virtually anytime. I Bonds' flexibility makes it possible to sell one bond without penalty (after the holding period) to buy another at a higher interest rate (as long as the annual purchasing limit is not a factor and taxes are considered).

Figure 166 shows the historical fixed return of I Bonds. After inflation adjustment, this becomes the real rate of return for the life of bond. Unlike TIPS, I Bonds can never have a negative real rate of return. Like TIPS, their history is short. Also like TIPS, when interest rates are low, they become less attractive. Still, their reliability and flexibility are always outstanding.

FIGURE 166

I Bonds rates based on date of issue. (Source: Treasury Direct)

Historically I Bond rates trail 10-year TIPS coupon rates by approximately 1%. This may put their average as low as 0.5% when excluding high rates shortly after introduction, but there is not much history to go on. Still, a lower rate in some cases can be offset by I Bonds' unique ability to upgrade (i.e., sell old and buy new) when rates are better.

I Bonds are unique in their ability to preserve value with no risk, hassle, or taxes. Until attempted, it's easy to underappreciate the difficulty of preserving real value with nearly absolute assurance. As shown later, I Bonds can play an important role in broader GI strategies.

Less Desirable Instruments

There are many other instruments, but each has one or more weaknesses, making them unsuitable for retirement GI. Some are well-suited for other circumstances (e.g., bond funds work well in systemic withdrawals); others are generally poor, given better alternatives. The most known of the less desirable GI instruments are briefly discussed below.

Keep in mind, the financial industry periodically creates new instruments to market to investors. Their goal is to boost their profits. It pays well for retirees to be skeptical. It's not rare for instruments to be crafted to hide disadvantages from unsuspecting buyers, especially excessive fees. Generally, the harder an instrument is to fully understand, and the harder the financial industry tries to sell it, the lower the likelihood it's suitable for retirement.

Bond Funds

Bond funds are a convenient and inexpensive way to invest in individual bonds, but the way they operate results in characteristics that are very different from individual bonds. Ultimately, bond funds can't provide GI.

Figure 167 shows the individual sources of price change within a TIPS index fund[65]. Looking at a breakdown of the fund's return, the coupon payments and inflation adjustments come directly from individual TIPS—the reliable portion of the income. However, the price-change component of the return is externally driven, primarily from interest rate changes. This results in volatility that individual TIPS don't have when held to maturity. Notice that, because of the price-change component, the total return is sometimes negative.

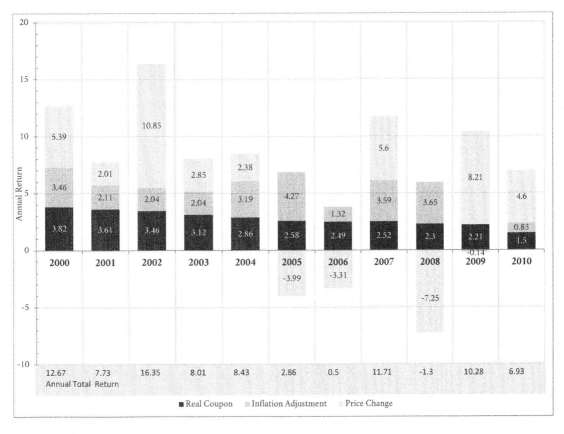

FIGURE 167

Source-of-return breakdowns of TIPS index funds between 2000 and 2010 (Source: TIAA-CREF)

Figure 168 shows the forward 10-year real return for three US-Treasury bond indexes and one corporate bond index. The variance is surprisingly large. Bond indexes have sequence-of-return risk just like stock indexes, although on a smaller scale. Only very short-term bond funds will have a reliable positive nominal return; no bond fund reliably has a positive *real* return. This volatility in real return prevents any bond funds from being a source of GI.

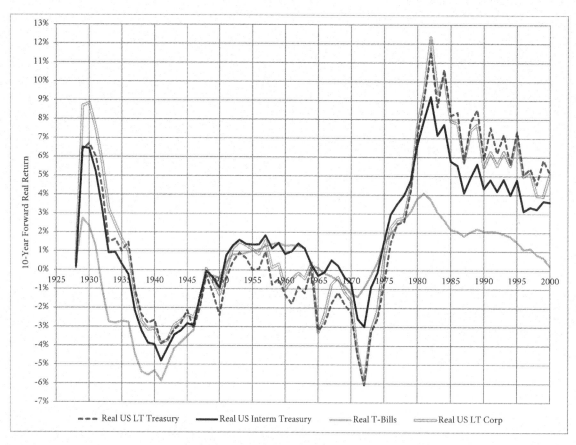

FIGURE 168

Annualized forward 10-year real returns for US bond indexes.

This volatility in bond funds may lead some to question their use within systemic withdrawals, given bonds are the ballast for the overall stock portfolio. The quick answer for now is that bond funds and stock funds empirically work well together, in large part because they are negatively correlated. A more through answer is given in Appendix B, which explores the option of using bond ladders in place of bond funds within systemic withdrawals.

Nominal Bonds, Certificates of Deposit, and Related Securities

Nominal bonds (i.e., conventional bonds with no inflation adjustment), certificates of deposit (CDs), and all similar debt instruments share the same simple flaw: they don't reliably keep up with inflation over the long term. Their income can be laddered to deliver guaranteed fixed income in nominal terms, but without inflation protection, the value of the income is not guaranteed (as documented in the framework discussion).

Inflation estimates are captured in bond prices, but not unexpected inflation. History shows unexpected inflation can be large. While inflation risk in this context may not be high, the data shows it's historically much higher than the risk of a pure systemic withdrawal solution without GI.

Any type of long-term laddered income must have inflation protection to provide real guaranteed income, which is why TIPS and I Bonds are the only recommended debt instruments.

Nominal Annuities

All nominal annuities including SPIAs have the same problem as nominal bonds: there is no inflation protection. Figure 161 in the framework discussion uses nominal annuities to illustrate the risk of inflation. While nominal annuities generally don't satisfy retirement needs, there are a couple of special cases where they might work well.

The first case is a retiree buying an annuity early in retirement with the goal of intentionally frontloading income, accepting that inflation will erode annuity value late in life. For example, a retiree may plan to travel more and pay off a mortgage early in retirement, making it okay for some income to be slowly eroded over time from inflation.

The second case is very late in retirement, when buying choices are limited (or nonexistent) for inflation-adjusted annuities. Also, inflation risk is much lower very late in retirement, due to a limited life expectancy. For example, a 90-year old retiree whose income has been inadequate may decide to boost it with a nominal SPIA.

These exceptions lack planning precision, deserving some caution, but should work well under the right conditions.

Variable Annuities

A variable annuity has a fixed-income portion and a variable-income portion. The variable-income portion is supported by a portfolio of stocks. While they are packaged to make annuities more appealing to retirees, there are better options than variable annuities.

An insurance company gains an inherent investment advantage over individual investors by creating a bond pool for varying life expectancies. This is the mortality premium of SPIAs. In contrast, an insurance company has no inherent advantage when it comes to managing a portfolio of stocks.

Complexity is often a guise for hiding high expenses. This appears to be the case with variable annuities. Robert Port, an attorney specializing in securities arbitration and litigation, sums up variable annuities well: "Advisers I respect tell me that except in very rare instances, there is almost always a cheaper, less complicated option than buying a variable annuity[66]."

Inflation adds another downside. While inflation protection is harder to analyze in a variable annuity, the portion of annuity income coming from bonds is certainly not inflation protected.

Finally, stock portfolios packaged and managed by investment companies cannot match the efficiency of the mechanisms recommended in this book for individual retirees.

Guaranteed Lifetime Withdrawal Benefit Rider

A Guaranteed Lifetime Withdrawal Benefit Rider (GLWB) is an extra rider that can be purchased with variable annuities. A GLWB guarantees a minimum income throughout retirement. While a GLWB may sound well-matched to retirement, it's not. GLWBs push harder to make annuities attractive to retirees, but as with all variable annuities there are better options in retirement.

To start with, GLWB fees are higher than the value they add. Vanguard is one of the top investment companies in the industry, known for its low fees. Its GLWB rider still carries a hefty 1.20% management fee (not including other fees), and this is much *lower* than its competitors. Fees are an expense added to the essential-income rate! It's safe to assume that any instrument with high fees and complexity is more in the seller's interest than the retiree's.

Also, if an insurance company doesn't have an "escape clause" written deep in its GLWB contract, then its risk of default from extra guarantees can only grow during a failure market. Not surprisingly, Vanguard separates itself from any liability, stating in its GLWB contract: "Product guarantees are subject to the claims-paying ability of the issuing insurance company."

Finally, as with variable annuities in general, the GLWB does not include inflation protection—the value of the guaranteed withdrawal amount slowly erodes over a long retirement.

Inflation-Adjusted Deferred Immediate Annuities

An Inflation-Adjusted Deferred Immediate Annuity (DIA) is an inflation-adjusted annuity that doesn't start paying out until much later, such as 20 or 30 years later. This sounds attractive, since deferring income is a valuable tool in long-term GI strategies; unfortunately, DIAs have a serious flaw preventing their recommendation.

The flaw is, inflation-adjustment doesn't start until payments begin. This means, for the deferred period, often 20 years or more, there are no inflation adjustments. This effectively cripples the viability of long-term DIAs in retirement because of inflation risk.

Figure 169 shows the power of using an inflation-adjusted DIA within a broader strategy, assuming a failure market. 50% of assets are put in a 25 years TIPS bond ladder; 12% are put in an inflation-adjusted DIA; the remaining 38% are in systemic withdrawals. The overall results are excellent with a 2.5% inflation rate over the first 25 years.

FIGURE 169

*Failure-market results allocating 50% for 25-Year TIPS ladder plus 12%
DIA assuming 2.5% inflation (over the 25 deferred years).*

Figure 170 shows the exact same strategy: everything is the same, except the inflation rate over the first 25 years was an unexpected 5% instead of the planned 2.5%. Notice that over the first 25 years when income was funded by the TIPS ladder, the income is exactly the same, but the problem surfaces when the DIA starts. When inflation performed as expected at 2.5%, the results easily supported a 3% essential-income rate; however, when inflation jumped to an unexpected 5%, the results failed to do so. Basically, real income can't be guaranteed with inflation-adjusted DIAs.

Initial	Start	End	A65	A66	A67	A68	A69	A70	A71	A72	A73	A74	A75	A76	A77	A78	A79	A80	A81	A82	A83	A84	A85	A86	A87	A88	A89	A90	A91	A92	A93	A94	A95	A96	A97	A98	A99	A00	A01	A02	A03	A04	%Left	Min	Avg	1st 10Y	MSWR
4.0%	1928	1967	4.4	4.0	3.9	3.8	3.9	3.9	3.9	4.1	4.3	3.8	3.9	3.9	3.8	3.7	3.7	3.8	3.9	4.3	3.9	3.8	3.8	3.8	4.1	4.2	4.2	3.3	4.0	4.1	4.1	3.7	4.1	4.1	4.1	4.1	4.1	4.1	4.1	4.1	4.1	4.1	27.9%	3.3	4.0%	4.0%	4.4
4.0%	1929	1968	3.9	3.7	3.7	3.7	3.8	3.8	3.8	4.0	3.7	3.7	3.7	3.7	3.6	3.6	3.7	3.8	4.0	3.7	3.7	3.7	3.7	3.8	3.9	3.9	3.8	3.7	3.9	3.8	3.3	3.8	4.1	3.8	4.1	3.9	4.0	4.1	4.1	4.1	4.1	4.1	24.7%	3.3	3.8%	3.8%	3.8
4.2%	1930	1969	3.9	3.8	3.8	3.9	3.9	4.0	4.3	3.8	3.9	3.9	3.8	3.7	3.8	3.9	3.9	4.5	4.0	3.9	3.9	3.9	4.2	4.2	4.3	4.2	4.8	4.3	4.2	3.8	4.3	4.3	4.3	4.3	4.3	4.3	4.3	4.3	4.3	4.3	4.3	4.3	19.7%	3.7	4.1%	3.9%	4.6
4.4%	1931	1970	3.9	3.9	4.1	4.1	4.4	4.8	4.1	4.3	4.2	4.1	3.9	3.9	4.1	4.3	4.8	4.2	4.1	4.0	4.1	4.3	4.4	4.4	4.3	5.0	5.1	4.4	4.1	4.4	4.5	4.3	4.5	4.3	4.5	4.5	4.5	4.5	4.5	4.5	4.5	4.5	18.4%	3.9	4.3%	4.2%	5.7
4.8%	1932	1971	4.2	5.1	5.0	5.4	5.5	5.0	5.2	5.2	5.1	4.6	4.5	4.9	5.1	5.4	4.9	4.6	4.5	4.7	4.9	4.9	5.0	4.8	5.4	5.5	5.5	4.5	4.8	4.8	4.8	4.8	4.8	4.8	4.8	4.8	4.8	4.8	4.8	4.8	4.8	4.8	20.3%	4.2	4.9%	5.0%	7.7
4.8%	1933	1972	4.9	4.8	5.2	5.5	4.8	5.0	5.0	4.8	4.4	4.3	4.6	5.0	5.3	4.8	4.5	4.4	4.7	4.8	4.8	5.0	4.9	5.3	5.5	5.5	5.1	4.8	4.8	4.7	4.8	4.6	4.8	4.8	4.8	4.8	4.8	4.8	4.7	4.8	4.8	4.5	17.4%	4.3	4.9%	4.9%	7.5
4.4%	1934	1973	4.1	4.4	4.8	4.1	4.2	4.2	4.1	3.9	3.9	4.0	4.2	4.7	4.1	4.0	4.0	4.1	4.2	4.2	4.3	4.2	5.0	5.1	5.0	4.8	5.0	4.4	4.4	4.5	4.3	4.3	4.5	4.5	4.5	4.5	4.5	4.5	4.3	4.5	4.4	3.3	10.3%	3.3	4.4%	4.2%	5.8
4.4%	1935	1974	4.5	4.8	4.1	4.2	4.2	4.1	3.9	3.9	4.0	4.2	4.7	4.1	4.0	4.0	4.0	4.2	4.2	4.3	4.2	4.8	5.1	5.0	4.7	5.1	5.1	4.3	4.5	4.2	4.4	4.4	4.5	4.4	4.5	4.5	4.4	4.4	4.2	4.5	3.4	3.0	5.8%	3.0	4.3%	4.2%	5.8
4.4%	1936	1975	4.4	3.9	4.0	4.0	3.9	3.9	3.9	3.9	4.0	4.3	4.0	3.9	3.9	3.9	4.0	4.0	4.1	4.0	4.7	4.9	4.9	4.5	5.0	5.1	4.9	4.4	4.2	4.2	4.4	4.5	4.3	4.5	4.5	4.4	4.2	4.3	4.1	3.4	2.9	3.1	6.5%	2.9	4.2%	4.0%	5.2
4.0%	1937	1976	3.7	3.8	3.8	3.7	3.7	3.7	3.7	3.8	4.1	3.8	3.7	3.7	3.7	3.8	3.9	3.9	3.9	4.4	4.6	4.6	4.3	4.7	4.8	4.7	4.9	3.9	4.0	4.1	4.1	4.1	4.1	4.1	4.1	4.1	4.1	4.1	3.2	3.0	3.0	3.2	9.4%	3.0	4.0%	3.8%	4.4
4.2%	1938	1977	4.3	4.3	4.1	3.9	3.9	4.2	4.4	4.8	4.2	4.0	4.0	4.1	4.2	4.2	4.3	4.2	4.8	4.9	4.9	4.7	5.0	5.0	5.0	5.1	5.0	4.3	4.3	4.3	4.3	4.3	4.3	4.3	4.3	4.3	4.3	3.8	3.0	3.4	3.6	3.3	10.3%	3.0	4.3%	4.2%	5.8
4.2%	1939	1978	4.0	4.0	3.8	3.9	4.0	4.2	4.6	4.0	3.9	3.9	4.0	4.1	4.1	4.2	4.1	4.7	4.9	4.8	4.5	4.9	5.0	4.9	5.1	5.0	5.0	4.3	4.3	4.3	4.3	4.3	4.3	4.2	4.3	4.3	3.5	3.0	3.1	3.6	3.3	3.2	9.0%	3.0	4.2%	4.0%	5.7
4.2%	1940	1979	4.0	3.9	3.9	4.0	4.2	4.7	4.1	3.9	3.9	4.0	4.1	4.1	4.2	4.1	4.7	4.8	4.8	4.5	4.8	4.9	4.9	5.0	4.9	5.0	5.0	4.3	4.3	4.3	4.3	4.3	4.3	4.2	4.3	3.6	3.0	3.2	3.3	3.5	3.2	3.2	9.3%	3.0	4.2%	4.0%	5.5
4.2%	1941	1980	3.9	3.9	4.2	4.4	4.8	4.3	4.0	4.0	4.1	4.3	4.3	4.3	4.2	4.7	4.9	4.8	4.6	4.9	4.9	5.0	5.1	4.9	5.0	5.1	5.1	4.3	4.3	4.3	4.3	4.1	4.2	4.1	3.6	3.0	3.1	3.4	3.2	3.3	3.2	3.2	9.4%	3.0	4.2%	4.2%	5.5
4.4%	1942	1981	4.2	4.6	4.8	5.2	4.7	4.4	4.3	4.5	4.6	4.5	4.6	4.5	4.9	5.1	5.0	4.8	5.1	5.1	5.0	5.2	5.1	5.1	5.2	5.2	5.2	4.5	4.5	4.4	4.3	4.2	4.3	3.5	3.2	3.2	3.4	3.4	3.2	3.5	3.4	3.2	9.0%	3.2	4.4%	4.6%	6.0
4.6%	1943	1982	4.4	4.7	5.0	4.5	4.2	4.2	4.3	4.4	4.4	4.4	4.3	4.9	5.0	5.0	4.7	5.0	5.1	5.0	5.1	5.0	5.1	5.2	5.4	5.2	5.4	4.6	4.4	4.2	4.3	4.2	3.6	3.2	3.4	3.4	3.3	3.3	3.2	3.4	3.2	3.2	9.5%	3.2	4.4%	4.5%	5.9
4.4%	1944	1983	4.3	4.7	4.1	4.0	4.0	4.0	4.1	4.1	4.2	4.1	4.6	4.8	4.7	4.4	4.8	4.8	4.8	4.9	4.8	4.9	5.0	5.1	5.0	5.2	5.2	4.3	4.2	4.2	4.2	3.4	3.1	3.2	3.5	3.3	3.2	3.3	3.2	3.3	3.3	3.4	11.0%	3.1	4.2%	4.2%	5.4
4.4%	1945	1984	4.5	4.0	3.9	3.9	3.9	4.0	4.0	4.0	4.0	4.4	4.7	4.5	4.2	4.7	4.7	4.7	4.9	4.7	4.7	4.9	5.1	4.8	5.2	5.2	4.8	4.0	4.1	4.0	3.4	3.1	3.2	3.2	3.3	3.2	3.2	3.2	3.1	3.3	3.4	3.2	9.1%	3.1	4.1%	4.1%	5.1
4.4%	1946	1985	3.9	3.9	3.8	3.9	3.9	3.9	3.9	3.9	4.1	4.3	4.2	4.0	4.3	4.4	4.3	4.7	4.4	4.5	4.7	4.8	4.7	5.0	5.1	4.7	4.5	3.9	3.9	3.2	3.1	3.1	3.2	3.1	3.1	3.1	3.1	3.1	3.1	3.3	3.2	3.2	9.0%	3.1	3.9%	4.0%	4.6
4.4%	1947	1986	4.0	3.9	4.0	4.1	4.1	4.2	4.0	4.5	4.7	4.5	4.2	4.7	4.7	4.7	4.8	4.7	4.8	4.8	5.0	4.8	5.1	5.2	4.8	4.7	4.7	4.0	3.3	3.1	3.1	3.2	3.2	3.1	3.2	3.2	3.1	3.2	3.3	3.4	3.4	3.4	10.6%	3.1	4.1%	4.2%	5.0
4.6%	1948	1987	4.1	4.2	4.3	4.3	4.3	4.2	4.7	4.9	4.8	4.4	4.8	4.8	4.8	5.0	4.8	4.9	5.0	5.1	4.9	5.2	5.4	4.9	4.9	5.0	4.9	3.5	3.2	3.2	3.4	3.3	3.3	3.2	3.3	3.2	3.2	3.4	3.3	3.7	3.6	3.3	9.5%	3.2	4.2%	4.4%	5.5
4.6%	1949	1988	4.2	4.3	4.3	4.4	4.3	4.8	4.9	4.8	4.5	4.8	4.9	4.8	5.0	4.9	4.9	5.0	5.2	5.0	5.2	5.4	5.0	4.9	5.0	5.0	4.3	3.2	3.3	3.4	3.4	3.2	3.3	3.3	3.3	3.4	3.4	3.4	3.5	4.0	3.4	3.4	10.8%	3.2	4.3%	4.6%	5.6
4.6%	1950	1989	4.2	4.2	4.2	4.1	4.6	4.8	4.7	4.3	4.7	4.7	4.7	4.9	4.7	4.8	4.9	5.0	4.9	5.1	5.3	4.9	4.9	4.9	4.9	4.3	4.0	3.2	3.4	3.3	3.2	3.2	3.3	3.2	3.4	3.5	3.3	3.6	3.5	3.5	3.5	3.4	11.2%	3.2	4.2%	4.5%	5.3
4.4%	1951	1990	4.1	4.1	4.0	4.5	4.7	4.6	4.3	4.7	4.7	4.6	4.8	4.6	4.7	4.8	4.9	4.7	5.0	5.1	4.7	4.7	4.8	4.7	4.2	3.9	4.0	3.3	3.2	3.2	3.2	3.2	3.2	3.2	3.6	3.3	3.5	3.7	3.3	3.7	3.6	3.1	7.8%	3.1	4.1%	4.4%	5.1
4.4%	1952	1991	4.1	4.0	4.5	4.7	4.5	4.3	4.5	4.7	4.6	4.7	4.5	4.6	4.7	4.9	4.7	5.0	5.1	4.7	4.6	4.7	4.7	4.1	3.9	4.0	4.0	3.2	3.2	3.2	3.2	3.1	3.2	3.3	3.4	3.5	3.5	3.3	3.3	3.8	3.1	3.2	9.3%	3.1	4.1%	4.5%	5.0
4.3%	1953	1992	4.0	4.4	4.6	4.5	4.2	4.5	4.6	4.5	4.7	4.4	4.6	4.7	4.8	4.7	4.8	4.9	4.6	4.4	4.5	4.5	4.0	3.9	3.9	4.0	3.9	3.1	3.1	3.1	3.1	3.1	3.4	3.2	3.6	3.6	3.2	3.4	3.4	3.2	3.3	3.3	10.3%	3.1	4.0%	4.4%	4.8
4.6%	1954	1993	4.5	4.7	4.5	4.3	4.6	4.7	4.6	4.8	4.5	4.6	4.8	4.9	4.7	5.0	5.0	4.7	4.7	4.6	4.6	4.2	4.0	4.0	4.1	4.0	4.0	3.2	3.2	3.2	3.2	3.3	3.3	3.4	3.7	3.3	3.4	3.5	3.2	3.4	3.4	3.4	10.8%	3.2	4.1%	4.6%	5.0
4.3%	1955	1994	4.2	4.1	4.0	4.2	4.2	4.2	4.3	4.2	4.2	4.3	4.5	4.3	4.7	4.8	4.3	4.3	4.4	4.3	3.9	3.9	3.9	3.9	3.9	3.9	3.9	3.1	3.0	3.1	3.2	3.1	3.3	3.3	3.2	3.3	3.3	3.0	3.1	3.4	3.4	3.1	8.8%	3.0	3.8%	4.2%	4.3
4.3%	1956	1995	4.0	3.9	4.1	4.2	4.1	4.2	4.1	4.2	4.2	4.4	4.2	4.6	4.7	4.2	4.2	4.3	4.3	3.9	3.8	3.9	3.9	3.9	3.9	3.9	3.9	3.0	3.1	3.2	3.1	3.2	3.4	3.1	3.4	3.4	3.0	3.2	3.2	3.5	3.2	3.3	10.2%	3.0	3.8%	4.1%	4.2
4.3%	1957	1996	3.9	4.1	4.2	4.1	4.3	4.1	4.2	4.3	4.5	4.2	4.6	4.7	4.2	4.2	4.2	4.2	3.9	3.9	3.9	3.9	3.9	3.9	3.9	3.9	3.9	3.1	3.2	3.1	3.3	3.3	3.2	3.2	3.5	3.0	3.2	3.3	3.3	3.4	3.5	3.4	11.0%	3.0	3.8%	4.2%	4.2
4.3%	1958	1997	4.5	4.6	4.5	4.7	4.4	4.5	4.6	4.7	4.6	4.8	4.8	4.5	4.4	4.5	4.5	4.0	3.9	3.9	4.0	3.9	3.9	3.9	3.9	3.9	3.9	3.3	3.2	3.4	3.6	3.3	3.5	3.6	3.2	3.4	3.5	3.7	3.4	4.0	3.9	4.0	14.4%	3.2	4.0%	4.6%	4.7
4.1%	1959	1998	4.2	4.1	4.2	4.1	4.1	4.2	4.5	4.2	4.6	4.7	4.2	4.2	4.2	4.2	3.9	3.8	3.8	3.9	3.8	3.8	3.8	3.8	3.8	3.9	4.0	3.1	3.4	3.4	3.2	3.3	3.5	3.0	3.4	3.4	3.4	3.3	3.6	3.9	4.0	3.8	12.9%	3.0	3.8%	4.3%	4.2
4.0%	1960	1999	4.0	4.2	4.0	4.1	4.2	4.4	4.2	4.5	4.6	4.1	4.1	4.1	4.1	3.8	3.7	3.7	3.8	3.7	3.7	3.7	3.8	3.7	3.8	3.9	3.8	3.2	3.3	3.1	3.2	3.2	3.0	3.1	3.4	3.4	3.2	3.6	3.5	4.0	3.8	3.8	13.0%	3.0	3.8%	4.2%	4.0
4.0%	1961	2000	4.3	4.1	4.2	4.3	4.5	4.2	4.5	4.6	4.2	4.1	4.2	4.2	3.8	3.7	3.7	3.8	3.8	3.7	3.7	3.8	3.7	3.8	3.9	3.9	4.0	3.4	3.2	3.2	3.4	3.0	3.3	3.3	3.7	3.4	3.6	3.8	3.9	4.1	4.0	3.6	11.7%	3.0	3.8%	4.3%	4.1
4.0%	1962	2001	4.0	4.0	4.1	4.3	4.0	4.4	4.5	4.1	4.0	4.0	4.0	3.8	3.7	3.7	3.7	3.7	3.7	3.7	3.7	3.7	3.8	3.9	3.8	4.0	4.0	3.1	3.2	3.2	3.0	3.1	3.3	3.4	3.4	3.6	3.6	3.9	3.8	4.1	3.7	3.5	11.3%	3.0	3.8%	4.1%	3.9
4.0%	1963	2002	4.2	4.3	4.5	4.3	4.5	4.6	4.2	4.1	4.2	4.1	3.8	3.7	3.7	3.8	3.8	3.7	3.7	3.7	3.7	3.8	3.9	3.8	4.0	4.1	3.9	3.2	3.4	3.0	3.2	3.3	3.6	3.3	3.8	3.8	3.9	4.0	4.0	3.9	3.8	3.0	8.5%	3.0	3.8%	4.3%	4.1
4.0%	1964	2003	4.2	4.4	4.1	4.5	4.5	4.2	4.1	4.1	4.1	3.8	3.7	3.7	3.8	3.7	3.7	3.7	3.7	3.7	3.7	3.9	3.8	3.9	4.1	3.9	4.0	3.4	3.0	3.2	3.4	3.4	3.4	3.6	3.9	4.0	3.9	4.1	3.7	4.0	3.2	3.5	11.4%	3.0	3.8%	4.2%	4.0
3.9%	1965	2004	4.3	4.1	4.3	4.5	4.0	4.0	4.0	4.0	3.7	3.6	3.7	3.7	3.7	3.7	3.7	3.7	3.7	3.7	3.8	3.8	3.9	4.0	3.9	4.0	4.0	3.0	3.2	3.2	3.5	3.2	3.7	3.6	4.1	3.9	4.0	3.8	3.7	3.3	3.7	3.6	11.7%	3.0	3.8%	4.0%	3.7
3.7%	1966	2005	4.0	4.2	4.3	3.9	3.8	3.9	3.9	3.7	3.5	3.6	3.7	3.7	3.6	3.7	3.7	3.6	3.7	3.7	3.7	3.8	3.9	3.7	3.9	4.0	3.7	3.0	3.2	3.3	3.2	3.4	3.6	3.8	3.9	3.9	3.6	3.7	3.0	3.7	3.6	3.4	10.6%	3.0	3.7%	3.9%	3.5
4.0%	1967	2006	4.5	4.5	4.1	4.0	4.1	4.0	3.8	3.7	3.7	3.7	3.7	3.7	3.7	3.7	3.7	3.7	3.8	3.8	3.9	4.0	3.9	3.9	4.1	3.8	3.9	3.3	3.5	3.2	3.7	3.7	4.0	3.9	4.1	3.9	3.8	3.2	3.7	4.0	3.8	3.8	12.8%	3.2	3.8%	4.0%	3.9
3.9%	1968	2007	4.3	3.9	3.9	3.9	3.9	3.7	3.5	3.6	3.7	3.7	3.6	3.6	3.6	3.5	3.7	3.7	3.7	3.7	3.8	3.7	3.8	3.8	3.7	3.8	3.8	3.1	3.0	3.2	3.3	3.6	3.6	3.7	3.6	3.5	2.9	3.3	3.3	3.5	3.4	3.0	8.7%	2.9	3.6%	3.8%	3.3
3.9%	1969	2008	3.8	3.8	3.8	3.8	3.7	3.5	3.5	3.6	3.5	3.5	3.5	3.5	3.5	3.6	3.7	3.7	3.7	3.7	3.7	3.7	3.8	3.6	3.7	3.8	3.8	2.9	3.1	3.1	3.4	3.3	3.6	3.2	3.4	2.9	3.1	3.3	3.1	3.5	3.1	2.7	3.6%	2.7	3.5%	3.7%	3.1
3.9%	1970	2009	4.0	4.1	4.0	3.7	3.6	3.7	3.7	3.7	3.7	3.7	3.7	3.7	3.7	3.9	3.8	4.0	4.1	3.9	4.0	4.2	3.9	4.1	4.3	4.5	4.2	3.8	3.9	4.0	4.1	4.1	4.0	4.0	3.7	4.0	4.0	4.0	4.0	4.0	2.9	3.0	7.7%	2.9	3.9%	3.8%	3.9
4.1%	1971	2010	4.2	4.1	3.8	3.7	3.8	3.8	3.8	3.8	3.8	3.8	3.8	3.8	3.9	3.9	4.0	4.1	4.0	4.0	4.1	3.9	4.2	4.3	4.5	4.3	4.6	3.9	4.2	4.1	4.2	4.0	4.1	3.5	4.2	4.2	4.0	4.2	3.8	3.0	3.1	3.1	9.0%	3.0	3.9%	3.8%	4.1
4.0%	1972	1928	4.1	3.8	3.7	3.7	3.7	3.7	3.7	3.7	3.7	3.7	3.7	3.8	3.8	3.9	4.0	3.9	4.0	4.1	3.9	4.1	4.3	4.4	4.2	4.6	4.6	4.1	4.1	4.1	4.0	3.9	3.6	3.9	4.1	4.0	4.0	3.9	2.9	3.1	3.2	3.4	11.0%	2.9	3.9%	3.8%	4.0
4.0%	1973	1929	3.8	3.7	3.7	3.8	3.7	3.7	3.7	3.7	3.7	3.7	3.8	3.8	3.9	4.0	3.9	4.0	4.1	3.8	4.0	4.2	4.5	4.2	4.5	4.6	4.7	4.0	4.1	3.9	4.0	3.4	4.0	4.0	4.1	4.1	3.8	2.9	3.0	3.3	3.6	2.9	6.7%	2.9	3.9%	3.7%	4.0
4.3%	1974	1930	3.9	3.9	4.0	4.0	3.9	4.0	4.0	3.9	4.1	4.2	4.2	4.4	4.6	4.4	4.5	4.6	4.3	4.6	4.7	4.8	4.7	4.9	5.0	5.1	5.1	4.4	4.3	4.3	3.9	4.2	4.4	4.3	4.4	4.3	3.2	3.6	3.7	4.4	3.4	2.8	5.3%	2.8	4.2%	4.0%	5.1
4.7%	1975	1931	4.3	4.6	4.5	4.3	4.3	4.3	4.2	4.4	4.6	4.5	4.9	5.0	4.8	4.9	5.0	4.7	5.0	5.0	5.1	5.0	5.3	5.2	5.4	5.4	5.4	4.6	4.7	4.2	4.6	4.6	4.6	4.6	4.6	3.6	3.7	4.0	4.3	3.6	3.0	2.7	2.0%	2.7	4.5%	4.4%	5.9
4.6%	1976	1932	4.3	4.2	4.1	4.1	4.1	4.0	4.2	4.3	4.3	4.5	4.7	4.5	4.5	4.7	4.3	4.7	4.8	4.9	4.7	5.0	5.1	5.3	5.3	5.3	5.2	4.5	4.2	4.4	4.6	4.4	4.6	4.3	3.4	3.6	3.7	4.4	3.3	3.0	2.7	2.7	1.2%	2.7	4.3%	4.2%	5.2
4.6%	1977	1933	4.1	4.0	4.0	4.0	4.0	4.1	4.2	4.2	4.4	4.5	4.3	4.4	4.5	4.2	4.5	4.7	4.8	4.5	4.8	4.9	5.2	5.1	5.2	5.1	5.1	4.1	4.4	4.4	4.4	4.4	4.3	3.3	3.7	3.8	4.2	3.3	2.8	2.7	2.7	2.7	1.7%	2.7	4.2%	4.1%	4.8
4.7%	1978	1934	4.1	4.1	4.1	4.0	4.1	4.2	4.2	4.4	4.6	4.3	4.4	4.5	4.2	4.5	4.7	4.8	4.6	4.9	4.9	5.2	5.2	5.2	5.1	5.2	4.8	4.4	4.5	4.3	4.5	4.2	3.4	3.5	4.0	4.3	3.3	2.9	2.7	2.7	2.7	2.7	1.2%	2.7	4.2%	4.2%	5.0
4.8%	1979	1935	4.2	4.1	4.1	4.2	4.3	4.3	4.5	4.6	4.4	4.5	4.6	4.3	4.5	4.7	4.8	4.6	5.0	5.0	5.1	5.2	5.3	5.1	5.2	5.0	5.1	4.5	4.4	4.5	4.3	3.4	3.6	3.8	4.5	3.4	3.0	2.7	2.7	2.7	2.7	2.7	2.6%	2.7	4.2%	4.3%	5.3
4.8%	1980	1936	4.2	4.1	4.2	4.3	4.3	4.5	4.5	4.4	4.5	4.5	4.2	4.5	4.6	4.8	4.5	4.9	5.0	5.1	5.1	5.2	5.1	5.1	4.7	5.1	5.1	4.4	4.5	4.2	3.3	3.4	3.7	4.2	3.6	3.2	2.7	2.7	3.0	3.1	3.3	3.3	9.2%	2.7	4.2%	4.3%	5.3
4.7%	1981	1937	4.1	4.2	4.3	4.3	4.5	4.7	4.4	4.5	4.7	4.3	4.6	4.7	4.9	4.6	4.9	5.0	5.2	5.1	5.2	5.1	5.2	4.9	5.2	5.3	5.1	4.5	4.4	3.5	3.7	3.8	4.4	3.5	3.2	2.7	2.7	3.2	3.0	3.3	3.4	2.7	4.3%	2.7	4.3%	4.4%	5.4
4.8%	1982	1938	4.3	4.4	4.4	4.7	4.8	4.6	4.6	4.8	4.4	4.7	4.8	5.0	4.7	5.0	5.0	5.2	5.3	5.3	5.1	5.3	5.1	5.3	5.3	5.3	5.3	4.4	3.6	3.7	4.0	4.3	3.6	3.3	2.8	2.8	3.2	3.2	3.3	3.8	2.8	2.9	5.6%	2.8	4.4%	4.6%	5.7
4.8%	1983	1939	4.2	4.2	4.3	4.5	4.3	4.3	4.4	4.2	4.4	4.5	4.6	4.4	4.7	4.8	5.0	5.0	5.1	4.9	5.0	4.7	5.1	5.1	5.0	5.1	4.8	3.4	3.5	3.6	4.2	3.4	3.0	2.7	2.7	2.7	2.7	2.8	3.1	2.7	2.7	2.7	1.7%	2.7	4.1%	4.3%	5.0
4.7%	1984	1940	4.1	4.2	4.3	4.2	4.2	4.3	4.1	4.3	4.3	4.5	4.3	4.5	4.5	4.9	4.9	4.9	4.8	4.8	4.4	4.9	5.0	4.8	5.0	4.8	4.0	3.4	3.6	4.0	3.4	3.2	2.8	2.8	3.2	3.1	3.2	3.5	2.7	3.0	2.8	2.7	3.4%	2.7	4.0%	4.3%	4.8
4.7%	1985	1941	4.3	4.4	4.2	4.3	4.3	4.2	4.3	4.4	4.5	4.3	4.5	4.6	4.8	4.9	4.9	4.7	4.9	4.4	4.8	4.9	4.9	4.9	4.8	4.2	4.2	3.6	4.1	3.4	3.2	2.8	2.9	3.2	3.2	3.2	3.4	2.8	2.8	2.9	2.7	2.7	2.1%	2.7	4.0%	4.3%	4.8
4.6%	1986	1942	4.2	4.1	4.1	4.2	4.0	4.2	4.2	4.3	4.2	4.3	4.4	4.7	4.7	4.7	4.6	4.7	4.4	4.7	4.8	4.7	4.9	4.6	4.1	4.2	4.3	4.0	3.4	3.2	2.7	2.7	3.1	3.0	3.2	3.4	2.7	2.9	2.7	2.7	2.7	2.7	1.7%	2.7	3.9%	4.2%	4.4
4.6%	1987	1943	4.0	4.0	4.1	4.0	4.0	4.1	4.2	4.1	4.3	4.3	4.5	4.5	4.5	4.4	4.5	4.2	4.6	4.6	4.5	4.7	4.5	4.0	4.1	4.2	4.5	3.2	2.9	2.7	2.7	2.7	2.7	2.9	3.2	2.7	2.7	2.7	2.7	2.7	2.4	1.7	0.0%	1.7	3.7%	4.1%	4.0
4.6%	1988	1944	4.2	4.2	4.0	4.2	4.2	4.4	4.2	4.4	4.4	4.7	4.7	4.7	4.6	4.7	4.3	4.7	4.8	4.7	4.8	4.7	4.2	4.2	4.3	4.8	4.1	3.2	2.9	3.0	3.2	3.2	3.2	3.5	2.9	3.1	2.9	2.7	2.7	2.7	2.7	2.7	4.0%	2.7	3.9%	4.3%	4.5
4.6%	1989	1945	4.2	4.0	4.1	4.2	4.3	4.1	4.3	4.3	4.7	4.6	4.7	4.5	4.6	4.3	4.6	4.7	4.7	4.7	4.5	4.0	4.2	4.2	4.7	4.1	4.0	2.7	2.8	3.1	3.1	3.2	3.4	2.7	3.0	2.8	2.7	2.7	2.7	2.7	2.7	2.7	3.5%	2.7	3.8%	4.3%	4.3
4.3%	1990	1946	3.9	4.0	4.1	4.2	4.0	4.3	4.3	4.5	4.6	4.5	4.4	4.5	4.2	4.5	4.6	4.5	4.7	4.4	4.0	4.1	4.2	4.5	4.0	3.9	3.6	3.0	3.1	3.0	3.2	3.4	2.9	3.0	3.0	2.7	2.7	2.7	2.7	2.8	3.0	2.7	3.7%	2.7	3.8%	4.3%	4.2
4.4%	1991	1947	4.3	4.4	4.6	4.3	4.6	4.6	4.8	4.8	4.8	4.7	4.7	4.5	4.7	4.8	4.7	4.8	4.7	4.2	4.2	4.5	4.8	4.2	4.0	3.9	3.9	3.2	3.2	3.4	3.8	3.1	3.2	3.1	3.1	2.8	2.8	3.1	3.2	4.0	3.2	3.1	6.4%	2.8	4.0%	4.6%	4.9
4.1%	1992	1948	4.2	4.3	4.1	4.3	4.3	4.6	4.6	4.6	4.5	4.5	4.2	4.5	4.5	4.5	4.6	4.5	4.0	4.0	4.2	4.6	4.1	3.9	3.8	3.8	3.9	3.0	3.2	3.5	3.0	3.0	3.0	2.9	2.7	2.7	2.9	3.0	3.2	3.0	2.9	2.7	4.7%	2.7	3.8%	4.4%	4.3
4.0%	1993	1949	4.2	4.0	4.3	4.3	4.5	4.5	4.5	4.5	4.5	4.2	4.5	4.5	4.5	4.5	4.4	3.9	4.0	4.1	4.5	4.0	3.8	3.5	3.7	3.8	3.7	3.1	3.5	2.8	2.9	2.9	2.8	2.7	2.7	2.7	2.9	3.0	2.8	2.7	2.7	2.7	3.4%	2.7	3.7%	4.4%	4.1
4.0%	1994	1950	4.0	4.2	4.2	4.4	4.4	4.5	4.2	4.3	4.0	4.3	4.4	4.3	4.4	4.3	3.9	3.9	4.1	4.3	3.9	3.8	3.7	3.7	3.8	3.8	3.9	3.4	2.9	2.9	2.9	2.8	2.7	2.7	2.9	3.0	3.2	3.0	2.9	2.9	2.9	2.9	5.8%	2.7	3.7%	4.2%	4.0
3.9%	1995	1951	4.4	4.4	4.5	4.5	4.5	4.5	4.5	4.3	4.5	4.5	4.5	4.5	4.4	3.9	4.0	4.2	4.5	4.0	3.8	3.7	3.8	3.9	3.9	4.1	4.4	2.9	3.0	3.0	2.9	2.8	2.9	2.9	3.2	3.8	3.1	3.0	2.9	3.1	3.2	3.1	8.9%	2.8	3.8%	4.5%	4.4
3.7%	1996	1952	4.2	4.3	4.3	4.4	4.3	4.3	4.0	4.3	4.3	4.3	4.3	4.2	3.8	3.9	4.0	4.3	3.9	3.7	3.5	3.7	3.7	3.7	3.8	4.2	3.7	2.9	2.8	2.8	2.7	2.7	2.8	2.9	3.5	2.9	2.8	2.8	2.8	2.9	2.9	2.8	6.4%	2.7	3.6%	4.3%	3.8
3.7%	1997	1953	4.3	4.3	4.3	4.2	4.3	3.9	4.2	4.3	4.2	4.3	4.1	3.7	3.8	3.9	4.2	3.8	3.7	3.6	3.7	3.7	3.7	3.8	4.1	3.7	3.7	2.9	2.8	2.7	2.7	2.8	3.0	3.5	3.0	2.9	2.8	2.9	2.9	3.1	3.0	2.9	7.0%	2.7	3.6%	4.3%	3.8
3.7%	1998	1954	4.2	4.2	4.0	4.1	3.8	4.0	4.1	4.0	4.2	4.0	3.7	3.7	3.8	4.0	3.7	3.7	3.5	3.5	3.7	3.7	3.7	3.9	3.6	3.7	3.7	2.7	2.7	2.7	2.8	2.8	3.1	2.8	2.8	2.7	2.7	2.8	2.8	2.8	2.7	2.8	6.3%	2.7	3.5%	4.1%	3.4
3.7%	1999	1955	4.2	4.0	4.0	3.8	4.0	4.1	4.0	4.1	4.0	3.7	3.7	3.8	4.0	3.7	3.7	3.5	3.6	3.7	3.7	3.7	3.9	3.6	3.7	3.7	3.5	2.7	2.7	2.8	2.8	3.1	2.8	2.8	2.8	2.8	2.8	2.8	2.8	2.8	3.0	3.0	8.1%	2.7	3.4%	4.0%	3.3
3.6%	2000	1956	4.0	4.1	3.8	4.0	4.1	4.0	4.1	4.0	3.7	3.7	3.8	4.0	3.7	3.6	3.5	3.5	3.6	3.6	3.6	3.8	3.5	3.6	3.5	3.5	3.5	2.7	2.7	2.7	2.9	2.7	2.7	2.7	2.7	2.7	2.7	2.7	2.7	2.8	2.8	2.7	4.1%	2.7	3.4%	4.0%	3.2
																																								Totals	9%	1.7	4.0%	4.2%	4.7%

FIGURE 170

Failure-market results allocating 50% for 25-Year TIPS ladder plus 12% DIA assuming 5% inflation (over the 25 deferred years).

This isn't a contrived example. In the US, starting in the late 1950s and continuing until the early 1970s, the 25-year annualized CPI rate consistently stayed over 5%. Since we can't fully rely on inflation maintaining a low average, we can't fully rely on an inflation-adjusted DIA performing well.

This flaw with DIAs is unfortunate, since they provide a powerful fulcrum for generating future income—an essential part of some strategies. The good news is, the type of inflation-adjusted DIA needed (with inflation-adjusted starting at the moment of purchase) can be simulated well enough using I Bonds combined with an inflation-adjusted SPIA (a topic covered later in the strategies). It's a little more work and might pay a little less, but the overall results are produced without inflation risk.

Similar to nominal annuities, a place where an inflation-adjusted DIA can be more safely used is late in retirement with a small deferred period (e.g., 5 years). This may be useful since a DIA can sometimes be purchased to start at an age higher than SPIAs are normally sold at, providing a unique option for rare circumstances.

STRATEGIC PITFALLS TO AVOID

When sorting through all the options for GI, it's easy to get lost in the decision forest amidst all the decision trees. Before covering the most viable strategies, this section points out strategic pitfalls to be aware of. The cases are not white and black, but they identify situations which should be approached with caution.

Again, everything works well during typical markets; it's for the failure market without norms that the most careful planning is required.

Over-Relying on a Stock Pool to Replenish GI

The maximum length of TIPS ladders is 30 years, although outliving a 30-year ladder is not unusual for today's retirees. To compensate, some retirees keep a separate pool of stocks in reserve to fund a second TIPS ladder late in life if they outlive the first one. Within a failure market, relying on a static pool of stocks to fund retirement after a ladder expires carries more risk than desired for GI. Why is explained below.

Allocating 10% of the portfolio value to the stock pool is reasonably common. Keep in mind, the higher the percentage allocated to stocks, the lower the effective withdrawal rate for a TIPS ladder, so retirees are strongly motivated to keep the percentage small. Based on historical stock performance, it's also reasonable to estimate the stock value will double in real terms approximately every 10 years. After 30 years, this estimate leaves the stock-pool value at 80% of the original portfolio—a very strong percentage providing much more than needed. The problem is, GI planning should be based on a failure market, not a typical market. Even the worst case in the Baseline Market doesn't adequately represent a failure market.

In a failure market, the stock pool may not be able to fund what's left of retirement after a TIPS ladder expires. The worst-case annualized 30-year real return in the failure-market benchmark is 0%, meaning the stock pool would not have grown over 30 years. Putting 10% of portfolio value (after no growth) into a 10-year bond ladder with a 2% coupon rate delivers an equivalent withdrawal rate of 1.1% of the original portfolio value. Essentially, the plan fails for this case.

The above problem cannot be solved by increasing the size of the stock pool. Putting 20% aside pushes the withdrawal for the first 30 years down, while still resulting in a withdrawal rate of only 2.2% of the original portfolio value for the last 10 years using the previous scenario. Nor can the problem be solved with different time periods (i.e., stocks for a 20-year period for the failure market actually lost over 3% of their real value).

The above assumptions are certainly harsh, but so must they be to justify the use of guaranteed income. No growth after 30 years is improbable, just as a failure market is improbable, but it fits in the domain of the failure-market benchmark. Notably, a TIPS ladder combined with a static stock pool might roughly have the same magnitude of risk as systemic withdrawals used alone, but with significantly less income on average.

The mechanics of systemic withdrawal have been refined to handle volatile markets well, so it's better to let those mechanics manage the stock portfolio. For example, systemic withdrawals using Prime Harvesting lower stock risk by capturing gains (i.e., buying more bonds) after strong growth. A static stock pool doesn't do this. It might work if the excess income was pulled off at appropriate times (e.g., using Prime Harvesting's trigger), but this essentially morphs back into something more kin to systemic withdrawals.

Wrong Timing of GI Purchases

The big advantage of waiting to purchase GI is more income is generated (i.e., GI gets cheaper). This is most notably true with annuities, where the mortality premium is continually growing, contributing to a higher payout. Using 2014 numbers, a retired couple delaying the purchase of an inflation-adjusted SPIA from 65 to 75 years of age boosted their payout from 4.01% to 5.75%...more than 40%. It's not surprising some retirees wait until past 70 before purchasing an SPIA. Unfortunately, there is risk in waiting, as I'll explain.

Assume a couple at age 65 is holding 100% of their assets in systemic withdrawals. The couple want to purchase an inflation-adjusted SPIA, but decide to wait until age 75 for a higher payout. SPIA prices can change, but the couple is comfortable with that risk, especially since current interest rates are low. The couple waits as planned, 10 years pass, then they invest in an SPIA, reaping the 40% higher payout. The problem is, the value of the portfolio may have dropped more than 40%, causing the net income level from investing in an SPIA to drop at age 75, not rise.

Figure 171 shows what happens to the withdrawal rate under the failure market by delaying the SPIA purchase. For simplicity, 100% of the portfolio is allocated to the SPIA at 75. Payout rates are again assumed to be 5.75% at age 75 (versus 4.01% at age 65). Compared to the 4.01% rate available at the start of retirement, the figure shows waiting 10 years lowered the annual payout approximately 20% of the time under the failure market. Again, these poor results are because the portfolio lost value while waiting for better rates. If the portfolio value drops by half, the effective payout is also halved (e.g., a 5.75% payout effectively becomes a 2.875% payout). For the retirement period starting in 1969 under the failure market, the effective payout after 10 years is only 2.4%, because the portfolio shrunk to less than 42% of its original value.

Start	End	A65	A66	A67	A68	A69	A70	A71	A72	A73	A74	A75	A76	A77	A78	A79	A80	A81	A82	A83	A84	A85	A86	A87	A88	A89	A90	A91	A92	A93	A94	A95	A96	A97	A98	A99	A00	A01	A02	A03	A04	%Left	Min	Avg	1st 10Y	MSWR
1928	1967	4.9	3.8	3.4	3.2	3.4	3.6	3.6	4.0	4.6	3.3	4.1	4.1	4.1	4.1	4.1	4.1	4.1	4.1	4.1	4.1	4.1	4.1	4.1	4.1	4.1	4.1	4.1	4.1	4.1	4.1	4.1	4.1	4.1	4.1	4.1	4.1	4.1	4.1	4.1	4.1	0%	3.2	4.0%	3.8%	4.4
1929	1968	3.4	3.1	3.1	3.1	3.2	3.2	3.3	3.7	3.1	3.1	3.5	3.5	3.5	3.5	3.5	3.5	3.5	3.5	3.5	3.5	3.5	3.5	3.5	3.5	3.5	3.5	3.5	3.5	3.5	3.5	3.5	3.5	3.5	3.5	3.5	3.5	3.5	3.5	3.5	3.5	0%	3.1	3.4%	3.2%	3.8
1930	1969	3.5	3.3	3.3	3.5	3.5	3.9	4.5	3.3	3.5	3.4	4.2	4.2	4.2	4.2	4.2	4.2	4.2	4.2	4.2	4.2	4.2	4.2	4.2	4.2	4.2	4.2	4.2	4.2	4.2	4.2	4.2	4.2	4.2	4.2	4.2	4.2	4.2	4.2	4.2	4.2	0%	3.3	4.1%	3.6%	4.6
1931	1970	3.5	3.6	4.1	4.1	4.9	6.0	4.1	4.5	4.4	4.1	5.8	5.8	5.8	5.8	5.8	5.8	5.8	5.8	5.8	5.8	5.8	5.8	5.8	5.8	5.8	5.8	5.8	5.8	5.8	5.8	5.8	5.8	5.8	5.8	5.8	5.8	5.8	5.8	5.8	5.8	0%	3.5	5.4%	4.3%	5.7
1932	1971	4.4	6.6	6.5	7.4	7.8	6.5	6.9	6.9	6.6	5.3	8.2	8.2	8.2	8.2	8.2	8.2	8.2	8.2	8.2	8.2	8.2	8.2	8.2	8.2	8.2	8.2	8.2	8.2	8.2	8.2	8.2	8.2	8.2	8.2	8.2	8.2	8.2	8.2	8.2	8.2	0%	4.4	7.8%	6.5%	7.7
1933	1972	6.1	5.9	6.9	7.8	5.9	6.5	6.4	5.9	4.8	4.7	6.3	6.3	6.3	6.3	6.3	6.3	6.3	6.3	6.3	6.3	6.3	6.3	6.3	6.3	6.3	6.3	6.3	6.3	6.3	6.3	6.3	6.3	6.3	6.3	6.3	6.3	6.3	6.3	6.3	6.3	0%	4.7	6.3%	6.1%	7.5
1934	1973	4.0	4.9	5.9	4.0	4.4	4.3	4.0	3.6	3.6	3.9	4.9	4.9	4.9	4.9	4.9	4.9	4.9	4.9	4.9	4.9	4.9	4.9	4.9	4.9	4.9	4.9	4.9	4.9	4.9	4.9	4.9	4.9	4.9	4.9	4.9	4.9	4.9	4.9	4.9	4.9	0%	3.6	4.7%	4.3%	5.8
1935	1974	5.0	5.9	4.0	4.4	4.3	4.1	3.6	3.6	3.9	4.4	5.6	5.6	5.6	5.6	5.6	5.6	5.6	5.6	5.6	5.6	5.6	5.6	5.6	5.6	5.6	5.6	5.6	5.6	5.6	5.6	5.6	5.6	5.6	5.6	5.6	5.6	5.6	5.6	5.6	5.6	0%	3.6	5.3%	4.3%	5.8
1936	1975	4.9	3.6	3.8	3.7	3.6	3.5	3.5	3.6	3.8	4.6	5.9	5.9	5.9	5.9	5.9	5.9	5.9	5.9	5.9	5.9	5.9	5.9	5.9	5.9	5.9	5.9	5.9	5.9	5.9	5.9	5.9	5.9	5.9	5.9	5.9	5.9	5.9	5.9	5.9	5.9	0%	3.5	5.4%	3.9%	5.2
1937	1976	3.1	3.2	3.2	3.1	3.0	3.0	3.1	3.2	4.0	3.2	4.4	4.4	4.4	4.4	4.4	4.4	4.4	4.4	4.4	4.4	4.4	4.4	4.4	4.4	4.4	4.4	4.4	4.4	4.4	4.4	4.4	4.4	4.4	4.4	4.4	4.4	4.4	4.4	4.4	4.4	0%	3.0	4.1%	3.2%	4.4
1938	1977	4.7	4.5	4.1	3.5	3.6	4.2	4.8	5.8	4.4	3.8	5.2	5.2	5.2	5.2	5.2	5.2	5.2	5.2	5.2	5.2	5.2	5.2	5.2	5.2	5.2	5.2	5.2	5.2	5.2	5.2	5.2	5.2	5.2	5.2	5.2	5.2	5.2	5.2	5.2	5.2	0%	3.5	5.0%	4.3%	5.8
1939	1978	3.9	3.7	3.3	3.4	3.7	4.2	5.3	3.9	3.6	3.5	4.1	4.1	4.1	4.1	4.1	4.1	4.1	4.1	4.1	4.1	4.1	4.1	4.1	4.1	4.1	4.1	4.1	4.1	4.1	4.1	4.1	4.1	4.1	4.1	4.1	4.1	4.1	4.1	4.1	4.1	0%	3.3	4.0%	3.9%	5.7
1940	1979	3.8	3.4	3.4	3.8	4.3	5.5	4.0	3.6	3.5	3.7	4.3	4.3	4.3	4.3	4.3	4.3	4.3	4.3	4.3	4.3	4.3	4.3	4.3	4.3	4.3	4.3	4.3	4.3	4.3	4.3	4.3	4.3	4.3	4.3	4.3	4.3	4.3	4.3	4.3	4.3	0%	3.4	4.2%	3.9%	5.5
1941	1980	3.5	3.5	4.2	4.9	5.9	4.5	3.9	3.8	4.1	4.5	5.2	5.2	5.2	5.2	5.2	5.2	5.2	5.2	5.2	5.2	5.2	5.2	5.2	5.2	5.2	5.2	5.2	5.2	5.2	5.2	5.2	5.2	5.2	5.2	5.2	5.2	5.2	5.2	5.2	5.2	0%	3.5	5.0%	4.3%	5.5
1942	1981	4.2	5.3	6.0	7.0	5.6	4.8	4.5	5.0	5.4	5.2	6.0	6.0	6.0	6.0	6.0	6.0	6.0	6.0	6.0	6.0	6.0	6.0	6.0	6.0	6.0	6.0	6.0	6.0	6.0	6.0	6.0	6.0	6.0	6.0	6.0	6.0	6.0	6.0	6.0	6.0	0%	4.2	5.8%	5.3%	6.0
1943	1982	4.9	5.6	6.5	5.0	4.4	4.2	4.5	4.9	4.9	4.9	5.9	5.9	5.9	5.9	5.9	5.9	5.9	5.9	5.9	5.9	5.9	5.9	5.9	5.9	5.9	5.9	5.9	5.9	5.9	5.9	5.9	5.9	5.9	5.9	5.9	5.9	5.9	5.9	5.9	5.9	0%	4.2	5.7%	5.0%	5.9
1944	1983	4.6	5.7	4.1	3.8	3.7	3.9	4.1	4.1	4.2	4.0	4.8	4.8	4.8	4.8	4.8	4.8	4.8	4.8	4.8	4.8	4.8	4.8	4.8	4.8	4.8	4.8	4.8	4.8	4.8	4.8	4.8	4.8	4.8	4.8	4.8	4.8	4.8	4.8	4.8	4.8	0%	3.7	4.6%	4.2%	5.4
1945	1984	5.0	3.8	3.6	3.6	3.6	3.8	3.8	3.9	3.8	4.8	5.7	5.7	5.7	5.7	5.7	5.7	5.7	5.7	5.7	5.7	5.7	5.7	5.7	5.7	5.7	5.7	5.7	5.7	5.7	5.7	5.7	5.7	5.7	5.7	5.7	5.7	5.7	5.7	5.7	5.7	0%	3.6	5.3%	4.0%	5.1
1946	1985	3.5	3.5	3.3	3.5	3.5	3.5	3.6	3.5	4.1	4.6	4.6	4.6	4.6	4.6	4.6	4.6	4.6	4.6	4.6	4.6	4.6	4.6	4.6	4.6	4.6	4.6	4.6	4.6	4.6	4.6	4.6	4.6	4.6	4.6	4.6	4.6	4.6	4.6	4.6	4.6	0%	3.3	4.4%	3.7%	4.6
1947	1986	3.7	3.6	3.8	4.1	4.0	4.2	3.9	5.1	5.6	5.2	6.0	6.0	6.0	6.0	6.0	6.0	6.0	6.0	6.0	6.0	6.0	6.0	6.0	6.0	6.0	6.0	6.0	6.0	6.0	6.0	6.0	6.0	6.0	6.0	6.0	6.0	6.0	6.0	6.0	6.0	0%	3.6	5.6%	4.3%	5.0
1948	1987	4.0	4.2	4.5	4.5	4.6	4.4	5.6	6.1	5.9	4.9	6.5	6.5	6.5	6.5	6.5	6.5	6.5	6.5	6.5	6.5	6.5	6.5	6.5	6.5	6.5	6.5	6.5	6.5	6.5	6.5	6.5	6.5	6.5	6.5	6.5	6.5	6.5	6.5	6.5	6.5	0%	4.0	6.1%	4.9%	5.5
1949	1988	4.4	4.7	4.7	4.8	4.5	6.0	6.2	6.0	5.2	6.0	7.7	7.7	7.7	7.7	7.7	7.7	7.7	7.7	7.7	7.7	7.7	7.7	7.7	7.7	7.7	7.7	7.7	7.7	7.7	7.7	7.7	7.7	7.7	7.7	7.7	7.7	7.7	7.7	7.7	7.7	0%	4.4	7.1%	5.3%	5.6
1950	1989	4.3	4.3	4.3	4.1	5.3	5.9	5.5	4.7	5.7	5.7	6.6	6.6	6.6	6.6	6.6	6.6	6.6	6.6	6.6	6.6	6.6	6.6	6.6	6.6	6.6	6.6	6.6	6.6	6.6	6.6	6.6	6.6	6.6	6.6	6.6	6.6	6.6	6.6	6.6	6.6	0%	4.1	6.2%	5.0%	5.3
1951	1990	4.0	4.1	3.9	5.2	5.7	5.4	4.5	5.5	5.6	5.3	6.5	6.5	6.5	6.5	6.5	6.5	6.5	6.5	6.5	6.5	6.5	6.5	6.5	6.5	6.5	6.5	6.5	6.5	6.5	6.5	6.5	6.5	6.5	6.5	6.5	6.5	6.5	6.5	6.5	6.5	0%	3.9	6.1%	4.9%	5.1
1952	1991	4.1	3.9	5.0	5.6	5.2	4.5	5.2	5.5	5.3	5.7	7.1	7.1	7.1	7.1	7.1	7.1	7.1	7.1	7.1	7.1	7.1	7.1	7.1	7.1	7.1	7.1	7.1	7.1	7.1	7.1	7.1	7.1	7.1	7.1	7.1	7.1	7.1	7.1	7.1	7.1	0%	3.9	6.6%	5.0%	5.0
1953	1992	3.8	4.9	5.3	5.0	4.2	5.2	5.3	5.0	5.6	4.9	6.3	6.3	6.3	6.3	6.3	6.3	6.3	6.3	6.3	6.3	6.3	6.3	6.3	6.3	6.3	6.3	6.3	6.3	6.3	6.3	6.3	6.3	6.3	6.3	6.3	6.3	6.3	6.3	6.3	6.3	0%	3.8	5.9%	4.9%	4.8
1954	1993	5.2	5.6	5.2	4.5	5.4	5.6	5.3	5.9	5.2	5.4	7.0	7.0	7.0	7.0	7.0	7.0	7.0	7.0	7.0	7.0	7.0	7.0	7.0	7.0	7.0	7.0	7.0	7.0	7.0	7.0	7.0	7.0	7.0	7.0	7.0	7.0	7.0	7.0	7.0	7.0	0%	4.5	6.6%	5.3%	5.0
1955	1994	4.3	4.1	3.7	4.2	4.4	4.3	4.7	4.2	4.4	4.6	6.0	6.0	6.0	6.0	6.0	6.0	6.0	6.0	6.0	6.0	6.0	6.0	6.0	6.0	6.0	6.0	6.0	6.0	6.0	6.0	6.0	6.0	6.0	6.0	6.0	6.0	6.0	6.0	6.0	6.0	0%	3.7	5.6%	4.3%	4.3
1956	1995	3.9	3.5	4.0	4.2	4.0	4.4	4.0	4.2	4.4	4.9	6.2	6.2	6.2	6.2	6.2	6.2	6.2	6.2	6.2	6.2	6.2	6.2	6.2	6.2	6.2	6.2	6.2	6.2	6.2	6.2	6.2	6.2	6.2	6.2	6.2	6.2	6.2	6.2	6.2	6.2	0%	3.5	5.7%	4.2%	4.2
1957	1996	3.6	4.1	4.3	4.1	4.5	4.1	4.3	4.5	5.1	4.4	5.7	5.7	5.7	5.7	5.7	5.7	5.7	5.7	5.7	5.7	5.7	5.7	5.7	5.7	5.7	5.7	5.7	5.7	5.7	5.7	5.7	5.7	5.7	5.7	5.7	5.7	5.7	5.7	5.7	5.7	0%	3.6	5.3%	4.3%	4.2
1958	1997	5.1	5.3	5.0	5.5	4.9	5.2	5.4	5.7	5.3	5.8	7.5	7.5	7.5	7.5	7.5	7.5	7.5	7.5	7.5	7.5	7.5	7.5	7.5	7.5	7.5	7.5	7.5	7.5	7.5	7.5	7.5	7.5	7.5	7.5	7.5	7.5	7.5	7.5	7.5	7.5	0%	4.9	6.9%	5.3%	4.7
1959	1998	4.2	4.0	4.4	4.0	4.1	4.4	5.0	4.3	5.3	5.5	7.2	7.2	7.2	7.2	7.2	7.2	7.2	7.2	7.2	7.2	7.2	7.2	7.2	7.2	7.2	7.2	7.2	7.2	7.2	7.2	7.2	7.2	7.2	7.2	7.2	7.2	7.2	7.2	7.2	7.2	0%	4.0	6.5%	4.5%	4.2
1960	1999	3.9	4.3	3.8	4.0	4.3	4.9	4.2	5.0	5.3	4.1	5.5	5.5	5.5	5.5	5.5	5.5	5.5	5.5	5.5	5.5	5.5	5.5	5.5	5.5	5.5	5.5	5.5	5.5	5.5	5.5	5.5	5.5	5.5	5.5	5.5	5.5	5.5	5.5	5.5	5.5	0%	3.8	5.2%	4.4%	4.0
1961	2000	4.6	4.0	4.2	4.5	5.0	4.4	5.1	5.4	4.3	4.1	5.5	5.5	5.5	5.5	5.5	5.5	5.5	5.5	5.5	5.5	5.5	5.5	5.5	5.5	5.5	5.5	5.5	5.5	5.5	5.5	5.5	5.5	5.5	5.5	5.5	5.5	5.5	5.5	5.5	5.5	0%	4.0	5.3%	4.6%	4.1
1962	2001	3.7	3.8	4.0	4.6	3.9	4.9	5.1	4.0	3.9	3.9	5.1	5.1	5.1	5.1	5.1	5.1	5.1	5.1	5.1	5.1	5.1	5.1	5.1	5.1	5.1	5.1	5.1	5.1	5.1	5.1	5.1	5.1	5.1	5.1	5.1	5.1	5.1	5.1	5.1	5.1	0%	3.7	4.9%	4.2%	3.9
1963	2002	4.3	4.6	5.0	4.5	5.1	5.4	4.2	4.1	4.3	4.1	5.4	5.4	5.4	5.4	5.4	5.4	5.4	5.4	5.4	5.4	5.4	5.4	5.4	5.4	5.4	5.4	5.4	5.4	5.4	5.4	5.4	5.4	5.4	5.4	5.4	5.4	5.4	5.4	5.4	5.4	0%	4.1	5.2%	4.6%	4.1
1964	2003	4.4	4.9	4.1	5.0	5.2	4.2	4.0	4.1	4.1	3.3	4.3	4.3	4.3	4.3	4.3	4.3	4.3	4.3	4.3	4.3	4.3	4.3	4.3	4.3	4.3	4.3	4.3	4.3	4.3	4.3	4.3	4.3	4.3	4.3	4.3	4.3	4.3	4.3	4.3	4.3	0%	3.3	4.3%	4.3%	4.0
1965	2004	4.6	4.0	4.7	5.0	3.8	3.7	3.8	3.7	3.1	2.8	2.9	2.9	2.9	2.9	2.9	2.9	2.9	2.9	2.9	2.9	2.9	2.9	2.9	2.9	2.9	2.9	2.9	2.9	2.9	2.9	2.9	2.9	2.9	2.9	2.9	2.9	2.9	2.9	2.9	2.9	0%	2.8	3.2%	3.9%	3.7
1966	2005	3.7	4.4	4.7	3.5	3.3	3.4	3.4	2.9	2.5	2.7	2.6	2.6	2.6	2.6	2.6	2.6	2.6	2.6	2.6	2.6	2.6	2.6	2.6	2.6	2.6	2.6	2.6	2.6	2.6	2.6	2.6	2.6	2.6	2.6	2.6	2.6	2.6	2.6	2.6	2.6	0%	2.5	2.8%	3.5%	3.5
1967	2006	5.0	5.2	4.0	3.9	4.0	3.9	3.2	3.1	3.1	3.1	3.5	3.5	3.5	3.5	3.5	3.5	3.5	3.5	3.5	3.5	3.5	3.5	3.5	3.5	3.5	3.5	3.5	3.5	3.5	3.5	3.5	3.5	3.5	3.5	3.5	3.5	3.5	3.5	3.5	3.5	0%	3.1	3.6%	3.9%	3.9
1968	2007	4.5	3.5	3.4	3.4	3.4	3.0	2.6	2.8	3.0	2.9	2.8	2.8	2.8	2.8	2.8	2.8	2.8	2.8	2.8	2.8	2.8	2.8	2.8	2.8	2.8	2.8	2.8	2.8	2.8	2.8	2.8	2.8	2.8	2.8	2.8	2.8	2.8	2.8	2.8	2.8	0%	2.6	2.9%	3.3%	3.3
1969	2008	3.3	3.2	3.2	3.2	3.0	2.5	2.5	2.8	2.6	2.5	2.4	2.4	2.4	2.4	2.4	2.4	2.4	2.4	2.4	2.4	2.4	2.4	2.4	2.4	2.4	2.4	2.4	2.4	2.4	2.4	2.4	2.4	2.4	2.4	2.4	2.4	2.4	2.4	2.4	2.4	0%	2.4	2.5%	2.9%	3.1
1970	2009	3.9	4.0	3.9	3.1	2.8	3.0	3.1	3.0	3.0	3.0	3.4	3.4	3.4	3.4	3.4	3.4	3.4	3.4	3.4	3.4	3.4	3.4	3.4	3.4	3.4	3.4	3.4	3.4	3.4	3.4	3.4	3.4	3.4	3.4	3.4	3.4	3.4	3.4	3.4	3.4	0%	2.8	3.4%	3.3%	3.9
1971	2010	4.2	4.1	3.3	2.9	3.2	3.3	3.2	3.2	3.2	3.2	3.6	3.6	3.6	3.6	3.6	3.6	3.6	3.6	3.6	3.6	3.6	3.6	3.6	3.6	3.6	3.6	3.6	3.6	3.6	3.6	3.6	3.6	3.6	3.6	3.6	3.6	3.6	3.6	3.6	3.6	0%	2.9	3.6%	3.4%	4.1
1972	1928	4.0	3.2	2.9	3.1	3.1	3.1	3.1	3.1	3.1	3.1	3.0	3.0	3.0	3.0	3.0	3.0	3.0	3.0	3.0	3.0	3.0	3.0	3.0	3.0	3.0	3.0	3.0	3.0	3.0	3.0	3.0	3.0	3.0	3.0	3.0	3.0	3.0	3.0	3.0	3.0	0%	2.9	3.1%	3.2%	4.0
1973	1929	3.3	3.0	3.1	3.2	3.1	3.1	3.1	3.1	3.1	3.1	3.1	3.1	3.1	3.1	3.1	3.1	3.1	3.1	3.1	3.1	3.1	3.1	3.1	3.1	3.1	3.1	3.1	3.1	3.1	3.1	3.1	3.1	3.1	3.1	3.1	3.1	3.1	3.1	3.1	3.1	0%	3.0	3.1%	3.1%	4.0
1974	1930	3.4	3.6	3.9	3.8	3.6	3.7	3.7	3.6	4.0	4.3	4.8	4.8	4.8	4.8	4.8	4.8	4.8	4.8	4.8	4.8	4.8	4.8	4.8	4.8	4.8	4.8	4.8	4.8	4.8	4.8	4.8	4.8	4.8	4.8	4.8	4.8	4.8	4.8	4.8	4.8	0%	3.4	4.5%	3.8%	5.1
1975	1931	4.7	5.4	5.0	4.7	4.6	4.6	4.3	4.9	5.4	5.2	6.1	6.1	6.1	6.1	6.1	6.1	6.1	6.1	6.1	6.1	6.1	6.1	6.1	6.1	6.1	6.1	6.1	6.1	6.1	6.1	6.1	6.1	6.1	6.1	6.1	6.1	6.1	6.1	6.1	6.1	0%	4.3	5.8%	4.9%	5.9
1976	1932	4.6	4.3	4.1	4.1	4.0	3.9	4.3	4.6	4.5	5.1	6.1	6.1	6.1	6.1	6.1	6.1	6.1	6.1	6.1	6.1	6.1	6.1	6.1	6.1	6.1	6.1	6.1	6.1	6.1	6.1	6.1	6.1	6.1	6.1	6.1	6.1	6.1	6.1	6.1	6.1	0%	3.9	5.7%	4.4%	5.2
1977	1933	4.0	3.8	3.8	3.9	3.7	4.0	4.3	4.2	4.8	5.1	5.8	5.8	5.8	5.8	5.8	5.8	5.8	5.8	5.8	5.8	5.8	5.8	5.8	5.8	5.8	5.8	5.8	5.8	5.8	5.8	5.8	5.8	5.8	5.8	5.8	5.8	5.8	5.8	5.8	5.8	0%	3.7	5.4%	4.2%	4.8
1978	1934	4.0	4.0	4.0	3.9	4.1	4.4	4.3	4.9	5.3	4.7	5.4	5.4	5.4	5.4	5.4	5.4	5.4	5.4	5.4	5.4	5.4	5.4	5.4	5.4	5.4	5.4	5.4	5.4	5.4	5.4	5.4	5.4	5.4	5.4	5.4	5.4	5.4	5.4	5.4	5.4	0%	3.9	5.2%	4.4%	5.0
1979	1935	4.2	4.1	4.0	4.3	4.5	4.5	5.0	5.4	4.9	5.0	5.6	5.6	5.6	5.6	5.6	5.6	5.6	5.6	5.6	5.6	5.6	5.6	5.6	5.6	5.6	5.6	5.6	5.6	5.6	5.6	5.6	5.6	5.6	5.6	5.6	5.6	5.6	5.6	5.6	5.6	0%	4.0	5.3%	4.6%	5.3
1980	1936	4.2	4.0	4.3	4.5	4.5	5.0	5.2	4.8	5.0	5.2	6.0	6.0	6.0	6.0	6.0	6.0	6.0	6.0	6.0	6.0	6.0	6.0	6.0	6.0	6.0	6.0	6.0	6.0	6.0	6.0	6.0	6.0	6.0	6.0	6.0	6.0	6.0	6.0	6.0	6.0	0%	4.0	5.7%	4.7%	5.3
1981	1937	4.0	4.3	4.6	4.6	5.1	5.6	4.9	5.2	5.5	4.6	5.7	5.7	5.7	5.7	5.7	5.7	5.7	5.7	5.7	5.7	5.7	5.7	5.7	5.7	5.7	5.7	5.7	5.7	5.7	5.7	5.7	5.7	5.7	5.7	5.7	5.7	5.7	5.7	5.7	5.7	0%	4.0	5.5%	4.8%	5.4
1982	1938	4.6	4.9	4.8	5.5	5.9	5.3	5.4	5.8	4.9	5.6	7.0	7.0	7.0	7.0	7.0	7.0	7.0	7.0	7.0	7.0	7.0	7.0	7.0	7.0	7.0	7.0	7.0	7.0	7.0	7.0	7.0	7.0	7.0	7.0	7.0	7.0	7.0	7.0	7.0	7.0	0%	4.6	6.5%	5.3%	5.7
1983	1939	4.4	4.3	4.7	5.0	4.6	4.7	4.9	4.3	4.8	5.0	6.4	6.4	6.4	6.4	6.4	6.4	6.4	6.4	6.4	6.4	6.4	6.4	6.4	6.4	6.4	6.4	6.4	6.4	6.4	6.4	6.4	6.4	6.4	6.4	6.4	6.4	6.4	6.4	6.4	6.4	0%	4.3	6.0%	4.7%	5.0
1984	1940	4.1	4.4	4.6	4.3	4.4	4.6	4.1	4.5	4.7	5.0	6.3	6.3	6.3	6.3	6.3	6.3	6.3	6.3	6.3	6.3	6.3	6.3	6.3	6.3	6.3	6.3	6.3	6.3	6.3	6.3	6.3	6.3	6.3	6.3	6.3	6.3	6.3	6.3	6.3	6.3	0%	4.1	5.8%	4.5%	4.8
1985	1941	4.5	4.8	4.4	4.5	4.7	4.2	4.6	4.8	5.2	4.6	5.8	5.8	5.8	5.8	5.8	5.8	5.8	5.8	5.8	5.8	5.8	5.8	5.8	5.8	5.8	5.8	5.8	5.8	5.8	5.8	5.8	5.8	5.8	5.8	5.8	5.8	5.8	5.8	5.8	5.8	0%	4.2	5.5%	4.6%	4.8
1986	1942	4.3	4.0	4.1	4.3	3.8	4.2	4.3	4.6	4.2	4.7	6.1	6.1	6.1	6.1	6.1	6.1	6.1	6.1	6.1	6.1	6.1	6.1	6.1	6.1	6.1	6.1	6.1	6.1	6.1	6.1	6.1	6.1	6.1	6.1	6.1	6.1	6.1	6.1	6.1	6.1	0%	3.8	5.7%	4.3%	4.4
1987	1943	3.9	3.9	4.0	3.7	3.9	4.1	4.3	4.0	4.5	4.5	5.8	5.8	5.8	5.8	5.8	5.8	5.8	5.8	5.8	5.8	5.8	5.8	5.8	5.8	5.8	5.8	5.8	5.8	5.8	5.8	5.8	5.8	5.8	5.8	5.8	5.8	5.8	5.8	5.8	5.8	0%	3.7	5.4%	4.1%	4.0
1988	1944	4.2	4.4	3.9	4.3	4.4	4.8	4.3	4.9	4.9	5.5	6.6	6.6	6.6	6.6	6.6	6.6	6.6	6.6	6.6	6.6	6.6	6.6	6.6	6.6	6.6	6.6	6.6	6.6	6.6	6.6	6.6	6.6	6.6	6.6	6.6	6.6	6.6	6.6	6.6	6.6	0%	3.9	6.1%	4.6%	4.5
1989	1945	4.2	3.8	4.1	4.3	4.5	4.1	4.6	4.7	5.5	5.4	6.5	6.5	6.5	6.5	6.5	6.5	6.5	6.5	6.5	6.5	6.5	6.5	6.5	6.5	6.5	6.5	6.5	6.5	6.5	6.5	6.5	6.5	6.5	6.5	6.5	6.5	6.5	6.5	6.5	6.5	0%	3.8	6.0%	4.5%	4.3
1990	1946	3.6	3.9	4.1	4.4	3.9	4.5	4.5	5.2	5.3	5.2	6.3	6.3	6.3	6.3	6.3	6.3	6.3	6.3	6.3	6.3	6.3	6.3	6.3	6.3	6.3	6.3	6.3	6.3	6.3	6.3	6.3	6.3	6.3	6.3	6.3	6.3	6.3	6.3	6.3	6.3	0%	3.6	5.8%	4.5%	4.2
1991	1947	4.7	4.9	5.3	4.6	5.4	5.4	5.8	5.9	5.9	5.6	7.0	7.0	7.0	7.0	7.0	7.0	7.0	7.0	7.0	7.0	7.0	7.0	7.0	7.0	7.0	7.0	7.0	7.0	7.0	7.0	7.0	7.0	7.0	7.0	7.0	7.0	7.0	7.0	7.0	7.0	0%	4.6	6.6%	5.4%	4.9
1992	1948	4.3	4.6	4.0	4.7	4.7	5.3	5.3	5.3	5.1	5.1	6.2	6.2	6.2	6.2	6.2	6.2	6.2	6.2	6.2	6.2	6.2	6.2	6.2	6.2	6.2	6.2	6.2	6.2	6.2	6.2	6.2	6.2	6.2	6.2	6.2	6.2	6.2	6.2	6.2	6.2	0%	4.0	5.9%	4.8%	4.3
1993	1949	4.4	3.9	4.5	4.6	5.1	5.2	5.2	5.0	5.1	4.2	5.4	5.4	5.4	5.4	5.4	5.4	5.4	5.4	5.4	5.4	5.4	5.4	5.4	5.4	5.4	5.4	5.4	5.4	5.4	5.4	5.4	5.4	5.4	5.4	5.4	5.4	5.4	5.4	5.4	5.4	0%	3.9	5.3%	4.7%	4.1
1994	1950	3.7	4.2	4.2	4.9	4.9	5.0	4.4	4.6	3.8	4.5	5.7	5.7	5.7	5.7	5.7	5.7	5.7	5.7	5.7	5.7	5.7	5.7	5.7	5.7	5.7	5.7	5.7	5.7	5.7	5.7	5.7	5.7	5.7	5.7	5.7	5.7	5.7	5.7	5.7	5.7	0%	3.7	5.4%	4.4%	4.0
1995	1951	4.8	4.8	5.2	5.2	5.2	5.0	5.1	4.5	5.1	5.1	6.4	6.4	6.4	6.4	6.4	6.4	6.4	6.4	6.4	6.4	6.4	6.4	6.4	6.4	6.4	6.4	6.4	6.4	6.4	6.4	6.4	6.4	6.4	6.4	6.4	6.4	6.4	6.4	6.4	6.4	0%	4.5	6.1%	5.0%	4.4
1996	1952	4.2	4.7	4.7	4.8	4.5	4.7	3.9	4.6	4.7	4.5	5.6	5.6	5.6	5.6	5.6	5.6	5.6	5.6	5.6	5.6	5.6	5.6	5.6	5.6	5.6	5.6	5.6	5.6	5.6	5.6	5.6	5.6	5.6	5.6	5.6	5.6	5.6	5.6	5.6	5.6	0%	3.9	5.4%	4.5%	3.8
1997	1953	4.7	4.7	4.7	4.4	4.5	3.6	4.4	4.6	4.4	4.6	5.7	5.7	5.7	5.7	5.7	5.7	5.7	5.7	5.7	5.7	5.7	5.7	5.7	5.7	5.7	5.7	5.7	5.7	5.7	5.7	5.7	5.7	5.7	5.7	5.7	5.7	5.7	5.7	5.7	5.7	0%	3.6	5.4%	4.5%	3.8
1998	1954	4.2	4.3	3.8	4.0	3.2	3.9	4.1	3.9	4.2	3.8	5.0	5.0	5.0	5.0	5.0	5.0	5.0	5.0	5.0	5.0	5.0	5.0	5.0	5.0	5.0	5.0	5.0	5.0	5.0	5.0	5.0	5.0	5.0	5.0	5.0	5.0	5.0	5.0	5.0	5.0	0%	3.2	4.7%	3.9%	3.4
1999	1955	4.3	3.8	3.9	3.3	3.9	4.1	3.9	4.1	3.8	2.9	3.1	3.1	3.1	3.1	3.1	3.1	3.1	3.1	3.1	3.1	3.1	3.1	3.1	3.1	3.1	3.1	3.1	3.1	3.1	3.1	3.1	3.1	3.1	3.1	3.1	3.1	3.1	3.1	3.1	3.1	0%	2.9	3.3%	3.8%	3.3
2000	1956	3.9	4.0	3.3	3.9	4.1	3.9	4.1	3.8	2.9	3.0	3.7	3.7	3.7	3.7	3.7	3.7	3.7	3.7	3.7	3.7	3.7	3.7	3.7	3.7	3.7	3.7	3.7	3.7	3.7	3.7	3.7	3.7	3.7	3.7	3.7	3.7	3.7	3.7	3.7	3.7	0%	2.9	3.7%	3.7%	3.2
																																								Totals	0%	2.4	5.1%	4.3%	4.7%

FIGURE 171

Failure market results transitioning from systemic withdrawal to inflation-adjust SPIA at age 75.

Guidelines for timing GI purchases are outlined later, but here the point is simple: there's risk in waiting to purchase GI. The risk isn't high and it doesn't show up under normal markets, but it's there under failure market conditions, which is what GI is meant to handle. The risk of not locking in income exists whether waiting to purchase an SPIA or waiting to build a TIPS bond ladder.

GI purchases should be timed to meet specific goals as part of a larger verified strategy, but shouldn't be timed based purely on payout amounts.

Fortifying Against Longevity Risk without an Income Floor

Generally, the largest risk of insufficient income comes late in retirement. With longevity risk, the longer one lives, the higher the risk of insufficient income.

One way to fortify against longevity risk is to leverage GI to boost income late in retirement. A deferred annuity (or better yet, a simulated deferred annuity as shown later) does exactly this. It provides extra income at the end of retirement. While this can work well, it does not fully address the risk of a failure market. Insufficient income can also be a problem early in retirement when using a variable-withdrawal strategy to gauge the current risk, independent of longevity risk.

Figure 172 shows the results in a failure market when 10% of the portfolio value is allocated to a DIA, which starts paying off at age 90. Income after 90 overall looks strong: the rate drops below 3% in only one year. Most noticeable though are low income rates regularly showing up much earlier in retirement. Income drops by 10% to fund the DIA, making the problem worse in early retirement. The key point is, deferring income to cover longevity risk without a complementary plan to provide an income floor earlier in retirement can lead to problems.

Initial	Start	End	A65	A66	A67	A68	A69	A70	A71	A72	A73	A74	A75	A76	A77	A78	A79	A80	A81	A82	A83	A84	A85	A86	A87	A88	A89	A90	A91	A92	A93	A94	A95	A96	A97	A98	A99	A00	A01	A02	A03	A04	%Left	Min	Avg	1st 10Y	MSWR
4.0%	1928	1967	4.4	3.4	3.1	2.9	3.1	3.2	3.2	3.6	4.1	3.0	3.2	3.2	3.0	2.8	2.8	3.0	3.2	4.1	3.1	2.9	2.9	3.0	3.6	3.9	3.9	6.2	7.9	8.1	8.1	7.2	8.1	8.1	8.1	8.1	8.1	8.1	8.1	8.1	8.1	8.1	62.8%	2.8	5.0%	3.4%	4.4
4.0%	1929	1968	3.1	2.8	2.8	2.8	2.9	2.9	3.0	3.3	2.8	2.8	2.8	2.8	2.5	2.5	2.8	2.9	3.4	2.8	2.8	2.7	2.8	3.0	3.1	3.2	3.0	7.1	7.5	7.2	6.3	7.4	8.0	7.4	8.1	7.6	7.7	8.1	8.1	8.1	8.1	8.1	55.7%	2.5	4.7%	2.9%	3.8
4.2%	1930	1969	3.2	3.0	3.0	3.2	3.2	3.5	4.1	3.0	3.2	3.1	3.0	2.8	2.9	3.1	3.2	4.5	3.3	3.1	3.1	3.2	3.9	3.9	4.2	4.0	5.3	8.4	8.3	7.3	8.5	8.5	8.4	8.5	8.5	8.5	8.5	8.5	8.5	8.5	8.5	8.5	44.4%	2.8	5.3%	3.2%	4.6
4.4%	1931	1970	3.2	3.2	3.7	3.7	4.4	5.4	3.7	4.1	4.0	3.7	3.2	3.2	3.6	4.1	5.2	3.9	3.6	3.4	3.7	4.1	4.4	4.4	4.1	5.9	6.1	8.6	8.0	8.7	8.9	8.5	8.9	8.4	8.9	8.9	8.9	8.9	8.9	8.9	8.9	8.9	41.3%	3.2	5.8%	3.9%	5.7
4.8%	1932	1971	4.0	5.9	5.9	6.7	7.0	5.9	6.2	6.2	5.9	4.8	4.7	5.6	6.0	6.8	5.6	4.8	4.7	5.0	5.5	5.6	5.9	5.2	6.8	7.0	6.9	8.9	9.6	9.6	9.6	9.6	9.6	9.6	9.6	9.6	9.6	9.6	9.6	9.6	9.6	9.6	45.6%	4.0	7.2%	5.8%	7.7
4.8%	1933	1972	5.5	5.3	6.2	7.0	5.3	5.9	5.8	5.3	4.3	4.2	4.9	5.8	6.6	5.2	4.5	4.3	5.0	5.4	5.4	5.8	5.5	6.6	7.0	6.9	6.1	9.5	9.6	9.3	9.6	9.1	9.6	9.6	9.6	9.6	9.6	9.6	9.4	9.6	9.5	8.9	39.1%	4.2	7.0%	5.5%	7.5
4.4%	1934	1973	3.6	4.4	5.3	3.6	4.0	3.9	3.6	3.2	3.2	3.5	4.0	5.1	3.7	3.4	3.3	3.6	4.0	4.0	4.1	4.0	5.7	5.9	5.9	5.3	5.9	8.8	8.6	8.9	8.5	8.5	8.9	8.9	8.9	8.9	8.9	8.9	8.5	8.9	8.8	6.3	23.1%	3.2	5.9%	3.8%	5.8
4.4%	1935	1974	4.5	5.3	3.6	4.0	3.9	3.7	3.2	3.2	3.5	4.0	5.0	3.7	3.4	3.3	3.5	3.9	4.0	4.1	3.8	5.4	5.9	5.7	5.1	5.9	5.9	8.4	8.9	8.3	8.6	8.6	8.9	8.6	8.9	8.9	8.7	8.6	8.3	8.9	6.4	5.4	13.1%	3.2	5.8%	3.9%	5.8
4.4%	1936	1975	4.4	3.2	3.4	3.3	3.2	3.2	3.2	3.2	3.4	4.1	3.3	3.2	3.2	3.2	3.5	3.5	3.7	3.4	5.0	5.6	5.6	4.6	5.7	5.9	5.5	8.7	8.2	8.3	8.7	8.9	8.5	8.9	8.9	8.8	8.1	8.4	8.1	6.5	5.4	5.7	14.6%	3.2	5.5%	3.5%	5.2
4.0%	1937	1976	2.8	2.9	2.9	2.8	2.7	2.7	2.8	2.9	3.6	2.9	2.8	2.8	2.8	3.0	3.1	3.2	3.1	4.4	4.8	4.8	4.1	5.0	5.3	5.1	5.5	7.6	7.9	8.1	8.1	8.0	8.1	8.1	8.1	8.1	8.0	8.1	6.1	5.4	5.6	5.9	21.2%	2.7	5.0%	2.9%	4.4
4.2%	1938	1977	4.2	4.1	3.7	3.2	3.2	3.8	4.3	5.2	4.0	3.4	3.3	3.6	4.0	4.0	4.1	3.9	5.3	5.6	5.5	5.0	5.9	5.9	5.8	5.9	5.7	8.5	8.5	8.5	8.5	8.5	8.5	8.5	8.5	8.5	8.5	7.2	5.6	6.4	6.9	6.2	23.1%	3.2	5.7%	3.9%	5.8
4.2%	1939	1978	3.5	3.3	3.0	3.1	3.3	3.8	4.8	3.5	3.2	3.2	3.3	3.6	3.7	3.9	3.6	5.0	5.5	5.2	4.7	5.5	5.8	5.5	5.9	5.7	5.7	8.5	8.5	8.4	8.5	8.5	8.5	8.2	8.5	8.5	6.6	5.6	5.8	7.0	6.3	5.9	20.2%	3.0	5.5%	3.5%	5.7
4.2%	1940	1979	3.4	3.1	3.1	3.4	3.9	5.0	3.6	3.2	3.2	3.3	3.6	3.7	3.8	3.6	5.0	5.4	5.3	4.7	5.4	5.6	5.6	5.9	5.5	5.8	5.9	8.5	8.5	8.5	8.5	8.4	8.4	8.3	8.5	6.9	5.6	5.9	6.3	6.6	6.1	5.9	21.0%	3.1	5.5%	3.5%	5.5
4.2%	1941	1980	3.2	3.2	3.8	4.4	5.3	4.1	3.5	3.4	3.7	4.1	4.1	4.2	4.0	5.1	5.5	5.3	4.9	5.5	5.6	5.7	5.9	5.5	5.9	5.9	5.9	8.5	8.5	8.5	8.4	8.0	8.3	8.1	6.8	5.5	5.7	6.3	6.0	6.3	6.1	5.9	21.1%	3.2	5.6%	3.9%	5.5
4.4%	1942	1981	3.8	4.8	5.4	6.3	5.0	4.3	4.1	4.5	4.9	4.7	4.9	4.5	5.6	5.9	5.7	5.2	5.9	5.9	5.9	6.3	6.0	6.0	6.3	6.3	6.2	8.9	8.9	8.6	8.4	8.3	8.5	6.6	5.9	6.1	6.3	6.3	6.0	6.7	6.4	5.9	20.2%	3.8	6.1%	4.8%	6.0
4.6%	1943	1982	4.4	5.0	5.9	4.5	4.0	3.8	4.1	4.4	4.4	4.4	4.2	5.5	5.8	5.7	5.0	5.8	5.9	5.8	6.1	5.9	6.1	6.2	6.7	6.2	6.7	9.2	8.7	8.3	8.5	8.2	6.9	6.0	6.3	6.5	6.2	6.2	6.1	6.5	6.1	6.1	21.4%	3.8	6.0%	4.5%	5.9
4.4%	1944	1983	4.1	5.1	3.7	3.4	3.3	3.5	3.7	3.7	3.8	3.6	4.9	5.3	5.1	4.4	5.2	5.4	5.3	5.6	5.2	5.6	5.9	6.1	5.8	6.3	6.3	8.4	8.2	8.1	8.1	6.4	5.8	5.9	6.6	6.2	6.0	6.2	6.1	6.3	6.3	6.4	24.7%	3.3	5.5%	3.8%	5.4
4.4%	1945	1984	4.5	3.4	3.2	3.2	3.2	3.4	3.4	3.5	3.4	4.3	5.0	4.7	4.0	5.0	5.1	5.0	5.5	5.0	5.1	5.5	5.9	5.4	6.2	6.3	5.4	7.9	8.1	7.8	6.3	5.7	5.9	6.1	6.2	5.9	5.9	6.0	5.8	6.3	6.4	5.9	20.4%	3.2	5.3%	3.6%	5.1
4.4%	1946	1985	3.2	3.2	3.0	3.2	3.2	3.2	3.2	3.2	3.7	4.1	4.0	3.5	4.2	4.4	4.2	5.0	4.4	4.6	5.0	5.4	5.0	5.7	6.1	5.1	4.7	7.6	7.6	6.0	5.7	5.7	5.9	5.8	5.8	5.8	5.8	5.7	5.8	6.3	5.9	5.9	20.3%	3.0	4.9%	3.3%	4.6
4.4%	1947	1986	3.3	3.2	3.4	3.7	3.6	3.8	3.5	4.6	5.0	4.7	4.0	5.0	5.0	5.0	5.3	5.0	5.2	5.4	5.7	5.4	6.1	6.2	5.2	5.1	5.0	7.7	6.2	5.7	5.8	5.9	5.9	5.8	6.0	6.0	5.8	6.0	6.2	6.3	6.5	6.3	23.9%	3.2	5.2%	3.9%	5.0
4.6%	1948	1987	3.6	3.8	4.1	4.1	4.1	4.0	5.0	5.5	5.3	4.4	5.3	5.4	5.3	5.7	5.3	5.5	5.8	5.9	5.6	6.3	6.7	5.6	5.5	5.7	5.5	6.6	6.0	6.1	6.3	6.2	6.2	6.1	6.3	6.0	6.1	6.5	6.2	7.2	6.9	6.2	21.5%	3.6	5.6%	4.4%	5.5
4.6%	1949	1988	4.0	4.2	4.2	4.3	4.1	5.4	5.6	5.4	4.7	5.4	5.5	5.4	5.8	5.5	5.6	5.8	6.2	5.7	6.3	6.7	5.8	5.6	5.8	5.7	4.1	6.1	6.3	6.4	6.3	6.1	6.3	6.2	6.2	6.3	6.5	6.4	6.7	7.8	6.4	6.4	24.4%	4.0	5.7%	4.7%	5.6
4.6%	1950	1989	3.9	3.9	3.9	3.7	4.8	5.3	5.0	4.2	5.1	5.1	5.0	5.5	5.0	5.3	5.5	5.9	5.5	6.0	6.4	5.5	5.5	5.5	5.5	4.1	3.4	6.1	6.4	6.2	6.1	6.1	6.2	6.0	6.3	6.6	6.3	6.8	6.7	6.7	6.7	6.5	25.3%	3.4	5.5%	4.5%	5.3
4.4%	1951	1990	3.6	3.7	3.5	4.7	5.1	4.9	4.1	5.0	5.0	4.8	5.2	4.8	5.0	5.3	5.5	5.1	5.9	6.0	5.1	5.1	5.3	5.1	3.8	3.2	3.3	6.2	6.1	5.9	6.0	5.9	5.9	6.0	6.9	6.3	6.6	7.1	6.2	7.2	6.9	5.8	17.6%	3.2	5.3%	4.4%	5.1
4.4%	1952	1991	3.7	3.5	4.5	5.0	4.7	4.1	4.7	5.0	4.8	5.1	4.7	4.9	5.1	5.5	5.0	5.7	6.0	5.0	4.9	5.1	5.1	3.7	3.2	3.3	3.5	6.0	5.9	5.9	5.9	5.8	6.0	6.3	6.3	6.7	6.6	6.3	6.3	7.2	5.8	6.0	21.0%	3.2	5.2%	4.5%	5.0
4.3%	1953	1992	3.4	4.4	4.8	4.5	3.8	4.7	4.8	4.5	5.0	4.4	4.8	5.0	5.2	5.0	5.4	5.6	4.8	4.4	4.6	4.7	3.5	3.1	3.2	3.3	3.2	5.7	5.8	5.8	5.7	5.8	6.4	6.0	7.0	6.9	6.1	6.5	6.4	5.9	6.3	6.2	23.1%	3.1	5.1%	4.4%	4.8
4.6%	1954	1993	4.7	5.0	4.7	4.1	4.9	5.0	4.8	5.3	4.7	4.9	5.2	5.5	5.0	5.7	5.9	5.0	5.0	4.9	4.8	3.9	3.4	3.4	3.7	3.5	3.4	6.0	6.0	5.9	6.1	6.3	6.2	6.4	7.2	6.3	6.3	6.7	5.9	6.5	6.4	6.3	24.3%	3.4	5.3%	4.8%	5.0
4.3%	1955	1994	3.9	3.7	3.3	3.8	4.0	3.9	4.2	3.8	4.0	4.1	4.7	4.1	5.0	5.2	4.1	4.1	4.3	4.1	3.2	3.1	3.1	3.2	3.2	3.1	3.1	5.7	5.6	5.7	6.0	5.7	6.3	6.3	6.1	6.2	6.2	5.6	5.8	6.4	6.3	5.8	19.8%	3.1	4.6%	3.9%	4.3
4.3%	1956	1995	3.5	3.2	3.6	3.8	3.6	4.0	3.6	3.8	4.0	4.4	3.9	4.8	5.0	4.0	3.9	4.1	4.1	3.2	3.0	3.1	3.2	3.1	3.1	3.1	3.1	5.6	5.7	5.9	5.8	6.0	6.3	5.8	6.3	6.3	5.6	5.9	5.9	6.7	6.0	6.2	23.0%	3.0	4.5%	3.7%	4.2
4.3%	1957	1996	3.2	3.7	3.9	3.7	4.1	3.7	3.9	4.1	4.6	4.0	4.9	5.0	4.0	3.9	4.0	4.0	3.2	3.1	3.1	3.2	3.2	3.1	3.1	3.1	3.1	5.7	6.0	5.8	6.2	6.2	6.0	6.1	6.7	5.6	5.9	6.2	6.2	6.3	6.7	6.4	24.7%	3.1	4.6%	3.9%	4.2
4.3%	1958	1997	4.6	4.8	4.5	5.0	4.4	4.7	4.9	5.1	4.8	5.2	5.4	4.5	4.3	4.6	4.5	3.5	3.1	3.2	3.3	3.2	3.2	3.2	3.2	3.2	3.2	6.3	6.1	6.5	6.9	6.2	6.7	6.8	6.0	6.4	6.6	7.2	6.3	7.8	7.6	7.8	32.4%	3.1	5.1%	4.8%	4.7
4.1%	1959	1998	3.8	3.6	4.0	3.6	3.7	4.0	4.5	3.9	4.8	5.0	3.9	3.8	3.9	3.9	3.1	2.9	3.0	3.1	3.0	3.0	3.0	3.0	3.0	3.1	3.3	5.8	6.3	6.3	6.0	6.2	6.7	5.6	6.3	6.5	6.5	6.3	6.8	7.6	7.8	7.3	29.1%	2.9	4.7%	4.1%	4.2
4.0%	1960	1999	3.5	3.9	3.4	3.6	3.9	4.4	3.8	4.5	4.8	3.7	3.6	3.7	3.6	3.0	2.8	2.8	2.9	2.8	2.8	2.8	2.9	2.8	2.9	3.2	3.0	6.0	6.3	5.7	6.0	6.1	5.4	5.8	6.4	6.5	5.9	6.8	6.6	7.9	7.4	7.3	29.3%	2.8	4.5%	3.9%	4.0
4.0%	1961	2000	4.1	3.6	3.8	4.1	4.5	4.0	4.6	4.9	3.9	3.7	3.8	3.8	3.0	2.8	2.8	3.0	2.9	2.8	2.8	2.9	2.8	2.9	3.2	3.2	3.4	6.3	5.9	6.1	6.5	5.4	6.2	6.3	7.2	6.3	7.0	7.2	7.5	8.0	7.9	6.9	26.4%	2.8	4.7%	4.1%	4.1
4.0%	1962	2001	3.3	3.4	3.6	4.1	3.5	4.4	4.6	3.6	3.5	3.5	3.5	2.9	2.7	2.8	2.8	2.8	2.8	2.8	2.8	2.8	2.9	3.1	3.0	3.3	3.4	5.7	6.0	6.1	5.4	5.7	6.3	6.3	6.3	7.0	6.8	7.6	7.2	8.1	7.1	6.7	25.4%	2.7	4.5%	3.8%	3.9
4.0%	1963	2002	3.9	4.1	4.5	4.1	4.6	4.9	3.8	3.7	3.9	3.7	3.0	2.8	2.8	2.9	2.9	2.8	2.8	2.8	2.8	2.9	3.2	3.0	3.4	3.7	3.2	6.1	6.4	5.4	6.0	6.2	6.9	6.2	7.3	7.2	7.6	7.7	7.7	7.6	7.3	5.6	19.1%	2.8	4.7%	4.1%	4.1
4.0%	1964	2003	4.0	4.4	3.7	4.5	4.7	3.8	3.6	3.7	3.7	3.0	2.8	2.8	2.9	2.8	2.8	2.8	2.8	2.8	2.8	3.1	3.0	3.2	3.6	3.2	3.4	6.3	5.5	5.9	6.3	6.5	6.3	7.0	7.5	7.9	7.5	8.0	7.2	7.8	5.9	6.7	25.6%	2.8	4.7%	3.9%	4.0
3.9%	1965	2004	4.1	3.6	4.2	4.5	3.4	3.3	3.4	3.3	2.8	2.5	2.7	2.7	2.7	2.7	2.7	2.7	2.7	2.7	2.9	2.9	3.2	3.3	3.1	3.3	3.5	5.4	5.9	6.1	6.6	6.0	7.1	7.0	8.0	7.6	7.7	7.2	7.1	6.2	7.1	6.9	26.3%	2.5	4.5%	3.5%	3.7
3.7%	1966	2005	3.3	4.0	4.2	3.2	3.0	3.1	3.1	2.6	2.3	2.4	2.6	2.6	2.5	2.6	2.6	2.5	2.6	2.7	2.6	3.0	3.2	2.8	3.1	3.3	2.6	5.6	6.0	6.2	5.9	6.5	6.9	7.2	7.5	7.6	6.8	7.1	5.4	7.1	7.0	6.4	23.8%	2.3	4.3%	3.1%	3.5
4.0%	1967	2006	4.5	4.7	3.6	3.5	3.6	3.5	2.9	2.8	2.8	2.8	2.8	2.8	2.8	2.8	2.8	2.8	3.0	2.9	3.1	3.3	3.2	3.2	3.6	2.9	3.2	6.2	6.7	6.1	7.1	7.1	7.9	7.6	8.1	7.5	7.4	6.1	7.1	7.9	7.3	7.2	28.8%	2.8	4.7%	3.5%	3.9
3.9%	1968	2007	4.1	3.2	3.1	3.1	3.1	2.7	2.3	2.5	2.7	2.6	2.4	2.4	2.4	2.3	2.6	2.7	2.7	2.8	2.9	2.8	2.9	3.0	2.7	2.9	3.0	5.7	5.5	5.9	6.2	6.9	7.0	7.1	6.8	6.6	5.4	6.2	6.2	6.7	6.5	5.6	19.5%	2.3	4.1%	2.9%	3.3
3.9%	1969	2008	3.0	2.9	2.9	2.9	2.7	2.3	2.3	2.5	2.3	2.3	2.3	2.3	2.3	2.4	2.7	2.6	2.7	2.8	2.7	2.8	2.9	2.5	2.7	2.9	2.9	5.4	5.7	5.8	6.5	6.3	7.0	5.9	6.4	5.4	5.8	6.2	5.8	6.7	5.7	4.8	8.1%	2.3	3.9%	2.6%	3.1
3.9%	1970	2009	3.5	3.6	3.5	2.8	2.5	2.7	2.8	2.7	2.7	2.7	2.7	2.7	2.8	3.1	3.0	3.3	3.7	3.2	3.4	4.0	3.2	3.7	4.2	4.6	4.0	7.3	7.5	7.9	8.0	8.0	7.8	7.7	7.1	7.7	7.8	7.8	7.8	7.8	5.3	5.4	17.3%	2.5	4.8%	3.0%	3.9
4.1%	1971	2010	3.8	3.7	3.0	2.6	2.9	3.0	2.9	2.9	2.9	2.9	2.9	3.0	3.2	3.1	3.3	3.6	3.3	3.4	3.7	3.2	3.8	4.1	4.6	4.1	4.8	7.5	8.2	8.1	8.3	7.8	8.1	6.6	8.1	8.2	7.8	8.2	7.4	5.5	5.7	5.8	20.3%	2.6	4.9%	3.0%	4.1
4.0%	1972	1928	3.6	2.9	2.6	2.8	2.8	2.8	2.8	2.8	2.8	2.8	2.8	3.0	3.0	3.2	3.4	3.2	3.4	3.7	3.1	3.7	4.1	4.4	4.0	4.8	4.8	8.0	8.0	8.1	7.7	7.6	6.9	7.6	8.1	7.8	7.9	7.5	5.4	5.8	5.9	6.4	24.7%	2.6	4.8%	2.9%	4.0
4.0%	1973	1929	3.0	2.7	2.8	2.9	2.8	2.8	2.8	2.8	2.8	2.8	3.0	2.9	3.2	3.4	3.2	3.3	3.7	3.0	3.5	4.0	4.5	3.8	4.7	4.8	5.1	7.8	8.1	7.5	7.7	6.5	7.7	7.7	8.0	8.0	7.2	5.4	5.4	6.2	6.8	5.4	15.1%	2.7	4.7%	2.8%	4.0
4.3%	1974	1930	3.1	3.2	3.5	3.4	3.2	3.3	3.3	3.2	3.6	3.9	3.8	4.4	4.8	4.3	4.5	4.9	4.1	4.9	5.0	5.4	5.0	5.5	5.7	6.0	6.0	8.6	8.5	8.5	7.6	8.3	8.6	8.4	8.6	8.4	6.0	6.8	7.1	8.7	6.3	5.1	12.0%	3.1	5.6%	3.4%	5.1
4.7%	1975	1931	4.2	4.9	4.5	4.2	4.1	4.1	3.9	4.4	4.9	4.7	5.5	5.8	5.3	5.5	5.7	5.0	5.8	5.9	6.1	5.8	6.5	6.3	6.8	6.8	6.8	9.2	9.4	8.3	9.2	9.1	9.2	9.1	9.2	6.8	7.1	7.9	8.5	6.9	5.4	4.8	4.4%	3.9	6.3%	4.4%	5.9
4.6%	1976	1932	4.1	3.9	3.7	3.7	3.6	3.5	3.9	4.1	4.1	4.6	5.0	4.5	4.7	5.0	4.1	5.0	5.4	5.5	5.0	5.9	5.9	6.4	6.5	6.6	6.2	9.0	8.3	8.8	9.0	8.7	9.1	8.4	6.4	6.9	7.2	8.6	6.3	5.6	4.8	4.8	2.8%	3.5	5.8%	3.9%	5.2
4.6%	1977	1933	3.6	3.4	3.4	3.5	3.3	3.6	3.9	3.8	4.3	4.6	4.1	4.3	4.6	3.9	4.5	5.0	5.4	4.6	5.4	5.6	6.2	6.1	6.3	6.0	6.0	8.0	8.7	8.7	8.6	8.6	8.4	6.2	7.1	7.3	8.1	6.3	5.1	4.8	4.8	4.8	3.8%	3.3	5.5%	3.7%	4.8
4.7%	1978	1934	3.6	3.6	3.6	3.5	3.7	4.0	3.9	4.4	4.8	4.2	4.4	4.7	4.0	4.6	5.0	5.4	4.9	5.5	5.6	6.2	6.3	6.3	6.0	6.2	5.4	8.7	8.9	8.5	8.9	8.2	6.4	6.7	7.7	8.5	6.3	5.3	4.8	4.8	4.8	4.8	2.7%	3.5	5.6%	3.9%	5.0
4.8%	1979	1935	3.8	3.7	3.6	3.9	4.1	4.1	4.5	4.9	4.4	4.5	4.8	4.1	4.7	5.0	5.4	4.8	5.8	5.7	6.1	6.3	6.5	6.1	6.3	5.8	6.1	9.0	8.8	8.9	8.5	6.4	7.0	7.2	8.9	6.5	5.4	4.8	4.8	4.8	4.8	4.8	5.8%	3.6	5.6%	4.1%	5.3
4.8%	1980	1936	3.8	3.6	3.9	4.1	4.1	4.5	4.7	4.3	4.5	4.7	4.0	4.6	4.9	5.3	4.7	5.5	5.7	6.0	6.0	6.2	6.0	5.9	5.1	6.1	6.1	8.6	8.9	8.2	6.3	6.5	7.2	8.1	6.8	6.1	4.8	4.8	5.4	5.7	6.2	6.3	20.7%	3.6	5.6%	4.2%	5.3
4.7%	1981	1937	3.6	3.9	4.1	4.1	4.6	5.0	4.4	4.7	5.0	4.1	4.8	5.0	5.5	4.8	5.6	5.7	6.2	6.1	6.2	6.0	6.3	5.6	6.2	6.4	6.0	9.0	8.6	6.7	7.2	7.4	8.6	6.6	6.1	4.8	4.8	5.9	5.4	6.2	6.5	4.8	9.7%	3.6	5.7%	4.4%	5.4
4.8%	1982	1938	4.1	4.4	4.3	5.0	5.3	4.8	4.9	5.2	4.4	5.0	5.3	5.7	5.0	5.9	5.9	6.3	6.5	6.4	6.1	6.4	5.9	6.4	6.6	6.4	6.4	8.7	7.0	7.2	7.8	8.5	7.0	6.2	5.1	5.1	6.1	6.0	6.2	7.4	5.2	5.3	12.6%	4.1	5.9%	4.7%	5.7
4.8%	1983	1939	4.0	3.9	4.2	4.5	4.1	4.2	4.4	3.9	4.3	4.5	4.9	4.3	5.0	5.2	5.8	5.9	5.9	5.5	5.7	5.0	5.9	5.9	5.9	6.0	5.4	6.3	6.7	7.0	8.2	6.3	5.6	4.8	4.8	4.8	4.8	5.2	5.8	4.8	4.8	4.8	3.9%	3.9	5.2%	4.2%	5.0
4.7%	1984	1940	3.7	4.0	4.1	3.9	4.0	4.1	3.7	4.1	4.2	4.5	4.1	4.6	4.7	5.5	5.5	5.5	5.2	5.3	4.3	5.5	5.8	5.4	5.7	5.3	3.5	6.4	6.8	7.7	6.4	6.0	5.0	5.1	6.0	5.8	6.1	6.6	4.8	5.6	5.0	4.8	7.6%	3.5	5.1%	4.0%	4.8
4.7%	1985	1941	4.1	4.3	4.0	4.1	4.2	3.8	4.1	4.3	4.7	4.1	4.7	4.8	5.4	5.5	5.5	5.1	5.5	4.3	5.3	5.6	5.5	5.6	5.3	3.9	4.0	7.0	8.1	6.3	6.0	5.0	5.3	6.0	6.0	6.1	6.5	5.0	5.2	5.3	4.8	4.8	4.8%	3.8	5.1%	4.2%	4.8
4.6%	1986	1942	3.9	3.6	3.7	3.9	3.4	3.8	3.9	4.1	3.8	4.2	4.3	5.0	5.0	5.1	4.8	5.0	4.3	5.0	5.2	5.1	5.5	4.9	3.6	3.9	4.1	7.7	6.3	5.9	4.8	4.8	5.8	5.5	6.0	6.5	4.8	5.3	4.8	4.8	4.8	4.8	3.9%	3.4	4.8%	3.8%	4.4
4.6%	1987	1943	3.5	3.5	3.6	3.3	3.5	3.7	3.9	3.6	4.1	4.1	4.6	4.7	4.7	4.4	4.5	3.9	4.8	4.9	4.6	5.1	4.7	3.3	3.6	3.9	4.6	6.1	5.4	4.8	4.8	4.8	4.8	5.3	5.9	4.8	4.8	4.8	4.8	4.8	4.3	2.6	0.0%	2.6	4.4%	3.7%	4.0
4.6%	1988	1944	3.8	4.0	3.5	3.9	4.0	4.3	3.9	4.4	4.4	5.0	5.0	5.1	4.8	5.0	4.2	5.0	5.3	5.0	5.2	5.0	3.8	3.9	4.2	5.2	3.7	5.9	5.4	5.4	5.9	5.9	6.1	6.6	5.4	5.7	5.3	4.8	4.8	4.8	4.8	4.8	9.1%	3.5	4.8%	4.1%	4.5
4.6%	1989	1945	3.8	3.4	3.7	3.9	4.1	3.7	4.1	4.2	5.0	4.9	5.0	4.6	4.8	4.1	4.9	5.1	5.0	5.0	4.6	3.5	3.8	4.0	5.0	3.7	3.3	4.8	5.1	5.8	5.7	5.9	6.5	4.8	5.4	5.1	4.8	4.8	4.8	4.8	4.8	4.8	7.8%	3.3	4.6%	4.1%	4.3
4.3%	1990	1946	3.2	3.5	3.7	4.0	3.5	4.1	4.1	4.7	4.8	4.7	4.4	4.5	3.9	4.6	4.8	4.6	5.0	4.4	3.3	3.6	4.0	4.7	3.5	3.1	2.5	5.4	5.7	5.6	5.9	6.3	5.3	5.5	5.5	4.9	4.8	4.8	4.8	5.2	5.6	4.8	8.4%	2.5	4.5%	4.0%	4.2
4.4%	1991	1947	4.2	4.4	4.8	4.1	4.9	4.9	5.2	5.3	5.3	5.0	5.1	4.6	5.1	5.3	5.1	5.3	5.1	3.8	4.0	4.5	5.3	4.0	3.4	3.2	3.2	6.1	6.1	6.3	7.4	5.7	5.9	5.8	5.8	5.1	5.1	5.8	5.9	7.7	5.9	5.7	14.4%	3.2	5.1%	4.8%	4.9
4.1%	1992	1948	3.9	4.1	3.6	4.2	4.2	4.8	4.8	4.8	4.6	4.6	4.0	4.6	4.7	4.6	4.8	4.5	3.4	3.5	3.8	4.8	3.6	3.1	2.9	3.0	3.1	5.6	6.0	6.6	5.4	5.5	5.5	5.3	4.8	4.8	5.4	5.5	6.0	5.6	5.4	4.8	10.5%	2.9	4.6%	4.4%	4.3
4.0%	1993	1949	4.0	3.5	4.1	4.1	4.6	4.7	4.7	4.5	4.6	3.8	4.5	4.6	4.5	4.6	4.3	3.2	3.4	3.6	4.5	3.3	2.9	2.3	2.6	2.9	2.8	5.7	6.6	5.2	5.4	5.3	5.0	4.8	4.8	4.9	5.3	5.5	5.0	4.9	4.8	4.8	7.7%	2.3	4.4%	4.2%	4.1
4.0%	1994	1950	3.3	3.8	3.8	4.4	4.4	4.5	4.0	4.1	3.4	4.1	4.3	4.1	4.4	4.1	3.1	3.2	3.6	4.1	3.2	2.9	2.7	2.8	2.9	2.9	3.2	6.4	5.4	5.4	5.4	5.2	4.8	4.8	5.4	5.4	6.1	5.4	5.3	5.4	5.4	5.4	13.1%	2.7	4.3%	4.0%	4.0
3.9%	1995	1951	4.3	4.3	4.7	4.7	4.7	4.5	4.6	4.1	4.6	4.6	4.5	4.6	4.4	3.2	3.4	3.9	4.6	3.4	2.9	2.7	2.9	3.1	3.1	3.6	4.3	5.4	5.6	5.4	5.4	5.1	5.3	5.4	6.1	7.3	5.7	5.4	5.4	5.7	5.9	5.7	20.1%	2.7	4.6%	4.5%	4.4
3.7%	1996	1952	3.8	4.2	4.2	4.3	4.1	4.2	3.5	4.1	4.2	4.1	4.2	4.0	2.9	3.1	3.3	4.1	3.1	2.6	2.3	2.6	2.7	2.7	3.0	3.8	2.6	5.3	5.2	5.1	4.8	4.8	5.2	5.3	6.6	5.3	5.2	5.2	5.2	5.4	5.3	5.2	14.3%	2.3	4.2%	4.1%	3.8
3.7%	1997	1953	4.2	4.2	4.2	4.0	4.1	3.2	4.0	4.1	4.0	4.1	3.7	2.7	2.9	3.2	3.9	3.0	2.7	2.5	2.6	2.8	2.8	3.0	3.7	2.6	2.7	5.3	5.2	4.8	4.9	5.2	5.5	6.6	5.6	5.3	5.2	5.3	5.4	5.8	5.6	5.3	15.8%	2.5	4.1%	4.0%	3.8
3.7%	1998	1954	3.8	3.9	3.4	3.6	2.9	3.5	3.7	3.5	3.8	3.4	2.7	2.8	3.0	3.5	2.8	2.6	2.3	2.3	2.6	2.6	2.8	3.2	2.4	2.6	2.6	4.8	4.8	4.8	5.0	5.2	5.7	5.2	5.2	4.8	4.9	5.2	5.1	5.2	4.9	5.2	14.2%	2.3	3.8%	3.5%	3.4
3.7%	1999	1955	3.9	3.4	3.5	3.0	3.5	3.7	3.5	3.7	3.4	2.6	2.7	2.9	3.4	2.8	2.6	2.3	2.4	2.6	2.6	2.7	3.2	2.4	2.6	2.6	2.3	4.8	4.8	5.0	5.2	5.7	5.2	5.1	5.1	5.2	5.2	5.2	5.2	5.2	5.4	5.4	18.3%	2.3	3.8%	3.4%	3.3
3.6%	2000	1956	3.5	3.6	3.0	3.5	3.7	3.5	3.7	3.4	2.6	2.7	2.9	3.4	2.6	2.4	2.3	2.3	2.4	2.4	2.5	3.0	2.3	2.4	2.3	2.3	2.3	4.8	4.8	4.9	5.3	4.8	4.8	4.8	4.8	4.8	4.8	4.8	4.8	5.0	5.0	4.8	9.2%	2.3	3.6%	3.3%	3.2
																																									Totals	20%	2.3	5.1%	3.9%	4.7%

FIGURE 172

Failure-market results from allocating 10% to longevity insurance starting at age 90.

A simple workaround for early shortages is to pull out more than systemic withdrawals recommends, knowing that deferred income will kick in later. This may work fine, but it exposes the GI plan to unknowns that can be avoided though better GI planning. The safest solution is to form a complete GI plan, helping to insure that there will be an income floor throughout retirement that satisfies essential income needs.

Too Much GI, Reducing Flexibility

A total reliance on GI probably has more risk than a total reliance on systemic withdrawals. Guaranteed income instruments generally lack flexibility, which can be a monumental disadvantage under the wrong conditions. The problem of flexibility is related to the problem of unexpected expenses discussed in the framework.

A systemic-withdrawal portfolio is usually to supply cash for unexpected expenses—a retiree need only pull out the extra money with future withdrawals compensating. In contrast, pulling out extra funds from a GI plan, if it can be done at all, typically disables the plan.

Consider a couple in their early 80s having a major unexpected expense requiring 10% of their assets. Using systemic withdrawals, the extra money can usually be withdrawn. In contrast, if the assets are in an SPIA, there is no provision to withdraw more. If the assets are in a TIPS bond ladder, the funds can be raised by selling the TIPS on the secondary market, although there is interest rate risk, and now the ladder is broken. Neither annuities nor bond ladders are good sources of emergency income.

However, I Bonds are an exception as an emergency-income source when held in large enough amounts (and for over one year), but they rarely comprise a substantial percentage of the overall portfolio. Plus, when sold, they can take a long time to replenish if held for other purposes (their use in providing an income floor is shown later).

In summary, retirees should not eliminate their financial flexibility by putting too much of their assets in annuities and bond ladders. I Bonds provide the most reliable hedge against emergency expenses. Still, systemic withdrawals provide the most pragmatic hedge against the unexpected: no upfront plan is required, plus surplus growth is often available.

Too Little GI with High Valuations

A very high valuation level, such as 3.5 and above, usually implies several things:

- The systemic-withdrawal portfolio's value is uncommonly high; more than one should expect.

- The risk of a substantial drop in portfolio value is much higher than average.

- It's an excellent time to convert part of the systemic-withdrawal portfolio to GI, capturing a portion of the unexpectedly high returns.

- When interest rates are also high, putting a portion of the portfolio into GI is exceptionally attractive, perhaps even compelling.

The common mistake is for retirees to increase their expectations of future stock returns when valuations are exceptionally high (e.g., think of market sentiments during the dot-com bubble), exactly when they should be decreasing expectations. While valuation levels are not a precise predictor of future returns, risk grows higher as valuation levels exceed 3.0, then exceptionally higher as valuation levels exceed 3.5.

In summary, when valuation levels are very high, it's a good time to trade in some of the inflated stock value for GI. More can be bought for less during an opportunity that may not come again.

The Most Viable Basic Strategies for Guaranteed Income

The focus now finally turns to the most viable GI strategies for retirement. These are the strategies later used to form the final recommendations.

This section can't address all the possibilities, but it gets to the root of how to appropriately use GI. Direct historical comparisons aren't included, because data isn't available, but detailed comparisons are made using representative payout rates of different strategies. Also, not all variations can be shown, but these strategies form the building blocks for many different plan combinations.

A Blanket of Inflation-Adjusted SPIAs

A blanket of inflation-adjusted SPIAs means locking in the desired rate from the start, ensuring the full retirement is protected. Using SPIAs alone from the beginning is simple and effective when affordable. It can even work when interest rates are low. However, this strategy can require a substantial percentage of total assets.

Figure 173 shows failure-market results using a blanket of inflation-adjusted SPIAs. The SPIA payout is 4.01% for a 65 year old couple, using October 2014 rates. A 3% essential-income rate is locked, requiring 75% of total assets. The problem is this leaves only 25% for systemic withdrawals, often insufficient for an affordable solution. However, looking at the annual income rates, the results are overall solid and generally consistent, considering the extreme conditions. Little is usually left at the end; however, this is often the case for a failure market even without GI (see Figure 159).

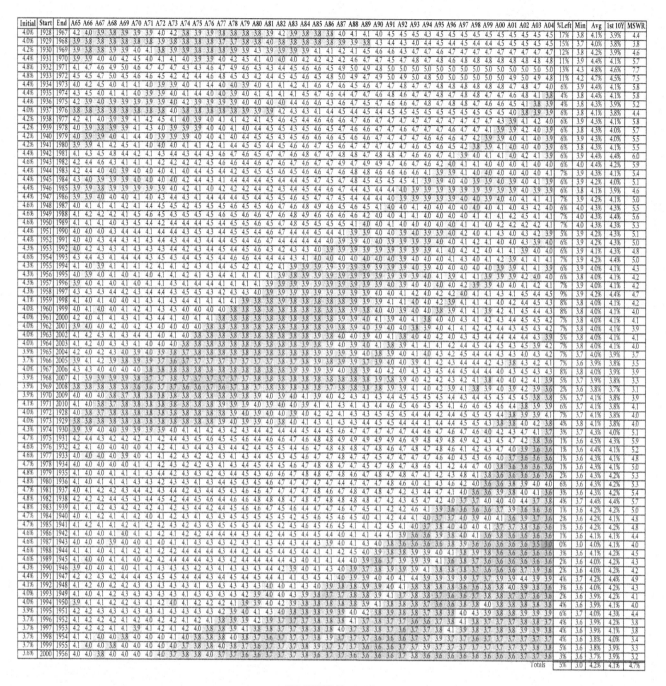

FIGURE 173

Failure-market results starting retirement at age 65 with 75% of portfolio in an inflation-adjusted SPIA and 25% in systemic withdrawals. The inflation-adjusted SPIA payout at 65 is 4.01%.

Figure 174 shows a similar example, but this time the SPIA payout is increased to 5.01% (from 4.01%). With the higher payout, only 60% of the portfolio is needed to lock in the same 3% essential-income rate, making the results much more affordable. The average annual income rate is significantly stronger, in part due to the higher percentage left in systemic withdrawals.

Initial	Start	End	A65	A66	A67	A68	A69	A70	A71	A72	A73	A74	A75	A76	A77	A78	A79	A80	A81	A82	A83	A84	A85	A86	A87	A88	A89	A90	A91	A92	A93	A94	A95	A96	A97	A98	A99	A00	A01	A02	A03	A04	%Left	Min	Avg	1st 10Y	MSWR
4.0%	1928	1967	5.0	4.5	4.4	4.3	4.4	4.4	4.4	4.6	4.8	4.3	4.4	4.4	4.3	4.2	4.2	4.3	4.4	4.8	4.4	4.3	4.3	4.3	4.6	4.7	4.7	4.6	5.4	5.4	5.4	5.0	5.4	5.4	5.4	5.4	5.4	5.4	5.4	5.4	5.4	5.4	28%	4.2	4.8%	4.5%	4.4
4.0%	1929	1968	4.4	4.2	4.2	4.2	4.3	4.3	4.3	4.5	4.2	4.2	4.2	4.2	4.1	4.1	4.2	4.3	4.5	4.2	4.2	4.2	4.2	4.3	4.4	4.4	4.3	5.0	5.2	5.1	4.6	5.2	5.4	5.2	5.4	5.2	5.3	5.4	5.4	5.4	5.4	5.4	25%	4.1	4.7%	4.3%	3.8
4.2%	1930	1969	4.4	4.3	4.3	4.4	4.4	4.6	4.8	4.3	4.4	4.4	4.3	4.2	4.3	4.4	4.4	5.0	4.5	4.4	4.4	4.4	4.7	4.7	4.9	4.8	5.4	5.6	5.6	5.1	5.6	5.6	5.6	5.6	5.6	5.6	5.6	5.6	5.6	5.6	5.6	5.6	20%	4.2	4.9%	4.4%	4.6
4.4%	1931	1970	4.4	4.4	4.6	4.6	5.0	5.4	4.6	4.8	4.8	4.6	4.4	4.4	4.6	4.8	5.3	4.7	4.6	4.5	4.6	4.8	5.0	5.0	4.8	5.6	5.7	5.7	5.4	5.7	5.8	5.6	5.8	5.6	5.8	5.8	5.8	5.8	5.8	5.8	5.8	5.8	18%	4.4	5.2%	4.7%	5.7
4.8%	1932	1971	4.8	5.6	5.6	6.0	6.1	5.6	5.8	5.8	5.6	5.1	5.1	5.5	5.7	6.0	5.5	5.1	5.1	5.2	5.4	5.5	5.6	5.3	6.0	6.1	6.1	5.8	6.1	6.1	6.1	6.1	6.1	6.1	6.1	6.1	6.1	6.1	6.1	6.1	6.1	6.1	20%	5.1	5.8%	5.6%	7.7
4.8%	1933	1972	5.4	5.4	5.8	6.1	5.4	5.6	5.6	5.4	4.9	4.9	5.2	5.6	5.9	5.3	5.0	4.9	5.2	5.4	5.4	5.6	5.4	5.9	6.1	6.1	5.7	6.1	6.1	6.0	6.1	5.9	6.1	6.1	6.1	6.1	6.1	6.1	6.0	6.1	6.1	5.8	17%	4.9	5.7%	5.4%	7.5
4.4%	1934	1973	4.6	5.0	5.4	4.6	4.8	4.7	4.6	4.4	4.4	4.6	4.8	5.3	4.6	4.5	4.5	4.6	4.8	4.8	4.8	4.8	5.5	5.6	5.6	5.4	5.6	5.8	5.7	5.8	5.6	5.6	5.8	5.8	5.8	5.8	5.8	5.8	5.6	5.8	5.8	4.6	10%	4.4	5.2%	4.7%	5.8
4.4%	1935	1974	5.0	5.4	4.6	4.8	4.7	4.6	4.4	4.4	4.6	4.8	5.2	4.6	4.5	4.5	4.6	4.7	4.8	4.8	4.7	5.4	5.6	5.5	5.3	5.6	5.6	5.6	5.8	5.6	5.7	5.7	5.8	5.7	5.8	5.8	5.7	5.7	5.6	5.8	4.7	4.3	6%	4.3	5.2%	4.8%	5.8
4.4%	1936	1975	5.0	4.4	4.5	4.5	4.4	4.4	4.4	4.4	4.5	4.8	4.5	4.4	4.4	4.4	4.6	4.6	4.6	4.5	5.2	5.5	5.5	5.0	5.5	5.6	5.4	5.7	5.5	5.6	5.7	5.8	5.6	5.8	5.8	5.8	5.5	5.6	5.4	4.8	4.2	4.4	6%	4.2	5.0%	4.5%	5.2
4.0%	1937	1976	4.2	4.3	4.3	4.2	4.2	4.2	4.2	4.3	4.6	4.3	4.2	4.2	4.2	4.3	4.4	4.4	4.4	5.0	5.1	5.1	4.8	5.2	5.4	5.3	5.4	5.2	5.4	5.4	5.4	5.4	5.4	5.4	5.4	5.4	5.4	5.4	4.6	4.3	4.4	4.5	9%	4.2	4.8%	4.3%	4.4
4.2%	1938	1977	4.9	4.8	4.6	4.4	4.4	4.7	4.9	5.3	4.8	4.5	4.5	4.6	4.8	4.8	4.8	4.7	5.4	5.5	5.4	5.2	5.6	5.6	5.6	5.6	5.5	5.6	5.6	5.6	5.6	5.6	5.6	5.6	5.6	5.6	5.6	5.1	4.4	4.7	4.9	4.6	10%	4.4	5.1%	4.7%	5.8
4.2%	1939	1978	4.6	4.5	4.3	4.4	4.5	4.7	5.1	4.6	4.4	4.4	4.5	4.6	4.6	4.7	4.6	5.2	5.4	5.3	5.1	5.4	5.6	5.4	5.6	5.5	5.5	5.6	5.6	5.6	5.6	5.6	5.6	5.5	5.6	5.6	4.8	4.4	4.4	5.0	4.6	4.5	9%	4.3	5.0%	4.5%	5.7
4.2%	1940	1979	4.5	4.4	4.4	4.5	4.7	5.2	4.6	4.4	4.4	4.5	4.6	4.6	4.7	4.6	5.2	5.4	5.4	5.1	5.4	5.5	5.5	5.6	5.4	5.6	5.6	5.6	5.6	5.6	5.6	5.6	5.6	5.6	5.6	4.9	4.4	4.5	4.6	4.8	4.6	4.5	9%	4.4	5.0%	4.6%	5.5
4.2%	1941	1980	4.4	4.4	4.7	5.0	5.4	4.8	4.6	4.5	4.6	4.8	4.8	4.9	4.8	5.3	5.4	5.4	5.2	5.4	5.5	5.5	5.6	5.4	5.6	5.6	5.6	5.6	5.6	5.6	5.6	5.4	5.6	5.4	4.9	4.3	4.4	4.7	4.5	4.6	4.6	4.5	9%	4.3	5.1%	4.8%	5.5
4.4%	1942	1981	4.7	5.1	5.4	5.8	5.2	4.9	4.8	5.0	5.2	5.1	5.2	5.0	5.5	5.6	5.5	5.3	5.6	5.6	5.6	5.8	5.7	5.7	5.8	5.8	5.8	5.8	5.8	5.7	5.6	5.6	5.6	4.8	4.5	4.6	4.7	4.7	4.5	4.8	4.7	4.5	9%	4.5	5.3%	5.2%	6.0
4.6%	1943	1982	5.0	5.2	5.6	5.0	4.8	4.7	4.8	5.0	5.0	5.0	4.9	5.4	5.6	5.5	5.2	5.6	5.6	5.6	5.7	5.6	5.7	5.8	6.0	5.8	6.0	6.0	5.7	5.6	5.6	5.5	4.9	4.5	4.7	4.8	4.6	4.6	4.6	4.8	4.6	4.6	9%	4.5	5.2%	5.0%	5.9
4.4%	1944	1983	4.8	5.3	4.6	4.5	4.5	4.6	4.6	4.6	4.7	4.6	5.2	5.4	5.3	5.0	5.3	5.4	5.4	5.5	5.3	5.5	5.6	5.7	5.6	5.8	5.8	5.6	5.5	5.5	5.5	4.7	4.4	4.5	4.8	4.6	4.5	4.6	4.6	4.6	4.6	4.7	11%	4.4	5.0%	4.7%	5.4
4.4%	1945	1984	5.0	4.5	4.4	4.4	4.4	4.5	4.5	4.6	4.5	4.9	5.2	5.1	4.8	5.2	5.3	5.2	5.4	5.2	5.3	5.4	5.6	5.4	5.8	5.8	5.4	5.4	5.4	5.3	4.7	4.4	4.5	4.6	4.6	4.5	4.5	4.5	4.4	4.6	4.7	4.5	9%	4.4	4.9%	4.6%	5.1
4.4%	1946	1985	4.4	4.4	4.3	4.4	4.4	4.4	4.4	4.4	4.6	4.8	4.8	4.6	4.9	5.0	4.9	5.2	5.0	5.0	5.2	5.4	5.2	5.5	5.7	5.3	5.1	5.2	5.2	4.5	4.4	4.4	4.5	4.4	4.4	4.4	4.4	4.4	4.4	4.6	4.5	4.5	9%	4.3	4.8%	4.5%	4.6
4.4%	1947	1986	4.5	4.4	4.5	4.6	4.6	4.7	4.6	5.0	5.2	5.1	4.8	5.2	5.2	5.2	5.4	5.2	5.3	5.4	5.5	5.4	5.7	5.8	5.3	5.3	5.2	5.3	4.6	4.4	4.4	4.5	4.5	4.4	4.5	4.5	4.4	4.5	4.6	4.7	4.8	4.7	11%	4.4	4.9%	4.8%	5.0
4.6%	1948	1987	4.6	4.7	4.8	4.8	4.8	4.8	5.2	5.4	5.4	5.0	5.4	5.4	5.4	5.5	5.4	5.4	5.6	5.6	5.5	5.8	6.0	5.5	5.4	5.5	5.4	4.8	4.5	4.6	4.7	4.6	4.6	4.6	4.6	4.5	4.6	4.8	4.6	5.0	4.9	4.6	10%	4.5	5.1%	5.0%	5.5
4.6%	1949	1988	4.8	4.9	4.9	4.9	4.8	5.4	5.5	5.4	5.1	5.4	5.4	5.4	5.6	5.4	5.5	5.6	5.8	5.5	5.8	6.0	5.6	5.5	5.6	5.5	4.8	4.6	4.6	4.7	4.7	4.6	4.6	4.6	4.6	4.7	4.8	4.7	4.8	5.3	4.7	4.7	11%	4.6	5.1%	5.2%	5.6
4.6%	1950	1989	4.7	4.7	4.7	4.6	5.1	5.4	5.2	4.9	5.3	5.3	5.2	5.4	5.2	5.4	5.4	5.6	5.4	5.7	5.8	5.4	5.4	5.4	5.4	4.8	4.5	4.6	4.7	4.6	4.6	4.6	4.6	4.5	4.7	4.8	4.6	4.9	4.8	4.8	4.8	4.8	11%	4.5	5.0%	5.0%	5.3
4.4%	1951	1990	4.6	4.6	4.6	5.1	5.3	5.2	4.8	5.2	5.2	5.1	5.3	5.1	5.2	5.4	5.4	5.3	5.6	5.7	5.3	5.3	5.4	5.3	4.7	4.4	4.5	4.6	4.6	4.5	4.5	4.5	4.5	4.5	4.9	4.6	4.8	5.0	4.6	5.0	4.9	4.4	8%	4.4	5.0%	5.0%	5.1
4.4%	1952	1991	4.6	4.6	5.0	5.2	5.1	4.8	5.1	5.2	5.1	5.3	5.1	5.2	5.3	5.4	5.2	5.5	5.7	5.2	5.2	5.3	5.3	4.6	4.4	4.5	4.6	4.5	4.5	4.5	4.5	4.4	4.5	4.6	4.7	4.8	4.8	4.6	4.6	5.1	4.4	4.5	9%	4.4	4.9%	5.0%	5.0
4.3%	1953	1992	4.5	5.0	5.1	5.0	4.7	5.1	5.1	5.0	5.2	5.0	5.1	5.2	5.3	5.2	5.4	5.5	5.1	5.0	5.0	5.1	4.6	4.4	4.4	4.5	4.4	4.4	4.4	4.4	4.4	4.4	4.7	4.5	5.0	4.9	4.6	4.8	4.7	4.5	4.6	4.6	10%	4.4	4.8%	5.0%	4.8
4.6%	1954	1993	5.1	5.2	5.1	4.8	5.2	5.2	5.1	5.4	5.1	5.2	5.3	5.4	5.2	5.5	5.6	5.2	5.2	5.2	5.1	4.7	4.5	4.5	4.6	4.6	4.5	4.5	4.5	4.5	4.6	4.6	4.6	4.7	5.0	4.6	4.7	4.8	4.5	4.8	4.7	4.7	11%	4.5	4.9%	5.2%	5.0
4.3%	1955	1994	4.7	4.6	4.5	4.7	4.8	4.7	4.9	4.7	4.8	4.8	5.1	4.8	5.2	5.3	4.8	4.8	4.9	4.8	4.4	4.4	4.4	4.4	4.4	4.4	4.4	4.4	4.4	4.4	4.5	4.4	4.6	4.6	4.6	4.6	4.6	4.4	4.4	4.7	4.7	4.4	9%	4.4	4.6%	4.8%	4.3
4.3%	1956	1995	4.6	4.4	4.6	4.7	4.6	4.8	4.6	4.7	4.8	5.0	4.7	5.1	5.2	4.8	4.7	4.8	4.8	4.4	4.3	4.4	4.4	4.4	4.4	4.4	4.4	4.4	4.4	4.5	4.4	4.5	4.7	4.4	4.7	4.7	4.4	4.5	4.5	4.8	4.5	4.6	10%	4.3	4.6%	4.7%	4.2
4.3%	1957	1996	4.4	4.6	4.7	4.6	4.8	4.6	4.7	4.8	5.0	4.8	5.2	5.2	4.8	4.7	4.8	4.8	4.4	4.4	4.4	4.4	4.4	4.4	4.4	4.4	4.4	4.4	4.5	4.4	4.6	4.6	4.5	4.6	4.8	4.4	4.5	4.6	4.6	4.7	4.8	4.7	11%	4.4	4.6%	4.8%	4.2
4.3%	1958	1997	5.0	5.1	5.0	5.2	5.0	5.1	5.2	5.3	5.1	5.3	5.4	5.0	4.9	5.0	5.0	4.6	4.4	4.4	4.5	4.4	4.4	4.4	4.4	4.4	4.4	4.6	4.6	4.8	4.9	4.6	4.8	4.9	4.5	4.7	4.8	5.0	4.7	5.3	5.2	5.3	14%	4.4	4.8%	5.2%	4.7
4.1%	1959	1998	4.7	4.6	4.8	4.6	4.6	4.8	5.0	4.7	5.1	5.2	4.7	4.7	4.7	4.7	4.4	4.3	4.3	4.4	4.3	4.3	4.3	4.3	4.3	4.4	4.5	4.4	4.7	4.7	4.5	4.6	4.8	4.4	4.7	4.8	4.8	4.6	4.9	5.2	5.3	5.1	13%	4.3	4.7%	4.8%	4.2
4.0%	1960	1999	4.6	4.7	4.5	4.6	4.7	5.0	4.7	5.0	5.1	4.6	4.6	4.6	4.6	4.3	4.2	4.2	4.3	4.2	4.2	4.2	4.3	4.2	4.3	4.4	4.3	4.5	4.6	4.4	4.5	4.6	4.3	4.4	4.7	4.8	4.5	4.9	4.8	5.4	5.2	5.1	13%	4.2	4.6%	4.8%	4.0
4.0%	1961	2000	4.8	4.6	4.7	4.8	5.0	4.8	5.0	5.2	4.7	4.6	4.7	4.7	4.3	4.2	4.2	4.3	4.3	4.2	4.2	4.3	4.2	4.3	4.4	4.4	4.5	4.7	4.5	4.6	4.8	4.3	4.6	4.6	5.0	4.7	5.0	5.1	5.2	5.4	5.4	4.9	12%	4.2	4.7%	4.8%	4.1
4.0%	1962	2001	4.5	4.5	4.6	4.8	4.6	5.0	5.0	4.6	4.6	4.6	4.6	4.3	4.2	4.2	4.2	4.2	4.2	4.2	4.2	4.2	4.3	4.4	4.3	4.5	4.5	4.4	4.5	4.6	4.3	4.4	4.6	4.7	4.7	5.0	4.9	5.2	5.1	5.4	5.0	4.8	11%	4.2	4.6%	4.7%	3.9
4.0%	1963	2002	4.7	4.8	5.0	4.8	5.0	5.2	4.7	4.6	4.7	4.6	4.3	4.2	4.2	4.3	4.3	4.2	4.2	4.2	4.2	4.3	4.4	4.3	4.5	4.6	4.4	4.6	4.7	4.3	4.5	4.6	4.9	4.6	5.1	5.1	5.2	5.3	5.3	5.2	5.1	4.4	8%	4.2	4.7%	4.8%	4.1
4.0%	1964	2003	4.8	5.0	4.6	5.0	5.1	4.7	4.6	4.6	4.6	4.3	4.2	4.2	4.3	4.2	4.2	4.2	4.2	4.2	4.2	4.4	4.3	4.4	4.6	4.4	4.5	4.7	4.3	4.5	4.7	4.8	4.7	5.0	5.2	5.4	5.2	5.4	5.0	5.3	4.5	4.8	11%	4.2	4.6%	4.7%	4.0
3.9%	1965	2004	4.8	4.6	4.9	5.0	4.5	4.5	4.5	4.5	4.2	4.1	4.2	4.2	4.2	4.2	4.2	4.2	4.2	4.2	4.3	4.3	4.4	4.5	4.4	4.5	4.6	4.3	4.5	4.6	4.8	4.5	5.0	5.0	5.4	5.2	5.3	5.1	5.0	4.6	5.0	4.9	12%	4.1	4.6%	4.5%	3.7
3.7%	1966	2005	4.5	4.8	4.9	4.4	4.3	4.4	4.4	4.2	4.0	4.1	4.2	4.2	4.1	4.2	4.2	4.1	4.2	4.2	4.2	4.3	4.4	4.2	4.4	4.5	4.2	4.4	4.5	4.6	4.5	4.8	4.9	5.1	5.2	5.2	4.9	5.0	4.3	5.0	5.0	4.7	11%	4.0	4.5%	4.4%	3.5
4.0%	1967	2006	5.0	5.1	4.6	4.6	4.6	4.6	4.3	4.2	4.2	4.2	4.2	4.2	4.2	4.2	4.2	4.2	4.3	4.3	4.4	4.5	4.4	4.4	4.6	4.3	4.4	4.6	4.8	4.6	5.0	5.0	5.4	5.2	5.4	5.2	5.2	4.6	5.0	5.4	5.1	5.1	13%	4.2	4.6%	4.5%	3.9
3.9%	1968	2007	4.8	4.4	4.4	4.4	4.4	4.2	4.0	4.1	4.2	4.2	4.1	4.1	4.1	4.0	4.2	4.2	4.2	4.2	4.3	4.2	4.3	4.3	4.2	4.3	4.3	4.4	4.3	4.5	4.6	4.9	5.0	5.0	4.9	4.8	4.2	4.6	4.6	4.8	4.8	4.4	9%	4.0	4.4%	4.2%	3.3
3.9%	1969	2008	4.3	4.3	4.3	4.3	4.2	4.0	4.0	4.1	4.0	4.0	4.0	4.0	4.0	4.1	4.2	4.2	4.2	4.2	4.2	4.2	4.3	4.1	4.2	4.3	4.3	4.2	4.4	4.4	4.8	4.6	5.0	4.5	4.7	4.2	4.4	4.6	4.4	4.8	4.4	4.0	4%	4.0	4.3%	4.1%	3.1
3.9%	1970	2009	4.6	4.6	4.6	4.2	4.1	4.2	4.2	4.2	4.2	4.2	4.2	4.2	4.2	4.4	4.3	4.5	4.6	4.4	4.5	4.8	4.4	4.6	4.9	5.0	4.8	5.1	5.2	5.4	5.4	5.4	5.3	5.3	5.0	5.3	5.3	5.3	5.3	5.3	4.2	4.3	8%	4.1	4.7%	4.3%	3.9
4.1%	1971	2010	4.7	4.6	4.3	4.2	4.3	4.3	4.3	4.3	4.3	4.3	4.3	4.3	4.4	4.4	4.5	4.6	4.5	4.5	4.6	4.4	4.7	4.8	5.0	4.8	5.1	5.2	5.5	5.4	5.6	5.3	5.4	4.8	5.5	5.5	5.3	5.5	5.2	4.3	4.4	4.4	9%	4.2	4.8%	4.3%	4.1
4.0%	1972	1928	4.6	4.3	4.2	4.2	4.2	4.2	4.2	4.2	4.2	4.2	4.2	4.3	4.3	4.4	4.5	4.4	4.5	4.6	4.4	4.6	4.8	5.0	4.8	5.1	5.1	5.4	5.4	5.4	5.3	5.2	4.9	5.2	5.4	5.3	5.4	5.2	4.2	4.4	4.5	4.7	11%	4.2	4.7%	4.2%	4.0
4.0%	1973	1929	4.3	4.2	4.2	4.3	4.2	4.2	4.2	4.2	4.2	4.2	4.3	4.3	4.4	4.5	4.4	4.5	4.6	4.3	4.6	4.8	5.0	4.7	5.1	5.1	5.3	5.3	5.4	5.2	5.3	4.8	5.3	5.3	5.4	5.4	5.1	4.2	4.3	4.6	4.9	4.2	7%	4.2	4.7%	4.3%	4.0
4.3%	1974	1930	4.4	4.4	4.6	4.5	4.4	4.5	4.5	4.4	4.6	4.7	4.7	5.0	5.1	4.9	5.0	5.2	4.8	5.2	5.2	5.4	5.2	5.4	5.5	5.7	5.7	5.7	5.6	5.6	5.2	5.6	5.7	5.6	5.7	5.6	4.5	4.9	5.0	5.7	4.7	4.1	5%	4.1	5.1%	4.5%	5.1
4.7%	1975	1931	4.9	5.2	5.0	4.9	4.8	4.8	4.7	5.0	5.2	5.1	5.4	5.6	5.4	5.4	5.5	5.2	5.6	5.6	5.7	5.6	5.9	5.8	6.0	6.0	6.0	6.0	6.0	5.6	6.0	5.9	6.0	5.9	6.0	4.9	5.0	5.4	5.6	4.9	4.3	4.0	2%	4.0	5.4%	5.0%	5.9
4.6%	1976	1932	4.8	4.7	4.6	4.6	4.6	4.6	4.7	4.8	4.8	5.0	5.2	5.0	5.1	5.2	4.8	5.2	5.4	5.4	5.2	5.6	5.6	5.8	5.9	5.9	5.8	5.8	5.6	5.8	5.9	5.7	5.9	5.6	4.7	4.9	5.0	5.7	4.6	4.4	4.0	4.0	1%	4.0	5.2%	4.8%	5.2
4.6%	1977	1933	4.6	4.5	4.5	4.6	4.5	4.6	4.7	4.7	4.9	5.0	4.8	4.9	5.0	4.7	5.0	5.2	5.4	5.0	5.4	5.5	5.8	5.7	5.8	5.7	5.7	5.4	5.7	5.7	5.7	5.7	5.6	4.6	5.0	5.1	5.5	4.6	4.1	4.0	4.0	4.0	2%	4.0	5.0%	4.7%	4.8
4.7%	1978	1934	4.6	4.6	4.6	4.6	4.6	4.8	4.7	5.0	5.1	4.9	5.0	5.1	4.8	5.0	5.2	5.4	5.2	5.4	5.5	5.8	5.8	5.8	5.7	5.8	5.4	5.7	5.8	5.6	5.8	5.5	4.7	4.8	5.3	5.6	4.6	4.2	4.0	4.0	4.0	4.0	1%	4.0	5.1%	4.8%	5.0
4.8%	1979	1935	4.7	4.6	4.6	4.7	4.8	4.8	5.0	5.2	5.0	5.0	5.1	4.8	5.1	5.2	5.4	5.1	5.6	5.5	5.7	5.8	5.9	5.7	5.8	5.6	5.7	5.8	5.8	5.8	5.6	4.7	5.0	5.1	5.8	4.8	4.3	4.0	4.0	4.0	4.0	4.0	3%	4.0	5.1%	4.9%	5.3
4.8%	1980	1936	4.7	4.6	4.7	4.8	4.8	5.0	5.1	4.9	5.0	5.1	4.8	5.0	5.2	5.4	5.1	5.4	5.5	5.7	5.7	5.8	5.7	5.6	5.3	5.7	5.7	5.7	5.8	5.5	4.6	4.8	5.0	5.5	4.9	4.6	4.0	4.0	4.3	4.4	4.6	4.6	9%	4.0	5.1%	4.9%	5.3
4.7%	1981	1937	4.6	4.7	4.8	4.8	5.0	5.2	5.0	5.1	5.2	4.8	5.1	5.2	5.4	5.1	5.5	5.5	5.8	5.7	5.8	5.7	5.8	5.5	5.8	5.8	5.7	5.8	5.7	4.8	5.0	5.2	5.7	4.8	4.6	4.0	4.0	4.5	4.3	4.6	4.8	4.0	4%	4.0	5.1%	5.0%	5.4
4.8%	1982	1938	4.8	5.0	4.9	5.2	5.4	5.1	5.2	5.3	5.0	5.2	5.4	5.5	5.2	5.6	5.6	5.8	5.9	5.8	5.7	5.8	5.6	5.8	5.9	5.8	5.8	5.7	5.0	5.0	5.3	5.6	5.0	4.6	4.1	4.1	4.6	4.5	4.6	5.2	4.2	4.2	6%	4.1	5.2%	5.2%	5.7
4.8%	1983	1939	4.8	4.7	4.9	5.0	4.8	4.9	5.0	4.7	4.9	5.0	5.2	4.9	5.2	5.3	5.6	5.6	5.6	5.4	5.5	5.2	5.6	5.6	5.6	5.7	5.4	4.7	4.8	5.0	5.5	4.7	4.4	4.0	4.0	4.0	4.0	4.2	4.4	4.0	4.0	4.0	2%	4.0	4.9%	4.9%	5.0
4.7%	1984	1940	4.6	4.8	4.8	4.7	4.8	4.8	4.6	4.8	4.9	5.0	4.8	5.0	5.1	5.4	5.4	5.4	5.3	5.4	4.9	5.4	5.6	5.4	5.5	5.4	4.6	4.7	4.9	5.3	4.7	4.5	4.1	4.1	4.5	4.4	4.6	4.8	4.0	4.4	4.1	4.0	3%	4.0	4.9%	4.8%	4.8
4.7%	1985	1941	4.8	4.9	4.8	4.8	4.9	4.7	4.8	4.9	5.1	4.8	5.1	5.1	5.4	5.4	5.4	5.3	5.4	4.9	5.4	5.5	5.4	5.5	5.4	4.7	4.8	5.0	5.4	4.7	4.5	4.1	4.2	4.5	4.5	4.6	4.8	4.1	4.2	4.2	4.0	4.0	2%	4.0	4.9%	4.9%	4.8
4.6%	1986	1942	4.7	4.6	4.6	4.7	4.5	4.7	4.7	4.8	4.7	4.9	4.9	5.2	5.2	5.3	5.1	5.2	4.9	5.2	5.3	5.3	5.4	5.2	4.6	4.7	4.8	5.3	4.7	4.5	4.0	4.0	4.4	4.3	4.5	4.8	4.0	4.2	4.0	4.0	4.0	4.0	2%	4.0	4.7%	4.7%	4.4
4.6%	1987	1943	4.6	4.6	4.6	4.5	4.6	4.6	4.7	4.6	4.8	4.8	5.0	5.1	5.1	5.0	5.0	4.7	5.1	5.2	5.0	5.3	5.1	4.5	4.6	4.7	5.0	4.6	4.2	4.0	4.0	4.0	4.0	4.2	4.5	4.0	4.0	4.0	4.0	4.0	3.8	3.0	0%	3.0	4.5%	4.7%	4.0
4.6%	1988	1944	4.7	4.8	4.6	4.7	4.8	4.9	4.7	5.0	5.0	5.2	5.2	5.3	5.1	5.2	4.9	5.2	5.4	5.2	5.3	5.2	4.7	4.7	4.9	5.3	4.6	4.5	4.2	4.3	4.5	4.5	4.6	4.8	4.2	4.4	4.2	4.0	4.0	4.0	4.0	4.0	4%	4.0	4.7%	4.9%	4.5
4.6%	1989	1945	4.7	4.5	4.6	4.7	4.8	4.6	4.8	4.9	5.2	5.2	5.2	5.0	5.1	4.8	5.2	5.3	5.2	5.2	5.0	4.6	4.7	4.8	5.2	4.6	4.5	4.0	4.1	4.4	4.4	4.5	4.8	4.0	4.3	4.1	4.0	4.0	4.0	4.0	4.0	4.0	3%	4.0	4.6%	4.9%	4.3
4.3%	1990	1946	4.4	4.6	4.6	4.8	4.6	4.8	4.8	5.1	5.1	5.1	5.0	5.0	4.7	5.0	5.1	5.0	5.2	5.0	4.5	4.6	4.8	5.1	4.6	4.4	4.1	4.3	4.4	4.4	4.5	4.7	4.2	4.3	4.3	4.0	4.0	4.0	4.0	4.2	4.4	4.0	4%	4.0	4.6%	4.8%	4.2
4.4%	1991	1947	4.9	5.0	5.1	4.8	5.2	5.2	5.3	5.4	5.4	5.2	5.3	5.0	5.3	5.4	5.3	5.4	5.3	4.7	4.8	5.0	5.4	4.8	4.5	4.4	4.4	4.6	4.6	4.7	5.2	4.4	4.5	4.4	4.4	4.1	4.1	4.4	4.5	5.3	4.5	4.4	6%	4.1	4.9%	5.2%	4.9
4.1%	1992	1948	4.7	4.8	4.6	4.9	4.9	5.1	5.1	5.1	5.0	5.0	4.8	5.0	5.1	5.0	5.1	5.0	4.5	4.6	4.7	5.1	4.6	4.4	4.3	4.3	4.4	4.4	4.5	4.8	4.3	4.3	4.3	4.2	4.0	4.0	4.2	4.3	4.5	4.4	4.2	4.0	5%	4.0	4.6%	4.9%	4.3
4.0%	1993	1949	4.8	4.6	4.8	4.8	5.0	5.1	5.1	5.0	5.0	4.7	5.0	5.0	5.0	5.0	4.9	4.4	4.5	4.6	5.0	4.5	4.3	4.0	4.2	4.3	4.2	4.4	4.8	4.2	4.2	4.2	4.1	4.0	4.0	4.0	4.2	4.3	4.1	4.0	4.0	4.0	3%	4.0	4.5%	4.9%	4.1
4.0%	1994	1950	4.5	4.7	4.7	5.0	5.0	5.0	4.8	4.8	4.5	4.8	4.9	4.8	5.0	4.8	4.4	4.4	4.6	4.8	4.4	4.3	4.2	4.2	4.3	4.3	4.4	4.7	4.2	4.2	4.2	4.2	4.0	4.0	4.2	4.3	4.6	4.3	4.2	4.2	4.2	4.2	6%	4.0	4.5%	4.8%	4.0
3.9%	1995	1951	4.9	4.9	5.1	5.1	5.1	5.0	5.0	4.8	5.0	5.0	5.0	5.0	5.0	4.4	4.5	4.7	5.0	4.5	4.3	4.2	4.3	4.4	4.4	4.6	4.9	4.2	4.4	4.3	4.2	4.1	4.2	4.2	4.6	5.1	4.4	4.3	4.2	4.4	4.5	4.4	9%	4.1	4.6%	5.0%	4.4
3.7%	1996	1952	4.7	4.9	4.9	4.9	4.8	4.9	4.6	4.8	4.9	4.8	4.9	4.8	4.3	4.4	4.5	4.8	4.4	4.2	4.0	4.2	4.2	4.2	4.3	4.7	4.2	4.2	4.2	4.1	4.0	4.0	4.2	4.2	4.8	4.2	4.2	4.2	4.2	4.2	4.2	4.2	6%	4.0	4.4%	4.8%	3.8
3.7%	1997	1953	4.9	4.9	4.9	4.8	4.8	4.4	4.8	4.8	4.8	4.8	4.6	4.2	4.3	4.4	4.7	4.3	4.2	4.1	4.2	4.2	4.2	4.3	4.6	4.2	4.2	4.2	4.2	4.0	4.0	4.2	4.3	4.8	4.4	4.2	4.2	4.2	4.2	4.4	4.4	4.2	7%	4.0	4.4%	4.8%	3.8
3.7%	1998	1954	4.7	4.7	4.5	4.6	4.3	4.6	4.6	4.6	4.7	4.5	4.2	4.2	4.3	4.6	4.2	4.2	4.0	4.0	4.2	4.2	4.2	4.4	4.1	4.2	4.2	4.0	4.0	4.0	4.1	4.2	4.4	4.2	4.2	4.0	4.0	4.2	4.1	4.2	4.0	4.2	6%	4.0	4.3%	4.5%	3.4
3.7%	1999	1955	4.7	4.5	4.6	4.3	4.6	4.6	4.6	4.6	4.5	4.2	4.2	4.3	4.5	4.2	4.2	4.0	4.1	4.2	4.2	4.2	4.4	4.1	4.2	4.2	4.0	4.0	4.0	4.1	4.2	4.4	4.2	4.1	4.1	4.2	4.2	4.2	4.2	4.2	4.3	4.3	8%	4.0	4.3%	4.5%	3.3
3.6%	2000	1956	4.6	4.6	4.3	4.6	4.6	4.6	4.6	4.5	4.2	4.2	4.3	4.5	4.2	4.1	4.0	4.0	4.1	4.1	4.1	4.3	4.0	4.1	4.0	4.0	4.0	4.0	4.0	4.0	4.2	4.0	4.0	4.0	4.0	4.0	4.0	4.0	4.0	4.1	4.1	4.0	4%	4.0	4.2%	4.5%	3.2
																																								Totals	9%	3.0	4.8%	4.8%	4.7%

FIGURE 174

Failure-market results starting retirement at age 65 with 60% of portfolio in an inflation-adjusted SPIA and 40% in systemic withdrawals. The inflation-adjusted SPIA payout at 65 is 5.01%.

A smaller essential-income rate will also lower the amount of required assets. For a 2% rate, 50% of the portfolio is needed upfront when the payout is 4.01% for total coverage. Only 40% is needed for total coverage when the payout is 5.01%. A lower essential-income rate makes a major difference in GI planning.

SPIAs are not flexible alone nor immune to default risk, plus they can eat up bequest value. Nevertheless, when they are used in moderation with systemic withdrawals, these concerns are much less significant. What they do, they do very well, which includes taking the pressure off systemic withdrawals in a poor market.

A Standby Bond Pool (Used Alone)

A standby bond pool is a holding place for assets, which guarantees that their real value is maintained for later use. It's a special form of GI. It's similar to the principle of locking in income from the start, but *value* is instead locked in. A standby bond pool keeps its value independent of markets and inflation. It's most effective when it also grows, although its growth rate is typically slow due to the cost of guaranteeing value.

A standby bond pool is used in one of three ways:

1. It can be a reserve for making up annual-income shortfalls (i.e., when systemic withdrawals don't deliver the essential-income rate).

2. It can be held long term, then sold to replenish an expired TIPS ladder (covered in the next section on building an extended TIPS ladder).

3. It can be held until later in life, then sold to purchase an SPIA (covered in a later section on simulating a DIA).

Either TIPS or I Bonds can be used to build a standby bond pool. I Bonds are an excellent instrument for locking in real value while maintaining flexibility, but with purchase limitations, a pool must usually be built over multiple years (with interim assets often held in a short-term bond index fund). TIPS also can work well building a bond pool when held in a tax-advantaged account. Only one maturity date or a few staggered ones (depending on intended use) need be purchased, without the complexity of a ladder. TIPS are less flexible than I Bonds, because they have interest-rate risk if sold before maturity, but pay better (e.g., 1% more) and have no purchase limit. Also, coupon payments must be reinvested (e.g., held in a bond fund until enough is accumulated to buy another TIPS). Depending on the circumstances, a combination of I Bonds and TIPS can also work well together. I Bonds can provide the flexibility (no interest-rate risk), while TIPS provide the growth. The only requirement for a standby bond pool is to ensure that real value is maintained, but growing at a slow rate magnifies its effectiveness.

Figure 175 shows the cumulative growth for a bond pool over time based on different interest rates. For example, a bond pool with a 2% real interest rate will increase in real value by 48.6% over 20 years. The same bond pool with a 1% interest rate increases in value by only 22%. Squeezing more out the bond pool's interest rate does pay off over long time periods.

Years	0.5% Interest	1% Interest	1.5% Interest	2% Interest	2.5% Interest	3% Interest	3.5% Interest
1	0.5%	1.0%	1.5%	2.0%	2.5%	3.0%	3.5%
2	1.0%	2.0%	3.0%	4.0%	5.1%	6.1%	7.1%
3	1.5%	3.0%	4.6%	6.1%	7.7%	9.3%	10.9%
4	2.0%	4.1%	6.1%	8.2%	10.4%	12.6%	14.8%
5	2.5%	5.1%	7.7%	10.4%	13.1%	15.9%	18.8%
6	3.0%	6.2%	9.3%	12.6%	16.0%	19.4%	22.9%
7	3.6%	7.2%	11.0%	14.9%	18.9%	23.0%	27.2%
8	4.1%	8.3%	12.6%	17.2%	21.8%	26.7%	31.7%
9	4.6%	9.4%	14.3%	19.5%	24.9%	30.5%	36.3%
10	5.1%	10.5%	16.1%	21.9%	28.0%	34.4%	41.1%
11	5.6%	11.6%	17.8%	24.3%	31.2%	38.4%	46.0%
12	6.2%	12.7%	19.6%	26.8%	34.5%	42.6%	51.1%
13	6.7%	13.8%	21.4%	29.4%	37.9%	46.9%	56.4%
14	7.2%	14.9%	23.2%	31.9%	41.3%	51.3%	61.9%
15	7.8%	16.1%	25.0%	34.6%	44.8%	55.8%	67.5%
16	8.3%	17.3%	26.9%	37.3%	48.5%	60.5%	73.4%
17	8.8%	18.4%	28.8%	40.0%	52.2%	65.3%	79.5%
18	9.4%	19.6%	30.7%	42.8%	56.0%	70.2%	85.7%
19	9.9%	20.8%	32.7%	45.7%	59.9%	75.4%	92.3%
20	10.5%	22.0%	34.7%	48.6%	63.9%	80.6%	99.0%
21	11.0%	23.2%	36.7%	51.6%	68.0%	86.0%	105.9%
22	11.6%	24.5%	38.8%	54.6%	72.2%	91.6%	113.2%
23	12.2%	25.7%	40.8%	57.7%	76.5%	97.4%	120.6%
24	12.7%	27.0%	43.0%	60.8%	80.9%	103.3%	128.3%
25	13.3%	28.2%	45.1%	64.1%	85.4%	109.4%	136.3%
26	13.8%	29.5%	47.3%	67.3%	90.0%	115.7%	144.6%
27	14.4%	30.8%	49.5%	70.7%	94.8%	122.1%	153.2%
28	15.0%	32.1%	51.7%	74.1%	99.6%	128.8%	162.0%
29	15.6%	33.5%	54.0%	77.6%	104.6%	135.7%	171.2%
30	16.1%	34.8%	56.3%	81.1%	109.8%	142.7%	180.7%

FIGURE 175

Cumulative growth for various interest rates over time.

Figure 176 shows the results of using a bond pool to make up income shortfalls during a failure market (other uses are explored in later sections). The bond pool is allocated 10% of total assets at the start of retirement. Its assumed real growth rate is relatively strong at 2%. The essential-income rate maintained is 3%. This means that any time systemic-withdrawal income (as determined using ECM) falls below 3%, the shortfall amount is pulled from the bond pool (this assumes some I Bonds are always available in small denominations to redeem flexibly). When systemic withdrawals stay above 3%, the bond pool is left untouched to grow. Although the internal accounting for the bond pool is not shown, few of the bond pool's assets are needed until later in retirement, allowing time for it to grow over 40% during the initial 20 years (with a little sometimes used early on to make up shortfalls).

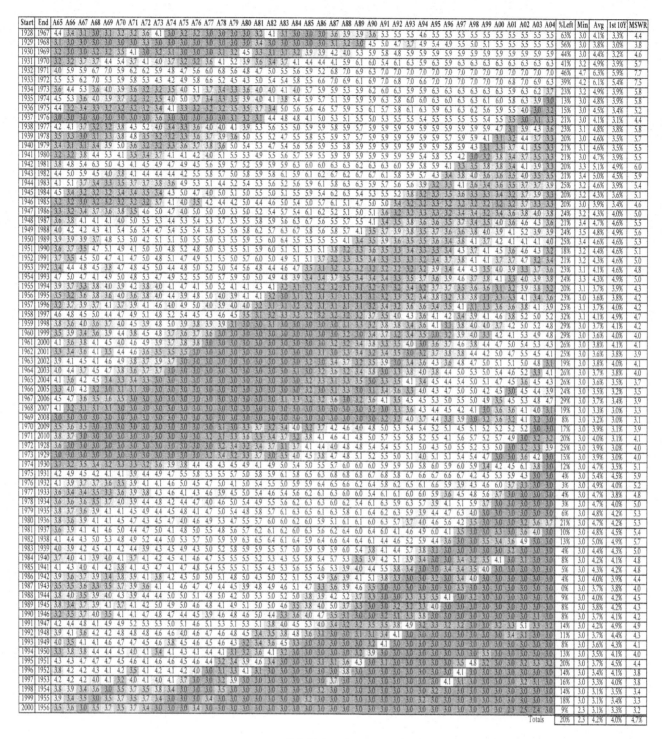

FIGURE 176

*Failure-market results with 10% in standby bond pool earning
2% and maintaining a 3% income floor.*

It's important to understand in Figure 176 that the bond pool successfully maintains the 3% essential-income rate using only 10% of total assets. The only exception is the last retirement period starting in year 2000, where the bond pool runs dry in the retiree's 101st year, although even in this case, assets are still left in the portfolio. Of course the overall income during the failure market is much lower than with SPIAs, often hovering at or right above 3%, but again only 10% is allocated to GI. Note that when the bond pool has only a 1% growth rate, sufficient income is still provided in all but three cases, with two of the three cases occurring after age 100. When making up small shortfalls in the essential-income rate, a little can go a long way.

A standby bond pool has one inherent disadvantage. The funds allocated to it no longer contribute to normal income. For example, if the portfolio on average generates 4% annually, putting 10% of assets in a standby bond pool immediately lowers systemic withdrawal average income to 3.6%. This drop in income is reflected in Figure 176. From the start, systemic withdrawals are immediately 10% smaller in every retirement period, because 10% was pulled out for the bond pool. The implication is, the power of a standby bond pool is partly due to sacrificing income from the start of retirement.

There are also instances where a bond pool doesn't work as well. As the essential-income rate exceeds 3%, a pool becomes less effective making up shortfalls. In addition, when interest rates are lower, the bond pool grows more slowly, again becoming less effective. Finally, for high net-worth individuals without sufficient funds in a tax-advantaged account, there is no way to build a completely adequate bond pool (i.e., I Bonds have purchase limits and TIPS have their inflation adjustments taxed).

Still, the general principle holds for many retirees. Allocating a small portion to a standby bond pool creates a flexible reserve for helping maintain essential-income requirements during a failure market. This is the least expensive approach to supplementing the essential-income rate using GI.

An Extended TIPS Ladder (Replenished by a Standby Bond Pool)

When a TIPS ladder is being built for 30-year or less retirement, no special strategy beyond building the ladder is required, but for many retirees, the target retirement period should be 40 years. How to reliably construct a 40-year TIPS ladder is shown below. While this is not the best option for most retirees seeking GI (why is shown), it will be the top choice for a few.

Handled properly, an extended TIPS ladder can provide a steady GI stream throughout retirement, like inflation-adjusted SPIAs. Their advantage over SPIAs is direct ownership of assets, including bequest value. Their disadvantage is higher cost (i.e., a lower payout without the mortality premium), plus more complexity to set up.

Previously, the pitfalls of using a stock pool to extend a 30-year TIPS ladder were explained. Here, the standby bond pool replaces the stock pool to remove the risk. When enough is set aside, a standby bond pool reliably replenishes a TIPS ladder with virtually no risk.

Here are the steps for setting up an extended TIPS ladder.

1. Pick the desired GI rate (e.g., 3%).

2. Estimate the real IRR for a 30-year TIPS ladder (see the previous section on TIPS for doing this).

3. Look up the 30-year ladder payout using the real IRR. For example, with a 2% IRR, the 30-year payout is 4.5%.

4. Similarly, look up the 40-year ladder payout using the same real IRR. For example, with a 2% IRR, the 40-year payout is 3.7%. *The retiree should be content with this overall payout to continue.*

5. Determine how much to allocate to the 30-year ladder by dividing the desired GI rate by the 30-year ladder payout. For example, a 3% desired payout divided by 4.5% (i.e., 30-year ladder payout) is a 66% allocation.

6. Similarly, determine the total allocation by dividing the desired GI rate by the 40-year ladder payout rate to. For example a 3% desired payout divided by 3.7% (i.e., 40-year ladder payout) is an 81% total allocation.

7. Build the 30-year TIPS ladder using its allocation (e.g., 66% of the portfolio).

8. Construct the standby bond pool using the difference between the total allocation and the 30-year ladder allocation (e.g., 81% minus 66% is 15% to construct the standby bond pool with I Bonds or TIPS).

9. What remains is allocated to systemic withdrawals (e.g., 19%, which is 100% minus 66% for TIPS ladder minus 15% for the standby bond pool).

10. After 30 years, when the first ladder expires, the assets in the standby bond pool are used to construct a second TIPS ladder of 10 years.

There are a couple of minor issues with the above, although the general idea is sound. The same interest rate cannot be guaranteed 30 years later, and the real IRR for a 10-year ladder is smaller. Neither of these are a problem for a short ladder that pays out mainly principal (e.g., the 10-year payout for a 2% IRR is 11.1%, and for a 1% IRR 10.6%). Also, the standby bond pool is assumed to earn the same return as the TIPS ladder. If the pool is constructed with TIPS, the return will actually be a little higher, because the average TIPS maturity is longer. However, if the pool is constructed with I Bonds, the return will often be lower (although there is the potential to sell and rebuy I Bonds as rates improve or buy some TIPS to compensate). Still, to virtually guarantee a bond pool of I Bonds will be large enough to match the same payout as the first TIPS ladder, the pool allocation should be boosted by 25% (e.g., an 18.75% allocation instead of 15%).

Figure 177 shows the failure-market results using a 40-year extended TIPS ladder with a 2% IRR to produce a 3% GI rate. The standby bond pool is assumed to earn the same as the TIPS ladder. While the payouts and percentage left in systemic withdrawals are not impressive, the goal is met for a 3% essential-income rate with an overall 2% real IRR for GI.

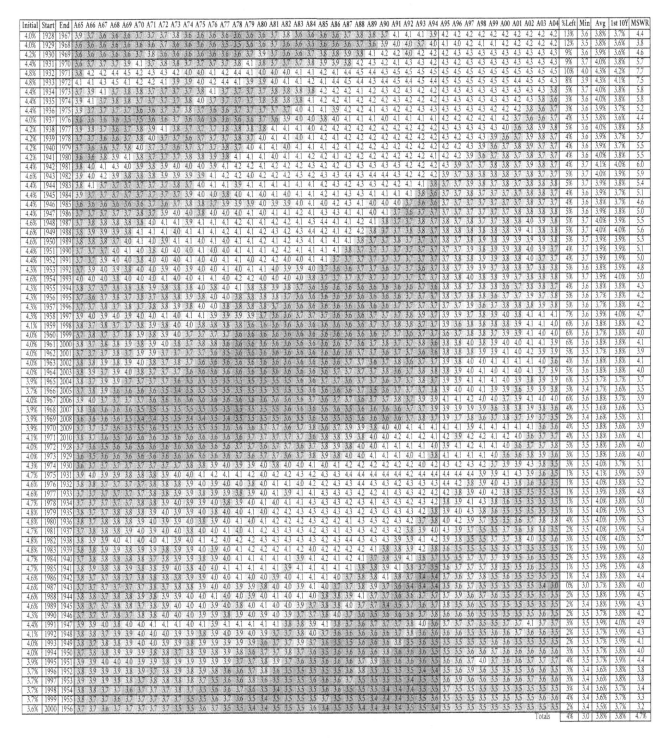

FIGURE 177

*Failure-market results for an extended 40-year TIPS ladder with a 2%
real IRR. The essential-income rate is 4%. A 30-year TIPS ladder is built
with 66% of assets, 15% goes into a standby bond pool funding a follow-up
10-year ladder (with the remaining 19% in systemic withdrawals).*

Figure 178 shows the same extended TIPS ladder case, but with a 3% IRR. This time, using the same steps for the extended ladder, 58% of the portfolio is allocated to the 30-year ladder, 11% to the bond pool, and the remaining 31% to systemic withdrawals. The results are much more attractive, but it's doubtful a retirees will ever see a 3% real IRR, essentially making this the best-case scenario.

FIGURE 178

Failure-market results for an extended 40-year TIPS ladder with a 3% real IRR. The essential-income rate is 3%. A 30-year TIPS ladder is built with 58% of assets, 11% goes into a standby bond pool funding a follow-up 10-year ladder (with the remaining 31% in systemic withdrawals).

A retiree is more likely to see a 1% real IRR. What may be surprising is a 40-year extended TIPS ladder with a 1% real IRR requires 100% of the portfolio to produce a 3% GI rate, with nothing left over for systemic withdrawals. This results in a 3% income rate for 40 years with no growth or flexibility—a clearly unaffordable solution.

This implies that unless interest rates are reasonably high, extended TIPS ladders are not viable in retirement. A 40-year TIPS ladder needs a real IRR of 2% just to look reasonably attractive. Of course, for shorter ladders, a smaller real IRR can work, but a shorter timeframe must be appropriate.

Generally, the results using an extended TIPS ladder are disappointing, but for many retirees with an aversion to SPIA, this is the only viable option for a fixed GI payout spanning a long retirement. To recap, it doesn't make sense to base a GI solution on a 30-year TIPS ladder when there is a significant probability of living past 30 years (e.g., an 18% chance for a 65 year old couple). It also doesn't make sense to use a stock pool to extend a 30-year TIPS ladder when the stocks in the pool are exposed to essentially more risk than in systemic withdrawals.

An extended TIPS ladder is a viable option only for rare times or rare retirees who prefer it.

A Simulated Deferred "Annuity" (Funded by a Standby Bond Pool)

A simulated deferred annuity removes the inflation risk associated with a DIA (as discussed under pitfalls), while still delivering the advantages of deferring income. There are two parts to this solution: the first is to safely maintain value over the deferred period using a standby bond pool; the second to wait for the deferred period (e.g., 20 years), then use the deferred assets in the pool to purchase an SPIA *or* build a 20-year TIPS ladder.

A simulated deferred annuity is not usually sufficient alone, but it's a powerful GI strategy that can be combined with others. Since the deferred assets are controlled by the retiree, there's flexibility to decide late in retirement how to use the bond pool assets. Still, the same inherent disadvantage remains: retirement income is immediately reduced because assets have been set aside. Also, there's an unknown, because the lock-in rate for a SPIA or TIPS ladder depends on the current interest rate at the time of purchase, although this can go either way. However, as previously mentioned, interest rates generally have less impact late in retirement (i.e., payouts come more from the principal).

Figure 179 shows a simulated deferred annuity, where the standby bond pool is converted at age 85 to a 20-year TIPS ladder.

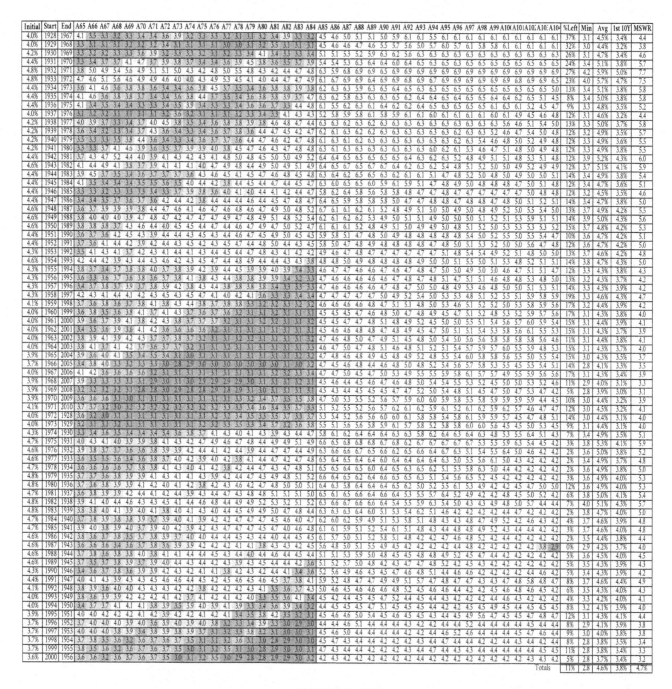

FIGURE 179

*Failure-market results including 1) 37.5% initially going into an inflation-adjusted SPIA with a
4.01% payout; 2) 10% going into a simulated DIA using a standby bond pool with a 2% IRR. At
age 85, the standby bond pool is used to construct a 20-year TIPS ladder with a 5.54% payout.*

Figure 180 shows the same simulated deferred annuity converted at age 85 to an inflation-adjusted SPIA.

Initial	Start	End	A65	A66	A67	A68	A69	A70	A71	A72	A73	A74	A75	A76	A77	A78	A79	A80	A81	A82	A83	A84	A85	A86	A87	A88	A89	A90	A91	A92	A93	A94	A95	A96	A97	A98	A99	A100	A101	A102	A103	A104	%Left	Min	Avg	1st 10Y	MSWR
4.0%	1928	1967	4.1	3.5	3.3	3.2	3.3	3.4	3.4	3.6	3.9	3.2	3.3	3.3	3.2	3.1	3.1	3.2	3.4	3.9	3.3	3.2	4.0	4.1	4.4	4.6	4.6	4.4	5.4	5.5	5.5	5.0	5.5	5.5	5.5	5.5	5.5	5.5	5.5	5.5	5.5	5.5	37%	3.1	4.3%	3.4%	4.4
4.0%	1929	1968	3.3	3.1	3.1	3.1	3.2	3.2	3.2	3.4	3.1	3.1	3.1	3.1	3.0	3.0	3.1	3.2	3.5	3.1	3.1	3.1	4.0	4.1	4.1	4.2	4.1	5.0	5.2	5.1	4.5	5.2	5.5	5.2	5.5	5.3	5.3	5.5	5.5	5.5	5.5	5.5	32%	3.0	4.1%	3.2%	3.8
4.2%	1930	1969	3.3	3.2	3.2	3.3	3.3	3.6	3.9	3.2	3.3	3.3	3.2	3.1	3.2	3.3	3.4	4.1	3.4	3.3	3.3	3.4	4.6	4.6	4.8	4.6	5.4	5.7	5.7	5.1	5.8	5.8	5.7	5.8	5.8	5.8	5.8	5.8	5.8	5.8	5.8	5.8	26%	3.1	4.5%	3.4%	4.6
4.4%	1931	1970	3.3	3.4	3.7	3.7	4.1	4.7	3.7	3.9	3.8	3.7	3.4	3.4	3.6	3.9	4.5	3.8	3.6	3.5	3.7	3.9	4.9	4.9	4.7	5.7	5.9	5.8	5.5	5.9	6.0	5.8	6.0	5.7	6.0	6.0	6.0	6.0	6.0	6.0	6.0	6.0	24%	3.4	4.8%	3.8%	5.7
4.8%	1932	1971	3.8	5.0	4.9	5.4	5.6	4.9	5.1	5.1	5.0	4.3	4.2	4.8	5.0	5.5	4.8	4.3	4.2	4.4	4.7	4.8	5.7	5.4	6.3	6.4	6.4	6.0	6.4	6.4	6.4	6.4	6.4	6.4	6.4	6.4	6.4	6.4	6.4	6.4	6.4	6.4	27%	4.2	5.6%	5.0%	7.7
4.8%	1933	1972	4.7	4.6	5.1	5.6	4.6	4.9	4.9	4.6	4.0	4.0	4.3	4.9	5.3	4.5	4.1	4.0	4.4	4.7	4.7	4.9	5.5	6.2	6.4	6.4	5.9	6.4	6.4	6.3	6.4	6.2	6.4	6.4	6.4	6.4	6.4	6.4	6.3	6.4	6.4	6.0	23%	4.0	5.5%	4.7%	7.5
4.4%	1934	1973	3.6	4.1	4.6	3.6	3.8	3.8	3.6	3.4	3.4	3.6	3.8	4.5	3.7	3.5	3.4	3.6	3.8	3.8	3.9	3.8	5.6	5.8	5.7	5.4	5.7	5.9	5.8	6.0	5.8	5.8	6.0	6.0	6.0	6.0	6.0	6.0	5.8	6.0	5.9	4.5	13%	3.4	4.8%	3.8%	5.8
4.4%	1935	1974	4.1	4.6	3.6	3.8	3.8	3.7	3.4	3.4	3.6	3.8	4.4	3.7	3.5	3.4	3.6	3.8	3.8	3.9	3.7	4.7	5.8	5.6	5.3	5.8	5.8	5.7	6.0	5.7	5.8	5.8	6.0	5.8	6.0	6.0	5.9	5.8	5.7	6.0	4.6	4.0	8%	3.4	4.8%	3.8%	5.8
4.4%	1936	1975	4.1	3.4	3.5	3.4	3.4	3.3	3.3	3.4	3.5	3.9	3.4	3.3	3.3	3.4	3.6	3.6	3.7	3.5	4.4	4.8	5.6	5.0	5.6	5.8	5.5	5.9	5.6	5.7	5.9	6.0	5.8	6.0	6.0	5.9	5.6	5.7	5.5	4.6	4.0	4.2	9%	3.3	4.6%	3.5%	5.2
4.0%	1937	1976	3.1	3.2	3.2	3.1	3.1	3.1	3.1	3.2	3.6	3.2	3.1	3.1	3.1	3.2	3.3	3.4	3.3	4.1	4.3	4.3	4.7	5.3	5.4	5.3	5.5	5.3	5.4	5.5	5.5	5.5	5.5	5.5	5.5	5.5	5.5	5.5	4.4	4.0	4.1	4.3	12%	3.1	4.3%	3.2%	4.4
4.2%	1938	1977	4.0	3.9	3.7	3.3	3.4	3.7	4.0	4.5	3.8	3.5	3.4	3.6	3.8	3.8	3.9	3.8	4.6	4.8	4.7	4.4	5.7	5.7	5.7	5.8	5.6	5.8	5.8	5.8	5.8	5.8	5.8	5.8	5.8	5.8	5.8	5.1	4.1	4.6	4.8	4.4	13%	3.3	4.7%	3.7%	5.8
4.2%	1939	1978	3.6	3.4	3.2	3.3	3.4	3.7	4.3	3.6	3.4	3.3	3.4	3.6	3.7	3.8	3.6	4.4	4.7	4.5	4.2	4.7	5.7	5.5	5.8	5.6	5.6	5.8	5.8	5.7	5.8	5.8	5.8	5.6	5.8	5.8	4.7	4.1	4.2	4.9	4.5	4.3	12%	3.2	4.6%	3.5%	5.7
4.2%	1940	1979	3.5	3.3	3.3	3.5	3.8	4.4	3.6	3.4	3.3	3.4	3.6	3.7	3.7	3.6	4.4	4.7	4.6	4.2	4.7	4.8	5.6	5.7	5.5	5.7	5.7	5.8	5.8	5.8	5.8	5.7	5.7	5.7	5.8	4.8	4.1	4.3	4.5	4.7	4.4	4.3	12%	3.3	4.6%	3.6%	5.5
4.2%	1941	1980	3.3	3.3	3.7	4.1	4.6	3.9	3.6	3.5	3.7	3.9	3.9	4.0	3.8	4.5	4.7	4.6	4.3	4.7	4.8	4.8	5.8	5.5	5.7	5.8	5.8	5.8	5.8	5.8	5.7	5.5	5.7	5.5	4.8	4.1	4.2	4.5	4.3	4.5	4.4	4.3	12%	3.3	4.7%	3.8%	5.5
4.4%	1942	1981	3.7	4.3	4.7	5.2	4.4	4.0	3.9	4.1	4.3	4.2	4.3	4.1	4.8	5.0	4.8	4.5	5.0	5.0	4.9	5.2	5.8	5.8	6.0	6.0	5.9	6.0	6.0	5.8	5.7	5.7	5.8	4.7	4.3	4.4	4.5	4.5	4.3	4.7	4.6	4.3	12%	3.9	4.9%	4.3%	6.0
4.6%	1943	1982	4.1	4.4	4.9	4.1	3.8	3.7	3.9	4.1	4.1	4.1	4.0	4.7	4.9	4.8	4.4	4.9	5.0	4.9	5.1	4.9	5.9	5.9	6.2	5.9	6.2	6.2	5.9	5.7	5.8	5.6	4.8	4.3	4.5	4.6	4.4	4.4	4.4	4.6	4.4	4.4	12%	3.7	4.8%	4.1%	5.9
4.4%	1944	1983	3.9	4.5	3.7	3.5	3.4	3.6	3.7	3.7	3.7	3.6	4.3	4.6	4.5	4.1	4.5	4.7	4.6	4.8	4.5	4.8	5.7	5.9	5.7	6.0	6.0	5.7	5.6	5.6	5.6	4.6	4.2	4.3	4.7	4.4	4.3	4.4	4.4	4.5	4.5	4.6	14%	3.4	4.6%	3.8%	5.4
4.4%	1945	1984	4.1	3.5	3.4	3.4	3.4	3.5	3.5	3.6	3.5	4.0	4.4	4.2	3.8	4.4	4.5	4.4	4.7	4.4	4.5	4.7	5.8	5.5	5.9	6.0	5.5	5.4	5.5	5.4	4.5	4.2	4.3	4.4	4.4	4.3	4.3	4.3	4.2	4.5	4.6	4.3	12%	3.4	4.4%	3.6%	5.1
4.4%	1946	1985	3.3	3.3	3.2	3.3	3.3	3.3	3.4	3.3	3.7	3.9	3.8	3.6	4.0	4.1	4.0	4.4	4.1	4.2	4.4	4.7	5.3	5.6	5.9	5.3	5.1	5.3	5.3	4.3	4.2	4.2	4.3	4.2	4.2	4.2	4.2	4.2	4.2	4.5	4.3	4.3	12%	3.2	4.2%	3.5%	4.6
4.4%	1947	1986	3.4	3.4	3.5	3.7	3.6	3.7	3.6	4.2	4.4	4.2	3.8	4.4	4.4	4.4	4.6	4.4	4.5	4.7	4.8	4.7	5.9	5.9	5.4	5.3	5.3	5.3	4.4	4.2	4.2	4.3	4.3	4.2	4.3	4.3	4.2	4.3	4.4	4.5	4.6	4.5	14%	3.4	4.4%	3.8%	5.0
4.6%	1948	1987	3.6	3.7	3.9	3.9	3.9	3.8	4.4	4.7	4.6	4.1	4.6	4.7	4.6	4.8	4.6	4.7	4.9	5.0	4.8	5.2	6.2	5.6	5.5	5.6	5.5	4.7	4.3	4.4	4.5	4.4	4.4	4.4	4.5	4.3	4.4	4.6	4.4	5.0	4.8	4.4	13%	3.7	4.6%	4.2%	5.5
4.6%	1949	1988	3.8	4.0	4.0	4.0	3.9	4.7	4.8	4.7	4.2	4.7	4.7	4.7	4.9	4.7	4.8	4.9	5.1	4.8	5.2	5.4	5.7	5.6	5.7	5.6	4.7	4.4	4.5	4.6	4.5	4.4	4.5	4.4	4.4	4.5	4.6	4.6	4.7	5.4	4.6	4.6	14%	3.9	4.7%	4.3%	5.6
4.6%	1950	1989	3.8	3.8	3.8	3.7	4.3	4.6	4.4	4.0	4.5	4.5	4.4	4.7	4.4	4.6	4.7	4.9	4.7	5.0	5.2	4.7	5.5	5.5	5.5	4.7	4.3	4.4	4.6	4.4	4.4	4.4	4.4	4.3	4.5	4.7	4.5	4.8	4.7	4.7	4.7	4.6	15%	3.7	4.6%	4.2%	5.3
4.4%	1951	1990	3.6	3.7	3.6	4.2	4.5	4.3	3.9	4.4	4.4	4.3	4.5	4.3	4.4	4.6	4.7	4.5	4.9	5.0	4.5	4.5	5.4	5.3	4.5	4.2	4.3	4.4	4.4	4.3	4.3	4.3	4.3	4.3	4.8	4.5	4.7	5.0	4.4	5.0	4.8	4.2	10%	3.6	4.5%	4.2%	5.1
4.4%	1952	1991	3.7	3.6	4.1	4.4	4.2	3.9	4.2	4.4	4.3	4.5	4.2	4.3	4.5	4.7	4.4	4.8	5.0	4.4	4.3	4.5	5.3	4.5	4.2	4.3	4.4	4.3	4.3	4.3	4.3	4.2	4.3	4.5	4.5	4.7	4.7	4.5	4.5	5.1	4.2	4.3	12%	3.6	4.4%	4.2%	5.0
4.3%	1953	1992	3.5	4.1	4.3	4.1	3.7	4.2	4.3	4.1	4.4	4.1	4.3	4.4	4.5	4.4	4.7	4.8	4.3	4.1	4.2	4.2	4.4	4.1	4.2	4.3	4.2	4.2	4.2	4.2	4.2	4.2	4.6	4.3	4.9	4.8	4.4	4.6	4.6	4.3	4.5	4.4	13%	3.7	4.3%	4.2%	4.8
4.6%	1954	1993	4.2	4.4	4.2	3.9	4.3	4.4	4.3	4.6	4.2	4.3	4.5	4.7	4.4	4.8	4.9	4.4	4.4	4.3	4.3	3.8	4.3	4.3	4.5	4.4	4.3	4.3	4.3	4.3	4.4	4.5	4.4	4.6	5.0	4.5	4.5	4.7	4.3	4.6	4.6	4.5	14%	3.8	4.4%	4.3%	5.0
4.3%	1955	1994	3.8	3.7	3.4	3.7	3.8	3.8	4.0	3.7	3.8	3.9	4.2	3.9	4.4	4.5	3.9	3.9	4.0	3.9	3.4	3.3	4.1	4.2	4.2	4.1	4.1	4.2	4.1	4.2	4.3	4.2	4.5	4.5	4.4	4.4	4.4	4.1	4.2	4.6	4.5	4.2	12%	3.3	4.1%	3.8%	4.3
4.3%	1956	1995	3.6	3.3	3.6	3.7	3.6	3.8	3.6	3.7	3.8	4.1	3.8	4.3	4.4	3.8	3.8	3.9	3.9	3.4	3.2	3.3	4.2	4.1	4.1	4.1	4.1	4.1	4.2	4.3	4.2	4.3	4.5	4.2	4.5	4.5	4.1	4.3	4.3	4.7	4.3	4.4	13%	3.2	4.0%	3.7%	4.2
4.3%	1957	1996	3.4	3.7	3.8	3.7	3.9	3.7	3.8	3.9	4.2	3.8	4.3	4.4	3.8	3.8	3.8	3.8	3.4	3.3	3.3	3.3	4.2	4.1	4.1	4.1	4.1	4.2	4.3	4.2	4.4	4.4	4.3	4.4	4.7	4.1	4.3	4.4	4.4	4.5	4.7	4.6	14%	3.3	4.1%	3.9%	4.2
4.3%	1958	1997	4.2	4.3	4.1	4.4	4.1	4.2	4.3	4.5	4.3	4.5	4.7	4.1	4.0	4.2	4.1	3.6	3.3	3.3	3.4	3.4	4.2	4.2	4.2	4.2	4.2	4.5	4.4	4.6	4.8	4.4	4.7	4.8	4.3	4.6	4.7	5.0	4.5	5.4	5.3	5.4	19%	3.3	4.3%	4.3%	4.7
4.1%	1959	1998	3.7	3.6	3.8	3.6	3.7	3.8	4.1	3.8	4.3	4.4	3.8	3.7	3.8	3.8	3.3	3.2	3.2	3.3	3.2	3.2	4.1	4.1	4.1	4.1	4.3	4.2	4.5	4.5	4.3	4.4	4.7	4.1	4.5	4.6	4.6	4.5	4.8	5.3	5.4	5.1	17%	3.2	4.1%	3.9%	4.2
4.0%	1960	1999	3.6	3.8	3.5	3.6	3.8	4.1	3.7	4.1	4.3	3.7	3.6	3.7	3.6	3.2	3.1	3.1	3.2	3.1	3.1	3.1	4.0	4.0	4.0	4.2	4.1	4.3	4.5	4.2	4.3	4.4	4.0	4.2	4.6	4.6	4.3	4.8	4.7	5.4	5.2	5.1	17%	3.1	4.0%	3.8%	4.0
4.0%	1961	2000	3.9	3.6	3.7	3.9	4.1	3.8	4.2	4.3	3.8	3.7	3.7	3.7	3.2	3.1	3.1	3.2	3.2	3.1	3.1	3.2	4.0	4.0	4.2	4.2	4.3	4.5	4.3	4.4	4.6	4.0	4.4	4.5	5.0	4.5	4.9	5.1	5.2	5.5	5.4	4.8	15%	3.1	4.1%	3.9%	4.1
4.0%	1962	2001	3.4	3.5	3.6	3.9	3.6	4.1	4.2	3.6	3.6	3.6	3.6	3.2	3.1	3.1	3.1	3.1	3.1	3.1	3.1	3.1	4.0	4.1	4.1	4.3	4.3	4.2	4.3	4.4	4.0	4.2	4.5	4.5	4.5	4.9	4.8	5.3	5.1	5.5	5.0	4.7	15%	3.1	4.0%	3.7%	3.9
4.0%	1963	2002	3.8	3.9	4.1	3.9	4.2	4.3	3.7	3.7	3.8	3.7	3.2	3.1	3.1	3.2	3.2	3.1	3.1	3.1	3.1	3.2	4.2	4.1	4.3	4.5	4.2	4.4	4.6	4.0	4.3	4.4	4.8	4.4	5.1	5.1	5.3	5.3	5.3	5.3	5.1	4.1	11%	3.1	4.1%	3.8%	4.1
4.0%	1964	2003	3.8	4.1	3.7	4.1	4.2	3.7	3.6	3.7	3.7	3.2	3.1	3.1	3.2	3.1	3.1	3.1	3.1	3.1	3.1	3.3	4.1	4.2	4.4	4.2	4.3	4.5	4.1	4.3	4.5	4.6	4.5	4.9	5.2	5.4	5.2	5.5	5.0	5.4	4.3	4.7	15%	3.1	4.1%	3.7%	4.0
3.9%	1965	2004	3.9	3.6	4.0	4.1	3.5	3.4	3.5	3.4	3.1	3.0	3.1	3.1	3.1	3.1	3.1	3.1	3.1	3.1	3.2	3.2	4.2	4.3	4.1	4.3	4.4	4.0	4.3	4.4	4.7	4.3	5.0	4.9	5.5	5.3	5.3	5.1	5.0	4.4	5.0	4.8	15%	3.0	4.0%	3.5%	3.7
3.7%	1966	2005	3.4	3.8	4.0	3.3	3.2	3.3	3.3	3.0	2.8	2.9	3.0	3.0	3.0	3.0	3.0	3.0	3.0	3.1	3.0	3.2	4.2	4.0	4.1	4.3	3.8	4.1	4.3	4.4	4.3	4.6	4.8	5.1	5.2	5.3	4.8	5.0	4.0	5.0	4.9	4.6	14%	2.8	3.9%	3.3%	3.5
4.0%	1967	2006	4.1	4.2	3.6	3.6	3.6	3.6	3.2	3.1	3.1	3.1	3.1	3.1	3.1	3.1	3.1	3.1	3.2	3.2	3.3	3.4	4.2	4.2	4.4	4.0	4.2	4.4	4.7	4.4	5.0	5.0	5.4	5.3	5.5	5.2	5.2	4.4	5.0	5.4	5.1	5.1	17%	3.1	4.1%	3.4%	3.9
3.9%	1968	2007	3.9	3.3	3.3	3.3	3.3	3.1	2.9	3.0	3.1	3.0	2.9	2.9	2.9	2.9	3.0	3.1	3.1	3.1	3.2	3.1	4.0	4.1	3.9	4.0	4.1	4.2	4.1	4.3	4.4	4.8	4.9	5.0	4.8	4.7	4.0	4.4	4.4	4.7	4.6	4.1	11%	2.9	3.7%	3.1%	3.3
3.9%	1969	2008	3.2	3.2	3.2	3.2	3.1	2.8	2.8	3.0	2.9	2.8	2.8	2.9	2.8	2.9	3.1	3.0	3.1	3.1	3.1	3.1	4.0	3.8	3.9	4.0	4.0	4.0	4.2	4.2	4.6	4.5	4.9	4.3	4.6	4.0	4.2	4.4	4.2	4.7	4.2	3.6	5%	2.8	3.6%	3.0%	3.1
3.9%	1970	2009	3.6	3.6	3.6	3.1	3.0	3.1	3.1	3.1	3.1	3.1	3.1	3.1	3.1	3.3	3.2	3.4	3.7	3.3	3.5	3.8	4.2	4.5	4.8	5.0	4.6	5.1	5.2	5.4	5.5	5.5	5.4	5.3	5.0	5.3	5.4	5.4	5.4	5.4	3.9	4.0	10%	3.0	4.2%	3.2%	3.9
4.1%	1971	2010	3.7	3.7	3.2	3.0	3.2	3.2	3.2	3.2	3.2	3.2	3.2	3.2	3.3	3.3	3.4	3.6	3.4	3.5	3.7	3.3	4.5	4.7	5.0	4.7	5.1	5.2	5.6	5.5	5.7	5.4	5.5	4.7	5.6	5.6	5.4	5.6	5.2	4.1	4.2	4.2	12%	3.0	4.2%	3.2%	4.1
4.0%	1972	1928	3.6	3.2	3.0	3.1	3.1	3.1	3.1	3.1	3.1	3.1	3.1	3.2	3.2	3.4	3.5	3.3	3.5	3.7	3.3	3.7	4.7	4.9	4.6	5.1	5.1	5.5	5.5	5.5	5.3	5.3	4.8	5.3	5.5	5.4	5.4	5.2	4.0	4.2	4.3	4.6	14%	3.0	4.2%	3.1%	4.0
4.0%	1973	1929	3.2	3.1	3.1	3.2	3.1	3.1	3.1	3.1	3.1	3.1	3.2	3.2	3.3	3.5	3.3	3.4	3.7	3.2	3.6	3.8	5.0	4.5	5.1	5.1	5.3	5.4	5.5	5.2	5.3	4.6	5.3	5.3	5.5	5.5	5.1	4.0	4.0	4.4	4.8	4.0	9%	3.1	4.1%	3.1%	4.0
4.3%	1974	1930	3.3	3.4	3.6	3.5	3.4	3.4	3.4	3.4	3.6	3.8	3.7	4.1	4.3	4.0	4.1	4.3	3.9	4.3	4.4	4.7	5.3	5.5	5.6	5.8	5.8	5.8	5.8	5.8	5.3	5.7	5.8	5.7	5.8	5.7	4.3	4.8	5.0	5.9	4.5	3.8	7%	3.4	4.6%	3.5%	5.1
4.7%	1975	1931	4.0	4.3	4.1	4.0	3.9	3.9	3.8	4.1	4.3	4.2	4.7	4.9	4.6	4.7	4.8	4.4	4.9	4.9	5.1	4.9	6.1	6.0	6.3	6.3	6.3	6.2	6.3	5.7	6.2	6.2	6.2	6.2	6.2	4.8	5.0	5.4	5.8	4.8	4.0	3.6	3%	3.6	5.1%	4.1%	5.9
4.6%	1976	1932	3.9	3.8	3.7	3.7	3.6	3.6	3.8	3.9	3.9	4.2	4.4	4.1	4.2	4.4	3.9	4.4	4.7	4.7	4.4	4.9	5.8	6.1	6.1	6.2	5.9	6.1	5.7	5.9	6.1	5.9	6.2	5.7	4.6	4.8	5.0	5.8	4.5	4.1	3.6	3.6	2%	3.6	4.8%	3.8%	5.2
4.6%	1977	1933	3.6	3.5	3.5	3.6	3.4	3.6	3.8	3.7	4.0	4.2	3.9	4.0	4.2	3.8	4.1	4.4	4.7	4.2	4.7	4.8	5.9	5.9	6.0	5.8	5.8	5.5	5.9	5.9	5.8	5.8	5.7	4.4	5.0	5.1	5.6	4.5	3.8	3.6	3.6	3.6	2%	3.4	4.6%	3.7%	4.8
4.7%	1978	1934	3.6	3.6	3.6	3.6	3.7	3.8	3.8	4.1	4.3	4.0	4.1	4.2	3.8	4.2	4.4	4.7	4.3	4.7	4.8	5.1	6.0	6.0	5.8	5.9	5.5	5.9	6.0	5.8	6.0	5.6	4.6	4.7	5.3	5.8	4.5	3.9	3.6	3.6	3.6	3.6	2%	3.6	4.6%	3.8%	5.0
4.8%	1979	1935	3.7	3.7	3.6	3.8	3.9	3.9	4.1	4.3	4.1	4.1	4.3	3.9	4.2	4.4	4.7	4.3	4.9	4.8	5.1	5.2	6.1	5.9	6.0	5.7	5.9	6.1	5.9	6.0	5.8	4.6	4.9	5.1	6.0	4.6	4.0	3.6	3.6	3.6	3.6	3.6	3%	3.6	4.7%	4.0%	5.3
4.8%	1980	1936	3.7	3.6	3.8	3.9	3.9	4.1	4.2	4.0	4.1	4.2	3.8	4.2	4.3	4.6	4.2	4.7	4.8	5.0	5.0	5.1	5.8	5.8	5.3	5.9	5.9	5.8	6.0	5.6	4.5	4.6	5.0	5.6	4.8	4.4	3.6	3.6	4.0	4.2	4.4	4.5	12%	3.6	4.6%	4.0%	5.3
4.7%	1981	1937	3.6	3.8	3.9	3.9	4.2	4.4	4.1	4.2	4.4	3.9	4.3	4.4	4.7	4.3	4.8	4.8	5.1	5.1	5.1	5.0	6.0	5.6	5.9	6.1	5.8	6.1	5.8	4.7	5.0	5.2	5.8	4.7	4.4	3.6	3.6	4.3	4.0	4.4	4.6	3.6	6%	3.6	4.7%	4.1%	5.4
4.8%	1982	1938	3.9	4.1	4.0	4.4	4.6	4.3	4.3	4.5	4.1	4.4	4.6	4.8	4.4	4.9	4.9	5.2	5.3	5.2	5.1	5.2	5.8	6.1	6.2	6.1	6.1	5.9	4.9	5.0	5.4	5.8	4.9	4.4	3.8	3.8	4.4	4.3	4.4	5.2	3.8	3.9	7%	3.8	4.8%	4.3%	5.7
4.8%	1983	1939	3.8	3.8	4.0	4.1	3.9	4.0	4.1	3.8	4.0	4.1	4.3	4.0	4.4	4.5	4.9	4.9	5.0	4.7	4.8	4.4	5.8	5.8	5.7	5.8	5.5	4.5	4.7	4.9	5.6	4.5	4.1	3.6	3.6	3.6	3.6	3.8	4.2	3.6	3.6	3.6	2%	3.6	4.4%	4.0%	5.0
4.7%	1984	1940	3.7	3.8	3.9	3.8	3.8	3.9	3.7	3.9	4.0	4.1	3.9	4.2	4.2	4.7	4.7	4.7	4.5	4.6	4.0	4.7	5.7	5.5	5.6	5.4	4.4	4.6	4.8	5.3	4.6	4.3	3.7	3.8	4.3	4.2	4.4	4.7	3.6	4.1	3.7	3.6	4%	3.6	4.3%	3.9%	4.8
4.7%	1985	1941	3.9	4.0	3.8	3.9	4.0	3.7	3.9	4.0	4.2	3.9	4.2	4.3	4.7	4.7	4.7	4.5	4.7	4.0	4.6	4.8	5.5	5.6	5.4	4.6	4.6	4.9	5.5	4.5	4.3	3.7	3.9	4.3	4.3	4.4	4.6	3.7	3.8	3.9	3.6	3.6	3%	3.6	4.4%	4.0%	4.8
4.6%	1986	1942	3.8	3.6	3.7	3.8	3.5	3.7	3.8	3.9	3.7	4.0	4.0	4.4	4.4	4.5	4.3	4.4	4.0	4.4	4.5	4.5	5.5	5.2	4.4	4.6	4.7	5.3	4.5	4.3	3.6	3.6	4.2	4.1	4.3	4.6	3.6	3.9	3.6	3.6	3.6	3.6	2%	3.5	4.2%	3.8%	4.4
4.6%	1987	1943	3.6	3.6	3.6	3.4	3.6	3.7	3.8	3.6	3.9	3.9	4.2	4.2	4.2	4.1	4.1	3.8	4.3	4.3	4.2	4.5	5.1	4.3	4.4	4.6	5.0	4.4	4.0	3.6	3.6	3.6	3.6	3.9	4.3	3.6	3.6	3.6	3.6	3.6	3.3	2.3	0%	2.3	3.9%	3.7%	4.0
4.6%	1988	1944	3.7	3.8	3.6	3.8	3.8	4.0	3.8	4.1	4.1	4.4	4.4	4.5	4.3	4.4	4.0	4.4	4.6	4.4	4.5	4.4	4.5	4.6	4.8	5.4	4.5	4.3	4.0	4.0	4.3	4.3	4.4	4.7	4.0	4.2	3.9	3.6	3.6	3.6	3.6	3.6	5%	3.6	4.2%	4.0%	4.5
4.6%	1989	1945	3.7	3.5	3.7	3.8	3.9	3.7	3.9	4.0	4.4	4.3	4.4	4.2	4.3	3.9	4.3	4.5	4.4	4.4	4.2	3.6	4.5	4.6	5.2	4.5	4.3	3.6	3.8	4.2	4.2	4.3	4.6	3.6	4.0	3.8	3.6	3.6	3.6	3.6	3.6	3.6	5%	3.5	4.1%	3.9%	4.3
4.3%	1990	1946	3.4	3.6	3.7	3.8	3.6	3.9	3.9	4.2	4.3	4.2	4.1	4.1	3.8	4.2	4.3	4.2	4.4	4.1	3.4	3.6	4.6	5.1	4.4	4.1	3.8	4.0	4.2	4.1	4.3	4.5	3.9	4.1	4.1	3.7	3.6	3.6	3.6	3.8	4.1	3.6	5%	3.4	4.0%	3.9%	4.2
4.4%	1991	1947	4.0	4.1	4.3	3.9	4.3	4.3	4.5	4.6	4.6	4.4	4.5	4.2	4.5	4.6	4.5	4.6	4.5	3.7	3.8	4.1	5.4	4.6	4.3	4.2	4.2	4.4	4.4	4.5	5.2	4.2	4.3	4.2	4.2	3.8	3.8	4.2	4.3	5.3	4.3	4.2	8%	3.7	4.4%	4.4%	4.9
4.1%	1992	1948	3.8	3.9	3.6	4.0	4.0	4.3	4.3	4.3	4.2	4.2	3.8	4.2	4.2	4.2	4.3	4.1	3.5	3.6	3.7	4.3	4.4	4.1	4.0	4.1	4.1	4.1	4.3	4.7	4.0	4.1	4.1	3.9	3.6	3.6	4.0	4.1	4.3	4.1	4.0	3.6	6%	3.5	4.0%	4.0%	4.3
4.0%	1993	1949	3.8	3.6	3.9	3.9	4.2	4.2	4.2	4.1	4.2	3.7	4.1	4.2	4.1	4.2	4.0	3.3	3.5	3.6	4.1	3.4	4.0	3.7	3.8	4.0	4.0	4.2	4.7	3.8	4.0	3.9	3.7	3.6	3.6	3.7	3.9	4.1	3.7	3.7	3.6	3.6	4%	3.3	3.9%	4.0%	4.1
4.0%	1994	1950	3.4	3.7	3.7	4.1	4.1	4.1	3.8	3.9	3.5	3.9	4.0	3.9	4.1	3.9	3.3	3.4	3.6	3.9	3.4	3.2	3.9	4.0	4.0	4.0	4.2	4.6	4.0	4.0	4.0	3.8	3.6	3.6	4.0	4.0	4.4	4.0	3.9	4.0	4.0	4.0	8%	3.2	3.9%	3.9%	4.0
3.9%	1995	1951	4.0	4.0	4.2	4.2	4.2	4.1	4.2	3.9	4.2	4.2	4.1	4.2	4.1	3.4	3.5	3.8	4.2	3.5	3.2	3.1	4.0	4.1	4.1	4.4	4.8	4.0	4.1	4.0	4.0	3.8	3.9	4.0	4.4	5.1	4.2	4.0	4.0	4.2	4.3	4.2	12%	3.1	4.0%	4.1%	4.4
3.7%	1996	1952	3.7	4.0	4.0	4.0	3.9	4.0	3.6	3.9	4.0	3.9	4.0	3.8	3.2	3.3	3.4	3.9	3.3	3.0	2.9	3.0	3.9	3.9	4.1	4.5	3.8	3.9	3.8	3.8	3.6	3.6	3.8	3.9	4.7	3.9	3.8	3.8	3.8	4.0	3.9	3.8	8%	2.9	3.8%	3.9%	3.8
3.7%	1997	1953	4.0	4.0	4.0	3.8	3.9	3.4	3.8	3.9	3.8	3.9	3.7	3.1	3.2	3.3	3.8	3.2	3.1	3.0	3.0	3.1	4.0	4.1	4.5	3.8	3.9	3.9	3.8	3.6	3.7	3.8	4.1	4.7	4.1	3.9	3.8	3.9	4.0	4.2	4.1	3.9	9%	3.0	3.8%	3.8%	3.8
3.7%	1998	1954	3.7	3.8	3.5	3.6	3.2	3.6	3.7	3.6	3.7	3.5	3.1	3.1	3.2	3.6	3.1	3.0	2.8	2.9	3.0	3.0	4.0	4.2	3.7	3.8	3.8	3.6	3.6	3.6	3.7	3.8	4.2	3.8	3.8	3.6	3.7	3.8	3.8	3.8	3.7	3.8	8%	2.8	3.6%	3.5%	3.4
3.7%	1999	1955	3.8	3.5	3.6	3.2	3.6	3.7	3.6	3.7	3.5	3.0	3.1	3.2	3.5	3.1	3.0	2.8	2.9	3.0	3.0	3.1	4.2	3.7	3.8	3.8	3.6	3.6	3.6	3.7	3.8	4.2	3.8	3.8	3.8	3.8	3.8	3.8	3.8	3.8	4.0	4.0	11%	2.8	3.6%	3.4%	3.3
3.6%	2000	1956	3.6	3.6	3.2	3.6	3.7	3.6	3.7	3.5	3.0	3.1	3.2	3.5	3.0	2.9	2.8	2.8	2.9	2.9	3.0	3.2	3.6	3.7	3.7	3.6	3.6	3.6	3.6	3.7	3.9	3.6	3.6	3.6	3.6	3.6	3.6	3.6	3.6	3.7	3.7	3.6	5%	2.8	3.5%	3.4%	3.2
																																								Totals	11%	2.3	4.3%	3.8%	4.7%

FIGURE 180

Failure-market results including 1) 37.5% initially going into an inflation-adjusted SPIA with a 4.01% payout; 2) 10% going into a simulated DIA using a standby bond pool with a 2% IRR. At age 85, the standby bond pool is used to purchase an SPIA with a 9.07% payout.

In both cases above, an inflation-adjusted SPIA is used at the start of retirement to lock in a 1.5% GI rate, requiring 37.5% of the total assets. Still, for both cases, the income is weak for the first 20 years due to the failure market and the 10% drop to fund the bond pool. After 20 years, deferred income kicks in, greatly improving income rates; how much depends on whether a TIPS ladder is built or an SPIA purchased. While a 20-year TIPS ladder doesn't pay out as much (locking in less GI) as the SPIA at 85, it does pays well enough to be the choice for those wanting to keep control of their assets, including their bequest value. Both examples show a few small shortages (i.e., less than 3% income) very late in retirement after age 100.

It's noteworthy that, in both examples, 52% of assets stay in systemic withdrawals, which reduces costs during typical times, and maintains flexibility.

In summary, a simulated deferred annuity effectively boosts income late in retirement, but should only be used in moderation due to the drag it exerts on early income.

A Valuation-Based Strategy for Timing Guaranteed-Income Purchases

Chapter 9 has already lain out a framework for identifying valuation levels; the same can be reapplied to GI to help time GI purchases. As shown earlier, delaying the purchase of GI boost the payout rate, but at the risk of losing portfolio value from the stock volatility of systemic-withdrawals. The end result can be a net loss in income. However, by leveraging valuations, a substantial portion of this timing risk can be sidestepped. Basically, valuations tell when GI purchases can be reasonably delayed and when they shouldn't be.

Here's a simple valuation strategy for purchasing GI: when valuation levels are at 3.0 and above, immediately lock in the desired GI rate. However, when valuation levels are below 3.0, lock in only half the desired amount now and wait until payouts are substantially higher to lock in the rest.

Two examples below apply valuations to timing GI purchases. In both cases, 100% of the portfolio is allocated to SPIAs to accentuate the effects of the strategy. The October 2014 payouts are again used: 4.01% for a couple at 65 years, 5.75% at 75 years, and 9.07% at 85 years.

Figure 181 shows failure-market results using the valuation strategy to delay (when valuations are attractive) SPIA purchases for 10 years. The outcome is significantly better than seen in Figure 171, which always delayed for 10 years (independent of the valuation). Valuations correctly avoided delaying GI purchases where it mattered most in 1929, the late 1960s, the early 1970s, and in 1999. Delaying resulted in a net loss of income only in one case: the 1971 retirement with a 10-year delay dropped income to 3.8%, compared to 4% from locking in at the beginning.

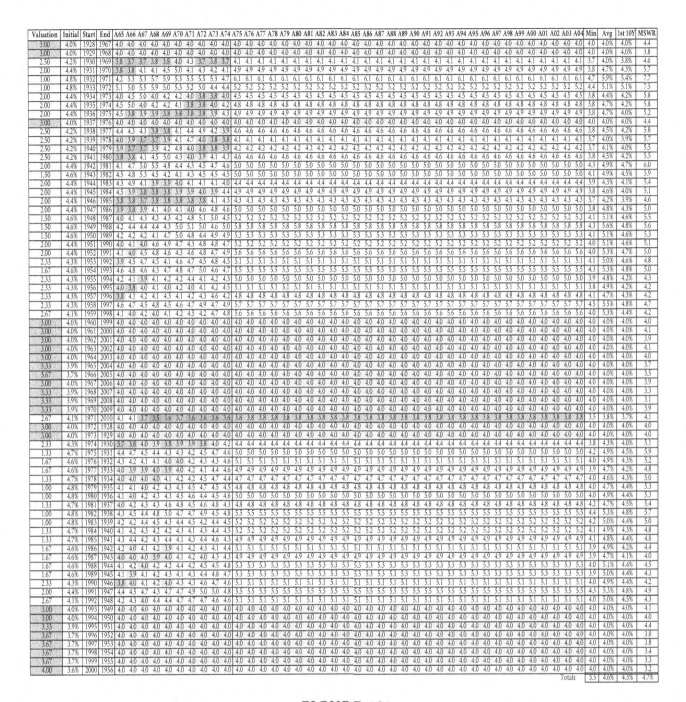

FIGURE 181

Failure-market results with valuation-based purchasing of SPIA. For valuation levels of 3 or above, purchase 100% at age 65. For valuation levels below 3, purchase 50% at 65 and 50% at 75.

Figure 182 shows the same example using a 20-year delay instead of the 10-year delay. The results are again consistent and strong, even a little better. Delaying never resulted in a loss of income.

Valuation	Initial	Start	End	A65	A66	A67	A68	A69	A70	A71	A72	A73	A74	A75	A76	A77	A78	A79	A80	A81	A82	A83	A84	A85	A86	A87	A88	A89	A90	A91	A92	A93	A94	A95	A96	A97	A98	A99	A00	A01	A02	A03	A04	Min	Avg	1st 10Y	MSWR
3.00	4.0%	1928	1967	4.0	4.0	4.0	4.0	4.0	4.0	4.0	4.0	4.0	4.0	4.0	4.0	4.0	4.0	4.0	4.0	4.0	4.0	4.0	4.0	4.0	4.0	4.0	4.0	4.0	4.0	4.0	4.0	4.0	4.0	4.0	4.0	4.0	4.0	4.0	4.0	4.0	4.0	4.0	4.0	4.0	4.0%	4.0%	4.4
3.00	4.0%	1929	1968	4.0	4.0	4.0	4.0	4.0	4.0	4.0	4.0	4.0	4.0	4.0	4.0	4.0	4.0	4.0	4.0	4.0	4.0	4.0	4.0	4.0	4.0	4.0	4.0	4.0	4.0	4.0	4.0	4.0	4.0	4.0	4.0	4.0	4.0	4.0	4.0	4.0	4.0	4.0	4.0	4.0	4.0%	4.0%	3.8
2.50	4.2%	1930	1969	3.8	3.7	3.7	3.8	3.8	4.0	4.3	3.7	3.8	3.7	3.7	3.6	3.6	3.7	3.8	4.5	3.9	3.7	3.7	3.8	4.7	4.7	4.7	4.7	4.7	4.7	4.7	4.7	4.7	4.7	4.7	4.7	4.7	4.7	4.7	4.7	4.7	4.7	4.7	4.7	3.6	4.3%	3.8%	4.6
2.00	4.4%	1931	1970	3.8	3.8	4.1	4.1	4.5	5.0	4.1	4.3	4.2	4.1	3.8	3.8	4.0	4.3	4.9	4.2	4.0	3.9	4.1	4.3	6.0	6.0	6.0	6.0	6.0	6.0	6.0	6.0	6.0	6.0	6.0	6.0	6.0	6.0	6.0	6.0	6.0	6.0	6.0	6.0	3.8	5.1%	4.2%	5.7
1.00	4.8%	1932	1971	4.2	5.3	5.3	5.7	5.9	5.3	5.5	5.5	5.3	4.7	4.6	5.1	5.4	5.8	5.1	4.7	4.6	4.8	5.1	5.1	7.0	7.0	7.0	7.0	7.0	7.0	7.0	7.0	7.0	7.0	7.0	7.0	7.0	7.0	7.0	7.0	7.0	7.0	7.0	7.0	4.6	6.1%	5.3%	7.7
1.00	4.8%	1933	1972	5.1	5.0	5.5	5.9	5.0	5.3	5.2	5.0	4.4	4.4	4.7	5.2	5.7	4.9	4.5	4.4	4.8	5.0	5.0	5.2	6.4	6.4	6.4	6.4	6.4	6.4	6.4	6.4	6.4	6.4	6.4	6.4	6.4	6.4	6.4	6.4	6.4	6.4	6.4	6.4	4.4	5.7%	5.0%	7.5
2.00	4.4%	1934	1973	4.0	4.5	5.0	4.0	4.2	4.2	4.0	3.8	3.8	4.0	4.2	4.9	4.1	3.9	3.9	4.0	4.2	4.2	4.3	4.2	5.2	5.2	5.2	5.2	5.2	5.2	5.2	5.2	5.2	5.2	5.2	5.2	5.2	5.2	5.2	5.2	5.2	5.2	5.2	5.2	3.8	4.7%	4.2%	5.8
2.00	4.4%	1935	1974	4.5	5.0	4.0	4.2	4.2	4.1	3.8	3.8	4.0	4.2	4.8	4.1	3.9	3.9	4.0	4.2	4.2	4.3	4.1	5.0	6.2	6.2	6.2	6.2	6.2	6.2	6.2	6.2	6.2	6.2	6.2	6.2	6.2	6.2	6.2	6.2	6.2	6.2	6.2	6.2	3.8	5.2%	4.2%	5.8
2.00	4.4%	1936	1975	4.5	3.8	3.9	3.9	3.8	3.8	3.8	3.8	3.9	4.3	3.9	3.8	3.8	3.8	4.0	4.0	4.1	3.9	4.8	5.1	6.4	6.4	6.4	6.4	6.4	6.4	6.4	6.4	6.4	6.4	6.4	6.4	6.4	6.4	6.4	6.4	6.4	6.4	6.4	6.4	3.8	5.2%	3.9%	5.2
3.00	4.0%	1937	1976	4.0	4.0	4.0	4.0	4.0	4.0	4.0	4.0	4.0	4.0	4.0	4.0	4.0	4.0	4.0	4.0	4.0	4.0	4.0	4.0	4.0	4.0	4.0	4.0	4.0	4.0	4.0	4.0	4.0	4.0	4.0	4.0	4.0	4.0	4.0	4.0	4.0	4.0	4.0	4.0	4.0	4.0%	4.0%	4.4
2.50	4.2%	1938	1977	4.4	4.3	4.1	3.8	3.8	4.1	4.4	4.9	4.2	3.9	3.9	4.0	4.2	4.2	4.3	4.2	5.0	5.1	5.1	4.8	6.2	6.2	6.2	6.2	6.2	6.2	6.2	6.2	6.2	6.2	6.2	6.2	6.2	6.2	6.2	6.2	6.2	6.2	6.2	6.2	3.8	5.3%	4.1%	5.8
2.50	4.2%	1939	1978	4.0	3.9	3.7	3.7	3.9	4.1	4.7	4.0	3.8	3.8	3.9	4.0	4.1	4.2	4.0	4.8	5.1	4.9	4.6	5.1	6.6	6.6	6.6	6.6	6.6	6.6	6.6	6.6	6.6	6.6	6.6	6.6	6.6	6.6	6.6	6.6	6.6	6.6	6.6	6.6	3.7	5.4%	3.9%	5.7
2.50	4.2%	1940	1979	3.9	3.7	3.7	3.9	4.2	4.8	4.0	3.8	3.8	3.9	4.0	4.1	4.1	4.0	4.8	5.0	5.0	4.6	5.0	5.1	6.6	6.6	6.6	6.6	6.6	6.6	6.6	6.6	6.6	6.6	6.6	6.6	6.6	6.6	6.6	6.6	6.6	6.6	6.6	6.6	3.7	5.4%	4.0%	5.5
2.50	4.2%	1941	1980	3.8	3.8	4.1	4.5	5.0	4.3	4.0	3.9	4.1	4.3	4.3	4.4	4.2	4.9	5.1	5.0	4.7	5.1	5.1	5.2	6.2	6.2	6.2	6.2	6.2	6.2	6.2	6.2	6.2	6.2	6.2	6.2	6.2	6.2	6.2	6.2	6.2	6.2	6.2	6.2	3.8	5.4%	4.2%	5.5
2.00	4.4%	1942	1981	4.1	4.7	5.0	5.5	4.8	4.4	4.3	4.5	4.7	4.6	4.7	4.5	5.1	5.3	5.2	4.9	5.3	5.3	5.3	5.5	7.0	7.0	7.0	7.0	7.0	7.0	7.0	7.0	7.0	7.0	7.0	7.0	7.0	7.0	7.0	7.0	7.0	7.0	7.0	7.0	4.3	6.0%	4.7%	6.0
1.50	4.6%	1943	1982	4.5	4.8	5.3	4.5	4.2	4.1	4.3	4.5	4.5	4.5	4.4	5.1	5.2	5.2	4.8	5.2	5.3	5.2	5.4	5.3	6.7	6.7	6.7	6.7	6.7	6.7	6.7	6.7	6.7	6.7	6.7	6.7	6.7	6.7	6.7	6.7	6.7	6.7	6.7	6.7	4.1	5.8%	4.5%	5.9
2.00	4.4%	1944	1983	4.3	4.9	4.1	3.9	3.9	4.0	4.1	4.1	4.1	4.0	4.7	5.0	4.9	4.5	4.9	5.0	5.0	5.1	4.9	5.1	6.5	6.5	6.5	6.5	6.5	6.5	6.5	6.5	6.5	6.5	6.5	6.5	6.5	6.5	6.5	6.5	6.5	6.5	6.5	6.5	3.9	5.5%	4.2%	5.4
2.00	4.4%	1945	1984	4.5	3.9	3.8	3.8	3.8	3.9	3.9	4.0	3.9	4.4	4.8	4.6	4.2	4.8	4.9	4.8	5.1	4.8	4.9	5.1	6.4	6.4	6.4	6.4	6.4	6.4	6.4	6.4	6.4	6.4	6.4	6.4	6.4	6.4	6.4	6.4	6.4	6.4	6.4	6.4	3.8	5.4%	4.0%	5.1
2.00	4.4%	1946	1985	3.8	3.8	3.7	3.8	3.8	3.8	3.8	3.8	4.1	4.3	4.2	4.0	4.4	4.5	4.4	4.8	4.5	4.6	4.8	5.0	5.7	5.7	5.7	5.7	5.7	5.7	5.7	5.7	5.7	5.7	5.7	5.7	5.7	5.7	5.7	5.7	5.7	5.7	5.7	5.7	3.7	5.0%	3.9%	4.6
2.00	4.4%	1947	1986	3.9	3.8	3.9	4.1	4.0	4.1	4.0	4.6	4.8	4.6	4.2	4.8	4.8	4.8	5.0	4.8	4.9	5.0	5.2	5.0	6.2	6.2	6.2	6.2	6.2	6.2	6.2	6.2	6.2	6.2	6.2	6.2	6.2	6.2	6.2	6.2	6.2	6.2	6.2	6.2	3.8	5.4%	4.2%	5.0
1.50	4.6%	1948	1987	4.0	4.1	4.3	4.3	4.3	4.2	4.8	5.1	5.0	4.5	5.0	5.0	5.0	5.2	5.0	5.1	5.2	5.3	5.1	5.5	7.6	7.6	7.6	7.6	7.6	7.6	7.6	7.6	7.6	7.6	7.6	7.6	7.6	7.6	7.6	7.6	7.6	7.6	7.6	7.6	4.1	6.3%	4.5%	5.5
1.50	4.6%	1949	1988	4.2	4.4	4.4	4.4	4.3	5.0	5.1	5.0	4.6	5.0	5.1	5.0	5.2	5.1	5.1	5.2	5.5	5.2	5.5	5.7	8.3	8.3	8.3	8.3	8.3	8.3	8.3	8.3	8.3	8.3	8.3	8.3	8.3	8.3	8.3	8.3	8.3	8.3	8.3	8.3	4.3	6.7%	4.7%	5.6
1.50	4.6%	1950	1989	4.2	4.2	4.2	4.1	4.7	5.0	4.8	4.4	4.9	4.9	4.8	5.1	4.8	5.0	5.1	5.3	5.1	5.4	5.6	5.1	6.5	6.5	6.5	6.5	6.5	6.5	6.5	6.5	6.5	6.5	6.5	6.5	6.5	6.5	6.5	6.5	6.5	6.5	6.5	6.5	4.1	5.7%	4.6%	5.3
2.00	4.4%	1951	1990	4.0	4.1	4.0	4.6	4.9	4.7	4.3	4.8	4.8	4.7	4.9	4.7	4.8	5.0	5.1	4.9	5.3	5.4	4.9	4.9	6.3	6.3	6.3	6.3	6.3	6.3	6.3	6.3	6.3	6.3	6.3	6.3	6.3	6.3	6.3	6.3	6.3	6.3	6.3	6.3	4.0	5.5%	4.6%	5.1
2.00	4.4%	1952	1991	4.1	4.0	4.5	4.8	4.6	4.3	4.6	4.8	4.7	4.9	4.6	4.7	4.9	5.1	4.8	5.2	5.4	4.8	4.7	4.9	6.4	6.4	6.4	6.4	6.4	6.4	6.4	6.4	6.4	6.4	6.4	6.4	6.4	6.4	6.4	6.4	6.4	6.4	6.4	6.4	4.0	5.6%	4.6%	5.0
2.33	4.3%	1953	1992	3.9	4.5	4.7	4.5	4.1	4.6	4.7	4.5	4.8	4.5	4.7	4.8	4.9	4.8	5.0	5.1	4.7	4.5	4.6	4.6	6.0	6.0	6.0	6.0	6.0	6.0	6.0	6.0	6.0	6.0	6.0	6.0	6.0	6.0	6.0	6.0	6.0	6.0	6.0	6.0	4.1	5.3%	4.5%	4.8
1.67	4.6%	1954	1993	4.6	4.8	4.6	4.3	4.7	4.8	4.7	5.0	4.6	4.7	4.9	5.1	4.8	5.2	5.3	4.8	4.8	4.7	4.7	4.2	5.7	5.7	5.7	5.7	5.7	5.7	5.7	5.7	5.7	5.7	5.7	5.7	5.7	5.7	5.7	5.7	5.7	5.7	5.7	5.7	4.2	5.2%	4.7%	5.0
2.33	4.3%	1955	1994	4.2	4.1	3.9	4.1	4.2	4.2	4.4	4.1	4.2	4.3	4.6	4.3	4.8	4.9	4.3	4.3	4.4	4.3	3.8	3.7	4.4	4.4	4.4	4.4	4.4	4.4	4.4	4.4	4.4	4.4	4.4	4.4	4.4	4.4	4.4	4.4	4.4	4.4	4.4	4.4	3.7	4.3%	4.2%	4.3
2.33	4.3%	1956	1995	4.0	3.8	4.0	4.1	4.0	4.2	4.0	4.1	4.2	4.5	4.2	4.7	4.8	4.2	4.2	4.3	4.3	3.8	3.7	3.7	4.3	4.3	4.3	4.3	4.3	4.3	4.3	4.3	4.3	4.3	4.3	4.3	4.3	4.3	4.3	4.3	4.3	4.3	4.3	4.3	3.7	4.2%	4.1%	4.2
2.33	4.3%	1957	1996	3.8	4.1	4.2	4.1	4.3	4.1	4.2	4.3	4.6	4.2	4.7	4.8	4.2	4.2	4.2	4.2	3.8	3.7	3.7	3.8	4.5	4.5	4.5	4.5	4.5	4.5	4.5	4.5	4.5	4.5	4.5	4.5	4.5	4.5	4.5	4.5	4.5	4.5	4.5	4.5	3.7	4.4%	4.2%	4.2
2.33	4.3%	1958	1997	4.6	4.7	4.5	4.8	4.5	4.6	4.7	4.9	4.7	4.9	5.0	4.5	4.4	4.6	4.5	4.0	3.7	3.8	3.9	3.8	4.8	4.8	4.8	4.8	4.8	4.8	4.8	4.8	4.8	4.8	4.8	4.8	4.8	4.8	4.8	4.8	4.8	4.8	4.8	4.8	3.7	4.6%	4.7%	4.7
2.67	4.1%	1959	1998	4.1	4.0	4.2	4.0	4.1	4.2	4.5	4.2	4.7	4.8	4.2	4.1	4.2	4.2	3.7	3.6	3.7	3.7	3.7	3.7	4.4	4.4	4.4	4.4	4.4	4.4	4.4	4.4	4.4	4.4	4.4	4.4	4.4	4.4	4.4	4.4	4.4	4.4	4.4	4.4	3.6	4.2%	4.3%	4.2
3.00	4.0%	1960	1999	4.0	4.0	4.0	4.0	4.0	4.0	4.0	4.0	4.0	4.0	4.0	4.0	4.0	4.0	4.0	4.0	4.0	4.0	4.0	4.0	4.0	4.0	4.0	4.0	4.0	4.0	4.0	4.0	4.0	4.0	4.0	4.0	4.0	4.0	4.0	4.0	4.0	4.0	4.0	4.0	4.0	4.0%	4.0%	4.0
3.00	4.0%	1961	2000	4.0	4.0	4.0	4.0	4.0	4.0	4.0	4.0	4.0	4.0	4.0	4.0	4.0	4.0	4.0	4.0	4.0	4.0	4.0	4.0	4.0	4.0	4.0	4.0	4.0	4.0	4.0	4.0	4.0	4.0	4.0	4.0	4.0	4.0	4.0	4.0	4.0	4.0	4.0	4.0	4.0	4.0%	4.0%	4.1
3.00	4.0%	1962	2001	4.0	4.0	4.0	4.0	4.0	4.0	4.0	4.0	4.0	4.0	4.0	4.0	4.0	4.0	4.0	4.0	4.0	4.0	4.0	4.0	4.0	4.0	4.0	4.0	4.0	4.0	4.0	4.0	4.0	4.0	4.0	4.0	4.0	4.0	4.0	4.0	4.0	4.0	4.0	4.0	4.0	4.0%	4.0%	3.9
3.00	4.0%	1963	2002	4.0	4.0	4.0	4.0	4.0	4.0	4.0	4.0	4.0	4.0	4.0	4.0	4.0	4.0	4.0	4.0	4.0	4.0	4.0	4.0	4.0	4.0	4.0	4.0	4.0	4.0	4.0	4.0	4.0	4.0	4.0	4.0	4.0	4.0	4.0	4.0	4.0	4.0	4.0	4.0	4.0	4.0%	4.0%	4.1
3.00	4.0%	1964	2003	4.0	4.0	4.0	4.0	4.0	4.0	4.0	4.0	4.0	4.0	4.0	4.0	4.0	4.0	4.0	4.0	4.0	4.0	4.0	4.0	4.0	4.0	4.0	4.0	4.0	4.0	4.0	4.0	4.0	4.0	4.0	4.0	4.0	4.0	4.0	4.0	4.0	4.0	4.0	4.0	4.0	4.0%	4.0%	4.0
3.33	3.9%	1965	2004	4.0	4.0	4.0	4.0	4.0	4.0	4.0	4.0	4.0	4.0	4.0	4.0	4.0	4.0	4.0	4.0	4.0	4.0	4.0	4.0	4.0	4.0	4.0	4.0	4.0	4.0	4.0	4.0	4.0	4.0	4.0	4.0	4.0	4.0	4.0	4.0	4.0	4.0	4.0	4.0	4.0	4.0%	4.0%	3.7
3.67	3.7%	1966	2005	4.0	4.0	4.0	4.0	4.0	4.0	4.0	4.0	4.0	4.0	4.0	4.0	4.0	4.0	4.0	4.0	4.0	4.0	4.0	4.0	4.0	4.0	4.0	4.0	4.0	4.0	4.0	4.0	4.0	4.0	4.0	4.0	4.0	4.0	4.0	4.0	4.0	4.0	4.0	4.0	4.0	4.0%	4.0%	3.5
3.00	4.0%	1967	2006	4.0	4.0	4.0	4.0	4.0	4.0	4.0	4.0	4.0	4.0	4.0	4.0	4.0	4.0	4.0	4.0	4.0	4.0	4.0	4.0	4.0	4.0	4.0	4.0	4.0	4.0	4.0	4.0	4.0	4.0	4.0	4.0	4.0	4.0	4.0	4.0	4.0	4.0	4.0	4.0	4.0	4.0%	4.0%	3.9
3.33	3.9%	1968	2007	4.0	4.0	4.0	4.0	4.0	4.0	4.0	4.0	4.0	4.0	4.0	4.0	4.0	4.0	4.0	4.0	4.0	4.0	4.0	4.0	4.0	4.0	4.0	4.0	4.0	4.0	4.0	4.0	4.0	4.0	4.0	4.0	4.0	4.0	4.0	4.0	4.0	4.0	4.0	4.0	4.0	4.0%	4.0%	3.3
3.33	3.9%	1969	2008	4.0	4.0	4.0	4.0	4.0	4.0	4.0	4.0	4.0	4.0	4.0	4.0	4.0	4.0	4.0	4.0	4.0	4.0	4.0	4.0	4.0	4.0	4.0	4.0	4.0	4.0	4.0	4.0	4.0	4.0	4.0	4.0	4.0	4.0	4.0	4.0	4.0	4.0	4.0	4.0	4.0	4.0%	4.0%	3.1
3.33	3.9%	1970	2009	4.0	4.0	4.0	4.0	4.0	4.0	4.0	4.0	4.0	4.0	4.0	4.0	4.0	4.0	4.0	4.0	4.0	4.0	4.0	4.0	4.0	4.0	4.0	4.0	4.0	4.0	4.0	4.0	4.0	4.0	4.0	4.0	4.0	4.0	4.0	4.0	4.0	4.0	4.0	4.0	4.0	4.0%	4.0%	3.9
2.67	4.1%	1971	2010	4.1	4.1	3.7	3.5	3.6	3.7	3.6	3.6	3.6	3.6	3.6	3.7	3.8	3.7	3.9	4.0	3.9	3.9	4.1	3.8	4.5	4.5	4.5	4.5	4.5	4.5	4.5	4.5	4.5	4.5	4.5	4.5	4.5	4.5	4.5	4.5	4.5	4.5	4.5	4.5	3.5	4.1%	3.6%	4.1
3.00	4.0%	1972	1928	4.0	4.0	4.0	4.0	4.0	4.0	4.0	4.0	4.0	4.0	4.0	4.0	4.0	4.0	4.0	4.0	4.0	4.0	4.0	4.0	4.0	4.0	4.0	4.0	4.0	4.0	4.0	4.0	4.0	4.0	4.0	4.0	4.0	4.0	4.0	4.0	4.0	4.0	4.0	4.0	4.0	4.0%	4.0%	4.0
3.00	4.0%	1973	1929	4.0	4.0	4.0	4.0	4.0	4.0	4.0	4.0	4.0	4.0	4.0	4.0	4.0	4.0	4.0	4.0	4.0	4.0	4.0	4.0	4.0	4.0	4.0	4.0	4.0	4.0	4.0	4.0	4.0	4.0	4.0	4.0	4.0	4.0	4.0	4.0	4.0	4.0	4.0	4.0	4.0	4.0%	4.0%	4.0
2.33	4.3%	1974	1930	3.7	3.8	4.0	3.9	3.8	3.9	3.9	3.8	4.0	4.2	4.1	4.5	4.7	4.4	4.5	4.7	4.3	4.7	4.8	5.0	5.9	5.9	5.9	5.9	5.9	5.9	5.9	5.9	5.9	5.9	5.9	5.9	5.9	5.9	5.9	5.9	5.9	5.9	5.9	5.9	3.8	5.1%	3.9%	5.1
1.33	4.7%	1975	1931	4.4	4.7	4.5	4.4	4.3	4.3	4.2	4.5	4.7	4.6	5.1	5.2	5.0	5.1	5.2	4.8	5.2	5.3	5.4	5.2	6.4	6.4	6.4	6.4	6.4	6.4	6.4	6.4	6.4	6.4	6.4	6.4	6.4	6.4	6.4	6.4	6.4	6.4	6.4	6.4	4.2	5.6%	4.5%	5.9
1.67	4.6%	1976	1932	4.3	4.2	4.1	4.1	4.0	4.0	4.2	4.3	4.3	4.6	4.8	4.5	4.6	4.8	4.3	4.8	5.0	5.1	4.8	5.3	6.6	6.6	6.6	6.6	6.6	6.6	6.6	6.6	6.6	6.6	6.6	6.6	6.6	6.6	6.6	6.6	6.6	6.6	6.6	6.6	4.0	5.6%	4.2%	5.2
1.67	4.6%	1977	1933	4.0	3.9	3.9	4.0	3.9	4.0	4.2	4.1	4.4	4.6	4.3	4.4	4.6	4.2	4.5	4.8	5.0	4.6	5.0	5.1	6.3	6.3	6.3	6.3	6.3	6.3	6.3	6.3	6.3	6.3	6.3	6.3	6.3	6.3	6.3	6.3	6.3	6.3	6.3	6.3	3.9	5.4%	4.1%	4.8
1.33	4.7%	1978	1934	4.0	4.0	4.0	4.0	4.1	4.2	4.2	4.5	4.7	4.4	4.5	4.6	4.2	4.6	4.8	5.0	4.7	5.1	5.1	5.5	6.6	6.6	6.6	6.6	6.6	6.6	6.6	6.6	6.6	6.6	6.6	6.6	6.6	6.6	6.6	6.6	6.6	6.6	6.6	6.6	4.0	5.6%	4.2%	5.0
1.00	4.8%	1979	1935	4.1	4.1	4.0	4.2	4.3	4.3	4.5	4.7	4.5	4.5	4.7	4.3	4.6	4.8	5.0	4.7	5.2	5.2	5.4	5.5	6.5	6.5	6.5	6.5	6.5	6.5	6.5	6.5	6.5	6.5	6.5	6.5	6.5	6.5	6.5	6.5	6.5	6.5	6.5	6.5	4.0	5.6%	4.4%	5.3
1.00	4.8%	1980	1936	4.1	4.0	4.2	4.3	4.3	4.5	4.6	4.4	4.5	4.6	4.2	4.6	4.7	5.0	4.6	5.1	5.2	5.4	5.4	5.5	6.7	6.7	6.7	6.7	6.7	6.7	6.7	6.7	6.7	6.7	6.7	6.7	6.7	6.7	6.7	6.7	6.7	6.7	6.7	6.7	4.0	5.7%	4.3%	5.3
1.33	4.7%	1981	1937	4.0	4.2	4.3	4.3	4.6	4.8	4.5	4.6	4.8	4.3	4.7	4.8	5.1	4.7	5.1	5.2	5.5	5.4	5.5	5.4	6.9	6.9	6.9	6.9	6.9	6.9	6.9	6.9	6.9	6.9	6.9	6.9	6.9	6.9	6.9	6.9	6.9	6.9	6.9	6.9	4.2	5.9%	4.5%	5.4
1.00	4.8%	1982	1938	4.3	4.5	4.4	4.8	5.0	4.7	4.7	4.9	4.5	4.8	5.0	5.2	4.8	5.3	5.3	5.5	5.6	5.6	5.4	5.6	7.3	7.3	7.3	7.3	7.3	7.3	7.3	7.3	7.3	7.3	7.3	7.3	7.3	7.3	7.3	7.3	7.3	7.3	7.3	7.3	4.4	6.2%	4.7%	5.7
1.00	4.8%	1983	1939	4.2	4.2	4.4	4.5	4.3	4.4	4.5	4.2	4.4	4.5	4.7	4.4	4.8	4.9	5.2	5.3	5.3	5.1	5.2	4.8	6.1	6.1	6.1	6.1	6.1	6.1	6.1	6.1	6.1	6.1	6.1	6.1	6.1	6.1	6.1	6.1	6.1	6.1	6.1	6.1	4.2	5.4%	4.4%	5.0
1.33	4.7%	1984	1940	4.1	4.2	4.3	4.2	4.2	4.3	4.1	4.3	4.4	4.5	4.3	4.6	4.6	5.1	5.1	5.1	4.9	5.0	4.4	5.1	6.4	6.4	6.4	6.4	6.4	6.4	6.4	6.4	6.4	6.4	6.4	6.4	6.4	6.4	6.4	6.4	6.4	6.4	6.4	6.4	4.1	5.5%	4.3%	4.8
1.33	4.7%	1985	1941	4.3	4.4	4.2	4.3	4.4	4.1	4.3	4.4	4.6	4.3	4.6	4.7	5.0	5.1	5.1	4.9	5.1	4.4	5.0	5.1	6.6	6.6	6.6	6.6	6.6	6.6	6.6	6.6	6.6	6.6	6.6	6.6	6.6	6.6	6.6	6.6	6.6	6.6	6.6	6.6	4.1	5.6%	4.4%	4.8
1.67	4.6%	1986	1942	4.2	4.0	4.1	4.2	3.9	4.1	4.2	4.3	4.1	4.4	4.4	4.8	4.8	4.9	4.7	4.8	4.4	4.8	4.9	4.9	6.4	6.4	6.4	6.4	6.4	6.4	6.4	6.4	6.4	6.4	6.4	6.4	6.4	6.4	6.4	6.4	6.4	6.4	6.4	6.4	3.9	5.4%	4.2%	4.4
1.67	4.6%	1987	1943	4.0	4.0	4.0	3.9	4.0	4.1	4.2	4.0	4.3	4.3	4.6	4.6	4.6	4.5	4.5	4.2	4.7	4.7	4.6	4.9	6.2	6.2	6.2	6.2	6.2	6.2	6.2	6.2	6.2	6.2	6.2	6.2	6.2	6.2	6.2	6.2	6.2	6.2	6.2	6.2	3.9	5.3%	4.1%	4.0
1.67	4.6%	1988	1944	4.1	4.2	4.0	4.2	4.2	4.4	4.2	4.5	4.5	4.8	4.8	4.9	4.7	4.8	4.4	4.8	5.0	4.8	4.9	4.8	6.1	6.1	6.1	6.1	6.1	6.1	6.1	6.1	6.1	6.1	6.1	6.1	6.1	6.1	6.1	6.1	6.1	6.1	6.1	6.1	4.0	5.4%	4.4%	4.5
1.67	4.6%	1989	1945	4.1	3.9	4.1	4.2	4.3	4.1	4.3	4.4	4.8	4.7	4.8	4.6	4.7	4.3	4.7	4.9	4.8	4.8	4.6	4.0	4.8	4.8	4.8	4.8	4.8	4.8	4.8	4.8	4.8	4.8	4.8	4.8	4.8	4.8	4.8	4.8	4.8	4.8	4.8	4.8	3.9	4.6%	4.3%	4.3
2.33	4.3%	1990	1946	3.8	4.0	4.1	4.2	4.0	4.3	4.3	4.6	4.7	4.6	4.5	4.5	4.2	4.6	4.7	4.6	4.8	4.5	3.9	4.0	5.0	5.0	5.0	5.0	5.0	5.0	5.0	5.0	5.0	5.0	5.0	5.0	5.0	5.0	5.0	5.0	5.0	5.0	5.0	5.0	3.9	4.7%	4.3%	4.2
2.00	4.4%	1991	1947	4.4	4.5	4.7	4.3	4.7	4.7	4.9	5.0	5.0	4.8	4.9	4.6	4.9	5.0	4.9	5.0	4.9	4.1	4.2	4.5	5.8	5.8	5.8	5.8	5.8	5.8	5.8	5.8	5.8	5.8	5.8	5.8	5.8	5.8	5.8	5.8	5.8	5.8	5.8	5.8	4.1	5.3%	4.7%	4.9
2.67	4.1%	1992	1948	4.2	4.3	4.0	4.4	4.4	4.7	4.7	4.7	4.6	4.6	4.2	4.6	4.6	4.6	4.7	4.5	3.9	4.0	4.1	4.7	5.8	5.8	5.8	5.8	5.8	5.8	5.8	5.8	5.8	5.8	5.8	5.8	5.8	5.8	5.8	5.8	5.8	5.8	5.8	5.8	3.9	5.1%	4.4%	4.3
3.00	4.0%	1993	1949	4.0	4.0	4.0	4.0	4.0	4.0	4.0	4.0	4.0	4.0	4.0	4.0	4.0	4.0	4.0	4.0	4.0	4.0	4.0	4.0	4.0	4.0	4.0	4.0	4.0	4.0	4.0	4.0	4.0	4.0	4.0	4.0	4.0	4.0	4.0	4.0	4.0	4.0	4.0	4.0	4.0	4.0%	4.0%	4.1
3.00	4.0%	1994	1950	4.0	4.0	4.0	4.0	4.0	4.0	4.0	4.0	4.0	4.0	4.0	4.0	4.0	4.0	4.0	4.0	4.0	4.0	4.0	4.0	4.0	4.0	4.0	4.0	4.0	4.0	4.0	4.0	4.0	4.0	4.0	4.0	4.0	4.0	4.0	4.0	4.0	4.0	4.0	4.0	4.0	4.0%	4.0%	4.0
3.33	3.9%	1995	1951	4.0	4.0	4.0	4.0	4.0	4.0	4.0	4.0	4.0	4.0	4.0	4.0	4.0	4.0	4.0	4.0	4.0	4.0	4.0	4.0	4.0	4.0	4.0	4.0	4.0	4.0	4.0	4.0	4.0	4.0	4.0	4.0	4.0	4.0	4.0	4.0	4.0	4.0	4.0	4.0	4.0	4.0%	4.0%	4.4
3.67	3.7%	1996	1952	4.0	4.0	4.0	4.0	4.0	4.0	4.0	4.0	4.0	4.0	4.0	4.0	4.0	4.0	4.0	4.0	4.0	4.0	4.0	4.0	4.0	4.0	4.0	4.0	4.0	4.0	4.0	4.0	4.0	4.0	4.0	4.0	4.0	4.0	4.0	4.0	4.0	4.0	4.0	4.0	4.0	4.0%	4.0%	3.8
3.67	3.7%	1997	1953	4.0	4.0	4.0	4.0	4.0	4.0	4.0	4.0	4.0	4.0	4.0	4.0	4.0	4.0	4.0	4.0	4.0	4.0	4.0	4.0	4.0	4.0	4.0	4.0	4.0	4.0	4.0	4.0	4.0	4.0	4.0	4.0	4.0	4.0	4.0	4.0	4.0	4.0	4.0	4.0	4.0	4.0%	4.0%	3.8
3.67	3.7%	1998	1954	4.0	4.0	4.0	4.0	4.0	4.0	4.0	4.0	4.0	4.0	4.0	4.0	4.0	4.0	4.0	4.0	4.0	4.0	4.0	4.0	4.0	4.0	4.0	4.0	4.0	4.0	4.0	4.0	4.0	4.0	4.0	4.0	4.0	4.0	4.0	4.0	4.0	4.0	4.0	4.0	4.0	4.0%	4.0%	3.4
3.67	3.7%	1999	1955	4.0	4.0	4.0	4.0	4.0	4.0	4.0	4.0	4.0	4.0	4.0	4.0	4.0	4.0	4.0	4.0	4.0	4.0	4.0	4.0	4.0	4.0	4.0	4.0	4.0	4.0	4.0	4.0	4.0	4.0	4.0	4.0	4.0	4.0	4.0	4.0	4.0	4.0	4.0	4.0	4.0	4.0%	4.0%	3.3
4.00	3.6%	2000	1956	4.0	4.0	4.0	4.0	4.0	4.0	4.0	4.0	4.0	4.0	4.0	4.0	4.0	4.0	4.0	4.0	4.0	4.0	4.0	4.0	4.0	4.0	4.0	4.0	4.0	4.0	4.0	4.0	4.0	4.0	4.0	4.0	4.0	4.0	4.0	4.0	4.0	4.0	4.0	4.0	4.0	4.0%	4.0%	3.2
																																											Totals	3.5	4.9%	4.2%	4.7%

FIGURE 182

Failure-market results with valuation-based purchasing of SPIA. For valuation levels of 3 or above, purchase 100% at age 65. For valuation levels below 3, purchase 50% at 65 and 50% at 85.

An indirect advantage of delaying GI is better opportunities for TIPS, not just an SPIA. TIPS are usually too expensive when building longer ladders, but they become reasonably priced for a 20-year ladder. When the bequest value is important, a delayed purchase is an especially opportune for building a TIPS ladder.

The consistent results shown using valuations are partly due to hedging: only half the desired GI rate is ever timed. As discussed in Chapter 9, valuations are best used in moderation. The same is seen with GI. The data show that results are poorer when valuations are ignored, but also that results are poorer when valuations are overemphasized by delaying 100% of a GI purchase instead of 50%.

A valid question remains as to whether valuations will correctly gauge yet-to-be-seen failure-market conditions? There is no way to know for sure. Not only is data limited, the domain is speculative risk. Ultimately, each retiree has to decide if using valuation hints provide a net advantage over no hints at all. For this case and a couple of others (e.g., setting the initial withdrawal rate), the opinion is, they are worth the level of concern they introduce, although the opposite conclusion was reached for using valuations within income harvesting: the details matter.

The next section uses this strategy along with others to form an overall recommendation for GI.

THE RECOMMENDATIONS: A COMBINATION OF STRATEGIES AND COSTS

The aim of GI here is to ensure an income floor greater than a retiree's essential-income rate. As shown, this doesn't mean 100% of the essential-income rate is locked in using GI — it's reasonable to rely on systemic withdrawals to meet a portion of the essential income needs in order to reduce the cost of GI and maintain flexibility. The key question then becomes, what combination of GI strategies and systemic withdrawals can reliably provide the essential-income rate under failure-market conditions for a reasonable cost? This answer is addressed in the primary recommendations.

Without compromises, planning quickly ends up in a corner without a satisfactory solution. Consider the following GI challenges. It's safer to lock in the full essential-income rate at the beginning of retirement, but this can be expensive, as is locking in from the beginning. Also, the cheapest and sometimes only affordable GI solution comes from an inflation-adjusted SPIA. The downside is that control of the associated assets is lost along with the bequest value, a problem for many retirees. Also, SPIAs depend on the solvency of their issuing insurance company, which raises a concern we'd rather not have to content with during a failure market. Moving away from an SPIA to a TIPS ladder gains the backing of the US government, but at a cost few retirees can afford for retirements over 30 years. I Bonds, another alternative, are exceptionally flexible as a backup solution, but generally insufficient for a primary solution, plus they are even more expensive than TIPS. None of these challenges with GI can be sidestepped by allocating additional assets. Additional assets lock in a higher rate of GI, by taking away from systemic withdrawals. Systemic withdrawals are the most flexible and strongest income source, and as such, hedge well against unexpected expenses, which, like failure markets, manifest in insufficient income. One risk of insufficient income is as bad as the other, plus the risk from both is unmeasurable. Ultimately, compromises are required for a pragmatic solution.

The best compromises cannot include absolute guarantees. The aim for GI then shouldn't be the absence of risk, but a substantial reduction in risk, well under what systemic withdrawal provides alone. This requires using GI in moderation, with compromises, alongside systemic withdrawals. Most retirees find that a small amount of risk is acceptable when the benefits are sizeable.

The following recommendations provide a balance between many compromises, boiling down a diverse set of options into a small set of straightforward choices, adaptable to many individual plans. Remember, these recommendations depend on affordability, specific to each retiree's circumstances and outlook. If a retiree can't find an affordable GI plan, then GI should not be used. Also keep in mind, these recommendation take into account the income-floor characteristics of ECM; however, enough data has been shown in this chapter to reasonably adapt the recommendations to a different variable-withdrawal strategies if preferred.

The primary recommendations follow:

1. A. When valuations are high at the start of retirement (i.e., the valuation level is 3 or above)

   a. Immediately lock in a *minimum* of 50% of the essential-income rate with inflation-adjusted SPIAs.

   B. Otherwise, when valuations are not high at the start of retirement (i.e., the valuation level is less than 3)

   a. Immediately lock in a *minimum* of 25% the essential-income rate with inflation-adjusted SPIAs.

   b. Around age 85, lock in another *minimum* of 25% of essential income with a TIPS ladder (or optionally another SPIA if there is no bequest motive), using systemic-withdrawal assets.

2. Optionally, for additional protection, at the start of retirement allocate 5% (or more) of total assets to a standby bond pool. This pool might be used later in life for income shortfalls, emergencies, purchasing an SPIA, or building a TIPS ladder.

3. Allocate the remaining assets to systemic withdrawals following best practices, with ECM (i.e., the best for failure markets) used in place of EM.

The above recommendations define the timing, the instruments, and the minimum percentage of the essential-income rate to lock in by purchasing GI. The minimum percentage might only barely supply the essential rate under the failure-market baseline. Whether or not to go higher, potentially locking in up to 100% of the essential-income rate, is an individual decision. Any retiree preferring not to use valuations can simply take the more conservative option: immediately lock in 50% or more of the essential-income rate.

Tests below show the results and costs of following the recommendations. Retirees can then decide where they fit on the spectrum of deploying GI, if at all.

To set the stage, Figure 183 shows systemic withdrawals results using ECM under failure-market conditions without GI. Only insufficient income is highlighted, which for this example is everything under 3%. Without GI, the figure shows 35 different retirement periods with income falling under 3%, with consistent shortages starting as early as 6 years into retirement. (Note the results would have been substantially worse using EM.)

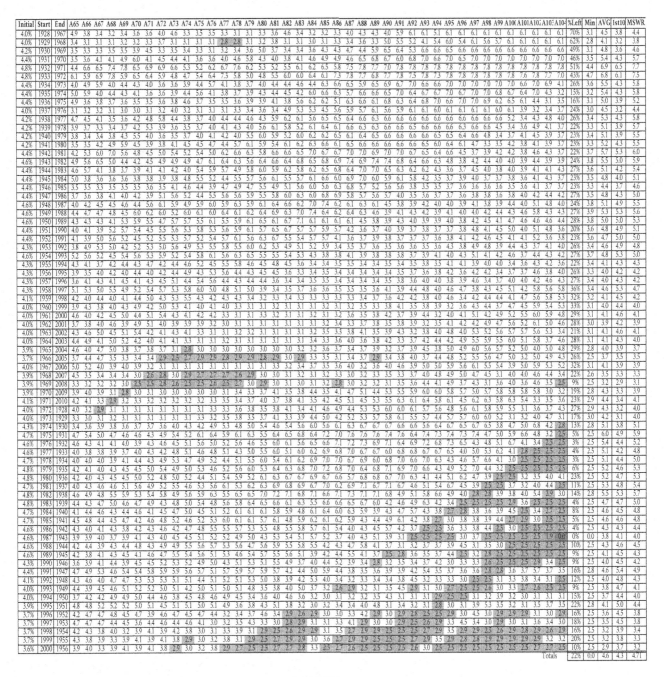

FIGURE 183

Systemic-withdrawal's failure-market benchmark with annual income below 3% highlighted.

Now the same failure-market scenario is considered using the *minimum* GI recommendations. Again the essential-income rate is 3%. As earlier, GI payout rates are assumed to be low: inflation-adjusted SPIA rates pay 4.01% for a couple at age 65; a 20-year TIPS ladder has a 1% real IRR generating a 5.54% payout (compared to an SPIA's 9.07% payout at age 85).

For this example the minimum recommendations translate to the following parameters for backtesting:

1. A. If the valuation level is 3 or above at the start of retirement
    - 50% of the essential-income rate is locked in with SPIAs. For the 3% essential-income rate, this means 1.5% is locked in annually by allocating 37.5% of total assets to an inflation-adjusted SPIAs with a 4.01% payout rate (i.e., 37.5% of 4.01% is 1.5%).

    B. Otherwise, when the valuation level is less than 3 at the start of retirement

    - 25% of essential-income rate is locked in with SPIAs. For the 3% essential-income rate, this means 0.75% is locked in by allocating 18.75% of total assets to an inflation-adjusted SPIA with a 4.01% payout rate (i.e., 18.75% of 4.01% is 0.75%).
    - At age 85, another 25% of essential income is locked in with a TIPS ladder, pulling the assets from systemic withdrawals. For the 3% essential-income rate, this means 0.75% is locked in using 13.5%* of total assets for a 20-year TIPS ladder with a payout of 5.54% based on a 1% real IRR (i.e., 13.5% of 5.54% is 0.75%).

2. No standby bond pool is used, keeping the GI solution to a minimum.

3. The remaining assets (depending on valuations either 62.5% or 67.75% of total assets) are allocated to systemic withdrawals using the recommended mechanics (e.g., 55% stocks, 40% tilt) with ECM.

Figure 184 shows results using the above minimum parameters on the failure market benchmark (with the right-hand columns showing the final allocation between systemic withdrawals, SPIAs, and TIPS). Considering the context, the results are solid. There is a strong improvement over the pure systemic-withdrawal results in Figure 183. Income drops below 3% in only 3 retirement periods, down from the 35 periods without GI. Of these, the portfolio fails once in the 1987 retirement, near age 103. For the other two shortages, the income dropped just below 3%, to 2.9%, but in both cases enough remaining funds were available to meet the essential rate. These results are important for two reasons. First, they identify a minimal solution for handling failure-market conditions. Second, they show only about 40% of total assets were required, even though interest rates were low, keeping approximately 60% in systemic withdrawals. This represents the minimum plan that should virtually always work.

---

*   The percentage of assets is fixed, so the actual lock-in rate relative to the start of retirement varies as the portfolio value grows or shrinks over 20 years. Locking in a constant rate instead doesn't fundamentally change the backtesting results.

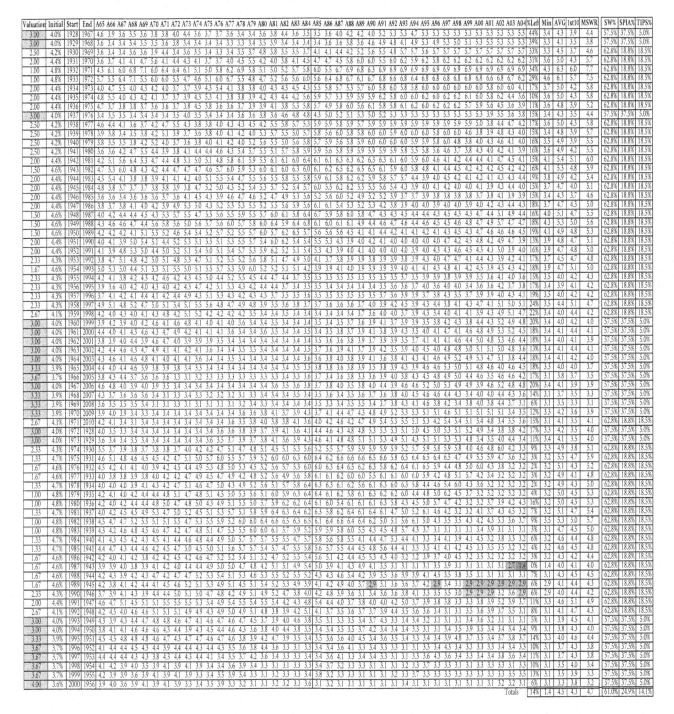

FIGURE 184

Failure-market results for basic GI recommendation when interest rates are low. Inflation-adjusted SPIA payout at 65 is 4.01%. 20-year TIPS ladder payout at age 85 is 5.54% based on a 1% real IRR. From 57.5% to 62.8% of total assets remain in systemic withdrawals.

Figure 185 shows the same scenario, but this time a moderate payout rate from higher interest rates is assumed. The same percentage of the portfolio is used as in the previous example, but because it buys more (i.e., GI is cheaper), a high percentage of the essential-income rate is locked in. The exact parameters follow:

1. If the valuation level is 3 or above at the start of retirement
    *   A 1.9% income rate is locked in annually by again allocating 37.5% of total assets to an inflation-adjusted SPIA with a 5.01% payout rate (37.5% of 5.01% is 1.9%).

2. Otherwise, when the valuation level is less than 3 at the start of retirement
    *   A 0.94% income rate is locked in annually by allocating 18.75% of total assets to an inflation-adjusted SPIA with a 5.01% payout rate (18.75% of 5.01% is 0.94%).
    *   At age 85, another 0.8% of income is locked in annually by allocating 13.5% of total assets to a 20-year TIPS ladder with a payout of 6.1%, based on a 2% real IRR (13.5% of 6.1% is 0.8%).

3. To keep the GI solution to a minimum, no standby bond pool is used.

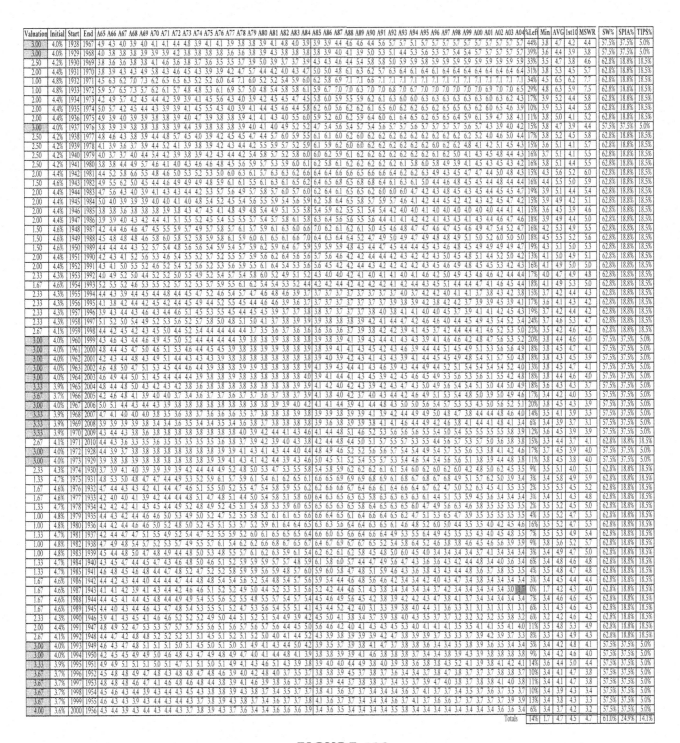

FIGURE 185

*Failure-market results for basic GI recommendation when interest rates are moderate.
Inflation-adjusted SPIA payout at 65 is 5.01%. 20-year TIPS ladder payout at age 85 is 6.1%
based on a 2% real IRR. From 57.5% to 62.8% of total assets remain in systemic withdrawals.*

319

This time, there is only one case where income drops under 3%, and not until age 104. Higher interest rates support locking in a higher percentage of essential income for the same cost (e.g., a 1.9% rate instead of 1.5% with high valuations). As expected, a higher GI payout rate improves total income throughout retirement. It's also notable that using another SPIA at age 85 instead of the TIPS ladder would have increased income above what is shown.

Of course, locking in a full 100% of essential income at the beginning of retirement eliminates the possibility of a shortage, but this guarantee comes at a much higher cost: 75% of the portfolio is needed for the first case above, and 60% for the second.

Another alternative for the second example is to again lock in only the minimal 1.5% initially, using 30% of the total assets (given the higher 5.01% payout rate). This would leave 70% in systemic withdrawals. Doing so produced very similar results, with again only the 1987 retirement period dropping below the 3% rate, but this time a year earlier at age 103.

Locking in 50% of the essential-income rate is the lower bound for effective GI, while locking in 100% is the upper bound. Between lies a spectrum: as the lock-in rate increases, failure-market risk lowers, but so does affordability. Putting 5% or more in a standby bond pool, drawing on it as needed, may be the lowest-cost approach for reducing risk beyond the minimum GI allocation, although it comes with the significant downside of immediately lowering income by 5%. The cost of GI is explored next in much more detail.

The preceding analysis is based on the failure-market benchmark, which is the target condition for GI. However, it's the Baseline Market that represents what today's retirees will likely encounter. The same two cases (shown in Figure 184 and Figure 185) can be retested using the Baseline Market, providing a different perspective and eventually a better understanding of GI costs.

Figure 186 shows the Baseline Market results matching the failure-market results in Figure 184 with the same parameters and GI payouts. Likewise, Figure 187 shows the Baseline Market results matching the failure-market results in Figure 185 with the same parameters and GI payouts. These two cases provide a realistic estimate of the type of income a retiree might expect in the future using the minimum GI recommendations with systemic withdrawals. (Returning to an earlier convention, these figures only highlight returns under 4%.)

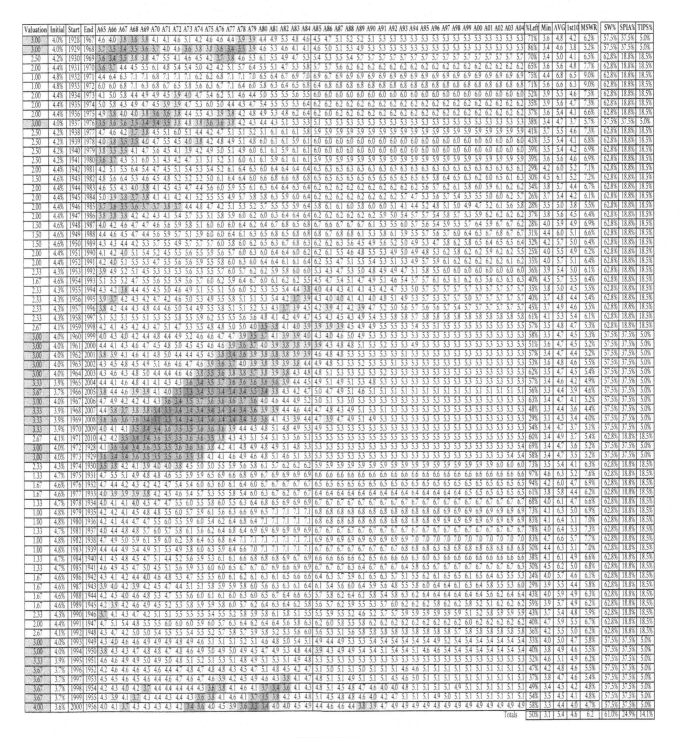

FIGURE 186

*Baseline Market results for basic GI recommendation when interest rates
are low. Inflation-adjusted SPIA payout at 65 is 4.01%. 20-year TIPS
ladder payout at age 85 is 5.54% based on a 1% real IRR.*

Valuation	Initial	Start	End	A65	A66	A67	A68	A69	A70	A71	A72	A73	A74	A75	A76	A77	A78	A79	A80	A81	A82	A83	A84	A85	A86	A87	A88	A89	A90	A91	A92	A93	A94	A95	A96	A97	A98	A99	A00	A01	A02	A03	A04	%Left	Min	AVG	1st10	MSWR	SW%	SPIA%	TIPS%
3.00	4.0%	1928	1967	5.0	4.4	4.1	3.9	4.1	4.5	4.5	5.0	5.4	4.6	5.0	5.0	4.8	4.3	4.3	4.8	5.3	5.7	5.2	4.9	4.9	5.1	5.4	5.6	5.6	5.4	5.7	5.7	5.7	5.7	5.7	5.7	5.7	5.7	5.7	5.7	5.7	5.7	5.7	5.7	71%	3.9	5.2	4.6	6.2%	57.5%	37.5%	5.0%
3.00	4.0%	1929	1968	4.1	3.9	3.8	3.9	4.0	4.1	4.4	5.0	4.0	4.2	4.2	4.0	3.8	3.9	4.3	4.9	5.7	4.9	4.5	5.0	5.4	5.5	5.3	5.7	5.7	5.7	5.7	5.7	5.7	5.7	5.7	5.7	5.7	5.7	5.7	5.7	5.7	5.7	5.7	5.7	86%	3.8	5.0	4.1	5.2%	57.5%	37.5%	5.0%
2.50	4.2%	1930	1969	4.6	3.7	4.0	4.0	4.8	5.7	4.3	4.8	4.7	4.4	3.9	3.9	4.8	5.5	6.3	5.7	5.1	4.9	5.5	5.6	5.6	5.8	5.6	5.9	5.9	5.9	5.9	5.9	5.9	5.9	5.9	5.9	5.9	5.9	5.9	5.9	5.9	5.9	5.9	5.9	70%	3.6	5.3	4.3	6.5%	62.8%	18.8%	18.5%
2.00	4.4%	1931	1970	3.8	3.9	4.6	4.7	5.7	6.3	5.0	5.6	5.6	5.2	4.4	4.5	5.3	5.9	6.6	5.7	5.2	4.8	5.5	6.0	5.9	6.0	5.9	6.4	6.4	6.4	6.4	6.4	6.4	6.4	6.4	6.4	6.4	6.4	6.4	6.4	6.4	6.4	6.4	6.4	65%	3.8	5.8	5.0	7.7%	62.8%	18.8%	18.5%
1.00	4.8%	1932	1971	4.6	6.5	6.5	7.3	7.3	7.0	7.3	7.3	7.3	6.4	6.4	7.0	7.3	7.3	7.2	6.7	6.6	6.9	7.2	7.1	7.0	7.1	7.1	7.1	7.1	7.1	7.1	7.1	7.1	7.1	7.1	7.1	7.1	7.1	7.1	7.1	7.1	7.1	7.1	7.1	75%	4.6	7.0	6.7	9.0%	62.8%	18.8%	18.5%
1.00	4.8%	1933	1972	6.1	6.1	7.0	7.3	6.5	7.0	6.9	6.7	6.0	5.8	6.5	6.9	7.3	6.6	6.1	6.0	6.5	6.0	6.7	7.0	6.6	7.0	7.0	7.0	7.0	7.0	7.0	7.0	7.0	7.0	7.0	7.0	7.0	7.0	7.0	7.0	7.0	7.0	7.0	7.0	71%	5.8	6.8	6.5	9.0%	62.8%	18.8%	18.5%
2.00	4.4%	1934	1973	4.3	5.2	6.0	4.6	5.1	5.1	4.7	4.1	4.2	4.8	5.6	6.4	5.3	4.8	4.6	5.2	5.7	5.8	5.7	6.3	6.3	6.3	6.3	6.3	6.3	6.3	6.3	6.3	6.3	6.3	6.3	6.3	6.3	6.3	6.3	6.3	6.3	6.3	6.3	6.3	52%	4.1	5.7	4.8	7.5%	62.8%	18.8%	18.5%
2.00	4.4%	1935	1974	5.2	6.0	4.5	5.1	4.9	4.7	4.1	4.1	4.8	5.5	6.2	5.2	4.6	4.5	4.9	5.2	5.7	5.7	5.5	6.5	6.5	6.5	6.5	6.5	6.5	6.5	6.5	6.5	6.5	6.5	6.5	6.5	6.5	6.5	6.5	6.5	6.5	6.5	6.5	6.5	35%	4.1	5.8	4.9	7.3%	62.8%	18.8%	18.5%
2.00	4.4%	1936	1975	5.1	3.9	4.2	4.2	4.0	3.8	3.8	4.0	4.6	5.7	4.5	4.1	4.0	4.4	5.0	5.1	5.5	5.0	6.4	6.6	6.5	6.2	6.5	6.5	6.5	6.5	6.5	6.5	6.5	6.5	6.5	6.5	6.5	6.5	6.5	6.5	6.5	6.5	6.5	6.5	37%	3.8	5.6	4.3	6.6%	62.8%	18.8%	18.5%
3.00	4.0%	1937	1976	3.9	3.9	3.9	3.9	3.8	3.9	4.2	5.1	4.2	4.0	3.9	4.2	4.6	4.6	4.8	4.7	5.5	5.7	5.7	5.7	5.7	5.4	5.7	5.7	5.7	5.7	5.7	5.7	5.7	5.7	5.7	5.7	5.7	5.7	5.7	5.7	5.7	5.7	5.7	5.7	38%	3.8	5.0	4.1	5.7%	57.5%	37.5%	5.0%
2.50	4.2%	1938	1977	4.9	4.8	4.4	3.9	3.9	4.7	5.3	6.2	5.2	4.6	4.4	4.9	5.3	5.3	5.4	5.3	6.3	6.3	6.0	6.2	6.2	6.2	6.2	6.2	6.2	6.2	6.2	6.2	6.2	6.2	6.2	6.2	6.2	6.2	6.2	6.2	6.2	6.2	6.2	6.2	41%	3.9	5.7	4.8	7.3%	62.8%	18.8%	18.5%
2.50	4.2%	1939	1978	4.2	3.9	3.7	4.7	4.2	4.0	4.4	5.0	5.1	5.3	5.0	6.2	6.3	6.3	6.1	6.3	6.2	6.2	6.2	6.2	6.2	6.2	6.2	6.2	6.2	6.2	6.2	6.2	6.2	6.2	6.2	6.2	6.2	6.2	6.2	6.2	6.2	6.2	6.2	6.2	43%	3.7	5.6	4.3	6.8%	62.8%	18.8%	18.5%
2.50	4.2%	1940	1979	4.0	3.7	4.3	4.9	5.8	4.7	4.3	4.1	4.4	5.1	5.2	5.2	5.1	6.1	6.3	6.3	6.1	6.3	6.2	6.2	6.2	6.2	6.2	6.2	6.2	6.2	6.2	6.2	6.2	6.2	6.2	6.2	6.2	6.2	6.2	6.2	6.2	6.2	6.2	6.2	39%	3.7	5.7	4.4	6.9%	62.8%	18.8%	18.5%
2.50	4.2%	1941	1980	3.8	3.9	4.5	5.3	6.1	5.2	4.5	4.4	4.9	5.2	5.2	5.4	5.2	6.1	6.3	6.3	6.1	6.3	6.2	6.2	6.2	6.2	6.2	6.2	6.2	6.2	6.2	6.2	6.2	6.2	6.2	6.2	6.2	6.2	6.2	6.2	6.2	6.2	6.2	6.2	39%	3.8	5.8	4.8	6.9%	62.8%	18.8%	18.5%
2.00	4.4%	1942	1981	4.4	5.2	5.7	6.6	5.6	4.9	4.7	5.2	5.6	5.6	5.4	6.3	6.6	6.5	6.1	6.6	6.6	6.6	6.6	6.6	6.6	6.6	6.6	6.6	6.6	6.6	6.6	6.6	6.6	6.6	6.6	6.6	6.6	6.6	6.6	6.6	6.6	6.6	6.6	6.6	29%	4.4	6.2	5.3	7.1%	62.8%	18.8%	18.5%
1.50	4.6%	1943	1982	5.0	5.8	6.6	5.5	4.8	4.7	5.0	5.4	5.4	5.4	5.2	6.3	6.6	6.5	6.1	6.8	7.0	6.8	7.0	7.0	6.8	6.8	6.8	6.8	6.8	6.8	6.8	6.8	6.8	6.8	6.8	6.8	6.8	6.8	6.8	6.8	6.8	6.8	6.8	6.8	30%	4.7	6.3	5.4	7.2%	62.8%	18.8%	18.5%
2.00	4.4%	1944	1983	4.8	5.7	4.5	4.2	4.1	4.7	5.0	5.1	5.1	6.1	5.7	6.3	6.5	6.5	6.6	6.6	6.5	6.1	6.2	6.6	6.5	6.5	6.3	6.5	6.4	5.8	6.0	6.5	6.4	6.0	6.2	6.2	6.4	6.5	6.5	6.5	6.5	6.5	6.5	6.5	34%	4.0	5.9	4.6	6.7%	62.8%	18.8%	18.5%
2.00	4.4%	1945	1984	5.2	4.1	3.9	3.9	4.3	4.3	4.4	4.3	5.4	5.7	5.7	5.9	6.0	6.0	6.1	6.2	6.6	6.5	6.5	6.5	6.5	6.5	6.0	4.9	5.6	5.9	6.0	5.7	5.5	5.8	6.3	6.3	6.5	6.5	6.5	6.5	6.5	6.5	6.5	6.5	26%	3.9	5.6	4.4	6.4%	62.8%	18.8%	18.5%
2.00	4.4%	1946	1985	3.9	3.8	3.7	3.8	3.9	3.9	3.9	4.6	5.0	4.8	4.4	5.2	5.5	5.4	5.9	5.7	5.7	6.1	6.5	6.1	6.3	6.2	6.1	6.3	6.5	5.3	4.4	4.7	5.5	5.1	5.3	5.3	6.3	6.5	5.8	6.1	6.1	6.1	6.1	6.1	28%	3.7	5.2	4.0	5.5%	62.8%	18.8%	18.5%
2.00	4.4%	1947	1986	4.0	3.9	4.0	4.4	4.4	4.5	4.3	5.6	5.9	5.7	5.2	6.0	6.1	6.1	6.4	6.1	6.5	6.6	6.4	6.4	6.4	6.4	6.2	5.7	6.0	6.0	5.6	6.1	6.4	6.4	6.4	6.4	3.7	3.9	5.8	4.9	7.1%	62.8%	18.8%	18.5%
1.50	4.6%	1948	1987	4.2	4.4	4.8	4.8	4.9	4.8	5.8	6.1	6.0	6.1	6.2	6.2	6.6	6.4	6.4	6.5	6.9	7.0	6.7	7.0	7.0	7.0	7.0	7.0	7.0	7.0	6.4	5.6	5.8	6.0	5.9	5.7	5.2	5.6	6.0	6.7	6.2	7.0	7.0	6.4	28%	4.2	6.1	5.1	6.9%	62.8%	18.8%	18.5%
1.50	4.6%	1949	1988	4.6	4.8	4.7	4.8	4.6	5.8	6.1	5.9	5.2	6.1	6.2	6.5	6.3	6.5	6.7	7.0	6.7	7.0	7.0	7.1	7.1	7.1	7.1	6.4	5.6	6.1	6.4	6.2	5.7	6.0	5.9	6.0	6.3	6.7	6.6	7.0	7.1	7.0	7.0	7.0	31%	4.6	6.2	5.3	6.6%	62.8%	18.8%	18.5%
1.50	4.6%	1950	1989	4.5	4.5	4.6	4.5	5.9	5.7	5.1	5.9	5.9	5.9	6.2	6.0	6.9	6.5	6.9	7.0	6.5	6.5	6.8	6.8	6.7	6.8	6.7	6.8	6.1	6.4	6.0	6.8	6.7	6.8	6.8	6.7	32%	4.4	5.9	5.2	6.4%	62.8%	18.8%	18.5%
2.00	4.4%	1951	1990	3.3	4.4	4.2	5.2	5.6	5.4	4.7	5.7	5.7	5.8	5.7	6.1	5.8	5.9	6.2	6.5	6.2	6.6	6.0	6.2	6.4	6.5	3.5	4.9	5.1	5.1	5.6	6.5	6.5	6.5	6.5	6.5	25%	4.2	5.7	5.1	6.4%	62.8%	18.8%	18.5%
2.00	4.4%	1952	1991	4.4	4.2	5.2	5.7	5.5	4.9	5.7	5.8	5.8	6.1	5.7	6.0	6.1	6.5	6.1	6.6	6.0	6.3	6.6	6.6	5.7	4.9	5.4	5.7	5.7	5.4	5.5	6.4	6.5	6.5	6.5	6.5	35%	4.2	5.9	5.3	6.4%	62.8%	18.8%	18.5%
2.33	4.3%	1953	1992	4.1	5.1	5.4	5.3	4.7	5.5	5.5	5.8	5.3	5.7	5.9	6.1	5.9	6.4	6.6	6.4	6.6	6.0	6.1	5.5	5.3	5.3	5.1	5.2	5.1	4.9	5.4	6.2	6.2	6.2	6.2	6.2	36%	4.1	5.7	5.2	6.1%	62.8%	18.8%	18.5%
1.67	4.6%	1954	1993	5.3	5.7	5.4	4.9	5.7	5.8	5.7	6.1	5.8	5.9	6.1	6.4	6.1	6.6	6.9	6.1	6.3	6.4	6.4	5.7	4.7	4.9	5.6	5.4	5.0	5.1	5.3	4.9	5.7	5.9	5.9	6.3	40%	4.7	5.9	5.6	6.4%	62.8%	18.8%	18.5%
2.33	4.3%	1955	1994	4.5	4.4	4.7	4.7	5.2	4.8	5.1	5.7	5.3	5.7	5.8	6.2	5.4	5.5	5.5	5.6	4.4	4.4	4.4	4.6	4.4	4.9	5.5	5.2	5.9	5.9	5.9	5.9	5.9	5.9	5.9	5.9	35%	3.9	5.2	4.7	5.5%	62.8%	18.8%	18.5%
2.33	4.3%	1956	1995	4.1	3.9	4.4	4.5	4.4	4.9	4.8	5.2	5.5	5.7	6.0	5.3	5.3	5.5	5.6	4.4	3.9	4.1	4.5	4.3	4.2	4.3	4.3	5.0	5.3	5.1	5.6	5.9	5.9	5.9	5.9	5.9	40%	3.9	5.0	4.6	5.4%	62.8%	18.8%	18.5%
2.33	4.3%	1957	1996	3.9	4.4	4.6	4.5	5.0	4.6	4.8	5.2	5.6	5.1	5.7	6.0	5.2	5.3	5.4	5.5	3.9	4.1	4.7	4.4	4.2	4.3	4.4	4.2	4.9	5.3	5.9	5.9	5.9	5.9	5.9	5.9	45%	3.9	5.1	4.8	5.4%	62.8%	18.8%	18.5%
2.33	4.3%	1958	1997	5.2	5.4	5.3	5.7	5.3	5.5	5.7	6.0	5.7	6.1	6.4	5.7	5.7	5.8	5.8	5.0	4.3	4.4	5.1	5.6	6.0	6.0	6.0	6.0	6.0	6.0	6.0	6.0	6.0	6.0	6.0	6.0	61%	4.3	5.5	5.6	6.1%	62.8%	18.8%	18.5%
2.67	4.1%	1959	1998	4.4	4.3	4.7	4.4	4.5	4.9	5.2	4.8	5.5	5.7	5.0	5.0	5.2	5.2	4.7	3.9	4.3	4.2	4.1	4.1	4.1	4.8	5.2	5.1	5.7	5.7	5.6	5.6	5.7	5.3	5.7	5.7	37%	3.7	5.0	4.8	5.3%	62.8%	18.8%	18.5%
3.00	4.0%	1960	1999	4.4	4.7	4.4	4.6	5.1	4.8	5.3	5.6	4.9	4.9	5.1	5.1	4.3	3.9	4.1	4.5	4.3	4.3	4.4	5.0	5.4	5.3	5.7	5.7	5.7	5.6	5.7	5.7	5.7	5.7	5.7	5.7	57%	3.9	5.1	4.9	5.3%	57.5%	37.5%	5.0%
3.00	4.0%	1961	2000	4.8	4.5	4.6	4.9	5.1	4.9	5.2	5.4	4.9	4.9	5.0	5.0	4.3	3.9	4.1	4.4	4.3	4.2	4.3	4.3	4.4	5.0	5.4	5.3	5.7	5.6	5.7	5.6	5.7	5.7	5.7	5.7	51%	3.9	5.1	4.9	5.2%	57.5%	37.5%	5.0%
3.00	4.0%	1962	2001	4.2	4.3	4.5	4.5	5.2	5.4	4.8	4.8	4.9	4.9	4.1	3.8	3.9	4.2	4.1	4.2	4.3	4.3	5.0	5.4	5.7	5.7	5.7	5.6	5.7	5.7	5.7	5.7	5.7	5.7	5.7	5.7	58%	3.8	5.0	4.7	5.2%	57.5%	37.5%	5.0%
3.00	4.0%	1963	2002	4.6	4.9	5.1	4.9	5.3	5.4	4.9	4.9	5.1	5.0	4.3	3.9	4.1	4.4	4.3	4.3	5.1	5.6	5.7	5.6	5.7	5.7	5.7	5.7	5.7	5.7	5.7	5.7	5.7	5.7	5.7	5.7	53%	3.9	5.1	5.0	5.5%	57.5%	37.5%	5.0%
3.00	4.0%	1964	2003	4.6	5.0	4.6	5.2	5.4	4.8	4.8	4.9	4.9	4.1	3.9	3.9	4.2	4.1	4.2	4.3	4.1	4.6	5.2	5.7	5.7	5.6	5.7	5.6	5.7	5.7	5.7	5.7	5.7	5.7	5.7	5.7	62%	3.9	5.1	4.8	5.4%	57.5%	37.5%	5.0%
3.33	3.9%	1965	2004	4.8	4.4	4.9	5.1	4.5	4.6	4.0	3.8	3.9	4.1	3.9	3.9	4.0	4.0	4.3	4.8	5.3	5.4	5.3	5.5	5.6	5.6	5.6	5.6	5.6	5.6	5.6	5.6	5.6	5.6	5.6	5.6	59%	3.7	5.0	4.5	4.9%	57.5%	37.5%	5.0%
3.67	3.7%	1966	2005	4.2	4.8	4.9	4.3	4.3	4.4	3.9	3.9	3.8	3.8	3.9	3.8	4.0	4.2	4.6	5.1	5.4	5.3	5.4	4.9	5.4	5.4	5.4	5.4	5.4	5.4	5.4	5.4	5.4	5.4	5.4	5.4	56%	3.7	4.8	4.3	4.6%	57.5%	37.5%	5.0%
3.00	4.0%	1967	2006	5.1	5.3	4.6	4.7	4.7	4.0	3.8	3.9	4.1	4.0	3.9	4.0	4.1	4.0	4.4	4.9	4.8	5.3	5.6	5.7	5.7	5.7	5.7	5.7	5.7	5.7	5.7	5.7	5.7	5.7	5.7	5.7	63%	3.8	5.1	4.5	4.9%	57.5%	37.5%	5.0%
3.33	3.9%	1968	2007	4.8	4.1	4.1	4.2	4.1	3.8	3.8	3.8	3.9	3.9	3.9	3.9	3.9	4.3	4.8	5.0	4.8	5.1	5.2	4.7	5.3	4.9	5.7	5.7	5.6	5.6	5.6	5.6	5.6	5.6	5.6	5.6	48%	3.7	4.8	4.0	4.0%	57.5%	37.5%	5.0%
3.33	3.9%	1969	2008	3.9	3.9	3.9	4.0	3.8	3.4	3.4	3.8	3.8	3.8	3.8	3.8	4.0	4.0	4.4	4.4	4.3	4.8	5.1	4.3	5.1	5.3	5.5	5.3	5.6	5.6	5.6	5.6	5.6	5.6	5.6	5.6	29%	3.4	4.7	3.8	4.0%	57.5%	37.5%	5.0%
3.33	3.9%	1970	2009	4.4	4.5	4.4	3.9	3.8	3.8	3.9	3.9	3.9	4.0	3.9	4.1	4.4	4.4	4.4	4.7	5.2	5.4	5.2	5.3	5.6	5.6	5.6	5.6	5.6	5.6	5.6	5.6	5.6	5.6	5.6	5.6	54%	3.8	5.0	4.1	5.4%	57.5%	37.5%	5.0%
2.67	4.1%	1971	2010	4.4	4.4	3.9	3.8	3.8	3.9	3.9	3.9	4.0	4.0	4.5	4.5	4.5	5.2	5.0	5.3	5.5	5.3	5.7	5.7	5.7	5.7	5.7	5.7	5.7	5.7	5.7	5.7	5.7	5.8	60%	3.5	5.1	3.8	5.4%	62.8%	18.8%	18.5%
3.00	4.0%	1972	1928	4.4	3.9	3.8	3.8	3.9	3.9	4.0	3.9	3.9	4.0	4.0	4.4	4.4	4.4	4.7	5.2	5.4	5.2	5.3	5.6	5.6	5.6	5.6	5.7	5.7	5.7	5.7	5.7	5.7	5.7	5.7	5.7	69%	3.8	5.1	4.0	5.2%	57.5%	37.5%	5.0%
3.00	4.0%	1973	1929	3.9	3.8	3.9	3.9	3.9	3.9	4.1	4.4	4.4	5.0	4.5	4.7	5.7	5.7	5.7	5.7	5.7	5.7	5.7	5.7	5.7	5.7	5.7	5.7	5.7	5.7	5.7	5.7	5.7	5.7	5.7	5.8	58%	3.8	5.1	3.9	5.2%	57.5%	37.5%	5.0%
2.33	4.3%	1974	1930	3.2	3.9	4.4	4.3	4.1	4.2	4.2	4.0	4.7	5.2	5.2	5.7	6.1	5.8	6.0	6.3	5.9	6.4	6.4	6.2	6.2	6.2	6.2	6.2	6.2	6.2	6.2	6.2	6.2	6.2	6.2	6.2	73%	3.7	5.7	4.3	6.3%	62.8%	18.8%	18.5%
1.33	4.7%	1975	1931	4.8	5.7	5.3	5.1	5.0	5.0	4.8	5.7	6.1	6.1	6.7	7.1	6.8	7.0	7.1	6.9	7.1	7.1	6.9	6.9	6.9	6.9	6.9	6.9	6.9	6.9	6.9	6.9	6.9	6.9	6.9	6.9	97%	4.8	6.5	5.4	7.6%	62.8%	18.8%	18.5%
1.67	4.6%	1976	1932	4.8	4.6	4.4	4.5	4.4	4.4	4.9	5.6	5.6	6.1	6.7	7.1	6.8	7.1	6.9	6.9	6.9	6.9	6.9	6.7	6.7	6.7	6.7	6.7	6.8	6.8	6.8	6.8	6.8	6.9	6.9	6.9	94%	4.4	6.3	4.9	6.9%	62.8%	18.8%	18.5%
1.67	4.6%	1977	1933	4.2	4.1	4.1	4.1	4.0	4.4	4.7	4.8	5.6	5.7	6.1	6.6	6.9	6.9	6.9	6.9	6.9	6.7	6.7	6.7	6.7	6.7	6.7	6.7	6.7	6.7	6.7	6.7	6.7	6.7	6.7	6.7	61%	4.0	6.0	4.6	6.2%	62.8%	18.8%	18.5%
1.33	4.7%	1978	1934	4.2	4.3	4.3	4.2	4.5	4.9	4.9	5.7	6.1	5.7	6.0	6.2	5.7	6.6	6.6	7.0	6.7	7.1	7.1	7.1	6.9	6.9	6.9	6.9	6.9	6.9	6.9	6.9	6.9	6.9	6.9	6.9	68%	4.2	6.3	4.9	6.6%	62.8%	18.8%	18.5%
1.00	4.8%	1979	1935	4.4	4.4	4.3	4.7	5.0	5.0	5.7	6.2	5.9	6.1	6.3	5.8	6.5	6.8	7.1	6.7	7.3	7.3	7.3	7.0	7.0	7.0	7.0	7.0	7.0	7.0	7.1	7.1	7.1	7.1	7.1	7.1	73%	4.3	6.5	5.2	6.9%	62.8%	18.8%	18.5%
1.00	4.8%	1980	1936	4.4	4.3	4.6	4.9	5.0	5.7	6.2	6.0	6.0	7.0	6.5	7.3	7.3	7.3	7.0	7.0	7.0	7.0	7.0	7.0	7.0	7.0	7.0	7.0	7.0	7.0	7.0	7.0	7.0	7.0	7.0	7.0	83%	4.3	6.6	5.3	7.0%	62.8%	18.8%	18.5%
1.33	4.7%	1981	1937	4.2	4.6	5.0	5.0	5.9	6.2	5.9	6.0	6.3	5.8	6.4	6.6	7.0	6.5	7.1	7.1	7.1	7.1	7.1	7.0	7.0	7.0	7.0	7.0	7.0	7.0	7.0	7.0	7.0	7.0	7.0	7.0	83%	4.2	6.6	5.3	7.3%	62.8%	18.8%	18.5%
1.00	4.8%	1982	1938	4.8	5.1	5.2	6.1	6.3	6.1	6.1	6.4	6.0	6.5	6.7	7.0	6.6	7.3	7.3	7.3	7.3	7.3	7.2	7.2	7.2	7.2	7.2	7.3	7.3	7.3	7.3	7.3	7.3	7.3	7.3	7.3	83%	4.8	6.9	5.9	7.7%	62.8%	18.8%	18.5%
1.00	4.8%	1983	1939	4.0	4.6	5.1	5.6	5.1	5.3	5.7	5.1	6.0	6.1	6.6	6.8	7.3	7.3	7.3	7.3	7.3	7.2	7.2	7.2	7.2	7.2	7.3	7.3	7.3	7.0	7.0	7.0	7.0	7.0	7.0	7.0	50%	4.6	6.6	5.3	7.0%	62.8%	18.8%	18.5%
1.33	4.7%	1984	1940	4.3	4.7	5.0	4.7	4.8	5.2	4.6	5.4	5.8	6.1	5.5	6.3	6.3	6.8	7.0	7.0	7.1	6.9	7.1	6.9	6.9	6.9	6.9	6.5	6.8	6.9	6.6	6.9	6.9	6.9	6.9	6.9	38%	4.3	5.9	4.8	6.4%	62.8%	18.8%	18.5%
1.33	4.7%	1985	1941	4.8	5.1	4.7	4.7	5.3	5.8	6.1	5.2	6.2	6.9	6.9	6.7	7.1	6.8	7.1	7.1	6.9	6.9	6.9	6.6	6.7	6.9	6.9	6.9	6.9	6.7	6.9	6.4	5.2	6.8	30%	4.7	6.4	5.2	6.8%	62.8%	18.8%	18.5%
1.67	4.6%	1986	1942	4.5	4.3	4.4	4.6	4.2	4.8	5.0	5.5	4.9	5.7	5.7	6.1	6.3	6.4	6.3	6.7	6.8	6.8	6.7	6.5	5.7	5.9	5.3	5.7	6.4	6.7	6.7	6.7	5.6	5.7	24%	3.9	5.8	4.8	6.1%	62.8%	18.8%	18.5%
1.67	4.6%	1987	1943	4.1	4.2	4.4	4.1	4.4	4.7	4.9	4.6	5.3	6.0	6.1	6.1	6.0	6.1	5.8	6.5	6.5	6.6	6.4	5.7	5.9	6.2	6.7	6.2	5.8	5.1	5.8	6.1	5.9	6.3	29%	4.1	5.8	4.6	5.8%	62.8%	18.8%	18.5%
1.67	4.6%	1988	1944	4.4	4.7	4.2	4.8	5.0	5.5	4.8	5.7	6.1	6.1	6.0	6.1	5.8	6.5	6.5	6.6	6.0	5.7	6.0	6.6	6.4	6.7	6.7	6.7	6.7	6.7	5.8	6.4	6.7	6.7	43%	4.2	6.1	5.1	6.3%	62.8%	18.8%	18.5%
1.67	4.6%	1989	1945	4.4	4.1	4.4	4.8	5.0	5.1	4.7	5.4	5.5	6.0	6.1	6.1	6.0	6.1	5.9	6.4	6.5	6.6	6.5	6.4	5.8	6.0	6.5	6.1	5.7	5.5	6.0	6.3	6.4	6.5	59%	4.1	5.9	5.0	5.9%	62.8%	18.8%	18.5%
2.33	4.3%	1990	1946	3.9	4.4	4.8	5.0	4.4	5.2	5.2	5.7	5.7	5.6	5.7	5.4	6.0	6.1	6.1	6.1	5.8	5.1	5.8	6.1	5.9	6.1	6.1	6.1	6.1	6.1	5.3	5.5	6.0	6.1	40%	3.9	5.6	4.5	6.0%	62.8%	18.8%	18.5%
2.00	4.4%	1991	1947	4.9	5.2	5.6	5.0	5.7	6.1	6.2	6.1	6.2	5.9	6.5	6.6	6.5	5.8	6.0	6.5	6.4	6.4	6.4	6.4	6.4	6.4	5.6	5.8	6.3	6.3	46%	4.9	6.2	5.2	6.7%	62.8%	18.8%	18.5%
2.67	4.1%	1992	1948	4.5	4.8	4.4	5.2	5.2	5.6	5.7	5.6	5.7	5.4	6.0	6.0	5.4	5.5	5.8	6.2	5.9	5.6	5.8	6.0	6.0	6.0	6.0	6.0	6.0	6.0	36%	4.4	5.7	5.2	6.2%	62.8%	18.8%	18.5%
3.00	4.0%	1993	1949	4.7	4.4	4.9	5.2	5.3	5.3	5.2	5.3	5.0	5.4	5.5	5.4	4.9	5.2	5.4	5.8	5.8	5.8	5.8	5.8	5.8	5.8	5.8	5.8	5.8	5.8	33%	4.4	5.4	5.0	5.3%	57.5%	37.5%	5.0%
3.00	4.0%	1994	1950	4.2	4.6	4.6	5.1	5.1	5.2	5.2	4.9	5.3	5.4	5.3	4.9	5.1	5.3	5.8	4.3	4.6	5.3	5.5	5.7	5.8	5.8	5.8	5.8	5.8	5.8	40%	4.3	5.4	4.9	6.0%	57.5%	37.5%	5.0%
3.33	3.9%	1995	1951	5.0	5.3	5.3	5.4	5.3	5.4	5.1	5.5	5.6	5.5	5.1	5.3	5.5	4.7	4.9	5.1	5.4	5.3	5.2	5.7	5.7	5.7	5.7	5.7	5.7	5.7	50%	5.0	5.5	5.3	6.2%	57.5%	37.5%	5.0%
3.67	3.7%	1996	1952	4.6	4.9	4.9	5.0	4.9	5.0	4.8	5.1	5.2	5.1	4.7	4.9	5.1	5.4	5.1	4.9	4.6	5.4	5.4	5.4	5.0	5.1	5.5	5.5	5.5	5.5	47%	4.6	5.2	4.9	5.4%	57.5%	37.5%	5.0%
3.67	3.7%	1997	1953	4.9	4.9	4.9	4.9	4.8	5.0	5.1	5.0	5.1	4.9	4.3	4.6	4.9	5.3	4.9	4.6	4.1	4.5	5.1	5.5	5.5	5.3	5.5	5.4	4.9	5.2	37%	4.1	5.1	4.9	5.4%	57.5%	37.5%	5.0%
3.67	3.7%	1998	1954	4.6	4.3	4.4	4.4	4.1	4.8	4.8	4.8	4.6	3.9	4.1	4.4	4.0	4.4	4.1	4.6	4.5	5.2	5.5	4.9	5.2	5.1	4.9	4.4	4.6	5.1	43%	3.8	4.8	4.6	4.8%	57.5%	37.5%	5.0%
3.67	3.7%	1999	1955	4.6	4.3	4.4	4.1	4.6	4.8	4.6	4.8	4.7	3.9	4.1	4.4	4.0	4.5	4.2	4.9	5.2	4.9	4.4	4.6	5.1	5.5	5.5	5.3	5.4	5.5	54%	3.9	4.9	4.5	4.8%	57.5%	37.5%	5.0%
4.00	3.6%	2000	1956	4.4	4.5	4.1	4.6	4.7	4.6	4.7	4.6	3.8	4.0	4.4	4.9	4.3	3.9	3.7	4.4	4.4	4.9	5.3	4.8	4.9	4.9	4.8	4.1	4.3	5.1	5.3	5.3	5.1	5.3	5.3	5.3	5.3	5.3	5.3	5.3	58%	3.7	4.7	4.4	4.7%	57.5%	37.5%	5.0%
Totals																																											50%	3.4	5.6	4.8	6.2	61.0%	24.9%	14.1%

FIGURE 187

Baseline Market results for basic GI recommendation when interest rates are moderate. Inflation-adjusted SPIA payout at 65 is 5.01%. 20-year TIPS ladder payout at age 85 is 6.1% based on a 2% real IRR.

To clearly see the typical cost of deploying GI, it's necessary to go one step further, directly comparing Baseline Market results with and without GI. The cost-comparison approach outlined back in Figure 162 is used; again, cost is the difference between annual income without GI and without GI, everything else being the same. A positive value identifies an increase in income from using GI; a negative value identifies a decrease in income from using GI.

Figure 188 shows this year-by-year cost difference for the first case with low GI payout rates. For example, the 0.3 value for the first year in the 1969 retirement is due to GI producing an income rate of 3.6%, versus 3.3% without GI. Likewise, 1968 shows a -0.2 value for the first year in the 1968 retirement, due to GI producing 0.2 less with an income rate of 4.4% versus 4.6% without GI. For perspective, a 0.1 difference translates to a $1000 difference for a portfolio starting with $1 million. Similarly, 1.0 would translate to a $10,000 difference for a year.

Valuation	Initial	Start	End	A65	A66	A67	A68	A69	A70	A71	A72	A73	A74	A75	A76	A77	A78	A79	A80	A81	A82	A83	A84
3.00	4.0%	1928	1967	-0.4	0.0	0.2	0.3	0.2	-0.1	-0.1	-0.4	-0.6	-0.1	-0.4	-0.4	-0.2	0.1	0.1	-0.3	-0.6	-0.8	-0.5	-0.3
3.00	4.0%	1929	1968	0.2	0.3	0.3	0.3	0.2	0.2	0.0	-0.4	0.2	0.1	0.1	0.2	0.3	0.3	0.1	-0.3	-0.8	-0.3	-0.1	-0.1
2.50	4.2%	1930	1969	0.1	0.1	0.1	0.0	0.0	-0.1	-0.3	0.0	-0.1	-0.1	0.0	0.1	0.1	-0.1	-0.3	-0.5	-0.3	-0.2	-0.2	-0.3
2.00	4.4%	1931	1970	0.1	0.1	-0.1	-0.1	-0.3	-0.5	-0.2	-0.3	-0.3	-0.2	-0.1	-0.1	-0.3	-0.4	-0.6	-0.3	-0.2	-0.1	-0.3	-0.4
1.00	4.8%	1932	1971	-0.1	-0.5	-0.5	-0.7	-0.7	-0.6	-0.7	-0.7	-0.7	-0.5	-0.3	-0.7	-0.7	-0.7	-0.7	-0.6	-0.6	-0.6	-0.7	-0.7
1.00	4.8%	1933	1972	-0.4	-0.4	-0.6	-0.7	-0.5	-0.6	-0.6	-0.6	-0.4	-0.4	-0.5	-0.6	-0.7	-0.6	-0.4	-0.4	-0.5	-0.6	-0.6	-0.6
2.00	4.4%	1934	1973	0.0	-0.2	-0.4	-0.1	-0.2	-0.2	-0.1	0.0	0.0	-0.1	-0.3	-0.5	-0.3	-0.1	-0.1	-0.2	-0.4	-0.4	-0.4	-0.4
2.00	4.4%	1935	1974	-0.2	-0.4	-0.1	-0.2	-0.2	-0.1	0.0	0.0	-0.1	-0.3	-0.5	-0.2	-0.1	-0.1	-0.2	-0.3	-0.3	-0.3	-0.3	-0.6
2.00	4.4%	1936	1975	-0.2	0.1	0.0	0.0	0.0	0.1	0.1	0.0	-0.1	-0.4	-0.1	0.0	0.0	-0.1	-0.2	-0.2	-0.3	-0.2	-0.5	-0.6
3.00	4.0%	1937	1976	0.3	0.3	0.3	0.3	0.3	0.3	0.3	0.1	-0.4	0.1	0.2	0.3	0.1	-0.1	-0.1	-0.3	-0.2	-0.7	-0.8	-0.8
2.50	4.2%	1938	1977	-0.2	-0.1	0.0	0.1	0.1	-0.1	-0.3	-0.5	-0.2	-0.1	-0.1	-0.2	-0.3	-0.3	-0.3	-0.3	-0.5	-0.5	-0.5	-0.4
2.50	4.2%	1939	1978	0.0	0.1	0.1	0.1	0.0	-0.1	-0.4	-0.1	0.0	0.0	-0.1	-0.2	-0.2	-0.3	-0.2	-0.5	-0.5	-0.5	-0.4	-0.5
2.50	4.2%	1940	1979	0.0	0.1	0.1	0.0	-0.2	-0.4	-0.1	0.0	0.0	-0.1	-0.2	-0.2	-0.2	-0.2	-0.4	-0.5	-0.5	-0.4	-0.5	-0.5
2.50	4.2%	1941	1980	0.1	0.1	-0.1	-0.3	-0.4	-0.2	-0.1	-0.1	-0.2	-0.2	-0.2	-0.3	-0.2	-0.4	-0.5	-0.5	-0.4	-0.5	-0.5	-0.5
2.00	4.4%	1942	1981	0.0	-0.2	-0.4	-0.6	-0.3	-0.2	-0.1	-0.2	-0.3	-0.3	-0.3	-0.3	-0.5	-0.6	-0.5	-0.4	-0.6	-0.6	-0.6	-0.6
1.50	4.6%	1943	1982	-0.2	-0.4	-0.6	-0.3	-0.1	-0.1	-0.2	-0.3	-0.3	-0.3	-0.2	-0.5	-0.6	-0.5	-0.4	-0.6	-0.6	-0.6	-0.6	-0.6
2.00	4.4%	1944	1983	-0.1	-0.4	-0.1	0.0	0.0	0.0	-0.1	-0.1	-0.1	-0.1	-0.4	-0.4	-0.4	-0.3	-0.5	-0.5	-0.5	-0.6	-0.5	-0.6
2.00	4.4%	1945	1984	-0.2	0.0	0.1	0.1	0.1	0.0	0.0	0.0	0.0	-0.3	-0.4	-0.3	-0.2	-0.4	-0.4	-0.4	-0.5	-0.4	-0.5	-0.6
2.00	4.4%	1946	1985	0.1	0.1	0.1	0.1	0.1	0.1	0.1	0.1	-0.1	-0.2	-0.1	0.0	-0.2	-0.3	-0.3	-0.4	-0.3	-0.4	-0.4	-0.5
2.00	4.4%	1947	1986	0.0	0.1	0.0	-0.1	-0.1	-0.1	0.0	-0.3	-0.4	-0.4	-0.2	-0.4	-0.4	-0.4	-0.5	-0.4	-0.5	-0.5	-0.6	-0.6
1.50	4.6%	1948	1987	0.0	-0.1	-0.1	-0.1	-0.2	-0.1	-0.4	-0.4	-0.4	-0.2	-0.4	-0.5	-0.5	-0.6	-0.5	-0.5	-0.6	-0.6	-0.6	-0.6
1.50	4.6%	1949	1988	-0.1	-0.1	-0.1	-0.1	-0.1	-0.4	-0.4	-0.4	-0.2	-0.4	-0.5	-0.5	-0.5	-0.5	-0.5	-0.6	-0.6	-0.6	-0.6	-0.6
1.50	4.6%	1950	1989	-0.1	-0.1	-0.1	-0.1	-0.3	-0.4	-0.3	-0.2	-0.4	-0.4	-0.4	-0.5	-0.4	-0.4	-0.5	-0.6	-0.5	-0.6	-0.6	-0.5
2.00	4.4%	1951	1990	0.0	0.0	0.0	-0.2	-0.3	-0.3	-0.1	-0.3	-0.4	-0.4	-0.4	-0.4	-0.4	-0.5	-0.5	-0.5	-0.6	-0.6	-0.5	-0.5
2.00	4.4%	1952	1991	0.0	0.0	-0.2	-0.4	-0.3	-0.2	-0.4	-0.4	-0.4	-0.4	-0.4	-0.4	-0.4	-0.5	-0.4	-0.6	-0.6	-0.5	-0.5	-0.6
2.33	4.3%	1953	1992	0.0	-0.2	-0.3	-0.3	-0.1	-0.3	-0.3	-0.3	-0.4	-0.3	-0.3	-0.4	-0.4	-0.4	-0.5	-0.5	-0.4	-0.4	-0.4	-0.5
1.67	4.6%	1954	1993	-0.3	-0.4	-0.3	-0.2	-0.4	-0.4	-0.4	-0.4	-0.4	-0.4	-0.4	-0.5	-0.4	-0.6	-0.6	-0.4	-0.5	-0.5	-0.5	-0.3
2.33	4.3%	1955	1994	-0.1	0.0	0.1	-0.1	-0.1	-0.1	-0.2	-0.1	-0.2	-0.3	-0.3	-0.3	-0.4	-0.5	-0.3	-0.3	-0.4	-0.3	-0.1	0.0
2.33	4.3%	1956	1995	0.0	0.1	0.0	-0.1	0.0	-0.2	-0.1	-0.1	-0.2	-0.3	-0.2	-0.4	-0.4	-0.3	-0.3	-0.3	-0.3	0.0	0.1	0.0
2.33	4.3%	1957	1996	0.1	-0.1	-0.1	-0.1	-0.2	-0.1	-0.1	-0.2	-0.3	-0.2	-0.4	-0.4	-0.2	-0.3	-0.3	-0.3	-0.1	0.1	0.0	-0.1
2.33	4.3%	1958	1997	-0.2	-0.3	-0.3	-0.3	-0.3	-0.3	-0.3	-0.4	-0.3	-0.4	-0.5	-0.3	-0.3	-0.4	-0.4	-0.2	0.0	-0.1	-0.2	-0.2
2.67	4.1%	1959	1998	0.0	0.0	-0.1	0.0	-0.1	-0.2	-0.2	-0.1	-0.3	-0.4	-0.2	-0.2	-0.2	-0.2	0.0	0.1	0.1	0.0	0.0	0.0
3.00	4.0%	1960	1999	0.0	-0.2	0.0	-0.1	-0.2	-0.4	-0.2	-0.6	-0.7	-0.3	-0.3	-0.4	-0.4	0.0	0.3	0.2	-0.1	0.0	0.1	0.0
3.00	4.0%	1961	2000	-0.3	-0.1	-0.1	-0.3	-0.4	-0.3	-0.5	-0.6	-0.3	-0.3	-0.4	-0.4	0.1	0.3	0.2	0.0	0.0	0.2	0.1	0.0
3.00	4.0%	1962	2001	0.1	0.0	-0.1	-0.3	-0.1	-0.5	-0.6	-0.3	-0.2	-0.3	-0.3	0.2	0.3	0.3	0.1	0.1	0.2	0.1	0.0	0.1
3.00	4.0%	1963	2002	-0.1	-0.3	-0.4	-0.3	-0.5	-0.7	-0.3	-0.3	-0.4	-0.4	0.1	0.3	0.2	0.0	0.1	0.1	0.0	0.0	0.1	-0.3
3.00	4.0%	1964	2003	-0.1	-0.4	-0.1	-0.5	-0.6	-0.3	-0.2	-0.3	-0.3	0.2	0.3	0.3	0.1	0.2	0.2	0.1	0.0	0.2	-0.1	-0.5
3.33	3.9%	1965	2004	-0.3	0.0	-0.3	-0.4	-0.1	-0.1	-0.1	-0.1	0.2	0.3	0.3	0.2	0.3	0.3	0.3	0.2	0.2	0.1	-0.3	-0.3
3.67	3.7%	1966	2005	0.1	-0.2	-0.3	0.0	0.1	0.0	0.0	0.3	0.4	0.4	0.3	0.3	0.3	0.3	0.3	0.3	0.1	-0.1	-0.1	-0.4
3.00	4.0%	1967	2006	-0.4	-0.5	-0.1	-0.1	-0.2	-0.2	0.2	0.3	0.3	0.2	0.2	0.3	0.2	0.2	0.2	0.0	-0.3	-0.2	-0.5	-0.7
3.33	3.9%	1968	2007	-0.2	0.2	0.2	0.1	0.2	0.3	0.4	0.4	0.3	0.3	0.4	0.3	0.3	0.3	0.3	0.1	0.1	-0.2	-0.4	-0.2
3.33	3.9%	1969	2008	0.3	0.3	0.3	0.2	0.4	0.6	0.4	0.4	0.4	0.4	0.4	0.4	0.4	0.3	0.2	0.2	0.0	-0.1	0.0	-0.2
3.33	3.9%	1970	2009	0.0	-0.1	0.0	0.3	0.4	0.3	0.3	0.3	0.3	0.3	0.2	0.3	0.0	-0.2	-0.2	-0.5	-0.6	-0.5	-0.6	-0.7
2.67	4.1%	1971	2010	-0.1	-0.1	0.1	0.2	0.2	0.1	0.1	0.1	0.1	0.1	0.1	0.0	-0.1	-0.1	-0.2	-0.3	-0.3	-0.3	-0.4	-0.3
3.00	4.0%	1972	1928	0.0	0.3	0.3	0.3	0.3	0.3	0.3	0.3	0.2	0.3	0.1	-0.1	-0.1	-0.4	-0.6	-0.4	-0.6	-0.6	-0.4	-0.7
3.00	4.0%	1973	1929	0.3	0.3	0.3	0.3	0.3	0.3	0.3	0.3	0.3	0.2	0.0	0.0	-0.4	-0.5	-0.4	-0.5	-0.6	-0.4	-0.6	-0.8
2.33	4.3%	1974	1930	0.1	0.1	0.0	0.0	0.0	0.0	0.0	0.0	-0.1	-0.2	-0.2	-0.4	-0.4	-0.4	-0.4	-0.5	-0.4	-0.5	-0.5	-0.5
1.33	4.7%	1975	1931	-0.1	-0.4	-0.3	-0.2	-0.2	-0.2	-0.1	-0.4	-0.4	-0.4	-0.6	-0.7	-0.6	-0.6	-0.7	-0.6	-0.7	-0.7	-0.7	-0.7
1.67	4.6%	1976	1932	-0.1	-0.1	-0.1	-0.1	-0.1	0.0	-0.2	-0.3	-0.3	-0.4	-0.5	-0.5	-0.5	-0.6	-0.4	-0.6	-0.6	-0.6	-0.6	-0.6
1.67	4.6%	1977	1933	0.0	0.0	0.0	0.0	0.0	-0.1	-0.1	-0.1	-0.3	-0.4	-0.3	-0.4	-0.4	-0.3	-0.5	-0.5	-0.6	-0.5	-0.6	-0.6
1.33	4.7%	1978	1934	0.0	0.0	0.0	0.0	-0.1	-0.2	-0.2	-0.4	-0.4	-0.4	-0.4	-0.5	-0.4	-0.5	-0.6	-0.7	-0.6	-0.7	-0.7	-0.7
1.00	4.8%	1979	1935	0.0	0.0	0.0	-0.1	-0.2	-0.2	-0.4	-0.5	-0.4	-0.4	-0.5	-0.4	-0.5	-0.6	-0.7	-0.6	-0.7	-0.7	-0.7	-0.7
1.00	4.8%	1980	1936	0.0	0.0	-0.1	-0.2	-0.2	-0.4	-0.4	-0.4	-0.4	-0.5	-0.3	-0.5	-0.6	-0.7	-0.5	-0.7	-0.7	-0.7	-0.7	-0.7
1.33	4.7%	1981	1937	0.0	-0.1	-0.2	-0.2	-0.4	-0.5	-0.4	-0.4	-0.5	-0.4	-0.5	-0.6	-0.6	-0.5	-0.7	-0.7	-0.7	-0.7	-0.7	-0.7
1.00	4.8%	1982	1938	-0.1	-0.2	-0.2	-0.4	-0.3	-0.4	-0.4	-0.5	-0.4	-0.5	-0.6	-0.7	-0.6	-0.7	-0.7	-0.7	-0.7	-0.7	-0.7	-0.7
1.00	4.8%	1983	1939	-0.1	-0.1	-0.2	-0.3	-0.2	-0.3	-0.3	-0.2	-0.4	-0.4	-0.5	-0.4	-0.6	-0.6	-0.7	-0.7	-0.7	-0.7	-0.7	-0.7
1.33	4.7%	1984	1940	0.0	-0.1	-0.2	-0.1	-0.1	-0.2	-0.1	-0.3	-0.4	-0.4	-0.3	-0.5	-0.5	-0.6	-0.6	-0.6	-0.7	-0.7	-0.6	-0.7
1.33	4.7%	1985	1941	-0.1	-0.2	-0.1	-0.2	-0.2	-0.1	-0.3	-0.4	-0.4	-0.3	-0.5	-0.5	-0.6	-0.6	-0.6	-0.6	-0.7	-0.6	-0.7	-0.7
1.67	4.6%	1986	1942	-0.1	0.0	0.0	-0.1	0.0	-0.1	-0.2	-0.3	-0.2	-0.3	-0.4	-0.4	-0.5	-0.5	-0.5	-0.5	-0.5	-0.6	-0.6	-0.6
1.67	4.6%	1987	1943	0.0	0.0	0.0	0.0	-0.1	-0.1	-0.2	-0.1	-0.3	-0.3	-0.4	-0.4	-0.4	-0.4	-0.4	-0.4	-0.5	-0.5	-0.5	-0.6
1.67	4.6%	1988	1944	-0.1	-0.1	0.0	-0.1	-0.2	-0.3	-0.1	-0.4	-0.4	-0.4	-0.5	-0.5	-0.5	-0.5	-0.5	-0.6	-0.6	-0.6	-0.6	-0.6
1.67	4.6%	1989	1945	-0.1	0.0	-0.1	-0.1	-0.2	-0.1	-0.3	-0.3	-0.4	-0.4	-0.4	-0.4	-0.4	-0.4	-0.5	-0.5	-0.5	-0.5	-0.5	-0.4
2.33	4.3%	1990	1946	0.1	0.0	-0.1	-0.2	-0.1	-0.2	-0.2	-0.3	-0.4	-0.4	-0.3	-0.4	-0.3	-0.4	-0.4	-0.4	-0.5	-0.4	-0.3	-0.3
2.00	4.4%	1991	1947	-0.2	-0.2	-0.3	-0.2	-0.4	-0.4	-0.4	-0.5	-0.5	-0.4	-0.5	-0.4	-0.5	-0.5	-0.5	-0.6	-0.5	-0.4	-0.4	-0.5
2.67	4.1%	1992	1948	-0.1	-0.1	0.0	-0.2	-0.2	-0.3	-0.3	-0.4	-0.3	-0.4	-0.3	-0.4	-0.4	-0.4	-0.4	-0.4	-0.3	-0.3	-0.4	-0.5
3.00	4.0%	1993	1949	-0.2	0.0	-0.3	-0.4	-0.5	-0.6	-0.6	-0.5	-0.6	-0.4	-0.6	-0.7	-0.6	-0.7	-0.6	-0.3	-0.5	-0.6	-0.8	-0.6
3.00	4.0%	1994	1950	0.1	-0.1	-0.1	-0.4	-0.4	-0.5	-0.4	-0.5	-0.3	-0.5	-0.6	-0.5	-0.6	-0.6	-0.3	-0.4	-0.6	-0.7	-0.4	-0.2
3.33	3.9%	1995	1951	-0.4	-0.4	-0.5	-0.6	-0.6	-0.6	-0.6	-0.4	-0.7	-0.7	-0.7	-0.7	-0.7	-0.4	-0.5	-0.7	-0.8	-0.7	-0.6	-0.5
3.67	3.7%	1996	1952	-0.1	-0.3	-0.3	-0.4	-0.3	-0.4	-0.2	-0.4	-0.5	-0.4	-0.5	-0.4	-0.2	-0.3	-0.4	-0.6	-0.4	-0.3	-0.1	-0.4
3.67	3.7%	1997	1953	-0.3	-0.3	-0.3	-0.3	-0.3	-0.2	-0.4	-0.4	-0.4	-0.4	-0.3	0.0	-0.1	-0.3	-0.6	-0.3	-0.1	0.2	-0.1	-0.4
3.67	3.7%	1998	1954	-0.1	-0.1	0.0	-0.1	0.2	-0.2	-0.3	-0.2	-0.3	-0.1	0.3	0.2	0.0	-0.4	0.0	0.2	0.3	0.2	-0.1	-0.1
3.67	3.7%	1999	1955	-0.1	0.0	0.0	0.2	-0.1	-0.2	-0.1	-0.3	-0.2	0.3	0.2	0.0	-0.4	-0.1	0.2	0.3	0.2	-0.1	-0.1	-0.5
4.00	3.6%	2000	1956	0.0	-0.1	0.2	-0.1	-0.2	-0.1	-0.2	-0.1	0.3	0.2	0.0	-0.3	0.0	0.3	0.4	0.3	0.0	0.0	-0.3	-0.6

Start	A85	A86	A87	A88	A89	A90	A91	A92	A93	A94	A95	A96	A97	A98	A99	A00	A01	A02	A03	A04	Bequest	AVG	1st 10Y%	Sum to 85	Sum to 105
1928	-0.3	-0.4	-0.6	-0.7	-0.7	-0.6	-0.8	-0.8	-0.8	-0.8	-0.8	-0.8	-0.8	-0.8	-0.8	-0.8	-0.8	-0.8	-0.8	-0.8	-32%	-0.5	-0.1	-4.3	-18.7
1929	-0.4	-0.6	-0.7	-0.7	-0.6	-0.8	-0.8	-0.8	-0.8	-0.8	-0.8	-0.8	-0.8	-0.8	-0.8	-0.8	-0.8	-0.8	-0.8	-0.8	-43%	-0.3	0.2	1.0	-13.7
1930	-0.8	-0.8	-0.9	-0.8	-0.9	-0.9	-0.9	-0.9	-0.9	-0.9	-0.9	-0.9	-0.9	-0.9	-0.9	-0.9	-0.9	-0.9	-0.9	-0.9	-25%	-0.5	0.0	-2.1	-20.3
1931	-0.6	-0.7	-0.6	-0.8	-0.8	-0.8	-0.8	-0.8	-0.8	-0.8	-0.8	-0.8	-0.8	-0.8	-0.8	-0.8	-0.8	-0.8	-0.8	-0.8	-18%	-0.5	-0.2	-4.7	-20.9
1932	-0.9	-0.9	-0.9	-0.9	-0.9	-0.9	-0.9	-0.9	-0.9	-0.9	-0.9	-0.9	-0.9	-0.9	-0.9	-0.9	-0.9	-0.9	-0.9	-0.9	-26%	-0.8	-0.6	-12.3	-31.1
1933	-0.8	-1.0	-1.0	-1.0	-1.0	-1.0	-1.0	-1.0	-1.0	-1.0	-1.0	-1.0	-1.0	-1.0	-1.0	-1.0	-1.0	-1.0	-1.0	-1.0	-17%	-0.8	-0.5	-11.0	-31.6
1934	-1.0	-1.0	-1.0	-1.0	-1.0	-1.0	-1.0	-1.0	-1.0	-1.0	-1.0	-1.0	-1.0	-1.0	-1.0	-1.0	-1.0	-1.0	-1.0	-1.0	-13%	-0.6	-0.1	-4.4	-23.9
1935	-0.8	-0.8	-0.8	-0.8	-0.8	-0.8	-0.8	-0.8	-0.8	-0.8	-0.8	-0.8	-0.8	-0.8	-0.8	-0.8	-0.8	-0.8	-0.8	-0.8	-9%	-0.5	-0.2	-4.5	-20.6
1936	-0.8	-0.6	-0.8	-0.8	-0.8	-0.8	-0.8	-0.8	-0.8	-0.8	-0.8	-0.8	-0.8	-0.8	-0.8	-0.8	-0.8	-0.8	-0.8	-0.8	-10%	-0.4	0.0	-2.3	-17.7
1937	-0.6	-0.8	-0.8	-0.8	-0.8	-0.8	-0.8	-0.8	-0.8	-0.8	-0.8	-0.8	-0.8	-0.8	-0.8	-0.8	-0.8	-0.8	-0.8	-0.8	-16%	-0.4	0.2	-0.4	-16.0
1938	-0.7	-0.7	-0.7	-0.7	-0.7	-0.7	-0.7	-0.7	-0.7	-0.7	-0.7	-0.7	-0.7	-0.7	-0.7	-0.7	-0.7	-0.7	-0.7	-0.7	-9%	-0.5	-0.1	-4.5	-18.1
1939	-0.6	-0.6	-0.6	-0.6	-0.6	-0.6	-0.6	-0.6	-0.6	-0.6	-0.6	-0.6	-0.6	-0.6	-0.6	-0.6	-0.6	-0.6	-0.6	-0.6	-13%	-0.4	0.0	-3.5	-16.0
1940	-0.6	-0.6	-0.6	-0.6	-0.6	-0.6	-0.6	-0.6	-0.6	-0.6	-0.6	-0.6	-0.6	-0.6	-0.6	-0.6	-0.6	-0.6	-0.6	-0.6	-21%	-0.4	0.0	-4.2	-16.7
1941	-0.7	-0.7	-0.7	-0.7	-0.7	-0.7	-0.7	-0.7	-0.7	-0.7	-0.7	-0.7	-0.7	-0.7	-0.7	-0.7	-0.7	-0.7	-0.7	-0.7	-11%	-0.5	-0.1	-5.5	-19.3
1942	-0.7	-0.7	-0.7	-0.7	-0.7	-0.7	-0.7	-0.7	-0.7	-0.7	-0.7	-0.7	-0.7	-0.7	-0.7	-0.7	-0.7	-0.7	-0.7	-0.6	-5%	-0.5	-0.3	-7.5	-21.1
1943	-0.9	-0.9	-0.9	-0.9	-0.9	-0.9	-0.9	-0.9	-0.9	-0.9	-0.9	-0.5	-0.8	-0.9	-0.7	-0.7	-0.6	-0.9	-0.6	-0.7	-3%	-0.6	-0.3	-8.1	-23.9
1944	-0.8	-0.8	-0.8	-0.8	-0.8	-0.8	-0.8	-0.8	-0.8	-0.7	-0.4	-0.5	-0.8	-0.7	-0.5	-0.6	-0.6	-0.7	-0.8	-0.8	0%	-0.5	-0.1	-5.8	-19.8
1945	-0.8	-0.8	-0.8	-0.8	-0.8	-0.8	-0.8	-0.8	-0.6	0.0	-0.4	-0.5	-0.6	-0.4	-0.3	-0.5	-0.2	-0.7	-0.8	-0.5	-2%	-0.4	0.0	-4.5	-16.0
1946	-0.8	-0.9	-0.9	-0.8	-0.8	-0.9	-0.9	-0.4	0.0	-0.1	-0.5	-0.3	-0.4	-0.4	-0.4	-0.3	-0.4	-0.9	-0.6	-0.8	-3%	-0.3	0.0	-2.7	-14.0
1947	-0.8	-0.8	-0.8	-0.8	-0.8	-0.8	-0.7	-0.2	-0.5	-0.6	-0.6	-0.4	-0.6	-0.6	-0.4	-0.6	-0.8	-0.8	-0.8	-0.8	2%	-0.5	-0.1	-5.8	-19.1
1948	-0.7	-0.7	-0.7	-0.7	-0.7	-0.4	0.0	-0.1	-0.4	-0.2	-0.2	-0.1	-0.3	0.0	-0.3	-0.6	-0.4	-0.7	-0.7	-0.4	-1%	-0.4	-0.2	-7.5	-15.9
1949	-0.6	-0.5	-0.6	-0.6	-0.2	0.1	-0.1	-0.2	-0.2	0.1	-0.1	0.0	-0.1	-0.2	-0.4	-0.3	-0.5	-0.6	-0.5	-0.5	0%	-0.4	-0.2	-8.0	-14.2
1950	-0.8	-0.8	-0.8	-0.5	0.0	-0.2	-0.5	-0.3	-0.2	-0.2	-0.3	-0.1	-0.6	-0.7	-0.5	-0.9	-0.9	-0.9	-0.9	-0.9	1%	-0.5	-0.2	-7.4	-18.1
1951	-0.8	-0.7	-0.4	-0.1	-0.2	-0.4	-0.4	-0.2	-0.3	-0.2	-0.2	-0.4	-0.8	-0.6	-0.8	-0.8	-0.6	-0.8	-0.8	-0.4	1%	-0.4	-0.2	-6.8	-16.7
1952	-0.8	-0.4	0.0	-0.3	-0.4	-0.4	-0.3	-0.3	-0.4	-0.1	-0.5	-0.7	-0.8	-0.8	-0.8	-0.8	-0.8	-0.8	-0.7	-0.8	3%	-0.5	-0.3	-7.5	-18.3
1953	-0.4	0.0	-0.2	-0.4	-0.3	-0.2	-0.3	-0.2	-0.1	-0.4	-0.7	-0.5	-0.7	-0.7	-0.7	-0.7	-0.7	-0.7	-0.7	-0.7	4%	-0.4	-0.2	-6.7	-16.4
1954	-0.1	-0.2	-0.5	-0.5	-0.3	-0.3	-0.4	-0.2	-0.6	-0.7	-0.7	-0.9	-1.0	-0.9	-0.9	-1.0	-0.6	-1.0	-1.0	-1.0	5%	-0.5	-0.3	-8.2	-21.1
1955	-0.2	-0.4	-0.3	-0.3	-0.3	-0.4	-0.3	-0.5	-0.8	-0.7	-1.0	-1.0	-1.0	-1.0	-1.0	-0.8	-1.0	-1.0	-1.0	-1.0	5%	-0.5	-0.1	-3.9	-18.0
1956	-0.4	-0.3	-0.2	-0.3	-0.3	-0.3	-0.6	-0.7	-0.7	-0.9	-1.0	-0.8	-1.0	-1.0	-0.7	-1.0	-1.0	-1.0	-1.0	-1.0	4%	-0.4	-0.1	-3.0	-17.4
1957	-0.2	-0.2	-0.2	-0.3	-0.2	-0.5	-0.8	-0.7	-1.0	-1.0	-0.9	-1.0	-1.0	-0.8	-1.0	-1.0	-1.0	-1.0	-1.0	-1.0	6%	-0.4	-0.1	-3.3	-17.8
1958	-0.3	-0.3	-0.3	-0.3	-0.5	-0.8	-0.8	-0.9	-0.9	-0.9	-0.9	-0.9	-0.9	-0.9	-0.9	-0.9	-0.9	-0.9	-0.9	-0.9	-1%	-0.5	-0.3	-5.7	-21.3
1959	-0.2	-0.2	-0.1	-0.5	-0.7	-0.6	-0.9	-0.9	-0.9	-0.9	-0.9	-0.7	-0.9	-0.9	-0.9	-0.9	-0.9	-0.9	-0.9	-0.9	0%	-0.4	-0.1	-2.1	-17.0
1960	-0.1	0.0	-0.4	-0.6	-0.5	-0.8	-0.8	-0.7	-0.8	-0.8	-0.7	-0.8	-0.8	-0.8	-0.8	-0.8	-0.8	-0.8	-0.8	-0.8	-14%	-0.4	-0.3	-3.4	-16.7
1961	0.1	-0.1	-0.5	-0.5	-0.7	-0.8	-0.7	-0.8	-0.8	-0.5	-0.8	-0.8	-0.8	-0.8	-0.8	-0.8	-0.8	-0.8	-0.8	-0.8	-9%	-0.4	-0.3	-3.1	-16.2
1962	-0.3	-0.5	-0.5	-0.8	-0.8	-0.7	-0.8	-0.8	-0.7	-0.8	-0.8	-0.8	-0.8	-0.8	-0.8	-0.8	-0.8	-0.8	-0.8	-0.8	-12%	-0.4	-0.2	-1.1	-15.6
1963	-0.5	-0.4	-0.7	-0.8	-0.7	-0.8	-0.8	-0.7	-0.8	-0.8	-0.8	-0.8	-0.8	-0.8	-0.8	-0.8	-0.8	-0.8	-0.8	-0.8	0%	-0.5	-0.4	-3.2	-18.0
1964	-0.5	-0.7	-0.8	-0.7	-0.8	-0.8	-0.7	-0.8	-0.8	-0.8	-0.8	-0.8	-0.8	-0.8	-0.8	-0.8	-0.8	-0.8	-0.8	-0.8	-13%	-0.4	-0.3	-2.0	-17.2
1965	-0.6	-0.6	-0.5	-0.7	-0.7	-0.4	-0.7	-0.7	-0.7	-0.7	-0.7	-0.7	-0.7	-0.7	-0.7	-0.7	-0.7	-0.7	-0.7	-0.7	-16%	-0.3	-0.1	0.3	-13.7
1966	-0.6	-0.4	-0.5	-0.6	-0.3	-0.6	-0.6	-0.6	-0.6	-0.6	-0.6	-0.6	-0.6	-0.6	-0.6	-0.6	-0.6	-0.6	-0.6	-0.6	-18%	-0.2	0.1	2.2	-9.9
1967	-0.6	-0.7	-0.8	-0.6	-0.8	-0.8	-0.8	-0.8	-0.8	-0.8	-0.8	-0.8	-0.8	-0.8	-0.8	-0.8	-0.8	-0.8	-0.8	-0.8	-20%	-0.4	0.0	-1.1	-16.3
1968	-0.4	-0.5	-0.2	-0.6	-0.6	-0.7	-0.7	-0.7	-0.7	-0.7	-0.7	-0.7	-0.7	-0.7	-0.7	-0.7	-0.7	-0.7	-0.7	-0.7	-12%	-0.3	0.2	3.2	-10.2
1969	-0.4	0.0	-0.4	-0.6	-0.7	-0.5	-0.7	-0.7	-0.7	-0.7	-0.7	-0.7	-0.7	-0.7	-0.7	-0.7	-0.7	-0.7	-0.7	-0.7	3%	-0.2	0.4	5.1	-7.9
1970	-0.6	-0.7	-0.7	-0.7	-0.7	-0.7	-0.7	-0.7	-0.7	-0.7	-0.7	-0.7	-0.7	-0.7	-0.7	-0.7	-0.7	-0.7	-0.7	-0.7	-15%	-0.4	0.2	-0.7	-15.5
1971	-0.9	-0.9	-0.9	-0.9	-0.9	-0.9	-0.9	-0.9	-0.9	-0.9	-0.9	-0.9	-0.9	-0.9	-0.9	-0.9	-0.9	-0.9	-0.9	-0.9	-8%	-0.5	0.1	-0.9	-19.1
1972	-0.8	-0.8	-0.8	-0.8	-0.8	-0.8	-0.8	-0.8	-0.8	-0.8	-0.8	-0.8	-0.8	-0.8	-0.8	-0.8	-0.8	-0.8	-0.8	-0.8	-22%	-0.4	0.3	-1.4	-17.1
1973	-0.8	-0.8	-0.8	-0.8	-0.8	-0.8	-0.8	-0.8	-0.8	-0.8	-0.8	-0.8	-0.8	-0.8	-0.8	-0.8	-0.8	-0.8	-0.8	-0.8	-16%	-0.4	0.3	-1.4	-17.2
1974	-0.8	-0.8	-0.8	-0.8	-0.8	-0.8	-0.8	-0.8	-0.8	-0.8	-0.8	-0.8	-0.8	-0.8	-0.8	-0.8	-0.8	-0.8	-0.8	-0.8	-10%	-0.5	0.0	-4.3	-19.9
1975	-1.0	-1.0	-1.0	-1.0	-1.0	-1.0	-1.0	-1.0	-1.0	-1.0	-1.0	-1.0	-1.0	-1.0	-1.0	-1.0	-1.0	-1.0	-1.0	-1.0	-12%	-0.7	-0.3	-9.2	-28.6
1976	-0.8	-0.8	-0.8	-0.8	-0.8	-0.8	-0.8	-0.8	-0.8	-0.8	-0.8	-0.8	-0.8	-0.8	-0.8	-0.9	-0.9	-0.9	-0.9	-0.9	-4%	-0.6	-0.2	-7.3	-24.4
1977	-0.9	-0.9	-0.9	-0.9	-0.9	-0.9	-0.9	-0.9	-0.9	-0.9	-0.9	-0.9	-0.9	-0.9	-0.9	-0.9	-0.9	-0.9	-0.9	-0.9	6%	-0.6	-0.1	-5.6	-23.7
1978	-0.9	-0.9	-0.9	-0.9	-0.9	-0.9	-0.9	-0.9	-0.9	-0.9	-0.9	-0.9	-0.9	-0.9	-0.9	-0.9	-0.9	-0.9	-0.9	-0.9	6%	-0.6	-0.2	-7.2	-25.9
1979	-1.0	-1.0	-1.0	-1.0	-1.0	-1.0	-1.0	-1.0	-1.0	-1.0	-1.0	-1.0	-1.0	-1.0	-1.0	-1.0	-1.0	-1.0	-1.0	-1.0	10%	-0.7	-0.2	-8.3	-28.9
1980	-1.0	-1.0	-1.0	-1.0	-1.0	-1.0	-1.0	-1.0	-1.0	-1.0	-1.0	-1.0	-1.0	-1.0	-1.0	-1.0	-1.0	-1.0	-1.0	-1.0	2%	-0.7	-0.3	-8.7	-28.9
1981	-0.9	-0.9	-0.9	-0.9	-0.9	-0.9	-0.9	-0.9	-0.9	-0.9	-0.9	-0.9	-0.9	-0.9	-0.9	-0.9	-0.9	-0.9	-0.9	-0.9	5%	-0.7	-0.3	-9.3	-27.2
1982	-0.9	-0.9	-0.9	-0.9	-0.9	-0.9	-0.9	-0.9	-0.9	-0.9	-0.9	-0.9	-0.9	-0.9	-0.9	-0.9	-0.9	-0.9	-0.9	-0.9	8%	-0.7	-0.4	-10.6	-28.6
1983	-1.1	-1.1	-1.1	-1.1	-1.1	-1.1	-1.1	-1.1	-1.1	-1.1	-1.1	-0.9	-1.1	-1.1	-1.1	-1.1	-1.1	-1.1	-1.1	-1.1	12%	-0.8	-0.3	-8.9	-30.8
1984	-1.0	-1.0	-1.0	-1.0	-0.8	-0.9	-1.0	-1.0	-1.0	-0.8	-0.6	-0.8	-1.0	-1.0	-1.0	-1.0	-1.0	-1.0	-1.0	-1.0	9%	-0.7	-0.2	-7.8	-26.2
1985	-0.9	-0.9	-0.9	-0.8	-0.8	-0.9	-0.9	-0.9	-0.8	-0.5	-0.8	-0.9	-0.9	-0.9	-0.9	-0.9	-0.9	-0.9	-0.9	-0.7	9%	-0.6	-0.2	-8.3	-26.0
1986	-0.9	-0.8	-0.5	-0.7	-0.8	-0.9	-0.8	-0.5	-0.2	-0.4	-0.8	-0.7	-0.9	-0.9	-0.8	-0.9	-0.9	-0.9	-0.4	-0.4	3%	-0.5	-0.1	-6.4	-20.6
1987	-0.8	-0.5	-0.6	-0.7	-1.0	-0.7	-0.5	-0.2	-0.5	-0.7	-0.8	-1.0	-1.0	-0.8	-0.9	-0.9	-0.6	-0.5	-0.4	-0.8	0%	-0.5	-0.1	-5.5	-19.1
1988	-0.6	-0.6	-0.8	-1.0	-0.8	-0.6	-0.5	-0.6	-0.9	-0.8	-1.0	-1.0	-1.0	-1.0	-1.0	-1.0	-0.5	-0.8	-1.0	-1.0	4%	-0.6	-0.2	-7.5	-23.7
1989	-0.9	-1.0	-1.2	-1.0	-0.8	-0.7	-1.0	-1.1	-1.1	-1.2	-1.2	-1.0	-1.2	-1.2	-1.0	-0.7	-0.6	-1.2	-1.2	-1.2	9%	-0.7	-0.2	-6.7	-26.9
1990	-0.8	-0.9	-0.8	-0.7	-0.4	-0.7	-0.9	-0.8	-0.9	-0.9	-0.9	-0.9	-0.9	-0.9	-0.6	-0.7	-0.9	-0.9	-0.9	-0.9	1%	-0.6	-0.2	-5.5	-22.0
1991	-0.9	-0.8	-0.7	-0.6	-0.8	-0.9	-0.9	-0.9	-0.9	-0.9	-0.9	-0.9	-0.9	-0.9	-0.8	-0.9	-0.9	-0.9	-0.9	-0.9	-1%	-0.6	-0.3	-8.3	-25.7
1992	-0.7	-0.5	-0.4	-0.6	-0.7	-0.7	-0.7	-0.7	-0.7	-0.7	-0.7	-0.7	-0.7	-0.7	-0.7	-0.7	-0.7	-0.7	-0.7	-0.7	1%	-0.5	-0.2	-6.1	-19.9
1993	-0.5	-0.2	-0.5	-0.8	-0.7	-0.8	-0.8	-0.8	-0.8	-0.8	-0.8	-0.6	-0.7	-0.8	-0.8	-0.8	-0.8	-0.8	-0.8	-0.8	-5%	-0.6	-0.4	-10.1	-24.9
1994	0.0	-0.1	-0.6	-0.6	-0.8	-0.8	-0.7	-0.8	-0.8	-0.6	-0.4	-0.4	-0.8	-0.8	-0.8	-0.8	-0.8	-0.8	-0.8	-0.8	-2%	-0.5	-0.3	-8.2	-21.4
1995	-0.8	-0.8	-0.8	-0.8	-0.8	-0.8	-0.8	-0.8	-0.8	-0.7	-0.8	-0.8	-0.8	-0.8	-0.8	-0.8	-0.8	-0.8	-0.8	-0.8	-16%	-0.7	-0.5	-11.6	-27.3
1996	-0.6	-0.6	-0.7	-0.7	-0.6	-0.7	-0.7	-0.6	-0.4	-0.4	-0.7	-0.7	-0.7	-0.7	-0.7	-0.7	-0.7	-0.7	-0.7	-0.7	-12%	-0.5	-0.3	-7.1	-19.7
1997	-0.4	-0.7	-0.7	-0.6	-0.7	-0.7	-0.6	-0.3	-0.3	-0.6	-0.7	-0.7	-0.7	-0.7	-0.7	-0.7	-0.7	-0.7	-0.7	-0.7	-7%	-0.4	-0.3	-5.4	-17.7
1998	-0.5	-0.7	-0.3	-0.5	-0.4	-0.3	0.0	0.0	-0.4	-0.7	-0.7	-0.7	-0.7	-0.5	-0.7	-0.7	-0.7	-0.7	-0.7	-0.7	-11%	-0.3	-0.1	-0.8	-11.1
1999	-0.7	-0.3	-0.5	-0.5	-0.3	0.0	-0.1	-0.4	-0.7	-0.7	-0.7	-0.5	-0.6	-0.7	-0.7	-0.7	-0.7	-0.7	-0.7	-0.7	-15%	-0.3	-0.1	-1.1	-11.7
2000	-0.2	-0.3	-0.3	-0.3	0.2	0.0	-0.4	-0.6	-0.6	-0.6	-0.6	-0.4	-0.6	-0.6	-0.6	-0.6	-0.6	-0.6	-0.6	-0.6	-21%	-0.2	0.0	-0.2	-8.7
																					Overall Average			-4.9	-19.7
																					Low-Valuation Avg			-6.1	-21.2
																					High-Valuation Avg			-2.3	-15.9

FIGURE 188

Annual cost of GI summary, based on 1% IRR using recommended GI solution with low rates, compared to 100% systemic withdrawal solution on Baseline Market and Portfolio.

Figure 189 shows the cost difference for the second case (with moderate GI payout rates), with and without GI.

Valuation	Initial	Start	End	A65	A66	A67	A68	A69	A70	A71	A72	A73	A74	A75	A76	A77	A78	A79	A80	A81	A82	A83	A84
3.00	4.0%	1928	1967	0.0	0.4	0.5	0.6	0.5	0.3	0.3	0.0	-0.3	0.3	0.0	0.0	0.2	0.5	0.5	0.1	-0.2	-0.4	-0.1	0.0
3.00	4.0%	1929	1968	0.6	0.7	0.7	0.7	0.6	0.6	0.4	0.0	0.6	0.5	0.5	0.6	0.7	0.7	0.5	0.0	-0.4	0.0	0.3	0.3
2.50	4.2%	1930	1969	0.3	0.3	0.3	0.2	0.2	0.0	-0.1	0.2	0.1	0.1	0.2	0.3	0.2	0.1	-0.1	-0.3	-0.1	0.0	0.0	-0.1
2.00	4.4%	1931	1970	0.3	0.3	0.1	0.1	-0.1	-0.3	0.0	-0.1	-0.1	0.0	0.1	0.1	-0.1	-0.2	-0.4	-0.1	-0.1	0.0	-0.1	-0.2
1.00	4.8%	1932	1971	0.1	-0.4	-0.3	-0.5	-0.5	-0.4	-0.5	-0.5	-0.5	-0.3	-0.3	-0.5	-0.5	-0.5	-0.5	-0.4	-0.4	-0.4	-0.5	-0.5
1.00	4.8%	1933	1972	-0.3	-0.3	-0.4	-0.5	-0.3	-0.4	-0.4	-0.4	-0.2	-0.2	-0.3	-0.4	-0.5	-0.4	-0.3	-0.2	-0.3	-0.4	-0.4	-0.4
2.00	4.4%	1934	1973	0.2	0.0	-0.2	0.1	0.0	0.0	0.1	0.2	0.2	0.0	-0.1	-0.3	-0.1	0.1	0.1	0.0	-0.2	-0.2	-0.2	-0.2
2.00	4.4%	1935	1974	0.0	-0.2	0.1	0.0	0.0	0.1	0.2	0.2	0.0	-0.1	-0.3	0.0	0.1	0.1	0.0	-0.1	-0.1	-0.1	-0.1	-0.4
2.00	4.4%	1936	1975	0.0	0.2	0.2	0.2	0.2	0.3	0.3	0.2	0.1	-0.2	0.1	0.2	0.2	0.1	0.0	0.0	-0.1	0.0	-0.3	-0.4
3.00	4.0%	1937	1976	0.7	0.6	0.6	0.7	0.7	0.7	0.7	0.5	-0.1	0.5	0.6	0.6	0.5	0.3	0.2	0.1	0.2	-0.3	-0.4	-0.4
2.50	4.2%	1938	1977	0.0	0.1	0.2	0.3	0.2	0.1	-0.1	-0.3	-0.1	0.1	0.1	0.0	-0.1	-0.1	-0.1	-0.1	-0.3	-0.3	-0.3	-0.2
2.50	4.2%	1939	1978	0.2	0.2	0.3	0.3	0.2	0.0	-0.2	0.1	0.2	0.2	0.1	0.0	0.0	-0.1	0.0	-0.3	-0.3	-0.3	-0.2	-0.3
2.50	4.2%	1940	1979	0.2	0.3	0.3	0.2	0.0	-0.2	0.1	0.2	0.2	0.1	0.0	0.0	-0.1	0.0	-0.3	-0.3	-0.3	-0.2	-0.3	-0.3
2.50	4.2%	1941	1980	0.3	0.3	0.1	-0.1	-0.3	-0.1	0.1	0.1	0.0	-0.1	-0.1	-0.1	-0.1	-0.3	-0.3	-0.3	-0.2	-0.3	-0.3	-0.3
2.00	4.4%	1942	1981	0.2	-0.1	-0.2	-0.4	-0.1	0.0	0.1	-0.1	-0.1	-0.1	-0.1	-0.1	-0.3	-0.4	-0.3	-0.3	-0.4	-0.4	-0.4	-0.4
1.50	4.6%	1943	1982	0.0	-0.2	-0.4	-0.1	0.1	0.1	0.0	-0.1	-0.1	-0.1	0.0	-0.3	-0.4	-0.4	-0.3	-0.4	-0.4	-0.4	-0.4	-0.4
2.00	4.4%	1944	1983	0.1	-0.2	0.1	0.2	0.2	0.2	0.1	0.1	0.0	0.1	-0.2	-0.3	-0.2	-0.1	-0.3	-0.3	-0.4	-0.4	-0.3	-0.4
2.00	4.4%	1945	1984	0.0	0.2	0.2	0.3	0.2	0.2	0.2	0.2	0.2	-0.1	-0.2	-0.1	0.0	-0.2	-0.2	-0.2	-0.3	-0.2	-0.3	-0.4
2.00	4.4%	1946	1985	0.3	0.3	0.3	0.3	0.3	0.3	0.2	0.3	0.1	0.0	0.0	0.2	-0.1	-0.1	-0.1	-0.2	-0.1	-0.2	-0.2	-0.4
2.00	4.4%	1947	1986	0.2	0.2	0.2	0.1	0.1	0.1	0.2	-0.1	-0.2	-0.2	-0.1	-0.2	-0.2	-0.3	-0.3	-0.3	-0.3	-0.4	-0.4	-0.4
1.50	4.6%	1948	1987	0.2	0.1	0.1	0.0	0.0	0.1	-0.2	-0.2	-0.2	-0.1	-0.3	-0.3	-0.3	-0.4	-0.3	-0.4	-0.4	-0.4	-0.4	-0.4
1.50	4.6%	1949	1988	0.1	0.1	0.1	0.0	0.1	-0.2	-0.2	-0.2	-0.1	-0.2	-0.3	-0.3	-0.4	-0.3	-0.3	-0.4	-0.4	-0.4	-0.4	-0.4
1.50	4.6%	1950	1989	0.1	0.1	0.1	0.1	-0.1	-0.2	-0.1	0.0	-0.2	-0.2	-0.2	-0.3	-0.2	-0.3	-0.3	-0.4	-0.3	-0.4	-0.4	-0.3
2.00	4.4%	1951	1990	0.2	0.2	0.2	-0.1	-0.1	-0.1	0.1	-0.1	-0.2	-0.2	-0.2	-0.2	-0.2	-0.3	-0.3	-0.3	-0.4	-0.4	-0.3	-0.3
2.00	4.4%	1952	1991	0.2	0.2	-0.1	-0.2	-0.1	0.0	-0.2	-0.2	-0.2	-0.2	-0.2	-0.2	-0.3	-0.3	-0.3	-0.4	-0.4	-0.3	-0.3	-0.4
2.33	4.3%	1953	1992	0.2	0.0	-0.1	-0.1	0.1	-0.1	-0.1	-0.1	-0.2	-0.1	-0.1	-0.2	-0.3	-0.2	-0.3	-0.3	-0.2	-0.2	-0.3	-0.3
1.67	4.6%	1954	1993	-0.1	-0.2	-0.1	0.0	-0.2	-0.2	-0.2	-0.2	-0.2	-0.2	-0.3	-0.3	-0.2	-0.4	-0.4	-0.3	-0.3	-0.3	-0.3	-0.1
2.33	4.3%	1955	1994	0.1	0.2	0.2	0.1	0.1	0.1	0.0	0.1	0.0	-0.1	-0.1	-0.1	-0.2	-0.3	-0.1	-0.1	-0.2	-0.1	0.1	0.2
2.33	4.3%	1956	1995	0.2	0.3	0.2	0.1	0.2	0.0	0.1	0.1	0.0	-0.1	0.0	-0.2	-0.2	-0.1	-0.1	-0.1	-0.1	0.2	0.3	0.2
2.33	4.3%	1957	1996	0.2	0.1	0.1	0.1	0.0	0.1	0.1	0.0	-0.1	0.0	-0.2	-0.2	-0.1	-0.1	-0.1	-0.1	0.1	0.3	0.2	0.1
2.33	4.3%	1958	1997	-0.1	-0.1	-0.1	-0.1	-0.1	-0.1	-0.1	-0.2	-0.1	-0.2	-0.3	-0.1	-0.1	-0.2	-0.2	0.0	0.2	0.1	0.0	0.0
2.67	4.1%	1959	1998	0.2	0.2	0.1	0.2	0.1	0.0	-0.1	0.0	-0.1	-0.2	0.0	0.0	0.0	0.0	0.2	0.3	0.2	0.2	0.2	0.2
3.00	4.0%	1960	1999	0.4	0.2	0.4	0.3	0.2	-0.1	0.2	-0.2	-0.3	0.0	0.0	0.0	0.0	0.4	0.7	0.6	0.3	0.4	0.5	0.4
3.00	4.0%	1961	2000	0.1	0.3	0.2	0.0	0.0	0.1	-0.1	-0.2	0.1	0.1	0.0	0.0	0.5	0.6	0.6	0.4	0.4	0.5	0.5	0.4
3.00	4.0%	1962	2001	0.5	0.4	0.3	0.0	0.3	-0.1	-0.2	0.1	0.2	0.1	0.1	0.5	0.7	0.6	0.5	0.5	0.5	0.5	0.4	0.5
3.00	4.0%	1963	2002	0.2	0.1	-0.1	0.1	-0.1	-0.3	0.0	0.0	0.0	0.0	0.5	0.6	0.6	0.4	0.5	0.5	0.4	0.4	0.5	0.1
3.00	4.0%	1964	2003	0.2	0.0	0.2	-0.1	-0.2	0.1	0.2	0.0	0.0	0.5	0.7	0.6	0.5	0.5	0.6	0.5	0.4	0.5	0.2	-0.1
3.33	3.9%	1965	2004	0.1	0.3	0.0	-0.1	0.3	0.3	0.2	0.2	0.6	0.7	0.7	0.6	0.6	0.6	0.6	0.6	0.6	0.5	0.1	0.1
3.67	3.7%	1966	2005	0.5	0.2	0.0	0.4	0.5	0.3	0.4	0.7	0.8	0.8	0.7	0.7	0.7	0.7	0.7	0.7	0.5	0.2	0.3	0.0
3.00	4.0%	1967	2006	0.0	-0.1	0.3	0.3	0.2	0.2	0.6	0.7	0.7	0.6	0.6	0.6	0.6	0.6	0.6	0.4	0.0	0.2	-0.1	-0.3
3.33	3.9%	1968	2007	0.2	0.5	0.6	0.5	0.5	0.7	0.8	0.8	0.7	0.7	0.8	0.7	0.7	0.7	0.6	0.5	0.5	0.2	0.0	0.2
3.33	3.9%	1969	2008	0.6	0.6	0.6	0.6	0.8	0.9	0.8	0.8	0.8	0.8	0.8	0.8	0.8	0.7	0.6	0.6	0.3	0.2	0.4	0.2
3.33	3.9%	1970	2009	0.4	0.3	0.3	0.7	0.8	0.7	0.6	0.7	0.7	0.6	0.6	0.6	0.4	0.2	0.2	-0.1	-0.3	-0.1	-0.2	-0.4
2.67	4.1%	1971	2010	0.1	0.1	0.3	0.3	0.3	0.3	0.3	0.3	0.3	0.3	0.3	0.2	0.1	0.1	-0.1	-0.1	-0.1	-0.1	-0.2	-0.1
3.00	4.0%	1972	1928	0.3	0.6	0.7	0.7	0.6	0.7	0.7	0.6	0.6	0.6	0.5	0.3	0.3	-0.1	-0.2	-0.1	-0.2	-0.3	-0.1	-0.4
3.00	4.0%	1973	1929	0.6	0.7	0.7	0.6	0.7	0.7	0.7	0.6	0.7	0.5	0.3	0.3	0.0	-0.1	0.0	-0.1	-0.3	0.0	-0.3	-0.4
2.33	4.3%	1974	1930	0.3	0.2	0.2	0.2	0.2	0.2	0.2	0.2	0.1	0.0	0.0	-0.2	-0.2	-0.2	-0.2	-0.3	-0.2	-0.3	-0.3	-0.3
1.33	4.7%	1975	1931	0.0	-0.2	-0.1	0.0	0.0	0.0	0.1	-0.2	-0.2	-0.2	-0.4	-0.5	-0.4	-0.4	-0.5	-0.4	-0.5	-0.5	-0.5	-0.5
1.67	4.6%	1976	1932	0.0	0.1	0.1	0.1	0.1	0.2	0.0	-0.1	-0.1	-0.3	-0.3	-0.3	-0.3	-0.4	-0.3	-0.4	-0.4	-0.4	-0.4	-0.4
1.67	4.6%	1977	1933	0.2	0.2	0.2	0.2	0.2	0.1	0.1	0.1	-0.1	-0.2	-0.1	-0.2	-0.2	-0.1	-0.3	-0.3	-0.4	-0.3	-0.4	-0.4
1.33	4.7%	1978	1934	0.2	0.2	0.2	0.2	0.1	0.0	0.0	-0.2	-0.3	-0.2	-0.2	-0.3	-0.2	-0.3	-0.4	-0.5	-0.4	-0.5	-0.5	-0.5
1.00	4.8%	1979	1935	0.2	0.2	0.2	0.1	0.0	0.0	-0.2	-0.3	-0.2	-0.2	-0.3	-0.2	-0.3	-0.4	-0.5	-0.4	-0.5	-0.5	-0.5	-0.5
1.00	4.8%	1980	1936	0.2	0.2	0.1	0.0	0.0	-0.2	-0.3	-0.2	-0.2	-0.3	-0.1	-0.3	-0.4	-0.5	-0.4	-0.5	-0.5	-0.5	-0.5	-0.5
1.33	4.7%	1981	1937	0.2	0.1	0.0	0.0	-0.2	-0.3	-0.2	-0.2	-0.3	-0.2	-0.3	-0.4	-0.4	-0.4	-0.5	-0.5	-0.5	-0.5	-0.5	-0.5
1.00	4.8%	1982	1938	0.0	0.0	0.0	-0.2	-0.3	-0.2	-0.3	-0.3	-0.2	-0.4	-0.4	-0.5	-0.4	-0.5	-0.5	-0.5	-0.5	-0.5	-0.5	-0.5
1.00	4.8%	1983	1939	0.1	0.1	0.0	-0.1	0.0	-0.1	-0.1	0.0	-0.2	-0.3	-0.3	-0.2	-0.4	-0.4	-0.5	-0.5	-0.5	-0.5	-0.5	-0.5
1.33	4.7%	1984	1940	0.2	0.1	0.0	0.1	0.0	-0.1	0.1	-0.1	-0.2	-0.2	-0.1	-0.3	-0.3	-0.4	-0.4	-0.4	-0.5	-0.5	-0.4	-0.5
1.33	4.7%	1985	1941	0.1	0.0	0.1	0.0	0.0	0.1	-0.1	-0.2	-0.2	-0.1	-0.3	-0.3	-0.4	-0.4	-0.4	-0.4	-0.5	-0.4	-0.5	-0.5
1.67	4.6%	1986	1942	0.1	0.2	0.2	0.1	0.2	0.1	0.0	-0.1	0.0	-0.1	-0.2	-0.3	-0.3	-0.3	-0.3	-0.3	-0.3	-0.4	-0.4	-0.4
1.67	4.6%	1987	1943	0.2	0.2	0.2	0.2	0.1	0.1	0.0	0.1	-0.1	-0.1	-0.2	-0.2	-0.2	-0.2	-0.3	-0.2	-0.3	-0.3	-0.3	-0.4
1.67	4.6%	1988	1944	0.1	0.1	0.2	0.1	0.0	-0.1	0.0	-0.2	-0.2	-0.3	-0.3	-0.3	-0.3	-0.3	-0.3	-0.4	-0.4	-0.4	-0.4	-0.4
1.67	4.6%	1989	1945	0.1	0.2	0.1	0.1	0.0	0.1	-0.1	-0.1	-0.2	-0.2	-0.2	-0.2	-0.3	-0.2	-0.3	-0.4	-0.3	-0.4	-0.3	-0.2
2.33	4.3%	1990	1946	0.3	0.2	0.1	0.0	0.1	-0.1	-0.1	-0.1	-0.2	-0.2	-0.1	-0.2	-0.1	-0.2	-0.2	-0.2	-0.3	-0.2	-0.1	-0.1
2.00	4.4%	1991	1947	0.0	-0.1	-0.1	0.0	-0.2	-0.2	-0.3	-0.3	-0.3	-0.2	-0.3	-0.2	-0.3	-0.4	-0.3	-0.4	-0.4	-0.2	-0.2	-0.3
2.67	4.1%	1992	1948	0.1	0.0	0.2	0.0	0.0	-0.1	-0.1	-0.2	-0.1	-0.2	-0.1	-0.2	-0.2	-0.2	-0.2	-0.2	-0.1	-0.1	-0.2	-0.3
3.00	4.0%	1993	1949	0.2	0.4	0.0	0.0	-0.1	-0.2	-0.2	-0.1	-0.2	0.0	-0.3	-0.3	-0.3	-0.3	-0.3	0.0	-0.1	-0.2	-0.4	-0.3
3.00	4.0%	1994	1950	0.5	0.2	0.2	0.0	-0.1	-0.1	0.0	-0.1	0.0	-0.1	-0.2	-0.1	-0.2	-0.2	0.1	0.0	-0.2	-0.4	-0.1	0.2
3.33	3.9%	1995	1951	0.0	0.0	-0.1	-0.2	-0.2	-0.2	-0.2	-0.1	-0.3	-0.3	-0.3	-0.4	-0.3	-0.1	-0.1	-0.3	-0.4	-0.3	-0.2	-0.1
3.67	3.7%	1996	1952	0.3	0.0	0.0	0.0	0.1	0.0	0.2	0.0	-0.1	0.0	-0.1	-0.1	0.2	0.1	0.0	-0.3	-0.1	0.1	0.3	0.0
3.67	3.7%	1997	1953	0.1	0.1	0.0	0.1	0.0	0.2	0.0	0.0	0.0	0.0	0.0	0.4	0.3	0.1	-0.2	0.0	0.2	0.5	0.3	0.0
3.67	3.7%	1998	1954	0.3	0.2	0.4	0.3	0.6	0.2	0.1	0.2	0.1	0.2	0.6	0.5	0.3	0.0	0.3	0.6	0.7	0.6	0.3	0.2
3.67	3.7%	1999	1955	0.2	0.4	0.3	0.6	0.2	0.2	0.2	0.1	0.2	0.6	0.5	0.3	0.0	0.3	0.6	0.7	0.5	0.3	0.2	-0.1
4.00	3.6%	2000	1956	0.4	0.3	0.6	0.2	0.2	0.2	0.2	0.3	0.7	0.6	0.4	0.1	0.4	0.6	0.8	0.7	0.4	0.4	0.1	-0.2

Start	A85	A86	A87	A88	A89	A90	A91	A92	A93	A94	A95	A96	A97	A98	A99	A00	A01	A02	A03	A04	Bequest	AVG	1st 10Y%	Sum to 85	Sum to 105
1928	0.1	0.0	-0.3	-0.3	-0.3	-0.3	-0.4	-0.4	-0.4	-0.4	-0.4	-0.4	-0.4	-0.4	-0.4	-0.4	-0.4	-0.4	-0.4	-0.4	-32%	-0.1	0.3	3.2	-3.7
1929	0.0	-0.2	-0.3	-0.4	-0.2	-0.4	-0.4	-0.4	-0.4	-0.4	-0.4	-0.4	-0.4	-0.4	-0.4	-0.4	-0.4	-0.4	-0.4	-0.4	-43%	0.0	0.5	8.5	1.3
1930	-0.6	-0.5	-0.6	-0.6	-0.7	-0.7	-0.7	-0.7	-0.7	-0.7	-0.7	-0.7	-0.7	-0.7	-0.7	-0.7	-0.7	-0.7	-0.7	-0.7	-25%	-0.3	0.2	1.6	-11.9
1931	-0.4	-0.4	-0.3	-0.6	-0.6	-0.6	-0.6	-0.6	-0.6	-0.6	-0.6	-0.6	-0.6	-0.6	-0.6	-0.6	-0.6	-0.6	-0.6	-0.6	-18%	-0.3	0.0	-0.9	-12.0
1932	-0.7	-0.6	-0.7	-0.7	-0.7	-0.7	-0.7	-0.7	-0.7	-0.7	-0.7	-0.7	-0.7	-0.7	-0.7	-0.7	-0.7	-0.7	-0.7	-0.7	-26%	-0.5	-0.4	-8.5	-22.0
1933	-0.6	-0.8	-0.8	-0.8	-0.8	-0.8	-0.8	-0.8	-0.8	-0.8	-0.8	-0.8	-0.8	-0.8	-0.8	-0.8	-0.8	-0.8	-0.8	-0.8	-17%	-0.6	-0.4	-7.2	-22.6
1934	-0.7	-0.7	-0.7	-0.7	-0.7	-0.7	-0.7	-0.7	-0.7	-0.7	-0.7	-0.7	-0.7	-0.7	-0.7	-0.7	-0.7	-0.7	-0.7	-0.7	-13%	-0.4	0.0	-0.6	-15.4
1935	-0.5	-0.5	-0.5	-0.5	-0.5	-0.5	-0.5	-0.5	-0.5	-0.5	-0.5	-0.5	-0.5	-0.5	-0.5	-0.5	-0.5	-0.5	-0.5	-0.5	-9%	-0.3	0.0	-0.7	-11.7
1936	-0.5	-0.4	-0.5	-0.5	-0.5	-0.5	-0.5	-0.5	-0.5	-0.5	-0.5	-0.5	-0.5	-0.5	-0.5	-0.5	-0.5	-0.5	-0.5	-0.5	-10%	-0.2	0.2	1.4	-8.7
1937	-0.3	-0.4	-0.4	-0.4	-0.4	-0.4	-0.4	-0.4	-0.4	-0.4	-0.4	-0.4	-0.4	-0.4	-0.4	-0.4	-0.4	-0.4	-0.4	-0.4	-16%	0.0	0.6	7.1	-1.0
1938	-0.4	-0.4	-0.4	-0.4	-0.4	-0.4	-0.4	-0.4	-0.4	-0.4	-0.4	-0.4	-0.4	-0.4	-0.4	-0.4	-0.4	-0.4	-0.4	-0.4	-9%	-0.2	0.1	-0.8	-9.2
1939	-0.4	-0.4	-0.4	-0.4	-0.4	-0.4	-0.4	-0.4	-0.4	-0.4	-0.4	-0.4	-0.4	-0.4	-0.4	-0.4	-0.4	-0.4	-0.4	-0.4	-13%	-0.2	0.2	0.2	-7.0
1940	-0.4	-0.4	-0.4	-0.4	-0.4	-0.4	-0.4	-0.4	-0.4	-0.4	-0.4	-0.4	-0.4	-0.4	-0.4	-0.4	-0.4	-0.4	-0.4	-0.4	-21%	-0.2	0.1	-0.4	-7.6
1941	-0.4	-0.4	-0.4	-0.4	-0.4	-0.4	-0.4	-0.4	-0.4	-0.4	-0.4	-0.4	-0.4	-0.4	-0.4	-0.4	-0.4	-0.4	-0.4	-0.4	-11%	-0.3	0.0	-1.7	-10.4
1942	-0.4	-0.4	-0.4	-0.4	-0.4	-0.4	-0.4	-0.4	-0.4	-0.4	-0.4	-0.4	-0.4	-0.4	-0.4	-0.4	-0.4	-0.4	-0.4	-0.3	-5%	-0.3	-0.1	-3.8	-12.0
1943	-0.6	-0.6	-0.6	-0.6	-0.6	-0.6	-0.6	-0.6	-0.6	-0.6	-0.6	-0.2	-0.5	-0.6	-0.5	-0.4	-0.3	-0.6	-0.4	-0.5	-3%	-0.4	-0.1	-4.3	-14.8
1944	-0.5	-0.5	-0.5	-0.5	-0.5	-0.5	-0.5	-0.5	-0.5	-0.5	-0.2	-0.2	-0.5	-0.4	-0.3	-0.4	-0.3	-0.4	-0.5	-0.5	0%	-0.3	0.1	-2.0	-10.8
1945	-0.5	-0.5	-0.5	-0.5	-0.5	-0.5	-0.5	-0.5	-0.3	0.2	-0.1	-0.2	-0.3	-0.1	-0.1	-0.2	0.1	-0.4	-0.5	-0.3	-2%	-0.2	0.1	-0.7	-7.1
1946	-0.5	-0.7	-0.7	-0.6	-0.5	-0.6	-0.6	-0.2	0.3	0.2	-0.2	0.0	-0.2	-0.1	-0.1	0.0	-0.2	-0.7	-0.4	-0.5	-3%	-0.1	0.2	1.1	-5.2
1947	-0.6	-0.6	-0.6	-0.6	-0.6	-0.6	-0.4	0.0	-0.2	-0.3	-0.3	-0.2	-0.4	-0.3	-0.1	-0.4	-0.6	-0.6	-0.6	-0.6	2%	-0.3	0.1	-2.1	-10.2
1948	-0.4	-0.4	-0.4	-0.4	-0.4	-0.1	0.3	0.2	-0.1	0.1	0.1	0.2	0.0	0.3	0.0	-0.3	-0.1	-0.4	-0.4	-0.2	-1%	-0.2	0.0	-3.8	-6.5
1949	-0.3	-0.2	-0.3	-0.3	0.1	0.4	0.2	0.1	0.1	0.3	0.2	0.3	0.2	0.1	-0.1	0.0	-0.2	-0.3	-0.2	-0.2	0%	-0.1	-0.1	-4.2	-4.6
1950	-0.5	-0.5	-0.5	-0.2	0.3	0.1	-0.2	0.0	0.1	0.1	-0.1	0.2	-0.3	-0.5	-0.3	-0.6	-0.6	-0.6	-0.6	-0.6	1%	-0.2	0.0	-3.7	-9.1
1951	-0.5	-0.5	-0.2	0.2	0.1	-0.2	-0.1	0.1	0.0	0.1	0.1	-0.1	-0.5	-0.3	-0.5	-0.5	-0.4	-0.5	-0.5	-0.2	1%	-0.2	0.0	-3.1	-7.8
1952	-0.5	-0.2	0.2	0.0	-0.2	-0.1	-0.1	0.0	-0.1	0.1	-0.3	-0.4	-0.5	-0.5	-0.5	-0.5	-0.5	-0.5	-0.5	-0.5	3%	-0.2	-0.1	-3.7	-9.3
1953	-0.2	0.3	0.1	-0.2	0.0	0.1	0.0	0.0	0.1	-0.1	-0.4	-0.3	-0.5	-0.5	-0.5	-0.5	-0.5	-0.5	-0.5	-0.5	4%	-0.2	-0.1	-3.0	-7.6
1954	0.1	0.0	-0.3	-0.2	0.0	-0.1	-0.2	0.1	-0.3	-0.5	-0.5	-0.7	-0.8	-0.7	-0.7	-0.8	-0.4	-0.8	-0.8	-0.8	5%	-0.3	-0.1	-4.4	-12.4
1955	0.0	-0.2	-0.1	0.0	0.0	-0.1	-0.1	-0.3	-0.6	-0.5	-0.8	-0.8	-0.8	-0.8	-0.8	-0.6	-0.8	-0.8	-0.8	-0.8	5%	-0.2	0.1	-0.2	-9.7
1956	-0.2	0.0	0.0	-0.1	-0.1	0.0	-0.4	-0.5	-0.5	-0.6	-0.8	-0.6	-0.8	-0.8	-0.5	-0.8	-0.8	-0.8	-0.8	-0.8	4%	-0.2	0.1	0.8	-9.1
1957	0.0	0.1	0.0	-0.1	0.1	-0.3	-0.5	-0.4	-0.7	-0.8	-0.7	-0.7	-0.8	-0.6	-0.8	-0.8	-0.8	-0.8	-0.8	-0.8	6%	-0.2	0.1	0.5	-9.5
1958	-0.1	0.0	-0.1	0.0	-0.3	-0.6	-0.5	-0.7	-0.7	-0.7	-0.7	-0.7	-0.7	-0.7	-0.7	-0.7	-0.7	-0.7	-0.7	-0.7	-1%	-0.3	-0.1	-2.0	-12.8
1959	0.0	0.0	0.1	-0.2	-0.4	-0.4	-0.7	-0.7	-0.6	-0.7	-0.7	-0.5	-0.7	-0.7	-0.7	-0.7	-0.7	-0.7	-0.7	-0.7	0%	-0.2	0.0	1.6	-8.7
1960	0.2	0.4	0.0	-0.2	-0.1	-0.4	-0.4	-0.4	-0.4	-0.4	-0.4	-0.4	-0.4	-0.4	-0.4	-0.4	-0.4	-0.4	-0.4	-0.4	-14%	0.0	0.1	4.1	-1.7
1961	0.5	0.2	-0.1	-0.1	-0.3	-0.4	-0.3	-0.4	-0.4	-0.1	-0.4	-0.4	-0.4	-0.4	-0.4	-0.4	-0.4	-0.4	-0.4	-0.4	-9%	0.0	0.1	4.4	-1.2
1962	0.0	-0.1	-0.1	-0.4	-0.4	-0.4	-0.4	-0.4	-0.3	-0.4	-0.4	-0.4	-0.4	-0.4	-0.4	-0.4	-0.4	-0.4	-0.4	-0.4	-12%	0.0	0.2	6.4	-0.6
1963	-0.1	-0.1	-0.4	-0.4	-0.3	-0.4	-0.4	-0.3	-0.4	-0.4	-0.4	-0.4	-0.4	-0.4	-0.4	-0.4	-0.4	-0.4	-0.4	-0.4	0%	-0.1	0.0	4.3	-3.0
1964	-0.1	-0.3	-0.4	-0.4	-0.4	-0.4	-0.3	-0.4	-0.4	-0.4	-0.4	-0.4	-0.4	-0.4	-0.4	-0.4	-0.4	-0.4	-0.4	-0.4	-13%	-0.1	0.1	5.5	-2.2
1965	-0.2	-0.3	-0.1	-0.3	-0.4	-0.1	-0.4	-0.4	-0.4	-0.4	-0.4	-0.4	-0.4	-0.4	-0.4	-0.4	-0.4	-0.4	-0.4	-0.4	-16%	0.0	0.3	7.8	1.3
1966	-0.2	0.0	-0.1	-0.3	0.0	-0.3	-0.3	-0.3	-0.3	-0.3	-0.3	-0.3	-0.3	-0.3	-0.3	-0.3	-0.3	-0.3	-0.3	-0.3	-18%	0.1	0.4	9.7	5.1
1967	-0.2	-0.3	-0.4	-0.2	-0.4	-0.4	-0.4	-0.4	-0.4	-0.4	-0.4	-0.4	-0.4	-0.4	-0.4	-0.4	-0.4	-0.4	-0.4	-0.4	-20%	0.0	0.3	6.4	-1.3
1968	0.0	-0.1	0.2	-0.2	-0.3	-0.4	-0.3	-0.4	-0.4	-0.4	-0.4	-0.4	-0.4	-0.4	-0.4	-0.4	-0.4	-0.4	-0.4	-0.4	-12%	0.1	0.6	10.7	4.8
1969	0.0	0.4	0.0	-0.2	-0.3	-0.1	-0.4	-0.4	-0.4	-0.4	-0.4	-0.4	-0.4	-0.4	-0.4	-0.4	-0.4	-0.4	-0.4	-0.4	3%	0.2	0.7	12.6	7.1
1970	-0.2	-0.4	-0.4	-0.4	-0.4	-0.4	-0.4	-0.4	-0.4	-0.4	-0.4	-0.4	-0.4	-0.4	-0.4	-0.4	-0.4	-0.4	-0.4	-0.4	-15%	0.0	0.6	6.8	-0.5
1971	-0.7	-0.7	-0.7	-0.7	-0.7	-0.7	-0.7	-0.7	-0.7	-0.7	-0.7	-0.7	-0.7	-0.7	-0.7	-0.7	-0.7	-0.7	-0.7	-0.7	-8%	-0.3	0.3	2.8	-10.8
1972	-0.4	-0.4	-0.4	-0.4	-0.4	-0.4	-0.4	-0.4	-0.4	-0.4	-0.4	-0.4	-0.4	-0.4	-0.4	-0.4	-0.4	-0.4	-0.4	-0.4	-22%	-0.1	0.6	6.1	-2.1
1973	-0.4	-0.4	-0.4	-0.4	-0.4	-0.4	-0.4	-0.4	-0.4	-0.4	-0.4	-0.4	-0.4	-0.4	-0.4	-0.4	-0.4	-0.4	-0.4	-0.4	-16%	-0.1	0.7	6.1	-2.2
1974	-0.5	-0.5	-0.5	-0.5	-0.5	-0.5	-0.5	-0.5	-0.5	-0.5	-0.5	-0.5	-0.5	-0.5	-0.5	-0.5	-0.5	-0.6	-0.6	-0.6	-10%	-0.3	0.2	-0.6	-11.1
1975	-0.7	-0.7	-0.7	-0.7	-0.7	-0.7	-0.7	-0.7	-0.7	-0.7	-0.7	-0.7	-0.7	-0.7	-0.7	-0.7	-0.7	-0.7	-0.7	-0.7	-12%	-0.5	-0.1	-5.4	-19.7
1976	-0.6	-0.6	-0.6	-0.6	-0.6	-0.6	-0.6	-0.6	-0.6	-0.6	-0.6	-0.6	-0.6	-0.6	-0.6	-0.6	-0.6	-0.6	-0.6	-0.6	-4%	-0.4	0.0	-3.5	-15.4
1977	-0.6	-0.6	-0.6	-0.6	-0.6	-0.6	-0.6	-0.6	-0.6	-0.6	-0.6	-0.6	-0.6	-0.6	-0.7	-0.7	-0.7	-0.7	-0.7	-0.7	6%	-0.4	0.1	-1.9	-14.8
1978	-0.7	-0.7	-0.7	-0.7	-0.7	-0.7	-0.7	-0.7	-0.7	-0.7	-0.7	-0.7	-0.7	-0.7	-0.7	-0.7	-0.7	-0.7	-0.7	-0.7	6%	-0.4	0.0	-3.4	-16.8
1979	-0.8	-0.8	-0.8	-0.8	-0.8	-0.8	-0.8	-0.8	-0.8	-0.8	-0.8	-0.8	-0.8	-0.8	-0.8	-0.8	-0.8	-0.8	-0.8	-0.8	10%	-0.5	0.0	-4.5	-19.9
1980	-0.7	-0.7	-0.7	-0.7	-0.7	-0.7	-0.7	-0.7	-0.7	-0.7	-0.7	-0.8	-0.8	-0.8	-0.8	-0.8	-0.8	-0.8	-0.8	-0.8	2%	-0.5	-0.1	-4.9	-19.8
1981	-0.6	-0.6	-0.6	-0.6	-0.6	-0.6	-0.6	-0.6	-0.6	-0.6	-0.6	-0.6	-0.6	-0.6	-0.6	-0.6	-0.6	-0.6	-0.6	-0.6	5%	-0.5	-0.1	-5.5	-18.1
1982	-0.6	-0.6	-0.6	-0.6	-0.6	-0.6	-0.6	-0.6	-0.6	-0.6	-0.6	-0.6	-0.6	-0.6	-0.6	-0.6	-0.6	-0.6	-0.6	-0.6	8%	-0.5	-0.2	-6.9	-19.3
1983	-0.8	-0.8	-0.8	-0.8	-0.8	-0.8	-0.8	-0.8	-0.9	-0.9	-0.9	-0.6	-0.9	-0.9	-0.9	-0.9	-0.9	-0.9	-0.9	-0.9	12%	-0.5	-0.1	-5.2	-21.9
1984	-0.7	-0.7	-0.7	-0.7	-0.5	-0.6	-0.7	-0.7	-0.7	-0.5	-0.4	-0.5	-0.7	-0.7	-0.7	-0.7	-0.7	-0.7	-0.7	-0.7	9%	-0.4	0.0	-4.0	-17.2
1985	-0.7	-0.7	-0.7	-0.5	-0.5	-0.7	-0.7	-0.7	-0.5	-0.3	-0.6	-0.7	-0.7	-0.7	-0.7	-0.7	-0.7	-0.7	-0.7	-0.5	9%	-0.4	0.0	-4.5	-17.0
1986	-0.6	-0.6	-0.3	-0.4	-0.5	-0.7	-0.6	-0.3	0.0	-0.2	-0.5	-0.5	-0.7	-0.7	-0.5	-0.7	-0.6	-0.7	-0.2	-0.1	3%	-0.3	0.1	-2.7	-11.6
1987	-0.5	-0.2	-0.3	-0.5	-0.7	-0.4	-0.3	0.1	-0.2	-0.4	-0.5	-0.7	-0.7	-0.5	-0.6	-0.7	-0.4	-0.2	-0.1	-0.5	0%	-0.3	0.1	-1.8	-10.3
1988	-0.3	-0.4	-0.6	-0.7	-0.5	-0.4	-0.2	-0.4	-0.6	-0.6	-0.7	-0.7	-0.7	-0.7	-0.7	-0.7	-0.3	-0.6	-0.7	-0.7	4%	-0.4	0.0	-3.7	-14.8
1989	-0.7	-0.7	-0.9	-0.8	-0.6	-0.5	-0.7	-0.8	-0.9	-0.9	-0.9	-0.7	-0.9	-0.9	-0.7	-0.5	-0.4	-0.9	-0.9	-0.9	9%	-0.5	0.0	-2.9	-18.5
1990	-0.5	-0.7	-0.5	-0.4	-0.1	-0.4	-0.6	-0.6	-0.7	-0.7	-0.7	-0.7	-0.7	-0.7	-0.4	-0.4	-0.7	-0.7	-0.7	-0.7	1%	-0.3	0.0	-1.7	-13.5
1991	-0.7	-0.6	-0.5	-0.3	-0.5	-0.7	-0.7	-0.7	-0.7	-0.7	-0.7	-0.7	-0.7	-0.7	-0.6	-0.7	-0.7	-0.7	-0.7	-0.7	-1%	-0.4	-0.2	-4.5	-16.9
1992	-0.4	-0.2	-0.2	-0.4	-0.5	-0.5	-0.5	-0.5	-0.5	-0.5	-0.5	-0.5	-0.5	-0.4	-0.5	-0.5	-0.5	-0.5	-0.5	-0.5	1%	-0.3	-0.1	-2.4	-11.1
1993	-0.1	0.2	-0.1	-0.4	-0.4	-0.4	-0.4	-0.4	-0.4	-0.4	-0.4	-0.2	-0.3	-0.4	-0.4	-0.4	-0.4	-0.4	-0.4	-0.4	-5%	-0.2	0.0	-2.6	-9.9
1994	0.4	0.2	-0.2	-0.2	-0.4	-0.4	-0.3	-0.4	-0.4	-0.3	0.0	0.0	-0.4	-0.4	-0.4	-0.4	-0.4	-0.4	-0.4	-0.4	-2%	-0.2	0.0	-0.7	-6.4
1995	-0.4	-0.4	-0.4	-0.4	-0.4	-0.4	-0.4	-0.4	-0.4	-0.4	-0.4	-0.4	-0.4	-0.4	-0.4	-0.4	-0.4	-0.4	-0.4	-0.4	-16%	-0.3	-0.2	-4.1	-12.3
1996	-0.3	-0.2	-0.3	-0.3	-0.2	-0.3	-0.3	-0.3	0.0	0.0	-0.3	-0.3	-0.3	-0.3	-0.3	-0.3	-0.3	-0.3	-0.3	-0.3	-12%	-0.1	0.0	0.4	-4.7
1997	-0.1	-0.3	-0.3	-0.2	-0.3	-0.3	-0.3	0.1	0.0	-0.2	-0.3	-0.3	-0.3	-0.3	-0.3	-0.3	-0.3	-0.3	-0.3	-0.3	-7%	-0.1	0.0	2.1	-2.7
1998	-0.1	-0.3	0.1	-0.1	0.0	0.0	0.4	0.4	-0.1	-0.3	-0.3	-0.3	-0.3	-0.1	-0.3	-0.3	-0.3	-0.3	-0.3	-0.3	-11%	0.1	0.2	6.7	3.9
1999	-0.3	0.1	-0.1	-0.1	0.0	0.4	0.3	0.0	-0.3	-0.3	-0.3	-0.1	-0.2	-0.3	-0.3	-0.3	-0.3	-0.3	-0.3	-0.3	-15%	0.1	0.3	6.4	3.3
2000	0.2	0.0	0.0	0.1	0.5	0.4	0.0	-0.2	-0.2	-0.2	-0.2	-0.1	-0.2	-0.2	-0.2	-0.2	-0.2	-0.2	-0.2	-0.2	-21%	0.2	0.4	7.3	6.3
																					Overall Average			0.0	-8.9
																					Low-Valuation Avg			-2.4	-12.5
																					High-Valuation Avg			5.2	-0.9

FIGURE 189

Annual cost of GI summary, based on 2% IRR using recommended GI solution with low rates, compared to 100% systemic withdrawal solution on Baseline Market and Portfolio.

For consistency, ECM is used in both cases (Figure 188 and Figure 189), to show the exact differences with and without GI, everything else being equal. However, a retiree would likely use EM when not using GI; therefore, to complete the picture, a similar set of tests use EM without GI compared to ECM with GI, with everything else the same.

Figure 190 shows this year-by-year cost difference for the first case (with low GI payout rates) using ECM with GI and EM without GI.

Valuation	Initial	Start	End	A65	A66	A67	A68	A69	A70	A71	A72	A73	A74	A75	A76	A77	A78	A79	A80	A81	A82	A83	A84	A85	A86	A87	A88	A89	A90	A91	A92	A93	A94	A95	A96	A97	A98	A99	A00	A01	A02	A03	A04	Bequest	AVG	1st 10Y%	Sum to 85	Sum to 105
3.00	4.0%	1928	1967	-1.5	-0.5	0.1	0.2	0.1	-0.5	-0.4	-1.3	-1.0	-0.4	-1.0	-0.8	-0.4	0.1	0.1	-0.6	-1.2	-0.8	-1.3	-0.5	-0.4	-0.9	-1.0	-0.9	-0.9	-1.0	-0.8	-0.8	-0.8	-0.8	-0.8	-0.8	-0.8	-0.8	-0.8	-0.8	-0.8	-0.8	-0.8	-0.8	-32%	-0.7	-0.5	-11.6	-27.8
3.00	4.0%	1929	1968	0.0	0.2	0.3	0.3	0.0	0.0	-0.4	-1.4	0.2	-0.1	0.0	0.1	0.3	0.3	-0.1	-1.0	-0.8	-1.0	-0.4	-0.3	-1.1	-1.1	-1.0	-0.8	-1.2	-0.8	-0.8	-0.8	-0.8	-0.8	-0.8	-0.8	-0.8	-0.8	-0.8	-0.8	-0.8	-0.8	-0.8	-0.8	-43%	-0.5	-0.1	-3.6	-20.5
2.50	4.2%	1930	1969	-0.1	0.1	0.0	-0.4	-0.3	-0.9	-1.1	-0.3	-0.7	-0.5	-0.3	0.1	0.1	-0.5	-1.3	-0.5	-1.1	-0.7	-0.5	-1.3	-1.2	-1.3	-1.1	-1.2	-0.9	-0.9	-0.9	-0.9	-0.9	-0.9	-0.9	-0.9	-0.9	-0.9	-0.9	-0.9	-0.9	-0.9	-0.9	-0.9	-25%	-0.7	-0.4	-10.3	-30.0
2.00	4.4%	1931	1970	0.0	0.0	-0.7	-0.7	-1.5	-0.9	-0.8	-1.4	-1.2	-0.6	-0.1	-0.2	-0.7	-1.3	-0.6	-1.3	-0.4	-0.2	-0.6	-1.2	-1.3	-1.3	-1.4	-0.8	-0.8	-0.8	-0.8	-0.8	-0.8	-0.8	-0.8	-0.8	-0.8	-0.8	-0.8	-0.8	-0.8	-0.8	-0.8	-0.8	-18%	-0.8	-0.8	-14.5	-32.8
1.00	4.8%	1932	1971	-0.4	-1.4	-1.5	-0.7	-0.7	-1.0	-0.7	-0.7	-0.7	-1.6	-1.6	-1.0	-0.7	-0.7	-0.8	-1.3	-1.4	-1.1	-0.9	-0.8	-0.9	-1.1	-0.9	-0.9	-0.9	-0.9	-0.9	-0.9	-0.9	-0.9	-0.9	-0.9	-0.9	-0.9	-0.9	-0.9	-0.9	-0.9	-0.9	-0.9	-26%	-1.0	-1.0	-19.8	-38.8
1.00	4.8%	1933	1972	-1.8	-1.7	-1.0	-0.7	-1.5	-1.0	-1.1	-1.3	-1.1	-0.9	-1.5	-1.1	-0.7	-1.4	-1.0	-0.7	-1.5	-1.4	-1.3	-1.0	-1.4	-1.0	-1.0	-1.0	-1.0	-1.0	-1.0	-1.0	-1.0	-1.0	-1.0	-1.0	-1.0	-1.0	-1.0	-1.0	-1.0	-1.0	-1.0	-1.0	-17%	-1.1	-1.2	-24.0	-45.2
2.00	4.4%	1934	1973	-0.3	-1.2	-1.2	-0.5	-0.9	-0.7	-0.4	-0.1	-0.1	-0.5	-1.3	-0.8	-0.9	-0.4	-0.2	-0.5	-1.4	-1.3	-1.4	-1.0	-1.0	-1.0	-1.0	-1.0	-1.0	-1.0	-1.0	-1.0	-1.0	-1.0	-1.0	-1.0	-1.0	-1.0	-1.0	-1.0	-1.0	-1.0	-1.0	-1.0	-13%	-0.9	-0.6	-15.1	-34.6
2.00	4.4%	1935	1974	-1.2	-1.2	-0.5	-0.9	-0.8	-0.4	0.0	-0.1	-0.5	-1.1	-1.0	-0.7	-0.3	-0.2	-0.5	-1.0	-1.2	-1.1	-0.6	-0.6	-0.8	-0.8	-0.8	-0.8	-0.8	-0.8	-0.8	-0.8	-0.8	-0.8	-0.8	-0.8	-0.8	-0.8	-0.8	-0.8	-0.8	-0.8	-0.8	-0.8	-9%	-0.8	-0.7	-13.9	-30.0
2.00	4.4%	1936	1975	-1.1	0.0	-0.2	-0.2	-0.1	0.1	0.1	-0.2	-0.6	-1.5	-0.4	-0.2	-0.1	-0.3	-0.7	-0.8	-1.0	-0.5	-0.8	-0.6	-0.8	-1.0	-0.8	-0.8	-0.8	-0.8	-0.8	-0.8	-0.8	-0.8	-0.8	-0.8	-0.8	-0.8	-0.8	-0.8	-0.8	-0.8	-0.8	-0.8	-10%	-0.6	-0.4	-8.8	-24.6
3.00	4.0%	1937	1976	0.3	0.1	0.2	0.2	0.3	0.3	0.2	-0.2	-1.3	-0.2	0.1	0.2	-0.1	-0.6	-0.6	-0.9	-0.6	-1.0	-0.8	-0.8	-1.0	-0.8	-0.8	-0.8	-0.8	-0.8	-0.8	-0.8	-0.8	-0.8	-0.8	-0.8	-0.8	-0.8	-0.8	-0.8	-0.8	-0.8	-0.8	-0.8	-16%	-0.5	0.0	-5.1	-21.1
2.50	4.2%	1938	1977	-1.1	-0.8	-0.5	0.0	0.0	-0.8	-1.4	-0.6	-1.1	-0.4	-0.3	-0.7	-1.0	-1.1	-1.2	-0.7	-0.5	-0.5	-0.5	-0.8	-0.7	-0.7	-0.7	-0.7	-0.7	-0.7	-0.7	-0.7	-0.7	-0.7	-0.7	-0.7	-0.7	-0.7	-0.7	-0.7	-0.7	-0.7	-0.7	-0.7	-9%	-0.7	-0.7	-13.8	-27.4
2.50	4.2%	1939	1978	-0.4	-0.1	0.1	0.0	-0.3	-0.9	-1.1	-0.6	-0.3	-0.2	-0.4	-0.9	-0.9	-1.1	-0.6	-0.6	-0.5	-0.5	-0.7	-0.5	-0.6	-0.6	-0.6	-0.6	-0.6	-0.6	-0.6	-0.6	-0.6	-0.6	-0.6	-0.6	-0.6	-0.6	-0.6	-0.6	-0.6	-0.6	-0.6	-0.6	-13%	-0.6	-0.4	-10.3	-22.8
2.50	4.2%	1940	1979	-0.3	0.1	0.0	-0.4	-1.0	-1.0	-0.7	-0.3	-0.2	-0.5	-0.9	-0.9	-1.1	-0.7	-0.6	-0.5	-0.5	-0.7	-0.5	-0.5	-0.6	-0.6	-0.6	-0.6	-0.6	-0.6	-0.6	-0.6	-0.6	-0.6	-0.6	-0.6	-0.6	-0.6	-0.6	-0.6	-0.6	-0.6	-0.6	-0.6	-21%	-0.6	-0.4	-11.2	-23.7
2.50	4.2%	1941	1980	0.0	-0.1	-0.8	-1.5	-0.6	-1.2	-0.6	-0.4	-0.8	-1.1	-1.0	-1.2	-0.6	-0.6	-0.5	-0.5	-0.7	-0.5	-0.5	-0.5	-0.7	-0.7	-0.7	-0.7	-0.7	-0.7	-0.7	-0.7	-0.7	-0.7	-0.7	-0.7	-0.7	-0.7	-0.7	-0.7	-0.7	-0.7	-0.7	-0.7	-11%	-0.7	-0.7	-13.8	-27.6
2.00	4.4%	1942	1981	-0.5	-1.2	-1.5	-0.6	-1.4	-0.8	-0.5	-0.8	-1.2	-1.0	-1.2	-0.7	-0.9	-0.6	-0.7	-1.0	-0.6	-0.6	-0.6	-0.6	-0.7	-0.7	-0.7	-0.7	-0.7	-0.7	-0.7	-0.7	-0.7	-0.7	-0.7	-0.7	-0.7	-0.7	-0.7	-0.7	-0.7	-0.7	-0.7	-0.9	-5%	-0.8	-1.0	-16.9	-30.8
1.50	4.6%	1943	1982	-1.0	-1.6	-1.0	-1.2	-0.5	-0.4	-0.6	-0.9	-0.9	-0.9	-0.6	-1.3	-1.0	-1.0	-1.4	-0.8	-0.6	-0.8	-0.6	-0.6	-0.9	-0.9	-0.9	-0.9	-0.9	-0.9	-0.9	-0.9	-0.9	-0.9	-0.9	-0.4	-1.0	-0.9	-1.1	-0.9	-0.5	-0.9	-0.1	-0.1	-3%	-0.8	-0.9	-17.8	-33.1
2.00	4.4%	1944	1983	-0.8	-1.5	-0.5	-0.1	-0.1	-0.3	-0.5	-0.6	-0.6	-0.3	-1.4	-1.0	-1.1	-1.3	-0.9	-0.7	-0.6	-0.6	-0.7	-0.6	-0.8	-0.8	-0.8	-0.8	-0.8	-0.8	-0.8	-0.8	-0.8	-0.8	-0.6	-1.0	-0.8	-0.9	-0.7	-1.0	-0.9	-0.9	-0.8	-0.8	0%	-0.8	-0.5	-14.3	-30.4
2.00	4.4%	1945	1984	-1.2	-0.2	0.1	0.1	-0.1	-0.2	-0.2	-0.4	-0.2	-1.2	-1.5	-1.3	-0.6	-1.3	-1.2	-1.2	-0.7	-1.1	-1.0	-0.6	-0.8	-0.8	-0.8	-0.8	-0.8	-0.8	-0.8	-0.8	-1.0	0.6	0.2	-0.5	-0.7	0.3	0.2	-0.4	0.5	-1.0	-0.8	0.5	-2%	-0.6	-0.4	-14.2	-22.3
2.00	4.4%	1946	1985	0.1	0.1	0.1	0.1	0.1	0.0	0.1	0.1	-0.6	-1.0	-0.8	-0.3	-1.1	-1.3	-0.9	-1.3	-1.1	-1.4	-1.1	-0.6	-1.2	-0.9	-0.9	-1.0	-1.2	-1.0	-1.0	0.1	0.4	0.3	-0.2	0.2	0.1	-0.1	-0.1	0.1	0.1	-0.9	-0.4	-0.6	-3%	-0.5	-0.1	-11.1	-19.1
2.00	4.4%	1947	1986	-0.1	0.0	-0.2	-0.5	-0.4	-0.6	-0.3	-1.5	-1.3	-1.5	-0.8	-1.2	-1.1	-1.0	-0.8	-1.0	-0.7	-0.6	-0.6	-0.6	-0.8	-0.8	-0.8	-0.8	-0.8	-0.8	-1.1	0.2	-0.5	-1.2	-1.0	-0.1	-1.1	-0.9	0.3	-0.8	-0.8	-0.8	-0.8	-0.8	2%	-0.7	-0.6	-14.8	-29.1
1.50	4.6%	1948	1987	-0.2	-0.4	-0.6	-0.6	-0.7	-0.5	-1.6	-1.5	-1.5	-0.6	-1.4	-1.4	-1.4	-1.0	-1.2	-1.0	-0.7	-0.6	-0.9	-0.6	-0.7	-0.8	-0.7	-0.7	-0.7	-0.6	0.7	0.5	-0.4	0.4	0.4	0.4	-0.3	0.4	0.3	-1.0	0.4	-0.7	-0.7	0.9	-1%	-0.5	-0.8	-18.5	-21.5
1.50	4.6%	1949	1988	-0.5	-0.7	-0.6	-0.7	-0.5	-1.6	-1.5	-1.5	-0.6	-1.5	-1.4	-1.4	-1.0	-1.3	-1.1	-0.9	-0.6	-0.9	-0.6	-0.6	-0.6	-0.7	-0.6	-0.6	-0.1	0.8	0.6	0.1	0.3	0.7	0.3	0.4	0.4	0.0	-0.7	0.0	-0.5	-0.6	0.5	0.8	0%	-0.5	-1.0	-19.7	-19.4
1.50	4.6%	1950	1989	-0.5	-0.4	-0.4	-0.4	-1.2	-1.6	-1.1	-0.6	-1.5	-1.4	-1.1	-1.4	-1.0	-1.4	-1.2	-0.9	-1.1	-0.7	-0.6	-1.1	-1.2	-1.2	-1.1	0.1	0.5	0.4	0.1	0.4	0.4	0.3	0.1	0.3	-0.5	-1.1	0.3	-0.9	-0.8	-0.3	0.2	0.6	1%	-0.6	-0.9	-19.6	-22.7
2.00	4.4%	1951	1990	-0.3	-0.3	-0.2	-1.1	-1.5	-1.1	-0.4	-1.4	-1.4	-1.4	-1.1	-1.3	-1.3	-1.0	-0.7	-1.0	-0.6	-0.6	-1.0	-0.8	-0.8	-0.9	-0.2	0.4	0.3	-0.2	0.0	0.3	0.1	0.1	0.1	-0.1	-0.8	-0.6	-0.8	-0.8	0.2	-0.8	-0.8	1.5	1%	-0.6	-0.9	-18.4	-22.2
2.00	4.4%	1952	1991	-0.4	-0.2	-1.2	-1.5	-1.4	-0.7	-1.5	-1.4	-1.4	-1.1	-1.4	-1.2	-1.0	-0.7	-1.0	-0.6	-0.6	-0.9	-0.9	-0.6	-0.8	-0.3	0.5	0.2	-0.3	-0.1	0.1	0.0	-0.4	0.2	-0.8	-1.1	-0.9	-0.8	-0.8	-0.8	-0.8	-0.8	0.8	-0.3	3%	-0.7	-1.1	-19.6	-26.7
2.33	4.3%	1953	1992	-0.3	-1.2	-1.5	-1.3	-0.6	-1.4	-1.3	-1.2	-1.1	-1.1	-1.2	-1.0	-0.7	-1.0	-0.5	-0.5	-0.8	-0.9	-0.7	-0.7	-0.2	0.5	0.3	-0.2	0.3	0.2	0.0	0.1	0.2	-0.2	-0.9	-0.6	-0.7	-0.7	-0.6	-0.7	-0.7	0.2	-0.7	-0.5	4%	-0.6	-1.1	-19.0	-24.3
1.67	4.6%	1954	1993	-1.3	-1.6	-1.2	-0.7	-1.4	-1.5	-1.1	-1.4	-1.1	-1.3	-1.3	-1.1	-1.3	-0.9	-0.6	-1.3	-1.2	-1.1	-1.1	0.3	0.4	0.4	0.0	0.1	0.2	0.1	-0.1	0.1	-0.3	-1.3	-1.0	-1.2	-1.0	-1.1	-1.1	-1.0	1.0	-1.0	-1.0	-0.9	5%	-0.8	-1.2	-22.1	-30.9
2.33	4.3%	1955	1994	-0.7	-0.4	-0.1	-0.7	-0.8	-0.5	-1.0	-0.5	-0.7	-1.0	-1.2	-0.8	-1.1	-0.7	-1.0	-0.8	-1.2	-0.8	0.2	0.3	0.1	-0.1	0.0	-0.1	-0.1	-0.3	-0.1	-0.3	-1.4	-0.6	-1.0	-1.0	-1.0	-1.0	-1.0	0.5	-0.6	-1.0	-1.0	-0.3	5%	-0.6	-0.6	-13.4	-23.8
2.33	4.3%	1956	1995	-0.4	0.0	-0.4	-0.6	-0.4	-0.9	-0.5	-0.6	-0.8	-1.3	-0.6	-1.2	-0.9	-0.8	-0.6	-0.8	-0.8	0.2	0.3	0.2	-0.2	-0.1	0.0	-0.2	-0.3	-0.1	-0.5	-1.4	-1.1	-1.4	-1.0	-1.0	-1.0	-1.0	0.4	-1.0	-1.0	-1.0	-1.0	-1.0	4%	-0.6	-0.6	-10.9	-25.0
2.33	4.3%	1957	1996	0.0	-0.7	-0.6	-0.6	-0.9	-0.6	-0.7	-1.0	-1.3	-0.7	-1.2	-0.9	-0.6	-0.6	-0.9	-0.7	0.1	0.3	0.2	0.1	-0.1	0.0	-0.1	-0.3	-0.1	-0.4	-1.5	-0.7	-1.1	-1.0	-1.1	-1.1	-1.0	0.3	-1.0	-1.0	-1.0	-1.0	-1.0	-1.0	6%	-0.6	-0.7	-11.3	-25.2
2.33	4.3%	1958	1997	-1.1	-1.4	-1.2	-1.2	-1.2	-1.4	-1.2	-0.9	-1.2	-0.8	-0.5	-1.2	-1.1	-1.1	-1.1	0.1	0.4	0.2	0.1	0.1	0.0	-0.1	-0.2	-0.1	-0.4	-1.3	-1.4	-0.9	-0.9	-1.0	-0.9	-0.9	-0.9	-0.9	-0.9	-0.9	-0.9	-0.9	-0.9	-0.9	-1%	-0.8	-1.2	-16.0	-31.9
2.67	4.1%	1959	1998	-0.6	-0.4	-0.8	-0.4	-0.7	-0.9	-1.2	-0.7	-1.1	-0.9	-0.6	-0.5	-0.6	-0.6	0.1	0.2	0.2	0.1	0.2	0.1	-0.2	-0.2	0.0	-0.5	-1.4	-1.0	-0.9	-0.9	-1.1	-1.0	-0.9	0.2	-0.9	-0.9	-0.9	-0.9	-0.9	-0.9	-0.9	-0.9	0%	-0.6	-0.8	-9.2	-24.5
3.00	4.0%	1960	1999	-0.5	-1.0	-0.5	-0.7	-0.9	-1.3	-0.8	-1.2	-0.9	-0.9	-0.7	-1.0	-0.9	0.1	0.4	0.3	0.0	0.1	0.2	0.0	-0.2	0.1	-0.5	-1.1	-1.0	-0.8	-0.8	-0.8	-0.8	-0.8	-0.8	-0.8	-0.8	-0.8	-0.8	-0.8	-0.8	-0.8	-0.8	-0.8	-14%	-0.6	-0.9	-10.3	-24.9
3.00	4.0%	1961	2000	-1.3	-0.6	-0.7	-1.1	-1.4	-0.9	-1.3	-1.1	-0.8	-0.6	-0.8	-0.7	0.2	0.4	0.3	0.1	0.1	0.3	0.2	0.0	0.2	-0.1	-1.2	-0.9	-1.0	-0.8	-0.9	-0.8	-0.8	-0.1	-0.8	-0.8	-0.8	-0.8	-0.8	-0.8	-0.8	-0.8	-0.8	-0.8	-9%	-0.6	-1.0	-9.7	-23.9
3.00	4.0%	1962	2001	-0.3	-0.5	-0.7	-1.3	-0.6	-1.3	-1.1	-0.8	-0.6	-0.8	-0.7	0.2	0.3	0.3	0.1	0.2	0.2	0.1	-0.1	0.0	-0.5	-1.3	-1.2	-0.8	-0.8	-0.8	-0.8	-0.8	-1.0	-0.8	-0.8	-0.8	-0.8	-0.8	-0.8	-0.8	-0.8	-0.8	-0.8	-0.8	-12%	-0.6	-0.8	-7.3	-23.9
3.00	4.0%	1963	2002	-0.9	-1.3	-1.3	-1.1	-1.2	-1.0	-1.0	-0.9	-1.2	-0.9	0.1	0.4	0.3	0.0	0.2	0.2	0.0	0.0	0.1	-0.3	-1.2	-0.9	-0.8	-0.8	-0.9	-0.8	-0.8	-1.0	-0.8	-0.8	-0.8	-0.8	-0.8	-0.8	-0.8	-0.8	-0.8	-0.8	-0.8	-0.8	0%	-0.7	-1.1	-10.1	-26.7
3.00	4.0%	1964	2003	-0.9	-1.5	-0.7	-1.3	-1.1	-1.0	-0.6	-0.8	-0.8	0.2	0.4	0.3	0.1	0.2	0.2	0.1	-0.1	0.1	-0.2	-1.3	-1.2	-1.0	-0.8	-0.8	-0.8	-0.8	-0.9	-0.8	-0.8	-0.8	-0.8	-0.8	-0.8	-0.8	-0.8	-0.8	-0.8	-0.8	-0.8	-0.8	-13%	-0.6	-0.9	-8.9	-25.4
3.33	3.9%	1965	2004	-1.2	-0.5	-1.3	-1.2	-0.5	-0.5	-0.4	-0.4	0.2	0.4	0.4	0.2	0.3	0.3	0.3	0.1	0.2	0.0	-0.7	-0.5	-1.1	-0.9	-1.1	-0.9	-0.7	-0.5	-0.7	-0.7	-0.7	-0.7	-0.7	-0.7	-0.7	-0.7	-0.7	-0.7	-0.7	-0.7	-0.7	-0.7	-16%	-0.5	-0.5	-4.9	-20.6
3.67	3.7%	1966	2005	-0.4	-1.2	-1.1	-0.4	-0.2	-0.4	-0.3	0.3	0.4	0.5	0.3	0.3	0.4	0.3	0.2	0.3	0.0	-0.5	-0.3	-1.0	-0.7	-1.0	-0.8	-0.6	-0.3	-0.6	-0.6	-0.6	-0.6	-0.6	-0.6	-0.6	-0.6	-0.6	-0.6	-0.6	-0.6	-0.6	-0.6	-0.6	-18%	-0.4	-0.3	-2.7	-15.8
3.00	4.0%	1967	2006	-1.4	-1.2	-0.7	-0.6	-0.7	-0.7	0.1	0.3	0.3	0.1	0.2	0.3	0.2	0.1	0.2	-0.2	-0.8	-0.5	-1.2	-0.9	-1.1	-1.0	-0.8	-1.1	-0.8	-0.8	-0.8	-0.8	-0.8	-0.8	-0.8	-0.8	-0.8	-0.8	-0.8	-0.8	-0.8	-0.8	-0.8	-0.8	-20%	-0.6	-0.4	-7.1	-23.6
3.33	3.9%	1968	2007	-1.2	0.0	0.0	-0.2	-0.1	0.3	0.5	0.4	0.3	0.3	0.4	0.3	0.3	0.3	0.3	-0.2	-0.1	-0.7	-1.2	-0.5	-1.3	-1.2	-0.1	-1.1	-0.9	-0.7	-0.9	-0.7	-0.7	-0.7	-0.7	-0.7	-0.7	-0.7	-0.7	-0.7	-0.7	-0.7	-0.7	-0.7	-12%	-0.4	0.0	-0.8	-16.7
3.33	3.9%	1969	2008	0.1	0.2	0.1	0.1	0.4	0.6	0.5	0.4	0.4	0.4	0.4	0.4	0.4	0.2	0.0	0.1	-0.5	-0.7	-0.3	-0.7	-1.3	0.0	-1.1	-1.1	-0.9	-1.1	-0.7	-0.7	-0.7	-0.7	-0.7	-0.7	-0.7	-0.7	-0.7	-0.7	-0.7	-0.7	-0.7	0.0	3%	-0.3	0.3	2.3	-12.9
3.33	3.9%	1970	2009	-0.6	-0.7	-0.6	0.2	0.4	0.3	0.2	0.2	0.2	0.2	0.0	0.2	-0.3	-0.8	-0.7	-1.2	-0.9	-1.2	-1.1	-0.7	-1.1	-0.7	-0.7	-0.7	-0.7	-0.7	-0.7	-0.7	-0.7	-0.7	-0.7	-0.7	-0.7	-0.7	-0.7	-0.7	-0.7	-0.7	-0.7	-0.7	-15%	-0.6	0.0	-6.9	-22.2
2.67	4.1%	1971	2010	-0.7	-0.6	0.1	0.3	0.2	0.0	0.1	0.1	0.0	0.0	0.0	-0.3	-0.6	-0.6	-1.2	-1.0	-1.2	-1.1	-0.8	-0.8	-0.9	-0.9	-0.9	-0.9	-0.9	-0.9	-0.9	-0.9	-0.9	-0.9	-0.9	-0.9	-0.9	-0.9	-0.9	-0.9	-0.9	-0.9	-0.9	-0.9	-8%	-0.7	0.0	-7.9	-26.1
3.00	4.0%	1972	1928	-0.6	0.3	0.4	0.3	0.2	0.2	0.3	0.3	0.1	0.3	-0.1	-0.7	-0.6	-1.3	-1.2	-1.3	-1.2	-1.0	-1.0	-0.8	-0.8	-0.8	-0.8	-0.8	-0.8	-0.8	-0.8	-0.8	-0.8	-0.8	-0.8	-0.8	-0.8	-0.8	-0.8	-0.8	-0.8	-0.8	-0.8	-0.8	-22%	-0.6	0.2	-7.6	-23.3
3.00	4.0%	1973	1929	0.2	0.3	0.3	0.1	0.2	0.2	0.2	0.1	0.2	0.0	-0.5	-0.4	-1.3	-1.2	-1.1	-1.3	-1.0	-0.6	-1.0	-0.8	-0.8	-0.8	-0.8	-0.8	-0.8	-0.8	-0.8	-0.8	-0.8	-0.8	-0.8	-0.8	-0.8	-0.8	-0.8	-0.8	-0.8	-0.8	-0.8	-0.8	-16%	-0.6	0.2	-7.5	-23.3
2.33	4.3%	1974	1930	0.0	0.0	-0.5	-0.3	-0.2	-0.3	-0.3	-0.2	-0.6	-0.9	-0.8	-1.2	-0.8	-1.1	-0.9	-0.6	-1.0	-0.5	-0.5	-0.5	-0.8	-0.8	-0.8	-0.8	-0.8	-0.8	-0.8	-0.8	-0.8	-0.8	-0.8	-0.8	-0.8	-0.8	-0.8	-0.8	-0.8	-0.8	-0.8	-0.8	-10%	-0.7	-0.3	-11.2	-26.8
1.33	4.7%	1975	1931	-0.7	-1.5	-1.1	-0.8	-0.6	-0.7	-0.4	-1.1	-1.6	-1.5	-1.1	-0.7	-1.0	-0.8	-0.7	-0.9	-0.7	-0.7	-0.7	-0.7	-1.0	-1.0	-1.0	-1.0	-1.0	-1.0	-1.0	-1.0	-1.0	-1.0	-1.0	-1.0	-1.0	-1.0	-1.0	-1.0	-1.0	-1.0	-1.0	-1.0	-12%	-0.9	-1.0	-17.9	-37.3
1.67	4.6%	1976	1932	-0.8	-0.6	-0.4	-0.4	-0.5	-0.2	-0.8	-1.1	-1.1	-1.3	-1.0	-1.3	-1.2	-0.9	-1.3	-0.6	-0.6	-0.6	-0.6	-0.6	-0.8	-0.8	-0.8	-0.8	-0.8	-0.8	-0.8	-0.8	-0.8	-0.8	-0.8	-0.8	-0.8	-0.8	-0.8	-0.9	-0.9	-0.9	-0.9	-0.9	-4%	-0.8	-0.7	-16.0	-33.1
1.67	4.6%	1977	1933	-0.2	-0.1	-0.1	-0.2	-0.1	-0.4	-0.6	-0.6	-1.2	-1.5	-0.9	-1.2	-1.3	-0.6	-1.3	-1.0	-0.6	-1.1	-0.6	-0.6	-0.9	-0.9	-0.9	-0.9	-0.9	-0.9	-0.9	-0.9	-0.9	-0.9	-0.9	-0.9	-0.9	-0.9	-0.9	-0.9	-0.9	-0.9	-0.9	-0.9	6%	-0.8	-0.5	-14.3	-32.4
1.33	4.7%	1978	1934	-0.2	-0.1	-0.2	-0.1	-0.5	-0.8	-0.7	-1.4	-1.6	-1.1	-1.2	-1.6	-0.7	-1.3	-1.2	-0.8	-1.1	-0.7	-0.7	-0.7	-0.9	-0.9	-0.9	-0.9	-0.9	-0.9	-0.9	-0.9	-0.9	-0.9	-0.9	-0.9	-0.9	-0.9	-0.9	-0.9	-0.9	-0.9	-0.9	-0.9	6%	-0.9	-0.7	-16.4	-35.1
1.00	4.8%	1979	1935	-0.2	-0.2	-0.1	-0.5	-0.7	-0.8	-1.4	-1.8	-1.1	-1.1	-1.6	-0.7	-1.5	-1.2	-0.9	-1.3	-0.7	-0.7	-0.7	-0.7	-1.0	-1.0	-1.0	-1.0	-1.0	-1.0	-1.0	-1.0	-1.0	-1.0	-1.0	-1.0	-1.0	-1.0	-1.0	-1.0	-1.0	-1.0	-1.0	-1.0	10%	-1.0	-0.8	-17.9	-38.5
1.00	4.8%	1980	1936	-0.2	-0.1	-0.4	-0.8	-0.7	-1.4	-1.7	-1.1	-1.2	-1.6	-0.6	-1.6	-1.4	-1.0	-1.4	-0.7	-0.7	-0.7	-0.7	-0.7	-1.0	-1.0	-1.0	-1.0	-1.0	-1.0	-1.0	-1.0	-1.0	-1.0	-1.0	-1.0	-1.0	-1.0	-0.2	-1.0	-1.0	-1.0	-1.0	-1.0	2%	-1.0	-0.9	-18.7	-38.1
1.33	4.7%	1981	1937	-0.2	-0.5	-0.9	-0.9	-1.5	-1.6	-1.2	-1.3	-1.5	-0.8	-1.4	-1.2	-0.8	-1.2	-0.7	-0.7	-0.7	-0.7	-0.7	-0.7	-0.9	-0.9	-0.9	-0.9	-0.9	-0.9	-0.9	-0.9	-0.9	-0.9	-0.9	-0.9	-0.9	-0.9	-0.9	-0.9	-0.9	-0.9	-0.9	-0.9	5%	-0.9	-1.0	-19.2	-37.1
1.00	4.8%	1982	1938	-0.5	-0.9	-0.8	-1.5	-1.7	-1.2	-1.3	-1.6	-0.9	-1.4	-1.3	-1.0	-1.4	-0.7	-0.7	-0.7	-0.7	-0.7	-0.7	-0.7	-0.9	-0.9	-0.9	-0.9	-0.9	-0.9	-0.9	-0.9	-0.9	-0.9	-0.9	-0.9	-0.9	-0.9	-0.9	-0.9	-0.9	-0.9	-0.9	-0.9	8%	-1.0	-1.2	-20.6	-38.6
1.00	4.8%	1983	1939	-0.4	-0.4	-0.8	-1.1	-0.7	-0.9	-1.0	-0.5	-1.1	-1.4	-1.5	-0.9	-1.4	-1.2	-0.8	-0.7	-0.7	-0.7	-0.7	-0.7	-1.1	-1.1	-1.1	-1.1	-1.3	-1.1	-1.1	-1.1	-1.1	-1.1	-1.1	0.9	-0.9	-1.1	-1.1	-1.1	-1.1	-1.1	-1.1	-1.0	12%	-0.9	-0.8	-17.7	-37.5
1.33	4.7%	1984	1940	-0.2	-0.6	-0.8	-0.5	-0.6	-0.8	-0.4	-0.9	-1.2	-1.5	-0.8	-1.5	-1.5	-1.0	-0.8	-0.8	-0.8	-0.7	-0.9	-0.7	-1.0	-1.0	-1.0	-1.0	-1.3	-1.1	-1.0	-1.0	-1.0	0.0	1.1	0.9	-1.0	-1.0	-1.0	-1.0	0.0	-1.0	-1.0	1.5	9%	-0.7	-0.8	-17.1	-28.5
1.33	4.7%	1985	1941	-0.6	-0.9	-0.5	-0.7	-0.9	-0.4	-1.0	-1.2	-1.6	-0.8	-1.6	-1.6	-1.1	-0.9	-0.9	-0.9	-0.7	-1.0	-0.7	-0.7	-0.9	-0.9	-0.9	-1.2	-1.2	-0.9	-0.9	-0.9	0.0	1.3	0.9	-0.7	-0.9	-0.9	-0.9	-0.3	-0.9	-0.9	1.3	2.4	9%	-0.7	-0.9	-18.6	-26.7
1.67	4.6%	1986	1942	-0.5	-0.2	-0.3	-0.6	-0.2	-0.5	-0.8	-1.0	-0.6	-1.1	-1.3	-1.3	-1.2	-1.1	-1.2	-1.0	-1.2	-0.8	-0.7	-0.7	-0.9	-1.0	0.0	-1.1	-1.2	-0.9	-1.1	0.9	1.2	1.4	0.1	0.7	-0.9	-0.9	0.8	-0.8	0.8	1.0	1.7	1.5	3%	-0.4	-0.6	-16.3	-15.1
1.67	4.6%	1987	1943	-0.1	-0.2	-0.3	-0.1	-0.4	-0.5	-0.9	-0.4	-1.1	-1.0	-1.5	-1.4	-1.4	-1.4	-1.3	-0.5	-1.0	-1.0	-1.2	-0.9	-1.2	0.3	-0.5	-1.2	-1.0	-0.5	0.8	0.9	1.2	0.5	0.3	-0.9	-1.0	0.7	0.1	0.6	1.5	1.6	1.3	0.8	0%	-0.3	-0.5	-16.5	-11.9
1.67	4.6%	1988	1944	-0.5	-0.6	-0.2	-0.6	-0.9	-1.1	-0.6	-1.5	-1.5	-1.3	-1.2	-1.2	-1.3	-1.0	-1.3	-0.8	-0.6	-0.9	-0.7	-0.8	-0.4	-0.9	-1.1	-1.0	-1.1	0.4	1.1	1.1	-0.5	0.1	-1.0	-1.0	-0.8	-1.0	0.0	1.1	1.8	1.4	-0.8	-1.0	4%	-0.5	-0.9	-18.5	-21.8
1.67	4.6%	1989	1945	-0.5	-0.1	-0.5	-0.7	-0.9	-0.5	-1.0	-1.0	-1.5	-1.4	-1.4	-1.4	-1.3	-0.8	-1.1	-0.9	-1.0	-0.9	-1.1	0.0	-1.1	-1.5	-1.2	-1.3	0.3	0.9	0.3	-0.5	-0.4	-1.2	-1.2	0.8	-1.2	0.3	1.4	1.4	1.3	-0.8	-1.2	-1.2	9%	-0.6	-0.8	-18.2	-24.0
2.33	4.3%	1990	1946	-0.1	-0.5	-0.6	-0.9	-0.5	-1.1	-1.0	-1.2	-1.2	-1.2	-1.3	-1.2	-0.5	-0.9	-0.8	-0.9	-0.6	-0.9	0.1	-0.5	-1.2	-0.9	-1.2	0.1	0.8	0.7	-0.7	-0.1	-0.9	-0.9	-0.3	-0.9	-0.9	0.7	1.5	1.2	-0.4	-0.9	-0.9	-0.9	1%	-0.6	-0.8	-15.8	-22.1
2.00	4.4%	1991	1947	-1.1	-1.1	-1.4	-0.9	-1.5	-1.5	-1.0	-1.0	-1.0	-1.1	-1.0	-1.3	-0.7	-0.6	-0.8	-0.6	-0.6	-0.5	-1.0	-0.7	-0.9	-1.1	-0.6	0.4	-0.1	-0.9	-0.9	-0.9	-0.9	-0.9	-0.9	-0.9	-0.9	1.3	1.2	-0.9	-0.9	-0.9	-0.9	-0.9	-1%	-0.8	-1.2	-19.4	-31.1
2.67	4.1%	1992	1948	-0.8	-1.0	-0.5	-1.2	-1.1	-1.0	-0.9	-0.9	-1.0	-0.9	-1.1	-0.7	-0.6	-0.7	-0.5	-0.6	-0.6	-0.9	-0.8	-0.5	-0.9	-0.3	0.5	-0.2	-0.7	-0.7	-0.7	-0.7	-0.7	-0.7	-0.7	-0.7	0.8	0.9	-0.7	-0.7	-0.7	-0.7	-0.7	-0.7	1%	-0.6	-0.9	-16.3	-25.7
3.00	4.0%	1993	1949	-1.1	-0.4	-1.2	-1.4	-1.2	-1.2	-1.2	-1.3	-1.2	-0.8	-1.0	-1.0	-1.0	-0.9	-1.0	0.0	-0.8	-1.1	-0.8	-1.1	0.0	0.7	0.5	-0.9	-0.5	-0.8	-0.8	-0.7	-0.8	-0.8	-0.5	1.2	0.6	-0.8	-0.8	-0.8	-0.8	-0.8	-0.8	-0.8	-5%	-0.7	-1.1	-19.7	-28.5
3.00	4.0%	1994	1950	-0.3	-0.8	-0.8	-1.4	-1.3	-1.3	-1.3	-1.3	-0.6	-1.2	-1.1	-1.2	-1.1	-1.2	0.0	-0.4	-1.2	-0.9	-0.2	0.5	0.7	0.9	0.1	0.0	-0.8	-0.8	-0.1	-0.8	-0.5	0.7	1.1	0.9	-0.8	-0.8	-0.8	-0.8	-0.8	-0.8	-0.8	-0.8	-2%	-0.6	-1.0	-17.3	-22.5
3.33	3.9%	1995	1951	-1.4	-1.4	-1.1	-1.1	-1.0	-1.1	-1.0	-1.2	-0.9	-0.8	-0.9	-0.7	-0.9	-1.2	-1.1	-0.9	-0.8	-1.0	-1.2	-0.7	-0.8	-0.8	-0.8	-0.8	-0.8	-0.8	-0.8	-0.8	-0.8	-0.3	-0.8	-0.8	-0.8	-0.8	-0.8	-0.8	-0.8	-0.8	-0.8	-0.8	-16%	-0.9	-1.1	-20.2	-35.5
3.67	3.7%	1996	1952	-0.9	-1.1	-1.1	-1.1	-1.2	-1.1	-0.6	-1.0	-0.9	-1.0	-0.9	-0.9	-0.1	-0.6	-1.0	-0.7	-1.0	0.0	0.5	0.0	-0.7	-0.8	-0.7	-0.7	-0.4	-0.7	-0.7	0.0	0.9	0.8	-0.7	-0.7	-0.7	-0.7	-0.7	-0.7	-0.7	-0.7	-0.7	-0.7	-12%	-0.6	-1.0	-14.9	-24.5
3.67	3.7%	1997	1953	-1.2	-1.3	-1.1	-1.2	-1.1	-0.6	-1.1	-1.0	-1.1	-1.0	-1.1	0.2	0.0	-0.7	-0.9	-0.4	0.4	0.7	0.6	-0.3	-0.4	-0.7	-0.7	-0.7	-0.7	-0.7	-0.2	1.0	0.7	-0.8	-0.7	-0.7	-0.7	-0.7	-0.7	-0.7	-0.7	-0.7	-0.7	-0.7	-7%	-0.6	-1.1	-12.2	-22.1
3.67	3.7%	1998	1954	-0.9	-1.0	-0.5	-0.7	0.0	-0.8	-1.0	-0.7	-1.2	-0.4	0.4	0.2	-0.1	-1.2	0.0	0.4	0.5	0.6	0.3	0.3	-1.0	-0.7	0.2	-0.8	-0.2	0.4	0.7	0.6	-0.7	-0.7	-0.7	-0.7	-0.7	-0.9	-0.7	-0.7	-0.7	-0.7	-0.7	-0.7	-11%	-0.4	-0.7	-6.0	-15.1
3.67	3.7%	1999	1955	-1.0	-0.6	-0.6	0.0	-0.7	-1.0	-0.6	-1.1	-0.6	0.4	0.1	-0.2	-1.2	-0.1	0.4	0.5	0.6	0.2	0.3	-1.0	-0.7	0.1	-0.9	-0.7	0.3	0.6	0.6	-0.6	-0.7	-0.7	-0.7	-0.9	-0.8	-0.7	-0.7	-0.7	-0.7	-0.7	-0.7	-0.7	-15%	-0.4	-0.6	-6.5	-16.2
4.00	3.6%	2000	1956	-0.7	-0.8	-0.1	-0.9	-1.1	-0.8	-1.1	-0.5	0.4	0.2	-0.1	-1.0	0.0	0.5	0.5	0.5	0.3	0.4	-0.7	-0.6	0.2	-0.6	-0.4	0.2	0.7	0.5	-0.8	-0.6	-0.6	-0.6	-0.6	-0.7	-0.6	-0.6	-0.6	-0.6	-0.6	-0.6	-0.6	-0.6	-21%	-0.3	-0.5	-5.5	-13.2
																																												Overall Average			-13.4	-26.3
																																												Low-Valuation Avg			-15.5	-27.8
																																												High-Valuation Avg			-8.5	-22.1

FIGURE 190

Annual cost of GI summary, based on 1% IRR using ECM recommended GI solution with low rates, compared to 100% systemic withdrawal EM solution on Baseline Market and Portfolio.

Figure 191 shows the cost difference for the second case (with moderate GI payout rates) using ECM with GI and EM without GI.

Valuation	Initial	Start	End	A65	A66	A67	A68	A69	A70	A71	A72	A73	A74	A75	A76	A77	A78	A79	A80	A81	A82	A83	A84	A85	A86	A87	A88	A89	A90	A91	A92	A93	A94	A95	A96	A97	A98	A99	A00	A01	A02	A03	A04	Bequest	AVG	1st 10Y%	Sum to 85	Sum to 105
3.00	4.0%	1928	1967	-1.1	-0.1	0.4	0.5	0.4	-0.1	0.0	-0.9	-0.7	0.0	-0.6	-0.4	0.0	0.5	0.5	-0.2	-0.8	-0.4	-0.9	-0.2	0.0	-0.5	-0.7	-0.5	-0.5	-0.7	-0.4	-0.4	-0.4	-0.4	-0.4	-0.4	-0.4	-0.4	-0.4	-0.4	-0.4	-0.4	-0.4	-0.4	-32%	-0.3	-0.2	-4.1	-12.8
3.00	4.0%	1929	1968	0.4	0.6	0.7	0.7	0.4	0.4	0.0	-1.0	0.6	0.3	0.4	0.5	0.7	0.7	0.3	-0.7	-0.4	-0.7	0.0	0.1	-0.7	-0.7	-0.6	-0.5	-0.8	-0.4	-0.4	-0.4	-0.4	-0.4	-0.4	-0.4	-0.4	-0.4	-0.4	-0.4	-0.4	-0.4	-0.4	-0.4	-43%	-0.1	0.3	3.9	-5.5
2.50	4.2%	1930	1969	0.1	0.3	0.2	-0.2	-0.1	-0.8	-0.9	-0.1	-0.5	-0.3	-0.1	0.3	0.2	-0.3	-1.1	-0.3	-0.9	-0.5	-0.3	-1.1	-1.0	-1.0	-0.8	-1.0	-0.7	-0.7	-0.7	-0.7	-0.7	-0.7	-0.7	-0.7	-0.7	-0.7	-0.7	-0.7	-0.7	-0.7	-0.7	-0.7	-25%	-0.5	-0.2	-6.6	-21.6
2.00	4.4%	1931	1970	0.2	0.2	-0.5	-0.5	-1.3	-0.7	-0.6	-1.2	-1.0	-0.4	0.1	0.0	-0.5	-1.1	-0.4	-1.1	-0.3	-0.1	-0.4	-1.0	-1.1	-1.0	-1.1	-0.6	-0.6	-0.6	-0.6	-0.6	-0.6	-0.6	-0.6	-0.6	-0.6	-0.6	-0.6	-0.6	-0.6	-0.6	-0.6	-0.6	-18%	-0.6	-0.6	-10.7	-23.9
1.00	4.8%	1932	1971	-0.2	-1.3	-1.3	-0.5	-0.5	-0.8	-0.5	-0.5	-0.5	-1.4	-1.4	-0.8	-0.5	-0.5	-0.6	-1.1	-1.2	-0.9	-0.7	-0.6	-0.7	-0.8	-0.7	-0.7	-0.7	-0.7	-0.7	-0.7	-0.7	-0.7	-0.7	-0.7	-0.7	-0.7	-0.7	-0.7	-0.7	-0.7	-0.7	-0.7	-26%	-0.7	-0.8	-16.0	-29.7
1.00	4.8%	1933	1972	-1.7	-1.6	-0.8	-0.5	-1.3	-0.8	-0.9	-1.1	-0.9	-0.7	-1.3	-0.9	-0.5	-1.2	-0.9	-0.5	-1.3	-1.2	-1.1	-0.8	-1.2	-0.8	-0.8	-0.8	-0.8	-0.8	-0.8	-0.8	-0.8	-0.8	-0.8	-0.8	-0.8	-0.8	-0.8	-0.8	-0.8	-0.8	-0.8	-0.8	-17%	-0.9	-1.0	-20.2	-36.2
2.00	4.4%	1934	1973	-0.1	-1.0	-1.0	-0.3	-0.7	-0.5	-0.2	0.1	0.1	-0.4	-1.1	-0.6	-0.7	-0.2	0.0	-0.3	-1.2	-1.1	-1.2	-0.8	-0.7	-0.7	-0.7	-0.7	-0.7	-0.7	-0.7	-0.7	-0.7	-0.7	-0.7	-0.7	-0.7	-0.7	-0.7	-0.7	-0.7	-0.7	-0.7	-0.7	-13%	-0.7	-0.4	-11.3	-26.1
2.00	4.4%	1935	1974	-1.0	-1.0	-0.3	-0.7	-0.6	-0.2	0.2	0.1	-0.4	-0.9	-0.8	-0.5	-0.1	0.0	-0.3	-0.8	-1.0	-0.9	-0.4	-0.4	-0.5	-0.5	-0.5	-0.5	-0.5	-0.5	-0.5	-0.5	-0.5	-0.5	-0.5	-0.5	-0.5	-0.5	-0.5	-0.5	-0.5	-0.5	-0.5	-0.5	-9%	-0.5	-0.5	-10.1	-21.1
2.00	4.4%	1936	1975	-0.9	0.1	0.0	0.0	0.1	0.3	0.3	0.0	-0.4	-1.3	-0.2	0.0	0.1	-0.1	-0.5	-0.6	-0.8	-0.3	-0.6	-0.4	-0.5	-0.8	-0.5	-0.5	-0.5	-0.5	-0.5	-0.5	-0.5	-0.5	-0.5	-0.5	-0.5	-0.5	-0.5	-0.5	-0.5	-0.5	-0.5	-0.5	-10%	-0.4	-0.2	-5.1	-15.6
3.00	4.0%	1937	1976	0.7	0.4	0.5	0.6	0.7	0.7	0.6	0.2	-1.0	0.2	0.5	0.5	0.3	-0.2	-0.3	-0.5	-0.2	-0.6	-0.4	-0.4	-0.7	-0.4	-0.4	-0.4	-0.4	-0.4	-0.4	-0.4	-0.4	-0.4	-0.4	-0.4	-0.4	-0.4	-0.4	-0.4	-0.4	-0.4	-0.4	-0.4	-16%	-0.2	0.4	2.4	-6.1
2.50	4.2%	1938	1977	-0.9	-0.6	-0.3	0.2	0.1	-0.6	-1.2	-0.4	-1.0	-0.2	-0.1	-0.5	-0.8	-0.9	-1.0	-0.5	-0.3	-0.3	-0.3	-0.6	-0.4	-0.4	-0.4	-0.4	-0.4	-0.4	-0.4	-0.4	-0.4	-0.4	-0.4	-0.4	-0.4	-0.4	-0.4	-0.4	-0.4	-0.4	-0.4	-0.4	-9%	-0.5	-0.5	-10.1	-18.5
2.50	4.2%	1939	1978	-0.2	0.0	0.3	0.2	-0.1	-0.8	-0.9	-0.4	-0.1	0.0	-0.2	-0.7	-0.7	-0.9	-0.4	-0.4	-0.3	-0.3	-0.5	-0.3	-0.4	-0.4	-0.4	-0.4	-0.4	-0.4	-0.4	-0.4	-0.4	-0.4	-0.4	-0.4	-0.4	-0.4	-0.4	-0.4	-0.4	-0.4	-0.4	-0.4	-13%	-0.3	-0.2	-6.6	-13.8
2.50	4.2%	1940	1979	-0.1	0.3	0.2	-0.2	-0.8	-0.8	-0.5	-0.1	0.0	-0.3	-0.7	-0.7	-1.0	-0.5	-0.5	-0.3	-0.3	-0.5	-0.3	-0.3	-0.4	-0.4	-0.4	-0.4	-0.4	-0.4	-0.4	-0.4	-0.4	-0.4	-0.4	-0.4	-0.4	-0.4	-0.4	-0.4	-0.4	-0.4	-0.4	-0.4	-21%	-0.4	-0.2	-7.4	-14.6
2.50	4.2%	1941	1980	0.2	0.1	-0.6	-1.3	-0.5	-1.1	-0.4	-0.2	-0.6	-1.0	-0.9	-1.0	-0.5	-0.5	-0.3	-0.3	-0.5	-0.3	-0.3	-0.3	-0.4	-0.4	-0.4	-0.4	-0.4	-0.4	-0.4	-0.4	-0.4	-0.4	-0.4	-0.4	-0.4	-0.4	-0.4	-0.4	-0.4	-0.4	-0.4	-0.4	-11%	-0.5	-0.5	-10.0	-18.7
2.00	4.4%	1942	1981	-0.3	-1.1	-1.3	-0.4	-1.2	-0.6	-0.3	-0.7	-1.0	-0.8	-1.0	-0.5	-0.7	-0.4	-0.5	-0.9	-0.4	-0.4	-0.4	-0.4	-0.4	-0.4	-0.4	-0.4	-0.4	-0.4	-0.4	-0.4	-0.4	-0.4	-0.4	-0.4	-0.4	-0.4	-0.4	-0.4	-0.4	-0.4	-0.4	-0.6	-5%	-0.5	-0.8	-13.2	-21.7
1.50	4.6%	1943	1982	-0.8	-1.4	-0.8	-1.0	-0.3	-0.2	-0.4	-0.7	-0.7	-0.7	-0.4	-1.1	-0.8	-0.9	-1.3	-0.6	-0.4	-0.6	-0.4	-0.4	-0.6	-0.6	-0.6	-0.6	-0.6	-0.6	-0.6	-0.6	-0.6	-0.6	-0.6	-0.1	-0.7	-0.6	-0.9	-0.6	-0.2	-0.6	0.1	0.1	-3%	-0.6	-0.7	-14.0	-24.0
2.00	4.4%	1944	1983	-0.6	-1.3	-0.3	0.1	0.1	-0.1	-0.3	-0.4	-0.5	-0.1	-1.2	-0.9	-0.9	-1.1	-0.7	-0.5	-0.5	-0.4	-0.5	-0.4	-0.5	-0.5	-0.5	-0.5	-0.5	-0.5	-0.5	-0.5	-0.5	-0.6	-0.4	-0.7	-0.5	-0.6	-0.5	-0.8	-0.6	-0.6	-0.5	-0.5	0%	-0.5	-0.3	-10.5	-21.4
2.00	4.4%	1945	1984	-1.0	0.0	0.2	0.3	0.0	0.0	0.0	-0.2	0.0	-1.0	-1.3	-1.1	-0.4	-1.1	-1.0	-1.0	-0.5	-0.9	-0.8	-0.4	-0.5	-0.5	-0.5	-0.5	-0.5	-0.5	-0.5	-0.5	-0.7	0.8	0.5	-0.2	-0.4	0.6	0.4	-0.1	0.8	-0.7	-0.5	0.7	-2%	-0.3	-0.2	-10.4	-13.4
2.00	4.4%	1946	1985	0.3	0.3	0.3	0.3	0.3	0.2	0.2	0.3	-0.4	-0.8	-0.7	-0.1	-1.0	-1.1	-0.7	-1.1	-0.9	-1.2	-0.9	-0.5	-0.9	-0.7	-0.7	-0.8	-0.9	-0.7	-0.7	0.3	0.7	0.6	0.1	0.5	0.3	0.2	0.2	0.4	0.3	-0.7	-0.2	-0.3	-3%	-0.3	0.1	-7.3	-10.3
2.00	4.4%	1947	1986	0.1	0.1	0.0	-0.3	-0.2	-0.4	-0.1	-1.3	-1.1	-1.3	-0.7	-1.0	-0.9	-0.9	-0.6	-0.9	-0.5	-0.5	-0.4	-0.4	-0.6	-0.6	-0.6	-0.6	-0.6	-0.6	-0.8	0.4	-0.2	-0.9	-0.7	0.1	-0.9	-0.6	0.6	-0.6	-0.6	-0.6	-0.6	-0.6	2%	-0.5	-0.4	-11.1	-20.2
1.50	4.6%	1948	1987	0.0	-0.2	-0.4	-0.5	-0.5	-0.3	-1.4	-1.3	-1.3	-0.5	-1.3	-1.2	-1.2	-0.8	-1.0	-0.9	-0.5	-0.4	-0.7	-0.4	-0.4	-0.5	-0.4	-0.4	-0.4	-0.3	1.0	0.8	-0.1	0.7	0.7	0.7	0.0	0.7	0.6	-0.7	0.7	-0.4	-0.4	1.1	-1%	-0.3	-0.6	-14.8	-12.1
1.50	4.6%	1949	1988	-0.3	-0.5	-0.4	-0.6	-0.3	-1.4	-1.3	-1.3	-0.5	-1.3	-1.2	-1.2	-0.9	-1.1	-0.9	-0.7	-0.4	-0.7	-0.4	-0.4	-0.3	-0.4	-0.3	-0.3	0.2	1.1	0.9	0.4	0.6	0.9	0.6	0.7	0.7	0.3	-0.4	0.3	-0.2	-0.3	0.8	1.1	0%	-0.2	-0.8	-15.9	-9.8
1.50	4.6%	1950	1989	-0.3	-0.2	-0.2	-0.2	-1.0	-1.4	-0.9	-0.4	-1.3	-1.2	-0.9	-1.2	-0.8	-1.3	-1.0	-0.7	-0.9	-0.5	-0.4	-0.9	-0.9	-0.9	-0.8	0.4	0.8	0.7	0.4	0.7	0.7	0.6	0.3	0.6	-0.2	-0.9	0.5	-0.6	-0.5	0.0	0.5	0.9	1%	-0.3	-0.7	-15.9	-13.7
2.00	4.4%	1951	1990	-0.1	-0.1	0.0	-1.0	-1.3	-0.9	-0.2	-1.2	-1.2	-1.2	-0.9	-1.1	-1.1	-0.8	-0.5	-0.8	-0.4	-0.4	-0.8	-0.6	-0.5	-0.7	0.0	0.7	0.6	0.0	0.3	0.6	0.4	0.4	0.4	0.2	-0.5	-0.3	-0.5	-0.5	0.4	-0.5	-0.5	1.7	1%	-0.3	-0.7	-14.7	-13.3
2.00	4.4%	1952	1991	-0.2	0.0	-1.1	-1.3	-1.2	-0.5	-1.3	-1.2	-1.2	-0.9	-1.2	-1.0	-0.9	-0.5	-0.9	-0.4	-0.4	-0.7	-0.7	-0.4	-0.5	-0.1	0.7	0.5	-0.1	0.2	0.3	0.3	-0.1	0.4	-0.6	-0.8	-0.6	-0.5	-0.5	-0.5	-0.5	-0.5	1.0	0.0	3%	-0.4	-0.9	-15.8	-17.7
2.33	4.3%	1953	1992	-0.1	-1.0	-1.3	-1.1	-0.4	-1.2	-1.1	-1.0	-0.9	-0.9	-1.0	-0.8	-0.6	-0.8	-0.3	-0.3	-0.6	-0.7	-0.6	-0.5	0.0	0.8	0.6	0.0	0.6	0.5	0.3	0.3	0.4	0.1	-0.6	-0.4	-0.5	-0.5	-0.4	-0.5	-0.5	0.4	-0.5	-0.3	4%	-0.4	-0.9	-15.3	-15.5
1.67	4.6%	1954	1993	-1.1	-1.4	-1.0	-0.5	-1.2	-1.3	-0.9	-1.2	-0.9	-1.1	-1.2	-0.9	-1.1	-0.7	-0.4	-1.2	-1.0	-0.9	-0.9	0.5	0.6	0.6	0.2	0.4	0.5	0.3	0.1	0.4	0.0	-1.1	-0.8	-1.0	-0.8	-0.9	-0.9	-0.8	1.2	-0.8	-0.8	-0.7	5%	-0.6	-1.0	-18.3	-22.2
2.33	4.3%	1955	1994	-0.5	-0.2	0.0	-0.5	-0.6	-0.3	-0.8	-0.3	-0.5	-0.8	-1.0	-0.6	-0.9	-0.5	-0.8	-0.6	-1.0	-0.6	0.4	0.5	0.3	0.1	0.2	0.2	0.2	0.0	0.1	-0.1	-1.2	-0.4	-0.8	-0.8	-0.8	-0.8	-0.8	0.7	-0.4	-0.8	-0.8	-0.1	5%	-0.4	-0.5	-9.7	-15.5
2.33	4.3%	1956	1995	-0.2	0.2	-0.2	-0.4	-0.2	-0.7	-0.3	-0.4	-0.6	-1.1	-0.4	-1.0	-0.7	-0.6	-0.4	-0.6	-0.6	0.4	0.5	0.4	0.0	0.2	0.2	0.0	-0.1	0.2	-0.3	-1.2	-0.9	-1.1	-0.8	-0.8	-0.8	-0.8	0.6	-0.8	-0.8	-0.8	-0.8	-0.8	4%	-0.4	-0.4	-7.1	-16.7
2.33	4.3%	1957	1996	0.1	-0.5	-0.4	-0.4	-0.7	-0.4	-0.5	-0.8	-1.1	-0.5	-1.0	-0.7	-0.5	-0.4	-0.7	-0.5	0.3	0.5	0.4	0.3	0.1	0.3	0.1	-0.1	0.2	-0.2	-1.2	-0.4	-0.8	-0.8	-0.9	-0.8	-0.8	0.5	-0.8	-0.8	-0.8	-0.8	-0.8	-0.8	6%	-0.4	-0.5	-7.5	-16.9
2.33	4.3%	1958	1997	-1.3	-1.2	-1.0	-1.0	-1.0	-1.2	-1.0	-0.7	-1.0	-0.6	-0.3	-1.0	-0.9	-0.9	-0.9	0.3	0.6	0.4	0.3	0.3	0.2	0.2	0.0	0.2	-0.2	-1.1	-1.1	-0.7	-0.7	-0.8	-0.7	-0.7	-0.7	-0.7	-0.7	-0.7	-0.7	-0.7	-0.7	-0.7	-1%	-0.6	-1.0	-12.3	-23.4
2.67	4.1%	1959	1998	-0.4	-0.2	-0.6	-0.2	-0.5	-0.7	-1.1	-0.6	-0.9	-0.7	-0.4	-0.3	-0.4	-0.4	0.3	0.4	0.3	0.3	0.4	0.3	0.0	0.0	0.2	-0.2	-1.1	-0.8	-0.7	-0.7	-0.8	-0.8	-0.7	0.4	-0.7	-0.7	-0.7	-0.7	-0.7	-0.7	-0.7	-0.7	0%	-0.4	-0.6	-5.5	-16.2
3.00	4.0%	1960	1999	-0.1	-0.6	-0.1	-0.3	-0.5	-1.0	-0.4	-0.8	-0.5	-0.6	-0.4	-0.6	-0.5	0.5	0.8	0.7	0.4	0.5	0.6	0.4	0.1	0.5	-0.1	-0.7	-0.6	-0.4	-0.4	-0.5	-0.4	-0.4	-0.5	-0.4	-0.4	-0.4	-0.4	-0.4	-0.4	-0.4	-0.4	-0.4	-14%	-0.2	-0.5	-2.8	-9.9
3.00	4.0%	1961	2000	-0.9	-0.2	-0.4	-0.8	-1.0	-0.5	-0.9	-0.7	-0.4	-0.2	-0.4	-0.3	0.6	0.7	0.7	0.5	0.5	0.6	0.6	0.4	0.6	0.2	-0.8	-0.5	-0.6	-0.4	-0.5	-0.4	-0.4	0.3	-0.4	-0.4	-0.4	-0.4	-0.4	-0.4	-0.4	-0.4	-0.4	-0.4	-9%	-0.2	-0.6	-2.2	-8.9
3.00	4.0%	1962	2001	0.1	-0.1	-0.3	-1.0	-0.2	-0.9	-0.7	-0.4	-0.2	-0.4	-0.3	0.5	0.7	0.6	0.5	0.6	0.5	0.5	0.3	0.4	-0.2	-0.9	-0.8	-0.4	-0.4	-0.5	-0.4	-0.4	-0.6	-0.4	-0.4	-0.4	-0.4	-0.4	-0.4	-0.4	-0.4	-0.4	-0.4	-0.4	-12%	-0.2	-0.4	0.2	-8.9
3.00	4.0%	1963	2002	-0.6	-0.9	-1.0	-0.7	-0.8	-0.6	-0.7	-0.6	-0.8	-0.5	0.5	0.7	0.7	0.4	0.6	0.6	0.4	0.4	0.5	-0.1	-0.8	-0.6	-0.5	-0.4	-0.5	-0.4	-0.4	-0.6	-0.4	-0.4	-0.4	-0.4	-0.4	-0.4	-0.4	-0.4	-0.4	-0.4	-0.4	-0.4	0%	-0.3	-0.7	-2.6	-11.7
3.00	4.0%	1964	2003	-0.6	-1.1	-0.4	-0.9	-0.7	-0.6	-0.2	-0.5	-0.5	0.5	0.8	0.6	0.5	0.5	0.6	0.5	0.3	0.4	0.1	-0.9	-0.8	-0.6	-0.4	-0.5	-0.4	-0.4	-0.5	-0.4	-0.4	-0.4	-0.4	-0.4	-0.4	-0.4	-0.4	-0.4	-0.4	-0.4	-0.4	-0.4	-13%	-0.3	-0.5	-1.4	-10.4
3.33	3.9%	1965	2004	-0.8	-0.2	-1.0	-0.9	-0.1	-0.1	-0.1	-0.1	0.6	0.8	0.8	0.6	0.6	0.6	0.6	0.5	0.6	0.4	-0.3	-0.1	-0.7	-0.6	-0.7	-0.5	-0.4	-0.2	-0.4	-0.4	-0.4	-0.4	-0.4	-0.4	-0.4	-0.4	-0.4	-0.4	-0.4	-0.4	-0.4	-0.4	-16%	-0.1	-0.2	2.6	-5.6
3.67	3.7%	1966	2005	0.0	-0.8	-0.8	0.0	0.2	-0.1	0.1	0.7	0.8	0.9	0.7	0.7	0.8	0.7	0.6	0.7	0.4	-0.2	0.1	-0.6	-0.3	-0.6	-0.4	-0.3	0.0	-0.3	-0.3	-0.3	-0.3	-0.3	-0.3	-0.3	-0.3	-0.3	-0.3	-0.3	-0.3	-0.3	-0.3	-0.3	-18%	0.0	0.1	4.8	-0.8
3.00	4.0%	1967	2006	-1.0	-0.8	-0.3	-0.2	-0.3	-0.3	0.5	0.7	0.7	0.5	0.6	0.6	0.6	0.5	0.6	0.2	-0.5	-0.1	-0.8	-0.5	-0.7	-0.6	-0.4	-0.7	-0.4	-0.4	-0.4	-0.4	-0.4	-0.4	-0.4	-0.4	-0.4	-0.4	-0.4	-0.4	-0.4	-0.4	-0.4	-0.4	-20%	-0.2	-0.1	0.4	-8.6
3.33	3.9%	1968	2007	-0.8	0.3	0.4	0.2	0.2	0.7	0.9	0.8	0.7	0.7	0.8	0.7	0.7	0.7	0.6	0.2	0.3	-0.3	-0.8	-0.1	-0.9	-0.8	0.3	-0.7	-0.6	-0.4	-0.5	-0.4	-0.4	-0.4	-0.4	-0.4	-0.4	-0.4	-0.4	-0.4	-0.4	-0.4	-0.4	-0.4	-12%	0.0	0.4	6.7	-1.7
3.33	3.9%	1969	2008	0.4	0.5	0.4	0.5	0.8	0.9	0.9	0.8	0.8	0.8	0.8	0.8	0.8	0.6	0.4	0.5	-0.2	-0.4	0.1	-0.3	-0.9	0.4	-0.7	-0.7	-0.5	-0.7	-0.4	-0.4	-0.4	-0.4	-0.4	-0.4	-0.4	-0.4	-0.4	-0.4	-0.4	-0.4	-0.4	0.3	3%	0.1	0.7	9.8	2.1
3.33	3.9%	1970	2009	-0.2	-0.3	-0.3	0.6	0.8	0.7	0.5	0.6	0.6	0.5	0.4	0.5	0.1	-0.4	-0.3	-0.8	-0.6	-0.8	-0.7	-0.4	-0.7	-0.4	-0.4	-0.4	-0.4	-0.4	-0.4	-0.4	-0.4	-0.4	-0.4	-0.4	-0.4	-0.4	-0.4	-0.4	-0.4	-0.4	-0.4	-0.4	-15%	-0.2	0.4	0.6	-7.2
2.67	4.1%	1971	2010	-0.5	-0.4	0.3	0.4	0.3	0.2	0.3	0.3	0.2	0.2	0.2	-0.1	-0.4	-0.4	-1.1	-0.8	-1.0	-0.9	-0.6	-0.6	-0.7	-0.7	-0.7	-0.7	-0.7	-0.7	-0.7	-0.7	-0.7	-0.7	-0.7	-0.7	-0.7	-0.7	-0.7	-0.7	-0.7	-0.7	-0.7	-0.7	-8%	-0.4	0.1	-4.2	-17.8
3.00	4.0%	1972	1928	-0.3	0.6	0.8	0.7	0.5	0.6	0.7	0.6	0.5	0.6	0.3	-0.3	-0.2	-1.0	-0.8	-1.0	-0.8	-0.7	-0.7	-0.5	-0.4	-0.4	-0.4	-0.4	-0.4	-0.4	-0.4	-0.4	-0.4	-0.4	-0.4	-0.4	-0.4	-0.4	-0.4	-0.4	-0.4	-0.4	-0.4	-0.4	-22%	-0.2	0.5	-0.1	-8.3
3.00	4.0%	1973	1929	0.5	0.7	0.7	0.4	0.6	0.6	0.6	0.4	0.6	0.3	-0.2	-0.1	-0.9	-0.8	-0.7	-0.9	-0.7	-0.2	-0.7	-0.4	-0.4	-0.4	-0.4	-0.4	-0.4	-0.4	-0.4	-0.4	-0.4	-0.4	-0.4	-0.4	-0.4	-0.4	-0.4	-0.4	-0.4	-0.4	-0.4	-0.4	-16%	-0.2	0.5	0.0	-8.3
2.33	4.3%	1974	1930	0.2	0.1	-0.3	-0.1	0.0	-0.1	-0.1	0.0	-0.4	-0.7	-0.6	-1.0	-0.6	-0.9	-0.7	-0.4	-0.8	-0.3	-0.3	-0.3	-0.5	-0.5	-0.5	-0.5	-0.5	-0.5	-0.5	-0.5	-0.5	-0.5	-0.5	-0.5	-0.5	-0.5	-0.5	-0.5	-0.5	-0.6	-0.6	-0.6	-10%	-0.4	-0.1	-7.5	-18.0
1.33	4.7%	1975	1931	-0.6	-1.3	-0.9	-0.6	-0.4	-0.5	-0.2	-0.9	-1.4	-1.3	-0.9	-0.5	-0.8	-0.6	-0.5	-0.7	-0.5	-0.5	-0.5	-0.5	-0.7	-0.7	-0.7	-0.7	-0.7	-0.7	-0.7	-0.7	-0.7	-0.7	-0.7	-0.7	-0.7	-0.7	-0.7	-0.7	-0.7	-0.7	-0.7	-0.7	-12%	-0.7	-0.8	-14.1	-28.4
1.67	4.6%	1976	1932	-0.7	-0.4	-0.2	-0.2	-0.3	0.0	-0.6	-0.9	-0.9	-1.2	-0.8	-1.1	-1.0	-0.7	-1.2	-0.4	-0.4	-0.4	-0.4	-0.4	-0.6	-0.6	-0.6	-0.6	-0.6	-0.6	-0.6	-0.6	-0.6	-0.6	-0.6	-0.6	-0.6	-0.6	-0.6	-0.6	-0.6	-0.6	-0.6	-0.6	-4%	-0.6	-0.5	-12.2	-24.1
1.67	4.6%	1977	1933	0.0	0.1	0.1	0.0	0.1	-0.2	-0.4	-0.4	-1.0	-1.3	-0.7	-1.0	-1.3	-0.4	-1.1	-0.8	-0.4	-0.9	-0.4	-0.4	-0.6	-0.6	-0.6	-0.6	-0.6	-0.6	-0.6	-0.6	-0.6	-0.6	-0.6	-0.6	-0.6	-0.6	-0.7	-0.7	-0.7	-0.7	-0.7	-0.7	6%	-0.6	-0.3	-10.6	-23.5
1.33	4.7%	1978	1934	0.0	0.1	0.0	0.1	-0.3	-0.6	-0.5	-1.2	-1.5	-0.9	-1.0	-1.4	-0.5	-1.1	-1.0	-0.6	-0.9	-0.5	-0.5	-0.5	-0.7	-0.7	-0.7	-0.7	-0.7	-0.7	-0.7	-0.7	-0.7	-0.7	-0.7	-0.7	-0.7	-0.7	-0.7	-0.7	-0.7	-0.7	-0.7	-0.7	6%	-0.7	-0.5	-12.6	-26.0
1.00	4.8%	1979	1935	0.0	0.0	0.1	-0.3	-0.3	-0.6	-1.2	-1.6	-0.9	-0.9	-1.4	-0.5	-1.3	-1.0	-0.7	-1.1	-0.5	-0.5	-0.5	-0.5	-0.8	-0.8	-0.8	-0.8	-0.8	-0.8	-0.8	-0.8	-0.8	-0.8	-0.8	-0.8	-0.8	-0.8	-0.8	-0.8	-0.8	-0.8	-0.8	-0.8	10%	-0.7	-0.6	-14.1	-29.5
1.00	4.8%	1980	1936	0.0	0.1	-0.2	-0.6	-0.5	-1.2	-1.6	-0.9	-1.0	-1.4	-0.4	-1.4	-1.2	-0.8	-1.3	-0.5	-0.5	-0.5	-0.5	-0.5	-0.7	-0.7	-0.7	-0.7	-0.7	-0.7	-0.7	-0.7	-0.7	-0.7	-0.7	-0.8	-0.8	-0.8	0.0	-0.8	-0.8	-0.8	-0.8	-0.8	2%	-0.7	-0.7	-14.9	-29.0
1.33	4.7%	1981	1937	0.0	-0.3	-0.7	-0.7	-1.3	-1.4	-1.0	-1.3	-1.3	-0.6	-1.2	-1.0	-0.6	-1.1	-0.5	-0.5	-0.5	-0.5	-0.5	-0.5	-0.6	-0.6	-0.6	-0.6	-0.6	-0.6	-0.6	-0.6	-0.6	-0.6	-0.6	-0.6	-0.6	-0.6	-0.6	-0.6	-0.6	-0.6	-0.6	-0.6	5%	-0.7	-0.9	-15.4	-28.0
1.00	4.8%	1982	1938	-0.4	-0.7	-0.6	-1.3	-1.5	-1.0	-1.2	-1.4	-0.7	-1.3	-1.1	-0.8	-1.2	-0.5	-0.5	-0.5	-0.5	-0.5	-0.5	-0.5	-0.6	-0.6	-0.6	-0.6	-0.6	-0.6	-0.6	-0.6	-0.6	-0.6	-0.6	-0.6	-0.6	-0.6	-0.6	-0.6	-0.6	-0.6	-0.6	-0.6	8%	-0.7	-1.0	-16.9	-29.3
1.00	4.8%	1983	1939	-0.2	-0.2	-0.6	-0.9	-0.5	-0.7	-0.8	-0.3	-0.9	-1.3	-1.3	-0.7	-1.2	-1.0	-0.6	-0.5	-0.5	-0.5	-0.5	-0.5	-0.8	-0.8	-0.8	-0.8	-0.8	-0.8	-0.8	-0.8	-0.9	-0.9	-0.9	1.2	-0.7	-0.9	-0.9	-0.9	-0.9	-0.9	-0.9	-0.8	12%	-0.7	-0.6	-14.0	-28.6
1.33	4.7%	1984	1940	0.0	-0.4	-0.6	-0.3	-0.5	-0.7	-0.2	-0.7	-1.0	-1.3	-0.6	-1.3	-1.3	-0.8	-0.6	-0.6	-0.6	-0.5	-0.7	-0.5	-0.7	-0.7	-0.7	-0.7	-1.0	-0.8	-0.7	-0.7	-0.7	0.3	1.3	1.2	-0.7	-0.7	-0.7	-0.7	0.3	-0.7	-0.7	1.8	9%	-0.5	-0.6	-13.3	-19.5
1.33	4.7%	1985	1941	-0.4	-0.7	-0.3	-0.5	-0.7	-0.2	-0.8	-1.0	-1.4	-0.6	-1.4	-1.4	-0.9	-0.7	-0.7	-0.7	-0.5	-0.8	-0.5	-0.5	-0.7	-0.7	-0.7	-0.9	-0.9	-0.7	-0.7	-0.7	0.3	1.5	1.1	-0.5	-0.7	-0.7	-0.7	-0.1	-0.7	-0.7	1.5	2.6	9%	-0.4	-0.7	-14.8	-17.7
1.67	4.6%	1986	1942	-0.3	0.0	-0.1	-0.4	0.0	-0.3	-0.6	-0.8	-0.4	-0.9	-1.1	-1.2	-1.0	-0.9	-1.0	-0.8	-1.0	-0.6	-0.5	-0.5	-0.6	-0.8	0.2	-0.8	-0.9	-0.7	-0.9	1.1	1.4	1.6	0.4	0.9	-0.7	-0.7	1.1	-0.6	1.1	1.2	1.9	1.8	3%	-0.2	-0.4	-12.6	-6.1
1.67	4.6%	1987	1943	0.1	0.0	-0.1	0.1	-0.2	-0.3	-0.7	-0.2	-0.9	-0.8	-1.3	-1.2	-1.2	-1.2	-1.2	-0.3	-0.8	-0.8	-1.0	-0.7	-0.9	0.6	-0.2	-1.0	-0.7	-0.2	1.0	1.2	1.5	0.8	0.6	-0.6	-0.7	1.0	0.4	0.8	1.7	1.9	1.6	1.1	0%	-0.1	-0.3	-12.8	-3.1
1.67	4.6%	1988	1944	-0.3	-0.4	0.0	-0.4	-0.7	-0.9	-0.5	-1.3	-1.3	-1.2	-1.0	-1.0	-1.1	-0.8	-1.1	-0.6	-0.4	-0.7	-0.5	-0.6	-0.1	-0.7	-0.9	-0.7	-0.8	0.6	1.4	1.3	-0.2	0.3	-0.7	-0.7	-0.5	-0.7	0.3	1.4	2.0	1.6	-0.5	-0.7	4%	-0.3	-0.7	-14.7	-12.9
1.67	4.6%	1989	1945	-0.3	0.1	-0.3	-0.5	-0.7	-0.3	-0.8	-0.8	-1.3	-1.2	-1.2	-1.2	-1.2	-0.6	-0.9	-0.8	-0.8	-0.8	-0.9	0.2	-0.9	-1.2	-0.9	-1.1	0.5	1.1	0.6	-0.2	-0.2	-0.9	-0.9	1.1	-0.9	0.6	1.7	1.6	1.5	-0.5	-0.9	-0.9	9%	-0.4	-0.6	-14.4	-15.6
2.33	4.3%	1990	1946	0.1	-0.3	-0.4	-0.7	-0.3	-1.0	-0.9	-1.0	-1.0	-1.0	-1.1	-1.0	-0.3	-0.7	-0.6	-0.7	-0.4	-0.7	0.3	-0.3	-0.9	-0.7	-0.9	0.4	1.1	1.0	-0.4	0.1	-0.7	-0.7	-0.1	-0.7	-0.7	0.9	1.7	1.5	-0.2	-0.7	-0.7	-0.7	1%	-0.3	-0.6	-12.0	-13.6
2.00	4.4%	1991	1947	-0.9	-1.0	-1.2	-0.7	-1.3	-1.3	-0.9	-0.8	-0.8	-0.9	-0.8	-1.1	-0.5	-0.5	-0.6	-0.4	-0.5	-0.3	-0.8	-0.5	-0.7	-0.9	-0.4	0.7	0.2	-0.7	-0.7	-0.7	-0.7	-0.7	-0.7	-0.7	-0.7	1.5	1.4	-0.7	-0.7	-0.7	-0.7	-0.7	-1%	-0.6	-1.0	-15.6	-22.3
2.67	4.1%	1992	1948	-0.6	-0.9	-0.3	-1.0	-0.9	-0.8	-0.7	-0.7	-0.8	-0.7	-0.9	-0.5	-0.4	-0.5	-0.3	-0.4	-0.4	-0.7	-0.6	-0.3	-0.6	0.0	0.7	0.0	-0.5	-0.5	-0.5	-0.5	-0.5	-0.5	-0.5	-0.5	1.0	1.2	-0.5	-0.5	-0.5	-0.5	-0.5	-0.5	1%	-0.4	-0.8	-12.6	-16.9
3.00	4.0%	1993	1949	-0.7	0.0	-0.9	-1.0	-0.8	-0.8	-0.8	-0.9	-0.8	-0.4	-0.7	-0.6	-0.7	-0.5	-0.7	0.3	-0.4	-0.7	-0.4	-0.8	0.4	1.1	0.9	-0.5	-0.2	-0.4	-0.4	-0.3	-0.4	-0.4	-0.1	1.6	1.0	-0.4	-0.4	-0.4	-0.4	-0.4	-0.4	-0.4	-5%	-0.3	-0.7	-12.2	-13.5
3.00	4.0%	1994	1950	0.1	-0.5	-0.5	-1.0	-1.0	-0.9	-0.9	-0.9	-0.3	-0.8	-0.7	-0.8	-0.7	-0.8	0.4	0.0	-0.8	-0.6	0.1	0.9	1.1	1.2	0.5	0.4	-0.4	-0.4	0.3	-0.4	-0.1	1.0	1.5	1.3	-0.4	-0.4	-0.4	-0.4	-0.4	-0.4	-0.4	-0.4	-2%	-0.2	-0.7	-9.8	-7.5
3.33	3.9%	1995	1951	-1.0	-1.0	-0.7	-0.7	-0.6	-0.7	-0.6	-0.9	-0.5	-0.4	-0.5	-0.4	-0.5	-0.9	-0.7	-0.5	-0.4	-0.6	-0.8	-0.3	-0.4	-0.4	-0.4	-0.4	-0.4	-0.4	-0.4	-0.4	-0.4	0.0	-0.4	-0.4	-0.4	-0.4	-0.4	-0.4	-0.4	-0.4	-0.4	-0.4	-16%	-0.5	-0.7	-12.7	-20.5
3.67	3.7%	1996	1952	-0.5	-0.8	-0.8	-0.7	-0.8	-0.7	-0.2	-0.6	-0.5	-0.6	-0.5	-0.6	0.3	-0.2	-0.6	-0.4	-0.7	0.4	0.9	0.4	-0.4	-0.4	-0.3	-0.3	0.0	-0.3	-0.3	0.3	1.3	1.2	-0.3	-0.3	-0.3	-0.3	-0.3	-0.3	-0.3	-0.3	-0.3	-0.3	-12%	-0.2	-0.6	-7.4	-9.5
3.67	3.7%	1997	1953	-0.8	-0.8	-0.8	-0.8	-0.8	-0.2	-0.7	-0.6	-0.7	-0.6	-0.8	0.6	0.4	-0.3	-0.5	-0.1	0.7	1.0	1.0	0.1	-0.1	-0.3	-0.3	-0.3	-0.3	-0.3	0.1	1.4	1.0	-0.4	-0.3	-0.3	-0.3	-0.3	-0.3	-0.3	-0.3	-0.3	-0.3	-0.3	-7%	-0.2	-0.7	-4.7	-7.1
3.67	3.7%	1998	1954	-0.5	-0.7	-0.1	-0.3	0.4	-0.4	-0.6	-0.3	-0.8	-0.1	0.7	0.5	0.2	-0.8	0.3	0.8	0.9	1.0	0.7	0.6	-0.6	-0.3	0.6	-0.4	0.2	0.7	1.1	1.0	-0.4	-0.3	-0.3	-0.3	-0.3	-0.5	-0.3	-0.3	-0.3	-0.3	-0.3	-0.3	-11%	0.0	-0.4	1.5	-0.1
3.67	3.7%	1999	1955	-0.7	-0.2	-0.3	0.4	-0.4	-0.6	-0.3	-0.7	-0.2	0.7	0.4	0.1	-0.8	0.3	0.8	0.9	0.9	0.6	0.6	-0.6	-0.3	0.5	-0.5	-0.3	0.6	1.0	1.0	-0.2	-0.3	-0.3	-0.3	-0.5	-0.4	-0.3	-0.3	-0.3	-0.3	-0.3	-0.3	-0.3	-15%	0.0	-0.2	1.0	-1.2
4.00	3.6%	2000	1956	-0.3	-0.4	0.3	-0.6	-0.7	-0.5	-0.7	-0.1	0.8	0.6	0.3	-0.6	0.4	0.8	0.9	0.9	0.7	0.8	-0.3	-0.2	0.6	-0.3	-0.1	0.6	1.0	0.9	-0.4	-0.2	-0.2	-0.2	-0.2	-0.4	-0.2	-0.2	-0.2	-0.2	-0.2	-0.2	-0.2	-0.2	-21%	0.0	-0.2	2.0	1.8

	Sum to 85	Sum to 105
Overall Average	-8.4	-15.4
Low-Valuation Avg	-11.9	-19.1
High-Valuation Avg	-1.0	-7.1

FIGURE 191

Annual cost of GI summary, based on 2% IRR using ECM recommended GI solution with low rates, compared to 100% systemic withdrawal EM solution on Baseline Market and Portfolio.

Across the four examples showing cost differences (Figure 188 through Figure 191), two columns, *Sum-to-85* and *Sum-to-105* respectively, show the sum of the real payout differences for the first 20 years and the full 40-year retirement. If the sum is positive, then GI generated more income than systemic withdrawals over the timeframe. For a starting portfolio of $1 million, a value of -5.0 means the GI solution produced $50,000 less real income spread over the time period than a pure systemic-withdrawal solution without GI. Likewise, an Overall Average of -19.7 at the bottom translates to the GI plans on average generating $197,000 less real income over the time periods. Along with the overall average at the bottom are the averages for those retirement periods starting with a low valuation and those starting with a high valuation—the results are both distinct and consistent.

A few conclusions can now be reached on the typical cost of GI. It's generally expensive, but the cost drops substantially under the right circumstances. The cost typically drops when starting valuation levels are high (e.g., over 3), and always drops when starting GI payouts are higher (e.g., over 5%). Valuations and payout rates are the two main determinants of the cost of GI.

A careful review of the numbers in Figure 188 and Figure 189 will show that when ECM is used both with and without GI, it's possible to conclude GI should always be used when valuation levels are above 3 and interest rates are reasonable. However, this is a somewhat artificial comparison. EM is the recommended variable-withdrawal strategy based on known risk; ECM is the recommended strategy based on planning for failure markets (i.e., speculative risk). Each plan needs its best strategy.

EM with no GI almost always performs better than ECM with GI. ECM with GI only twice came out ahead (i.e., 1969 and 2000) when starting payouts were moderate (see Figure 191). ECM with GI never outpaced EM without GI when interest rates were low (see Figure 190). Based purely on known market risk, GI can be justified only if both the valuation level and interest rates are clearly high, but this is rare.

The results reflect the original assumption: the justification for GI is mostly based on speculative risk, not known risk.

However, focusing on *average* life expectancies, spanning approximately the first 20 years after retirement, GI more often boosts the income level when interest and starting valuations are generally high. This is reflected in the "Sum to 85". These numbers provide a little more justification for using GI based on known risk with high valuations, but the original assumption still holds (i.e., the motivation for GI is mostly speculative risk).

How do these cost differences change when a larger percentage of GI is used? In each case, the cost difference generally grows or shrinks in proportion to the assets allocated to GI. If twice as much is allocated to GI (e.g., 60% instead of 30%) then the income difference in either direction would roughly double what is shown.

Here's a short summary. GI is generally expensive, but its cost lowers as interest rates and valuations rise. When interest rates and valuation levels are both high, then GI is probably always affordable. It becomes an attractive buy. When valuation levels are very high, like 3.5 or above, but interest rates aren't high, GI should be seriously considered (i.e., it's often affordable), although the data is not conclusive on the costs. If valuations are low and interest rates are high, then GI is still expensive and less affordable, but perhaps not very expensive. With both low valuations and low interest rates, GI is very expensive and usually only affordable to retirees who have substantial extra assets and a low tolerance for risk.

A few details and special cases complete the recommendations.

- If valuation levels are very low (e.g., less than 2.0) and GI is desired, then a reasonable alternative is to delay all GI purchases until later in retirement, but this comes with a small amount of additional risk. Even if valuation levels are not low (e.g., 2.6), there is no dire risk from waiting longer before doing the initial lock-in of GI. The purpose of the recommendations is to show how to reliably counter failure-market risk—the domain of GI—but at the same time, failure-market risk remains small.

- If the essential-income rate is very high (e.g., 4%) and valuation levels are also high, typically a retiree can only handle a failure-market scenario by downsizing to a lower essential-income rate.

- Any time the initial withdrawal rate with GI is significantly higher (e.g., 20% higher) than without GI, the higher GI payout will likely produce more income over the first 20 years of retirement, making it a more attractive option. This may be due to poor valuations, high interest rates, or a combination of both.

- For smaller portfolios, I Bonds may be able to substitute for a TIPS ladder, providing a simpler and more flexible solution.

- Early retirees will usually be better off waiting until after age 60 before considering GI (Figure 192, explained below, makes this clearer by examining the effect of lower payout rates).

- Some may wonder if valuations should be monitored when delaying GI. For example, instead of waiting until 85 to add a TIPS ladder, a ladder could be built any time after age 75 based on valuations and interest rates. This is logical and may be worthwhile, but keep in mind that it stretches the capability of valuations. Also, the specifics haven't been verified.

- When selling systemic withdrawal assets to fund GI purchases, the assets sold are typically selected in proportion to their current asset allocation (e.g., if 35% of the portfolio is in bonds, then 35% of the assets sold will be bonds). With an excess of bonds, however, due to Prime Harvesting's management, it's also reasonable to pull more from the bonds.

- What may stand out as an omission is a discussion of gold. Duke's Campbell Harvey provides an excellent assessment of gold in several papers downloadable from his website[67]. The bottom line is, gold is not recommended here because there is insufficient data to verify its use in retirement portfolios. Nevertheless, keeping a small amount in a diversified commodity fund appears to be a reasonable hedge.

As a final refinement for a few, when the essential-income rate is above 3%, it becomes necessary to generalize the recommendations (this was ignored before to simplify the discussion, plus most retirees will have an essential-income rate less than 3%). It turns out for rates over 3%, the minimal percentage (i.e., 50%) of the essential-income rate to lock in starts to creep upward, because systemic withdrawals contribute a smaller percentage to the overall essential-income rate.

Figure 192 provides the general solution, listing the minimal percentage to lock in according to the essential-income rate. For example, for an essential-income rate of 3.4%, the minimal percentage to be locked in is 70%. Like before, this lock-in may be all done at the start of retirement, or split between the start and 20 years later when valuations are attractive.

Figure 192 also shows the percentage of assets potentially required to support the minimum percentage of essential-income rate based on a specific GI payout rate. For example an essential-income rate of 3% with a 4% GI payout rate requires 38% (rounded) of the portfolio at the start of retirement with high valuations. Likewise, a 2% essential-income rate with a 4.5% payout requires 22% of the portfolio with high valuations. Less than the stated percentage is required when valuations are not high. Nevertheless, the portfolio percentages convey the effect of the essential-income rate and payout rate.

Figure 192 also indirectly approximates the maximum supportable essential-income rate, given that the maximum recommended GI allocation is 70% (leaving only 30% for systemic withdrawals). For example, a 5% initial GI payout rate can support at most a 3.8% essential-income rate without requiring more than 70% of the total portfolio (again with high valuations); likewise it takes a 6% payout rate using 67% of total assets to be able to support a 4% essential-income rate conforming to the recommendations.

Essential-Income Rate	Minimum Percentage of Essential-Income Rate to Lock In	Percentage of Assets Potentially Required for GI Initial GI Payout Rate						
		3.0%	3.5%	4%	4.50%	5%	5.50%	6%
1.0%	50%	17%	14%	13%	11%	10%	9%	8%
1.1%	50%	18%	16%	14%	12%	11%	10%	9%
1.2%	50%	20%	17%	15%	13%	12%	11%	10%
1.3%	50%	22%	19%	16%	14%	13%	12%	11%
1.4%	50%	23%	20%	18%	16%	14%	13%	12%
1.5%	50%	25%	21%	19%	17%	15%	14%	13%
1.6%	50%	27%	23%	20%	18%	16%	15%	13%
1.7%	50%	28%	24%	21%	19%	17%	15%	14%
1.8%	50%	30%	26%	23%	20%	18%	16%	15%
1.9%	50%	32%	27%	24%	21%	19%	17%	16%
2.0%	50%	33%	29%	25%	22%	20%	18%	17%
2.1%	50%	35%	30%	26%	23%	21%	19%	18%
2.2%	50%	37%	31%	28%	24%	22%	20%	18%
2.3%	50%	38%	33%	29%	26%	23%	21%	19%
2.4%	50%	40%	34%	30%	27%	24%	22%	20%
2.5%	50%	42%	36%	31%	28%	25%	23%	21%
2.6%	50%	43%	37%	33%	29%	26%	24%	22%
2.7%	50%	45%	39%	34%	30%	27%	25%	23%
2.8%	50%	47%	40%	35%	31%	28%	25%	23%
2.9%	50%	48%	41%	36%	32%	29%	26%	24%
3.0%	50%	50%	43%	38%	33%	30%	27%	25%
3.1%	55%	57%	49%	43%	38%	34%	31%	28%
3.2%	60%	64%	55%	48%	43%	38%	35%	32%
3.3%	65%		61%	54%	48%	43%	39%	36%
3.4%	70%		68%	60%	53%	48%	43%	40%
3.5%	75%			66%	58%	53%	48%	44%
3.6%	80%				64%	58%	52%	48%
3.7%	85%				70%	63%	57%	52%
3.8%	90%					68%	62%	57%
3.9%	95%						67%	62%
4.0%	100%							67%
4.1%	100%							68%
4.2%	100%							70%

FIGURE 192

The generalized minimum percentage of assets required to lock-in the essential-income rate based on payout rate.

If the essential-income rate cannot be supported, then GI is not a viable option unless the retiree downsizes expenses. If systemic-withdrawals, without GI, also can't support the essential-income rate, then downsizing is the only option conforming to the recommendations.

THE TOLL OF ANNUITY-FREE GI SOLUTIONS

If there's too much perceived risk of using valuations to plan for a failure market, then a retiree can ignore them (always locking in the full GI rate at the start of retirement). If there's too much perceived risk depending on systemic withdrawals to contribute half of the essential-income rate in a failure market, then a higher rate can be locked in. If there's too much perceived risk of using SPIAs, then an annuity-free GI solution can be used.

In every case above, there is a risk, and the ability to lower it, but doing so will raise the cost of GI, sometimes by a large amount. This is why looking at the data has been so important in finding the right balance. Below, more focus is put on the common case of avoiding annuities, specifically SPIAs, for whatever reason.

A review of the previous survey of the most viable GI strategies shows that an extended TIPS ladder is the only complete end-to-end solution without annuities. Of course, a normal TIPS ladder without being extended can be used when planning for 30 years or less, but a ladder must match the retirement length, and 40 years is the baseline case (i.e., it's the most difficult, and needed frequently enough). Unfortunately, an extended TIPS ladder for 40-year retirement is almost always very expensive.

Figure 193 shows the failure-market results for a 40-year extended TIPS ladder assuming a 1% IRR for the ladders and the supporting standby bond pool. As before, a 3% essential-income rate is assumed, so 1.5% is locked in at the beginning of retirement. After 20 years, the first ladder terminates and the bond pool then funds the second ladder, again locking in 1.5%. To stay with only the basics, no valuations are used to delay part of the lock-in percentage. With the low interest rate, this is one of the most difficult GI cases. This is the same case covered in Figure 184 using the primary recommendations (and as before, only annual income less than 3% is highlighted).

FIGURE 193

Failure-market results for two back-to-back 20-year TIPS ladders assuming a 1% IRR. 53% of total assets remain in systemic withdrawals.

What's important in the above example is that the extended TIPS ladder does work successfully overall under a failure market, even with a low interest rate. There are quite a few cases that drop a little under 3%, but at most down to 2.8%. Pulling out a little extra to satisfy the essential rate makes up the shortfalls (based on the remaining percentage at the end of retirement). There is only one clear failure: the 1987 retirement period runs out of money around age 103 when pulling out extra income to meet the essential-income rate.

Figure 194 shows the same example using the Baseline Market. What stands out is that the income is still low even under expected market conditions—the numbers are exceptionally poor. The average income under the Baseline Market is 4.2% compared to 3.8% under the failure market, not a big difference. The average adhering to the earlier recommended solution (with SPIAs) for the same cases is 5.4%. For the same case, a pure systemic withdrawal solution goes up to 6%. The price for this near riskless completely government-backed solution is immense.

FIGURE 194

*Baseline Market results for two back-to-back 20-year TIPS ladders assuming
a 1% IRR. 53% of total assets remain in systemic withdrawals.*

Figure 195 shows the typical costs in detail, comparing the above TIPS solution to the pure systemic withdrawal solution using EM. Again, the cost can be seen to be exceedingly high. Assuming a starting portfolio value of $1 million, the average GI cost is $744,000 in real income distributed over a 40-year retirement. This translates on average to $18,600 annually in extra cost for an extended TIPS ladder to guarantee half of a 3% essential-income rate.

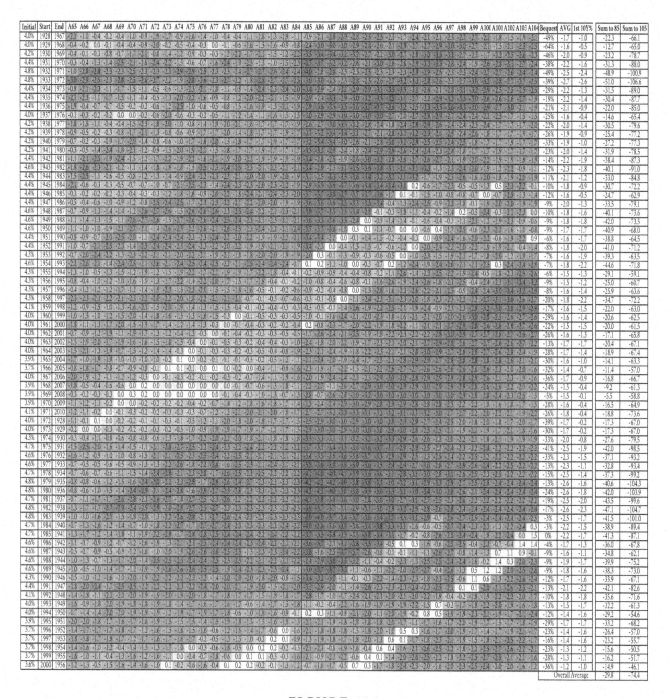

FIGURE 195

*Annual cost of GI summary, based on 1% IRR comparing minimum solution
with extended TIPS ladder to pure systemic withdrawal solution.*

Even with a much higher 2% IRR for an extended TIPS ladder, the cost still translates on average to $14,500 annually. Contrast these numbers to the average cost of the earlier recommended solution, which is $6500 annually with a 1% IRR, and $3850 annually with a 2% IRR.

Why is the TIPS ladder so expensive? In part because the quality of the guaranteed income stream is incomparable: it's a US-backed inflation-protected bond. Another reason is that earlier guarantees (i.e., at the start of retirement) cost more, and longer guarantees (i.e., 40 years) cost more. Also, TIPS don't have the mortality premium of SPIAs, which makes a sizable difference. The bottom line is, TIPS ladders work in failure markets, but they are almost always too expensive for most retirees.

The expense can be lowered by waiting a few years before implementing a TIPS solution. Each year a TIPS ladder is extended decreases the income rate by about 0.1%. So, a delay of 10 years can increase the income rate a full 1%, e.g., from 3.5% to 4.5%. Delaying is especially attractive when valuations are low. However, the wait is long, and retirees who are determined to use TIPS usually don't have much risk tolerance.

A foolproof TIPS solution requires either paying too much, or dying early. It's this experience of being forced into a corner through risk avoidance that makes the earlier recommendations with limited SPIAs more attractive (and perhaps worth a second look by those on the fence).

EXAMPLES AND APPLICATION

The below scenarios include examples of retirees following the recommendations, or changing the recommendations to suit their own preferences. What works for one retiree may not for another.

All assets are assumed to be in tax-advantaged accounts except where noted. Also, the following default parameters are used for systemic withdrawals.

- 55% Stocks using Evanson 10x10, HR-8x12, or Triad portfolio.

- 45% Bonds using Short-Term Treasuries, Intermediate Treasuries, and TIPS

- Prime Harvesting

- EM without GI, and ECM with GI, both with a 150% income cap.

- 30% or 40% tilt for setting the initial withdrawal rate.

SPIAs are always inflation-adjusted.

Case 1: Wants GI, Bequest Motive, Unattractive Valuations

A couple start retirement at age 65. Both are risk averse, desire the extra protection of GI, and can afford it. They also have children and want to leave a bequest. They are planning a 40-year retirement. Their essential-income rate is 3.2%. The current valuation level is 3.1.

With the high valuation level and SPIAs paying well at 4.8%, the couple immediately locks in 2% annually for life (i.e., 65% of their essential-income rate) by putting 42% of their total assets in an SPIA. They also allocate 5% to a standby bond.

The rest of the couple's assets (53% of total) go into the recommended systemic-withdrawal 40-year plan. Their initial withdrawal rate with a 3.1 valuation level is 4% using a 30% tilt (after taking off 5% for the longer 40-year plan when referring back to Figure 141).

Given 53% of their portfolio is allocated to systemic withdrawals with a 4% payout and 42% is allocated to a SPIA with a 4.8% payout, their total starting annual income is ((4% * 0.53) + (4.8% * 0.42)) = 4.14%.

The standby bond pool will be kept in reserve.

Case 2: Wants GI, No Bequest Motive, Moderate Valuations

A single male starts retirement at age 65. He is highly risk averse, desires the extra protection of GI, and can afford it; on the other hand he desires strong retirement income to fund an active retirement. He has no plans for a bequest. His essential-income rate is 2.8%. The current valuation level is 2.7.

SPIAs are paying well at 5.5% for a single male, so he immediately locks in the full 2.8% of his essential-income rate by putting 51% of total assets in an SPIA. No assets are allocated to a standby bond pool. He understands the option of allocating less to GI, but he is more comfortable locking in his full essential-income rate since his SPIA payout is high and he has no bequest motive.

The rest of the assets (49% of total) go into the recommended systemic-withdrawal 30-year plan using the Evanson 10x10 portfolio. (A 30-year systemic-withdrawal plan is reasonable because the retiree plans to later lock in another SPIA, going beyond the essential-income rate, which will cover longevity risk.) The initial income rate using systemic withdrawals for a 2.7 valuation level is 4.4% using a 30% tilt.

Given 49% of his portfolio is allocated to systemic withdrawals with a 4.4% payout, and 51% is allocated to a SPIA with a 5.5% payout, the initial annual income rate is ((4.4% * 0.49) + (5.5% * 0.51)) = 4.96%.

Around age 80, or possibly sooner if valuations are high, he plans to take approximately half of the remaining systemic withdrawal assets and put them in another SPIA to boost income higher and hire a part-time assistant. The rest of the portfolio stays in systemic withdrawals for flexibility.

Case 3: Wants GI, Bequest Motive, Attractive Valuations

A single female starts retirement at age 63. She is moderately risk averse, desires the extra protection of GI, and can afford it. She is also highly motivated to leave a bequest to her children. She is planning a 40-year retirement. Her essential-income rate is 3.2%. The current valuation level is 2.1.

With valuations very low, there is little risk from stocks, but she still prefers to lock in a 1% rate by putting 21% of total assets into an SPIA paying out 4.75%. She also allocates 5% to a standby bond for added protection.

The rest of the assets (74% of total) go into a systemic-withdrawal 40-year plan with a 40% tilt for setting the initial withdrawal rate. A 40% tilt, compared to 30%, partly compensates for the income lost from the standby bond pool. The initial withdrawal rate for a 2.1 valuation level using a 40% tilt is 4.7% (after taking off 5% for the 40-year retirement).

Given that 74% of her portfolio is allocated to systemic withdrawals with a 4.7% payout, and 21% is allocated to a SPIA with a 4.75% payout, the initial annual income rate is ((4.7% * 0.74) + (4.75% * 0.21)) = 4.47%.

The plan is to lock in another 1% of income at age 85 by building a 20-year TIPS ladder using a portion of the systemic withdrawal assets (the rest of the systemic-withdrawal assets stay in place to build a larger bequest). The standby bond pool will be kept in reserve.

Case 4: Wants GI, Bequest Motive, SPIA Aversion, Unattractive Valuations, Low Interest Rates

A couple start retirement at age 65. Both are highly risk averse, desire the extra protection of GI but are firmly against the use of SPIAs (their neighbor recently died soon after purchasing a large annuity). They are planning a 40-year retirement. They also desire to leave a bequest to their children. Their essential-income rate is 3.1%. The current valuation level is 2.9. They understand that their criteria are difficult to satisfy.

The interest rate is also low, so an extended 40-year TIPS ladder only delivers 2.8% annually from a 0.5% IRR. This is an unappealing payout that is less than the essential-income rate. Since the couple is unwilling to invest in SPIAs, they decide instead to put 15% of total assets in a Standby Bond Pool and wait until a TIPS ladder becomes affordable. (This may not be the best plan, but they feel secure with the bond pool.)

The rest of the assets (85% of total) go into a systemic-withdrawal 40-year plan with a 30% tilt for setting the initial withdrawal rate. Because they are nervous about stocks, they also want to lower the systemic-withdrawal stock allocation from the recommended 55% to 45%, requiring income be dropped another 5% using Figure 141 (in addition to the 5% for the 40-year retirement). The initial income rate using systemic withdrawals for a 2.9 valuation level using a 30% tilt is 3.9% (after taking off 10%).

Given that 85% of their portfolio is allocated to systemic withdrawals with a 3.9% payout, the initial annual income rate is (3.9% * 0.85) = 3.3%, not much above the essential-income rate of 3.1%, but acceptable for the couple (although many retirees would consider this GI unaffordable).

When interest rates improve (or the ladder length shortens enough from aging) the couple plans to build a TIPS bond ladder. Their goal is to have at least a 3.5% payout from the TIPS ladder based on the years left in retirement (which might require an extended ladder over 30 years). They also want to keep 30% in systemic withdrawals for flexibility and to increase their bequest value, although they believe they will probably die well before the TIPS ladder matures. When and how the bond pool will be used depends on what happens. A little might be used to supplement insufficient income, but the primarily aim is to build a TIPS ladder (or second ladder if spanning over 30 years).

Case 5: Wants GI, Barely Sufficient Assets, No Bequest Motive, Attractive Valuations, Low Interest Rates

A couple start retirement at age 64. Both are risk averse, desire the extra protection of GI, but can afford only a minimal amount. Leaving a bequest is not a significant motivation. They are planning for a 40-year retirement. Their essential-income rate is 4%. After a recent market drop, the current valuation level is 1.8.

With the attractive valuation level and SPIAs paying out only 4.2% for the couple, they immediately lock in only 1% (i.e., 25% of their essential-income rate) by putting 24% of their total assets in an SPIA.

The rest of the couple's assets (76% of total) go into the recommended systemic-withdrawal plan. Their initial income rate using systemic withdrawals for a 1.8 valuation level is 4.47% using a 30% tilt (after taking off 5% for the 40-year plan).

Given that 76% of their portfolio is allocated to systemic withdrawals with a 4.47% payout, and 24% is allocated to a SPIA with a 4.2% payout, the initial annual income rate is ((4.47% * 0.76) + (4.2% * 0.24)) = 4.4%.

They plan is to wait for higher SPIA rates (and hopefully strong portfolio growth), eventually putting up to 70% of total assets in SPIAs, spread over one or two more purchases. They will keep at least 30% in systemic withdrawal for flexibility.

Case 6: Wants GI, No Affordability, Unattractive Valuations, Low Interest Rates

Due to health problems a couple retire early at age 62. They are moderately risk averse, desire the extra protection of GI, but have limited funds. They are planning a 40-year retirement. They would like to leave some assets for their children, but their main concern is maintaining their quality of life. Their essential-income rate is 3.9%. The current valuation level is high at 3.4.

With low interest rate and an early retirement age, an SPIA is paying only 3.6%, under the essential-income rate. A TIPS ladder is even worse. Setting aside funds in a standby bond pool will lower the payout further when they are already short on funds. However, they feel they are walking a tightrope with high valuations—they may be forced to downsize but choose to accept some risk exposure to see if better options open up.

Because of valuations, they decide to lock in 1% annually by putting 28% of their total assets in an SPIA. This is less than the recommend amount with high valuations, but GI is really not affordable for them. They also allocate 10% to a standby bond pool even though they are short on assets, because they like its flexibility and ability to preserve asset value in case the market drops.

The rest of the couple's assets (62% of total) temporarily go into the recommended systemic-withdrawal 40-year plan. Their initial income rate for systemic withdrawals starting with a 3.4 valuation level is 3.9% using a 30% tilt (after taking off 5% for the 40-year plan).

Given that 62% of their portfolio is allocated to systemic withdrawals with a 3.9% payout, and 28% is allocated to an SPIA with a 3.6% payout, their total starting income is ((3.9% * 0.62) + (3.6% * 0.28)) = 3.4%. This is significantly short of their 3.9 essential-income rate.

Their plan is to overdraw as needed from systemic withdraws for a few years, pulling out enough to meet their essential-income rate (the odds are still in their favor). They hope that interest rates will improve, but SPIA payouts will still rise as they age. Their goal is to lock in an SPIA payout of 4.3%, then keep a remaining 30% of total assets in systemic withdrawals for flexibility and a potential bequest. If the stock market holds its value, this plan should support an overall 4% or better income rate, which they would be content with.

If they cannot reach their goal by age 72 (i.e., 10 years), they will sell their house and move closer to their children, generally downsizing to reduce living expenses to match expected income.

Case 7: Wants GI, Ample Assets, Taxable Account, SPIA Aversion, Bequest Motive

After selling their business, a couple start retirement at age 68 with the bulk of their assets in a taxable account. Both are risk averse, desiring the safety of GI, but do not like SPIAs. They want to leave a large portion of the assets to their children, perhaps passing some on early over time. They are planning a 35-year retirement. Their essential-income rate is low at 1.6%. The current valuation level is 3.1.

There are no strong GI options available: SPIAs are off the list, TIPS are not tax efficient and rates aren't attractive, and enough I Bonds can't be purchased in a reasonable time period to meet their needs. Compromises are required.

The couple accept that a significant portion of the assets should be kept in systemic withdrawals, which provides growth and an excellent inflation hedge. They allocate 60% to systemic withdrawals, but choose the minimal stock percentage of 35%.

Their initial income rate using systemic withdrawals for a 3.1 valuation level is 3.7%, using a 30% tilt (after deducting 2.5% for the 35-year plan (i.e., half the 5% deduction for the 40-year plan)) and another 10% for the lower stock allocation.

Given that 60% of their portfolio is allocated to systemic withdrawals with a 3.7% payout, the initial annual income rate is (3.7% * 0.60) = 2.2%. This is likely more than enough for the couples' annual income needs.

The other 40% of their assets they allocate to a standby bond pool. Although they plan to buy I Bonds annually, there are too many assets in the bond pool to make this a complete solution. The bulk of the bond pool's assets are distributed across a diverse set of low-cost tax-advantaged bond index funds, including TIPS and municipal bonds. They prefer to manage their own assets, but are considering a fee-only advisor to find better alternatives for their bond pool, potentially including individual municipal bonds. With the recent sale of their business and a desire to pass on assets, they also plan to seek the advice of an estate-planning attorney.

Case 8: GI Neutral, Ample Assets, Bequest Motive

A single female starts retirement at age 65. She is moderately risk averse but unsure if the extra protection of GI is worth the overall cost. Still, she has ample assets. She is also motivated to leave a bequest to her children. She is planning a 40-year retirement. Her essential-income rate is 3.1%. The current valuation level is 2.8.

With valuations a little on the high side, she decides to lock in a 0.75% income rate by putting 16% of total assets into an SPIA paying out 4.7%.

The rest of the assets (84% of total) go into a systemic-withdrawal 40-year plan. The initial income rate using systemic withdrawals for a 2.9 valuation level using a 40% tilt is 4.2% (after 5% off for the 40-year plan).

Given 84% of her portfolio is allocated to systemic withdrawals with a 4.2% payout, and 16% is allocated to a SPIA with a 4.7% payout, the initial annual income rate is ((4.2% * 0.84) + (4.7% * 0.16)) = 4.3%.

She is unsure about purchasing more GI later in life. She plans to keep an eye on valuations and reevaluate around age 75.

Case 9: GI Neutral, Ample Assets, Potential Income Frontloading

A couple start retirement at age 65. Both are unsure if the extra protection of GI is worth the overall cost, but they can generally afford it. They would like to leave a bequest, but a fulfilling retirement is their first priority. They are planning a 40-year retirement. They intend to travel a lot during their first 5 years in retirement, so they want extra income for these years. Their essential-income rate is 3.2%. The current valuation level is 2.6.

They put 5% of assets in a standby bond pool to boost income for first 5 years for travel. Another 5% goes in a standby bond pool as an extra hedge.

The rest of the couple's assets (90% of total) go into systemic withdrawals. Their initial income rate for a 2.6 valuation level is 4.4% using a 40% tilt (after 5% off for the 40-year plan).

Given that 90% of their portfolio is allocated to systemic withdrawals with a 4.4% payout, the initial annual income rate is (4.4% * 0.90) = 4%. However, 5% of the bond pool is allocated to boosting the income rate by approximately 1% for the first 5 years, making the first year's income 5%.

Case 10: GI Neutral, Later GI Revaluation, Bequest Motive

A single female starts retirement at age 61. She is comfortable with systemic withdrawal, in part because the valuation level is moderate at 2.4. She is also motivated to leave a bequest to her children. She is planning a 40-year retirement. Her essential-income rate is 3.2%.

All of her assets go into the recommended systemic-withdrawal 40-year plan. Their initial income rate using systemic withdrawals for a 2.4 valuation level is 4.5% using a 40% tilt (after 5% off for the 40-year plan).

Later, 15 years into retirement at age 76, stocks have done well. The valuation level is now 3.5, which causes her to reevaluate. Interest rates are also moderately high with a 2% real IRR. She decides to lock in 70% of her essential-income rate using a 30-year TIPS Ladder using under half of her systemic withdrawal assets. She also gives away 10% of her total assets as an early inheritance to her children and grandchildren. The remainder of her portfolio stays in systemic withdrawals.

Case 11: GI Neutral, Assets Shortfall, No Bequest Motive, Attractive Valuations

A couple start retirement at age 65. Both are mildly risk averse and unsure about purchasing GI. They also have an asset shortfall. A bequest is not a significant motivation. Their essential-income rate is 5%. After a recent market drop, the current valuation level is 1.6. They are planning for a 40-year retirement.

They go with 100% systemic withdrawals with a 50% tilt for setting the initial withdrawal rate to produce a 5.2% initial withdrawal rate (after 5% off for the 40-year plan).

They will pull out at least 5%, even if EM recommends a lower rate, but if they consistently overdraw for several years. Then they will downsize and trim their spending to align with their income.

They plan to purchase an SPIA when rates reach 5.5%. How much to allocate to the SPIA depends on portfolio growth and their age, but they will maintain at least 30% in systemic withdrawals.

Case 12: GI Neutral, Moderate Valuations, Early Retirement

A single male starts retirement at age 50. He is not risk averse. He wants to leave a bequest to friends and family. His essential-income rate is 3.2%. The current valuation level is 2.4. He is planning for a 50-year retirement.

He allocates 5% to a standby bond pool for unexpected expenses.

The rest of the assets (95% of total) go into the recommended systemic-withdrawal 50-year plan. The initial income rate using systemic withdrawals for a 2.4 valuation level is 4.3% using a 30% tilt (after 5% off for the 50-year plan).

Given that 95% of his portfolio is allocated to systemic withdrawals with a 4.3% payout, the initial annual income rate is (4.3% * 0.95) = 4.1%.

Case 13: GI Neutral, Unattractive Valuations, Later GI Revaluation

A couple start retirement at age 62. They don't consider GI currently affordable because the valuation level is moderate at 2.3 and they have a high essential-income rate of 4.1%. Leaving a bequest is a secondary goal. They are planning for a 40-year retirement.

They put 100% of their assets in systemic withdrawals, with a 40% tilt, to produce a 4.5% initial withdrawal rate (after 5% off for the 40-year plan).

9 years into retirement, the market has performed below average, causing their annual income from EM to drop their essential-income rate to 4.1%. They are concerned that their income may drop further due to economic turmoil, even though valuation levels are now attractive at 1.6.

They reevaluate, and find SPIA rates to be much higher at 71, but their real portfolio value has dropped. They eventually decide to put 50% of the assets in an SPIA to lock in a 2.5% annual income rate, which is 60% of the essential-income rate. This boosts their current income up to 4.5%.

While the immediate gain may be small given the likely cost to future income and bequest value, they enjoy the immediate rise in income and sleep much better, having 60% of the essential-income rate guaranteed for life.

Case 14: GI Neutral in a Potential Market Bubble

A single male starts retirement at age 63. He is usually comfortable with systemic withdrawals, but valuation levels are extremely high at 3.8, indicating a possible stock bubble. His bequest motivation is secondary. His essential-income rate is 2.7%.

After reviewing the numbers, he decides to allocate 57% of assets to an SPIA with a payout of 4.7%, to lock in 100% of his essential-income rate. He also allocates 10% to a standby bond pool.

The rest of the assets (33% of total) go into the recommended systemic-withdrawal 40-year plan, but with only 35% allocated to stocks. The initial income rate using systemic withdrawals for a valuation level of 4 is only 3.2% (after 15% off for the lower stock allocation and the long retirement).

Given that 33% of his portfolio is allocated to systemic withdrawals with a 3.2% payout, and 57% is allocated to a SPIA with a 5.5% payout, the initial annual income rate is ((3.2% * 0.33) + (4.7% * 0.57)) = 3.7%.

After a market correction (which might take years) the plan is to restart systemic withdrawals with new parameters and the recommended stock percentage. At the same time, the assets in the standby bond pool will be put back into systemic withdrawals.

The key to trying to time the market using valuations is to never put the portfolio in an unsustainable position, since it might take a decade or more for markets to adjust.

Case 15: GI Averse

A couple start retirement at age 65. They are not risk averse. They believe the cost of GI almost always makes it unaffordable. Their essential-income rate is 3.3%. The current valuation level is 2.7. They are planning a 30-year retirement.

They put 100% of their assets into a systemic-withdrawal plan using the Triad portfolio, increasing their initial stock allocation to 65% of assets (preferring the likely boost in returns for the minimal increase in risk).

Their initial income rate with systemic withdrawals for a 2.7 valuation level is 4.5% with a 40% tilt, and 4.7% with a 50% tilt. They select 4.6% as their initial rate.

FINAL THOUGHTS

A moderate amount of guaranteed income applied well can substantially reduce speculative risk for those who find it affordable, which is an individual decision.

While this chapter dwells on the possibility of failure markets, keep in mind that the Baseline Market provides the best estimate of what to expect in retirement. Whether a failure market will occur in the next 50 or even 100 years is unknowable in the realm of speculative risk.

Living well has risks, as does investing well. Fortunately, foreknowledge is not a requirement for either. To invest well, we plan thoughtfully, applying best practices, hedging only those risks deemed worth the cost. A retiree can iterate on a plan until satisfied within the bounds of what there is to work with. This can't eliminate all the unknowns, but the final plan should be as good as anyone can expect, which should be satisfying. Then there is no more that must be done, except to virtually forget about your portfolio. Checking back in once a year is good enough.

THE POINT

Enjoy your retirement!

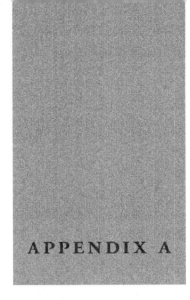

THE HISTORICAL DATASETS

Following are the sources of the datasets used in this book.

1. Ibbotson's Stocks, Bonds, Bills, and Inflation Yearbook (2011)

    This is the primary dataset, given its unique breakdown into stock asset classes. Total-return data from 1928 to 2010 is used. The following asset classes are included.

    a. SBBI Data Series Large Company Stocks (CRSP Deciles 1-2—S&P 500 Composite)
    b. SBBI Data Series Small Company Stocks (primarily 5th quintile of NYSE)
    c. Mid-Cap Stocks (CRSP Deciles 3-5 from NYSE, AMEX, and NASDAQ)
    d. Low-Cap Stocks (CRSP Deciles 6-8 from NYSE, AMEX, and NASDAQ)
    e. Micro-Cap Stocks (CRSP Deciles 9-10 from NYSE, AMEX, and NASDAQ)
    f. Total-Market (CRSP Deciles 1-10 from NYSE, AMEX, and NASDAQ)
    g. Fama-French Large Growth Stocks (NYSE/AMEX/NASDAQ)
    h. Fama-French Large Value Stocks (NYSE/AMEX/NASDAQ)
    i. Fama-French Small Growth Stocks (NYSE/AMEX/NASDAQ)
    j. Fama-French Small Value Stocks (NYSE/AMEX/NASDAQ)
    k. Long-Term High-Grade Corporate Bonds
    l. Long-Term Government Bonds (20-Year Maturity)
    m. Intermediate-Term Government Bonds (5-Year Maturity)
    n. US Treasury Bills (30-Day Maturity)

2. Robert Shiller's Dataset (http://www.econ.yale.edu/~shiller/data/ie_data.xls)

    Yale's Professor Shiller generously makes available the historical data from his book *Irrational Exuberance*. The data includes the S&P Composite returns for stock prices, the 10-Year Treasury Index (GS10) for bond prices, and the CPI-U (Consumer Price Index-All Urban Consumers) for inflation adjustments. All data goes back to 1871.

3. Global Financial Data's United Kingdom Datasets

The following UK indexes are used. All calculations are done in British pounds (there is no exchange-rate conversions to US dollars). This better reflects the characteristics of the UK market.

a. UK FTSE All-Share Return Index (w/GFD extension) 1694–2012
b. United Kingdom Total Return Bills Index 1800-2011
c. UK FT-Actuaries PE Ratio (w/GFD extension) 1927–2012

Because the older historical numbers do not reflect modern markets, backtesting with the UK datasets only goes back to 1923.

Earnings are derived from the FT-Actuaries' P/E data, so that CAPE-10 and PeakCAPE-10 can be calculated from the annual earnings and the closing price data (inflation adjusted).

The UK inflation numbers[68] are independent from the datasets.

4. Global Financial Data's Japan Datasets

The following Japanese indexes are used. All calculations are done in Japanese yen, as opposed to US dollars—again, this better reflects the characteristics of the Japan market.

a. Japan Topix Total Return Index 1920-2012
b. Japan Total Return Bills Index 1882-2012

Japanese inflation numbers[69] are independent from the datasets. Because hyperinflation essentially destroyed Japan's market value during the 1940s after the end of World War II, backtesting with the Japan datasets only goes back to 1950.

5. Simba's Data

Simba's dataset includes international mutual fund data going back to 1972. It's publicly available at the Bogleheads website (www.bogleheads.org). Simba, known by his Bogleheads username, generously pulled this data together from public sources into a single spreadsheet.

INCORPORATING TIPS LADDERS INTO SYSTEMIC WITHDRAWALS

This book separates guaranteed income strategies from systemic withdrawal strategies. Their goals are different and their instruments are usually different. However, this appendix examines a special case of using a TIPS ladder within systemic withdrawal.

Bond funds are assumed within a systemic-withdrawal portfolio. They are easy to manage, flexible, and generally work well. Still, bond funds have volatility, which leads to the key question: should a TIPS ladder* with no volatility be used in place of bond funds within systemic withdrawals?

Figure 196 compares systemic-withdrawal results using a bond fund to systemic withdrawal using TIPS ladders with varying payout rates (i.e., 1%, 2%, 3%, and 4%). The initial bond allocation is 50%. The only difference is where the bond allocation resides: either in bond funds or a TIPS ladder.

---

* Applying bond ladders within systemic withdrawals is not a new idea. Stephen Huxley and J. Burns recommend it in their book, *Asset Dedication* (2004). Paul Grangaard in his book, *The Grangaard Strategy*, has similar recommendations.

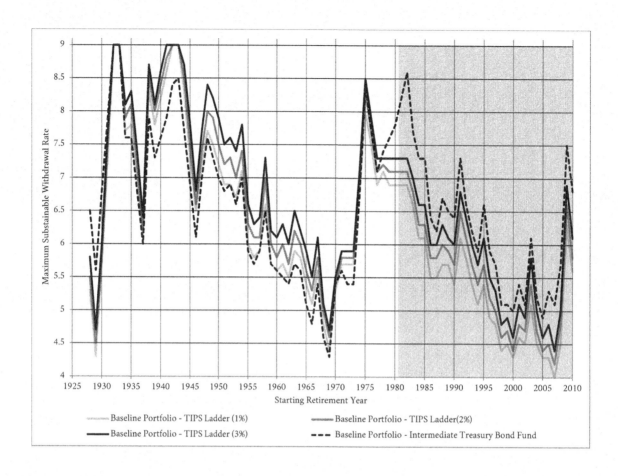

FIGURE 196

*30-year systemic-withdrawal comparison based on simulated TIPS bond ladders (of
varying real returns) versus intermediate-bond index fund. For retirements after 1981
the missing data is simulated (i.e., the data is wrapped, from 2010 back to 1928.)*

Generally, the results of the comparison are mixed. Before 1930, the bond fund performs best. From 1930 to 1980, a TIPS ladder generally performs best. Then after 1980, the bond fund again performs best.

Of course, the higher the TIPS payout, the better the performance, but the ladder payout was not a deciding factor on which approach performed best.

Focusing on the worst retirement period provides a little more insight into the comparison. Bond indexes did better during the most difficult stock periods (e.g., 1929, 2000, 2007) while a TIPS bond ladder did better during the overall worst retirement period (i.e., 1969), when high inflation was a strong factor. Another perspective is that the TIPS ladder did best during the unexpected inflation of the 1970s and early 1980s, while the bond index did best during bear stock markets due to their negative correlation with stocks.

The results aren't substantially different when testing with annual rebalancing, or testing different retirement lengths. Also, the same inconclusive results are seen with Shiller's data and UK data: TIPS ladders tended to underperform during market crises, but did better during periods of high inflation. However, TIPS ladders did consistently better with Japan's data. Ultimately, no definitive conclusion can be reached without more data.

Without a clear winner, the tie vote goes to sticking with bond funds. They are simpler and more flexible within systemic withdrawals.

Still, using a TIPS ladder within systemic withdrawal remains a viable approach (especially when TIPS rates are very high). For those interested, the procedure is outlined below.

- Take approximately 75% of bond assets and build a TIPS bond ladder to match the current withdrawal rate (or initial withdrawal rate). Build the ladder as far out as it can go. To gain better yields, the ladder might start a few years out (e.g., a starting ladder to cover income for years 3 through 12). The remaining 25% of the bond allocation goes into the normal bond funds (i.e., short, intermediate, TIPS).
  - All ladder income goes to withdrawals; note that with Prime Harvesting, stocks are never bought in retirement, only sold. This means all coupon payments are applied to each year's annual withdrawal. Also, maturing bonds are applied to the annual withdrawal.
  - The ladder doesn't have to deliver exact amounts, but it can provide a base amount.
  - If income from the ladder is short, assets in the bond fund make up the difference.
  - If income from the ladder exceeds the withdrawal amount, the excess is rolled into a bond fund.
- Each time Prime Harvesting sells stock to replenish bonds, a portion (e.g., 75%) of the assets go to building the ladder further out, with the rest going into the bond fund. When stocks are doing well, how far out the retiree wants to build the ladder is a personal choice (e.g., 15 years, 20 years).

On a related note, when interest rates are high and systemic withdrawal bond levels are high, I Bonds also make an attractive repository for systemic-withdrawal bonds.

About the Author from the Author

My investing philosophy has evolved over 20 years of study, only starting to mature in the last decade. It took the writing of this book to complete my education on investing during retirement.

Bachelor's and Master's degrees in Computer Science, as well as many years of problem solving, helped with the analysis for this book. I've been fortunate to work at many institutions including Cisco Systems, IBM, Bell Laboratories, and Lawrence Livermore National Laboratory, plus several smaller outfits, including one successful startup. Modeling and simulation experience from many sectors of the technology industry made financial modeling easier. My first exposure to Monte Carlo techniques goes back to 1979 as an undergraduate working on an IBM 1130 under the helpful guidance of Professor Chandler.

If You Like This Book

If you like this book, please tell others about it in reviews, online discussion groups, blogs, reader comments, etc. Reader support is a key factor to any book's success in today's publishing world.

Supporting this book will enable others like it to be written.

REFERENCES

1. Luigi Zingales. "Preventing Economists' Capture." 2013. http://faculty.chicagobooth.edu/luigi.zingales/papers/research/Preventing_Economists_Capture.pdf.

2. Campbell Harvey, Yan Liu, and Heqing Zhu. ". . . and the Cross-Section of Expected Returns." 2014. https://people.duke.edu/~charvey/research.htm. Working Paper.

3. "Evidence-based Practice." Wikipedia. https://en.wikipedia.org/wiki/Evidence-based_practice

4. "2011 Risks and Process of Retirement Survey Report." Society of Actuaries: Key Findings and Issues: Longevity; June, 2012. https://www.soa.org/files/research/projects/research-key-finding-longevity.pdf.

5. John H Cochrane. "New Facts in Finance." 1999. NBER Working Papers 7169, National Bureau of Economic Research, Inc.

6. Jim C. Otar. *Unveiling the Retirement Myth*. Toronto, 2009. www.aftcast.com

7. "FIRECalc®: How Long Will Your Money Last?" July, 2011. FIRECalc: A Different Kind of Retirement Calculator. http://www.firecalc.com.

8. Nicolas M Granger, Douglas Greenig, Campbell R. Harvey, Sandy Rattray, and David Zou. "Rebalancing Risk." October 3, 2014. Available at SSRN: http://ssrn.com/abstract=2488552 or http://dx.doi.org/10.2139/ssrn.2488552.

9. John J. Spitzer and Sandeep Singh. "Is Rebalancing a Portfolio During Retirement Necessary?" June 2007. Journal of Financial Planning. http://www.retailinvestor.org/pdf/SpitzerSingh.pdf.

10. http://www.bogleheads.org/wiki/Withdrawal_Methods.

11. Jonathan T. Guyton. "Decision Rules and Portfolio Management for Retirees: Is the 'Safe' Initial Withdrawal Rate Too Safe?" October 2004. FPA Journal.

12. Jonathan T. Guyton and William J. Klinger. "Decision Rules and Maximum Initial Withdrawal Rates." March 2006. Journal of Financial Planning. http://www.cornerstonewealthadvisors.com/files/08-06_WebsiteArticle.pdf

13. William J. Klinger. "Using Decision Rules to Create Retirement Withdrawal Profiles." August 2007. Journal of Financial Planning.

14. Zachary Parker. "Income-Harvesting Strategy: Achieving Inflation-Adjusted Income from a Lump-Sum Asset." 2008. Journal of Financial Planning.

15. Gerald R. Weiss. "Dynamic Rebalancing." 2001. Journal of Financial Planning, 14, 100–108. 131.

16. David Lee. "Omega Strategy (not)." http://daveleemn.tripod.com/omega_strategy.htm.

17. Wikipedia. http://en.wikipedia.org/wiki/Ray_Lucia.

18. Paul A. Grangaard. *The Grangaard Strategy: Invest Right during Retirement.* Perigee, 2003.

19. Paul A. Grangaard. http://www.thegrangaardstrategy.com.

20. Wade D. Pfau and Michael E. Kitces. "Reducing Retirement Risk with a Rising Equity Glide-Path." September 12, 2013. http://papers.ssrn.com/sol3/papers.cfm?abstract_id=2324930

21. William P. Bengen, "Determining Withdrawal Rates Using Historical Data." October 1994. Journal of Financial Planning: 14–24.

22. Jonathan T. Guyton and William J. Klinger. "Decision Rules and Maximum Initial Withdrawal Rates." March 2006. Journal of Financial Planning. www.cornerstonewealthadvisors.com/files/08-06_WebsiteArticle.pdf

23. Darla Mercado. "15 Transformational Advisors." June 12, 2013. http://www.investmentnews.com/article/20130612/FREE/130619962

24. Peter Ponzo. http://www.gummy-stuff.org/sensible_withdrawals.htm

25. Robert C. Carlson. *The New Rules of Retirement: Strategies for a Secure Future.* 2005. Wiley.

26. David Blanchett, Maciej Kowara, and Peng Chen. "Optimal Withdrawal Strategy for Retirement-Income Portfolios." September, 2012. Working Paper. http://corporate.morningstar.com/us/documents/ResearchPapers/OptimalWithdrawalStrategyRetirementIncomePortfolios.pdf.

27. Wade Pfau, "Will 2000-era retirees experience the worst retirement outcomes in U.S. History? A progress report after 10 years." November 2010. The Journal of Investing.

28. E. Arias United States life tables, 2007. National vital statistics reports; vol 59 no 9. National Center for Health Statistics. 2011. http://www.cdc.gov/nchs/data/nvsr/nvsr59/nvsr59_09.pdf

29. David Blanchett, Maciej Kowara, and Peng Chen. "Optimal Withdrawal Strategy for Retirement-Income Portfolios." Working Paper. http://corporate.morningstar.com/us/documents/ResearchPapers/OptimalWithdrawalStrategyRetirementIncomePortfolios.pdf.

30. Ty Bernicke. "Reality Retirement Planning: A New Paradigm for an Old Science." June 2005. Journal of Financial Planning.

31. "Models of Spending as Retirement Progresses." July, 2014. http://www.bogleheads.org/wiki/Models_of_spending_as_retirement_progresses.

32. Elroy Dimson, Paul Marsh, and Mike Staunton. Credit Suisse Global Investment Returns Yearbook. 2014.

33. Elroy Dimson, Paul Marsh, and Mike Staunton. Credit Suisse Global Investment Returns Yearbook. 2013.

34. Elroy Dimson, Paul Marsh, and Mike Staunton. Credit Suisse Global Investment Returns Yearbook. 2013.

35. Philippe Jorion. "The Long-Term Risks of Global Stock Markets." http://merage.uci.edu/~jorion/papers/risk.pdf. 2003.

36. Gerald P. Dwyer. "Federal Reserve Bank of Atlanta." January, 2011. International Dimensions of the Financial Crisis of 2007 and 2008. https://www.frbatlanta.org/cenfis/publications/notesfromthevault/1101.aspx

37. Wade Pfau. "Does International Diversification Improve Safe Withdrawal Rates?" March 4, 2014. http://www.advisorperspectives.com

38. Elroy Dimson, Paul Marsh, and Mike Staunton. Credit Suisse Global Investment Returns Yearbook. 2011.

39. E. F Fama and K. R. French. "Common risk factors in the returns on stocks and bonds". February 1993. Journal of Financial Economics, Vol. 33 No. 1.

40. Wade D. Pfau. "An International Perspective on Safe Withdrawal Rates from Retirement Savings: The Demise of the 4 Percent Rule?" September 2010. www3.grips.ac.jp/~pinc/data/10-12.pdf

41. "Invest Simple with Lazy Portfolios." http://www.marketwatch.com/lazyportfolio

42. "Bogleheads: Spreadsheet for Backtesting (includes TrevH's Data)." https://www.bogleheads.org/forum/viewtopic.php?t=2520

43. Jason Zweig. *Your Money and Your Brain: How the New Science of Neuroeconomics Can Help Make You Rich.* 2007. Simon & Schuster.

44. Ronald Q Doeswijk, Trevin W. Lam, and Laurens A.P. Swinkels. "Strategic Asset Allocation: The Global Multi-Asset Market Portfolio 1959-2011." 2014. Financial Analysts Journal.

45. National Bureau of Economic Research. http://www.nber.org/digest/may02/w8680.html

46. Stephanie Braming. "Emerging Markets: Essential Sources of Global Economic Growth." August 2010. http://sicav.williamblairfunds.com/resources/docs/Fund-Literature/White-Papers/Emerging_Markets.pdf

47. Felix Schindler. "Long-Term Benefits from Investing in International Securitized Real Estate." 2011. International Real Estate Review, Vol. 14 No. 1.

48. Eterna Investment Management Global Real Estate Team White Paper Series. May 25, 2011. http://www.eterna.ca/pdfs/egreif-white-paper-cross-asset-correlations.pdf

49. Eduardo Roca. "How Globally Contagious Was the Recent US Real Estate Market Crisis?" www98.griffith.edu.au/dspace/bitstream/handle/10072/42408/74259_1.pdf

50. Graeme Newell. "The Investment Characteristics and Benefits of Asian REITs for Retail Investors." November 2012. Asia Pacific Real Estate Association Limited.

51. Michael C. Hudgins. "Brave New Worlds: Revisiting the strategic case for global REITs." April 2010. JP Morgan.

52. K. Geert Rouwenhorst. "Local return factors and turnover in emerging stock markets." July 1998. School of Management, Yale University.

53. Nusret Cakici and Sinan Tan. "Size, Value, and Momentum in Emerging Market Stock Returns." 15 April 2012. Fordham University.

54. Wade Pfau. "Can We Predict the Sustainable Withdrawal Rate for New Retirees?" May 2011. National Graduate Institute for Policy Studies. http://mpra.ub.uni-muenchen.de/30877

55. Joachim Klement. "Does the Shiller-PE work in emerging markets?" Revised version. July 22nd, 2012. http://samuelssonsrapport.se/wp-content/uploads/SSRN-id2088140.pdf

56. Mebane Faber. *Global Value: How to Spot Bubbles, Avoid Market Crashes, and Earn Big Returns in the Stock Market*. March, 2014. The Idea Farm.

57. "2011 Risks and Process of Retirement Survey Report." June 2012. Society of Actuaries: Key Findings and Issues: Longevity.

58. Phil DeMuth and Ben Stein. *Yes, You Can Still Retire Comfortably!: The Baby-Boom Retirement Crisis and How to Beat It*. August 2, 2005. New Beginnings Press.

59. Wade Pfau. "How Do I Build a TIPS Bond Ladder for Retirement Income?" December 19, 2013. http://retirementresearcher.com/how-do-i-build-a-tips-bond-ladder-for-retirement-income

60. "Bogleheads. Wade Pfau's TIPS Ladder Guide." http://www.bogleheads.org/forum/viewtopic.php?t=128677

61. The Wall Street Journal Market Data Center. Treasury Inflation-Protected Securities. http://online.wsj.com/mdc/public/page/2_3020-tips.html

62. Economic Research: Federal Reserve Bank of St. Louis. https://research.stlouisfed.org/fred2/

63. William C. Dudley, Jennifer Roush, and Michelle Steinberg Ezer. "The Case for TIPS: An Examination of the Costs and Benefits." July 2009. FRBNY Economic Policy Review. http://www.newyorkfed.org/research/epr/09v15n1/0907dudl.pdf

64. Joe Tomlinson. "How Safe are Annuities?" August 14, 2012. www.advisorperspectives.com/newsletters12/How_Safe_are_Annuities.php

65. Brett Hammond. "Investment Insights: Inflation-Linked Bonds For Long-Term Diversification." September 30, 2010. http://www1.tiaa-cref.org/public/about/news/comm_009.html

66. Robert Powell. "Variable annuities: right or wrong for you?" Nov 16, 2013. http://www.marketwatch.com/story/variable-annuities-right-or-wrong-for-you-2013-11-16

67. "Campbell R. Harvey's Homepage." http://people.duke.edu/~charvey/

68. Grahame Allen, Jim O'Donoghue, and Louise Goulding. "Consumer Price Inflation since 1750." March 10, 2004. Economic Trends, No. 604. U.K. Office for National Statistics.

69. Lawrence H. Officer and Samuel H. Williamson, "What Was the Japan GDP or CPI Then?" 2011. MeasuringWorth. http://www.measuringworth.com/japandata/

INDEX

CPSIA information can be obtained
at www.ICGtesting.com
Printed in the USA
BVOW04s2101010118

504135BV00004B/6/P